NEW JERSEY

Past and Present

Joanne Mattern

rosen publishing's
rosen
central®

New York

Published in 2010 by The Rosen Publishing Group, Inc.
29 East 21st Street, New York, NY 10010

First Edition

Library of Congress Cataloging-in-Publication Data

Mattern, Joanne, 1963–
New Jersey: past and present / Joanne Mattern.—1st ed.
    p. cm.—(The United States: past and present)
Includes bibliographical references and index.
ISBN 978-1-4358-3525-2 (library binding)
ISBN 978-1-4358-8500-4 (pbk)
ISBN 978-1-4358-8501-1 (6 pack)
1. New Jersey—Juvenile literature. I. Title.
F134.3.M386 2010
974.9—dc22

2009026985

Manufactured in the United States of America

CPSIA Compliance Information: Batch #LW10YA: For Further Information contact Rosen Publishing, New York, New York at 1-800-237-9932

On the cover: Top left: Danforth, Cooke & Company's Locomotive and Machine Works was one of the many locomotive factories in Paterson during the 1800s. Top right: Lucy the Elephant, located in the seaside community of Margate, is one of New Jersey's most unusual tourist attractions. Bottom: Bradley Beach is one of the family-friendly attractions along the New Jersey shore and a great place to cool off on a hot summer day.

Contents

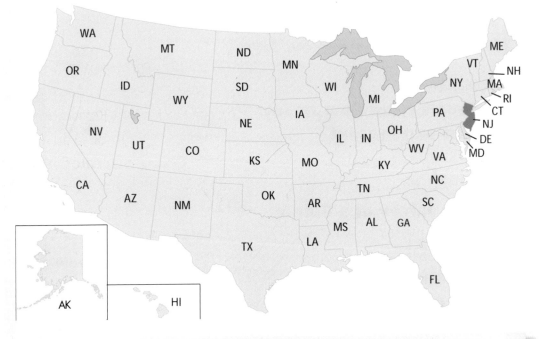

New Jersey's location near the big cities of Philadelphia and New York, along with its Atlantic coastline, have made it one of the most populous and vital states in the nation.

Introduction

New Jersey is one of the smallest states in the United States, but it is big in history and cultural importance. It was one of the original thirteen colonies, and it went on to become one of the original thirteen states. From its earliest days, when it was settled by Native Americans, to its growth as a center of industry, New Jersey has been a diverse and fascinating state. Today the state features big cities, rural farms, sprawling suburbs, and a variety of places and people.

New Jersey's location has made it a vital part of American history. George Washington marched through New Jersey, and several important battles were fought in the state during the American Revolution. The state's coastal location has helped it become a hub of industry and a destination for tourists. In addition, New Jersey is located near two major U.S. cities, New York and Philadelphia. This has helped it grow into a populous and important part of the United States.

Over the centuries, New Jersey has grown from a rural area of woodlands, fields, and swamps to a state with a variety of businesses and fascinating people. New Jersey residents have become famous all over the world for their accomplishments in music, the arts, politics, and science. Some of the world's most important inventions were created in New Jersey, and many popular music works were inspired by life in the state. Let's take a closer look at New Jersey and discover its secrets.

Chapter 1

THE GEOGRAPHY OF NEW JERSEY

Almost every state in the United States is bigger than New Jersey. New Jersey measures only 8,204 square miles (21,248 square kilometers), which ranks it forty-seventh in total area among the U.S. states. It borders New York State to the north, but the other three sides of the state are surrounded by water. The Hudson River, New York Bay, and the Atlantic Ocean create New Jersey's eastern border. The Delaware River separates the state from Pennsylvania and Delaware on the west, and the Delaware Bay and Atlantic Ocean border the state on the south.

Geographic Regions

New Jersey is divided into four main geographic regions. Despite the size of the state, there is a great deal of diversity within its natural landscape.

The Atlantic Coastal Plain

New Jersey's largest natural region is the Atlantic Coastal Plain. This area covers the central and southern parts of the state. The Atlantic Coastal Plain also includes much of New Jersey's 127 miles (204 km)

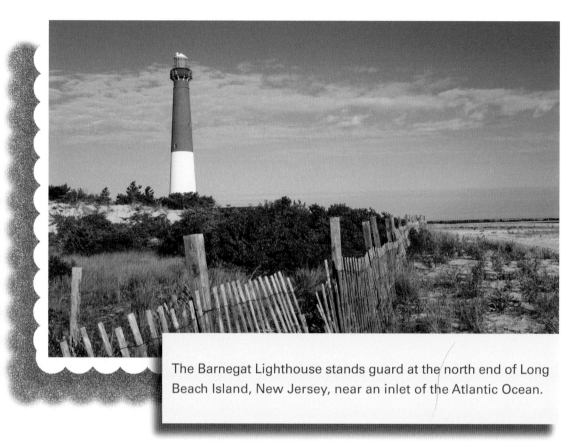

The Barnegat Lighthouse stands guard at the north end of Long Beach Island, New Jersey, near an inlet of the Atlantic Ocean.

of coastline. The coastline contains many barrier islands to the east of the mainland.

Most of the land in this region is low and flat, without any tall mountains. The land in the southwestern part of the state is very fertile, while the eastern part is made up of pine forests and salt-water marshes. The Atlantic Coastal Plain also includes the Pinelands, or Pine Barrens, which is a large area of bogs, swamps, marshes, and pine forests in the southern part of the state. Because of the large number of unusual plants and animals that live in the Pine Barrens, the U.S. Congress established the area as the country's first National Reserve in 1978.

The Piedmont

The Piedmont is a narrow area about 20 miles (32 km) wide, which cuts a swath across the northern part of New Jersey, just above the Coastal Plain. It covers only about one-fifth of the state, but it includes the state's major rivers like the Hudson, Raritan, Ramapo, and Passaic. The Piedmont is mainly filled with low hills and some ridges. However, the land drops sharply where the Passaic River flows over a cliff and into a canyon in the Watchung Mountains. This spot is called the Great Falls and is the second highest waterfall east of the Mississippi River. It is surpassed only by New York's Niagara Falls.

The Piedmont also includes a wide, tall area of cliffs called the Palisades, located along the Hudson River. South of the Palisades are two wetlands, the Meadowlands and the Great Swamp.

The Highlands

New Jersey's Highlands are northwest of the Piedmont. This area is sometimes called the New England Upland. The Highlands region features many lakes that were created thousands of years ago when a glacier moved through the area. These lakes include Lake Hopatcong, Budd Lake, and Greenwood Lake. Along with lakes, the Highlands feature thick forests and rocky ridges.

The Appalachian Ridge and Valley Region

The northwestern corner of New Jersey is known as the Appalachian Ridge and Valley Region. This area is rugged and mountainous. The Kittatinny Mountains are located here and include High Point, the

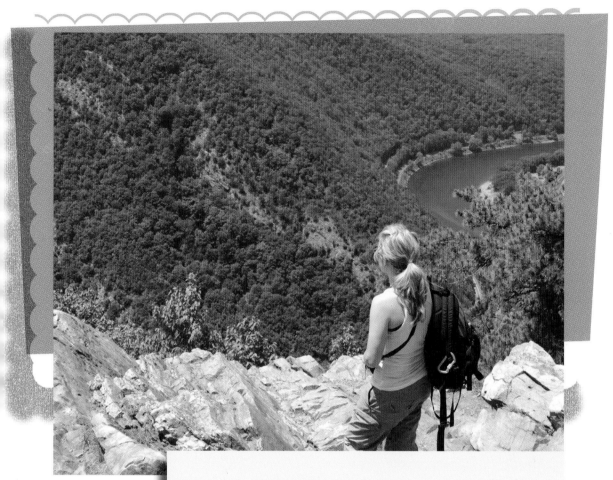

The stunning natural beauty of the Delaware Water Gap makes it a popular place for hiking and camping.

highest place in New Jersey. The fertile land supports many dairy farms and apple orchards.

The Delaware River flows through this region and has carved a deep gorge in the Kittatinny Mountains, which are part of the Appalachian chain. This gorge is called the Delaware Water Gap and features rock walls more than 1,200 feet (366 meters) deep.

Animal Life

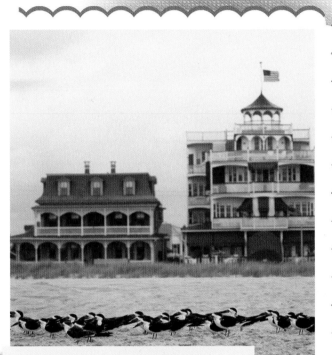

A flock of black skimmers gather on the beach in Cape May, New Jersey. The state is home to a variety of shore birds.

More than five hundred species of animals call New Jersey home. The state's forests include a large population of white-tailed deer and black bears. Some smaller mammals include chipmunks, skunks, squirrels, foxes, opossums, raccoons, and muskrats.

New Jersey is home to a wide variety of birds. Songbirds, such as cardinals, robins, chickadees, and finches, live in the area. The state also has a large population of shore birds, including sandpipers, gulls, and herons, along with other water birds, such as geese and ducks. Raptors, or birds of prey, like hawks and bald eagles are also found in the state. New Jersey is located along a major migration route for birds, the Atlantic Flyway. Every year, thousands of birds fly over the state as they migrate from north to south and back again.

New Jersey has many reptiles and amphibians. Many species of frogs live in the lakes, ponds, and streams, which also provide a home for painted turtles, spotted turtles, and eastern snapping turtles. Garter snakes and other types of snakes are common in fields and woods.

PAST AND PRESENT

Deer Invasion

White-tailed deer have always called New Jersey home. Two hundred years ago, before so many people crowded into the state, deer were free to roam the fields and forests. During that time, wolves and mountain lions also lived in New Jersey. These large animals preyed upon deer and helped keep the population under control.

Things changed as more and more people settled in New Jersey. Wolves, mountain lions, and other large predators left when they lost their habitats to the construction of homes, businesses, and highways. The deer, however, learned to adapt to these new conditions. Without large predators to keep them under control, the deer population exploded in the late 1900s. The deer moved into suburban areas, where they found plenty of food in people's backyard gardens.

Although white-tailed deer are beautiful, they have become pests to many people in New Jersey. They threaten gardens and can severely harm forests by eating new seedlings. They also carry a parasite called the deer tick, which can spread to pets and humans and cause a serious illness called Lyme disease. Deer can also pose a serious and potentially deadly risk to automobile drivers. Deer are a huge danger on the highways, since they often dart in front of cars, especially at dusk or at night when they are hard to see. There are about ten thousand deer-car collisions in New Jersey every year. Since a full-grown deer can weigh about 200 pounds (90 kilograms), hitting one can destroy a car and cause serious injuries, and even death, to the car's occupants.

New Jersey's government has tried several ways to control the deer population, including controlled sport hunting of deer in certain parts of the state. However, hunting is not allowed in the suburbs and other heavily populated areas. Without natural predators to keep the population under control, it seems that the presence of deer in New Jersey will continue to be both a beauty and a menace for years to come.

The waters in and around New Jersey are full of animal life. Humpback whales and fin whales swim off the Atlantic Coast, and dolphins and seals sometimes swim near the southern shore and in the waters of the Delaware Bay. Large fish, such as largemouth bass, catfish, trout, pike, perch, and pickerel, swim in New Jersey's lakes, while bluefish, flounder, striped bass, and mackerel swim in the ocean. Occasionally, sharks are seen in ocean waters as well.

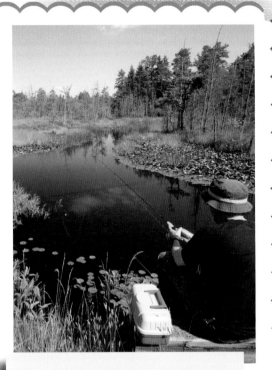

Many narrow streams wind through the thick plant life in New Jersey's Pine Barrens.

Plant Life

New Jersey has a wide variety of plant life. More than eight hundred species of plants live in the Pine Barrens, including some rare plants that can be found nowhere else. One of these rare plants is the curly-grass fern. New Jersey's forests are filled with hardwood trees, such as oak, maple, beech, and dogwood. The state also includes many evergreen forests filled with a variety of pine trees. The state's forests and swamps also contain many types of shrubs, including the spicebush and mountain laurel.

Among New Jersey's wildflowers are black-eyed Susans, daisies, violets, and buttercups. Marshy areas feature rare flowers like jack-in-the-pulpit, swamp pink, and lady's slipper.

Chapter 2

The History of NEW JERSEY

New Jersey's first residents arrived about ten thousand years ago. Archaeologists have found the sites of camping areas along the Atlantic Ocean that were left by ancient fishermen.

Native American Settlers

The Native Americans who lived in New Jersey were called the Lenape, or Delaware Indians. The Lenape lived in permanent settlements but traveled with the seasons to make use of natural resources. During the spring, they planted gardens around their homes, which were wigwams and longhouses made of saplings and bark. In summer, they caught oysters, clams, and fish at the shore. When fall came, they harvested their crops, which included corn, beans, and squash. The Lenape survived the winter by hunting deer, raccoons, squirrels, and bears, and eating food they had stored from the harvest.

The Europeans Arrive

In 1524, an Italian explorer named Giovanni da Verrazano, sailing for France, became the first European to explore the coast of New Jersey. However, his visit did not last long, and he did not have much

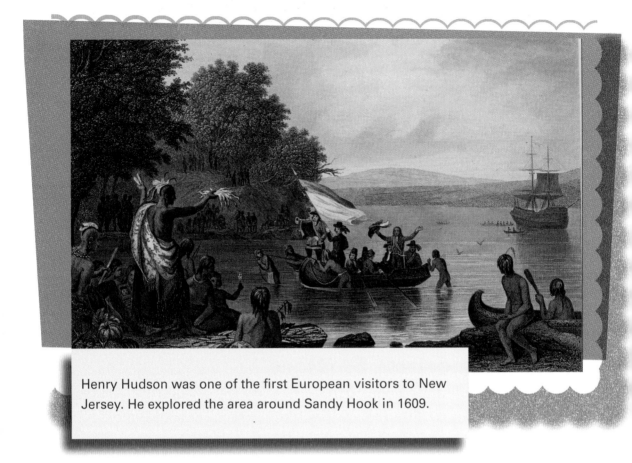

Henry Hudson was one of the first European visitors to New Jersey. He explored the area around Sandy Hook in 1609.

contact with the Lenape. The Native Americans' first real contact with Europeans came in 1609, when Henry Hudson sailed into the area. Hudson was an English captain sailing for the Netherlands. Hudson traded with the Lenape, and although one of his crew members was killed by an arrow, his efforts opened the area to exploration by other Europeans.

Soon Dutch and Swedish colonists settled in New Jersey. The Dutch called their colony New Netherland, and the Swedes called their colony New Sweden. The settlers set up trading posts, where they gave goods to the Lenape in exchange for furs. The settlers then shipped the furs to Europe, where they sold for a lot of money. The fur trade became so profitable that fighting broke out between the Dutch and the Swedes. By 1655 the Dutch, under Governor Peter Stuyvesant, had forced the Swedes to surrender control of New Jersey.

The Dutch claim to New Jersey did not last long. In 1664, Great Britain took control of all the lands held by the Dutch. Great Britain's Duke of York gave the area between the Hudson and Delaware rivers to Lord John Berkeley and Sir George Carteret. Carteret had been the governor of a British island called Jersey, so he decided to name his new territory after that island. From then on, the land was called New Jersey.

Great Britain opened New Jersey to colonists. To attract people, Great Britain offered colonists religious and political freedom. People who were persecuted for their beliefs eagerly left Great Britain to start a new life in the New World. The Quakers were one of the religious groups that arrived. In 1675, Lord Berkeley sold his share of the colony to two Quakers, Edward Byllynge and John Fenwick. Because of this sale, the colony was divided into two portions, West Jersey and East Jersey. West Jersey became the first Quaker colony in America, with its own government and capital. However, there were so many disputes between East Jersey and West Jersey that in 1702 Great Britain's Queen Anne took over the two colonies and united them into one royal colony.

Although New Jersey offered freedom to settlers from Europe, it was not so generous to the Native Americans. The Lenape suffered greatly because of the European influx. Thousands of Lenape died of European diseases, and fighting broke out over land ownership and settlement. The Lenape wanted to preserve the forests for hunting,

In 1851, artist Emanuel Gottlieb Leutze created this painting, *Washington Crossing the Delaware,* a famous image of the American Revolution.

while the European settlers were determined to clear the land for farms, mines, and towns. By the late 1750s, most of the Lenape had left New Jersey and moved to areas in New York and Pennsylvania.

The American Revolution

New Jersey, like the other American colonies, had many problems with the rule of Great Britain. In 1776, the colonies banded together to form the United States and fight for their independence. Much of the ammunition and guns used by General George Washington's troops were made in New Jersey's ironworks, and a large part of the army's food was grown on New Jersey's farms.

Washington himself led the Continental Army through New Jersey. On December 25, 1776, he brought his troops across the Delaware River and attacked British and Hessian troops the next day. Known as the Battle of Trenton, this surprise attack was a great victory for the Continental Army. Washington's crossing of the Delaware is depicted in a famous painting by Emanuel Leutze and is still commemorated today. Other vital Revolutionary battles also occurred in New Jersey, including the Battle of Monmouth in 1778. Finally, in 1783, the United States won the war. New Jersey became the third state to ratify, or approve, the U.S. Constitution in December 1787.

New Jersey and Industry

After the Revolution, New Jersey became an industrial leader. The Great Falls of the Passaic River was a natural spot for mills because the water could power the machinery. The city of Paterson, built at the Great Falls in the early 1800s, became an important factory town, manufacturing cotton cloth. Later, in 1840, Paterson became a center for manufacturing silk, which gave the town a new nickname: Silk City.

Other cities also became important industrial centers. Newark, Jersey City, and Hoboken all developed into important factory towns in the northern part of the state, while several areas in southern New Jersey became well known for glasswork factories. Food and drink became popular industries, too. In 1869, Welch's Grape Juice Company began making juice from grapes in Vineland. That same year, Joseph Campbell used New Jersey's plentiful tomato crops in his new canning plant in Camden. That plant eventually grew into the Campbell Soup Company.

The water power provided by the Great Falls made Paterson an important industrial city in the 1700s and 1800s.

New Jersey's location near the water and between New York City and Philadelphia made it a natural center for the shipping and

Nike Missiles at the Ready

During World War II (1939–1945), the Soviet Union and the United States were allies, fighting on the same side. However, almost as soon as the war ended, deep mistrust and escalating tension between the two powerful nations led to a different kind of conflict, the Cold War. The United States and the Soviet Union feared that one nation would attack the other, triggering another worldwide conflict. Each built up a powerful arms system that included different types of long-range missiles, as well as a defensive system against unexpected attacks.

During the 1950s, the U.S. government built a number of Nike missile bases in New Jersey as a defense against enemy attacks. Nike missiles were radar-guided and designed to intercept and destroy any incoming Soviet bombers. They were meant to be a last line of defense against Soviet airplanes carrying bombs. Because these missiles could only travel a short distance, all of the bases were located near major targets. Missile bases in northern New Jersey were designed to protect New York City, while bases in southern New Jersey guarded Philadelphia.

Nike bases included underground bomb chambers that housed up to twenty-four missiles. The bases, often located in suburban areas, were off limits to visitors. They were protected by rows of barbed-wire fences and patrolled by guard dogs and soldiers.

By 1974, the fear of a military attack by the Soviet Union had decreased, and technology had improved and surpassed the Nike missiles. In 1974, the entire Nike system was deactivated and closed down. The government sealed the bomb tunnels shut and abandoned the bases.

Today, some of the missile bases are still empty ruins, while others have been redeveloped into neighborhoods. One base, in Livingston, has been preserved and renamed Riker Hill Park. This base is open to the public and is a place where visitors can learn about a little-known part of New Jersey's military history.

railroad industries. In 1827, Thomas Rogers began building steam locomotives in Paterson, and the city soon became a center for locomotive manufacturing. Shipyards flourished along the coast and rivers. Shipping of goods expanded even more once canals and railroads connected New Jersey to New York and Philadelphia. New Jersey's cities became major destinations for a flood of European immigrants during the late 1800s and early 1900s. These immigrants, many of whom came from Italy, Poland, Ireland, and Germany, found work in New Jersey's factories, railroads, and shipyards.

World War II made New Jersey's industries even more prosperous. The state was a major producer of ammunition, tanks, chemicals, battleships, airplane engines, and communications equipment.

A Changing Landscape

New Jersey's cities, towns, and farms changed dramatically after World War II. A housing boom after the war, along with the more widespread ownership of cars, made it possible for people to move out of the cities and into the suburbs. Farmland was turned into housing developments, as people decided to trade crowded city living for more space in the country. The areas around New York City and Philadelphia became especially popular and were soon filled with new suburban communities.

New Jersey's cities were changing, too. As people and industries left the cities, many faced hard times. Crime rates rose and so did unemployment and poverty. Cities, including Camden and Newark, became run-down. Finally, in the 1980s, efforts began to revive these cities and other urban communities. The government provided money to build new housing and attract businesses back to urban

Fans gather at Giants Stadium in New Jersey's Meadowlands Sports Complex to watch the New York Giants play. The stadium is a popular site for sports events and other gatherings.

areas. Tourist attractions, such as an aquarium in Camden and the Prudential Center Arena in Newark, were built to bring people back into the cities. The Meadowlands Sports Complex became home to several professional teams, and casinos opened in Atlantic City. These efforts have helped, but there is still a lot of work to be done.

Today, New Jersey is a vibrant state. There are still many industries there. In particular, New Jersey has become an important center for the communications and high-tech industries. Cities and towns are a mix of different ethnic groups, all working together to make the state the best it can be.

Chapter 3

THE GOVERNMENT OF NEW JERSEY

The state capital of New Jersey is Trenton. Most of the state's political business takes place there. New Jersey's government is set up in a way that is similar to the U.S. government. Like the federal government, New Jersey's government is divided into three branches. These branches are the executive branch, the legislative branch, and the judicial branch. The three-branch system divides powers and responsibilities, and it provides a system of checks and balances to ensure fairness. Each branch of government can change or halt the actions of the others, so no one branch can have too much power.

The Executive Branch

The executive branch makes sure that state laws are enforced, and it runs public affairs. New Jersey's executive branch includes the governor, the attorney general, the treasurer, and the secretary of state. In 2010, the office of lieutenant governor becomes a new part of the executive branch. The job of the lieutenant governor is to assist the governor and take over the job should the governor be unable to perform his or her duties.

As the leader of the executive branch, the governor is the head of the state's government. He or she is elected every four years

The stately home called Drumthwacket is the official residence of New Jersey's governor. It was built in 1835 in Princeton, New Jersey.

and may not serve more than two terms. Some of the governor's responsibilities are preparing the state's budget, serving as commander in chief of the state's militia, creating state programs, and appointing other state officials.

The governor is the only member of the executive branch who is elected. He or she appoints the other executive officials. The attorney general works closely with the courts to make sure that the state's court system runs smoothly. The treasurer controls the state's finances. The secretary of state oversees many different departments of the government.

The executive branch includes a number of departments. Each department focuses on a specific issue. Some of New Jersey's state departments are natural resources, health, transportation, and human resources.

The Legislative Branch

The job of the legislative branch is to write and pass laws. New Jersey's legislature has two houses, the senate and the general assembly, which meet and do their work in Trenton.

New Jersey's legislature meets at the New Jersey State House in Trenton. It has been the site of many important speeches, such as Governor Jon Corzine's budget address in March 2006.

The state senate is the upper house of the legislature. There are forty senators in this house. New Jersey is divided into legislative districts; each district has a senator to represent it. Senators are usually elected every four years. However, if a senator's term begins with a new decade, it is only two years long. Along with making and passing state laws, the Senate is responsible for approving the governor's appointments. The lower house is the general assembly. The general assembly has eighty members. Each member of the general assembly is elected for a two-year term.

Any member of the legislature can suggest a new law by writing a bill. Bills are debated and voted on by all members of the legislature. If a bill receives enough votes, it goes to the governor. The governor

PAST AND PRESENT

The Governor's Changing Role

The role of New Jersey's governor has changed over the years. When Great Britain put John Berkeley and George Carteret in charge of the colony of New Jersey in 1664, it also gave them the right to appoint a governor. No election was held. Instead, Carteret appointed his cousin Philip to be New Jersey's first governor in 1665. The governor of New Jersey continued to be an appointed position until 1702. Then Queen Anne of England named Edward Hyde as the first royal governor of New Jersey. Hyde was already royal governor of New York, and the two colonies shared a governor until 1738.

Governing the colony was a difficult job. The governor had to respond to the will of the people, but he also had to run the colony according to British wishes. After the American colonies declared their independence in 1776, colonist William Livingston replaced New Jersey's royal governor. Livingston had little real power and few responsibilities because the colonists were nervous about giving too much power to just one person. Instead, the state's legislature had most of the power.

By the mid-1800s, the state government had become so complicated that lawmakers realized the governor had to take on more responsibilities. A new state constitution in 1844 addressed the problem, giving more power to the governor. According to the new constitution, the governor would no longer be appointed but instead would be elected by popular vote and serve a three-year term.

In 1947, the governor's term was lengthened to four years, which remains the term length today. At that time, the governor also received increased veto powers, and all state commissions were reorganized under the governor and the executive branch. Today, the governor enjoys a lot more power and responsibility than his or her predecessors did three hundred years ago. New Jersey's governor also has to manage a lot more money than in the past: In 2008, the state budget totaled more than $33 billion!

can accept the bill, send it back to the legislature for changes, or reject the idea altogether by vetoing it. If the governor vetoes a bill, it can still become law if two-thirds of both the senate and the general assembly vote to override the veto.

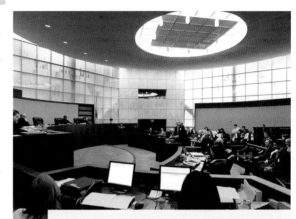

New Jersey's supreme court listens as a lawyer addresses the court. The supreme court decides which laws are constitutional in the state.

The Judicial Branch

The judicial branch is the state's court system. New Jersey's highest court is the state supreme court. The supreme court includes one chief justice and six associate justices. These judges are responsible for resolving cases involving constitutional issues. In other words, the court decides if laws follow the state constitution. The supreme court's decisions are final and cannot be appealed or changed.

A number of courts fall under the supreme court. Thirty-five judges serve on the superior courts in New Jersey. These courts are divided into a tax court, a criminal court, a civil court, and a family court. Members of New Jersey's supreme court and superior courts are appointed to seven-year terms by the governor. The state senate must approve these appointments. Judges can be reappointed once, and they are allowed to serve until they are seventy years old.

New Jersey has many lower courts. Most towns have their own municipal courts, which hold trials. Each county also has a county court.

Chapter 4

THE INDUSTRIES OF NEW JERSEY

Service industries provide the major part of New Jersey's economy. However, other industries, including manufacturing, the military, tourism, agriculture, and fishing, are also important parts of the job sector in the state.

Service

The service industry makes up the largest part of New Jersey's economy. About 66 percent of the state's workers are employed in this industry, providing important services. These workers include government employees, doctors, nurses, teachers, bankers, salespeople, telecommunications specialists, and computer programmers. Prudential, one of the nation's major insurance and financial companies, is headquartered in New Jersey. The state also has several major medical centers, including the Robert Wood Johnson University Hospital and the Hackensack University Medical Center.

Tourism is an important part of New Jersey's service industry. Its beaches are a top tourist attraction. New Jersey also has large amusement parks, such as Six Flags Great Adventure, as well as several ski areas in the northern part of the state. Atlantic City is one of the nation's premier gambling centers. These tourist centers,

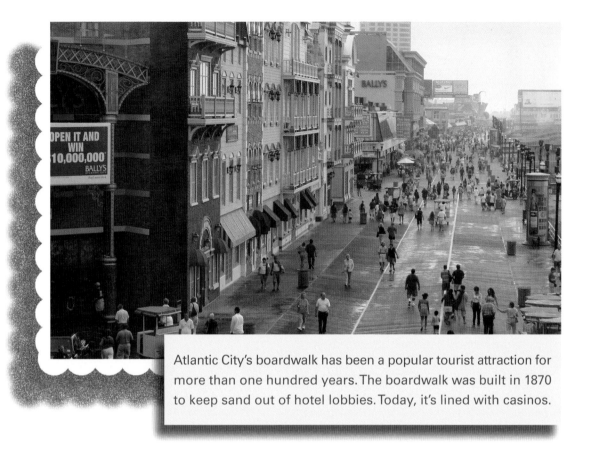

Atlantic City's boardwalk has been a popular tourist attraction for more than one hundred years. The boardwalk was built in 1870 to keep sand out of hotel lobbies. Today, it's lined with casinos.

along with other attractions around the state, provide jobs for many workers. Tourists bring business to hotels, restaurants, state parks, casinos, retail stores, and other businesses in the state.

Manufacturing

Manufacturing is the second largest industry in New Jersey. The state produces a variety of products, including medicine, chemicals, food items, machinery, electronics, and printed materials. New Jersey leads the United States in manufacturing petrochemicals, plastics, and pharmaceutical and personal health care products. Its

New Jersey in Motion Pictures

New Jersey was the center of the film industry long before Hollywood began producing movies. In the early 1900s, the movie industry was primarily located in Fort Lee, New Jersey. At that time, all movies were silent, and most featured romance and adventure. Many of the silent movie stars of the day, including Lillian Gish, Douglas Fairbanks, and Mary Pickford, lived in the Fort Lee area.

One of the most popular movie serials was *The Perils of Pauline*. These action movies, which appeared in installments, featured a heroine who was always in terrible danger at the end of every episode. Often, poor Pauline was left dangling off a high cliff. These scenes were filmed along the cliffs of the Palisades and created a new word—"cliffhanger"—to describe a story that ended suddenly, with the hero or heroine in great danger.

Fort Lee's days in the spotlight did not last long. In 1910, director D. W. Griffith filmed the first movie in Hollywood. Directors and performers came to prefer California to New Jersey because California had warm weather all year long, which made it easier to film there. By 1925, all major film production companies had left New Jersey.

Although it is no longer the center of the industry, New Jersey continues to have a place in movie-making today. Because of its location near New York City, such films as *School of Rock* (2003) and *War of the Worlds* (2005), have been filmed in the state.

New Jersey's Palisades are named after the wooden walls around medieval castles.

factories also make products like glassware and cans used in food packaging. One of the state's tastiest products is M&M's candy. The Mars Company, which makes M&M's and many candy bars, is headquartered in Hackettstown.

New Jersey's manufacturing industry includes laboratories and companies that specialize in research and development of new products. Several scientific and pharmaceutical companies have their headquarters in New Jersey, including Bell Laboratories, Johnson & Johnson, and Merck.

Military

New Jersey is home to several important military bases. These include McGuire Air Force Base, Fort Dix, and the Naval Air Engineering Station in Lakehurst. More than forty-three thousand people, both military personnel and other government workers, have jobs on these military bases. In addition, the U.S. Coast Guard trains its men and women at a center in the seaside town of Cape May.

Fishing

New Jersey's location along the Atlantic Ocean provides the state with a small but vital fishing industry. Clams are the top maritime product. Two-thirds of all clams harvested in the United States come from New Jersey's waters. The state is also an important producer of oysters, which are harvested along the Atlantic Ocean and Delaware Bay. Squid, blue crabs, and lobsters are harvested offshore as well, while the ocean provides larger fish, such as tuna, flounder, and swordfish.

Agriculture

New Jersey's cranberry bogs produce millions of pounds of this sour fruit every year.

Even though New Jersey is called the Garden State, only about 1 percent of its industry is agriculture. However, this small industry produces many tasty foods. New Jersey farmers grow flowers, vegetables like corn, eggplant, bell peppers, and tomatoes, and nursery plants. The state also produces a variety of fruits, including cranberries, blueberries, plums, peaches, apples, melons, and pears. New Jersey also has farms that produce dairy products and eggs.

Mining

At one time, the mining of iron and zinc was a very important industry in New Jersey, especially in the northwestern part of the state. Although its iron and zinc mines were closed many years ago, New Jersey still has several sand and gravel beds that supply materials for the construction industry. In addition, mines in central New Jersey provide materials used in fertilizers, while the northwestern part of the state has several granite quarries.

Chapter 5

PEOPLE FROM NEW JERSEY: PAST AND PRESENT

From musicians to astronauts, athletes to scientists, New Jersey has been the birthplace or home of many famous Americans. Here are just a few of the talented people who have called New Jersey home.

Buzz Aldrin (1930–) Edwin "Buzz" Aldrin was born in Cedarville and later lived in Montclair. An astronaut on the historic Apollo 11 mission, he was the second person to walk on the moon on July 20, 1969. Aldrin recently celebrated the fortieth anniversary of his moonwalk and published a book about his life, *Magnificent Desolation: The Long Journey Home from the Moon.*

William "Count" Basie (1904–1984) Count Basie was born in Red Bank in 1904 and began playing piano and drums as a child. He became one of the most famous jazz and swing musicians of all time. He continued to lead his orchestra almost until his death in 1984. The Count Basie Theater in Red Bank was named in his honor.

Judy Blume (1938–) Author Judy Blume was born and grew up in Elizabeth. After she started a family, she began writing humorous novels about ordinary children dealing with the problems of growing up. Many of her books are set in the New Jersey suburbs, including the classic novel *Are You There God? It's Me, Margaret.*

Buzz Aldrin followed crewmate Neil Armstrong to become the second man to walk on the moon on July 20, 1969.

Jon Bon Jovi (1962–) The future rock star was born John Francis Bongiovi Jr. in Perth Amboy. Bon Jovi grew up in New Jersey and started playing in clubs when he was sixteen. He and his band, also called Bon Jovi, released their first album in 1984 and became one of rock music's most popular acts. Along with performing such classic songs as "Livin' on a Prayer," "Bad Medicine," and "I'll Be There for You," Bon Jovi has appeared in several movies and is active in charity work. He lives in New Jersey and Manhattan with his wife and four children.

Mary Higgins Clark (1927–) Born in the Bronx, New York, Mary Higgins Clark moved to New Jersey as an adult and raised a family there. Her first suspense novel, *Where Are the Children?*, was published in 1975. Clark continued writing books and had more than eighty million copies of her novels in print by 2007. She lives in Saddle River.

Grover Cleveland (1837–1908)

Born in 1837 in Caldwell, Grover Cleveland is the only native New Jerseyan ever elected U.S. president. He was the only president to serve two non-consecutive terms, starting in 1884 and 1892. In addition, Cleveland is the only president who married in the White House.

Stephen Crane (1871–1900)

Born in 1871 in Newark, Stephen Crane became a well-known poet and novelist. He started his career as a newspaper reporter but is best known for his classic novel about the Civil War, *The Red Badge of Courage*.

Albert Einstein's equations revolutionized physics. He was a professor at Princeton University.

Tom Cruise (1962–) Actor

Tom Cruise was born in Syracuse, New York. He settled in Glen Ridge, New Jersey, during his teens and attended that town's high school. Cruise starred in the classic 1983 film *Risky Business* and went on to become a huge Hollywood star. He is especially known for his *Mission Impossible* action films.

Albert Einstein (1879–1955) Born in Germany in 1879,

Albert Einstein revolutionized the world of science when he

New Jersey's Inventors

Many inventors have lived and worked in New Jersey. For one hundred years or more, individual people created most inventions. Samuel Morse and Alfred Vail perfected the telegraph in Morristown in 1838, working on the estate of Morse's father. Robert Johnson and George Seabury invented the first adhesive bandage in 1870. John Holland invented the first practical submarine in 1878. The submarine ran on gasoline above the water and electricity under the water.

New Jersey's most famous inventor is undoubtedly Thomas Edison. Although he was born in Ohio, Edison did most of his work in his laboratories in West Orange and Menlo Park. He patented more than one thousand inventions during his lifetime. Some of his most noteworthy creations were the phonograph in 1877 and the incandescent lightbulb in 1879. Edison also invented the first electric power plant so that homes and businesses could receive electric current.

In the 1900s, New Jersey continued to be an important invention center. Yet fewer inventions were credited to individuals. Instead, corporations patented most of them. In 1948, New Jersey's Bell Laboratories invented the transistor, which allowed radios and other electronic equipment to be made much smaller. Bell Labs was also responsible for the first telecommunications satellite, invented in 1962. Color television was developed in New Jersey, too, thanks to RCA and Princeton Labs in 1953.

Today, New Jersey's large companies and labs have teams of employees to invent, develop, test, and market their products. It takes a lot of money to produce a new drug or technology. It's rare that one person has the finances to develop a new product on his or her own. Even if one person is responsible for a new idea, he or she often sells the rights to a corporation to develop and market it. With the support of their companies, today's innovative New Jerseyans are developing new products in high-speed communications, computer technology, energy, agriculture, disease detection, and more. The state's pharmaceutical companies, such as Merck & Co. and Bristol-Myers Squibb, develop new medicines every year. In New Jersey, as in the rest of the world, inventions have become big business.

published his theory of relativity in 1905. Einstein, who was Jewish, fled Germany in 1933 when the Nazis were rising to power. He came to settle in Princeton, where he lived and worked until his death in 1955.

Anne Hathaway (1982–) One of today's most popular actresses, Anne Hathaway was born in Brooklyn, New York, but grew up in Millburn, New Jersey. She began acting in high school and made her first professional appearances at Millburn's acclaimed Paper Mill Playhouse. Audiences discovered Hathaway when she starred in the Disney films *The Princess Diaries* and *Ella Enchanted*. She went on to play adult roles in such movies as *Brokeback Mountain*, *The Devil Wears Prada*, and *Rachel Getting Married*, for which she was nominated for an Academy Award.

Lauryn Hill (1975–) Lauryn Hill was born in South Orange in 1975, and she still lives in New Jersey. The award-winning singer and producer worked with the band the Fugees, which also included another South Orange resident, Wyclef Jean. She has also performed as a solo hip-hop artist, winning five Grammy Awards for her album *The Miseducation of Lauryn Hill*.

Jonas Brothers Kevin (1987–), Joe (1989–), and Nick Jonas (1992–) grew up in Wyckoff. Nick began performing on Broadway as a child and later teamed up with Kevin and Joe to form the hugely popular band the Jonas Brothers. The brothers have played to sold-out audiences all over the world and regularly appear on the Disney Channel.

Jonathan Stuart Leibowitz (1962–) Better known by his professional name, Jon Stewart, this comedian was born in New York City in 1962 but grew up and attended high school in Lawrenceville. After a few years playing comedy clubs in the New York area, Stewart rose to national fame as host of *The Daily Show*, which blends humor with top news stories and politics. Stewart has also hosted the Academy Awards and written several best-selling books.

After her start as a rap singer, Queen Latifah is now also a popular actress and commercial spokesperson.

Thomas Nast (1840–1902)
Thomas Nast was born in Germany in 1840. Working for New York newspapers, he became one of the most influential political cartoonists of the late nineteenth century. He is credited with creating the image of Santa Claus that we recognize today. Nast lived in Morristown until his death in 1902.

Dana Owens (1970–) Dana Owens, whose stage name is Queen Latifah, was born in Newark and grew up in Irvington and Wayne. She became one of the first female rap stars, projecting the image of a powerful, confident woman. She later starred in several major motion pictures, including the musical *Chicago*.

Duane Charles "Bill" Parcells (1941–) Born in Englewood, Parcells is one of professional football's most influential coaches. Parcells coached the New York Giants from 1983 to 1991 and the New York Jets from 1997 to 1999. (Both teams play in New Jersey.) Parcells led the Giants to two Super Bowl victories and the New England Patriots to one Super Bowl win. He has also worked with the Dallas Cowboys and the Miami Dolphins.

Rocker Bruce Springsteen used his experiences growing up on the Jersey shore to influence his music.

Frank Sinatra (1915–1998)

Frank Sinatra was born in Hoboken in 1915. He became one of the most popular singers in U.S. history. He also appeared in several major movies and won an Academy Award for his portrayal of a soldier in the classic 1953 film *From Here to Eternity*. Sinatra's musical career lasted from the 1940s into the 1990s.

Bruce Springsteen (1949–) Bruce Springsteen is a New Jersey native who became a major figure in rock-and-roll music. He was born in Freehold in 1949 and lived in New Jersey for most of his life. Springsteen's musical career began in nightclubs in the shore town of Asbury Park, and much of his music reflects his working-class, New Jersey background.

John Travolta (1954–) John Travolta was born in Englewood in 1954 and grew up in this New York City suburb. He first became popular for his role on the 1970s TV series *Welcome Back, Kotter* and went on to star in many popular movies, including *Saturday Night Fever* in 1977. More recently, Travolta appeared in *Hairspray* and *The Taking of Pelham 1 2 3*. He also voiced the character Bolt in the 2008 animated movie of the same name.

Timeline

10,000 BCE   The first Native Americans arrive in New Jersey.

1524   Giovanni da Verrazano becomes the first European to explore the New Jersey coast.

1609   Henry Hudson explores the Hudson River and the area around Sandy Hook.

1618   Dutch settlers set up a trading post in Bergen, the first permanent European settlement in New Jersey.

1664   Great Britain takes control of New Jersey.

1665   Lord John Berkeley and Sir George Carteret split New Jersey into East Jersey and West Jersey.

1702   East Jersey and West Jersey are united as one colony.

1776   General George Washington crosses the Delaware River on December 25 and surprises and defeats Hessian soldiers guarding Trenton.

1778   British and colonial armies fight the Battle of Monmouth.

1787   New Jersey becomes the third state to ratify the U.S. Constitution.

1790   Trenton becomes New Jersey's capital.

1858   The first dinosaur skeleton found in North America is discovered in Haddonfield.

1879   Thomas Edison invents the lightbulb in his Menlo Park laboratory.

1884   New Jersey native Grover Cleveland is elected U.S. president.

1912   Woodrow Wilson is elected president of the United States.

1947   New Jersey adopts its present constitution.

1967   Riots in Newark kill twenty-six people and cause more than $10 million in damage.

1976   Casino gambling is legalized in Atlantic City.

1999   Hurricane Floyd causes major flooding throughout the state.

2007   New Jersey lawmakers repeal the death penalty in the state.

State motto	"Liberty and Prosperity"
State capital	Trenton
State flower	Common violet
State bird	Eastern goldfinch
State animal	Horse
State insect	Honeybee
State dinosaur	*Hadrosaurus foulkii*
State tree	Red oak
State fruit	Blueberry
State shell	Knobbed whelk
State folk dance	Square dance
Statehood date and number	December 18, 1787; third state
State nickname	Garden State
Total area and U.S. rank	8,204 square miles (21,248 sq km); forty-seventh largest state
Population	8,414,350 (2000 census)

State Flag

State Seal

Length of coastline	127 miles (204 km) on the Atlantic Ocean
Highest elevation	High Point at Kittatinny Mountain, 1,803 ft (550 m)
Lowest elevation	Sea level at the Atlantic Ocean
Major rivers	Delaware River, Hudson River, Passaic River, Raritan River, Ramapo River, Hackensack River
Major lakes	Lake Mohawk, Lake Hopatcong, Budd Lake, Greenwood Lake
Hottest temperature recorded	110 degrees Fahrenheit (43 degrees Celsius) at Runyon, on July 10, 1936
Coldest temperature recorded	-34°F (-37°C) at River Vale, on January 4, 1904
Origin of state name	Named after the British Isle of Jersey
Chief agricultural products	Nursery plants and flowers, blueberries, peaches, cranberries, bell peppers, tomatoes, dairy, poultry and eggs
Major industries	Science and technology, manufacturing, communications, pharmaceuticals, financial services, tourism, transportation

Eastern goldfinch

Common violet

agriculture The practice of farming.

casino An establishment where people go to gamble.

colony A distant territory that is owned by a parent nation.

constitution Basic laws that establish and run a government and that guarantee certain rights to the citizens of that government.

ethnic Related to a group of people sharing a common and distinctive culture, religion, language, or national identity.

executive The branch of government that runs public affairs and carries out the laws.

federal Having to do with the national government.

fertile Capable of growing plants.

gorge A deep valley with steep, rocky sides.

immigrant A person who leaves one country to live in another country.

judicial Having to do with judges and courts.

legislature A group of people who have the power to make laws.

locomotive A vehicle that runs along railway tracks and is powered by steam, diesel fuel, or electricity.

militia A form of military that consists of citizens who can serve in case of an emergency.

missile A weapon that can be projected to strike a distant target.

native Belonging to a place by birth.

patent A legal document stating that one has exclusive rights to manufacture and sell an invention.

petrochemical A chemical that is derived from petroleum or natural gas; examples are gasoline and kerosene.

pharmaceutical Having to do with drugs that are used for medical reasons.

populous Having a large number of people occupying a region.

settler A person who comes to live in an area.

territory A geographic area belonging to a government.

FOR MORE INFORMATION

Advocates for New Jersey History
William Trent House
15 Market Street
Trenton, NJ 08611
Web site: http://njhistoryadvocates.org
This organization works to increase public awareness of historical events and sites all over New Jersey.

New Jersey Historical Society
52 Park Place
Newark, NJ 07102
(973) 596-8500
Web site: http://www.jerseyhistory.org
The New Jersey Historical Society produces many exhibits and programs, and its Web site contains articles and photos about important events and people in the state.

New Jersey State House
125 West State Street
Trenton, NJ 08625
(609) 777-2719
Web site: http://www.njleg.state.nj.us/legislativepub/visitingstatehouse.asp
The New Jersey State House is the home of New Jersey's government and provides many interesting facts about the legislature and its importance.

New Jersey State Museum
205 West State Street
Trenton, NJ 08608-1001
(609) 292-6464
Web site: http://www.state.nj.us/state/museum/index.htm
Located in the capital city of Trenton, this museum houses collections in archaeology and ethnology, natural history, cultural history, and fine art. Highlights include Native American artifacts and exhibits on colonial and Revolutionary War history.

Preservation New Jersey

30 South Warren Street

Trenton, NJ 08608

(609) 392-6409

Web site: http://www.preservationnj.org

This nonprofit organization is dedicated to the preservation of New Jersey's historic resources, communities, and landscapes.

Washington Crossing State Park

355 Washington Crossing-Pennington Road

Titusville, NJ 08560-1517

(609) 737-0623

Web site: http://www.state.nj.us/dep/parksandforests/parks/washcros.html

Exhibits in the visitor center explore the Revolutionary War with an emphasis on the military campaign known as the "Ten Crucial Days." The events of these ten days, December 25, 1776, through January 3, 1777, include George Washington's crossing of the Delaware River and the battles of Trenton and Princeton. The Web site provides a virtual tour of the park.

Waterloo Village, Allamuchy Mountain State Park

Waterloo Road

Stanhope, NJ

Web site: http://www.state.nj.us/dep/parksandforests/parks/allamuch.html

Waterloo Village is a restored nineteenth-century village along the banks of the Morris Canal. It has a number of historic buildings, including barns, meeting houses, sawmills, gristmills, and homes. A re-created Lenape settlement is located on an island at one end of the village. The village is currently undergoing capital improvements, but it is expected to reopen to the public when the projects are complete.

Web Sites

Due to the changing nature of Internet links, Rosen Publishing has developed an online list of Web sites related to the subject of this book. This site is updated regularly. Please use this link to access this list:

http://www.rosenlinks.com/uspp/njpp

Adkins, Jan. *Thomas Edison*. New York, NY: DK Publishing, 2009.

Blume, Judy. *Are You There God? It's Me, Margaret*. New York, NY: Atheneum/Richard Jackson Books, 2001.

Cameron, Eileen. *G Is for Garden State: A New Jersey Alphabet*. Chelsea, MI: Sleeping Bear Press, 2004.

Dalton, Anne. *The Lenape of Pennsylvania, New Jersey, Delaware, Wisconsin, and Ontario*. New York, NY: PowerKids Press, 2005.

Dixon, Franklin W. *Boardwalk Bust* (Hardy Boys: Undercover Brothers). New York, NY: Aladdin Paperbacks, 2005.

Doak, Robin. *New Jersey: 1609–1776* (Voices from Colonial America). Washington, DC: National Geographic, 2005.

Doherty, Craig A., and Katherine M. Doherty. *New Jersey* (The Thirteen Colonies). New York, NY: Facts on File, 2005.

Dubois, Muriel L. *The New Jersey Colony*. Mankato, MN: Capstone Press, 2006.

Fairbanks, Randy. *The Weird Club: The Search for the Jersey Devil*. New York, NY: Sterling, 2007.

Holme, Jennifer L. *Penny from Heaven*. New York, NY: Yearling, 2007.

Kent, Deborah. *New Jersey* (America the Beautiful. Third Series). New York, NY: Scholastic, 2008.

Moragne, Wendy, and Tamra B. Orr. *New Jersey* (Celebrate the States). New York, NY: Marshall Cavendish, 2009.

Orr, Tamra B. *A Primary Source History of the Colony of New Jersey* (Primary Sources of the Thirteen Colonies and the Lost Colony). New York, NY: Rosen Publishing Group, Inc., 2006.

Redmond, Shirley-Raye. *The Jersey Devil*. Detroit, MI: Kidhaven Press, 2009.

Rumsch, Breann. *Grover Cleveland* (United States Presidents). Edina, MI: ABDO Publishing, 2009.

Scholl, Elizabeth J. *New Jersey* (From Sea to Shining Sea). Brookfield, CT: Children's Press, 2008.

Schumacher, Julie. *The Book of One Hundred Truths*. New York, NY: Delacorte Press, 2006.

Sterngass, Jon, and Matthew Kachur. *New Jersey* (Discover Life in the Thirteen Colonies). New York, NY: Children's Press, 2004.

Bender, Donald E. "Nike Missile Sites in New Jersey." 1999. Retrieved May 12, 2009 (http://alpha.fdu.edu/~bender/NYmsg.html).

Dirks, Tim. "The Perils of Pauline (1914)." Filmsite.org, 2009. Retrieved May 20, 2009 (http://www.filmsite.org/peri.html).

Ditmire, Susan. "Native People of New Jersey." June 6, 2000. Retrieved August 3, 2009 (http://www.usgennet.org/usa/nj/state/Lenape.htm).

Famous New Jerseyans. "Home page." Retrieved May 22, 2009 (http://www.famousnewjerseyans.com/index.html).

Fort Lee Film Commission. "Work of the Commission." FortLeeFilm.org, 2009. Retrieved May 15, 2009 (http://www.fortleefilm.org/work.html).

Hangout NJ: The Next Generation. "NJ Governors: The History of the Governorship." NJ.gov, 2009. Retrieved May 15, 2009 (http://www.nj.gov/hangout_nj/government_governors.html).

Magoun, Alexander B. *David Sarnoff Research Center: RCA Labs to Sarnoff Corporation.* Mount Pleasant, SC: Arcadia Publishing, 2003.

Moran, Mark. *Weird NJ: Your Travel Guide to New Jersey's Local Legends and Best Kept Secrets.* New York, NY: Sterling, 2006.

New Jersey's Great Northwest Skylands. "Mines, Metal and Men." NJSkylands.com, 2009. Retrieved May 15, 2009 (http://www.njskylands.com/hsmines.htm).

NJDEP Division of Fish and Wildlife. "Wildlife Populations: White-Tailed Deer." NJ.gov, 2009. Retrieved May 10, 2009 (http://www.nj.gov/dep/dsr/trends2005/pdfs/wildlife-whitetail.pdf).

Read, Phillip M. *Paterson.* Mount Pleasant, SC: Arcadia Publishing, 2003.

Shea, Martha Esposito, and Mike Mathis. *Campbell Soup Company.* Mount Pleasant, SC: Arcadia Publishing, 2002.

INDEX

About the Author

Joanne Mattern lives in New York State, less than a mile from the New Jersey border, and she visits the state daily. Mattern has traveled extensively throughout New Jersey and has visited many of its attractions and sites of natural beauty. She enjoys history, nature, travel, and discovering new places and interesting stories. She has written more than two hundred nonfiction books for children and works in her local library. Mattern also enjoys spending time with her husband, four children, and a menagerie of pets.

Photo Credits

Cover (top left) Library of Congress Prints and Photographs Division; cover (top right), pp. 3, 6, 13, 21, 22, 26, 27, 30, 31, 39, 41 (left) Wikipedia; cover (bottom) William Thomas Cain/Getty Images; p. 4 © GeoAtlas; p. 7 © Richard Cummins/SuperStock; p. 9 © www.istockphoto.com/Richard Mirro; p. 10 © Arthur Morris/Visuals Unlimited, Inc.; p. 12 © www.istockphoto.com/John Mroz; pp. 14, 17 The New York Public Library/Art Resource, NY; p. 16 © The Metropolitan Museum of Art/Art Resource, NY; p. 20 Bernie Nunez/Getty Images; pp. 23, 25 © AP Images; p. 28 © Tony Linck/SuperStock; p. 32 NASA; p. 33 AFP/Getty Images; p. 36 Peter Kramer/Getty Images; p. 37 Richard McCaffrey/Michael Ochs Archive/Getty Images; p. 40 (left) Courtesy of Robesus, Inc.; p. 41 (right) © www.istockphoto.com/Constance McGuire.

Designer: Les Kanturek; Editor: Andrea Sclarow;
Photo Researcher: Amy Feinberg

Compensation

Twelfth Edition

Jerry M. Newman
State University of New York–Buffalo

Barry Gerhart
University of Wisconsin–Madison

George T. Milkovich
Cornell University

Mc
Graw
Hill
Education

COMPENSATION, TWELFTH EDITION

Published by McGraw-Hill Education, 2 Penn Plaza, New York, NY 10121. Copyright © 2017 by McGraw-Hill Education. All rights reserved. Printed in Singapore. Previous editions © 2014, 2011, and 2008. No part of this publication may be reproduced or distributed in any form or by any means, or stored in a database or retrieval system, without the prior written consent of McGraw-Hill Education, including, but not limited to, in any network or other electronic storage or transmission, or broadcast for distance learning.

Some ancillaries, including electronic and print components, may not be available to customers outside the United States.

This book is printed on acid-free paper.

6 7 8 9 MPM 21 20 19

ISBN   978-1-259-53272-6
MHID   1-259-53272-0

Senior Vice President, Products & Markets: *Kurt L. Strand*
Managing Director: *Susan Gouijnstook*
Vice President, Content Production & Technology Services: *Kimberly Meriwether David*
Director: *Michael Ablassmeir*
Brand Managers: *Anke Weekes/Laura Hurst Spell*
Product Developer: *Laura Hurst Spell*
Digital Product Analyst: *Sankha Basu*
Executive Program Manager: *Faye M. Herrig*
Content Project Manager: *Mary Jane Lampe*
Content Project Managers (Assessment): *Evan Roberts/Keri Johnson*
Buyer: *Jennifer Pickel*
Content Licensing Specialists: *Lori Slattery/Deanna Dausener*
Cover Designer: *Studio Montage*
Compositor: *MPS Limited*
Typeface: *10/12 Times Lt Std*
Printer: *Markono Print Media Pte Ltd*

All credits appearing on page or at the end of the book are considered to be an extension of the copyright page.

Library of Congress Cataloging-in-Publication Data
Milkovich, George T., | Newman, Jerry M., | Gerhart, Barry A., author.
     Compensation / George T. Milkovich, Cornell University, Jerry M. Newman, State University of New
     York/Buffalo, Barry Gerhart, University of Wisconsin/Madison.
     Twelfth ed. | New York, NY: McGraw-Hill Education, [2017]
     LCCN 2015041046 | ISBN 9781259532726 (alk. paper)
     LCSH: Compensation management.
     LCC HF5549.5.C67 M54 2017 | DDC 658.3/2—dc23
     LC record available at http://lccn.loc.gov/2015041046

The Internet addresses listed in the text were accurate at the time of publication. The inclusion of a website does not indicate an endorsement by the authors or McGraw-Hill Education, and McGraw-Hill Education does not guarantee the accuracy of the information presented at these sites.

www.mhhe.com

Table of Contents

About the Authors

JERRY M. NEWMAN

Dr. Jerry Newman is a SUNY Distinguished Professor at State University of New York–Buffalo. His interests are in the area of human resource management, with particular emphasis on compensation and rewards. He is author of the book *My Secret Life on the McJob: Lessons in Leadership Guaranteed to Supersize Any Management Style* (McGraw-Hill, 2007). This book was selected as one of the twelve "Best of 2007" by *The Wall Street Journal*. Newman is also coauthor with George Milkovich of earlier editions of *Compensation,* a best-in-class-book for McGraw-Hill since 1984. His article, "Compensation Lessons from the Fast Food Trenches" (*WorldatWork, March 2007*, pp. 22–27), was chosen as SNAPS National feature article winner in 2008. He is also author of approximately 100 articles on compensation and rewards, performance management, and other HR issues. In more than 30 years of consulting, Jerry has worked with such companies as Cummins Engine, AT&T, Graphic Controls, Hewlett-Packard, RJR Nabisco, Sorrento Cheese, McDonalds, and A & W Root Beer. Dr. Newman is a recipient of nine teaching awards, including the SUNY Chancellor's Award for Excellence in teaching. He loves to work with students, so send him an e-mail sometime!

BARRY GERHART

Barry Gerhart is the Bruce R. Ellig Distinguished Chair in Pay and Organizational Effectiveness, School of Business, University of Wisconsin–Madison. Professor Gerhart received his B.S. in Psychology from Bowling Green State University and his Ph.D. in Industrial Relations from the University of Wisconsin–Madison. He serves on the editorial boards of the *Academy of Management Journal, Industrial and Labor Relations Review, International Journal of Human Resource Management, Journal of Applied Psychology, Journal of World Business, Management and Organization Review, Management Revue,* and *Personnel Psychology.* Professor Gerhart is a past recipient of the Scholarly Achievement Award, the International Human Resource Management Scholarly Achievement Award (twice), and the Heneman Career Achievement Award, all from the Human Resources Division, Academy of Management. He is also a Fellow of the Academy of Management. Professor Gerhart has served previously as a department chair and/or area coordinator at Cornell, Vanderbilt, and Wisconsin. He has held visiting appointments at Bayreuth University, King's College London, and Copenhagen Business School.

GEORGE T. MILKOVICH

George T. Milkovich is the M. P. Catherwood Emeritus Professor at the Industrial Labor Relations School, Cornell University. For more than 40 years he has studied and written about how people get paid and what difference it makes. Milkovich served on several editorial boards and received many awards for his research contributions. He received the Keystone Award for Lifetime Achievement from the WorldatWork Association and the Distinguished Career Contributions Award from the Academy of Management, and he is a Fellow in both the Academy of Management and the National Academy of Human Resources. He chaired the National Academy of Sciences Committee on Performance and Pay. Milkovich is one of the founders of the Center for Advanced HR Studies, a research and development partnership of leading corporations and Cornell's ILR School. He also advised numerous companies around the world on their compensation strategies, received three outstanding teacher awards, and was a visiting professor at several international universities in Europe and Asia. Milkovich conducted executive seminars in many countries and served on advisory boards of leading academic/research centers in the United States and China.

Preface

A few books can change your life. Our book may not be one of them. However, if you read it, you will better understand that *pay matters*. After all, you can't pick up a newspaper, power up a computer, or read a blog today without someone talking about compensation. The Great Recession had major ramifications for pay. Some folks had their hours cut and/or their pay frozen or reduced. Why? Because it's a way to cut compensation costs (though not necessarily the benefits portion of compensation costs) without laying off workers. Others, of course, were laid off and lost their jobs, income, and benefits. The recession also focused attention on executive compensation. As the government bailed out the financial industry, newspapers were reporting large bonuses going to the very employees who helped cause the financial disaster. With the end of the recession, we saw employers put less emphasis on cutting labor costs and more emphasis on hiring (sometimes even in the United States). However, job growth was initially quite modest. Why? Employers have become increasingly careful about adding new workers because they want to keep costs under control and they don't want to have to reduce the workforce if they guess wrong about increasing product demand (and the need for more workers). But competition for some types of workers has increased and wages, salaries, and benefits have likewise increased for such workers, meaning that employers must continually evaluate and benchmark their pay to be competitive.

Pay also matters around the globe. For example, if you are a Russian cosmonaut, you can earn a bonus of $1,000 for every space walk you take (technically known as "extravehicular activity," or EVA), up to three per space trip. A contract listing specific tasks to be done on a space mission permits you to earn up to $30,000 above the $20,000 you earn while you are on the ground. (In contrast to the Russian cosmonauts, wealthy Americans are lining up to pay $15 million [plus an additional $20 million airfare] to the Russian Space Agency for their own personal EVA.) Conclusion: *Pay matters.*

If you read this book, you will also better understand that *what you pay for matters.* Many years ago, when Green Giant discovered too many insect parts in the pea packs from one of its plants, it designed a bonus plan that paid people for finding insect parts. Green Giant got what it paid for: insect parts. Innovative Green Giant employees brought insect parts from home to add to the peas just before they removed them and collected the bonus.

The Houston public school district also got what it paid for when it promised teachers bonuses of up to $6,000 if their students' test scores exceeded targets. Unfortunately, several teachers were later fired when it was discovered that they had leaked answers to their students and adjusted test scores.

Such problems are global. A British telephone company paid a cash bonus to operators based on how quickly they completed requests for information. Some operators discovered that the fastest way to complete a request was to give out a wrong number or—even faster—just hang up on the caller. "We're actually looking at a new bonus scheme," says an insightful company spokesperson. Conclusion: *What you pay for matters.*

If you read this book, you will also learn that *how you pay matters.* Motorola trashed its old-fashioned pay system that employees said guaranteed a raise every six months if you were still breathing. The new system paid for learning new skills and working in teams. Sound good? It wasn't. Employees resented those team members who went off for six weeks of training at full pay while remaining team members picked up their work. Motorola was forced to get rid of its new-fashioned system, too.

Microsoft employees were also grumbling. More were leaving; top recruits were going elsewhere. The lackluster performance of Microsoft stock was depressing the value of the eye-popping stock options the company routinely doled out. What to do? Rather than stock options, Microsoft changed its pay system to give employees actual shares of stock with a value that was immediately known. This move increased the value of employees' pay and eliminated the risk they faced from the stock performance. What did Microsoft get? Happier, more expensive people. No word yet on product innovation, customer satisfaction, or even quality of new hires. Conclusion: *How you pay matters.*

We live in interesting times. Anywhere you look on the globe today, economic and social pressures are forcing managers to rethink how people get paid and what difference it makes. Traditional approaches to compensation are being questioned. But what is being achieved by all this experimentation and change? We have lots of fads and fashions, but how much of it is folderol?

In this book, we strive to cull beliefs from facts, wishful thinking from demonstrable results, and opinions from research. Yet when all is said and done, managing compensation is part science, but also part art.

ABOUT THIS BOOK

This book focuses on the strategic choices in managing compensation. We introduce these choices, real-world issues that managers confront from New York to New Zealand and all points between, in the total compensation model in Chapter 1. This model provides an integrating framework that is used throughout the book. Major compensation issues are discussed in the context of current theory, research, and practice. The practices illustrate new developments as well as established approaches to compensation decisions.

Each chapter contains at least one *e-Compensation box* to point you to some of the vast compensation information on the Internet. Real-life *Your Turn* cases ask you to apply the concepts and techniques discussed in each chapter. For example, the Your Turn in Chapter 9 draws on Professor Newman's experience when he worked undercover for 14 months in seven fast-food restaurants. The case takes you into the gritty details of the employees' behaviors (including Professor Newman's) during rush hour, as they desperately work to satisfy the customers' orders and meet their own performance targets set by their manager. You get to recommend which rewards will improve employees' performance (including Professor Newman's) and customers' satisfaction. We tackle major compensation issues from three sides: theory, research, and practice—no problem can survive that onslaught!

The authors also publish *Cases in Compensation,* an integrated casebook designed to provide additional practical skills that apply the material in this book. The casebook is available directly from the authors (e-mail: cases.in.compensation@gmail.com). Completing the integrated case will help you develop skills readily transferable to future jobs and assignments. Instructors are invited to e-mail for more information on how *Cases in Compensation* can help translate compensation research and theory into practice and build competencies for on-the-job decisions.

But *caveat emptor!* "Congress raises the executive minimum wage to $565.15 an hour," reads the headline in the satirical newspaper *The Onion* (www.onion. com, "America's Finest News Source"). The article says that the increase will help executives meet the federal standard-of-easy-living. "Our lifestyles are expensive to maintain," complains one manager. Although the story in *The Onion* may clearly be fiction, sometimes it is more difficult to tell. One manager told us that when she searched for this textbook in her local bookstore, store personnel found the listing in their information system—under fiction!

WHAT'S NEW

All chapters have been revised, in recognition of ongoing changes at organizations and in their competitive environments around the world. Many examples are provided of the current pay strategies or practices used in specific, named companies. Some of these are well established and successful (Apple, IBM, Microsoft, Merrill Lynch, Nucor, Toyota), some face real problems (American Airlines, Best Buy, General Motors), and others are using unique practices (Google, Whole Foods). Whenever possible, we observe how the challenges faced by these companies have evolved over time. This edition continues to emphasize the importance of total compensation and its relevance for achieving sustainable competitive advantage. It reinforces our conviction that beyond *how much* people are paid, *how* they are paid really matters. Managing pay means ensuring that the right people get the right pay for achieving objectives in the right way. Greater emphasis is given to theoretical advances and evidence from research. Throughout the book we translate this evidence into guidance for improving the management of pay.

ACKNOWLEDGMENTS

In addition to our bookstore shopper, many people have contributed to our understanding of compensation and to the preparation of this textbook. We owe a special, continuing debt of gratitude to our students. In the classroom, they motivate and challenge us, and as returning seasoned managers, they try mightily to keep our work relevant:

Kenneth Abosch
Hewitt Associates

Stephanie Argentine
Rich Products

Patrick Beall
Lockheed Martin

Joseph Bruno
Kodak

Karee Buerger
Hewitt Associates

Federico Castellanos
IBM EMEA

Cindy Cohen
Impac

Andrew Doyle
Oppenheimer Fund

Brian Dunn
Maclagan

Bruce Ellig
Author

Thomas Fentner
Health Now

Rich Floersch
McDonald's USA

Beth Florin
Clark Consulting

Richard Frings
Johnson & Johnson

Takashi Fujiwara
Mitsubishi

Yuichi Funada
Toshiba

Ted Grasela
Cognigen

Thomas Gresch
General Motors

Peter Hearl
YUM Brands (emeritus)

Lada Hruba
Bristol Meyers Squibb

Richard Ivey
KFC

Tae-Jin Kim
SK Group

Joe Kreuz
Advantage Professionals

Hiroshi Kurihara
Fuji Xerox

Christian LeBreton
IBM EMEA

Mitch Linnick
IBM

Tony Marchak
IBM EMEA

Masaki Matsuhashi
Toshiba

Randy McDonald
IBM

Nancy McGough
Room & Board

Matt Milkovich
Registry Nursing

Michael Milkovich
Warecorp

Sarah Milkovich
Jet Propulsion Laboratory

Sonja Milkovich
Sled Dog Software

Pat Murtha
Pizza Hut

David Ness
Medtronic

Erinn Newman
American Express

Kelly Newman
Presbyterian Residence

Terrie Newman
HR Foundations

Stephen O'Byrne
Shareholder Value Advisors

Tony Ragusa
Stereo Advantage

Jaime Richardson
GE Healthcare

Lindsay Scott
Lindsay Scott & Associates

Jason Sekanina
Linear Technology

Rich Severa
Accretive Partners & Strategies LLC

Diana Southall
HR Foundations

Cassandra Steffan
Frito-Lay

Masanori Suzuki
Google Japan

Ichiro Takemura
Toshiba

Richard Their
Xerox

Jan Tichy
Merck

Andrew Thompson
Link Group Consultants

Jose Tomas
Burger King

Karen Velkey
Northrop Grumman

Ian Ziskin
Northrop Grumman

Our universities—Cornell, Buffalo, and Wisconsin—provide forums for the interchange of ideas among students, experienced managers, and academic colleagues. We value this interchange. Other academic colleagues also provided helpful comments on this and previous editions of the book. We particularly thank:

Tom Arnold
Westmoreland Community College

Lubica Bajzikova
Comenius University, Bratislava

Stuart Basefsky
Cornell University

Glenda Barrett
University of Maryland
University College

Melissa Barringer
University of Massachusetts

Rebecca Bennett
Louisiana Tech University

Matt Bloom
University of Notre Dame

James T. Brakefield
Western Illinois University

Timothy Brown
San Jose State University

Lisa Burke
University of Tennessee–Chattanooga

Wayne Cascio
University of Colorado–Denver

Dennis Cockrell
Washington State University–Pullman

H. Kristi Davison
University of Mississippi

Lee Dyer
Cornell University

Allen D. Engle Sr.
Eastern Kentucky University

Ingrid Fulmer
Rutgers University

Luis Gomez-Mejia
Arizona State University

Thomas Hall
Penn State University

Kevin Hallock
Cornell University

Robert Heneman
Ohio State University

Vandra Huber
University of Washington

Greg Hundley
Purdue

Debra D. Kuhl
Pensacola State College

Frank Krzystofiak
SUNY–Buffalo

David I. Levine
University of California–Berkeley

Frank B. Markham
University of Mississippi

Janet Marler
SUNY–Albany

Patrenia McAbee
Delaware County Community
College

Atul Mitra
Northern Iowa University

Michael Moore
Michigan State University

Bahaudin Mujtaba
Nova Southeastern University

Teresa S. Nelson
Butler County Community College

Bryan J. Pesta
Cleveland State University

Richard Posthuma
University of Texas at El Paso

Janez Prasnikar
University of Ljubljana

Vlado Pucik
IMD

Hesan Ahmed Quazi
Nanyang Business School

Sara Rynes
University of Iowa

Dow Scott
Loyola University Chicago

Jason Shaw
University of Minnesota

Thomas Stone
Oklahoma State University

Warren Scott Stone
University of Arkansas at Little Rock

Michael Sturman
Cornell University

Ningyu Tang
Shanghai Jiao Tong University

Thomas Li-Ping Tang
Middle Tennessee State University

Tom Timmerman
Tennessee Tech University

Charlie Trevor
University of Wisconsin

Zhong-Ming Wang
Zhejiang University

Yoshio Yanadori
University of British Columbia

Tae Seok Yang
Western Illinois University

Nada Zupan
University of Ljubljana

Introducing the Pay Model and Pay Strategy

Why do we work? If we are fortunate, our work brings meaning to our lives, challenges us in new and exciting ways, brings us recognition, and gives us the opportunity to interact with interesting people and create friendships. Oh yes—we also get a paycheck. Here in Part One of your book, we begin by talking about what we mean by "pay" and how paying people in different ways can influence them and, in turn, influence organization success. Wages and salaries, of course, are part of compensation, but so too, for some employees, are bonuses, health care benefits, stock options, and/or work/life balance programs.

Compensation is one of the most powerful tools organizations have to influence their employees. Managed well, it can play a major role in organizations successfully executing their strategies through their employees. We will see how companies like Whole Foods, Nucor, the SAS Institute, Microsoft, Google, and others use compensation to attract, motivate, and retain the right employees to execute their strategies. We will also see how companies like Apple sell premium products at attractive price points, to an important degree by using suppliers that have low labor costs. Managed less well, as bankruptcies at General Motors, Chrysler, Lehman Brothers, and American Airlines (which stated that it needed to reduce labor costs by $1.25 billion per year to be competitive), for example, might indicate, compensation decisions can also come back to haunt you. In Part One, we describe the compensation policies and techniques that organizations use and the multiple objectives they hope to achieve by effectively managing these compensation decisions.

Although compensation has its guiding principles, we will see that "the devil is in the details" and how any compensation program is specifically designed and implemented will help determine its success. We want you to bring a healthy skepticism when you encounter simplistic or sweeping claims about whether a particular way of managing compensation does or does not work. For example, organizations, in general, benefit from pay for performance, but there are many types of pay for performance programs and it is not always easy to design and implement a program that has the intended consequences (and avoids *unintended* consequences). So, general principles are helpful, but only to a point.

Thus, in Part One, our aim is to also help you understand how compensation strategy decisions interact with the specific context of an organization (e.g., its business and human resource strategies) to influence organization success. We emphasize that good theory and research are fundamental to not only understanding compensation's likely effects, but also to developing that healthy skepticism we want you to have toward simplistic claims about what works and what does not.

The Pay Model

COMPENSATION: DOES IT MATTER? (OR, "SO WHAT?")

Why should you care about compensation? Do you find that life goes more smoothly when there is at least as much money coming in as going out? (Refer, for example, to the lyrics for the Beatles' song "Money.")[1] They say something like: it's true money doesn't buy everything, but if money can't buy it, I can't use it. OK, maybe something of an exaggeration, but.... Yes? Well, of course, it is the same for companies. It really does help to have as much money coming in (actually, more is better) as going out. Until recently, workers at Chrysler got total compensation (i.e., wages plus benefits) of about $76 per hour, whereas U.S. workers at Toyota received $48 per hour and the average total compensation per hour in U.S. manufacturing was $25 (and $16 in Korea, $3 in Mexico). It is one thing to pay more than your competitors if you get something more (e.g., higher productivity and/or quality) in return. But, Chrysler was not. So, the "strategy" was not sustainable. It ended up going through bankruptcy, being bought out by Fiat, and then reducing worker compensation costs as part of its strategy for return to competitiveness. Specifically, Chrysler took steps (as part of its bankruptcy plan) to bring its hourly labor costs down to about $49 more recently.[2]

General Motors (GM), like Chrysler, has, for decades, paid its workers well—too well perhaps for what it received in return. So what? Well, in 1970, GM had 150 U.S. plants and 395,000 hourly workers. In sharp contrast, GM now has 40 U.S. manufacturing plants and 51,000 U.S. hourly workers.[3] In June 2009, GM, like Chrysler, had to file for bankruptcy (avoiding it for a while thanks to loans from the U.S. government—i.e., you, the taxpayer). Not all of GM's problems were compensation related. Of course, building too many vehicles that consumers did not want was also a problem. But, having labor costs higher than the competition, without corresponding advantages in efficiency, quality, and customer service, does not seem to have served GM or its stakeholders well. Its stock price peaked at $93.62/share in April 2000. Its market value was about $60 billion in 2000. That shareholder wealth was wiped out in bankruptcy. Think of the billions of dollars the U.S. taxpayer had to put into GM. Think of all the jobs that have been lost over the years and the effects on communities that have lost those jobs.

On the other hand, Nucor Steel pays its workers very well relative to what other companies inside and outside of the steel industry pay. But Nucor also has much higher productivity than is typical in the steel industry. The result: Both the company and its workers do well. Apple Computer is able to keep prices for its iPad and iPhone lower than otherwise by outsourcing manufacturing to China in facilities owned by the Hon Hai Precision Industry Co., Ltd (Foxconn), a Taiwanese company. (See Chapter 7.) As we will see later, doing so generates billions (yes, billions with a "b") of dollars in cost savings per year. Google and Facebook are companies that are known for paying very well. So far, that seems to have worked in that their high pay allows them to be very selective in who they hire and who they keep and they would say that their talent rich strategy has helped them to foster growth and innovation.

Wall Street financial services firms and banks used **incentive** plans that rewarded people for developing "innovative" new financial investment vehicles and for taking risks to earn themselves and their firms a lot of money.[4] That is what happened—until several years ago. Then, the markets discovered that many such risks had gone bad. Blue Chip firms such as Lehman Brothers slid quickly into bankruptcy, whereas others like Bear Stearns and Merrill Lynch survived to varying degrees by finding other firms (J.P. Morgan and Bank of America, respectively) to buy them. The issue has not gone away. Recently, U.S. Federal Reserve officials have "made it clear that they believe bad behavior at banks goes deeper than a few bad apples and are advising firms to track warning signs of excessive risk taking and other cultural breakdowns." In the words of one Fed official, "Risk takers are drawn to finance like they are to Formula One racing." An important driver of risk taking among traders and others is the incentive system that encourages them to be "confident and aggressive" and that often results in those who thrive under this incentive rising to top leadership positions at the banks.[5]

Does greater expertise in the design and execution of compensation plans play a role in controlling excessive risk taking and other problematic behaviors and encouraging a more positive culture? Congress and the president seemed to think so, because in hopes of avoiding a similar financial crisis in the future they put into place legislation, the Troubled Asset Relief Program (TARP), which included restrictions on executive pay designed to discourage executives from taking "unnecessary and excessive risks." Another commentator agreed. In an opinion piece in *The Wall Street Journal,* entitled "How Business Schools Have Failed Business," the former director of corporate finance policy at the United States Treasury argued that misaligned incentives were a major cause of the global financial crisis (see above) and he wondered how many of the business schools that educated top executives and directors included a course on how to design compensation systems. His answer: not many. Our book, we hope, can play a role in helping to better educate you, the reader, about the design of compensation systems, both for managers and for workers.

How people are paid affects their behaviors at work, which affect an organization's success.[7] For most employers, compensation is a major part of total cost, and often it is the single largest part of operating cost. These two facts together mean that well-designed compensation systems can help an organization achieve and sustain competitive advantage. On the other hand, as we have recently seen, poorly designed compensation systems can likewise play a major role in undermining organization success.

COMPENSATION: DEFINITION, PLEASE

How people view compensation affects how they behave. It does not mean the same thing to everyone. Your view probably differs, depending on whether you look at compensation from the perspective of a member of society, a stockholder, a manager, or an employee. Thus, we begin by recognizing different perspectives.

Society

Some people see pay as a measure of justice. For example, a comparison of earnings between men and women highlights what many consider inequities in pay decisions. In 2013, among full-time workers in the United States, U.S. Bureau of Labor Statistics data indicate that women earned 82 percent of what men earned, up from 62 percent in 1979.[8] If women had the same education, experience, and union coverage as men and also worked in the same industries and occupations, the ratio would increase, but most evidence suggests that no more than one-half of the gap would disappear. Thus, under even a best case scenario, such adjustments would increase the women/men earnings ratio to as high as about 90 percent, still leaving a sizable gap.[9] Society has taken an interest in such earnings differentials. One indicator of this interest is the introduction of laws and regulation aimed at eliminating the role of discrimination in causing them.[10] (See Chapter 17.)

Benefits given as part of a total compensation package may also be seen as a reflection of equity or justice in society. Employers spend about 44 cents for benefits on top of every dollar paid for **wages** and **salaries**.[11] Individuals and businesses in the United States spend $2.9 trillion per year, or 17.4 percent of its economic output (gross domestic product) on health care.[12] Nevertheless, roughly 41 million people in the United States (14 percent of the population) have no health insurance.[13] (The Affordable Care Act of

2010 is aimed at increasing coverage and one projection is the number of uninsured will decrease to 23 million by 2023.)[14] A major reason is that the great majority of people (who are under the age of 65 and not below the poverty line) obtain health insurance through their employers, but small employers, which account for a substantial share of employment, are much less likely than larger employers to offer health insurance to their employees. As a result, 8 in 10 of the uninsured in the United States are from working families.[15] Given that those who do have insurance typically have it through an employer, it also follows then that as the unemployment rate increases, health care coverage declines further. Some users of online dating services provide information on their employer-provided health care insurance. Dating service "shoppers" say they view health insurance coverage as a sign of how well a prospect is doing in a career.

Job losses (or gains) in a country over time are partly a function of relative labor costs (and productivity) across countries. People in the United States worry about losing manufacturing jobs to Mexico, China, and other nations. (Increasingly, white collar work in areas like finance, computer programming, and legal services is also being sent overseas.) Exhibit 1.1 reveals that the hourly compensation (wages plus benefits) for Mexican manufacturing work ($6.82) are about 19 percent of those paid in the United States ($36.34). China's estimated $3.38 per hour is about 9 percent of the U.S. rate. However, the value of what is produced also needs to be considered. Productivity in China is about 22 percent of that of U.S. workers, whereas Mexican worker productivity is 30 percent of the U.S. level.[16] Finally, if low wages are the goal, there always seems to be somewhere that is lower. Some companies (e.g., Coach) are now moving work from China because its hourly wage, especially after recent increases, is not as low as in countries like Vietnam, India, and the Philippines. However, for other companies such as Foxconn, which builds iPhones and iPads for Apple, even with rapid increases in wages in China, labor costs remain very low in China compared to those in the United States and other advanced economies and Foxconn appears to be poised to continue having a larger presence in China.[17] (We return to the topic of international comparisons in Chapter 7 and Chapter 16.)

EXHIBIT 1.1 Hourly Compensation Costs for Production Workers in Manufacturing and Economy-wide Productivity (Gross Domestic Product, GDP, per Employed Person), in U.S. Dollars

	Hourly Compensation Cost	**Productivity (GDP per employee)**
China	3.38	15,250
Mexico	6.82	20,275
Czech Republic	12.17	26,781
United States	36.34	68,374
Germany	49.98	42,343

Source: Hourly Compensation Cost: The Conference Board. International Comparisons of Hourly Compensation Costs in Manufacturing, 2013. December 2014. Productivity: The World Bank. http://data.worldbank.org/indicator/SL.GDP.PCAP.EM.KD. Extracted February 3, 2015.

Notes: Compensation includes wages and benefits. The most recent Conference Board compensation cost was $3.07 (in 2012) for China. The estimate for China was obtained by inflating the Conference Board estimates based on data from the National Bureau of Statistics of China. Productivity is gross domestic product (GDP), in constant 1990 PPP $, divided by total employment in the economy. Purchasing power parity (PPP) GDP is GDP converted to 1990 constant international dollars using PPP rates. An international dollar has the same purchasing power over GDP that a U.S. dollar has in the United States.

Some consumers know that pay increases often lead to price increases. They do not believe that higher labor costs benefit them. But other consumers lobby for higher wages. While partying revelers were collecting plastic beads at New Orleans' Mardi Gras, filmmakers were showing video clips of the Chinese factory that makes the beads. In the video, the plant manager describes the punishment (5 percent reduction in already low pay) that he metes out to the young workers for workplace infractions. After viewing the video, one reveler complained, "It kinda takes the fun out of it."[18]

Stockholders

Stockholders are also interested in how employees are paid. Some believe that using stock to pay employees creates a sense of ownership that will improve performance, which will, in turn, increase stockholder wealth. But others argue that granting employees too much ownership dilutes stockholder wealth. Google's stock plan cost the company $600 million in its first year of operation. So people who buy Google stock are betting that this $600 million will motivate employees to generate more than $600 million in extra revenue.

Stockholders have a particular interest in executive pay.[19] (Executive pay will be discussed further in Chapter 14.)[20] To the degree that the interests of executives are aligned with those of shareholders (e.g., by paying executives on the basis of company performance measures such as shareholder return), the hope is that company performance will be higher. There is debate, however, about whether executive pay and company performance are strongly linked in the typical U.S. company.[21] In the absence of such a linkage, concerns arise that executives can somehow use their influence to obtain high pay without necessarily performing well. Exhibit 1.2 provides descriptive data on chief executive officer (CEO) compensation. Note the large numbers (total annual compensation of about $10 million to $11 million, depending on whether one uses the median or mean) and also that the bulk of compensation (stock-related) is connected to shareholder return or other performance measures (bonus). As such, one would expect changes in CEO wealth and shareholder wealth to be, generally speaking, aligned. To be sure, there are overpaid executives who earn a lot and produce little

EXHIBIT 1.2

Annual Compensation of Chief Executive Officers, 200 Largest (by revenues) U.S. Public Companies

Compensation Component	Median	Mean
Salary	$ 1,100,000	$ 1,161,343
Bonus	$ 2,139,014	$ 2,866,328
Other	$ 184,674	$ 284,929
Stock granted + (estimated) value of stock options granted	$ 6,198,613	$ 6,754,191
Total Annual Compensation	$10,130,520	$11,066,790

Source: Original data from S&P Capital IQ; USA TODAY research, as reported in Barbara Hansen and Mark Hannan. Millions by millions, CEO pay goes up. USA TODAY, April 4, 2014 http://www.usatoday.com/story/money/business/2014/04/03/2013-ceo-pay/7200481/.

Notes: Based on 200 Standard & Poor's 500 companies that filed proxies with the Securities and Exchange Commission between January 1 and March 27, 2014. Mean (but not median) compensation components sum to equal total annual compensation.

in return for shareholders (or other stakeholders such as employees). However, the assessment of whether an executive is being paid appropriately for performance is not as simple as it may seem:

> Consider the example of Richard Fairbank, the CEO of Capital One, as reported in the annual Wall Street Journal/Mercer CEO Compensation Survey (April 13, 2006). In 2005, Capital One shareholders earned a one-year return of 2.7 percent, and over five years, had earned a return of 5.8 percent. The survey reported that Fairbank received $249.3 million in total direct compensation from Capital One in 2005. This large lump sum, compared with a relatively small shareholder return number, implies a lack of alignment between shareholder return and CEO compensation that was widely reported in the popular press. However, most of the $249.3 million received by Fairbank arose from the exercise of stock options granted to him in 1995 (and that expired in 2005, forcing him to exercise them or lose them). Over that longer time period (1995–2005), shareholder wealth at Capital One increased by $23 billion, for a cumulative shareholder return of 802 percent.[22]

As the example indicates, the answer to how strongly CEO pay and shareholder return are related depends to some degree on how carefully the timing and measurement of performance are addressed. One study, which sought to address this issue found a strong relationship ($\Delta R^2 = .35$, $\Delta R = .59$) over time between total shareholder return and a new, corresponding concept, CEO return (i.e., change in CEO wealth). Exhibit 1.3 shows how CEO wealth changes in response to changes in shareholder wealth.

Although CEO and shareholder interests appear to be significantly aligned on average, there are important exceptions and it is certainly an ongoing challenge to ensure that executives act in the best interest of shareholders. For example, during the meltdown in the financial services industry, top executives at Bear Stearns and Lehman Brothers regularly exercised stock options and sold stock during the 2000 to 2008 period prior to the meltdown. One estimate is that these stock-related gains plus bonus payments generated $1.4 billion for the top five executives at Bear Stearns and $1 billion for those at Lehman Brothers during the 2000–2008 period. "Thus, while the long-term shareholders in their firms were largely decimated, the executives' performance-based compensation kept them in positive territory." The problem here is that shareholders paid a huge penalty for what appears to have been overly aggressive risk-taking by executives, but the executives, in contrast, did quite well because of "their ability to claim large amounts of compensation based on short-term results."[23]

Shareholders can influence executive compensation decisions in a variety of ways (e.g., through shareholder proposals and election of directors in proxy votes). In addition, the Dodd–Frank Wall Street Reform and Consumer Protection Act was signed into law in 2010.

EXHIBIT 1.3
Chief Executive Officer (CEO) Return and Shareholder Return

Shareholder Return	Shareholder Return in $ (change in wealth)	CEO Return in $ (change in wealth)
25th percentile	−198 milion	−0.7 million
Median	+163 million	+9.5 million
75th percentile	+553 million	+21.6 million

Source: A. Nyberg, I. S. Fulmer, B. Gerhart, and M. A. Carpenter, "Agency Theory Revisited: CEO Returns and Shareholder Interest Alignment," *Academy of Management Journal*, 53 (2010), pp. 1029–1049.

Among its provisions is "say on pay," which requires public companies to submit their executive compensation plan to a vote by shareholders. The vote is not binding. However, companies seem to be intent on designing compensation plans that do not result in negative votes. In addition, clawback provisions (designed to allow companies to reclaim compensation from executives in some situations) are available under Dodd-Frank and have also been adopted in stronger form by some companies.[24]

Managers

For managers, compensation influences their success in two ways. First, it is a major expense that must be managed. Second, it is a major determinant of employee attitudes and behaviors (and thus, organization performance). We begin with the cost issue. Competitive pressures, both global and local, force managers to consider the affordability of their compensation decisions. Labor costs can account for more than 50 percent of total costs. In some industries, such as financial or professional services and in education and government, this figure is even higher. However, even within an industry, labor costs as a percent of total costs vary among individual firms. For example, small neighborhood grocery stores, with labor costs between 15 percent and 18 percent, have been driven out of business by supermarkets that delivered the same products at a lower cost of labor (9 percent to 12 percent). Supermarkets today are losing market share to the warehouse club stores such as Sam's Club and Costco, who enjoy an even lower cost of labor (4 percent to 6 percent), even though Costco pays above-average wages for the industry.

Exhibit 1.4 compares the hourly pay rate for retail workers at Costco to that at Walmart and Sam's Club (which is owned by Walmart). Each store tries to provide a unique shopping experience. Walmart and Sam's Club compete on low prices, with Sam's Club being a "warehouse store" with especially low prices on a narrower range of products, often times sold in bulk. Costco also competes on the basis of low prices, but with a mix that includes more high-end products aimed at a higher customer income segment. To compete in this segment, Costco appears to have chosen to pay higher wages, perhaps as a way to attract and retain a higher quality workforce.[25] Indeed, in a recent annual report, Costco states, "With respect to expenses relating to the compensation of our employees, our philosophy is not to seek to minimize the wages and benefits that they earn. Rather, we believe that achieving our longer-term objectives of reducing employee turnover and enhancing employee satisfaction requires maintaining compensation levels that are better than the industry average for much of our workforce." By comparison, Walmart simply states in a recent annual report that they "experience significant turnover in associates [i.e., employees] each year."[26] Based on Exhibit 1.4, Costco is quite successful, relative to its competitors, in terms of employee retention, customer satisfaction, and the efficiency with which it generates sales (see revenue per square foot and revenue per employee). So, although its labor costs are higher than those of Sam's Club and Walmart, it appears that this model works for Costco because it helps gain an advantage over its competitors.

Thus, rather than treating pay only as an expense to be minimized, a manager can also use it to influence employee behaviors and to improve the organization's performance. High pay, as long as it can be documented that it brings high returns through

EXHIBIT 1.4 Pay Rates at Retail Stores, Customer Satisfaction, Employee Turnover, and Sales/Square Ft.

	Starting Wage	Wage after 4 Years	Average Cashier Wage	Customer Satisfaction (100 = highest)	Employee Annual Turnover	Stores	Revenues	Store Size Average (square ft.)	Number of Employees	Revenue per Square ft.	Revenues per Employee
Costco	$11.00	$20.89	$16.00	84	20%	663	$110.2 billion	143,288	195,000	$1,160	$565,190
Sam's Club	$10.00	$15.00[a]	$ 9.08	80	50%	632	$ 57.2 billion	132,911	—	$ 680	—
Walmart	$ 8.40	$12.57	$10.00	77	50%	4,203	$279.4 billion	156,793	—	$ 424	—
Walmart + Sam's Club						10,942	$476.3 billion	100,621	1,200,000	$ 433	$396,912

Sources: Starting Wage, Employee Annual Turnover, and Wage after 4 Years from Liza Featherstone, "Wage Against the Machine," *Slate*, June 27, 2008; "The Costco Craze." CNBC Television Report, April 26, 2012; Brad Stone. "Costco CEO Craig Jelinek Leads the Cheapest, Happiest Company in the World," *Business Week*, June 06, 2013. www.businessweek.com. Customer Satisfaction Data from American Customer Satisfaction Index™. http://www.theacsi.org/. Extracted May 17, 2012. Store Size, Number of Employees from 2014 Costco and 2014 Walmart annual reports. Average Cashier Wage from www.glassdoor.com, extracted February 4, 2015.

Notes: Separate turnover data unavailable for Sam's Club. Overall Walmart turnover rate is thus used.

[a]Estimated.

its influences on employees, can be a successful strategy. As our Costco (versus Sam's Club and Walmart) example seems to suggest, the way people are paid affects the quality of their work and their attitude toward customers.[27] It may also affect their willingness to be flexible, learn new skills, or suggest innovations. On the other hand, people may become interested in unions or legal action against their employer based on how they are paid. This potential to influence employees' behaviors, and subsequently the productivity and effectiveness of the organization, means that the study of compensation is well worth your time, don't you think?[28]

Employees

The pay individuals receive in return for the work they perform and the value they create is usually the major source of their financial security. Hence, pay plays a vital role in a person's economic and social well-being. Employees may see compensation as a *return in an exchange* between their employer and themselves, as an **entitlement** for being an employee of the company, as an incentive to decide to take/stay in a job and invest in performing well in that job, or as a reward for having done so. Compensation can be all of these things.[29]

The importance of pay is apparent in many ways. Wages and benefits are a major focus of labor unions efforts to serve their members' interests. (See Chapter 14.) The extensive legal framework governing pay, including minimum wage, living wage, overtime, and nondiscrimination regulations, also points to the central importance of pay to employees in the employment relationship. (See Chapter 17.) Next, we turn to how pay influences employee behaviors.

Incentive and Sorting Effects of Pay on Employee Behaviors

Pay can influence employee **motivation** and behavior in two ways. First, and perhaps most obvious, pay can affect the motivational intensity, direction, and persistence of current employees. Motivation, together with employee **ability** and work/organizational design (which can help or hinder employee performance), determines employee behaviors such as performance. We will refer to this effect of pay as an **incentive effect**, the degree to which pay influences individual and aggregate motivation among the employees we have at any point in time.

However, pay can also have an indirect, but important, influence via a **sorting effect** on the composition of the workforce.[30] That is, different types of pay strategies may cause different types of people to apply to and stay with (i.e., self-select into) an organization. In the case of pay structure/level, it may be that higher pay levels help organizations to attract more high-quality applicants, allowing them to be more selective in their hiring. Similarly, higher pay levels may improve employee retention. (In Chapter 7, we will talk about when paying more is most likely to be worth the higher costs.)

Less obvious perhaps, it is not only how much, but *how* an organization pays that can result in sorting effects.[31] Ask yourself: Would people who are highly capable and have a strong work ethic and interest in earning a lot of money prefer to work in an organization that pays employees doing the same job more or less the same amount, regardless of their performance? Or, would they prefer to work in an organization where their pay can be much higher (or lower) depending on how they perform? If you chose the latter answer, then you believe that sorting effects matter. People differ regarding which type of pay arrangement they prefer. The question for organizations is simply this: Are you using the pay policy that will attract and retain the types of employees you want? Keep in mind that high performers have more alternative job opportunities and that more opportunities, all else equal (e.g., if they are not paid more for their higher performance), translate into higher turnover, a likely significant problem to the degree it is the high performers leaving, especially to the degree that high performers in particular roles create a disproportionately high amount of value for organizations.[32] This also raises the issue of dealing with outside offers that employees receive. We know that a substantial share of employee turnover results from receiving unsolicited outside offers. (In other words, turnover is not always in response to dissatisfaction. Sometimes, it is driven by opportunity.) These are likely to be some of the most valuable employees and thus policy and practice on dealing with outside offers (hopefully informed by research) is important.[33]

Let's take a look at one especially informative study conducted by Edward Lazear regarding incentive and sorting effects.[34] Individual worker productivity was measured before and after a glass installation company switched one of its plants from a salary-only (no pay for performance) system to an individual incentive plan under which each employee's pay depended on his/her own performance. An overall increase in plant productivity of 44 percent was observed comparing before and after. Roughly one-half of this increase was due to individual employees becoming more productive. However, the remaining one-half of the productivity gain was not explained by this fact. So, where did the other one-half of the gain come from? The answer: Less productive workers were less likely to stay under the new individual incentive system because it was less favorable to them. When they left, they tended to be replaced by more productive workers (who were happy to have the chance to make more money than they might make elsewhere). Thus, focusing only on the incentive effects of pay (on current workers) can miss the other major mechanism (sorting) by which pay decisions influence employee behaviors.

The pay model that comes later in this chapter includes compensation policies and the **objectives** (efficiency, fairness, compliance) these are meant to influence. Our point here is that compensation policies work through employee incentive and sorting effects to either achieve or not achieve those objectives.

Global Views—*Vive la Différence*

In English, *compensation* means something that counterbalances, offsets, or makes up for something else. However, if we look at the origin of the word in different languages, we get a sense of the richness of the meaning, which combines entitlement, return, and reward.[35]

In China, the traditional characters for the word "compensation" are based on the symbols for logs and water; compensation provides the necessities in life. In the recent past, the state owned all enterprises and compensation was treated as an entitlement. In today's China, compensation takes on a more subtle meaning. A new word, *dai yu,* is used. It refers to how you are being treated—your wages, benefits, training opportunities, and so on. When people talk about compensation, they ask each other about the *dai yu* in their companies. Rather than assuming that everyone is entitled to the same treatment, the meaning of compensation now includes a broader sense of returns as well as entitlement.[36]

"Compensation" in Japanese is *kyuyo,* which is made up of two separate characters (*kyu* and *yo*), both meaning "giving something." *Kyu* is an honorific used to indicate that the person doing the giving is someone of high rank, such as a feudal lord, an emperor, or a samurai leader. Traditionally, compensation is thought of as something given by one's superior. Today, business consultants in Japan try to substitute the word *hou-syu,* which means "reward" and has no associations with notions of superiors. The many allowances that are part of Japanese compensation systems translate as *teate,* which means "taking care of something." *Teate* is regarded as compensation that takes care of employees' financial needs. This concept is consistent with the family, housing, and commuting allowances that are still used in many Japanese companies.[37]

These contrasting ideas about compensation—multiple views (societal, stockholder, managerial, employee, and even global) and multiple meanings (returns, rewards, entitlement)—add richness to the topic. But they can also cause confusion unless everyone is talking about the same thing. So let's define what we mean by "compensation" or "pay" (the words are used interchangeably in this book):

> **Compensation** refers to all forms of financial returns and tangible services and benefits employees receive as part of an employment relationship.

FORMS OF PAY

Exhibit 1.5 shows the variety of returns people receive from work. They are categorized as **total compensation** and **relational returns.** The relational returns (learning opportunities, status, challenging work, and so on) are psychological.[38] Total compensation returns are more transactional. They include pay received directly as cash (e.g., base,

EXHIBIT 1.5 Total Returns for Work

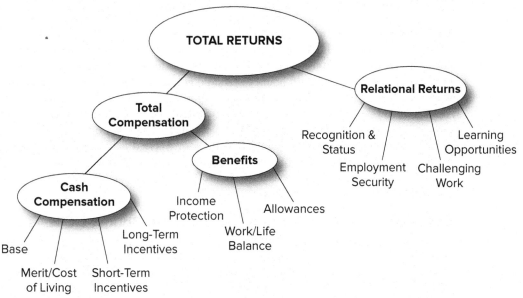

merit, incentives, cost-of-living adjustments) and indirectly as benefits (e.g., pensions, medical insurance, programs to help balance work and life demands, brightly colored uniforms).[39] So pay comes in different forms, and programs to pay people can be designed in a wide variety of ways. WorldatWork has a Total Rewards Model that is similar and includes compensation, benefits, work-life, performance/recognition, and development/career opportunities.[40] The importance of monetary rewards as a motivator relative to other rewards (e.g., intrinsic rewards such as how interesting the work is) has long been a topic of interest, as have the conditions under which money is more or less important to people (and even whether money is sometimes too important to people).[41] Although scholars and pundits have sometimes debated which is more important, (and have sometimes argued that money does not motivate or even that it demotivates) our reading of the research indicates that both types of rewards are important and that it is usually not terribly productive to debate which is more important.[42] It will no doubt come as little surprise that we will focus on monetary rewards (total compensation) in a book called *Compensation.* Whatever other rewards employees value, it is our experience that they expect to be paid for their work, that how and how much they are paid affects their attitudes, performance, and job choice, as well as their standard of living. These effects of compensation on employees (as well as the cost of employee compensation) have major implications for how successfully organizations can execute their strategies and achieve their goals, as we will see.

Cash Compensation: Base

Base wage is the cash compensation that an employer pays for the work performed. Base wage tends to reflect the value of the work or skills and generally ignores differences attributable to individual employees. For example, the base wage for machine operators may be $20 an hour. However, some individual operators may receive more because of their experience and/or performance. Some pay systems set base wage as a function of the skill or education an employee possesses; this is common for engineers and schoolteachers.[43]

A distinction is often made in the United States between wage and salary, with **salary** referring to pay for employees who are **exempt** from regulations of the Fair Labor Standards Act (FLSA) and hence do not receive overtime pay.[44] Managers and professionals usually fit this category. Their pay is calculated at an annual or monthly rate rather than hourly, because hours worked do not need to be recorded. In contrast, workers who are covered by overtime and reporting provisions of the Fair Labor Standards Act—*nonexempts*—have their pay calculated as an hourly wage. Some organizations, such as IBM, Eaton, and Walmart, label all base pay as "salary." Rather than dividing employees into separate categories of salaried and wage earners, they believe that an "all-salaried" workforce reinforces an organizational **culture** in which all employees are part of the same team. However, merely changing the terminology does not negate the need to comply with the FLSA.

Cash Compensation: Merit Increases/Merit Bonuses/COLAs

A cost of living adjustment (COLA) to base wages may be made on the basis of changes in what other employers are paying for the same work, changes in living costs, or changes in experience or skill. Such provisions are less common than in the past as employers continually try to control fixed costs and link pay increases to individual and/or company performance.

Merit increases are given as increments to base pay and are based on performance.[45] According to surveys, 90 percent of U.S. firms use merit pay increases.[46] An assessment (or rating) of recent past performance is made, with or without a formal performance evaluation. In recent years, merit increase budgets (or average merit increases) have been just under 3 percent, creeping up to 3 percent most recently. Survey data indicate that, on average, an outstanding performer receives a 4.4 percent increase, an average performer a 2.8 percent increase, and a poor performer a 0.4 percent increase.[47] Finally, companies increasingly use merit bonuses. As with merit increases, *merit bonuses* are based on a performance rating but, unlike merit increases, are paid in the form of a lump sum rather than becoming (a permanent) part of the base salary.[48] Merit bonuses may now be more important than traditional merit increases. "Indeed, merit bonuses now appear to account for more of the pay-performance relationship than do the traditional and most often discussed form of [pay for individual performance], merit pay."[49] In companies that use merit bonuses and among those workers who receive them, the average annual merit bonus in recent years has been about 5 percent for hourly employees, 6 percent for lower level salaried employees, and 13 percent for higher level (but below officers/executives) salaried employees, all much larger than the more often discussed recent merit increase pools of around 3 percent.[50] We return to this issue in Chapter 18.

Cash Compensation: Incentives

Incentives also tie pay increases to performance.[51] However, incentives differ from merit adjustments. First, incentives do not increase the base wage and so must be reearned each pay period. Second, the potential size of the incentive payment will generally be known beforehand. Whereas merit pay programs evaluate past performance of an individual and then decide on the size of the increase, what must happen in order to receive the incentive payment is called out very specifically ahead of time. For example, a Toyota salesperson knows the **commission** on a Land Cruiser versus a Prius prior to making the sale. The larger commission he or she will earn by selling the Land Cruiser is the incentive to sell a customer that car rather than the Prius. Third, an incentive program relies on an objective measure of performance (e.g., sales), whereas a merit increase program typically relies on a subjective rating of performance. Although both merit pay and incentives try to influence performance, incentives explicitly try to influence future behavior whereas merit recognizes (rewards) past behavior, which is hoped to influence future behavior. The incentive-reward distinction is a matter of timing.

Incentives can be tied to the performance of an individual employee, a team of employees, a total business unit, or some combination of individual, team, and unit. The performance objective may be expense reduction, volume increases, customer satisfaction, revenue growth, return on investments, increase in stock value—the possibilities are endless. Prax Air, for example, uses return on capital (ROC). For every quarter that a 6 percent ROC target is met or exceeded, Prax Air awards bonus days of pay. An 8.6 percent ROC means 2 extra days of pay for that quarter for every employee covered by the program. An ROC of 15 percent means 8.5 extra days of pay.

Because incentives are one-time payments, they do not permanently increase labor costs. When performance declines, incentive pay automatically declines, too. Consequently, incentives (and sometimes merit bonuses also) are frequently referred to as **variable pay.**

Long-Term Incentives

Incentives may be short- or long-term. Long-term incentives are intended to focus employee efforts on multiyear results. Typically they are in the form of stock ownership or options to buy stock at a fixed price (thus leading to a monetary gain to the degree the stock price later goes up). The belief underlying stock ownership is that employees with a financial stake in the organization will focus on long-term financial objectives: return on investment, market share, return on net assets, and the like. Bristol-Myers Squibb grants stock to selected "Key Contributors" who make outstanding contributions to the firm's success. Stock options are often the largest component in an executive pay package. Some companies extend stock ownership beyond the ranks of managers and professionals. Intel, Google, and Starbucks, for example, offer stock options to all their employees.[52]

Benefits: Income Protection

Exhibit 1.5 showed that benefits, including income protection, work/life services, and allowances, are also part of total compensation. Some income protection programs are legally required in the United States; employers must pay into a fund that provides income replacement for workers who become disabled or unemployed. Employers also make half the contributions to Social Security. (Employees pay the other half.) Different countries have different lists of mandatory benefits.

Medical insurance, retirement programs, life insurance, and savings plans are common benefits. They help protect employees from the financial risks inherent in daily life. Often companies can provide these protections to employees more cheaply than employees can obtain them for themselves. In the United States, employers spend roughly $611 billion per year on health care costs, or about 21 percent of all U.S. health care expenditures. Among employers that provide health insurance, the cost to provide family coverage is $16,834 per year per employee (the average employer pays $12,011 of that and the average employee pays the remaining $4,283).[53] Given the magnitude of such costs, it is no surprise that employers have sought to rein in or reduce benefits costs. One approach has been to shift costs to employees (e.g., having employees pay a larger share of health insurance premiums).[54] Some companies have allowed their benefits costs to get so far out of control that more drastic action has been taken. For example, as noted, companies like Chrysler, GM, and American Airlines have recently gone through bankruptcy, which has been used to reduce benefits costs and labor costs more generally. GM benefits costs had gotten so high that it was sometimes described as a pension and health care provider that also makes cars.

Benefits: Work/Life Balance

Programs that help employees better integrate their work and life responsibilities include time away from work (vacations, jury duty), access to services to meet specific needs (drug counseling, financial planning, referrals for child and elder care), and flexible work arrangements (telecommuting, nontraditional schedules, nonpaid time off). Responding to the changing demographics of the workforce (two-income families or single parents who need work-schedule flexibility so that family obligations can be met), many U.S. employers are giving a higher priority to these benefit forms. Medtronic, for example, touts its Total Well-Being Program that seeks to provide "resources for growth—mind, body, heart, and spirit" for each employee. Health and wellness, financial rewards and security, individual and family well-being, and a fulfilling work environment are part of this "total well-being."[55] Medtronic believes that this program permits employees to be "fully present" at work and less distracted by conflicts between their work and nonwork responsibilities.

Benefits: Allowances

Allowances often grow out of whatever is in short supply. In Vietnam and China, housing (dormitories and apartments) and transportation allowances are frequently part of the pay package. Sixty years after the end of World War II–induced food shortages, some Japanese companies still continue to offer a "rice allowance" based on the number of an employee's dependents. Almost all foreign companies in China discover that housing, transportation, and other allowances are expected.[56] Companies that resist these allowances must come up with other ways to attract and retain employees. In many European countries, managers assume that a car will be provided—only the make and model are negotiable.[57]

Total Earnings Opportunities: Present Value of a Stream of Earnings

Up to this point we have treated compensation as something received at a moment in time. But a firm's compensation decisions have a temporal effect. Say you have a job offer of $50,000. If you stay with the firm five years and receive an annual increase of 4 percent, in five years you will be earning $60,833 a year. For your employer, the five-year cost commitment of the decision to hire you turns out to be $331,649 in cash. If you add in an additional 30 percent for benefits, the decision to hire you implies a commitment of over $430,000 from your employer. Will you be worth it? You will be after this course.

A present-value perspective shifts the comparison of today's initial offers to consideration of future bonuses, merit increases, and promotions. Sometimes a company will tell applicants that its relatively low starting offers will be overcome by larger future pay increases. In effect, the company is selling the present value of the future stream of earnings. But few candidates apply that same analysis to calculate the future increases required to offset the lower initial offers. Hopefully, everyone who reads Chapter 1 will now do so.

Relational Returns from Work

Why do Google millionaires continue to show up for work every morning? Why does Andy Borowitz write the funniest satirical news site on the web (*www.borowitzreport .com*) for free? There is no doubt that nonfinancial returns from work have a substantial effect on employees' behavior.[58] Exhibit 1.4 includes such relational returns from work as recognition and status, employment security, challenging work, and opportunities to learn. Other forms of relational return might include personal satisfaction from successfully facing new challenges, teaming with great co-workers, receiving new uniforms, and the like.[59] Such factors are part of the total return, which is a broader umbrella than total compensation.

The Organization as a Network of Returns

Sometimes it is useful to think of an organization as a network of returns created by all these different forms of pay, including total compensation and relational returns. The challenge is to design this network so that it helps the organization to succeed. As in the case of rowers pulling on their oars, success is more likely if all are pulling in unison rather than working against one another. In the same way, the network of returns is more likely to be useful if bonuses, development opportunities, and promotions all work together.

So the next time you walk in an employer's door, look beyond the cash and health care offered to search for all the returns that create the network. Even though this book focuses on compensation, let's not forget that compensation is only one of many factors affecting people's decisions about work. (You might enjoy listening to Roger Miller's song, "Kansas City Star," or Chely Wright's "It's the Song" for some other reasons people choose their work.)

A PAY MODEL

The pay model shown in Exhibit 1.6 serves as both a framework for examining current pay systems and a guide for most of this book. It contains three basic building blocks: (1) the compensation objectives, (2) the policies that form the foundation of the compensation system, and (3) the techniques that make up the compensation system. Because objectives drive the system, we will discuss them first.

Compensation Objectives

Pay systems are designed to achieve certain objectives. The basic objectives, shown at the right side of the model, include efficiency, fairness, ethics, and compliance with laws and regulations. *Efficiency* can be stated more specifically: (1) improving performance, increasing quality, delighting customers and stockholders, and (2) controlling labor costs.

Compensation objectives at Medtronic and Whole Foods are contrasted in Exhibit 1.7. Medtronic is a medical technology company that pioneered cardiac pacemakers. Its compensation objectives emphasize performance, business success, minimizing fixed costs, and attracting and energizing top talent.

Whole Foods is the nation's largest organic- and natural-foods grocer. Its markets are a "celebration of food": bright, well-stocked, and well-staffed.[60] The company describes its commitment to offering the highest quality and least processed foods as a shared responsibility. Its first compensation objective is ". . . committed to increasing shareholder value."

EXHIBIT 1.6   The Pay Model

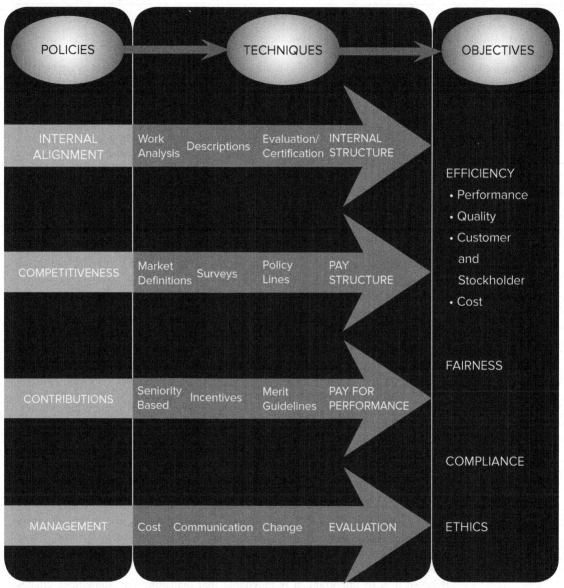

POLICIES → TECHNIQUES → OBJECTIVES

INTERNAL ALIGNMENT | Work Analysis | Descriptions | Evaluation/ Certification | INTERNAL STRUCTURE

COMPETITIVENESS | Market Definitions | Surveys | Policy Lines | PAY STRUCTURE

CONTRIBUTIONS | Seniority Based | Incentives | Merit Guidelines | PAY FOR PERFORMANCE

MANAGEMENT | Cost | Communication | Change | EVALUATION

EFFICIENCY
• Performance
• Quality
• Customer and Stockholder
• Cost

FAIRNESS

COMPLIANCE

ETHICS

Fairness is a fundamental objective of pay systems.[61] In Medtronic's objectives, fairness means "ensure fair treatment" and "recognize personal and family well-being." Whole Foods's pay objectives discuss a "shared fate." In their egalitarian work culture, pay beyond base wages is linked to team performance, and employees have some say about who is on their team.

EXHIBIT 1.7   **Pay Objectives at Medtronic and Whole Foods**

Medtronic	Whole Foods
Support Medtronic mission and increased complexity of business	We are committed to increasing long-term shareholder value.
Minimize increases in fixed costs	Profits are earned every day through voluntary exchange with our customers.
Attract and engage top talent	
Emphasize personal, team, and Medtronic performance	Profits are essential to create capital for growth, prosperity, opportunity, job satisfaction, and job security.
Recognize personal and family total well-being	Support team member happiness and excellence.
Ensure fair treatment	We share together in our collective fate.

The fairness objective calls for fair treatment for all employees by recognizing both employee contributions (e.g., higher pay for greater performance, experience, or training) and employee needs (e.g., a fair wage as well as fair procedures). *Procedural fairness* refers to the process used to make pay decisions.[62] It suggests that the way a pay decision is made may be equally as important to employees as the results of the decision.

Compliance as a pay objective means conforming to federal and state compensation laws and regulations. If laws change, pay systems may need to change, too, to ensure continued compliance. As companies go global, they must comply with the laws of all the countries in which they operate.

Ethics

Asian philosophy gives us the concept of yin and yang—complementary opposites rather than substitutes or trade-offs. It is not yin *or* yang; part of yin is in yang, and part of yang is in yin. So it is with objectives in the pay model. It is not efficiency versus fairness versus compliance. Rather, it is all three simultaneously. All three must be achieved. The tension of working toward all objectives at once creates fertile grounds for ethical dilemmas.

Ethics means the organization cares about how its results are achieved.[63] Scan the websites or lobby walls of corporate headquarters and you will inevitably find statements of "Key Behaviors," "Our Values," and "Codes of Conduct." One company's code of conduct is shown in Exhibit 1.8. The challenge is to put these statements into daily practice. The company in the exhibit is the formerly admired, now reviled, Enron, whose employees lost their jobs and pensions in the wake of legal and ethical misdeeds by those at the top.

Because it is so important, it is inevitable that managing pay sometimes creates ethical dilemmas. Manipulating results to ensure executive bonus payouts, misusing (or failing to understand) statistics used to measure competitors' pay rates, re-pricing or backdating stock options to increase their value, encouraging employees to invest a portion of their wages in company stock while executives are bailing out, offering just enough pay to get a new hire in the door while ignoring the relationship to co-workers' pay, and shaving the hours recorded in employees' time card—these are all too common examples of ethical lapses.

EXHIBIT 1.8   Enron's Ethics Statement

Foreword

"As officers and employees of Enron Corp., its subsidiaries, and its affiliated companies, we are responsible for conducting the business affairs of the companies in accordance with all applicable laws and in a moral and honest manner. . . . We want to be proud of Enron and to know that it enjoys a reputation for fairness and honesty and that it is respected. . . . Enron's reputation finally depends on its people, on you and me. Let's keep that reputation high."

July 1, 2000
Kenneth L. Lay
Chairman and Chief Executive Officer

Values

Respect	We treat others as we would like to be treated ourselves. We do not tolerate abusive or disrespectful treatment. Ruthlessness, callousness, and arrogance don't belong here.
Integrity	We work with customers and prospects openly, honestly, and sincerely. When we say we will do something, we will do it; when we say we cannot or will not do something, then we won't do it.
Communication	We have an obligation to communicate. Here, we take the time to talk with one another . . . and to listen.
Excellence	We are satisfied with nothing less than the very best in everything we do. . . . The great fun here will be for all of us to discover just how good we can really be.

Source: *www.thesmokinggun.com.*

Some, but not all, compensation professionals and consultants remain silent during ethical misconduct and outright malfeasance. Absent a professional code, compensation managers must look to their own ethics—and the pay model, which calls for combining the objectives of efficiency and fair treatment of employees as well as compliance.[64]

There are probably as many statements of pay objectives as there are employers. In fact, highly diversified firms such as General Electric and Eaton, which operate in multiple lines of businesses, may have different **pay objectives** for different business units. At General Electric, each unit's objectives must meet GE overall objectives.

Objectives serve several purposes. First, they guide the design of the pay system. If an objective is to increase customer satisfaction, then incentive programs and merit pay might be used to pay for performance. Another employer's objective may be to develop innovative new products. Job design, training, and team building may be used to reach this objective. The pay system aligned with this objective may include salaries that are at least equal to those of competitors (external competitiveness) and that go up with increased skills or knowledge (internal alignment). This pay system could be very different from our first example, where the focus is on increasing customer satisfaction. Notice that policies and techniques are the means to reach the objectives.

In summary, objectives guide the design of pay systems. They also serve as the standards for judging the success of the pay system. If the objective is to attract and retain the best and the brightest skilled employees, but they are leaving for higher-paying jobs elsewhere, the system may not be performing effectively. Although there may be many nonpay reasons for such turnover, objectives provide standards for evaluating the effectiveness of a pay system.[65]

Four Policy Choices

Every employer must address the policy decisions shown on the left side of the pay model: (1) internal alignment, (2) external competitiveness, (3) employee contributions, and (4) management of the pay system. These policies are the foundation on which pay systems are built. They also serve as guidelines for managing pay in ways that accomplish the system's objectives.

Internal Alignment

Internal alignment refers to comparisons among jobs or skill levels inside a single organization. Jobs and people's skills are compared in terms of their relative contributions to the organization's business objectives. How, for example, does the work of the programmer compare with the work of the systems analyst, the software engineer, and the software architect? Does one contribute to solutions for customers and satisfied stockholders more than another? What about two marketing managers working in different business units of the same organization? Internal alignment pertains to the pay rates both for employees doing equal work and for those doing dissimilar work. In fact, determining what is an appropriate difference in pay for people performing different work is one of the key challenges facing managers. Whole Foods tries to manage differences with a salary cap that limits the **total cash** compensation (wages plus bonuses) of any executive to 19 times the average cash compensation of all full-time employees. The cap originally started at eight times the average. However, attraction and retention problems were cited as a need for raising the cap several times since. (Note that the cap does not include stock options.)

Pay relationships within the organization affect all three compensation objectives. They affect employee decisions to stay with the organization, to become more flexible by investing in additional training, or to seek greater responsibility. By motivating employees to choose increased training and greater responsibility in dealing with customers, internal pay relationships indirectly affect the capabilities of the workforce and hence the efficiency of the entire organization. Fairness is affected through employees' comparisons of their pay to the pay of others in the organization. Compliance is affected by the basis used to make internal comparisons. Paying on the basis of race, gender, age, or national origin is illegal in the United States.

External Competitiveness

External competitiveness refers to pay comparisons with competitors. *How much* do we wish to pay in comparison to what other employers pay?

Many organizations claim their pay systems are market-driven, that is, based almost exclusively on what competitors pay. "Market driven" gets translated into practice in different ways.[66] Some employers may set their pay levels higher than their competition, hoping to attract the best applicants. Of course, this assumes that someone is able to identify and hire the "best" from the pool of applicants. And what is the appropriate market? When, for example, should international pay rates be considered? Should the pay of software engineers in New Delhi or Minsk influence pay for engineers in Silicon Valley or Boston?

External competitiveness decisions—both how much and what forms—have a two-fold effect on objectives: (1) to ensure that the pay is sufficient to attract and retain employees—if employees do not perceive their pay as competitive in comparison to what other organizations are offering for similar work, they may be more likely to leave—and (2) to control labor costs so that the organization's prices of products or services can remain competitive in a global economy.

Employee Contributions

How much emphasis should there be on paying for performance? Should one programmer be paid differently from another if one has better performance and/or greater seniority? Or should there be a **flat rate** for programmers? Should the company share any profits with employees? Share with all employees, part-time as well as full-time?

The emphasis to place on **employee contributions** (or nature of **pay mix**) is an important policy decision since it directly affects employees' attitudes and work behaviors. Eaton and Motorola use pay to support other "high-performance" practices in their workplaces.[67] Both use team-based pay and corporate profit-sharing plans. Starbucks emphasizes stock options and sharing the success of corporate performance with the employees. General Electric uses different performance-based pay programs at the individual, division, and companywide level. Performance-based pay affects fairness in that employees need to understand the basis for judging performance in order to believe that their pay is fair.

What mix of pay forms—base, incentives, stock, benefits—do our competitors use in comparison to the pay mix we use? Whole Foods combines base pay and **team incentives** to offer higher pay if team performance warrants. Nucor targets base pay below market, but targets total cash compensation (including profit sharing and gain-sharing/plant production bonuses) at well above the market median. Medtronic sets its base pay to match its competitors but ties bonuses to performance. It offers stock to all its employees based on overall company performance.[68] Further, Medtronic believes that its benefits, particularly its emphasis on programs that balance work and life, make it a highly attractive place to work. It believes that *how* its pay is positioned and *what forms* it uses create an advantage over competitors.

The external competitiveness and employee contribution decisions should be made jointly. Clearly, an above-market compensation level is most effective and sustainable when it exists together with above-market employee contributions to productivity, quality, customer service, or other important strategic objectives.

Management

A policy regarding management of the pay system is the last building block in our model. Management means ensuring that the *right people* get the *right pay* for *achieving the right objectives in the right way*. The greatest system design in the world is useless without competent management.

Managing compensation means answering the "So What" question. So what is the impact of this policy, this technique, this decision? Although it is possible to design a system that is based on internal alignment, external competitiveness, and employee contributions, what difference does it make? Does the decision help the organization achieve its objectives?[69]

The ground under compensation management has shifted. The traditional focus on how to administer various techniques is long gone, replaced by more strategic thinking—managing pay as part of the business. It goes beyond simply managing pay as an expense to better understanding and analyzing the impact of pay decisions on people's behaviors and organizations' success. The impact of pay decisions on expenses is one result that is easily measured and well understood. But other measures—such as pay's impact on attracting and retaining the right people, and engaging these people productively—are not yet widely used in the management of compensation. Efforts to do so are increasing and the perspective is shifting from "How To" toward trying to answer the "So What" question.[70] Ease of measurement is not the same as importance; costs are easy to measure (and, of course, important), so there is a tendency to focus there. Yet, the consequences of pay, although often less amenable to measurement, are nonetheless just as important.

Pay Techniques

The remaining portion of the pay model in Exhibit 1.6 shows the techniques that make up the pay system. The exhibit provides only an overview since techniques are discussed throughout the rest of the book. Techniques tie the four basic policies to the pay objectives.

Uncounted variations in **pay techniques** exist; many are examined in this book. Most consultant firms tout their surveys and techniques on their web pages. You can obtain updated information on various practices by simply surfing the web.

e-Compensation

World at Work (*www.worldatwork.org*) provides information on its compensation-related journals and special publications, as well as short courses aimed at practitioners. The Society of Human Resource Management (*www.shrm.org*) also offers compensation-related information as well as more general human resource management (HRM) information. The society's student services section offers guidance on finding jobs in the field of human resources. Both sites are good sources of information for people interested in careers in HRM. Information on pay trends in Europe is available from the European Industrial Relations Observatory (http://www.eurofound.europa.eu/observatories/eurwork). The International Labour Organization (*www.ilo.org*) maintains a database that can be browsed either by subject (conditions of employment) or country (*http://www.ilo.org/travail/info/fs/lang–en/index.htm*). Over 2,000 articles are listed in their "wages" subheading, including such information as the minimum wage in Vanuatu. Cornell University's Industrial and Labor Relations School offers a "research portal" for articles of interest in human resource management (http://guides.library.cornell.edu/hrm). The Employee Benefits Research Institute (EBRI) includes links to other benefits sources on its website (*www.ebri.org*). Every chapter in this book also mentions interesting websites. Use them as a starting point to search out others.

BOOK PLAN

Compensation is such a broad and compelling topic that several books are devoted to it. The focus of this book is on the design and management of compensation systems. To aid in understanding how and why pay systems work, our pay model provides the structure for much of the book. Chapter 2 discusses how to formulate and execute a compensation strategy. We analyze what it means to be strategic about how people are paid and how compensation can help achieve and sustain an organization's competitive advantage.[71]

The pay model plays a central role in formulating and implementing an organization's pay strategy. The model identifies four basic policy choices that are the core of the pay strategy. After we discuss strategy, the next sections of the book examine each of these policies in detail. Part 2 on *internal alignment* (Chapters 3 through 6) examines pay relationships within a single organization. Part 3 (Chapters 7 and 8) examines *external competitiveness*—the pay relationships among competing organizations—and analyzes the influence of market-driven forces.

Once the compensation rates and structures are established, other issues emerge. How much should we pay each individual employee? How much and how often should a person's pay be increased and on what basis—experience, seniority, or performance? Should pay increases be contingent on the organization's and/or the employee's performance? How should the organization share its success (or failure) with employees? These are questions of *employee contributions,* the third building block in the model, covered in Part 4 (Chapters 9 through 11).

In Part 5, we cover employee services and benefits (Chapters 12 and 13). How do benefits fit in the company's overall compensation package? What choices should employees have in their benefits? In Part 6, we cover systems tailored for special groups—sales representatives, executives, contract workers, unions (Chapters 14 and 15)—and we provide more detail on global compensation systems (Chapter 16). Part 7 concludes with information essential for *managing the compensation system.* The government's role in compensation is examined in Chapter 17. Chapter 18 includes understanding, communicating, budgeting, and evaluating results.

Even though the book is divided into sections that reflect the pay model, pay decisions are not discrete. All of them are interrelated. Together, they influence employee behaviors and organization performance and can create a pay system that can be a source of competitive advantage.

Throughout the book our intention is to examine alternative approaches. We believe that rarely is there a single correct approach; rather, alternative approaches exist or can be designed. The one most likely to be effective depends on the circumstances. We hope that this book will help you become better informed about these options, how to evaluate and select the most effective ones, and how to design new ones. Whether as an employee, a manager, or an interested member of society, you should be able to assess the effectiveness and fairness of pay systems.

CAVEAT EMPTOR—BE AN INFORMED CONSUMER

Most managers do not read research. They do not subscribe to research journals; they find them too full of jargon and esoterica, and they see them as impractical and irrelevant.[72] However, a study of 5,000 HR managers compared their beliefs to the research evidence in several areas and identified seven common and important misconceptions held by managers.[73] The study authors concluded that being unaware of key research findings may prove costly to organizations. For example, when it comes to motivating workers, organization efforts may be somewhat misguided if they do not know that "Money is the crucial incentive . . . no other incentive or motivational technique comes even close to money with respect to its instrumental value."[74]

So it pays to read the research. There is no question that some studies are irrelevant and poorly performed. But if you are not a reader of research literature, you become prey for the latest business self-help fad. Belief, even enthusiasm, is a poor substitute for informed judgment. Therefore, we end the chapter with a consumer's guide to research that includes three questions to help make you a critical reader—and a better-informed decision maker.

1. Is the Research Useful?

How useful are the variables in the study? How well are they measured? For example, many studies purport to measure organization performance. However, performance may be accounting measures such as return on assets or cash flow, financial measures such as earnings per share, operational measures such as scrap rates or defect indicators, or qualitative measures such as customer satisfaction. It may even be the opinions of compensation managers, as in, "How effective is your gain-sharing plan?" (Answer choices are "highly effective," "effective," "somewhat," "disappointing," "not very effective." "Disastrous" is not usually one of the choices.) The informed consumer must ask, Does this research measure anything useful?

2. Does the Study Separate Correlation from Causation?

Once we are confident that the variables are useful and accurately measured, we must be sure that they are actually related. Most often this is addressed through the use of statistical analysis. The **correlation coefficient** is a common measure of association and indicates how changes in one variable are related to changes in another. Many research studies use a statistical analysis known as *regression analysis*. One output from a regression analysis is the R^2. The R^2 is a squared correlation and tells us what percentage of the variation in the outcome variable is accounted for by the variables we are using to predict or explain.

But even if there is a relationship, correlation does not ensure causation. For example, just because a manufacturing plant initiates a new incentive plan and the facility's performance improves, we cannot conclude that the incentive plan caused the improved performance. Perhaps new technology, **reengineering,** improved marketing, or the general expansion of the local economy underlies the results. The two changes are associated or related, but causation is a tough link to make.

Too often, case studies, benchmarking studies of best practices, or consultant surveys are presented as studies that reveal cause and effect. They do not. Case studies are descriptive accounts whose value and limitations must be recognized. Just because the best-performing companies are using a practice does not mean the practice is causing the performance. IBM provides an example of the difficulty of deciding whether a change is a cause or an effect. Years ago, IBM pursued a no-layoff policy. While IBM was doing well, the no-layoff policy was cited as part of the reason. Later, when performance declined, IBM eventually ended the no-layoff policy as a partial response. Did the policy contribute to company success at one time, but not later due to changing circumstances? Did it always act as a drag on company success? Or, was it a mistake to get rid of it? Causality is difficult to infer as we do not know what would have happened had IBM never had the policy and/or if they had it and kept it (versus ending it). Perhaps because of such challenges in inference, compensation research often does attempt to answer questions of causality. Yet, good policy decisions rest on making good causal inferences.[75] Thus, we need to strive to overcome the challenges to answer key questions such as: How does the use of performance-based pay influence employee ability and motivation, customer satisfaction, product quality, and company performance?

3. Are There Alternative Explanations?

Consider a hypothetical study that attempts to assess the impact of a performance-based pay program. The researchers measure performance by assessing quality, productivity, customer satisfaction, employee satisfaction, and the facility's performance. The final step is to see whether future periods' performance improves over this period's. If it does, can we safely assume that it was the incentive pay that caused performance? Or is it equally likely that the improved performance has alternative explanations, such as the fluctuation in the value of currency or perhaps a change in leadership in the facility?

In this case, causality evidence seems weak. Alternative explanations exist. If the researchers had measured the performance indicators several years prior to and after installing the plan, then the evidence of causality is only a bit stronger. Further, if the researchers repeated this process in other facilities and the results were similar, then the preponderance of evidence is stronger yet. Clearly, the organization is doing something right, and incentive pay is part of it.

The best way to establish causation is to account for competing explanations, either statistically or through control groups. The point is that alternative explanations often exist. And if they do, they need to be accounted for to establish causality. It is very difficult to disentangle the effects of pay plans to clearly establish causality. However, it is possible to look at the overall pattern of evidence to make judgments about the effects of pay.

So we encourage you to become a critical reader of all management literature, including this book. As Hogwarts' famous Professor Alaster Moody cautions, be on "constant vigilance for sloppy analysis masquerading as research."[76]

Your **Turn**

The Role of Labor Costs in Retail Electronics

Let's get started with trying to assess the degree to which compensation is an important cause of company success (or lack of success) in two different competitive environments.

First, let's consider the case of consumer electronics and the experiences of Circuit City and Best Buy. Circuit City had traditionally used a commission pay plan that paid off big for experienced, high-performing salespeople. Top salespeople knew the products and kept up to date and customers knew that they could get expert advice at Circuit City. The strategy differentiated Circuit City from archrival Best Buy, which featured self-service stores with huge inventories, but less expert salespeople. Best Buy hired young, less-experienced people and offered lower wages and smaller bonuses. However, Best Buy's sales and total shareholder returns soared past those of Circuit City. Subsequently, Circuit City laid off 3,900 top-earning salespeople in 2003 and replaced them with 2,100 less-experienced people who received lower wages and smaller bonuses. Circuit City said it could no longer afford to pay big commissions to its sales staff while its rivals paid less.[77]

In 2007, Circuit City fired 3,400 of its highest-paid store employees and began to replace them with lower-paid workers in hopes of reducing labor costs. In the following quarter, Circuit City reported that the company lost money. Some commentators attributed the loss to the fact that Circuit City had gotten rid of many of its most experienced and highly trained employees, which they believed translated into a poorer customer experience and, in turn, lower revenues and profits.

For example, according to *BusinessWeek*, "In the world of pricey consumer electronics, where customer service is arguably as important as quality products, Circuit City Stores is missing the mark and further eroding its profits." However, a company spokesman said that only a few salespeople per store were affected by the workforce reductions and that many of the employees affected worked as customer service representatives or in the warehouses. As such, he questioned whether the cuts had significantly affected the in-store customer experience and thus whether the cuts had caused the decline in the company's performance. Eventually, the bottom fell out of Circuit City's profits and stock price and it had to liquidate, closing its over 500 stores (resulting in over 30,000 employees losing their jobs).[78]

Now consider the next part of the story. Best Buy itself subsequently sought to further cut its own labor costs by essentially demoting 8,000 senior sales associates to positions that could pay half as much. A question was whether the Best Buy pay-level cuts would have the same consequences as what one person described as the "disastrous personnel moves" made at Circuit City just a few years ago.[79] Apparently, Best Buy did not see it that way. Subsequently, Best Buy announced that it would close 50 stores and also cut 400 corporate jobs in an effort to cut $800 million in costs. Why is Best Buy aggressively cutting costs? *USA Today* stated that Best Buy "is trying to avoid the fate of Circuit City, which went out of business in 2009. (See also Radio Shack.) It faces slower sales of expensive items like TVs, plus increased competition from Amazon.com and discount stores such as Walmart and Target.[80] Employment at the headquarters has been an ongoing target and is now around 5,000 employees, down from its peak of 9,000 in the mid-2000s. After those cuts, store closings, and pay cuts, Best Buy next (in 2014) cut employment by around 2,000 in its stores and regional offices. However, the cuts are being made in a way that Best Buy hopes will minimize any negative impact on the customer experience. Most of the cuts target middle managers, many of whom have six-figure salaries and who supervise product categories at more than a dozen stores each. That will leave fewer middle managers (spread more thinly across more stores) and give more responsibility to the store managers who will now have the "full ability to run their (respective) stores." The cuts, which target regional offices rather than stores and employees who directly help shoppers, are intended to minimize the impact on customer service inside stores, while helping Best Buy continue to lower costs as it continues to successfully compete on price (and service) against Amazon, Walmart, Target, and others with low cost structures.

Here are data on stock prices and customer satisfaction for Circuit City, Best Buy, and two other competitors, Amazon and Walmart.

	Opening Stock Price				Customer Satisfaction (ASCI Index)			
Year	Circuit City	Best Buy	Amazon	Walmart	Circuit City	Best Buy	Amazon	Walmart
2000	48	26	82	68			84	73
2001	16	18	16	53			84	75
2002	29	32	11	58			88	74
2003	7	18	19	51	73	72	88	75
2004	9	36	53	53	73	72	84	73
2005	14	37	45	54	72	72	87	72
2006	23	47	48	46	70	71	87	72
2007	19	50	37	47	69	76	88	68
2008	4	44	96	47	71	74	86	70
2009	0	28	51	56	72	74	86	71
2010	*	40	136	53	*	77	87	73
2011	*	34	181	54	*	77	86	70
2012	*	24	176	60				
2013	*	12	257	69	*	77	88	71
2014	*	41	398	79	*	77	86	68
2015	*	39	309	86				

ASCI = American Customer Satisfaction Index™, http://www.theacsi.org/. ASCI scores for Circuit City and Best Buy not available prior to 2003.
*Circuit City no longer in business.

QUESTIONS:

1. Thinking back to our discussion in the chapter section, *Caveat Emptor*—Be An Informed Consumer, evaluate whether the replacement of highly paid workers with lower-paid workers did or did not cause Circuit City to perform so poorly. How confident are you in your evaluation? Why?
2. Do you believe that the compensation changes at Best Buy are a major reason for its current difficulties?
3. Why are Walmart, Sam's Club, and Costco doing better than Best Buy (and Circuit City)? Do they have high pay?
4. Are there larger problems in the competitive landscape for Best Buy that cannot be solved by compensation strategy changes alone? When customers look to buy electronics, what options do they have other than Best Buy and why would they choose these options over Best Buy? Where do customers "test drive" the product and where do they buy it? Can compensation changes address these challenges? Explain.
5. Is Best Buy focusing too much or too little on cost reduction? Explain.

Summary   The model presented in this chapter provides a structure for understanding compensation systems. The three main components of the model are the compensation objectives, the policy decisions that guide how the objectives are going to be achieved, and the techniques that make up the pay system and link the policies to the objectives. The following sections of the book examine each of the four policy decisions—internal alignment, external competitiveness, employee performance, and management—as well as the techniques, new directions, and related research.

Two questions should constantly be in the minds of managers and readers of this text. First, why do it this way? There is rarely one correct way to design a system or pay an individual. Organizations, people, and circumstances are too varied. But a well-trained manager can select or design a suitable approach. Second, so what? What does this technique do for us? How does it help achieve our goals? If good answers to the "so-what" question are not apparent, there is no point to the technique. Adapting the pay system to meet the needs of the employees and helping to achieve the goals of the organization is what this book is all about.

The basic premise of this book is that compensation systems do have a profound impact. Yet, too often, traditional pay systems seem to have been designed in response to some historical but long-forgotten problem. The practices continue, but the logic underlying them is not always clear or even relevant. The next generation pay systems hopefully will be more flexible—designed to achieve specific objectives under changing conditions.

Review Questions

1. How do differing perspectives affect our views of compensation?
2. What is your definition of compensation? Which meaning of compensation seems most appropriate from an employee's view: return, reward, or entitlement? Compare your ideas with someone with more experience, someone from another country, someone from another field of study.
3. What is the "network of returns" that your college offers your instructor? What returns do you believe make a difference in teaching effectiveness? What "returns" would you change or add to increase the teaching effectiveness?
4. What are the four policy issues in the pay model? What purposes do the objectives in the pay model serve?
5. List all the forms of pay you receive from work. Compare your list to someone else's list. Explain any differences.
6. Answer the three questions in the *Caveat Emptor—Be An Informed Consumer* section for any study or business article that tells you how to pay people.

Endnotes   1. Written by Jenny Bradford and Berry Gordy Jr. Performed by The Beatles on *The Beatles' Second Album* (1964).

2. Brent Snavely, "Labor Costs to Be Sticking Point of UAW Talks with Automakers," *Los Angeles Times,* July 8, 2011. Chris Woodyard, "VW Exec Knows of No Talks to Unionize

Tennessee Plant," *USA Today,* August 1, 2011. Jerry Hirsch, "Automakers Plan to Hire Thousands of Workers This Year," *Los Angeles Times,* January 12, 2012.

3. General Motors Annual Reports (10-K), filed February 27, 2012 and February 6, 2014, with the SEC.

4. W. G. Sanders and D. C. Hambrick, "Swinging for the Fences: The Effects of CEO Stock Options on Company Risk Taking and Performance," *Academy of Management Journal* 50 (2007), pp. 1055–1078; Cynthia E. Devers, Gerry McNamara, Robert M. Wiseman, and Mathias Arrfelt, "Moving Closer to the Action: Examining Compensation Design Effects on Firm Risk," *Organization Science* 19 (July–August 2008), pp. 548–566.

5. Emily Glazer and Christina Rexrode. "As Regulators Focus on Culture, Wall Street struggles to define it," *The Wall Street Journal,* February 2, 2015. p. A1.

6. Michael Jacobs, "Opinion: How Business Schools Have Failed Business," *The Wall Street Journal,* April 24, 2009. For a similar view, see also Alan S. Blinder, "Crazy Compensation and the Crisis," *The Wall Street Journal,* May 28, 2009. (Mr. Blinder is a former vice chairman of the Federal Reserve Board.)

7. B. Gerhart and M. Fang, "Pay, Intrinsic Motivation, Extrinsic Motivation, Performance, and Creativity in the Workplace: Revisiting Long-held Beliefs," *Annual Review of Organizational Psychology and Organizational Behavior* 2 (2015), pp. 489–521; B. Gerhart and M. Fang, "Pay for (Individual) Performance: Issues, Claims, Evidence and the Role of Sorting Effects," *Human Resource Management Review* 24 (2014), 41–52; K. F. Hallock, *Pay: Why People Earn What They Earn and What You Can Do Now to Make More.* Cambridge: Cambridge University Press, 2012; N. Gupta and J. D. Shaw, "Employee Compensation: The Neglected Area of HRM Research," *Human Resource Management Review,* 24(1), 2014, 1–4; G. E. Ledford, "The Changing Landscape of Employee Rewards: Observations and Prescriptions," *Organizational Dynamics,* 43(3), 2014, pp. 168–179; B. Gerhart, S. L. Rynes, and I. S. Fulmer, "Pay and Performance: Individuals, Groups, and Executives," *Academy of Management Annals* 3 (2009), pp. 251–315; B. Gerhart and S. L. Rynes, *Compensation: Theory, Evidence, and Strategic Implications* (Thousand Oaks, CA: Sage, 2003); James H. Dulebohn and Stephen E. Werling, "Compensation Research: Past, Present, and Future," *Human Resource Management Review* 17 (2007), pp. 191–207; Steve Werner and Stephanie Ward, "Recent Compensation Research: An Eclectic Review," *Human Resource Management Review* 14 (2004), pp. 201–227; S. L. Rynes, B. Gerhart, and K. A. Minette, "The Importance of Pay in Employee Motivation: Discrepancies between What People Say and What They Do," *Human Resource Management* 43 (2004), pp. 381–394.

8. U.S. Bureau of Labor Statistics, "Highlights of Women's Earnings in 2013," Report 1051. December 2014. Chart 1 and Table 1.

9. B. Gerhart, "Gender Differences in Current and Starting Salaries: The Role of Performance, College Major, and Job Title," *Industrial and Labor Relations Review* 43 (1990), pp. 418–433; G. G. Cain, "The Economic Analysis of Labor-Market Discrimination: A Survey," in *Handbook of Labor Economics,* O. Ashenfelter and R. Layard, eds (New York: North-Holland, 1986), pp. 694–785; F. D. Blau and L. M. Kahn, "The Gender Pay Gap: Have Women Gone as Far as They Can?" *Academy of Management Perspectives,* February 2007, pp. 7–23.

10. U.S. Department of Labor, Bureau of Labor Statistics, "Highlights of Women's Earnings in 2010," *Report 1031,* July 2011; Francine D. Blau and Lawrence M. Kahn, "The Gender Pay Gap: Have Women Gone as Far as They Can?" *Academy of Management Perspectives* 21 (February 2007), pp. 7–23.

11. "Employer Costs for Employer Compensation," *www.bls.gov.* Extracted March 12, 2009.

12. Robert Peardec, "Health Spending Rises Only Modestly," *New York Times,* December 4, 2014, p. A22.

13. The Henry J. Kaiser Foundation, "The Uninsured: A Primer—Key Facts About Health Insurance and the Uninsured in America," December 05, 2014. http://kff.org/uninsured /report/the-uninsured-a-primer/.

14. Centers for Medicare and Medicaid Services, "National Health Expenditures Data," NHE Fact Sheet. May 5, 2014. www.cms.gov.

15. The National Coalition on Health Care, "Health Insurance Coverage," *www.nchc.org/facts /coverage.shtml.* Extracted May 22, 2009.

16. GDP per head, US $, constant prices, constant PPPs, reference year 2005. OECD. StatExtracts. Stats.OECD.org. Extracted May 16, 2012.

17. John Gapper and Barney Jopson, "Coach to Cut Output in China," *Financial Times,* May 13, 2011; Ben Blanchard, "Foxconn to Raise Wages again at China Plant," www.reuters .com. Retrieved October 19, 2010; Joe Manget and Pierre Mercier, "As Wages Rise, Time to Leave China?" *Bloomberg Businessweek,* December 1, 2010; Shai Oster, "China's Rising Wages Propel U.S. Prices," *The Wall Street Journal,* May 9, 2011. Tim Worstall, "Apple's Foxconn to Double Wages Again," *Forbes,* May 28, 2012.

18. David Redmon, director, *Mardi Gras: Made in China, www.mardigrasmadeinchina.com /news.html;* B. Powell and D. Skarbek, "Sweatshops and Third World Living Standards: Are the Jobs Worth the Sweat?" *Journal of Labor Research,* Spring 2006, pp. 263–290.

19. L. Bebchuk and J. M. Fried, *Pay without Performance* (Cambridge, MA: Harvard University Press, 2004); M. J. Conyon, "Executive Compensation and Incentives," *Academy of Management Perspectives* 21 (February 2006), pp. 25–44; S. N. Kaplan, "Are CEOs Overpaid?" *Academy of Management Perspectives* 22(2), 2008, pp. 5–20; J. P. Walsh, "CEO Compensation: The Responsibilities of the Business Scholar to Society," *Academy of Management Perspectives* 22(2), 2008, pp. 26–33; A. J. Nyberg, I. S. Fulmer, B. Gerhart, and M. A. Carpenter, "Agency Theory Revisited: CEO Returns and Shareholder Interest Alignment," *Academy of Management Journal* 53 (2010), pp. 1029–1049.

20. Information on executive pay can be found in the following sources: Bruce R. Ellig, *The Complete Guide to Executive Compensation* (New York: McGraw-Hill, 3rd ed., 2014); I. S. Fulmer, "Labor Market Influences on CEO Compensation," *Personnel Psychology* 62, pp. 659–696; B. Gerhart, S. L. Rynes, and I. S. Fulmer, "Pay and Performance: Individuals, Groups, and Executives," *Academy of Management Annals* 3 (2009), pp. 251–315; C. Frydman and D. Jenter, "CEO Compensation," *Annual Review of Financial Economics* 2, (2010), pp. 75–102; K. J. Murphy, "Executive Compensation," in *Handbook of Labor Economics,* vol. 3B, O. C. Ashenfelter and David Card, eds. (Amsterdam: Elsevier/North Holland, 2009).

21. C. E. Devers, A. A. Cannella, G. P. Reilly, and M. E. Yoder, "Executive Compensation: A Multidisciplinary Review of Recent Developments," *Journal of Management* 33 (2007), pp. 1016–1072; I. S. Fulmer, "The Elephant in the Room: Labor Market Influences on CEO Compensation," *Personnel Psychology,* in press; A. Nyberg, I. S. Fulmer, B. Gerhart, and M. A. Carpenter, "Agency Theory Revisited: CEO Returns and Shareholder Interest Alignment," *Academy of Management Journal,* 53 (2010), pp. 1029–1049.

22. A. Nyberg, I. S. Fulmer, B. Gerhart, and M. A. Carpenter, "Agency Theory Revisited: CEO Returns and Shareholder Interest Alignment," *Academy of Management Journal* 53 (2010), p. 1032.

23. Lucian Bebchuk, Alma Cohen, and Holger Spamann, "Paid to Fail," Project Syndicate, March 2010. www.project–syndicate.com. Extracted May 18, 2012; Lucian Bebchuk

et al., "The Wages of Failure: Executive Compensation at Bear Stearns and Lehman 2000–2008," *Yale Journal on Regulation* 27, pp. 257–282.

24. Joann S. Lublin, "Firms Feel 'Say on Pay' Effect: Companies Work Harder to Win Shareholder Votes on Executive Compensation," *The Wall Street Journal,* May 2, 2011; Gretchen Morgenson, "When Shareholders Make Their Voices Heard," *The New York Times,* April 7, 2012; Steven M. Davidoff, "After $2 Billion Loss, Will JPMorgan Move to Claw Back Pay?" *The New York Times,* May 14, 2012. dealbook.nytimes.com/2012/05/14/after-2-billion-trading-loss-will-jpmorgan-claw-back-pay. Extracted May 18, 2012.

25. Wayne F. Cascio, "The High Cost of Low Wages," *Harvard Business Review* 84 (December 2006), p. 23; Liza Featherstone, "Wage against the Machine," *Slate,* June 27, 2008.

26. Costco 10-K (annual report), filed October 14, 2011; Walmart 10-K (annual report), filed March 27, 2012.

27. Jerry Newman, *My Secret Life on the McJob* (New York: McGraw-Hill, 2007); Edward Lawler III, *Treat People Right! How Organizations and Individuals Can Propel Each Other into a Virtuous Spiral of Success* (San Francisco: Jossey-Bass, 2003).

28. K. Bartol and E. Locke, "Incentives and Motivation," Chap. 4 in *Compensation in Organizations,* S. Rynes and B. Gerhart, eds. (San Francisco: Jossey-Bass, 2000), pp. 104–150; B. Gerhart, S. L. Rynes, and I. S. Fulmer, "Pay and Performance: Individuals, Groups, and Executives," *Academy of Management Annals* 3 (2009), pp. 251–315.

29. Edward E. Lawler III, *Pay and Organizational Effectiveness: A Psychological View* (New York: McGraw-Hill, 1971). T. L. P. Tang, "The Meaning of Money Revisited," *Journal of Organizational Behavior*, 13(2), (1992), pp. 197–202.

30. E. P. Lazear, "Salaries and Piece Rates," *Journal of Business* 59, 1986, pp. 405–431; B. Gerhart and G. T. Milkovich, "Employee Compensation: Research and Practice," in *Handbook of Industrial & Organizational Psychology,* 2nd ed., M. D. Dunnette and L. M. Hough, eds. (Palo Alto, CA: Consulting Psychologists Press, 1992); B. Gerhart and S. L. Rynes, *Compensation: Theory, Evidence, and Strategic Implications* (Thousand Oaks: Sage, 2003).

31. D. M. Cable and T. A. Judge, "Pay Preferences and Job Search Decisions: A Person-Organization Fit Perspective," *Personnel Psychology* 47 (1994), pp. 317–348; C. B. Cadsby, F. Song, and F. Tapon, "Sorting and Incentive Effects of Pay-for-Performance: An Experimental Investigation," *Academy of Management Journal* 50 (2007), pp. 387–405; C. Q. Trank, S. L. Rynes, and R. D. Bretz, Jr., "Attracting Applicants in the War for Talent: Differences in Work Preferences Among High Achievers," *Journal of Business and Psychology* 16 (2001), pp. 331–345; C. O. Trevor, B. Gerhart, and J. W. Boudreau, "Voluntary Turnover and Job Performance: Curvilinearity and the Moderating Influences of Salary Growth and Promotions," *Journal of Applied Psychology* 82 (1997), pp. 44–61; A. Salamin and P. W. Hom, "In Search of the Elusive U-Shaped Performance-Turnover Relationship: Are High Performing Swiss Bankers More Liable to Quit?" *Journal of Applied Psychology* 90 (2005), pp. 1204–1216; J. D. Shaw and N. Gupta, "Pay System Characteristics and Quit Patterns of Good, Average, and Poor Performers," *Personnel Psychology* 60 (2007), pp. 903–928; B. Schneider, "The People Make the Place," *Personnel Psychology* 40 (1987), pp. 437–453; A. Nyberg, "Retaining Your High Performers: Moderators of the Performance-Job Satisfaction-Voluntary Turnover Relationship," *Journal of Applied Psychology* 95 (2010), pp. 440–453; J. D. Shaw, B. Dineen, R. Fang, and R. F. Vellella, "Employee-Organization Exchange Relationships, HRM Practices, and Quit Rates of Good and Poor Performers," *Academy of Management*

Journal 52 (2009), pp. 1016–1033. M. Lynn, R. J. Kwortnik, and M. C. Sturman, "Voluntary Tipping and the Selective Attraction and Retention of Service Workers in the USA: An Application of the ASA Model," *International Journal of Human Resource Management* 22 (2011), pp. 1887–1901; T. Dohmen and A. Falk, "Performance Pay and Multidimensional Sorting: Productivity, Preferences, and Gender." *The American Economic Review* 2011, pp. 556–590; B. Gerhart and M. Fang, "Pay for (Individual) Performance: Issues, Claims, Evidence and the Role of Sorting Effects," *Human Resource Management Review* 24, 2014, 41–52; B. D. Blume, R. S. Rubin, and T. T. Baldwin, "Who Is Attracted to an Organisation Using a Forced Distribution Performance Management System? *Human Resource Management Journal*, 23(4), 2013, pp. 360–378; W. J. Becker and R. Cropanzano, "Dynamic Aspects of Voluntary Turnover: An Integrated Approach to Curvilinearity in the Performance-Turnover Relationship," *Journal of Applied Psychology* 96 (2011), pp. 233–246; B. W. Swider, W. R. Boswell, and R. D. Zimmerman, "Examining the Job Search—Turnover Relationship: The Role of Embeddedness, Job Satisfaction, and Available Alternatives," *Journal of Applied Psychology* 96 (2011), pp. 432–441.

32. O'Boyle EH, Aguinis H. 2012. The best and the rest: revisiting the norm of normality of individual performance. *Personnel Psychology* 65:79–119; Beck JW, Beatty AS, Sackett PR. 2014. On the distribution of job performance: the role of measurement characteristics in observed departures from normality. *Personnel Psychology*, 67:531–66. Aguinis, H., & O'Boyle, E. (2014). Star Performers in Twenty-First Century Organizations. *Personnel Psychology*, 67(2), 313–350. Aguinis, H., O'Boyle, E., Gonzalez-MulÉ, E., & Joo, H. (2014). Cumulative Advantage: Conductors and Insulators of Heavy-tailed Productivity Distributions and Productivity Stars. *Personnel Psychology*.

33. T. H. Lee, B. Gerhart, I. Weller, and C. O. Trevor, "Understanding Voluntary Turnover: Path-Specific Job Satisfaction Effects and the Importance of Unsolicited Job Offers," *Academy of Management Journal*, 51 (2008), pp. 651–671; W. I. MacKenzie Jr, B. S. Klaas, and J. A. McClendon, "Information Use in Counter-Offer Decisions: An Examination of Factors That Influence Management Counter-Offer Decisions," *Journal of Labor Research* 33(3), 2012, 370–387.

34. E. Lazear, "Performance Pay and Productivity," *American Economic Review* 90 (2000), pp. 1346–1361.

35. Atul Mitra, Matt Bloom, and George Milkovich, "Crossing a Raging River: Seeking Far-Reaching Solutions to Global Pay Challenges," *WorldatWork Journal* 22(2), Second Quarter 2002; Mark Fenton-O'Creevy, "HR Practice: Vive la Différence," *Financial Times,* October 2002, pp. 6–8; Mansour Javidan, Peter Dorman, Mary Sully deLuque, and Robert House, "In the Eye of the Beholder: Cross Cultural Lessons in Leadership from Project GLOBE," *Academy of Management Perspectives,* February 2006, pp. 67–90.

36. Anne Tsui and Chung-Ming Lau, *The Management of Enterprises in the People's Republic of China* (Boston: Kluwer Academic, 2002).

37. Sanford Jacoby, *The Embedded Corporation: Corporate Governance and Employment Relations in Japan and the United States* (Princeton, NJ: Princeton University Press, 2004); Yoshio Yanadori, "Minimizing Competition? Entry-Level Compensation in Japanese Firms," *Asia Pacific Journal of Management* 21 (December 2004), pp. 445–467.

38. Chun Hui, Cynthia Lee, and Denise M. Rousseau, "Psychological Contract and Organizational Citizenship Behavior in China: Investigating Generalizability and Instrumentality," *Journal of Applied Psychology* 89 (2004), pp. 311–321; N. Conway and R. Briner, *Understanding Psychological Contracts at Work: A Critical Evaluation of Theory and Research* (Oxford: Oxford University Press, 2005); WorldatWork has

developed a total rewards model, described in Jean Christofferson and Bob King, "The 'It' Factor: A New Total Rewards Model Leads the Way," *Workspan,* April 2006.

39. "Brightly Colored Uniforms Boost Employee Morale," *The Onion* 36(43), November 30, 2000.

40. Jean Christofferson and Bob King, "New Total Rewards Model," *Workspan,* April 2006, pp. 1–8.

41. F. Herzberg, "One More Time: How Do You Motivate Employees?" *Harvard Business Review,* September–October 1987, pp. 5–16. E. L. Deci, R. Koestner, and R. M. Ryan, "A Meta-Analytic Review of Experiments Examining the Effects of Extrinsic Rewards on Intrinsic Motivation," *Psychological Bulletin* 25 (1999), pp. 627–668. R. Eisenberger and J. Cameron, "Detrimental Effects of Reward: Reality or Myth?" *American Psychologist* 51 (1996), pp. 1153–1166. D. Pink, *Drive: The Surprising Truth about What Motivates Us* (New York, NY: Penguin Group, 2009); S. E. DeVoe, J. Pfeffer, and B. Y. Lee, "When Does Money Make Money More Important? Survey and Experimental Evidence," *Industrial & Labor Relations Review* 66(5), 2013, pp. 1078–1096; T. L. P. Tang, R. Luna-Arocas, I. Q. Pardo, and T. L. N. Tang, "Materialism and the Bright and Dark Sides of the Financial Dream in Spain: The Positive Role of Money Attitudes—The Matthew Effect," *Applied Psychology*, 63(3), 2014, pp. 480–508; J. Chen, T. L. P. Tang, and N. Tang, "Temptation, Monetary Intelligence (Love of Money), and Environmental Context on Unethical Intentions and Cheating," *Journal of Business Ethics*, 123(2), 2014, pp. 197–219; B. Gerhart and S. L. Rynes, *Compensation: Theory, Evidence, and Strategic Implications* (Thousand Oaks: Sage, 2003), Chapter 3; Edward E. Lawler III, *Pay and Organizational Effectiveness: A Psychological View* (New York: McGraw-Hill, 1971).

42. Gerhart, B. & Fang, M. (2015). Intrinsic Motivation, Pay for Performance, and Effectiveness (in the Workplace): Theories and Evidence. *Annual Review of Organizational Psychology and Organizational Behavior*; Cerasoli PC, Nicklin JM, Ford MT. 2014. Intrinsic motivation and extrinsic incentives jointly predict performance: a 40-year meta-analysis. *Psychol. Bull.* 140:980–1008. Ledford, G.E. Jr., Fang, M., & Gerhart, B. (2013). Negative Effects of Extrinsic Rewards on Intrinsic Motivation: More Smoke than Fire. *World at Work Journal* 22(2), 17–29. Grandey, A. A., Chi, N. W., & Diamond, J. A. (2013). Show me the money! Do financial rewards for performance enhance or undermine the satisfaction from emotional labor? Personnel Psychology, 66(3), 569–612; M. Fang and B. Gerhart, "Does Pay for Performance Diminish Intrinsic Interest? A Workplace Test Using Cognitive Evaluation Theory and the Attraction-Selection-Attrition Model," *International Journal of Human Resource Management,* 2012; M. Gagné and E. L. Deci, "Self-Determination Theory and Work Motivation," *Journal of Organizational Behavior* 26 (2005), pp. 331–362.

43. Allan Odden and Carolyn Kelley, *Paying Teachers for What They Know and Do: New and Smarter Compensation Strategies to Improve Schools,* 2nd ed. (Thousand Oaks: Corwin Press, 2002); Ralph Blumenthal, "Houston Ties Teachers' Pay to Test Scores," *The New York Times,* January 13, 2006, p. A12.

44. U.S. Department of Labor, Fair Labor Standards Act, *http://www.dol.gov/compliance /laws/comp-flsa.htm.*

45. B. Gerhart and M. Fang, "Pay for (Individual) Performance: Issues, Claims, Evidence and the Role of Sorting Effects," *Human Resource Management Review*, 24, 2014, pp. 41–52; S. L. Rynes, B. Gerhart, and L. Parks, "Personnel Psychology: Performance Evaluation and Pay for Performance," *Annual Review of Psychology* 56 (2005), pp. 571–600; R. L. Heneman, *Merit Pay: Linking Pay Increases to Performance Ratings* (New York: Addison-Wesley, 1992); G. Milkovich and A. Wigdor, *Pay for Performance: Evaluating*

Performance Appraisal and Merit Pay (Washington, DC: National Academy Press, 1991); M. C. Sturman, C. O. Trevor, J. W. Boudreau, and B. Gerhart, "Is It Worth It to Win the Talent War? Evaluating the Utility of Performance-Based Pay," *Personnel Psychology* 56 (2003), pp. 997–1035; Michael Sturman, "How Versus How Much You Pay: The Effects of Various Pay Components on Future Performance," working paper, Hotel School, Ithaca, NY: 2006; John J. Schaubroeck, Jason D. Shaw, and Michelle K Duffy, "An Under-Met and Over-Met Expectations Model of Employee Reactions to Merit Raises," *Journal of Applied Psychology* 93 (2008), pp. 424–434; S. E. Scullen, P. K. Bergey, and L. Aiman-Smith, "Forced Distribution Rating Systems and the Improvement of Workforce Potential: A Baseline Simulation," *Personnel Psychology* 58 (2005), pp. 1–32.

46.   WorldatWork, *2008–2009 Salary Budget Survey* (Scottsdale).

47.   Mercer 2011/2012 U.S. Compensation Planning Survey report; AON Hewitt Survey—U.S. Salary Increases 1991/1992 and 2011/2012; *WorldatWork, 2014–2015 Salary Budget Survey*.

48.   A. J. Nyberg, J. R. Pieper, and C. O. Trevor (forthcoming), "Pay-for-Performance's Effect on Future Employee Performance Integrating Psychological and Economic Principles Toward a Contingency Perspective," *Journal of Management*. B. Gerhart and M. Fang, "Pay for (Individual) Performance: Issues, Claims, Evidence and the Role of Sorting Effects," *Human Resource Management Review*, 24, 2014, pp. 41–52; AON Hewitt Survey—U.S. Salary Increases 1991/1992 and 2011/2012.

49.   B. Gerhart and M Fang, "Pay for (Individual) Performance: Issues, Claims, Evidence and the Role of Sorting Effects," *Human Resource Management Review* 24, 2014, pp. 41–52.

50.   *Ibid.* WorldatWork, "Compensation Programs and Practices 2012," *Scottsdale*, 2012. See also K. Abosch, *Why Can't (Won't) We Differentiate*. Presentation at Wisconsin School of Business, University of Wisconsin-Madison, May 2012.

51.   D. G. Jenkins, Jr., A. Mitra, N. Gupta, and J. D. Shaw, "Are Financial Incentives Related to Performance? A Meta-analytic Review of Empirical Research," *Journal of Applied Psychology* 83, 1998, pp. 777–787; Steve Kerr, "The Best Laid Incentive Plans," *Harvard Business Review,* January 2003; Michael C. Sturman and J. C. Short, "Lump Sum Bonus Satisfaction: Testing the Construct Validity of a New Pay Satisfaction Dimension," *Personnel Psychology* 53, 2000, pp. 673–700; A. D. Stajkovic and F. Luthans, "A Meta-Analysis of the Effects of Organizational Behavior Modification on Task Performance, 1975–1995," *Academy of Management Journal*, 40, 1997, pp. 1122–1149; T. M. Nisar, "Bonuses and Investment in Intangibles," *Journal of Labor Research,* Summer 2006, pp. 381–396; W. F. Whyte, *Money and Motivation: An Analysis of Incentives in Industry* (New York: Harper Brothers, 1955); E. E. Lawler III, *Pay and Organizational Effectiveness: A Psychological View* (New York: McGraw-Hill, 1971); D. Roy, "Quota Restriction and Gold Bricking in a Machine Shop," *American Journal of Sociology* 57, 1952, pp. 427–442; B. Gerhart and S. L. Rynes, *Compensation: Theory, Evidence, and Strategic Implications* (Thousand Oaks: Sage, 2003).

52.   Cory Rosen, John Case, and Martin Staubus, "Every Employee an Owner," *Harvard Business Review,* June 2005, pp. 123–130; Ben Dunford, John Boudreau, and Wendy Boswell, "Out of the Money: The Impact of Underwater Stock Options on Executive Job Search," *Personnel Psychology* 58 (2005), pp. 67–101; Bartolome Deya-Tortella, Luis R. Gomez-Mejia, Julio E. DeCastro, and Robert M. Wiseman, "Incentive Alignment or Perverse Incentives? A Behavioral View of Stock Options," *Management Research* 3(2), 2005, 109–120.

53.   Centers for Medicare and Medicaid Services. National Health Expenditures Data. NHE Fact Sheet. Table 5. May 5, 2014. www.cms.gov; Kaiser Family Foundation/Health

Research & Educational Trust (HRET), *2014 Employer Health Benefits Survey.* September 10, 2014. http://kff.org/report-section/ehbs-2014-summary-of-findings/.

54. Barbara Mannino, "Employees Get Pinched: Health Insurance Costs More," May 9, 2012. http://www.foxbusiness.com/personal-finance/2012/03/09/employees-get-pinched-health -insurance-costs-more/. Extracted May 17, 2012.

55. *www.medtronic.com.*

56. Mei Fong, "A Chinese Puzzle," *The Wall Street Journal,* August 16, 2004, p. B1.

57. The websites for the International Labour Organization (*www.ilo.org*) and the European Industrial Relations Observatory On-Line (*www.eiro.eurofound.ie*) publish news of developments in HR in Europe. Also see Paul Boselie and Jaap Paauwe, *HR Function Competencies in European Companies* (Ithaca, NY: CAHRS Working Paper, 2005).

58. Gary P. Latham, *Work Motivation: History, Theory, Research, and Practice* (Thousand Oaks: Sage, 2007); A. H. Maslow, "A Theory of Human Motivation," *Psychological Review* 50 (1943), pp. 370–396; F. Herzberg, B. Mausner, R. O. Peterson, and D. F. Capwell, *Job Attitudes: Review of Research and Opinion* (Pittsburgh: Psychological Service of Pittsburgh, 1957); B. Gerhart and S. L. Rynes, *Compensation: Theory, Evidence, and Strategic Implications* (Thousand Oaks: Sage, 2003): R. Sage, G. Kanfer, G. Chen, and R. D. Pritchard, eds., *Motivation: Past, Present, and Future* (New York: Taylor and Francis, 2008).

59. Austin Collins, "Pay in Theoretical Physics," *California Institute of Technology Newspaper,* May 23, 1997, p. 3; Richard P. Feynman, *The Pleasure of Finding Things Out* (Cambridge, MA: Helix Books, 1999); "Brightly Colored Uniforms Boost Employee Morale," *The Onion* 36 (43), November 30, 2000; Just Racz, *50 Jobs Worse Than Yours* (New York: Bloomsbury, 2004).

60. Charles Fishman, "The Anarchist's Cookbook," *Fast Company,* July 2004, *http://www .fastcompany.com/magazine/84/wholefoods.html.* Further information on each company's philosophy and way of doing business can be deduced from their websites: *www .medtronic.com* and *www.wholefoods.com.*

61. Readers of earlier editions of this book will note that "fairness" is substituted for "equity." The word "equity" has taken on several meanings in compensation, e.g., stock ownership and pay discrimination. We decided that "fairness" better conveyed our meaning in this book.

62. Charlie O. Trevor and David L. Wazeter, "A Contingent View of Reactions to Objective Pay Conditions: Interdependence Among Pay Structure Characteristics and Pay Relative to Internal and External Referents," *Journal of Applied Psychology* 91 (2006), pp. 1260–1275; Quinetta M. Roberson and Jason A. Colquitt, "Shared and Configural Justice: A Social Network Model of Justice in Teams," *Academy of Management Review* 30(3), 2005, pp. 595–607; Don A. Moore, Philip E. Tetlock, Lloyd Tanlu, and Max H. Bazerman, "Conflicts of Interest and the Case of Auditor Independence: Moral Seduction and Strategic Issue Cycling," *Academy of Management Review* 31(1), 2006, pp. 10–29; Maurice E. Schweitzer, Lisa Ordonez, and Bambi Douma, "Goal Setting as a Motivator of Unethical Behavior," *Academy of Management Journal* 47(3), 2004, pp. 422–432; Vikas Anand, Blake E. Ashforth, and Mahendra Joshi, "Business as Usual: The Acceptance and Perpetuation of Corruption in Organizations," *Academy of Management Executive* 19(4), 2005, pp. 9–22.

63. John W. Budd and James G. Scoville, eds., *The Ethics of Human Resources and Industrial Relations* (Ithaca: Cornell University Press, 2004); Richard M Locke, Fei Qin, and Alberto Brause, "Does Monitoring Improve Labor Standards? Lessons from Nike," *Industrial & Labor Relations Review* 61 (2007), p. 3.

64. "Academy of Management Code of Ethical Conduct," *Academy of Management Journal* 48(6), 2005, pp. 1188–1192; Barrie E. Litzky, Kimberly A. Eddleston, and Deborah L. Kidder, "The Good, the Bad, and the Misguided: How Managers Inadvertently Encourage Deviant Behaviors," *Academy of Management Perspectives* 20(1), February 2006, pp. 91–103; Frederic W. Cook, "Compensation Ethics: An Oxymoron or Valid Area for Debate?" Featured speech at ACA International Conference Workshop, 1999; Stuart P. Green, *Lying, Cheating, and Stealing: A Moral Theory of White-Collar Crime* (Boston: Oxford University Press, 2006); Tom Stone, "Ethics in HRM," Oklahoma State HR Conference, May 2005. See *www.shrm.org/ethics/code-of-ethics/asp*. Stone identifies an integrity test at *www.hoganassessments.com* and *www.epredix.com*. The site for the Ethics Resource Center is *www.ethics.org*. The Josephson Institute of Ethics publishes online their pamphlet *Making Ethical Decisions, www.josephsoninstitute.org*.

65. Michael Gibbs and Wallace Hendricks, "Do Formal Pay Systems Really Matter?" *Industrial & Labor Relations Review,* October 2004, pp. 71–93; John Boudreau and Pete Ramstad, *Beyond Cost-Per-Hire and Time to Fill: Supply-Chain Measurement for Staffing.* (Los Angeles: Center for Effective Organizations, 2006); Christopher Collins, Jeff Ericksen, and Matthew Allen, *HRM Practices, Workforce Alignment, and Firm Performance* (Ithaca: CAHRS Working Paper, 2005).

66. *Market Pricing: Methods to the Madness* (Scottsdale: WorldatWork, 2002).

67. Rosemary Batt, "Managing Customer Services: Human Resource Practices, Quit Rates, and Sales Growth," *Academy of Management Journal* 45(3), 2002, pp. 587–597; Paul Osterman, "The Wage Effects of High Performance Work Organization in Manufacturing," *Industrial and Labor Relations Review,* January 2006, pp. 187–204; Patrick Wright, Timothy Gardner, Lisa Moynihan, and Mathew Allen, "The Relationship between HR Practices and Firm Performance: Examining Causal Order," *Personal Psychology,* Summer 2005, pp. 409–446; Robert D. Mohr and Cindy Zoghi, "High-Involvement Work Design and Job Satisfaction," *Industrial & Labor Relations Review* 61 (2008), p. 275; Eileen Appelbaum, Thomas Bailey, Peter Berg, and Arne Kalleberg, *Manufacturing Advantage: Why High Performance Work Systems Pay Off* (Ithaca: Cornell University Press, 2000).

68. Mary Graham, Rick Welsh, and George Mueller, "In the Land of Milk and Money: One Dairy Farm's Strategic Compensation System," *Journal of Agribusiness* 15(2), 1997, pp. 171–188.

69. J. Paauwe, *HRM and Performance: Unique Approaches in Order to Achieve Long-term Viability* (Oxford: Oxford University Press, 2004).

70. John Boudreau and Pete Ramstad, *Beyond Cost-Per-Hire and Time to Fill: Supply-Chain Measurement for Staffing* (Los Angeles: Center for Effective Organizations, 2006); Ed Lawler, Dave Ulrich, Jac Fitz-Enz, and James Madden, *HR Business Process Outsourcing* (San Francisco: Jossey-Bass, 2004); D. Scott, D. Morajda, T. McMullen, and R. Sperling, "Evaluating Pay Program Effectiveness," *WorldatWork Journal* 15(2) (Second Quarter 2006), pp. 50–59; S. Raza, *Optimizing Human Capital Investments for Superior Shareholder Returns* (New York: Hewitt Associates, 2006); M. Huselid and B. Becker, "Improving HR Analytical Literacy: Lessons from Moneyball," Chapter 32 in M. Losey, S. Meisinger, and D. Ulrich, *The Future of Human Resource Management* (Hoboken: Wiley, 2005).

71. Y. Yanadori and J. H. Marler, "Compensation Strategy: Does Business Strategy Influence Compensation in High-Technology Firms?" *Strategic Management Journal,* 27 (2006), pp. 559–570.

72. Jeffrey Pfeffer and Robert Sutton, "Management Half-Truth and Nonsense: How to Practice Evidence-Based Management," *California Management Review,* Spring 2006; Denise Rousseau, "Is There Such a Thing as 'Evidence-Based Management'?" *Academy of Management Review* 31(2) 2006, pp. 258–269; Sara L. Rynes, Amy E. Colbert, and Kenneth G. Brown, "HR Professionals' Beliefs About Effective Human Resource Practices: Correspondence Between Research and Practice," *Human Resource Management* 41(2), Summer 2002, pp. 149–174; Sara L. Rynes, Amy E. Colbert, and Kenneth G. Brown, "Seven Common Misconceptions About Human Resource Practices: Research Findings Versus Practitioner Beliefs," *Academy of Management Executive* 16(3) 2002, pp. 92–102.

73. Sara L. Rynes, Amy E. Colbert, and Kenneth G. Brown, "Seven Common Misconceptions About Human Resource Practices: Research Findings versus Practitioner Beliefs," *Academy of Management Executive* 16(3), 2002, pp. 92–102.

74. E. A. Locke, D. B. Feren, V. M. McCaleb, et al., "The Relative Effectiveness of Four Ways of Motivating Employee Performance," in *Changes in Working Life,* K. D. Duncan, M. M. Gruenberg, and D. Wallis, eds. (New York: Wiley, 1980), pp. 363–388. See also S. L. Rynes, B. Gerhart, and L. Parks, "Personnel Psychology: Performance Evaluation and Pay-for-Performance," *Annual Review of Psychology* 56 (2005), pp. 571–600.

75. B. Gerhart, "Modeling Human Resource Management—Performance Linkages," in P. Boxall, J. Purcell, and P. Wright, eds., *The Oxford Handbook of Human Resource Management* (Oxford: Oxford University Press, 2007); P. M. Wright, T. M. Gardner, L. M. Moynihan, and M. R. Allen, "The Relationship between HR Practices and Firm Performance: Examining the Causal Order," *Personnel Psychology* 52 (2005), pp. 409–446.

76. J. K. Rowling, *Harry Potter and the Goblet of Fire* (London: Scholastic, 2000).

77. Carlos Tejada and Gary McWilliams, "New Recipe for Cost Savings: Replace Expensive Workers," *The Wall Street Journal,* June 11, 2003, pp. 1, A12.45.

78. Amy Joyce, "Circuit City's Job Cuts Backfiring, Analysts Say," *Washington Post,* May 2, 2007, p. D1; David Bogoslaw, "Circuit City Gets Crushed," *BusinessWeek,* December 2, 2007.

79. Mary Ellen Lloyd, "Best Buy's Store-Staffing Changes Draw Circuit City Comparisons," *The Wall Street Journal,* April 15, 2009.

80. "Best Buy Announces Locations for Store Closings." *USA Today,* April 15, 2012.

Strategy: The Totality of Decisions

You probably think you can skip this chapter. After all, what can be so challenging about a compensation strategy? How about this for a strategy: We'll let the market decide what we need to pay people! Unfortunately, a dose of reality quickly reveals that employers do not behave so simply. Even if they did, deciphering what "the market" has "decided" requires an investment in information search and cognitive processing. Information has a cost, and in processing information, people are only "boundedly rational" (to use a term coined by Herbert Simon).

SIMILARITIES AND DIFFERENCES IN STRATEGIES

In Exhibit 2.1 we compare compensation strategies at Google, Nucor, and Merrill Lynch. Google is a popular Internet search engine company. Nucor is a pioneer in recycling steel scrap and other metallics into steel products, including rebar, angles, rounds, channels, flats, sheet, beams, plate, and other products. Merrill Lynch, now part of Bank of America, a financial services organization that has had an eventful several years, advises companies and clients worldwide. We will focus primarily on financial advisors ("brokers") at Merrill Lynch. (See Your Turn: Merrill Lynch at the end of this chapter.) All three are innovators in their industry. Their decisions on the five

EXHIBIT 2.1   Three Compensation Strategies

	Google	Nucor	Merrill Lynch
Objectives	Emphasis on innovation Commitment to cost containment Recognize contributions Attract and reward the best	Focus on customer Most productive Highest quality	Focus on customer Attract, motivate, and retain the best talent Fair, understandable policies and practices
Internal Alignment	Minimize hierarchy Everyone wears several hats Emphasize collaboration	Succeed by working together No defined career paths, but many opportunities	Pay fairly internally Job sized on four factors: knowledge/skill, complexity, business impact, strategic value
Externally Competitive	Market leader in pay and benefits Unique benefits	Below market for base Market leader for total cash compensation	Market competitive in base and benefits Market competitive in incentive/bonus and stock
Employee Contributions	Recognize individual contributions Significant stock programs	Bonuses based on plant production and company profits	Financial advisors work under a strong incentive system based on client wealth management fees/ commissions and total wealth of their client base
Management	Love employees, want them to know it	Not for everyone No-layoff practice, but income fluctuates	Understandable, consistent message

dimensions of compensation strategy are both similar and different. All three formulate their pay strategy to support their business strategy. All three emphasize outstanding employee performance and commitment. However, there are major differences.

Google, while in fact one of the largest companies in the world with a market value of about $350 billion, positions itself as still being, at heart, the feisty start-up populated by nerds and math whizzes. It offers all its employees such generous stock options that many of them have become millionaires. Its benefits are "way beyond the basics" compared to its competitors. (Yes, there is a free lunch, a gym, a grand piano, bocce courts, a bowling alley, and roller hockey in the parking lot. There is also food: 25 cafés in the company, all free.) Not surprisingly, Google was named the best company to work for by *Fortune* in 2007, 2008, 2012, 2013, and 2014 (and in the top four in 2009, 2010, and 2011). Google has traditionally downplayed cash compensation (base plus bonus), but again the current reality is different. For example, Google was recently ranked #1 on Glassdoor's list of Top Companies for Compensation & Benefits.[1] According to Glassdoor, the mean salary for a senior software engineer at Google is $162,637, compared to the national average of $106,675. A few years ago, Google implemented an across the board 10% increase in base pay, reportedly based on employee survey results indicating that Google employees "consider salary more important than bonuses or equity."[2] Google also believes in pay for performance. Laszlo Bock, its Head of People Operations, in his 2015 book, *Work Rules!*, recommends that organizations "Pay unfairly (it's more fair!)" Bock explains that a small percentage of employees create a large percentage of the value and that their pay must recognize their disproportionate contributions.

At Nucor Steel, the emphasis is on high productivity, high quality, and low cost products. Nucor provides an opportunity for those who are willing to work hard to make a lot of money by helping the company be productive and profitable. Consider that in a good year, an hourly worker can make $75,000 or more per year. That compares to an average annual wage in U.S. manufacturing of about $44,000. In addition, Nucor has had no layoffs, even when sales dropped from $23.7 billion in 2008 to $11.2 billion in 2009. Thus, when Nucor says in its corporate mission that it succeeds by "working together" and that all of its customers are important (including employees), its actions show it takes these words seriously.

Merrill Lynch pay objectives are straightforward: to attract, motivate, and retain the best talent. Merrill Lynch relies heavily on the human capital of its employees to compete. One of its segments is Global Markets and Investment Banking, an area where a lot of money can be made, but also where a lot of money can be lost, as we saw during the financial crisis late in the last decade. Our focus here is on the Global Wealth Management segment and its key group, financial advisors (brokers). For every $100 million in client assets under management, about $1 million in fees and commissions are generated.[3] A financial advisor at Merrill Lynch would keep roughly one-half of this amount (referred to as "production"), or about $500,000. A financial associate with client assets of $40 million would keep a somewhat smaller portion, roughly $170,000. There are separate incentives for team production and for adding new clients.[4]

Merrill Lynch went through a turbulent period, having been acquired by Bank of America in a deal brokered by the U.S. Treasury Department. However, unlike its former key competitors like Lehman Brothers, which entered bankruptcy, and Bear Stearns, which appears to have lost its identity within J.P. Morgan after being acquired, Merrill Lynch has retained its separate identity and is structured as a wholly owned subsidiary of Bank of America. Its compensation approach for brokers, its key employee group, remains essentially unchanged.[5]

The aggressive pay-for-performance approach at Merrill Lynch was traditionally seen as a key factor in generating substantial wealth both for shareholders and for many of its employees over the years. However, that same aggressive pay-for-performance approach at Merrill Lynch (and at its competitors), most notably in the Global Markets and Investment Banking segment is now seen as a key factor in the "meltdown" in the financial industry. A widely held view is that this aggressive approach led to too much risk-taking (e.g., in areas of the business like subprime lending and currency trading) and consequently the downfall of firms in the financial industry. So, the same aggressive approach that was seen as the core of a culture that generated substantial wealth for Merrill Lynch shareholders, and many employees, subsequently was identified as the culprit in the downfall of Merrill Lynch and its peers. What about going forward? *Forbes Magazine* included an article a few years after the acquisition called "Here's Why Bank of America Loves Merrill Lynch."[6] It reported that net income for the most recent quarter (not for the entire year) from the brokerage unit alone, which then employed about 18,000 financial advisors, was $547 million. Consider that Bank of America overall had 282,000 employees and a total quarterly profit of $1.45 billion. Merrill Lynch's disproportionate (to its size) contribution to Bank of America's profitability has continued.[7] You will have an opportunity to consider this and other issues at Merrill Lynch further in the Your Turn section at the end of this chapter.

These three companies are in very different businesses facing different conditions, serving different customers, and employing different talent. So the differences in their pay strategies may not surprise you. Pay strategies can also differ among companies competing for the same talent and similar customers.[8]

Different Strategies within the Same Industry

Google, Microsoft, and SAS all compete for software engineers and marketing skills. In its earlier years, Microsoft adopted a very similar strategy to Google's, except its employees "put some skin in the game"; that is, they accepted less base pay to join a company whose stock value was increasing exponentially.[9] But when its stock quit performing so spectacularly, Microsoft shifted its strategy to increase base and bonus to the 65th percentile from the 45th percentile of competitors' pay. It still retained its strong emphasis on (still nonperforming) stock-related compensation, but eliminated its longstanding, broad-based stock option plan in favor of stock grants. Its benefits continue to lead the market. More recently, Microsoft, as CNET put it, "took another step toward middle age" by "significantly scaling back its stock awards for employees, replacing that with cash." CNET describes this shift as "implicitly acknowledging that its stock performance isn't enough [any more] to retain top talent." Microsoft has gone from being #8 on the first (1998) list of 100 Best Companies to Work For to being #86 on the 2014 list.[10]

SAS Institute, the world's largest privately owned software company, takes a very different approach. It emphasizes its work/life programs over cash compensation and gives only limited bonuses and no stock awards. Like Google, SAS is regularly one of the top companies on the 100 Best Companies to Work For list (e.g., #1 in 2011, #3 in 2012 , #2 in 2013, #2 in 2014). SAS headquarters in Cary, North Carolina, include free onsite child care centers, subsidized private schools for children of employees, doctors on site for free medical care, plus recreation facilities.[11] Working more than 35 hours per week is discouraged. By removing as many of the frustrations and distractions of day-to-day life as possible, SAS believes people will focus on work when they are at work and won't burn out. SAS feels, for example, that programming code written by someone working a 35-hour week will be better than that written by tired employees. Google so far retains the excitement of a start-up, Microsoft has morphed into "the new Boeing—a solid place to work for a great salary."[12] SAS emphasizes its work/family programs and work/nonwork balance.

So, all these examples illustrate the variance in strategic perspectives among companies in different industries (Google, Nucor, Merrill Lynch) and even among companies in the same industry (Google, Microsoft, SAS).

Different Strategies within the Same Company

Sometimes different business units within the same corporation will have very different competitive conditions, adopt different business strategies, and thus fit different compensation strategies. The business units at United Technologies include Otis Elevator, Pratt & Whitney aircraft engines, Sikorsky Aircraft, Climate Controls/Security, Aerospace, and Building/Industrial Systems. These businesses face very different competitive conditions. The Korean company SK Holdings has even more variety in its business units. They include a gasoline retailer, a cellular phone manufacturer, and SK Construction. SK has different compensation strategies aligned to each of its very different businesses.[13]

A simple, "let the market decide our compensation" approach doesn't work internationally either. In many nations, markets do not operate as in the United States or may not even exist. People either do not—or in some cases, cannot—easily change employers. In China, central Asia, and some eastern European countries, markets for labor are just emerging. Even in some countries with highly developed economies, such as Germany and France, the labor market is highly regulated. Consequently, there is less movement of people among companies than is common in the United States, Canada, or even Korea and Singapore.[14]

The point is that a strategic perspective on compensation is more complex than it first appears. So we suggest that you continue to read this chapter.

STRATEGIC CHOICES

Strategy refers to the fundamental directions that an organization chooses.[15] An organization defines its strategy through the tradeoffs it makes in choosing what (and what not) to do. Exhibit 2.2 ties these strategic choices to the quest for competitive advantage.

EXHIBIT 2.2   **Strategic Choices**

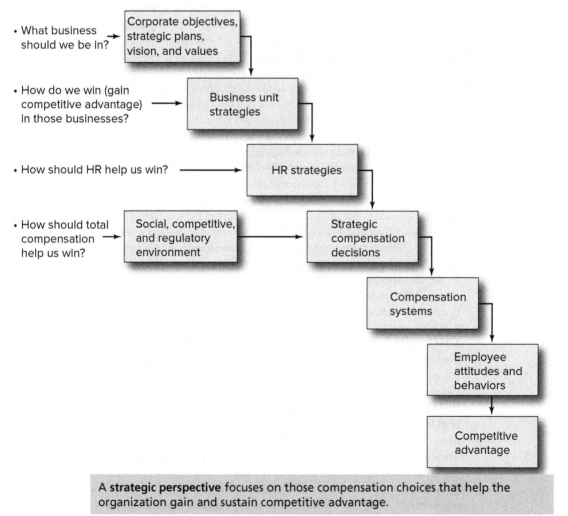

A **strategic perspective** focuses on those compensation choices that help the organization gain and sustain competitive advantage.

At the corporate level, the fundamental strategic choice is: *What business should we be in?* At the business unit level, the choice shifts to: *How do we gain and sustain competitive advantage in this business?* At the function level the strategic choice is: *How should total compensation help this business gain and sustain competitive advantage?* The ultimate purpose—the "so what?"—is to gain and sustain competitive advantage.

SUPPORT BUSINESS STRATEGY

A currently popular theory found in almost every book and consultant's report tells managers to tailor their pay systems to align with the organization's business strategy. The rationale is based on contingency notions. That is, differences in a firm's business strategy should be supported by corresponding differences in its human resource strategy, including compensation. The underlying premise is that the greater the alignment, or fit, between the organization and the compensation system, the more effective the organization.[16]

Exhibit 2.3 gives an example of how compensation systems might be tailored to three general business strategies. The **innovator** stresses new products and short response time to market trends. A supporting compensation approach places less emphasis on evaluating skills and jobs and more emphasis on incentives designed to encourage innovations. The **cost cutter's** efficiency-focused strategy stresses doing more with less by minimizing costs, encouraging productivity increases, and specifying in greater detail exactly how jobs should be performed. The **customer-focused** business strategy stresses delighting customers and bases employee pay on how well they do this.

Other business strategy frameworks rely on similar ideas. In Michael Porter's strategy work, firms that cut costs would be said to follow a *cost leadership* strategy, while

EXHIBIT 2.3   Tailor the Compensation System to the Strategy

Strategy	Business Response	HR Program Alignment	Compensation Systems
Innovator: Increase Product Complexity and Shorten Product Life Cycle	• Product Leadership • Shift to Mass Customization • Cycle Time	• Committed to Agile, Risk-Taking, Innovative People	• Reward Innovation in Products and Processes • Market-Based Pay • Flexible—Generic Job Descriptions
Cost Cutter: Focus on Efficiency	• Operational Excellence • Pursue Cost-Effective Solutions	• Do More with Less	• Focus on Competitors' Labor Costs • Increase Variable Pay • Emphasize Productivity • Focus on System Control and Work Specifications
Customer Focused: Increase Customer Expectations	• Deliver Solutions to Customers • Speed to Market	• Delight Customer, Exceed Expectations	• Customer Satisfaction Incentives • Value of Job and Skills Based on Customer Contact

those that seek to provide a unique and/or innovative product or service at a premium price are said to follow a *differentiation* strategy. Likewise, Miles and Snow refer to *defenders* as those that operate in stable markets and compete on cost, whereas *prospectors* are more focused on innovation, new markets, and so forth.[17] These are known as generic strategy frameworks. Conventional wisdom would be that competing on cost requires lower compensation, whereas competing through innovation is likely to be more successful with high-powered incentives/pay for performance.

Most firms, however, do not have generic strategies. Instead, as our discussion below suggests, they tend to have aspects of cost and innovation. Likewise, compensation strategies do not necessarily line up neatly with generic business strategies.[18] Lincoln Electric, Nucor, and Southwest Airlines rely heavily on cost leadership in their strategies, but pay their employees well above market (e.g., using stock and profit sharing plans) when firm performance is strong. SAS follows a customer and innovation strategy, but uses little in the way of pay for performance. If you think about it, if a particular business strategy automatically meant that a particular pay strategy would work best, there would not be much need for managers. These generic business strategy and pay strategy ideas are a good starting point.[19] But, to do better than its competitors, a firm must consider how to fashion its own unique way of adding value through matching its business strategy and pay strategy.[20]

How do Google, Nucor, and Merrill Lynch fit into these generic business strategies? Look again at Exhibit 2.3. At first pass, Google might be an innovator and Merrill Lynch customer focused. Nucor is an innovator in its capability to recycle scrap steel while also being a dedicated cost cutter and productivity-focused. Yet managers in these companies would probably say that their company is a combination of all three descriptors. Merrill Lynch is also an innovator in financial investment derivatives and seeks to control costs. So like our discussion of yin and yang in Chapter 1, the reality for each company is a unique blending of all three strategies.

It also follows that when business strategies change, pay systems should change, too. A classic example is IBM's strategic and cultural transformation. For years, IBM placed a strong emphasis on internal alignment. Its well-developed job evaluation plan, clear hierarchy for decision making, work/life balance benefits, and policy of no layoffs served well when the company dominated the market for high-profit mainframe computers. But it did not provide flexibility to adapt to competitive changes in the new century. A redesigned IBM no longer sells the PCs they popularized. Instead, IBM describes its current strategy as having a "focus on the high-growth, high-value segments of the IT industry." It notes, for example, that it "has exited commoditizing businesses like personal computers and hard disk drives." IBM describes its current global capabilities as including "services, software, hardware, fundamental research and financing" and that this "broad mix of businesses and capabilities are combined to provide business insight and solutions for the company's clients."[21] Exhibit 2.4 depicts IBM's "New Blue" approach to executing its strategy. A new business strategy meant a new compensation strategy. At IBM, this meant streamlining the organization by cutting layers of management, redesigning jobs to build in more flexibility, increasing incentive pay to more strongly differentiate on performance, and keeping a constant eye on costs. IBM changed its pay strategy and system to support its changed business strategy.

EXHIBIT 2.4   IBM's Strategic Principles and Priorities in Strategy Execution

Principles	Priorities
1. The marketplace is the driving force behind everything.	1. Delivering business value
2. At our core, we are a technology company with an overriding commitment to quality.	2. Offering world-class open infrastructure
	3. Developing innovative leadership technology
3. Our primary measures of success are customer satisfaction and shareholder value.	4. Exploiting new profitable growth opportunities
4. We operate as an entrepreneurial organization with a minimum of bureaucracy and a never-ending focus on productivity.	5. Creating brand leadership and a superior customer experience
	6. Attracting, motivating, and retaining the best talent in our industry
5. We never lose sight of our strategic vision.	
6. We think and act with a sense of urgency.	
7. Outstanding, dedicated people make it happen, particularly when they work together as a team.	
8. We are sensitive to the needs of all employees and to the communities in which we operate.	

Source: Adapted from IBM. © IBM Corporation.

SUPPORT HR STRATEGY

Although a compensation strategy that supports the business strategy implies alignment between compensation and overall HR strategies, this topic is important enough that we want to explicitly deal with it. In the literature on so-called high-performance work-systems (HPWS) and HR strategy, Boxall and Purcell find an increasingly common "very basic theory of performance" being used, which they refer to as "AMO theory":

$$P = f(A,M,O)$$

P is performance, which is specified to be a function (f) of three factors: A is **ability,** M is **motivation,** and O is **opportunity.**[22] In other words, the **AMO** logic is that HR systems will be most effective when roles are designed to allow employees to be involved in decisions and have an opportunity to make an impact, when employee ability is developed through selective hiring and training and development, and when the compensation system motivates employees to act on their abilities and take advantage of the opportunity to make a difference. (It is also common to refer to O part as E, for environment.) Compensation (through incentive and sorting effects) is the key to attracting, retaining, and motivating employees with the abilities necessary to execute the business strategy and handle greater decision-making responsibilities. Compensation is also the key to motivating them to fully utilize those abilities. As such, higher pay levels and pay for performance are often part of such a HPWS.

Consider alignment between compensation and other aspects of HR at SAS. Rather than being sold in a one-time transaction, SAS's software is licensed. This is part of a business strategy by which SAS gets ongoing and substantial feedback from customers

EXHIBIT 2.5 Fit Between HR Strategy and Compensation Strategy and Effectiveness

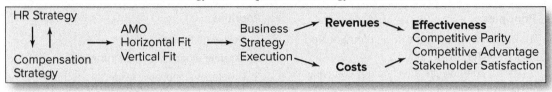

Horizontal Fit: Fit of Compensation Strategy with overall HR Strategy
Vertical Fit: Fit of Compensation Strategy and HR Strategy with the Business Strategy
AMO = Ability, Motivation, Opportunity

regarding how products can be continually improved and also regarding what new products customers would like. To support this long-term customer relationship, SAS seeks to have low employee turnover. Its heavy emphasis on benefits in compensation seems to be helpful in retaining employees. SAS also gets many job applications, which allows it to be very selective in its hiring. That no doubt helps build a highly able workforce and allows selection of those who fit SAS's emphasis on teamwork and idea sharing. The de-emphasis on pay for individual performance probably reduces the risk that competition among employees will undermine this objective. As we discuss in the next section, Whole Foods also is team-based. Unlike SAS, however, it relies heavily on pay for performance. But, it is team performance that matters. (Contrast the de-emphasis on differences in individual performance at SAS and Whole Foods with the very different approach—strong emphasis on individual pay for performance—that seems to fit the business and HR strategies of companies such as General Electric, Nucor Steel, Lincoln Electric, and Merrill Lynch.) How effective can a compensation strategy be in supporting business strategy if it is at cross-purposes with the overall HR strategy? While reading about Whole Foods below, ask yourself how well its reliance on teams and giving workers wide decision latitude would work with a different compensation strategy. Such a mismatch happens surprisingly often.[23]

Compensation strategy and HR strategy are central to successful business strategy execution. Exhibit 2.5 seeks to capture that idea, the importance of AMO and fit. It also makes the very simple, but very important, observation that all of this comes down to effects on either revenues or costs. Compensation strategy, HR strategy, and business strategy ultimately seek to decrease costs or increase revenues, relative to competitors.[24] At the same time, key stakeholders (e.g., employees, customers, shareholders) must be happy with their "deal" or relationship with the company. To the extent all of this happens, effectiveness is more likely to follow.

THE PAY MODEL GUIDES STRATEGIC PAY DECISIONS

Let us continue our discussion of Whole Foods. The competitive advantage of Whole Foods is apparent with the first visit to one of its grocery stores, described as "a mouth-watering festival of colors, smells, and textures; an homage to the appetite."[25] What started out in 1978 as a small health food store in Austin, Texas, has, through strategic decisions, grown to become the world's leading natural and organic foods supermarket whose objective is to change the way Americans eat. Along the way, Whole Foods' managers have designed a total compensation system to support the company's phenomenal growth (from 10,000 "team members" and $900 million in sales in 1996 to 67,000 "team members" and sales of $14.2 billion today) while remaining true to company founder John Mackey's vision for the company.

Using our pay model, let us consider the five strategic compensation choices facing Whole Foods managers.

1. *Objectives:* How should compensation support the business strategy and be adaptive to the cultural and regulatory pressures in a global environment? (Whole Foods objectives: Increase shareholder value through profits and growth; go to extraordinary lengths to satisfy and delight customers; seek and engage employees who are going to help the company make money—every new hire must win a two-thirds vote from team members before being given a permanent position.)

2. *Internal Alignment:* How differently should the different types and levels of skills and work be paid within the organization? [Whole Foods: Store operations are organized around eight to ten self-managed teams; these teams make the types of decisions (e.g., what products to order and stock) that are often reserved for managers. Egalitarian, shared-fate philosophy means that executive salaries do not exceed 19 times the average pay of full-time employees (the ratio used to be 8 times; note that for top executives, salary typically accounts for well under one-half of total compensation); all full-time employees qualify for stock options, and 94 percent of the company's options go to nonexecutive employees.]

3. *External Competitiveness:* How should total compensation be positioned against competitors? (Whole Foods: Offer a unique deal compared to competitors.) What **forms of compensation** should be used? (Whole Foods: Provide health insurance for all full-time employees and 20 hours of paid time a year to do volunteer work.)

4. *Employee Contributions:* Should pay increases be based on individual and/or team performance, on experience and/or continuous learning, on improved skills, on changes in cost of living, on personal needs (housing, transportation, health services), and/or on each business unit's performance? [Whole Foods: A shared fate—every four weeks the performance of each team is measured in terms of revenue per hour worked, which directly affects what they get paid. (This is one reason why staffers are given some say in who gets hired—co-workers want someone who will help them make money!)]

5. *Management:* How open and transparent should the pay decisions be to all employees? Who should be involved in designing and managing the system? (Whole Foods: "No-secrets" management: Every store has a book listing the previous year's pay for every employee including executives; "You Decide"—employees recently voted to pick their health insurance rather than having one imposed by leadership.)

These decisions, taken together, form a pattern that becomes an organization's compensation strategy.

Stated versus Unstated Strategies

All organizations that pay people have a compensation strategy. Some may have written compensation strategies for all to see and understand. Others may not even realize they have a compensation strategy. Ask a manager at one of these latter organizations about its compensation strategy and you may get a pragmatic response: "We do whatever it takes." Its compensation strategy is inferred from the pay decisions it has made.[26] Managers in all organizations make the five strategic decisions discussed earlier. Some do it in a rational, deliberate way, while others do it more chaotically—as ad hoc responses to pressures from the economic, sociopolitical, and regulatory context in which the organization operates. But in any organization that pays people, there is a compensation strategy at work.

DEVELOPING A TOTAL COMPENSATION STRATEGY: FOUR STEPS

Developing a compensation strategy involves four simple steps, shown in Exhibit 2.6. While the steps are simple, executing them is complex. Trial and error, experience, and insight play major roles. Research evidence can also help.[27]

EXHIBIT 2.6 Key Steps in Formulating a Total Compensation Strategy

1. **Assess Total Compensation Implications**
   Business Strategy and Competitive Dynamics
   HR Strategy
   Culture/Values
   Social and Political Context
   Employee/Union Needs
   Other HR Systems

2. **Map a Total Compensation Strategy**
   Objectives
   Alignment
   Competitiveness
   Contributions
   Management

3. **Implement Strategy**
   Design System to Translate Strategy into Action
   Choose Techniques to Fit Strategy

4. **Reassess**
   Realign as Conditions Change
   Realign as Strategy Changes

Step 1: Assess Total Compensation Implications

Think about any organization's past, present, and—most vitally—its future. What factors in its business environment have contributed to the company's success? Which of these factors are likely to become more (or less) important as the company looks ahead? Exhibit 2.6 classifies the factors as competitive dynamics, culture/values, social and political context, employee/union needs, and other HR systems.

Business Strategy and Competitive Dynamics—Understand the Business

This first step includes an understanding of the specific industry in which the organization operates and how the organization plans to compete in that industry. This corresponds with the first two decisions in Exhibit 2.2: What business should we be in, and how do we win in that business?[28] To cope with the turbulent competitive dynamics, focus on what factors in the business environment (i.e., changing customer needs, competitors' actions, changing labor market conditions, changing laws, globalization) are important today. What will be important in the future?

What is your company's strategy? How do you compete to win? How should the compensation system support that strategy? Learn to gauge the underlying dynamics in your business (or build relationships with those who can). We have already discussed aligning different compensation strategies with different business strategies using the examples of cost cutter, customer centered, and innovator (Exhibit 2.3). But be cautious: As we have already pointed out, reality is more complex and chaotic. Organizations are innovators *and* cost cutters *and* customer centered. All three, and more. The orderly image conveyed in the exhibits does not adequately capture the turbulent competitive dynamics underlying this process.[29]

Competitive dynamics can be assessed globally.[30] However, comparing pay among countries is complex. In Chapter 1, we noted differences in hourly labor costs and productivity (output per dollar of wages) among countries. But as we shall see in Chapter 16 on global pay, countries also differ on the average length of the workweek, the average number of paid holidays, the kinds of national health care and retirement programs, and even how pay is determined. Nevertheless, managers must become knowledgeable about competitive conditions both globally and locally.

HR Strategy: Pay as a Supporting Player or Catalyst for Change?

As noted earlier, the pay strategy is also influenced by how it fits with other HR systems in the organization.[31] Whatever the overall HR strategy, a decision about the prominence of pay in that HR strategy is required. Pay can be a supporting player, as in the high-performance approach, or it can take the lead and be a catalyst for change. Whatever the role, compensation is embedded in the total HR approach.[32]

So, the compensation implications of all the above factors—the organization's business strategy, global competitive dynamics, culture and values, the sociopolitical context, employee preferences, and how pay fits with other HR systems—all are necessary to formulate a compensation strategy.

EXHIBIT 2.7 Medtronic Values

Written more than 30 years ago, our mission statement gives purpose to our work, describes the values we live by, and is the motivation behind every action we take.

1. To contribute to human welfare by application of biomedical engineering in the research, design, manufacture, and sale of instruments or appliances that alleviate pain, restore health, and extend life.

2. To direct our growth in the areas of biomedical engineering where we display maximum strength and ability; to gather people and facilities that tend to augment these areas; to continuously build on these areas through education and knowledge assimilation; to avoid participation in areas where we cannot make unique and worthy contributions.

3. To strive without reserve for the greatest possible reliability and quality in our products; to be the unsurpassed standard of comparison and to be recognized as a company of dedication, honesty, integrity, and service.

4. To make a fair profit on current operations to meet our obligations, sustain our growth, and reach our goals.

5. To recognize the personal worth of employees by providing an employment framework that allows personal satisfaction in work accomplished, security, advancement opportunity, and means to share in the company's success.

6. To maintain good citizenship as a company.

Culture/Values

A pay system reflects the values that guide an employer's behavior and underlie its treatment of employees. The pay system mirrors the company's image and reputation. As we noted in Chapter 1, most companies publish a values statement on their websites. Medtronic publishes theirs in 24 languages. Part of it is in Exhibit 2.7. Medtronic's value #5 recognizes employees' worth by fostering "personal satisfaction in work accomplished, security, advancement opportunity, and means to share in the company's success." Its compensation strategy reflects this value by including work/life balance programs for security, incentives, and stock ownership to share the company's success.

But there are some skeptics out there. Mission statements have been described as "an assemblage of trite phrases" which impressed no one.[33] In contrast, Johnson and Johnson considers its statement its "moral compass" and "recipe for business success."[34]

Social and Political Context

Context refers to a wide range of factors, including legal and regulatory requirements, cultural differences, changing workforce demographics, expectations, and the like. These also affect compensation choices. In the case of Whole Foods, its business is very people-intensive. Consequently, Whole Foods managers may find that an increasingly diverse workforce and increasingly diverse forms of pay (child care, chemical dependency counseling, educational reimbursements, employee assistance programs) may add value and be difficult for competitors (other supermarkets) to imitate.

Because governments are major stakeholders in determining compensation, lobbying to influence laws and regulations can also be part of a compensation strategy. In the United States, employers will not sit by while Congress considers taxing employee benefits. Similarly, the European Union's "social contract" is a matter of interest.[35] And in China, every foreign company has undoubtedly discovered that building relationships with government officials is essential. So, from a strategic perspective, managers of compensation may try to shape the sociopolitical environment as well as be shaped by it.

Employee Preferences

The simple fact that employees differ is too easily overlooked in formulating a compensation strategy. Individual employees join the organization, make investment decisions, interact with customers, design new products, assemble components, and so on. Individual employees receive the pay. A major challenge in the design of next-generation pay systems is how to better satisfy individual needs and preferences. Offering more choice is one approach. Older, highly paid workers may wish to defer taxes by putting their pay into retirement funds, while younger employees may have high cash needs to buy a house, support a family, or finance an education. Dual-career couples who have double family coverage may prefer to use more of their combined pay for child care, automobile insurance, financial counseling, or other benefits such as flexible schedules. Employees who have young children or dependent parents may desire dependent care coverage.[36] Whole Foods, in fact, as described in its annual report each year, holds an employee vote every three years to determine the nature of their benefits program.

Based on the opinions of 10,000 U.S. workers, Hudson found that:

- Nearly three out of four U.S. workers claim to be satisfied with their compensation, yet a large portion of the same sample (44%) say they would change their mix of cash and benefits if given the chance.

- When given their choice of unconventional benefits, most employees would select a more flexible work schedule (33%) or additional family benefits (22%), including parental leaves and personal days, over job training (13%) or supplemental insurance (16%).

- One in five workers say better health care benefits would make them happier with their compensation package. On the other hand, 41 percent said that the single thing that would make them happier is more money.[37]

Choice Is Good. Yes, No, Maybe?[38]

Contemporary pay systems in the United States do offer some choices. Flexible benefits and choices among health care plans and investment funds for retirement are examples. As we saw earlier, Whole Foods employees vote on the benefits they want. Netflix employees can choose the mix of stock options and salary. General Mills similarly allows many employees to swap several weeks' salary for stock awards. The company believes that allowing employees their choice adds value and is difficult for other companies to imitate—it is a source of competitive advantage for General Mills. Whether or not this belief is correct remains to be studied.

Some studies have found that people do not always choose well. They do not always understand the alternatives, and too many choices simply confuse them. Thus, the value added by offering choices and satisfying preferences may be offset by the expense of communicating and simply confusing people.[39]

In addition to possibly confusing employees, unlimited choice would be a challenge to design and manage. Plus, it would meet with disapproval from the U.S. Internal

Revenue Service (health benefits are not viewed by the IRS as income). Offering greater choice to employees in different nations would require meeting a bewildering maze of codes and regulations. On the other hand, the U.S. federal government, including the IRS, already offers its employees a bit of choice in their work schedules. Forty-three percent avail themselves of the option to take compensatory time off for extra hours worked. In contrast, U.S. private sector workers covered by the Fair Labor Standards Act (i.e., **nonexempt** employees) must be paid time-and-a-half overtime if they work over 40 hours in a week. A compensatory time option is not permitted.[40]

Union Preferences

Pay strategies need to take into account the nature of the union-management relationship.[41] Even though union membership among private-sector workers in the United States is now less than 10 percent of the workforce, union influence on pay decisions remains significant, especially in key sectors (e.g., manufacturing, health care, education). Union preferences for different forms of pay (e.g., protecting retirement and health care plans) and their concern with job security affect pay strategy.

Unions' interests can differ. In Denver, Colorado, a merit pay plan was developed collaboratively by the Denver Public Schools and the Denver Classroom Teachers Association, the local union affiliate. Teachers approved the agreement by a 59 to 41 percent vote, and Denver voters approved a $25 million property tax increase to pay for it. Conversely, many teachers in Springfield, Massachusetts, left for neighboring, higher-paying school districts in part because the district wanted to impose a merit pay plan.[42]

Compensation deals with unions can be costly to change. The U.S. auto companies negotiated "The Jobs Bank" program that began in 1984 with the United Auto Workers. Employees who were no longer needed to make cars continued to get paid until they were needed again. Some received up to $100,000 a year, including benefits. Their job: Do nothing but wait for a job to open. But for a number of people, those jobs never materialized. In various cities around the U.S., about 15,000 employees showed up at 6 a.m. each day and stayed until 2:30 p.m. with 45 minutes off for lunch. Some volunteered for approved community projects or took classes. Jerry Mellon claims, "They paid me like $400,000 over 6 years to learn how to deal blackjack."[43] Readers may wonder if the Jobs Bank was a compensation strategy that trumped the business strategy. No wonder GM eventually bought its way out of the Bank. No wonder GM recently found it necessary to go through bankruptcy.

Step 2: Map a Total Compensation Strategy

The compensation strategy is made up of the elements in the pay model: objectives, and the four policy choices of alignment, competitiveness, contributions, and management. Mapping these decisions is Step 2 in developing a compensation strategy.

Mapping is often used in marketing to clarify and communicate a product's identity. A strategic map offers a picture of a company's compensation strategy. It can also clarify the message that the company is trying to deliver with its compensation system.

Exhibit 2.8 maps the compensation strategies of Microsoft and SAS. The five dimensions are subdivided into a number of descriptors rated on importance. These ratings are from your fearless (read "tenured") authors. They are not ratings assigned

EXHIBIT 2.8   Contrasting Maps of Microsoft and SAS

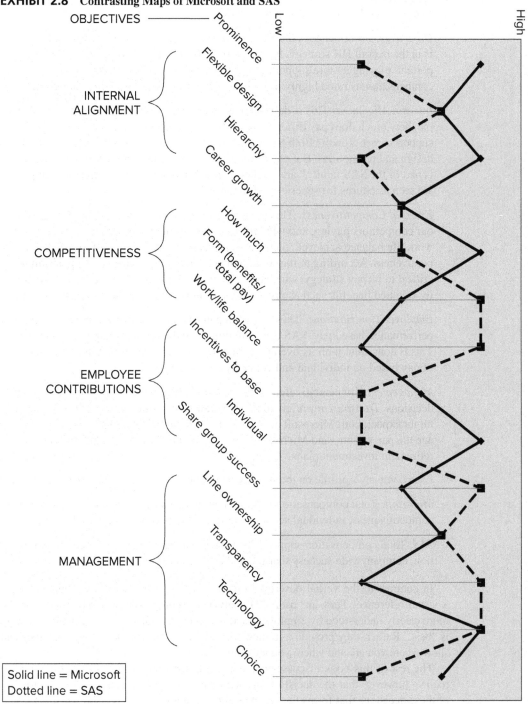

Solid line = Microsoft
Dotted line = SAS

by managers in the companies. The descriptors used under each of the strategy dimensions can be modified as a company sees fit.

Objectives: Prominence is the measure of how important total compensation is in the overall HR strategy. Is it a catalyst, playing a lead role? Or is it less important, playing a more supporting character to other HR programs? At Microsoft, compensation is rated highly prominent, whereas at SAS it is more supportive.

Internal Alignment: This is described as the degree of internal hierarchy. For example, how much does pay differ among job levels and how well does compensation support career growth? Both SAS and Microsoft use pay to support flexible work design and promotions. But pay differences at SAS, whose philosophy is "Everyone is part of the SAS family," are smaller than at Microsoft, where differences in pay are seen as returns for superior performance.

External Competitiveness: This includes comparisons on two issues. How much are our competitors paying, and what forms of pay are they using? The importance of work/life balance achieved via benefits and services is also part of external competitiveness. According to the strategy map, Microsoft's **competitive position** is critical to its pay strategy, whereas SAS competes on work/family balance in family-oriented benefits such as private schools and doctors on the company's campus.

Employee Contributions: These two companies take a very different approach to performance-based pay. SAS uses only limited individual-based performance pay. This is consistent with its overall egalitarian approach. Microsoft makes greater use of pay based on individual and company performance.

Management: Ownership refers to the role non-HR managers play in making pay decisions. *Transparency* refers to openness and communication about pay. As one might expect, both Microsoft and SAS rate high on the use of technology to manage the pay system, and Microsoft offers greater choices in their health care and retirement investment plans.

Each company's profile on the strategy map reflects its main message or "pay brand":

Microsoft: Total compensation is prominent, with a strong emphasis on market competitiveness, individual accomplishments, and performance-based returns.

SAS: Total compensation supports its work/life balance. Competitive market position, companywide success sharing, and egalitarianism are the hallmarks.

In contrast to the verbal description earlier in this chapter, strategic maps provide a visual reference. They are useful in analyzing a compensation strategy that can be more clearly understood by employees and managers.[44] Maps *do not* tell which strategy is "best." Rather, they provide a framework and guidance. Just like a road map, they can show where you are and where you are going.[45]

The rest of this book discusses compensation decisions in detail. It is important to realize, however, that the decisions in the pay model work in concert. It is the totality of these decisions that forms the compensation strategy.

Steps 3 and 4: Implement and Reassess

Step 3 in Exhibit 2.6 is to implement the strategy through the design and execution of the compensation system. The compensation system translates strategy into practice—and into people's bank accounts.

Step 4, Reassess and Realign, closes the loop. This step recognizes that the compensation strategy must change to fit changing conditions. Thus, periodic reassessment is needed to continuously learn, adapt, and improve. The results from using the pay system need to be assessed against the objectives we are trying to achieve.

SOURCE OF COMPETITIVE ADVANTAGE: THREE TESTS

Developing and implementing a pay strategy that is a source of sustained competitive advantage is easier said than done. Not all compensation decisions are strategic or a source of competitive advantage. Three tests determine whether a pay strategy is a source of advantage: (1) Is it aligned? (2) Does it differentiate? (3) Does it add value?

Align

Alignment of the pay strategy includes three aspects, as we have already discussed: (1) align with the business strategy, (2) align externally with the economic and sociopolitical conditions, and (3) align internally within the overall HR system. Alignment is probably the easiest test to pass.

Differentiate

Some believe that the only thing that really matters about a strategy is how it is different from everyone else's. If the pay system is relatively simple for any competitor to copy, then how can it possibly be a source of competitive advantage? The answer, according to the advocates of the strategic approach, is in how the pay system is managed. This rhetoric is appealing, but the evidence to support it is slim.[46]

The map profiles in Exhibit 2.8 show how Microsoft and SAS differ in their strategies. One uses pay as a strong signal; the other uses pay to support its "work/family balance" HR strategy. Both organizations claim to have organization cultures that value performance, yet their compensation strategies differ.

Are they difficult to imitate? Probably, since each strategy is woven into the fabric of the company's overall HR strategy. Copying one or another dimension of a strategy means ripping apart the overall approach and patching in a new one. So, in a sense, the alignment test (weaving the fabric) helps ensure passing the differentiation test. Microsoft's use of stock awards for all employees—often worth considerably more than people's base pay—is difficult for its competitors to copy. SAS's work-family-balance (like Medtronic's total-presence-at-the-workplace strategy) is difficult to copy. It may be relatively easy to copy any individual action a competitor takes (i.e., grant stock options to more employees or offer more choice in their health insurance). But the strategic perspective implies that it is the *way* programs fit together and fit the overall organization that is hard to copy. Simply copying others by blindly benchmarking best practices amounts to trying to get in and/or stay in the race, not win it.[47] (Of course, being in the race, or achieving competitive parity, may be a major improvement for some organizations.)

e-Compensation: Compensation Consultants

Compensation consultants are major players, and practically every organization uses at least one for data and advice. So learning more about the services these consultants offer is useful. Go to the website of at least two of them. You can choose from the consulting firms listed below or find others.

Fred Cook *www.fredericwcook.com*
Hay *www.haygroup.com*
Mercer *www.mercer.com*
Aon Hewitt *www.hewittassociates.com*
Towers Watson *www.towersperrin.com*
Clark Consulting *www.clarkconsulting.com*
McLagan *www.mclagan.com*

1. Compare consultants. From their websites, construct a chart comparing their stated values and culture and their business strategies, and highlight the services offered.

2. Critically assess whether their strategies and services are unique and/ or difficult to imitate. Which one would you select (based on the web information) to help you formulate a company's total compensation strategy?

3. Based on the web information, which one would you prefer to work for? Why?

4. Be prepared to share this information with others in class.

Return on the Investment: If everyone does a great job on this e-Compensation, you will all have useful information on consultants.

For more background, see Lewis Pinault, *Consulting Demons: Inside the Unscrupulous World of Global Corporate Consulting* (New York: Harpers Business, 2000), and Fred Cook, "A Personal Perspective of the Consulting Profession," *ACA News,* October 1999, pp. 35–43.

Add Value

Organizations continue to look for the return they are getting from their incentives, benefits, and even base pay. Compensation is often a company's largest controllable expense. Since consultants and a few researchers treat different forms of pay as investments, the task is to come up with ways to calculate the return on those investments (ROI). But this is a difficult proposition. As one writer put it, "It is easier to count the bottles than describe the wine."[48] Costs are easy to fit into a spreadsheet, but any value created as a result of those costs is difficult to specify, much less measure.[49] Current attempts to do so are described in Chapter 18, Management.

Trying to measure an ROI for any compensation strategy implies that people are "human capital," similar to other factors of production. Many people find this view dehumanizing. They argue that viewing pay as an investment with measurable returns diminishes the importance of treating employees fairly.[50] In Chapter 1 we discussed the need to keep all objectives, including efficiency and fairness, in mind at the same time. No doubt about it, of the three tests of strategy—align, differentiate, add value—the last is the most difficult.

Are there advantages to an innovative compensation strategy? We do know that in products and services, first movers (innovators) have well-recognized advantages that can offset the risks involved—high margins, market share, and mindshare (brand recognition).[51] But we do not know whether such advantages accrue to innovators in total compensation. What, if any, benefits accrued to Microsoft, one of the first to offer very large stock options to all employees, once its competitors did the same thing? What about General Mills, who was among the first to offer some managers a choice of more stock options for smaller base pay? Does a compensation innovator attract more and better people? Induce people to stay and contribute? Are there cost advantages? Studies are needed to find the answers.

"BEST PRACTICES" VERSUS "BEST FIT"?

The premise of any strategic perspective is that if managers align pay decisions with the organization's strategy and values, are responsive to employees and union relations, and are globally competitive, then the organization is more likely to achieve competitive advantage.[52] The challenge is to design the "fit" with the environment, business strategy, and pay plan. The better the fit, the greater the competitive advantage.

But not everyone agrees. In contrast to the notion of strategic fit, some believe that (1) a set of **best-pay practices** exists and (2) these practices can be applied universally across situations. Rather than having a better fit between business strategy and compensation plans that yields better performance, they say that best practices result in better performance with almost any business strategy.[53]

These writers believe that adopting best-pay practices allows the employer to gain preferential access to superior employees. These superior employees will in turn be the organization's source of competitive advantage. The challenge here is to select from various recommended lists which are "the" best practices.[54] Which practices truly are the best? We believe that research over the past few years is beginning to point the way to improve our choices.

GUIDANCE FROM THE EVIDENCE

There is consistent research evidence that the following practices do matter to the organization's objectives.

- *Internal alignment:* Both smaller and larger pay differences among jobs inside an organization can affect results. Smaller internal pay differences and larger internal pay differences can both be a "best" practice. Which one depends on the context; that is, the fit with business strategy, other HR practices, the organization culture, and so on.[55]

- *External competitiveness:* Paying higher than the average paid by competitors can affect results. Is higher competitive pay a "best" practice? Again, it depends on the context.

- *Employee contributions:* Performance-based pay can affect results. Are performance incentives a "best" practice? Once more, it depends on the context.[56]

- *Managing compensation:* Rather than focusing on only one dimension of the pay strategy (e.g., pay for performance or internal pay differences), all dimensions need to be considered together.[57]
- *Compensation strategy:* Finally, embedding compensation strategy within the broader HR strategy affects results. Compensation does not operate alone; it is part of the overall HR perspective.[58]

So, specific pay practices appear to be more beneficial in some contexts than in others.[59] Thus, best practice versus best fit does not appear to be a useful way to frame the question. A more useful question is, *What practices pay off best under what conditions?* Much of the rest of this book is devoted to exploring this question.

VIRTUOUS AND VICIOUS CIRCLES

A group of studies suggests specific conditions to look at when making strategic pay decisions. One study examined eight years of data from 180 U.S. companies.[60] The authors reported that while *pay levels* (external competitiveness) differed among these companies, they were not related to the companies' subsequent financial performance. However, when combined with differences in the size of bonuses and the number of people eligible for stock options, then pay levels were related to future financial success of the organizations. This study concluded that it is not only *how much* you pay but also *how* you pay that matters.[61]

Think of pay as part of a circle. Exhibit 2.9 suggests that performance-based pay works best when there is success to share. An organization whose profits or market share is increasing is able to pay larger bonuses and stock awards. And paying these bonuses fairly improves employee attitudes and work behaviors, which in turn improves their performance.[62] The circle gains upward momentum.[63] Employees receive returns that compensate for the risks they take. And they behave like owners, since they are sharing in the organization's success.

EXHIBIT 2.9 Virtuous and Vicious Circles

(A) Virtuous Circle

Organization Performance Increasing → Pay for Performance → Risk-Return Balance → Ownership Culture

Upward Momentum, Continuous Improvement

(B) Vicious Circle

Organization Performance Decreasing → Pay for Performance → Risk-Return Imbalance → Ownership Culture

Downward Momentum, Continuous Difficulties

Additionally, there are several studies that analyzed pay strategies as part of the "high-performance workplace" approaches discussed earlier. This research focused on specific jobs and workplaces, such as sales and service representatives in call-service centers and jobs in factories.[64] They indicate that performance-based pay that shares success with employees does improve employee attitudes, behaviors, performance—especially when coupled with the other "high-performance" practices. One study even reported that the effects of the compensation strategy equaled the impact of all the other practices [high involvement, teams, selective hiring, and training programs] combined.[65] These findings are near and dear to our hearts. So other "high-performance" HR practices also become factors that support improved performance and the virtuous circle.

It cannot have escaped your attention that circles can also gain momentum going downward to become a vicious circle. As shown in Exhibit 2.9, when organization performance declines, performance-based pay plans do not pay off; there are no bonuses, and the value of stock declines—with potentially negative effects on organization performance. Declining organization performance increases the risks facing employees—risks of still smaller bonuses, demotions, wage cuts, and even layoffs. Unless the increased risks are offset by larger returns, the risk-return imbalance will reinforce declining employee attitudes and speed the downward spiral. Unfortunately, we do not yet know what compensation practices can be used to shift an organization caught in a downward spiral into an upward one.

Perhaps we believe so strongly that pay matters and that studying it in the workplace is beneficial, that this is what we see—believing is seeing. So, caution and more evidence are required. Nevertheless, these studies do seem to indicate that performance-based pay may be a best practice, under the right circumstances. (Could performance-based pay sometimes be a "worst practice"? Yes, when incentive systems don't pay off and they alienate employees or lead to government investigation of possible stock option manipulation.) Additionally, we do not have much information about how people perceive various pay strategies. Do all managers "see" the total compensation strategy at Merrill Lynch or Google the same way? Some evidence suggests that if you ask 10 managers about their company's HR strategy, you get 10 different answers. If the link between the strategy and people's perceptions is not clear, then maybe we are using evidence to build on unstable ground.

Your **Turn**   Merrill Lynch

During the financial crisis at the end of the last decade, Merrill Lynch was acquired by Bank of America for $50 billion. The reason for the acquisition was that Merrill Lynch was unsure it could survive the crisis on its own.

Bank of America received government assistance during the financial crisis from (and was thus covered by) TARP (the Troubled Asset Relief Program). So too then was Merrill Lynch. One initial consequence of TARP coverage was that some employees, including some high-level, high-revenue generating employees, began to leave larger financial institutions like Merrill Lynch/Bank of America to go to so-called "boutique" financial services firms, which had not received TARP money and thus were not covered by TARP restrictions on compensation. Another initial reaction was an increase in base salary levels and a decrease in bonus levels, apparently in response to all of the negative publicity bonuses had received and as a way to get around TARP restrictions. One senior executive at a company receiving TARP money and now paying smaller bonuses and bigger salaries, however, questioned whether the TARP-induced greater emphasis on base pay made sense: So, "You're going to overpay them regularly, instead of just sometimes?"[66]

However, now that some time has passed, the economy has recovered (somewhat), and the stock market has bounced back, Merrill Lynch (as we saw earlier) and other financial services companies are making money again. At Merrill Lynch, there is always a lot of action and discussion around compensation strategy. Merrill introduced a plan to expand its number of financial advisors by 8% (about 1,200 people). Where would they come from? Other firms? How would Merrill get them to move? By offering unusually high up-front signing bonuses and decentralizing authority to make such offers. Traditionally, top brokers from other firms can receive 1.5 times their pay at the firm they are leaving.[67] Merrill was not the only firm looking to add top brokers. Indeed, what was described as a "bidding war" broke out, and signing bonuses were reported to have gone as high as three to four times previous pay in some cases.[68] Why the bidding war? "Wealth management firms make the bulk of their profits on the top 10 percent of their producers" according to compensation attorney Katten Muchin.[69] And, very wealthy clients tend to be more loyal to their advisors than to the advisors' firms.

At Merrill, there are some concerns among financial advisors. First, in the non-Merrill part of Bank of America, brokers are under a discretionary bonus system rather than an (objective) incentive system where pay is based on a formula. Merrill financial advisors fear that Bank of America wants to extend that system to cover them. Second, and likely related, non-Merrill brokers at B of A are expected to cross-sell—in other words, to push products sold by other parts of the bank. The opportunities for such synergies are typically seen as a source of competitive advantage for a large, diversified financial intsitution such as B of A. However, cross-selling performance (and cooperation) is difficult to assess objectively. Thus, subjective evaluations are likely necessary. Merrill brokers appear to be opposed to cross-selling, both because they are concerned it could undermine their relationships with their clients and they prefer to have their pay determined by objective measures.[70]

QUESTIONS:

1. What is the likely result of bidding wars of this type for top brokers? Will most firms benefit? Who will be the winners and losers? What about the brokers?

2. Explain why there is such a strong relationship between pay and performance for brokers. Why isn't this true of many other jobs?

3. Should Bank of America change its compensation strategy to include more subjective assessments of performance and a greater emphasis on cross-selling? What effect might this have on its success in the bidding war for top brokers?

4. In chapter 1, we talked about incentive and sorting effects of pay strategies. Describe the incentive and sorting effects at Merrill Lynch and how changes to the compensation strategy might affect them.

Still Your **Turn**   Mapping Compensation Strategies

Take any organization that you know—current employer, business school, the place you interned, a friend's employer. Look at Exhibit 2.8, "Contrasting Maps of Microsoft and SAS." Map your organization's compensation strategy then compare it to that of Microsoft and SAS.

1. Summarize the key points of your company's strategy.
2. What are the key differences compared to the strategies of Microsoft and SAS?

Or ask several managers in the *same* organization to map that organization's compensation strategy. You may need to assist them. Then compare the managers' maps.

3. Summarize the key similarities and differences.
4. Why do these similarities and differences occur?
5. How can maps be used to clarify and communicate compensation strategies to leaders? To employees?

Summary

Managing total compensation strategically means fitting the compensation system to the business and environmental conditions. We believe the best way to proceed is to start with the pay model—the objectives and four policy choices—and take the steps discussed in the chapter: (1) assess implications for the total compensation of your organization's situation; (2) map out the compensation objectives and four policy choices to achieve them (internal alignment, external competitiveness, employee contributions, and management); (3) translate these policies into the workplace via the compensation system and implement it; and (4) reassess by comparing your results against the pay objectives. And continue to learn, adapt, and improve. Sound simple? It isn't. The major challenge in managing total compensation is to understand how your pay system can add value and make the organization more successful. We believe that research is beginning to offer useful evidence-based guidance, with the promise of more to come.

Review Questions

1. Select a familiar company or analyze the approach your college uses to pay teaching assistants or faculty. Infer its compensation strategy using the five dimensions (objectives, alignment, competitiveness, employee considerations, and management). How does your company or school compare to Microsoft and MerrillLynch? What business strategy does it seem to "fit" (i.e., cost cutter, customer centered, innovator, or something else)?

2. Contrast the essential differences between the best-fit and best-practices perspectives.

3. Reread Exhibit 2.7. Discuss how those values might be reflected in a compensation system. Are these values consistent with "Let the market decide"?

4. Three tests for any source of competitive advantage are align, differentiate, and add value. Discuss whether these tests are difficult to pass. Can compensation really be a source of competitive advantage?

5. Set up a debate over the following proposition: Nonfinancial returns (great place to work, opportunities to learn, job security, and flexible work schedules) are more important (i.e., best practice) than pay.

Endnotes

1. Top Companies for Compensation & Benefits. glassdoor.com. Extracted February 5, 2015.

2. Martin Peers, "Searching Google for Pay," *The Wall Street Journal,* November 11, 2010. Laszlo Bock. *Work Rules!* 2015. New York: Grand Central Publishing. Laszlo Bock. Google's 10 things to transform your team and your workplace. *Fortune,* March 5, 2015.

3. Jed Horowitz, "Analysis: Broker Bonus Bidding War Comes at a Cost," *NewsDaily,* April 10, 2012. www.newsdaily.com. Extracted April 14, 2012.

4. Payout Grids 2012. www.onwallstreet.com/global/payout_grids.html. Extracted April 17, 2012.

5. David Mildenbers, "Bank of America's Merrill Adds $5 Billion to Deposits in Month," *www.Bloomberg.com,* June 5, 2009. Accessed June 11, 2009. "Merrill Tweaks Advisor Pay for 2015." Merrill core pay gird unchanged, even as firm increases incentives for new clients and asset-based business and eliminates grandfathering provisions on mass affluent households. December 11, 2014. http://wealthmanagement.com; Michael Wursthorn. "Brokerages to Advisers: Follow the Carrot in 2015," *The Wall Street Journal*, December 19, 2014. www.wsj.com.

6. Halah Touryalai, "Here's Why Bank of America Loves Merrill Lynch," *Forbes,* April 19, 2012. www.forbes.com. Extracted April 20, 2012.

7. Michael Wursthorn, "Merrill Contributes More to Bank of America's Bottom Line," The *Wall Street Journal,* January 15, 2015. www.wsj.com.

8. Timothy M. Gardner, "Interfirm Competition for Human Resources: Evidence from the Software Industry," *Academy of Management Journal* 48(2), 2005, pp. 237–256; Yoshio Yanadori and Janet Marler, "Compensation Strategy: Does Business Strategy Influence Compensation in High Technology Firms?" *Strategic Management Journal,* June 2006, pp. 559–570.

9. An *option* is the opportunity to buy stock at a set price. If the value of shares increases, then the option has value (market price minus the set option price). Awards grant employees stock whose value is its market price. Later chapters discuss stock options and awards in detail. See Kevin F. Hallock and Craig A. Olson, "The Value of Stock Options to Non-Executive Employees," Working paper, Institute of Labor and Industrial Relations, University of Illinois Urbana/Champaign, January 2006.

10. Jay Greene, "Microsoft Boosts Cash Compensation for Employees," CNET News. http://news.cnet.com. Extracted March 11, 2012.

11. "SAS Institute," Stanford Business School case; Also, "SAS: The Royal Treatment," *60 Minutes,* October 13, 2002.

12. Rich Karlgaard, "Microsoft's IQ Dividend," *The Wall Street Journal,* July 28, 2004, p. A13; Holman W. Jenkins, Jr., "Stock Options Are Dead, Long Live Stock Options," *The Wall Street Journal,* July 16, 2003.

13. M. Treacy and F. Wiersma, *The Discipline of Market Leaders* (Reading, MA: Addison-Wesley, 1997).

14. Daniel Vaughan-Whitehead, "Wage Reform in Central and Eastern Europe," in *Paying the Price,* Daniel Vaughn-Whitehead, ed. (New York: St. Martin's Press, 2000); Marshall Meyer, Yuan Lu, Hailin Lan, and Xiaohui Lu, "Decentralized Enterprise Reform: Notes on the Transformation of State-Owned Enterprises," in *The Management of Enterprises in the People's Republic of China,* Anne S. Tsui and Chung-Ming Lau, eds. (Boston, MA: Kluwer Academic, 2002), pp. 241–274; Mei Fong, "A Chinese Puzzle," *The Wall Street Journal,* August 16, 2004, p. B1.

15. Michael Porter, "What Is Strategy?" *Harvard Business Review,* November–December 1996, pp. 61–78. Deepak K. Datta, James P. Guthrie, and Patrick M. Wright, "Human Resource Management and Labor Productivity: Does Industry Matter?" *Academy of Management Journal* 48(5), 2005, pp. 135–145; Yoshio Yanadori and Janet Marler, "Compensation Strategy: Does Business Strategy Influence Compensation in High Technology Firms?" *Strategic Management Journal* (June 2006), pp. 559–570; Henry Mintzberg, "Five Tips for Strategy," in *The Strategy Process: Concepts and Contexts,* Henry Mintzberg and James Brian Quinn, eds. (Englewood Cliffs, NJ: Prentice-Hall, 1992); J. E. Delery and D. H. Doty, "Models of Theorizing in Strategic Human Resource Management," *Academy of Management Journal* 39(4), 1996, pp. 802–835; Edilberto F. Montemayor, "Congruence between Pay Policy and Competitive Strategy in High-Performing Firms," *Journal of Management* 22(6), 1996, pp. 889–908; B. Gerhart, "Pay Strategy and Firm Performance," in *Compensation in Organizations: Current Research and Practice,* S. L. Rynes and B. Gerhart, eds. (San Francisco, CA: Jossey-Bass, 2000); Barry Gerhart and Sara Rynes, *Compensation: Theory, Evidence, and Strategic Implications* (Thousand Oaks, CA: Sage, 2003).

16. For a comprehensive reviews of theory and research on this topic, see Luis R. Gomez-Mejia, Pascual Berrone, and Monica Franco-Santos. *Compensation and Organizational Performance.* Armonk, NY: M.E. Sharpe, 2010 and Luis R. Gomez-Mejia and David B. Balkin. *Compensation, Organizational Strategy, and Firm Performance.* Cincinnati, OH: South-Western, 1992.

17. Michael E. Porter, *Competitive strategy* (New York: Free Press, 1980); R. E. Miles and C. C. Snow, *Organizational Strategy, Structure, and Process* (New York: McGraw-Hill, 1978).

18. George T. Milkovich, "A Strategic Perspective on Compensation," *Research in Personnel and Human Resources Management* 6 (1988), pp. 263–268; B. Gerhart and S. L. Rynes, *Compensation: Theory, Evidence, and Strategic Implications* (Thousand Oaks, CA: Sage, 2003).

19. Y. Yanadori and J. H. Marler, "Compensation Strategy: Does Business Strategy Influence Compensation in High-Technology Firms?" *Strategic Management Journal* 27 (2006), pp. 559–570; N. Rajagopalan, "Strategic Orientations, Incentive Plan Adoptions, and Firm Performance: Evidence From Electrical Utility Firms," *Strategic Management Journal* 18 (1996), pp. 761–785; Luis R. Gomez-Mejia and David B. Balkin, *Compensation, Organization Strategy, and Firm Performance* (Cincinnati, OH: South-Western, 1992); B. Gerhart, "Compensation Strategy and Organizational Performance," in *Compensation in Organizations,* S. L. Rynes and B. Gerhart, eds., Frontiers of Industrial and Organizational Psychology series (San Francisco, CA: Jossey-Bass, 2000).

20. B. Gerhart, C. Trevor, and M. Graham, "New Directions in Employee Compensation Research," in G. R. Ferris, ed., *Research in Personnel and Human Resources Management,* 1996, pp. 143–203.

21. IBM, "Our Strategy," *www.ibm.com/investor/strategy/* Extracted May 22, 2009.

22. Peter Boxall and John Purcell, *Strategy and Human Resource Management,* 2nd ed. (Basingstoke and New York: Palgrave MacMillan, 2007); Rosemary Batt, "Managing Customer Services: Human Resource Practices, Quit Rates, and Sales Growth," *Academy of Management Journal* 45 (2002), pp. 587–597; Eileen Appelbaum, Thomas Bailey, Peter Berg, and Arne Kalleberg, *Manufacturing Advantage: Why High Performance Work Systems Pay Off* (Ithaca, NY: Cornell Universty Press, 2000); I. S. Fulmer, B. Gerhart, and K. S. Scott, "Are the 100 Best Better? An Empirical Investigation of the Relationship Between Being A 'Great Place to Work' and Firm Performance," *Personnel Psychology* 56, (2003) pp. 965–993; H. C. Katz, T. A. Kochan, and M. R. Weber, "Assessing the Effects of Industrial Relations Systems and Efforts to Improve the Quality of Working Life on Organizational Effectiveness," *Academy of Management Journal* 28 (1985), pp. 509–526; Mark A. Huselid, "The Impact of Human Resource Management Practices on Turnover, Productivity, and Corporate Financial Performance," *Academy of Management Journal* 38 (1995), 635–672; John Paul Macduffie, "Human Resource Bundles and Manufacturing Performance: Organizational Logic and Flexible Production Systems in the World Auto Industry," *Industrial and Labor Relations Review* 48 (1995), 197–221. For a review, see B. Gerhart, "Horizontal and Vertical Fit in Human Resource Systems," in *Perspectives on Organizational Fit,* C. Ostroff and T. Judge, eds., SIOP Organizational Frontiers series (New York: Lawrence Erlbaum Associates, 2007).

23. P. M. Wright, G. McMahan, S. Snell, and B. Gerhart, "Comparing Line and HR Executives' Perceptions of HR Effectiveness: Services, Roles, and Contributions," *Human Resource Management* 40 (2001), pp. 111–124.

24. B. Becker and B. Gerhart, "The Impact of Human Resource Management on Organizational Performance: Progress and Prospects," *Academy of Management Journal* 39 (1996), pp. 779–801.

25. Charles Fishman, "The Anarchist's Cookbook," *Fast Company,* July 2004, *http://www.fastcompany.com/magazine/84/wholefoods.html,* July 2004; Whole Foods Market, Inc. Annual Repor (Form 10-K), November 26, 2008, *www.sec.gov.*

26. H. Mintzberg, "Crafting Strategy," *Harvard Business Review* (July–August 1970), pp. 66–75.

27. M. Brown, M. C. Sturman, and M. Simmering, "Compensation Policy and Organizational Performance: The Efficiency, Operational, and Financial Implications of Pay Levels and Pay Structure," *Academy of Management Journal* 46 (2003), pp. 752–762; Yoshio Yanadori and Janet Marler, "Compensation Strategy: Does Business Strategy Influence Compensation in High Technology Firms?" *Strategic Management Journal,* June 2006, pp. 559–570.

28. Timothy M. Gardner, "Interfirm Competition for Human Resources: Evidence from the Software Industry," *Academy of Management Journal* 48(2), 2005, pp. 237–256; H. Mintzberg, "Crafting Strategy," *Harvard Business Review* (July–August 1970), pp. 66–75.

29. S. Chatterjee, "Core Objectives: Clarity in Designing Strategy," *California Management Review* 47(2), 2005, pp. 33–49.

30. M. Bloom and G. Milkovich, "Strategic Perspectives on International Compensation and Reward Systems," in *Research and Theory in Strategic HRM: An Agenda for the Twenty-First Century,* Pat Wright, et al., eds. (Greenwich, CT: JAI Press, 1999); M. Bloom, G. Milkovich, and A. Mitra, "International Compensation: Learning from How Managers Respond to Variations in Local Host Contexts," *International Journal of Human Resource Management* (Special Issue, 2003); Allen D. Engle, Sr., and Mark Mendenhall, "Transnational Roles and Transnational Rewards: Global Integration in Executive Compensation," presentation at International HR conference, Limerick, Ireland, June 2003; Paul Evans, Vlado Pucik, and Jean-Louis Barsoux, *The Global Challenge* (New York: McGraw-Hill, 2002); *Global Rewards: A Collection of Articles from WorldatWork* (Scottsdale, AZ: WorldatWork, 2005).

31. George Milkovich and Thomas A. Mahoney, "Human Resource Planning Models: A Perspective," *Human Resource Planning* 1(1) (1978), pp. 1–18.

32. Rosemary Batt, Alexander J. S. Colvin, and Jeffrey Keefe, "Employee Voice, Human Resource Practices, and Quit Rates: Evidence from the Telecommunications Industry," *Industrial and Labor Relations Review* 55(4), July 2002, pp. 573–594; A. Colvin, R. Batt, and H. Katz, "How High Performance HR Practices and Workforce Unionization Affect Managerial Pay," *Personnel Psychology* 54 (2001), pp. 903–934; Paul Osterman, "The Wage Effects of High Performance Work Organization in Manufacturing," *Industrial and Labor Relations Review* (January 2006), pp. 187–204.

33. Study by Christopher K. Bart cited in Steven Greenhouse, "The Nation: Mission Statements; Words that Can't Be Set to Music," *The New York Times,* February 13, 2000.

34. *www.jnj.com/our_company/our_credo* in more than 50 languages!

35. See the website for Federation of European Employers, at *www.fedee.com.* Also, Watson Wyatt Worldwide, "Strategic Rewards: Managing through Uncertain Times," survey report (2001–2002).

36. Jason Shaw, Michelle Duffy, Atul Mitra, Daniel Lockhart, and Matthew Bowler, "Reactions to Merit Pay Increases: A Longitudinal Test of a Signal Sensitivity Perspective," *Journal of Applied Psychology* 88 (2003), pp. 538–544; Loretta Chao, "For Gen Xers, It's Work to Live," *The Wall Street Journal,* November 29, 2005, p. B6; Eduardo Porter, "Choice Is Good. Yes, No or Maybe?" *The New York Times,* March 27, 2005, p. WK12; Melissa Barringer and George Milkovich, "Employee Health Insurance Decisions in a Flexible Benefit Environment," *Human Resource Management* 35 (1996), pp. 293–315; M. P. Patterson, "Health Benefit Evolutions for the 21st Century: Vouchers and Other Innovations?" *Compensation and Benefits Review* 32(4), July/August 2000, pp. 6–14.

37. Hudson, *Rising Above the Average: Hudson's 2007 Compensation and Benefits Report.* Hudson's research also examines employee attitudes about traditional and nontraditional pay and benefit programs, including performance management, consumer-driven healthcare, and total-reward strategies. The full data set breaks down the findings by various demographics including employer type, occupational sector, age, gender, race, income, company size, managerial status, and others. *www.hudson-index.com.*

38. Eduardo Porter, "Choice Is Good. Yes, No or Maybe?" *The New York Times,* March 27, 2005, p. WK12.

39. S. S. Iyengar, R. E. Wells, and B. Schwartz, "Doing Better but Feeling Worse: Looking for the 'Best' Job Undermines Satisfaction," *Psychological Science* 17(2), 2003, pp. 143–150; R. Chua and S. S. Iyengar, "Empowerment through Choice?: A Critical Analysis of the Effects of Choice in Organizations" in *Research on Organizational Behavior,* B. Shaw and M. Kramer, eds. (Oxford, UK: Elsevier, in press).

40. Karen Strossel, "Make My (Mother's) Day . . ." *The Wall Street Journal,* May 12, 2006, p. A13; John Deckop, Kimberly Merriman, and Gary Blau, "Impact of Variable Risk Preferences on the Effectiveness of Control by Pay," *Journal of Occupational and Organizational Psychology* 77 (2004), pp. 63–80.

41. Morris M. Kleiner, Jonathan S. Leonard, and Adam M. Pilarski, "How Industrial Relations Affects Plant Performance: The Case of Commercial Aircraft Manufacturing," *Industrial and Labor Relations Review* 55(2), January 2002, pp. 195–218; Sean Karimi and Gangaram Singh, "Strategic Compensation: An Opportunity for Union Activism," *Compensation and Benefits Review,* March/April 2004, pp. 62–67; Henry S. Faber, "Union Success in Representation Elections: Why Does Unit Size Matter?" *Industrial and Labor Relations Review* 54(2), 2001, pp. 329–348.

42. Maria Sacchetti, "Teachers Study Merit Proposal," *Boston Globe*, August 8, 2005; Karla Dial, "Denver Voters Approve Merit Pay for Teachers," *School Reform News,* December 1, 2005.

43. Jeffrey McCracken, "Detroit's Symbol of Dysfunction: Paying Employees Not to Work," *The Wall Street Journal,* March 1, 2006, p. A1, A12; Lauren Etter, "Is General Motors Unraveling?" *The Wall Street Journal,* April 8, 2006, p. A7; "GM Offers Huge Employee Buyout," Associated Press, March 22, 2006.

44. George Milkovich and Carolyn Milkovich, *Cases in Compensation,* 9th ed. (Santa Monica, CA: Milkovich, 2004), p. 8; Aaron Chatterji and David Levine, "Breaking Down the Wall of Codes: Evaluating Non-Financial Performance Measurement," *California Management Review* 48(2), Winter 2006, pp. 29–51.

45. W. Chan Kim and Renee Mauborgne, "Pursuing the Holy Grail of Clear Vision," *Financial Times,* August 6, 2002, p. 8; Robert S. Kaplan and David P. Norton, "Having Trouble with Your Strategy? Then Map It," *Harvard Business Review,* September–October 2000, pp. 167–176; S. Chatterjee, "Core Objectives: Clarity in Designing Strategy," *California Management Review* 47(2), 2005.

46. L. Bossidy, R. Charman, and C. Burck, *Execution: The Discipline of Getting Things Done* (New York: Crown Business Publishers, 2002); R. Preston McAffee, *Competitive Solutions: The Strategist's Toolkit* (Princeton, NJ: Princeton University Press, 2005).

47. J. Pfeffer, "When It Comes to 'Best Practices,' Why Do Smart Organizations Occasionally Do Dumb Things?" *Organizational Dynamics* 25 (1997), pp. 33–44; J. Pfeffer, *The Human Equation: Building Profits by Putting People First* (Boston, MA: Harvard Business School Press, 1998); Barry Gerhart, Charlie Trevor, and Mary Graham, "New Directions in Employee Compensation Research," in G. R. Ferris, ed., *Research in Personnel and Human Resources Management,* vol. 14 (Greenwich, CT: JAI Press, 1996), pp. 143–203.

48. Samir Raza, "Optimizing Human Capital Investments for Superior Shareholder Returns," *Valuation Issues,* 2006, *www.valuationissues.com;* M. Huselid and B. Becker, "Improving HR Analytical Literacy: Lessons from Moneyball," chapter 32 in M. Losey, S. Meisinger, and D. Ulrich, *The Future of Human Resource Management* (Hoboken, NJ: Wiley, 2005); Lindsay Scott, "Managing Labor Costs Using Pay-for-Performance," Lindsay Scott & Associates, Inc., *www.npktools.com,* 2006; Thomas Stewart, *Intellectual Capital: The New Wealth of Organizations* (New York: Currency, 1997); D. Scott, D. Morajda, and T. McMullen, "Evaluating Pay Program Effectiveness," *WorldatWork Journal,* First Quarter 2006; D. Scott, T. McMullen, and R. Sperling, "Evaluating Pay Program Effectiveness: A National Survey of Compensation and Human Resource Professionals," *WorldatWork Journal* 15(2), Second Quarter 2006, pp. 50–59.

49. Richard Donkin, "Measuring the Worth of Human Capital," *Financial Times,* November 7, 2002; Peter F. Drucker, "They're Not Employees, They're People," *Harvard Business Review,* February 2002, pp. 70–77; Stephen Gates, *Value at Work: The Risks and Opportunities of Human Capital Measurement and Reporting* (New York: Conference Board, 2002).

50. John Boudreau and Pete Ramstad, "Beyond Cost-per-Hire and Time to Fill: Supply-Chain Measurement for Staffing," Working Paper T04-16 (468) (Los Angeles, CA: Center for Effective Organizations, 2006).

51. Connie Willis, *Bellwether* (London: Bantam Books 1996); M. Gladwell, *The Tipping Point: The Next Big Thing* (Boston, MA: Little, Brown, 2000).

52. J. Purcell, "Best Practices and Best Fit: Chimera or Cul-de-Sac?" *Human Resources Management Journal* 9(3), pp. 26–41.

53. B. Gerhart, "Pay Strategy and Firm Performance," in *Compensation in Organizations: Current Research and Practice,* S. Rynes and B. Gerhart, eds. (San Francisco, MA:

Jossey-Bass, 2000); B. Gerhart and G. Milkovich, "Employee Compensation," in *Handbook of Industrial and Organization Psychology,* 3rd ed., M. Dunnette and L. Hough, eds. (Palo Alto, CA: Consulting Psychologists Press, 1992).

54. P. K. Zingheim and J. R. Schuster, *Pay People Right!* (San Francisco, CA: Jossey-Bass, 2000); J. Pfeffer, "Seven Practices of Successful Organizations," *California Management Review* 49(2), 1998, pp. 96–124; E. Lawler, *Rewarding Excellence* (San Francisco, CA: Jossey-Bass, 2000).

55. Jason Shaw, Michelle Duffy, Atul Mitra, Daniel Lockhart, and Matthew Bowler, "Reactions to Merit Pay Increases: A Longitudinal Test of a Signal Sensitivity Perspective," *Journal of Applied Psychology* 88 (2003), pp. 538–544; M. Bloom and G. Milkovich, "Relationships Among Risk, Incentive Pay, and Organization Performance," *Academy of Management Journal* 41(3), 1998, pp. 283–297; Charlie O. Trevor and David L. Wazeter, "A Contingent View of Reactions to Objective Pay Conditions: Interdependence Among Pay Structure Characteristics and Pay Relative to Internal and External Referents," *Journal of Applied Psychology,* in press; Charlie Trevor, Barry Gerhart, and Greg Reilly, "Decoupling Explained and Unexplained Pay Dispersion to Predict Organizational Performance," presentation at Academy of Management meeting Atlanta, Georgia, August 11–16, 2006; Matthew C. Bloom, "The Performance Effects of Pay Structures on Individuals and Organizations," *Academy of Management Journal* 42(1), 1999, pp. 25–40; Mark Brown, Michael C. Sturman, and Marcia Simmering, "Compensation Policy and Organizational Performance: The Efficiency, Operational, and Financial Implications of Pay Levels and Pay Structure," *Academy of Management Journal* 46 (2003), pp. 752–762; E. P. Lazear, *Personnel Economics* (Cambridge, MA: MIT Press, 1995).

56. Brian Becker and Mark Huselid, "High Performance Work Systems and Firm Performance: A Synthesis of Research and Managerial Implications," in *Research in Personnel and Human Resource Management,* G. R. Ferris, ed. (Greenwich, CT: JAI Press, 1997); Stephen H. Wagner, Christopher P. Parker, and Neil D. Christiansen, "Employees that Think and Act Like Owners: Effects of Ownership Beliefs and Behaviors on Organizational Effectiveness," *Personnel Psychology,* Winter 2003, pp. 847–871; M. C. Sturman, C. O. Trevor, J. W. Boudreau, and B. Gerhart, "Is It Worth It to Win the Talent War? Evaluating the Utility of Performance-Based Pay," *Personnel Psychology* 56 (2003), pp. 997–1035; A. D. Stajkovic, and F. Luthans, "Differential Effects of Incentive Motivators on Work Performance," *Academy of Management Journal* (44), 2001, pp. 580–590; Jeffrey B. Arthur and Christopher L. Huntley, "Ramping Up the Organizational Learning Curve: Assessing the Impact of Deliberate Learning on Organizational Performance under Gainsharing," *Academy of Management Journal* 48(6), 2005, pp. 1159–1170.

57. Edilberto F. Montemayor, "Congruence between Pay Policy and Competitive Strategy in High-Performing Firms," *Journal of Management* 22(6), 1996, pp. 889–908; L. R. Gomez-Mejia and D. B. Balkin, *Compensation, Organization Strategy, and Firm Performance* (Cincinnati, OH: Southwestern, 1992); Charlie Trevor, Barry Gerhart, and Greg Reilly, "Decoupling Explained and Unexplained Pay Dispersion to Predict Organizational Performance," presentation at Academy of Management meeting, Atlanta, Georgia, August 11–16, 2006.

58. Mark A. Huselid, Brian E. Becker, and Richard W. Beatty, *The Workforce Scorecard* (Boston, MA: Harvard Business School Press, 2005); David Ulrich and Wayne Brockbank, *The HR Value Proposition* (Boston, MA: Harvard Business School Press, 2005); Brian Becker, Mark Huselid, and Dave Ulrich, *The HR Scorecard: Linking People, Strategy, and Performance* (Boston, MA: Harvard Business School Press, 2001); Rosemary Batt, Virginia Doellgast, and Hyunji Kwon, *The U.S. Call Center Industry 2004: National Benchmarking Report—Strategy, HR Practices, and Performance* (Ithaca, NY: Industrial and Labor Relations School, 2005); D. Scott, D. Morajda, and T. McMullen, "Evaluating Pay Program Effectiveness," *WorldatWork Journal,* First Quarter 2006; and D. Scott, T. McMullen, and R. Sperling, "Evaluating Pay Program Effectiveness: A National Survey of Compensation and Human Resource Professionals," *WorldatWork Journal* 15(2), Second Quarter 2006, pp. 50–59; B. Becker and M. Huselid, "High Performance Work Systems and Firm Performance: A Synthesis of Research and Managerial Implications," in *Research in Personnel and Human Resources,* G. Ferris, ed. (Greenwich, CT: JAI Press, 1997); Paul Osterman, "The Wage Effects of High Performance Work Organization in Manufacturing," *Industrial and Labor Relations Review,* January 2006, pp. 187–204.

59. Deepak K. Datta, James P. Guthrie, and Patrick M. Wright, "Human Resource Management and Labor Productivity: Does Industry Matter?" *Academy of Management Journal* 48(5), pp. 135–145.

60. K. Murphy and M. Jensen, "It's Not How Much You Pay, But How," *Harvard Business Review,* May–June 1990, pp. 138–149.

61. B. Gerhart and G. Milkovich, "Organization Differences in Managerial Compensation and Financial Performance," *Academy of Management Journal* 90(33), pp. 663–691.

62. Barry Gerhart and Sara Rynes, *Compensation: Theory, Evidence, and Strategic Implications* (Thousand Oaks, CA: Sage, 2003).

63. Bartolome Deya-Tortella, Luis R. Gomez-Mejia, Julio O. DeCastro, and Robert M. Wiseman, "Incentive Alignment or Perverse Incentives?" *Management Research* 3(2), 2005; Stephane Renaud, Sylvie St-Onge, and Michel Magnan, "The Impact of Stock Purchase Plan Participation on Workers' Individual Cash Compensation," *Industrial Relations,* January 2004, pp. 120–147; Ingrid Smithey Fulmer, Barry Gerhart, and Kimberly Scott, "Are the 100 Best Better? An Empirical Investigation of the Relationship between Being a 'Great Place to Work' and Firm Performance," *Personnel Psychology* 56 (2003), pp. 965–993; S. Werner and H. Tosi, "Other People's Money: The Effects of Ownership on Compensation Strategy," *Academy of Management Journal* 38(6), pp. 1672–1691.

64. Rosemary Batt, Virginia Doellgast, and Hyunji Kwon, *The U.S. Call Center Industry 2004: National Benchmarking Report—Strategy, HR Practices, and Performance* (Ithaca, NY: Industrial and Labor Relations School, 2005); Rosemary Batt, Alexander J. S. Colvin, and Jeffrey Keefe, "Employee Voice, Human Resource Practices, and Quit Rates: Evidence from the Telecommunications Industry," *Industrial and Labor Relations Review* 55(4), July 2002, pp. 573–594; N. Bloom and J. Van Reenen, "Discussion Paper No. 716," *London School of Economics,* March 2006.

65. Brian Becker and Mark Huselid, "High Performance Work Systems and Firm Performance: A Synthesis of Research and Managerial Implications," in *Research in Personnel and Human Resource Management,* G. R. Ferris, ed. (Greenwich, CT: JAI Press, 1997).

66. Martha Graybow, "Wall Street Faces Pay Conundrum Amid TARP Rules," May 28, 2009. *www.reuters.com.*

67. Joseph Giannone and Jed Horowitz, "Merrill Lynch Uses Unusually Large Signing Bonuses to Attract Star Brokers," *Huffington Post,* April 15, 2011. Extracted April 14, 2012.

68. Michael Wursthorn, "Merrill Contributes More to Bank of America's Bottom Line," *The Wall Street Journal,* January 15, 2015. www.wsj.com.

69. Jed Horowitz, "Analysis: Broker Bonus Bidding War Comes at a Cost," *NewsDaily,* April 10, 2012. www.newsdaily.com. Extracted April 14, 2012.

70. John Carney, "New Worries over Broker Pay at Bank of America," *NetNet,* September 7, 2011. www.cnbc.com. Extracted April 16, 2012; John Carney, "Bank of America's Darnell Seeks to Reassure Nervous Merrill Brokers," *NetNet,* September 8, 2011. www.cnbc.com. Extracted April 16, 2012.

Part Two

Internal Alignment: Determining the Structure

According to the U.S. Department of Labor's Bureau of Labor Statistics (BLS), Occupational Employment Statistics, there are large differences in pay as a function of position/job. The average annual pay for a licensed practical nurse working at a hospital is $42,280. For a registered nurse working at a hospital, it is $70,590. For physicians and surgeons, average annual pay is $191,580. A separate survey, the Medscape General Surgeon Report, finds substantial differences in pay among physicians: $176,000 for family practice, $295,000 for general surgery, and $413,000 for orthopedics. Turning to soccer (or what most countries outside of the United States call football), we see that position once again matters. The Los Angeles Galaxy won the MLS Cup recently. Their highest paid forward, Robbie Keane, earned $4.5 million and their highest paid midfielder, Landon Donovan, earned $4.5 million. (David Beckham, another midfielder, retired from the Galaxy, had earned $6.5 million.) What about the highest paid defender on the Galaxy? That was Omar Gonzalez at $1,000,000 (a major increase from the $197,000 he earned a few years ago). A look at the 10 highest paid players in MLS finds that there are seven forwards, three midfielders, and no defenders. (Omar Gonzalez is the 12th highest paid player.) Why does position matter so much when it comes to pay? Why don't hospitals and soccer teams just pay all types of "jobs" the same? In the examples above, can one get promoted to earn more money? For example, can a registered nurse become a physician? Can a defender move up to midfielder and then to forward? What about at law firms and consulting firms? Can an associate become a partner? If so, what is the payoff?

EXHIBIT II.1   The Pay Model

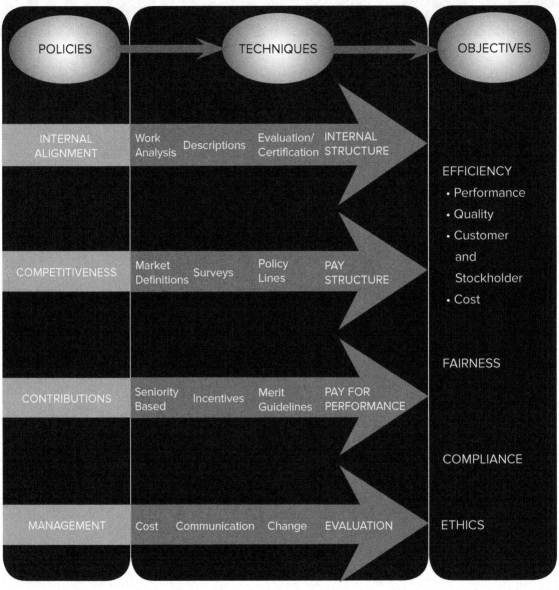

Chapter **Three**

Defining Internal Alignment

Chapter Outline

For the kingdom of heaven is like a householder who went out early in the morning to hire laborers for his vineyard. And having agreed with the laborers for a denarius a day, he sent them into his vineyard. And about the third hour, he went out and saw others standing . . . idle; and he said to them, "Go you also into the vineyard, and I will give you whatever is just." And again he went out about the ninth hour, and did as before . . . But about the eleventh hour he went out and found others . . . and he said to them, "Go you also into the vineyard." When evening came, the owner said to his steward, "Call the laborers, and pay them their wages, beginning from the last even to the first." When the first in their turn came . . . they also received each his denarius. . . . They began to murmur against the householder, saying, "These last have worked a single hour, and thou hast put them on a level with us, who have borne the burden of the day's heat." But answering them, he said, "Friend, I do thee no injustice; take what is thine and go."[1]

Matthew's parable raises age-old questions about internal alignment and pay structures within a single organization.[2] The laborers felt that those "who have borne the burden of the day's heat" should be paid more than those who worked fewer hours. But apparently the householder was looking at an individual's needs. He ignored (1) the content of the work, (2) the skills and knowledge required to perform it, and (3) its relative value for achieving the organization's objectives. These three are common bases for today's pay structure. And if the procedures to determine the structure are not acceptable to the parties involved, today's employees murmur, too. That murmuring translates into turnover, an unwillingness to try new technologies, even indifference to the quality of the grapes or the customer's satisfaction with them. This chapter examines internal alignment and its consequences.

JOBS AND COMPENSATION

As we just saw in the Part Two Introduction, pay varies significantly according to the job. We will see in this chapter that organizations design their pay structures around jobs and job levels and that, in many organizations, an employee's pay (and by implication, their pay growth over time) depends on both the nature of the job and the job level (and thus promotion rate).[3]

COMPENSATION STRATEGY: INTERNAL ALIGNMENT

Setting objectives is our first issue in a strategic approach to pay. Our second issue, **internal alignment,** addresses relationships *inside* the organization. Matthew doesn't tell us how the work in the vineyard was organized. Perhaps laborers worked in teams: Some trimmed while others tied the vines. Does trimming require more judgment than tying? How do the responsibilities and pay of the trimmer relate to the responsibilities and pay of the tier, the householder's cook, or the steward? Internal alignment addresses the logic underlying these relationships. The relationships form a pay structure that should *support the organization strategy, support the work flow,* and *motivate behavior toward organization objectives.*

> **Internal alignment,** often called *internal equity,* refers to the pay relationships among different jobs/skills/competencies within a single organization.[4]

Exhibit 3.1 shows a structure for engineering work at a division of Lockheed Martin, the world's largest defense contractor. Lockheed also builds rockets, shuttles, and Martian rovers for NASA. Lockheed has the contract to build the next shuttle that will take manned flights back to the moon and on to Mars. The six levels in Lockheed's structure range from entry to consultant. You can see the relationships in the descriptions of each level. Decisions on how to pay each level create a **pay structure.**

> **Pay structure** refers to the array of pay rates for different work or skills within a single organization. The *number of levels,* the *differentials* in pay between the levels, and the *criteria* used to determine those differences describe the structure.

EXHIBIT 3.1 **Engineering Structure at Lockheed Martin**

Engineer
Limited use of basic principles and concepts. Develops solutions to limited problems. Closely supervised.

Senior Engineer
Full use of standard principles and concepts. Provides solutions to a variety of problems. Under general supervision.

Systems Engineer
Wide applications of principles and concepts, plus working knowledge of other related disciplines. Provides solutions to a wide variety of difficult problems. Solutions are imaginative, thorough, and practicable. Works under only very general direction.

Lead Engineer
Applies extensive expertise as a generalist or specialist. Develops solutions to complex problems that require the regular use of ingenuity and creativity. Work is performed without appreciable direction. Exercises considerable latitude in determining technical objectives of assignment.

Advisor Engineer
Applies advanced principles, theories, and concepts. Contributes to the development of new principles and concepts. Works on unusually complex problems and provides solutions that are highly innovative and ingenious. Works under consultative direction toward predetermined long-range goals. Assignments are often self-initiated.

Consultant Engineer
Exhibits an exceptional degree of ingenuity, creativity, and resourcefulness. Applies and/or develops highly advanced technologies, scientific principles, theories, and concepts. Develops information that extends the existing boundaries of knowledge in a given field. Often acts independently to uncover and resolve problems associated with the development and implementation of operational programs.

Supports Organization Strategy

Lockheed decided that six levels of engineering work would support the company's strategy of researching, designing, and developing advanced technology systems.

Supports Work Flow

Work flow refers to the process by which goods and services are delivered to the customer. The pay structure ought to support the efficient flow of that work and the design of the organization.[5] For example, financial service firms in the United States traditionally offer investment advice and products through client centers. At Merrill Lynch, customer associates used to take all calls from clients or new prospects and route them to financial advisors (FAs). If the caller wanted a specific transaction, such as purchasing a stock, mutual fund, or certificate of deposit, the customer associate passed the information on to an FA who was legally certified to make the purchase. No one at Merrill Lynch "owned" a client. Personal long-term relationships were not emphasized.

But Merrill Lynch recognized that its clients' investment needs varied, depending on their net worth, among other factors. Ultra-high-net-worth individuals with more than $25 million to invest were not interested in CDs or stock transactions. They wanted advice specific to their circumstances from someone they knew and trusted. And rather than waiting for calls from these people, the FAs should initiate calls to them. That would help build the long-term relationship around adding value to clients' investments. Merrill Lynch also noticed that meeting the needs of these high-net-worth clients was very profitable (i.e., higher margins on the fees and the products).[6] So Merrill Lynch redesigned the flow of work to better reflect its clients' needs—and increase its profits.

Merrill Lynch divided its clients into five groups based on net worth: investor, emerging affluent, affluent, high net worth, and ultra high net worth (the "whales"). Then it revamped its job structure to match. The work of financial advisor was divided into five job levels, ranging from assistant vice president, investments (AVPI), to senior vice president, investments (SVPI). These new job levels were defined by the amount of client assets the advisor manages and the expertise and knowledge the advisor possesses. Building those long-term relationships with the "whales" requires complex interactions. The smaller ("investor") clients are still buying stocks, bonds, and CDs through the financial advisor centers. Newly trained and experienced FAs are now building relationships with individuals in the various client groups. In addition to the financial advisor centers, Merrill Lynch also created private banking hubs to serve clients with very high net worth.

To support the new financial advisor job structure, Merrill Lynch designed a new pay structure. The differential in base pay between the entry level financial advisor and the top level (the SVPI) is about 8 to 1. Aggressive bonus and stock incentives are a substantial part of the new pay structure. The pay difference between entry level FAs, AVPIs, and SVPIs was a major issue—just as it is for Lockheed engineers, health care workers, soccer players, and the laborers in the vineyard.

Motivates Behavior

Internal pay structures are part of the network of returns discussed in Chapter 1: pay increases for promotions, more challenging work, and greater responsibility as employees move up in the structure. The challenge is to design structures that will engage people to help achieve organization objectives. Merrill Lynch financial advisors work to meet the specific needs of their clients by building long-term relationships. Lockheed engineers work together to share knowledge with each other and with their customers. Is taking on a "bigger" job worth it? Does it pay off to take more training to get promoted? It will in a well-designed pay structure.

The structure ought to make clear the relationship between each job and the organization's objectives. This is an example of **"line-of-sight."** Employees should be able to "see" the links between their work, the work of others, and the organization's objectives. And the structure ought to be fair to employees. The vineyard owner's internal pay structure may have been aligned with his business strategy, but the employee dissatisfaction raises concerns about its fairness to employees.

STRUCTURES VARY AMONG ORGANIZATIONS

An internal pay structure can be defined by (1) the number of *levels* of work, (2) the pay *differentials* between the levels, and (3) the *criteria or bases* used to determine those levels and differentials.

EXHIBIT 3.2
Career
Bands at GE
Healthcare

Source: GE Healthcare.

GE Band	Nature of Work
Associate	Front line, administrative and secretarial
Professional	Developing professional
Lead Professional	Team leader, supervisor, or experienced individual contributor
Senior Professional	Manager or seasoned professional
Executive	Key member of management team and/or individual contributor with major impact on business
	Driven by job scope, accountability, and skills

Number of Levels

One feature of any pay structure is its hierarchical nature: the number of levels and reporting relationships. Some are more hierarchical, with multiple levels; others are compressed, with few levels.[7] The stated goal of GE Healthcare is to provide "transformational medical technologies and services that are shaping a new age of patient care." One of their many product lines is magnetic resonance imaging (MRI). In comparison to Lockheed's six levels for engineering alone (Exhibit 3.1), GE Healthcare uses five broad levels, described in Exhibit 3.2, to cover all professional and executive work, including engineering. GE Healthcare would probably fit the Lockheed Martin structure into two or three levels.

Differentials

The pay differences among levels are referred to as **differentials.** If we assume that an organization has a compensation budget of a set amount to distribute among its employees, there are a number of ways it can do so. It can divide the budget by the number of employees to give everyone the same amount. The Moosewood Restaurant in Ithaca, New York, adopts this approach. But few organizations in the world are that egalitarian. In most, pay varies among employees.[8] Work that requires more knowledge or skills, is performed under unpleasant working conditions, or adds more value is usually paid more.[9] Exhibit 3.3 shows the percent differentials traditionally attached to Lockheed Martin's engineering structure. (Actual pay levels are now somewhat higher for the entire structure.) Northrup Grumman uses a similar six-level engineering structure with similar differentials. One intention of these differentials is to motivate people to strive for promotion to a higher-paying level. As Exhibit 3.3 shows, the same basic structure, in terms of percent differentials, can be paired with different pay level policies. For example, although a lead engineer gets paid more in the structure on the right, the percent differential between the lead engineer and systems engineer is the same in both (28 percent).

Criteria: Content and Value

Work content and its value are the most common bases for determining internal structures. **Content** refers to the work performed in a job and how it gets done (tasks, behaviors, knowledge required, etc.). **Value** refers to the worth of the work: its relative contribution to the organization objectives. A structure based on content typically

EXHIBIT 3.3 Pay Structure at Lockheed Martin, under Two Alternative Pay Level Policies

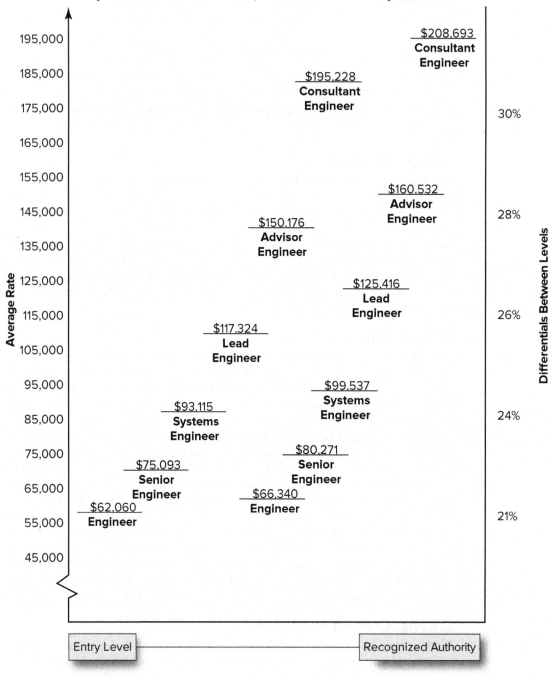

ranks jobs on skills required, complexity of tasks, problem solving, and/or responsibility. In contrast, a structure based on the value of the work focuses on the *relative contribution* of these skills, tasks, and responsibilities to the organization's goals. While the resulting structures may be the same, there are important differences. In addition to relative contribution, external market value may also be included (i.e., what competitors pay for this job). Or it may include rates agreed upon through collective bargaining, or even legislated rates (minimum wage). In centrally planned economies such as Cuba, job values in all organizations are set by a government agency. Following the now-discarded approaches of the former Soviet Union and China, Cuba's government dictates a universal structure: 8 levels for industrial workers, 16 levels for technical and engineering work, and 26 levels for government employees.

Use Value and Exchange Value

Use value reflects the value of goods or services an employee produces in a job. **Exchange value** is whatever wage the employer and employee agree on for a job. Think about IBM software engineers living in Bangalore, Kiev, and Purchase, New York. Their work content is very similar across all locations. Now think about them working together on the same project—same company, same job content, same internal job. They have the same use value. Wage rates in Bangalore and Kiev are a lot less than in Purchase, New York. The jobs' exchange value varies.[10] For promotions, IBM treats these jobs as being at the same level in the structure. But the external markets in India, the Ukraine, and the United States yield very different pay rates.

The difference between exchange value and use value also surfaces when one firm acquires another. IBM's acquisition of PricewaterhouseCoopers (PWC), where consultants were the lifeblood of the company, is a case in point. At the time, IBM was moving from being a computer company to a provider of information technology solutions whose applications were broader than the IT department. PWC consultants could help IBM's marketing teams engage with clients at a higher organization level. The use value of the PWC consultants within IBM differed from their use value within PWC (how they contributed to IBM or PWC objectives). So, similar marketing jobs in two different companies may be valued differently based on how they contribute to organization objectives. Alternatively, the same work content in the same company (IBM's software engineers) may have different exchange value based on different geographies.

Job- and Person-Based Structures

A **job-based structure** relies on the work content—tasks, behaviors, responsibilities. A **person-based structure** shifts the focus to the employee: the *skills, knowledge, or competencies* the employee possesses, whether or not they are used in the employee's particular job. The engineering structure at Lockheed Martin (Exhibit 3.1) uses the work performed as the criterion. GE Healthcare (Exhibit 3.2) uses the individual employees' competencies/knowledge required at each level of work.

In the real workplace, it is often hard to describe a job without reference to the jobholder's knowledge and skills. Conversely, it is hard to define a person's job-related knowledge or competencies without referring to work content. So rather than a job- *or* person-based structure, reality includes both job *and* person.

WHAT SHAPES INTERNAL STRUCTURES?

The major factors that shape internal structures are shown in Exhibit 3.4. We categorize them as *external* and *organization* factors, even though they are connected and interact. Exactly how they interact is not always well understood. As we discuss the factors, we will also look at various theories.[11]

Economic Pressures

Adam Smith was an early advocate of letting economic market forces influence pay structures. He was the first to ascribe both an exchange value and a use value to human resources. Smith faulted the new technologies associated with the Industrial

EXHIBIT 3.4
What Shapes Internal Structures?

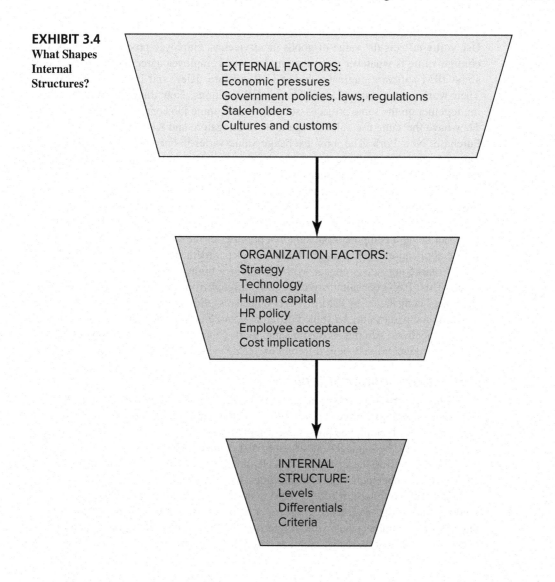

EXTERNAL FACTORS:
Economic pressures
Government policies, laws, regulations
Stakeholders
Cultures and customs

ORGANIZATION FACTORS:
Strategy
Technology
Human capital
HR policy
Employee acceptance
Cost implications

INTERNAL STRUCTURE:
Levels
Differentials
Criteria

Revolution for increasing the use value of labor without a corresponding increase in exchange value (i.e., higher wages).

Karl Marx took this criticism even further.[12] He said that employers unfairly pocketed the **surplus value** created by the difference between use and exchange value. He urged workers to overthrow capitalistic systems to become owners themselves and reap the full use value of their labor.

A countering theory put forth in the last half of the 19th century, **marginal productivity,** says that employers do in fact pay use value.[13] Unless an employee can produce a value equal to the value received in wages, it will not be worthwhile to hire that worker. One job is paid more or less than another because of differences in relative productivity of the job and/or differences in how much a consumer values the output. In the short run especially, interesting things can happen. For example, some nurses (specifically, nurse anesthetists) now earn $140,000 to $170,000 per year, more than many family practice and pediatrics doctors.[14] These nurses earn less than physician anesthesiologists ($300,000+), but can perform many of the same tasks. Not surprisingly, they are in high demand. Surgeons may be fine with the situation because it removes a possible constraint on being able to do surgery. One wonders about the views of primary care doctors. Hence, differences in productivity provide a rationale for the internal pay structure.

In addition to supply and demand for labor, supply and demand for products and services also affect internal structures.[15] Turbulent changes, either in competitors' products/services (as in the rise of the Internet for making purchases) or in customers' tastes (as in the popularity of fuel-efficient vehicles), force organizations to redesign work flow and force employees to continuously learn new skills. Unpredictable external conditions require pay structures that support agile organizations and flexible people.[16]

Government Policies, Laws, and Regulations

In the United States, equal employment legislation forbids pay systems that discriminate on the basis of gender, race, religion, or national origin. The Equal Pay Act and the Civil Rights Act require "equal pay for equal work," with work considered equal if it requires equal skill, equal effort, and equal responsibility and is performed under equal working conditions. An internal structure may contain any number of levels, with differentials of any size, as long as the criteria for setting them are not gender, race, religion, or national origin.

Much pay-related legislation attempts to regulate economic forces to achieve social welfare objectives. The most obvious place to affect an internal structure is at the minimums (minimum-wage legislation) and maximums (special reporting requirements for executive pay). But legislation also aims at the differentials. A contemporary U.S. example is the "living wage."[17] A number of U.S. cities require minimum hourly wage rates well above what federal law requires. The anticipated outcome of such legislation is a flatter, more compressed structure of wage rates in society.

External Stakeholders

Unions, stockholders, and even political groups have a stake in how internal pay structures are determined. Unions are the most obvious case. Most unions seek smaller pay differences among jobs and seniority-based promotions as a way to promote solidarity among members.

One specific comparison often used is the ratio of CEO pay to that of the average or entry level worker. Indeed, the new Dodd-Frank law will require public U.S. companies to report such a ratio. Estimates vary by what data are used, but they range from CEO pay that is 110 times to over 500 times the pay for manufacturing jobs.[18] The AFL-CIO website (*http://www.aflcio.org/Corporate-Watch/Paywatch-2014*) has a tool called Executive Pay Watch. For example, it reports a CEO-to-worker pay ratio of 331. (The degree to which employees compare their pay to that of their CEO is not known, as no systematic data have been reported.)

Cultures and Customs

National Public Radio host and author Garrison Keillor defines culture by what songs we know in common—camp songs, religious hymns, the big hits of the year we were 15. A General Mills executive says culture is the foods we eat. A more academic definition of culture is "the mental programming for processing information that people share in common."[19] Shared mind-sets may judge what size pay differential is fair. In ancient Greece, Plato declared that societies are strongest when the richest earned a maximum of four times the lowest pay. Aristotle favored a five-times limit. In 1942, President Franklin Roosevelt proposed a maximum wage: a 100 percent tax on all income above 10 times the minimum wage.

Historians note that in 14th-century western Europe, the Christian church endorsed a **"just wage" doctrine,** which supported the existing class structure. The doctrine was an effort to end the economic and social chaos resulting from the death of one-third of the population from plague. The resulting shortage of workers gave ordinary people power to demand higher wages, much to the dismay of church and state. Market forces such as skills shortages (higher exchange value) were explicitly denied as appropriate determinants of pay structures. Today, advocates of the living wage are trying to change societal judgments about what wage is just.

Even today, cultural factors play a role in shaping pay structures. Many traditional Japanese employers place heavy emphasis on experience in their internal pay structures. But pressures from global competitors plus an aging workforce have made age-based pay structures very expensive. Consequently, some Japanese employers are shifting older employees to lower-paying business units, emphasizing performance and downplaying seniority.[20] (This change is particularly irksome; as the authors have grown older, the wisdom of basing pay on age has become more and more obvious to us!)

Organization Strategy

You have already read how organization strategies influence internal pay structures. The belief is that pay structures that are not aligned with the organization strategy may become obstacles to the organization's success. However, aligned structures today may become an obstacle tomorrow. So aligned, yet adaptable, may be required.

Organization Human Capital

Human capital—the education, experience, knowledge, abilities, and skills required to perform the work—is a major influence on internal structures.[21] The greater the value added by the skills and experience, the more pay those skills will command. Lockheed's structure pays consultant engineers more than lead or senior engineers because the human capital required in the consultant engineer job brings a greater return to Lockheed. It is more crucial to Lockheed's success.

Organization Work Design

Technology used in producing goods and services influences the *organizational design,* the *work* to be performed, and the *skills/knowledge* required to perform the work. The technology required to produce precision military hardware differs from that used to develop and manufacture plastics. These differences contribute to the different structures observed at Lockheed and GE Healthcare.

Multiple structures often exist within the same organization for different types of work. For example, Northrup Grumman has supervisory, engineering, technical, administrative, and non-exempt structures, each having five to six base-pay groupings/levels.

The design of organizations is undergoing profound changes. A lot of people who work in organizations are not employees of these organizations. They may be employed by either a supplier (e.g., an IT services supplier such as IBM or Hewlett-Packard or a circuit designer such as Primarion) or perhaps a *temporary* work supplier (e.g., Accountemps, Manpower Services). Or, they may be working under a temporary contract for a limited amount of time or on a limited project. The security guards, software engineers, or accountants may be supplied by **outsourcing** specialists. Pay for these employees is based on the internal structure of their home employer (e.g., IBM or Accountemps) rather than of the workplace at which they are currently located. Another major work design change is **delayering**.[22] Entire levels of work have disappeared. Just weeks after arriving at Hewlett Packard, new CEO Mark Hurd began hearing complaints about HP's sluggish response to customer needs. He discovered that internal organization layers were delaying responses. HP cut levels of management from 11 to 8 and customers immediately applauded the reduced response time.[23] Delayering can cut unnecessary, noncontributing work. It can also add work to other jobs, enlarging them. Through the use of self-managed work teams in production work, entire levels of supervisory jobs are removed and the responsibility for more decisions is delegated to the teams.[24] This will change a job's value and the job structure.

Overall HR Policies

The organization's other human resource policies also influence internal pay structures. Most organizations tie money to promotions to induce employees to apply for higher-level positions.[25] If an organization has more levels, it can offer more promotions, but there may be smaller pay differences between levels. The belief is that more frequent promotions (even without significant pay increases) offer a sense of "career progress" to employees.[26]

Internal Labor Markets: Combining External and Organization Factors

Internal labor markets combine both external and organizational factors. Internal labor markets refer to the rules and procedures that (1) determine the pay for the different jobs within a single organization and (2) allocate employees among those different jobs.[27] In the organization depicted in Exhibit 3.5, individuals are recruited only for entry-level jobs (an engineer would be hired right out of college; a senior engineer would have a few years' experience). They are later promoted or transferred to other jobs inside the organization. Because the employer competes in the external market for people to fill these **entry jobs,** their pay must be high enough to attract a pool of qualified applicants. In contrast, pay for jobs filled via transfer and promotions is connected to external market forces, but the connection is less direct. External factors are dominant influences on pay for entry jobs, but the differences for nonentry jobs tend to reflect internal factors.[28]

Employee Acceptance: A Key Factor

Employees judge the fairness of their pay through comparisons with the compensation paid to others for work related in some fashion to their own.[29] Accordingly, an important factor influencing the internal pay structure is its *acceptability to the*

EXHIBIT 3.5
Illustration of an Internal Labor Market

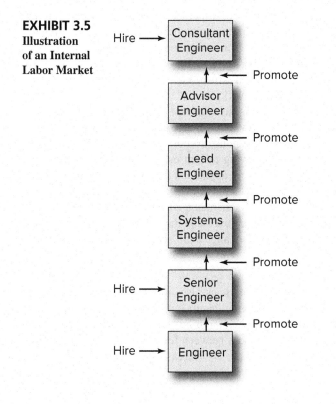

employees involved.[30] Employees make multiple pay comparisons to assess the fairness of an internal pay structure. They compare both with other jobs in the same internal structure and with the pay for their job in the external market (i.e., at competing employers).[31]

Two sources of fairness are important: the procedures for determining the pay structure, called **procedural justice;** and the results of those procedures—the pay structure itself—called **distributive justice.**

Suppose you are given a ticket for speeding. *Procedural justice* refers to the process by which a decision is reached: the right to an attorney, the right to an impartial judge, and the right to receive a copy of the arresting officer's statement. *Distributive justice* refers to the fairness of the decision: guilty. Researchers report that employees' perceptions of procedural fairness significantly influence their acceptance of the results; employees and managers are more willing to accept low pay if they believe that the way this result was obtained was fair. This research also suggests that pay procedures are more likely to be perceived as fair (1) if they are consistently applied to all employees, (2) if employees participated in the process, (3) if appeals procedures are included, and (4) if the data used are accurate. Nevertheless, a later study raises a question about the usefulness of employee participation.[32] In a low-wage company, there was no connection between employee participation and pay fairness. It may be that employees were paid so low that no amount of participation could overcome their dissatisfaction. So rather than tossing aside the idea of participation, it may be that in extreme cases (very low wages), a pay raise may trump participation.

Applied to internal structures, procedural justice addresses how design and administration decisions are made and whether procedures are applied in a consistent manner. Distributive justice addresses whether the actual pay differences among employees are acceptable.

Pay Structures Change

Pay structures change in response to external factors such as skill shortages. Over time, distorted pay differences may become accepted as equitable and customary; efforts to change them are resisted. Thus, pay structures established for organizational and economic reasons at an earlier time may be maintained for cultural or political reasons. It may take another economic jolt to overcome the resistance. Then new norms form around the new structure. This "change-and-congeal" process does not yet support the continuous changes occurring in today's economy.[33] New norms for employee acceptance will probably need to include recognition that people must get used to constant change, even in internal pay relationships.

The pay for airport security screeners relative to other airport jobs illustrates the change-and-congeal process. Prior to 9/11, airport screeners were paid about $5.50 an hour with no benefits. Recent immigrants, some undocumented, and relatively unskilled people were hired to screen travelers and their luggage. The people working at the airport Starbucks or the newspaper shop may have been earning more than the screeners. After the 9/11 attack, the Transportation Security Administration (TSA) took over airport security and screening. Wages are now comparable to police and fire protection jobs.[34] Employees in other airport jobs have had to revise their comparisons to the security jobs.[35]

STRATEGIC CHOICES IN DESIGNING INTERNAL STRUCTURES

Aligned pay structures support the way the work gets done, fit the organization's business strategy, and are fair to employees. Greater internal alignment—fit—is more likely to lead to success. Misaligned structures become obstacles. They may still motivate employee behavior, but it may be undesirable behavior. Jeff Goldblum's mathematician character may never have stolen the dinosaur egg in *Jurassic Park* if he had been given the pay raise he felt he deserved.

But what does it mean to fit or tailor the pay structure to be internally aligned? Two strategic choices are involved: (1) how specifically tailored to the organization's design and work flow to make the structure and (2) how to distribute pay throughout the levels in the structure.

Tailored versus Loosely Coupled

A low-cost, customer-focused business strategy such as that followed by McDonald's or Walmart may be supported by a closely tailored structure. Jobs are well defined with detailed tasks or steps to follow. You can go into a McDonald's in Cleveland, Prague, or Shanghai and find they all are very similar. Their pay structures are, too. There are seven jobs in each McDonald's (under supervisors and managers). All are very well defined in order to eliminate variance in how they are performed. Cooking french fries takes nine steps. It seems hard to make a mistake in these jobs.[36] It is also hard to be the very best french fryer in the whole company. Differences in pay among jobs are very small.

In contrast to McDonald's, 3M's business strategy requires constant product innovation and short product-design-to-market cycle times. The 3M competitive environment is turbulent and unpredictable. No steps at all are laid out. 3M engineers may work on several teams developing several products at the same time. 3M's pay structures are more loosely linked to the organization in order to provide flexibility.

Hierarchical versus Egalitarian and Layered versus Delayered Structures

Pay structures can range from hierarchical to egalitarian. Exhibit 3.6 clarifies the differences. Egalitarian structures have fewer levels and/or smaller differentials between adjacent levels and between the highest- and lowest-paid workers.

Structures can also be said to vary from layered to delayered. In Exhibit 3.7, the layered structure has eight different levels, with relatively small between-level differentials in comparison to the delayered structure, which has only three levels. The layered structure is more hierarchical than the delayered structure and less egalitarian in terms of number of levels; the multiple levels would include detailed descriptions of work done at each level and outline who is responsible for what. Hierarchies send the message that the organization values the differences in work content, individual skills, and contributions to the organization.[37]

EXHIBIT 3.6
Hierarchical versus Egalitarian Structures

	Hierarchical ⟷	Egalitarian
Levels	Many	Fewer
Differentials	Large	Small
Criteria	Person or job	Person or job
Supports:	Close fit	Loose fit
Work Organization	Individual performers	Teams
Fairness	Performance	Equal treatment
Behaviors	Opportunities for promotion	Cooperation

EXHIBIT 3.7
Layered versus Delayered Structures

Layered	Delayered
Chief Engineer	Chief Engineer
Engineering Manager	
Consulting Engineer	
Senior Lead Engineer	
Lead Engineer	Consulting Engineer
Senior Engineer	
Engineer	
Engineer Trainee	Associate Engineer

In the delayered structure, several levels of job titles are removed so that all employees at all levels become responsible for a broader range of tasks but also have greater freedom (with less close supervision) to determine how best to accomplish what is expected of them. The delayered structure is more egalitarian in that it sends the message that all employees are valued equally. Employees are less closely supervised and they are given more autonomy (less close supervision), in hopes of allowing them to exercise independent thought, initiative, and action. The assumption is that more equal treatment will improve employee satisfaction, support cooperation, and therefore affect workers' performance. Of course, if there are fewer levels in a delayered structure and if the difference between the lowest and highest compensation in the organization is the same as in a layered structure (as shown in Exhibit 3.7), then the pay differentials between levels would actually be larger in the delayered structure, not smaller. To more completely fit the egalitarian criteria laid out in Exhibit 3.6, the delayered structure in Exhibit 3.7 would need to raise the pay of the Associate Engineer and bring down the pay of the Chief Engineer, relative to the layered structure. That would decrease overall pay differentiation (variance/dispersion) between employees, making it more egalitarian. For example, at Costco, CEO James Sinegal tries to maintain his cash compensation (base plus bonus) at 8 times the average of Costco unionized employees. Likewise, John Mackey at Whole Foods maintains his at 19 times. (See Exhibit 3.8.) They believe the more delayered structure better fits their emphasis on cooperative employee teams. (Both CEOs nevertheless typically have high total compensation due to the value of their stock options.)

EXHIBIT 3.8

Employee
Wages and
Executive
Salary Cap at
Whole Foods

Fiscal Year	Employee Hourly Wage	Employee Annual Wage	Multiple	Executive Salary Cap
2014	$19.16	$39,853	19	$757,200
2013	18.89	39,289	19	746,500
2012	18.63	38,747	19	736,200
2011	18.24	37,947	19	721,000
2010	17.84	37,107	19	705,037

Source: Proxy Statement, Whole Foods, December 30, 2014.

Notes: Average hourly wage is the total cash compensation of all full-time team members in a fiscal year divided by the total hours worked by all such team members in that year. Average annual wage is the product of the average hourly wage and 2,080 hours. The company uses 2,080 hours in the calculation as it represents the product of 40 hours per week and a 52-week year.

Yet egalitarian structures are not problem-free. For example, Ben and Jerry's Homemade, purveyors of premium ice cream, tried to maintain a ratio of only 7 to 1. (When the company started, the spread was 5 to 1.) The relatively narrow differential reflected the company's philosophy that the prosperity of its production workers and its management should be closely linked. However, it eventually became a barrier to recruiting. Ben and Jerry's was forced to abandon this policy to hire an accounting manager and a new CEO. And only when the company was acquired by Unilever did the press report the value of Ben and Jerry's stock, which netted cofounders Ben Cohen $19 million and Jerry Greenfield $42 million—far beyond the 7-to-1 ratio.

Still, it is hard to be against anything called "egalitarian." If we instead use the word "averagism," as Chinese workers do when describing the pay system under socialism's state-owned enterprises, where maximum differentials of 3 to 1 were mandated, some of the possible drawbacks of this approach become clear.[38] Equal treatment (i.e., a lack of pay for performance, either through within-grade or between-grade pay growth) can mean that the more knowledgeable and high-performing employees—the stars—feel underpaid. They may quit to go to an employer that better recognizes their contributions with higher pay (i.e., there is the risk of a negative sorting effect) or simply refuse to do anything (e.g., because of negative incentive effects and/or perceptions of inequity) that is not specifically required of them. Their change in behavior will lower overall performance. So a case can be made for both egalitarian and hierarchical structures.

Keep in mind, though, that the choice is rarely either/or. Rather, the differences are a matter of degree: Levels can range from many to few, differentials can be large or small, and the criteria can be based on the job, the person, or some combination of the two.

GUIDANCE FROM THE EVIDENCE

Before managers recommend a pay structure for their organizations, we hope they will not only look at organization strategy, work flow, fairness, and employee motivation, but also look at the research. Both economists and psychologists have something to tell us about the effects of various structures.

Equity Theory: Fairness

As we noted earlier, employees judge the equity (fairness) of their pay by making multiple comparisons.[39] Evidence based on a study of 2,000 school teachers suggests that teachers are more likely to feel their internal pay structures are fair when they are paid relatively highly within the structure. They will also feel pay structures are fair even when they are relatively low in the internal structure if they work in a high-paying school district. Applying these findings to Lockheed's engineers, advisors, and consultant engineers, we would assume they are more likely to say the internal structure is fair if they are in one of the higher pay levels. Engineers at lower levels will think Lockheed's structure is fair only if Lockheed pays more than its aerospace defense industry competitors. What we don't know is how the lead engineer with 10 years experience will judge the pay structure if Lockheed hires new people into lead engineer jobs with only 5 years of experience. This event is unlikely to occur with unionized teachers' pay structures, but it is very common in other organizations.

So the research suggests that employees judge the fairness of their organization's internal pay structure by making multiple comparisons:

- Comparing to jobs similar to their own (internal equity),
- Comparing their job to others at the same employer (internal equity), and
- Comparing their jobs' pay against external pay levels (external equity).

What evidence do we have on the degree to which employees make internal and external equity comparisons? Exhibit 3.9 provides some data. Among the organizations surveyed, external and internal pay comparisons appear to be about equally common, at least in terms of which types of comparisons employees raise with managers.[40] Note that about one-quarter to one-third of the organizations report that employees raise these comparisons frequently or constantly. Thus, it appears that a job as a compensation professional requires not only designing a compensation system that supports the organization's objectives but also being able to explain to employees on a regular and ongoing basis the rationale for the compensation system choices.

EXHIBIT 3.9 How Often Do Employees Express Concerns about the Lack of Internal or External Equity/Fairness?

	Internal Equity/Fairness			External Equity/Fairness		
	Frequently or Constantly	Occasionally	Seldom or Never	Frequently or Constantly	Occasionally	Seldom or Never
Base Pay Amount	21%	45%	34%	28%	51%	22%
Base Pay Merit Increases	27%	45%	28%	24%	42%	34%

Source: Adapted from Dow Scott, Tom McMullen, and Mark Royal. *WorldatWork Journal*. Fourth Quarter, 2011, pp. 50–64. Survey of 568 compensation professionals (primarily mid-level to senior-level).

The results from these comparisons depend in part on the *accuracy* of employee knowledge of other employees' jobs, internal structures, and external pay levels.[41] Teachers' pay schedules are generally public knowledge, but this is seldom the case in private sector organizations like Lockheed. Evidence from 30-year-old research shows employees often are misinformed about their relative standing in the pay structure.[42] Equity theory could support either egalitarian or hierarchical structures, depending on the comparisons and the accuracy of information about them.

It is important to be clear that the terms *equity* and *equal* are not interchangeable. Outcomes such as pay can be unequal across employees, but pay can nevertheless be perceived as equitable or fair, if those perceived as making larger performance contributions are the ones receiving higher pay. Equity theory says that people compare the ratio of their own outcomes (e.g., pay, status, enjoyment) to inputs (e.g., effort, ability, performance) with the outcome to input ratio of as noted above, one or more comparison others (internal, external, or themselves in a past or future situation). Perceived equity results if the ratios are very similar. The ratios can be similar despite differences in pay if performance differences are perceived to exist.[43]

A study of a wide range of organizations, found that those having larger pay differentials among top executives experienced slightly higher executive turnover, perhaps because of perceptions on inequity. A 1 standard deviation increase in the size of pay differentials was associated with 2% to 6% lower average tenure among executives. However, the study did not examine the degree to which pay differentials were based on performance and the performance levels of those leaving was also not examined. Thus, we cannot make an assessment of the perceived equity implications and we also don't know what (if any) kind of sorting effect (whether it was high or low performers who were more likely to leave) large versus small pay differentials had. We only know that turnover was higher in organizations having larger pay differentials. Other studies have also reported that greater pay dispersion is related to higher turnover among executives, but again the performance of the leavers and stayers has not typically been compared.[44]

Tournament Theory (and Pay Dispersion): Motivation and Performance

Economists have focused more directly on the motivational effects of structures as opposed to people's perceptions of structures. Consider, for example, a golf tournament where the prizes total, say, $100,000. How that $100,000 is distributed affects the performance of all players in the tournament. Compare a 3-prize schedule of $60,000, $30,000, and $10,000 with a 10-prize schedule of $19,000, $17,000, $15,000, $13,000, and so on. According to **tournament theory,** *all* players will play better in the first tournament, where the prize differentials are larger.[45] There is some evidence to support this. Raising the total prize money by $100,000 in the Professional Golf Association tournament lowered each player's score, on average, by 1.1 strokes over 72 holes.[46] And the closer the players got to the top prize, the more their scores were lowered. (Note to nongolfers: A lower score is an improvement.)

Applying these results to organization structures, the greater the differential between your salary and your boss's salary, the harder you (and everyone else but the boss) will work. If Lockheed pays its advisor engineers $125,000 and its consultant engineers $162,000, the tournament model says that increasing the consultants' pay to $200,000 will cause everyone (except the consultants) to work harder. Rather than resenting the big bucks going to the consultants, engineers at all levels will work harder to be a "winner," that is, get promoted to the next level on the way to becoming consultants themselves. Within limits, the bigger the prize for getting to the next level of the structure, the greater the motivational impact of the structure. Several studies support tournament theory. One reported that giving larger raises with a promotion increases effort and reduces absenteeism.[47] Others find that performance improves with larger differentials at the top levels of the structure. The "winner-take-all" idea springs from these studies.[48]

Differentiation and Dispersion in Teams

But what about team settings?[49] Virtually all the research that supports hierarchical structures and tournament theory is on situations where individual performance matters most (auto racing, bowling, golf tournaments) or, at best, where the demand for cooperation among a small group of individuals is relatively low (professors, stockbrokers, truck drivers).[50]

In contrast to individual performers, team sports provide a setting where both an individual player's performance as well as the cooperative efforts of the entire team make a difference.[51] Using eight years of data on major league baseball, Matt Bloom found that teams with small differences in player salaries did better than those with large differentials. In addition to affecting team performance, egalitarian structures had a sizable effect on individual players' performance, too. A mediocre player improved more on a team with an egalitarian structure than on a team with a hierarchical structure. It may also be that the egalitarian pay structure reflects a more flexible, supportive organization culture in which a mediocre player is given the training and support needed to improve.

Although the baseball study was important in providing a paradigm for studying the effects of pay dispersion (egalitarian versus hierarchical pay), one potential issue is that baseball is not a sport characterized by a great deal of interdependence nor is it a sport where there is much in the way of (discretionary) cooperative effort. A later study was conducted using hockey teams, a setting where there is substantial task interdependence and a player does have discretion regarding cooperative behavior. The hockey study found that teams that differentiated salaries more greatly as a function of individual performance (as opposed to factors not related to performance) did better, in large part because such teams were more successful in attracting and retaining the most talented players. In other words, larger differentials based on performance generated positive sorting effects. Without differentials based on performance, the most talented players go elsewhere to play.[52] Also, it is important to remember that *equal* and *equitable* mean different things. Equal pay may actually be seen as inequitable (unfair), especially by stronger performers.[53] Other studies similarly suggest that the performance consequences of dispersion depend on contingency factors such as the basis (how justifiable) of dispersion and also the degree (too much or too little may be less effective).[54] However, there continues to be a debate about the effects of dispersion and the moderating role of contextual factors.[55]

e-Compensation

Salaries for players and teams in Major League Baseball and the National Hockey League are listed at *http://www.usatoday.com/sports/mlb/salaries/ and http://www.usatoday.com/sports/nhl/salaries/.* Pick some of your favorite teams and compare the highest- and lowest-paid players on the team. Based on the differentials, which teams do the models and research discussed in this chapter predict will have the better record?

Information on team standings is available at USA Today and other sources. Question: Would you bet your tuition on the relationship between player salary differentials on a team and the team's performance? (What about player salary levels and/or the relationship between player performance and pay as the basis for predicting team success?)

Institutional Theory: Copy Others and Conform

Sometimes internal pay structures are adopted because they have been called a "best practice."[56] Organizations simply copy or imitate others. Recent examples of such "benchmarking" behavior include the rush to outsource jobs, to emphasize teams, to de-emphasize individual contributions, and to shift to a **competency-based pay system,** often with little regard to whether any of these practices fit the organization or its employees and add value.

Institutional theory sees firms as responding/conforming to normative pressures in their environments so as to gain legitimacy and to reduce risk. As such, institutional theory, predicts that very few firms are "first movers"; instead, they copy innovative practices after innovators have learned how to make the practices work. The potential drawback of such mimetic behavior is that what aligns with the strategy of another organization may not align with the organization's own strategy. And according to the resource-based view of the firm, it is not possible to out-perform one's competitors if you simply imitate their practices.[57] However, as noted earlier, for a firm that is performing worse than competitors, learning from other organizations, which may entail some imitation, may be quite useful in achieving competitive parity and may represent a significant improvement for the firm.

(More) Guidance from the Evidence

Exhibit 3.10 summarizes the effects attributed to internally aligned structures. The impact of internal structures depends on the context in which they operate.

- More hierarchical structures are related to greater performance when the work flow depends on individual contributors (e.g., consulting and law practices, surgical units, stockbrokers, even university researchers).
- High performers quit less under more hierarchical systems when pay is based on performance rather than seniority and when people have knowledge of the structure.

EXHIBIT 3.10
Some
Consequences
of an Internally
Aligned
Structure

Pay structure

- Undertake training
- Increase experience
- Reduce turnover
- Facilitate career progression
- Facilitate performance
- Reduce pay-related grievances
- Reduce pay-related work stoppages

- More egalitarian structures are related to greater performance when close collaboration and sharing of knowledge are required (e.g., firefighting and rescue squads, manufacturing teams, global software design teams). The competition fostered in the "winner-take-all" tournament hierarchies appears to have negative effects on performance when the work flow and organization design require teamwork.
- The impact of any internal structure on organization performance is affected by the other dimensions of the pay model; pay levels (competitiveness), employee performance (contributions), and employee knowledge of the pay structure (management).[58]

Beyond these points, much remains to be studied. There is practically no research on the optimal size of the promotional increase or its effects on behavior, satisfaction, or performance. Nor is much known about whether more frequent promotions with minimal change in the nature of the work are better (or worse) than less frequent promotions with major changes in work. Informal expectations often develop at each workplace. ("You can expect to get promoted here after about three years, and a 10 percent raise usually goes with it.") In universities, promotion from assistant to associate professor tends to occur after six years, although there is no norm on accompanying pay increases. In Japanese pay structures, promotion from associate to *kakaricho* occurs after five years in a company. Similar norms exist in the military. Little is known about how these rules of thumb develop and what their original logic was. But they do matter. Promotions sooner (or later) than expected, accompanied by a larger (or smaller) pay increase, send a powerful message.

So what should be the size of the pay differentials among the engineering levels within Lockheed? To answer this question, we would need to understand how differentials within the **career path** support Lockheed's business strategy and work flow, whether the differentials motivate engineers to contribute to Lockheed's success, and whether they are considered fair by the engineers. The next several chapters discuss how to manage these internal structures.

CONSEQUENCES OF STRUCTURES

Let's turn again to that "so-what" question and the pay model. Why worry about internal alignment at all? Why not simply pay employees whatever it takes to get them to take a job and to show up for work every day? Why not let external market forces or what competitors are paying determine internal wage differentials? Or why not let a government agency decide?

Efficiency

Research shows that an aligned structure can lead to better organization performance.[59] If the structure does not motivate employees to help achieve the organization's objectives, then it is a candidate for redesign.

Internal pay structures imply future returns. The size of the differentials between the entry level in the structure and the highest level can encourage employees to remain with the organization, increase their experience and training, cooperate with co-workers, and seek greater responsibility.[60]

Chapter 2 raised the strategy question, Do you want to be difficult to imitate? We already noted that the number of levels and titles in a career path may be rewarding beyond the pay attached to the titles. Microsoft added a "distinguished engineer" title to its structure. The consulting firm McKinsey and Company added an "associate partner." Their rationale was that employees are motivated by these more frequent steps in the career ladder. These are new titles and levels that are not yet reflected in the external market.

Fairness

Writers have long agreed that departures from an acceptable wage structure will occasion turnover, grievances, and diminished motivation.[61] But that is where the agreement ends. One group argues that if fair (i.e., sizable) differentials among jobs are not paid, individuals may harbor ill will toward the employer, resist change, change employment if possible, become depressed, and "lack that zest and enthusiasm which makes for high efficiency and personal satisfaction in work."[62] Others, including labor unions, argue for only small differentials within pay levels and for similar work, in the belief that more egalitarian structures support cooperation and commitment and improve performance. As with all rules, there are exceptions. For example, in U.S. professional sports like baseball and hockey, players are unionized, yet the players' unions do not strive for egalitarian pay. To the contrary, these unions have, over the years, negotiated strongly for free agent rights for players, which allows for individual players, especially the top performers, to achieve high salaries, much higher than those of average players.

Compliance

As with any pay decision, internal pay structures must comply with the regulations of the countries in which the organization operates.

While the research on internal alignment is very informative, there is still a lot we do not know. What about the appropriate number of levels, the size of the differentials, and the criteria for advancing employees through a structure? We believe the answers lie in understanding the factors discussed in this chapter: the organization's strategic intent, its design and work flow, human capital, and the external conditions, regulations, and customs it faces. We also believe that aligning the pay structure to fit the organization's conditions is more likely to lead to competitive advantage for the organization and a sense of fair treatment for employees. On the other hand, sometimes people take the notion of internal alignment too far. At a Houston oil company, official policy was that wall hangings were related to position in the structure. Top brass got original art, while employees at the bottom of the structure got photos of the company's oil refineries. One analyst commented, "It was so level specific that you could tell immediately upon entering an office the minimum salary level of that person."[63]

Your **Turn** So You Want to Lead an Orchestra!

Peter Drucker calls orchestras an example of an organization design that will become increasingly popular in the 21st century, in that they employ skilled and talented people, joined together as a team to create products and services. Drucker may hear what he wants to hear. Others say orchestras are autocratic. The conductor dictates what is played and how it is played. Rather than basking in the glow of orchestral teamwork, jokes like the following are common among orchestra members: *Q. Why do so many people take an instant dislike to the viola? A. It saves time.*

Job descriptions for orchestras look simple: Play the music. *(Q. How is lightning like a keyboardist's fingers? A. Neither strikes the same place twice.)* Violins play violin parts; trumpets play trumpet parts. Yet one study reported that job satisfaction for orchestra members ranks below that of prison guards. However, orchestra members were more satisfied than operating room nurses and hockey players.

Exhibit 1 shows the pay structure for a regional chamber orchestra. *(Q. How can you make a clarinet sound like a French horn? A. Play all the wrong notes.)* The pay covers six full orchestra concerts, one Caroling by Candlelight event, three Sunday Chamber Series concerts, several Arts in Education elementary school concerts, two engagements for a flute quartet, and one Ring in the Holidays brass event as well as the regularly scheduled rehearsals. *(Q. How can you tell when a trombonist is playing out of tune? A. When the slide is moving.)*

1. Describe the orchestra's pay structure in terms of levels, differentials, and job- or person-based approach.

2. Discuss what factors may explain the structure. Why does violinist I receive more than the oboist and trombonist? Why does the principal trumpet player earn more than the principal cellist and principal clarinetist but less than the principal viola and principal flute players? What explains these differences? Does the relative supply versus the demand for violinists compare to the supply versus the demand for trombonists? Is it that violins play more notes?

3. What is the pay differential between the principal viola and next highest paid viola? What about between the principal trumpet and the next highest paid trumpet? Why these differentials between the principal and other? Why aren't they larger? Smaller? Why is the differential between trumpet players different than between the viola players?

4. How well do equity and tournament models apply? Do custom and tradition play any role? What about institutional theory?

EXHIBIT 1 Orchestra Compensation Schedule

Instrument	Fee	Instrument	Fee
Violin, Concertmaster	$6,970	Violin I	$2,483
Principal Bass and Conductor	5,070	Violin I	2,483
Principal Viola	5,036	Violin I	2,483
Principal Flute	4,337	Violin II	2,483
Principal Trumpet	4,233	Violin II	2,483
Principal Cello	4,181	Viola	2,483
Principal Clarinet	4,146	Violin II	1,975
Trumpet	3,638	Viola	2,212
Principal Oboe	3,615	Oboe	2,206
Principal Violin II	3,488	Trombone	2,137
Principal Horn	3,390	Viola	2,033
Keyboard I	3,361	Violin II/Viola	1,784
Cello	3,228	Cello	1,634
Principal Percussion	3,049	Clarinet	1,548
Violin I	2,899	Horn	1,548
Cello	2,882	Flute	1,455
Principal Bassoon	2,824	Keyboard II	1,392
Violin I	2,685	Bassoon	1,265
		Violin II	1,178

Still Your **Turn**

(If You Don't Want to Lead the Orchestra...)

Use another example of how different jobs/skills get paid differently and how lines of career progression operate. You can use the health care or sports examples from the Part II introduction earlier. Or, you can choose another example. You can use the pay structure in Exhibit 3-11 at Pennsylvania Power & Light that was negotiated with the International Brotherhood of Electrical Workers (IBEW). Address the same general questions raised above in the orchestra example regarding the size of pay differentials and why they exist.

EXHIBIT 3.11 Pay Structure for Selected Job Families, Pennsylvania Power & Light

Annual Salary (Min)	Annual Salary (Max)	Pay Grade	Bookkeeping	Coal Equipment Operator	Nuclear Plant Operator	Electrical Equipment Repair	Technician Effluents	Technician Radiation Protection
36,660	43,992	1	Clerk Cash Receipts					
40,352	47,684	2					Handyman Effluents	
43,992	51,376	3						
47,684	55,016	4						
51,376	58,656	5		Coal Equipment Operator I			Helper Effluents	
55,016	62,348	6				Electrical Equipment Repair 3rd Class		
58,656	65,988	7					Effluents Technician I	
62,348	69,680	8		Coal Equipment Operator II				
65,988	73,320	9	Cash Receipts Leader	Coal Equipment Operator III		Electrical Equipment Repair 2nd Class		
69,680	77,012	10						
73,320	80,652	11	Bookkeeper	Coal Equipment Operator IV			Effluents Technician II	
77,012	84,344	12	Bookkeeper Senior					

(Continued)

EXHIBIT 3.11 *(continued)*

Annual Salary (Min)	Annual Salary (Max)	Pay Grade	Bookkeeping	Coal Equipment Operator	Nuclear Plant Operator	Electrical Equipment Repair	Technician Effluents	Technician Radiation Protection
80,652	87,984	13				Electrical Equipment Repair 1st Class		Radiation Protection Technician Junior
84,344	91,676	14						
87,984	95,368	15				Electrical Equipment Repair Leader		Radiation Protection Technician Senior
91,676	99,008	16			Nuclear Plant Oper Trainee			
95,368	102,700	17						
103,220	103,220	18			Nuclear Plant Oper			
113,568	113,568	19						

Source: Agreement between Local Union No. 1600 of the International Brotherhood of Electrical Workers, AFL–CIO, and Pennsylvania Power and Light Company. Pay rates shown are effective May 9, 2016. http://www.dol.gov/olms/regs/compliance/cba/pdf/2014/private/K9292.pdf.

Still (yes, still) Your **Turn**   (NCAA)

The NCAA has a 14-year contract with CBS and Turner Sports under which they pay the NCAA $10.8 billion, or $720 billion per year, for the right to broadcast the NCAA men's basketball tournament. The players do not get paid. Some receive scholarships. There is currently a legal challenge to the status quo of not paying the players. Recently, the five power conferences in the NCAA decided to increase the value of a scholarship by additionally providing a cost-of-living stipend of $200 to $400 per month to pay for expenses beyond tuition, books, and housing. Is that enough? Or, should players be paid as employees and paid an amount that is more consistent with the revenue they generate for their universities?

After considering that issue, consider next the question of how such a system should be designed. Develop a pay strategy to have at the ready (a contingency plan) in case players are to be paid like employees in the future. In evaluating design options, take into account the following issues raised by NCAA men's basketball tournament analysts (and former college and pro basketball stars) Kenny Smith, Charles Barkley, and Clark Kellogg. Kenny Smith believes players should get paid, but only if they graduate. Charles Barkley believes that it would be unfair, even discrimination, to pay basketball players, but not fencers, gymnast, softball players, and swimmers. Barkley also warns against letting college athletes sign sponsorship deals (e.g., with shoe or apparel companies). He says it would ruin team chemistry. He says that if he is an offensive lineman and the quarterback "is making money and I'm not, I'm not blocking for him." Clark Kellog believes players should get paid, in part, because the time commitment has grown to be so large, in season and off-season. He notes that it is not possible to even have a summer job anymore. Another analyst, former college coach, Bill Raftery, is concerned that paying players would make for even less parity in NCAA college sports because the small schools may not be able to afford to pay their players and/or to pay them as much as larger schools.

In summary, please address the following three questions:

1. Should NCAA athletes get paid as employees?
2. If NCAA athletes are paid as employees, either because of legal action or colleges/universities deciding on their own to change the system, how should the pay strategy be designed to "work" and avoid the potential pitfalls identified above?
3. What would your pay strategy design cost and how would it be funded? What impact would the required level of funding have on colleges and universities? How would athletes outside of sports such as basketball and football be affected?

Sources: Matthew Futterman, "The Debate Continues: Should the Players Get Paid?" *The Wall Street Journal*. March 19, 2015, pp. D8; Steve Berkowitz, "NCAA Increases Value of Scholarships in Historic Vote," *USA Today*, January 17, 2015.

Summary   This chapter discusses internal alignment and how it affects employees, managers, and employers. Internal alignment refers to the pay relationships among jobs/skills/competencies within a single organization. The potential consequences of internal pay structures are vital to organizations and individuals. Recent research plus experience offers guidance concerning the design and management of internal pay structures.

Pay structures—the array of pay rates for different jobs within an organization—are shaped by societal, economic, organizational, and other factors. Employees judge a structure to be fair by comparing to other jobs within the organization and to what competitors pay for jobs similar to theirs. Acceptance by employees of the pay differentials among jobs is a key test of an equitable pay structure. Such structures are part of the network of returns offered by organizations. They offer career paths to higher-paying jobs and a sense of achievement.

Keep the goals of the entire compensation system in mind when thinking about internal pay structures. There is widespread experience and increasing research to support the belief that differences in internal pay structures, coupled with the other dimensions of compensation systems, influence people's attitudes and work behaviors and therefore the success of organizations.

Review Questions

1. Why is internal alignment an important policy in a strategic perspective of compensation?
2. Discuss the factors that influence internal pay structures. Based on your own experience, which ones do you think are the most important? Why?
3. Internal structures are part of the incentives offered in organizations. Look into any organization: your college, workplace, or the grocery store where you shop. Describe the flow of work. How is the job structure aligned with the organization's business, the work flow, and its objectives? How do you believe it influences employee behaviors?
4. What is the "just-wage" doctrine? Can you think of any present-day applications?
5. A typical structure within colleges is instructor, assistant professor, associate professor, full professor. Is this egalitarian or hierarchical? What added information would you need to decide? What behaviors by the faculty do you believe the structure influences? Is it aligned? Difficult to copy? Does it add value?

Endnotes

1. *Matthew* 20: 1–16.
2. For a history of the different standards for pay, see Thomas Mahoney, *Compensation and Reward Perspectives* (Burr Ridge, IL: Irwin, 1979); G. Milkovich and J. Stevens, "From Pay to Rewards: 100 Years of Change," *ACA Journal* 9(1) (2000), pp. 6–18; D. F. Schloss, *Methods in Industrial Remuneration* (New York: Putnam's, 1892).
3. Peter Doeringer and Michael Piore, *Internal Labor Markets and Manpower Analysis* (Armonk, NY: Sharpe, 1985). Edward P. Lazear, *Personnel Economics* (Cambridge: MIT Press). One study, for example, found that education level and work experience explained about 30 percent of the variance in salaries in a large company. Job level explained an additional 50 percent of the variance in salaries. See B. Gerhart and G. T. Milkovich, "Salaries, Salary Growth, and Promotions of Men and Women in a Large Private Firm," in *Pay Equity: Empirical Inquiries,* R. Michael and H. Hartmann, eds. (Washington, D.C.: National Academy Press, 1989).

4. "Equity" could refer to stock, to some perceived balance of effort and rewards, and/or pay discrimination (gender equity). We believe "internal alignment" better reflects the meaning and importance underlying pay structures.

5. H. Kenneth Doerr, Tali Freed, Terence Mitchell, Chester Schriesheim, and Xiaohua (Tracy) Zhou, "Work Flow Policy and Within-Worker and Between-Workers Variability in Performance," *Journal of Applied Psychology* 89(5), 2004, pp. 911–921.

6. Kristen McNamara, "Push Is on to Advise the Very Wealthy," *The Wall Street Journal,* May 27, 2006, p. B4.

7. James Brian Quinn, Philip Anderson, and Sydney Finkelstein, "Leveraging Intellect," *Academy of Management Executive* 19(4), 2005, pp. 78–94.

8. Researchers use a statistic called the *gini coefficient* to describe the distribution of pay. A gini of zero means everyone is paid the identical wage. The higher the gini coefficient (maximum = 1), the greater the pay differentials among the levels.

9. Dale T. Mortensen, *Wage Dispersion: Why Are Similar Workers Paid Differently?* (Cambridge, MA: MIT Press, 2005); Barry Gerhart and Sara Rynes, *Compensation: Theory, Evidence, and Strategic Implications* (Thousand Oaks, CA: Sage, 2003); Robert Gibbons and Michael Waldman, "A Theory of Wage and Promotion Dynamics Inside Firms," *Quarterly Journal of Economics,* November 1999, pp. 1321–1358; George Baker, Michael Gibbs, and Bengt Holmstrom, "The Internal Economics of the Firm: Evidence from Personnel Data," *Quarterly Journal of Economics* (November 1994), pp. 881–919; M. Bloom and G. Milkovich, "Money, Managers, and Metamorphosis," in D. Rousseau and C. Cooper, eds., *Trends in Organizational Behavior,* 3rd ed. (New York: Wiley, 1996).

10. David Kirkpatrick, "The Net Makes It All Easier—Including Exporting U.S. Jobs," *Fortune,* May 26, 2003, p. 146.

11. Yoshio Yanadori, "Cascading Model of Compensation Management: The Determinants of Compensation of Top Executives and Employees," Vancouver, BC: Sauder School of Business working paper, January 2006.

12. C. Tucker, ed., *The Marx-Engels Reader* (New York: Norton, 1978).

13. Allan M. Carter, *Theory of Wages and Employment* (Burr Ridge, IL: Irwin, 1959).

14. Jacob Goldstein, "Some Nurses Land Higher Salaries Than Primary Care Doctors," *The Wall Street Journal,* June 18, 2008.

15. Dana Matlioli, "Help-Wanted: Senior-Level Job, Junior Title, Pay," *The Wall Street Journal,* April 12, 2008.

16. B. Gerhart and G. Milkovich, "Employee Compensation," in *Handbook of Industrial and Organization Psychology, vol. 3,* M. Dunnette and L. Hough, eds. (Palo Alto, CA: Consulting Psychologists Press, 1992); S. Brown and K. Eisenhardt, *Competing on the Edge: Strategy and Structured Chaos* (Boston, MA: Harvard Business Press, 1998); George Baker, Michael Gibbs, and Bengt Holmstrom, "The Internal Economics of the Firm: Evidence from Personnel Data," *Quarterly Journal of Economics,* November 1994, pp. 881–919; Michael Gibbs, "Incentive Compensation in a Corporate Hierarchy," *Journal of Accounting and Economics* 19 (1995), pp. 247–277.

17. Scott Adams and David Neumark, "The Effects of Living Wage Laws: Evidence from Failed and Derailed Living Wage Campaigns," NBER working paper 11342, May 2005.

18. Two articles in the same issue of *Workspan,* June 2006, report ratios of 531 versus 400 percent. For a ratio of 104, see *Fortune,* July 16, 2006, p. 81; Eric Dash, "Off to the Races Again, Leaving Many Behind," *The New York Times,* April 9, 2006, Section 3 (entire section on Executive Pay: A Special Report); also see "Pay for Performance? Sometimes, but Not Always," p. 6 of section.

19. G. Hoefstede, *Culture's Consequences: International Differences in Work Relationships and Values* (Thousand Oaks, CA: Sage, 1980); R. Donkin, "The Pecking Order's Instinctive Appeal," *Financial Times,* August 23, 2002; A. Mitra, M. Bloom, and G. Milkovich, "Crossing a Raging River: Seeking Far-Reaching Solutions to Global Pay Challenges," *WorldatWork Journal* 11(2), Second Quarter 2002; F. Trompenaars, *Riding the Waves of Culture: Understanding Diversity in Global Business* (Burr Ridge, IL: Irwin, 1995); J. Brockner, Y. Chen, K. Leung, and D. Skarlick, "Culture and Procedural Fairness: When the Effects of What You Do Depend on How You Do It," *Administrative Science Quarterly* 45 (2000), pp. 138–159; Thomas Li-Ping Tang, Vivenne Wai-Mei Luk, and Randy K. Chiu, "Pay Differentials in the People's Republic of China: An Examination of Internal Equity and External Competitiveness," *Compensation and Benefits Review* 32(3), May/June 2000, pp. 43–49.

20. Yoshio Yanadori, "Minimizing Competition? Entry-Level Compensation in Japanese Firms," *Asia Pacific Journal of Management* 21 (December 2004), pp. 445–467.

21. D. Levine, D. Belman, G. Charness, et al., *The New Employment Contract: How Little Wage Structures at U.S. Employers Have Changed* (Kalamazoo, MI: Upjohn, 2001).

22. Raghuram G. Rajan and Julie Wulf, "The Move from Tall to Flat: How Corporate Hierarchies Are Changing," working paper, Wharton, August 2003.

23. Pui-Wing Tam, "Hurd's Big Challenge at H-P: Overhauling Corporate Sales," *The Wall Street Journal,* April 3, 2006, pp. A1, A13.

24. Rosemary Batt, Alexander J. S. Colvin, and Jeffrey Keefe, "Employee Voice, Human Resource Practices, and Quit Rates: Evidence from the Telecommunications Industry," *Industrial and Labor Relations Review* 55(4), July 2002, pp. 573–594; Wayne F. Cascio, "Strategies for Responsible Restructuring," *Academy of Management Executive* 19(4), 2005, pp. 39–50.

25. Paul Schumann, Dennis Ahlburg, and Christine B. Mahoney, "The Effects of Human Capital and Job Characteristics on Pay," *Journal of Human Resources* 29(2), 1994, pp. 481–503; A. Kohn, *Punished by Rewards: The Trouble with Gold Stars, Incentive Plans, A's, Praise and Other Bribes* (Boston, MA: Houghton Mifflin, 1993); Jerald Greenberg and Suzy N. Ornstein, "High Status Job Titles as Compensation for Underpayment: A Test of Equity Theory," *Journal of Applied Psychology* 68(2), 1983, pp. 285–297.

26. Specialized studies of competitors' pay structures are conducted by some consulting firms. These are discussed in Chapter 8.

27. Thomas A. Mahoney, "Organizational Hierarchy and Position Worth," *Academy of Management Journal,* December 1979, pp. 726–737; Barry Gerhart and Sara Rynes, *Compensation: Theory, Evidence, and Strategic Implications* (Thousand Oaks, CA: Sage, 2003).

28. John Sutherland, "Wages In and Voluntary Quits From an Establishment Internal Labour Market," *Applied Economics* 34 (2002), pp. 395–400; Philip Moss, "Earnings Inequality and the Quality of Jobs," in *Corporate Governance and Sustainable Prosperity,* W. Lazonick and M. O'Sullivan, eds. (New York: Macmillan, 2001); Erica L. Groshen and David I. Levine, "The Rise and Decline (?) of U.S. Internal Labor Markets," Research Paper No. 9819 (New York Federal Reserve Bank, 1998); S. Bacharach and E. Lawler, "Political Alignments in Organizations," Chapter 4 in *Research in the Sociology of Organizations,* vol. IV., Sam Bacharach and Stephen Mitchell, eds. (Greenwich, CT: JAI Press, 1998).

29. E. Robert Livernash, "The Internal Wage Structure," in *New Concepts in Wage Determination,* G. W. Taylor and F. C. Pierson, eds. (New York: McGraw-Hill, 1957), pp. 143–172.

30. T. Judge and H. G. Heneman III, "Pay Satisfaction," in *Compensation in Organizations: Current Research and Practice,* S. Rynes and B. Gerhart, eds. (San Francisco, CA: Jossey-

Bass, 2000); Robert Folger and Mary Konovsky, "Effects of Procedural and Distributive Justice on Reactions to Pay Raise Decisions," *Academy of Management Journal,* March 1989, pp. 115–130; M. L. Williams, M. A. McDaniel, and N. Nguyen, "A Meta-Analysis of the Antecedents and Consequences of Pay Level Satisfaction," *Journal of Applied Psychology* 91 (2006), pp. 392–413.

31. Charlie O. Trevor and David L. Wazeter, "A Contingent View of Reactions to Objective Pay Conditions: Interdependence among Pay Structure Characteristics and Pay Relative to Internal and External Referents," *Journal of Applied Psychology,* 91, 2006, pp. 1260–1275.

32. Frederick P. Morgeson, Michael A. Campion, and Carl P. Maertz, "Understanding Pay Satisfaction: The Limits of a Compensation System Implementation," *Journal of Business & Psychology* 16(1), Fall 2001, pp. 133–163.

33. Paula England, Paul Allison, Yuxiao Wu, and Mary Ross, "Does Bad Pay Cause Occupations to Feminize, Does Feminization Reduce Pay, and How Can We Tell with Longitudinal Data?" presented at annual meeting of the American Sociological Association, August 2004, San Francisco, CA.

34. Aaron Smith, "TSA officers 'desperate' to unionize," CNN.com. http://money.cnn.com/2010/11/24/news/economy/tsa_screener_union/index.htm. Extracted May 20, 2012.

35. "Federal Uniformed Police: Selected Data on Pay, Recruitment, and Retention at 13 Police Forces in the Washington, D.C. Metropolitan Area," GAO-03-658, June 13, 2003.

36. This statement does not apply to professors who work in McDonald's while on sabbatical. See Jerry Newman, *My Secret Life on the McJob* (New York: McGraw-Hill, 2007).

37. Elliot Jaques, "In Praise of Hierarchies," *Harvard Business Review,* January–February 1990, pp. 32–40; Matthew C. Bloom, "The Performance Effects of Pay Structures on Individuals and Organizations," *Academy of Management Journal* 42(1), 1999, pp. 25–40.

38. Daniel Z. Ding, Keith Goodall, and Malcolm Warner, "The End of the 'Iron Rice-Bowl': Whither Chinese Human Resource Management?" *International Journal of Human Resource Management* 11(2), April 2000, pp. 217–236; Thomas Li-Ping Tang, Vivenne Wai-Mei Luk, and Randy K. Chiu, "Pay Differentials in the People's Republic of China: An Examination of Internal Equity and External Competitiveness," *Compensation and Benefits Review* 32(3), May/June 2000, pp. 43–49; Li Hua Wang, "Pay Policies and Determination in China," working paper, Northwestern University, 2003.

39. E. E. Lawler, *Pay and Organizational Effectiveness: A Psychological View* (New York: McGraw-Hill, 1971); T. A. Mahoney, *Compensation and Reward Perspectives* (Homewood, IL: Irwin, 1979); Charlie O. Trevor and David L. Wazeter, "A Contingent View of Reactions to Objective Pay Conditions: Interdependence Among Pay Structure Characteristics and Pay Relative to Internal and External Referents," *Journal of Applied Psychology,* 91, 2006, pp. 1260–1275; E. Lawler III, *Treat People Right! How Organizations and Individuals Can Propel Each Other into a Virtuous Spiral of Success* (San Francisco, CA: Jossey-Bass, 2003).

40. For more evidence on employee pay comparisons and their consequences, see the following sources. P. S. Goodman, "An Examination of Referents Used in the Evaluation of Pay," *Organizational Behavior and Human Performance* 12 (1974), pp. 170–95; C. O. Trevor and D. L. Wazeter, "A Contingent View of Reactions to Objective Pay Conditions: Interdependence among Pay Structure Characteristics and Pay Relative to Internal and External Referents," *Journal of Applied Psychology* 91 (2006), pp. 1260–1275; M. M. Harris, F. Anseel, and F. Lievens, "Keeping Up with the Joneses: A Field Study of the Relationships among Upward, Lateral, and Downward Comparisons and Pay Level Satisfaction," *Journal of Applied Psychology* 93, no. 3 (May 2008), pp. 665–673; Gordon D. A. Brown, Jonathan Gardner, Andrew J. Oswald, Jing

Qian, "Does Wage Rank Affect Employees' Well-Being?" *Industrial Relations* 47, no. 3 (July 2008), p. 355; D. Card, A. Mas, E. Moretti, and E. Saez, Inequality at Work: The Effect of Peer Salaries on Job Satisfaction. Working Paper 16396, National Bureau of Economic Research, September 2010.

41. Jason Shaw and Nina Gupta, "Pay System Characteristics and Quit Rates of Good, Average, and Poor Performers," University of Kentucky working paper, May 2006.

42. George Milkovich and P. H. Anderson, "Management Compensation and Secrecy Policies," *Personnel Psychology* 25 (1972), pp. 293–302.

43. J. S. Adams, "Toward an Understanding of Inequity," *Journal of Abnormal and Social Psychology* 67(5), 1963, pp. 422–436. C.O. Trevor, G. Reilly, and B. Gerhart, "Reconsidering Pay Dispersion's Effect on the Performance of Interdependent Work: Reconciling Sorting and Pay Inequality," *Academy of Management Journal* 55, 2012, pp. 585–610.

44. J. G. Messersmith, J. P. Guthrie, Y. Y. Ji, and J. Y. Lee, "Executive Turnover: The Influence of Dispersion and Other Pay Characteristics," *Journal of Applied Psychology* 96, 2011, pp. 457–469.

45. B. E. Becker and M. A. Huselid, "The Incentive Effects of Tournament Compensation Systems," *Administrative Science Quarterly* 37 (1992), pp. 336–350; E. Lazear and S. Rosen, "Rank-Order Tournaments as Optimum Labor Contracts," *Journal of Political Economy* 89 (1981), pp. 841–864; Matthew C. Bloom, "The Performance Effects of Pay Structures on Individuals and Organizations," *Academy of Management Journal* 42(1), 1999, pp. 25–40; Michael L. Bognanno, "Corporate Tournaments," *Journal of Labor Economics* 19(2), 2001, pp. 290–315; B. L. Connelly, L. Tihanyi, T. R. Crook, and K. A. Gangloff, "Tournament Theory: Thirty Years of Contests and Competitions," *Journal of Management*, 40(1), 2014, pp. 16–47.

46. R. G. Ehrenberg and M. L. Bognanno, "The Incentive Effects of Tournaments Revisited: Evidence from the European PGA Tour," *Industrial and Labor Relations Review* 43 (1990), pp. 74S–88S; Tor Eriksson, "Executive Compensation and Tournament Theory: Empirical Tests on Danish Data," *Journal of Labor Economics,* April 1999, pp. 262–280.

47. E. P. Lazear, *Personnel Economics* (Cambridge, MA: MIT Press, 1995).

48. Robert H. Frank and Philip J. Cook, *The Winner-Take-All Society: Why the Few at the Top Get So Much More Than the Rest of Us* (New York: Penguin, 1996).

49. Pfeffer, Jeffrey & Langton, Nancy. The Effect of Wage Dispersion on Satisfaction, Productivity, and Working Collaboratively: Evidence from College and University Faculty. Administrative Science Quarterly, 1993, 38, 382–407; Edward P. Lazear, "Pay Equality and Industrial Politics," *Journal of Political Economy*, 97(3), 1989, pp. 561–580.

50. Shaw, J. D., & Gupta, N. 2007. Pay system characteristics and quit patterns of good, average, and poor performers. Personnel Psychology, 60, 903–928.

51. Matthew C. Bloom, "The Performance Effects of Pay Structures on Individuals and Organizations," *Academy of Management Journal* 42(1), 1999, pp. 25–40; J. M. Beus and D. S. Whitman, "Almighty Dollar or Root of All Evil? Testing the Effects of Money on Workplace Behavior," *Journal of Management*, 0149206314565241.

52. C. O. Trevor, G. Reilly, and B. Gerhart, "Reconsidering Pay Dispersion's Effect on the Performance of Interdependent Work: Reconciling Sorting and Pay Inequality," *Academy of Management Journal,* 2012, 55, 585–610.

53. C. O. Trevor, G. Reilly, and B. Gerhart, "Reconsidering Pay Dispersion's Effect on the Performance of Interdependent Work: Reconciling Sorting and Pay Inequality," *Academy of Management Journal* 55 (2012), pp. 585–610; Y. Garbers and U. Konradt, "The Effect of Financial Incentives on Performance: A Quantitative Review of Individual

and Team-Based Financial Incentives," *Journal of Occupational and Organizational Psychology*, 87(1), 2014, 102–137; E. E. Lawler, *Pay and Organizational Effectiveness: A Psychological View* (New York: McGraw-Hill, 1971).

54. H. Yang and B. S. Klaas, "Pay Dispersion and the Financial Performance of the Firm: Evidence from Korea," *International Journal of Human Resource Management* 22 (2011), pp. 2147–2166; J. W. Fredrickson, A. Davis-Blake, and W. M. G. Sanders, "Sharing the Wealth: Social Comparisons and Pay Dispersion in the CEO's Top Team," *Strategic Management Journal* 31 (2010), pp. 1031–1055; C. Anderson and C. E. Brown, "The Functions and Dysfunctions of Hierarchy," *Research in Organizational Behavior* 30 (2010), pp. 55–89; M. J. Pearsall, M. S. Christian, and A. P. J. Ellis, "Motivating Interdependent Teams: Individual Rewards, Shared Rewards, or Something in Between," *Journal of Applied Psychology* 95 (2010), pp. 183–191; S. Kepes, J. E. Delery, and N. Gupta, "Contingencies in the Effects of Pay Range on Organizational Effectiveness," *Personnel Psychology* 62(3), 2009, pp. 497–531.

55. J. D. Shaw, "Pay Dispersion," *Annual Review of Organizational Psychology and Organizational Behavior*, 1(1), 2014, pp. 521–544; P. E. Downes and D. Choi, "Employee Reactions to Pay Dispersion: A Typology of Existing Research." *Human Resource Management Review*, 24(1), 2014, pp. 53–66; A. Bucciol, N. J. Foss, and M. Piovesan, "Pay Dispersion and Performance in Teams," *PloS one*, 9(11), 2014, p. e112631; Y. Yanadori and V. Cui, "Creating Incentives for Innovation? The Relationship between Pay Dispersion in R&D Groups and Firm Innovation Performance," *Strategic Management Journal* 34(12), 2013, pp. 1502–1511.

56. P. S. Tolbert and L. G. Zucker, "Institutionalization of Institution Theory," in *Handbook of Organization Studies,* G. Glegg, C. Hardy, and W. Nord, eds. (London: Sage, 1996), pp. 175–199; M. Barringer and G. Milkovich, "A Theoretical Exploration of the Adoption and Design of Flexible Benefit Plans: A Case of HR Innovation," *Academy of Management Review* 23(2), 1998, pp. 305–324.

57. Jay B. Barney, "Firm Resources and Sustained Competitive Advantage," *Journal of Management* 17, (1991), pp. 99–120.

58. M. Brown, M. C. Sturman, and M. Simmering, "Compensation Policy and Organizational Performance: The Efficiency, Operational, and Financial Implications of Pay Levels and Pay Structure," *Academy of Management Journal* 46 (2003), pp. 752–762; Jason Shaw and Nina Gupta, "Pay System Characteristics and Quit Rates of Good, Average, and Poor Performers," University of Kentucky working paper, May 2006.

59. M. Brown, M. C. Sturman, and M. Simmering, "Compensation Policy and Organizational Performance: The Efficiency, Operational, and Financial Implications of Pay Levels and Pay Structure," *Academy of Management Journal* 46 (2003), pp. 752–762.

60. Edward Lazear, "Labor Economics and Psychology of Organization," *Journal of Economic Perspectives* 5 (1991), pp. 89–110; David Wazeter, "Determinants and Consequences of Pay Structures," Ph.D. dissertation, Cornell University, 1991.

61. E. Robert Livernash, "The Internal Wage Structure," in *New Concepts in Wage Determination,* G. W. Taylor and F. C. Pierson, eds. (New York: McGraw-Hill, 1957), pp. 143–172.

62. Elliot Jaques, "In Praise of Hierarchies," *Harvard Business Review* (January–February 1990), pp. 32–46.

63. Jared Sandberg, "Apportioning Furniture by Rank Can Stir Up Anger, Envy, Rebellion," *The Wall Street Journal,* November 10, 2004, p. B1.

Job Analysis

Three people sit in front of their keyboards scanning their monitors. One is a customer representative in Ohio, checking the progress of an order for four dozen web-enabled cell phones from a retailer in Texas, who just placed the four dozen into his shopping cart on the company's website. A second is an engineer logging in to the project design software for the next generation of these phones. Colleagues in China working on the same project last night (day in China) sent some suggestions for changes in the new design; the team in the United States will work on the project today and have their work waiting for their Chinese colleagues when they come to work in the morning. A third employee, in Ireland, is using the business software recently installed worldwide to analyze the latest sales reports. In today's workplace, people working for the same company no longer need to be down the hallway from one another. They can be on-site and overseas. Networks and business software link them all. Yet all their jobs are part of the organization's internal structure.

If pay is to be based on work performed, some way is needed to discover and describe the differences and similarities among these jobs—observation alone is not enough. **Job analysis** is that systematic method. Two products result from a job analysis. A *job description* is the list of tasks, duties, and responsibilities that make up a job. These are observable actions. A *job specification* is the list of knowledge, skills, abilities, and other characteristics that are necessary for an individual to have to perform the job. Thus, the description focuses on the job and the specification focuses on the person.

STRUCTURES BASED ON JOBS, PEOPLE, OR BOTH

Exhibit 4.1 outlines the process for constructing a work-related internal structure. No matter the approach, the process begins by looking at people at work. Job-based structures look at what people are doing and the expected outcomes; skill- and competency-based structures look at the person. However, the underlying purpose of each phase of

EXHIBIT 4.1   **Many Ways to Create Internal Structure**

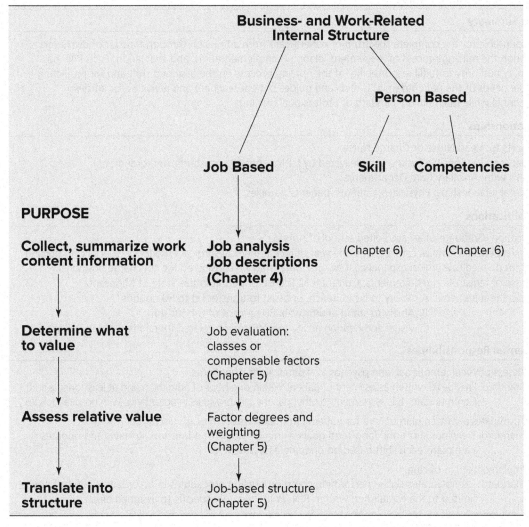

the process, called out in the left-hand side of the exhibit, remains the same for both job- and person-based structures: (1) collect and summarize work content information that identifies similarities and differences, (2) determine what to value, (3) assess the relative value, and (4) translate the relative value into an internal structure. (The blank areas in the person-based structure will be filled in when we get to Chapter 6.) This chapter and the next focus on the job-based structure.[1]

Exhibit 4.2 is part of a job description for a registered nurse. The job summary section provides an overview of the job. The section on relationships to other jobs demonstrates where the job fits in the organization structure: which jobs are

EXHIBIT 4.2   Contemporary Job Description for Registered Nurse

Job Title: Registered Nurse
Job Summary
Accountable for the complete spectrum of patient care from admission through transfer or discharge through the nursing process of assessment, planning, implementation, and evaluation. Each R.N. has primary authority to fulfill responsibility of the nursing process on the assigned shift and for projecting future needs of the patient/family. Directs and guides patient teaching and activities for ancillary personnel while maintaining standard of professional nursing.
Relationships
Reports to: Head Nurse or Charge Nurse. Supervises: Responsible for the care delivered by L.P.N.s, nursing assistants, and orderlies. Works with: Ancillary Care Departments. External relationships: Physicians, patients, patients' families.
Qualifications

Education: Graduate of an accredited school of nursing.
Work experience: Critical care requires one year of recent medical/surgical experience (special care nursing preferred), medical/surgical experience (new graduates may be considered for noncharge positions).
License or registration requirements: Current R.N. license or permit in the State of Minnesota.
Physical requirements: A. Ability to bend, reach, or assist to transfer up to 50 pounds.
                              B. Ability to stand and/or walk 80 percent of 8-hour shift.
                              C. Visual and hearing acuity to perform job-related functions.

Essential Responsibilities

1. Assess physical, emotional, and psychosocial dimensions of patients.
   Standard: Provides a written assessment of patient within one hour of admission and at least once a shift. Communicates this assessment to other patient care providers in accordance with hospital policies.
 	
2. Formulates a written plan of care for patients from admission through discharge.
   Standard: Develops short-and long-term goals within 24 hours of admission. Reviews and updates care plans each shift based on ongoing assessment.
 	
3. Implements plan of care.
   Standard: Demonstrates skill in performing common nursing procedures in accordance with but not limited to the established written R.N. skills inventory specific to assigned area.

Note: Additional responsibilities omitted from exhibit.

supervised by this jobholder, which job supervises this jobholder, and the nature of any internal and external relationships.

The section on essential responsibilities elaborates on the summary: "Provides a written assessment of patient within one hour of admission and at least once a shift." Collecting information on these essential responsibilities is the heart of job analysis.

JOB-BASED APPROACH: MOST COMMON

Exhibit 4.3 shows how job analysis and the resulting job description fit into the process of creating an internal structure. Job analysis provides the underlying information. It identifies the content of the job. This content serves as input for describing and valuing work.

> **Job analysis** is the systematic process of collecting information that identifies similarities and differences in the work.

Exhibit 4.3 also lists the major decisions in designing a job analysis: (1) Why are we performing job analysis? (2) What information do we need? (3) How should we collect it? (4) Who should be involved? (5) How useful are the results?

Why Perform Job Analysis?

Potential uses for job analysis have been suggested for every major human resource function. Often the type of job analysis data needed varies by function. For example, identifying the skills and experience required to perform the work clarifies hiring and promotion standards and identifies training needs. In performance evaluation, both employees and supervisors look to the required behaviors and results expected in a job to help assess performance. IBM recently identified every role (490 in all) performed by its 300,000-plus workers, managers, and executives. For example, IBM's vice president for learning has the roles of learning leader and manager. IBM also measures and monitors 4,000 skill sets.[2]

An internal structure based on job-related information provides both managers and employees a work-related rationale for pay differences. Employees who understand

EXHIBIT 4.3   Determining the Internal Job Structure

Internal work relationships within the organization	Job analysis The systematic process of collecting information that identifies similarities and differences in the work	Job descriptions Summary reports that identify, define, and describe the job as it is actually performed	Job evaluation Comparison of jobs within an organization	Job structure An ordering of jobs based on their content or relative value

Some Major Decisions in Job Analysis

- Why perform job analysis?
- What information is needed?
- How to collect information?
- Who to involve?
- How useful are the results?

this rationale can see where their work fits into the bigger picture and can direct their behavior toward organization objectives. Job analysis data also help managers defend their decisions when challenged.

In compensation, job analysis has two critical uses: (1) It establishes similarities and differences in the work contents of the jobs, and (2) it helps establish an internally fair and aligned job structure. If jobs have equal content, then in all likelihood the pay established for them will be equal (unless they are in different geographies). If, on the other hand, the job content differs, then the differences, along with the market rates paid by competitors, are part of the rationale for paying jobs differently.

The key issue for compensation decision makers is still to ensure that the data collected are useful and acceptable to the employees and managers involved. As the arrows in Exhibit 4.3 indicate, collecting job information is only an interim step, not an end in itself.

JOB ANALYSIS PROCEDURES

Exhibit 4.4 summarizes some job analysis terms and their relationship to each other. Job analysis usually collects information about specific tasks or behaviors.[3] A group of tasks performed by one person makes up a *position.* Identical positions make a *job,* and broadly similar jobs combine into a **job family.**[4]

EXHIBIT 4.4 Job Analysis Terminology

JOB FAMILY

Grouping of related jobs with broadly similar content; e.g., marketing, engineering, office support, technical.

JOB

Group of tasks performed by one person that make up the total work assignment of that person; e.g., customer support representative.

TASK

Smallest unit of analysis, a specific statement of what a person does; e.g., answers the telephone.
Similar tasks can be grouped into a task dimension; e.g., responsible for ensuring that accurate information is provided to the customer.

The U.S. federal government, one of the biggest users of job analysis data, has developed a step-by-step approach to conducting **conventional job analysis**.[5] The government's procedures, shown in Exhibit 4.5, include developing preliminary information, interviewing jobholders and supervisors, and then using the information to create and verify job descriptions. The picture that emerges from reading the steps in the exhibit is of a very stable workplace where the division from one job to the next is clear, with little overlap.

In this workplace, jobs follow a steady progression in a hierarchy of increasing responsibility, and the relationship between jobs is clear. So is how to qualify for promotion into a higher-level job. While some argue that such a traditional, stable structure is a shrinking part of the workplace landscape, such structures nevertheless persist, in varying degrees, in many large organizations.[6] Thus, the federal Department of Labor's description of conventional job analysis provides a useful "how-to" guide.

WHAT INFORMATION SHOULD BE COLLECTED?

As Exhibit 4.5 suggests, a typical analysis starts with a review of information already collected in order to develop a framework for further analysis. Job titles, major duties, task dimensions, and work flow information may already exist. However, it may no longer be accurate. So the analyst must clarify existing information, too.

Generally, a good job analysis collects sufficient information to adequately identify, define, and describe a job. Exhibit 4.6 lists some of the information that is usually collected. The information is categorized as "related to the job" and "related to the employee."

Job Data: Identification

Job titles, departments, the number of people who hold the job, and whether it is exempt from the Fair Labor Standards Act are all examples of information that identifies a job.

While a job title may seem pretty straightforward, it may not be. An observer of the U.S. banking system commented that "every employee over 25 seems to be a vice president." A study accuses the U.S. government of creating more new job titles in a recent six-year period than in the preceding 30 years.[7] Some of the newer positions include deputy to the deputy secretary, principal assistant deputy undersecretary, and associate principal deputy assistant secretary. Most of these titles were created at the highest levels of government service, often to attract a specific person with unique skills. Our personal favorite is at the Jet Propulsion Laboratory in Pasadena, California, where the head of the Interplanetary Network Directorate is, naturally, the director of the Directorate.[8] On the other hand, your tax dollars were at one point paying the wages of 484 deputy assistant secretaries, 148 associate assistant secretaries, 220 assistant assistant secretaries, and 82 deputy assistant assistant secretaries.

Job Data: Content

This is the heart of job analysis. Job content data involve the elemental tasks or units of work, with emphasis on the purpose of each task. An excerpt from a job analysis questionnaire that collects task data is shown in Exhibit 4.7. The inventory describes the job aspect of communication in terms of actual tasks, such as "read technical publications" and "consult with co-workers." The inventory takes eight items to cover

EXHIBIT 4.5 Conventional Job Analysis Procedures

Step	Things to Remember or Do
1. Develop preliminary job information	a. Review existing documents in order to develop an initial "big-picture" familiarity with the job: its main mission, its major duties or functions, work flow patterns. b. Prepare a preliminary list of duties that will serve as a framework for conducting the interviews. c. Make a note of major items that are unclear or ambiguous or that need to be clarified during the data-gathering process.
2. Conduct initial tour of work site	a. The initial tour is designed to familiarize the job analyst with the work layout, the tools and equipment that are used, the general conditions of the workplace, and the mechanics associated with the end-to-end performance of major duties. b. The initial tour is particularly helpful in those jobs where a firsthand view of a complicated or unfamiliar piece of equipment saves the interviewee the thousand words required to describe the unfamiliar or technical. c. For continuity, it is recommended that the first-level supervisor-interviewee be designated the guide for the job-site observations.
3. Conduct interviews	a. It is recommended that the first interview be conducted with the first-level supervisor, who is considered to be in a better position than the jobholders to provide an overview of the job and how the major duties fit together. b. For scheduling purposes, it is recommended that no more than two interviews be conducted per day, each interview lasting no more than three hours.
Notes on selection of interviewees	a. The interviewees are considered subject-matter experts by virtue of the fact that they perform the job (in the case of job incumbents) or are responsible for getting the job done (in the case of first-level supervisors). b. The job incumbent to be interviewed should represent the *typical* employee who is knowledgeable about the job (*not* the trainee who is just learning the ropes *or* the outstanding member of the work unit). c. Whenever feasible, the interviewees should be selected with a view toward obtaining an appropriate race/sex mix.
4. Conduct second tour of work site	a. The second tour of the work site is designed to clarify, confirm, and otherwise refine the information developed in the interviews. b. As in the initial tour, it is recommended that the same first-level supervisor-interviewee conduct the second walk-through.
5. Consolidate job information	a. The consolidation phase of the job study involves piecing together into one coherent and comprehensive job description the data obtained from several sources: supervisor, jobholders, on-site tours, and written materials about the job. b. Past experience indicates that one minute of consolidation is required for every minute of interviewing. For planning purposes, at least five hours should be set aside for the consolidation phase. c. A subject-matter expert should be accessible as a resource person to the job analyst during the consolidation phase. The supervisor-interviewee fills this role. d. The job analyst should check the initial preliminary list of duties and questions—all must be answered or confirmed.
6. Verify job description	a. The verification phase involves bringing all the interviewees together for the purpose of determining if the consolidated job description is accurate and complete. b. The verification process is conducted in a group setting. Typed or legibly written copies of the job description (narrative description of the work setting *and* list of task statements) are distributed to the first-level supervisor and the job incumbent interviewees. c. Line by line, the job analyst goes through the entire job description and makes notes of any omissions, ambiguities, or needed clarifications. d. The job analyst collects all materials at the end of the verification meeting.

EXHIBIT 4.6
Typical Data
Collected for
Job Analysis

Data Related to Job

Job Identification	Job Content
Title	Tasks
Department in which job is located	Activities
Number of people who hold job	Constraints on actions
	Performance criteria
	Critical incidents
	Conflicting demands
	Working conditions
	Roles (e.g., negotiator, monitor, leader)

Data Related to Employee

Employee Characteristics	Internal Relationships	External Relationships
Professional/technical knowledge	Boss and other	Suppliers
Manual skills	superiors	Customers
Verbal skills	Peers	Regulatory
Written skills	Subordinates	Professional industry
Quantitative skills		Community
Mechanical skills		Union/employee groups
Conceptual skills		
Managerial skills		
Leadership skills		
Interpersonal skills		

"obtain technical information" and another seven for "exchange technical information." In fact, the task inventory from which the exhibit is excerpted contains 250 items and covers only systems and analyst jobs. New task-based questions need to be designed for each new set of jobs.

In addition to the emphasis on the task, the other distinguishing characteristic of the inventory in the exhibit is the emphasis on the objective of the task, for example, "read technical publications to keep current on industry" and "consult with co-workers to exchange ideas and techniques." **Task data** reveal the actual work performed and its purpose or outcome.

Employee Data

We can look at the kinds of behaviors that will result in the outcomes. Exhibit 4.6 categorizes employee data as employee characteristics, internal relationships, and external relationships. Exhibit 4.8 shows how communication can be described with verbs (e.g., negotiating, persuading). The verbs chosen are related to the employee characteristic being identified (e.g., bargaining skills, interpersonal skills). The rest of the statement helps identify whether the behavior involves an internal or external relationship. So both Exhibit 4.7 and Exhibit 4.8 focus on communication, but they come at it with different approaches.

EXHIBIT 4.7 Communication: Task-Based Data

1. Mark the circle in the "Do This" column for tasks that you currently perform.

2. At the end of the task list, write in any unlisted tasks that you currently perform.

3. Rate each task that you perform for relative time spent by marking the appropriate circle in the "Time Spent" column.

   Please use a No. 2 pencil and fill all circles completely.

Time spent in current position — Do This / Very small amount / Much below average / Below average / Slightly below average / About average / Slightly above average / Above average / Much above average / Very large amount

PERFORM COMMUNICATION ACTIVITIES	Do This	Time Spent (1–9)
Obtain technical information		
421. Read technical publications about competitive products.	◯	①②③④⑤⑥⑦⑧⑨
422. Read technical publications to keep current on industry.	◯	①②③④⑤⑥⑦⑧⑨
423. Attend required, recommended, or job-related courses and/or seminars.	◯	①②③④⑤⑥⑦⑧⑨
424. Study existing operating systems/programs to gain/maintain familiarity with them.	◯	①②③④⑤⑥⑦⑧⑨
425. Perform literature searches necessary to the development of products.	◯	①②③④⑤⑥⑦⑧⑨
426. Communicate with system software group to see how their recent changes impact current projects.	◯	①②③④⑤⑥⑦⑧⑨
427. Study and evaluate state-of-the-art techniques to remain competitive and/or lead the field.	◯	①②③④⑤⑥⑦⑧⑨
428. Attend industry standards meetings.	◯	①②③④⑤⑥⑦⑧⑨
Exchange technical information		
429. Interface with coders to verify that the software design is being implemented as specified.	◯	①②③④⑤⑥⑦⑧⑨
430. Consult with co-workers to exchange ideas and techniques.	◯	①②③④⑤⑥⑦⑧⑨
431. Consult with members of other technical groups within the company to exchange new ideas and techniques.	◯	①②③④⑤⑥⑦⑧⑨
432. Interface with support consultants or organizations to clarify software design or courseware content.	◯	①②③④⑤⑥⑦⑧⑨

Source: Excerpted from Control Data Corporation's Quantitative Job Analysis. Used by permission.

The excerpt in Exhibit 4.8 is from the **Position Analysis Questionnaire (PAQ)**, which groups work information into seven basic factors: information input, mental processes, work output, relationships with other persons, job context, other job characteristics, and general dimensions. Similarities and differences among jobs are described in terms of these

EXHIBIT 4.8 Communication: Behavioral-Based Data

Section 4 Relationships with Others	*Code Importance to This job (1)*
This section deals with different aspects of interaction between people involved in various kinds of work.	N Does not apply 1 Very minor 2 Low 3 Average 4 High 5 Extreme

4.1 Communication

Rate the following in terms of how important the activity is to the completion of the job. Some jobs may involve several or all of the items in this section.

4.1.1 Oral (communicating by speaking)

99 _____ Advising (dealing with individuals in order to counsel and/or guide them with regard to problems that may be resolved by legal, financial, scientific, technical, clinical, spiritual, and/or professional principles)

100 _____ Negotiating (dealing with others in order to reach an agreement on solution, for example, labor bargaining, diplomatic relations, etc.)

101 _____ Persuading (dealing with others in order to influence them toward some action or point of view, for example, selling, political campaigning, etc.)

102 _____ Instructing (the teaching of knowledge or skills, in either an informal or a formal manner, to others, for example, a public school teacher, a machinist teaching an apprentice, etc.)

103 _____ Interviewing (conducting interviews directed toward some specific objective, for example, interviewing job applicants, census taking, etc.)

104 _____ Routine information exchange job related (the giving and/or receiving of *job-related* information of a routine nature, for example, ticket agent, taxicab dispatcher, receptionist, etc.)

105 _____ Nonroutine information exchange (the giving and/or receiving of *job-related* information of a nonroutine or unusual nature, for example, professional committee meetings, engineers discussing new product design, etc.)

106 _____ Public speaking (making speeches or formal presentations before relatively large audiences, for example, political addresses, radio/TV broadcasting, delivering a sermon, etc.)

4.1.2 Written (communicating by written/printed material)

107 _____ Writing (for example, writing or dictating letters, reports, etc., writing copy for ads, writing newspaper articles, etc.; do *not* include transcribing activities described in item 4.3 but only activities in which the incumbent creates the written material)

Source: E. J. McConnick, P. R. Jeanneret, and R. C. Mecham, *Position Analysis Questionnaire,* copyright © 1969 by Purdue Research Foundation, West Lafayette, IN 47907. Reprinted with permission.

seven factors, rather than in terms of specific aspects unique to each job.[9] The communication behavior in this exhibit is part of the relationships-with-other-persons factor.

The entire PAQ consists of 194 items. Its developers claim that these items are sufficient to analyze any job. However, you can see by the exhibit that the reading level is quite high. A large proportion of employees need help to get through the whole thing.

EXHIBIT 4.9
The McFry Nine-Step Program

Source: Jerry Newman, *My Secret Life on the McJob,* (New York: McGraw-Hill, 2007).

1. Open a bag of fries.
2. Fill basket about half full (at McDonald's, a machine does this step because we humans might make a mistake. At most places, the task is manual.)
3. Place basket in deep fryer.
4. Push timer button to track cooking time.
5. Play Pavlov's dog—remove basket from fryer when buzzer rings and tip so fries go into holding tray. Be careful; this takes two hands, and hot grease can be flying about. Don't spill even a drop of grease on the floor or you will be skating—not walking—in it for the rest of the day.
6. Salt fries.
7. Push another button that signals when seven minutes are up, the "suggested holding time" for fries.
8. Check screen for size fries requested on next order.
9. Fill the corresponding fry container with fries and place in holding bin.

Another, more nuanced view of "communication" focuses on the nature of the interactions required plus knowledge underlying them. Interactions are defined as the knowledge and behaviors involved in searching, monitoring, and coordinating required to do the work. Some interactions are transactional—routine; "do it by the book." The nine steps of a McFry job, shown in Exhibit 4.9, seem transactional to us. Other interactions are more tacit—complex and ambiguous. Work content that involves more tacit interactions is believed to add greater value than more transactional tasks.[10]

The content of communications that occurs between the Merrill Lynch financial advisor and a client to complete a stock transaction differs substantively from that between a Merrill Lynch senior vice president investor and client who aims to build a long-term relationship to manage a client's $10 million in assets. Communication in both settings includes interactions with clients, but "building long-term relationships" versus "complete transactions" reveals substantive differences in content.

However appealing it may be to rationalize job analysis as the foundation of all HR decisions, collecting all of this information for so many different purposes is very expensive. In addition, the resulting information may be too generalized for any single purpose, including compensation. If the information is to be used for multiple purposes, the analyst must be sure that the information collected is accurate and sufficient for each use. Trying to be all things to all people often results in being nothing to everyone.

"Essential Elements" and the Americans With Disabilities Act

In addition to the job description having sections that identify, describe, and define the job, the **Americans With Disabilities Act (ADA)** requires that **essential elements** of a job—those that cannot be reassigned to other workers—must be specified for jobs covered by the legislation. If a job applicant can perform these essential elements, it is assumed that the applicant can perform the job. After that, reasonable accommodations must be made to enable an otherwise-qualified handicapped person to perform those elements.[11]

ADA regulations state that "essential functions refers to the fundamental job duties of the employment position the individual with a disability holds or desires." The difficulty of specifying essential elements varies with the discretion in the job and with the stability of the job. Technology changes tend to make some tasks easier for all people, including those with disabilities, by reducing the physical strength or mobility required to do them. Unfortunately, employment rates for people with disabilities are still low.

The law does not make any allowances for special pay rates or special benefits for people with disabilities. Say, for example, a company subsidizes paid parking for its employees. An employee who does not drive because of a disability requests that the employer provide the cash equivalent of the parking subsidy as a reasonable accommodation so that the money can be used to pay for alternative transportation.

While the law does not require any particular kind of analysis, many employers have modified the format of their job descriptions to specifically call out the essential elements. A lack of compliance places an organization at risk and ignores one of the objectives of the pay model.

Level of Analysis

The job analysis terms defined in Exhibit 4.4 are arranged in a hierarchy. The level at which an analysis begins influences whether the work is similar or dissimilar. The three jobs described in the beginning of the chapter—customer representative, engineer, account analyst—all involve use of computers, but a closer look showed that the jobs are very different. At the job-family level bookkeepers, tellers, and accounting clerks may be considered to be similar jobs, yet at the job level they are very different. An analogy might be looking at two grains of salt under a microscope versus looking at them as part of a serving of french fries. If job data suggest that jobs are similar, the jobs must be paid equally; if jobs are different, they can be paid differently.[12]

> **e-Compensation**
> Many companies post a sample of job openings on their websites. Compare the job postings from several companies. How complete are the job descriptions included with the postings? Are "essential elements" listed? Are job titles specific or generic? Can you get any sense of a company's culture from its job postings?

Does this mean that the microscopic approach is best? Not necessarily. Many employers find it difficult to justify the time and expense of collecting task-level information, particularly for flexible jobs with frequently changing tasks. They may collect just enough job-level data to make comparisons in the external market for setting wages. However, the ADA's essential-elements requirement for hiring and promotion decisions seems to require more detail than what is required for pay decisions. Designing career paths, staffing, and legal compliance may also require more detailed, finely grained information.

Using broad, generic descriptions that cover a large number of related tasks closer to the job-family level in Exhibit 4.4 is one way to increase flexibility. Two employees working in the same broadly defined jobs may be doing entirely different sets of related tasks. But for pay purposes, they may be doing work of equal value. Employees in these broadly defined jobs can switch to other tasks that fall within the same broad range without the bureaucratic burden of making job transfer requests and wage adjustments. Thus, employees can more easily be matched to changes in the work flow. Recruiter, compensation analyst, and training specialist could each be analyzed as a separate, distinct job, or could all be combined more broadly in the category "HR associate."

Still, a countervailing view deserves consideration. A promotion to a new job title is part of the organization's network of returns. Reducing the number of titles may reduce the opportunities to reinforce positive employee behavior. E*Trade experienced an increase in turnover after it retitled jobs. It reduced its vice presidents and directors to 85, down from around 170 before the retitling.[13] Moving from the federal government job of assistant secretary to that of associate assistant secretary (or reverse) may be far more meaningful than people outside Washington, DC, imagine.

HOW CAN THE INFORMATION BE COLLECTED?

Conventional Methods

The most common way to collect job information is to ask the people who are doing a job to fill out a questionnaire. Sometimes an analyst will interview the jobholders and their supervisors to be sure they understand the questions and that the information is correct. Or the analyst may observe the person at work and take notes on what is being done.

Exhibit 4.10 shows part of a job analysis questionnaire. Questions range from "Give an example of a particularly difficult problem that you face in your work. Why does it occur? How often does it occur? What special skills and/or resources are needed to solve this difficult problem?" to "What is the nature of any contact you have with individuals or companies in countries other than the United States?" These examples are drawn from the Complexity of Duties section of a job analysis questionnaire used by 3M. Other sections of the questionnaire are Skills/Knowledge Applied (19 to choose from), Impact This Job Has on 3M's Business, and Working Conditions. It concludes by asking respondents how well they feel the questionnaire has captured their particular job.

The advantage of conventional questionnaires and interviews is that the involvement of employees increases their understanding of the process. However, the results are only as good as the people involved. If important aspects of a job are omitted, or if the jobholders themselves either do not realize or are unable to express the importance of certain aspects, the resulting job descriptions will be faulty. If you look at the number of jobs in an organization, you can see the difficulty in expecting a single analyst to understand all the different types of work and the importance of certain job aspects. Different people have different perceptions, which may result in differences in interpretation or emphasis. The whole process is open to bias and favoritism.[14] As a result of this potential subjectivity, as well as the huge amount of time the process takes, conventional methods have given way to more quantitative (and systematic) data collection.

Quantitative Methods

Increasingly, employees are directed to a website where they complete a questionnaire online.[15] Such an approach is characterized as **quantitative job analysis (QJA),** since

EXHIBIT 4.10   **3M's Structured Interview Questionnaire**

I. Job Overview	
Job Summary	What is the main purpose of your job? (Why does it exist and what does the work contribute to 3M?) 　　Examples:　To provide secretarial support in our department by performing office and administrative duties. 　　　　　　　To purchase goods and services that meet specifications at the least cost. 　　　　　　　To perform systems analysis involved in the development, installation, and maintenance of 　　　　　　　computer applications. Hint: It may help to list the duties first before answering this question.
Duties and Respon-sibilities	What are your job's main duties and responsibilities? (These are the major work activities that usually take up a significant amount of your work time and occur regularly as you perform your work.)
	In the spaces below, list your job's five most important or most frequent duties. Then, in the boxes, estimate the percentage of the time you spend on each duty each day.	**Percentage of Time Spent** (Total may be less than but not more than 100%)
	1.	

II. Skills/Knowledge Applied	
Formal Training or Education	What is the level of formal training/education that is needed to start doing your job? 　　Example: High School, 2 Year Vo-Tech in Data Processing. Bachelor of Science in Chemistry. In some jobs, a combination of education and job-related experience can substitute for academic degrees. 　　Example: Bachelor's Degree in Accounting or completion of 2 years of general business plus 3–4 years' work 　　　　　　experience in an accounting field.

Experience	Months:		Years:	None
	What important skills, competencies, or abilities are needed to do the work that you do? (Please give examples for each skill that you identify.)			
Skills/ Compet- encies	**A. Coordinating Skills** (such as scheduling activities, organizing/maintaining records)			
	Are coordinating skills required?　　☐ Yes　　☐ No　　　　If yes, give examples of specific skills needed			
	Example			
	B. Administrative Skills (such as monit...			

III. Complexity of Duties	
Structure and Variation of Work	How processes and tasks within your work are determined, and how you do them are important to understanding your work at 3M. Describe the work flow in your job. Think of the major focus of your job or think of the work activities on which you spend the most time.
	1.　From whom/where (title, not person) do you receive work?
	2.　What processes or tasks do you perform to comple...
Problem Solving and Analysis	3.
	Give an example of a particularly difficult problem that you face in your work.
	Why does it occur?
	How often does it occur?
	What special skills and/or resources are needed to solve this difficult problem?

VI. General Comments	
General Comments	What percentage of your job duties do you feel was captured in this questionnaire? 　　☐ 0–25%　　　　☐ 26–50%　　　　☐ 51–75%　　　　☐ 76–100%
	What aspect of your job was not covered adequately by this questionnaire?

statistical analysis of the results is possible. Exhibits 4.7 and 4.8 are excerpts from quantitative questionnaires. In addition to facilitating statistical analysis of the results, quantitative data collection allows more data to be collected faster.

A questionnaire typically asks jobholders to assess each item in terms of whether or not that particular item is part of their job. If it is, they are asked to rate how important it is and the amount of job time spent on it. The responses can be machine-scored, similar to the process for a multiple-choice test (only there are no wrong answers), and the results can be used to develop a profile of the job. Questions are grouped around five compensable factors (discussed in Chapter 5): knowledge, accountability, reasoning, communication, and working conditions. Knowledge is further subcategorized as range of depth, qualifications, experience, occupational skills, management skills, and learning time. Assistance is given in the form of prompting questions and a list of jobs whose holders have answered each question in a similar way. Results can be used to prepare a job profile based on the compensable factors. If more than one person is doing a particular job, results of several people in the job can be compared or averaged to develop the profile. Profiles can be compared across jobholders in both the same and different jobs.

Some consulting firms have developed quantitative inventories that can be tailored to the needs of a specific organization or to a specific family of jobs, such as data/information processing jobs.[16] Many organizations find it practical and cost-effective to modify these existing inventories rather than to develop their own analysis from ground zero. But, remember, as we have said, the results depend on the quality of the inputs. Here, the items on the questionnaire matter. If important aspects of a job are omitted or if the jobholders themselves do not realize the importance of certain aspects, the resulting job descriptions will be faulty. In one study, the responses of high-performing stockbrokers on amounts of time spent on some tasks differed from those of low performers. The implication is that any analysis needs to include good performers to ensure that the work is usefully analyzed.[17]

Who Collects the Information?

Collecting job analysis information through one-on-one interviews can be a thankless task. No matter how good a job you do, some people will not be happy with the resulting job descriptions. In the past, organizations often assigned the task to a new employee, saying it would help the new employee become familiar with the jobs of the company. Today, if job analysis is performed at all, human resource generalists and supervisors do it. The analysis is best done by someone thoroughly familiar with the organization and its jobs and trained in how to do the analysis properly.[18]

Who Provides the Information?

The decision on the source of the data (jobholders, supervisors, and/or analysts) hinges on how to ensure consistent, accurate, useful, and acceptable data. Expertise about the work resides with the jobholders and the supervisors; hence, they are the principal sources. For key managerial/professional jobs, supervisors "two levels above" have also been suggested as valuable sources since they may have a more strategic view of how jobs fit in the overall organization. In other instances, subordinates and employees in other jobs that interface with the job under study are also involved.

The number of incumbents per job from which to collect data probably varies with the stability of the job, as well as the ease of collecting the information. An ill-defined or changing job will require either the involvement of more respondents or a more careful selection of respondents. Obviously, the more people involved, the more time-consuming and expensive the process, although computerization helps mitigate these drawbacks.

Whether through a conventional analysis or a quantitative approach, completing a questionnaire requires considerable involvement by employees and supervisors. Involvement can increase their understanding of the process, thereby increasing the likelihood that the results of the analysis will be acceptable.[19] But it also is expensive.

What about Discrepancies?

What happens if the supervisor and the employees present different pictures of the jobs? While supervisors, in theory, ought to know the jobs well, they may not, particularly if jobs are changing. People actually working in a job may change it. They may find ways to do things more efficiently, or they may not have realized that certain tasks were supposed to be part of their jobs.

3M had an interesting problem when it collected job information from a group of engineers. The engineers listed a number of responsibilities that they viewed as part of their jobs; however, the manager realized that those responsibilities actually belonged to a higher level of work. The engineers had enlarged their jobs beyond what they were being paid to do. No one wanted to tell these highly productive employees to slack off. Instead, 3M looked for additional ways to reward these engineers rather than bureaucratize them.

What should the manager do if employees and their supervisors do not agree on what is part of the job? Differences in job data may arise among the jobholders as well. Some may see the job one way, some another. The best answer is to collect more data. Enough data are required to ensure consistent, accurate, useful, and acceptable results. Holding a meeting of multiple jobholders and supervisors in a focus group to discuss discrepancies and then asking both employees and supervisors to sign off on the revised results helps ensure agreement on, or at least understanding of, the results. Disagreements can be an opportunity to clarify expectations, learn about better ways to do the job, and document how the job is actually performed. Discrepancies among employees may even reveal that more than one job has been lumped under the same job title.

Top Management (and Union) Support Is Critical

In addition to involvement by analysts, jobholders, and their supervisors, support of top management is absolutely essential. Support of union officials in a unionized workforce is as well. They know (hopefully) what is strategically relevant. They must be alerted to the cost of a thorough job analysis, its time-consuming nature, and the fact that changes will be involved. For example, jobs may be combined; pay rates may be adjusted. If top managers (and unions) are not willing to seriously consider any changes suggested by job analysis, the process is probably not worth the bother and expense.

JOB DESCRIPTIONS SUMMARIZE THE DATA

So now the job information has been collected, maybe even organized. But it still must be summarized and documented in a way that will be useful for HR decisions, including job evaluation (Chapter 5). As noted previously, that summary of the job is the **job description.** The job description provides a "word picture" of the job. Let us return to Exhibit 4.2, our job description for a registered nurse. It contains information on the tasks, people, and things included. Trace the connection between different parts of the description and the job analysis data collected. The job is identified by its title and its relationships to other jobs in the structure. A job summary provides an overview of the job. The section on essential responsibilities elaborates on the summary. It includes the tasks. Related tasks may be grouped into task dimensions.

This particular job description also includes very specific standards for judging whether an essential responsibility has been met—for example, "Provides a written assessment of patient within one hour of admission and at least once a shift." A final section lists the qualifications necessary in order to be hired for the job. These are the **job specifications** that can be used as a basis for hiring—the knowledge, skills, and abilities required to adequately perform the tasks. But keep in mind that the summary needs to be relevant for pay decisions and thus must focus on similarities and differences in content.

Using Generic Job Descriptions

To avoid starting from scratch (if writing a job description for the first time) or as a way to cross-check externally, it can be useful to refer to generic job descriptions that have not yet been tailored to a specific organization. One readily accessible source is the Occupational Information Network, or O*NET (*www.onetcenter.org*). Exhibit 4.11 shows the information O*NET provides using the job of computer programmer as an example.

e-Compensation

Use O*NET to find the knowledge, skills, and other characteristics needed to be a computer programmer (or an occupation of your choice).

Go to *http://online.onetcenter.org/*
Choose: Find Occupations
Enter the occupation name into space under "Keyword or O*NET-SOC code"
Click on "go"
Then click on the name of the occupation to see the knowledge, skills, etc. required.
Would this information from O*NET be useful to you if you needed to write job descriptions in your organizations?

Describing Managerial/Professional Jobs

Descriptions of managerial/professional jobs often include more detailed information on the nature of the job, its scope, and accountability. One challenge is that an individual manager will influence the job content.[20] Professional/managerial job descriptions must capture the relationship between the job, the person performing it, and the organization objectives—how the job fits into the organization, the results expected, and what the person performing it brings to the job. Someone with strong information systems and finance

EXHIBIT 4.11   O*NET Code Connector

Source: National Center for O*NET Development, U.S. Department of Labor, Employment and Training Administration, *http://www.onetcodeconnector.org/ccreport/15-1021.00.*

expertise performing the compensation manager's job will probably shape it differently, based on this expertise, than someone with strong negotiation and/or counseling expertise.

Exhibit 4.12 excerpts this scope and accountability information for a nurse manager. Rather than emphasizing the tasks to be done, this description focuses on the accountabilities (e.g., "responsible for the coordination, direction, implementation, evaluation, and management of personnel and services; provides leadership; participates in strategic planning and defining future direction").

Verify the Description

The final step in the job analysis process is to verify the accuracy of the resulting job descriptions (step 6 in Exhibit 4.5). Verification often involves the jobholders as well as their supervisors to determine whether the proposed job description is accurate and complete. The description is discussed, line by line, with the analyst, who makes notes of any omissions, ambiguities, or needed clarifications (an often excruciating and thankless task). It would have been interesting to hear the discussion between our nurse from 100 years ago, whose job is described in Exhibit 4.13, and her supervisor.

EXHIBIT 4.12
Job Description for a Manager

Title: Nurse Manager

Department: ICU

Position Description:

Under the direction of the Vice President of Patient Care Services and Directors of Patient Care Services, the Nurse Manager assumes 24-hour accountability and responsibility for the operations of defined patient specialty services. The Nurse Manager is administratively responsible for the coordination, direction, implementation, evaluation, and management of personnel and services. The Nurse Manager provides leadership in a manner consistent with the corporate mission, values, and philosophy and adheres to policies and procedures established by Saint Joseph's Hospital and the Division of Patient Care Services. The Nurse Manager participates in strategic planning and defining future direction for the assigned areas of responsibility and the organization.

Qualification:

Education: Graduate of accredited school of nursing. A bachelor's degree in nursing or related field required. Master's degree preferred. Current license in State of Wisconsin as a Registered Nurse, Experience: A minimum of three years' clinical nursing is required. Minimum of two years' management experience or equivalent preferred.

EXHIBIT 4.13
Job Description for Nurse 100 Years Ago

In addition to caring for your 50 patients each nurse will follow these regulations:

1. Daily sweep and mop the floors of your ward, dust the patient's furniture and window sills.
2. Maintain an even temperature in your ward by bringing in a scuttle of coal for the day's business.
3. Light is important to observe the patient's condition. Therefore, each day, fill kerosene lamps, clean chimneys, and trim wicks. Wash the windows once a week.
4. The nurse's notes are important in aiding the physician's work. Make your pens carefully, you may whittle nibs to your individual taste.
5. Each nurse on the day duty will report every day at 7 a.m. and leave at 8 p.m. except on the Sabbath on which day you will be off from 12:00 noon to 2:00 p.m.
6. Graduate nurses in good standing with the director of nurses will be given an evening off each week for courting purposes, or two evenings a week if you go regularly to church.
7. Each nurse should lay aside from each pay day a goodly sum of her earnings for her benefit during her declining years, so that she will not become a burden. For example, if you earn $30 a month you should set aside $15.
8. Any nurse who smokes, uses liquor in any form, gets her hair done at a beauty shop, or frequents dance halls will give the director good reason to suspect her worth, intentions, and integrity.
9. The nurse who performs her labors and serves her patients and doctors faithfully and without fault for a period of five years will be given an increase by the hospital administration of five cents a day, provided there are no hospital debts that are outstanding.

The job description paints a vivid picture of expectations at that time, although we suspect the nurse probably did not have much opportunity for input regarding the accuracy of the job description.

JOB ANALYSIS: BEDROCK OR BUREAUCRACY?

HRNet, an Internet discussion group related to HR issues, provoked one of its largest responses ever with the query, "What good is job analysis?" Some felt that managers have no basis for making defensible, work-related decisions without it. Others called the process a bureaucratic boondoggle. Yet job analysts are an endangered species. Many employers, as part of their drive to contain expenses, no longer have job analysts. The unknown costs involved are too difficult to justify.

One expert writes, "Whenever I visit a human resources department, I ask whether they have any [job analysis]. I have not had a positive answer in several years, except in government organizations."[21] Yet if job analysis is the cornerstone of human resource decisions, what are such decisions based on if work information is no longer rigorously collected?

This disagreement centers on the issue of flexibility. Many organizations today are using fewer employees to do a wider variety of tasks in order to increase productivity and reduce costs. Reducing the number of different jobs and cross-training employees can make work content more fluid and employees more flexible.[22]

Generic job descriptions that cover a larger number of related tasks (e.g., "associate") can provide flexibility in moving people among tasks without adjusting pay. Employees may be more easily matched to changes in the work flow; the importance of flexibility in behavior is made clear to employees.

Traditional job analysis that makes fine distinctions among levels of jobs has been accused of reinforcing rigidity in the organization. Employees may refuse to do certain tasks that are not specifically called out in their job descriptions. It should be noted, however, that this problem mainly arises where employee relations are already poor. In unionized settings, union members may "work to the rules" (i.e., not do anything that is not specifically listed in their job descriptions) as a technique for putting pressure on management.

In some organizations, analyzing work content is now conducted as part of work flow and supply chain analysis. **Supply chain analysis** looks at how an organization does its work: activities pursued to accomplish specific objectives for specific customers. A "customer" can be internal or external to the organization. So Starbucks, in its continuous quest for improved service, frets over "average wait time." If the time to put that Venti Double Chocolate Chip Frappuccino Blended Creme in your hand is increased because customers in front of you are musing over the new CD for sale at the register, you may decide that the Dunkin' Donuts across the street might be a better choice. Starbucks shaved 20 seconds off its wait time by redesigning the barista job to include "floating." Floaters walk the queue, take your order, mark the cup, and hand the cup to the barista who will actually fill your order—all before you get to the cash register. Floaters also "communicate" with the customers to make the experience enjoyable. Notice that as part of a work flow study, job analysis is conducted to understand the work and how it adds value. Is the barista job content now different with the floating tasks? Yes. We will face the issue of whether to pay floaters differently in later chapters.[23]

JOB ANALYSIS AND GLOBALIZATION

Job Analysis and Susceptibility to Offshoring

Offshoring refers to the movement of jobs to locations beyond a country's borders. Historically, manual, low-skill jobs were most susceptible to offshoring. As we saw in Chapter 1, there are substantial differences in hourly compensation costs across countries for manufacturing workers; this has played an important role in companies' decisions about where to locate production operations. Similar differences in cost in other low-skill occupations (e.g., in call centers) have had similar ramifications. (So, when you call for an airline reservation or help with your printer, you may well reach someone in another country.) Of course, as we also noted, labor cost is only part of the story. There are productivity differences across countries as well, meaning that lower labor costs may in some cases be offset by lower productivity. Availability of workers with needed education and skills is another potential constraint. Proximity to customers is yet another issue. Sometimes that argues for moving offshore, sometimes it does not.

Increasingly, susceptibility to offshoring is no longer limited to low-skill jobs. White- collar jobs are also increasingly at risk. Is there a way to systematically measure which jobs are most susceptible to offshoring? The U.S. Bureau of Labor Statistics has attempted to do just this with respect to service-providing occupations. Exhibit 4.14 shows the list of occupations it found to have the highest and lowest susceptibility to offshoring. The offshoring susceptibility scores are based on the sum of scores on the four items shown. So, jobs are most susceptible to outsourcing when inputs and outputs can easily be transmitted electronically, little interaction with other workers is required, little local knowledge is required, and the work can be routinized.

Interestingly, highly susceptible jobs include not only those that require little education and training, such as data entry keyers and telemarketers, but also computer programmers and tax preparers. Turning to jobs with low susceptibility to outsourcing, we see various managerial positions and also positions where local knowledge is required (e.g., marketing managers presumably need to know consumer preferences in particular regions of the world) or where being "on the ground" (literally, in the case of landscape architects) is necessary.

To our knowledge, the system for assessing susceptibility to offshoring has not been rigorously validated to see how well it predicts actual offshoring of occupations. Nevertheless, as Exhibit 4.14 indicates, growth rates (in the United States) for jobs on the highly susceptible list are generally small or negative, while jobs on the low susceptibility list have shown strong growth. Unless the two sets of jobs have different growth rates across countries, the differential growth rates seem consistent with the possibility that jobs on the highly susceptible list have lower growth rates, at least in part because they have experienced greater offshoring. Also, there are certainly numerous examples of jobs on the highly susceptible list (e.g., data entry keyers, telemarketers, and computer programmers) being offshored. In Chapter 7, we return to the topic of offshoring to discuss labor cost and effectiveness ramifications.

EXHIBIT 4.14   Susceptibility of Occupations to Offshoring and Projected Employment Growth

Susceptibility Score	Occupation	Projected 10-Year Employment Growth
	Highest Susceptibility to Offshoring	
16	Computer programmers	−4%
16	Pharmacy technicians	32%
16	Parts salespersons	−2%
16	Telephone operators	−4.9%
16	Billing and posting clerks and machine operators	−39%
16	Computer operators	4%
16	Data entry keyers	−25%
16	Word processors and typists	−5%
15	Tax preparers	−11%
15	Medical transcriptionists	−9%
15	Telemarketers	14%
15	Payroll and timekeeping clerks	−10%
15	Proofreaders and copy markers	6%
	Lowest Susceptibility to Offshoring	
6	Chief executives	2%
6	General and operations managers	1%
6	Administrative services managers	12%
6	Computer and information systems managers	16%
6	Wholesale and retail buyers, except farm products	0%
6	Computer systems analysts	29%
6	Landscape architects	16%
6	Industrial engineers	21%
6	Animal scientists	9%
6	Advertising sales agents	21%
5	Advertising and promotions managers	6%
5	Marketing managers	15%
5	Sales managers	10%
5	Public relations managers	17%
5	Engineering managers	7%
5	Natural science managers	12%
5	Management analysts	22%
5	Civil engineers	18%
5	Art directors	9%
4	Environmental engineers	26%

Offshoring susceptibility questions (maximum score = 16, minimum score = 4)?

1. To what degree can the inputs and outputs of the occupation be transmitted electronically?

Very low degree (1 point)	Low degree (2 points)	High degree (3 points)	Very high degree (4 points)

2. To what degree do the duties of this occupation require interaction with other types of workers?

Very low degree (1 point)	Low degree (2 points)	High degree (3 points)	Very high degree (4 points)

3. To what degree is knowledge of social and cultural idiosyncrasies, or other local knowledge, needed to carry out the tasks of this occupation?

Very low degree (4 point)	Low degree (3 points)	High degree (2 points)	Very high degree (1 points)

4. To what degree can the work of the occupation be routinized or handled by following a script?

Very low degree (1 point)	Low degree (2 points)	High degree (3 points)	Very high degree (4 points)

Source: Roger J. Moncarz, Michael G. Wolf, and Benjamin Wright, "Service-Providing Occupations, Offshoring and The Labor Market." *Monthly Labor Review*, December 2008, pp. 71–86.

Job Analysis Information and Comparability across Borders

As firms spread work across multiple countries, there is an increasing need to analyze jobs to either maintain consistency in job content or else be able to measure the ways in which jobs are similar and different. For example, for a software development team to work equally effectively with programmers in the United States and India, the job descriptions and job specifications need to be measured and understood. One potential challenge is that norms or perceptions regarding what is and what is not part of a particular job may vary across countries. However, a study of three different jobs (first-line supervisor, general office clerk, and computer programmer) in the United States, China, Hong Kong, and New Zealand found that ratings of the importance and amount of work activities and job requirements were "quite similar" across countries, suggesting that job analysis information "is likely to transport quite well across countries."[24]

JUDGING JOB ANALYSIS

Beyond beliefs about its usefulness—or lack thereof—for satisfying both employees and employers, there are several ways to judge job analysis.

Reliability

If you measure something tomorrow and get the same results you got today, or if I measure and get the same result you did, the measurement is considered to be reliable. This doesn't mean it is right—only that repeated measures give the same result. **Reliability** is a measure of the consistency of results among various analysts, various methods, various sources of data, or over time. Reliability is a necessary, but not sufficient, condition for **validity.**

The mean correlation between work content ratings of jobs from two different raters, a typical way to estimate reliability, is .083.[25] So, using a single rater to conduct a job analysis typically results in very poor reliability. By using multiple raters and taking their average rating, the reliability increases. With 5 raters, it is .312. With 15 raters, it is .488. These are still not terribly high reliabilities and indicate that the outcome of a job analysis depends to an important degree on who conducts it. There is higher reliability between professional job analysts and also when more specific tasks are rated (as opposed to more general job requirements or knowledge and skill requirements).[26] Research on employee and supervisor agreement in job analysis information is mixed.[27] For instance, experience may change an employee's perceptions about a job since the employee may have found new ways to do it or added new tasks to the job. The supervisor may not realize the extent of change. In such cases, the job the employee is actually doing may not be the same as the job originally assigned by the supervisor. Differences in performance seem to influence reliability. Other research finds that reliability is lower for jobs that are more interdependent with other jobs, and have more autonomy/are less routine.[28] To date, no studies have found that gender and race differences affect reliability.[29] Obviously, the way to increase reliability in a job analysis is to understand and reduce sources of difference. Quantitative job analysis helps do this. But we need to be sure that we do not eliminate the richness of responses while eliminating the differences. Sometimes there really may be more than one job. Training can also improve reliability.[30]

See the section "Reliability of Job Evaluation Techniques" in Chapter 6 for further details on how reliability can affect pay outcomes.

Validity

Does the analysis create an accurate portrait of the work? There is almost no way of showing statistically the extent to which an analysis is accurate, particularly for complex jobs. No gold standard exists; how can we know? Consequently, *validity* examines the convergence of results among sources of data and methods. If several job incumbents, supervisors, and peers respond in similar ways to questionnaires, then it is more likely that the information is valid. However, a sign-off on the results does not guarantee the information's validity.[31] It may mean only that all involved were sick to death of the process and wanted to get rid of the analyst so they could get back to work.

Acceptability

If job holders and managers are dissatisfied with the initial data collected and the process, they are not likely to buy into the resulting job structure or the pay rates attached to that structure. An analyst collecting information through one-on-one interviews or observation is not always accepted because of the potential for subjectivity and favoritism. One writer says, "We all know the classic procedures. One [worker] watched and noted the actions of another . . . at work on [the] job. The actions of both are biased and the resulting information varied with the wind, especially the political wind."[32] However, quantitative computer-assisted approaches may also run into difficulty, especially if they give in to the temptation to collect too much information for too many purposes. After four years in development, one application ran into such severe problems due to its unwieldy size and incomprehensible questions that managers simply refused to use it.

Currency

To be valid, acceptable, and useful (see below), job information must be up to date. Some jobs stay relatively stable over time, while others may change in important ways, even over short time periods. As Exhibit 4.15 shows, most organizations report that they have up-to-date job information, but a substantial portion report that job information is not up to date. That can not only hinder compensation practice and decision-making, but also employee selection, training, and development. Most organizations do not engage in any regular (e.g., annual or biannual) updating of job analysis information, instead being more likely to update job information when the significant changes are believed to have occurred or when the job is being re-evaluated for compensation purposes.[33] It may be useful to develop a systematic protocol for evaluating when job information needs to be updated.[34]

Usefulness

Usefulness refers to the practicality of the information collected. For pay purposes, job analysis provides work-related information to help determine how much to pay for a job—it helps determine whether the job is similar to or different from other jobs. If job analysis does this in a reliable, valid, and acceptable way and can be used to make pay decisions, then it is useful.[35]

EXHIBIT 4.15 Updated Job Descriptions

How many jobs in your organization have up-to-date position, job, or role descriptions in place?

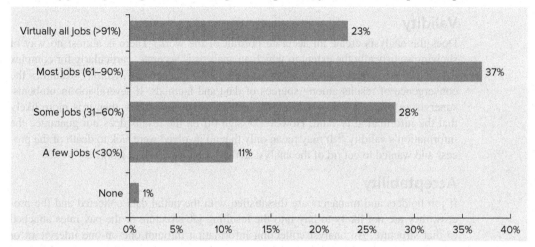

Source: "Job Evaluation and Market-Pricing Practices," *World at Work* © Reprinted with permission from *WorldatWork*. Content is licensed for use by purchaser only. No part of this article may be reproduced, excerpted or redistributed in any form without express written permission from WorldatWork.

As we have noted, some see job analysis information as useful for multiple purposes, such as hiring and training. But multiple purposes may require more information than is required for pay decisions. The practicality of all-encompassing quantitative job analysis plans, with their relatively complex procedures and analysis, remains in doubt. Some advocates get so taken with their statistics and computers that they ignore the role that judgment must continue to play in job analysis. Dunnette's point, made more than 25 years ago, still holds true today: "I wish to emphasize the central role played in all these procedures by human judgment. I know of no methodology, statistical technique or objective measurements that can negate the importance of, nor supplement, rational judgment."[36]

A Judgment Call

In the face of all the difficulties, time, expense, and dissatisfaction, why on earth would you as a manager bother with job analysis? Because work-related information is needed to determine pay, and differences in work determine pay differences. There is no satisfactory substitute that can ensure the resulting pay structure will be work-related or will provide reliable, accurate data for making and explaining pay decisions.

If work information is required, then the real issue should be, How much detail is needed to make these pay decisions? The answer is, Enough to help set individual employees' pay, encourage continuous learning, increase the experience and skill of the work force, and minimize the risk of pay-related grievances. Omitting this detail and contributing to an incorrect and costly decision by uninformed managers can lead to unhappy employees who drive away customers with their poor service, file lawsuits, or complain about management's inability to justify their decisions. The response to inadequate analysis ought not to be to dump the analysis; rather, the response should be to obtain a more useful analysis.

Your **Turn**   The Customer-Service Agent

Read the accompanying article on a day in the work life of Bill Ryan. Then write a job description for the job of customer-service agent. Use the exhibits in this chapter to guide you in deciding what information in the story is relevant for job analysis.

1. Does the day diary include sufficient information?
2. Identify the specific information in the article that you found useful.
3. What additional information do you require? How would that information help you?

Pick a teammate (or the instructor will assign one) and exchange job descriptions with your teammate.

1. How similar/different are the two descriptions? You and your teammate started with exactly the same information. What might explain any differences?
2. What process would you go through to understand and minimize the differences?
3. What are some of the relational returns of the job?

Bill Ryan often deals with difficult people. It's what he gets paid for. He's one of 30 customer-service agents at Half.com, an online marketplace owned by eBay Inc., the Internet auction company. Like eBay, Half.com attempts to match buyers and sellers in a vast flea market featuring millions of products ranging from trading cards to camcorders. But unlike eBay, there's no bidding. Half.com lists items only at fixed prices. If you see something you like, pay the price and it's yours.

The other big difference with eBay is that for most of the products listed on Half.com, there's no way for buyers and sellers to interact directly. Usually there's no need to. To make a purchase, buyers use their credit cards or checking accounts to pay Half.com, which then automatically credits the amount to the seller's card or account—minus a transaction fee. Once the payment is made, the seller ships the product.

Despite a well-oiled system, however, questions arise. Things can go wrong. A purchased item doesn't arrive, or isn't in the condition the buyer expected. Or maybe an interesting product is listed but its description isn't clear.

And that's where Mr. Ryan and his colleagues come in, handling the buckets of e-mail and intermittent phone calls from curious, addled, and upset users. They pass information between buyers and sellers, answer questions, and resolve the occasional dispute. Half.com says that fewer than 1 percent of the site's transactions require customer service's involvement. But with more than 15 million items for sale—well, you do the math.

In fact, the customer-service department receives about 1,500 to 2,000 e-mails a day, of which nearly a third are complaints about transactions. The rest are mostly questions about the goods and how the site works. Mr. Ryan himself on a typical day fields between 60 and 100 e-mails and half a dozen phone calls. The calls are the most stressful. "People panic and they want answers," Mr. Ryan says. "If they are calling, they are not happy."

For Half.com—as well as most other e-commerce companies—customer-service agents like Mr. Ryan are the crucial link between the faceless website and the consumer. And how they deal with the public can make or break a business. As Half.com's vice president for operations, says, "It costs too much to get a new customer only to fumble the relationship away." Half.com wouldn't discuss salaries. But Mr. Ryan and his colleagues, who are split into two shifts covering 8 a.m. to midnight, seven days a week, say they're satisfied with their wages, which include quarterly bonuses.

What he likes about the work, Mr. Ryan says, is the kind of customer problem that requires research and deep digging to find the resolution. What he sometimes doesn't like about his work are the routine questions that generate stock responses. Here's a day in Mr. Ryan's work life:

THE ANSWER MAN

8 AM Mr. Ryan strolls into the Half.com office in Plymouth Meeting, Pa., a short drive from his home. The company's single-story gray building is a former tire factory in this colonial-era industrial town on the outskirts of Philadelphia. Mr. Ryan works in a low-slung, black cubicle toward the back of the office, his space sparsely decorated.

The atmosphere at Half.com is decidedly young and casual. Jeans are the uniform. Mr. Ryan certainly fits in, though at 32 he's a few years older than most of his cubicle mates.

He started doing strictly customer service, answering customer e-mails. Now he also does what the company calls "trust and safety work": investigating fraud and looking for things on the site that are "funky." For instance, when Half.com receives a complaint from a buyer about a seller, it's Mr. Ryan's job to contact both parties and make sure there is no fraud occurring.

This day, because the site has received a high volume of e-mails, he's on regular customer-service duty. After checking the few internal e-mail messages he receives each day, he gets right to work. Mr. Ryan downloads his first batch of 10 e-mails for the day. He says it usually takes him about an hour to get through 10 messages.

8:10 AM The first e-mail is from a woman interested in buying an audio book on CD that she saw listed on the site. She wants to know whether the CD will work on her DVD player. But since she doesn't specify the exact listing, Mr. Ryan is stuck. He can't search for it among all the listings or contact the seller. The best he can do is suggest that she send him an item number so he can contact the seller with her question.

8:15 AM The next e-mail comes from a user who sold the Diana Krall CD "When I Look in Your Eyes," but lost the buyer's shipping information. The seller is concerned that a delay in her shipment will give the buyer reason to give her a negative rating on the site. After each purchase is made, the buyer gets a chance to rate the seller's performance on a scale from 1 to 5—"poor" to "excellent." Every rating sellers collect is displayed along with their user name next to subsequent items they list. Just one negative rating can ruin a seller's reputation, depending on how many sales he or she has made overall.

Mr. Ryan tracks down the details on this particular transaction in the Half.com user database. He identifies the buyer and writes an e-mail to explain that the seller lost the shipping address and "wants to let you know they are sorry for the inconvenience." He then e-mails the buyer's shipping address to the seller.

Mr. Ryan says he doesn't find the e-mails tedious. "There is such a variety of topics to respond to," he says. "I never get 50 of the same questions in a row." But, a few e-mails later, he shrugs with disapproval. The user's question could easily have been answered by going to the help section of the website: "Do I include shipping in the sale price or is it added later?"

Says Mr. Ryan, "It's a general question. I like the detailed research questions." Mr. Ryan pastes in an answer from a database of stock responses the customer-service team has put together. He then tacks onto the end of the e-mail a salutation that he draws from a list of suggested message closers provided by Half.

com. The list, the company says, makes it easier for the agents to write so many e-mails. For this message, Mr. Ryan chooses, "It was my pleasure to assist you."

GOT JUICE

9:30 AM After answering a few more messages, it's time for a coffee break. Mr. Ryan says he drinks two cups of coffee a day, a habit he picked up since starting at Half.com.

"A year ago I wouldn't have touched the stuff," he says. He heads to the kitchen, which is just down the hall from his desk. The well-lit room is stocked with free cappuccino, juice, soda, fruit, cereal, cookies, and other munchies. The cafeteria also doubles as a lounge with a satellite television playing ESPN, a Foosball table, and a ping-pong table. This early in the morning, however, most people are interested in the coffee.

9:48 AM An e-mail arrives from a Half.com colleague in charge of the stock-answer database. He writes that a response Mr. Ryan submitted on how users can sign up for direct deposit—linking their Half.com transactions with their checking accounts—would be included in the database. "There are so many things we don't have responses to," Mr. Ryan says. "It makes everyone's life easier to have the [database]."

9:50 AM The first 10 e-mails are done. Mr. Ryan downloads 10 more. One is from a father who several days earlier ordered the latest Sony PlayStation for his son's birthday and is concerned because it hasn't arrived yet. Half.com's policy is that if a buyer hasn't received an item within 30 days of the purchase, he or she can lodge an official complaint. The PlayStation seller is thus a long way from the delivery deadline. Nevertheless, as a courtesy, Mr. Ryan sends the seller an e-mail asking whether he can provide a shipping date and tracking number that Mr. Ryan can pass on to the restless father.

Half.com believes that help like this—beyond the requirements of its own rules—separates its customer-service approach from that of other companies. When the company was starting out, says Training Supervisor Ed Miller, customer service tried to respond to as many messages as it could, as fast as possible. What the company learned, however, is that "customers don't mind if you take a little more time to answer their specific question." Instead of just firing off e-mails, Half.com now sees it as important to personalize each message. Even with the personalization, Half.com says it responds to most messages within 24 hours.

Communications with customers have a consistent and pleasant tone. E-mail messages should conform to the "grandmother rule." Each message should "make sense to my grandmother."

10:10 AM Bathroom break.

10:15 AM "All right," Mr. Ryan says eagerly, returning to his desk. He cracks his knuckles and starts typing.

A buyer who purchased a video game two months ago but never received it writes to thank Half.com for "hounding" the seller to send him the item. But he wants a refund. Mr. Ryan verifies the buyer's version of events in Half.com's records, then refunds the buyer's money and charges the seller's account for the amount of the sale. Mr. Ryan sends e-mails to both parties informing them of his action. Half.com's rules say that when an official complaint has been lodged the other party has five days in which to respond. In this case, the seller didn't respond, so the buyer won the dispute by default.

10:25 AM Snack time. Mr. Ryan breaks into a high-energy Balance bar—a little nourishment to get him ready for what comes next.

WRECKING CREW

10:30 AM Time to knock down some walls. Lively human-resources worker Alicia DiCiacco invites

Mr. Ryan and his colleagues to pick up sledge-hammers and knock through a wall at the end of the office. Half.com's staff has doubled in the past year, and the company is expanding into adjacent space in the old tire factory. Everyone in the office takes turns whacking at the wall. Some of the younger males dish out screams of "I'm not going to take it any more!" and "Where's the Pink Floyd?!"—a reference to the 1970s rock album "The Wall" by Pink Floyd.

Mr. Ryan eats up the office energy. "It's exciting to work here," he says. "We're growing. We had the second launch of the site. [Half.com expanded its product line in April]. We're doing construction. It's good to come to work when the company is doing well."

11:15 AM Finished with another batch of 10 e-mails, he downloads 10 more, including two separate queries from customers who can't redeem special introductory coupons Half.com offers to new users.

11:47 AM Mr. Ryan gets an e-mail from a seller responding to a message from Half.com. A potential buyer has asked Half.com whether the seller's 75-cent copy of Carolyn Davidson's Harlequin romance "The Midwife" is a paperback or hardcover. Half.com forwarded the question to the seller, who now is writing back to say it's a paperback.

Mr. Ryan sends two e-mails: one to the buyer, answering his question, and one to the seller, thanking him for the information.

12:10 PM Lunch. Mr. Ryan eats his turkey wrap in the company cafeteria with some colleagues and heads back to his desk by 1 p.m.

1:06 PM E-mail from a user who can't find the new Stephen King novel on Half.com. The site is supposed to list all new books from major publishers, even if no one is selling them. That way, if a user is interested, he or she can put it on a wish list and the site will automatically e-mail him or her when a copy has been posted for sale.

Mr. Ryan searches for the book meticulously, checking by title, author and publisher's ISBN number. Once he's sure the book isn't listed, he e-mails Matt Walsh, who is in charge of fixing catalog errors. Mr. Ryan then e-mails the user and instructs him to check back at the site soon.

1:21 PM First phone call of the day. Because Half.com prefers to conduct customer service on e-mail, to keep its costs down, it doesn't display its phone number on its website. Still, persistent users get the number through directory assistance or other sources.

This caller, an agitated buyer of the video "Valley Girl," a 1983 comedy starring Nicolas Cage, says she received a damaged tape. She has lodged an official complaint against the seller on the website, but the seller hasn't responded. Mr. Ryan tells her that the five days the seller has to respond aren't up yet. He assures her that if the seller doesn't respond within the allotted time, he will refund her money and charge the seller's account. Until then, there's nothing Mr. Ryan can do except comfort the caller with apologies and explanations.

In the event that the seller disputes the buyer's claim about the tape, Half.com is still likely to grant a refund, especially on such an inexpensive item. Half.com makes it clear, however, that its customer-service team keeps a close watch on users' complaints, looking out for fraudulent refund requests. If Half.com suspects foul play, it doesn't grant refunds so easily.

2:02 PM A seller of the video "I Know What You Did Last Summer" got the package returned, marked address unknown. Mr. Ryan looks up the buyer's information in the user database and e-mails him, asking for an updated address to forward to the seller. He then e-mails the seller, telling him the address should be on its way shortly.

2:21 PM He downloads 10 more e-mails.

HOME STRETCH

2:30 PM The day is starting to get long, at least to an observer. But Mr. Ryan says sitting still all day doesn't cramp his style. "Sometimes it's tough to work at a desk, but it doesn't really bother me," he says. "I work out after work, and that really loosens things up."

3 PM Bathroom break.

3:15 PM With the clock ticking toward quitting time, Mr. Ryan hunkers down to finish his last batch of e-mails. It's more of the same: a user unsure how Half.com works; a seller who wants to list a 1976 edition of "The Grapes of Wrath" but can't figure out where to put it on the site; a buyer who wants a book shipped second-day air, even though the order was already placed.

3:30 PM A call from a buyer interrupts Mr. Ryan's streak of dispensing e-mails. The buyer felt the quality of a book she bought was not up to snuff. The book, a $2 copy of Danielle Steel's "Secrets," apparently had a torn cover. The buyer is upset, but Mr. Ryan remains calm, calling on skills he learned in a one-day seminar called "Dealing With Difficult People." In the class, which he took before coming to Half.com, he learned to paraphrase what the customer is saying to make sure he understands the complaint. Mr. Ryan also takes care to speak clearly with a strong sense of empathy. At one point he says, "I understand your frustration." When he explains that the buyer will have to wait some time for a final resolution of the matter, he makes sure to preface it with a heartfelt "I'm sorry to let you know . . ." An observer listening to Mr. Ryan gets the sense that he is not acting.

"If you don't understand what they are saying, then you have a problem," he says. Though he can't satisfy this customer then and there, he promises to talk to his supervisor and to call her back tomorrow with more information.

4 PM The day is done. Mr. Ryan finishes his last e-mail, closes up his desk and shoves on home. A new shift of workers picks up where Mr. Ryan left off, toiling from 4 p.m. to 12 a.m. When they finish, the customer-service staff in eBay's facility in Salt Lake City will take over. Tomorrow, Mr. Ryan will be back on duty at 8 a.m., downloading his first 10 e-mails.

Source: Alex Frangos, *The Wall Street Journal*, July 16, 2001.

Summary   Encouraging employee behaviors that help achieve an organization's objectives and fostering a sense of fairness among employees are two hallmarks of a useful internal pay structure. One of the first strategic pay decisions is how much to align a pay structure internally compared to aligning it to external market forces. Do not be misled. The issue is *not* achieving internal alignment versus alignment with external market forces. Rather, the strategic decision focuses on sustaining the optimal balance of internally aligned and externally responsive pay structures that helps the organization achieve its mission. *Both are required.* This part of the book focuses on one of the first decisions managers face in designing pay systems: how much to emphasize pay structures that are internally aligned with the work performed, the organization's structure, and its strategies. Whatever the choice, the decision needs to support (and be supported by) the organization's overall human resource strategy.

Next, managers must decide whether job and/or individual employee characteristics will be the basic unit of analysis supporting the pay structure. This is followed by deciding what data will be collected, what method(s) will be used to collect the information, and who should be involved in the process.

A key test of an effective and fair pay structure is acceptance of results by managers and employees. The best way to ensure acceptance of job analysis results is to involve employees as well as supervisors in the process. At the minimum, all employees should be informed of the purpose and progress of the activity.

If almost everyone agrees about the importance of job analysis, does that mean everyone does it? Of course not. Unfortunately, job analysis can be tedious and time-consuming. Often the job is given to newly hired compensation analysts, ostensibly to help them learn the organization, but perhaps there's also a hint of "rites of passage" in such assignments.

Alternatives to job-based structures such as **skill-based** or **competency-based systems** are being experimented with in many firms. The premise is that basing structures on these other criteria will encourage employees to become more flexible, and thus fewer workers will be required for the same level of output. This may be the argument, but as experience increases with the alternatives, managers are discovering that they can be as time consuming and bureaucratic as job analysis. Bear in mind, job content remains the conventional criterion for structures.

Review Questions

1. Job analysis has been considered the cornerstone of human resource management. Precisely how does it support managers making pay decisions?
2. What does job analysis have to do with internal alignment?
3. Describe the major decisions involved in job analysis.
4. Distinguish between task data and behavioral data.
5. What is the critical advantage of quantitative approaches over conventional approaches to job analysis?
6. How would you decide whether to use job-based or person-based structures?
7. Why do many managers say that job analysis is a colossal waste of their time and the time of their employees? Are they right?

Endnotes

1. Stanley Bing, *100 Bullshit Jobs . . . And How to Get Them* (New York: HarperCollins, 2006); Justin Racz, *50 Jobs Worse Than Yours* (New York: Bloomsbury, 2004). Our personal favorite is the ride operator at the "It's a Small World" ride at Disney.
2. Robert J. Grossman, "IBM's HR Takes a Risk," *HR Magazine*, April 2007.
3. Michael T. Brannick, Edward L. Levine, and Frederick P. Morgeson, *Job and Work Analysis: Methods, Research, and Applications for Human Resource Management*, 2nd ed. (Los Angeles, CA: Sage, 2007).
4. E. J. McCormick, "Job and Task Analysis," in *Handbook of Industrial and Organizational Psychology*, M. D. Dunnette, ed. (Chicago, IL: Rand McNally, 1976), pp. 651–696; Robert J. Harvey, "Job Analysis," in *Handbook of Industrial and Organizational Psychology*, vol. 2, M. D. Dunnette and L. Hough, eds. (Palo Alto, CA: Consulting Psychologists Press, 1991), pp. 72–157.

5. Particularly valuable sources of information on job analysis definitions and methods are U.S. Department of Labor, Manpower Administration, *Revised Handbook for Analyzing Jobs* (Washington, DC: U.S. Government Printing Office, 1992); Robert J. Harvey, "Job Analysis," in *Handbook of Industrial and Organizational Psychology,* vol. 2, M. D. Dunnette and L. Hough, eds. (Palo Alto, CA: Consulting Psychologists Press, 1991), pp. 72–157; Brenda Lister, *Evaluating Job Content* (Scottsdale, AZ: WorldatWork, 2006).

6. Wayne Cascio, "Strategies for Responsible Restructuring," *Academy of Management Executive* 19(4), 2005, pp. 39–50; Janet Marler, Melissa Barringer, and George Milkovich, "Boundaryless and Traditional Contingent Employees: Worlds Apart," *Journal of Organizational Behavior* 23 (2002), pp. 425–453.

7. Paul C. Light, *The True Size of Government* (Washington, DC: Brookings Institute, 1999); Candice Prendergast, "The Role of Promotion in Inducing Specific Human Capital Acquisition," *Quarterly Journal of Economics,* May 1993, pp. 523–534.

8. Dan Neil, "All Rays Lead to Pasadena," *Los Angeles Times,* February 5, 2006.

9. Much of the developmental work and early applications of the PAQ were done in the 1960s and 1970s. See, for example, E. J. McCormick, "Job and Task Analysis," in *Handbook of Industrial and Organizational Psychology,* M. D. Dunnette, ed. (Chicago, IL: Rand McNally, 1976), pp. 651–696; E. J. McCormick et al., "A Study of Job Characteristics and Job Dimensions as Based on the Position Analysis Questionnaire," Occupational Research Center, Purdue University, West Lafayette, IN, 1969. The PAQ is distributed by PAQ Services, www.paq.com; see PAQ's website and newsletters for recent discussions.

10. Thomas H. Davenport, "The Coming Commoditization of Processes," *Harvard Business Review,* June 2005, pp. 101–108.

11. *Benefits Compliance: An Overview for the HR Professional* (Scottsdale, AZ: WorldatWork, 2006).

12. V. L. Huber and S. R. Crandall, "Job Measurement: A Social-Cognitive Decision Perspective," in *Research in Personnel and Human Resources Management,* vol. 12, Gerald R. Ferris, ed. (Greenwich, CT: JAI Press, 1994), pp. 223–269; Juan I. Sanchez, I. Prager, A. Wilson, and C. Viswesvaran, "Understanding within-Job Title Variance in Job-Analytic Ratings," *Journal of Business and Psychology* 12 (1998), pp. 407–419.

13. Susanne Craig, "E*Trade Lowers Corporate Titles," in "Move That Could Spur Departures," *The Wall Street Journal,* September 6, 2001, pp. C1, C14.

14. Theresa M. Glomb, John D. Kammeyer-Mueller, and Maria Rotundo, "Emotional Labor Demands and Compensating Wage Differentials," *Journal of Applied Psychology* 89(4), 2004, pp. 700–714; Juan I. Sanchez and Edward L. Levine, "Is Job Analysis Dead, Misunderstood, or Both? New Forms of Work Analysis and Design," in *Evolving Practices in Human Resource Management: Responses to a Changing World of Work,* A. I. Kraut and A. K. Korman, eds. (San Francisco, CA: Jossey-Bass, 1999), pp. 43–68.

15. R. Reiter-Palmon, M. Brown, D. Sandall, C. Buboltz, and T. Nimps, "Development of an O*NET Web-Based Job Analysis and Its Implementation in the U.S. Navy: Lessons Learned," *Human Resources Management Review* 16 (2006), pp. 294–309.

16. Towers Perrin has done a lot of research on this issue. See its website at www.towers.com; "Joint Compensation Study: Technical Occupational Analysis Questionnaire," Control Data Business Advisors, Minneapolis, 1985.

17. Juan I. Sanchez and Edward L. Levine, "Accuracy or Consequential Validity: Which Is the Better Standard for Job Analysis Data?" *Journal of Organizational Behavior* 21 (2000), pp. 809–818; W. C. Borman, D. Dorsey, and L. Ackerman, "Time-Spent Responses and Time Allocation Strategies: Relations with Sales Performance in a Stockbroker Sample," *Personnel Psychology* 45 (1992), pp. 763–777.

18. Richard Arvey, Emily M. Passino, and John W. Lounsbury, "Job Analysis Results as Influenced by Sex of Incumbent and Sex of Analyst," *Journal of Applied Psychology* 62(4), 1977, pp. 411–416.

19. V. L. Huber and S. R. Crandall, "Job Measurement: A Social-Cognitive Decision Perspective," in *Research in Personnel and Human Resources Management,* vol. 12, Gerald R. Ferris, ed., (Greenwich, CT: JAI Press, 1994), pp. 223–269.

20. David Levine, Dale Belman, Gary Charness, Erica Groshen, and K. C. O'Shaughnessy, *Changes in Careers and Wage Structures at Large American Employers* (Kalamazoo, MI: Upjohn Institute, 2003).

21. See commentary by Charlie Fay in "The Future of Salary Management," *Compensation and Benefits Review,* July/August 2001, p. 10.

22. Allen I. Kraut, Patricia R. Pedigo, D. Douglas McKenna, and Marvin D. Dunnette, "The Role of the Manager: What's Really Important in Different Management Jobs," *Academy of Management Executive* 19(4), 2005, pp. 122–129; Lee Dyer and Richard A. Shafer, "From HR Strategy to Organizational Effectiveness," in *Strategic Human Resources Management in the Twenty-First Century,* Suppl. 4, Patrick M. Wright, Lee D. Dyer, John W. Boudreau, and George T. Milkovich, eds. (Stamford, CT: JAI Press, 1999).

23. S. Steven Gray, "Coffee on the Double," *The Wall Street Journal,* April 12, 2005, pp. B1–B7; Kenneth H. Doerr, Tali Freed, Terence Mitchell, Chester Schriesheim, and Xiaohua (Tracy) Zhou, "Work Flow Policy and Within-Worker and Between-Workers Variability in Performance," *Journal of Applied Psychology,* October 2004, pp. 911–921.

24. Paul Taylor, Wen-Dong Li, Kan Shi, and Walter Borman, "The Transportability of Job Information Across Countries," *Personnel Psychology* 61 (2008), pp. 69–111.

25. Erich Dierdorff and Mark Wilson, "A Meta-Analysis of Job Analysis Reliability," *Journal of Applied Psychology,* August 2003, pp. 635–646. Dierdorff and Wilson did not report the mean correlation between two raters. We used the Spearman-Brown Prophecy formula to compute it based on their other reported results. The formula is available in any psychometrics book, including J. C. Nunnally, *Psychometric Theory,* 2nd ed. (New York: McGraw-Hill, 1978).

26. [ibid]; Erich C. Dierdorff and Frederick P. Morgeson, "Effects of Descriptor Specificity and Observability on Incumbent Work Analysis Ratings," *Personnel Psychology* 62 (2009), pp. 601–628.

27. Juan I. Sanchez and E. L. Levine, "The Impact of Raters' Cognition on Judgment Accuracy: An Extension to the Job Analysis Domain," *Journal of Business and Psychology* 9 (1994), pp. 47–57; Juan I. Sanchez and Edward L. Levine, "Accuracy or Consequential Validity: Which Is the Better Standard for Job Analysis Data?" *Journal of Organizational Behavior* 21 (2000), pp. 809–818; Frederick P. Morgeson and Michael A. Campion, "Accuracy in Job Analysis: Toward an Inference-Based Model," *Journal of Organizational Behavior* 21 (2000), pp. 819–827; Erich Dierdorff and Mark Wilson, "A Meta-Analysis of Job Analysis Reliability," *Journal of Applied Psychology,* August 2003, pp. 635–646.

28. Erich C. Dierdorff and Frederick Morgeson, "Consensus in Role Requirements: The Influence of Discrete Occupational Context on Role Expectations," *Journal of Applied Psychology* 92 (2007), pp. 1228–1241.

29. Richard Arvey, Emily M. Passino, and John W. Lounsbury, "Job Analysis Results as Influenced by Sex of Incumbent and Sex of Analyst," *Journal of Applied Psychology* 62(4), 1977, pp. 411–416; Sara L. Rynes, Caroline L. Weber, and George T. Milkovich, "Effects of Market Survey Rates, Job Evaluation, and Job Gender on Job Pay," *Journal of Applied Psychology* 74(1), 1989, pp. 114–123.

30. Filip Lievens and Juan I. Sanchez, "Can Training Improve the Quality of Inferences Made by Raters in Competency Modeling? A Quasi-Experiment," *Journal of Applied Psychology* 92 (2008), pp. 812–819.

31. Juan I. Sanchez and E. L. Levine, "The Impact of Raters' Cognition on Judgment Accuracy: An Extension to the Job Analysis Domain," *Journal of Business and Psychology* 9 (1994), pp. 47–57; Juan I. Sanchez and Edward L. Levine, "Accuracy or Consequential Validity: Which Is the Better Standard for Job Analysis Data?" *Journal of Organizational Behavior* 21 (2000), pp. 809–818; Frederick P. Morgeson and Michael A. Campion, "Accuracy in Job Analysis: Toward an Inference-Based Model," *Journal of Organizational Behavior* 21 (2000), pp. 819–827.

32. E. M. Ramras, "Discussion," in Proceedings of Division of Military Psychology Symposium: Collecting, Analyzing, and Reporting Information Describing Jobs and Occupations, 77th Annual Convention of the American Psychological Association, Lackland Air Force Base, TX, September 1969, pp. 75–76; Tony Simons and Quinetta Roberson, "Why Managers Should Care About Fairness: The Effects of Aggregate Justice Perceptions on Organizational Outcomes," *Journal of Applied Psychology,* June 2003, pp. 432–443.

33. WorldatWork, "Job Evaluation and Market-Pricing Practices," www.worldatwork.org/waw/adimLink?id=31378, 2009.

34. P. Bobko, P. L. Roth, and M. A. Buster, "A Systematic Approach for Assessing the Currency ('Up-To-Dateness') of Job-Analytic Information," *Public Personnel Management* 37 (2008), pp. 261–277.

35. Edward L. Levine, Ronald A. Ash, Hardy Hall, and Frank Sistrunk, "Evaluation of Job Analysis Methods by Experienced Job Analysts," *Academy of Management Journal* 26(2), 1983, pp. 339–348.

36. M. D. Dunnette, L. M. Hough, and R. L. Rosse, "Task and Job Taxonomies as a Basis for Identifying Labor Supply Sources and Evaluating Employment Qualifications," in *Affirmative Action Planning,* George T. Milkovich and Lee Dyer, eds. (New York: Human Resource Planning Society, 1979), pp. 37–51.

Job-Based Structures and Job Evaluation

Chapter Outline

Job-Based Structures: Job Evaluation

Defining Job Evaluation: Content, Value, and External Market Links
  Content and Value
  Linking Content with the External Market
  Technical and Process Dimensions

"How-to": Major Decisions
  Establish the Purpose
  Single versus Multiple Plans
  Choose among Job Evaluation Methods

Job Evaluation Methods
  Ranking
  Classification
  Point Method

Who Should Be Involved?
  The Design Process Matters

The Final Result: Structure

Balancing Chaos and Control

Your Turn: Job Evaluation at Whole Foods

As soon as my daughter turned 14, she absolutely refused to go shopping with me. At first I thought it was because I like to hum along with the mall music. But she says it is because I embarrass her when I interrogate assistant store managers about how they are paid—more precisely, how their pay compares to that of the stock clerks, managers, and regional managers in the same company. My daughter claims I do this everywhere I go. *Compensationitis,* she calls it. And I know it's contagious, because a colleague grills his seatmates on airplanes. He's learned the pay rates for American Airlines captains who pilot Boeing 737s versus those who pilot the A330 Airbus.

How does any organization go about valuing work? The next time you go to the supermarket, check out the different types of work there: store manager, produce manager, front-end manager, deli workers, butchers, stock clerks, checkout people, bakers—the list is long, and the work surprisingly diverse. If you managed a supermarket, how would you value work? But be careful—*compensationitis* is contagious, and it can embarrass your friends.

This chapter and the next one discuss techniques used to value work. Both chapters focus on "how-to"—the specific steps involved. Job evaluation techniques are discussed in this chapter. Person-based techniques, both skill-based and competency-based, are discussed in Chapter 6. All these techniques are used to design pay structures that will influence employee behavior and help the organization sustain its competitive advantage.

JOB-BASED STRUCTURES: JOB EVALUATION

Exhibit 5.1 is a variation on Exhibit 4.1 in the previous chapter. It orients us to the process used to build a job-based internal structure. Our job analysis and job descriptions (Chapter 4) collected and summarized work information. In this chapter, the focus is on what to value in the jobs, how to assess that value, and how to translate it into a **job-based structure.** Job evaluation is a process for determining **relative value.**

> **Job evaluation** is the process of systematically determining the relative worth of jobs to create a job structure for the organization. The evaluation is based on a combination of job content, skills required, value to the organization,

EXHIBIT 5.1   **Many Ways to Create Internal Structure**

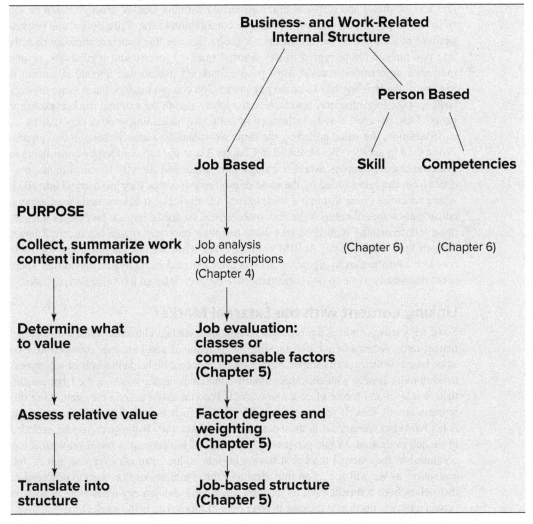

organizational culture, and the external market. This potential to blend organizational forces and external market forces is both a strength and a challenge of job evaluation.

DEFINING JOB EVALUATION: CONTENT, VALUE, AND EXTERNAL MARKET LINKS

Content and Value

We noted in Chapter 3 that **content** refers to what work is performed and how it gets done. Perspectives differ on whether job evaluation is based on **job content** or job value. Internal alignment based on content orders jobs on the basis of the skills required for the jobs and the duties and responsibilities associated with the jobs. A structure based on job value orders jobs on the basis of the relative contribution of the skills, duties, and responsibilities of each job to the organization's goals. But can this structure translate directly into pay rates, without regard to the external market, government regulations, or any individual negotiation process? Most people think not. Recall that internal alignment is just one of the building blocks of the pay model. Job content matters, but it is not the only basis for pay. Job value may also include the job's value in the external market (*exchange value*). Plus, pay rates may be influenced by collective bargaining or other negotiations.

In addition, the value added by the same work may be more (or less) in one organization than in another. We observed in Chapter 3 that the value added by consultants in PricewaterhouseCoopers, where earnings were generated directly by consultants, may differ from the value added by the same consultants now that they are merged into IBM, where revenues come through a wide variety of services. At PricewaterhouseCoopers, consultants were critical to organization objectives. At IBM, they are less so. As a result, those who remained with IBM may have had their base pay frozen but received larger bonuses until their base pay fit IBM's structure. So, while we talk about internal job value based on contributions to organization objectives, external market value may differ. There is not necessarily a one-to-one correspondence between internal job value and pay rates.

Linking Content with the External Market

Some see job evaluation as a process for linking job content and internal value with external market rates. Aspects of job content (e.g., skills required and customer contacts) take on value based on their relationship to market wages. Because higher skill levels or willingness to work more closely with customers usually commands higher wages in the labor market, then skill level and nature of customer contacts become useful criteria for establishing differences among jobs. If some aspect of job content, such as stressful working conditions, is not related to wages paid in the external labor market, then that aspect may be excluded in the job evaluation. In this perspective, the value of job content is based on what it can command in the external market; it has no intrinsic value.[1] But not everyone agrees. Job evaluation, as we will see, is an important tool for organizations that wish to differentiate themselves from competitors if, for example, their particular strategy relies more heavily on certain jobs or skills than is the case in other organizations (i.e., in the market).

EXHIBIT 5.2
Assumptions
Underlying
Different
Views of Job
Evaluation

Aspect of Job Evaluation	Assumption
Assessment of job content	Content has intrinsic value outside external market.
Assessment of relative value	Stakeholders can reach consensus on value.
External market link	Value cannot be determined without external market.
Measurement	Honing instruments will provide objective measures.
Negotiation	Negotiating brings rationality to a social/political process; establishes rules of the game and invites participation.

Technical and Process Dimensions

Researchers, too, have their own perspective on job evaluation. Some say that if job evaluation can be made sufficiently rigorous and systematic (objective, numerical, generalizable, documented, and reliable), then it can be judged according to technical standards. Just as with employment tests, the reliability, validity, and usefulness of job evaluation plans can be compared. (We cover these issues in Chapter 6.)

Those using job evaluation to make pay decisions sometimes see things differently. They see job evaluation also as a process that helps gain acceptance of pay differences among jobs—an administrative procedure through which the parties become involved and committed. Its statistical validity is not the only issue. Its usefulness also comes from providing a framework for give-and-take—an exchange of views. Employees, union representatives, and managers haggle over "the rules of the game" for determining the relative value of work. If all participants agree that skills, effort, responsibilities, and working conditions are important, then work is evaluated based on these factors. As in sports and games, we are more willing to accept the results if we accept the rules and believe they are applied fairly.[2] This interpretation is consistent with the history of job evaluation, which began as a way to bring peace and order to an often-chaotic and dispute-riven wage-setting process between labor and management.[3]

Exhibit 5.2 summarizes the assumptions that underlie the perspectives on job evaluation. Some say the content of jobs has intrinsic value that the evaluation will uncover; others say the only fair measure of job value is found in the external market. Some say contemporary job evaluation practices are just and fair; others say they are just fair. "Beneath the superficial orderliness of job evaluation techniques and findings, there is much that smacks of chaos."[4] We try to capture all these perspectives in this chapter.

"HOW-TO": MAJOR DECISIONS

Exhibit 5.3 shows job evaluation's role in determining the internal structure. You already know that the process begins with job analysis, in which the information on jobs is collected, and that job descriptions summarize the information and serve as input for the evaluation. The exhibit calls out some of the major decisions in the job evaluation process. They are (1) establish the purpose(s), (2) decide on single versus multiple plans, (3) choose among alternative methods, (4) obtain involvement of relevant stakeholders, and (5) evaluate the usefulness of the results.

EXHIBIT 5.3
Determining
an Internally
Aligned Job
Structure

> **Internal Alignment: Work Relationships within the**
> **Organization $\rightarrow$ Job Analysis $\rightarrow$ Job Description $\rightarrow$ Job Evaluation $\rightarrow$**
> **Job Structure**
>
> ---
>
> **Some Major Decisions in Job Evaluation**
>
> - Establish purpose of evaluation.
> - Decide whether to use single or multiple plans.
> - Choose among alternative approaches.
> - Obtain involvement of relevant stakeholders.
> - Evaluate plan's usefulness.

Establish the Purpose

Job evaluation is part of the process for establishing an internally aligned pay structure. Recall from Chapter 2 that a structure is aligned if it supports the organization strategy, fits the work flow, is fair to employees, and motivates their behavior toward organization objectives.

- *Supports organization strategy:* Job evaluation aligns with the organization's strategy by including what it is about work that adds value—that contributes to pursuing the organization's strategy and achieving its objectives. Job evaluation helps answer, How does this job add value?[5]
- *Supports work flow:* Job evaluation supports work flow in two ways. It integrates each job's pay with its relative contributions to the organization, and it helps set pay for new, unique, or changing jobs.
- *Is fair to employees:* Job evaluation can reduce disputes and grievances over pay differences among jobs by establishing a workable, agreed-upon structure that reduces the role of chance, favoritism, and bias in setting pay.
- *Motivates behavior toward organization objectives:* Job evaluation calls out to employees what it is about their work that the organization values, what supports the organization's strategy and its success. It can also help employees adapt to organization changes by improving their understanding of what is valued in their new assignments and why that value may have changed. Thus, job evaluation helps create the network of rewards (promotions, challenging work) that motivates employees.

If the purpose of the evaluation is not called out, it becomes too easy to get lost in complex procedures, negotiations, and bureaucracy. The job evaluation process becomes the end in itself instead of a way to achieve an objective. Establishing its purpose can help ensure that the evaluation actually is a useful systematic process.

Single versus Multiple Plans

Rarely do employers evaluate all jobs in the organization at one time. More typically, a related group of jobs, for example, manufacturing, technical, or administrative, will be the focus. As we saw in Chapter 3, for example, Northrup Grumman has four different structures. Many employers design different evaluation plans for different types of work. They do so because they believe that the work content is too diverse to be usefully evaluated by one plan. For example, production jobs may vary in terms of manipulative skills, knowledge of statistical quality control, and working conditions. But these tasks and skills may not be relevant to engineering and finance jobs. Rather, the nature of the contacts with customers may be relevant. Consequently, a single, universal plan may not be acceptable to employees or useful to managers if the work covered is highly diverse. Even so, there are some plans that have been successfully applied across a wide breadth and depth of work. The most prominent examples include the Hay plan (more on this later) and the **Position Analysis Questionnaire** (discussed in Chapter 4).

Benchmark Jobs—A Sample

To be sure that all relevant aspects of work are included in the evaluation, an organization may start with a sample of **benchmark (key) jobs.** In Exhibit 5.4, benchmark jobs would be identified for as many of the levels in the structure and groups of related jobs (administrative, manufacturing, technical) as possible. The heavy shading in the exhibit marks the benchmark jobs.

A benchmark job has the following characteristics:

- Its contents are well known and relatively stable over time.
- The job is common across a number of different employers. It is not unique to a particular employer.
- A reasonable proportion of the work force is employed in this job.

A representative sample of benchmark jobs will include the entire domain of work being evaluated—administrative, manufacturing, technical, and so on—and capture the diversity of the work within that domain.

EXHIBIT 5.4   **Benchmark Jobs**

Managerial Group	Technical Group	Manufacturing Group	Administrative Group
		Assembler I Inspector I	
Vice Presidents	Head/Chief Scientist	Packer	Administrative Assistant
Division General Managers	Senior Associate Scientist	Material Handler Inspector II	Principal Administrative Secretary
Managers	Associate Scientist	Assembler II	Administrative Secretary
Project Leaders	Scientist	Drill Press Operator Rough Grinder	Word Processor
Supervisors	Technician	Machinist I Coremaker	Clerk/Messenger

Note: More heavily shaded jobs have been selected as benchmarks.

Diversity in the work can be thought of in terms of depth (vertically) and breadth (horizontally). The *depth of work* in most organizations probably ranges from strategic leadership jobs (CEOs, general directors) to the filing and mail distribution tasks in entry-level office jobs. Horizontally, the *breadth of work* depends on the nature of business. Relatively similar work can be found in specialty consulting firms (e.g., compensation or executive search firms). The breadth of work performed in some multinational conglomerates such as General Electric mirrors the occupations in the entire nation. GE includes jobs in businesses spanning financial services, entertainment (NBC), aircraft engines, medical instruments, power systems, and home appliances.

Typically, a job evaluation plan is developed using benchmark jobs, and then the plan is applied to the remaining nonbenchmark jobs. Selecting benchmark jobs from each level ensures coverage of the entire work domain, thus helping to ensure the accuracy of the decisions based on the job evaluation.

The number of job evaluation plans used hinges on how detailed an evaluation is required to make pay decisions and how much it will cost. There is no ready answer to the question of "one plan versus many." Current practice (not always the best answer for the future, since practice is based on the past) is to use separate plans for major domains of work: top-executive/leadership jobs, managerial/professional jobs, operational/technical jobs, and office/administrative jobs. Open the door on some organizations and you will find additional plans for sales, legal, engineers/scientists, and skilled trades.

The costs associated with all these plans (including time) give impetus to the push to simplify job structures (reduce titles and levels). Some employers, notably Hewlett-Packard, simplify by using a single plan with a core set of common factors for all jobs and additional factors specific to particular occupational or functional areas (finance, manufacturing, software and systems, sales).

Choose among Job Evaluation Methods

Ranking, classification, and **point method** are the most common job evaluation methods, though uncounted variations exist. Research over 40 years consistently finds that different job evaluation plans generate different pay structures. So the method you choose matters.

Exhibit 5.5 compares the methods. They all begin by assuming that a useful job analysis has been translated into job description methods.

EXHIBIT 5.5
Comparison of
Job Evaluation
Methods

	Advantage	Disadvantage
Ranking	Fast, simple, easy to explain.	Cumbersome as number of jobs increases. Basis for comparisons is not called out.
Classification	Can group a wide range of work together in one system.	Descriptions may leave too much room for manipulation.
Point	Compensable factors call out basis for comparisons. Compensable factors communicate what is valued.	Can become bureaucratic and rule-bound.

JOB EVALUATION METHODS

A survey of roughly 1,000 members of WorldatWork, the association for compensation professionals, asked the primary job evaluation method used in their organizations. As Exhibit 5.6 indicates, the most common response was—"Well, not really any job evaluation method." Rather, **market pricing** was overwhelmingly chosen (67% to 73%, depending on the job level) as the primary method of job evaluation. What is market pricing? We will return to this topic in more detail later, especially in Chapter 8. For now, think of market pricing as directly matching as many of your own organization's jobs as possible to jobs described in the external pay surveys you use. To the extent that such matches can be made, the pay rate for your job will be based on the survey data. Internal equity is greatly de-emphasized (as is the organization's strategy—more on this in Chapter 8).

Note that Exhibit 5.6 does indicate that somewhere between 1 in 3 and 1 in 4 organizations continue to use traditional job evaluation approaches as their *primary* methods. Further, it is likely that job evaluation is also used widely even in organizations that rely primarily on market pricing because it is usually not possible to directly match all jobs to market survey jobs. Thus, job evaluation is still needed and we now discuss three job evaluation methods, with most of our attention given to point or point factor approaches.

Ranking

Ranking simply orders the job descriptions from highest to lowest based on a global definition of relative value or contribution to the organization's success. Ranking is simple, fast, and easy to understand and explain to employees; it is also the least expensive method, at least initially. However, it can create problems that require difficult and potentially expensive solutions because it doesn't tell employees and managers what it is about their jobs that is important.

Two ways of ranking are common: **alternation ranking** and **paired comparison.** *Alternation ranking* orders job descriptions alternately at each extreme. Agreement is reached among evaluators on which jobs are the most and least valuable (i.e., which is a 10, which is a 1), then the next most and least valued (i.e., which is a 9, which is a 2), and so on, until all the jobs have been ordered. The *paired comparison* method uses a

EXHIBIT 5.6
Primary
Method of Job
Evaluation

Source: WorldatWork,
"Job Evaluation
and Market-Pricing
Practices," December
2013.

	What is the *primary* method of job evaluation used by your organization?		
	Market Pricing	**Point Factor**	**All Other**
Senior Management	73%	16%	13%
Middle Management	69%	18%	13%
Professional	70%	18%	12%
Sales	70%	16%	14%
Administrative	67%	18%	15%
Production	67%	15%	18%

Note: "All Other" includes ranking, paired-comparison, and job component methods. Number of respondents ranged from 947 to 1,120 organizations.

EXHIBIT 5.7
Paired
Comparison
Ranking

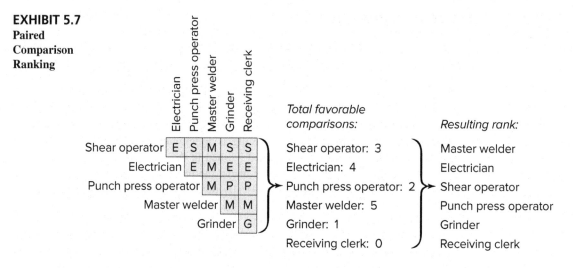

matrix to compare all possible pairs of jobs. Exhibit 5.7 shows that the higher-ranked job is entered in the cell of the matrix. When all comparisons have been completed, the job most frequently judged "more valuable" becomes the highest-ranked job, and so on.

Alternation-ranking and paired-comparison methods may be more reliable (produce similar results consistently) than simple ranking. Nevertheless, ranking has drawbacks. The criteria on which the jobs are ranked are usually so poorly defined, if they are specified at all, that the evaluations become subjective opinions that are impossible to justify in strategic and work-related terms. Further, evaluators using this method must be knowledgeable about every single job under study. The numbers alone turn what should be a simple task into a formidable one—50 jobs require 1,225 comparisons—and as organizations change, it is difficult to remain knowledgeable about all jobs. Some organizations try to overcome this difficulty by ranking jobs within single departments and merging the results. However, even though the ranking appears simple, fast, and inexpensive, in the long run the results are difficult to defend and costly solutions may be required to overcome the problems created.

Classification

Picture a bookcase with many shelves. Each shelf is labeled with a paragraph describing the kinds of books on that shelf and, perhaps, one or two representative titles. This same approach describes the **classification method of job evaluation.** A series of classes covers the range of jobs. Class descriptions are the labels. A job description is compared to the class descriptions to decide which class is the best fit for that job. Each class is described in such a way that the "label" captures sufficient work detail yet is general enough to cause little difficulty in slotting a job description onto its appropriate "shelf" or class. The classes may be described further by including titles of benchmark jobs that fall into each class.

Determining the number of classes and writing class descriptions to define the boundaries between each class (e.g., how many bookshelves and what distinguishes each from the other—fiction, nonfiction, mysteries, biographies, etc.) are something of an art form. One way to begin is to find the natural breaks or changes in the work content. At Lockheed, the engineering work discussed in previous chapters has obvious natural breaks between engineers (individual contributors) and lead engineers (responsible for overall projects). But how many classes within each of these make sense? Exhibit 5.8 shows classifications used by Clark Consulting to conduct salary surveys of engineering salaries at many different employers. Managerial work includes three classes, while there are five classes of individual contributors. Information to guide the writing of class descriptions can come from managers, job incumbents, job descriptions, and career progression considerations.

Writing class descriptions can be troublesome when jobs from several job families are covered by a single plan. Although greater specificity of the class definition improves the reliability of evaluation, it also limits the variety of jobs that can easily be classified. For example, class definitions written with sales jobs in mind may make it difficult to slot office or administrative jobs and vice versa. One issue with the job classification method is that trying to include a diverse set of jobs in one class can result in vagueness of job descriptions, leaving a lot of room for "judgment."[6] Including titles of benchmark jobs for each class can help make the descriptions more concrete.

In practice, with a classification method, the job descriptions not only are compared to the class descriptions and benchmark jobs but also can be compared to each other to be sure that jobs within each class are more similar to each other than to jobs in adjacent classes.

The end result is a job structure made up of a series of classes with a number of jobs in each. All these comparisons are used to ensure that this structure is based on the organization strategy and work flow, is fair, and focuses behaviors on desired results. The jobs within each class are considered to be equal (similar) work and will be paid equally. Jobs in different classes should be dissimilar and may have different pay rates.

The Wall Street Journal once compiled a list of the 10 most unusual U.S. government jobs. It included Smokey Bear's manager, a Supreme Court seamstress (job responsibility: keeping the Supremes in stitches), a gold stacker, condom tester, currency reconstructor, and Air Force art curator. The Office of Personnel Management publishes The Classifiers Handbook (45 pages) and Introduction to the Position Classification Standards (73 pages), which together provide instructions on how to classify jobs into the General Schedule.[7] Visit the site to discover the level of detail in the government's approach. Contrast that with "Big Blue" (IBM), which puts its complete classification plan on a single page.

Point Method

Point methods have three common characteristics: (1) compensable factors, with (2) factor degrees numerically scaled, and (3) weights reflecting the relative importance of each factor.[8] Each job's relative value, and hence its location in the pay structure, is determined by the total points assigned to it.

Point plans are the most commonly used job evaluation approach in the United States and Europe. They represent a significant change from ranking and classification methods in that they make explicit the criteria for evaluating jobs: *compensable factors.*[9]

EXHIBIT 5.8 Classifications for Engineering Work Used by Clark Consulting

Engineer 1	Engineer 2	Engineer 3	Engineer 4	Engineer 5	Eng Mgr 1	Eng Mgr 2	Eng Mgr 3
Participates in development, testing, and documentation of software programs. Performs design and analysis tasks as a project team member. Typical minimum requirements are a bachelor's degree in a scientific or technical field or the equivalent and up to two years of experience.	Develops, tests, and documents software programs of a more difficult nature. Assists in the development of assignments and schedules. Typical minimum requirements are a bachelor's degree in a scientific or technical field and two years to four years of experience or a master's degree and up to two years of experience.	Develops project plans, functional specifications, and schedules. Designs and performs analysis on complex programs and systems. Assists in determining product needs and enhancements. Typical minimum requirements are a bachelor's degree in engineering, computer science, or related technical field and four to six years of experience or a master's degree and two to four years of experience.	Acts as project engineer for complex programs in design, development, and analysis. Proposes new ideas and products and guides their implementation. Provides technical direction in area of specialty on major products. Typical minimum requirements are a bachelor's degree in engineering, computer science, or a related technical field and six or more years of experience or a master's degree and four to six years of experience.	Provides technical direction and advice to management in long-range planning for new areas of technological research. Designs, researches, and develops new systems while providing guidance to support staff. Typical minimum requirements are a bachelor's degree in engineering, computer science, or a related technical field and ten or more years of experience or a master's degree and six years or more of experience.	Supervises the design and development of software products or systems and related schedules and costs. Participates in developing management policies for software group. Typically manages up to 10 employees performing similar tasks. First level of management with human resource responsibilities.	Establishes work environment for development or implementation of complete products and programs. Develops long-range plans, schedules, and cost objectives. Typically manages 10 to 25 employees, including first-level managers. (May be from multiple disciplines.)	Develops long-range strategy for a product family including positioning, marketing, and pricing. Manages engineering product group to ensure timely delivery of high-quality products. Typically manages over 25 employees from multiple disciplines.

Compensable factors are based on the strategic direction of the business and how the work contributes to these objectives and strategy. The factors are scaled to reflect the degree to which they are present in each job and weighted to reflect their overall importance to the organization. Points are then attached to each **factor weight.** The total points for each job determine its position in the job structure.

There are eight steps in the design of a point plan.

1. Conduct job analysis.
2. Determine compensable factors.
3. Scale the factors.
4. Weight the factors according to importance.
5. Select criterion pay structure.
6. Communicate the plan and train users.
7. Apply to nonbenchmark jobs.
8. Develop online software support.

1. Conduct Job Analysis

Just as with ranking and classification, point plans begin with job analysis. Typically a representative sample of jobs, that is, benchmark jobs, is drawn for analysis. The content of these jobs is the basis for defining, **scaling,** and weighting the compensable factors.

2. Determine Compensable Factors

Compensable factors play a pivotal role in the point plan. These factors reflect how work adds value to the organization. They flow from the work itself and the strategic direction of the business.

> **Compensable factors** are those characteristics in the work that the organization values, that help it pursue its strategy and achieve its objectives.

To select compensable factors, an organization asks itself, What is it about the work that adds value? Organizations can often begin with existing compensable factor frameworks, which we discuss below. Exhibit 5.9 provides and example of a compensable factor called job controls and complexity. Organizations can then adapt existing compensable factors and/or add new ones that are more specific to their strategies. For example, one company decided to include decision making, which is somewhat similar to job controls and complexity in Exhibit 5.9, as a compensable factor. The definition of *decision making* is three-dimensional: (1) the risk and complexity (hence the availability of guidelines to assist in making the decisions), (2) the impact of the decisions, and (3) the time that must pass before the impact is evident.

In effect, this firm determined that its competitive advantage depends on decisions employees make in their work. And the relative value of the decisions depends

EXHIBIT 5.9 Compensable Factor Example: Job Controls and Complexity (3 of the 8 levels)

Factor Definition: The amount and type of direction received, the complexity of work, and the nature of the work within a job.

Level 1

• Employee does not deviate from detailed directions given by the supervisor and guides; e.g., standard operating procedures (SOPs), handbooks, and reference manuals.

AND

• Tasks are clear-cut and related. There is little choice in deciding what to do or how to do it. The level of complexity is low.

AND

• Work relieves others in the unit/office of simple, repetitive tasks. The work has minimal impact outside of the immediate organizational unit.

Level 4

• Employee either (a) carries out work with minimal supervision (i.e., the supervisor sets only goals, priorities, and deadlines; and the employee uses guidelines that cover most situations), **or** (b) the employee follows the supervisor's directions on methods and desired results but modifies methods to resolve unforeseen situations and problems.

AND

• Processes, procedures, or software very from one assignment to the next, although assignments are related in function and objective. Based on the assignment, the employee must use diverse but conventional methods, techniques, or approaches.

AND

• Work product or service affects the accuracy, reliability, or acceptability of further processes or services.

Level 8

• Employee works (a) with only administrative and policy direction **and** (b) must make decisions based on broadly stated guidelines that lack specificity or proven validity, e.g., general policy statements, basic laws, or scientific theory. The employee defines objectives, plans work, and develops new method or hypotheses that have led to recognition as a technical authority.

AND

• Work requires many different processes and methods applied to an established administrative or professional field. Problems are typically the result of unusual circumstances, variations in approach, and incomplete or conflicting data. The employee must interpret data and refine methods to complete assignments.

AND

• Work affects the work of other experts, influences important professional or administrative activities of the establishment, or impacts the well being of many groups of people.

Source: U.S. Bureau of Labor Statistics. May 2013 (Revised). National Compensation Survey: Guide for Evaluating Your Firm's Jobs and Pay. Note: The Job Controls and Complexity factor has 8 levels, 3 of which are shown here.

on their risk, their complexity, and their impact on the company. Hence, this firm is signaling to all employees that jobs will be valued based on the nature of the decisions required by employees in those jobs. Jobs that require riskier decisions with greater impact have a higher relative worth than jobs that require fewer decisions with less consequence.

To be useful, compensable factors should be

- Based on the strategy and values of the organization.
- Based on the work performed.
- Acceptable to the stakeholders affected by the resulting pay structure.

Based on the Strategy and Values of the Organization

The leadership of any organization is the best source of information on where the business should be going and how it is going to get there. Clearly, the leaders' input into factor selection is crucial. If the business strategy involves providing innovative, high-quality products and services designed in collaboration with customers and suppliers, then jobs with greater responsibilities for product innovation and customer contacts should be valued higher. Or if the business strategy is more Walmart-like, "providing goods and services to delight customers at the lowest cost and greatest convenience possible," then compensable factors might include impact on **cost containment,** customer relations, and so on.

Compensable factors reinforce the organization's culture and values as well as its business direction and the nature of the work. If the direction changes, then the compensable factors may also change. For example, strategic plans at many companies call for increased globalization. Procter & Gamble and 3M include a "multinational responsibilities" factor in their managerial job evaluation plan. In this example, multinational responsibilities are defined in terms of the type of responsibility, (in developing policies and strategies, whether the role is assisting, leading, or having full responsibility, including approval authority) the percent of time devoted to international issues, and the number of countries covered. Do you suppose that managers at 3M or P&G got raises when Czechoslovakia, Yugoslavia, and the Soviet Union rearranged themselves into a greater number of smaller, independent countries?

Factors may also be eliminated if they no longer support the business strategy. The railway company Burlington Northern revised its job evaluation plan to omit the factor "number of subordinates supervised." It decided that a factor that values increases to staff runs counter to the organization's objective of reducing bureaucracy and increasing efficiency. Major shifts in the business strategy are not daily occurrences, but when they do occur, compensable factors should be reexamined to ensure they are consistent with the new directions.[10]

Based on the Work Itself

Employees and supervisors are experts in the work actually done in any organization. Hence, it is important to seek their answers to what should be valued in the work itself. Some form of documentation (i.e., job descriptions, job analysis, employee and/or supervisory focus groups) must support the choice of factors. Work-related documentation helps gain acceptance by employees and managers, is easier to understand, and can withstand a variety of challenges to the pay structure. For example, managers may argue that the salaries of their employees are too low in comparison to those of other employees or that the salary offered a job candidate is too low. Union leaders may wonder why one job is paid differently from another. Allegations of **pay discrimination** may be raised. Employees, line managers, union leaders, and compensation managers must understand and be able to explain why work is paid differently or the same. Differences in factors that are obviously based on the work itself provide that rationale or even diminish the likelihood of the challenges arising.

Reliable and Valid

See the Chapter 4 and Chapter 6 discussions of reliability and validity.

Acceptable to the Stakeholders

Acceptance of the compensable factors used to slot jobs into the pay structure may depend, at least in part, on tradition. For example, people who work in hospitals, nursing homes, and child care centers make the point that responsibility for people is used less often as a compensable factor, and valued lower, than responsibility for property.[11] This omission may be a carryover from the days when nursing and child care service were provided by family members, usually women, without reimbursement. People now doing these jobs for pay say that properly valuing a factor for people responsibility would raise their wages. So the question is, acceptable to whom? The answer ought to be the stakeholders.

Using Existing Standardized Plans or Adapting Factors from Existing Plans

The use of existing, standardized plans (e.g., the HayGroup plan described below) offers the advantage of being able to compare the relative scope, content, and internal value of jobs in the organization to similar jobs in other organizations, which can be very helpful in deciding on what to pay jobs relative to similar jobs in other organizations. However, as noted, to the degree that job value and pay are to be uniquely tailored to the organization's strategy and values, the job evaluation system will also need to be tailored. Although a wide variety of factors are used in standard existing plans, the factors tend to fall into four generic groups: skills required, effort required, responsibility, and working conditions. These four were used more than 60 years ago in the **National Electrical Manufacturers Association (NEMA) plan** and are also included in the Equal Pay Act (1963) to define equal work. Many of these early point plans, such as those of the **National Metal Trades Association (NMTA)** and NEMA, and the Steel Plan, were developed for manufacturing and/or office jobs. Since then, point plans have also been applied to managerial and professional jobs. The **National Compensation Survey (NCS),** available from the U.S. Bureau of Labor Statistics (BLS), uses as compensable factors knowledge, job controls/complexity, contacts, and physical environment, and can be applied to a wide range of jobs. The NCS can be used by employers to match their jobs to jobs in the (free and publicly available) BLS pay surveys.[12]

The *Hay Group Guide Chart—Profile Method*[SM], used by more than 8,000 employers worldwide (including 150 of the 500 largest U.S. corporations), is perhaps the most widely used. This methodology considers work to be a process in which knowledge/skill/ability is applied to various issues and challenges in order to create an output that is of value to the organization (see Exhibit 5.10).

The three Hay factors—know-how, problem solving and accountability—use Guide Charts to quantify the requirement for each factor in more detail. Exhibit 5.11 summarizes the basic definitions of the three Hay factors. A fourth factor, working conditions, can be applied where appropriate or required by law.

In Exhibit 5.12, the Hay factor Know-How is considered in terms of the depth and breadth of specialized knowledge (A to H scale) required, the amount of "managerial" capability to plan/organize/coordinate/integrate resources to achieve results (T to V scale), and the degree of communicating and influencing skills required to achieve results through interacting with others (1 to 3 scale). The cell that corresponds to the right level of all three dimensions for the job being evaluated is located on the Guide Chart and this gives the points allocated for this factor. In the exhibit, the Factory Manager gets 400 points for Know-How. A similar process utilizes Guide Charts for Problem Solving and Accountability to determine the points for those factors which leads to a total point score for the job.

How Many Factors?

A remaining issue to consider is how many factors should be included in the plan. Some factors may have overlapping definitions or may fail to account for anything unique in the criterion chosen. In fact, the NEMA plan explicitly states that the

EXHIBIT 5.10

Hay Group, Role of Compensable Factors of Accountability, Problem Solving, and Know-How

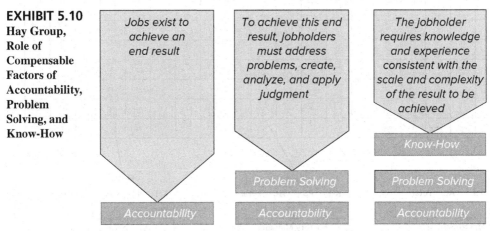

The Hay Group method uses three universal compensable elements to measure the relative size of jobs

EXHIBIT 5.11
Hay Group,
Compensable
Factors
Definitions

Know-how: the sum total of all knowledge and skill, however acquired, required to do the job competently.
Know-How typically has three dimensions:

- Practical, technical, and specialized knowledge & skill (includes depth and breadth)
- Planning, organizing, coordinating, and integrating knowledge
- Communicating and influencing skills

Problem solving: measure the nature and complexity of the issues and challenges that the job has to face.
Problem Solving typically has two dimensions:

- Environment—the availability of guidance for the thinking in terms of policies, procedures, guidelines and instructions, along with the degree of definition around the problems
- Challenge—the inherent complexity of the issues and the thought process required

Accountability: the measured impact that the job is designed to have on the success of the enterprise.
Accountability typically has two dimensions:

- Freedom to Act—the delegated authority vested in the job to act, approve or make decisions
- Impact—the magnitude and nature of the impact that the job has on the organization's ability to achieve its mandate

EXHIBIT 5.12 **Hay Group, Compensable Factors Scoring**

			T. Task 1	T. Task 2	T. Task 3	I. Minimal 1	I. Minimal 2	I. Minimal 3	II. Related 1	II. Related 2	II. Related 3	III. Diverse 1	III. Diverse 2	III. Diverse 3	IV. Broad 1	IV. Broad 2	IV. Broad 3	V. Total 1	V. Total 2	V. Total 3
	A Primary		38	43	50	50	57	66	66	76	87	87	100	115	115	132	152	152	175	200
			43	50	57	57	66	76	76	87	100	100	115	132	132	152	175	175	200	230
			50	57	66	66	76	87	87	100	115	115	132	152	152	175	200	200	230	264
	B Elementary Vocational		50	57	66	66	76	87	87	100	115	115	132	152	152	175	200	200	200	264
			57	66	76	76	87	100	100	115	132	132	152	175	175	200	230	230	264	304
			66	76	87	87	100	115	115	132	152	152	175	200	200	230	264	264	304	350
	C Vocational		66	76	87	87	100	115	115	132	152	152	175	200	200	230	264	264	304	350
			76	87	100	100	115	132	132	152	175	175	200	230	230	264	304	304	350	400
			87	100	115	115	132	152	152	175	200	200	230	264	264	304	350	350	400	460
	D Advanced Vocational		87	100	115	115	132	152	152	175	200	200	230	264	264	304	350	350	400	460
			100	115	132	132	152	175	175	200	230	230	264	304	304	350	400	400	460	528
			115	132	152	152	175	200	200	230	264	264	304	350	350	400	460	460	528	608
	E Professional/Basic Specialized		115	132	152	152	175	200	200	230	264	264	304	350	350	400	460	460	528	608
			132	152	175	175	200	230	230	264	304	304	350	400	400	460	528	528	608	700
			152	175	200	200	230	264	264	304	350	350	400	460	460	528	608	608	700	800
	F Seasoned Professional		152	175	200	200	230	264	264	304	350	350	400	460	460	528	608	608	700	800
			175	200	230	230	264	304	304	350	400	400	460	528	528	608	700	700	800	920
			200	230	264	264	304	350	350	400	460	460	528	608	608	700	800	800	920	1056
	G Specialized Mastery		200	230	264	264	304	350	350	400	460	460	528	608	608	700	800	800	920	1056
			230	264	304	304	350	400	400	460	528	528	608	700	700	800	920	920	1056	1216
			264	304	350	350	400	460	460	528	608	608	700	800	800	920	1056	1056	1216	1400

(Left axis label: Professional /Technical Skills & Knowledge. Top spanning header: Planning, Organizing, Coordinating, and Integrating.)

DI1

KH	PS	AC	Total
132			

Electrician

FII3

KH	PS	AC	Total
400			

Factory Manager

G-IV3

KH	PS	AC	Total
800			

VP Operations

▮ = unlikely combination

compensable factor experience should be correlated with education. One writer calls this the "illusion of validity"—we want to believe that the factors are capturing divergent aspects of the job and that both are important.[13] It has long been recognized that factors overlap or are highly correlated, raising the concern about double counting the value of a factor. Indeed, in the Hay plan, problem solving is calculated as a percentage of Know-How. So, by definition, one builds on the foundation established by the other. It is a central principle of the Hay plan that the factors are not independent—the reason that a know-how is required is because of the problems that have to be solved in order to achieve the results that are required (accountability)—and that the relative proportions of the factors that come together in a job provide important insights in to the job. This notion of relative proportions is the *Profile* concept in the *Hay Group Guide Chart—Profile Method.*

Another challenge is called "small numbers." If even one job in our benchmark sample has a certain characteristic, we tend to use that factor for the entire work domain. Unpleasant working conditions are a common example. If even one job is performed in unpleasant working conditions, it is tempting to make those conditions a compensable factor and apply it to all jobs. Once a factor is part of the system, other workers are likely to say their jobs have it, too. For example, office staff may feel that ringing telephones or leaky toner cartridges constitute stressful or hazardous conditions.

In one plan, a senior manager refused to accept a job evaluation plan unless the factor working conditions was included. The plan's designer, a recent college graduate, showed through statistical analysis that working conditions did not vary enough among 90 percent of the jobs to have a meaningful effect on the resulting pay structure. Nevertheless, the manager pointed out that the recent grad had never worked in the plant's foundry, where working conditions were extremely meaningful. In order to get the plan accepted by the foundry workers, the working-conditions factor was included.

This situation is not unusual. In one study, a 21-factor plan produced the same rank order of jobs that could be generated using only 7 of the factors. Further, the jobs could be correctly slotted into pay classes using only three factors. Yet the company decided to keep the 21-factor plan because it was "accepted and doing the job." Research as far back as the 1940s demonstrates that the skills dimension explains 90 percent or more of the variance in job evaluation results; three factors generally account for 98 to 99 percent of the variance.[14] Nevertheless, as we demonstrate in Chapter 6, even under such circumstances where reliability is high, the job evaluation points assigned to at least some jobs can vary depending on the choice of raters or factors.

3. Scale the Factors

Once the factors are determined, scales reflecting the different degrees within each factor are constructed. Each degree may also be anchored by the typical skills, tasks, and behaviors taken from the benchmark jobs that illustrate each factor degree. Exhibit 5.13 shows NMTA's scaling for the factor of knowledge.

Most **factor scales** consist of four to eight degrees. In practice, many evaluators use extra, undefined degrees such as plus and minus around a scale number. So what starts

EXHIBIT 5.13
Factor
Scaling—
National
Metal Trades
Association

1. Knowledge
This factor measures the knowledge or equivalent training required to perform the position duties.

1st Degree

Use of reading and writing, adding and subtracting of whole numbers; following of instructions; use of fixed gauges, direct reading instruments, and similar devices; where interpretation is not required.

2nd Degree

Use of addition, subtraction, multiplication, and division of numbers including decimals and fractions; simple use of formulas, charts, tables, drawings, specifications, schedules, wiring diagrams; use of adjustable measuring instruments; checking of reports, forms, records, and comparable data; where interpretation is required.

3rd Degree

Use of mathematics together with the use of complicated drawings, specifications, charts, tables; various types of precision measuring instruments. Equivalent to 1 to 3 years' applied trades training in a particular or specialized occupation.

4th Degree

Use of advanced trades mathematics, together with the use of complicated drawings, specifications, charts, tables, handbook formulas; all varieties of precision measuring instruments. Equivalent to complete accredited apprenticeship in a recognized trade, craft, or occupation; or equivalent to a 2-year technical college education.

5th Degree

Use of higher mathematics involved in the application of engineering principles and the performance of related practical operations, together with a comprehensive knowledge of the theories and practices of mechanical, electrical, chemical, civil, or like engineering field. Equivalent to completing four years of technical college or university education.

Source: HayGroup, personal communication, August 10, 2012. Copyright © 2004 *Hay Acquisition Company I, Inc.* All rights reserved.

as a 5-degree scale—1, 2, 3, 4, 5—ends up as a 15-degree scale, with −1, 1, 1+, −2, 2, 2+, and so on. The reason for adding plus/minus is that users of the plan believe more degrees are required to adequately differentiate among jobs. If we are trying to design 15 levels into the job structure but the factors use only three or five degrees, such users may be right.[15] However, all too often inserting pluses and minuses gives the illusion of accuracy of measurement that is simply not the case.

Another major issue in determining degrees is whether to make each degree equidistant from the adjacent degrees (**interval scaling**). For example, the difference between the first and second degrees in Exhibit 5.13 should approximate the difference between the fourth and fifth degrees, since the differences in points will be the same. In contrast, the intervals in the U.S. government plan range from 150 to 200 points.

The following criteria for scaling factors have been suggested: (1) Ensure that the number of degrees is necessary to distinguish among jobs, (2) use understandable terminology, (3) anchor degree definitions with benchmark-job titles and/or work behaviors, and (4) make it apparent how the degree applies to the job.

4. Weight the Factors According to Importance

Once the degrees have been assigned, the factor weights can be determined. Factor weights reflect the relative importance of each factor to the overall value of the job. Different weights reflect differences in importance attached to each factor by the employer. For example, the National Electrical Manufacturers Association plan weights education at 17.5 percent; another employer's association weights it at 10.6 percent; a consultant's plan recommends 15.0 percent; and a trade association weights education at 10.1 percent.

Weights are often determined through an advisory committee that allocates 100 percent of the value among the factors.[16] In the illustration in Exhibit 5.14, a committee allocated 40 percent of the value to skill, 30 percent to effort, 20 percent to responsibility, and 10 percent to working conditions. Each factor has two subfactors, with five degrees each. In the example for the bookstore manager, the subfactor mental skill gets half the 40 percent given to skill and the subfactor experience gets the other half: 4 degrees of mental skill times 20 equals 80 points, and 3 degrees of experience times 20 equals another 60 points.[17]

5. Select Criterion Pay Structure

Contemporary job evaluation often supplements committee judgment for determining weights with statistical analysis.[18] The committee members recommend the *criterion pay structure,* that is, a pay structure they wish to duplicate with the point

EXHIBIT 5.14   Job Evaluation Form

Job **bookstore manager**		
Check one: ☒ Administrative		
☐ Technical		

Compensable Factors	Degree × Weight = Total		
Skill: (40%)	1 2 3 4 5		
Mental	X (degree 4)	20%	80
Experience	X (degree 2)	20%	60
Effort: (30%)			
Physical	X (degree 1)	15%	30
Mental	X (degree 4)	15%	60
Responsibility: (20%)			
Effect of Error	X (degree 4)	10%	40
Inventiveness/ Innovation	X (degree 2)	10%	30
Working Conditions: (10%)			
Environment	X (degree 1)	5%	5
Hazards	X (degree 1)	5%	5
			310

plan. The criterion structure may be the current rates paid for benchmark jobs, market rates for benchmark jobs, rates for jobs held predominantly by males (in an attempt to eliminate gender bias), or union-negotiated rates.[19] Once a criterion structure is agreed on, statistical modeling techniques are used to determine the weight for each factor and the factor scales that will reproduce, as closely as possible, the chosen structure. The statistical approach is often labeled **policy capturing** to differentiate it from the **committee a priori judgment** approach. Not only do the weights reflect the relative importance of each factor, but research clearly demonstrates that the weights influence the resulting pay structure.[20] Thus, selecting the appropriate pay rates to use as the criteria is critical. The job evaluation and its results are based on it.[21]

Perhaps the clearest illustration can be found in municipalities. Rather than using market rates for firefighters, some unions have successfully negotiated a link between firefighters' pay and police rates. So the criterion structure for firefighters becomes some percentage of whatever wage structure is used for police. We describe this process in more detail in Chapter 8.

6. Communicate the Plan and Train Users

Once the job evaluation plan is designed, a manual is prepared so that other people can apply the plan. The manual describes the method, defines the compensable factors, and provides enough information to permit users to distinguish varying degrees of each factor. The point of the manual is to allow users who were not involved in the plan's development to apply the plan as its developers intended. One measure of success in this training would be high (inter)rater reliability. Users will also require training on how to apply the plan and background information on how the plan fits into the organization's total pay system. An **appeals process** may also be included so that employees who feel their jobs are unfairly evaluated have some recourse. Employee acceptance of the process is crucial if the organization is to have any hope that employees will accept the resulting pay as fair. In order to build this acceptance, communication to all employees whose jobs are part of the process used to build the structure is required. This communication may be done through informational meetings, websites, or other methods.

7. Apply to Nonbenchmark Jobs

Recall that the compensable factors and weights were derived using a sample of benchmark jobs. The final step is to apply the plan to the remaining jobs. If the policy-capturing approach described above (and in Chapter 9) is used, then an equation can be used to translate job evaluation points into salaries. This can be done by people who were not necessarily involved in the design process but have been given adequate training in applying the plan. Increasingly, once the plan is developed and accepted, it becomes a tool for managers and HR specialists. They evaluate new positions that may be created or reevaluate jobs whose work content has changed. They may also be part of panels that hear appeals from murmuring employees.

8. Develop Online Software Support

Online job evaluation is widely used in larger organizations. It becomes part of a Total Compensation Service Center for managers and HR generalists to use. The U.S.

State Department, with more than 50,000 employees in 180 countries, uses the "Link. Evaluate" systems. Accessed online by over 400 users worldwide, the time to process an evaluation has been cut from 3 months to 48 hours.[22]

WHO SHOULD BE INVOLVED?

If the internal structure's purpose is to aid managers—and if ensuring high involvement and commitment from employees is important—those managers and employees with a stake in the results should be involved in the process of designing it. A common approach is to use committees, task forces, or teams that include representatives from key operating functions, including nonmanagerial employees. In some cases, the group's role is only advisory; in others, the group designs the evaluation approach, chooses compensable factors, and approves all major changes. Organizations with unions often find that including union representatives helps gain acceptance of the results. Union-management task forces participated in the design of a new evaluation system for the federal government. However, other union leaders believe that philosophical differences prevent their active participation. They take the position that collective bargaining yields more equitable results. So the extent of union participation varies. No single perspective exists on the value of active participation in the process, just as no single management perspective exists.

Exhibit 5.15 shows further results from the survey of WorldatWork members discussed earlier. We see that compensation professionals (i.e., usually compensation analysts, sometimes also those at a higher levels such as the compensation manager) are primarily responsible for most job evaluations for most jobs. Although that holds true for senior management jobs as well, we see that the higher level compensation manager is more likely to be charged with the job evaluation in this case and that consultants also play a much larger role here.

The Design Process Matters

Research suggests that attending to the fairness of the design process and the approach chosen (job evaluation, skill/competency-based plan, and market pricing), rather than focusing solely on the results (the internal pay structure), is likely to achieve employee and management commitment, trust, and acceptance of the results. The absence of

EXHIBIT 5.15 Who Typically Conducts the Job Evaluation?

	Compensation Analyst	Compensation Manager	Consultant	Senior Management	Employee Committee
Senior Management	22%	45%	33%	13%	3%
Middle Management, Professional, Sales, Administrative, Production	64%	27%	3%	2%	4%

Source: *WorldatWork*, "Job Evaluation and Market-Pricing Practices," February 2009.

Note: Number of respondents ranged from 911 to 1,119 organizations.

e-Compensation

O*Net, the Occupational Information Network, is the U.S. Department of Labor's database that identifies and describes occupations; worker knowledge, skills, and abilities; and workplace requirements for jobs across the country in all sectors of the economy. For more information, visit O*Net's website: *www .onetcenter.org.*

How can public sector agencies use this information? Go to an occupation that is of interest to you. Compare the information offered by the Department of Labor to the job-opening descriptions you looked at for specific companies (Chapter 4's e-Compensation).

Why are they different? What purpose does each serve?

participation may make it easier for employees and managers to imagine ways the structure might have been rearranged to their personal liking. Two researchers note, "If people do not participate in decisions, there is little to prevent them from assuming that things would have been better, 'if I'd been in charge.' "[23]

Additional research is needed to ascertain whether the payoffs from increased participation offset potential costs (time involved to reach consensus, potential problems caused by disrupting current perceptions, etc.). We noted earlier that no amount of participation overcomes low wages. In multinational organizations the involvement of both corporate compensation and country managers raises the potential for conflict due to their differing perspectives. Country managers may wish to focus on the particular business needs in their markets, whereas corporate managers may want a system that operates equally well (or poorly) across all countries. The country manager has operating objectives, does not want to lose key individuals, and views compensation as a mechanism to help accomplish these goals; corporate adopts a worldwide perspective and focuses on ensuring that decisions are consistent with the overall global strategy.

Appeals/Review Procedures

No matter what the technique, no job evaluation plan anticipates all situations. It is inevitable that some jobs will be incorrectly evaluated—or at least employees and managers may suspect that they were. Consequently, review procedures for handling such cases and helping to ensure procedural fairness are required. In the past, the compensation manager handled reviews, but increasingly teams of managers and even peers are used. Sometimes these reviews take on the trappings of formal grievance procedures (e.g., documented complaints and responses and levels of approval). Problems may also be handled by managers and the employee relations generalists through informal discussions.[24]

When the evaluations are completed, approval by higher levels of management is usually required. An approval process helps ensure that any changes that result from evaluating work are consistent with the organization's operations and directions.

"I Know I Speak for All of Us When I Say I Speak for All of Us"

One study found that more powerful departments in a university were more successful in using the appeals process to change the pay or the classification of a job than were weaker departments.[25] This is consistent with other research that showed that a powerful member of a **job evaluation committee** could sway the results.[26] Consequently, procedures should be judged for their susceptibility to political influences. "It is the decision-making process, rather than the instrument itself, that seems to have the greatest influence on pay outcomes," writes one researcher.[27]

THE FINAL RESULT: STRUCTURE

The final result of the job analysis–job description–job evaluation process is a *structure,* a **hierarchy** of work. As shown in Exhibit 5.3 at the beginning of this chapter, this hierarchy translates the employer's internal alignment policy into practice. Exhibit 5.16 shows four hypothetical job structures within a single organization. These structures were obtained via different approaches to evaluating work. The jobs are arrayed within four basic functions: managerial, technical, manufacturing, and administrative. The managerial and administrative structures were obtained via a point job evaluation plan; the technical and manufacturing structures, via two different person-based plans (Chapter 6). The manufacturing plan was negotiated with the union. The exhibit illustrates the results of evaluating work: structures that support a policy of internal alignment.

Organizations commonly have multiple structures derived through multiple approaches that apply to different functional groups or units (see Exhibit 5.17). Although some employees in one structure may wish to compare the procedures used in another structure with their own, the underlying premise in practice is that internal alignment

EXHIBIT 5.16 Resulting Internal Structures—Job, Skill, and Competency Based

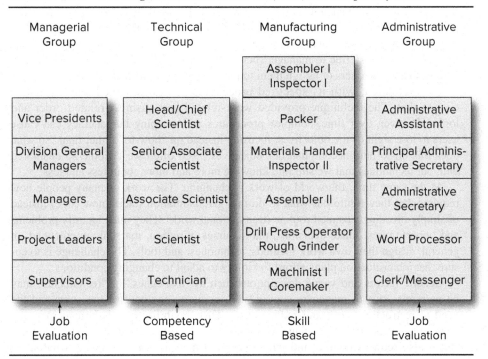

Managerial Group	Technical Group	Manufacturing Group	Administrative Group
		Assembler I Inspector I	
Vice Presidents	Head/Chief Scientist	Packer	Administrative Assistant
Division General Managers	Senior Associate Scientist	Materials Handler Inspector II	Principal Administrative Secretary
Managers	Associate Scientist	Assembler II	Administrative Secretary
Project Leaders	Scientist	Drill Press Operator Rough Grinder	Word Processor
Supervisors	Technician	Machinist I Coremaker	Clerk/Messenger
↑ Job Evaluation	↑ Competency Based	↑ Skill Based	↑ Job Evaluation

EXHIBIT 5.17
Number of Pay
Structures in
Organizations

Number of Pay Structures	Frequency
1	23%
2	16%
3	11%
4	9%
5 or more	41%

Source: WorldatWork. *Compensation Programs and Practices*. January 2015.

$N = 513$ organizations

is most influenced by fair and equitable treatment of employees doing similar work in the same skill/knowledge group.

BALANCING CHAOS AND CONTROL

Looking back at the material we have covered in the past three chapters (determining internal alignment, job analysis, job evaluation), you may be thinking that we have spent a lot of time and a lot of our organization's money to develop techniques. But we have yet to pay a single employee a single dollar. Why bother with all this? Why not just pay whatever it takes and get on with it?

Prior to the widespread use of job evaluation, employers in the 1930s and 1940s did just that, and got irrational pay structures—the legacy of decentralized and unco-ordinated wage-setting practices. Pay differences were a major source of unrest among workers. American Steel and Wire, for example, had more than 100,000 pay rates. Em-ployment and wage records were rarely kept; only the foreman knew with any accu-racy how many workers were employed in his department and the rates they received. Foremen were thus "free to manage," but they used wage information to vary the day rate for favored workers or assign them to jobs where piece rates were loose.

Job evaluation, with its specified procedures and documented results, helped change that. The technique provided work-related and business-related order and logic. However, over time, complex procedures and creeping bureaucracy can cause users to lose sight of the objectives, focusing instead on "how-to" rather than "so what does this do to help accomplish our objectives." Too often we become so enamored with our techniques that we slip into knowing more and more about less and less.

At the same time, the world of work is changing. The work of many people now requires that they figure out what to do in a given situation (tacit knowledge) instead of simply invoking a canned routine (transactional work). They must identify problems and opportunities, make decisions, plan courses of action, marshal support, and, in general, design their own work methods, techniques, and tools. The challenge is to en-sure that job evaluation plans afford flexibility to adapt to changing conditions.

Generic factors and vague descriptions such as "associates" or "technicians" may be very attractive to managers coping with increased competitive pressures and the need to restructure work and reduce costs. This flexibility avoids bureaucracy and leaves managers "free to manage"—just like the American Steel and Wire foremen. But it also reduces control and guidelines, and this in turn may make it harder to ensure that people are treated fairly. Some balance between chaos and control is required. History suggests that when flexibility without guidelines exists, chaotic and irrational pay rates too frequently result. Removing inefficient bureaucracy is important, but balanced guidelines are necessary to ensure that employees are treated fairly and that pay decisions help the organization achieve its objectives.

Your **Turn**   Job Evaluation at Whole Foods

Rather than wait until you are next in a supermarket to check out the different types of work, we brought some of the jobs at Whole Foods Market to you. Now that you have some background in job evaluation, it is time to try it out. As a first step, Whole Foods has done job analysis and prepared job descriptions. The results are shown below. Now a job structure is needed. The manager has assigned this job to you.

1. Divide into teams of four to six each. Each team should evaluate the jobs (i.e., assign job evaluation points to each job) and prepare a job structure based on its evaluation. Assign titles to each job, and show your structure by title and job letter. A broad hint: Recall from our discussion of Whole Foods' business and pay strategy that teams play an important role.
2. Your team should describe the process it went through to arrive at that job structure. The job evaluation techniques and compensable factors used should be described, and the reasons for selecting them should be stated.
3. Each team should put its job structure (i.e., points assigned to each job) on the board. Comparisons can then be made among job structures of the various teams. What is the average correlation between columns of job evaluation points from different teams? Is this correlation high enough to obtain a sufficient level of reliability? (You may wish to skip ahead to the section "Reliability of Job Evaluation Techniques" in Chapter 6 and pay special attention to the example of how even "high" reliability may not eliminate important salary differences that result from whose ratings are used.) Does the job evaluation method used appear to affect the results? Do the compensable factors chosen affect the results? Does the process affect the results?
4. Evaluate the job descriptions. What parts of them were most useful? How could they be improved?

JOB A (Team Member, Deli)[28]

Kind of Work

Provide excellent customer service. Follow and comply with all applicable health and sanitation procedures. Prepare food items: sandwiches, slice deli meats and cheeses. Prepare items on station assignment list and as predetermined. Stock and rotate products, stock supplies and paper goods in a timely basis; keep all utensils stocked. Check dates on all products in stock to ensure freshness and rotate when necessary. Use waste sheets properly, as directed. Operate and sanitize all equipment in a safe and proper manner. Comply with and follow Whole Foods Market Safety Procedures. Follow established Weights and Measures procedures (tares). Answer the phone and pages to department quickly and with appropriate phone etiquette. Practice proper use of knives, slicer, trash compactor, baler (must be 18 years of age or older), and all other equipment used during food preparation and cleanup. Perform other duties as assigned, and follow through on supervisor requests in a timely manner.

Requirements

- Some deli experience preferred.
- Clear and effective communicator.
- Patient and enjoys working and mentoring people.
- Ability to perform physical requirements of position.
- Ability to learn proper use of knives, slicer, baler (must be 18 years of age or older) and all other equipment used during food preparation and cleanup.
- Ability to work well with others as a team.
- Knowledge of all relevant Whole Foods Market policies and standards.
- Understands and can communicate quality goals to customers.

JOB B (Cashier)

Kind of Work

Assist and focus on customers during entire checkout process. Perform all cash register functions according to established procedures. Maintain a positive company image by providing courteous, friendly, and efficient customer service. Check out customer groceries efficiently and accurately. Pass entry-level PLU code test. Maintain a professional demeanor at all times. Stock registers with supplies as needed. Follow proper check-receiving procedure. Clean, stock, and detail front-end area with special attention to own register. Change journal tapes and ribbon as needed. Walk produce department at the beginning of every shift to identify and learn new produce codes. Comply with all posted state health and safety codes.

Requirements

- Excellent communication skills necessary for good customer and team relations.

- Ability to work well with others.
- Ability to learn proper use of baler (must be 18 or older).
- Desire to learn and grow.
- Ability to work in a fast-paced environment, with a sense of urgency.
- Understanding the importance of working as a team.
- Good math skills.
- Patience.

JOB C (Team Leader, Prepared Foods)

Kind of Work

Reports to store team leader and to associate store team leader. Provides overall management and supervision of the Prepared Foods Department. Responsible for team member hiring, development, and terminations. Also responsible for profitability, expense control, buying/merchandising, regulatory compliance, and special projects as assigned. Complete accountability for all aspects of department operations. Consistently communicate and model Whole Foods vision and goal. Interview, select, train, develop, and counsel team members in a manner that builds and sustains a high-performing team and minimizes turnover. Make hiring and termination decisions with guidance of store team leader. Establish and maintain a positive work environment. Manage inventory to achieve targeted gross profit margin. Manage the ordering process to meet Whole Foods Market quality standards. Maintain competitive pricing and achieve targeted sales. Establish and maintain positive and productive vendor relationships. Develop and maintain creative store layout and product merchandising in support of regional and national vision. Establish and maintain collaborative and productive working relationships. Model and cultivate effective inter-department and inter-store communication. Provide accurate, complete information in daily, weekly, monthly, annual, and "ad hoc" management reports. Maintain comprehensive knowledge of, and ensure compliance with, relevant regulatory rules and standards.

Requirements

- Two years relevant experience as a team leader, assistant team leader, supervisor, or buyer.
- Thorough knowledge of products, buying, pricing, merchandising, and inventory management.
- Excellent verbal and written communication skills.
- Strong organizational skills.
- Knowledge of all relevant Whole Foods Market policies and standards.
- Computer skills.

JOB D (Team Member, Prepared Foods)

Kind of Work

Perform all duties and responsibilities of Prepared Foods Team Member. Provide excellent customer service. Assist team leader in nightly team operations. Report all actions of team members that violate policies or standards to the team leader or associate team leader. Mentor and train team members. Maintain quality standards in production and counter display. Comply with all applicable health and safety codes. Help implement and support all regional programs.

Requirements

- Minimum 6 months' retail food production experience, or equivalent.
- Overall knowledge of both front and back of the house operations.
- Comprehensive product knowledge.
- Comprehensive knowledge of quality standards.
- Excellent organizational skills.
- Excellent interpersonal skills, and ability to train others.
- Demonstrated decision-making ability, and leadership skills.

- Ability to perform physical requirements of position.
- Able to work a flexible schedule based on the needs of the store.

JOB E (Team Member, Kitchen)

Kind of Work

Performs all duties related to dishwashing: unloading kitchen deliveries and cleaning all dishes, utensils, pots, and pans. May be prep work. Maintain food quality and sanitation in kitchen. Maintain a positive company image by being courteous, friendly, and efficient. Wash and sanitize all dishes, utensils, and containers. Assist with proper storage of all deliveries. Rotate and organize products. Perform prep work as directed. Provide proper ongoing maintenance of equipment. Maintain health department standards when cleaning and handling food. Perform deep-cleaning tasks on a regular basis. Take out all of the garbage and recycling materials. Sweep and wash floors as needed.

Requirements

- Entry-level position.
- Able to perform physical requirements of job.
- Practices safe and proper knife skills.
- Ability to work box baler (must be 18 years of age or older).
- Works well with others and participates as part of a team.

JOB F (Team Member II, Stock and Display)

Kind of Work

Performs all functions related to breaking down deliveries and moving back stock to floor. Assists in organizing and developing promotional displays; maintains back room, training entry-level grocery clerks. Trained and capable of operating any of the subdepartments as needed. Maintains and ensures retail standards during their shift. Responsible for implementing team's break schedule. Performs all duties and responsibilities of grocery team member. Builds displays and requests appropriate signage. Supervises shift to ensure standards are maintained. Implements break schedule for shift. Responsible for problem solving in team leader or associate team leader's absence. Fully responsible for completion of all opening or closing checklists. Responsible for checking in deliveries.

Requirements

- Minimum one-year retail grocery experience, or equivalent.
- Proficient in math skills (addition, subtraction, multiplication, and division).
- Ability to perform physical requirements of position.
- Ability to properly use baler (must be 18 years of age or older).
- Able to direct team members and implement break schedule.
- Ability to work well with others.

JOB G (Associate Team Leader, Prepared Foods)

Kind of Work

Reports directly to Prepared Foods Team Leader. Assists in overall management and supervision of the Prepared Foods Department. Can be responsible for team member hiring, development, and terminations. Also responsible for profitability, expense control, buying/merchandising, regulatory compliance, and special projects as assigned. Complete accountability for all assigned aspects of department operations. Consistently communicate and model Whole Foods vision and goals. Assist in the interview, selection, training, development, and counseling of team members in a manner that builds and sustains a high-performing team and minimizes turnover. Discuss hiring and termination decisions with guidance of others. Establish and maintain a positive work environment. Manage inventory to achieve targeted gross profit margin. Manage

the ordering process to meet Whole Foods Market quality standards, maintain competitive pricing, and achieve targeted sales. Develop and maintain creative store layout and product merchandising in support of regional and national vision. Establish and maintain collaborative and productive working relationships. Model and cultivate effective inter-department and inter-store communication. Provide accurate, complete information in daily, weekly, monthly, annual, and "ad hoc" management reports. Maintain comprehensive knowledge of, and ensure compliance with, relevant regulatory rules and standards.

Requirements

- One to two years of department experience, or industry equivalent.
- Analytical ability and proficiency in math needed to calculate margins, monitor profitability, and manage inventory.
- Clear and effective communicator.
- Patient and enjoys working and mentoring people.
- Strong organizational skills.
- Knowledge of all relevant Whole Foods Market policies and standards.
- Computer skills.

JOB H (Regional Team Leader)

Kind of Work

Rotate among stores. Assist and support the store team leader with all store functions. Interview, select, evaluate, counsel, and terminate team members. Coordinate and supervise all store products and personnel. Follow through on all customer and team member questions and requests. Evaluate customer service and resolve complaints. Operate the store in an efficient and profitable manner. Have a firm understanding of store financials and labor budgets. Establish and achieve sales, labor, and contribution goals. Review department schedules and research productivity improvements. Order store equipment and supplies in a timely manner. Enforce established food safety, cleaning, and maintenance procedures. Inspect store; ensure cleanliness; visit off-hours for consistency. Maintain accurate retail pricing and signage. Ensure that product is cross-merchandised in other departments. Coordinate, supervise, and report physical inventory. Analyze product transfers, waste, and spoilage. Manage expenses to maximize the bottom line. Provide, maintain, and safety-train team members on all equipment and tools. Resolve safety violations and hazards immediately. Maintain store security and ensure that opening and closing procedures are followed. Show EVA improvement over a designated period. Leverage sales growth to improve store profitability. Assist in handling liability claims and minimize their occurrence. Establish and maintain good community relations. Create a friendly, productive, and professional working environment. Communicate company goals and information to team members. Ensure and support team member development and training. Evaluate team member duties, dialogues, raises, and promotions. Keep regional leadership informed of all major events that affect the store. Ensure store policies and procedures are followed. Visit the competition on a regular basis and react to current industry trends.

Requirements

- A passion for retailing.
- Complete understanding of Whole Foods Market retail operations.
- Strong leadership and creative ability.
- Management and business skills with financial expertise.
- Well organized with excellent follow through.
- Detail oriented with a vision and eye for the big picture.
- Self-motivated and solution oriented.
- Excellent merchandising skills and eye for detail.

- Ability to delegate effectively and use available talent to the best advantage.
- Strong communicator/motivator; able to work well with others and convey enthusiasm.
- Ability to maintain good relationships with vendors and the community.
- Can train and inspire team members to excellence in all aspects of the store.
- Ability to make tough decisions.
- Love and knowledge of natural foods.
- Strong computer skills.

JOB I (Team Member, Stock and Display)

Kind of Work

Performs all functions related to breaking down deliveries and moving back stock to floor. May assist in organizing and developing promotional displays; maintains back room. Stock and clean grocery shelves, bulk bins, frozen and dairy case. Maintain back stock in good order. Sweep floors and face shelves throughout the store. Comply with all applicable health and safety codes. Provide excellent customer service. Log and expedite customers' special orders. Retrieve special orders for customers by request and offer service out to car. Respond to all grocery pages quickly and efficiently. Build displays and request appropriate signage.

Requirements

- Retail grocery or natural foods experience a plus.
- Proficient in math skills (addition, subtraction, multiplication, and division).
- Ability to learn basic knowledge of all products carried in department.
- Ability to perform physical requirements of position.
- Proper and safe use of box cutter, baler (must be 18 years of age or older), and all equipment.
- Ability to work well with others.

Summary

The differences in the rates paid for different jobs and skills affect the ability of managers to achieve their business objectives. Differences in pay matter. They matter to employees, because their willingness to take on more responsibility and training, to focus on adding value for customers and improving quality of products, and to be flexible enough to adapt to change all depend at least in part on how pay is structured for different levels of work. Differences in the rates paid for different jobs and skills also influence how fairly employees believe they are being treated. Unfair treatment is ultimately counterproductive.

So far, we have examined the most common approach to designing pay differences for different work: job evaluation. In the next chapter, we will examine several alternative approaches. However, any approach needs to be evaluated for how useful it is.

Job evaluation has evolved into many different forms and methods. Consequently, wide variations exist in its use and how it is perceived. This chapter discussed some of the many perceptions of the role of job evaluation and reviewed the criticisms leveled at it. No matter how job evaluation is designed, its ultimate use is to help design and manage a work-related, business-focused, and agreed-upon pay structure.

Review Questions

1. How does job evaluation translate internal alignment policies (loosely coupled versus tight fitting) into practice? What does (a) organization strategy and objectives, (b) flow of work, (c) fairness, and (d) motivating people's behaviors toward organization objectives have to do with job evaluation?

2. Why are there different approaches to job evaluation? Think of several employers in your area (the college, hospital, retailer, 7-Eleven, etc.). What approach would you expect them to use? Why?

3. What are the advantages and disadvantages of using more than one job evaluation plan in any single organization?

4. Why bother with job evaluation? Why not simply market price? How can job evaluation link internal alignment and external market pressures?

5. Consider your college or school. What are the compensable factors required for your college to evaluate jobs? How would you go about identifying these factors? Should the school's educational mission be reflected in your factors? Or are the more generic factors used in the Hay plan okay? Discuss.

6. You are the manager of 10 people in a large organization. All of them become very suspicious and upset when they receive a memo from the HR department saying their jobs are going to be evaluated. How do you try to reassure them?

Endnotes

1. Maeve Quaid, *Job Evaluation: The Myth of Equitable Assessment* (Toronto: University of Toronto Press, 1993); David W. Belcher, *Wage and Salary Administration* (New York: Prentice-Hall, 1955); *Job Evaluation: Methods to the Process* (Scottsdale, AZ: WorldatWork, 2006); Donald P. Schwab, "Job Evaluation and Pay Setting: Concepts and Practices," *in Comparable Worth: Issues and Alternatives,* E. Robert Livernash, ed. (Washington, DC: Equal Employment Advisory Council, 1980), pp. 49–77.

2. M. A. Konovsky, "Understanding Procedural Justice and Its Impact on Business Organizations," *Journal of Management* 26(3), 2000, pp. 489–511; B. H. Sheppard, R. J. Lewicki, and J. W. Minton, *Organizational Justice: The Search for Fairness in the Workplace* (New York: Macmillan, 1992); Frederick P. Morgeson, Michael A. Campion, and Carl P. Maertz, "Understanding Pay Satisfaction: The Limits of a Compensation System Implementation," *Journal of Business and Psychology* 16(1), Fall 2001, pp. 133–149.

3. E. Robert Livernash, "Internal Wage Structure," in *New Concepts in Wage Determination,* George W. Taylor and Frank C. Pierson, eds. (New York: McGraw-Hill, 1957).

4. M. S. Viteles, "A Psychologist Looks at Job Evaluation," *Personnel* 17 (1941), pp. 165–176.

5. Robert L. Heneman and Peter V. LeBlanc, "Developing a More Relevant and Competitive Approach for Valuing Knowledge Work," *Compensation and Benefits Review,* July/August 2002, pp. 43–47; Robert L. Heneman and Peter V. LeBlanc, "Work Valuation Addresses Shortcomings of Both Job Evaluation and Market Pricing," *Compensation and Benefits Review,* January/February 2003, pp. 7–11.

6. Howard Risher and Charles Fay, *New Strategies for Public Pay* (Saratoga Springs, NY: AMACOM, 2000). The Office of Personnel Management (OPM) does special studies on the Federal Civil Service. They are on the OPM's website at www.opm.gov/studies/index.htm.

7. www.opm.gov/fedclass/clashnbk.pdf. www.opm.gov/fedclass/gsintro.pdf.

8. Factor comparison, another method of job evaluation, bears some similarities to the point method in that compensable factors are clearly defined and the external market is linked to the job evaluation results. However, factor comparison is used by less than 10 percent of employers that use job evaluation. The method's complexity makes it difficult to explain to employees and managers, thus limiting its usefulness.

9. John Kilgour, "Job Evaluation Revisited: The Point Factor Method," *Compensations Benefits Review,* June/July 2008, 37–46.

10. Robert L. Heneman, "Job and Work Evaluation: A Literature Review," *Public Personnel Management,* Spring 2003; Robert L. Heneman and Peter V. LeBlanc, "Work Valuation Addresses Shortcomings of Both Job Evaluation and Market Pricing," *Compensation and Benefits Review,* January/February 2003, pp. 7–11; C. Ellis, R. Laymon, and P. LeBlanc, "Improving Pay Productivity with Strategic Work Valuation," *WorldatWork,* Second Quarter 2004, pp. 56–65.

11. M. K. Mount and R. A. Ellis, "Investigation of Bias in Job Evaluation Ratings of Comparable Worth Study Participants," *Personnel Psychology* 40 (1987), pp. 85–96; Morley Gunderson, "The Evolution and Mechanics of Pay Equity in Ontario," *Canadian Public Policy,* vol. XXVIII, Suppl. 1 (2002), pp. S117–S131.

12. See http://www.bls.gov/ncs/ocs/sp/ncbr0004.pdf.

13. D. F. Harding, J. M. Madden, and K. Colson, "Analysis of a Job Evaluation System," *Journal of Applied Psychology* 44 (1960), pp. 354–357.

14. See a series of studies conducted by C. H. Lawshe and his colleagues published in the *Journal of Applied Psychology* from 1944 to 1947. For example, C. H. Lawshe, "Studies in Job Evaluation: II. The Adequacy of Abbreviated Point Ratings for Hourly Paid Jobs in Three Industrial Plants," *Journal of Applied Psychology* 29 (1945), pp. 177–184. Also see Theresa M. Welbourne and Charlie O. Trevor, "The Roles of Departmental and Position Power in Job Evaluation," *Academy of Management Journal* 43 (2000), pp. 761–771.

15. Tjarda Van Sliedregt, Olga F. Voskuijl, and Henk Thierry, "Job Evaluation Systems and Pay Grade Structures: Do They Match?" *International Journal of Human Resource Management* 12(8), December 2001, pp. 1313–1324; R. M. Madigan and D. J. Hoover, "Effects of Alternative Job Evaluation Methods on Decisions Involving Pay Equity," *Academy of Management Journal,* March 1986, pp. 84–100.

16. John R. Doyle, Rodney H. Green, and Paul A. Bottomley, "Judging Relative Importance: Direct Rating and Point Allocation Are Not Equivalent," *Organizational Behavior and Human Decision Processes* 70(1), April 1997, pp. 65–72.

17. Some contemporary job evaluation plans include the factor weight directly in each factor scale. So rather than a 1 to 5 scale for each factor, each factor has a unique scale. An illustration: The weight or relative importance of skill/knowledge is 40 percent; each degree on a 1 to 5 scale is worth 40 points. The point range is 40 to 200. In practice, statistically modeling values for factor scales often yields more results.

18. Paul M. Edwards, "Statistical Methods in Job Evaluation," *Advanced Management,* December 1948, pp. 158–163.

19. Paula England, "The Case for Comparable Worth," *Quarterly Review of Economics and Finance* 39 (1999), pp. 743–755; N. Elizabeth Fried and John H. Davis, *Developing Statistical Job-Evaluation Models* (Scottsdale, AZ: WorldatWork, 2004); M. Gunderson, "The Evolution and Mechanics of Pay Equity in Ontario," *Canadian Public Policy,* vol. XXVIII, Suppl. 1 (2002), pp. S117–S131.

20. M. K. Mount and R. A. Ellis, "Investigation of Bias in Job Evaluation Ratings of Comparable Worth Study Participants," *Personnel Psychology* 40 (1987); Tjarda Van Sliedregt, Olga F. Voskuijl, and Henk Thierry, "Job Evaluation Systems and Pay Grade Structures: Do They Match?" *International Journal of Human Resource Management* 12(8), December 2001, pp. 1313–1324; Judith M. Collins and Paul M. Muchinsky, "An Assessment of the Construct Validity of Three Job Evaluation Methods: A Field Experiment," *Academy of Management Journal* 36(4), 1993, pp. 895–904; Robert M. Madigan and David J. Hoover, "Effects of Alternative Job Evaluation Methods on Decisions Involving Pay Equity," *Academy of Management Journal* 29 (1986), pp. 84–100.

21. The importance of appropriate criterion pay structure is particularly relevant in "pay equity studies" to assess gender bias. (*Canadian Telephone Employees Association et al. v. Bell Canada*; Canada Equal Wages Guidelines, 1986).

22. See www.link.hrsystems.com. Also see www.npktools.com.

23. Carl F. Frost, John W. Wakely, and Robert A. Ruh, *The Scanlon Plan for Organization Development: Identity, Participation, and Equity* (East Lansing, MI: Michigan State Press, 1974); E. A. Locke and D. M. Schweiger, "Participation in Decision Making: One More Look," *Research in Organization Behavior* (Greenwich, CT: JAI Press, 1979); G. J. Jenkins, Jr., and E. E. Lawler III, "Impact of Employee Participation in Pay Plan Development," *Organizational Behavior and Human Performance* 28 (1981), pp. 111–128; Frederick P. Morgeson, Michael A. Campion, and Carl P. Maertz, "Understanding Pay Satisfaction: The Limits of a Compensation System Implementation," *Journal of Business and Psychology* 16(1), Fall 2001, pp. 133–149; R. Crepanzano, *Justice in the Workplace: Vol. 2. From Theory to Practice* (Mahwah, NJ: Lawrence Erlbaum Associates, 2000); R. Folger and R. Crepanzano, *Organizational Justice and Human Resource Management* (Thousand Oaks, CA: Sage, 1998).

24. B. Carver and A. A. Vondra, "Alternative Dispute Resolution: Why It Doesn't Work and Why It Does," *Harvard Business Review,* May–June 1994, pp. 120–129.

25. Theresa M. Welbourne and Charlie O. Trevor, "The Roles of Departmental and Position Power in Job Evaluation," *Academy of Management Journal* 43 (2000), pp. 761–771.

26. N. Gupta and G. D. Jenkins, Jr., "The Politics of Pay," paper presented at the annual meeting of the Society for Industrial and Organizational Psychology, Montreal, 1992.

27. Vandra Huber and S. Crandall, "Job Measurement: A Social-Cognitive Decision Perspective," in *Research in Personnel and Human Resources Management,* vol. 12, Gerald R. Ferris, ed. (Greenwich, CT: JAI Press, 1994).

28. The job titles used here may differ from those used at Whole Foods.

Person-Based Structures

History buffs tell us that some form of job evaluation was in use when the pharaohs built the pyramids. Chinese emperors managed the Great Wall construction with the assistance of job evaluation. In the United States, job evaluation in the public sector came into use in the 1880s, when Chicago reformers were trying to put an end to patronage in government hiring and pay practices. To set pay based not on your connections but instead on the work you did was a revolutionary old idea.

The logic underlying job-based pay structures flows from scientific management, championed by Frederick Taylor in the early 20th century. Work was broken into a series of steps and analyzed so that the "one best way," the most efficient way to perform every element of the job (right down to how to shovel coal), could be specified. Strategically, Taylor's approach fit with mass production technologies that were beginning to revolutionize the way work was done.

Taylorism still pervades our lives. Not only are jobs analyzed and evaluated in terms of the "best way" (i.e., McFry's nine steps, Exhibit 4.9), but cookbooks and software manuals specify the methods for baking a cake or using a program as a series of simple, basic steps. Golf is analyzed as a series of basic tasks that can be combined successfully to lower one's handicap. At work, at play, in all daily life, "Taylor's thinking so permeates the soil of modern life we no longer realize it is there."[1]

In today's organizations, the work is also analyzed with an eye toward increasing competitiveness and success. Routine work (**transactional work**) is separated from more complex work (**tacit work**). Investment bankers can isolate routine transactions—even routine analysis of financial statements—from more complex analysis and problem solving required to make sound investment recommendations to clients. Legal work such as patent searches, entering documents into readable databases, even vetting simple contracts can be broken out from more complex client relationships. The more routine work generates lower revenues and requires less knowledge. People doing this work are likely paid less than people doing the more complex work that yields greater profits.

Once fragmented, work processes can be rebundled into new, different jobs.[2] Pay structures based on each person's skills/knowledge/experience offer flexibility to align talent with continuously redesigned workplaces. A few years ago, machine operators on Eaton's assembly line needed to know how to operate one machine; now, as part of a manufacturing cell, they are members of self-managing teams. Eaton assembly lines now require people to be multiskilled, continuously learning, flexible, and possess problem-solving and negotiating skills. The search is on for pay systems that support the fragmented and rebundled work flows. Routine work may even be outsourced, though outsourcing a McFryer is not on the horizon.

More complex work requires pay systems that support continuous learning, improvement, and flexibility. Person-based structures hold out that promise. Person-based approaches are the topic of this chapter. At the end of this chapter, we shall discuss the usefulness of the various job-based and person-based approaches for determining internal structures.

Exhibit 6.1 points out the similarities in the logic underlying job-based versus people-based approaches. No matter the basis for the structure, a way is needed to (1) collect and summarize information about the work, (2) determine what is of value to the organization, (3) quantify that value, and (4) translate that value into an internal structure.

PERSON-BASED STRUCTURES: SKILL PLANS

The majority of applications of **skill-based pay** have been in manufacturing, where the work often involves teams, multiskills, and flexibility. An advantage of a skill-based plan is that people can be deployed in a way that better matches the flow of work, thus avoiding bottlenecks as well as idle hands.[3]

Types of Skill Plans

Skill plans can focus on *depth* (specialists in corporate law, finance, or welding and hydraulic maintenance) and/or *breadth* (generalists with knowledge in all phases of operations including marketing, manufacturing, finance, and human resources).

Specialist: Depth

The pay structures for your elementary or high school teachers were likely based on their knowledge as measured by education level. A typical teacher's contract specifies a series of steps, with each step corresponding to a level of education. A bachelor's degree in education is step 1 and is the minimum required for hiring. To advance a

EXHIBIT 6.1 **Many Ways to Create Internal Structure**

Business- and Work-Related Internal Structure

Person Based

	Job Based	Skill	Competencies
PURPOSE			
Collect, summarize work content information	Job analysis Job descriptions (Chapter 4)	**Skill analysis (Chapter 6)**	Core competencies (Chapter 6)
Determine what to value	Job evaluation: classes or compensable factors (Chapter 5)	**Skill blocks**	Competency sets
Assess relative value	Factor degrees and weighting (Chapter 5)	**Certification process**	Behavioral descriptors
Translate into structure	Job-based structure (Chapter 5)	**Person-based structure (Chapter 6)**	Person-based structure (Chapter 6)

> **Skill-based structures** link pay to the depth or breadth of the skills, abilities, and knowledge a person acquires that are relevant to the work. Structures based on skill pay individuals for all the skills for which they have been certified regardless of whether the work they are doing requires all or just a few of those particular skills. The wage attaches to the person. In contrast, a job-based plan pays employees for the job to which they are assigned, regardless of the skills they possess.

step to higher pay requires additional education. Each year of seniority also is associated with a pay increase. The result can be that two teachers may receive different pay rates for doing essentially the same job—teaching English to high school juniors. The pay is based on the knowledge of the individual doing the job (measured by number of college credits and years of teaching experience) rather than on job content or output (performance of students).[4] The presumption is that more knowledge will translate into higher teaching effectiveness.

Generalist/Multiskill Based: Breadth

As with teachers, employees in a **multiskill system** earn pay increases by acquiring new knowledge, but the knowledge is specific to a range of related jobs. Pay increases come with certification of new skills, rather than with job assignments. Employees can then be assigned to any of the jobs for which they are certified, based on the flow of work. An example from Balzers Tool Coating makes the point. This company coats cutting tools by bombarding them with metal ions. The coating keeps the edge sharper longer. Originally, eight different jobs were involved in the coating process. Everyone started at the same rate, no matter the job to which the person was assigned. Employees received cross-training in a variety of jobs, but without a specific training path or level. Different locations started new people in different jobs. In order to put some order into its system and make better use of its employees, Balzers moved to a skill-based plan for all its hourly workers, including administrative and sales employees. Its new structure included four different levels, from fundamental to advanced. Exhibit 6.2 shows the new structure and the skill blocks in each level. New employees are hired into the fundamental level. Fundamental skills include familiarity with company forms and procedures, basic product knowledge, safety, basic computer usage, and so on. An employee starting at the bottom Fundamental level (100%) can increase his/her salary by 93 percent if s/he acquires every skill at each level, including the top Advanced level (193%) of the structure. Thus, a new employment starting at $10/hour could increase his/her pay to $19.30/hour by acquiring skills.

Once they have been certified in all the skills at the fundamental level, they receive a pay increase of 7% and move to the basic skill level. For each additional skill-block

EXHIBIT 6.2 Skill Ladder at Balzers Tool Coating

Grade Pay Range	Administration	Sales	Tool	Machine
Advanced 150–193%	Office administration	Inside sales	Incoming inspection	Service Arc technology
Inter-mediate 136–179%	Blueprint expediting	Customer service pricing–B	Outgoing inspection shipping	Evaporation technology coating
Basic 107–164%	Software pricing file/route general office	Van driver licensing packing courier	Receiving racking packing fixturing	Degas stripping cleaning blasting
Fundamental	Fundamental	Fundamental	Fundamental	Fundamental

Note: Pay range is expressed as a percentage of entry pay (100%) at the Fundamental level.

certification at this level, pay is increased by 5% to 6%. Basic-level employees can be assigned to any of the tasks for which they are certified; they will be paid at their highest certification rate. The same approach is used at the intermediate and advanced levels. A person certified at the very top of the structure could be assigned to any of the tasks in the structure. The advantage to Balzers is workforce flexibility and, hence, staffing assignments that can be better matched to the work flow.[5] The advantage to employees is that the more they learn, the more they earn.

The system at Balzers differs from the system for teachers in that the responsibilities assigned at Balzers can change drastically over a short period of time, whereas teachers' basic responsibilities do not vary on a day-to-day basis. Additionally, the Balzers system is designed to ensure that all the skills are clearly work-related. Training improves skills that the company values. In contrast, a school district has no guarantee that courses taken improve teaching skills (or students' knowledge and performance).

Purpose of the Skill-Based Structure

Skill-based structures can be evaluated using the objectives already specified for an internally aligned structure: supports the organization strategy, supports work flow, is fair to employees, and directs their behavior toward organization objectives.

Supports the Strategy and Objectives

The skills on which to base a structure need to be directly related to the organization's objectives and strategy. In practice, however, the "line of sight" between changes in the specific work skills (fundamental to advanced) required to operate the Balzers coaters and increased shareholder returns is difficult to make clear. In some cosmic sense, we know that these operating skills matter, but the link to the plant's performance is clearer than the link to corporate goals.

Supports Work Flow

The link here is clearer. One of the main advantages of a skill-based plan is that it facilitates matching people to a changing work flow.[6] For example, one national hotel chain moves many of its people to the hotel's front desk between 4 p.m. and 7 p.m., when the majority of guests check in. After 7 p.m., these same employees move to the food and beverage service area to match the demand for room service and dining room service. By ensuring that guests will not have to wait long to check in or to eat, the hotel believes it can provide a high level of service with fewer staff.

Is Fair to Employees

Employees like the potential of higher pay that comes with learning. And by encouraging employees to take charge of their own development, skill-based plans may give them more control over their work lives.

However, favoritism and bias may play a role in determining who gets first crack at the training necessary to become certified at higher-paying skill levels. Employees complain that they are forced to pick up the slack for those who are out for training. Additionally, the courts have not yet been asked to rule on the legality of having two people do the same task but for different (skill-based) pay.

Motivates Behavior Toward Organization Objectives

Person-based plans have the potential to clarify new standards and behavioral expectations. The fluid work assignments that skill-based plans permit encourage employees to take responsibility for the complete work process and its results, with less direction from supervisors.[7] If less direction from supervisors is needed, then fewer supervisors may likewise be needed. Indeed, research at nine manufacturing plants concluded that the number of managers in plants under skill-based pay was as much as 50 percent lower compared to traditional plants.[8] Having fewer supervisors can result in substantial labor cost savings, but, of course, supervisors can see this potential consequence as well, which can certainly dampen their enthusiasm for skill-based pay and the often related practice of using teams and moving some decision responsibility from supervisors to workers.[9]

"HOW TO": SKILL ANALYSIS

Exhibit 6.3 depicts the process for determining a skill-based structure. It begins with an analysis of skills, which is similar to the task statements in a job analysis. Related skills can be grouped into a **skill block**; skill blocks can be arranged by levels into a skill structure. To build the structure, a process is needed to describe, certify, and value the skills.

Exhibit 6.3 also identifies the major **skill analysis** decisions: (1) What is the objective of the plan? (2) What information should be collected? (3) What methods should be used? (4) Who should be involved? (5) How useful are the results for pay purposes? These are exactly the same decisions as in job analysis.

EXHIBIT 6.3 Determining the Internal Skill-Based Structure

> **Skill analysis** is a systematic process of identifying and collecting information about skills required to perform work in an organization.

What Information to Collect?

There is far less uniformity in the use of terms in person-based plans than there is in job-based plans. Equipment manufacturer FMC assigns points and groups skills as foundation, core electives, and optional electives. Its plan for technicians is more fully developed in Exhibit 6.4.

- Foundation skills include a quality seminar, videos on materials handling and hazardous materials, a three-day safety workshop, and a half-day orientation. All foundation skills are mandatory and must be certified to reach the Technician I level.
- Core electives having to do with the facility's operations (e.g., fabrication, welding, painting, finishing, assembly, inspection) are necessary. Each skill is assigned a point value.
- Optional electives are additional specialized competencies ranging from computer applications to team leadership and consensus building.

To reach Technician I (114% of entry level pay), 40 core elective points (of 370) must be certified, in addition to the foundation competencies. To reach Technician II, an additional 100 points of core electives must be certified, plus one optional elective.

A fully qualified Technician IV (certified in the foundations, 365 points of core electives, and 5 optional electives) is able to perform all work in any cell at the facility. Technician IV earns 162% of what an entry-level employee earns no matter what task they are doing. FMC's approach should look familiar to any college student: required courses, required credits chosen among specific categories, and optional electives. There is a minor difference, of course—FMC employees get paid for passing these courses, whereas college students pay to take courses!

The FMC plan illustrates the kind of information that underpins skill-based plans: very specific information on every aspect of the production process. This makes the plans particularly suited for continuous-flow technologies where employees work in teams.

Whom to Involve?

Employee involvement is almost built into skill-based plans. Employees and managers are the source of information on defining the skills, arranging them into a hierarchy, bundling them into skill blocks, and certifying whether a person actually possesses the skills. At Balzers and FMC, a committee consisting of managers from several sites developed the skill listing and certification process for each of the four skill ladders, with input from employees.

EXHIBIT 6.4 **FMC's Technician Skill-Based Structure**

Foundations

Quality course
Shop floor control
Materials handling
Hazardous materials video
Safety workshop
Orientation workshop

Core Electives

Skills	Points	Skills	Points
Longeron Fabrication	10	Leak Check/Patch Weld	5
Panel Fabrication	15	Final Acceptance Test	10
Shell Fabrication	15	Welding Inspection	15
End Casting Welding	20	Flame Spraying	15
Finishing—Paint	20	Assembly Inspection	5
Finishing—Ablative/Autoclave	20	Safe % Arm Assembly	15
Finishing—Surface Prep	10	MK 13 Machining	25
MK 13 Assembly	15	MK 14 Machining	25
MK 14 Assembly	15	Tool Setup	10
Finishing Inspection	15	NC1 Inspection	30
Machining Inspection	5	Degrease	10
Pad Welding	20	Guide Rail Assembly	5
		Receiving Inspection	5

Optional Electives

Maintenance	Career Development
Logistics—JIT	Group Decision Making
Plant First Aid	Public Relations
Geometric Tolerancing	Group Facilitator
Computer—Lotus	Training
Computer—dBASE III	Group Problem Solving
Computer—Word Processing	Administration
Assessment Center	Plant Security
Consensus Building	

Hourly wage

	Entry	Tech I	Tech II	Tech III	Tech IV
	100%				
	105%				
	114%				
	124%				
	138%				
	162%				

Tech I: Foundation all mandatory; 40 Core electives
Tech II: Foundation; 140 Core electives; Optional elective
Tech III: Foundation; 240 Core electives; 3 Optional electives
Tech IV: Foundation; 365 Core electives; 5 Optional electives

Note: Pay range is expressed as a percentage of entry pay (100%) at the Entry level.

Establish Certification Methods

Organizations may use peer review, on-the-job demonstrations, or tests to certify that employees possess skills and are able to apply them. Honeywell evaluates employees during the six months after they have learned the skills. Leaders and peers are used in the certification process. Still other companies require successful completion of formal courses. However, we do not need to point out to students that sitting in the classroom doesn't guarantee that anything is learned. School districts address this issue in a variety of ways. Some will certify for any courses; others only for courses in the teacher's subject area. However, no districts require evidence that the course and certification improve teaching effectiveness.

Newer skill-based applications appear to be moving away from an on-demand review and toward scheduling fixed review points in the year. Scheduling makes it easier to budget and control payroll increases. Other changes include ongoing recertification, which replaces the traditional one-time certification process and helps ensure skills are kept fresh, and removal of certification (and accompanying pay) when a particular skill is deemed obsolete.[10] However, it can be difficult to change certification procedures once a system is in place. TRW Automotive faced this problem in regard to using formal classes for its Mesa, Arizona, airbag facility. TRW felt that some employees were only putting in "seat time." Yet no one was willing to take the responsibility for refusing to certify, since an extra sign-off beyond classroom attendance had not been part of the original system design.

Many plans require that employees be recertified, since the skills may get rusty if they are not used frequently. At its Ome facility in Tokyo, where Toshiba manufactures laptops, all team members are required to recertify their skills every 24 months. Those who fail have the opportunity to retrain and attempt to recertify before their pay rate is reduced. However, the pressure to keep up to date and avoid obsolescence is intense.

Outcomes of Skill-Based Pay Plans: Guidance from Research and Experience

Skill-based plans are generally well accepted by employees because it is easy to see the connection between the plan, the work, and the size of the paycheck. Consequently, the plans provide strong motivation for individuals to increase their skills.[11] "Learn to earn" is a popular slogan used with these plans. One study connected the ease of communication and understanding of skill-based plans to employees' general perceptions of being treated fairly by the employer.[12] The design of the certification process is crucial in this perception of fairness. Two of the three studies to look at whether productivity is higher under skill-based pay concluded that it is. One of these studies found that most of the reported effect on productivity was due to higher worker flexibility (e.g., employee ability to work in teams, to perform multiple jobs, to be self-managed, to make better use of technology). The same study also found that employee attitudes were more positive under skill-based pay than under more traditional systems.[13] Another study found that younger, more educated employees with strong growth needs, organizational commitment, and a positive attitude toward workplace innovations were more successful in acquiring new skills.[14] Nevertheless, for reasons not made clear, the study's authors recommend allocating training opportunities by seniority.

Skill-based plans become increasingly expensive as the majority of employees become certified at the highest pay levels. As a result, the employer may have an average wage higher than competitors who are not using skill-based plans. Unless the increased flexibility permits leaner staffing, the employer may experience higher labor costs. Some employers are combating this by requiring that employees stay at a rate a certain amount of time before they can take the training to move to a higher rate. Motorola abandoned its skill-based plan because at the end of three years, everyone had topped out (by accumulating the necessary skill blocks). TRW, too, found that after a few years, people at two airbag manufacturing plants on skill-based systems had all **topped out.** They were flexible and well trained. So now what? What happens in the next years? Does everybody automatically receive a pay increase? Do the work processes get redesigned? In a firm with labor-intensive products, the increased labor costs under skill-based plans may become a source of competitive disadvantage.

So what kind of workplace seems best suited for a skill-based plan? Early researchers on skill-based plans found that about 60 percent of the companies in their original sample were still using skill-based plans seven years later. One of the key factors that determined a plan's success was how well it was aligned with the organization's strategy. Plans were more viable in organizations that follow a cost-cutter strategy (see Chapter 2)— doing more with less. The reduced numbers of highly trained, flexible employees that skill-based pay promises fit this strategy very well.[15]

On the other hand, it has also been argued that the higher labor costs under skill-based pay (estimated as between 10 and 15 percent) mean that it may be a better fit to companies in industries where labor costs are a small share of total costs, such as paper and forest products, chemicals, and food processing. If labor costs are 15 percent of total costs and skill-based pay translates into labor costs higher by 10 percent, then total costs would be higher by 1.5 percent due to skill-based pay.[16] The question then is whether this increase in labor costs is more than offset by gains in productivity, quality, customer responsiveness, flexibility, or worker retention, for example.

A final question is whether a multiskilled "jack-of-all-trades" might really be the master of none. Some research suggests that the greatest impact on results occurs immediately after just a small amount of increased flexibility.[17] Greater increments in flexibility achieve fewer improvements. There may be an optimal number of skills for any individual to possess. Beyond that number, productivity returns are less than the pay increases. Additionally, some employees may not be interested in giving up the job they are doing. Such a "camper" creates a bottleneck for rotating other employees into that position to acquire those skills. Organizations should decide in advance whether they are willing to design a plan to work around campers or whether they will force campers into the system.

The bottom line is that skill-based approaches may be only short-term initiatives for specific settings. Unfortunately, the longitudinal study of survival rates discussed above does not address the 40 percent of cases where skill-based pay did not survive beyond six years.

PERSON-BASED STRUCTURES: COMPETENCIES

As with job evaluation, there are several perspectives on what **competencies** are and what they are supposed to accomplish. Are they a skill that can be learned and developed, or are they a trait that includes attitudes and motives? Do competencies focus on the minimum requirements that the organization needs to stay in business, or do they focus on outstanding performance? Are they characteristics of the organization or of the employee? Unfortunately, the answer to all of these questions is "yes."[18] A lack of consensus means that competencies can be a number of things; consequently, they stand in danger of becoming nothing.

By now you should be able to draw the next exhibit (Exhibit 6.5) yourself. The top part shows the process of using competencies to address the need for internal alignment by creating a **competency-based structure**. All approaches to creating a structure begin by looking at the work performed in the organization. While **skill-** and **job-based systems** hone in on information about specific tasks, competencies take the opposite approach. They try to abstract the underlying, broadly applicable knowledge, skills, and behaviors that form the foundation for success at any level or job in the organization. These are the *core competencies*. Core competencies are often linked to mission statements that express an organization's philosophy, values, business strategies, and plans.

Competency sets translate each core competency into action. For the core competency of *business awareness,* for example, competency sets might be related to organizational understanding, cost management, third-party relationships, and ability to identify business opportunities.

Competency indicators are the observable behaviors that indicate the level of competency within each set. These indicators may be used for staffing and evaluation as well as for pay purposes.

EXHIBIT 6.5   Determining the Internal Competency-Based Structure

Internal Alignment: Work Relationships Within the Organization	→	Core Competencies	→	Competency Sets	→	Behavioral Descriptors	→	Competency-Based Structure
Basic Decisions								

- What is objective of plan?
- What information to collect?
- What methods are used to determine and certify competencies?
- Who is involved?
- How useful for pay purposes?

EXHIBIT 6.6 TRW Human Resources Competencies

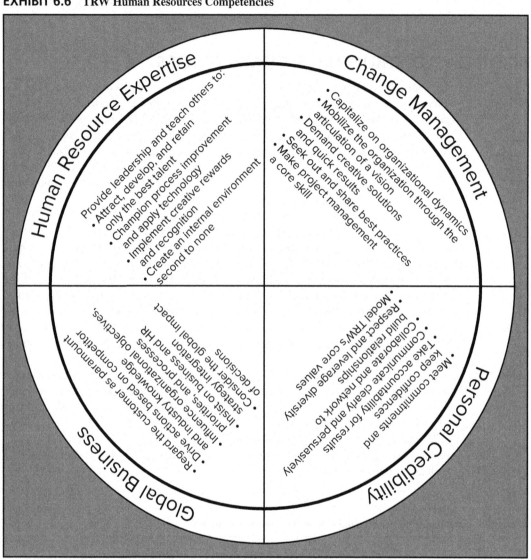

TRW's competency model for its human resource management department, shown in Exhibit 6.6, includes the four core competencies considered critical to the success of the business.[19] All HR employees are expected to demonstrate varying degrees of these competencies. However, not all individuals would be expected to reach the highest level in all competencies. Rather, the HR function should possess all levels of mastery of all the core competencies within the HRM group. Employees would use the model as a guide to what capacities the organization wants people to develop.

EXHIBIT 6.7   Sample Behavioral Competency Indicators

Impact and Influence: The intention to persuade, convince, or influence to have a specific impact. It includes the ability to anticipate and respond to the needs and concerns of others. *"Impact and Influence" is one of the competencies considered "most critical."*

Level	Behaviors
0: Not shown	• Lets things happen • Quotes policy and issues instruction
1: Direct persuasion	• Uses direct persuasion in a discussion or presentation • Appeals to reason; uses data or concrete examples • Does not adapt presentation to the interest and level of the audience • Reiterates the same points when confronted with opposition
2: Multiple attempts to persuade	• Tries different tactics when attempting to persuade without necessarily making an effort to adapt to the level or interest of an audience (e.g., making two or more different arguments or points in a discussion)
3: Builds trust and fosters win-win mentality (expected performance level)	• Tailors presentations or discussions to appeal to the interest and level of others • Looks for the "win-win" opportunities • Demonstrates sensitivity and understanding of others in detecting underlying concerns, interests, or emotions, and uses that understanding to develop effective responses to objections
4: Multiple actions to influence	• Takes more than one action to influence, with each action adapted to the specific audience (e.g., a group meeting to present the situation, followed by individual meetings) • May include taking a well-thought-out unusual action to have a specific impact
5: Influences through others	• Uses experts or other third parties to influence • Develops and maintains a planned network of relationships with customers, internal peers, and industry colleagues • When required, assembles "behind the scenes" support for ideas regarding opportunities and/or solving problems

---

Source: Reprinted from *Raising the Bar: Using Competencies to Enhance Employee Performance* with permission from the American Compensation Association (ACA), 14040 N. Northsight Blvd., Scottsdale, AZ, USA 85260; telephone (602) 483-8352. © ACA.

The *competency indicators* anchor the degree of a competency required at each level of complexity of the work. Exhibit 6.7 shows five levels of competency indicators for the competency *impact and influence*. These behavioral anchors make the competency more concrete. The levels range from "uses direct persuasion" at level 1 to "uses experts or other third parties to influence" at level 5. Sometimes the behavioral anchors might include scales of the intensity of action, the degree of impact of the action, its complexity, and/or the amount of effort expended. Scaled competency indicators are similar to job analysis questionnaires and degrees of compensable factors, discussed in previous chapters.

Defining Competencies

As supporters of planet Pluto have discovered, definitions matter. Because competencies are trying to get at what underlies work behaviors, there is a lot of fuzziness in defining them. Early conceptions of competencies focused on five areas:

1. Skills (demonstration of expertise)
2. Knowledge (accumulated information)
3. Self-concepts (attitudes, values, self-image)
4. Traits (general disposition to behave in a certain way)
5. Motives (recurrent thoughts that drive behaviors)[20]

As experience with competencies has grown, organizations seem to be moving away from the vagueness of self-concepts, traits, and motives. Instead, they are placing greater emphasis on business-related descriptions of behaviors "that excellent performers exhibit much more consistently than average performers." Competencies are becoming "a collection of observable behaviors (not a single behavior) that require no inference, assumption or interpretation."[21] Exhibit 6.7 shows behavioral anchors for the competency: Impact and Influence. Comparison with examples of compensable factors used in job evaluation from Chapter 5—Decision Making (Exhibit 5.9) and Multinational Responsibilities (Exhibit 5.10)—reveal the greater behavioral orientation of competencies. However, differences can be rather small. For example, "consult with technical experts" anchors level 6 of the job evaluation Decision Making compensable factor in Exhibit 5.9 and "uses experts" anchors the Impact and Influence behavioral competency shown in Exhibit 6.7.

Purpose of the Competency-Based Structure

Do competencies help support an internally aligned structure? Using our by-now familiar yardstick, how well do competencies support the organization strategy and work flow, treat employees fairly, and motivate their behavior toward organization objectives?

Organization Strategy

The main appeal of competencies is the direct link to the organization's strategy. The process of identifying competencies starts with the company leadership deciding what will spell success for the company. It resembles identifying compensable factors as part of job evaluation.

Frito-Lay, which has used competency-based structures for over 10 years, lists four competencies for managerial work, shown in Exhibit 6.8. Frito-Lay believes four are required in managerial work: leading for results, building work-force effectiveness, leveraging technical and business systems, and doing it the right way. The top of the exhibit shows the levels. At the first level, exhibiting the competency affects the team. At the next level, it has an impact across teams. And at the highest level, it has an impact on the entire location.

EXHIBIT 6.8 Frito-Lay Managerial Competencies

Competency Dimension	Behaviors
Leading for results	Using initiative and influence with others to drive results and promote continuous improvement.
Building workforce effectiveness	Coaching individual development and building capability of operational, project, or cross-functional teams to achieve business results.
Leveraging technical and business systems	Acquiring and applying a depth and/or breadth of knowledge, skills, and experience to achieve functional excellence.
Doing it the right way	Modeling, teaching, and coaching company values.

Source: Nancy Jagmin, "Assessing and Rewarding Competencies: The Ten-Year Tune-up at Frito-Lay," presentation for Center for Organization Effectiveness, April 2003, Marina del Rey, CA.

Work Flow

As you can judge from reading the previous exhibits, competencies are chosen to ensure that all the critical needs of the organization are met. For example, it is common practice to note: "These skills are considered important for all professionals but the weighting of importance and the level of proficiency varies for different positions, organizations, and business conditions."[22] So while the skills-based plans are tightly coupled to today's work, competencies more loosely apply to work requiring more tacit knowledge such as in managerial and professional work.

Fair to Employees

Advocates of competencies say they can empower employees to take charge of their own development. By focusing on optimum performance rather than average performance, competencies can help employees maintain their marketability.[23] However, critics of competencies worry that the field is going back to the middle of the last century, when basing pay on personal characteristics was standard practice.[24] Basing pay on race or gender seems appalling today, yet it was standard practice at one time. Basing pay on someone's judgment of another person's integrity raises a similar flag. Trying to justify pay differences based on inferred personal competencies creates risks that need to be managed.

> **e-Compensation**
>
> Look again at the Your Turn at the end of Chapter 4. How much do you think Bill Ryan, the customer service representative, is paid? Go to *www.salary.com* and search for some information. How does your job description for Mr. Ryan's job compare to those on salary.com? Does it matter?

Motivate Behavior Toward Organization Objectives

Competencies in effect provide guidelines for behavior and keep people focused. They can also provide a common basis for communicating and working together. This latter possibility has become increasingly important as organizations go global, and as employees with widely differing viewpoints and experiences fill leadership positions in these global organizations.

---

e-compensation

Go to www.shrm.org/hrcompetencies. Examine the competencies identified as important to be successful for human resource professionals and how they vary according to career stage. Consider how you would use this competency information in paying human resource professionals.

"HOW-TO": COMPETENCY ANALYSIS

The bottom part of Exhibit 6.5 shows the basic decisions in creating a competency-based structure.[25] The first decision, and by far the most important, is to clarify the objective of the plan.

Objective

We have already pointed out that one of the pitfalls of competency systems is trying to do too many things with ill-suited systems. Competencies may have value for personal development and communicating organization direction. However, the vagueness and subjectivity (what exactly *are* this person's motives?) make competencies a "risky foundation for a pay system."[26] The competency structure may exist on paper by virtue of the competency sets and scaled behavioral indicators but bear little connection to the work employees do. In contrast, companies like Frito-Lay have been using theirs for 10 years. Perhaps paying for competencies is the only way to get people to pay attention to them.

What Information to Collect?

A number of schemes for classifying competencies have been proposed.[27] One of them uses three groups:

1. *Personal characteristics:* These have the aura of the Boy Scouts about them: trustworthy, loyal, courteous. In business settings, the relevant characteristics might be personal integrity, maturity of judgment, flexibility, and respect for others. Employees are expected to come in the door with these characteristics and then develop and demonstrate them in increasingly complex and ambiguous job situations.

2. *Visionary:* These are the highest-level competencies. They might be expressed as possessing a global perspective, taking the initiative in moving the organization in new directions, and able to articulate the implications for the organization of trends in the marketplace, in world events, in the local community.

3. *Organization specific:* Between the above two groups are the competencies that are tied specifically to the particular organization and to the particular function where they are being applied. They generally include leadership, customer orientation,

functional expertise (e.g., able to leap tall buildings and explain the difference between competencies and compensable factors), and developing others—whatever reflects the company values, culture, and strategic intent.

At 3M, for example, competencies were developed internally for its global executives.[28] Behavioral anchors are used to rate an executive on each of these competencies. There are three competency areas: Fundamental (ethics and integrity, intellectual capability), Essential (customer orientation, developing people, inspiring others, business health and results), and Visionary (global perspective, vision and strategy, nurturing innovation, building alliances, organizational agility). Executives' ratings on these competencies are used to assess and develop executives worldwide. Because 3M relies heavily on promotion from within, competency ratings help develop executive talent for succession planning. Again, the link to development is clear; the link to pay is less clear.

Because they stem from each organization's mission statement or its strategy to achieve competitive advantage, you might conclude that the core competencies would be unique for each company. In fact, they are not. One analysis showed that most organizations appear to choose from the same list of 20 core competencies (Exhibit 6.9).[29] What does appear to differ among organizations is how they apply competencies.

EXHIBIT 6.9
The Top 20
Competencies

Achievement orientation
Concern of quality
Initiative
Interpersonal understanding
Customer service orientation
Influence and impact
Organization awareness
Networking
Directiveness
Teamwork and cooperation
Developing others
Team leadership
Technical expertise
Information seeking
Analytical thinking
Conceptual thinking
Self-control
Self-confidence
Business orientation
Flexibility

This parallels an issue in the strategy chapter (Chapter 2): There may be only slight differences in the words, but the actions differ. It is the actions that are the source of competitive advantage. 3M, for example, is known for innovation. Its competency, nurturing innovation, is defined as "Creates and sustains an environment that supports experimentation, rewards risk taking, reinforces curiosity, and challenges the status quo through freedom and openness without judgment. Influences the future to 3M's advantage." This competency, especially in terms of how 3M uniquely executes it, is thought to be a key to 3M's competitive advantage.

Whom to Involve?

Like compensable factors, competencies are derived from the executive leadership's beliefs about the organization and its strategic intent. However, anecdotal evidence indicates that not all employees understand that connection. Employees at one bank insisted that processing student tuition loans was a different competency from processing auto loans. The law department at Polaroid generated a list of over 1,000 competencies it felt were unique to the law department and that created value for the organization. (Is it possible that Polaroid, since bankrupt, would have been better served by devoting more time and energy to the effect of digital photography on film-based cameras?)

Exhibit 6.10 shows part of the competencies used by a major toy company. This is one of eight competencies for the marketing department. Other departments have separate competencies. Notice the mind-numbing level of detail. While this approach may be useful for career development, it is doubtful that all this information is useful, much less necessary, for compensation purposes. The initial promise of simplicity and flexibility in person-based systems remains unfulfilled.

Establish Certification Methods

The heart of the person-based plan is that employees get paid for the relevant skills or competencies they possess, whether or not those skills are used. Skill-based plans assume that possessing these skills will make it easier to match work flow with staffing levels, so whether or not an individual is *using* a particular skill on a particular day is not an issue. Competency-based plans assume—what? That all competencies are used all the time? The assumptions are not clear. What is clear, however, is the requirement that if people are to be paid based on their competencies, then there must be some way to demonstrate or certify to all concerned that a person possesses that level of competency. Although consultants discuss competencies as compatible with 360-degree feedback and personal development, they are silent on objectively certifying whether a person possesses a competency.

Resulting Structure

Recall that internal structures are described in terms of number of levels, pay differentials, and criterion on which the job structure is based. In practice, competency-based structures generally are designed with relatively few levels—four to six—and relatively wide differentials for increased flexibility. Exhibit 6.11 depicts the toy company's structures based on the four phases (levels) shown in Exhibit 6.10. Such a generic structure could be applied to almost any professional work, even the work of a university faculty.

EXHIBIT 6.10 Product Development Competency for Marketing Department at a Toy Company

Manages the product development process by:

- Analyzing and evaluating marketplace to identify niches/opportunities
- Evaluating product/concepts
- Developing marketing strategies
- Coordinating and evaluating research/testing
- Generating product recommendations and obtaining management support
- Driving product schedules/activities

Phase I: Baseline Expectation

- Analyzes market/competitive data (e.g., TRST, NPD) and provides top-line trend analysis, with supervision
- Evaluates products/concepts (see Toy Viability competency)
- Contributes to product brainstorming sessions
- Oversees market research activities and ensures timely completion
- Obtains Account Management input to the product development effort
- Develops and implements marketing strategy, with supervision: product, positioning, pricing/financial, promotion, packaging, merchandising, and advertising
- Facilitates cost reductions to achieve price/profit goals; ensures execution of cost meeting next steps
- Ensures adherence to product schedules
- Coordinates licensor approval of product concept/models

Phase II: Competent/Proficient

- Monitors and analyzes market/competitive data (e.g., TRST, NPD) with minimal supervision, and provides recommendations for product development opportunities
- Makes substantial contributions in product brainstorming sessions
- Analyzes market research results and makes appropriate product recommendations
- Partners with Account Management group to obtain their buy-in to the product development effort
- Develops and implements marketing strategy, with minimal supervision
- Drives cost reductions to achieve price/profit goals
- Drives product schedules and resolves product scheduling issues (late delivery, late debug)
- Negotiates with licensors to obtain product approvals

Phase III: Advanced/Coach

- Independently monitors and analyzes market/competitive data (e.g., TRST, NPD), provides recommendations for product development opportunities, and coaches others to do so
- Leads and facilitates formal product brainstorming sessions
- Coaches others in analyzing market research results and making product recommendations
- Develops innovative marketing plans (e.g., new channels of distribution, niche markets)
- Independently develops and implements marketing strategy, and coaches others to do so
- Identifies/evaluates cost reduction opportunities, and coaches others to do so
- Identifies and implements product schedule improvement tactics
- Coaches others to manage product schedules
- Shares product ideas/strategies with other teams/categories

Phase IV: Expert/Mentor

- Reviews/approves recommendations for product development opportunities
- Provides short- and long-term vision and goals for developing the corporate product portfolio across categories or brands
- Reviews/approves marketing strategy, and proactively adjusts strategy in response to internal/external changes
- Approves cost reduction recommendations
- Anticipates critical issues that may impact product schedules and develops alternate plans
- Ensures on-strategy delivery

EXHIBIT 6.11
Toy Company's
Structure
Based on
Competencies

Level	Phase	Title
4	Expert	Visionary; Champion; Executive
3	Advanced	Coach; Leader
2	Resource	Contributor; Professional
1	Proficient	Associate

Competencies and Employee Selection and Training/Development

In Chapter 2, we noted that human resource strategies can be thought of as influencing effectiveness through their impact on workforce ability, motivation, and ability to contribute (AMO). In the case of competencies, there is clear evidence that ability (broadly defined to include personality traits) is related to general competencies. Like Exhibit 6.9, Exhibit 6.12 shows a set of generic competencies, called the Great Eight, that seem to capture in an efficient way the themes found in the array of competency frameworks available. What Exhibit 6.12 adds are hypotheses regarding how these competencies relate to the individual characteristics of personality ("Big Five"), motivation, and ability. So, for example, based on Exhibit 6.12, if we wish to have managers who are competent in leading and deciding, we need to select or train and develop people high in need for power, need for control, and who have extroverted personalities. Failure to adequately screen employees on these individual characteristics would not only put more pressure on training and development, but also potentially de-motivate employees who are seeking to acquire and demonstrate these competencies, but who may not be well-suited to do so. Competency-based pay would be less likely to succeed in this situation.

Guidance (and Caution)[30] from the Research on Competencies

While the notion of competencies may have value in identifying what distinguishes typical from truly outstanding performance, there is debate on whether competencies can be translated into a measurable, objective basis for pay. Competencies often morph into compensable factors. But, that can cause difficulties if they were not developed for that purpose.

Thus far, research is limited. An area of research with potential application to competencies deals with human capital and knowledge management.[31] Viewing the competencies of employees as a portfolio similar to a diversified investment portfolio highlights the fact that some competencies deliver greater returns than others. The focus then changes to managing existing competencies and developing new ones in ways that maximize the overall returns to the organization.[32] Only one study has analyzed the competencies/performance relationship for managers. Managers' competencies were related to their performance ratings, but there was no relationship to unit-level performance.[33] (Perhaps future studies will report different results.) As organizations globalize, they may rebalance their values and perspectives to allow a global strategy to function.[34] They seek the right balance among the range and depth of cultural, functional, and product competencies in the global organization. But this is speculative and remains to be translated into pay practices.

EXHIBIT 6.12   Titles and High-Level Definitions of the Great Eight Competencies™

Factor	Competency Domain Title	Competency Domain Definition	Hypothesized Big Five, Motivation, and Ability Relationships[a]
1	Leading and deciding	Takes control and exercises leadership. Initiates action, gives direction, and takes responsibility.	Need for power and control, extroversion
2	Supporting and cooperating	Supports others and shows respect and positive regard for them in social situations. Puts people first, working effectively with individuals and tams, clients, and staff. Behaves consistently with clear personal values that complement those of the organization.	Agreeableness
3	Interacting and presenting	Communicates and networks effectively. Successfully persuades and influences these. Relates to others in a confident, relaxed manner.	Extroversion, general mental ability
4	Analyzing and interpreting	Shows evidence of clear analytical thinking. Gets to the heart of complex problems and issues. Applies own expertise effectively. Quickly takes on new technology. Communicates well in writing.	General mental ability, openness to new experience
5	Creating and conceptualizing	Works well in situations requiring openness to new ideas and experiences. Seeks out learning opportunities. Handles situations and problems with innovation and creativity. Thinks broadly and strategically. Supports and drives organizational change.	Openness to new experience, general mental ability
6	Organizing and executing	Plans ahead and works in a systematic and organized way. Follows directions and procedures. Focuses on customer satisfaction and delivers a quality service or product to the agreed standards.	Conscientiousness, general mental ability
7	Adapting and coping	Adapts and responds well to change. Manages pressure effectively and copes well with setbacks.	Emotional stability
8	Enterprising and performing	Focuses on results and achieving personal work objectives. Works best when work is related closely to results and the impact of personal efforts is obvious. Shows an understanding of business, commerce, and finance. Seeks opportunities for self-development and career advancement.	Need for achievement, negative agreeableness

[a] Where more than one predictor is shown, the second is expected to be of lesser importance than the first. The competency titles and definitions are taken from the SHL Universal Competency Framework™ Profiler and Designer Cards (copyright © 2004 by SHL Group plc, reproduced with permission of the copyright holder). These titles may be freely used for research purposes subject to due acknowledgment of the copyright holder.

Source: Dave Bartram, SHL Group, "The Great Eight Competencies: a Criterion-Centric Approach to Validation," *Journal of Applied Psychology* 90(6), 2005, pp. 1185–1203.

Note. More detailed definitions of each of the Great Eight are provided by the competency component level of the SHL Universal Competency Framework™.

The basic question remains: Is it appropriate to pay you for what I believe you are *capable of doing* versus what you are doing? Isn't it likely to be more effective, for pay purposes, to focus on what is easily measurable and directly related to organizational success (i.e., knowledge and skills that are job/performance related)? Also, a question raised earlier is whether competency-based systems are more susceptible to discrimination based on individual employee demographic characteristics.

ONE MORE TIME: INTERNAL ALIGNMENT REFLECTED IN STRUCTURES (PERSON-BASED OR JOB-BASED)

Now that we have spent three chapters examining all the trees, let's look again at the forest. The purpose of job- and person-based procedures is really very simple—to design and manage an internal pay structure that helps the organization succeed.

As with job-based evaluation, the final result of the person-based plan is an internal structure of work in the organization. This structure should reflect the organization's internal alignment policy (loosely versus tightly linked, egalitarian versus hierarchical) and support its business operations. Further, managers must ensure that the structure *remains* internally aligned by reassessing work/skills/competencies when necessary. Failure to do so risks pay structures that open the door to bias and potentially unethical and misdirected behavior.

In practice, when evaluating higher-value, nonroutine work, the distinction between job- versus person-based approaches blurs. The focus is on what factors (*both* job and person) create value for the organization. The person influences the job content in managerial and professional work. Skill-based fits more easily with manufacturing work.[35] Yet caution is advised: Much of the work required in contemporary manufacturing cells requires tacit, nonroutine knowledge (problem solving, interacting, negotiating).

ADMINISTERING AND EVALUATING THE PLAN

Whatever plan is designed, whether job-based or person-based, a crucial issue is the fairness of its administration. Just as with job evaluation, sufficient information should be available to apply the plan, such as definitions of compensable factors, degrees, or details of skill blocks, competencies, and certification methods. Increasingly, online tools are available for managers to learn about these plans and apply them.[36] We have already mentioned the issue of employee understanding and acceptance. Communication and employee involvement are crucial for acceptance of the resulting pay structures. See Chapter 18 for more discussion of pay communication.

There is vast research literature on job evaluation compared to person-based structures. Most of it focuses on the procedures used rather than the resulting structure's usefulness in motivating employee behaviors or achieving organization objectives. In virtually all the studies, job-based evaluation is treated as a measurement device; the research assesses its reliability, validity, costs, and its compliance with laws and regulations. Any value added by job evaluation (e.g., reducing pay dissatisfaction, improving employees' understanding of how their pay is determined) has been largely ignored.[37] In contrast, research on person-based structures tends to focus on their effects on behaviors and organization objectives and ignores questions of reliability and validity.

Reliability of Job Evaluation Techniques

A reliable evaluation would be one where different evaluators produce the same results. Most studies report high agreement when different people rank-order jobs—correlations between .85 and .96.[38] This is important because in practice, several different people usually evaluate jobs. The results should not depend on which person did the evaluation. However, even with what are normally considered to be "high" reliabilities (e.g., .90 or greater), practically important differences in assigned salaries can result when different people or groups assign job evaluation points. Consider the example in Exhibit 6.13. Two different sets of raters evaluated 9 jobs (Jobs A through I). In Chapter 8, we will see how job evaluation points can be translated into predicted salary rates using a pay policy line. In the present example, the pay policy line is Predicted Salary = $4,800 + $360 * Job Evaluation Points. Do we get the same predicted salaries regardless of whether we use Group 1 versus Group 2 as the job evaluation raters? The answer is a clear NO. For example, in the case of Job G, the predicted salary is $28,800 higher based on Group 1's job evaluation scores. That is despite the fact that the correlation between the Group 1 and Group 2 columns of job evaluation ratings (the inter-rater reliability) is high ($r = .94$). Some of the difference in predicted salaries is due to Group 1 giving out lower levels of job evaluation points on average. However, even when we eliminate that difference between the groups, as in the right side of Exhibit 6.13, there remain predicted salary differences of an uncomfortably large size. And, remember that each job has multiple employees. Thus, many employees will be affected. Now, an important caveat is that, as we saw in Chapter 5 and as we will discuss in Chapter 8, most organizations are now using market pricing, where many jobs are matched directly to jobs in pay surveys to determine salaries. In such cases, job evaluation results often have less influence on salaries. Nevertheless, it is important to remember that when job evaluation points do play a significant role in salary setting (e.g., for non-benchmark jobs, those jobs that cannot be directly matched to pay survey jobs), even seemingly high reliability between different raters may still leave room for very different resulting salaries.

Reliability can be improved by using evaluators who are familiar with the work and trained in the job evaluation process. Some organizations use group consensus to increase reliability. Each evaluator makes a preliminary independent evaluation. Then, they discuss their results until consensus emerges. Consensus certainly appears to make the results more acceptable. However, some studies report that results obtained through consensus were not significantly different from those obtained either by independent evaluators or by averaging individual evaluators' results. Others report that a forceful or experienced person on the committee can sway the results. So can knowledge about the job's present salary level.[39] These reliabilities for job evaluation scores are higher than those we saw in Chapter 4 for job analysis ratings. One possible reason is that those conducting job evaluation may already know the pay for the jobs, which may result in greater consistency across raters. Another factor is that job evaluation research has often had raters rely on job descriptions to assign job evaluation ratings. That

EXHIBIT 6.13   Differences in Salaries Despite "High" (.94) Interrater Reliability

	Original Data						Equate Mean Job Evaluation Points across Group 1 and Group 2[a]					
	Job Evaluation Points		Predicted Salary		Salary		Job Evaluation Points		Predicted Salary		Salary	
Job	Group 1	Group 2	Group 1	Group 2	Difference	Job	Group 1	Group 2	Group 1	Group 2	Difference
A	70	85	$ 30,000	$35,400	–$ 5,400	A	70	120	$ 30,000	$ 48,000	–$18,000
B	85	65	$ 35,400	$28,200	$ 7,200	B	85	100	$ 35,400	$ 40,800	–$ 5,400
C	200	180	$ 76,800	$69,600	$ 7,200	C	200	215	$ 76,800	$ 82,200	–$ 5,400
D	130	85	$ 51,600	$35,400	$ 16,200	D	130	120	$ 51,600	$ 48,000	$ 3,600
E	65	50	$ 28,200	$22,800	$ 5,400	E	65	85	$ 28,200	$ 35,400	–$ 7,200
F	135	105	$ 53,400	$42,600	$ 10,800	F	135	140	$ 53,400	$ 55,200	–$ 1,800
G	215	135	$ 82,200	$53,400	$ 28,800	G	215	170	$ 82,200	$ 66,000	$16,200
H	300	240	$112,800	$91,200	$ 21,600	H	300	275	$112,800	$103,800	$ 9,000
I	130	70	$ 51,600	$30,000	$ 21,600	I	130	105	$ 51,600	$ 42,600	$ 9,000
Mean	148	113	$ 58,000	$45,400		Mean	148	148	$ 58,000	$ 58,000	
Sum[b]					$124,200	Sum[b]					$75,600

Predicted salary = $4,800 + $360 * Job evaluation points

[a] Added 35 points to the Group 2 job evaluation score for each job.

[b] Sum of absolute values of differences.

196

(working from the same job description rather than starting "from scratch" with each evaluator observing jobs) may again result in greater consistency. In any case, as we have seen, even high reliabilities in job evaluation can still produce different pay rates for jobs that vary as a function of the rater/raters.

As part of efforts to reduce costs, job evaluation committees are disappearing. Instead, managers do the evaluations online as part of the organization's "HR Toolkit" or "shared services." The reliability and validity of the results obtained this way have not been studied.

Validity

Validity refers to the degree to which the evaluation assesses what it is supposed to—the relative worth of jobs to the organization. Validity of job evaluation has been measured in two ways: (1) the degree of agreement between rankings that resulted from the job evaluation with an agreed-upon *ranking of benchmarks* used as the criterion, and (2) by **"hit rates"**—the degree to which the job evaluation plan matches (hits) an agreed-upon *pay structure for benchmark jobs*. In both cases, the predetermined, agreed-upon ranking or pay structure is for benchmark jobs. It can be established by organization leadership or be based on external market data, negotiations with unions, or the market rates for benchmarks held predominantly by men (to try to eliminate any gender discrimination reflected in the market), or some combination of these.

Many studies report that when different job evaluation plans are compared to each other, they generate *very similar rankings* of jobs but *very low hit rates*—they disagree on how much to pay the jobs.[40] One study that looked at three different job evaluation plans applied to the same set of jobs reported similar rank order among evaluators using each plan but substantial differences in the resulting pay.[41] Some studies have found pay differences of up to $427 per month ($750/per month in today's dollars, or $9,000 a year) depending on the method used.

So it is clear that the definition of validity needs to be broadened to include impact on pay decisions. How the results are judged depends on the standards used. For managing compensation the correct standard is the pay structure—what jobholders get paid—rather than simply the jobs' rank order.

Studies of the degree to which different job evaluation plans produce the same results start with the assumption that if different approaches produce the same results, then those results must be "correct," that is, valid. But in one study, three plans all gave the same result (they were reliable) but all three ranked a police officer higher than a detective. They were not valid.[42] TV fans know that in U.S. police departments, the detectives outrank the uniforms. What accounts for the reliability of invalid plans? Either the compensable factors did not pick up something deemed important in the detectives' jobs or the detectives have more power to negotiate higher wages. So while these three plans gave the same results, they would have little acceptance among detectives.

You may wonder why any manager or employee cares about such details? Is this an example of compensation specialists inventing work for themselves? Not if your organization is facing challenges by dissatisfied employees or their lawyers. To miss this point is to place your organization at risk.[43]

Acceptability

Several methods are used to assess and improve employee acceptability. An obvious one is to include a *formal appeals process*. Employees who believe their jobs are evaluated incorrectly should be able to request reanalysis and/or skills reevaluation. Most firms respond to such requests from managers, but few extend the process to all employees unless it is part of a union-negotiated grievance process.[44] *Employee attitude surveys* can assess perceptions of how useful evaluation is as a management tool. Ask employees whether their pay is related to their job and how well they understand what is expected in their job.[45]

BIAS IN INTERNAL STRUCTURES

The continuing differences in jobs held by men, women, and people of color, and the accompanying pay differences, have focused attention on internal structures as a possible source of discrimination. Much of this attention has been directed at job evaluation as both a potential source of bias against women and a mechanism to reduce bias.[46] It has been widely speculated that job evaluation is susceptible to gender bias—jobs held predominantly by women are undervalued simply because of the jobholder's gender. But evidence does not support this proposition.[47] Additionally, there is no evidence that the job *evaluator's* gender affects the results.

In contrast to the gender of the jobholder or the evaluator, the evidence on compensable factors and bias is less clear. One study found that compensable factors related to job content (such as contact with others and judgment) did reflect bias against work done predominantly by women, but factors pertaining to employee requirements (such as education and experience) did not.[48]

Wages Criteria Bias

The second potential source of bias affects job evaluation indirectly, through the current wages paid for jobs. If job evaluation is based on the current wages paid and the jobs held predominantly by women are underpaid, then the results simply mirror bias in the current pay rates.[49] Since many job evaluation plans are purposely structured to mirror the existing pay structure, it is not surprising that current wages influence the results of job evaluation. One study of 400 compensation specialists revealed that market data had a substantially larger effect on pay decisions than did job evaluations or current pay data.[50] This study is a unique look at several factors that may affect pay structures.

Several recommendations seek to ensure that job evaluation plans are bias-free, including the following:

1. Define the compensable factors and scales to include the content of jobs held predominantly by women. For example, working conditions may include the noise and stress of office machines and the repetitive movements associated with the use of computers.
2. Ensure that factor weights are not consistently biased against jobs held predominantly by women. Are factors usually associated with these jobs always given less weight?
3. Apply the plan in as bias-free a manner as feasible. Ensure that the job descriptions are bias-free, exclude incumbent names from the job evaluation process, and train diverse evaluators.

At the risk of pointing out the obvious, all issues concerning job evaluation also apply to skill-based and competency-based plans. For example, the acceptability of the results of skill-based plans can be studied from the perspective of measurement (reliability and validity) and administration (costs, simplicity). The various points in skill certification at which errors and biases may enter into judgment (e.g., different views of skill-block definitions, potential favoritism toward team members, defining and assessing skill obsolescence) and whether skill-block points and evaluators make a difference all need to be studied. In light of the detailed bureaucracy that has grown up around job evaluation, we confidently predict a growth of bureaucratic procedures around person-based plans, too. In addition to bureaucracy to manage costs, the whole approach to certification may be fraught with potential legal vulnerabilities if employees who fail to be certified challenge the process. Unfortunately, no studies of gender effects in skill-based or competency-based plans exist. Little attention has been paid to assessor training or validating the certification process. Just as employment tests used for hiring and promotion decisions must be demonstrably free of illegal bias, it seems logical that certification procedures used to determine pay structures would face the same requirement.

THE PERFECT STRUCTURE

Exhibit 6.14 contrasts job-, skill-, and competency-based approaches. Pay increases are gained via promotions to more responsible jobs under job-based structures or via the acquisition of more-valued skills/competencies under the person-based structures. Logically, employees will focus on how to get promoted (experience, performance) or on how to acquire the required skills or competencies (training, learning).

Managers whose employers use job-based plans focus on placing the right people in the right job. A switch to skill-/competency-based plans reverses this procedure. Now, managers must assign the right work to the right people, that is, those with the right skills and competencies. A job-based approach controls costs by paying only as much as the work performed is worth, regardless of any greater skills the employee may possess. So, as Exhibit 6.14 suggests, costs are controlled via job rates or work assignments and budgets.

In contrast, skill-/competency-based plans pay employees for the highest level of skill/competency they have achieved *regardless of the work they perform.* This maximizes flexibility. But it also encourages all employees to become certified at top rates. Unless an employer can either control the rate at which employees can certify skill/competency mastery or employ fewer people, the organization may experience higher labor costs than do competitors using job-based approaches. The key is to offset the higher rates with greater productivity. One consulting firm claims that an average company switching to a skill-based system experiences a 15 to 20 percent increase in wage rates, a 20 to 25 percent increase in training and development costs, and initial *increases* in head count to allow people to cross-train and move around.[51] Another study found costs were no higher.[52]

In addition to having potentially higher rates and higher training costs, skill/competency plans may become as complex and burdensome as job-based plans.

EXHIBIT 6.14   Contrasting Approaches

	Job Based	Skill Based	Competency Based
What is valued	Compensable factors	Skill blocks	Competencies
Quantify the value	Factor degree weights	Skill levels	Competency levels
Mechanisms to translate into pay	Assign points that reflect criterion pay structure	Certification and price skills in external market	Certification and price competencies in external market
Pay structure	Based on job performed/ market	Based on skills certified/market	Based on competency developed/market
Pay increases	Promotion	Skill acquisition	Competency development
Managers' focus	Link employees to work promotion and placement cost control via pay for job and budget increase	Utilize skills efficiently Provide training Control costs via training, certification, and work assignments	Be sure competencies add value Provide competency-developing opportunities Control costs via certification and assignments
Employee focus	Seek promotions to earn more pay	Acquire skills	Acquire competencies
Procedures	Job analysis job evaluation	Skill analysis skill certification	Competency analysis competency certification
Advantages	Clear expectations sense of progress pay based on value of work performed	Continuous learning flexibility reduced work force	Continuous learning flexibility lateral movement
Limitations	Potential bureaucracy potential inflexibility	Potential bureaucracy requires cost controls	Potential bureaucracy requires cost controls

Additionally, questions still remain about a skill/competency system's compliance with the U.S. Equal Pay Act.

So where does all this come out? What is the best approach to pay structures, and how will we know it when we see it? The answer is, it depends. The best approach may be to provide sufficient ambiguity (loosely linked internal alignment) to afford flexibility to adapt to changing conditions. Too generic an approach may not provide sufficient detail to make a clear link between pay, work, and results; too detailed an approach may become

rigid. Bases for pay that are too vaguely defined will have no credibility with employees, will fail to signal what is really important for success, and may lead to suspicions of favoritism and bias.

This chapter concludes our section on internal alignment. Before we move on to external considerations, let's once again address the issue of, So what? Why bother with a pay structure? The answer should be, because it supports improved organization performance. An internally aligned pay structure, whether strategically loosely linked or tightly fitting, can be designed to (1) help determine pay for the wide variety of work in the organization, and (2) ensure that pay influences peoples' attitudes and work behaviors and directs them toward organization objectives.

Your **Turn**   Climb the Legal Ladder

Several years ago, Sullivan & Cromwell, a large New York law firm with offices around the world, raised its starting salary for law school graduates to $160,000, up from $145,000 the previous year. But, at Sullivan & Cromwell, like at many firms, starting salaries have not increased since. Indeed, some firms have cut salaries and/or jobs. *The New York Times* reported that law firms experienced a decline in their services following the financial crisis. In fact, Dewey & LeBoeuf, founded in 1909, which just a few years ago had 2,500 employees (including 1,400 attorneys) in 26 offices around the world, recently filed for bankruptcy. Although the root cause can be debated, one point of view is that the firm embraced unfettered growth (including a large merger in 2007) and also engaged in aggressive "poaching" of attorneys from other firms by offering large, multiyear, guaranteed pay packages. When business declined, they were stuck with large fixed compensation costs and also, some would argue, a weakened culture, making it difficult to rally the troops. Indeed, most partners, once they felt things were going downhill, defected to other firms. In such firms, top partners might earn 9 times what some other partners earn. In contrast to the Dewey & LeBoeuf approach, many law firms still follow the traditional law firm approach to compensation, which is a lock-step model where partners are paid to an important degree based on seniority within a narrower band where the highest paid partners make 4 or 5 times as much as some other partners. Talent is largely groomed from within, as opposed to significant poaching of attorneys from other firms. Most large firms, including Sullivan & Cromwell, use pay structures with six to eight levels from associate to partner. The associate's level is typically based on experience plus performance (see Exhibit 1). In the world of associate attorneys, performance is measured as billable hours. So the associates who meet or exceed the expected billable hours advance to the next level each year. Similar to the tenure process in academic settings, after six to eight years associates are expected to become partners or "find opportunities elsewhere." The likelihood of making partner differs among firms, but the norm seems to be less than one-third of the associates make it. Associates are expected to bill around 2,200 hours per year. That works out to six hours a day 365 days per year. Sullivan & Cromwell partners reportedly earn an average of $2.97 million a year.

Clients are billed about $250/hour for each associate. (Some partners' billing rates in New York firms have now hit $1,000 per hour.) So if associates hit or exceed their targets, they generate $550,000 annually ($250 times 2,200 hours). Many firms also use performance bonuses for associates. At Sullivan & Cromwell, associate bonuses ranged from $30,000 to $65,000 a few years ago. More recently, as Exhibit 1 shows, bonuses have gone higher. *The New York Times* described the recent overall trend as "Big Law Firms Bring Back Hefty Bonuses for Associates," which is attributed to "a recovery for corporate America in driving legal work on mergers and acquisitions, stock and bond offerings, and intellectual property matters." One observers also suggested that "law firms are adopting a version of the Wall Street pay model, which links bonuses to overall profitability of the firms." Another observer stated that "What we are continuing to see is law firms are looking for talent who can handle files on their own and bring high value to corporate clients."

1. Think about the research evidence discussed in the book. Would you expect the Sullivan & Cromwell associates to feel their pay structure is fair? What comparisons would they likely make? What work behaviors would you expect Sullivan & Cromwell's pay structure to motivate? Explain.

2. What about associates who joined the firm four years ago? If the salaries for new associates increased by $20,000, what would you recommend for other levels in the structure? Explain.

EXHIBIT 1 Pay Structure at a Law Firm	Associate Base Salary		Bonus Range		Bonus Discretionary
	Year		Low	High	
	1st	$160,000	$0	$15,000	Yes
	2nd	170,000	0	25,000	Yes
	3rd	185,000	0	50,000	Yes
	4th	210,000	0	65,000	Yes
	5th	230,000	0	80,000	Yes
	6th	250,000	0	90,000	Yes
	7th	267,500	0	100,000	Yes
	8th	290,000	0	100,000	Yes

3. Partners make around 10 times the highest-paid associates. A *Wall Street Journal* writer laments that law firms form "giant pyramids . . . (in which) associates at the bottom funnel money to partners at the top." What is missing from the writer's analysis? Hint: Speculate about the likely differences in content and value of the work performed by partners compared to associates. Any parallels to Merrill Lynch's FAs and SVPIs?

4. A few years ago, Sullivan & Cromwell announced that year-end bonuses would be cut in half, with a maximum of $17,500 for early-career associates and $32,500 for eighth-year associates. In the following two years, bonuses were cut further. However, the trend was then reversed with bonuses subsequently being increased (to range from $30,000 to $65,000 for associates), and more recently, as Exhibit 1 shows, there are further increases in bonuses. What drives these bonus decisions and how they vary over time? How does this bonus variability over time compare to variability in salaries over time at Sullivan & Cromwell? What explains the difference in the way salaries and bonuses are managed over time?

5. How does the Sullivan & Cromwell approach to compensation differ from that of Dewey & LeBoeuf? What are the advantages and disadvantages of each approach?

Sources: www.infirmation.com, www.sullcrom.com; Lindsey Fortado, "Linklaters Becomes Latest Law Firm to Cut Starting Lawyer Pay," Bloomberg.com, April 30, 2009; "The American Lawyer," *The AmLaw* 100, April 2009; Susan Beck, "Are Blue-Chip New York Firms Losing Their Balance?" *Law.com*, April 30, 2009; "Heavy Lies the Crown: Associate Cuts Were the Story in 2008. Are Partners Next?" *American Lawyer*, February 2009; "Sullivan & Cromwell Halves Associate Bonuses," *JD Journal*, December 19, 2008. Nathan Koppel and Vanessa O'Connell. "Pay Gap Widens at Big Law Firms as Partners Chase Star Attorneys." *Wall Street Journal*, February 8, 2011. Peter Lattman. "Dewey & LeBoeuf Files for Bankruptcy." *New York Times*. May 28, 2012. David Lat and Elie Mystal. "Breaking: Sullivan & Cromwell Announces (Paltry) Spring Bonuses." April 26, 2012. http://abovethelaw.com. Accessed June 1, 2012. Debra Cassens Weiss, "Sullivan & Cromwell Pays Spring Bonuses; Blog Deems them 'Small Change." *ABA Journal*. April 27, 2012. Matthew Goldstein. "Big Law Firms Bringing Back Hefty Bonuses for Associates." *New York Times*. December 3, 2014, p. B1; Staci Zaretsky. "Associate Bonus Watch: Sullivan & Cromwell Bonuses Are Here!" December 10, 2014. http://abovethelaw.com/2014/12/associate-bonus-watch-sullivan-crowell-matches-davis-polk/. Accessed February 7, 2015; "2015 LawCrossing Salary Survey of Lawyer Salaries in Best Law Firms." http://www.lawcrossing.com/article/900043256/2015-LawCrossing-Salary-Survey-of-Lawyer-Salaries-in-Best-Law-Firms/. Accessed February 7, 2015.

Summary   This section of the book examines pay structures within an organization. The premise underlying internal alignment is that internal pay structures need to be aligned with the organization's business strategy and objectives, the design of the work flow, a concern for the fair treatment of employees, and the intent of motivating employees. The work relationships within a single organization are an important part of internal alignment.

The structures are part of the web of incentives within organizations. They affect satisfaction with pay, the willingness to seek and accept promotions to more responsible jobs, the effort to keep learning and undertake additional training, and the propensity to remain with the employer. They also reduce the incidence of pay-related grievances.

The techniques for establishing internally aligned structures include job analysis, job evaluation, and person-based approaches for skill-/competency-based plans. But, in practice, aspects of both jobs and people are used. Although viewed by some as bureaucratic burdens, these techniques can aid in achieving the objectives of the pay system when they are properly designed and managed. Without them, our pay objectives of improving competitiveness and fairness are more difficult to achieve.

We have now finished the first part of the book. We discussed the techniques used to establish internal alignment as well as its effects on compensation objectives. The next part of the book focuses on the next strategic issue in our pay model: external competitiveness.

Review Questions

1. What are the pros and cons of having employees involved in compensation decisions? What forms can employee involvement take?

2. Why does the process used in the design of the internal pay structure matter? Distinguish between the processes used to design and administer a person-based and a job-based approach.

3. If you were managing employee compensation, how would you recommend that your company evaluate the usefulness of its job evaluation or person-based plans?

4. Based on the research on job evaluation, what are the sources of possible gender bias in skill-/competency-based plans?

5. How can a manager ensure that job evaluation or skill-/competency-based plans support a customer-centered strategy?

Endnotes
1. Robert Kanigel, *The One Best Way* (New York: Viking, 1997).
2. M. Marchington, D. Grimshaw, J. Rubery, and H. Willmott, eds., *Fragmenting Work: Blurring Organizational Boundaries and Disordering Hierarchies* (New York: Oxford University Press, 2004).
3. N. Gupta and J. D. Shaw, "Successful Skill-Based Pay Plans," in *The Executive Handbook of Compensation: Linking Strategic Rewards to Business,* C. Fay, D. Knight, and M. A. Thompson, eds. (New York: Free Press, 2001); Laurie Bienstock and Sandra McLellan, "Job Leveling in a Changing Environment," *WorldatWork Journal,* Fourth Quarter 2002, pp. 37–44.

4. The Consortium for Public Research in Education at the University of Wisconsin (*www .wcer.wisc.edu/cpre/tcomp/research*) publishes research on teachers' pay and analysis of emerging issues; see A. Milanowski, "The Varieties of Knowledge and Skill-Based Pay Design: A Comparison of Seven New Pay Systems for K–12 Teachers," Working Paper TC-01-2, University of Wisconsin, Wisconsin Center for Education Research, Consortium for Policy Research in Education, Madison, 2001; Steve Farkas, Jean Johnson, Ann Duffett, et al., *Stand by Me: What Teachers Really Think about Unions, Merit Pay, and Other Professional Matters* (New York: Public Agenda, 2003).

5. Diana Southall and Jerry Newman, *Skill-Based Pay Development* (Buffalo, NY: HR Foundations, 2000).

6. G. Douglas Jenkins Jr., Gerald E. Ledford Jr., Nina Gupta, and D. Harold Doty, *Skill-Based Pay* (Scottsdale, AZ: American Compensation Association, 1992).

7. B. Murray and B. Gerhart, "An Empirical Analysis of a Skill-Based Pay Program and Plant Performance Outcomes," *Academy of Management Journal* 41 (1998), pp. 68–78.

8. Gerald Ledford, "Factors Affecting the Long-Term Success of Skill-Based Pay," *WorldatWork Journal,* First Quarter, 2008, pp. 6–18; Judy Canavan, "Overcoming the Challenge of Aligning Skill-Based Pay Levels to the External Market," *WorldatWork Journal,* First Quarter (2008), pp. 18–24.

9. Rosemary Batt, "Who Benefits From Teams? Comparing Workers, Supervisors, and Managers," *Industrial Relations,* 43 (2004), pp. 183–212.

10. Gerald E. Ledford, Jr., "Three Case Studies of Skill-Based Pay: An Overview," *Compensation and Benefits Review,* March/April 1991, pp. 11–23; Gerald Ledford, "Factors Affecting the Long-Term Success of Skill-Based Pay," *WorldatWork Journal,* First Quarter (2008), pp. 6–18.

11. Erich C. Dierdorff and Eric A. Surface, "If You Pay for Skills, Will They Learn? Skill Change and Maintenance Under a Skill-Based Pay System," *Journal of Management* 34 (2008), pp. 721–743.

12. Cynthia Lee, Kenneth S. Law, and Philip Bobko, "The Importance of Justice Perceptions on Pay Effectiveness: A Two-Year Study of a Skill-Based Pay Plan," *Journal of Management* 25(6), 1999, pp. 851–873.

13. K. Parent and C. Weber, "Case Study: Does Paying for Knowledge Pay Off?" *Compensation and Benefits Review,* September–October 1994, pp. 44–50; B. Murray and B. Gerhart, "An Empirical Analysis of a Skill-Based Pay Program and Plant Performance Outcomes," *Academy of Management Journal* 41 (1998), pp. 68–78; A. Mitra, N. Gupta, and J. D. Shaw, "A Comparative Examination of Traditional and Skill-based Pay Plans," *Journal of Managerial Psychology* 26, (2010), pp. 278–296.

14. Kenneth Mericle and Dong-One Kim, "Determinants of Skill Acquisition and Pay Satisfaction under Pay-for-Knowledge Systems," Working Paper Series, Institute of Industrial Relations, University of California, Berkeley, *www.iir.berkeley.edu/ncw/,* 1996; Steve Farkas, Jean Johnson, Ann Duffett, et al., *Stand by Me: What Teachers Really Think about Unions, Merit Pay, and Other Professional Matters* (New York: Public Agenda, 2003), *www.publicagenda.org.*

15. Jason D. Shaw, Nina Gupta, Atul Mitra, and Gerald E. Ledford Jr., "Success and Survival of Skill-Based Pay Plans," *Journal of Management,* February 2005, pp. 28–49.

16. Gerald Ledford, "Factors Affecting the Long-Term Success of Skill-Based Pay," *WorldatWork Journal,* First Quarter (2008), pp. 6–18.

17. N. Fredric Crandall and Marc J. Wallace, Jr., "Paying Employees to Develop New Skills," in Howard Risher, ed., *Aligning Pay and Results* (New York: American Management Association, 1999).

18. Patricia Zingheim, Gerald E. Ledford, Jr., and Jay R. Schuster, "Competencies and Competency Models: Does One Size Fit All?" *ACA Journal,* Spring 1996, pp. 56–65.
19. TRW Corporate Competency Model.
20. Lyle M. Spencer Jr. and Signe M. Spencer, *Competence at Work* (New York: Wiley, 1993).
21. William M. Mercer, *Competencies, Performance and Pay* (New York: William M. Mercer, 1995).
22. TRW Corporate Competency Model.
23. James T. Kochanski and Howard Risher, "Paying for Competencies: Rewarding Knowledge, Skills, and Behaviors," in *Aligning Pay and Results,* Howard Risher, ed. (New York: American Management Association, 1999).
24. C. A. Bartlett and Sumantra Ghoshal, "The Myth of the Generic Manager: New Personal Competencies for New Management Roles," *California Management Review* 40(1), 1997, pp. 92–105.
25. For a comprehensive discussion of best practices in competency modeling in compensation and other areas of human resources, see M. A. Campion, A. A. Fink, B. J. Ruggeberg, L. Carr, G. M. Phillips, and R. B. Odman. "Doing Competencies Well: Best Practices in Competency Modeling," *Personnel Psychology* 64 (2011), pp. 225–262.
26. Edward E. Lawler III, "From Job-Based to Competency-Based Organizations," *Journal of Organizational Behavior* 15 (1994), pp. 3–15.
27. Patricia K. Zingheim and Jay R. Schuster, "Reassessing the Value of Skill-Based Pay: Getting the Runaway Train Back on Track," *WorldatWork Journal* 11(3), Third Quarter 2002.
28. Margaret E. Allredge and Kevin J. Nilan, "3M's Leadership Competency Model: An Internally Developed Solution," *Human Resource Management* 39 (Summer/Fall 2000), pp. 133–145.
29. Patricia Zingheim, Gerald E. Ledford, Jr., and Jay R. Schuster, "Competencies and Competency Models," in American Compensation Association, *Raising the Bar: Using Competencies to Enhance Employee Performance* (Scottsdale, AZ: American Compensation Association, 1996).
30. T. H. Stone, B. D. Webster, and S. Schoonover, "What Do We Know About Competency Modeling?" *International Journal of Selection and Assessment,* 21(3), 2013, pp. 334–338.
31. Scott A. Snell, David P. Lepak, and Mark A. Youndt, "Managing the Architecture of Intellectual Capital," in *Strategic Human Resources Management in the Twenty-First Century,* Suppl. 4, Patrick M. Wright, Lee E. Dyer, John W. Bodreau, and George T. Milkovich, eds. (Stamford, CT: JAI Press, 1999).
32. Robert L. Heneman and Peter V. Leblanc, "Developing a More Relevant and Competitive Approach for Valuing Knowledge Work," *Compensation and Benefits Review,* July/August 2002, pp. 43–47; James R. Bowers, "Valuing Work—An Integrated Approach," Chapter 16 in Charles H. Fay, Michael A. Thompson, and Damien Knight, eds., *The Executive Handbook on Compensation—Linking Strategic Rewards to Business Performance* (New York: Free Press, 2001).
33. A. R. Levenson, W. A. Van der Stede, and S. G. Cohen, "Measuring the Relationship between Managerial Competencies and Performance," *Journal of Management* 32(3), 2006, pp. 360–380.
34. Allen D. Engle Sr. and Mark E. Mendenhall, "Spinning the Global Competency Cube: Toward a Timely Transnational Human Resource Decision Support System," working paper, Eastern Kentucky University, Richmond, KY, 2000.
35. Jason D. Shaw, Nina Gupta, Atul Mitra, and Gerald E. Ledford Jr., "Success and Survival of Skill-Based Pay Plans," *Journal of Management,* February 2005, pp. 28–49.

36. *HRJob Evaluation Software, Online Job Classification, Web. NPKTools* (part of CompXpert compensation analysis suite), *www.npktools.com*.

37. An exception is the study cited in A. R. Levenson, W. A. Van der Stede, and S. G. Cohen, "Measuring the Relationship Between Managerial Competencies and Performance," *Journal of Management* 32(3), 2006, pp. 360–380.

38. Tjarda van Sliedregt, Olga F. Voskuijl, and Henk Thierry, "Job Evaluation Systems and Pay Grade Structures: Do They Match?" *International Journal of Human Resource Management* 12(8), December 2001, pp. 1313–1324.

39. Erich C. Dierdorff and Mark A. Wilson, "A Meta-Analysis of Job Analysis Reliability," *Journal of Applied Psychology,* August 2003, pp. 635–646; Vandra Huber and S. Crandall, "Job Measurement: A Social-Cognitive Decision Perspective," in *Research in Personnel and Human Resources Management,* vol. 12, Gerald R. Ferris, ed. (Greenwich, CT: JAI Press, 1994), pp. 223–269; Sheila M. Rutt and Dennis Doverspike, "Salary and Organizational Level Effects on Job Evaluation Ratings," *Journal of Business and Psychology,* Spring 1999, pp. 379–385.

40. R. M. Madigan and D. J. Hoover, "Effects of Alternative Job Evaluation Methods on Decisions Involving Pay Equity," *Academy of Management Journal,* March 1986, pp. 84–100.

41. D. Doverspike and G. Barrett, "An Internal Bias Analysis of a Job Evaluation Instrument," *Journal of Applied Psychology* 69 (1984), pp. 648–662; Kermit Davis, Jr., and William Sauser, Jr., "Effects of Alternative Weighting Methods in a Policy-Capturing Approach to Job Evaluation: A Review and Empirical Investigation," *Personnel Psychology* 44 (1991), pp. 85–127.

42. Judith Collins and Paul M. Muchinsky, "An Assessment of the Construct Validity of Three Job Evaluation Methods: A Field Experiment," *Academy of Management Journal* 36(4), 1993, pp. 895–904; Todd J. Maurer and Stuart A. Tross, "SME Committee vs. Field Job Analysis Ratings: Convergence, Cautions, and a Call," *Journal of Business and Psychology* 14(3), Spring 2000, pp. 489–499.

43. Examples abound. A recent one is the pay equity settlement by Bell Canada, discussed in Chapter 17. See Pay Equity Information Centre at *www.equityic.ca* and "CEP Reaches $104 million pay Equity Settlement at Bell," *www.cep.ca/human_rights/equity/bell /equityrelease_e.pdf.*

44. D. Lipsky and R. Seeber, "In Search of Control: The Corporate Embrace of Alternative Dispute Resolution," *Journal of Labor and Employment Law* 1(1), Spring 1998, pp. 133–157.

45. Hudson Employment Index, *www.hudson-index.com/node.asp?SID56755.*

46. D. J. Treiman and H. I. Hartmann, eds., *Women, Work and Wages: Equal Pay for Jobs of Equal Value* (Washington, DC: National Academy of Sciences, 1981); H. Remick, *Comparable Worth and Wage Discrimination* (Philadelphia, PA: Temple University Press, 1984); Morley Gunderson, "The Evolution and Mechanics of Pay Equity in Ontario," *Canadian Public Policy* 28(1), 2002, pp. S117–S126; Deborah M. Figart, "Equal Pay for Equal Work: The Role of Job Evaluation in an Evolving Social Norm," *Journal of Economic Issues,* March 2000, pp. 1–19.

47. D. Schwab and R. Grams, "Sex-Related Errors in Job Evaluation: A 'Real-World' Test," *Journal of Applied Psychology* 70(3), 1985, pp. 533–559; Richard D. Arvey, Emily M. Passino, and John W. Lounsbury, "Job Analysis Results as Influenced by Sex of Incumbent and Sex of Analyst," *Journal of Applied Psychology* 62(4), 1977, pp. 411–416.

48. Michael K. Mount and Rebecca A. Ellis, "Investigation of Bias in Job Evaluation Ratings of Comparable Worth Study Participants," *Personnel Psychology,* Spring 1987, pp. 85–96.

49. D. Schwab and R. Grams, "Sex-Related Errors in Job Evaluation: A 'Real-World' Test," *Journal of Applied Psychology* 70(3), 1985, pp. 533–559.

50. S. Rynes, C. Weber, and G. Milkovich, "The Effects of Market Survey Rates, Job Evaluation, and Job Gender on Job Pay," *Journal of Applied Psychology* 74 (1989), pp. 114–123.

51. N. Fredric Crandall and Marc J. Wallace Jr., "Paying Employees to Develop New Skills," in *Aligning Pay and Results,* Howard Risher, ed. (New York: American Management Association, 1999); B. Murray and B. Gerhart, "An Empirical Analysis of a Skill-Based Pay Program and Plant Performance Outcomes," *Academy of Management Journal* 41 (1998), pp. 68–78.

52. Howard Risher, ed., *Aligning Pay and Results* (New York: American Management Association, 1999).

External Competitiveness: Determining the Pay Level

In Part Two, our focus was on the internal structure or relative value organizations and markets assigned to different jobs. In Part Three, we continue with that focus, but also examine how organizations choose their overall pay level and how and why different organizations choose different levels. For example, Organization A and Organization B may have the same relative pay (i.e., the same internal structure) for the jobs of engineer and senior engineer (e.g., a 20% difference in value), but Organization A may choose a particular pay level for the two jobs (e.g., $60,000 and $72,000, respectively), while Organization B may choose a higher pay level for the two jobs (e.g., $70,000 and $84,000, respectively). To identify organization pay-level differences, we can focus in on a single job. Let's use the job of software engineer. According to Glassdoor. com, as your textbook goes to press, the average national salary is $90,374. But, companies differ. Google's average salary for a software engineer is $127,814, whereas the (national) average at IBM is 85,359 and at Lockheed Martin it is $79,909. Now, some part of that salary differential is likely geographic/cost of living related because Glassdoor data also indicate that the average software engineer in San Jose, CA ("Silicon Valley") earns $108,83 versus $80,938 in Austin, TX and $71,329 in Nashville, TN. However, it is not all geographic/cost of living based (or tech versus others) because even when we look only at tech companies (consider why tech companies would pay more) and only salaries of software engineers in Silicon Valley, company pay levels still differ: Google ($127,878), Cisco Systems ($117,691), Intel ($115,677), Apple ($110,973), Qualcomm ($101,212). Some part of the remaining difference could be due to some organizations having more experienced and knowledgeable software engineers. In a similar vein, some organizations may have more challenging and more autonomous software engineer jobs, for which they feel higher pay levels are necessary to attract and retain more experienced and knowledgeable software engineers. Or, perhaps some organizations have lower base salaries because they are higher on other forms of compensation (e.g., bonuses, stock awards/options, benefits). In other words, they differ in "how" they pay, the topic of future chapters in Part Four. These are strategic pay decisions that organizations must consider and that we now focus on.

EXHIBIT III.1 Who Makes How Much?

Name	Age	Place	Job	Earnings
Shaun Hoolahan	53	Opportunity, Montana	Petroleum Engineering Consultant	134,100
Gerry Smith	66	Fairbanks, Alaska	Oil Industry Inspector	130,000
Karla Turney	33	North Liberty, Iowa	Clinical Pharmacist	104,472
Cheryl Mcpherson	44	Sayreville, New Jersey	Pediatric Nurse	85,000
Annmarie McCoy	47	Riverside, California	Special Education Teacher	80,800
Jerry Li	31	New York City,New York	Aircraft Maintenance Technician	75,000
Yvonne Lander	43	Dayton, Ohio	Truck Driver	75,000
Mark Mcdevitt	57	Phoenix Arizona	Banquet Captain	66,000
Dawn Hoover	41	Fairhope, Alabama	Relief Veterinarian	65,000
Jeremy Hurd	36	Box Elder, South Dakota	School Principal	60,500
Mathew Wolfe	36	North Canton, Ohio	Fisheries Biologist	56,000
Lyn Barela	59	Berthold, North Dakota	Speech and Language Pathologist	52,500
Lee Chapman	56	Bloomington, Indiana	Firefighter	52,000
Lara Kibler	33	Lincoln, Nebraska	English Teacher	48,248
Valerie Leffler	50	Richland Center, Wisconsin	Cheese Worker	46,800
Leslie Lindsay	49	Round Rock, Texas	ESL Coordinator and Teacher	46,500
Monica Johnson	45	Columbia, South Carolina	Deputy Sheriff	44,200
Anna Norton	39	Cary, North Carolina	Operations Manager	40,000
Stephanie Juliano	33	Rio Rancho, New Mexico	Mental Health Counselor	31,200
Bob Jensen	61	Lewiston, Idaho	Glazier	29,000
Caleb Ogborn	29	Lawrence, Kansas	Sign Technician	28,000
Starr Mikkelson	37	Idaho Falls, Idaho	Montessori Teacher	26,000
Roslyn Guillory Phillip	48	Lake Charles, Louisiana	Security Guard	25,000
Heather Proctor	39	Malvern, Arkansas	Short-Oder Cook	19,000
Kristen Schuett	42	Loveland, Colorado	Riding Instructor	18,000
Gloria Ross	62	St.Louis, Missouri	Obituary Writer	13,000

Source: What People Earn, *Parade,* April 13, 2014.

In Part Four, we will look at how much individuals within specific jobs and organizations earn. We can provide a quick preview. Let us now shift (for now) from software engineers to Miley Cyrus. She earned an estimated $76.5 million last year. Estimated earnings for other notables in the entertainment business include Sandra Bullock ($63 million), Beyonce ($57 million), Bruno Mars ($38 million), Matthew McConaughey ($19 million), and Daniel Radcliff (Blimey, Harry!, $17 million). Not quite as glamorous perhaps, but not too shabby either, *Human Resource Executive* reported that the top-paid HR executive of last year (among companies where an HR executive was among the five highest paid executives) Abilio Gonzalez, Solera Holdings Inc., earned $5,045,298. (We have not been able to verify as of yet whether he used our compensation book when he was in college, or if he feels what he learned from our book was the key to his success. However, we suspect this must have been the case. Is there really any other plausible explanation?)

Further examples of earnings are shown in Exhibit III.1. There are "real" people on this list. It's kind of interesting to think about why these people get paid what they do. Why don't they get paid more? Why not less? What would they do if they were paid more or paid less? How well would their employers (where the person is not self-employed) do if they raised or lowered pay for these people and others in their jobs or other jobs? These are the kinds of questions we will now address.

External competitiveness is the term we use to describe the "how much to pay" and "*how* to pay" questions. It is the next strategic decision in the total pay model, as shown in Exhibit III.2. Two aspects of pay translate external competitiveness into practice: (1) how much to pay relative to competitors—whether to pay more than competitors, to match what they pay, or to pay less—and (2) what mix of base, bonus, stock options, and benefits to pay relative to the pay mix of competitors. In a sense, "what forms" to pay (base, bonus, benefits) are the pieces of the pie. "How much" is the size of the pie. External competitiveness includes both questions.

As we shall see in the next two chapters, a variety of answers exist. Chapter 7 discusses choosing the external competitiveness policy, the impact of that choice, and related theories and research. Chapter 8 has two parts: First, it discusses how to translate competitiveness policy into pay level and forms. Second, it discusses how to integrate information on pay levels and forms with the internal structure from Part One.

EXHIBIT III.2 The Pay Model

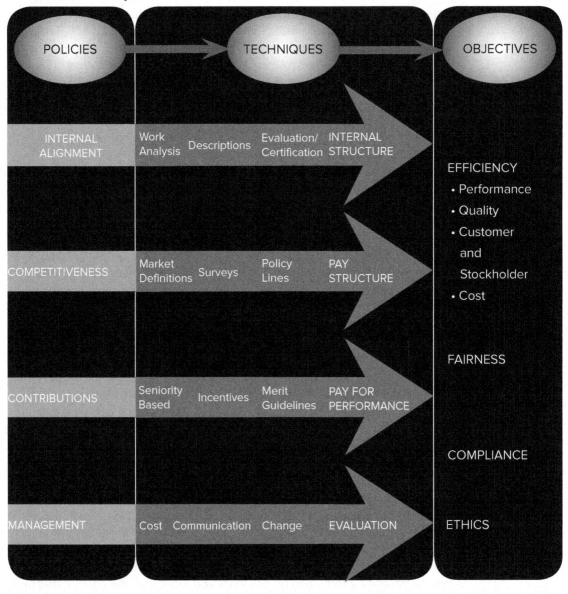

Defining Competitiveness

January is always a good month for travel agents in Ithaca, New York. In addition to the permanent population eager to flee Ithaca's leaden skies, graduating students from Ithaca's two colleges are traveling to job interviews with employers across the country—at company expense, full fare, no Saturday-night stayovers required. When they return from these trips, students compare notes and find that even for people receiving the same degree in the same field from the same college, the offers vary from company to company. What explains the differences? Location has an effect: Firms in San Francisco and New York City make higher offers. The work also has an effect: In HR, for example, jobs in employment pay a little less than jobs in compensation and employee relations. (Now aren't you glad you didn't drop this course?) And the industry to which the different firms belong has an effect: Pharmaceuticals, brokerage houses, and petroleum firms tend to offer more than consumer products, insurance, and heavy-manufacturing firms.[1]

Students would like to attribute these differences to themselves: differences in grades, courses taken, interviewing skills, and so on. But the same company makes the identical offer to most of its candidates at the school. So it is hard to make the case that an individual's qualifications totally explain the offers. Why would companies extend identical offers to most candidates? And why would different companies extend different offers? This chapter discusses these choices and what difference they make for the organization.

Pay levels at firms are not completely static. They also can adjust over time to changing market conditions and/or business strategies. The unemployment rate has dropped significantly in recent years, making for increased competition among retailers to hire and retain hourly workers. As a result, Gap, Walmart, and Target all raised their lowest wage rate recently to $9/hour, with Gap and Walmart stating that they will soon raise minimum wages again to $10/hour.[2] (The federally mandated minimum wage is currently $7.25/hour, but higher in some states and cities.)

Health insurance company Aetna, Inc. also announced a plan to increase its lowest wage, to $16/hour, which would affect about 12 percent of its workers and represent an increase of as much as one-third to some of those workers. A Deutsche Bank economist explained this increase as being due to the tightening of the labor market: "We are getting to the stage where companies can no longer find the right workers." However, Aetna's chief executive officer also cited a strategic rationale: "We're preparing out company for a future where we're going to have a much more consumer-oriented business" and for that reason Aetna wants to have "a better and more informed work force."[3]

The sheer number of economic theories related to compensation can make this chapter heavy going. Another difficulty is that the reality of pay decisions doesn't necessarily match the theories. The key to this chapter is to always ask, So what? How will this information help me?

COMPENSATION STRATEGY: EXTERNAL COMPETITIVENESS

In Part Two of the book, Internal Alignment, we looked at comparisons *inside* the organization. In **external competitiveness,** our second pay policy, we look at comparisons *outside* the organization—comparisons with other employers that hire people with the same skills. A major strategic decision is whether to mirror what competitors are paying or to design a pay package that may differ from competitors but better fits the business strategy.

External competitiveness is expressed in practice by (1) setting a **pay level** that is above, below, or equal to that of competitors; and (2) determining the **pay mix** relative to those of competitors.

> **External competitiveness** refers to the pay relationships among organizations—the organization's pay relative to its competitors.
>
> **Pay level** refers to the *average* of the array of rates paid by an employer:
>
> (base + bonuses + benefits + value of stock holdings) / number of employees
>
> **Pay mix** refers to the various types of payments, or pay forms, that make up total compensation.

Both pay-level and pay-mix decisions focus on two objectives: (1) control costs and increase revenues and (2) attract and retain employees.

Control Costs and Increase Revenues

Pay-level decisions have a significant impact on expenses. Other things being equal, the higher the pay level, the higher the labor costs:

> Labor costs = (pay level) times (number of employees)

Furthermore, the higher the pay level relative to what competitors pay, the greater the relative costs to provide similar products or services. So you might think that all organizations would pay the same job the same rate. However, as we saw in the opening to Part Three, they do not. Why would Google pay more than IBM for software engineers? What would any company pay above whatever minimum amount is required to hire engineers or other employees?

Paying employees above market can be an effective or ineffective strategy. It all depends on what the organization gets in return and whether that return translates into revenues that exceed the cost of the strategy. Let's look at a few examples. Exhibit 7.1 compares labor costs at the U.S. Big Three automakers with those at two Japanese automakers (Toyota, Honda) in the United States. It also compares what the companies get in return. As of 2007, U.S. automakers had higher labor costs, but lower reliability and lower road test performance ratings on average. GM and Chrysler (now Fiat Chrysler Auto, stock ticker: FCAU) subsequently went through bankruptcy. One might infer that the Big Three's pay-level strategy has not worked for it. (In Chapter 1, we also noted the huge drop in employment among U.S. producers like GM.) As part of that process and also as a result of government involvement, agreements were reached with the United Auto Workers to reduce labor costs to make them competitive with Japanese producers. Indeed, there has not been an increase in base salaries since 2007. The Big Three have long preferred profit sharing to increasing their fixed labor costs. As Exhibit 7.1 indicates, as of 2014, labor costs for Ford, GM, and Chrysler were significantly lower than previously.

EXHIBIT 7.1 Comparing Compensation Costs and Outcomes across Automakers and Time in the United States

	2007		2014				
	Ford GM Chrysler	Toyota Honda	Ford	GM	Chrysler	Toyota	Honda
Average hourly total compensation	$73	$48	$59[a]	$59[a]	$49[a]	$55[a]	$50[a]
Hourly wages	$29	$15-$26				$15-$26	$15-$26
Hourly wages (Tier 1)			$29	$29	$29		
Hourly wages (Tier 2)			$16-$19.50	$16-$19.50	$16-$19.50		
% of workers in Tier 2			20%	20%	42%		
Car Quality and Reliability/ Dependability							
Consumer reports							
Road-test performance (higher is better)	59	77	72	71	73	72	71
Reliability (higher is better)	43	77	34	51	35	76	67
J.D. Power Vehicle Dependability Study, problems per 100 vehicles (lower is better)	143	114	140	133	155	114	114
Productivity							
Total labor hours per vehicle	32.2	31.2	*	*	*	*	*

*Total labor hours per vehicle is hours for assembly, stamping, engine, and transmission. These data are no longer publicly available. Two-tier wages came into effect in 2007.

[a]Average hourly total compensation projections must consider at least four factors: (1) The Big Three have negotiated two-tier wage structures with the United Auto Workers, which have newly hired workers starting at a maximum wage of $19/hour. Fiat Chrysler has 42% of its production workers being paid the lower tier 2 wage versus a maximum of 20% at General Motors and Ford. (2) The Japanese producers also have a lower starting wage (compared to their average wage). Thus, average total compensation costs will depend on how many new versus experienced hires are employed in the future. (3) Legacy costs for the Big Three have, as of 2009, been taken "off the books" through an agreement with the United Auto Workers (UAW), under which the UAW are given a lump sum payment and/or stock and assume responsibility for pension and retiree health care obligations. That is a major reason why total compensation cost at Ford, General Motors, and Chrysler has declined. (4) Profit sharing and other bonuses affect labor cost. In early 2015, profit sharing payments for full-time hourly production workers were $9,000 at General Motors, $8,300 at Ford, and $2,250 at Fiat Chrysler.

Sources: Oliver Wyman, The Harbour ReportTM, North America 2008, www.oliverwyman.com; Consumer Reports, April 2008 and April 2015; David Leonhardt, "$73 an hour: Adding it up." *New York Times*, December 10, 2008; Chris Woodyard, "VW Exec Knows of no Talks to Unionize Tennessee Plant." *USA Today*, August 1, 2011; Nick Bunkley, "Group Predicts 28% Gain in Carmaking Jobs by 2015." *New York Times*, November 29, 2011; Diane Brady, "Record Profits, But Still Mixed Success at GM." *Bloomberg Business Week*, February 16, 2012; David Barkholz, "Can UAW Fix Tier 2 Disparity? Return to Pattern Bargaining Unlikely." *Automotive News*, March 8, 2015; Keith Naughton, "Detroit Worker Bonuses Approach Records on Rising Profits." *Bloomberg Business.*, February 13, 2015.

Notes: Average hourly total compensation includes wages and benefits. For 2007, it also includes legacy costs for Ford, GM, and Chrysler: retiree health care and pension payments.

As we go to press with your textbook, DaimlerChrysler and the UAW have tentatively reached agreement on a new four-year contract that includes salary increases for the first time in approximately 10 years. Tier 1 workers would receive approximately 3 % salary increases in years 1 and 3 and lump sum payments (i.e., salaries would not increase) of 4 % in years 2 and 4 of the contract. Tier 2 workers would receive larger salary increases that would narrow the pay differential with Tier 1 workers, but not eliminate it. Profit sharing and other bonus plans, which help control fixed labor costs, would play as larger or larger a role compared to past contracts. (Traditionally, the UAW seeks to negotiate the same contract with the remaining Big Three. By the time you read this, details of the final agreement should be available for you to look up and discuss. See the end of chapter Your Turn.)

The harder question to answer is whether the quality and performance of the cars will also become more competitive. The picture for the Big Three is mixed. There have been improvements in vehicle road test performance, but less success has been achieved in dealing with reliability problems. In a global competitive market, automakers have a choice as to where to locate production to best achieve cost, productivity, and quality goals.[4] Consider where new automobile plants in North America have or are being built since 2005. In the United States, the last announced new plant was 2008 (opened in 2011) by Volkswagen in Chattanooga, TN. Prior to that, since 2005, there have been three other plants opened in the United States, all in the South (Alabama, Mississippi, Georgia), all non-union. In contrast, since 2005, seven new plants in Mexico have been opened or announced, with six of those being since 2011, the year of the last new U.S. plant. Mexico has lower labor costs (Volkswagen estimates they are 50% lower than in Tennessee, which are already lower than in the northern states and lower than in Germany, where Volkswagen is headquartered) than does the United States. It also has free trade agreements that give it duty-free access to markets that represent about 60 percent of the world's economic output. Automakers seem to feel they are able to also achieve vehicle production efficiency and quality goals as well, something to which much effort is devoted.[5]

Exhibit 7.2 traces the history of two "legacy" airlines, USAir and American, and relative newcomer, Southwest. As in the automobile industry, we can look at what employees cost and what the airlines receive in return that would help drive revenues. American was the last major airline to go through bankruptcy, entering in 2011 and exiting in late 2013, which included a proposed merger (subsequently executed) with USAir. Note that by 2014, the new combined company had lower labor costs and lower operating costs per available seat mile (ASM) than Southwest. With consolidation and a healthier profit outlook for the airline industry overall, there are signs that American (and others) will face increasing pressures from employees to increase wages and salaries and thus labor costs. In 2000, USAir and American trailed Southwest in terms of efficiency, with overall operating costs of 14 cents per ASM, almost double that of Southwest at 7.7 cents per ASM. Likewise, USAir had labor costs per ASM roughly double (5.5 cents versus 2.8 cents) that of Southwest Airlines. American, while not having labor costs as high as those of USAir, still had a significantly higher cost structure than Southwest. USAir and other so-called legacy airlines realized that they needed to move their costs lower to compete with Southwest. (Question: What would labor costs and operating income be at American and USAir in 2000 if their labor cost/ASM had been the same as Southwest's?) By 2008, both USAir

EXHIBIT 7.2 Revenues, Capacity, Operating Costs, and Labor Costs of USAir, American, and Southwest Airlines

	2000 American	2000 USAir	2000 Southwest	2008 American	2008 USAir	2008 Southwest	2014 American (including former USAir)	2014 Southwest
Revenues (in millions)	$19,703	$9,269	$5,650	$23,696	$12,118	$11,023	$30,802	$18,605
Operating Costs (in millions)	$18,322	$9,322	$4,628	$25,750	$13,918	$10,574	$31,885	$16,380
Labor Costs (in millions)	$6,783	$3,637	$1,683	$6,044	$2,231	$3,340	$8,508	$5,434
Employees	93,951	43,467	29,274	70,900	32,671	35,499	94,400	46,278
Available Seat Miles (ASM) (in millions)	167,286	59,910	59,910	163,600	74,151	102,271	237,522	98,437
Labor Costs/Revenues	34.4%	39.2%	29.8%	25.5%	18.4%	30.3%	27.6%	29.2%
Labor Costs/Employees	$0.072	$0.084	$0.058	$0.085	$0.068	$0.094	$0.090	$0.117
Operating Costs/ASM	$0.110	$0.156	$0.077	$0.157	$0.188	$0.103	$0.134	$0.166
Labor Costs/ASM	$0.041	$0.061	$0.028	$0.037	$0.030	$0.033	$0.036	$0.055
Retiree Pension and Health Care Liabilities					Reduced		Not reduced	
Operating Income (in millions)	$1,381	($53)	$1,021	($2,054)	($1,800)	$449	($1,083)	$2,225
Customer Complaints (per 100,000)	3.5	2.6	0.5	1.3	2.0	0.3	2.1	0.5
American Customer Satisfaction Index®	63	62	70	62	54	79	66	78

Sources: Financial data come from company 10-K reports, available at www.sec.gov. Annual data on customer complaints are from the U.S. Department of Transportation and appear each year in the February issue of *American Travel Consumer Reports*, available at http://www.dot.gov/airconsumer/air-travel-consumer-reports. American Customer Satisfaction Index® is available at http://www .theacsi.org/.

Notes: For 2014, only mainline data were used for American because labor cost was not reported for combined regional and mainline operations. For 2000, the number of employees at American came from U.S. Bureau of Transportation Statistics. In 10-K reports, labor cost data may appear as salaries, wages, and benefits. USAir filed for bankruptcy in 2002. American filed for bankruptcy in 2011. The two airlines officially announced their merger in December 2013. USAir, during its bankruptcy, was able to reduce retiree-related costs. So far, American has not been able to do so, apparently because courts have judged the airline is able to compete without reducing such costs. For 2014, American financial data are post-merger, thus including data on both the former American Airlines and the former USAir.

and American had made considerable progress, at least with respect to labor costs, basically drawing even with Southwest on labor cost per ASM. Indeed, labor costs/revenues in 2008 were lower than at Southwest (though only Southwest had positive operating income). Part of USAir's success in reducing labor costs was due to it going through bankruptcy in 2002 (the first major airline to do so, subsequently followed by all others) and using that as an opportunity to reduce pay and benefits costs. However, American (including the former USAir) remains at a disadvantage with respect to the passenger experience. In all years, Southwest has had many fewer customer complaints and higher customer satisfaction. If anything, Southwest's advantage in customer satisfaction seemed to have increased between 2000 and 2008 as USAir and American cut costs. By 2014, Southwest's advantage on the customer experience was not as large, but remained substantial. As such, Southwest may continue to be a better bet going forward due to its continued advantage in terms of the customer experience. It is not necessarily how much it pays that is the key. Rather, it can be argued that it is its ability to pay competitively and get a great deal in return from its employees. Southwest has been widely studied for its total compensation strategy, which includes employee profit sharing and stock, but also having fun at work and strong employee relations. Southwest is unique in the airline industry both for its 42 consecutive years of profitability (compare, for example, USAir's consecutive years of losses, from 1989 to 1999) and as the lone major airline not to go through bankruptcy. However, there is growing concern that Southwest's labor costs may become a problem. It will be interesting to see what the future brings in the airline industry for companies using different compensation and human resource approaches.

Attract and Retain the Right Employees

One company may pay more because it believes its higher-paid engineers are more productive than those at other companies. Their engineers may be better trained; maybe they are more innovative in dreaming up new applications. Maybe they are less likely to quit, thus saving the company recruiting and training costs. Another company may pay less because it is differentiating itself on nonfinancial returns—more challenging and interesting projects, possibility of international assignments, superior training, more rapid promotions, or even greater job security. Different employers set different pay levels; that is, they deliberately choose to pay above or below what others are paying for the same work. That is why there is no single "going rate" in the labor market for a specific job.[6]

Not only do the rates paid for similar jobs vary among employers, but a single company may set a different pay level for different job families.[7] The company in Exhibit 7.3 illustrates the point. The *top chart* shows that this particular company pays about 2 percent above the market for its entry-level engineer. (Market is set at zero in the exhibit.) However, it pays 13 percent above the market for most of its marketing jobs and over 25 percent above the market for marketing managers. Office personnel and technicians are paid below the market. So this company uses very different pay levels for different job families.

These data are based on comparisons of **base wage.** When we look at **total compensation** in the bottom of the exhibit, a different pattern emerges. The company still has a different pay level for different job families. But when bonuses, stock options, and benefits are included, only marketing managers remain above the market. Every

EXHIBIT 7.3 A Single Company's Market Position May Differ Depending on Whether Comparing Base Pay or Total Compensation

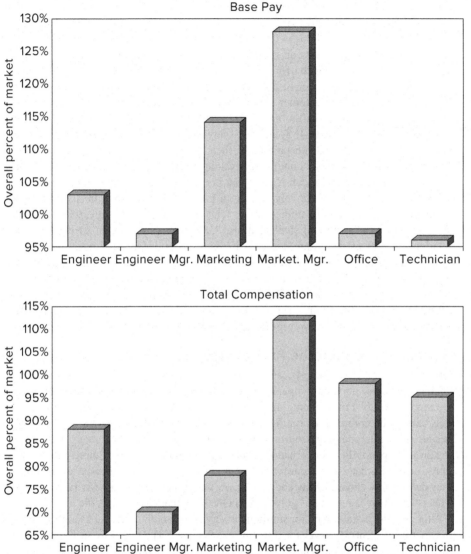

other job family is now substantially below the market. Engineering managers take the deepest plunge, from only 2 percent below the market to over 30 percent below.[8]

The exhibit, based on actual company data, makes two points. First, companies often set different pay-level policies for different job families. Second, how a company compares to the market depends on what competitors it compares to and what pay forms are included. It is not clear whether the company in the exhibit deliberately chose to emphasize marketing managers and deemphasize engineering in its pay plan or if it is paying the price for not hiring one of you readers to design its plan.[9] Either way, the point is, people love to talk about "the market rate" as if a single rate exists for any job, with the implication that organizations are constrained to pay that same rate to their own employees in that job. Nevertheless, Exhibit 7.4 instead shows that organizations can and do vary in how closely they match the "going rate." There is no single "going mix" of pay forms, either. Exhibit 7.4 compares the pay mix for the same job (software marketing manager) at two companies in the same geographic area. Both companies offer about the same total compensation. Yet the percentages allocated to base, bonuses, benefits, and options are very different.

WHAT SHAPES EXTERNAL COMPETITIVENESS?

Exhibit 7.5 shows the factors that affect decisions on pay level and pay mix. The factors include (1) competition in the *labor market* for people with various skills; (2) competition in the *product and service markets,* which affects the financial condition of the organization; and (3) characteristics unique to each organization and its employees, such as its business strategy, technology, and the productivity and experience of its workforce. These factors act in concert to influence pay-level and pay-mix decisions.

LABOR MARKET FACTORS

Economists describe two basic types of markets: the **quoted price** and the **bourse.** Stores that label each item's price or ads that list a job opening's starting wage are examples of quoted-price markets. You cannot name your own price when you order from Amazon, but Priceline says you can. However, Priceline does not guarantee that your price will be accepted, whereas an Amazon order arrives in a matter of days. In contrast with Amazon's quoted price, eBay allows haggling over the terms and conditions until an agreement is reached; eBay is a *bourse.* Graduating students usually find themselves in a quoted-labor market, though minor haggling may occur.[10] In both the bourse and the quoted market, employers are the buyers and the potential employees are the sellers. If the inducements (total compensation) offered by the employer and the skills offered by the employee are mutually acceptable, a deal is struck. It may be formal contracts negotiated by unions, professional athletes, and executives, or it may be a brief letter or maybe only the implied understanding of a handshake. All this activity makes up the labor market; the result is that people and jobs match up at specified pay rates.

How Labor Markets Work

Theories of labor markets usually begin with four basic assumptions:

1. Employers always seek to maximize profits.
2. People are homogeneous and therefore interchangeable; a business school graduate is a business school graduate is a business school graduate.
3. The pay rates reflect all costs associated with employment (e.g., base wage, bonuses, holidays, benefits, even training).
4. The markets faced by employers are competitive, so there is no advantage for a single employer to pay above or below the market rate.

EXHIBIT 7.4
Two
Companies:
Same Total
Compensation,
Different
Mixes

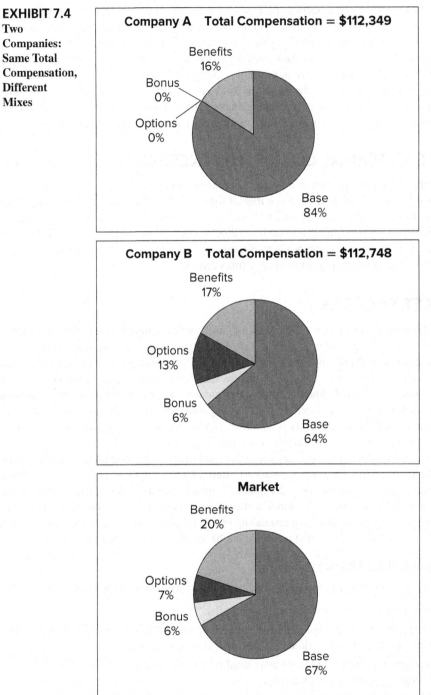

EXHIBIT 7.5 What Shapes External Competitiveness?

Although these assumptions oversimplify reality, they provide a framework for understanding labor markets. As we shall see later, as reality forces us to change our assumptions, our theories change too.

Organizations often claim to be "market-driven"; that is, they pay competitively with the market or even are market leaders. Understanding how markets work requires analysis of the demand and supply of labor. The demand side focuses on the actions of the employers: how many new hires they seek and what they are willing and able to pay new employees. The supply side looks at potential employees: their qualifications and the pay they are willing to accept in exchange for their services.

Exhibit 7.6 shows a simple illustration of demand and supply for business school graduates. The vertical axis represents pay rates from $25,000 to $80,000 a year. The horizontal axis depicts the number of business school graduates in the market. The line

EXHIBIT 7.6
Supply and Demand for Business School Graduates in the Short Run

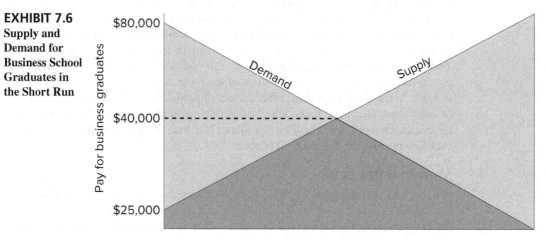

labeled "Demand" is the sum of *all* employers' hiring preferences for business graduates at various pay levels. At $80,000, only a small number of business graduates will be hired because only a few firms are able to afford them. At $25,000, companies can afford to hire a large number of business graduates. However, as we look at the line labeled "Supply," we see that there aren't enough business graduates willing to be hired at $25,000. In fact, only a small number are willing to work for $25,000. As pay rates rise, more graduates become interested in working, so the labor supply line slopes upward. *The market rate is where the lines for labor demand and labor supply cross.* In this illustration, the interaction among all employers and all business graduates determines the $40,000 market rate. Because any single employer can hire all the business graduates it wants at $40,000 and all business graduates are of equal quality (i.e., assumption 2 above), there is no reason for any wage other than $40,000 to be paid.

Labor Demand

If $40,000 is the market-determined rate for business graduates, how many business graduates will a specific employer hire? The answer requires an analysis of **labor demand.** In the short term, an employer cannot change any other factor of production (i.e., technology, capital, or natural resources). Thus, its level of production can change only if it changes the level of human resources. Under such conditions, a single employer's demand for labor coincides with the **marginal product of labor.**

> The **marginal product of labor** is the additional output associated with the employment of one additional person, with other production factors held constant.
>
> The **marginal revenue of labor** is the additional revenue generated when the firm employs one additional person, with other production factors held constant.

Marginal Product

Assume that two business graduates form a consulting firm that provides services to 10 clients. The firm hires a third person, who brings in four more clients. The marginal product (the change in output associated with the additional unit of labor) of the third person is four clients. But adding a fourth employee generates only two new clients. This diminishing marginal productivity results from the fact that each additional employee has a progressively smaller share of the other factors of production with which to work. In the short term, these other factors of production (e.g., office space, number of computers, telephone lines, hours of clerical support) are fixed. Until these other factors are changed, each new hire produces less than the previous hire. The amount each hire produces is the marginal product.

Marginal Revenue

Now let's look at marginal revenue. Marginal revenue is the money generated by the sale of the marginal product, the additional output from the employment of one additional person. In the case of the consulting firm, it's the revenues generated by each

EXHIBIT 7.7   **Supply and Demand at the Market and Individual Employer Level**

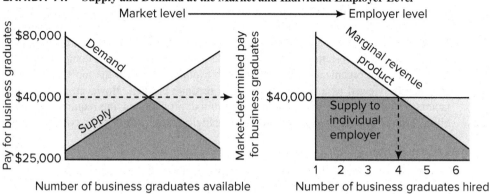

additional hire. If each new client generates $20,000 in revenue, then if the third employee has four clients, that will generate $80,000 in additional revenue. But perhaps the fourth employee will only be able to bring two clients, or $40,000, in additional revenue. This $40,000 is exactly the wage that must be paid that fourth employee. So the consulting firm will break even on the fourth person but will lose money if it hires beyond that. Recall that our first labor market theory assumption is that employers seek to maximize profits. Therefore, the employer will continue to hire until the marginal revenue generated by the last hire is equal to the costs associated with employing that person. Because other potential costs will not change in the short run, the level of demand that maximizes profits is that level at which the marginal revenue of the last hire is equal to the wage rate for that hire.

Exhibit 7.7 shows the connection between the labor market model and the conditions facing a single employer. On the left is the *market level* supply and demand model from Exhibit 7.6, showing that pay level ($40,000) is determined by the interaction of *all employers'* demands for business graduates. The right side of the exhibit shows supply and demand for an *individual employer.* At the market-determined rate ($40,000), the individual employer can hire as many business graduates as it wants. Therefore, supply is now an unlimited horizontal line. However, the demand line still slopes downward. The two lines intersect at 4. For this employer, the market-determined wage rate ($40,000) equals the marginal revenue of the fourth hire. The marginal revenue of the fifth graduate is less than $40,000 and so will not add enough revenue to cover costs. The point on the graph at which the incremental income generated by an additional employee equals the wage rate is the *marginal revenue product.*

A manager using the marginal revenue product model must do only two things: (1) Determine the pay level set by market forces, and (2) determine the marginal revenue generated by each new hire. This will tell the manager how many people to hire. Simple? Of course not.

The model provides a valuable analytical framework, but it oversimplifies the real world. In most organizations, it is almost impossible to quantify the goods or services produced by an individual employee, since most production is through joint efforts of employees with a variety of skills. Even in settings that use piece rates (i.e., 50 cents for each soccer ball sewn), it is hard to separate the contributions of labor from those of other resources (efficient machines, sturdy materials, good lighting, and ventilation).

So neither the marginal product nor the marginal revenue is directly measurable. However, managers do need some measure that reflects value. In the last two chapters, we discussed compensable factors, skill blocks, and competencies. If compensable factors define what organizations value, then job evaluation reflects the job's contribution and may be viewed as a proxy for marginal revenue product. However, compensable factors are usually defined as input (skills required, problem solving required, responsibilities) rather than value of output. This same logic applies to skills and competencies.

Labor Supply

Now let us look more closely at the assumptions about the behavior of potential employees. This model assumes that many people are seeking jobs, that they possess accurate information about all job openings, and that no barriers to mobility (discrimination, licensing provisions, or union membership requirements) exist.[11]

Just as with the analysis of labor demand, these assumptions greatly simplify the real world. As the assumptions change, so does the supply. For example, the upward sloping supply assumes that as pay increases, more people are willing to take a job. But if unemployment rates are low, offers of higher pay may not increase supply— everyone who wants to work is already working. If competitors quickly match a higher offer, the employer may face a higher pay level but no increase in supply. For example, when Giant Foods raised its hourly pay $1 above the minimum wage in the Chicago area, Wendy's and Burger King quickly followed suit. The result was that the supermarket was paying more for the employees it already had but was still shorthanded. Although some firms find lowering the job requirements and hiring less-skilled workers a better choice than raising wages, this choice incurs increased training costs (which were included in assumption 3).

MODIFICATIONS TO THE DEMAND SIDE

The story is told of the economics professor and the student who were strolling through campus. "Look," the student cried, "there's a $100 bill on the path!"

"No, that cannot be," the wiser head replied. "If there were a $100 bill, someone would have picked it up."

The point of the story is that economic theories must frequently be revised to account for reality. When we change our focus from *all* the employers in an economy to a *particular* employer, models must be modified to help us understand what actually occurs. A particularly troublesome issue for economists is why an employer would pay more than what theory states is the market-determined rate. Exhibit 7.8 looks at three modifications to the model that address this phenomenon: compensating differentials, efficiency wage, and signaling.

Compensating Differentials

More than 200 years ago, Adam Smith argued that individuals consider the "whole of the advantages and disadvantages of different employments" and make decisions

EXHIBIT 7.8
Labor Demand Theories and Implications

Theory	Prediction	So What?
Compensating Differentials	Work with negative characteristics requires higher pay to attract/retain workers.	Job evaluation and compensable factors must capture these negative characteristics.
Efficiency Wage	Above-market wage/pay level will improve efficiency by attracting higher-ability workers (sorting effect, Chapter 1) and by discouraging shirking (incentive effect, Chapter 1) because of risk of losing high-wage job. A high-wage policy may substitute for intense monitoring (e.g., use of many supervisors).	The payoff to a higher wage depends on the employee selection system's ability to validly identify the best workers. See the appendix at chapter end on utility. An efficiency wage policy may require the use of fewer supervisors.
Sorting & Signaling	Pay policies signal to applicants the attributes that fit the organization. Applicants may signal their attributes (e.g., ability) by the investments they have made in themselves.	How much, but also how (e.g., pay mix and emphasis on performance) will influence attraction-selection-attrition and resulting workforce composition.
Job Competition	Job requirements may be relatively fixed. Thus, workers may compete for jobs based on their qualifications, not based on how low of a wage (wage competition) they are willing to accept. Thus, wages are sticky downward. See also internal labor markets.	As hiring difficulties increase, employers should expect to spend more to (a) train new hires, (b) to increase compensation, or (c) search/recruit more.

based on the alternative with the greatest "net advantage."[12] If a job has negative characteristics—that is, if the necessary training is very expensive (medical school), job security is tenuous (stockbrokers, CEOs), working conditions are disagreeable (highway construction), or chances of success are low (professional sports)—then employers must offer higher wages to compensate for these negative features.

Such **compensating differentials** explain the presence of various pay rates in the market. Although the notion is appealing, it is hard to document, due to the difficulties in measuring and controlling all the factors that go into a net-advantage calculation.

Efficiency Wage

According to **efficiency-wage theory,** high wages may increase efficiency and actually lower labor costs if they:

1. Attract higher-quality applicants.
2. Lower turnover.

3. Increase worker effort.

4. Reduce **"shirking"** (what economists say when they mean "screwing around"). The higher the wage, the less likely it is that an employee would be able to find another job that pays as well. Also, the risk of losing one's high-paying job depends on how likely it is that you can be replaced. One indicator is the unemployment rate. (Karl Marx referred to the unemployed as a "reserve army" that employers can use to replace current workers.) Thus, efficiency wage predicts that high effort will be most likely and shirking less likely to the degree that the wage premium is high and the unemployment rate is high.

5. Reduce the need to supervise employees (academics say "monitoring").

So, basically, efficiency increases by hiring better employees or motivating present employees to work smarter or harder. The underlying assumption is that pay level determines effort—again, an appealing notion that is difficult to document. Later in this chapter (see the appendix), we show how something called **utility theory** can help compare the costs and benefits of different pay-level policies. We will also discuss how business strategy plays a role in pay-level choice.

There is some research on efficiency-wage theory, however.[13] One study looked at shirking behavior by examining employee discipline and wages in several auto plants. Higher wages were associated with lower shirking, measured as the number of disciplinary layoffs. However, the authors of the study were unable to say whether it was cut enough to offset the costs of the higher wage.[14]

Research shows that higher wages actually do attract more qualified applicants.[15] But higher wages also attract more unqualified applicants. Few companies evaluate their recruiting programs well enough to show whether they do in fact choose only superior applicants from the larger pool. So an above-market wage does not guarantee a more productive workforce.

Does an above-market wage allow an organization to operate with fewer supervisors? Some research evidence says yes. A study of hospitals found that those that paid high wages to staff nurses employed fewer nurse supervisors.[16] The researchers did not speculate on whether the higher wages attracted better nurses or caused average nurses to work harder. They also did not say whether the hospital was able to reduce its overall nursing costs.

An organization's **ability to pay** is related to the efficiency wage model. Firms with greater profits than competitors are able to share this success with employees. This could be done via "leading" competitors' pay levels and/or via bonuses that vary with profitability. Academics see this as "rent sharing." **Rent** is a return (profits) received from activities that are in excess of the minimum (pay level) needed to attract people to those activities.[17] Pay levels at more profitable firms were about 15 percent greater than at firms with lower profits, according to one study.[18]

Notice that the discussion so far has dealt with pay level only. What forms to pay—the mix question—is virtually ignored in these theories. The simplifying assumption is that the pay level includes the value of different forms. Abstracted away is the distinct possibility that some people find more performance-based bonus pay or better health insurance more attractive. Signaling theory is more useful in understanding pay mix.

Sorting and Signaling

Sorting, introduced in Chapter 1, is the effect that pay strategy has on the composition of the workforce—who is attracted and who is retained. Signaling is a closely related process that underlies the sorting effect. Signaling theory holds that employers deliberately design pay levels and pay mix as part of a strategy that signals to both prospective and current employees the kinds of behaviors that are sought.[19] Viewed through a marketing lens, how much to pay and what pay forms are offered establishes a "brand" that sends a message to prospective employees, just like brands of competing products and services.[20]

A policy of paying below the market for **base pay** yet offering generous bonuses or training opportunities sends a different signal, and presumably attracts different people, than does a policy of matching the market wage and offering no performance-based pay. An employer that combines lower base pay with high bonuses may be signaling that it wants employees who are risk takers. Its pay policy helps communicate expectations.

Check out Exhibit 7.4 again. It shows a breakdown of forms of pay for two competitors, as well as their relationship to the market. The pay mix at company A emphasizes base pay (84%) more than does the mix at company B (64%) or the market average (67%). Company A pays no bonuses, no stock options, and somewhat lighter benefits. Company B's mix is closer to the market average. What is the message that A's pay mix is communicating? Which message appeals to you, A's or B's? The astute reader will note that at A, you can earn the $112,349 with very little apparent link to performance. Maybe just showing up is enough. At B, earning the $112,748 requires performance bonuses and stock options as well. Riskier? Why would anyone work at B without extra returns for the riskier pay? Without a premium, how will B attract and retain employees? Perhaps with more interesting projects, flexible schedules, or more opportunity for promotions—all part of B's "total pay brand."

A study of college students approaching graduation found that both pay level and pay mix affected their job decisions.[21] Students wanted jobs that offered high pay, but they also showed a preference for individual-based (rather than team-based) pay, fixed (rather than variable) pay, job-based (rather than skill-based) pay, and flexible benefits. Job seekers were rated on various personal dimensions—materialism, confidence in their abilities, and risk aversion—that were related to pay preferences. Pay level was most important to materialists and less important to those who were risk-averse. So applicants appear to select among job opportunities based on the perceived match between their personal dispositions and the nature of the organization, as signaled by the pay system. Both pay level and pay mix send a signal, which results in sorting effects (i.e., who joins and who stays with the organization).

Signaling works on the supply side of the model, too, as suppliers of labor signal to potential employers. People who are better trained, have higher grades in relevant courses, and/or have related work experience signal to prospective employers that they are likely to be better performers. (Presumably they signal with the same degree of accuracy as employers.) So both characteristics of the applicants (degrees, grades, experience) and organization decisions about pay level (lead, match, lag) and mix (higher bonuses, benefit choices) act as signals that help communicate.

MODIFICATIONS TO THE SUPPLY SIDE (ONLY TWO MORE THEORIES TO GO)

Two theories shown in Exhibit 7.9—**reservation wage** and **human capital**—focus on understanding employee behavior: the supply side of the model.

Reservation Wage

Economists are renowned for their great sense of humor. So it is not surprising that they describe pay as "noncompensatory." What they mean is that job seekers have a reservation wage level below which they will not accept a job offer, no matter how attractive the other job attributes. If pay level does not meet their minimum standard, no other job attributes can make up (i.e., compensate) for this inadequacy. Other theorists go a step further and say that some job seekers—satisfiers—take the first job offer they get where the pay meets their reservation wage. A reservation wage may be above or below the market wage. The theory seeks to explain differences in workers' responses to offers. Reservation levels likely exist for pay forms, too, particularly for health insurance. A young high school graduate recently told us, "If I can't find a job that includes health insurance, I will probably go to college."

Human Capital

The theory of human capital, perhaps the most influential economic theory for explaining pay-level differences, is based on the premise that higher earnings flow to those who improve their potential productivity by investing in themselves (through additional education, training, and experience).[22] The theory assumes that people are in fact paid at the value of their marginal product. Improving productive abilities by investing in training or even in one's physical health will increase one's marginal product. In general, the value of an individual's skills and abilities is a function of the time, expense, and effort to acquire them. Consequently, jobs that require long and expensive training (engineering, physicians) should receive higher pay than jobs that require less investment (clerical work, elementary school

EXHIBIT 7.9
Labor Supply Theories and Implications

Theory	Prediction	So What?
Reservation Wage	Job seekers won't accept jobs if pay is below a certain wage, no matter how attractive other job aspects.	Pay level will affect ability to recruit. Pay must meet some minimum level.
Human Capital	General and specific skills require an investment in human capital. Firms will invest in firm-specific skills, but not general skills. Workers must pay for investment in general skills.	Skill/ability requires investment by workers and firms. There must be a sufficient return (e.g., pay level) on investment for the investment to take place. Workers, for example, must see a payoff to training.

teaching).[23] As pay level increases, the number of people willing to make that investment increases, thereby creating an upward-sloping supply. In fact, different types of education do get different levels of pay. In the United Kingdom, new graduates with a degree in math, law, or economics will earn around 25 percent more than job seekers their age who do not have a college degree. An extra year of education adds about $4,200 per year.

A number of additional factors affect the supply of labor.[24] Geographic barriers to mobility among jobs, union requirements, lack of information about job openings, the degree of risk involved, and the degree of unemployment also influence labor markets. Also, nonmonetary aspects of jobs (e.g., time flexibility) may be important aspects of the return on investment.

PRODUCT MARKET FACTORS AND ABILITY TO PAY

The supply and demand for labor are major determinants of an employer's pay level. However, any organization must, over time, generate enough revenue to cover expenses, including compensation. It follows that an employer's pay level is constrained by its ability to compete in the product/service market. So product market conditions to a large extent determine what the organization can afford to pay.

Product demand and the degree of competition are the two key product market factors. Both affect the ability of the organization to change what it charges for its products and services. If prices cannot be changed without decreasing sales, then the ability of the employer to set a higher pay level is constrained.

Product Demand

Although labor market conditions (and legal requirements) put a floor on the pay level required to attract sufficient employees, the product market puts a lid on the maximum pay level that an employer can set. If the employer pays above the maximum, it must either pass on to consumers the higher pay level through price increases or hold prices fixed and allocate a greater share of total revenues to cover labor costs.

Degree of Competition

Employers in highly competitive markets, such as manufacturers of automobiles or generic drugs, are less able to raise prices without loss of revenues. At the other extreme, single sellers of a Lamborghini or a breakthrough cancer treatment are able to set whatever price they choose. However, too high a price often invites the eye of government regulators.

Other factors besides product market conditions affect pay level. Some of these have already been discussed. The productivity of labor, the technology employed, the level of production relative to plant capacity available—all affect compensation decisions. These factors vary more across than within industries. The technologies employed and consumer preferences may vary among auto manufacturers, but the differences are relatively small compared to the differences between the technology and product demand of auto manufacturers versus those of the oil or financial industry.

A Different View: What Managers Say

Discussions with managers provide insight into how all of these economic factors translate into actual pay decisions. In one study, a number of scenarios were presented in which unemployment, profitability, and labor market conditions varied.[25] Managers were asked to make wage adjustment recommendations for several positions. Level of unemployment made almost no difference. One manager was incredulous at the suggestion that high unemployment should lead to cutting salaries: "You mean take advantage of the fact that there are a lot of people out of work?" The company's profitability was considered a factor for higher management in setting the overall pay budget but not something managers consider for individual pay adjustments. What it boiled down to was "whatever the chief financial officer says we can afford!" They thought it shortsighted to pay less, even though market conditions would have permitted lower pay. In direct contradiction to efficiency-wage theory, managers believed that problems attracting and keeping people were the result of poor management rather than inadequate compensation. They offered the opinion that, "Supervisors try to solve with money their difficulties with managing people."[26]

Of course, what managers say that they would do in a hypothetical situation is not necessarily what they would do when they actually experience a situation. Nor are their views or decisions necessarily the same as those of managers in other companies that do things differently. In this same vein, what managers think is not always what their employees think. As we write this, the unemployment rate is higher than it has been in two decades and companies are indeed making pay cuts, either outright or by requiring employees to take days off (often called furloughs) without pay. Another common cut is reducing contributions to 401k retirement plans. Other companies are imposing pay freezes.[27] With respect to employee retention, a national survey found that pay was the most often cited reason (51%) among high-performing employees for leaving, whereas relationship with supervisor was cited only 1 percent of the time by such employees. Employers, however, somewhat underestimated the role of pay (with 45% citing its role versus 51% of employees) and they very much overestimated the role of relationship with supervisor (with 31% citing its role versus 1% of employees).[28]

Segmented Supplies of Labor and (Different) Going Rates

However, faced with significant competition, a number of employers have cut pay. As we saw earlier, the U.S. airline industry is a notable example. Significant differences in wages paid around the world and the ease of offshoring work have also led many companies to consider this action.[29] Other options to reduce labor costs include segmenting the source of labor.

People Flow to the Work

Consider how a hospital staffs and pays its nursing positions and what each method costs. The number of nurses the hospital needs on each shift depends on the number of patients. To deal with fluctuating patient numbers, the hospital uses four different sources of nurses, as shown in Exhibit 7.10.

The segmented supply results in nurses working the same jobs side by side on the same shift, but earning significantly different pay and/or benefits and having different

EXHIBIT 7.10 Different Sources of Labor, Nurse Types

Nurse Type	Description	Relative Hourly Wage	Benefits?	Fee Paid by Hospital to Agency?
Regular	Full-time employees	100%	Yes	No
Pool	On call, part-time employees	132%	No	No
Registry	Agency employees who can work for multiple area hospitals. Benefits paid by agency.	150%	Yes	Yes
Travelers	Agency employees from outside the area who are sent on extended assignments (e.g., six months) to hospitals around the country. Benefits paid by agency.	150%	Yes	Yes

relationships with the hospital and the other nurses and health care professionals. This is a case of people flowing to the work. The hospital cannot send its nursing work to other cities or other nations.

Work Flows to the People—On-Site, Off-Site, Offshore

Apriso, a Long Beach, California, company, designs and installs computer-assisted manufacturing software that is used in factories around the world. When Apriso competes for a project, the bid is structured in part on the compensation paid to people in different locations. Apriso can staff the project with employees who are on-site (in Long Beach), off-site (contract employees from throughout the United States), or off-shore. Design engineers in Long Beach earn about twice as much as those in Krakow, Poland. Apriso can "mix and match" its people from different sources. Which source Apriso includes in its bid depends on many factors: customer preferences, time schedules, the nature of the project. To put together its bids, Apriso managers need to know pay levels and pay mix of forms not only in the market in Long Beach but also in other locations, including Krakow, Shanghai, Vancouver, and Bangalore. (We return to this topic later in this chapter.)

There are three points ("so whats?") to take with you from this discussion:

1. Reality is complex and theories abstract. It is not that our theories are useless. They simply abstract away the detail, clarifying the underlying factors that help us understand how reality works. Theories of market dynamics, the interaction of supply and demand, form a useful foundation.

2. The segmented sources of labor means that determining pay levels and pay mix increasingly requires understanding market conditions in different, even worldwide, locations.

3. Managers also need to know the jobs required to do the work, the tasks to be performed, and the knowledge and behaviors required to perform them (sound like job analysis?) so that they can bundle the various tasks to send to different locations.

ORGANIZATION FACTORS

Although product and labor market conditions create a range of possibilities within which managers create a policy on external competitiveness, organizational factors influence pay-level and pay-mix decisions, too.[30]

Industry and Technology

The industry in which an organization competes influences the technologies used. Labor-intensive industries such as education and health care tend to pay lower than technology-intensive industries such as petroleum or pharmaceuticals, whereas professional services such as consulting firms pay high. In addition to differences in technology across industries affecting compensation, the introduction of new technology *within an industry* influences pay levels. The next time you are waiting in line at the supermarket, think about the pay the checkout person gets. The use of universal product codes, scanners, scales built into the counter, even do-it-yourself checkout lanes have reduced the skills required of checkers. As a result, their average pay has declined over time.[31]

Qualifications and experience tailored to particular technologies is important in the analysis of labor markets. Machinists and millwrights who build General Electric diesel locomotives in Erie, Pennsylvania, have very different qualifications from machinists and millwrights who build Boeing airplanes in St. Louis.[32]

Employer Size

There is consistent evidence that large organizations tend to pay more than small ones. A study of manufacturing firms found that firms with 100 to 500 workers paid 6 percent higher wages than did smaller firms; firms of more than 500 workers paid 12 percent more than did the smallest firms.[33] This relationship between organization size, ability to pay, and pay level is consistent with economic theory that says that talented individuals have a higher marginal value in a larger organization because they can influence more people and decisions, thereby leading to more profits. Compare the advertising revenue that former late nigh host David Letterman was able to bring to CBS versus the potential revenue to station WBNS if his late-night show was only seen on WBNS in Athens, Ohio. No matter how cool he was in Athens, WBNS could not generate enough revenue to be able to afford to pay Mr. Letterman his multimillion dollar salary; CBS could. However, theories are less useful in explaining why practically everyone at bigger companies such as CBS, including janitors and compensation managers, is paid more. It seems unlikely that everyone has Letterman's impact on revenues.

People's Preferences

What pay forms (health insurance, eye care, bonuses, pensions) do employees really value? Better understanding of employee preferences is increasingly important in determining external competitiveness. Markets, after all, involve both employers' and employees' choices.[34] However, there are substantial difficulties in reliably measuring preferences. In response to the survey question "What do you value most in your work?" who among us would be so crass as to (publicly) rank money over cordial co-workers or challenging assignments? Researchers find that people place more importance on pay than they are willing to admit.[35]

Organization Strategy

A variety of pay-level and pay-mix strategies exist. Some employers adopt a low-wage, no-services strategy; they compete by producing goods and services with the lowest total compensation possible. Nike and Reebok reportedly do this. Both rely heavily on outsourcing to manufacture their products. Nike, for example, outsources 99 percent of its footwear production to independent contract suppliers in China, Vietnam, Indonesia, and Thailand, all of which have much lower labor costs than found in the United States. Others select a low-wage, high-services strategy. Marriott offers its low-wage room cleaners a hotline to social workers who assist with child care and transportation crises. English and citizenship courses are available for recent immigrants. Seminars cover how to manage one's paycheck and one's life. Still other employers use a high-wage, high-services approach. Medtronic's "fully present at work" approach, discussed in Chapter 2, is an example of high wage, high services. Obviously, these are extremes on a continuum of possibilities. One study found that like the company in Exhibit 7.3, a variety of pay-level strategies exist within some organizations. Pay levels that lead competition are used in jobs that most directly impact the organization's success (research and development and marketing in pharmacy companies). In jobs with less impact (human resource management and manufacturing), pay levels reflect a "meet competition" policy.

As noted earlier, efficiency wage argues that some firms, for a variety of reasons (e.g., their technology depends more heavily on having higher-quality workers or it is more difficult to monitor employee performance) do indeed have efficiency reasons to pay higher wages. Higher pay levels, either for the organization as a whole or for critical jobs, may be well-suited to particular strategies, such as higher value-added customer segments.[36] (Recall our example of Costco from Chapter 1.) Similarly, evidence suggests that organizations making greater use of so-called high-performance work practices (teams, quality circles, total quality management, job rotation) and computer-based technology and having higher-skilled workers also pay higher wages.[37] This is consistent with our discussion in Chapter 2 about the need for human resources practices designed to encourage ability, motivation, and opportunity to contribute (AMO) to reinforce each other. The observable benefits of higher wages may include: higher **pay satisfaction,** improved attraction and retention of employees, and higher quality, effort, and/or performance.[38] Ultimately, higher wages must bring something in return (e.g., higher productivity, quality, and/or innovation). Otherwise, a firm's ability to compete and survive is in question. (See our discussion of General Motors and the U.S. automobile industry in Chapter 1 and elsewhere in this chapter.) Evidence shows that in manufacturing, productivity (defined as sales value of production divided by employee hours worked) is positively correlated ($r = .45$) with hourly wage level.[39] Thus, the relationship, while far from perfect, is meaningful in manufacturing.

RELEVANT MARKETS

Economists take "the market" for granted—as in "The market determines wages." But managers at St. Luke's and Apriso realize that defining the **relevant markets** is a big part of figuring out how and how much to pay.

Although the notion of a single homogeneous labor market may be a useful analytical device, each organization operates in many labor markets, each with unique demand and supply. Some, as in the case of hospitals, face segmented supplies for the same skills in the same market. Others, such as Apriso, think more broadly about which markets to use as sources of talent. They seek to answer the question, What is the right pay to get the right people to do the right things?

Consequently, managers must define the markets that are relevant for pay purposes and establish the appropriate competitive positions in these markets. The three factors usually used to determine the relevant labor markets are the occupation (skill/knowledge required), geography (willingness to relocate, commute, or become virtual employees), and competitors (other employers in the same product/service and labor markets).

Defining the Relevant Market

How do employers choose their relevant markets? Surprisingly little research has been done on this issue. But if the markets are incorrectly defined, the estimates of competitors' pay rates will be incorrect and the pay level and pay mix inappropriately established.

> **e-Compensation**
> Select several companies that you believe might be labor market competitors (e.g., Microsoft, Oracle, IBM; or Johnson & Johnson, Merck, Pfizer). Compare their job postings on their Web sites. Do any of the companies list salaries for their jobs? Do they quote a single salary? Do they allow room for haggling?

Two studies do shed some light on this issue.[40] They conclude that managers look at both *competitors*—their products, location, and size—and the *jobs*—the skills and knowledge required and their importance to the organization's success (e.g., lawyers in law firms, software engineers at Microsoft). So depending on its location and size, a company may be deemed a relevant comparison even if it is not a product market competitor. We will see an example in Chapter 8 when we look at how Google and Microsoft define their relevant markets for paying executives.

The data from product market competitors (as opposed to labor market competitors) are likely to receive greater weight when:

1. Employee skills are specific to the product market (recall the differences in Boeing millwrights versus GE locomotive millwrights).
2. Labor costs are a large share of total costs.

3. Product demand is responsive to price changes. That is, people won't pay $4 for a bottle of Leinenkugel; instead, they'll go to Trader Joe's for a bottle of Charles Shaw wine, a.k.a. "two-buck Chuck" (the best $2 wine we have ever tasted).[41]

4. The supply of labor is not responsive to changes in pay (recall the earlier low-wage, low-skill example).

Globalization of Relevant Labor Markets: Offshoring and Outsourcing

We will discuss globalization and international issues more fully in Chapter 16. For now, we note that work flowing to lower wage locations is not new. Historically, clothing (needle trades) and furniture jobs flowed from New England to southern states. Nor is work flowing across national borders new. First, it was low-skill and low-wage jobs (clothing and Mardi Gras beads) from the U.S. to China and Central America; then higher-paid blue collar jobs (electronics, appliances); now it is service and professional jobs (accounting, legal, engineering, radiology). Vastly improved communication and software connectivity have accelerated these trends. For example, programming code and radiographic images can now be transported in an instant across the world.

In Chapter 4, we discussed characteristics of jobs (e.g., easily routinized, inputs/outputs easily transmitted electronically, little need for interaction with other workers, little need for local knowledge such as unique social and cultural factors) that are thought to increase susceptibility to offshoring (i.e., moving jobs to other countries). Here, we discuss why firms use offshoring, as well as challenges in doing so.

Several years ago, IBM found that a computer programmer (one of the occupations reported in Chapter 4 to be most susceptible to offshoring) in the United States with three to five years of experience cost $56 per hour in total compensation. In China, a similarly qualified programmer cost $12.50 per hour.[42] Based on these data, IBM estimated that it could save $168 million per year by shifting some of these programmer jobs to countries like China, India, and Brazil. That sort of savings is difficult to ignore, especially when competing firms are either based in lower labor cost countries (e.g., Infosys in India) or are offshoring or expanding operations there.

As noted, offshoring is also happening to lawyers and financial services jobs. In Mumbai, India, Pangea3 LLC employs Indian lawyers to do legal work for Wall Street banks. Whereas starting associates in the United States might bill more than $200 per hour, similar lawyers in India might bill something closer to $75 to $100 per hour. One estimate is that 35,000 U.S. legal jobs will be moved offshore by 2010 and another 79,000 will move by 2015.[43] In financial services, Copal Partners of India has seen large increases in its business as Wall Street firms not only outsource or offshore "back office" work (e.g., processing of transactions), but increasingly also production of research reports, trading recommendations, and so forth. Citigroup now employs over 20,000 people in India and Deutsche Bank has about 6,000. According to one observer, "There's a huge amount of grunt work that has been done by $250,000-a-year Wharton M.B.A.s" but "some of that stuff, it's natural to outsource it."[44] It is possible that more sophisticated jobs will increasingly follow.

While large differences in labor costs cannot simply be ignored, there are other factors to consider in deciding where jobs will be.[45] First, as we saw in Chapter 1, countries with lower average labor costs also tend to have lower average productivity. So, a company must assure itself that labor costs savings will not be neutralized by lower productivity. There may also be other risks. For example, going back to the case of manufacturing, consulting firm AMR Research found that, in the case of China, theft of intellectual property and product quality were major concerns and higher in China than any other country. In fact, China was ranked the riskiest country on 9 of 15 risk factors.[46] AMR observes that while some of the potential costs of these risks are difficult to quantify, they can be of great potential harm, for example, if they affect the value of brands and corporate reputation. Second, agency theory, which we discuss later, tells us that companies must devote resources to systems that monitor worker effort or output. This, as well as coordination of efforts, can be more difficult and more costly when geographic or cultural distance is great (and time zones different), even with advances in technology.[47] Third, customers' reactions must be considered. For example, Delta Air Lines Inc. decided to stop using call centers in India to handle sales and reservations, despite the fact that call-center workers in India earn roughly $500 a month (about one-sixth of U.S.–based call center workers). Delta said that customers had trouble communicating with India-based representatives. Delta's CEO explained that "Customer acceptance of call centers in foreign countries is low" and that "Our customers are not shy about letting us have that feedback."[48] Fourth, if labor costs are the driving force behind placing jobs, one must ask for how long the labor cost advantage at a significantly lower wage even will hold and whether sufficiently qualified employees will continue to be available as other companies also tap into this pool of labor. However, nothing is forever, and labor cost savings from offshoring and/or outsourcing can, of course, have a substantial effect on profits for many years before the cost advantage becomes small enough to be offset by other factors. We return to this issue in Chapter 16.

A compelling example is Apple's manufacturing strategy for its iPad and iPhone. The labor cost savings that Apple realizes by outsourcing assembly of these products to Foxconn is many billions of dollars compared to what it would cost to do assembly in the United States. Exhibit 7.11 shows that under Scenario 1, assembly of the iPhone and iPad in the United States would decrease operating income by $8.0 billion (24%). Under Scenario 2, operating income would be decreased by $14.8 billion (44%). Thus, if these products were assembled in the States, Apple would need to either (a) tell shareholders that profits (and thus shareholder return) will be reduced by billions of dollars, or (b) pass along the increased cost to the consumer, which, unless demand is inelastic (unlikely) would result in lower sales and thus, once again, lower profits and shareholder return.

EXHIBIT 7.11 Effect of Labor Costs (China versus U.S.) on Apple Operating Income

Operating Income, 2011	$33,790,000,000				

iPhone Units Sold, 2011	Labor Cost Difference per Unit United States–China		Total Labor Cost Difference United States–China		
72,293,000	Estimate 1[a]	$65.00	$4,699,045,000		
72,293,000	Estimate 2[b]	$158.57	$11,463,501,010		

iPad Units Sold, 2011	Labor Cost Difference per Unit United States - China		Total Labor Cost Difference United States - China		
33,394,000	Estimate[c]	$100.00	$3,339,400,000		

			Added Labor Cost, 2011, if iPhone and iPad Assembled in United States	% of Operating Income	New Operating Income	New Operating Income (% change)
Scenario 1 (Using iPhone labor cost Estimate 1)			$8,038,445,000	24%	$25,751,555,000	−24%
Scenario 2 (Using iPhone labor cost Estimate 2)			$14,802,901,010	44%	$18,987,098,990	−44%

[a]Charles Duhigg and Keith Bradsher. "How the U.S. Lost Out on iPhone Work." *The New York Times*, January 21, 2012.

[b]Julie Froud, Sukhdev Johal, Adam Leaver, and Karel Williams. "Apple Business Model: Financialization across the Pacific." University of Manchester, Centre for Research in Socio-Cultural Change, Working Paper No. 111. April 2012.

[c]Source: Tim Winstall. "If Apple Onshored iPad Production it Would Create 67,000 American Manufacturing Jobs! "Forbes.com, December 18, 2011. http://www.forbes.com/sites/timworstall/2011/12/18 /if-apple-onshored-ipad-production-it-would-create-67000-american-manufacturing-jobs. Extracted May 21, 2012.

COMPETITIVE PAY POLICY ALTERNATIVES

Compensation theories offer some help in understanding the variations in pay levels we observe among employers. They are less helpful in understanding differences in the mix of pay forms. Relevant markets are shaped by pressures from the labor and product markets and the organization. But so what? How, in fact, do managers set pay-level and pay-mix policy, and what difference does it make? In the remainder of this chapter, we will discuss those two issues.

Recall that pay level is the average of the array of rates inside an organization. There are three conventional pay-level policies: to lead, to meet, or to follow competition. Newer policies emphasize flexibility: among policies for different employee groups, among pay forms for individual employees, and among elements of the employee relationship that the company wishes to emphasize in its external competitiveness policy.

What Difference Does the Pay-Level Policy Make?

The basic premise is that the competitiveness of pay will affect the organization's ability to achieve its compensation objectives, and this in turn will affect its performance.[49] The probable effects of alternative policies are shown in Exhibit 7.12 and discussed in more detail below. The problem with much pay-level research is that it focuses on base pay and ignores bonuses, incentives, options, employment security, benefits, or other forms of pay. Yet the exhibits and discussion in this chapter should have convinced you that base pay represents only a portion of compensation. Comparisons on base alone can mislead. In fact, many managers believe they get more bang for the buck by allocating dollars away from base pay and into variable forms that more effectively shape employee behavior.[50]

General Mills, for example, seeks to pay at the 50th percentile of base salary (among consumer packaged goods companies) but at the 75th percentile for total cash (base salary variable pay) for managers if they have superior performance.[51] As Exhibit 7.13 shows, this seems to be a common strategy.

Pay with Competition (Match)

Given the choice to match, lead, or lag, the most common policy is to match rates paid by competitors.[52] Managers historically justify this policy by saying that failure to

EXHIBIT 7.12 Probable Relationships Between External Pay Policies and Objectives

	Compensation Objectives				
Policy	Ability to Attract	Ability to Retain	Contain Labor Costs	Reduce Pay Dissatisfaction	Increase Productivity
Pay above market (lead)	+	+	?	+	?
Pay with market (match)	=	=	=	=	?
Pay below market (lag)	−	?	+	−	?
Hybrid policy	?	?	+	?	+
Employer of choice	+	+	+	−	?

EXHIBIT 7.13 Competitive Pay Policy Objectives, Base Salary, and Total Cash

Base Salary Target

What Is Your Organization's *Base Salary* Target (or Goal) Compared to the Relevant Labor Market?

	<25th Percentile	25th–40th Percentile	40th–60th Percentile	60th–75th Percentile	>75th Percentile	Varies/Do Not Have a Target
Senior Management (n = 1,034)	0%	1%	73%	14%	3%	9%
Middle Management (n = 1,045)	0%	1%	85%	7%	2%	5%
Professional (n = 1,042)	1%	1%	86%	6%	2%	4%
Sales (n = 1,037)	1%	1%	85%	6%	1%	7%
Administrative (n = 1,037)	1%	2%	86%	6%	1%	5%
Production (n = 835)	0%	3%	84%	6%	1%	6%

Total Cash Target

What Is Your Organization's *Total Cash* Target (or Goal) Compared to the Relevant Labor Market?

	<25th Percentile	25th–40th Percentile	40th–60th Percentile	60th–75th Percentile	>75th Percentile	Varies/Do Not Have a Target
Senior Management (n = 1,037)	0%	1%	50%	24%	5%	20%
Middle Management (n = 1,041)	0%	1%	61%	18%	3%	18%
Professional (n = 1,035)	0%	1%	64%	14%	2%	18%
Sales (n = 1,896)	0%	1%	63%	15%	3%	18%
Administrative (n = 1,033)	0%	2%	65%	13%	2%	18%
Production (n = 837)	0%	3%	63%	12%	2%	20%

Source: "Job Evaluation and Market-Pricing Practices," *WorldatWork* © Reprinted with permission from *WorldatWork*. Content is licensed for use by purchaser only. No part of this article may be reproduced, excerpted or redistributed in any form without express written permission from WorldatWork.

match competitors' rates would cause murmuring among present employees and limit the organization's ability to recruit. Many nonunionized companies tend to match or even lead competition in order to discourage unions. A **pay-with-competition policy** tries to ensure that an organization's wage costs are approximately equal to those of its product competitors and that its ability to attract applicants will be approximately equal to its labor market competitors.

Classical economic models predict that employers meet competitive wages. While this avoids placing an employer at a disadvantage in pricing products, it may not provide a competitive advantage in its labor markets.

Lead Pay-Level Policy

A **lead pay-level policy** maximizes the ability to attract and retain quality employees and minimizes employee dissatisfaction with pay. It may also offset less attractive features of the work, à la Adam Smith's "net advantage." Combat pay premiums paid to military personnel offset some of the risk of being fired upon.[53] The higher pay offered by brokerage firms offsets the risk of being fired when the market tanks.

As noted earlier, sometimes an entire industry can pass high pay rates on to consumers if pay is a relatively low proportion of total operating expenses or if the industry is highly regulated. But what about specific firms within a high-pay industry? For example, Merrill Lynch adheres to a pay leadership position for financial analysts *in its industry*. Do any advantages actually accrue to Merrill Lynch? If all firms in the industry have similar operating expenses, then the lead policy must provide some competitive advantage to Merrill Lynch that offsets the higher costs.

A number of researchers have linked high wages to ease of attraction, reduced vacancy rates and training time, and better-quality employees.[54] Research also suggests that high pay levels reduce turnover and absenteeism.[55] Exhibit 7.14 summarizes several studies on the degree to which higher pay is associated with lower quits (turnover). These studies suggest that pay level can have a substantial influence on quit rates. As noted above, pay satisfaction helps explain the influence of pay level on quits. Exhibit 7.15 shows the relationship of pay satisfaction with turnover (quits) and also determinants of pay satisfaction. In addition to pay level, we see, consistent with equity theory, that fairness/justice perceptions, both distributive (based on how much they receive) and procedural (what process was used to decide how much), matter.[56] Nevertheless, there is no simple relationship between pay-level and financial performance. Several studies have found that the use of variable pay (bonuses and long-term incentives) is related to an organization's improved financial performance but that pay level is not.[57] We have conjectured that pay level is so important that paying "too low" or "too high" for any extended period has such significant potential drawbacks that organizations do not differentiate much on pay level (alone). It may be that high pay levels only have beneficial effects on performance when the pay level itself depends on performance (i.e., there a high pay level AND strong pay for performance).[58]

A lead policy can also have negative effects. It may force the employer to increase wages of current employees too, to avoid internal misalignment and murmuring. Additionally, a lead policy may mask negative job attributes that contribute to high turnover later on (e.g., boring assignments or hostile colleagues). Remember the managers' view mentioned earlier that high turnover was more likely to be a managerial problem than a compensation problem.[59]

Lag Pay-Level Policy

A policy of paying below-market rates may hinder a firm's ability to attract potential employees. But if a **lag pay-level policy** is coupled with the promise of higher future returns (e.g., stock ownership in a high-tech start-up firm), this combination may

EXHIBIT 7.14
Effect of Pay Levels on Quits, Organization Level Studies

Elasticity = % change in y/ % change in x

Study	Sample	Results	Elasticity
Riddell, *Industrial Relations,* 2011	390 firms in Greater Toronto, 6 occupational groups	A 10% increase in ratio of firm pay to market pay associated with quit rate going from .106 to .953, a 10.1% reduction	−1.01
Falch, *American Economic Review* (May 2011)	161 primary and secondary schools in Norway	Schools having teacher "shortage" and located in far north eligible to pay teachers wage premium of 10%. Introduction (also studied its removal) of 10% wage premium associated with quit rate going from .18 to .12, a 35% reduction	−3.50
Siebert & Zubanov, *Academy of Management Journal* (2009)	325 retail clothing stores in the United Kingdom	A 10% increase in ratio of store wage/county wage associated with separation rate going from .0500 to .0364, a 28% reduction	−2.78
Shaw, Delery, Jenkins, Gupta, *Academy of Management Journal* (1998)	227 trucking companies in the United States	Regression coefficient (beta) = −.31 for quits on pay level. A 10% increase in average annual pay level ($34,912 to $38,403) associated with quit rate going from .256 to .200, a 22% reduction	−2.20
Raff & Summers, *Journal of Labor Economics* (1987)	Ford Motor Company in 1914	Increasing daily wage 100%, from $2.50 to $5.00, associated with turnover reduction from 370% to 54%, an 85% reduction	−0.85

increase employee commitment and foster teamwork, which may increase productivity. How long this promise works, in the face of flat or declining stock markets, is unknown. Unmet expectations probably have negative effects. Additionally, it is possible to lag competition on pay level but to lead on other returns from work (e.g., hot assignments, desirable location, outstanding colleagues, cool tools, work/life balance).

Different Policies for Different Employee Groups

In practice, many employers go beyond a single choice among the three policy options. They may vary the policy for different occupational families, as did the company in Exhibit 7.3. They may vary the policy for different forms of pay, as did the companies in Exhibit 7.4. They may also adopt different policies for different business units that face very different competitive conditions.

Not by Pay Level Alone: Pay-Mix Strategies

Thus far, we have devoted limited attention to pay-mix policies. Some obvious alternatives include *performance driven, market match, work/life balance,* and *security.*

EXHIBIT 7.15 Pay Satisfaction Correlations with Determinants and Consequences

Meta-Analysis	Dependent Variable	Independent Variable	K (# studies)	N (# employees)	Correlation
Judge et al., *Journal of Vocational Behavior* (2010)	Pay Satisfaction	Pay Level	48	15,576	.23
Williams et al., *Journal of Applied Psychology* (2006)	Pay Satisfaction	Pay Level	64	29,574	.29
	Pay Satisfaction	Perceived Pay Discrepancy	64	29,754	−.54
	Pay Satisfaction	Distributive Justice	10	6,595	.79
	Pay Satisfaction	Procedural Justice	8	2,291	.42
	Turnover/Quits	Pay Satisfaction	9	1,362	−.17
	Turnover Intention	Pay Satisfaction	37	15,893	−.31

Notes: Correlation is ρ, the correlation corrected for artifacts (e.g., unreliability in the independent and/or dependent variable). Perceived pay discrepancy = Perceived amount should be paid minus the perceived amount actually paid. Both studies (Judge et al., 2010 and Williams et al., 2006) are meta-analyses that use primary studies conducted at the individual/employee level of analysis.

Exhibit 7.16 illustrates these four alternatives. Compared to the other three, incentives and stock ownership make up a greater percent of total compensation in *performance-driven* policies. The *market match* simply mimics the pay mix competitors are paying. How managers actually make these mix decisions is a ripe issue for more research.

How managers position their organization's pay against competitors is changing. Some alternatives that are emerging focus on total returns from work (beyond financial returns) and offering people choices among these returns. Rather than "flexible," perhaps a better term would be "fuzzy" policies.

Such pay-mix policy alternatives exist among enterprises in other countries, too. Apache Footware, located in Quingyuan, China, offers base plus bonus, which matches local practice. It also offers benefits that include a new medical clinic, housing for married couples, a school, sports facilities, and a shopping mall. Steve Chen, Apache's chief executive, states, "It's not just about pay, it's about lifestyle. We're building a community so people will stay." (Reminiscent of SAS, whose strategy was discussed in Chapter 2 In contrast, Top Form Undergarment Wear, located in the same region, phased out its employee housing. It opted to pay employees over 20 percent higher base pay than local practice. Top Form executive Charles Lee says, "Workers need to have a life of their own. They are not children. We pay them more and let each worker decide what is best for them."[60]

Employer of Choice/Shared Choice

Some companies compete based on their overall reputation as a place to work, beyond pay level and pay mix. For example, IBM compares within the information technology

EXHIBIT 7.16 Pay-Mix Policy Alternatives

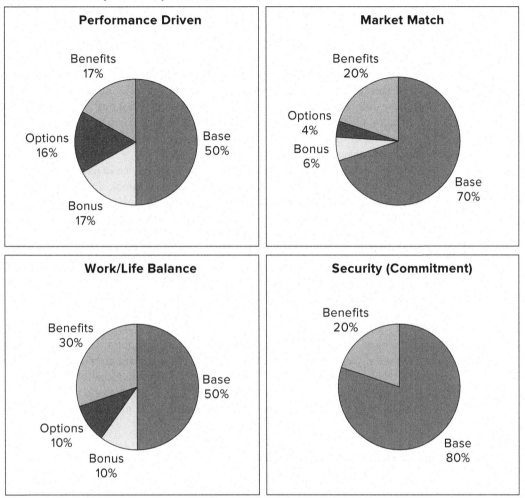

marketplace and positions its pay "among the best" in this group. Further, it claims to "strongly differentiate based on business and individual results." It leads the market with its strong emphasis on performance. IBM also offers extensive training opportunities, challenging work assignments, and the like. In a sense, **"employer of choice"** corresponds to the brand or image the company projects as an employer.

Shared choice begins with the traditional alternatives of lead, meet, or lag. But it then adds a second part, which is to *offer employees choices* (within limits) in the pay mix. This "employee-as-customer" perspective is not all that revolutionary, at least in the United States. Many employers offer choices on health insurance (individual versus dependent coverage), retirement investments (growth or value), and so on. (See flexible benefits in Chapter 13. See also Chapter 2 for how Whole Foods uses an employee vote every three years in choosing its benefits package.) More advanced software is making the employee-as-customer approach more feasible. Mass customization—being able to select among a variety of features—is routine when purchasing a new laptop or auto. It is now possible with total compensation, too. Does offering people choices matter? One risk is that employees will make "wrong" choices that will jeopardize their financial well-being (e.g., inadequate health insurance). Another is the "24 jars of jam" dilemma. Supermarket studies report that offering consumers a taste of just a few different jams increases sales. But offering a taste of 24 different jams decreases sales. Consumers feel overwhelmed by too many choices and simply walk away. Perhaps offering employees too many choices of different kinds of pay will lead to confusion, mistakes, and dissatisfaction.[61]

An example of a company that does give employees a choice in pay mix is Netflix. Each November, employees have their performance evaluations. In December, each employee chooses how much compensation to receive in cash and how much to receive in stock options. Roughly two-thirds of Netflix employees choose 100% cash. Of the remaining one-third, the average share of compensation taken in the form of stock options is 7 to 8%. (The share allocated to options was initially restricted, but no longer is. So, these results may change.) The apparent preference among most employees for cash rather than (more risky) options at Netflix is consistent with agency theory, which is covered in Chapter 9.[62]

Pitfalls of Pies

The pie charts in Exhibit 7.16 contrast various pay mix policies. However, thinking about the mix of pay forms as pieces in a pie chart has limitations. These are particularly clear when the value of stock is volatile. The pie charts in Exhibit 7.17 show how a well-known software company's mix changed after a major stock market decline (stock prices plummeted 50 percent within a month). Base pay went from 47 to 55

EXHIBIT 7.17 Volatility of Stock Value Changes Total Pay Mix

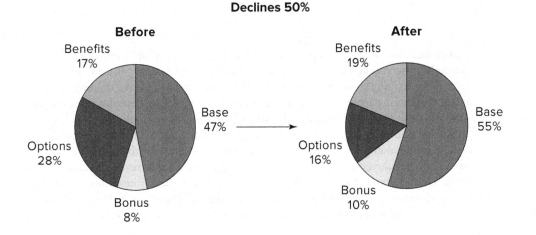

**Stock Value
Declines 50%**

Before — Benefits 17%, Base 47%, Bonus 8%, Options 28%

After — Benefits 19%, Base 55%, Bonus 10%, Options 16%

EXHIBIT 7.18
Dashboard:
Total Pay Mix
Breakdown vs.
Competitors*

Stock Options Base Salary Benefits Bonus Perquisites
79%   95%   103%   113%   122%

90 100 110
80   120
70   130
60   140
50 Total Compensation 150
        102%

*100 = Chosen market position, e.g., market median

percent of total compensation, whereas the value of stock options fell from 28 to 16 percent. (The reverse has happened in this company, too.) The mix changed even though the company made no overt decision to change its pay strategy. But wait, it can get worse. One technology company was forced to disclose that three-quarters of all its stock options were "under water," that is, exercisable at prices higher than the market price. Due to stock market volatility, the options had become worthless to employees. So what is the message to employees? To competitors? The company's intended strategy has not changed, but in reality the mix has changed. So the possible volatility in the value of different pay forms needs to be anticipated.

Some companies prefer to report the mix of pay forms using a "dashboard," as depicted in Exhibit 7.18. The dashboard changes the focus from emphasizing the relative importance of each form within a single company to comparing each form by itself to the market (many companies). In the example, the value of stock options is 79 percent of competitors' median, base pay is at 95 percent of competitors' median, and overall total compensation is 102 percent of (or 2 percent above) the market median. Pies, dashboards—different focus, both recognizing the importance of the mix of pay forms.

Keep in mind that the mix employees receive differs at different levels in the internal job structure. Exhibit 7.19 shows the different mix of base, cash incentives, and stock programs Merrill Lynch pays at different organization levels. Executive leadership positions receive less than 10 percent in base, about 20 percent in stock, and the rest in annual incentives. This compares to 50 percent in base, 40 percent in annual incentives, and 10 percent in stock for midlevel manager/professional positions, and 80 percent base, 20 percent incentives, and no stock for entry- and lower-level jobs. While the percentages vary among organizations, greater emphasis on performance (through incentives and stock) at higher levels is common practice. This is based on the belief that jobs at higher levels in the organization have greater opportunity to influence organization performance.

EXHIBIT 7.19
Merrill Lynch's
Pay Mix Varies
within the
Structure

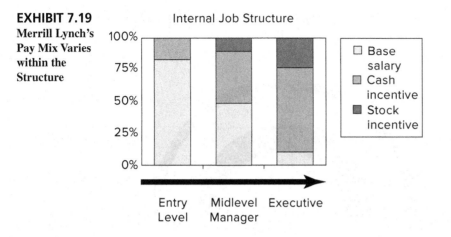

Internal Job Structure

CONSEQUENCES OF PAY-LEVEL AND PAY-MIX DECISIONS: GUIDANCE FROM THE RESEARCH

Earlier we noted that external competitiveness has two major consequences: It affects (1) operating expenses and (2) employee attitudes and work behaviors. Exhibit 7.20 summarizes these consequences, which have been discussed throughout this chapter.

Efficiency

A variety of theories make assumptions about the effects of relative pay levels on an organization's efficiency. Some recommend lead policies to diminish shirking and permit hiring better-qualified applicants. Others—such as marginal productivity theory—recommend matching. One study, using utility theory, concluded that a lag pay-level policy was the best choice for bank tellers.[63] However, as we will see, utility theory tells us that for higher impact jobs, the conclusion could differ. No research suggests under what circumstances managers should choose which pay-mix alternative.

EXHIBIT 7.20
Some
Consequences
of Pay Levels

Which Policy Achieves Competitive Advantage?

Research on the effect of pay-level policies is difficult because companies' stated policies often do not correspond to reality. For example, HR managers at 124 companies were asked to define their firm's target pay level. All 124 of them reported that their companies paid above the median![64]

Beyond opinions, there is little evidence of the consequences of different policy alternatives. We do know that pay level affects costs; we do not know whether any effects it might have on productivity or attracting and retaining employees are sufficient to offset costs. Nor is it known how much of a pay-level variation makes a difference to employees; will 5 percent, 10 percent, or 15 percent be a noticeable difference? Although lagging competitive pay could have a noticeable reduction in short-term labor costs, it is not known whether this savings is accompanied by a reduction in the quality and performance of the workforce. It may be that an employer's pay level will not gain any competitive *advantage;* however, the wrong pay level may put the organization at a serious *disadvantage.* Similarly, we simply do not know the effects of the different pay-mix alternatives or the financial results of shifting the responsibility for choosing the mix to employees. Perhaps it is the message communicated by pay mix and levels that is the key to achieving competitive advantage.

So where does this leave the manager? In the absence of convincing evidence, the least-risk approach may be to set both pay level and pay mix to match competition. An organization may adopt a lead policy for skills that are critical to its success, a match policy for less-critical skills, and a lag policy for jobs that are easily filled in the local labor market. An obvious concern with flexible policies is to achieve some degree of business alignment and fair treatment for employees among the choices. (The appendix to this chapter shows how utility analysis can help evaluate pay-level strategies.)

Fairness

Satisfaction with pay is directly related to the pay level: More is better.[65] But employees' sense of fairness is also related to how others are paid. A friend at Stanford claims that if all but one of the faculty in their business school got $1,000,000 and one person received $1,000,001, the others would all be lined up at the dean's office demanding an explanation. Employers have many choices about how and where to invest their resources. Even if the decision is made to invest in improving people's feelings about fairness of their pay, there is little research to tell us this will improve employees' overall feeling about fair treatment in the workplace.[66]

Compliance

It's not enough to say that an employer must pay at or above the legal minimum wage. Provisions of prevailing wage laws and equal rights legislation must also be met. In fact, we will return to the subject of market wages again when we discuss pay discrimination and the concept of "living wage." In addition to pay level, various pay forms are also regulated. Pensions and health care are considered part of every citizen's economic security and are regulated to some degree in most countries. This is discussed again when we look at international practices and benefits. Employers must also exercise caution when sharing salary information to avoid antitrust violations.[67]

No matter the competitive pay policy, it needs to be translated into practice. The starting point is measuring the market through use of a salary survey. For this, we turn to the next chapter.

Your **Turn**   Two-Tier Wages

In Chapter 7, we talked about the implications of different pay-level strategies for costs and revenues. We saw examples both of employers seeking to control/reduce pay levels and of employers increasing pay levels. Here, we continue our earlier discussion on how U.S. automakers have used two-tier wage structures to control labor costs and consider what might happen going forward. Also important is their use of profit sharing as a way to keep fixed labor costs under control and making labor costs move more in line with profitability, so that labor costs decline when profits decline and labor costs increase when profits increase. That reduces the problem of having high, fixed labor costs when the company is under financial duress.

As we saw earlier, a two-tier wage structure allows a company to pay new hires at a lower wage. The average hourly wage for Tier 1 workers is about $29 versus a maximum of $19.50 for Tier 2 workers. The average hourly total compensation is roughly $59 for Tier 1 workers versus about $35 for Tier 2 workers.

As recently as the late 1990s, the automobile industry (including both domestic and overseas owned U.S. producers) employed 1,000,000 people in the United States. That number dropped to 550,000 during the recession and bankruptcies of late last decade. Now, the Center for Automotive Research projects that employment could grow to 650,000 in 2012 and could be more than 750,000 by 2015.[68] Of course, the Big Three are expected to account for a minority share of that employment total, a big change from the old days. Currently, the Big Three have about 137,000 hourly jobs combined.

At the GM plant in Orion Township, Michigan, about 100 workers sort parts to be used on the assembly line to build the Chevrolet Sonic. What is notable is that these workers are not GM employees but rather (UAW-represented) employees of an outside supplier. Their average hourly labor cost is about $20/hour, lower not only than that of Tier I GM workers, but also lower than Tier 2 GM workers. As a result of using a significant number of lower cost Tier 2 workers and (even lower cost) outside supplier workers, GM is expected to be able to reduce the labor cost per vehicle from $1,160 to $710. All told, GM could save as much as $72 million per year.[69]

Here are some questions to consider:

1. To what extent is the renewed job growth in the automobile industry in the United States due to the use of two-tier wages?

2. To the degree job growth (and increased car sales that come from more competitive labor costs) is based on two tier-wage structures; how sustainable is this approach? Consider, for example, that Fiat and Chrysler CEO Sergio Marchionne stated in 2011 that "Long term, (the system) is not a viable structure. It creates two classes of workers within the plant. It doesn't work in the same direction we are working ... to get this organization to work in unison."[70] Why would Mr. Marchionne make this statement? What are the potential drawbacks of a two-tier structure? When would we expect any such drawbacks to materialize?

3. What about the use of non-GM workers at the Chevy Sonic plant? What might Mr. Marchionne think about that approach?

4. Will the two-tier wage structure go away in the near future? Summarize the pressures to eliminate it as well as the pressures to keep it. Be sure to consider labor costs and productivity of workers and plants at other companies and in other parts of the world. Auto worker Gary Walkowicz, a member of the UAW bargaining committee at Ford's Dearborn Truck assembly plant, estimates that Ford could convert its 14,685 Tier 2 workers to Tier 1 wages for $335 million per year. The UAW will likely point out that is a small fraction of the $6.9 billion North American profit earned by Ford the previous year. Your thoughts?

5. You may wish to do some research on the new Volkswagen plant in Chattanooga, Tennessee, the last one built in the United States. Also, consider that the *Automotive News* estimates that the Ford Fiesta (a competitor to the Chevy Sonic) plant in Cuautitlán, Mexico may have labor costs as low as $150 per vehicle.[71] Recall also our earlier discussion of where automobile production plants in North America have been built in recent years (as well as where they have not been built).

6. More recently, Fiat Chrysler CEO Sergio Marchionne referred to the two-tier wage structure as "impossible" and described it as "almost offensive." However, Mr. Marchionne's actual plan may not be to eliminate the two-tier structure entirely. As we saw earlier in the chapter, it appears that base pay differences will remain between the two tiers. However, consistent with suggestions made by Mr. Marchionne leading up to contract negotiations, Tier 2 worker pay may move nearer or even equal that of Tier 1 workers when the company's profits are high through larger profit sharing payments for Tier 2 workers. By the time you read this, details on the new contracts between the UAW and each of the Big Three American car companies should be available. Gather the key facts and evaluate how well the new contracts will serve the interests of the companies and those of the workers (which are similar, yet different).[72]

7. How do you think the UAW and the workers it represents will react to Mr. Marchionne's plan? Consider the global competitive market forces we have identified and consider also the degree to which worker interests in keeping and creating jobs and achieving higher wages (and/or total compensation) are in line with Fiat Chrysler's interests. How large have profit-sharing payments for workers been at Fiat Chrysler and at Ford and GM in recent years? Why would the companies wish to raise pay levels using these sorts of payments rather than via increases to base wages? How will the UAW and workers likely react? Explain.

Summary   One reviewer of this book told us that "There are three important contributions of this chapter: (1) that there is no 'going rate' and so managers make conscious pay-level and pay-mix decisions influenced by several factors; (2) that there are both product market and labor market competitors that impact the pay-level and pay-mix decisions; and (3) that alternative pay-level and pay-mix decisions have different consequences." That is a great summary of the key points.

The pay model used throughout this book emphasizes strategic policy issues: objectives, alignment, competitiveness, contributions, and management. Policies need to be designed to achieve specific pay objectives. This part of the book is concerned with external competitiveness, or pay comparisons among organizations. Does Apple Computer pay its accountants the same wage that Florida Power pays its accountants? Probably not. Different companies pay different rates; the average of the overall array of rates in an organization constitutes the pay level. Different companies also use different forms of pay. To achieve the objectives stipulated for the pay system, both the pay level and the pay mix must be properly positioned relative to competitors. Each integrated job structure or career path within the organization may have its own competitive position in the market. The next chapter considers the decisions involved and the variety of techniques available to implement those decisions.

Before we proceed, let us reemphasize that the major reason we are interested in the external competitiveness policy—pay level and mix of pay forms—is that it has profound consequences on the organization's objectives. Theories and practical experience support this belief. But as we have also noted, more research is needed to guide us in making decisions. We have clearly established that differences among organizations' competitive policies and their pay levels and forms exist. We have examined the factors that determine these differences. What remains to be better understood is the potential effects of various policies.

Review Questions

1. Distinguish policies on external competitiveness from policies on internal alignment. Why is external competitiveness so important?
2. What factors shape an organization's external competitiveness?
3. What does marginal revenue product have to do with pay?
4. What pay level does the efficiency wage predict? Does the theory accurately predict organization behavior? Why or why not?
5. What is a relevant market? What difference does it make when determining people's pay?
6. Can you think of any companies that follow a lag and/or lead policy? Why do they believe it pays to pay differently? Can you think of any companies that follow performance driven and/or work/life balance policies?

Appendix 7-A

Utility Analysis

One way to quantify and think about the effects of a compensation program is to use utility analysis. We define *utility* as the dollar value created by increasing revenues and/or decreasing costs by changing one or more human resource practices.[73] Utility analysis has most typically been used to analyze the payoff to making more valid employee hiring/selection decisions. Compensation plays a major role here because a higher pay level may increase an organization's ability to hire and keep the best talent. In addition, as our discussion of sorting effects in Chapter 1 suggested, differences in pay mix may also have major effects. For example, a pay mix that emphasizes performance-based pay may also have an impact by being especially attractive to high performers. In the broader picture, compensation decisions can be analyzed by modeling the cost and value created by different pay-level and pay-mix strategies. What does each strategy cost and what does it do for revenues via attraction, selection, and retention of a workforce that has a particular level of ability and motivation? Here, we will use a very basic form of utility analysis, which focuses only on the quality of the workforce initially hired.

To estimate utility in this basic approach, we model it as a function of several parameters:

$$u = r \times SDy \times Z - C/SR$$

where:

u = utility (revenue − cost) per hire per year.

r = validity coefficient, the correlation between criterion, y, and one or more pre-employment assessments used to make hiring decisions. It is the accuracy of our predictions regarding which applicants will perform well as employees.

SDy = standard deviation of the dollar value of different employee performance levels. In essence, this parameter measures the value of high performance versus average or low performance in a job. (This parameter would be higher for jobs like CEO, actors, athletes, attorneys, real estate brokers, and consultants where star performers can generate much more profit than weaker performers and lower for most lower-skill or highly structured jobs, where performance differences are less consequential.) Although accuracy of utility estimates depends on accurate estimation of SDy, we will use a very rough rule of thumb here to keep things more manageable: SDy equals 40% of salary.

Z = mean standard score (z distribution, mean = 0, SD =1) of those hired on the predictor used to select/hire employees.

C = cost per applicant. Note that in the utility formula, C is divided by the selection ratio. Thus, C/SR becomes large (and drives the utility estimate lower) as either cost per applicant increases or our selectivity increases (i.e., SR decreases). For example, a cost per applicant of \$200 and a selection ratio of .5 yields \$200/.5 = \$400, but a cost per applicant of \$200 and a selection ratio of .05 yields \$200/.05 = \$4,000. Thus, there is a trade-off between the gains from increasing average hire quality (Z) and the cost of being more selective in hiring to achieve this higher quality.

SR = selection ratio, which is hires/applicants.

It is important to note how Z changes as we become more selective (lower SR) in our hiring. Based on the standard normal distribution function:

SR	Z
5%	2.06
10%	1.75
20%	1.40
50%	0.80
80%	0.35
100%	0.00

In other words, if we hire all (100%) of applicants, our average z (Z) score would be .00, indicating that the average quality of our hires would be the same as the average quality of the applicant pool. However, if we are more selective and hire only 20% of our applicants, then our average quality will be much higher, 1.40. At a still higher selectivity of 5%, our applicant pool would be 2.06 standard deviations above the mean.

Let us assume we are filling a position that will cost us a salary of $100,000 under our new selective hiring approach (versus $90,000 under the old system). If we are able to increase the quality of our hires to $Z = 2.06$ through selective hiring, what would the impact be on utility? Assume that the average cost per applicant is $200. (Some applicants can be screened out quickly and cheaply, while other applicants will require higher costs to do more intensive screening.)

Old Selection Strategy

SR = .50 ($Z = .80$), $r = .40$, $SD = \$50,000$, $cost = \$200$
u = .40 × \$50,000 × .80 − \$200/.50 = \$15,600/hire

New Selection Strategy

SR = .05 ($Z = 2.06$), $r = .40$, $SD = \$50,000$, $cost = \$100$
u = .40 × \$50,000 × 2.06 − \$200/.05 = \$37,200/hire

In other words, our new, more selective hiring approach yields a utility gain of $37,200 − $15,600 = $21,500 per hire.

But hold on. We are paying a $10,000 higher salary to enable us to be more selective in our hiring in the new approach. Thus, the utility gain is instead $21,500 − $10,000 = $11,500. Further, benefits, on average, add about another 40 cents on top of every dollar of direct pay. So, perhaps we should use 1.4 × $10,000 + $14,000 as the incremental compensation cost of the new selection strategy. The incremental utility would then be $21,500 − $14,000 = $7,500 per hire.[74]

Of course, our conclusion depends entirely on the estimates and assumptions we put into the model. Paying more will, of course, not always generate higher utility. It really depends on the situation and the organization's strategy. More accurate estimates of utility of compensation can be obtained by following more complex models that have been developed.[75] Estimates obtained with these models would very likely change and be more accurate because they more fully recognize sorting effects (including retention patterns of high and low performers) and gains and losses to compensation decisions that accumulate over time. We have tried to keep things simpler here in the interest of introducing some basic ideas and logic.

Your **Turn**

Combining Pay Survey and Job Evaluation Data

Return to the job evaluation scores and job structure you created for Whole Foods in the Your Turn at the end of Chapter 5. To prepare for Chapter 8, where the internal job structure is combined with external market (pay survey) data to develop actual rates of pay for jobs (a pay structure), it will be helpful for you to now begin to become familiar with pay survey data. The U.S. Bureau of Labor Statistics provides Occupational Employment Statistics. For this exercise, we will use "National Industry-Specific Occupational Employment and Wage Estimates for the Grocery Stores industry (NAICS 445100–Grocery Stores). Use the following link.[76]

http://www.bls.gov/oes/current/naics4_445100.htm

Look for occupations that appear to match the occupations from Whole Foods.[77] As examples, consider:

11-9051 Food Service Managers
41-2011 Cashiers
43-5081 Stock Clerks

For each occupation, click on its name to show 10th, 25th, 50th (median), 75th, and 90th percentile wage levels for the occupation.

QUESTIONS:

1. What pay level (e.g., 50th or other) would you recommend be used for the Whole Foods jobs? Would you use the same pay level for all jobs? Explain.

2. How strongly do relative job evaluation points and relative survey pay correspond? For example, what is the ratio of job evaluation points you assigned to Job B (Cashier) and Job F (Team Member, Stock and Display) in the Chapter 5 Your Turn? What is the ratio of survey pay from Occupational Employment Statistics for 41-2011 Cashiers and 43-5081 Stock Clerks? Are the two ratios the same? (In Chapter 8, we will discuss why these ratios, one based on internal worth and the other based on external worth, may differ.) If these two ratios or other ratios you compute using other Whole Foods/pay survey jobs differ, which ratio (internal, based on job evaluation, or external, based on the pay survey) would you recommend be emphasized or receive priority in setting actual pay?

3. What are the limitations of the Occupational Employment Statistics data?

Endnotes

1. Erica Groshen, "Five Reasons Why Wages Vary Among Employers," *Industrial Relations* 30 (1991), pp. 350–381; B. Gerhart and S. Rynes, *Compensation: Theory, Evidence and Strategic Implications* (Thousand Oaks, CA: Sage, 2003); B. Gerhart and G. Milkovich, "Organization Differences in Managerial Compensation and Financial Performance," *Academy of Management Journal* 33 (1990), pp. 663–691.

2. Steven Greenhouse, "Gap to Raise Minimum Hourly Pay," *The New York Times.* February 19, 2014; Hiroko Tabuchimarch, "Target Plans to Raise Pay to at Least $9 an Hour," *The New York Times.* March 19, 2015, p. B5.

3. Anna Wilde Mathews and Theo Francis, "Aetna Sets Wage Floor: $16 an Hour," *Wall Street Journal.* January 13, 2015, p. B1.

4. Dudley Althaus and William Boston, "Trade Pacts Given Mexico an Edge," *Wall Street Journal,* March 18, 2015, p. A1.

5. William Boston, "In Germany, Mexican Workers Learn Audi's Ways," *Wall Street Journal.* March 18, 2015, p. A11.

6. The National Association of Colleges and Employers, Bethlehem, PA, publishes a quarterly survey of starting-salary offers to college graduates; data are reported by curriculum, by functional area, and by degree at *www.naceweb.org.* It is one of several sources employers may use to establish the offers they extend to new graduates.

7. Adapted from our analysis of CHiPS data set, by arrangement with Clark Consulting, Boston, MA.

8. C. Trevor and M. Graham, "Deriving the Market Wage: Three Decision Areas in the Compensation Survey Process," *WorldatWork* 9(4), 2000, pp. 69–77.

9. Barry Gerhart and George Milkovich, "Employee Compensation: Research and Practice," in *Handbook of Industrial and Organizational Psychology,* 2nd ed., M. D. Dunnette and L. M. Hought, eds. (Palo Alto, CA: Consulting Psychologists Press, 1992).

10. Barry Gerhart and Sara Rynes, "Determinants and Consequences of Salary Negotiations by Male and Female MBA Graduates," *Journal of Applied Psychology* 76(2), 1991, pp. 256–262.

11. Morris M. Kleiner, *Licensing Occupations: Ensuring Quality or Restricting Competition?* (Kalamazoo, MI: Upjohn Institute, 2006).

12. Thomas A. Mahoney, *Compensation and Reward Perspective* (Burr Ridge, IL: Irwin, 1979), p. 123.

13. David Levine, Dale Belman, Gary Charness, et al., *Changes in Careers and Wage Structures at Large American Employers* (Kalamazoo, MI: Upjohn Institute, 2001); David I. Levine, D. Belman, Gary Charness, et al., *The New Employment Contract: Evidence About How Little Wage Structures Have Changed* (Kalamazoo, MI: Upjohn Institute, 2001); Edward P. Lazear, *Personnel Economics* (New York: Wiley, 1998); Carl M. Campbell III, "Do Firms Pay Efficiency Wages? Evidence With Data at the Firm Level," *Journal of Labor Economics* 11(3), 1993, pp. 442–469.

14. Peter Cappelli and Keith Chauvin, "An Interplant Test of the Efficiency Wage Hypothesis," *Quarterly Journal of Economics,* August 1991, pp. 769–787.

15. L. Rynes and J. W. Boudreau, "College Recruiting in Large Organizations: Practice, Evaluation, and Research Implications," *Personnel Psychology* 39 (1986), pp. 729–757.

16. E. Groshen and A. B. Krueger, "The Structure of Supervision and Pay in Hospitals," *Industrial and Labor Relations Review,* February 1990, pp. 134S–146S.

17. P. Milgrom and J. Roberts, *Economics, Organizations, and Management* (Englewood Cliffs, NJ: Prentice-Hall, 1992).

18. A. K. G. Hildreth and A. Oswald, "Rentsharing and Wages: Evidence From Company and Establishment Panels," *Journal of Labor Economics* 15 (1997), pp. 318–337.

19. C. O. L. H. Porter, D. E. Conlon, and Allison Barber, "The Dynamics of Salary Negotiations: Effects on Applicants' Justice Perceptions and Recruitment Decisions," *The International Journal of Conflict Management* 15(3), 2005, pp. 273–303; A. VanVinnen, "Person-Organization Fit: The Match Between Newcomers' and Recruiters' Preferences for Organization Cultures," *Personnel Psychology* 53 (2000), pp. 115–125.

20. Christopher J. Collins and Jian Han, "Exploring Applicant Pool Quantity and Quality: The Effects of Early Recruitment Practice Strategies, Corporate Advertising, and Firm Reputation," *Personnel Psychology,* Autumn 2004, pp. 685–717.

21. Daniel M. Cable and Timothy A. Judge, "Pay Preferences and Job Search Decisions: A Person-Organization Fit Perspective," *Personnel Psychology,* Summer 1994, pp. 317–348.

22. Gary S. Becker, *Human Capital* (Chicago, IL: University of Chicago Press, 1975); Barry Gerhart, "Gender Differences in Current and Starting Salaries: The Role of Performance, College Major, and Job Title," *Industrial and Labor Relations Review* 43 (1990), pp. 418–433; Robert Bretz, C. Quinn Trank, and S. L. Rynes, "Attracting Applicants in the War for Talent: Differences in Work Preferences Among High Achievers," *Journal of Business and Psychology* 16 (2002), pp. 331–345.

23. Occupational earnings information for the United States is available at www.bls.govloes/curent/os_nat.htm. Earnings by education level is available at www.bls.gov/cps/earnings.htm#demographic.

24. George F. Dreher and Taylor Cox, Jr., "Labor Market Mobility and Cash Compensation: The Moderating Effects of Race and Gender," *Academy of Management Journal* 43(5), 2000, pp. 890–900.

25. Peter Drucker, "They're Not Employees, They're People," *Harvard Business Review,* February 2002, pp. 70–77; David I. Levine, "Fairness, Markets, and Ability to Pay: Evidence From Compensation Executives," *American Economic Review,* December 1993, pp. 1241–1259; B. Klaas, "Containing Compensation Costs: Why Firms Differ in Their Willingness to Reduce Pay," *Journal of Management* 25(6), 1999, pp. 829–850.

26. David I. Levine, "Fairness, Markets, and Ability to Pay: Evidence From Compensation Executives," *American Economic Review,* December 1993, p. 1250.

27. Dana Mattioli, "Salary Cuts: Ugly, But It Could Be Worse," *The Wall Street Journal,* April 9, 2009; Matthew Quinn, "Survey: One in Four Companies Has Frozen Salaries," *Workforce Management,* February 9, 2009.

28. Watson Wyatt, "Aligning Rewards With the Changing Employment Deal," *WorldatWork,* 2007, www.watsonwyatt.com.

29. "National Wages Council Recommends the Restructuring of Wage System for Competitiveness—Ministers and Top Civil Servants to Lead With Wage Cuts," *Singapore Straits,* May 22, 2003; Marek Szwejczewski and Sri Srikanthan, "The Risks of Outsourcing: Unexpected Consequences," *Financial Times,* April 14, 2006, p. 8; Thomas Friedman, *The World Is Flat* (New York: Farrar, Straus and Giroux, 2006); "CEO's Marital Duties Outsourced to Mexican Groundskeeper," *The Onion* 39(48), December 10, 2003, p. 1.

30. Erica L. Groshen and David Levine, *The Rise and Decline (?) of Employer Wage Structures* (New York: Federal Reserve Bank, 2000).

31. John W. Budd and Brian P. McCall, "The Grocery Stores Wage Distribution: A Semi-Parametric Analysis of the Role of Retailing and Labor Market Institutions," *Industrial and Labor Relations Review* 54(2A), 2001, pp. 484–501.

32. D. M. Raff, "The Puzzling Profusion of Compensation Systems in the Interwar Automobile Industry," Working Paper, NBER, 1998. Raff attributes the fantastic diversity of compensation programs for blue-collar employees (firm-based, piece rate, companywide, team-based) to differences in technology employed among competitors.

33. Walter Oi and Todd L. Idson, "Firm Size and Wages," in *Handbook of Labor Economics,* O. Ashenfelter and D. Card, eds. (Amsterdam: North Holland, 1999), pp. 2165–2214.

34. H. Heneman and T. Judge, "Pay and Employee Satisfaction," in *Compensation in Organizations: Current Research and Practice,* S. L. Rynes and B. Gerhart, eds. (San Francisco, CA: Jossey-Bass, 2000); T. R. Mitchell and A. E. Mickel, "The Meaning of Money: An Individual Differences Perspective," *Academy of Management Review* 24 (1999), pp. 568–578; Watson Wyatt, *Playing to Win: Strategic Rewards in the War for Talent* (New York: Watson Wyatt, 2001); Hudson Employment Index, *Transforming Pay Plans: 2006 Compensation and Benefits Report, www.hudson-index.com/node.asp?SID=6755.*

35. Sara L. Rynes, Amy E. Colbert, and Kenneth G. Brown, "HR Professionals' Beliefs about Effective Human Resource Practices: Correspondence between Research and Practice," *Human Resource Management* 41(2), Summer 2002, pp. 149–174; Sara L. Rynes, Amy E. Colbert, and Kenneth G. Brown, "Seven Common Misconceptions about Human Resource Practices: Research Findings Versus Practitioner Beliefs," *Academy of Management Executive* 16(3), 2002, pp. 92–102.

36. Larry W. Hunter, "What Determines Job Quality in Nursing Homes?" *Industrial 8 Labor Relations Review* 53, (2000) pp. 463–481; Rosemary Batt, "Explaining Intra-Occupational Wage Inequality in Telecommunications Services: Customer Segmentation, Human Resource Practices, and Union Decline," *Industrial and Labor Relations Review* 54 (2A), 2001, pp. 425–449.

37. P. Osterman, "The Wage Effects of High Performance Work Organization in Manufacturing," *Industrial and Labor Relations Review* 59 (2006), pp. 187–204.

38. A. E. Barber and R. D. Bretz Jr., "Compensation, Attraction and Retention," in *Compensation in Organizations,* S. L. Rynes and B. Gerhart, eds. (San Francisco, CA: Jossey-Bass, 2000), pp. 32–60; S. C. Currall, A. J. Towler, T. A. Judge, and L. Kohn, "Pay Satisfaction and Organizational Outcomes," *Personnel Psychology* 58 (2005), pp. 613–640; H. G. Heneman III and T. A. Judge, "Compensation Attitudes," in *Compensation in Organizations,* S. L. Rynes and B. Gehart, eds. (San Francisco, CA: Jossey-Bass, 2000); M. L. Williams, M. A. McDaniel, and N. T. Nguyen, "A Meta-Analysis of the Antecedents and Consequences of Pay Level Satisfaction," *Journal of Applied Psychology* 91 (2006), pp. 392–413; B. Gerhart and S. L. Rynes, *Compensation: Theory, Evidence, and Strategic Implications* (Thousand Oaks, CA: Sage, 2003); B. S. Klaas and J. A. McCledon, "To Lead, Lag, or Match: Estimating the Financial Impact of Pay Level Policies," *Personnel Psychology* 49 (1996), pp. 121–141.

39. Mark C. Long, Kristin M. Dziczek, Daniel D. Luria, and Edith A. Wiarda, "Wage and Productivity Stability in U. S. Manufacturing Plants," *Monthly Labor Review* 131(5), 2008, pp. 24–36.

40. Charlie Trevor and M. E. Graham, "Deriving the Market Wage: Three Decision Areas in the Compensation Survey Process," *WorldatWork Journal* 9(4), 2000, pp. 69–77.

41. Trader's Joe's, *http://www.traderjoes.com/product_categories.html#Booze,* August 31, 2009.

42. William M. Bulkeley, "IBM Documents Give Rare Look at Sensitive Plans on 'Offshoring,'" *The Wall Street Journal,* January 19, 2004.

43. Nira Sheth and Nathan Koppel, "With Times Tight, Even Lawyers Get Outsourced," *The Wall Street Journal,* November 26, 2008.

44. Heather Timmons, "Cost-Cutting in New York, But a Boom in India," *The New York Times,* August 12, 2008.

45. P. J. Dowling, M. Festing, and A. D. Engle, Sr., *International Human Resource Management,* 5th ed. (London: Thomson Learning, 2008).

46. Peter Engardio, "China Losing Luster With U.S. Manufacturers," *BusinessWeek,* November 26, 2008.

47. Kendall Roth and Sharon O'Donnell, "Foreign Subsidiary Compensation Strategy: An Agency Theory Perspective," *Academy of Management Journal* 39 (1996), pp. 678–703.

48. Paulo Prada and Niraj Shethapril, "Delta Air Ends Use of India Call Centers," *The Wall Street Journal,* April 18, 2009.

49. Margaret Williams, Michael McDaniels, and Njung Nguyen, "A Meta-Analysis of the Antecedents and Consequences of Pay Level Satisfaction," *Journal of Applied Psychology,* March 2006, pp. 392–413; David I. Levine, "Fairness, Markets, and Ability to Pay: Evidence from Compensation Executives," *American Economic Review,* December 1993, pp. 1241–1259.

50. See, for example, any of the surveys conducted by leading consulting firms: Hewitt, *www. hewitt.com;* Wyatt Watson, *www.watsonwyatt.com;* Hay, *www.haygroup.com;* Mercer, *www.mercer.com;* Towers Perrin, *www.towersperrin.com;* Executive Alliance, *www. executivealliance.com.*

51. Laura Johnson and Darrell Cira, "Taking the Best Path to Implementing a Global Pay Structure: The General Mill's Experience," paper at WorldatWork Conference, Seattle, WA, June 1, 2009.

52. Brian S. Klaas and John A. McClendon, "To Lead, Lag, or Match: Estimating the Financial Impact of Pay Level Policies," *Personnel Psychology* 49 (1996), pp. 121–140.

53. Robert Kaplan, *Imperial Grunts* (New York: Random House, 2005).

54. B. Gerhart and S. Rynes, *Compensation: Theory, Evidence and Strategic Implications* (Thousand Oaks, CA: Sage, 2003).

55. Robert Bretz, J. W. Boudreau, W. R. Boswell, and T. A. Judge, "Personality and Cognitive Ability as Predictors of Job Search Among Employed Managers," *Personnel Psychology* 54 (2001), pp. 25–50; Charlie Trevor, Barry Gerhart, and John Boudreau, "Voluntary Turnover and Job Performance: Curvilinearity and the Moderating Influences of Salary Growth and Promotions," *Journal of Applied Psychology* 82 (1997), pp. 44–61; A. L. Heavey, J. A. Holwerda, and J. P. Hausknecht, "Causes and Consequences of Collective Turnover: A Meta-analytic Review," *Journal of Applied Psychology*, 98(3), 2013, p. 412.

56. R. Folger and M. A. Konovsky, "Effects of Procedural and Distributive Justice on Reactions to Pay Raise Decisions," *Academy of Management Journal* 32 (1989), pp. 115–30; J. Greenberg, "Determinants of Perceived Fairness of Performance Evaluations," *Journal of Applied Psychology* 71 (1986), pp. 340–342.

57. B. Gerhart and G. Milkovich, "Organizational Differences in Managerial Compensation and Financial Performance," *Academy of Management Journal* 33 (1990), pp. 663–691; M. Bloom and J. Michel, "The Relationships among Organization Context, Pay, and Managerial Turnover," *Academy of Management Journal* 45 (2002), pp. 33–42; M. Bloom and G. Milkovich, "Relationships among Risk, Incentive Pay, and Organization Performance," *Academy of Management Journal* 41(3), 1998, pp. 283–297; B. Hall and J. Liebman, "Are CEOs Really Paid Like Bureaucrats?" *Quarterly Journal of Economics,* August 1998, pp. 653–691. Variable pay is discussed in Chapters 9 through 11. "Variable" indicates that the pay increase (bonus) is not added to base pay; hence, it is not part of fixed costs but is variable, since the amount may vary next year.

58. B. Gerhart and G. Milkovich, "Organizational Differences in Managerial Compensation and Financial Performance," *Academy of Management Journal* 33 (1990), pp. 663–691.

59. David I. Levine, "Fairness, Markets, and Ability to Pay: Evidence from Compensation Executives," *American Economic Review,* December 1993, pp. 1241–1259.

60. Mei Fong, "A Chinese Puzzle," *The Wall Street Journal,* August 16, 2005, p. B1.

61. L. Gaughan and J. Kasparek, "Employees as Customers: Using Market Research to Manage Compensation and Benefits," *Workspan* (9), 2000, pp. 31–38; M. Sturman, G. Milkovich, and J. Hannon, "Expert Systems' Effect on Employee Decisions and Satisfaction," *Personnel Psychology* (1997), pp. 21–34; J. Shaw and S. Schaubrock, "The Role of Spending Behavior Patterns in Monetary Rewards," Working Paper, University of Kentucky, 2001; S. Dubner, "Calculating the Irrational in Economics," *The New York Times,* June 28, 2003.

62. Reed Hastings, "How to Set Your Employees Free," *Bloomberg Businessweek*, April 12, 2012; Jeffrey Goldfarb and Reynolds Holding, "Incentives Play Role in Success of Netflix," *The New York Times,* May 8, 2011; National Center for Employee Ownership Report, "Equity Compensation Case Study: Netflix," November–December 2007; David F. Larcker, Allan McCall, and Brian Tayan, "Equity on Demand: The Netflix Approach to Compensation," Stanford Graduate School of Business, Case CG-19, January 15, 2010.

63. Brian Klaas and John A. McClendon, "To Lead, Lag, or Match: Estimating the Financial Impact of Pay Level Policies," *Personnel Psychology* 49 (1996), pp. 121–140; M. C. Sturman, C. O. Trevor, J. W. Boudreau, and B. Gerhart, "Is It Worth It to Win the Talent War? Evaluating the Utility of Performance-Based Pay," *Personnel Psychology* 56 (2003), pp. 997–1035.

64. Barry Gerhart and George Milkovich, "Employee Compensation: Research and Practice," in *Handbook of Industrial and Organizational* Psychology, 2nd ed., M. D. Dunnette and L. M. Hough, eds. (Palo Alto, CA: Consulting Psychologists Press, 1992).

65. H. Heneman and T. Judge, "Pay and Employee Satisfaction," in *Compensation in Organizations: Current Research and Practice,* S. Rynes and B. Gerhart, eds. (San Francisco, CA: Jossey-Bass, 2000).

66. B. Gerhart and S. Rynes, *Compensation Theory, Evidence and Strategic Implications* (Thousand Oaks, CA: Sage, 2003).

67. Kris Maher, "Nurses Win Settlement Over Wages," *The Wall Street Journal,* March 9, 2009, p. A6.

68. Mike Colias and David Barholz, "How a Small Car Is Helping Rewrite Labor Costs in a U.S. Plant," *Automotive News,* July 11, 2011. www.autonews.com. Extracted July 15, 2011.

69. Greg Gardner, "Pact Shrinks Pay Gap for Entry-level GM Workers," *Detroit Free Press,* September 11, 2011.

70. Jerry Hirsch, "Automakers Plan to Hire Thousands of Workers this Year," *Los Angeles Times*, January 12, 2012.

71. Colias and Barholz, "How a Small Car Is Helping . . ."

72. Mark Clothier, "Marchionne Says UAW's Two-Tiered Wage System 'Almost Offensive.'" www.bloomberg.com. January 12, 2015; Christina Rogers, "Fiat Chrysler CEO Takes Aim at Two-Tier Wages for UAW Workers," www.wsj.com. January 12, 2015; Mike Colias, David Barkholz, and Nick Bunkley, "Is High-Paying Tier 1 at Risk in UAW Talks?" *Automotive News.* March 23, 2015.

73. Wayne F. Cascio and John W. Boudreau, "Investing in People: Financial Impact of Human Resource Initiatives" (Upper Saddle River, NJ: Financial Times Press, 2008); H. E. Brogden, "When Testing Pays Off," *Personnel Psychology* 2 (1949), pp. 171–185; J. W. Boudreau and C. J. Berger, "Decision-Theoretic Utility Analysis Applied to Employee Separations and Acquisitions," *Journal of Applied Psychology* [monograph] 73 (1985), pp. 467–481; J. W. Boudreau, "Utility Analysis for Decisions in Human Resource Management, in *Handbook of Industrial and Organizational Psychology,* 2nd ed., M. D. Dunnette and L. M. Hough, eds. (Palo Alto, CA: Consulting Psychologists Press, 1991); I. S. Fulmer and R. E. Ployhart, "Our Most Important Asset": A Multidisciplinary/

Multilevel Review of Human Capital Valuation for Research and Practice," *Journal of Management*, doi: 0149206313511271. November 2013.

74. The accuracy of utility estimates depends on whether higher-quality applicants actually accept job offers. To the degree they do not, the Z parameter estimate will be biased upward, biasing utility estimates upward as well. Kevin R. Murphy, "When Your Top Choice Turns You Down: Effect of Rejected Offers on the Utility of Selection Tests," *Psychological Bulletin* 99 (1986), pp. 133–138. Compensation level is one way to increase the probability of job offer acceptance.

75. B. S. Klaas and J. A. McCledon, "To Lead, Lag, or Match: Estimating the Financial Impact of Pay Level Policies," *Personnel Psychology* 49 (1996), pp. 121–141; M. C. Sturman, C. O. Trevor, J. W. Boudreau, and B. Gerhart, "Is It Worth It to Win the Talent War? Evaluating the Utility of Performance-Based Pay," *Personnel Psychology* 56 (2003), pp. 997–1035.

76. If the link is broken, go to www.bls.gov and search for "NAICS 445100."

77. As we will see later, matching is more complex than we will treat it here and must be done well (i.e., with careful attention to the comparability and relative value of jobs in the survey versus jobs in our organization) to avoid significant mistakes in setting rates of pay for jobs. Here, we will temporarily put that important issue aside in the interest of simply becoming familiar with one example of survey data.

Designing Pay Levels, Mix, and Pay Structures

In its 2015 proxy statement, Lincoln Electric described its goals for executive compensation relative to its competition:

"Base pay is targeted at the 45th percentile...while target total cash compensation (which includes an annual bonus that incorporates aggressive financial targets) is set at the 65th percentile of the market...Long-term compensation is set at the 50th percentile...Although not targeted to a specific competitive level, we believe our benefits...are at the market median and our executive perquisites are below the market median."

In the last chapter, we discussed market and organization factors that influence these policies. Now we examine in more details the tools and strategies managers use to determine pay levels, mix of forms, and structures.

MAJOR DECISIONS

The major decisions in setting externally competitive pay and designing the corresponding pay structures are shown in Exhibit 8.1. They include (1) specify the employer's competitive pay policy, (2) define the purpose of the survey, (3) select relevant market competitors, (4) design the survey, (5) interpret survey results and construct the market line, (6) construct a pay policy line that reflects external pay policy, and (7) balance competitiveness with internal alignment through the use of **ranges,** flat rates, and/or bands. This is a lengthy list. Think of Exhibit 8.1 as a road map through this chapter. The guideposts are the major decisions you face in designing a pay structure. Don't forget to end with, So what? "So what" means ensuring that pay structures both support business success and treat employees fairly.

SPECIFY COMPETITIVE PAY POLICY

The first decision, determining the external competitive pay policy, was covered in the previous chapter. Translating any external pay policy into practice requires information on the external market. Surveys provide the data for translating that policy into pay levels, pay mix, and structures.

EXHIBIT 8.1 Determining Externally Competitive Pay Levels and Structures

External Competitiveness: Pay Relationships Among Organizations $\rightarrow$	Specify Policy $\rightarrow$	Select Market $\rightarrow$	Design Survey $\rightarrow$	Draw Policy Lines $\rightarrow$	Merge Internal & External Pressures $\rightarrow$	Competitive Pay Levels, Mix, and Structures

Some Major Decisions in Pay-Level Determination

- Specify pay-level policy.
- Define purpose of survey.
- Specify relevant market.
- Design and conduct survey.
- Interpret and apply result.
- Design grades and ranges or bands.

A **survey** is the systematic process of collecting and making judgments about the compensation paid by other employers.

THE PURPOSE OF A SURVEY

An employer conducts or participates in a survey for a number of reasons: (1) to adjust the pay level in response to changing rates paid by competitors, (2) to set the mix of pay forms relative to that paid by competitors, (3) to establish or price a pay structure, (4) to analyze pay-related problems, or (5) to estimate the labor costs of product/service market competitors.

Adjust Pay Level—How Much to Pay?

Most organizations make adjustments to employees' pay on a regular basis. Such adjustments can be based on the overall movement of pay rates caused by the competition for people in the market. Adjustments may also be based on performance, ability to pay, or terms specified in a contract.

Adjust Pay Mix—What Forms?

Adjustments to the different forms of pay competitors use (base, bonus, stock, benefits) and the relative importance they place on each form occur less frequently than adjustments to overall pay level. It is not clear (without good research) why changes to the pay mix occur less frequently than changes in the pay level. Perhaps the high costs of redesigning a different mix create a barrier. Perhaps inertia prevails. More likely, insufficient attention has been devoted to mix decisions. That is, the mix organizations use may have been based on external pressures such as health-care costs, stock values, government regulations, union demands, and what others did. Yet some pay forms may affect employee behavior more than others. So good information on total compensation, the mix of pay competitors use, and costs of various pay forms is increasingly important.

Adjust Pay Structure?

Many employers use market surveys to validate their own job evaluation results. For example, job evaluation may place purchasing assistant jobs at the same level in the job structure as some secretarial jobs. But if the market shows vastly different pay rates for the two types of work, most employers will recheck their evaluation process to see whether the jobs have been properly evaluated. Some may even establish a separate structure for different types of work. IBM sets pay according to market conditions for each separate occupation (finance, engineering, law). Thus, the job structure that results from internal job evaluation may not match competitors' pay structures in the external market. Reconciling these two pay structures is a major issue.

Rather than integrating an internal and external structure, some employers go straight to market surveys to establish their internal structures. Such "market pricing" mimics competitors' pay structures. Accurate market data are increasingly important as organizations move to more generic work descriptions (associate, leader) that focus on the person's skill as well as the job. Former relationships between job evaluation points and dollars may no longer hold. Accurate information and informed judgment are vital for making all these decisions.

Study Special Situations

Information from specialized surveys can shed light on specific pay-related problems. A special study may focus on a targeted group such as patent attorneys, retail sales managers, secretaries, or software engineers. Unusual increases in an employer's turnover in specific jobs may require focused market surveys to find out if market changes are occurring.[1]

Estimate Competitors' Labor Costs

Survey data are used as part of employers' broader efforts to gather **"competitive intelligence."**[2] To better understand how competitors achieve their market share and price their products/services, companies seek to examine (i.e., benchmark) practices, costs, and so forth against competitors, including in the area of compensation. One source of publicly available labor cost data is the Employment Cost Index (ECI), one of four types of salary surveys published regularly by the Department of Labor on its website at *www.bls.gov/ncs/*.[3] The ECI measures quarterly changes in employer costs for compensation. The index allows a firm to compare changes in its average costs to an all-industry or specific-industry average. However, this comparison may have limited value because industry averages may not reflect relevant competitors.[4]

SELECT RELEVANT MARKET COMPETITORS

We are up to the third of our major decisions shown in Exhibit 8.1: Specify relevant markets. To make decisions about pay level, mix, and structures, a relevant labor market must be defined that includes employers who compete in one or more of the following areas:

1. The same occupations or skills
2. Employees within the same geographic area
3. The same products and services[5]

Exhibit 8.2 shows how Microsoft and Google select relevant market competitors in establishing executive compensation. Both explicitly include product market ("technology") and labor market competitors. The geographic level is national or international.

Exhibit 8.3 shows how qualifications interact with geography to define the scope of relevant labor markets. As the importance and the complexity of the qualifications increase, the geographic limits also increase.[6] Competition tends to be national or international for managerial and professional skills (as in Exhibit 8.2) but local or regional for clerical and production skills.

However, these generalizations do not always hold true. In areas with high concentrations of scientists, engineers, and managers (e.g., Boston or San Jose/Silicon Valley), the primary market comparison may be regional, with national data used only secondarily. As Exhibit 8.4 shows, pay differentials vary among localities. A job that averages $80,930 nationally can pay from $58,300 in Jackson, Mississippi to $93,900 in San Jose, California. However, some larger firms

EXHIBIT 8.2 External Competitiveness Strategy for Top Executives, Microsoft and Google

MICROSOFT
Peer Group

Technology Peer Group. These are companies operating in the information technology industry that focus on producing software or hardware or providing online services, and that employ work forces with skill sets and professional backgrounds similar to those of our work force.

Dow 30 Peer Group. Generally, these are large, diversified companies with significant international operations. As an industry and worldwide business leader, they compete for senior executive talent with top companies across a variety of other industries, not just those in the information technology industry.

We give greater weight to the pay levels and practices of our technology peers because they more closely represent the labor market in which we compete for key talent.

Technology Peer Group		Dow 30 Peer Group		
Accenture	IBM*	3M	DuPont	Procter & Gamble
Adobe Systems	Intel*	Alcoa	ExxonMobil	Travelers Companies
Amazon	Oracle	American Express	General Electric	United Technologies
Apple	SAP	AT&T	Home Depot	UnitedHealth Group
BlackBerry	Symantec	Bank of America	JP Morgan Chase	Verizon
Cisco Systems*	Yahoo!	Boeing	Johnson & Johnson	Wal-Mart
Facebook		Caterpillar	McDonald's	Walt Disney
Google		Chevron	Merck	
Hewlett-Packard*		Coca-Cola	Pfizer	

* Technology companies in the Technology Peer Group are omitted from the Dow 30 Peer Group to avoid duplication.

Market Position Target

Cash compensation target	"below median" (2008 proxy. No clear statement in more recent proxies)
Equity award target	"above median" (2008 proxy. No clear statement in more recent proxies.)

GOOGLE
Peer Group

We considered peers to be companies that met at least three of the following criteria:
- High-technology or media company
- Key talent competitor
- High-growth, with a minimum of 50 percent of Google's revenue growth and/or headcount growth over the previous two-year period
- $10 billion or more in annual revenues
- $50 billion or more in market capitalization

Based on these criteria, the Leadership Development and Compensation Committee selected the following companies as peer companies:

Amazon.com, Inc.	Hewlett-Packard Company	Oracle Corporation
Apple Inc.	International Business Machines	Qualcomm, Inc.
Cisco Systems, Inc.	Corporation	The Walt Disney Company
eBay, Inc.	Intel Corporation	Yahoo! Inc.
Facebook, Inc.	Microsoft Corporation	

EXHIBIT 8.2 *(Continued)*

Yahoo! did not meet three of our five criteria. However, we chose to retain Yahoo! because it met the two most important criteria (it is a key talent competitor and is in the high-technology industry).

While peer group analysis provides a benchmark for our named executive officers' current roles, we also consider job opportunities our named executive officers could take if they were to leave Google. While we have not lost any named executive officer to other companies thus far, we intend to remain competitive with their potential opportunities. Therefore, we also benchmark compensation levels for our named executive officers against the following:

- CEO roles at other S&P 100 companies
- Founder and CEO roles at start-ups

We review CEO compensation levels and trends across companies in the S&P 100 using SEC filings. We benchmark start-up compensation based on publicly available data on start-up success rates and published survey data on start-up CEO earnings. Our executive compensation decisions are informed by market data in addition to reviews of individual roles and performance.

Market Position Target

Element of Compensation	Percentile (2008)	Percentile (2011)	Percentile (2014)
Base Salary	50th to 70th	90th	90th
Target Total Cash	75th	90th to 95th	90th
Target Equity	90th	90th to 95th	90th to 95th

Source: Microsoft 2008, 2011, and 2015 Proxy Statements; Google 2008, 2011, and 2014 Proxy Statements. Available at www.sec.gov.

ignore local market conditions.[7] Instead, they emphasize internal alignment across geographic areas to facilitate the use of virtual teams. But it turns out that team members in different locations compare their pay. What a surprise.

Some writers argue that if the skills are tied to a particular industry—as underwriters, actuaries, and claims representatives are to insurance, for example—it makes sense to define the market on an industry basis, and some research agrees.[8] If accounting, sales, or clerical skills are not limited to one particular industry, then industry considerations are less important. From the perspective of cost control and ability to pay, including competitors in the product/service market is crucial.[9] However, this becomes a problem when the major competitors are based in countries with far lower pay rates, such as China or Mexico. But a segmented labor supply (see Chapter 7) requires multiple country comparisons.[10] Legal regulations, tax policies, and customs vary among countries. Because of tax laws, managers in Korea and Spain receive company credit cards to use for personal expenses (groceries, clothing). In the United States, these purchases count as taxable income, but they do not in Korea and Spain.

While the quantity of data available for international comparisons is improving, using the data to adjust pay still requires a lot of judgment. Labor markets are just emerging in some regions (China, Russia). Historically, state planning agencies set nationwide wage rates, so there was no need for surveys.[11] Japanese companies share information among themselves but not with outsiders, so no surveys are available.[12]

But even with good international survey data, judgment is still required. For example, while salaries at international companies in developing economies are low by U.S., Western

EXHIBIT 8.3   Relevant Labor Markets by Geographic and Employee Groups

Geographic Scope	Production	Office and Clerical	Technicians	Scientists and Engineers	Managerial Professional	Executive
Local: Within relatively small areas such as cities or Metropolitan Statistical Areas (e.g., Dallas metropolitan area)	Most likely	Most likely	Most likely			
Regional: Within a particular area of the state or several states (e.g., oil-producing region of southwestern United States)	Only if in short supply or critical	Only if in short supply or critical	Most likely	Likely	Most Likely	
National: Across the country				Most likely	Most likely	Most likely
International: Across several countries				Only for critical skills or those in very short supply	Only for critical skills or those in very short supply	Sometimes

EXHIBIT 8.4
Pay Differences by Location: Annual Wage by Metro Area, Computer Programmer

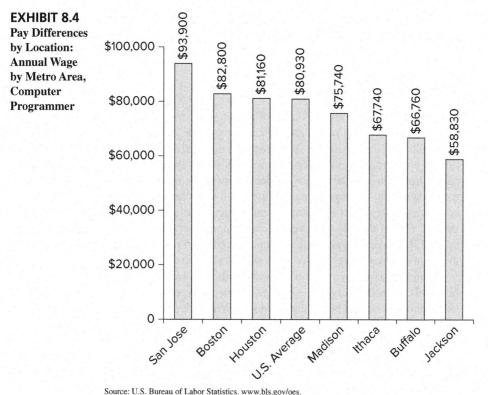

Source: U.S. Bureau of Labor Statistics. www.bls.gov/oes.

European, and Japanese standards, they are often very high compared to salaries at domestic companies in those countries. Pay practices of foreign companies can disrupt emerging local markets in developing economies.[13] IBM software engineers in India told us that while they are paid very well by Indian standards, they feel underpaid compared to IBM engineers in the United States who work on the same projects.[14]

Fuzzy Markets

Walk through a bay of cubicles (plastered with *Dilbert* cartoons) at Yahoo! and you are likely to find former kindergarten teachers, software engineers, and sales representatives all collaborating on a single team. Yahoo! combines technology, media, and commerce into one company. What is the relevant labor market? Which firms should be included in Yahoo!'s surveys?

Even within traditional companies, unique talent is required for unique jobs. West Publishing, a provider of legal information to law firms, designed the position of Senior Director of Future Vision Services. The holder of this mouthful title is responsible for ensuring that West's customers (litigious lawyers) increase their purchases over the Web plus increase their satisfaction with West's services. The job was filled by a software engineer with e-commerce, marketing, and theater experience. Try finding that job in the market. These new organizations and jobs fuse together diverse knowledge and experience, so "relevant" markets appear more like "fuzzy" markets.[15] Organizations with unique jobs and structures face the double bind of finding it hard to get comparable market data at the same time they are placing more emphasis on external market data.

DESIGN THE SURVEY

Consulting firms offer a wide choice of ongoing surveys covering almost every job family and industry group imaginable. Their surveys are getting better and better.[16] While we would like to attribute this to the fact that our textbook has improved the sophistication of compensation education (the first edition of our book was published in 1985, and at least some of those early readers ought to be in power positions by now), it is more likely that the improvement is the result of technological advances. Increasingly, consultants offer clients the option of electronically accessing the consultants' survey databases. Clients then do whatever special analysis they need. General Electric conducts most of its market analysis in this manner. Exhibit 8.5 provides some factors to consider in designing a pay survey and/or in choosing a pay survey vendor/consultant.[17]

Designing a survey requires answering the following questions: (1) Who should be involved in the survey design? (2) How many employers should be included? (3) Which jobs should be included? and (4) What information should be collected?

Who Should Be Involved?

In most organizations, the responsibility for managing the survey lies with the compensation manager. But since compensation expenses have a powerful effect on profitability, including managers and employees on the task forces makes sense.

Outside consulting firms are typically used as third-party protection from possible "price-fixing" lawsuits. Suits have been filed alleging that the direct exchange of survey data violates Section 1 of the Sherman Act, which outlaws conspiracies in restraint of trade. Survey participants may be guilty of price fixing if the overall effect of the information exchange is to *interfere with competitive prices* and *artificially hold down wages.* Identifying participants' data by company name is considered price fixing.[18]

How Many Employers?

There are no firm rules on how many employers to include in a survey. Large firms with a lead policy may exchange data with only a few (6 to 10) top-paying competitors.[19] Merrill Lynch aims for the 75th percentile among 11 peer financial firms. A small organization in an area dominated by two or three employers may decide to survey only smaller competitors. National surveys conducted by consulting firms often include more than 100 employers. Clients of these consultants often stipulate special analyses that report pay rates by selected industry groups, geographic region, and/or pay levels (e.g., top 10 percent).

Publicly Available Data

In the United States, the **Bureau of Labor Statistics (BLS)** is the major source of publicly available compensation (cash, bonus, and benefits but not stock ownership) data. The BLS publishes extensive information on various occupations.

EXHIBIT 8.5   **Getting the Most Out of Pay Surveys**

Look for communication from survey vendor	The vendor should communicate regularly, not just when it is time to collect data and later provide the survey results. Also, a sure way to tell if survey data are credible is if the vendor follows up with questions about pay data you submitted. There should be stringent quality assurance mechanisms in place.
Focus on your specific business needs	Ideally, the survey should provide data on at least 75 percent of the positions you want to price. Be sure that the survey includes organizations that are your specific labor market competitors—those specific organizations from which you hire employees and to which you most often lose employees. (Of course, product market competitors should also be included.)
Look for easy access to data	The data should come in the format (hard copy, PDF, Excel) that works best for you. Increasingly, data can be accessed at any time. The ability to tailor analyses by running custom reports that capture specific peer groups is important as is the recency of the data and/or the ability to accurately age the data.
Avoid time-consuming data input	Participation in a survey can take anywhere from one hour to several weeks, depending on the complexity and efficiency of data collection. Work with your human resource information system group to estimate the time and cost of responding to a survey. Make sure you are not required to submit data that will not appear in the survey results.
Stretch your salary budget	Participate in free surveys. Check job boards for salary information. Talk to recruiters to get real-time information on the latest market movements. Also, of course, participation (i.e., providing data) in a survey typically reduces the cost of purchasing the survey results.
Antitrust issues—use caution	Make sure that the survey is managed by a third party, pay information provided to participants is at least three months old, at least five participants report data for each survey question, data are weighted so that no single company accounts for more than 25 percent of any single data point. Always consult legal counsel with questions.
Look for added value	Events like job matching meetings and presentations of survey results provide participants the opportunity to meet peers, network, and learn from one another.

Source: Adapted from Rebecca Toman and Kristine Oliver, "Ways to Get the Most out of Salary Surveys," *Workspan*, February 2011, 17–21.

While some private firms may track the rate of change in BLS data as a cross-check on other surveys, the data are often not specific enough to be used alone. Tailoring analysis to specific industry segments, select companies, and specific job content is not feasible.

"Word of Mouse"

Once upon a time individual employees had a hard time comparing their salaries to others'. Information was gathered haphazardly, via word of mouth. Today, a click of the mouse (or trackpad) makes a wealth of data available to everyone. Employees are comparing their compensation to data from the BLS or Salary.com or occupation-specific websites.[20] This ease of access means that managers must be able to explain (defend?) the salaries paid to employees compared to those a mouse click away. Whole Foods confronted this issue via an "open book" list of last year's pay of all employees.[21] Unfortunately, the quality of much salary data on the Web is highly suspect. Few of the sites (except the BLS, of course) offer any information on how the data were collected, what pay forms are included, and so on. Most are based on information volunteered by site users. Some popular websites even misuse the cost-of-living index when making geographic salary comparisons.[22] On the other hand, Salary.com includes a compensation glossary, identifies where the site's information comes from, and explains what the statistics mean. Put in programmer for Birmingham, Alabama, and you will be asked to choose from 43 job descriptions. Exhibit 8.6 shows the Salary.com results for just three

EXHIBIT 8.6
Free Salary Survey Data on the Web for Computer Programmer from U.S. Bureau of Labor Statistics, and Salary.com

	Percentile		
	25th	**50th**	**75th**
Bureau of Labor Statistics			
National			
Computer programmer	$57,940	$ 76,140	$ 97,760
Boston, MA			
Computer programmer		$ 82,800	
Salary.com			
Salary			
National			
Programmer I	$ 51,016	$ 57,141	$ 64,781
Programmer III	$ 79,807	$ 88,886	$ 98,405
Programmer V	$ 99,743	$110,411	$122,516
Boston, MA			
Programmer I	$ 55,098	$ 61,712	$ 69,964
Programmer III	$ 86,191	$ 95,997	$106,278
Programmer V	$107,722	$119,244	$132,317
Salary.com			
Salary + Bonus			
National			
Programmer I	$ 51,578	$ 58,218	$ 6,339
Programmer III	$ 81,431	$ 91,428	$102,472
Programmer V	$102,831	$115,675	$130,669
Boston, MA			
Programmer I	$ 55,705	$ 62,875	$ 71,646
Programmer III	$ 87,946	$ 98,742	$110,670
Programmer V	$111,057	$124,929	$141,122

Bureau of Labor Statistics data from www.bls.gov/ncs/ocs.

Note: The 50th percentile is the median. Median salaries differ from mean salaries for computer programmers reported earlier in the chapter.

of those programmer jobs, both at the national level and in Birmingham. (Glassdoor. com is another website that can provide this sort of detailed salary-by-job description data.) By comparison, all programmer positions are included in a single category in the BLS survey, making it all but impossible to get a good match.

Many Surveys (But Few That Are Validated)

Opinions about the value of consultant surveys are rampant; research is not. Do Hay, Mercer, Towers Watson, and Aon Hewitt surveys yield significantly different results? The fact that companies typically use three or more surveys (for all job types) suggests that different surveys do, in fact, imply different pay levels.[23] Many firms select one survey as their primary source and use others to cross-check or "validate" the results. Some employers routinely combine the results of several surveys and weight each survey in this composite according to somebody's judgment of the quality of the data reported.[24] No systematic study of the effects of differences in market definition, participating firms, types of data collected, quality of data, analysis performed, and/ or results is available. Issues of sample design and statistical inference are seldom considered. For staffing decisions, employment test designers report the test's performance against a set of standards (reliability, validity, etc.). Job evaluation's reliability and validity (or lack of) has been much studied and debated. Yet for market surveys and analysis, similar standards do not exist.[25] Without reliability and validity metrics, survey data are open to challenge.

---

e-Compensation 1

For a demonstration of online surveys, go to *www.haypaynet.com* or *www. salary.com* or *www.bls.gov/bls/blswage.htm.* How do the sites compare? Do they give information on which employers are included and which ones are not? Where do their data come from? Do the sites tell you? Which would you use to design a pay system? Explain.

Which Jobs to Include?

There are several approaches to selecting jobs for inclusion.

Benchmark-Job Approach

In Chapter 5 we noted that benchmark jobs have stable job content, are common across different employers, and include sizable numbers of employees. If the purpose of the survey is to price the entire structure, then benchmark jobs can be selected to include the entire job structure—all key functions and all levels, just as in job evaluation. In Exhibit 8.7, the more heavily shaded jobs in the structures are benchmark jobs. Benchmark jobs are chosen from as many levels in each of these structures as can be matched with the descriptions of the benchmark jobs that are included in the survey. Exhibit 8.8 indicates that about one in three organizations are able to match over 80 percent of jobs to salary survey jobs, with the remaining organizations report less success in matching.

EXHIBIT 8.7 Benchmarks

EXHIBIT 8.8
Percentage of Jobs in Organizations That Match to Salary Survey Jobs

Source: "Job Evaluation and Market-Pricing Practices," A Survey Brief by WorldatWork, February 2009.

The degree of match between the survey's benchmark jobs and each company's benchmark jobs is assessed by various means. One approach, benchmark conversion/survey leveling is discussed below. As another example, the Hay Group has installed the same job evaluation plan in many companies that participate in its surveys. Consequently, jobs in different organizations can be compared on their job evaluation points and the distribution of points among the compensable factors. Other surveys simply ask participants to check the degree of match (e.g., my company's job is of moderately less value, slightly less value, equal value, etc.). A good survey will include this information in its results. A consultant friend insists that when the compensation manager of a company changes, the job matches change, too.

Low-High Approach

If an organization is using skill-competency-based structures or generic job descriptions, it may not have benchmark jobs to match with jobs at competitors who use a traditional job-based approach. Market data must be converted to fit the skill or competency structure. The simplest way to do this is to identify the lowest- and highest-paid benchmark jobs for the relevant skills in the relevant market and to use the wages for these jobs as anchors for the skill-based structures. Work at various levels within the structure can then be slotted between the anchors. For example, if the entry market rate for operator A is $12 per hour and the rate for a team leader is $42 per hour, then the rate for operator B can be somewhere between $12 and $42 per hour.[26]

The usefulness of this approach depends on how well the extreme benchmark jobs match the organization's work and whether they really do tap the entire range of skills. Hanging a pay system on two pieces of market data raises the stakes on the accuracy of those data.

Benchmark Conversion/Survey Leveling

In cases where the content (e.g., job description) of an organization's jobs does not sufficiently match that of jobs in the salary survey, an effort can be made to quantify the difference via **benchmark conversion.** If an organization uses job evaluation, then its job evaluation system can be applied to the survey jobs. The magnitude of difference between job evaluation points for internal jobs and survey jobs provides an estimate of their relative value and thus guidance for adjusting the market data. (Again, a judgment.)

What Information to Collect?

Three basic types of data typically are requested: (1) information about the organization, (2) information about the total compensation system, and (3) specific pay data on each incumbent in the jobs under study. Exhibit 8.9 lists the basic data elements and the logic for including them. No survey includes all the data that will be discussed. Rather, the data collected depend on the purpose of the survey and the jobs and skills included.

Organization Data

This information reflects the similarities and differences among organizations in the survey. Surveys of executive and upper-level positions include financial and reporting relationships data, since compensation for these jobs is more directly related to the organization's financial performance. Typically, financial data are simply used to group firms by size, expressed in terms of sales or revenues, rather than to analyze competitors' performance. These data are used descriptively to report pay levels and mix by company size. The competitors' data have not been used to compare competitors' productivity (revenues to compensation) or labor costs.

But this is changing. The increased gathering of "competitive intelligence" is changing the type of organization data collected and the way it gets used. Metrics of organization performance such as turnover and revenues are being collected. Some surveys such as Clark and Radford collect turnover data. Other outcomes such as

EXHIBIT 8.9 Possible Survey Data Elements and Rationale

Basic Elements	Examples	Rationale
Nature of Organization		
Identification	Company, name, address, contact person	Further contacts
Financial performance	Assets, sales, profits, cash flow	Indicates nature of product/service markets, ability to pay, size, and financials
Size	Profit centers, product lines	Importance of specific job groups
	Total number of employees	Impact on labor market
Structure	Organizational charts	Indicates how business is organized
	Percent of employees at each level	Indicates staffing pattern
Nature of Total Compensation System		
Cash forms used	Base pay, pay-increase schedules, long- and short-term incentives, bonuses, cost-of-living adjustments, overtime and shift differentials	Indicate the mix of compensation offered; used to establish a comparable base
Noncash forms used	Benefits and services, particularly coverage and contributions to medical and health insurance and pensions	
Incumbent and Job		
Date	Date survey data in effect	Update to current date
Job	Match generic job description	Indicates degree of similarity with survey's key jobs
	Reporting levels	Scope of responsibilities
Individual	Years since degree, education, date of hire	Indicates training tenure
Pay	Actual rates paid to each individual, total earnings, last increase, bonuses, incentives	
HR Outcomes		
Productivity	Revenues/employee Revenues/labor costs	Reflect organization performance and efficiency
Total labor costs	Number of employees × (average wages + benefits)	Major expense
Attraction	Yield ratio: Number accepting offers/Number of job offers	Reveals recruiting success, a compensation objective
Retention	Turnover rate: Number of high or low performers who leave/Number of employees	Reveals outflow of people, which is related to a compensation objective
Employee views	Total pay satisfaction	Reveals what employees think about their pay

earnings per share, market share, customer satisfaction, employee pay satisfaction, and recruiting yield ratios are not included. Financial data are gathered from other, often publicly available sources (e.g., Google Financial, Thompson Financial). Examples include metrics on organization success (revenues, net income, customer satisfaction), turnover (voluntary quit rates), and recruiting (yield ratios).[27]

Total Compensation Data

Information on all types of pay forms is required to assess the total pay package and competitors' practices.[28] The list shown in Exhibit 8.9 reveals the range of forms that could be included in each company's definition of total compensation. As a practical matter, it can be hard to include *all* the pay forms. Too much detail on benefits, such as medical coverage deductibles and flexible work schedules, can make a survey too cumbersome. Alternatives range from a brief description of a benchmark benefit package to including only the most expensive and variable benefits to an estimate of total benefit expenses as a percentage of total labor costs. Three alternatives—base pay, total cash (base, profit sharing, bonuses), and total compensation (total cash plus benefits and **perquisites**)—are the most commonly used measures of compensation. Exhibit 8.10 draws the distinction between these three alternatives and highlights the usefulness and limitations of each. Exhibit 8.11 shows some results of conducting a pay survey that includes these three measures on a sample of engineers.

A: *Base pay.* This is the amount of *cash* the competitors decided *each job and incumbent* is worth. A company might use this information for its initial observations of how "good" the data appear to fit a range of jobs. The market line A is based on base pay.

B: *Total cash.* This is base plus bonus—line B in the exhibit. Total cash measures reveal competitors' use of performance-based cash payments.

C: *Total compensation.* This includes total cash plus stock options and benefits. Total compensation reflects the total overall value of the employee (performance, experience, skills, etc.) plus the value of the work itself.

EXHIBIT 8.10 Advantages and Disadvantages of Measures of Compensation

Base pay	Tells how competitors are valuing the work in similar jobs	Fails to include performance incentives and other forms, so will not give true picture if competitors offer low base but high incentives.
Total cash (base + bonus)	Tells how competitors are valuing work; also tells the cash pay for performance opportunity in the job	All employees may not receive incentives, so it may overstate the competitors' pay; plus, it does not include long-term incentives.
Total compensation (base + bonus + stock options + stock awards + benefits)	Tells the total value competitors place on this work	All employees may not receive all the forms. Be careful: Don't set base equal to competitors' total compensation. Risks high fixed costs.

EXHIBIT 8.11 **Pay Survey Results for Different Measures of Compensation**

Survey Job	A: Base, Wtd Mean	B: Cash, Wtd Mean	C: Total Comp, Wtd Mean
Tech A	$22,989	$24,554	$30,831
Sr Tech	$37,748	$42,510	$51,482
Eng 1	$46,085	$48,289	$56,917
Eng 3	$73,134	$81,285	$112,805
Eng 5	$102,415	$112,587	$179,449
Mgr 1	$95,260	$115,304	$188,509
Mgr 3	$134,173	$171,030	$378,276

It is no surprise that for all seven jobs, total compensation is higher than base pay alone or base plus bonus. However, the variability and magnitude of the difference may be a surprise: from $7,842 (34 percent) for the job of technician A to $244,103.38 (182 percent) for the job of manager 3. Base pay is, on average, only 35 percent of total compensation for the manager 3s in this survey. So the measure of compensation is an important decision. Misinterpreting competitors' pay practices can lead to costly mispricing of pay levels and structures.

INTERPRET SURVEY RESULTS AND CONSTRUCT A MARKET LINE

Survey data today are typically exchanged online. Technology has made processing data and spitting out reports easy. The greatest challenge of total compensation surveys is to understand how to evaluate the information. In the best total compensation projects, each firm sees the survey as a customizable database project where they can specify the characteristics of the employers and jobs to analyze.

After the survey data are all collected, the next step is to analyze the results and use statistics to construct a **market pay line.** More than 20 years ago, Belcher interviewed compensation professionals to discover how survey data are actually analyzed. He reported:

> Every organization uses its own methods of distilling information from the survey; uses different surveys for different purposes; and uses different methods for company surveys. I could find no commonality in these methods of analysis by industry, by firm size, or by union presence. For example, some did nothing except read the entire survey, some emphasized industry data, others geographic competitors (commuting distances), some made comparisons with less than five competitors, some emphasized only large firms, others threw out the data from large firms.[29]

His conclusion still holds today. We hope this diversity reflects flexibility in dealing with a variety of circumstances and the use of improved compensation software. We worry that it reflects expediency and a lack of business- and work-related logic.

Verify Data

A common first step is to check the *accuracy* of the job matches, and then check for anomalies (i.e., an employer whose data are substantially out of line from data of others), age of data, and the nature of the organizations (e.g., industry, size—State Farm Insurance versus Google). Exhibit 8.12 is an excerpt from the survey used to prepare Exhibit 8.13. The survey was conducted at the behest of FastCat, a small start-up familiar to many readers. While there were a number of jobs included in the survey, we use information for just one job—engineer 1—to illustrate. As you can see, surveys do not make light reading. However, they contain a wealth of information. To extract that information, step through the portal . . . to being the FastCat analyst.[30]

Accuracy of Match (and Improving the Match)

Part A of the survey contains the description of the survey job. For jobs that match perfectly, things are easy. However, in most cases, the match is either poor or not perfect. In the latter case, one does not need to make a yes/no (all or nothing) decision. Rather, if the company job is sufficiently close to the survey job, especially on the most fundamental aspects, the benchmark conversion/survey leveling approach discussed earlier in this chapter can be used; that is, multiply the survey data by some factor that the analyst judges to be the difference between the company job and the survey job.[31] One way to execute this process is to conduct a job evaluation of the organization's benchmark job and the corresponding survey job and then determine their relative values.

Anomalies

Part B of the survey shows actual engineer 1 salaries. Perusal of salary data gives the analyst a sense of the quality of the data and helps identify any areas for additional consideration. For example, Part B of Exhibit 8.12 shows that no engineer 1 at company 1 receives stock options, and five receive no bonuses. The bonuses range from $500 to $4,000. (Because there are 585 engineer 1s in this survey, we have not included all their salary information.) Individual-level data provide a wealth of information about specific practices. Understanding minimums, maximums, and what percent actually receive bonuses and/or options is essential. Unfortunately, many surveys provide only summary information such as company averages.

EXHIBIT 8.12 Survey Data

A. Job Description: Engineer 1

Participates in development, testing, and documentation of software programs. Performs design and analysis tasks as a project team member. Typical minimum requirements are a bachelor's degree in a scientific or technical field or the equivalent and up to two years of experience.

B. Individual Salary Data (partial data; for illustration only)

Job	Base	Bonus	Total Cash	Stock Option	Benefits	Total Comp
Engineer 1					JE Points:	50
					Number of Incumbents:	585
Company 1						
Engineer 1	$79,000	$500	$79,500	$0	$8,251	$87,751
Engineer 1	$65,500	$2,500	$68,000	$0	$8,251	$76,251
Engineer 1	$65,000	$0	$65,000	$0	$8,251	$73,251
Engineer 1	$58,000	$4,000	$62,000	$0	$8,251	$70,251
Engineer 1	$57,930	$3,000	$60,930	$0	$8,251	$69,181
Engineer 1	$57,200	$2,000	$59,200	$0	$8,251	$67,451
Engineer 1	$56,000	$1,100	$57,100	$0	$8,251	$65,351
Engineer 1	$54,000	$0	$54,000	$0	$8,251	$62,251
Engineer 1	$52,500	$0	$52,500	$0	$8,251	$60,751
Engineer 1	$51,500	$1,500	$53,000	$0	$8,251	$61,251
Engineer 1	$49,000	$3,300	$52,300	$0	$8,251	$60,551
Engineer 1	$48,500	$0	$48,500	$0	$8,251	$56,751
Engineer 1	$36,500	$0	$36,500	$0	$8,251	$44,751
Company 2						
Engineer 1	$57,598	$0	$57,598	$28,889	$8,518	$95,004
Engineer 1	$57,000	$0	$57,000	$31,815	$8,518	$97,332
Engineer 1	$55,000	$0	$55,000	$20,110	$8,518	$83,628

C. Company Data (partial data; for illustration only)

	# Incumbents		Base	Short Term	Total Cash	LTI	Benefits	Total Comp
Company 1								
	13	Avg.	56,202.31	1,376.92	57,579.23	0.00	8,250.89	65,830.12
		Min.	36,500.00	0.00	36,500.00	0.00	8,250.89	44,750.89
		Max.	79,000.00	4,000.00	79,500.00	0.00	8,250.89	87,750.89
Company 2								
	13	Avg.	52,764.80	1,473.56	54,238.36	21,068.91	8,517.56	83,824.83
		Min.	47,376.20	0.00	50,038.33	4,878.98	8,517.56	65,416.54
		Max.	57,598.21	3,716.89	58,494.01	31,814.83	8,517.56	97,332.39
Company 4								
	2		56,004.00	0.00	56,004.00	0.00	9,692.56	65,696.56
			55,016.00	0.00	55,016.00	0.00	9,692.56	64,708.56
		Avg.	55,510.00	0.00	55,510.00	0.00	9,692.56	65,202.56
Company 8								
	14	Avg.	54,246.00	4,247.21	58,493.21	0.00	7,204.50	65,697.71
		Min.	45,000.00	860.00	48,448.00	0.00	7,204.50	55,363.50
		Max.	62,000.00	8,394.00	68,200.00	0.00	7,204.50	75,404.50
Company 12								
	35	Avg.	50,459.34	1,123.26	51,582.60	1,760.05	7,693.11	61,035.76
		Min.	42,000.00	0.00	43,092.00	0.00	7,693.11	52,606.26
		Max.	64,265.00	1,670.89	65,935.89	9,076.52	7,693.11	73,629.00
Company 13								
	5	Avg.	48,700.80	400.00	49,100.80	2,050.00	8,001.00	59,152.20
		Min.	45,456.00	0.00	45,456.00	0.00	8,001.00	53,458.00
		Max.	54,912.00	2,000.00	54,912.00	8,506.00	8,001.00	66,507.00
Company 14								
	10	Avg.	44,462.40	863.43	45,325.83	0.00	7,337.00	52,662.83
		Min.	37,440.00	372.95	37,812.95	0.00	7,337.00	45,149.95
		Max.	47,832.00	1,197.12	49,029.12	0.00	7,337.00	56,366.12

(Continued)

EXHIBIT 8.12   (*Continued*)

	# Incumbents		Base	Short Term	Total Cash	LTI	Benefits	Total Comp
Company 15								
	71	Avg.	49,685.92	8,253.61	57,939.52	1,762.97	8,404.00	68,106.48
		Min.	44,900.00	0.00	49,022.00	0.00	8,404.00	57,426.00
		Max.	57,300.00	14,132.00	68,357.00	63,639.00	8,404.00	125,471.00
Company 51								
	4	Avg.	46,193.88	1,399.75	47,593.63	41,954.39	7,640.89	97,188.90
		Min.	42,375.06	0.00	44,988.75	20,518.14	7,640.89	75,159.23
		Max.	48,400.04	2,985.31	51,385.35	74,453.00	7,640.89	133,479.24
Company 57								
	226	Avg.	44,091.57	1,262.43	45,354.00	0.00	6,812.00	52,166.00
		Min.	38,064.00	0.00	39,372.00	0.00	6,812.00	46,184.00
		Max.	60,476.00	2,179.00	62,655.00	0.00	6,812.00	69,467.00
Company 58								
	107	Avg.	44,107.18	1,367.04	45,474.21	0.00	6,770.00	52,244.21
		Min.	36,156.00	0.00	37,569.00	0.00	6,770.00	44,339.00
		Max.	57,600.00	2,147.00	58,913.00	0.00	6,770.00	65,683.00
Company 59								
	71	Avg.	44,913.63	1,152.85	46,066.48	0.00	6,812.00	52,878.48
		Min.	39,156.00	407.00	40,473.00	0.00	6,812.00	47,285.00
		Max.	57,000.00	1,639.00	57,407.00	0.00	6,812.00	64,219.00

D. Summary Data for Engineer 1

Base Salary		Total Cash		Total Compensation		Bonuses	Stock Options
Wtd Mean:	$46,085.21	Wtd Mean:	$48,289.66	Wtd Mean:	$56,917.08	Avg: 2,370.59	Avg: 16,920.18
Mean:	$49,092.71	Mean:	$50,940.53	Mean:	$65,524.22	As a % of Base:	As a % of Base:
50th:	$45,000.00	50th:	$46,422.00	50th:	$53,271.00	5.18%	33.96%
25th:	$42,600.00	25th:	$43,769.00	25th:	$50,593.11	% Who Receive:	% Who Receive:
75th:	$48,500.00	75th:	$51,854.04	75th:	$60,750.89	92.99%	8.38%

EXHIBIT 8.13 **Frequency Distributions**

Frequency and Value of Base Wages for Engineer 1 (*n* = 585)

Money (in $1,000)

Frequency and Value of Total Compensation for Engineer 5 (*n* = 719)

Money (in intervals of $10,000)

Part C of Exhibit 8.12 provides company data. Again, the first step is to look for anomalies:

1. *Does any one company dominate?* If so (i.e., company 57), a separate analysis of the largest company's data will isolate that employer's pay practices and clarify the nature of its influence.

2. *Do all employers show similar patterns?* Probably not. In our survey, base pay at company 1 ranges from $36,500 to $79,000 for a single job. This raises the possibility that this company might use broad bands (discussed later in this chapter). While seven of the companies have a bonus-to-base-pay ratio of around 2 to 3

percent, company 15 pays an average bonus of $8,254 for a bonus-to-base ratio of over 6 percent.

3. *Outlwiers*? Company 51 gives one of its engineers options valued at $74,453 on top of base pay. An analyst may consider dropping a company with such an atypical pay practice. The question is, What difference will it make if certain companies are dropped? What difference will it make if they are included?

The best way to answer questions on anomalies is to do an analysis of them alone. They may have deliberately differentiated themselves with pay as part of their strategy. Learning more about competitors that differentiate can offer valuable insights. Combining outliers' pay data with their financials may reveal that the most successful competitors also use larger bonuses for their engineers.

Part D at the bottom of Exhibit 8.12 contains summary data: five different measures of base pay, cash, and total compensation, as well as the percent of engineers who receive bonuses and options. The data suggest that most of FastCat's competitors use bonuses but are less likely to use options for this particular job. Summary data help abstract the survey information into a smaller number of measures for further statistical analysis. Statistics help FastCat get from pages of raw data (Exhibit 8.12) to graphs of actual salaries (Exhibit 8.13) and from there to a market line that reflects its competitive pay policy.

Statistical Analysis

While the statistics necessary to analyze survey data, including **regression,** are covered in basic statistics classes, a number of websites are probably more fun. Our favorite lets us click anywhere we want on a graph to see how adding that new data point (the mouse click) changes a regression line.[32] A useful first step in our analysis is to look at a frequency distribution of the pay rates.

Frequency Distribution

Exhibit 8.13 shows two frequency distributions created from the data in the Exhibit 8.12 survey. The top one shows the distribution of the base wages for the 585 engineer 1s in increments of $1,000. The second one shows the *total compensation* for 719 engineer 5s in increments of $10,000. (The wide range of dollars—from under $90,000 to over $900,000—is the reason that many surveys switch to logs of dollars for higher-level positions.) Frequency distributions help visualize information and may highlight anomalies. For example, the base wage above $79,000 may be considered an outlier. Is this a unique person? Or an error in reporting the data? A phone call (or e-mail) to the survey provider may answer the question.

Shapes of frequency distributions can vary. Unusual shapes may reflect problems with job matches, widely dispersed pay rates, or employers with widely divergent pay policies. If the data look reasonable at this point, one wag has suggested that it is probably the result of two large errors that offset one another.

EXHIBIT 8.14   Statistical Measures to Analyze Survey Data

Measure	What Does It Tell Us?	Advantage/Disadvantage
Central Tendency		
Mode	Most commonly occurring rate.	Must draw frequency distribution to calculate it.
Mean	Sum all rates and divide by number of rates. If have only company (rather than individual) data, wage of largest employer given same weight as smallest employer.	Commonly understood (also called the "average"). However, if have only company data, will not accurately reflect actual labor market conditions.
Median	Order all data points from highest to lowest; the one in the middle is the median.	Minimizes distortion caused by outliers.
Weighted mean	If have only companywide measures (rather than individual measures), the rate for each company is multiplied by the number of employees in that company. Total of all rates is divided by total number of employees.	Gives equal weight to each individual's wage. Captures size of supply and demand in market.
Variation		
Standard deviation	How tightly all the rates are clustered around the mean.	Tells how similar or dissimilar the market rates are from each other. A small SD means they are tightly bunched at center; a large SD means rates are more spread out.
Quartiles and percentiles	Order all data points from lowest to highest, then convert to percentages.	Common in salary surveys; frequently used to set pay ranges or zones.

Central Tendency

A measure of **central tendency** reduces a large amount of data into a single number. Exhibit 8.14 defines commonly used measures. The distinction between "mean" and "weighted mean" is important. If only company averages are reported in the survey, a *mean* may be calculated by adding each company's base wage and dividing by the number of companies. While use of the mean is common, it may not accurately reflect actual labor market conditions, since the base wage of the largest employer is given the same weight as that of the smallest employer. *Weighted mean* is calculated by adding the base wages for all 585 engineers in the survey and then dividing by 585 ($46,085). A weighted mean gives equal weight to *each individual employee's* wage.

Variation

The distribution of rates around a measure of central tendency is called *variation*. The two frequency distributions in Exhibit 8.13 show very different patterns of variation. Variation tells us how the rates are spread out in the market. *Standard deviation* is probably the most common statistical measure of variation, although its use in salary surveys is rare.

Quartiles and *percentiles* are more common measures in salary survey analysis. Recall from the chapter introduction that someone's policy was "to be in the 75th percentile nationally." This means that 75 percent of all pay rates are *at or below* that point and 25 percent are *above*. Quartiles (25th and 75th percentiles) are often used to set pay ranges. More on pay ranges later.

Update the Survey Data

Because they reflect decisions of employers, employees, unions, and government agencies, wages paid by competitors are constantly changing. Additionally, competitors adjust their wages at different times. Universities typically adjust to match the academic year. Unionized employers adjust on dates negotiated in labor agreements. Some employers operating in competitive locations (e.g., Minsk, Shanghai) update every quarter or even every month. Many employers adjust each employee's pay on the anniversary of the employee's date of hire. Even though these changes do not occur smoothly and uniformly throughout the year, as a practical matter we assume that they do. Therefore, a survey that requires three months to collect and analyze is probably outdated before it is available. The pay data are usually updated (a process often called *aging* or *trending*) to forecast the competitive rates for the future date when the pay decisions will be implemented.

The amount to update is based on several factors, including historical trends in the labor market, prospects for the economy in which the employer operates, and the manager's judgment, among others. Some recommend using the **Consumer Price Index (CPI).** We do not. The CPI measures the rate of change in prices for goods and services in the product market, not wage changes in labor markets. Chapter 18 has more information on this distinction.

Exhibit 8.15 illustrates updating. In the example, the base pay rate of $45,000 collected in the survey was in effect at January 1 of the current year—already in the past. The compensation manager will use this information for pay decisions that go into effect on January 1 of the plan year. So if base pay has been increasing by approximately 5 percent annually, and we assume that the future will be like the past, the rate is multiplied by 105 percent to account for the change expected by the end of the current year (to $47,250) and then by an additional percentage to estimate pay rates for the plan year.

Construct a Market Pay Line

Look again at Exhibit 8.11. It shows the results of the FastCat analyst's decisions on which salary survey jobs to include that are judged to closely match internal benchmark jobs (the seven jobs on the x [horizontal] axis), which companies to include and which measures of pay to use. For each of the compensation metrics, a line has been drawn connecting the pay for the seven jobs. Jobs are ordered on the horizontal axis according to their position (i.e., number of job evaluation points) in the internal structure. Thus, the line trends upward to create a market line.

EXHIBIT 8.15 **Choices for Updating Survey Data Reflect Pay Policy**

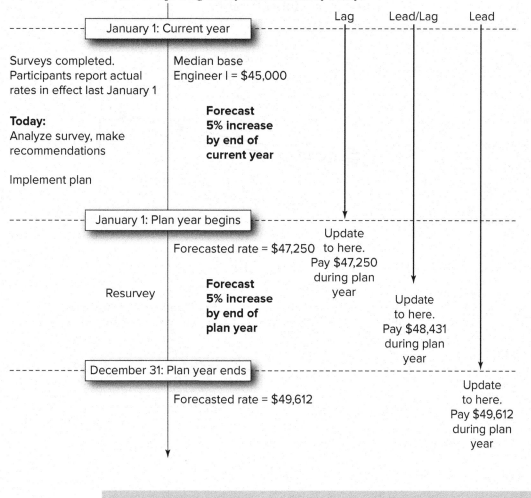

A **market line** links a company's benchmark jobs on the horizontal axis (internal structure) with market rates paid by competitors (market survey) on the vertical axis. It summarizes the distribution of going rates paid by competitors in the market.

A market line may be drawn freehand by connecting the data points, as was done in Exhibit 8.11, or statistical techniques such as regression analysis may be used. Regression generates a straight line that best fits the data by minimizing the variance around the line. Exhibit 8.16 shows the regression lines that use the pay survey data in Exhibit 8.11 as the dependent variable(s) and the job evaluation points of matched FastCat jobs as the independent variable. Compare the data tables in Exhibit 8.11 and Exhibit 8.16. Exhibit 8.11 shows the market rates for survey jobs. Exhibit 8.16 shows the job evaluation points for the FastCat jobs that match these survey jobs plus the

EXHIBIT 8.16 From Regression Results to a Market Line

PREDICTED AND ACTUAL PAY

Job B Job F   Job G   Job H   Job J   Job M   Job P

Survey Job	Matching FastCat Job*	FastCat JEPts	Predicted Base, Wtd Mean	Predicted Cash, Wtd Mean	Predicted Total Comp
Tech A	B	10	$23,057	$20,543	−$1,330
Sr Tech	F	25	$34,361	$35,116	$31,172
Eng 1	G	50	$53,199	$59,404	$85,343
Eng 3	H	75	$72,038	$83,692	$139,514
Eng 5	J	100	$90,876	$107,980	$193,685
Mgr 1	M	125	$109,715	$132,268	$247,856
Mgr 3	P	150	$128,553	$156,556	$302,027*

*We thought it best to leave it to an expert (you) to decide which FastCat job/job title is a good match for each survey job, if you are using *Cases in Compensation* with your textbook.

regression's statistical "prediction" of each pay measure for each job. The actual base pay for the survey job Tech A is $22,989 (Exhibit 8.11); the "predicted" base pay for the job is $23,058 (Exhibit 8.16).

In Exhibit 8.17, we focus in on the regression results that use base pay from the survey as the dependent variable. The diamonds are the actual results of the survey and the solid line is the regression result. Regression smoothes large amounts of data while minimizing variations. As the number of jobs in the survey increases, the advantage of the straight line that regression provides becomes clear.

Setting Pay for Benchmark and Non-benchmark Jobs

Setting pay for benchmark jobs is straightforward to the degree that good matches with survey jobs are found. Once it is known what other organizations

EXHIBIT 8.17 Understanding Regression

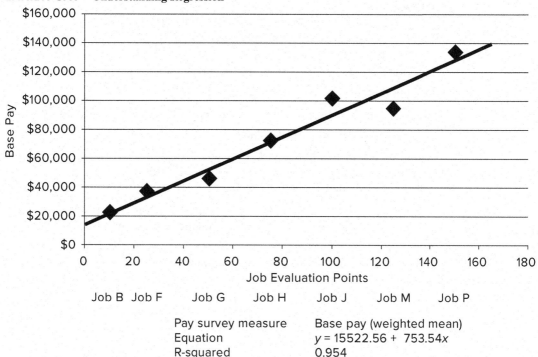

Pay survey measure	Base pay (weighted mean)
Equation	$y = 15522.56 + 753.54x$
R-squared	0.954

pay for each job, a pay level can be chosen that is a function of what other organizations pay and what role the job plays in executing the strategy of one's own organization. For nonbenchmark jobs (i.e., those jobs for which there is no good match among jobs included in the pay survey), the market pay lines in Exhibit 8.16 are especially useful. For example, take a job, Job Z, that has no match, but for which we have assigned a job evaluation points score of 110. How might we estimate its base pay? From Exhibit 8.16, we know that FastCat Job J has 100 job evaluation points and matches a survey job, Eng 5, that has a base pay of $90,876. So, one approach is to pay Job Z 110/100 × $90,876 = $99,964. Or, we can use the market survey line regression equation shown in Exhibit 8.17. The predicted base pay = $15,522.56 + $753.54 (110 job evaluation points) = $98,412. The results are close, but not identical. (Remember, the regression line smoothes the relationship, resulting in a small difference in predicted base pay.) So, our market line is very valuable. Even though only benchmark jobs in our company can be directly matched to the survey, the market line allows us to estimate the market pay for nonbenchmark jobs. (See also our earlier discussion of survey leveling.)

Before we leave survey data analysis, we must emphasize that not all survey results look like our examples and that not all companies use these statistical and analytical techniques. There is no one "right way" to analyze survey data. It has been our intent

e-Compensation 2
Calculating a Market Line Using Regression Analysis
Regression analysis uses the mathematical formula for a straight line:
$y = a + bx$, where

y = dollars

x = job evaluation points

a = the y value (in dollars) at which $x = 0$ (i.e., the straight line crosses the y axis)

b = the slope of the regression line

Using the dollars from the market survey data and the job evaluation points from the internal structure, replicate our Exhibits 8.16 and 8.17 results.
The market line can be written as

Pay for job A = a + (b × job evaluation points for job A)
Pay for job B = a + (b × job evaluation points for job B)

and so on.
Regression estimates the values of *a* and *b* in an efficient manner, so errors of prediction are minimized.

to provide some insight into the kinds of calculations that are useful and the assumptions that underlie salary surveys.

We are now beyond the halfway point of this long chapter. May we suggest that it might be a good time to consider resorting to the Puking Pastilles, one of the Weasleys' Wizarding Wheezes described in the fifth Harry Potter book? The Puking Pastilles make you just ill enough to convince your professor to give you an extension on an assignment before you magically recover to enjoy your illicit time off.[33]

Combine Internal Structure and External Market Rates

At this point, two parts of the total pay model have merged. Their relationship to each other can be seen in Exhibit 8.18.[34]

- The *internally aligned structure* (developed in Chapters 3–6) is shown on the horizontal (*x*) axis. For this illustration, our structure consists of jobs A through P. Jobs B, F, G, H, J, M, and P are the seven benchmark jobs that have been matched in the survey. Jobs A, C, D, E, I, K, L, N, and O have no direct matching jobs in the salary survey.
- The salaries paid by relevant competitors for those benchmark jobs, as measured by the survey—*the external competitive data*, are shown on the vertical (*y*) axis.

These two components—internal alignment and external competitiveness—come together in the pay structure. The pay structure has two aspects: the *pay-policy line* and *pay ranges*.

EXHIBIT 8.18
Develop Pay
Grades

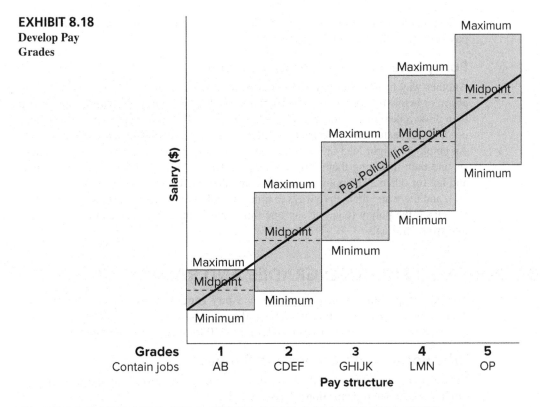

FROM POLICY TO PRACTICE: THE PAY-POLICY LINE
==

There are several ways to translate external competitive policy into practice. You have already made some of the choices that help you do this.

Choice of Measure

If Lincoln Electric practices what it claims at the beginning of the chapter, then we would expect Lincoln Electric to use the 45th percentile for base pay and the 65th percentile for total cash compensation as compensation measures in its regression.

Updating

Look again at Exhibit 8.15. The arrows on the right side of the exhibit show how updating survey data reflects policy. If the company chooses a "match" policy but then updates survey data to the end of the current year/start of the plan year and keeps this rate in effect throughout the plan year, the company will actually be lagging the market. It will match its desired market pay level only at the beginning of the plan year. The market rates continue to rise throughout the year; the company's rates do not.

Aging the market data to a point halfway through the plan year (middle arrow in Exhibit 8.15) is called *lead/lag*. The original survey rates are updated to the end of the current year plus half the projected amount for the plan year ($48,431). An employer who wants to lead the market may age data to the *end* of the plan year ($49,612) and pay at this rate throughout the plan year.

Policy Line as Percent of Market Line

Another way to translate pay-level policy into practice is to simply *specify a percent* above or below the regression line (market line) that an employer intends to match and then draw a new line at this higher (or lower) level. This **pay-policy line** would carry out a policy statement, "We lead the market by 10 percent." Other possibilities exist. An employer might lead by including only a few top-paying competitors in the analysis and then matching them ("pay among the leaders") or lead for some job families and lag for others. The point is that there are alternatives among competitive pay policies, and there are alternative ways to translate policy into practice. If the practice does not match the policy (e.g., we say one thing but do another), then employees receive the wrong message.

FROM POLICY TO PRACTICE: GRADES AND RANGES

The next step is to design **pay grades** and **pay ranges.** These analyses are usually done with base pay data, since base pay reflects the basic value of the work rather than performance levels of employees (see Exhibit 8.10 for a comparison of metrics).

Why Bother with Grades and Ranges?

Grades and ranges offer flexibility to deal with pressures from external markets and differences among organizations. These include:

1. *Differences in quality (skills, abilities, experience) among individuals applying for work* (e.g., Microsoft may have stricter hiring requirements for engineers than does FastCat, even though job descriptions appear identical).
2. *Differences in the productivity or value of these quality variations* (e.g., the value of the results from a software engineer at Microsoft probably differs from that of the results of a software engineer at Best Buy).
3. *Differences in the mix of pay forms competitors use* (e.g., Oracle uses more stock options and lower base compared to IBM).

In addition to offering flexibility to deal with these external differences, an organization may use differences in rates paid to employees on the same job. *A pay range exists whenever two or more rates are paid to employees in the same job.* Hence, ranges provide managers the opportunity to:

1. Recognize individual performance differences with pay.
2. Meet employees' expectations that their pay will increase over time, even in the same job.
3. Encourage employees to remain with the organization.

From an internal alignment perspective, the range reflects the differences in performance or experience that an employer wishes to recognize with pay. From an external competitiveness perspective, the range is a control device. A range maximum sets the lid on what the employer is willing to pay for that work; the range minimum sets the floor.

In Chapter 11, we will see that many organizations use a merit increase grid or salary increase matrix, which uses two factors, employee performance rating and position in the salary range, to guide pay increases. The goal is to continually adjust employee pay so that it is appropriately positioned relative to the market. Thus, an employee with consistently high performance ratings should move above the market median and **range midpoint,** whereas an employee with consistently average performance should be near the range midpoint.

Develop Grades

The first step in building flexibility into the pay structure is to group different jobs that are considered substantially equal for pay purposes into a grade. Grades enhance an organization's ability to move people among jobs with no change in pay. In Exhibit 8.18, the jobs are grouped into five grades on the horizontal axis.

The question of which jobs are substantially equal and therefore slotted into one grade requires the analyst to reconsider the original job evaluation results. Each grade will have its own pay range, and *all the jobs within a single grade will have the same pay range.* Jobs in different grades (e.g., jobs C, D, E, and F in grade 2) should be dissimilar from those in other grades (grade 1 jobs A and B) and will have a different pay range.

Although grades permit flexibility, they are challenging to design. The objective is for all jobs that are similar for pay purposes to be placed within the same grade. If jobs with relatively close job evaluation point totals fall on either side of grade boundaries, the magnitude of difference in the salary treatment may be out of proportion to the magnitude of difference in the value of the job content. Resolving such dilemmas requires an understanding of the specific jobs, career paths, and work flow in the organization, as well as considerable judgment.

Establish Range Midpoints, Minimums, and Maximums

Grades group job evaluation data on the horizontal axis; ranges group salary data on the vertical axis. Ranges set upper and lower pay limits for all jobs in each grade. A range has three salient features: a midpoint, a minimum, and a maximum. Exhibit 8.19 is an enlargement of grade 2 in Exhibit 8.18, which contains the engineer 1 job. The

EXHIBIT 8.19
Range Midpoint, Minimum, and Maximum

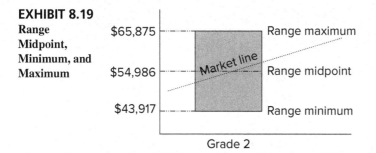

midpoint is $54,896. This is the point where the pay-policy line crosses the center of the grade. The range for this grade has been set at 20 percent above and 20 percent below the midpoint. Thus, all FastCat engineer 1s are supposed to receive a salary higher than $43,917 but lower than $65,875.[35]

What Size Should the Range Be?

The size of the range is based on some judgment about how the ranges support career paths, promotions, and other organization systems. Top-level management positions commonly have ranges of 30 to 60 percent above and below the midpoint; entry to midlevel professional and managerial positions, between 15 and 30 percent; office and production work, 5 to 15 percent. Larger ranges in the managerial jobs reflect the greater opportunity for individual discretion and performance variations in the work.

Some compensation managers use the actual survey rates, particularly the 75th and 25th percentiles, as maximums and minimums. Others ensure that the proposed range includes at least 75 percent of the rates in the survey data. Still others establish the minimum and maximum separately, with the amount between the minimum and the midpoint a function of how long it takes a new employee to become fully competent. Short training time may translate to minimums much closer to the midpoints. The maximum becomes the amount above the midpoint that the company is willing to pay for sustained performance on the job. In the end, the size of the range is based on judgment that weighs all these factors.

Overlap

Exhibit 8.20 shows two extremes in overlap between adjacent grades. The high degree of overlap and low midpoint differentials in Exhibit 8.20(a) indicate small differences in the value of jobs in the adjoining grades. Being promoted from one grade to another may include a title change but not much change in pay. The smaller ranges in Exhibit 8.20(b) create less overlap, which permits the manager to reinforce a promotion into a new grade with a larger pay increase. The downside is that there may be fewer opportunities for promotion.

Promotion Increases Matter

The size of differentials between grades should support career movement through the structure. A managerial job would typically be at least one grade higher than the jobs it

EXHIBIT 8.20
Range Overlap

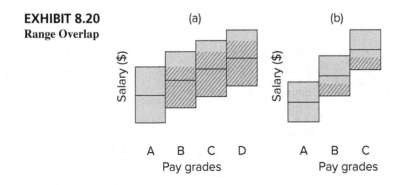

supervises. Although a 15 percent pay differential between manager and employee has been offered as a rule of thumb, large overlap and possible overtime in some jobs but not in managerial jobs can make it difficult to maintain manager–employee differentials. We are cautious about such rules of thumb. They are often ways to avoid thinking about what makes sense.

What is the optimal overlap between grades? It ought to be large enough to induce employees to seek promotion into a higher grade. However, there is virtually no research to indicate how much of a differential is necessary to influence employees to do so. Tracing how an employee might move through a career path in the structure (e.g., from engineer 1 to engineer 2 . . . to manager 3) and what size pay increases will accompany that movement will help answer that question.

Not all employers use grades and ranges. Skill-based plans establish single *flat rates* for each skill level regardless of performance or seniority. And many collective bargaining contracts establish single flat rates for each job (i.e., all senior machinists II receive $17.50 per hour regardless of performance or seniority). This flat rate often corresponds to some midpoint on a survey of that job. And increasingly, *broad bands* (think "really fat ranges") are being adopted for even greater flexibility.

FROM POLICY TO PRACTICE: BROAD BANDING

Exhibit 8.21 collapses salary grades into only a few broad bands, each with a sizable range. This technique, known as **broad banding,** consolidates as many as four or five traditional grades into a single band with one minimum and one maximum. Because the band encompasses so many jobs of differing values, a range midpoint is usually not used.[36]

Contrasts between ranges and broad bands are highlighted in Exhibit 8.22. Supporters of broad bands list several advantages over traditional approaches. First, broad bands provide flexibility to define job responsibilities more broadly. They support redesigned, downsized, or boundaryless organizations that have eliminated layers of managerial jobs. They foster cross-functional growth and development in

EXHIBIT 8.21
From Grades to Bands

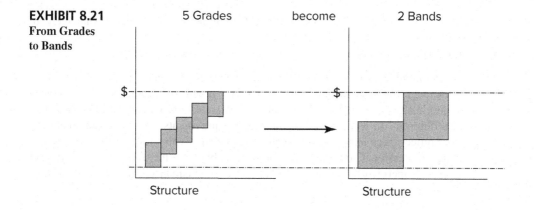

5 Grades   become   2 Bands

Structure   Structure

EXHIBIT 8.22
Contrasts
Between
Ranges and
Bands

Ranges Support:	Bands Support:
Some flexibility within controls	Emphasis on flexibility within guidelines
Relatively stable organization design	Global organizations
Recognition via titles or career progression	Cross-functional experience and lateral progression
Midpoint controls, comparatives	Reference market rates, shadow ranges
Controls designed into system	Controls in budget, few in system
Give managers "freedom with guidelines"	Give managers "freedom to manage" pay
To 150 percent range-spread	100–400 percent spread

these new organizations. Employees can move laterally across functions within a band in order to gain depth of experience. Companies with global operations such as 3M and Medtronic use bands to move managers among worldwide assignments. The emphasis on lateral movement with no pay adjustments helps manage the reality of fewer promotion opportunities in flattened organization structures. The flexibility of banding eases mergers and acquisitions since there are not a lot of levels to argue over.[37]

Broad bands are often combined with more traditional salary administration practices by using midpoints, **"zones,"** or other control points within bands.[38] Perhaps the most important difference between the grades-and-ranges and broad-banding approaches is the location of the controls. The grade-and-range approach has guidelines and controls designed right into the pay system. Range minimums, maximums, and midpoints ensure consistency across managers. Managers using bands have only a total salary budget limiting them. But as experience with bands has advanced, guidelines and structure are increasingly designed into them (e.g., reference market rates or shadow ranges).

Bands may add flexibility: Less time will be spent judging fine distinctions among jobs. But perhaps the time avoided judging jobs will now be spent judging individuals, a prospect managers already try to avoid. How will an organization avoid the appearance of salary treatment based on personality and politics rather than objective criteria? Ideally, with a well-thought-out performance management system.

Banding takes two steps:

1. *Set the number of bands.* Merck uses six bands for its entire pay structure. Band titles range from "contributor" to "executive." A unit of General Electric replaced 24 levels of work with 5 bands. Usually bands are established at the major "breaks," or differences, in work or skill/competency requirements. Titles used to label each band reflect these major breaks, such as "associate" (entry-level individual contributor), "professional" (experienced, knowledgeable team member), "leader" (project or group supervisor), "director," "coach," or even "visionary." The challenge is how

much to pay people who are in the same band but in different functions performing different work.

2. *Price the bands: reference market rates.* The four bands in Exhibit 8.23 (associates, professionals, lead professionals, senior professionals) include multiple job families within each band, for example, finance, purchasing, engineering, marketing, and so on. It is unlikely that General Electric pays associates and professionals with business degrees the same as associates and professionals with engineering degrees. Usually external market differences exist, so the different functions or groups within bands are priced differently. As the pop-out in Exhibit 8.23 depicts, the three job families (purchasing, finance, and engineering) in the professional band have different *reference rates,* drawn from survey data.

EXHIBIT 8.23   **Reference Rates Within Bands**

You might say that this is beginning to look a lot like grades and ranges within each band. You would be correct. The difference is that ranges traditionally serve as controls, whereas reference rates act as guides. Today's guides grow to tomorrow's bureaucracy.

Flexibility-Control

Broad banding encourages employees to seek growth and development by moving cross-functionally (e.g., from purchasing to finance). The assumption is that this cross-fertilization of ideas will benefit the organization. Hence, career moves within bands are more common than between bands. According to supporters, the principal payoff of broad banding is this flexibility. But flexibility is one side of the coin; chaos and favoritism is the other. Banding presumes that managers will manage employee pay to accomplish the organization's objectives (and not their own) and treat employees fairly. Historically, this is not the first time managers have sought greater flexibility. Indeed, the rationale for using grades and ranges was to reduce inconsistencies and favoritism in previous generations. The challenge today is to take advantage of flexibility without increasing labor costs or leaving the organization vulnerable to charges of inconsistent or illegal practices.

BALANCING INTERNAL AND EXTERNAL PRESSURES: ADJUSTING THE PAY STRUCTURE

Up until now, we have made a distinction between the job structure and the pay structure. A **job structure** orders jobs on the basis of internal factors (reflected in job evaluation or skill certification). The **pay structure,** on the other hand, is anchored by the organization's external competitive position and reflected in its pay-policy line.

Reconciling Differences

The problem with using two standards (internal and external) to create a structure is that they are likely to result in two different structures. The order in which jobs are ranked on internal versus external factors may not agree. Differences between market structures and rates and job evaluation rankings warrant a review of the basic decisions in evaluating and pricing a particular job. This may entail a review of the job analysis, the evaluation of the job, or the market data for the job in question. Often this reanalysis solves the problem. Sometimes, however, discrepancies persist. Survey data may be discarded, or benchmark-job matches may be changed.

One study of how differences are actually reconciled found that managers weigh external market data more heavily than internal job evaluation data. In light of all the judgments that go into internal evaluation, market data are often considered to be more objective.[39] Yet this chapter and research show that market data are also based on judgment.

Sometimes differences arise because a shortage of a particular skill has driven up the market rate. But reclassifying such a job into a higher salary grade, where it will remain long after the supply/demand imbalance has been corrected, creates additional problems. Creating a special range that is clearly designated as *market responsive* may be a better approach. Decisions made on the basis of expediency may undermine the integrity of the pay decisions.

MARKET PRICING

Some organizations adopt pay strategies that emphasize external competitiveness and deemphasize internal alignment. In fact, we saw in Chapter 5 that this approach is now quite common. Indeed, it has been said that "the core change" in compensation in recent years "is the diminished concern with internal salary relationships."[40] Called *market pricing,* this approach sets pay structures almost exclusively on external market rates.[41] Market pricers match a large percentage of their jobs with market data and collect as much market data as possible. The competitive rates for jobs for which external market data are available are calculated; then the remaining (nonbenchmark) jobs are blended into the pay hierarchy created by the external rates ("rank to market"). Pfizer, for example, begins with job analysis and job descriptions. This is immediately followed by market analysis and pricing for as many jobs as possible. After that, the few remaining (nonbenchmark) jobs are blended in and the internal job relationships are reviewed to be sure they are "*reasonable in light of organization work flow and other uniqueness.*" The final step is pricing the nonbenchmark jobs. This is done by comparing the value of these jobs to the Pfizer jobs already priced in the market.

Market pricing goes beyond using benchmark jobs and slotting nonbenchmarks. The objective of market pricing is to base most, if not all, of the internal pay structure on external rates, breaking down the boundaries between the internal organization and the external market forces. Some companies even match all forms of pay for each job to its competitors in the market. For example, if the average rate for a controller job is $150,000, then the company pays $150,000. If 60 percent of the $150,000 is base pay, 20 percent is annual bonus, 5 percent is stock options, and 15 percent is benefits, the company matches not only the amount but also this mix of pay forms. Another $150,000 job, say, director of marketing, may have a different pattern among market competitors, which is also matched.

Business Strategy (More Than "Follow the Leader")

Pure market pricing carried to this extreme ignores internal alignment completely. Gone is any attempt to align internal pay structures with the business strategy and the work performed. Rather, the internal pay structure is aligned with competitors' decisions as reflected in the market. In a very real sense, the decisions of its competitors determine an organization's pay.

Why should competitors' pay decisions be the sole or even primary determinant of another company's pay structure? If they are, then *how much or what mix of forms* a company pays is no longer a potential source of competitive advantage. It is not unique, nor is it difficult to imitate. The implied assumption is that little value is added through internal alignment.

Any unique or difficult-to-imitate aspects of the organization's pay structure, which may have been based on unique technology or the way work is organized, are deemphasized by market pricers. Fairness is presumed to be reflected by market rates; employee behavior is presumed to be reinforced by totally market-priced structures, which are the very same as those of competitors.

In contrast, an organization may choose to differentiate its pay strategy from that of its competitors to better execute its own strategy.[42] We saw earlier that organizations may choose different overall pay levels, depending on their business strategy. We also saw earlier that an organization may choose to pay some of its jobs above market, but other jobs at or below market.[43] For example, according to resource dependence theory, employees who are more central to strategy execution in terms of their criticality in obtaining resources from the environment would be expected to be paid better relative to the market than would other employees. For example, in a study of universities, it was found that private universities, which rely more on private fundraising to operate, paid their chief development (fundraising) officers more than did public universities, which rely more on state funds. On the other hand, public universities, which typically rely more heavily on athletic programs to build alumni relations, paid their athletic directors more than did private universities.[44] Other evidence shows that in capital intensive and highly diversified firms, where finance expertise is especially important, compensation for managers in finance jobs was higher relative to market than for other jobs on average. Likewise, managers in marketing were paid more in firms with large expenditures on marketing and advertising, and managers in research in development were paid more relative to market than other managers in firms focusing on product innovation.[45]

In sum, the process of balancing internal and external pressures is a matter of judgment made with an eye on the pay system objectives. De-emphasizing internal alignment may lead to unfair treatment among employees and inconsistency with the strategy and fundamental culture of the organization. Neglecting external competitive pay practices, however, will affect both the ability to attract applicants and the ability to retain valued employees. External pay relationships also directly impact labor costs and hence the ability to compete in the product/service market. Thus, while differentiating pay strategy from competitors can lead to competitive advantage, the reasons for being different must be clearly reasoned and articulated. Otherwise, being different may only lead to lack of competitiveness in the product market or labor market, hindering organization success and strategy execution.

REVIEW

The end of Part Two of the textbook is a logical spot for a midterm exam. Exhibit 8.24 has been designed to help you review.

EXHIBIT 8.24
Open-Book
Midterm Exam

Answer true or false to the following questions:

You know you are spending too much time working on compensation when you:

- Use "pay mix" and "external competitiveness" when you e-mail home for money.
- Think that paying for lunch requires a strategic approach.
- Ask your date to specify his or her competencies.
- Think that copying your classmate's answers on this exam is "gathering competitive intelligence."
- Can explain the difference between traditional pay grades and ranges and new broad bands with shadow ranges.
- Believe your answer to the above.
- Would cross the street to listen to economists and psychologists discuss the "likely effects of alternative external competitiveness policies."
- Consider your Phase II assignment a wonderful opportunity to increase your human capital.
- Think adding points to your project grade creates a "balanced scorecard."
- Are willing to pay your instructor to teach any other course.
- Are surprised to learn that some people think a COLA is a soft drink.
- Turn your head to listen rather than roll your eyes when someone talks about being "incentivized" with pay.
- Believe that instead of your mom, "the market" knows best.

How did you do? Good. Now let's move on to the next chapters.

Your Turn

Google's Evolving Pay Strategy

In Chapter 2, we talked about how Microsoft had changed its pay strategy to rely less on stock options, more on stock grants, and then to rely less on stock grants and more on cash as its product cycle phase changed from growth to maintenance and its stock price growth slowed. Google went public in 1994 and its stock price, already at around $100/share at that point, then rose rapidly (a great big understatement), peaking at around $370* in November 2007. However, as of May 2012, Google's stock price was right around $300 (with a 52-week high of about $335). As a result, Google was subjected to comments such as "Google isn't the hot place to work" and has "become the safe place to work" (per Robert Greene, who recruits engineers for start-ups such as Facebook).[46] Perhaps following in the footsteps of Microsoft, Google announced that it was giving a 10 percent across the board increase in salary. Not stock options. Not stock grants (but, see below). Salary.[47] The cost of the salary increase was estimated by Barclay's to be $400 million.[48]

*Google's stock split in 2014. Thus, the pre-2014 stock price values mentioned here have been adjusted by multiplying them by .50.

"Analysts say Google is facing what all Silicon Valley companies struggle with when they graduate from start-up status and into the realm of Big Tech."[49] With or without the 10 percent increase, one report says that Google was "paying computer science majors just out of college as much as $20,000 more than it was paying a few months ago" and that salary "is so far above the industry average that start-ups cannot match Google's salaries."[50] (Actually, one might ask how many non-start-ups are likely to match such salaries.)

It is also noteworthy that Google repriced 7.64 million stock options in 2009. Of 20,200 total employees, 15,642 took advantage of the opportunity to replace their existing options, which had an average exercise price of $522, with new options having an exercise price of $308.57.[51] By one estimate, Google was on a path to spend $2 billion on stock-related compensation in 2011.[52] Subsequently, Google moved from stock options to restricted stock units for employees. The latter are actual grants of stock and are restricted in the sense that employees need to remain with Google for a minimum amount of time.

As of early 2015, Google's stock price was around $560, so employee stock-related wealth has soared. That goes along with their high salaries (see above and also the beginning of Part Three of your text) and their well-known extensive benefits. (Recall from Chapter 2 that they regularly top Fortune's list of Best Companies to Work For.)

QUESTIONS:

1. What is Google's pay level? How do you define and measure its pay level? How well is it captured by salary alone?

2. Does your answer to the above question depend on what point in time it is answered? For example, what was Google's pay level the day before it repriced employee stock options? What was Google's pay level the day after it repriced employee stock options? And now?

3. Why did Google reprice its stock options and also give a 10 percent salary increase (in an era when 2 to 3 percent annual salary increase budgets are the norm)? Is it because its business strategy and/or product life cycle changed? Is it because it was concerned that employees' perceived value of compensation did not match what Google was spending?

4. Do you think Google has made the right choices in changing its compensation strategy? How much do these changes cost? How do these costs compare to Google's total costs and operating income? Are these increased compensation costs likely to be a good investment? In other words, will they pay for themselves (and more)? Explain.

5. Will Google's pay strategy work "forever"? Consider the evolution of Microsoft's pay strategy as its growth slackened. Should Google prepare for a similar future? If so, when and what sort of actions should they take to prepare?

Still Your **Turn**   Word-of-Mouse: Dot-Com Comparisons

More compensation information is available than ever before. Click on the website *www.salary.com* or on *www.glassdoor.com*. These websites, which we have used in the opening to Part Three and in the present chapter, provide pay data on hundreds of jobs in cities all over the

United States in many different industries. Identify several jobs of interest to you, such as accountant, financial analyst, product manager, or stockbroker. Select specific cities or use the U.S. national average. Obtain the median, the 25th and 75th percentile base wage, and total cash compensation rates for each job. Then consider the following questions:

1. Which jobs are paid more or less? Is this what you would have expected? Why or why not? What factors could explain the differences in the salaries?
2. Do the jobs have different bonuses as a percentage of their base salaries? What could explain these differences?
3. Do the data include the value of stock options? What are the implications of this?
4. Read the job descriptions. Are they accurate descriptions for jobs that you would be applying for? Why or why not? Are there jobs for which you cannot find an appropriate match? Why do you think this is the case?
5. If you are majoring in computer science, you may find that some surveys include data on software developers, but not software engineers (and vice versa). How similar are these jobs and can you use data on one of these job titles to estimate pay rates for the other title? Also, where does the job of computer programmer fit in?
6. Check out pay levels for these types of jobs in your school's career office. How does the pay for jobs advertised in your career office differ from the pay levels on salary.com? Why do you think these differences exist?
7. How could you use this information while negotiating your salary in your job after graduation? What data would you provide to support your "asking price"? What factors will influence whether or not you get what you ask for?
8. What is the relevant labor market for these jobs? How big are the differences between salaries in different locations?
9. For each job, compare the median salary to the low and high averages. How much variation exists? What factors might explain this variation in pay rates for the same job?
10. Look for a description of how these salary data are developed. Do you think it provides enough information? Why or why not? Discuss some of the factors that might impair the accuracy of these data. What are the implications of using inaccurate salary data for individuals or companies?
11. With this information available for free, why would you bother with consultants' surveys?
12. If you were a manager, how would you justify paying one of your employees either higher or lower than the results shown on this website?

Summary   This chapter has detailed the decisions and techniques that go into setting pay levels and mix and designing pay structures. Most organizations survey other employers' pay practices to determine the rates competitors pay. An employer using the survey results considers how it wishes to position its total compensation in the market: to lead, to match, or to follow competition. This policy decision may be different for different business units and even for different job groups within a single organization. The policy on competitive position is translated into practice by setting pay-policy lines; these serve as reference points around which pay grades and ranges or bands are designed.

The use of grades and ranges or bands recognizes both external and internal pressures on pay decisions. No single "going rate" for a job exists in the market; instead, an array of rates exists. This array results from conditions of demand and supply, variations in the quality of employees, and differences in employer policies and practices. It also reflects the fact that employers differ in the values they attach to the jobs and people. And, very importantly, it reflects differences in the mix of pay forms among companies.

Internally, the use of ranges is consistent with variations in the discretion in jobs. Some employees will perform better than others; some employees are more experienced than others. Pay ranges permit employers to recognize these differences with pay.

Managers are increasingly interested in broad banding, which offers even greater flexibility than grades and ranges to deal with the continuously changing work assignments required in many successful organizations. Broad banding offers freedom to adapt to changes without requiring approvals. However, it risks self-serving and potentially inequitable decisions on the part of the manager. Recently, the trend has been toward approaches with greater flexibility to adapt to changing conditions. Such flexibility also makes mergers and acquisitions easier and global alignment possible.

Let us step back for a moment to review what has been discussed and preview what is coming. We have examined two strategic components of the total pay model. A concern for internal alignment means that analysis and perhaps descriptions and evaluation are important for achieving a competitive advantage and fair treatment. A concern for external competitiveness requires competitive positioning, survey design and analysis, setting the pay-policy line (how much and what forms), and designing grades and ranges or broad bands. The next part of the book is concerned with employee contributions—paying the people who perform the work. This is perhaps the most important part of the book. All that has gone before is a prelude, setting up the pay levels, mix, and structures by which people are to be paid. It is now time to pay the people.

Review Questions

1. Which competitive pay policy would you recommend to an employer? Why? Does it depend on circumstances faced by the employer? Which ones?

2. How would you design a survey for setting pay for welders? How would you design a survey for setting pay for financial managers? Do the issues differ? Will the techniques used and the data collected differ? Why or why not?

3. What factors determine the relevant market for a survey? Why is the definition of the relevant market so important?

4. What do surveys have to do with pay discrimination?

5. Contrast pay ranges and grades with bands. Why would you use either? Does their use assist or hinder the achievement of internal alignment? External competitiveness?

Endnotes   1. Consulting firms' websites list their specialized surveys. See, for example, Clark Consulting's Total Compensation Survey of the computer and semiconductor industries, *www.clarkconsulting.com;* Hewitt, *www.hewitt.com;* Towers Perrin, *www.towers.com /towers/services_products/TowersPerrin/online.htm;* Hay, *www.haypaynet.com;* Radford's "Total Compensation Survey and Overall Practices Report," *www.radford.com/rbss/index. html;* Wyatt Watson, *www.watsonwyatt.com;* Mercer, *www.mercer.com;* or McLagan Partners executive compensation surveys at *www.mclagan.com.*

2. Donna Cavallini and Sabrina Pacifici, "Competitive Intelligence: A Selective Resource Guide," *www.llrx.com/features/ciguide.htm,* 2006; "Analyze This: The Evolution of Competitive Intelligence Products for the Legal Profession," *www.llrx.com/features /analyzethis.htm,* 2006.

3. Joseph R. Meisenheimer II, "Real Compensation, 1979 to 2003: Analysis from Several Data Sources," *Monthly Labor Review,* May 2005, pp. 3–22; *National Compensation Survey: Guide for Evaluating Your Firm's Jobs and Pay, www.bls.gov/ncs/ocs/sp /ncbr0004.pdf,* 2005.

4. Sara L. Rynes and G. T. Milkovich, "Wage Surveys: Dispelling Some Myths About the 'Market Wage,'" *Personnel Psychology,* Spring 1986, pp. 71–90; B. Gerhart and S. Rynes, *Compensation: Theory, Evidence, and Strategic Implications* (Thousand Oaks, CA: Sage, 2003).

5. Charlie Trevor and Mary E. Graham, "Deriving the Market Wage Derivatives: Three Decision Areas in the Compensation Survey Process," *WorldatWork Journal* 9(4), 2000, pp. 69–77; Brian Klaas and John A. McClendon, "To Lead, Lag, or Match: Estimating the Financial Impact of Pay Level Policies," *Personnel Psychology* 49 (1996), pp. 121–140.

6. F. Theodore Malm, "Recruiting Patterns and the Functioning of the Labor Markets," *Industrial and Labor Relations Review* 7 (1954), pp. 507–525; "Job Evaluation and Market Pricing Practices," *WorldatWork,* February 2009.

7. Andrew Klein, David G. Blanchflower, and Lisa M. Ruggiero, "Pay Differentials Hit Employees Where They Live," *Workspan,* June 2002, pp. 36–40; Stephen Ohlemacher, "Highest Wages in East, Lowest in South," U.S. Census Bureau, *www.census.gov/hhes /www/saipe/index.html,* 2005.

8. Charlie Trevor and Mary E. Graham, "Deriving the Market Wage Derivatives: Three Decision Areas in the Compensation Survey Process," *WorldatWork Journal* 9(4), 2000, pp. 69–77.

9. Barry Gerhart and George Milkovich, "Employee Compensation," in *Handbook of Industrial and Organizational Psychology,* 2d ed., M. D. Dunnette and L. M. Hough, eds. (Palo Alto, CA: Consulting Psychologists Press, 1992); B. Gerhart and S. Rynes, *Compensation: Theory, Evidence, and Strategic Implications* (Thousand Oaks, CA: Sage, 2003).

10. Beyond the U.S. consultants, international organizations also do surveys. See Income Data Services' website (*www.incomesdata.co.uk*). Also see William M. Mercer's "International Compensation Guidelines 2006" (information on 61 nations) or their European Total Rewards Survey 2006 at *www.mercerhr.com/totalrewardseurope;* Towers Perrin's "Global Surveys," and Organization Resource Counselors online survey for positions in countries ranging from Azerbaijan to Yugoslavia (*www.orcinc.com*). The Mercer and Towers Perrin website addresses are provided in footnote 1.

11. M. Bloom, G. Milkovich, and A. Mitra, "International Compensation: Learning from How Managers Respond to Variations in Local-Host Conditions," *International Journal of Human Resource Management,* December 2003, pp. 1350–1367.

12. Yoshio Yanadori, "Minimizing Competition? Entry-Level Compensation in Japanese Firms," *Asia Pacific Journal of Management* 21 (2004), pp. 445–467.

13. Daniel Vaughn-Whitehead, *Paying the Price: The Wage Crisis in Central and Eastern Europe* (Handmill Hampshire, UK: McMillin Press Ltd., 1998).

14. M. Bloom, G. Milkovich, and A. Mitra, "International Compensation: Learning from How Managers Respond to Variations in Local-Host Conditions," *International Journal of Human Resource Management,* December 2003, pp. 1350–1367.

15. Michael Wanderer, "Dot-Comp: A 'Traditional' Pay Plan with a Cutting Edge," *WorldatWork Journal,* Fourth Quarter 2000, pp. 15–24.

16. For consultants' websites, see footnotes 1 and 10 in this chapter. Also see WorldatWork's *2006–2007 Survey Handbook and Directory* (Scottsdale, AZ: WorldatWork, 2006).

17. See also R. J. Greene, "Compensation Surveys: The Rosetta Stones of Market Pricing," *WorldatWork Journal*, First Quarter 2014, pp. 23–31.

18. In response to a lawsuit, the Boston Survey Group agreed to publish only aggregated (rather than individual employee) information and not categorize information by industry. Eight hospitals in Utah made the mistake of exchanging information on their *intentions* to increase starting pay offers. They were charged with keeping entry-level wages for registered nurses in the Salt Lake City area artificially low. As part of the legal settlement, no health care facility in Utah can design, develop, or conduct a wage survey. They can respond in writing (only) to a written request for information for wage survey purposes from a third party, but only after the third party provides written assurance that the survey will be conducted with particular safeguards. *District of Utah U.S. District Court v. Utah Society for Healthcare Human Resources Administration, et al.,* 59 Fed. Reg. 14,203 (March 25, 1994). The resulting guidelines may buy legal protection, but they also give up control over the decisions that determine the quality and usefulness of the data. Prohibiting exchange of industry data eliminates the ability to make industry or product market comparisons. This might not be important in nursing or clerical jobs, but industry groups are important in comparisons among competitors.

19. Chockalingam Viswesvaran and Murray Barrick, "Decision-Making Effects on Compensation Surveys: Implications for Market Wages," *Journal of Applied Psychology* 77(5), 1992, pp. 588–597.

20. John A. Menefee, "The Value of Pay Data on the Web," *Workspan,* September 2000, pp. 25–28.

21. Charles Fishman, "The Anarchist's Cookbook," *Fast Company,* July 2004, Issue 84.

22. Some websites treat the federal government's Consumer Price Index as a measure of the cost of living in an area. It is not. The Consumer Price Index measures the rate of *change* in the cost of living in an area. So it can be used to compare how quickly prices are rising in one area versus another, but it cannot be used to compare living costs between two different areas.

23. "Job Evaluation and Market-Pricing Practices," *WorldatWork* report, February 2009.

24. Sara L. Rynes and G. T. Milkovich, "Wage Surveys: Dispelling Some Myths about the 'Market Wage,'" *Personnel Psychology,* Spring 1986, pp. 71–90; Frederic Cook, "Compensation Surveys Are Biased," *Compensation and Benefits Review,* September–October 1994, pp. 19–22.

25. Samir Raza, "Optimizing Human Capital Investments for Superior Shareholder Returns," *Valuation Issues* 2006 (*www.valuationissues.com*); M. Huselid and B. Becker, "Improving HR Analytical Literacy: Lessons from Moneyball," Chap. 32 in *The Future of Human Resource Management,* M. Losey, S. Meisinger, and D. Ulrich, eds. (Hoboken, NJ: Wiley, 2005); Lindsay Scott, "Managing Labor Costs Using Pay-for-Performance," *Lindsay Scott*

8 Associates, Inc., *www.npktools.com*, 2006; J. Fitzens, *How to Measure HRM* (New York: McGraw-Hill, 2002). Also see the website of the Saratoga Institute *www.pwcservices.com /saratoga-institute/default.htm* and *www.hudson-index.com/node.asp?SID=6755.*

26. Years-since-degree (YSD), or maturity curves, commonly used for scientists, are discussed in Chapter 14, Special Groups.

27. Donna Cavallini and Sabrina Pacifici, "Competitive Intelligence: A Selective Resource Guide," *www.llrx.com/features/ciguide.htm,* 2006; "Analyze This: The Evolution of Competitive Intelligence Products for the Legal Profession," *www.llrx.com/features /analyzethis.htm,* 2006. Additional information is available through the Sarasota Institute, *www.pwcservices.com/saratoga-institute/default.htm,* and the Society of HR Management, *www.shrm.org.*

28. Joseph R. Rich and Carol Caretta Phalen, "A Framework for the Design of Total Compensation Surveys," *ACA Journal,* Winter 1992–1993, pp. 18–29.

29. Letter from D. W. Belcher to G. T. Milkovich, in reference to D. W. Belcher, N. Bruce Ferris, and John O'Neill, "How Wage Surveys Are Being Used," *Compensation and Benefits Review,* September–October 1985, pp. 34–51.

30. Users of Milkovich and Gerhart's *Cases in Compensation,* edition 11.1e, will recognize the software company FastCat. The casebook offers the opportunity for hands-on experience. For more information, contact the authors at casesincompensation@gmail .com.

31. Margaret A. Coil, "Salary Surveys in a Blended-Role World," in *2003–2004 Survey Handbook and Directory* (Scottsdale, AZ: WorldatWork, 2002), pp. 57–64.

32. For an online tutorial in statistics, go to *www.robertniles.com;* for reading on the bus, try Larry Gonick and Woollcott Smith, *Cartoon Guide to Statistics* (New York: Harper Perennial, 1993); for the fun stuff, see e-Compensation 2 in this chapter.

33. J. K. Rowling, *Harry Potter and the Order of the Phoenix* (New York: Scholastic, 2003).

34. Brian Hinchcliffe, "Juggling Act: Internal Equity and Market Pricing," *Workspan,* February 2003, pp. 42–45.

35. An alternative formula for calculating minimum is midpoint/[100% 1 (1/2 range)] and for calculating maximum is minimum 11 (range 3 minimum). This approach gives a result different from that obtained by adding 20 percent above and below the midpoint. The important points are to be consistent in whatever approach you choose and to be sure other users of the survey are apprised of how range minimums and maximums are calculated.

36. Charles Fay, Eric Schulz, Steven Gross, and David VanDeVoort, "Broadbanding, Pay Ranges and Labor Costs," *WorldatWork Journal,* Second Quarter 2004, pp. 8–24; Gene Baker and Joe Duggan, "Global Banding Program and a Consultant's Critique," *WorldatWork Journal,* Second Quarter 2004, pp. 24–35; Kenan S. Abosch and Beverly Hmurovic, "A Traveler's Guide to Global Broadbanding," *ACA Journal,* Summer 1998, pp. 38–47.

37. "Life with Broadbands," ACA Research Project, 1998; "Broad Banding Case Study: General Electric," *WorldatWork Journal,* Third Quarter 2000, p. 43.

38. Kenan S. Abosch and Janice S. Hand, *Broadbanding Models* (Scottsdale, AZ: American Compensation Association, 1994); Charles Fay, Eric Schulz, Steven Gross, and David VanDeVoort, "Broadbanding, Pay Ranges and Labor Costs," *WorldatWork Journal,* Second Quarter 2004, pp. 8–24; Gene Baker and Joe Duggan, "Global Banding Program and a Consultant's Critique," *WorldatWork Journal,* Second Quarter 2004, pp. 24–35.

39. S. Rynes, C. Weber, and G. Milkovich, "Effects of Market Survey Rates on Job Evaluation, and Job Gender on Job Pay," *Journal of Applied Psychology* 74 (1989), pp. 114–123.

40. Howard Risher, "Second Generation Banded Salary Systems," *WorldatWork Journal* 16(1), 2007, p. 20.

41. *Market Pricing: Methods to the Madness* (Scottsdale, AZ: WorldatWork, 2002); "Job Evaluation and Market-Pricing Practices," *www.worldatwork.com,* accessed February 2009.

42. B. Gerhart and S. L. Rynes, *Compensation: Theory, Evidence, and Strategic Implications* (Thousand Oaks, CA: Sage, 2003); B. Gerhart, C. Trevor, and M. Graham, "New Directions in Employee Compensation Research," in G. R. Ferris, ed., *Research in Personnel and Human Resources Management* (Greenwich, CT: JAI Press, 1996), pp. 143–203.

43. Y. Yanadori and S.C. Kang, "Intra-firm Differentiation of Compensation Systems: Evidence from U.S. High-Technology Firms," *Human Resource Management Journal* 21 (2011), pp. 236–257.

44. Jeffrey Pfeffer and Alison Davis-Blake, "Understanding Organizational Wage Structures: A Resource Dependence Approach," *Academy of Management Journal* 30 (1987), pp. 437–455.

45. Mason Carpenter and James Wade, "Micro-Level Opportunity Structures as Determinants of Non-CEO Executive Pay," *Academy of Management Journal* 45 (2002), pp. 1085–1103.

46. Amir Efrati and Pui-Wing Tam, "Google Battles to Keep Talent," *The Wall Street Journal,* November 10, 2010.

47. Ibid.

48. Rolfe Winkler, "The High Cost of Googling Growth," *The Wall Street Journal,* October 15, 2011. B16.

49. "David Goldman. Google's Fight to Keep its Top Minds," *CNNMoney.com*, November 10, 2010.

50. "Claire Cain Miller and Jenna Wortham. Silicon Valley Hiring Perks: Meals, iPads and a Cubicle for Spot," *New York Times,* March 26, 2011.

51. Andrew Ross Sorkin, "Google Reprices 7.6 Million Employee Stock Options," *The New York Times,* March 11, 2009; Martin Peers, "Searching Google for Pay," *The Wall Street Journal,* November 11, 2010.

52. Rolfe Winkler, "The High Cost of Googling Growth," *The Wall Street Journal,* October 15, 2011. B16.

Employee Contributions: Determining Individual Pay

The first two sections of the pay model outlined in **Exhibit IV.1** essentially deal with fairness. Alignment, covered in Part Two, is all about internal fairness: describing jobs and determining their worth relative to each other based on content of the jobs and impact on the organization's objectives. Part Three extended fairness to the external market. It's not enough that jobs within a company are treated fairly in comparison to each other; we also need to look at external competitiveness with similar jobs in other companies. This raises questions of conducting salary surveys, setting pay policies, and arriving at competitive pay levels and equitable pay structures. This fourth part of the book finally brings people into the pay equation. How do we design a pay system so that individual contributors are rewarded according to their value to the organization? Let's hope the following example isn't a role model for today's practices:

> Another 4th dynasty tomb, beautifully carved and painted with vibrantly colored scenes, belonging to a priest of the royal cult and senior scribe named Kay. A fascinating glimpse into an ancient economic exchange is offered by the inscription at the entrance to this tomb, which reads: It is the tomb makers, the draftsmen, the craftsmen, and the sculptors who made my tomb. I paid them in bread and beer and made them take an oath that they were satisfied.
>
> ———Zahi Hawass, *Mountains of the Pharaohs: The Untold Story of the Pyramid Builders* (Cairo: American University in Cairo Press, 2006, p. 136)

How much should one employee be paid relative to another when they both hold the same jobs in the same organization? If this question is not answered satisfactorily, all prior efforts to evaluate and price jobs may have been in vain. For example, the compensation manager determines that all customer service representatives (CSRs) should be paid between $28,000 and $43,000.

EXHIBIT IV.1 **The Pay Model**

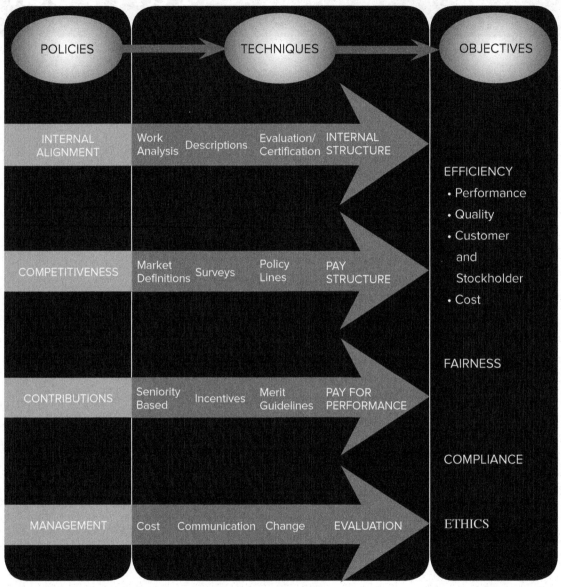

But where in that range is each individual paid? Should a good CSR be paid more than a poor one? If the answer is yes, how should performance be measured and what should be the differential reward? Similarly, should the CSR with more years of experience (i.e., higher seniority) be paid more than one with less time on the job? Again, if the answer is yes, what is the tradeoff between seniority and performance in assigning pay raises? Should Wesley, the compensation manager's son-in-law, be paid more just because he is family? What are the legitimate factors to consider in the reward equation? As Exhibit IV.1 suggests, all of these questions involve the concept of employee contribution. For the next three chapters, we will be discussing different facets of employee contribution.

Chapter 9 asks whether companies should invest in pay-for-performance plans. In other words, does paying for performance result in higher performance? The answer may seem obvious, but there are many ways to complicate this elegant notion.

Chapter 10 looks at actual pay-for-performance plans. The compensation arena is full of programs that promise to link pay and performance. We identify these plans and discuss their relative advantages and disadvantages.

Chapter 11 acknowledges that performance can't always be measured objectively. What do we do to ensure that subjective appraisal procedures are as free from error as possible? Much progress has been made here, and we provide a tour of the different strategies for measuring performance.

Pay-for-Performance: The Evidence

The primary focus of Part Three was on determining the worth of jobs, independent of who performed those jobs. **Job analysis, job evaluation,** and **job pricing** all have a common theme. They are techniques to identify the value a firm places on its jobs. Now we introduce people into the equation. Now we declare that different people performing the same job may add different value to the organization. Wesley is a better programmer than Kelly. Erinn knows more programming languages than Ian. Who should get what?

If you stop and think about it, employment is about a contract. When you accept a job you agree to perform work—complete tasks—in exchange for rewards. Sometimes this contract is simple. You agree to cut your neighbor's grass for 15 dollars. When you're done she pays you the money. As we grow up the contracts become more complex. Your first job after college will involve a contract, although the terms of that contract won't be spelled out fully. You will sign an agreement to perform tasks to the satisfaction of your employer. Rarely are the "satisfaction" terms clearly defined upfront. You hope you'll get feedback along the way that helps make the performance standards more apparent. In exchange, the contract reads, you will receive a certain amount of pay. Let's hope it's a big number, after all you had to suffer through reading this book in preparation for the big job. That should be worth quite a bit right there! But you might be a bit disappointed in the rest of the contract because it's rare that any other rewards besides money will be mentioned at all. You take it on faith that the employer will do right by you beyond just the monetary component of the job.

At the extreme of employment contracts are those between an employer and a union representing workers (Chapter 15). Unionized employees aren't willing to take it on faith that the employer will provide fair compensation for work performed. Some union contracts are hundreds of pages long and specify in the tiniest detail what a worker will get as rewards under different work conditions.

Whether the employment contract is simple or complex, though, we still struggle with both sides of the agreement. How do we decide if a worker is performing the job satisfactorily and how much should we pay for that performance?

Entering people into the compensation equation greatly complicates the compensation process. People don't behave like robots. Believe us, the auto industry has tried replacing people with robots. On some jobs, like welding car parts together, robots work just fine. You can tighten a bolt and oil a joint. But for most jobs it's easier and cheaper to do things the old-fashioned way—with people. And designing a performance and reward system so people support what the company is trying to accomplish, well, that's the challenge. Indeed, there is growing evidence that the way we design HR practices, like performance management, strongly affects the way employees perceive the company. Well-known organizations like the Container store and Costco both pay more and have more sophisticated performance tracking methods that lead to happier employees.[1] And this directly affects corporate performance.[2] The simple (or not so simple, as we will discuss) process of implementing a performance appraisal system that employees find acceptable goes a long way toward increasing trust for top management.[3] And that new performance appraisal and reward system has an impact on other parts of HR. The pool of people we recruit and select from changes as our HR system changes. In Chapter 2, we talked about sorting effects. Not everyone "appreciates" an incentive system or even a merit-based pay system. People who prefer less performance-based pay systems will "sort themselves" out of organizations with these pay practices and philosophies. Either they won't respond to recruitment ads, or, if already employed, may go so far as to seek employment elsewhere.[4] So as we discuss pay and performance in Chapters 9 to 11, remember that there are other important outcomes that also depend on building good performance measurement tools.

In Chapter 1, we talked about compensation objectives complementing overall human resource objectives and both of these helping an organization achieve its overall strategic objectives. But this begs the question, "How does an organization achieve its overall strategic objectives?" In this part of the book, we argue that organizational success ultimately depends on human behavior. Why did the San Francisco Giants do so well in 2014? Madison Bumgarner had a spectacular regular season followed by a better World Series pitching performance. That's behavior in its simplest and purest form! Our compensation decisions and practices should be designed to increase the likelihood that employees will behave in ways that help the organization achieve its strategic objectives. This chapter is organized around employee behaviors. First, we identify the four kinds of behaviors organizations are interested in. Then we note what theories say about our ability to motivate these behaviors. And, finally, we talk about our success, and sometimes lack thereof, in designing compensation systems to elicit these behaviors.

WHAT BEHAVIORS DO EMPLOYERS CARE ABOUT? LINKING ORGANIZATION STRATEGY TO COMPENSATION AND PERFORMANCE MANAGEMENT

The simple answer is that employers want employees to perform in ways that lead to better organizational performance. Exhibit 9.1 shows how organizational strategy is the guiding force that determines what kinds of employee behaviors are needed.

As an illustration, Nordstrom's department stores are known for extremely good quality merchandise and high levels of customer satisfaction—this is the organization strategy they use to differentiate themselves from competitors. Nordstrom's success isn't a fluke. You can bet that some of their corporate goals, strategic business unit goals (SBU goals, where a strategic business unit might be a store), department-level goals, and indeed individual employee goals are linked to pleasing customers and selling high-quality products. The job of Human Resources is to devise policies and practices (and compensation falls in this mix) that lead employees (the last box in Exhibit 9.1) to behave in ways that ultimately support corporate goals. Walk into a Nordstrom, you see employees politely greeting you, helping without suffocating, and generally making the shopping experience a pleasant one. These are behaviors that support Nordstrom's strategic plan. Every organization, whether they realize it or not, has human resource practices that can either work together or conflict with each other in trying to generate positive employee behaviors. One way of looking at this process is evident from Exhibit 9.2.

Let's use an example from the classroom. You have to make a presentation tomorrow. Twenty percent of your grade depends on it (the reward). Do you have the ability? Can you speak clearly, be interesting, and send a good message? Are you motivated? Maybe this class isn't important to you? Maybe the finale of "Walking Dead" is on TV and you're hooked on good Zombie shows? And is the environment right? One of the authors was making a presentation a few years ago in

EXHIBIT 9.1 The Cascading Link Between Organization Strategy and Employee Behavior

Indonesia and an earthquake hit. Kind of ruined the speech! Wanting to succeed isn't enough. Having the ability but not the motivation also isn't enough. Many a player with lots of talent doesn't have the motivation to endure thousands of hours of repetitive drills, or to endure weight training and general physical conditioning. Even with both ability and motivation, a player's work environment (both physical and political) must be free of obstacles. A home run hitter drafted by a team with an enormous ball park (home run fences set back much farther from home plate) might never reach his full potential. The same thing is true in more traditional jobs. Success depends on finding people with ability—that's the primary job of recruitment, selection, and training. Once good people are hired, they need to be motivated to behave in ways that help the organization. (Note, part of selection is also to hire motivated people, so the triangles interact with each other, as denoted by the three-pronged arrow in the center of Exhibit 9.2.) This is where compensation enters the picture. Pay and other rewards should reinforce desired behaviors. But so, too, should performance management, by making sure that what is expected of employees, and what is measured in regular performance reviews, is consistent with what the compensation practices are doing. And perhaps most important of all, the culture of the organization (i.e., the informal rules and expectations that are evident in any company) should point in the same direction. Finally, HR needs to establish policies and practices that minimize the chances that outside "distractors" hinder performance.

In the 1980s, Nabisco was slow to recognize customer demand for "soft batch" cookies. Why? They had a centralized organization structure that took a long time to get sales information up to the top decision makers. No matter how much ability or

EXHIBIT 9.2
The Big Picture or Compensation Can't Do It Alone!

Behavior = $f(M, A, E)$ where M = Motivation
A = Ability
E = Environment

Selection

Ability triangle

Recruitment   Training

Performance Management   Organizational Design

Motivation Triangle   Environmental Obstacle Triangle

Compensation   Culture   Org. Development   HR Planning

Environmental Obstacles:
Unions, Economic Conditions, Public Policy/Legislation

motivation the sales staff has, it's hard to sell cookies the public doesn't want. What did Nabisco do? They decentralized (organization design) the company, creating divisions responsible for different product lines. Now when sales people say consumer preferences are changing, response is much more rapid. Similarly, if we don't recognize changing **skill requirements** (human resource planning), it's hard to set up revised training programs or develop compensation packages to reward these new skills instantly. Knowing in advance about needed changes makes timely completion easier. As a further illustration, if we have inefficient processes (e.g., too many steps in getting approval for change), organization development (process to change the way a company operates) can free up motivated workers to use their skills.

The key lesson from Exhibit 9.2 is an important one: Compensation can't do it all alone. Try changing behavior by developing a compensation system to reward that behavior. If you haven't selected the right people, if they don't have the necessary training, if you aren't measuring performance, and if it's not part of the culture to do things that way, you're destined for failure. When you're out working in HR, and your boss asks you to "fix" something (e.g., pay, performance appraisal), make sure the change fits with what other programs are trying to do. Otherwise trouble lurks.

So, what behaviors does compensation need to reinforce? First, our compensation should be sufficiently attractive to make recruiting and hiring good potential employees possible (attraction).[5] Second, we need to make sure the good employees stay with the company (retention). The recession of 2008–2010, that still has a lingering impact today, severely tested companies' layoff strategy. Losing money? Layoff workers! But sometimes laying off workers means cutting future stars. Some wiser companies kept costs down by cutting salaries temporarily. Caterpillar, FedEx, Black and Decker, *The New York Times,* and the State of Pennsylvania all decided to trim salaries rather than resort to layoffs.[6] If we can succeed at these first two things, we can then concentrate on building further knowledge and skills (develop skills). And, finally, we need to find ways to motivate employees to perform well on their jobs—to take their knowledge and abilities and apply them in ways that contribute to organizational performance.

For example, whether we've developed a sound compensation package can only be determined by the impact on performance. We can't tell if our compensation system helps recruit and select good employees if we don't know how to measure what constitutes *good.* We can't tell if employees are building the kinds of knowledge base they need if we can't measure knowledge accumulation. We can't reward performance if we can't measure it! As a simple example, think about companies where piece-rate systems are used to pay people. Recently, one of the authors went to a saw mill, looking for wood to build a dining room table. Talks with the manager revealed they used a simple piece-rate system to motivate workers. For every board foot of lumber cut using giant saws, workers were paid a fixed amount. There is little ambiguity in this measure of performance, and this makes it easy to create a strong link between units of performance and amount of compensation. One of the biggest recent advances in compensation strategy has been to document and extend this link between ease of measuring performance and the type of compensation system that works best.

EXHIBIT 9.3 Performance Measurement Relationship to Compensation Strategy

		Variability in Corporate Performance	
		Low Variability	High Variability
Variability and ability to measure individual performance	Unstable and unclear performance measures	Situation A Provide a wide array of awards beyond just money. Include significant incentive component.	Situation B Provide a wide array of awards beyond just money. Emphasize base pay with low-incentive portion.
	Stable and clear performance measures	Situation C Emphasize monetary rewards with large-incentive component.	Situation D Emphasize monetary rewards: large base pay with low-incentive portion.

Let's take a minute to talk about each of the cells in Exhibit 9.3. They help explain why incentives work in some situations and not in others.[7] The columns in Exhibit 9.3 divide companies into those with widely variable performance from year to year and those with much more stable performance across time. What might cause wide swings in corporate performance? Often this occurs when something in the corporation's external environment (we call these environmental obstacles in Exhibit 9.2) fluctuates widely. A perfect example is gas prices today. Airlines are reporting record profits, not because they've done anything particularly well, but rather because they can get airline fuel that costs far less than even a year ago.[8] It probably wouldn't be fair, and employees would certainly object, if a large part of pay were incentive-based in this kind of environment. Lack of employee control translates into perceptions of unfair treatment if pay is tied to these uncontrollable things. Situations B and D both suggest that a low-incentive component is appropriate in organizations with highly variable annual performance. Conversely, as situations A and C indicate, larger-incentive components are appropriate in companies with stable annual performance.

The rows in Exhibit 9.3 note that individual employee performance also can vary. Some jobs are fairly stable, with expectations fairly consistent across time. What I do today is basically the same thing I did yesterday. And tomorrow looks like a repeat too! In other jobs, though, there might be high fluctuation in the kinds of things expected of employees, and employees willing to be flexible and adjust to changing demand are much in demand for these jobs. Here, using incentive pay exclusively might not work. Incentive systems are notorious for getting people to do exactly what is being incentivized. Pay me big money to sell suits, and that's just what I'm going to do. You want me to handle customer returns, too? No way, not unless the compensation system rewards a broader array of duties. Evidence suggests that companies are best able to get employees to adjust, be flexible, and show commitment when a broader array of rewards, rather than just money, is part of the compensation package.[9] For example, why does Lincoln Electric (a major producer of welding machines) out-produce other companies in the same industry year after year? Normally we think it's because the company has a well-designed incentive system that links to level of production. Certainly this is a big factor! But when you talk to people at Lincoln Electric, they suggest that part of the success comes from other forms of reward, including the strong commitment to job security—downsizing simply isn't part of the vocabulary there—that reinforces a willingness to try new technologies and new work processes (a culture that supports innovation). Situation A, with low variability in corporate performance but unclear performance measures for employees, describes the kind of reward package that fits these job and organizational performance characteristics.

When we distill all of this, what can we conclude? We think the answer depends on how we respond to the following four questions:

1. How do we attract good employment prospects to *join* our company?
2. How do we *retain* these good employees once they join?
3. How do we get employees to *develop skills* for current and future jobs?
4. How do we get employees to *perform well* while they are here?

First, how do we get good people to join our company? How did Nike get Lebron James to serve as a corporate spokesperson? Part of the answer is cold hard cash—90 million dollars guaranteed before Lebron had even played his first NBA game. But it isn't always just about the money. Lebron asked for and got artistic input on the products designed by Nike.[10] Even when the decision doesn't involve millions of dollars, the long-run success of any company depends on getting good people to accept employment. One particularly good study of this very question found that job characteristics (including rewards and tasks/abilities required) and recruiter behaviors were key elements in the decision to join a company.[11]

Second, the obvious complement to the decision to join is the decision to stay. How do we retain employees? It doesn't do much good to attract exceptional employees to our company only to lose them a short time later. Once our compensation practices get a good employee in the door, we need to figure out ways to ensure it's not a revolving door. Max Scherzer left the Detroit Tigers, a perennial pick for a Division title, to play with the Washington Nationals. Was it the $210,000,000 contract, including a $50,000,000 signing bonus, and an annual average salary of $30,000,000. Or was it because the Washington Nationals are favored to win the World Series? What does it take to retain key people? Money?[12] Or are other rewards important? And does their absence lead us to use money as the great neutralizer?

Third, we also must recognize that what we need employees to do today may change. Literally, overnight! A fast-changing world requires employees who can adjust more quickly. How do we get employees, traditionally resistant to change, to willingly develop skills that may not be vital on the current job but are forecast to be critical in the future. Another compensation challenge!

Finally, we want employees to do well on their current jobs. This means performing—and performing well—tasks that support our strategic objectives. What motivates employees to succeed? The compensation challenge is to design rewards that enhance job performance.

WHAT DOES IT TAKE TO GET THESE BEHAVIORS? WHAT THEORY SAYS

Another way of phrasing these same questions is to ask, "What motivates employees?" For example, we know that people differ in the importance they attribute to money. We all know someone who just isn't motivated by the almighty dollar. But even for these people, it's possible to design a pay system that is appreciated—one in which the effort-pay link is evident. The point is we can't even assume that money is everyone's prime motivator. Is it any wonder, then, that figuring out the motivation equation is a major pastime for compensation experts?[13] In the simplest sense, *motivation* involves three elements: (1) what's important to a person, and (2) offering it in exchange for some (3) desired behavior. As to the first element, what's important to employees, data suggest employees prefer pay systems that are influenced by individual performance, changes in cost of living, seniority, and the market rate, to name the most important factors.[14] To narrow down specific employee preferences, though, there has been some work on what's called **flexible compensation.** Flexible compensation is based on the idea that only the individual employee knows what package of rewards would best suit personal needs. Employees who hate risk could opt for more base pay and less incentive pay. Tradeoffs between pay and benefits could also be selected. The key ingredient in this new concept is careful cost analysis to make sure the dollar cost of the package an employee selects meets employer budgetary limits.[15] Absent widespread adoption of flexible compensation systems, we need to answer these three questions the old-fashioned way—by going back to theories of motivation to see what "makes people tick."

In Exhibit 9.4 we briefly summarize some of the important motivation theories.[16] These theories try to answer the three questions we posed above: what's important, how do we offer it, and how does it help deliver desired behaviors. Pay particular attention to the "So What?" column, in which we talk about the ways theory suggests employee behavior is delivered.

Some of the theories in Exhibit 9.4 focus on content—identifying what is important to people. Maslow's and Herzberg's theories, for example, both fall in this category. People have certain needs, such as physiological, security, and self-esteem, that influence behavior. Although neither theory is clear on how these needs are offered and how they help deliver behavior, presumably if we offer rewards that satisfy one or more needs, employees will behave in desired ways. These theories often drive compensation decisions about the breadth and depth of compensation offerings. Flexible compensation, with employees choosing from a menu of pay and benefit choices, clearly is driven by the issue of needs. Who best knows what satisfies needs? The employee! So let employees choose, within limits, what they want in their reward package.

A second set of theories, best exemplified by expectancy theory, equity theory, and agency theory, focus less on need states and more on the second element of motivation—companies provide rewards in exchange for desired employee behaviors.[17] Many of our compensation practices recognize the importance of a fair exchange. We evaluate jobs using a common set of compensable factors (Chapter 5) in part to let employees know that an explicit set of rules governs the evaluation process. We collect salary survey data

EXHIBIT 9.4 Motivation Theories

Theory	Essential Features	Predictions About Performance-Based Pay	So What?
Maslow's need hierarchy	People are motivated by inner needs. Needs form a hierarchy from most basic (food and shelter) to higher-order (e.g., self-esteem, love, self-actualization). Needs are never fully met; they operate cyclically. Higher-order needs become motivating after lower-order needs have been met. When needs are not met, they become frustrating.	1. Base pay must be set high enough to provide individuals with the economic means to meet their basic living needs. 2. An at-risk program will not be motivating since it restricts employees' ability to meet lower-order needs. 3. Success-sharing plans may be motivating to the extent they help employees pursue higher-order needs.	A. Performance-based pay may be demotivating if it impinges upon employees' capacity to meet daily living needs. B. Incentive pay is motivating to the extent it is attached to achievement, recognition, or approval.
Herzberg's two-factor theory	Employees are motivated by two types of motivators: hygiene factors and satisfiers. Hygiene, or maintenance, factors in their absence prevent behaviors, but in their presence cannot motivate performance. They are related to basic living needs, security, and fair treatment. Satisfiers, such as recognition, promotion, and achievement, motivate performance.	1. Base pay must be set high enough to provide individuals with the economic means to meet hygiene needs, but it cannot motivate performance. 2. Performance is obtained through rewards—payments in excess of that required to meet basic needs. 3. Performance-based pay is motivating to the extent it is connected with meeting employees' needs for recognition, pleasure attainment, achievement, and the like. 4. Other factors such as interpersonal atmosphere, responsibility, type of work, and working conditions influence the efficacy of performance-based pay.	A. Pay level is important—must meet minimum requirements before performance-based pay can operate as motivator. B. Security plans will induce minimum, but not extra, performance. Success-sharing plans will be motivating. At-risk plans will be demotivating. C. Other conditions in the working relationship influence the effectiveness of performance-based pay.

Expectancy	Motivation is the product of three perceptions: expectancy, instrumentality, and valence. **Expectancy** is employees' assessment of their ability to perform required job tasks. **Instrumentality** is employees' beliefs that requisite job performance will be rewarded by the organization. **Valence** is the value employees attach to the organization rewards offered for satisfactory job performance.	1. Job tasks and responsibilities should be clearly defined. 2. The pay-performance link is critical. 3. Performance-based pay returns must be large enough to be seen as rewards. 4. People choose the behavior that leads to the greatest reward.	A. Larger incentive payments are better than smaller ones. B. Line of sight is critical—employees must believe they can influence performance targets. C. Employee assessments of their own ability are important—organizations should be aware of training and resource needs required to perform at target levels.
Equity	Employees are motivated when perceived outputs (i.e., pay) are equal to perceived inputs (e.g., effort, work behaviors). A disequilibrium in the output-to-input balance causes discomfort. If employees perceive that others are paid more for the same effort, they will react negatively (e.g., shirk) to correct the output-to-input balance.	1. The pay-performance link is critical; increases in performance must be matched by commensurate increases in pay. 2. Performance inputs and expected outputs must be clearly defined and identified. 3. Employees evaluate the adequacy of their pay via comparisons with other employees.	A. Performance measures must be clearly defined, and employees must be able to affect them through work behaviors. B. If payouts do not match expectations, employees will react negatively. C. Fairness and consistency of performance-based pay across employees in an organization is important. D. Since employees evaluate their pay-effort balance in comparison to other employees, relative pay matters.

(Continued)

EXHIBIT 9.4 *(Continued)*

Theory	Essential Features	Predictions about Performance-Based Pay	So What?
Reinforcement	Rewards reinforce (i.e., motivate and sustain) performance. Rewards must follow directly after behaviors to be reinforcing. Behaviors that are not rewarded will be discontinued.	1. Performance-based payments must follow closely behind performance. 2. Rewards must be tightly coupled to desired performance objectives. 3. Withholding payouts can be a way to discourage unwanted behaviors.	A. Timing of payouts is very important.
Goal setting	Challenging performance goals influence greater intensity and duration in employee performance. Goals serve as feedback standards to which employees can compare their performance. Individuals are motivated to the extent that goal achievement is combined with receiving valued rewards.	1. Performance-based pay must be contingent upon achievement of important performance goals. 2. Performance goals should be challenging and specific. 3. The amount of the incentive reward should match the goal difficulty.	A. Line-of-sight is important; employees must believe they can influence performance targets. B. Performance targets should be communicated in terms of specific, difficult goals. C. Feedback about performance is important. D. Performance-based payouts should be contingent upon goal achievement.
Agency	Pay directs and motivates employee performance. Employees prefer static wages (e.g., a salary) to performance-based pay. If performance can be accurately monitored, payments should be based upon satisfactory completion of work duties. If performance cannot be monitored, pay should be aligned with achieving organizational objectives.	1. Performance-based pay must be tightly linked to organizational objectives. 2. Employees dislike risky pay and will demand a wage premium (e.g., higher total pay) in exchange for accepting performance-based pay. 3. Performance-based pay can be used to direct and induce employee performance.	A. Performance-based pay is the optimal compensation choice for more complex jobs where monitoring employees' work is difficult. B. Performance targets should be tied to organizational goals. C. Use of performance-based pay will require higher total pay opportunity.

(Chapter 8) because we want the exchange to be fair compared to external standards. We design incentive systems (Chapter 10) to align employee behavior with the needs (desired behaviors) of the organization. All of these pay decisions, and more, owe much to understanding how the employment exchange affects employee motivation.

Expectancy theory argues that people behave as if they cognitively evaluate what behaviors are possible (e.g., the probability that they can complete the task) in relation to the value of rewards offered in exchange. According to this theory, we choose behaviors that yield the most satisfactory exchange. Equity theory also focuses on what goes on inside an employee's head. Not surprisingly, equity theory argues that people are highly concerned about equity, or fairness of the exchange process. Employees look at the exchange as a ratio between what is expected and what is received. Some theorists say we judge transactions as fair when others around us don't have a more (or less) favorable balance between the give and get of an exchange.[18] Even greater focus on the exchange process occurs in the last of this second set of theories, agency theory.[19] Here, employees are depicted as agents who enter an exchange with principals—the owners or their designated managers. It is assumed that both sides to the exchange seek the most favorable exchange possible and will act opportunistically if given a chance (e.g., try to "get by" with doing as little as possible to satisfy the contract). Compensation is a major element in this theory, because it is used to keep employees in line: Employers identify important behaviors and important outcomes and pay specifically for achieving desired levels of each. Such incentive systems penalize employees who try to shirk their duties by giving proportionately lower rewards.

At least one of the theories summarized in Exhibit 9.4 focuses on the third element of motivation: desired behavior. Identifying desired behaviors—and goals expected to flow from these behaviors—is the emphasis of a large body of goal-setting research. Most of this research says that how we set goals (the process of goal setting, the level and difficulty of goals, etc.) can influence the performance levels of employees.[20] For example, workers assigned "hard" goals consistently do better than workers told to "do your best."[21]

A final theory purports to integrate motivation theories under a broad umbrella. Called self-determination theory (SDT), this approach believes that employees are motivated not only by reward systems and pay grades, examples of extrinsic motivators, but also by intrinsic motivators. Anything that promotes our sense of autonomy, competence, and relatedness is believed to generate the highest quality motivation and level of engagement.[22]

WHAT DOES IT TAKE TO GET THESE BEHAVIORS? WHAT PRACTITIONERS SAY

In the past, compensation people didn't ask this question very often. Employees learned what behaviors were important as part of the socialization process or as part of the performance management process.[23] If it was part of the culture to work long hours, you quickly learned this. One of our daughters worked as a business consultant for Accenture, a very large consulting company. She learned quickly that 70 to 80 hour work weeks were fairly common. Sure, she had very good wages for someone with a bachelor's degree in biology and no prior business experience, but it didn't take long to burn out when weeks of long hours turned into months. If your performance appraisal at the end of the year stressed certain types of behaviors, or if your boss said certain things were important to her, then the signals were pretty clear: Do these things! Compensation might have rewarded people for meeting these expectations, but usually the compensation package wasn't designed to be one of the signals about expected performance. Not true today![24] Now compensation people talk about pay in terms of a neon arrow flashing "Do these things." Progressive companies ask, "What do we want our compensation package to do? How, for example, do we get our product engineers to take more risks?" Compensation is then designed to support this risk-taking behavior. Compensation people will also tell you, though, that money isn't everything.

e-Compensation
The International Society for Performance Improvement has web information on performance journals, strategies for improving performance, and conferences covering the latest research on performance improvement techniques. Go to the society's website, *www.ispi.org*.

In fact, compensation is but one of many rewards that influence employee behavior. Sometimes this important point is missed by compensation experts. Going back at least to Henry Ford, we tend to look at money as the great equalizer. Job boring? No room for advancement? Throw money at the problem! Depending on the survey you consult, workers highly value such other job rewards as empowerment, recognition, and opportunities for advancement.[25] Entire books, for example, illustrate hundreds of ways to give meaningful recognition to employees.[26] And there is growing sentiment for letting workers choose their own "blend" of rewards from the 13 we note in Exhibit 9.5. We may be overpaying in cash *and* missing the opportunity to let employees construct both a more satisfying and less-expensive reward package. Known as flexible compensation, this idea introduced earlier is based on the notion of different rewards having different dollar costs associated with them. Armed with a fixed sum of

EXHIBIT 9.5 **Components of a Total Reward System**

1. Compensation	Wages, commissions, and bonuses
2. Benefits	Vacations, health insurance
3. Social interaction	Friendly workplace
4. Security	Stable, consistent position and rewards
5. Status/recognition	Respect, prominence due to work
6. Work variety	Opportunity to experience different things
7. Workload	Right amount of work (not too much, not too little)
8. Work importance	Work is valued by society
9. Authority/control/autonomy	Ability to influence others; control own destiny
10. Advancement	Chance to get ahead
11. Feedback	Receive information helping to improve performance
12. Work conditions	Hazard free
13. Development opportunity	Formal and informal training to learn new knowledge skills/abilities

money, employees move down the line, buying more or less of the 13 rewards as their needs dictate.[27] While widespread use of this type of system may be a long time in the future, the cafeteria approach still underscores the need for integration of rewards in compensation design.

If we don't think about the presence or absence of rewards other than money in an organization, we may find the compensation process producing unintended consequences. Consider the following three examples, which show how compensation decisions have to be integrated with total reward system decisions:

Example 1: McDonald's recently completed a worldwide "employment branding" exercise. Their goal was to find out what people liked about jobs at McDonald's and feature these rewards in the recruitment strategy for new employees. Three things emerged as strengths at McDonald's: (1) an emphasis on family and friends in a social work environment; (2) flexibility in work assignments and work schedules; and (3) development of skills that helped launch future careers.[28]

Example 2: This example comes from airline industry leader Southwest Airlines.[29] Southwest Airlines promotes a business culture of fun and encourages employees to find ways to make their jobs more interesting and relevant to them personally. All this is accomplished without using incentives as a major source of competitive advantage. Indeed, pay at Southwest isn't any higher than for competitor airlines, yet it's much easier to recruit top people there. Fun, a good social environment, is a reward!

Example 3: Consider the relationship between the different forms of compensation and another of the general rewards listed in Exhibit 9.5: security. Normally, we think of security in terms of job security. Drastic reductions in middle-management layers during the downsizing decade of the 1980s increased employee concerns about job security and probably elevated the importance of this reward to employees today. Maybe that's why new millenial workers are concerned not only about employment risk but also about compensation at risk. There is evidence that compensation at risk (pay based on incentives rather than base pay that is secure) leaves many employees less satisfied both with their pay level and with the process used to determine pay.[30] Security as an issue, it appears, is creeping into the domain of compensation. It used to be fairly well established that employees would make more this year than they did last year, and employees counted on such *security* to plan their purchases and other economic decisions. The trend today is toward less stable and less secure compensation packages. The very design of compensation systems today contributes to instability and insecurity. And that in turn leads some potential employees to reject a firm or some current employees to decide it's time to leave. Exhibit 9.6 outlines the different types of wage components.

Notice that Exhibit 9.6 generally orders compensation components from least risky to most risky for employees. We define risky in terms of stability of income or the ability to accurately predict income level from year to year. Base pay is, at least as far as there are any guarantees, the guaranteed portion of income, as long as employees remain employed. There have been very few years since the Depression when base wages did not rise or at least stay the same.[31] Across the board increases, cost-of-living increases, and merit increases all help the base pay component increase on a regular basis. Of course,

EXHIBIT 9.6 Wage Components

Wage Component	Definition	Level of Risk to Employee
Base pay	The guaranteed portion of an employee's wage package.	As long as employment continues, this is the secure portion of wages.
Across-the-board increase	Wage increase granted to all employees, regardless of performance. Size related to some subjective assessment of employer about ability to pay. Typically an add-on to base pay in subsequent years.	Some risk to employee since at discretion of employer. But not tied to performance differences, so risk lower in that respect.
Cost-of-living increase	Same as across-the-board increase, except magnitude based on change in cost of living (e.g., as measured by the Consumer Price Index [CPI]).	Same as-across-the-board increases.
Merit pay	Wage increase granted to employee as function of some assessment of employee performance. Adds on to base pay in subsequent years.	Two types of risk faced by employees. Size of total merit pool at discretion of employer (risk element), and individual portion of pool depends on performance, which also is not totally predictable.
Merit bonused (aka lump sum bonus)	As with merit pay, granted for individual performance. Does not add into base pay, but is distributed as a one-time bonus.	Three types of risks faced here. Both types mentioned under merit pay, plus not added into base—requires annually "re-earning" the added pay.
Individual incentive	Sometimes this variable pay is an add-on to a fixed base pay. The incentive component ties increments in compensation directly to extra individual production (e.g., commission systems, piece rate). While measures of performance are typically subjective with merit and lump-sum components, this form of variable pay differs because measures of performance are objective (e.g., sales volume).	Most risk compensation component if sole element of pay, but often combined with a base pay. No or low fixed-base pay means each year employee is dependent upon number of units of performance to determine pay.
Success-sharing plans	A generic category of pay add-on (variable pay) which is tied to some measure of group performance, not individual performance. Not added into base pay. Distinguished from risk-sharing plans, below, because employees share in any success—performance above standard—but are not penalized for performance below standard.	All success-sharing plans have risks noted in above pay components plus the risk associated with group performance measures. Now individual worker is also dependent upon the performance of others included in the group.

EXHIBIT 9.6   *(Continued)*

Wage Component	Definition	Level of Risk to Employee
• Profit sharing	Add-on linked to group performance (team, division, total company) relative to exceeding some financial goal.	Profit measures are influenced by factors beyond employee control (e.g., economic climate, accounting write-offs). Less control means more risk.
• Gain sharing	Differs from profit sharing in that goal to exceed is not financial performance of organization but some cost index (e.g., labor cost is most common, might also include scrap costs, utility costs).	Less risk to individual than profit sharing because performance measure is more controllable.
Risk sharing plans	Generic category of pay add-on (variable pay) that differs from success sharing in that employee not only shares in the successes but also is penalized during poor performance years. Penalty is in the form of lower total compensation in poor corporate performance years. Reward, though, is typically higher than that for success-sharing programs in high performance years.	Greater risk than success-sharing plans. Typically, employees absorb a "temporary" cut in base pay. If performance targets are met, this cut is neutralized by one component of variable pay. Risk to employee is increased though because even base pay is no longer totally predictable.

there always has to be an exception to the rule—and the Great Recession of 2008–2010 spawned many corporate base wage cuts. The next seven components are distinguished by increasing levels of uncertainty for employees. In fact, risk-sharing plans actually include a provision for cuts in base pay that are only recaptured in years when the organization meets performance objectives. At E.I. du Pont de Nemours & Company all employees put 6 percent of their salaries at risk and are paid a sliding percent of this based on how close the firm comes to its annual goals. If the company achieves less than 80 percent of goal, there is no pay increase. In the 80 to 100 range the increase is 3 to 6 percent. At 101 to 150 percent, increases are very lucrative to "pay for" employees taking a risk in the first place—7 to 19 percent range.[32]

All of this discussion of risk is only an exercise in intellectual gymnastics unless we add one further observation: Over the last several decades, companies have been moving more toward compensation programs higher on the risk continuum. Of 1001 companies reporting in a World at Work survey, 92 percent linked pay increases (increases in base wages) to individual performance. Further, 84 percent reported using variable pay (not built into base pay) that also linked to individual performance.[33] New forms of pay are less entitlement-oriented and more linked to the uncertainties of individual, group, and corporate performance.[34] Employees increasingly are expected to bear a share of the risks that businesses have solely born in the past. It's not entirely clear what impact this shifting of risk will have in the long run, but some experts are already voicing concerns that efforts to build employee loyalty and commitment may be an early casualty of these new pay systems.[35] Indeed, recent surveys show engagement levels for employees have fallen across the globe.[36] Some research suggests that employees may need a risk premium (higher pay) to stay and perform in a company with pay at risk.[37] Even a premium might not work for employees who are particularly risk-averse. Security-driven employees actually might accept lower wages if they come in a package that is more stable.[38] To explore what impact these new forms of pay have, the remainder of this chapter summarizes what we know about the ability of different compensation components to motivate the four general behaviors we noted earlier.

---

e-Compensation
IOMA is the Institute of Management and Administration. It specializes in finding studies from a wide variety of places that discuss different aspects of pay for performance. The index for IOMA's website is at *www.ioma.com.*

DOES COMPENSATION MOTIVATE BEHAVIOR?

Now let's look at the role of compensation in motivating the four types of behavior outlined earlier: the decision to join, to stay, to develop skills, and to perform well.

Do People Join a Firm Because of Pay?

Level of pay and pay system characteristics influence a job candidate's decision to join a firm, but this shouldn't be too surprising.[39] Pay is one of the more visible rewards in the whole recruitment process. We know, for example, that high ability applicants do select companies because they provide pay for good performance.[40] This so-called sorting effect has been shown both for good employees choosing a company and for bad employees leaving a company - all because they do (or don't) like the pay system being used.[41] Job offers spell out the level of compensation and may even include discussions about the kind of pay such as bonuses and profit-sharing participation. Less common are statements such as "You'll get plenty of work variety," or "Don't worry about empowerment," or "The workload isn't too heavy."[42] These other rewards are subjective and tend to require actual time on the job before we can decide if they are positive or negative features of the job. Not so for pay. Being perceived as more objective, it's more easily communicated in the employment offer.

Recent research suggests job candidates look for organizations with reward systems that fit their personalities.[43] Below we outline some of the ways that "fit" is important.

Person Characteristics	Preferred Reward Characteristics
Materialistic	Relatively more concerned about pay level[44]
Low self-esteem	Want large, decentralized organization with little pay for performance[45]
Risk takers	Want more pay based on performance[46]
Risk-averse	Want less performance-based pay[47]
Individualists ("I control my destiny")	Want pay plans based on individual performance, not group performance[48]

None of these relationships is particularly surprising. People are attracted to organizations that fit their personalities. Evidence suggests talented employees are attracted to companies that have strong links between pay and performance.[49] One way to get this linkage is to give employees some control over the rewards they received. Thirty years ago no company ceded this control to employees. Now almost all major companies allow employees to have some reward choice. And the impact of reward choice is positive: up to 40 percent improvement in performance but only if the choices available are attractive to employees.[50]

It's not a big jump, then, to suggest organizations should design their reward systems to attract people with desired personalities and values. For example, if we need risk takers, maybe we should design reward systems that have elements of risk built into them.

Do People Stay in a Firm (or Leave) Because of Pay?

There is clear evidence that poor performers are more likely to leave an organization than are good performers.[51] How does pay affect this relationship? Much of the equity theory research in the 1970s documented that workers who feel unfairly treated in pay react by leaving the firm for greener pastures.[52] This is particularly true under incentive conditions. Turnover is much higher for poor performers when pay is based on individual performance (a good outcome!). Conversely, group incentive plans may lead to more turnover of better performers—clearly an undesirable outcome. When AT&T shifted from individual to team-based incentives a number of years ago, star performers either reduced their output or quit. Out of 208 above-average performers, only one continued to report performance increases under the group incentive plan. The rest felt cheated because the incentives for higher individual performance were now spread across all group members.[53]

Clearly, pay can be a factor in decisions to stay or leave. Data suggest dissatisfaction with pay can be a key factor in turnovers.[54] Too little pay triggers feelings of unfair treatment. Result? Turnover. Supporting this, pay that employees find reasonable can help reduce turnover.[55] Even the way we pay has an impact on turnover. Evidence suggests that some employees are uncomfortable with pay systems that put any substantial future earnings at risk or pay systems that link less to personal effort and more to group effort.[56] Another recent study found superior performing employees were less likely to leave if they received bonuses. No such positive result was found with pay increases (thus changing base pay).[57] We need to make sure, as one critic has noted, that we don't let our design of new reward systems rupture our relationships with existing employees.[58] Recent efforts to use different types of compensation as a tool for retaining workers have focused on what is called *scarce talent*. For example, information technology employees have been scarce for much of the past decade, at least. One way to retain these workers is to develop a variable-pay component for each project. For example, reports of variable pay linked to individual length of stay on a project, to peer ratings, and to project results suggest that this pay-for-performance combination may appeal to scarce talent.[59]

The next time you go into an Applebee's restaurant, think about how the company uses compensation to reduce turnover. In an industry where manager turnover hovers around 50 percent, Applebee's allows general managers to earn as much as $30,000 above base salary for hitting sales, profitability, and customer satisfaction targets. To discourage turnover, this extra compensation is deferred for two years.[60]

Besides money, other rewards also influence the decision to stay (retention) in a firm. According to one recent study, the rewards that "work" to help retain employees in the tough economic times we face in the middle of this decade are as follows:[61]

Rewards That Lead People to Stay	Description
Job satisfaction	Work enjoyment
Pay and benefits	Self-explanatory
Social	Coworkers are fun
Organizational commitment	Not a job jumper; loyal
Organizational prestige	Respect afforded company in industry, region

Source: John P. Hausknecht, Julianne Rodda, and Michael J. Howard, "Targeted Employee Retention: Performance-Based and Job-Related Differences in Reported Reasons for Staying," *Human Resource Management* 48(2), 2009, pp. 269–288.

Do Employees More Readily Agree to Develop Job Skills Because of Pay?

We don't know the answer to this question. Skill-based pay (Chapter 6) is intended, at least partially, to pay employees for learning new skills—skills that hopefully will help employees perform better on current jobs and adjust more rapidly to demands on future jobs. For example, the U.S. Army pays ROTC cadets in college to learn new languages. Hot spots like the Mideast command monthly premiums of $100 to $250 per month.[62] Anyone know Farsi (spoken in Iran)?

We do know that one complaint about skill-based pay centers on cost implications. More employees request training, spurred by the promise of skill-based increments. Poorly administered plans, allowing more people to acquire certification in a skill than are actually required, creates cost inefficiencies. This leads to plan abandonment. So is the net result positive? Whether the promise of skill-based pay is fulfilled is unclear. Evidence is starting to accumulate that pay for skill may not increase productivity, but it does focus people on believing in the importance of quality and in turning out significantly higher quality products.[63]

Do Employees Perform Better on Their Jobs Because of Pay?

We'll be the first to admit that no matter what stand you take on this question, someone is going to disagree with you. Pfeffer reports that hundreds of studies and dozens of systematic reviews show that rewards motivate performance.[64] Mercer recently released a global study indicating which rewards motivate performance. A well-designed plan linking pay to behaviors of employees generally results in better individual and organizational performance.[65] One particularly good study looked at the HR practices of over 3,000 companies.[66] One set of questions asked: (1) Did the company have a formal appraisal process, (2) Was the appraisal tied to the size of pay increases, and (3) Did performance influence who would be promoted? Organizations significantly above the mean (by one standard deviation) on these and other "high-performance work practices" had annual sales that averaged $27,000 more per employee. So rewarding employees for performance pays off. Even more recently, WorldatWork surveyed 1,001 companies and 92 percent claimed they used individual performance to determine salary increases. Further, 84 percent also used variable pay that was tied to performance.[67]

In another comprehensive review, Heneman reports that 40 of 42 studies looking at merit pay show performance increases when pay is tied to performance.[68] Looking at this from the opposite direction, both Towers Watson and Aon Hewitt, two of the top compensation consulting firms, reported that high performers received significantly higher merit increases than average performers (4.7 percent vs. 3.2 percent and 3.5 percent vs. 2.4 percent, respectively).[69] One study of 841 union and nonunion companies found gain-sharing and profit-sharing plans (both designed to link pay to performance) increased individual and team performance 18 to 20 percent.[70] How, though, does this translate into corporate performance? A review of 26 studies gives high marks to profit-sharing plans: Organizations with such plans had 3.5 to 5 percent higher annual performance.[71] Gerhart and Milkovich took the performance-based pay question one step further. Across 200 companies they found a 1.5-percent increase in return on assets for every 10-percent increase in the size of a bonus.[72] Further, they found that the variable portion of pay had a stronger impact on individual and corporate performance than did the level of base pay.

If all this research isn't enough to convince you, consider Google's position on the matter. In recent speeches the top HR person at Google, Laszlo Bock, says the people you hire and the way you treat them (the rewards) make for happier and more productive workers. With evangelical zeal he advocates transparency in communications, obtainable goal setting, and less hierarchical organizations (fewer levels so employees can empower themselves to grow and learn).[73]

Conversely, numerous critics, led by Alfie Kohn, argue that incentives are both morally and practically wrong.[74] The moral argument suggests that incentives are flawed because they involve one person controlling another. The counterargument to this notes that employment is a reciprocal arrangement. In periods of low unemployment especially, workers can choose whether they want to work under compensation systems with strong pay-for-performance linkages (as in the case of incentive systems). We do know that applicants aren't totally risk-averse. There are circumstances when they will prefer an incentive component to compensation rather than a totally fixed salary. Generally, if the incentive depends on individual performance, applicants find the company more attractive. Team-based incentives, in contrast, are less attractive.

Kohn also suggests that incentive systems can actually harm productivity, a decidedly negative practical outcome. His rationale is based on citations mostly from laboratory studies where subjects work in isolation on a task for either pay or no pay. His conclusion, based heavily on the work of Deci and colleagues, is that rewarding a person for performing a task reduces interest in that task—**extrinsic rewards** (money) reduce intrinsic rewards (enjoyment of the task for its own sake).[75] Critics of this interpretation point out at least two important flaws in Kohn's conclusions.[76] First, the pragmatics of business demand that some jobs be performed— indeed, many jobs—that aren't the most intrinsically interesting. Although Target may be a great store for shopping, spending day after day stocking shelves with towels and other nonbreakables falls far down the intrinsic-interest scale.[77] If incentives are required for real-world jobs to be completed and thus to create value for an organization and its consumers, so be it. This may simply be one of the costs of doing business. Second, Kohn's studies frequently looked at people in isolation. In the real world people interact with each other, know who is performing and who isn't, and react to this when rewards are allocated. Without any link to performance, the less-motivated employees will eventually recognize that harder work isn't necessary. These issues raise the basic question, "Should we tie pay to performance?" One view says, "Not always." Employers are less likely to offer performance-based pay when the job involves multitasking, important quality control issues, or team work. In all three cases performance is harder to measure, and employers shy away from linking pay as a consequence.[78] Alternatively, we could break the issue down to a series of questions.

The first question perhaps should focus on an obvious but often overlooked issue: Do employees think any link at all should be made between pay and performance? Substantial evidence indicates that management and workers alike believe pay should be tied to performance. Dyer and colleagues asked 180 managers from 72 different companies to rate nine possible factors in terms of the importance they should receive in determining the size of salary increases.[79] This group believed the most important factor for salary increases should be job performance. Following close behind is a factor that presumably would be picked up in job evaluation (nature of job) and a motivational variable (amount of effort expended).

Other research supports these findings.[80] Both college students and a second group of managers ranked job performance as the most important variable in allocating pay raises. Another way to make the pay-for-performance argument is to look at the ways HR professionals try to cut costs. At the top of the list: Create greater distinction between high and low performers![81] In other words, really pay for performance! Once we move away from the managerial ranks, though, other groups express a different view of the pay-performance link. The role that performance levels should assume in determining pay increases is less clear-cut for blue-collar workers.[82] As an illustration, consider the frequent opposition to compensation plans that are based on performance (i.e., incentive piece-rate systems). Unionized workers prefer seniority rather than performance as a basis for pay increases.[83] Part of this preference may stem from a distrust of subjective performance measurement systems. Unions ask, "Can management be counted on to be fair?" In contrast, seniority is an objective index for calculating increases. Some evidence also suggests that women might prefer allocation methods not based on performance.[84]

It's probably a good thing that, in general, workers believe pay should be tied to performance, because the research we've reported suggests this link makes a difference.[85] And the difference may translate into bottom-line results! In a study of over 3,000 companies, convincing evidence showed that linking pay to performance has a positive impact on the bottom line. Over a five-year period such practices can increase per-employee sales by as much as $100,000.[86]

How does this performance improvement occur? One view suggests that linking pay to performance occurs through two mechanisms, an incentive effect and a sorting effect.[87] Incentive effect means pay can motivate people to perform better. Sorting effect means people sort themselves by what is important to them. So if Company X pays for performance, and you don't want to play by those rules (i.e., work harder or smarter to perform better) you sort yourself out, most easily by leaving Company X and finding another company with different rules for getting rewards. Lazear provides important evidence of the sorting effect. Employees in an auto glass installation company increased productivity 44 percent when pay practices switched from salaries to individual incentives. The interesting hook in this study was a separate analysis of employees who were present before and after the shift versus those who left and were replaced. Half of the 44 percent increase came from increased productivity of the "stayers." The other half though was due to the sorting effect. Less productive workers left and were replaced by more productive workers.[88]

Many meta-analyses (reviews of pay for performance research that use statistical tools to estimate the magnitude of pay's impact on performance) demonstrate the incentive effect of pay. Strong evidence suggests that linking pay to performance does increase motivation of workers and lead to improved performance. Locke and colleagues analyzed studies where individual incentives were introduced into actual work settings. Productivity increased on average 30 percent![89] A host of other meta-analyses draw similar conclusions—money does motivate performance.

Choice of pay systems (pay increases based on performance or some other attribute like seniority) also influence productivity through the sorting effect—people sort themselves into or out of organizations based on a preference for being paid based on personal performance or some something else.[90] Of course, the most obvious sorting factor is ability. Higher ability individuals are attracted to companies that will pay for performance, thus recognizing their greater contribution.[91] High performers will also leave firms that don't reward their performance (pay for something like seniority rather than performance) and go to those that do. Coming at this from a different angle, data also suggest that some people make job choices based on effort aversion. "Find me a job where I don't have to work hard!" Obviously jobs where high performance is expected are less likely to be attractive to these prospective employees.[92]

When we look at pay and group performance (instead of individual performance), the evidence is mixed. In general, though, we think group pay (whether the group is a team or an entire organization) leads to small (relative to individual pay for performance) productivity increases. On average, that productivity increase is about 4 to 5 percent. A recent study suggests that, to be effective, group incentives need to be paired with complementary HR practices. Specifically, group incentives work if you have implemented a team-based structure where members monitor team performance and personally sanction "free riders."[93]

Compensation experts estimate that every dollar spent on any performance-based pay plan yields $2.34 more in organizational earnings.[94] Put differently, there is further documented evidence that every 10 percent increase in the bonus paid to employees yields a 1.5 percent increase in ROA (return on assets) to the firm.[95]

Before we rush out and develop a variable-pay component to the compensation package, though, we should recognize that such plans can, and do, fail. Sometimes

EXHIBIT 9.7
Sears Makes
a Mistake

Strategic Goal	Supporting Compensation Component as Translated for Tire and Auto Centers	Unintended Consequence
Cut costs by $600 million, provide facelift to stores, cut prices, make every employee focus on profits.	Set high quotas for generating dollars from repairs and back up with commissions.	The California Consumer Affairs Division went undercover posing as customers. On 34 of 38 undercover runs, Sears charged an average of $235 for unnecessary repairs.

the failure arises, ironically, because the incentive works too well, leading employees to exhibit rewarded behaviors to the exclusion of other desired behaviors. Exhibit 9.7 documents one such embarrassing incident that haunted Sears for much of the early 1990s.[96]

Apparently the Sears example is no fluke. Other companies have found poorly implemented incentive pay plans can hurt rather than help. Green Giant, for example, used to pay a bonus based on insect parts screened in its pea-packing process. The goal, of course, was to cut the number of insect parts making their way into the final product (anyone planning on vegetables for dinner tonight?). Employees found a way to make this incentive system work for them. By bringing insect parts from home, inserting, and inspecting, their incentive dollars rose. Clearly, the program didn't work as intended. Experts contend this is evidence that the process wasn't managed well. Just a few days ago, the first author was working with an oil drilling company. They attached a sizeable incentive to the compensation of geologists if they could reduce the time to explore for a well site and set up the drilling operation. They couldn't figure out why so many more wells were being reported as dry (no oil) than had been the case historically![97] What does this mean in terms of design?

DESIGNING A PAY-FOR-PERFORMANCE PLAN

A recent survey of HR professionals indicates widespread use of different pay-for-performance plans Exhibit 9.8. Our pay model suggests effectiveness is dependent on three things: efficiency, equity, and compliance in designing a pay system.

Efficiency

Efficiency involves three general areas of concern.

Strategy

Does the pay-for-performance plan support corporate objectives? For example, is the plan cost-effective, or are we making payouts that bear no relation to improved performance on the bottom line? Similarly, does the plan help us improve quality of service? Some pay-for-performance plans are so focused on quantity of performance

EXHIBIT 9.8
Compensation
Programs Used
in Past 12
Months

	2009	2010	2011	2012	2013
Market adjustments/increase to base salary	37%	35%	60%	69%	72%
Sign-on/hiring bonus	64%	50%	62%	66%	69%
Employee referral bonus	66%	55%	62%	62%	62%
Spot bonus (individual)	39%	36%	48%	51%	53%
Noncash recognition and rewards	–	38%	41%	50%	52%
Retention/stay bonus	34%	26%	34%	41%	44%
Stock grant programs	20%	18%	25%	28%	28%
Paying above market	21%	14%	19%	27%	29%
Stock option program	20%	17%	22%	24%	22%
Project milestone/completion bonus	15%	12%	19%	21%	24%
Special cash bonus/group incentives	15%	12%	19%	21%	24%
Exempt overtime pay or time off	11%	9%	15%	20%	22%
Separate salary structures	11%	7%	15%	19%	20%
Larger merit increase budgets	3%	4%	14%	10%	9%

Source: "WorldatWork 2013–2014 Salary Budget Survey."

as a measure that we forget about quality. Defect rates rise. Customers must search for someone to handle a merchandise return. A number of things happen that aren't consistent with the emphasis on quality that top organizations insist upon.

The plan also should link well with HR strategy and objectives. If other elements of our total HR plan are geared to select, reinforce, and nurture risk-taking behavior, we don't want a compensation component that rewards the status quo. Be careful, though. Fannie Mae changed its performance metrics from return on assets and cost management to total earnings and earnings per share. No problem, you say? What if the CEO of Fannie Mae is part of the "team" that writes legislation, so he helped sculpt the laws to fit his company's strategy. He got rich, and helped start the huge financial collapse of 2008–2010.[98]

Finally, we address the most difficult question of all—how much of an increase makes a difference? What does it take to motivate an employee? Is 4 percent, the recent average of pay increases, really enough to motivate higher performance?[99] While there are few hard data on this question, most experts agree that employees don't begin to consider changing behavior unless payouts are at least 10 percent higher, with 15 to 20 percent more likely to evoke the desired response.[100]

Structure

Is the structure of the organization sufficiently decentralized to allow different operating units to create flexible variations on a general pay-for-performance plan? For example, IBM adapted performance reviews to the different needs of different units, and the managers in them, resulting in a very flexible system. In this new system, midpoints for pay grades don't exist. Managers get a budget, some training on how to conduct reviews, and a philosophical mandate: Differentiate pay for stars relative to average performers, or risk losing stars. Managers are given a number of performance dimensions. Determining which dimensions to use for which employees is totally a personal decision. Indeed, managers who don't like reviews at all can input merit increases directly, anchored only by a brief explanation for the reason.[101] Different operating units may have different competencies and different competitive advantages. We don't want a rigid pay-for-performance system that detracts from these advantages, all in the name of consistency across divisions.

Standards

Operationally, the key to designing a pay-for-performance system rests on standards. Specifically, we need to be concerned about the following:

Objectives: Are they specific yet flexible? Can employees see that their behavior influences their ability to achieve objectives (called the "line-of-sight" issue in industry)?

Measures: Do employees know what measures (individual appraisals, peer reviews of team performance, corporate financial measures, etc.) will be used to assess whether performance is sufficiently good to merit a payout?

Eligibility: How far down the organization will the plan run? Companies like PepsiCo and Starbucks believe all employees should be included. Others think only top management can see how their decisions affect the bottom line.

Funding: Will you fund the program out of extra revenue generated above and beyond some preset standard? If so, what happens in a bad year? Many employees become disillusioned when they feel they have worked harder but economic conditions or poor management decisions conspire to cut or eliminate bonuses.

Equity/Fairness

Our second design objective is to ensure that the system is fair to employees. Two types of fairness are concerns for employees. The first type is fairness in the *amount* that is distributed to employees. Not surprisingly, this type of fairness is labeled *distributive justice*.[102] Does an employee view the amount of compensation received as fair? As we discussed earlier in the section on equity theory, perceptions of fairness here depend on the amount of compensation actually received relative to input (e.g., productivity) compared against some relevant standard. Notice that several of the components of this equity equation are frustratingly removed from the control of the typical supervisor or manager working with employees. A manager has little influence over the size of an employee's paycheck. It is influenced more by external market conditions, pay-policy decisions of the organization, and the occupational choice made by the employee. Indeed, recent research suggests that employees may look at the relative distribution of pay. For example, some major league baseball teams have met with mixed success in trying to buy stars via the free-agent market. Some speculate that this creates feelings of inequity among other players. Some evidence suggests that narrower ranges for pay differences may actually have positive impacts on overall organizational performance.[103]

Managers have somewhat more control over the second type of equity. Employees are also concerned about the fairness of the *procedures* used to determine the amount of rewards they receive. Employees expect *procedural justice*.[104] Evidence suggests that organizations using fair procedures and having supervisors who are viewed as fair in the means they use to allocate rewards are perceived as more trustworthy and command higher levels of commitment.[105] Some research even suggests that employee satisfaction with pay may depend more on the procedures used to determine pay than on the actual level distributed.[106]

A key element in fairness is communications. Employees want to know in advance what is expected of them. They want the opportunity to provide input into the standards or expectations. And, if performance is judged lacking relative to these standards, they want a mechanism for appeals. The importance of open communications also extends to upper management. In firms that practice greater transparency of pay practices. Executives perform better when told what the linkage is between pay and performance.[107] In a union environment, this is the grievance procedure. Something similar needs to be set up in a nonunion environment.[108] As evidence, only 15 percent of employees who feel well informed indicate they are considering leaving their company. This jumps to 41 percent who think about leaving if they feel poorly informed about the way the pay system operates.[109]

Compliance

Finally, our pay-for-performance system should comply with existing laws. We want a reward system that maintains and enhances the reputation of our firm. Think about the companies that visit a college campus. For some of these companies, students naturally gravitate to interview opportunities—the interview schedule fills very quickly indeed. Why? Because of reputation.[110] We tend to undervalue the reward value of a good reputation. To guard this reputation, we need to make sure we comply with compensation laws.

Your **Turn**   Burger Boy

This is a true case. Jerry Newman (second author of this book) spent 14 months working in seven fast-food restaurants. He wrote about his experiences in the book *My Secret Life on the McJob* (McGraw-Hill, 2007). This is a description of events in one store . . . labeled here Burger Boy.

Person	Job Title	Base Salary	Other Wage Information	Avg Hrs/Wk
Otis	Assistant Store Manager	34k	Exempt (no overtime pay)	55
Leon	Shift Supervisor	23k	Nonexempt	55
Marge	Crew Member (fries)	$6.25/hr	Nonexempt	30
Me	Cook	$6.50/hr	Nonexempt	20
Chuck	Drive-thru Window	$7.00/hr	Nonexempt	30
Lucy	Sandwich Assembler	$7.00/hr	Nonexempt	35

It's a hot Friday in Florida, and lunch rush is just beginning. Chuck is working the pay window and is beginning to grouse about the low staffing for what is traditionally the busiest day of the week. "Where the heck is LaVerne?" he yells to no one. Chuck has only worked here for six weeks but has prior experience at another Burger Boy. Marge, typically working the fries station (the easiest job at this Burger Boy), has been pressed into service on the front drive-thru window because 2 of 10 scheduled workers have called in sick. She can handle the job when business is slow, but she clearly is getting flustered as more cars enter the drive-thru line. I'm cooking, my third day on job, but my first one alone. I've worked the grill for 10 years as a volunteer at Aunt Rosie's Womens Fastpitch Softball Tournament, but nothing prepared me for the volume of business we will do today. By 11:30 I've got the grill full of burgers. Lucy is going full speed trying to keep up with sandwich assembly and wrapping. She's the best assembler the place has and would be a supervisor if she could just keep from self-destructing. Yesterday she lit a can of vegetable spray with a lighter and danced around the floor, an arc of flame shooting out from the can. She thinks this is funny. Everyone else thinks she's nuts. But she's rumored to be a friend of the manager, Nancy, so everyone keeps quiet.

"Marge, you've got to get moving girl. The line's getting longer. Move girl, move," shouts Otis, unfazed by the fact that Marge really isn't good enough to work the window and clearly is showing signs of heavy stress. "I'll help her," chimes in Chuck. "I can work the pay window, then run up front to help Marge when she gets way behind." Otis says nothing and goes back to the office where he begins to count the morning receipts for the breakfast rush.

My job as cook also includes cooking baked potatoes in the oven and cooking chicken in the pressure cooker, so I have little time to do anything besides stay on top of my job. Finally, at noon, in comes Leon. He will replace Otis at three, but for now he is a sorely needed pair of hands on the second sandwich assembly board. Leon looks over at me and shouts above the din, "Good job, Jerry. Keeping up with Friday rush on your third cooking day. Good job." That's the first compliment I've received in the two weeks I've worked here, so I smile at the unexpected recognition. By 12:30 we're clearly all frazzled. Even with Chuck's help, Marge falls farther behind. She is now making mistakes on orders in efforts to get food out the drive-thru window quickly. Otis comes barreling up front from the office and shouts for everyone to hear: "We're averaging 3:05 (minutes) on drive time. Someone's in trouble if we don't get a move on." He says this while staring directly at Marge. Everyone knows that drive times (the amount of time from an order being placed until the customer receives it) should be about 2:30 (two minutes, thirty seconds). In my head I do some mental math. The normal staffing for a Friday is 13 people (including management). Because of absenteeism we're working with eight, including Otis and Leon. By noon Marge is crying, but she stays at it. And finally things begin to slow at 1 p.m. We know rush is officially over when Lucy tells Leon she's "going to the can." This starts a string of requests for rest breaks that are interrupted by Otis, "All right, for God's sake. Here's the order of breaks." He points to people in turn, with me being next to last, and Marge going last. After Lucy, Chuck is second, and the others fill in the gap ahead of me. When my turn finally comes I resolve to break quickly, taking only 6 minutes instead of the allotted 10. When I return Otis sneers at me and chides, "What was that, about a half hour?" I snap, I'm angry, and let him know it. "If I could tell time, would I be working fast food?" Now I realize I've done the unforgivable, sassing my boss. But I'm upset, and I don't care. My only care is I've just claimed fast food is work for dummies, and I absolutely don't believe this. But as I said, I was mad. Otis looks me over, staring at my face, and finally decides to let out a huge bellow, "You're ok, Newman. Good line!"

It's now 2:10 and Marge has told Otis twice that she has to leave. Her agreement with the store manager at the time of hire was that she would leave no later than 2:30 every day. Her daughter gets off the school bus at 2:45, and she must meet her at that time. Otis ignores her first request, and is nowhere to be seen when, at 2:25, Marge looks around frantically and pleads to no one in particular, "What should I do? I have to leave." I look at her and declare, "Go. I will tell Otis when he comes out again." Marge leaves. Ten minutes later we have a mini-surge of customers. Leon yells, "Where the hell is Marge? That's it; she's out of here tomorrow. No more chances for her." When he's done ranting, I explain the details of Marge's plight. Angrily Leon stomps back to the manager's office and confronts Otis. The yelling quickly reaches audible levels. Everyone in the store, customers included, hear what is quickly broadening into confrontations about other unresolved issues:

Leon: "I'm sick of coming in here and finding nothing stocked. Otis, it's your job to make sure the lunch shift (roughly 10 a.m.–2 p.m.) stocks items in their spare time. It never happens and I'm sick of it. Now you tell me you're leaving and sticking me with a huge stocking job."

Otis: "I'm sick of your whining, Leon. I work 50–60 hours a week. I'm sick of working 10–12 hours a day for crappy wages. You want things stocked . . . you do it. I'm going home and try to forget this place."

With that Otis drops what he has in his hands, a printout of today's receipts so far, and walks out the door. Leon swears, picks up the spreadsheet, and storms back to the office. I finish my shift and happily go home. No more Burger Boy for this burger boy.

1. What appear to be the problems at this Burger Boy?
2. How many of these problems could be explained by compensation issues?
3. How many other problems could be lessened with diligent use of rewards other than pay?
4. Are hours of work a reward? What might explain why I was happy to be working 20 hours per week, but Chuck was unhappy with 30 hours per week? How might schedules be used as a reward?

Summary   Why not admit it? We don't know what makes people tick! Reading this chapter should prove that we have more questions unanswered than we have supposed truths. We know that employee performance depends upon some blend of skill, knowledge, and motivation. If any of these three ingredients is missing, performance is likely to be suboptimal. This chapter concentrates on the motivation component of this performance triangle. Rewards must help organizations attract and retain employees; they must make high performance an attractive option for employees; they must encourage employees to build new skills and gradually foster commitment to the organization. A tall order, you say! The problem is especially big because we are just starting to realize all the different things that can serve as rewards (or punishments) for employees. This chapter outlines 13 rewards and makes a strong case that fair administration of these rewards can lead a company to higher performance levels.

Review Questions

1. A father decides to put his two sons to work landscaping. The business involves going to a customer's home and providing landscaping services (cut grass, edge sidewalk, pull weeds in flower beds, prune bushes and trees, rake leaves). Rather than paying a flat wage, the father decides to pay an incentive according to the following schedule (average across all lawns).

Task	Piece Rate Incentive per Person	Physical Effort	Time to Complete per Person	Charge to Customer
Cut grass	$4	Easy	.4 hr	$30
Edge sidewalk	$1	Easy	.1 hr	$ 5
Pull weeds	$6	Very Hard	.5 hr	$40
Prune bushes, etc.	$5	Hard	.5 hr	$30
Rake leaves	$5	Hard	.5	$25

At the end of the second week under this arrangement the boys are quarreling with each other and not happy with their dad. All of the disagreements revolve around the incentive system. What might be the problems?

2. Father Michael's Wraps (pitas, wraps, flat breads) is experiencing turnover in the range of 100 percent. Most of this occurs in the first 18 months of employment. How would you determine if this turnover rate is high? How would you justify to your boss that lower turnover is strategically important? What would you look at in both pay and other forms of rewards to identify ways of reducing turnover? Justify your choices based on your reading of this chapter.

3. Eric Dempsey Associates (EDA) is a relatively small public relations/advertising firm in western New York. It recently shifted its strategic plan to focus almost exclusively on clients who generate $200,000 or more in revenue for the firm. There are six employees in the firm who focus exclusively on business development, identifying new client prospects and making "pitches" to these prospects about ways that EDA can help them. While the payout for landing these prospects is high, averaging four times the revenue of the typical EDA client in the past, the likelihood of getting these new clients is considerably lower. In the past the development associates (as they are called) were paid heavily on incentive pay (4 percent of revenue generated by clients landed by the associate) along with a base pay that was 95 percent of the market rate for comparable jobs in western New York. What changes do you think should be made in compensation to reflect changes in the strategic plan of EDA?

4. Companies focus heavily on cost-saving strategies to be competitive today. Identify both monetary and nonmonetary ways of cost saving that would be relevant to a compensation person's job.

5. You supervise in a company that is a low payer relative to competitors. What things do you have control over to increase the likelihood that workers will feel fairly treated?

Endnotes

1. Rachael Feintzeig, "Container store bets on $50,000 retail worker," Wall Street Journal, October 15, 2014. B6.

2. Ingrid Smithey Fulmer, Barry Gerhart, and Kimberly Scott, "Are the 100 Best Better? An Empirical Investigation of the Relationship Between Being a Great Place to Work and Firm Performance," *Personnel Psychology* 56 (2003), pp. 965–993.

3. Bonnie G. Mani, "Performance Appraisal Systems, Productivity, and Motivation: A Case Study," *Public Personnel Management* 31(2), 2000, pp. 141–159; R. Mayer and J. Davis, "The Effect of the Performance Appraisal System on Trust for Management," *Journal of Applied Psychology* 84(1) (1999), pp. 123–136.

4. Barry Gerhart, Sara L. Rynes, and Ingrid Smithey Fulmer, "Pay and Performance: Individuals, Groups and Executives," in A. P. Brief and J. P. Walsh, *Academy of Management Annals,* vol. 3 (Mahwah, NJ: Lawrence Erlbaum, forthcoming).

5. Matthew Bidwell and J. R. Keller, "Within or Without? How Firms Combine Internal and External Labor Markets to Fill Jobs." *Academy of Management Journal* 57(4), 2014, pp. 1035–1055; Sara L. Rynes, Kenneth G. Brown, and Amy E. Colbert, "Seven Common Misconceptions about Human Resource Practices: Research Findings Versus Practitioner Beliefs," *Academy of Management Executive* 16(3), 2002, pp. 92–102; Brian Becker and Barry Gerhart, "The Impact of Human Resource Management on Organizational Performance: Progress and Prospects," *Academy of Management Journal* 39 (4), 1996, pp. 779–801.

6. Sue Kirchoff and Del Jones, "Caterpillar Joins Other Companies Cutting Pay," Reuters, December 23, 2008, p. B1; Jena McGregor, "Cutting Salaries Instead of Jobs." *BusinessWeek,* June 8, 2009, pp. O46–O48.

7. This table extrapolates the findings from two studies: Matthew C. Bloom and George T. Milkovich, "The Relationship among Risk, Incentive Pay, and Organizational Performance," *Academy of Management Journal* 14(3), 1998, pp. 283–297; Anne Tsui, Jone L. Pearce, Lyman W. Porter, and Angela M. Tripoli, "Alternative Approaches to the Employee-Organization Relationship: Does Investment in Employees Pay Off?" *Academy of Management Journal* 40(5), 1997, pp. 1089–1121.

8. Andrew Ross Sorkin, "Mergers Pare Competition at 30,000 Feet," *The New York Times*, March 24, 2015, B1.

9. Anne Tsui, Jone L. Pearce, Lyman W. Porter, and Angela M. Tripoli, "Alternative Approaches to the Employee-Organization Relationship: Does Investment in Employees Pay Off?" *Academy of Management Journal* 40(5), 1997, pp. 1089–1121.

10. http://lesterslegends.com/ten-biggest-endorsement-deals-athletic-history/, accessed March 31, 2015.

11. Krista L. Uggerslev, Neil E. Fassina, and David Kraichy, "Recruiting Through the Stages: A Meta-analytic Test of Predictors of Applicant Attraction at Different Stages of the Recruitment Process," *Personnel Psychology*. Autumn 65(3), 2012, pp. 597–660.

12. http://www.spotrac.com/mlb/washinton-nationals/max-scherzer/, accessed March 31, 2015.

13. Sanford E. Devoe, Jeffrey Pfeffer, and Byron Y. Lee, "When Does Money Make Money More Important? Survey and Experimental Evidence," *Industrial and Labor Relations Review* 66(5), 2013, pp. 1078–1097.

14. A. Mamman, M. Sulaiman, and A. Fadel, "Attitude to Pay Systems: An Exploratory Study Within and Across Cultures," *International Journal of Human Resource Management* 7(1), 1996, pp. 101–121.

15. IOMA, "Are You Ready to Serve Cafeteria Style Comp?" *Pay for Performance Report,* June 2000, pp. 1, 13.

16. For an excellent discussion of developments in motivation theory, see the special topic forum, including the following articles in the 2004 issue of *Academy of Management Review* 29(2): R. Steers, R. Mowday, and D. Shapiro, "The Future of Work Motivation," pp. 379–387; E. Locke and G. Latham, "What Should We Do about Motivation Theory? Six Recommendations for the Twenty-First Century," pp. 388–403; Y. Fried and L. H. Slowik, "Enriching Goal-Setting Theory with Time: An Integrated Approach," pp. 404–422; and M. Seo, L. Barrett, and J. Bartunek, "The Role of Affective Experience in Work Motivation," pp. 423–438.

17. Barry Gerhart, Sara L. Rynes, and Ingrid Smithey Fulmer, "Pay and Performance: Individuals, Groups and Executives," in *Academy of Management Annals,* vol. 3, A. P. Brief and J. P. Walsh, eds. (Mahwah, NJ: Lawrence Erlbaum, 2009).

18. J. S. Adams, "Toward an Understanding of Inequity," *Journal of Abnormal and Social Psychology* 67 (1963), pp. 422–436; J. S. Adams, "Injustice in Social Exchange," in *Advances in Experimental Social Psychology,* vol. 2, L. Berkowitz, ed. (New York: Academic Press, 1965); R. Cosier and D. Dalton, "Equity Theory and Time: A Reformulation," *Academy of Management Review* 8 (1983), pp. 311–319.

19. B. Oviatt, "Agency and Transaction Cost Perspectives on the Manager-Shareholder Relationship: Incentives for Congruent Interests," *Academy of Management Review* 13 (1988), pp. 214–225.

20. D. Knight, C. Durham, and E. A. Locke, "The Relationship of Team Goals, Incentives, and Efficacy to Strategic Risk, Tactical Implementation, and Performance," *Academy of Management Journal* 44(2), 2001, pp. 326–338.

21. E. A. Locke, K. N. Shaw, L. M. Saari, and G. P. Latham, "Goal Setting and Task Performance: 1969–1980," *Psychological Bulletin* 90 (1981), pp. 125–152.

22. Richard M. Ryan and Edward L. Deci, "Self-Regulation and the Problem of Human Autonomy: Does Psychology Need Choice, Self-Determination, and Will?" *Journal of Personality* 74(6), December 2006, pp. 1557–1586.

23. M. R. Louis, B. Z. Posner, and G. N. Powell, "The Availability and Helpfulness of Socialization Practices," *Personnel Psychology* 36 (1983), pp. 857–866; E. H. Schein, "Organizational Socialization and the Profession of Management," *Industrial Management Review* 9 (1968), pp. 1–16.

24. P. Zingheim and J. Schuster, "Creating a High-Performance Culture by Really Paying for Performance," in IOMA, *Complete Guide to Best Practices in Pay for Performance,* 2005, pp 1.17–1.22.

25. Byron Wine, Shawn Gilroy, and Donald Hantula, "Temporal (In) Stability of Employee Preferences for Rewards," *Journal of Organizational Behavior Management* 32(1), 2012, pp. 58–64.

26. Bob Nelson, *1501 Ways to Reward Employees*, (New York: Workman Publishing, 2012).

27. J. Tropman, *The Compensation Solution: How to Develop an Employee-Driven Rewards System* (San Francisco, CA: Jossey-Bass, 2001).

28. Jerry M. Newman, Richard Floersch, and Mike Balaka, "Employment Branding at McDonalds: Leveraging Rewards for Positive Outcomes," Workspan, March 2012. pp. 20–24.

29. N. Stein, "America's Most Admired Companies," *Fortune,* March 3, 2003, pp. 81–87; J. Pfeffer, "Six Dangerous Myths about Pay," *Harvard Business Review,* May–June 1998, pp. 109–119.

30. K. Brown and V. Huber, "Lowering Floors and Raising Ceilings: A Longitudinal Assessment of the Effects of an Earnings-at-Risk Plan on Pay Satisfaction," *Personnel Psychology* 45 (1992), pp. 279–311. Elena Belogolovsky and Peter A Bamberger, "Signaling in Secret: Pay for Performance Incentive and Sorting Effects of Pay Secrecy,"

Academy of Management Journal, 57(6), 2014, pp. 1706–1733; B. Gerhart, S. L. Rynes, and I. S. Fulmer, "Pay and Performance: Individuals, Groups, and Executives," *Academy of Management Annals*, 3 (2009), pp. 251–315.

31. Please note, though, most of the declines experienced in base pay have occurred since 1980.

32. http://www.payscale.com/research/US/Employer=E.I._Du_Pont_De_Nemours_%26_Co_ (DuPont)/Salary, accessed March 31, 2015.

33. *WorldatWork, 2012* WorldatWork Compensation programs and practices 2012 (2012, October) (Scottsdale, AZ).

34. IOMA, *Complete Guide to Best Practices in Pay for Performance* (Newark, NJ: BNA Subsidiaries, 2005), pp. 1.8–1.10; J. R. Schuster and P. K. Zingheim, *The New Pay: Linking Employee and Organizational Performance* (New York: Lexington Books, 1992).

35. Mercer, "What's Working Survey." http://inside-employees-mind.mercer.com/global. Visited April 24, 2012.

36. Aon Hewitt, "Trends in Global Employee Engagement," www.aon.com/attachments/ thoughtleadership/Trends_Global_Employee_Engagement_Final.pdf visited April 24, 2012.

37. Ibid.

38. D. M. Cable and T. A. Judge, "Pay Preferences and Job Search Decisions: A Person-Organization Fit Perspective," *Personnel Psychology* 47 (1994), pp. 317–348.

39. Julie Wayne & Wendy Casper, "Why Does Firm Reputation in Human Resource Policies Influence College Students? The Mechanisms Underlying Job Pursuit Intentions," *Human Resource Management* 51(1), 2012, pp. 121–142; Sara Rynes, Barry Gerhart, and Kathleen Minette, "The Importance of Pay in Employee Motivation: Discrepancies between What People Say and What They Do," *Human Resource Management* 43(4), Winter 2004, pp. 381–394; S. L. Rynes, K. G. Brown, and A. E. Colbert, "Seven Common Misconceptions about Human Resource Practices: Research Findings Versus Practitioner Beliefs," *Academy of Management Executive* 16(2), 2002, pp. 92–103; E. E. Lawler, *Pay and Organizational Effectiveness: A Psychological View* (New York: McGraw-Hill, 1971); E. E. Lawler and G. D. Jenkins, "Strategic Reward Systems" in *Handbook of Industrial and Organizational Psychology*, M. D. Dunnette and L. M. Hough, eds. (Palo Alto, CA: Consulting Psychologist Press, 1992), pp. 1009–1055; W. Mobley, *Employee Turnover: Causes, Consequences and Control* (Reading, MA: Addison-Wesley, 1982).

40. E. Lazear, "Performance Pay and Productivity," *The American Economic Review*, 90 (2000), pp. 1346–1361.

41. Barry Gerhart and Meiyu Fang, "Pay for (Individual) Performance: Issues, Claims, Evidence and the Role of Sorting Effects," *Human Resource Management Review 24(1)*, March 2014, pp. 41–52.

42. David A. Comerford and Peter A. Ubel, "Effort Aversion: Job Choice and Compensation Decisions Overweight Effort," *Journal of Economic Behavior & Organization* 92, August 2013, pp. 152–162.

43. D. M. Cable and T. A. Judge, "Pay Preferences and Job Search Decisions: A Person-Organization Fit Perspective," *Personnel Psychology* 47 (1994), pp. 317–348.

44. Ibid.

45. D. B. Turban and T. L. Keon, "Organizational Attractiveness: An Interactionist Perspective," *Journal of Applied Psychology* 78 (1993), pp. 184–193.

46. D. M. Cable and T. A. Judge, "Pay Preferences and Job Search Decisions: A Person-Organization Fit Perspective," *Personnel Psychology* 47 (1994), pp. 317–348; A. Kohn, *Punished by Rewards: The Trouble With Gold Stars, Incentive Plans, A's, Praise and Other Bribes* (Boston, MA: Houghton-Mifflin, 1993).

47. Cable and Judge, Ibid.

48. Cable and Judge, Ibid.

49. T. R. Zenger, "Why Do Employers Only Reward Extreme Performance? Examining the Relationships among Performance Pay and Turnover," *Administrative Science Quarterly* 37 (1992), pp. 198–219.

50. B. Gerhart, S. L. Rynes, and I. S. Fulmer, "Pay and Performance: Individuals, Groups, and Executives," *The Academy of Management Annals*, 3 (2009), pp. 251–315.

51. Barry Gerhart and Meiyu Fang, "Pay for (Individual) Performance: Issues, Claims, Evidence and the Role of Sorting Effects." *Human Resource Management Review Volume* 24(1), March 2014, pp. 41–52; Chi-Sum Wong and Kenneth Law, "The Effects of Leader and Follower Emotional Intelligence on Performance and Attitude: An Exploratory Study," *Leadership Quarterly* 13(3), 2002, pp. 243–274; David A. Harrison, Meghna Virick, and Sonja William, "Working Without a Net: Time, Performance, and Turnover Under Maximally Contingent Rewards," *Journal of Applied Psychology* 81(4), 1996, pp. 331–345.

52. Arran Caza, Matthew W. McCarter, and Gregory Northcraft, "Performance Benefits of Reward Choice: A Procedural Justice Perspective." *Human Resource Management Journal*, forthcoming; M. R. Carrell and J. E. Dettrich, "Employee Perceptions of Fair Treatment," Personnel Journal 55 (1976), pp. 523–524.

53. A. Weiss, "Incentives and Worker Behavior: Some Evidence," in *Incentives, Cooperation and Risk Sharing*, H. R. Nalbantian, ed. (Totowa, NJ: Rowan & Littlefield, 1987), pp. 137–150.

54. Susan Warren, "The Transient Workers," *The Wall Street Journal*, October 28, 2002, p. R4; R. Heneman and T. Judge, "Compensation Attitudes: A Review and Recommendations for Future Research," in *Compensation in Organizations: Progress and Prospects*, S. L. Rynes and B. Gerhart, eds. (San Francisco, CA: New Lexington Press, 1999).

55. P. W. Hom and R. W. Griffeth, *Employee Turnover* (Cincinnati, OH: Southwestern, 1995); M. Kim, "Where the Grass Is Greener: Voluntary Turnover and Wage Premiums," *Industrial Relations* 38 (October 1999), p. 584.

56. Barry Gerhart and Meiyu Fang, "Pay for (Individual) Performance: Issues, Claims, Evidence and the Role of Sorting Effects." *Human Resource Management Review Volume* 24(1), March 2014, pp. 41–52; D. M. Cable and T. A. Judge, "Pay Preferences and Job Search Decisions: A Person-Organization Fit Perspective," *Personnel Psychology* 47 (1994), pp. 317–348.

57. S. Salamin and P. Hom, "In Search of the Elusive U-Shaped Performance-Turnover Relationship: Are High Performing Swiss Bankers More Liable to Quit?" *Journal of Applied Psychology* 90(6), 2005, pp. 1–9.

58. A. Kohn, *Punished by Rewards: The Trouble With Gold Stars, Incentive Plans, A's, Praise and Other Bribes* (Boston, MA: Houghton-Mifflin, 1993).

59. P. Zingheim and J. R. Shuster, *Pay People Right* (San Francisco, CA: Jossey-Bass, 2000); J. Boudreau, M. Sturman, C. Trevor, and B. Gerhart, "Is It Worth It to Win the Talent War? Using Turnover Research to Evaluate the Utility of Performance-Based Pay," Working Paper 99–06, Center for Advanced Human Resource Studies, Cornell University, 2000.

60. Allison Perlik, "Payback Time," *Restaurants and Institutions*, Chicago, January 15, 2003, pp. 22–29.

61. IOMA, "Top-Notch Retention Strategies for These Tight-Money Times," *Pay for Performance Report* (Newark, NJ: BNA Subsidiaries, 2002), p. 2.

62. Aamer Madhani, "ROTC Recruits Paid to Command New Languages," *USA Today*, December 23, 2008, p. B1.

63. IOMA, "Report on Salary Surveys," BNA Subsidiaries, Newark: NJ, May 1997, p. 14; Kevin J. Parent and Caroline L. Weber, "Does Paying for Knowledge Pay Off?" *Compensation and Benefits Review,* September 1994, pp. 44–50.

64. J. Pfeffer, *The Human Equation: Building Profits by Putting People First* (Boston, MA: Harvard Business School Press, 1998).

65. R. L. Heneman, *Strategic Reward Management: Design, Implementation, and Evaluation* (Greenwich, CT: Information Age Publishing, 2002); W. N. Cooke, "Employee Participation Programs, Group Based Incentives, and Company Performance," *Industrial and Labor Relations Review* 47 (1994), pp. 594–610; G. W. Florkowski, "The Organizational Impact of Profit Sharing," *Academy of Management Review* 12 (1987), pp. 622–636; R. Heneman, *Merit Pay: Linking Pay Increases to Performance Ratings* (Reading, MA: Addison-Wesley, 1992); J. L. McAdams and E. J. Hawk, *Organizational Performance and Rewards* (Phoenix, AZ: American Compensation Association, 1994); D. McDonaly and A. Smith, "A Proven Connection: Performance Management and Business Results," *Compensation and Benefits Review,* January–February 1995, pp. 59–64; G. T. Milkovich, "Does Performance-Based Pay Really Work? Conclusions Based on the Scientific Research," unpublished document for 3M, 1994; G. Milkovich and C. Milkovich, "Strengthening the Pay Performance Relationship: The Research," *Compensation and Benefits Review,* May–June 1992, pp. 53–62.

66. Mark A. Huselid, "The Impact of Human Resource Management Practices on Turnover, Productivity, and Corporate Financial Performance," *Academy of Management Journal* 38(3), 1995, pp. 635–672.

67. Barry Gerhart and Meiyu Fang, "Pay for (Individual) Performance: Issues, Claims, Evidence and the Role of Sorting Effects," *Human Resource Management Review* 24(1), March 2014, pp. 41–52.

68. *Merit Pay: Linking Pay Increases to Performance Ratings* (Reading, MA: Addison-Wesley, 1992).

69. Towers Watson, "Moderate Pay Raises on Tap for U.S. Workers, Towers Watson Survey Finds," http://www.towerswatson.com/press/7856. August 24, 2012.

70. W. N. Cooke, "Employee Participation Programs, Group Based Incentives and Company Performance: A Union–Non Union Comparison," *Industrial and Labor Relations Review* 47(4), 1994, pp. 594–610.

71. D. L. Kruse, *Profit Sharing: Does It Make a Difference?* (Kalamazoo, MI: Upjohn Institute, 1993).

72. B. Gerhart and G. Milkovich, "Organizational Differences in Managerial Compensation and Financial Performance," *Academy of Management Journal* 33 (1990), pp. 663–690.

73. Christopher Mims, "At Google, the Science of Working," *The Wall Street Journal,* March 30, 2015, p. b1; Laszlo Bock, *Work Rules!: Insights from Inside Google That Will Transform How You Live and Lead Hardcover* (New York: Twelve Publishing, 2015).

74. A. Kohn, *Punished by Rewards. The Trouble with Gold Stars, Incentive Plans, A's, Praise and Other Bribes* (Boston, MA: Houghton-Mifflin, 1993).

75. E. Deci, R. Ryan, and R. Koestner, "A Meta-Analytic Review of Experiments Examining the Effects of Extrinsic Rewards on Intrinsic Motivation," *Psychological Bulletin,* 125(6), 1999, pp. 627–668.

76. R. McKensie and D. Lee, *Managing Through Incentives* (New York: Oxford University Press, 1998); R. Eisenberger and J. Cameron, "Detrimental Effects of Rewards," *American Psychologist,* November 1996, pp. 1153–1156.

77. The second author knows this all too well, based on the daily venting of his daughter, a short-term Target employee.

78. Vera Brencic, and John B. Norris, "On-the-Job Tasks and Performance Pay: A Vacancy-Level Analysis," *Industrial and Labor Relations Review* 63(3), 2010, pp. 511–544.

79. L. Dyer, D. P. Schwab, and R. D. Theriault, "Managerial Perceptions Regarding Salary Increase Criteria," *Personnel Psychology* 29 (1976), pp. 233–242.

80. J. Fossum and M. Fitch, "The Effects of Individual and Contextual Attributes on the Sizes of Recommended Salary Increases," *Personnel Psychology* 38 (1985), pp. 587–603.

81. IOMA, *Complete Guide to Best Practices in Pay for Performance* (Newark, NJ: BNA Subsidiaries, 2005), pp. 1–5.

82. L. V. Jones and T. E. Jeffrey, "A Quantitative Analysis of Expressed Preferences for Compensation Plans," *Journal of Applied Psychology* 48 (1963), pp. 201–210; Opinion Research Corporation, *Wage Incentives* (Princeton, NJ: Opinion Research Corporation, 1946); Opinion Research Corporation, *Productivity from the Worker's Standpoint* (Princeton, NJ: Opinion Research Corporation, 1949).

83. D. Koys, T. Keaveny, and R. Allen, "Employment Demographics and Attitudes That Predict Preferences for Alternative Pay Increase Policies," *Journal of Business and Psychology* 4 (1989), pp. 27–47.

84. Emily Grijalva, Daniel A Newman, Louis Tay M. Brent Donnellan, P.D. Harms, Richard W. Robins and Taiyi Yan, "Gender Differences in Narcissism: A Meta-Analytic Review." Psychological Bulletin, 2015, 141(2), 261–310. B. Major, "Gender, Justice and the Psychology of Entitlement," *Review of Personality and Social Psychology* 7 (1988), pp. 124–148.

85. IOMA, "Incentive Pay Programs and Results: An Overview" (Newark, NJ: Institute of Management and Administration, May 1996), p. 11; G. Green, "Instrumentality Theory of Work Motivation," Journal of Applied Psychology 53 (1965), pp. 1–25; R. D. Pritchard, D. W. Leonard, C. W. Von Bergen, Jr., and R. J. Kirk, "The Effects of Varying Schedules of Reinforcement on Human Task Performance," Organizational Behavior and Human Performance 16 (1976), pp. 205–230; D. P. Schwab and L. Dyer, "The Motivational Impact of a Compensation System on Employee Performance," Organizational Behavior and Human Performance 9 (1973), pp. 215–225; D. Schwab, "Impact of Alternative Compensation Systems on Pay Valence and Instrumentality Perceptions," Journal of Applied Psychology 58 (1973), pp. 308–312.

86. Mark A. Huselid, "The Impact of Human Resource Management Practices on Turnover, Productivity, and Corporate Financial Performance," *Academy of Management Journal* 38(3), 1995, pp. 635–673.

87. Barry Gerhart, Sara L. Rynes, and Ingrid Smithey Fullmer, "Pay and Performance: Individuals, Groups and Executives," in *Academy of Management Annals,* vol. 3, A. P. Brief and J. P. Walsh, eds. (Newark, NJ: Lawrence Erlbaum, 2009).

88. E. Lazear, "Performance Pay and Productivity." *American Economic Review* 90(6), 2000, 1346–1361.

89. E. A. Locke, D. B. Feren, V. M. McCaleb, K. N. Shaw, and A. T. Denny, "The Relative Effectiveness of Four Methods of Motivating Employee Performance" in Changes in Working Life, K. D. Duncan, M. M. Gruenberg, and D. Wallis, eds. (New York: Wiley, 1980), pp. 363–388.

90. B. Gerhart and G. T. Milkovich, "Employee Compensation: Research and Practice," in *Handbook of Industrial & Organizational Psychology,* 2nd ed., M. D. Dunnette and L. M. Hough, eds. (Palo Alto, CA: Consulting Psychologists Press, 1992).

91. C. Q. Trank, S. L. Rynes, and R. D. Bretz, Jr., "Attracting Applicants in the War for Talent: Differences in Work Preferences Among High Achievers," *Journal of Business and Psychology* 16 (2001), pp. 331–345.

92. David A. Comerford and Peter A. Ubel, "Effort Aversion: Job Choice and Amount of Effort Required in Work." *Journal of Economic Behavior and Organizations* 92(8), August 2013, 152–162.

93. Derek Jones, Panu Kalmi, and Antii Kauhanen, "Teams, Incentive Pay, and Productive Efficiency: Evidence from a Food-Processing Plant," *Industrial and Labor Relations Review* 63(4), 2010, pp. 606–626.

94. J. McAdams and E. Hawk, "Organizational Performance and Rewards," *ACA Journal* 3(3), 1994, pp. 28–34.

95. B. Gerhart and G. Milkovich, "Organizational Differences in Managerial Compensation and Financial Performance," *Academy of Management Journal* 33 (1990), pp. 663–690.

96. K. Kelly and E. Schine, "How Did Sears Blow This Gasket?" *BusinessWeek,* June 29, 1992, p. 38.

97. Jerry Newman, personal correspondence, April 5, 2015.

98. G. Morenson and J. Rosner, *Reckless Endangerment: How Outsized Ambition, Greed, and Corruption Led to Economic Armageddon,* Time Magazine books, 2011.

99. Richard Metcalf, "A Modest Raise," *Albuquerque Tribune,* October 6, 2002, p. C1.

100. IOMA, "When Are Bonuses High Enough to Improve Performance?" *IOMA* (Newark, NJ: Institute of Management and Administration, November 1996), p. 12.

101. A. Richter, "Paying the People in Black at Big Blue," *Compensation and Benefits Review,* May/June 1998, pp. 51–59.

102. John Thibaut and Laurens Walker, *Procedural Justice: A Psychological View* (Hillsdale, NJ: Wiley, 1975).

103. M. Bloom, "The Performance Effects of Pay Dispersion on Individuals and Organizations," *Academy of Management Journal* 4(1), 1999, pp. 25–40.

104. Joel Brockner, "Making Sense of Procedural Fairness: How High Procedural Fairness Can Reduce or Heighten the Influence of Outcome Favorability," *Academy of Management Review* 27(1), 2002, pp. 58–76.

105. Robert Folger and Mary Konovsky, "Effects of Procedural and Distributive Justice on Reactions to Pay Raise Decisions," *Academy of Management Journal* 32(1), March 1989, pp. 155–130.

106. S. Alexander and M. Ruderman, "The Role of Procedural and Distributive Justice in Organizational Behavior," *Social Justice Research* 1 (1987), pp. 177–198.

107. Gus Defranco, "The Effect of Disclosure on the Pay-Performance Relation." *Journal of Accounting and Public Policy*, 32, 2013, 117–136.

108. G. S. Leventhal, J. Karuza, and W. R. Fry, "Beyond Fairness: A Theory of Allocation Preferences," in *Justice and Social Interaction,* G. Mikula, ed. (New York: Springer Verlag, 1980), pp. 167–218.

109. IOMA, *Complete Guide to Best Practices in Pay for Performance* (Newark: NJ: Institute of Management and Administration, 2005).

110. K. B. Stone, B. A. Backhaus, and K. Heiner, "Exploring the Relationship between Corporate Social Performance and Employer Attractiveness," *Business and Society,* September 2002, pp. 28–41.

Pay-for-Performance Plans

Chapter Outline

WHAT IS A PAY-FOR-PERFORMANCE PLAN?

Good question! Many different compensation practices are lumped under the name **pay-for-performance.** When your Mom told you last summer she would give you 20 dollars to cut the grass, that's a pay-for-performance plan! When you didn't do a very good job because you were rushing to make a pick up game on the local court, and she paid you anyway, that's still a pay-for-performance plan, just not a very good one. Indeed it sounds like your Mom learned about pay-for-performance from many of the managers we've met—don't distinguish between good and bad performance and pay everyone about the same.

Listen long enough and you will hear about **incentive plans, variable pay plans, compensation at risk, earnings at risk, success sharing, risk sharing,** and others.

Sometimes these names are used interchangeably. They shouldn't be. The major thing all these names have in common is a shift in thinking about compensation. We used to think of pay as primarily an entitlement. If you went to work and did well enough to avoid being fired, you were entitled to the same size check as everyone else doing the same job as you. Pay-for-performance plans signal a movement away from entitlement . . . sometimes a very *slow* movement toward pay that varies with some measure of individual or organizational performance. Of the pay components we discussed in Chapter 9, only base pay and across-the-board increases don't fit the pay-for-performance category. Curiously, though, many of the surveys on pay for performance tend to omit the grandfather of all these plans, **merit pay.**

Despite this omission, merit pay is still a pay-for-performance plan used for more than three-quarters of all exempt, clerical, and administrative employees.[1] In comparison, variable pay of some form (individual or group incentive pay) is offered by 95 percent of all companies, up from 51 percent in 1991 (see Exhibit 10.1 for other forms of variable pay).[2]

Exhibit 10.1 illustrates the wide variety of variable-pay plans in use today. What used to be primarily a compensation tool for top management is gradually becoming more prevalent for lower-level employees, too. Exhibit 10.2 indicates that variable pay is commanding a larger share of total compensation for all employee groups.

The greater interest in variable pay probably can be traced to two trends. First, the increasing competition from foreign producers forces American firms to cut costs and/or increase productivity. Well-designed variable-pay plans have a proven track record in motivating better performance and helping cut costs. Plus, variable pay is, by definition, a variable cost. No profits, or poor profits, means no extra pay beyond base pay—when times are bad, compensation is lower.[3] Second, today's fast-paced business environment means that workers must be willing to adjust what they do and how they do it. There are new technologies, new work processes, and new work relationships. All these require workers to adapt in new ways and with a speed that is unparalleled. Failure to move quickly means market

EXHIBIT 10.1 Use of Different Variable Payment Plan Types

Type of Plan	Percent of Companies with Plan						
	1998	1999	2002	2007	2010	2012	2014
Special recognition plans	51	59	34	72	58	42	65
Stock option plans	46	43	40	34	20	26	30/63*
Individual incentive plans	35	39	38	36	39	39	38
Cash profit sharing	22	23	18	24	19	19	16
Gainsharing plans	20	18	11	10	33	N/A	9
Team awards	17	15	8	17	26	26	28

Source: 2014, 2012, and 2010 data from WorldatWork and Vivient Consulting, "Private Company Incentive Pay Practices Survey" January 2012 2007 data are from US Compensation Planning Survey, Mercer Human Resource Consulting; 2005 data are from *www.hewitt.com* as reported in IOMA, *Complete Guide to Best Practices in Pay for Performance,* 2005, pp. 1–8; 2002 data are from IOMA, "Latest Data—What's Hot and What's Not in PFP," *Pay for Performance Report,* May 2002, p. 11, and IOMA, "Variable Pay Popularity," *Pay for Performance Report,* January 2003, p. 8; 1996–1999 data are from IOMA, "The Goods and Evils of Variable-Based Pay," *Pay for Performance Report,* July 2000, p. 12.

*exempt and executive employee participation respectively

EXHIBIT 10.2
Base versus
Variable Pay

	Percentage of Total Compensation Today				
	2004	**2005**	**2009**	**2010**	**2014***
Variable Pay as a percentage of payroll	9.5	11.4	12	11.8	8–17

Sources: 2014 World at Work and Vivient Consulting Survey; 2009 and 2010 data are from 2010 data from WorldatWork and Vivient Consulting, "Private Company Incentive Pay Practices Survey" January 2012. 2005 data are from *www.hewitt.com* survey as reported in IOMA.

*Executives, not included in this range, are at 46%

share goes to competitors. If this happens, workers face possible layoffs and terminations. To avoid this scenario, compensation experts are focusing on ways to design reward systems so that workers will be able—and willing—to move quickly into new jobs and new ways of performing old jobs. The ability and incentive to do this come partially from reward systems that more closely link worker interests with the objectives of the company.[4]

DOES VARIABLE PAY IMPROVE PERFORMANCE RESULTS? THE GENERAL EVIDENCE

As the evidence pointed out in Chapter 9, pay-for-performance plans, those that introduce variability into the level of pay you receive, seem to have a positive impact on performance if designed well. Notice that we have qualified our statement that variable-pay plans can be effective *if they are designed well.* Too often though the plans have too small a payout for the work expected, unattainable (or too easy) goals, outdated or inaccurate metrics, or even too many metrics making it hard to determine what is important.[5] In the next sections, we talk about issues in design and the impacts they can have.

SPECIFIC PAY-FOR-PERFORMANCE PLANS: SHORT TERM

Merit Pay

A **merit pay** system links increases in base pay (called *merit increases*) to how highly employees are rated on a performance evaluation. Chapter 11 covers performance evaluation, but as a simple illustration consider the following typical merit pay setup:

	Well Above Average	Above Average	Average	Below Average	Well Below Average
Performance rating	1	2	3	4	5
Merit pay increase	5%	4%	3%	1%	0%

At the end of a performance year, the employee is evaluated, usually by the direct supervisor. The performance rating, 1 to 5 in the above example, determines the size of the increase added into base pay. This last point is important. In effect, what you do this year in terms of performance is rewarded *every year* you remain with your employer. By building into base pay, the dollar amount, just like the Energizer bunny, keeps on going! With compounding, this can amount to tens of thousands of dollars over an employee's work career.[6]

Increasingly, merit pay is under attack. Not only is it expensive, but many argue it doesn't achieve the desired goal: improving employee and corporate performance.[7] In a thorough review of merit pay literature, though, Heneman concludes that merit pay does have a small, but significant, impact on performance.[8] High performance ratings are nearly always statistically related to high merit increases and the reverse holds too. Departments and strategic business units with better merit pay programs have higher subsequent performance.[9] And removal of merit pay appears to result in lower subsequent performance, as well as lower satisfaction among top performers. A final argument for merit pay centers on the sorting effect we discuss throughout our sections on variable pay impacts. People who don't want to have their pay tied to performance don't accept jobs at such companies or leave when pay for performance is implemented. This sorting leaves a residual workforce that is more productive and more responsive to merit rewards.[10]

Meanwhile, at the state/municipal levels, public schools in Minnesota, Ohio, Denver, and Philadelphia led the way to merit pay for teachers.[11] In Cincinnati, for example, teachers are held accountable for things they control: good professional practices. Teachers argue they should be held to standards similar to doctors: not a promise of a long healthy life but a promise that the highest professional standards will be followed. To assess teacher professional practices in Cincinnati, six evaluations are conducted over the school year, four by a trained teacher evaluator (essentially a trained teacher) and two by a building administrator. The size of pay increases is directly linked to performance during these observational reviews.[12] Perhaps because of these pioneers, in 2006 Congress appropriated $99 million per annum to school districts, charter schools, and states on a competitive basis to fund development and implementation of principal and teacher performance-related pay programs.[13] In another vein, the public sector is also experimenting with bonuses for better student test scores. Teachers who show improved student scores can receive up to $8,000 in annual bonuses in Chicago and up to $15,000 in Nashville.[14] Be careful what you wish for, though! New York state teachers and principals recently were caught cheating on the grading process for regents' exams. The lure of bonuses totaling as much as $3,500 for teachers, and increased funding for principals' schools if pass rates improved, was too tempting.[15]

Of course, we could always design a system like that used in South Korea, a country whose students consistently outperform ours. Teachers in private schools often are paid on incentive. The dollar amount can be staggering if you're judged to be a good teacher. Kim Hi-Koon is an after school tutor who makes 4 million per year because of his performance. He teaches three hours of lectures then spends 50 or so hours tutoring students online, developing lesson plans, and writing texts.[16]

If we want merit pay to live up to its potential, it needs to be managed better.[17] This requires a complete overhaul of the way we allocate raises: improving the accuracy of performance ratings, allocating enough merit money to truly reward performance, and making sure the size of the merit increase differentiates across performance levels. To illustrate the latter point, consider the employee who works hard all year, earns a 5 percent increase as our guidelines above indicate, and compares herself with the

EXHIBIT 10.3
Relative Cost
Comparisons

	Merit Pay		Merit Bonus
Base pay	$50,000		$50,000
Year 1 payout 5%	(2,500)	5%	(2,500)
New base pay	52,500		50,000
Extra cost total	2,500		2,500
Year 2 payout 5%	($2,625 = .05 × 52,500)	5%	(2,500 =.05 × 50,000)
New base pay	55,125 (52,500 + 2,625)		50,000
Extra cost total	5,125		5,000
After 5 years:			
Year 5 payout	3,039		2,500
New base pay	63,814		50,000

average performer who coasts to a 3 percent increase. First we take out taxes on that extra 2 percent. Then we spread the raise out over 52 paychecks. It's only a slight exaggeration to suggest that the extra money won't pay for a good cup of coffee. Unless we make the reward difference larger for every increment in performance, many employees are going to say, "Why bother?"

Merit Bonuses Aka Lump-Sum Bonuses

Merit bonuses are thought to be a substitute for merit pay. Based on employee or company performance, employees receive an end-of-year bonus that does not build into base pay. Because employees must earn this increase every year, it is viewed as less of an entitlement than merit pay. As Exhibit 10.3 indicates, merit bonuses can be considerably less expensive than merit pay over the long run.

Notice how quickly base pay rises under a merit pay plan. After just five years, base pay is almost $14,000 higher than it is under a merit bonus plan. It should be no surprise that cost-conscious firms report switching to merit bonuses. It also should be no surprise that employees aren't particularly fond of merit bonuses. After all, the intent of merit is to cause shock waves in an entitlement culture. By giving merit for several years, a company is essentially freezing base pay. Gradually this results in a repositioning relative to competitors. The message becomes loud and clear: "Don't expect to receive increases in base pay year after year—new rewards must be earned each year." Consider the bonus system developed by Prometric Thomson Learning call centers, which register candidates for computerized tests. The centers have very clear targets that yield specific employee bonuses, as shown in Exhibit 10.4. At Prometric, each day is a new day when it comes to earning bonuses.

Individual Spot Awards

Technically, **spot awards** should fall under pay-for-performance plans. About 35 percent of all companies use spot awards.[18] And an impressive 74 percent of companies in one survey reported that these awards were either highly or moderately effective.[19] Usually these payouts are awarded for exceptional performance, often on

EXHIBIT 10.4   Customer Service Bonus Scheme at Prometric Thomson Learning Call Centers

Performance Measure	Minimum Performance	Bonus	Target Performance	Bonus	Superior Performance	Bonus
Average call wait	<32 min/day	0.5%	<28 min/day	1%	<20 min/day	1.75%
Average talk time	3 min 50 sec	.5	<3 min 20 sec	1	3 min	1.75
Attendance	2 occurrences	.5	1 occurrence	1	0 occurrence	1.75
Quality	As monitored	.5	As monitored	1	As monitored	0.75
Total Bonus		2%		4%		7%

special projects or for performance that so exceeds expectations as to be deserving of an add-on bonus. The mechanics are simple: After the fact, someone in the organization alerts top management to the exceptional performance. If the company is large, there may be a formal mechanism for this recognition, and perhaps some guidelines on the size of the spot award (so named because it is supposed to be awarded "on the spot"). Smaller companies may be more casual about recognition and more subjective about deciding the size of the award. The University of California at San Francisco's Pharmacy School has a pretty typical spot award program. Awards of up to $225 are given for such behaviors as "effectively resolved a complaint situation," or "went beyond the expected by staying late to get a grant out on time."[20]

Individual Incentive Plans

These plans differ from the merit and lump sum payments because they offer a promise of pay for some objective, preestablished level of performance. For example, offering students financial incentives for getting better grades actually works. These students end up having better first and second year grade point averages. The "bribe" worked even better for impatient students. Yeah, we know, get on with the story.[21]

On a more suspect note, reports indicate a large part of the income for some doctors in linked to incentives given by the pharmaceutical industry. For the last five months of last year the pharmaceutical industry paid 3.5 million to doctors, simply for considering their drugs!

All incentive plans have one common feature: an established standard against which worker performance is compared to determine the magnitude of the incentive pay. For individual incentive systems, this standard is compared against individual worker performance. Because it's often difficult to find good, objective individual measures, individual incentive plans don't work for every job. How, for example, would you come up with an incentive plan for construction laborers? Maybe if they did the same thing all day the task wouldn't be difficult: Your goal is to dig 5 feet of trench, 2 feet wide by 18 inches deep, every hour. But construction laborers aren't limited to shovel jobs. They also help pour concrete, assist carpenters and masons framing buildings, etc. The job is too complex for an individual incentive plan. Even a repetitive job like working on an assembly line isn't well-suited to individual incentives. One of us (Newman) used to work on a Ford assembly line building Lincolns. Even if we wanted to build faster to make more money, the line went by with a new car frame every 55 seconds. No room for individual differences here, we would argue.

EXHIBIT 10.5
Individual
Incentive Plans

		Method of Rate Determination	
		Units of production per time period	*Time period per unit of production*
Relationship between Production Level and Pay	*Pay constant function of production level*	(1) Straight piecework plan	(2) Standard hour and Bedeaux plans
	Pay varies as function of production level	(3) Taylor differential piece-rate system Merrick multiple piece-rate system	(4) Halsey 50-50 method Rowan plan Gantt plan

Despite this constraint, a number of different individual incentive plans exist. Their differences can be reduced to variation along two dimensions and can be classified into one of four cells, as illustrated in Exhibit 10.5.

The first dimension on which incentive systems vary is in the **method of rate determination.** Plans set up a rate based either on units of production per time period or on time period per unit of production. On the surface, this distinction may appear trivial, but, in fact, the deviations arise because tasks have different cycles of operation.[22] Short-cycle tasks, those that are completed in a relatively short period of time, typically have as a standard a designated number of units to be produced in a given time period. For example, a book distributor we worked with had an incentive plan for packers. Number of books packed is a short cycle task, with only seconds taken to get a book from a supply stack and place in a shipping box. For long-cycle tasks, this would not be appropriate. It is entirely possible that only one task or some portion of it may be completed in a day. Consequently, for longer-cycle tasks, the standard is typically set in terms of time required to complete one unit of production. Individual incentives are based on whether or not workers complete the task in the designated time period. Auto mechanics work off a blue book that tells how long, for example, a fuel injection system should take to replace. Finish faster than the allotted time and the full pay is awarded.

The second dimension on which individual incentive systems vary is the *specified relationship between production level and wages.* The first alternative is to tie wages to output on a one-to-one basis, so that wages are some constant function of production. In contrast, some plans vary wages as a function of production level. For example, one common alternative is to provide higher dollar rates for production above the standard than for production below the standard.

Each of the plans discussed in this section has as a foundation a standard level of performance determined by some form of time study or job analysis completed by an industrial engineer or trained personnel administrator. The variations in these plans occur in either the way the standard is set or the way wages are tied to output. As in Exhibit 10.5, there are four general categories of plans:

1. *Cell 1:* The most frequently implemented incentive system is a **straight piecework system.** Rate determination is based on units of production per time period, and wages vary directly as a function of production level. The major advantages of this type of system are that it is easily understood by workers and, perhaps consequently, is more readily accepted than some of the other incentive systems.

2. *Cell 2:* Two relatively common plans set standards based on time per unit and tie incentives directly to level of output: (1) **standard hour plans** and (2) **Bedeaux plans.** A standard hour plan is a generic term for plans setting the incentive rate based on completion of a task in some expected time period. A common example we introduced earlier can be found in any neighborhood gasoline station or automobile repair shop. Let us assume that you need a new transmission. The estimate you receive for labor costs is based on the mechanic's hourly rate of pay, multiplied by a time estimate for job completion derived from a book listing average time estimates for a wide variety of jobs. If the mechanic receives $40 per hour and a transmission is listed as requiring four hours to be removed and replaced, the labor cost would be $160. All this is determined in advance of any actual work. Of course, if the mechanic is highly experienced and fast, the job may be completed in considerably less time than indicated in the book. However, the job is still charged as if it took the quoted time to complete. The "surplus" money is split between the employee and the service station. Standard hour plans are more practical than straight piecework plans for long-cycle operations and jobs that are nonrepetitive and require numerous skills for completion.[23]

3. A *Bedeaux* plan provides a variation on straight piecework and standard hour plans. Instead of timing an entire task, a Bedeaux plan requires division of a task into simple actions and determination of the time required by an average skilled worker to complete each action. After the more detailed time analysis of tasks, the Bedeaux system functions similarly to a standard hour plan.

4. *Cell 3:* The two plans included in cell 3 provide for variable incentives as a function of units of production per time period. Both the **Taylor plan** and the **Merrick plan** provide different piece rates, depending on the level of production relative to the standard. The Taylor plan establishes two piecework rates. One rate goes into effect when a worker exceeds the published standard for a given time period. This rate is set higher than the regular wage incentive level. A second rate is established for production below standard, and this rate is lower than the regular wage.

   The Merrick system operates in the same way, except that three piecework rates are set: (1) high for production exceeding 100 percent of standard; (2) medium for production between 83 and 100 percent of standard; and (3) low for production less than 83 percent of standard. Exhibit 10.6 compares these two plans.

5. *Cell 4:* The three plans included in cell 4 provide for variable incentives linked to a standard expressed as a time period per unit of production. The three plans include the Halsey 50–50 method, the Rowan plan, and the Gantt plan.

The **Halsey 50–50 method** derives its name from the shared split between worker and employer of any savings in direct cost. An allowed time for a task is determined via time study. The savings from completion of a task in less than the standard time are allocated 50–50 (most frequent division) between the worker and the company.

EXHIBIT 10.6
The Taylor and Merrick Plans

- Piece-rate standard: 10 units/hour
- Standard wage: $5/hour
- Piecework rate:

Output (Units/hour)	Taylor		Merrick	
	Rate per Unit	Wage	Rate per Unit	Wage
7	$.50	$3.50	$.50	$3.50
8	$.50	$4.00	$.50	$4.00
9	$.50	$4.50	$.60	$5.40
10	$.50	$5.00	$.60	$6.00
11	$.70	$7.70	$.70	$7.70
12 +	Calculations at same rate as for 11 units.			

The **Rowan plan** is similar to the Halsey plan in that an employer and employee both share in savings resulting from work completed in less than standard time. The major distinction in this plan, however, is that a worker's bonus increases as the time required to complete the task decreases. For example, if the standard time to complete a task is 10 hours and it is completed in 7 hours, the worker receives a 30 percent bonus. Completion of the same task in 6 hours would result in a 40 percent bonus above the hourly wage for each of the 6 hours.

The **Gantt plan** differs from both the Halsey and the Rowan plans in that the standard time for a task is purposely set at a level requiring high effort to complete. Any worker who fails to complete the task in the standard time is guaranteed a preestablished wage. However, for any task completed in standard time or less, earnings are pegged at 120 percent of the time saved. Consequently, workers' earnings increase faster than production whenever standard time is met or exceeded.

Individual Incentive Plans: Advantages and Disadvantages

We already mentioned that incentive plans can lead to unexpected, and undesired, behaviors. Certainly Sears, our example in Chapter 9, did not want the public relations nightmare of having mechanics sell unnecessary repairs, but the incentive program encouraged that type of behavior. Please don't think Sears is an isolated example. Workers in a subsidiary of Caterpillar were placed on an incentive system to find problems with rail cars that could be repaired and charged back to their respective owners. Under pressure employees—just like at Sears—manufactured problems (smashing brakes with hammers, ruining wheels with chisels) and then making the "repairs."[24] This is a common problem with incentive plans: Employees and managers end up in conflict because the incentive system often focuses only on one small part of what it takes for the company to be successful.[25] Employees, being rational, do more of what the incentive system pays for. Sales staff provide a perfect example. Try developing a unit-based sales system that doesn't prioritize products by offering different levels of incentives. In this case the smart salesperson sells the easiest product to unload (e.g., discounted and bargain prices products).[26] As a sad example, New York teachers and administrators were put on an incentive system to get student pass rates and

EXHIBIT 10.7 Advantages and Disadvantages of Individualized Incentive Plans

Advantages

1. Substantial impact that raises productivity, lowers production costs, and increases earnings of workers.

2. Less direct supervision is required to maintain reasonable levels of output than under payment by time.

3. In most cases, systems of payment by results, if accompanied by improved organizational and work measurement, enable labor costs to be estimated more accurately than under payment by time. This helps costing and budgetary control.

Disadvantages

1. Greater conflict may emerge between employees seeking to maximize output and managers concerned about deteriorating quality levels.

2. Attempts to introduce new technology may be resisted by employees concerned about the impact on production standards.

3. Reduced willingness of employees to suggest new production methods for fear of subsequent increases in production standards.

4. Increased complaints that equipment is poorly maintained, hindering employee efforts to earn larger incentives.

5. Increased turnover among new employees discouraged by the unwillingness of experienced workers to cooperate in on-the-job training.

6. Elevated levels of mistrust between workers and management.

Source: Michael Coates, *Psychology and Organizations, Heineman Themes in Psychology* (Boston, MA: Heineman, 2001); T. Wilson, "Is It Time to Eliminate the Piece Rate Incentive System?" *Compensation and Benefits Review* 24(2), 1992, pp. 43–49; Pinhas Schwinger, *Wage Incentive Systems* (New York: Halsted, 1975).

graduation numbers up. Both these rates increased, not because of better performance, but because standards were lowered so the incentive would be paid out.[27] Exhibit 10.7 outlines some of the other problems, as well as advantages, with individual incentive plans.

Individual Incentive Plans: Examples

Even though incentive systems are less popular than they used to be, there are still notable successes. Of course, most sales positions have some part of pay based on commissions, a form of individual incentive. One of today's biggest success stories is the merger of individual incentives with efforts to reduce health care costs. For example, Jet Blue deposits 400 dollars into employee health reimbursement accounts for participating in various activities such as smoking cessation programs or running in ironman contests. In general, health incentives are on the rise: 57 percent of companies used them in 2009 while 75 percent are expected to use them this year.[28] Perhaps the longest-running success with individual incentives, going back to before World War I, belongs to a company called Lincoln Electric. In Exhibit 10.8, the compensation package for factory jobs at Lincoln Electric is described. Notice how the different pieces fit together. This isn't a case of an incentive plan operating in a vacuum. All the pieces of the compensation and reward package fit together. Both culture and the performance review system support the different pay components. Lincoln Electric's success is so striking that it's the subject of many case analyses.[29]

EXHIBIT 10.8   Lincoln Electric's Compensation System

Description of culture	Reservoir of trust. Long history of employment stability even during severe economic downturns. Employees with 3+ years' seniority are guaranteed (on 1 year renewable basis) at least 75 percent full-time work for that year. In exchange, employees agree to flexible assignment across jobs.
Base wages	Market rate determined. Time study department sets piece rate so that average worker can earn market rate.
Bonus (short term)	Board of directors sets year-end bonus pool as function of company performance. Employee's share in pool is function of semiannual performance review (see below).
Incentive (long term)	Employees share in long-term company successes/failures in form of **employee stock ownership plan (ESOP).** Employees now own 28 percent of outstanding stock shares.
Performance review	Employees rated on four factors: (1) dependability, (2) quality, (3) output, (4) ideas and cooperation in comparison to others in department. To ensure against rating inflation, the average score in department cannot exceed 100.

TEAM INCENTIVE PLANS: TYPES

When we move away from individual incentive systems and start focusing on people working together, we shift to **group incentive plans.** The group might be a work team. It might be a department. Or we might focus on a division or the whole company. Or it might even be a pirate ship! Around 1750 Captain Henry Morgan, infamous pirate, recruited and motivated his men using a simple group incentive plan: an even split of all "booty" captured (of course, after distribution of shares to Captain Morgan and his top men). "No prey, no pay" was an early tagline, and it worked: A good day for a pirate was 1000 pounds, far more than the 13–33 pounds earned by merchant seamen in more legitimate vessels.[30] The basic concept is still the same, though. A standard is established against which worker performance (in this case, team performance) is compared to determine the magnitude of the incentive pay. With the focus on groups, now we are concerned about group performance in comparison against some standard, or level, of expected performance. The standard might be an expected level of operating income for a division. Or the measure might be more unusual, as at Litton Industries (now a part of Northrop Grumman Corp). One division has a team variable-pay measure that is based on whether customers would be willing to act as a reference when Litton solicits other business. The more customers willing to do this, the larger the team's variable pay.[31] In a second study, four food processing plants moved to team-based structures and implements team incentive plans. The team incentive component resulted in productivity increases of 9–20 percent.[32] Some group incentive plans have even higher success goals—like winning a war. Napoleon took over an army that was underfed and demoralized. He developed one of the earliest profit sharing plans by promising soldiers a share of any bounty achieved. When Napoleon defeated Italians in what is now the Piedmont region, he demanded gold and silver from the defeated foe. Morale soared when Napoleon then shared this with his troops.

Despite an explosion of interest in teams and team compensation, many of the reports from the front lines are not encouraging.[33] Companies report they generally are not satisfied with the way their team compensation systems work. Failures of team incentive schemes can be attributed to at least five causes.[34] First, one of the problems with team compensation is that teams come in many varieties. There are full-time teams (work group organized as a team). There are part-time teams that cut across functional departments (experts from different departments pulled together to improve customer relations). There are even full-time teams that are temporary (e.g., cross-functional teams pulled together to help ease the transition into a partnership or joint venture).

With so many varieties of teams, it's hard to argue for one consistent type of compensation plan. Unfortunately, we still seem to be at the stage of trying to find the one best way. Maybe the answer is to look at different compensation approaches for different types of teams. Perhaps the best illustration of this differential approach for different teams comes from Xerox.

Xerox has a **gain-sharing plan** that pays off for teams defined at a very broad level, usually at the level of a strategic business unit. For smaller teams, primarily intact work teams (e.g., all people in a department or function), there are group rewards based on supervisory judgments of performance. Units that opt to have their performance judged as teams (it is also possible to declare that a unit wouldn't be fairly judged if team measures were used) have managers who judge the amount to be allocated to each team based on the team's specific performance results. For new teams, the manager might also decide how much of the total will go to each individual on the team. More mature teams do individual allocations on their own. In Xerox's experience, these teams start out allocating equal shares, but as they evolve the teams allocate based on each worker's performance. Out of about 2,000 work teams worldwide at Xerox, perhaps 100 have evolved to this level of sophistication. For problem-solving teams and other temporary teams, Xerox has a reward component called the Xerox Achievement Award. Teams must be nominated for exceptional performance. A committee decides which teams meet a set of predetermined absolute standards. Even contributors outside the core team can share in the award. If nominated by team members, extended members who provide crucial added value are given cash bonuses equal to those of team members.

A second problem with rewarding teams is called the "level problem." If we define teams at the very broad level—the whole organization being an extreme example—much of the motivational impact of incentives can be lost. As a member of a 1,000-person team, I'm unlikely to be at all convinced that my extra effort will significantly affect our team's overall performance. Why, then, should I try hard? Conversely, if we let teams get too small, other problems arise. TRW found that small work teams competing for a fixed piece of incentive awards tend to gravitate to behaviors that are clearly unhealthy for overall corporate success. Teams hoard star performers, refusing to allow transfers even for the greater good of the company. Teams are reluctant to take on new employees for fear that time lost to training will hurt the team—even when the added employees are essential to long-run success. Finally, bickering arises when awards are given. Because teams have different performance objectives, it is difficult to equalize for difficulty when assigning rewards. Inevitably, complaints arise.[35]

The last three major problems with team compensation involve the three Cs: *complexity, control,* and *communications.* Some plans are simply too complex. Xerox's

Houston facility had a gain-sharing plan for teams that required understanding a three-dimensional performance matrix. Employees (and these authors!) threw their hands up in dismay when they tried to understand the "easy-to-follow directions." In contrast, Xerox's San Diego unit has had great success with a simple program called "bet the boss." Employees come to the boss with a performance-saving idea and bet their hard effort against the boss's incentive that they can deliver. Such plans have a simplicity that encourages employee buy-in. With a good line of sight as it's called, employees can see a clear link between their effort and the rewards they receive.

The second C is control. Praxair, a worldwide provider of gases (including oxygen) extracted from the atmosphere, works hard to make sure all its team pay comes from performance measures under the control of the team. If mother nature ravages a construction site, causing delays and skyrocketing costs, workers aren't penalized with reduced team payouts. Such uncontrollable elements are factored into the process of setting performance standards. Indeed, experts assert that this ability to foretell sources of problems and adjust for them is a key element in building a team pay plan.[36] Key to the control issue is the whole question of fairness. Are the rewards fair given our ability to produce results? Recent research suggests that this perception of fairness is crucial.[37] With it, employees feel it is appropriate to monitor all members of the group—slackers beware! Without fairness, employees seem to have less sense of responsibility for the team's outcomes.[38]

The final C is a familiar factor in compensation successes and failures: communication. Team-based pay plans simply are not well communicated. Employees asked to explain their plans often flounder because more effort has been devoted to designing the plan than to deciding how to explain it. Conversely, the more transparent the plan, the more employees trust management and respond positively to the incentive effects of the plan.

Although there is much pessimism about team-based compensation, many companies still seek ways to reward groups of employees for their interdependent work efforts. Companies that do use team incentives typically set team performance standards based on productivity improvements (38 percent of plans), customer satisfaction measures (37 percent), financial performance (34 percent), or quality of goods and services (28 percent).[39] For example, Kraft Foods uses a combination of financial measures (e.g., income from operations and cash flow) combined with measures designed to gauge success in developing managers, building diversity, and adding to market share.[40] Exhibit 10.9 summarizes some of these measures.

As Exhibit 10.9 suggests, the range of performance measures for different types of corporate objectives is indeed impressive.[41] For example, if the corporate objective is to reward short term performance, the measures outlined in Exhibit 10.10 could be used.

Historically, financial measures have been the most widely used performance indicator for large group incentive plans. Increasingly, though, top executives express concern that these measures do a better job of communicating performance to stock analysts than to managers trying to figure out how to improve operating effectiveness.[42]

Whatever our thinking is about appropriate performance measures, the central point is still that we are now concerned about group performance. This presents both problems and opportunities. As Exhibit 10.11 illustrates, we need to decide which type of group

EXHIBIT 10.9 A Sampling of Performance Measures

Customer-Focused Measures	Financially Focused Measures
Time-to-Market Measures	**Value Creation**
• On-time delivery	• Revenue growth
• Cycle time	• Resource yields
• New product introductions	• Profit margins
	• Economic value added
Customer Satisfaction Measures	**Shareholder Return**
• Market share	• Return on invested capital
• Customer satisfaction	• Return on sales/earnings
• Customer growth and retention	• Earnings per share
• Account penetration	• Growth in profitability
Capability-Focused Measures	**Internal Process-Focused Measures**
Human Resource Capabilities	**Resource Utilization**
• Employee satisfaction	• Budget-to-actual expenses
• Turnover rates	• Cost-allocation ratios
• Total recruitment costs	• Reliability/rework
• Rate of progress on developmental plans	• Accuracy/error rates
• Promotability index	• Safety rates
• Staffing mix/head-count ratio	
Other Asset Capabilities	**Change Effectiveness**
• Patents/copyrights/regulations	• Program implementation
• Distribution systems	• Teamwork effectiveness
• Technological capabilities	• Service/quality index

EXHIBIT 10.10 Private Company Bonus Performance Measures

Measure	Percent of Companies Using
Sales	24
Operating income	24
Net income/EPS	28
Service quality/returns	23
Customer satisfaction	28
Operational efficiency	28

Source: WorldatWork and Vivien Consulting, "Private Company Incentive Pay Practices," http://www.worldatwork.org/waw/adimLink?id=74763 2014, Accessed April 10, 2015.

EXHIBIT 10.11 Types of Variable-Pay Plans: Advantages and Disadvantages

Plan Type	What Is It?	Advantages	Disadvantages	Why?
Cash profit sharing	• Award based on organizational profitability • Shares a percentage of profits (typically above a target level of profitability) • Usually an annual payout • Can be cash or deferred 401(k)	• Simple, easily understood • Low administrative costs	• Profit influenced by many factors beyond employee control • May be viewed as an entitlement • Limited motivational impact	• To educate employees about business operations • To foster teamwork or "one-for-all" environment
Stock ownership or options	• Award of stock shares or options	• Option awards have minimal impact on the financial statements of the company at the time they are granted • If properly communicated, can have powerful impact on employee behavior • Tax deferral to employee	• Indirect pay/performance link • Employees may be required to put up money to exercise grants	• To recruit top-quality employees when organization has highly uncertain future (i.e., start-ups, high-tech, or biotech industries) • To address employee retention concerns
Balanced scorecard	• Awards that combine financial and operating measures for organization, business unit, and/or individual performance • Award pool based on achieving performance targets	• Communicates organizational priorities	• Performance criteria may be met, but if financial targets are not met, there may be a reduced payout or no payout at all • Can be complex	• To focus employees on need to increase shareholder value • To focus employees on organization, division, and/or individual goals • To link payouts to a specific financial and/or operational target

	• Multiple performance measures may include: 1. Nonfinancial/operating: quality improvements, productivity gains, customer service improvements 2. Financial: EPS, ROE, ROA, revenues		
Productivity/gain sharing	• Awards that share economic benefits of improved productivity, quality, or other measurable results • Focus on group, plant, department, or division results • Designed to capitalize on untapped knowledge of employees	• Clear performance–reward links • Productivity and quality improvements • Employee's knowledge of business increases • Fosters teamwork, cooperation	• Can be administratively complicated • Unintended effects, like drop-off in quality • Management must "open the books" • Payouts can occur even if company's financial performance is poor	• To support a major productivity/quality initiative (such as TQM or reengineering) • To foster teamwork environment • To reward employees for improvements in activities that they control
Team/group incentives	• Awards determined based on team/group performance goals or objectives • Payout can be more frequent than annual and can also extend beyond the life of the team • Payout may be uniform for team/group members	• Reinforces teamwork and team identity/results • Effective in stimulating ideas and problem-solving • Minimizes distinctions between team members • May better reflect how work is performed	• May be difficult to isolate impact of team • Not all employees can be placed on a team • Can be administratively complex • May create team competition • Difficult to set equitable targets for all teams	• To demonstrate an organizational commitment to teams • To reinforce the need for employees to work together to achieve results

Source: From Kenan S. Abosch, "Variable Pay: Do We Have the Basics in Place?" *Compensation and Benefits Review*, 30(4) 1998, pp. 12–22. Compensation and Benefits Review by American Management Association.

incentive plan best fits our objectives. Indeed, we should even ask if an incentive plan is appropriate. Recent evidence, for example, suggests that firms high on business risk and those with uncertain outcomes, are better off not having incentive plans at all—corporate performance is higher.[43]

Comparing Group and Individual Incentive Plans

In this era of heightened concern about productivity, we frequently are asked if setting up incentive plans really boosts performance. As we noted in Chapter 9, the answer is yes. And individual—rather than group—incentives win the productivity "medal." We also are asked, though, which is better in a specific situation—group or individual incentive plans. Often this is a misleading question. Individual incentives yield higher productivity gains, but group incentives often are right in situations where team coordination is the issue. One study found that changing from individual incentives to gain sharing resulted in a decrease in grievances and a fairly dramatic increase in product quality (defects per 1,000 products shipped declined from 20.93 to 2.31).[44]

As we noted in Exhibit 10.11, things like the type of task, the organizational commitment to teams, and the type of work environment may preclude one or the other type of incentive plan. Exhibit 10.12 provides a guide for when to choose group or individual plans. When forced to choose the type of plan with greater productivity "pep," experts agree that individual incentive plans have better potential for—and probably better track records in—delivering higher productivity. Group plans suffer from what

EXHIBIT 10.12   **The Choice between Individual and Group Plans**

Characteristic	Choose an Individual Plan when . . .	Choose a Group Plan when . . .
Performance measurement	Good measures of individual performance exist. Task accomplishment not dependent on performance of others.	Output is group collaborative effort. Individual contributions to output cannot be assessed.
Organizational adaptability	Individual performance standards are stable. Production methods and labor mix relatively constant.	Performance standards for individuals change to meet environmental pressures on relatively constant organizational objectives. Production methods and labor mix must adapt to meet changing pressures.
Organizational commitment	Commitment strongest to individual's profession or superior. Supervisor viewed as unbiased and performance standards readily apparent.	High commitment to organization built upon sound communication of organizational objectives and performance standards.
Union status	Nonunion; unions promote equal treatment. Competition between individuals inhibits "fraternal" spirit.	Union or nonunion; unions less opposed to plans that foster cohesiveness of bargaining unit and which distribute rewards evenly across group.

Source: WorldatWork and Vivient Consulting, 2012. "Private Company Incentive Pay Practice Survey." Reprinted with permission.

is called the *free-rider problem.* See if this sounds familiar: You are a team member on a school project and at least one person doesn't carry his or her share of the load. Yet, when it comes time to divide the rewards, they are typically shared equally. Problems like this caused AT&T to phase out many of its team reward packages. Top-performing employees quickly grew disenchanted with having to carry free riders. End result— turnover of the very group that is most costly to lose.

Research on free riders suggests that the problem can be lessened through use of good performance measurement techniques. Specifically, free riders have a harder time loafing when there are clear performance standards. Rather than being given instructions to "do your best," poorer performers who were asked to deliver specific levels of performance at a specific time actually showed the most performance improvement.[45]

Large Group Incentive Plans

When we get beyond a small work team and try to incentivize large groups, there are generally two types of plans. Gain-sharing plans use operating measures to gauge performance. Profit sharing plans use financial measures.

Gain-Sharing Plans

Our discussion of team-based compensation often mentioned gain-sharing plans as a common component. As the name suggests, employees share in the gains in these types of group incentive plans. With profit-sharing plans (surprise) the sharing involves some form of profits. Realistically, though, most employees feel as if little they can do will affect profits; that's something top-management decisions influence more. So gain sharing looks at cost components of the income ledger and identifies savings over which employees have more impact (e.g., reduced scrap, lower labor costs, reduced utility costs). It was just this type of thinking that led the United States Post Office to an annual cost avoidance of $497 million under its gain-sharing plan.[46] Other studies of gain sharing report similar positive results. Indeed, the empirical evidence on gain sharing appears to be quite favorable.[47] One study of 1,600 employees in an auto parts company showed gain sharing over five years reduced labor, material, tool purchase, scrap, rework, and supply costs. The total savings were $15 million over the five-year period. Absenteeism (20%) and grievances (50%) also decreased.[48]

In a particularly good study of a major retailer, stores with gain-sharing incentives had 4.9 percent higher sales, 3.4 percent higher customer satisfaction, and 4.4 percent higher profit than stores without the incentive plan. In our experience these effects are pretty typical of gain-sharing plans—improvements in the 4–5 percent range. Keep in mind, though, gain-sharing plans can lead to the sorting effect we talked about in Chapter 9. Good employees want to be rewarded for their individual effort and performance. Changes to group plans, like gain-sharing, can lead to turnover. Just ask AT&T. They found that very high and very low performing individuals had much higher turnover rates under gain-sharing than other employees.[49] The following issues are key elements in designing a gain-sharing plan:[50]

1. *Strength of reinforcement:* What role should base pay assume relative to incentive pay? Incentive pay tends to encourage only those behaviors that are rewarded. For

example, try returning an unwanted birthday present to a store that pays its sales force solely for new sales. Tasks carrying no rewards are only reluctantly performed (if at all).

2. *Productivity standards:* What standard will be used to calculate whether employees will receive an incentive payout? Almost all group incentive plans use a historical standard. A historical standard involves choice of a prior year's performance to use for comparison with current performance. But which baseline year should be used? If too good (or too bad) a comparison year is used, the standard will be too hard (or easy) to achieve, with obvious motivational and cost effects. One possible compromise is to use a moving average of several years (e.g., the average for the past five years, with the five-year block changing by one year on an annual basis).

   One of the major problems with historical standards is that changing environmental conditions can render a standard ineffective. For example, consider the ice cream company that based profit sharing on a financial measure that had been easily achieved the prior year. What they didn't expect was a dramatic increase in milk costs. It was clear by the third month of the fiscal year that the goal wasn't going to be met, and grumblings amongst employees were mounting. The targets were adjusted and ice cream makers rejoiced.[51] Such problems are particularly insidious during economic swings and for organizations facing volatile economic climates. Care must be taken to ensure that the link between performance and rewards is sustained. This means that environmental influences on performance, which are not controllable by plan participants, should be factored out when identifying incentive levels.

3. *Sharing the gains split between management and workers:* Part of the plan must address the relative cuts between management and workers of any profit or savings generated. This also includes discussion of whether an emergency reserve (gains withheld from distribution in case of future emergencies) will be established in advance of any sharing of profits.

4. *Scope of the formula:* Formulas can vary in the scope of inclusions for both the labor inputs in the numerator and the productivity outcomes in the denominator.[52] Recent innovations in gain-sharing plans largely address broadening the types of productivity standards considered appropriate. Given that organizations are complex and require more complex measures, performance measures have expanded beyond traditional financial measures. For example, with the push for greater quality management, we could measure retention of customers or some other measure of customer satisfaction. Similarly, other measures include delivery performance, safety, absenteeism, turnaround time, and number of suggestions submitted. Four specific examples are:[53]

Performance Measure	Goal	Monthly Incentive Bonus
Error/Damage rate	20 per 10,000 units	To be Determined
Customer Dissatisfaction	1 per 100,000 lbs	TBD
Productivity Measure	10,000 lb/month	TBD
Cost	.1 lb below quota	TBD

5. Great care must be exercised with such alternative measures, though, to ensure that the behaviors reinforced actually affect the desired bottom-line goal. Getting workers to expend more effort, for example, might not always be the desired behavior. Increased effort may bring unacceptable levels of accidents. It may be preferable to encourage cooperative planning behaviors that result in more efficient work.

6. *Perceived fairness of the formula:* One way to ensure the plan is perceived as fair is to let employees vote on whether implementation should go forward. This and union participation in program design are two elements in plan success.[54]

7. *Ease of administration:* Sophisticated plans with involved calculations of profits or costs can become too complex for existing company information systems. Increased complexities also require more effective communications and higher levels of trust among participants.

8. *Production variability:* One of the major sources of problems in group incentive plans is failure to set targets properly. At times the problem can be traced to volatility in sales. Large swings in sales and profits, not due to any actions by workers, can cause both elation (in good times) and anger (in bad times). As stated above, a good plan ensures that environmental influences on performance, which are not controllable by plan participants, should be factored out when identifying incentive levels. The second author once worked with an ice cream producer that experienced huge unexpected increases in milk costs. End result? The original profit goal was unattainable. To their credit, the company adjusted the profit target to reflect the uncontrollable cost change. One alternative would be to set standards that are relative to industry performance. To the extent data are available, a company could trigger gain sharing when performance exceeds some industry norm. The obvious advantage of this strategy is that economic and other external factors hit all firms in the industry equally hard. If our company performs better, relatively, it means we are doing something as employees to help achieve success.

Exhibit 10.13 illustrates three different formulas that can be used as the basis for gain-sharing plans. The numerator, or input factor, is always some labor cost variable, expressed in either dollars or actual hours worked; the denominator is some output measure such as net sales or value added. Each of the plans determines employees' incentives based on the difference between the current value of the ratio and the ratio in some agreed-upon base year. The more favorable the current ratio relative to the historical

EXHIBIT 10.13   **Three Gain-Sharing Formulas**

	Scanlon Plan (Single Ratio Volume)	Rucker Plan	Improshare
Numerator of ratio (input factor)	Payroll costs	Labor cost	Actual hours worked
Denominator of ratio (output factor)	Net sales (plus or minus inventories)	Value added	Total standard value hours

EXHIBIT 10.14 Examples of a Scanlon Plan

2010 Data (base year) for Alton, Ltd.		
Sales value of production (SVOP)	=	$10,000,000
Total wage bill	=	4,000,000
Total wage bill/SVOP	=	4,000,000/10,000,000 = .40 = 40%
Operating Month, March 2012		
SVOP	=	$950,000
Allowable wage bill	=	.40 ($950,000) = $380,000
Actual wage bill (August)	=	$330,000
Savings	=	$ 50,000
50,000 available for distribution as a bonus.		

standard, the larger the incentive award.[55] The three primary types of gain-sharing plans, differentiated by their focus on either cost savings (the numerator of the equation) or some measure of revenue (the denominator of the equation), are noted below.

Scanlon Plan

Scanlon plans are designed to lower labor costs without lowering the level of a firm's activity. Incentives are derived as a function of the ratio between labor costs and **sales value of production (SVOP).**[56] The SVOP includes sales revenue and the value of goods in inventory. To understand how these two figures are used to derive incentives under a Scanlon plan, see Exhibit 10.14

In practice, the $50,000 bonus in Exhibit 10.14 is not all distributed to the workforce. Rather, 25 percent is distributed to the company, 75 percent of the remainder is distributed as bonuses, and the other 25 percent is withheld and placed in an emergency fund to reimburse the company for any future months when a "negative bonus" is earned (i.e., when the actual wage bill is greater than the allowable wage bill). The excess remaining in the emergency pool is distributed to workers at the end of the year.

To look at the impact of Scanlon plans, consider the retail chain that adopted a Scanlon plan in six of its stores and compared results against six control stores chosen for their similarity.[57] Presence of a Scanlon plan led to stores having higher customer satisfaction, higher sales, and lower turnover.

---

e-Compensation

HR Guide provides information about gain-sharing plans, including critiques of plans and statistical studies. The website is at *http://www.hr-guide.com/data/G443.htm*

Rucker Plan

The **Rucker plan** involves a somewhat more complex formula than a Scanlon plan for determining worker incentive bonuses. Essentially, a ratio is calculated that expresses the value of production required for each dollar of total wage bill. Consider the following illustration:[58]

1. Assume accounting records show that the company expended $.60 worth of electricity, materials, supplies, and so on, to produce $1.00 worth of product. The value added is $.40 for each $1.00 of sales value. Assume also that 45 percent of the value added was attributable to labor; a productivity ratio (PR) can be allocated from the formula in item 2.

2. *PR* (labor) $\times$ .40 $\times$ .45 = 1.00. Solving yields *PR* = 5.56.

3. If the wage bill equals $100,000, the *expected* production value is the wage bill ($100,000) $\times$ *PR* (5.56) = $555,556.

4. If *actual* production value equals $650,000, then the savings (actual production value minus expected production value) is $94,444.

5. Since the labor contribution to value added is 45 percent, the bonus to the workforce should be .45 $\times$ $94,444 = $42,500.

6. The savings are distributed as an incentive bonus according to a formula similar to the Scanlon formula—75 percent of the bonus is distributed to workers immediately and 25 percent is kept as an emergency fund to cover poor months. Any excess in the emergency fund at the end of the year is then distributed to workers.

Implementation of the Scanlon/Rucker Plans

Two major components are vital to the implementation and success of a Rucker or Scanlon plan: (1) a productivity norm and (2) effective worker committees. Development of a productivity norm requires both effective measurement of base-year data and acceptance by workers and management of this standard for calculating bonus incentives. Effective measurement requires that an organization keep extensive records of historical cost relationships and make them available to workers or union representatives to verify cost accounting figures. Acceptance of these figures, assuming they are accurate, requires that the organization choose a base year that is neither a "boom" nor a "bust" year. The logic is apparent. A boom year would reduce opportunities for workers to collect bonus incentives. A bust year would lead to excessive bonus costs for the firm. The base year chosen also should be fairly recent, allaying worker fears that changes in technology or other factors would make the base year unrepresentative of a given operational year.

The second ingredient of Scanlon/Rucker plans is a series of worker committees (also known as productivity committees or bonus committees). The primary function of these committees is to evaluate employee and management suggestions for ways to improve productivity and/or cut costs. Operating on a plantwide basis in smaller firms, or a departmental basis in larger firms, these committees have been highly successful in eliciting suggestions from employees. It is not uncommon for the suggestion rate to be above that found in companies with standard suggestion incentive plans.[59]

Scanlon/Rucker plans foster this type of climate, and that is perhaps the most vital element of their success. Numerous authorities have pointed out that these plans have the best chance for success in companies with competent supervision, cooperative union-management attitudes, strong top-management interest and participation in the development of the program, and management open to criticism and willing to discuss different operating strategies.[60] It is beyond the scope of this discussion to outline specific strategies adopted by companies to achieve this climate, but the key element is a belief that workers should play a vital role in the decision-making process.

Similarities and Contrasts Between Scanlon and Rucker Plans

Scanlon and Rucker plans differ from individual incentive plans in their primary focus. Individual incentive plans focus primarily on using wage incentives to motivate higher performance through increased effort. While this is certainly a goal of the Scanlon/Rucker plans, it is not the major focus of attention. Rather, given that increased output is a function of group effort, more attention is focused on organizational behavior variables. The key is to promote faster, more intelligent, and more acceptable decisions through participation. This participation is won by developing a group unity in achieving cost savings—a goal that is not stressed, and is often stymied, in individual incentive plans.

Even though Scanlon and Rucker plans share this common attention to groups and committees through participation as a linking pin, there are two important differences between the two plans. First, Rucker plans tie incentives to a wide variety of savings, not just the labor savings focused on in Scanlon plans.[61] Second, this greater flexibility may help explain why Rucker plans are more amenable to linkages with individual incentive plans.

Improshare

Improshare (Improved Productivity through Sharing) is a gain-sharing plan that has proved easy to administer and to communicate.[62] First, a standard is developed that identifies the expected hours required to produce an acceptable level of output. This standard comes either from time-and-motion studies conducted by industrial engineers or from a base-period measurement of the performance factor. Any savings arising from production of the agreed-upon output in fewer than the expected hours is shared by the firm and by the workers.[63] For example, if 100 workers can produce 50,000 units over 50 weeks, this translates into 200,000 hours (40 hours × 50 weeks) for 50,000 units, or 4 hours per unit. If we implement an Improshare plan, any gains resulting in less than 4 hours per unit are shared 50–50 between employees and management (wages times number of hours saved).[64]

One survey of 104 companies with an Improshare plan found a mean increase in productivity during the first year of 12.5 percent.[65] By the third year the productivity gain rose to 22 percent. A significant portion of this productivity gain was traced to reduced defect rates and downtime (e.g., repair time).

Profit-Sharing Plans

Profit sharing seems to have a pretty consistent impact on productivity about equal to that of gain sharing. One study of 6 million employees across 275 firms found 3.5–5.0 percent higher profits in companies that used profit sharing than in those that didn't.[66]

Productivity was much higher in plans where payouts were that year than in plans where payment was deferred (as in profit sharing used for a pension program). Also, these plans worked much better in smaller (less than 775 employees) companies.

Even in companies that don't have profit sharing plans, many variable-pay plans still require a designated profit target to be met before any payouts occur. Our experience with chief executive officers is that they have a hard time giving employees extra compensation if the company isn't also profiting. Thus, many variable-pay plans have some form of profit "trigger" linked to revenue growth or profit margins or some measure of shareholder return such as earnings per share or return on capital. Despite modestly positive results, profit sharing continues to be popular because the focus is on the measure that matters most to the most people: a predetermined index of profitability. When payoffs are linked to such measures, employees spend more time learning about financial measures and the business factors that influence them.

On the downside, most employees don't feel their jobs have a direct impact on profits. A small cog in a big wheel is difficult to motivate very well. For example, before the big crunch in the auto industry Ford Motor and GM gave profit sharing checks of about $7,500, compared to $2,250 at Fiat-Chrysler.[67] You can bet the Chrysler employees wondered if their counterparts at Ford and GM were working more than three times as hard. If you guessed that they blamed the difference on bad management decisions, you're right on target. Over the past four years total Ford bonuses, including quality bonuses and one time lump sums, have been $43,200 dollars, compare to $39,250 at GM.[68] This admittedly smaller disparity also has GM employees grumbling a bit.

The trend in recent variable-pay design is to combine the best of gain-sharing and profit-sharing plans.[69] The company will specify a funding formula for any variable payout that is linked to some profit measure. As experts say, the plan must be self-funding. Dollars going to workers are generated by additional profits gained from operational efficiency. Along with having the financial incentive, employees feel they have a measure of control. For example, an airline might give an incentive for reductions in lost baggage, with the size of the payout dependent on hitting profit targets. Such a program combines the need for fiscal responsibility with the chance for workers to affect something they can control.

Earnings-at-Risk Plans

We probably shouldn't separate **earnings-at-risk plans** as a distinct category. In fact, any incentive plan could be an at-risk plan. Think of incentive plans as falling into one of two categories: success sharing or risk sharing. In success-sharing plans, employee base wages are constant and variable pay adds on during *successful years*. If the company does well, you receive a predetermined amount of variable pay. If the company does poorly, you simply forgo any variable pay—there is no reduction in your base pay, though. In a risk-sharing plan, base pay is reduced by some amount relative to the level that would be offered in a success-sharing plan. AmeriSteel's at-risk plan is typical of risk-sharing plans. Base pay was reduced 15 percent across the board in year 1. That 15 percent was replaced with a .5 percent increase in base pay for every 1 percent increase in productivity beyond 70 percent of the prior year's productivity. This figure would leave workers whole (no decline in base pay) if they only matched the prior year's productivity. Each additional percent improvement in productivity yielded a 1.5 percent increase in base wages. Everyone in AmeriSteel, from the CEO on down, is in this type of plan and the result has been an 8 percent improvement in productivity.[70]

Clearly, at-risk plans shift part of the risk of doing business from the company to the employee. The company hedges against the devastating effects of a bad year by mortgaging part of the profits that would have accrued during a good year. Not surprisingly, a key element of incentive design these days is to identify possible risks and incorporate design features that minimize them.[71] At-risk plans appear to be met with decreases in satisfaction with both pay in general and the process used to set pay.[72] In turn, this can result in higher turnover.

Group Incentive Plans: Advantages and Disadvantages

Clearly, group pay-for-performance plans are gaining popularity in today's team-based environment. Other factors play a role, though. One factor with intriguing implications suggests that group-based plans, particularly gain-sharing plans, cause organizations to evolve into learning organizations.[73] Apparently the suggestions employees are encouraged to make (how to do things better in the company) gradually evolve from first-order learning experiences of a more routine variety (maintenance of existing ways of doing things) into suggestions that exhibit second-order learning characteristics—suggestions that help the organization break out of existing patterns of behavior and explore different ways of thinking and behaving.[74]

Exhibit 10.15 outlines some of the general positive and negative features of group pay-for-performance plans.[75]

EXHIBIT 10.15   Group Incentive Plans: Advantages and Disadvantages

---

Advantages

1. Positive impact on organization and individual performance of about 5 to 10 percent per year.
2. Easier to develop performance measures than it is for individual plans.
3. Signals that cooperation, both within and across groups, is a desired behavior.
4. Teamwork meets with enthusiastic support from most employees.
5. May increase participation of employees in decision-making process.

Disadvantages

1. Line-of-sight may be lessened, that is employees may find it more difficult to see how their individual performance affects their incentive payouts.
2. May lead to increased turnover among top individual performers who are discouraged because they must share with lesser contributors.
3. Increases compensation risk to employees because of lower income stability. May influence some applicants to apply for jobs in firms where base pay is a larger compensation component.

EXHIBIT 10.16   Corporate Examples of Group Incentive Plans

GE Information systems	A team-based incentive that also links to individual payouts. Team and individual performance goals are set. If the team hits its goals, the team members earn their incentive only if they also hit their individual goals. The team incentive is 12 to 15 percent of monthly base pay.
Corning Glass	A gain-sharing program (goal sharing) where 75 percent of the payout is based on unit objectives such as quality measures, customer satisfaction measures, and production targets. The remainder is based on Corning's return on equity.
3M	Operates with an earnings-at-risk plan. Base pay is fixed at 80 percent of market. Employees have a set of objectives to meet for pay to move to 100 percent of market. Additionally, there is a modest profit-sharing component.
DuPont Fibers	Earnings-at-risk plan where employees receive reduced pay increases over 5 years resulting in 6 percent lower base pay. If department meets annual profit goal, employees collect all 6 percent. Variable payout ranges from 0 (reach less than 80% of goal) to 19 percent (150% of goal).

Group Incentive Plans: Examples

All incentive plans, as we noted earlier, can be described by common features: (1) the size of the group that participates in the plan, (2) the standard against which performance is compared, and (3) the payout schedule. Exhibit 10.16 illustrates some of the more interesting components of plans for leading companies.

EXPLOSIVE INTEREST IN LONG-TERM INCENTIVE PLANS

All of the individual and group plans we have discussed thus far focus on short time horizons for performance and payouts. Usually the time horizon is a year or less. Now we shift to variable pay plans where the time horizon is longer than a year. Such programs force executives to think long term, and develop strategic plans that don't sacrifice tomorrow's riches for today's small gains.

Exhibit 10.17 shows different types of **long-term incentives** and their definitions. These plans are also grouped by the level of risk faced by employees having these incentives, as well as the expected rewards that might come from them.

Long-term incentives (LTIs) focus on performance beyond the one-year time line used as the cutoff for short-term incentive plans. Recent explosive growth in long-term plans appears to be spurred in part by a desire to motivate longer-term value creation.[76] One analysis of over 200 empirical studies of the relation between stock ownership and financial performance casts a gloomy pallor indeed. There is very little empirical evidence that stock ownership by management leads to better corporate performance.[77] There is some evidence, though, that stock ownership is likely to increase internal growth, rather than more rapid external diversification.[78]

All this talk about stock options neglects the biggest change in recent memory. As of June 2005 companies were required to report stock options as an expense.[79] Prior

EXHIBIT 10.17 Long-Term Incentives and Their Risk/Reward Tradeoffs

Level One: Low Risk/Reward

1. *Time-based restricted stock:* An award of shares that actually are received only after the completion of a predefined service period. Employees who terminate employment before the restriction lapses must return their shares to the company.

2. *Performance-accelerated restricted stock:* Restricted stock granted only after attainment of specified performance objectives.

3. *Stock purchase plan:* Opportunity to buy shares of company stock either at prices below market price or with favorable financing.

Level Two: Medium Risk/Reward

4. *Time-vested stock option:* This is what most stock options are—the right to purchase stock at a specified price for a fixed time period.

5. *Performance-vested restricted stock:* This is a grant of stock to employees upon attainment of defined performance objective(s).

6. *Performance-accelerated stock option:* An option with a vesting schedule that can be shortened if specific performance criteria are met.

Level Three: High Risk/Reward

7. *Premium-priced stock option:* A stock option that has an exercise price about market value at the time of grant. This creates an incentive for employees to create value for the company, see the stock price rise, and thus be eligible to purchase the stock.

8. *Indexed stock option:* An option whose exercise price depends on what peer companies' experiences are with stock prices. If industry stock prices are generally rising, it would be difficult to attribute any similar rise in specific improvements beyond general industry improvement.

9. *Performance-vested stock option:* One that vests only upon the attainment of a predetermined performance objective.

to this date, generally accepted accounting rules didn't require options to be reported as an overhead cost. They were (wrongly) viewed as a free good under old accounting rules.[80] Think about the executive issued 500,000 shares with a vesting period of five years (the shares can be bought in five years). After five years, the CEO can purchase the stock at the initial-offer price (if the market price is now lower than that, the stock option is said to be "underwater" and is not exercised).[81] If the executive bought the shares, they were typically issued from a pool of unissued shares. The money paid by the CEO was treated like money paid by any investor . . . found money? Not really. Options diluted the per-share earnings because they increase the denominator applied to net profits used to figure per-share earnings. (OK, OK we promise, no more accounting terms!) Cases like Enron, which did not expense options, gave an unrealistic picture of profits and helped to elevate stock prices. The publicity from this case increased pressure to change accounting rules and led to the changes that began affecting most companies in 2006.[82] Microsoft asserts that it will still continue to offer stock options to rank and file employees, but insiders admit that the modest movement in their stock prices have lessened the appeal of this vehicle for retaining top talent. No more instant multi-millionaires like the roaring 90s.[83] As a direct result of the changing rules, some companies, like Coca Cola, Dell Inc., Aetna Inc., Pfizer Inc., McDonald's Corp., Time Warner Inc., ExxonMobil Corp., and Microsoft Corp either stopped granting options or only grant them to executives.[84]

Employee Stock Ownership Plans (ESOPs)

Some companies believe that employees can be linked to the success or failure of a company in yet another way—through employee stock ownership plans.[85] At places like PepsiCo, Lincoln Electric, DuPont, Coca-Cola, and others, the goal is to increase employee involvement in the organization, and hopefully this will influence performance. Toward this end, employees own 28 percent of the stock at Lincoln Electric. At Worthington Industries, an oft-praised performer in the steel industry, employees augment wages by 40–100 percent between profit sharing and stock ownership.[86]

Despite these high-profile adoptions, ESOPs don't make sense as an incentive. First, the effects are generally long-term. How I perform today won't have much of an impact on the stock price at the time I exercise my option.[87] Nor does my working harder mean more for me. Indeed, we can't predict very well what makes stock prices rise and this is the central ingredient in the reward component of ESOPs. So if the performance measure is too complex to figure out, how can we control our own destiny? Sounds like ESOPs do poorly on two of the three Cs we mentioned earlier as causing incentive plans to fail. Why then do about 9,500 companies have ESOPs covering more than 10 million employees with holdings of over $600 billion in the stock's of their companies?[88] The answer may well be that ESOPs foster employee willingness to participate in the decision-making process.[89] And a company that takes advantage of that willingness can harness a considerable resource—the creative energy of its workforce.

If we just look at the impact of ESOPs on productivity or financial outcomes, leaving aside the positive effect on employee participation, the results are very modest. ESOPs have little impact on productivity or profit.[90] Critics of ESOP argue that companies don't use these programs effectively. If more firms would combine ESOPs with high goal setting, improved employee communication with management, and greater participation in decision making by employees, maybe ESOPs would have more positive results.[91]

Performance Plans (Performance Share and Performance Unit)

Performance plans typically feature corporate performance objectives for a time three years in the future. They are driven by financial earnings or return measures, and they pay out for meeting or exceeding specific goals.

Broad-Based Option Plans (BBOPs)

For the past 15 years broad-based option plans represented a growing trend. BBOPs are stock grants: The company gives employees shares of stock over a designated time period. The strength of BBOPs is their versatility. Depending on the way they are distributed to employees, they can either reinforce a strong emphasis on performance (performance culture) or inspire greater commitment and retention (ownership culture) of employees. There is growing evidence that the incentive effect of BBOPs is relatively small, and declines as the number of employees included grows. The smaller size of the effect in larger plans is explained by the free rider effect—"I can coast and get the same size benefit as others, and not get caught!"[92] Some of the best-known companies in the country offer stock grants to employees at all levels: Southwest Airlines, Chase Manhattan, DuPont, General Mills, Procter & Gamble, PepsiCo, Merck, Eli Lilly, Kimberly-Clark, Microsoft, and Amazon.com.[93] For example, Starbucks has a stock grant program called Beanstock, and all employees who work at least 500 hours per year, up to the level of vice president, are eligible (broad-based participation).[94] If company performance goals are reached, all employees receive equal stock grants worth somewhere between 10 and 14 percent of their earnings. The grants vest 20 percent each year, and the option expires 10 years after the grant date. This program exists to send the clear signal that all employees, especially the two-thirds who are part-timers, are business partners. This effort to create a culture of ownership is viewed as the primary reason Starbucks has turnover that is only a fraction of the usually high turnover in the retail industry.

Colliding with this trend, though, is increasing shareholder pushback against equity awards for all but the top 1 percent of employees. The public simply doesn't believe that lower level employees can affect stock price with their performance! Bowing to this pressure, Coca-Cola is eliminating stock options for all but the top 1 percent. They will shift to cash awards for performance instead.[95]

Combination Plans: Mixing Individual and Group

It's not uncommon for companies to use both individual and group incentives. The goal is to both motivate individual behavior and to insure that employees work together, where needed, to promote team and corporate goals. These combination programs start with standard individual (e.g., performance appraisal, quantity of output) and group measures (e.g., profit, operating income). Variable pay level depends on how well individuals perform and how well the company (or division/strategic business unit) does on its macro (e.g., profit) measures. A typical plan might call for a 75–25 split. Seventy-five percent of the payout is based on how well the individual worker does, the other portion is dependent on corporate performance. An alternative might be a completely **self-funding plan,** often favored by CEOs who don't like to make payouts when the company loses money. These plans specify that payouts only occur after the company reaches a certain profit target. Then variable payouts for individual, team, and company performance are triggered.

Your **Turn**

Most of the Your Turns in earlier chapters asked you to apply your knowledge of a specific chapter to answer a real world question. Now we are going to move one step further and give you information about two companies that operate in the same industry—Airlines. American Airlines and Delta both make information available about base wages and profit sharing.* Below we provide base wages and profit sharing information obtained from multiple sources. These data are only for Airline pilots. The pilot is the number one authority, and in charge, in the cockpit of an airplane. Mistakes and heroic good decisions are likely to be attributed to the pilot in most circumstances. In this exercise we would like you to deduce what these two airlines believe about:

1. The importance of base wages relative to variable pay (profit sharing)
2. The likely behavioral impact of profit sharing in this case, assuming the payout is based on overall net revenue of the organization. Some impacts might be positive or negative. What is your assessment of the use of profit sharing, given what we've said about when to use such a compensation tool?
3. How important is seniority in each of these situations? Should the importance be more or less? Why?
4. Do these airlines pay for skill acquisition? What data do you have to support your position? Should skill acquisition be rewarded?
5. Do you have any predictions about attraction and retention for each company?
6. Does the external environment influence any of your answers?

	2014 Wage Figures Represent Base plus Profit Sharing					
American	Type of Plane					
	777	767	757	A319	A 320	E190
12 years' experience	230	195	195	181	181	123
2 years' experience	212	180	180	167	167	113
Delta						
12 years' experience	270	255	226	209	209	139
2 years' experience	250	236	207	194	194	129

Note:

1. American Airlines Base Wages are 7 percent above market. They pay no profit sharing for pilots.
2. Delta wages include a 16 percent profit sharing bonus for 2014.

*These numbers, although taken for published sources, are solely for educational purposes and may not accurately represent current compensation practices at these airlines.

Summary   Pay-for-performance plans can work. But as this chapter demonstrates, the design and effective administration of these plans is key to their success. Having a good idea is not enough. The good idea must be followed up by sound practices that recognize rewards can, if used properly, shape employee behavior.

Review Questions

1. As VP of HR at Pilsner Roofing, the eleventh largest roofing company in the world, you are experiencing turnover problems with the employees who actually install roofs (roofers). General Manager Roy Cranston has asked you to fix the problem. While your primary emphasis might be on having a competitive base pay, you need to decide if there is anything you can do in the incentive department. Before you can make this decision, what information would you like about (a) pay (base + incentive) at major competitors, (b) the nature of the turnover, and (c) next year's labor budget?

2. How is an earnings-at-risk plan different from an ordinary gain-sharing or profit-sharing plan? How might earnings-at-risk plans affect attraction and retention of employees? How does the 2008–2010 recession affect the viability of earnings-at-risk plans?

3. You own Falzer's Tool Coating Company, a high-tech firm specializing in the coating of cutting tools (e.g., drill bits, cutting blades) to provide longer life before resharpening is needed. You are concerned that the competition continues to develop new coating methods and new applications of coating in different industries. You want to create a work environment where employees offer more new product ideas and suggest new industries where these ideas might be applied. What type of compensation plan will you recommend? What are some of the problems you need to be aware of?

4. Why do the new accounting standards make stock options less popular?

5. You are the teacher in a class where team project account for 25 percent of course grades. Each student is assigned to a team and that team is responsible for all team assignments. Student come to you and complain bitterly about one of their members who does absolutely nothing. You know this will affect your teaching ratings if you don't do something about it. What should you do?

Appendix **10-A**

Profit-Sharing (401k) at Walgreens

Many of our employees say Walgreens 401(k) plan, called the Walgreens Profit-Sharing Plan, is the No. 1 benefit Walgreens offers. That's because you benefit from the company's success through an annual match that is one of the highest match rates in American business.

Here's how it works: After you have 90 days of service with the company and have worked an average of 20 hours per week, you have the opportunity to contribute up to 50 percent of your annual salary to the Profit-Sharing Plan, up to the IRS limit. The company matches the first 2 percent of your contributions with a guaranteed match of $2 for every $1 you contribute. There's also the possibility of an additional match based on company profits for the year. The great thing about our plan is that as long as the company's profits grow, so does your retirement account.

Endnotes

1. American Management Association, "Merit Raises Remain Popular among Fortune 1000," *Compflash* (December 1994), p. 6.

2. Data are from a WorldatWork/Vivient consulting "Private Company Incentive Pay Practices Survey" 2012, PayScale Research Report: 2015 "Compensation Best Practices Report."

3. Kenan S. Abosch, "Rationalizing Variable Pay Plans," in Lance A. Berger and Dorothy Berger, *The Compensation Handbook* (New York: McGraw-Hill, 2008), pp. 227–238.

4. Jeffrey Arthur and Lynda Aiman-Smith, "Gainsharing and Organizational Learning: An Analysis of Employee Suggestions Over Time," *Academy of Management Journal* 44(4), 2001, pp. 737–754.

5. Christopher W. Cabrera, *Game the plan* (Austin, TX: River Grove Books, 2014).

6. Jerry M. Newman and Daniel J. Fisher, "Strategic Impact Merit Pay," *Compensation and Benefits Review* (July/August 1992), pp. 38–45.

7. Jonathan Day, Paul Mang, Ansgar Richter, and John Roberts, "Has Pay for Performance Had Its Day?" *McKinsey Quarterly* 25(2), 2002, pp. 6–54.

8. Robert Heneman, *Merit Pay: Linking Pay Increases to Performance Ratings* (Reading, MA: Addison-Wesley, 1992).

9. R. E. Kopelman and L. Reinharth, "Research Results: The Effect of Merit-Pay Practices on White Collar Performance," *Compensation Review* 14(4), 1982, pp. 30–40.

10. Barry Gerhart and Meiyu Fang, "Pay for (Individual) Performance: Issues, Claims, Evidence and the Role of Sorting Effects," *Human Resource Management Review* 24(1), 41–52. S. L. Rynes, B. Gerhart, and L. Parks, "Personnel Psychology: Performance Evaluation and Pay for Performance," *Annual Review of Psychology* 56 (2005) 56, pp. 571–600.

11. Hanover Research Institute, "Best Practices in Teacher Pay for Performance Models." December 2012, Hanover Research institute. Sam Dillon, "Long Reviled, Merit Pay Gains Among Teachers," *The New York Times,* June 18, 2007, www.NYTimes.com, accessed June 29, 2009.

12. Cincinnati Federation of Teachers, "Teacher Quality Update," www.cft-aft.org/prof /tqa_comp3.html, August 2000.

13. Michael Podgursky and Matthew Springer, "Teacher Performance Pay: A Review," The National Center for Performance Incentives, November 2006.

14. Greg Toppo, "Teachers Take Test Scores to Bank," *USA Today,* October 22, 2008, p. A1.

15. www.huffingtonpost.com/2011/07/18/merit-based-teacher-bonus_n_901679.html visited May 2, 2012.

16. Amanda Ripley, "The $4 Million Teacher," *Wall Street Journal*, August 3, 2013, p. C1.

17. Myrna Hellerman and James Kochanski, "Merit Pay," in *The Compensation Handbook,* 5th ed., Lance A. Berger and Dorothy Berger, eds. (New York: McGraw-Hill, 2008), pp. 85–93; D. Eskew and R. L. Heneman, "A Survey of Merit Pay Plan Effectiveness: End of the Line for Merit Pay or Hope for Improvement," in *Strategic Reward Management,* R. L. Heneman, ed. (Greenwich, CT: Information Age Publishing, 2002).

18. IOMA, "Incentives Are Gaining Ground," *Complete Guide to Best Practices in Pay for Performance* (Newark NJ: Institute of Management & Administration, 2005), pp. 1–8.

19. IOMA, *2002 Incentive Pay Programs and Results* (Newark NJ: Institute of Management and Administration, May 2002), p. 13.

20. UCSF School of Pharmacy, Office of the Associate Dean for Administration Personnel Unit, "Spot Awards," http://pharmacy.ucsf.edu/personnel/spot.html, July 6, 2009.

21. Yvonne Oswald and Uschi Backes-Gellner, "Learning for a Bonus: How Financial Incentives Interact with Preferences," *Journal of Public Economics* 118, October 2014, pp. 52–61.

22. E. A. Locke, D. B. Feren, V. M. McCaleb, et al., "The Relative Effectiveness of Four Methods of Motivating Employee Performance," in *Changes in Working Life,* K. D. Duncan, M. M. Gruenberg, and D. Wallis, eds. (New York: Wiley, 1980), pp. 363–388; R. A. Guzzo, R. D. Jette, and R. A. Katzell, "The Effects of Psychologically Based Intervention Programs on Worker Productivity: A Meta-Analysis," *Personnel Psychology* 38 (1985), pp. 275–291.

23. Thomas Patten, *Pay, Employee Compensation, and Incentive Plans* (New York: Macmillan, 1977).

24. James R. Hagerty and Bob Tita, "Workers Say Train Repairs Were Often Bogus." *Wall Street Journal*, July 21, 2014, p. B1.

25. Thomas Wilson, "Is It Time to Eliminate the Piece Rate Incentive System?" *Compensation and Benefits Review,* March–April 1992, pp. 43–49.

26. Christopher W. Cabrera, *Game the Plan* (Austin, TX: River Grove Books, 2014).

27. www.huffingtonpost.com/2011/07/18/merit-based-teacher-bonus_n_901679.html; accessed May 12, 2012.

28. Lauren Weber, "A health check for wellness programs." Wall Street Journal, October 8, 2014. B1.

29. Christopher W. Cabrera, *Game the Plan* (Austin, TX: River Grove Books, 2014). Daniel Eisenberg, "Where People Are Never Let Go," *Time,* June 18, 2001, p. 40; Kenneth Chilton, "Lincoln Electric's Incentive System: A Reservoir of Trust," *Compensation and Benefits Review,* November–December 1994, pp. 29–34.

30. Christopher W. Cabrera, *Game the Plan* (Austin, TX: River Grove Books, 2014).

31. Jon Katzenbach and Douglas Smith, *The Wisdom of Teams* (New York: HarperCollins, 1993).

32. Christopher W. Cabrera, *Game the Plan* (Austin, TX: River Grove Books, 2014). Derek C. Jones, Panu Kalmi, and Antti Kauhanen, "Teams, Incentive Pay, and Productive Efficiency: Evidence from a Food-Processing Plant," *Industrial & Labor Relations Review* 4, vol. 63 (2010), pp. 606–626.

33. Barry Gerhart, Sara L. Rynes, and Ingrid Smithey Fulmer, "Pay and Performance: Individuals, Groups and Executives," *Academy of Management Annals*, 2009, 3(1), 251–315. K. Dow Scott, Jane Floyd, Philip G. Benson, and James W. Bishop, "The Impact of the Scanlon Plan on Retail Store Performance," *WorldatWork* 11(3), 2002, pp. 18–27.

34. Barry Gerhart, Sara L. Rynes, and Ingrid Smithey Fullmer, "Pay and Performance: Individuals, Groups and Executives," in *Academy of Management Annals,* vol. 3, A. P. Brief and J. P. Walsh, eds. (Newark NJ: Lawrence Erlbaum, forthcoming).

35. Conversation with Thomas Ruddy, manager of research, Xerox Corporation, 1997.

36. John G. Belcher, *Results Oriented Variable Pay System* (New York: AMACOM, 1996); Steven E. Gross, *Compensation for Teams* (New York: AMACOM, 1995).

37. Theresa M. Welbourne, David B. Balkin, and Luis R. Gomez-Mejia, "Gainsharing and Mutual Monitoring: A Combined Agency-Organizational Justice Interpretation," *Academy of Management Journal* 38(3), 1995, pp. 881–899.

38. D. Terpstra and A. Honoree, "The Relative Importance of External, Internal, Individual, and Procedural Equity to Pay Satisfaction," *Compensation and Benefits Review,* November–December 2003, pp. 67–78.

39. Rachel Emma Silverman, "Are You Happy in Your Job? Bosses Push Weekly Surveys." Wall *Street Journal*, December 3, 2014, p. B1. American Management Association, "Team-Based Pay: Approaches Vary, But Produce No Magic Formulas," *Compflash,* April 1994, p. 4.

40. Elena Belogolovsky and Peter A. Bamberger, "Signaling in Secret: Pay for Performance and the Incentive and Sorting Effects of Pay Secrecy." *Academy of Management Journal* 57(6), 2014, pp. 1706–1733. Conversation with Sharon Knight, director of compensation, and Martha Kimber, manager of compensation, both at Kraft Foods, 1997.

41. John G. Belcher, *Results Oriented Variable Pay System* (New York: AMACOM, 1996).

42. Personal communication to Jerry Newman from an anonymous client, 2013. F. McKenzie and M. Shilling, "Ensuring Effective Incentive Design and Implementation," *Compensation and Benefits Review,* May–June 1998, pp. 57–65.

43. M. Bloom and G. Milkovich, "Relationships among Risk, Incentive Pay, and Organizational Performance," *Academy of Management Journal* 11(3), 1998, pp. 283–297.

44. L. Hatcher, T. L. Ross, "From Individual Incentives to an Organization-Wide Gain-Sharing Plan: Effects on Teamwork and Product Quality," *Journal of Organizational Behavior* 12 (1991), pp. 169–183.

45. American Management Association, "Team-Based Pay: Approaches Vary, but Produce No Magic Formulas," *Compflash,* April 1994, p. 4.

46. G. K. Shives and K. D. Scott, "Gainsharing and EVA: The U.S. Postal Experience," *WorldatWork Journal,* First Quarter 2003, pp. 1–30.

47. B. Gerhart and G. Milkovich, "Employee Compensation: Research and Practice," in *Handbook of Industrial & Organizational Psychology,* 2nd Edition, M. D. Dunnette and L. M. Hough, eds. (Palo Alto, CA: Consulting Psychologists Press, Inc., 1992); T. M. Welbourne and L. Gomez-Mejia, "Gain sharing: A critical review and a future research agenda," *Journal of Management* 21 (1995), pp. 559–609.

48. J. B. Arthur and G. S. Jelf, "The Effects of Gain Sharing on Grievance Rates and Absenteeism Over Time," *Journal of Labor Research* 20 (1999), pp. 133–145.

49. A. Weiss, "Incentives and Worker Behavior: Some Evidence," in *Incentives, Cooperation and Risk Taking,* H. R. Nalbantian, ed. (Lanham, MD: Rowman & Littlefield, 1987).

50. Some of these issues are addressed at *www.hr-guide.com/data/G443.htm,* retrieved July 17, 2006.

51. Robert Masternak, "How to Make Gainsharing Successful: The Collective Experience of 17 Facilities," *Compensation and Benefits Review,* September–October 1997, pp. 43–52.

52. John G. Belcher, "Gainsharing and Variable Pay: The State of the Art," *Compensation and Benefits Review,* May/June 1994, pp. 50–60.

53. John Belcher, "Design Options for Gain Sharing," unpublished paper, American Productivity Center, 1987.

54. D. Kim, "Determinants of the Survival of Gainsharing Programs," *Industrial and Labor Relations Review* 53(1), 1999, pp. 21–42.

55. A. J. Geare, "Productivity from Scanlon Type Plans," *Academy of Management Review* 1(3), 1976, pp. 99–108.

56. Ibid.

57. K. D. Scott, J. Floyd, and P. Benson, "The Impact of the Scanlon Plan on Retail Store Performance," *WorldatWork Journal* 11(3), 2002, pp. 4–13.

58. T. H. Patten, *Pay: Employee Compensation and Incentive Plans* (New York: Free Press, 1977); P. Schwinger, *Wage Incentive Systems* (New York: Halsted, 1975).

59. Matthew H. Roy and Sanjiv S. Dugal, "Using Employee Gainsharing Plans to Improve Organizational Effectiveness," *International Journal* 3, vol. 12, (2005), pp. 250–259.

60. B. Graham-Moore and T. Ross, *Productivity Gainsharing* (Englewood Cliffs, NJ: Prentice-Hall, 1983).

61. J. Newman, "Selecting Incentive Plans to Complement Organizational Strategy," in *Current Trends in Compensation Research and Practice,* L. Gomez-Mejia and D. Balkin, eds. (Englewood Cliffs, NJ: Prentice-Hall, 1987).

62. Marhsall Fein, "Improshare: A Technique for Sharing Productivity Gains with Employees," in *The Compensation Handbook,* M. L. Rock and L. A. Berger, eds. (New York: McGraw-Hill, 1993), pp. 158–175.

63. R. Kaufman, "The Effects of Improshare on Productivity," *Industrial and Labor Relations Review* 45(2), 1992, pp. 311–322.

64. Darlene O'Neill, "Blending the Best of Profit Sharing and Gainsharing," *HR Magazine,* March 1994, pp. 66–69.

65. John D. Stoll, UAW's Rands Press to Close Pay Gap," *Wall Street Journal*, March 23, 2015, p. B2. D. L. Kruse, *Profit Sharing: Does It Make a Difference?* (Kalamazoo, MI: Upjohn Institute for Employment Research, 1993).

66. Ford data appears at *www.chryslerforum.com/m_346/mpage_1/key_/tm.htm* and GM data appears at *search.yahoo.com/search?ei=utf-8ʃr=slv8-ˉp=GM%20profit%20sharing%20 payout%202005;.* accessed July 18, 2006.

67. http://www.detroitnews.com/story/business/autos/2015/06/14/profit-sharing/71222980/.

68. http://www.detroitnews.com/story/business/autos/2015/06/14/profit-sharing/71222980/.

69. Daniel P. Moynihan, "Designing Compensation Plans to Manage Today's Risk Environment," *Compensation & Benefits Review* 1, vol. 43 (January 1, 2011), pp. 17–22.

70. K. Brown and V. Huber, "Lowering Floors and Raising Ceilings: A Longitudinal Assessment of the Effects of an Earnings-at-Risk Plan on Pay Satisfaction," *Personnel Psychology* 45 (1992), pp. 279–311.

71. S. E. Gross and D. Duncan, "Gainsharing Plan Spurs Record Productivity and Payouts at AmeriSteel," *Compensation and Benefits Review,* November–December 1998, pp. 46–50.

72. R. Renn and W. K. Barksdale, "Earnings-at-Risk Incentive Plans: A Performance, Satisfaction, and Turnover Dilemma," *Compensation and Benefits Review,* July–August 2001, pp. 68–73.

73. P. M. Senge, *The Fifth Discipline: The Art and Practice of the Learning Organization* (New York: Doubleday, 1990).

74. Jeffrey Arthur and Lynda Aiman-Smith, "Gainsharing and Organizational Learning: An Analysis of Employee Suggestions Over Time," *Academy of Management Journal* 44(4), 2001, pp. 737–754.

75. T. H. Hammer and R. N. Stern, "Employee Ownership: Implications for the Organizational Distribution of Power," *Academy of Management Journal* 23 (1980), pp. 78–100.

76. B. J. Hall, "What You Need to Know about Stock Options," *Harvard Business Review,* March–April 2000, pp. 121–129.

77. D. R. Dalton, S. T. Certo, and R. Roengpitya, "Meta-Analyses of Financial Performance and Equity: Fusion or Confusion?" *Academy of Management Journal* 46(1), 2003, pp. 13–26.

78. Barry Gerhart, "Pay Strategy and Firm Performance," in *Compensation in Organizations: Progress and Prospects,* S. Rynes and B. Gerhart, eds. (San Francisco: New Lexington Press, 1999).

79. Wikipedia, "Employee Stock Option," *en.wikipedia.org/wiki/Employee_stock_option;* retrieved July 24, 2006.

80. W. Zellner, "An Insider's Tale of Enron's Toxic Culture," *BusinessWeek,* March 31, 2003, pp. 16.

81. T. Buyniski and B. Harsen, "The Cancel and Regrant: A Roadmap for Addressing Underwater Options," *Compensation and Benefits Review,* January–February 2002, pp. 28–32.

82. T. McCoy, "Emerging Option to Stock Options," *Pay for Performance Report* (Newark, NJ: Institute of Management & Administration, June 2001), p. 2.

83. Nick Wingfield, "Microsoft to Boost Cash Pay for Employees," *The Wall Street Journal,* April 2, 2012, B5.

84. Mike Esterl and Joanne Lublin, "Coke Scales Back Stock Options," *Wall Street Journal,* October 2, 2014, p. B1. "Expensing Stock Options: The Rule Is Final—Or Is it?," *http://accounting.smartpros.com/x49842.xml;* accessed July 24, 2006.

85. Fortune Magazine, Best Companies to work For. URL visited May 22, 2012 http://money.cnn.com/magazines/fortune/bestcompanies/snapshots/1586.html.

86. IOMA, "Stock Options Motivate," *Pay for Performance Report,* May 1996, p. 3.

87. IOMA, "Another Pan of Stock Option Plans," *Pay for Performance Report,* January 1999, p. 11.

88. Staff, "An *ESOP* to the Workers," *Economist,* April 14, 2007, pp. 26–28.

89. Ibid.

90. J. Blasi, M. Conte, and D. Kruse, "Employee Stock Ownership and Corporate Performance Among Public Companies," *Industrial and Labor Relations Review* 50 (1996), pp. 60–66.

91. J. Blasi, D. Kruse, J. Sesil, and M. Kroumova, "An Assessment of Employee Ownership in the United States with Implications for the EU," *International Journal of Human Resource Management* 14 (2003), pp. 893–919.

92. Kim E. Han and Paige Quimet, "Broad-Based Employee Stock Ownership: Motives and Outcomes," *Journal of Finance,* 69(3), 2014, pp. 1273–1319.

93. R. Buckman, "Microsoft Uses Stock Options to Lift Morale," *The Wall Street Journal,* April 26, 2000, p. A3.

94. http://lifeat.sbux.com/BeanStock2011Reward.htm visited May 22, 2012.

95. Mike Esterl and Joanne Lublin, "Coke Scales Back Stock Options," *Wall Street Journal,* October 2, 2014, p. B1. S. Burzawa, "Broad-Based Stock Options Are Used to Attract, Retain, and Motivate Employees," *Employee Benefit Plan Review,* July 1998, pp. 46–50.

Performance Appraisals

Chapter Outline

Here's What Performance Appraisals Are Really Like:
Attention: Human Resources—submission of performance review for Joe Smith

Joe Smith, my assistant programmer, can always be found hard at work in his cubicle. Joe works independently, without wasting company time talking to colleagues. Joe never thinks twice about assisting fellow employees, and he always finishes given assignments on time. Often Joe takes extended measures to complete his work, sometimes skipping coffee breaks. Joe is an individual who has absolutely no vanity in spite of his high accomplishments and profound knowledge in his field. I firmly believe that Joe can be

classed as a high-caliber employee, the type which cannot be
dispensed with. Regards,

Project Leader

---

e-mail to Attention: Human Resources

Joe Smith was reading over my shoulder while I wrote the report sent to you
earlier today. Kindly read only the odd numbered lines [1, 3, 5, etc.] for my true
assessment of his ability.

Regards,
Project Leader

Chapters 9 and 10 covered the merits of pay-for-performance plans. A key element
of these plans is one or more measures of performance. Most companies use multiple measures of performance to link to pay increases and bonuses, as shown in
Exhibit 11.1. Sometimes these measures are subjective and yield ratings that don't
represent employee performance, as in the example above; sometimes this measure is
objective and quantifiable. Blue Cross–Blue Shield of New Jersey, for example, uses
data from insurance claims (number of tests ordered, treatments administered, drugs
prescribed) to compare doctors with their peers.[1] Certainly, when we are measuring
performance for a group incentive plan, objective financial measures may be readily
available. As we move down to the level of the individual and the team, these "hard"
measures are not as readily available. Despite this, some organizations are guilty of
"criterion deficiency"—using objective measures that don't truly represent all of the

EXHIBIT 11.1
Number of
Performance
Measures
Companies Use
to Determine
Pay for
Performance

Source: WorldatWork 2014–2015 Salary Budget Survey.

key dimensions of the job. A secretary who is measured solely on words per minute in word processing would complain, legitimately, that he or she does other things that are far more vital to job performance. This chapter discusses in more detail the difficulties of measuring performance, particularly when we use subjective procedures.

THE ROLE OF PERFORMANCE APPRAISALS IN COMPENSATION DECISIONS

The first use of merit ratings apparently took place in a Scottish cotton mill around 1800. Wooden cubes, indicating different levels of performance, were hung above worker stations as a visible signal of who was doing well.[2] Some 200 years later, the Iraqi national soccer team reported that bad performance frequently led to torture of players during the Saddam Hussein reign. While performance reviews don't usually lead to such questionable outcomes, they are used for a wide variety of decisions in organizations—only one of which is to guide the allocation of merit increases. Unfortunately, as we will discover, the link between performance ratings and these outcomes is not always as strong as we would like. In fact, it's common to make a distinction between performance judgments and performance ratings.[3] Performance ratings—the things we enter into an employee's permanent record—are influenced by a host of factors besides the employee behaviors observed by raters. Such things as organization values (e.g., valuing technical skills or interpersonal skills more highly), competition among departments, differences in status between departments, economic conditions (labor shortages which make for less willingness to terminate employees for poor performance)—all influence the way raters rate employees. There is even some evidence that much of job performance ratings can be attributed to a general performance factor (after accounting for error) that is present across a wide variety of jobs and situations.[4] Is it any wonder then that employees often voice frustration about the appraisal process?[5] A survey of 2,600 employees nationwide yielded the following rather disheartening conclusions:

39 percent felt their performance goals weren't clearly defined.

39 percent felt they didn't know how their performance was evaluated.

45 percent didn't believe their last performance review guided them on how to improve.

45 percent didn't think the reviews could differentiate among good, average, and poor performers.

48 percent didn't think doing a good job was recognized.[6]

This dissatisfaction makes a difference. Employees unhappy with the appraisal process were less satisfied with their firms, less satisfied with their pay, less committed, and more likely to turn over.[7] One trending approach by companies to deal with this is to conduct "Pulse" surveys as often as three times per week. Employers want to catch problems before they fester.[8] Perhaps the biggest complaint of all from employees (and managers too) is that appraisals are too subjective. And lurking behind subjectivity, always, is the possibility of unfair treatment by a supervisor. A good leader is key to making an employee believe that pay is linked to individual performance.[9] Is it any surprise that the subject of **performance metrics** is one of the hottest areas of study in both academic and business organizations? Critics of subjective measures want performance measures (metrics) that are fair to employees and reflect value for the organization.

Performance Metrics

Huge advances in the development of metrics have been made over the past 15 years. The first observation is that pay for performance programs evolve along multiple dimensions. First, is the measure (metric) results-oriented (e.g., financial measures, physical output, or sales being good examples) or behaviorally oriented (e.g., customer or supervisory ratings)? Second, does the measure focus on individual employees or aggregation up to team or even total organization?[10] Weaving these two issues together in an example, at the individual level (in this case, for an employee) finding good results-oriented measures is very difficult. Some reliable estimates suggest that between 13 percent of the time (hourly workers) and 70 percent of the time (managerial employees), employee performance is tied to quantifiable or results-oriented measures.[11] Just because something is quantifiable, though, doesn't mean it is an objective measure of performance. And this problem extends to even higher levels of analysis (e.g, firm level). As any accounting student knows, financial measures are arrived at through a process that involves some subjective decision making. Which year we choose to take write-offs for plant closings, for example, affects the bottom line reported to the public. Such potential for subjectivity has led some experts to warn that so-called objective data can be deficient (**criterion deficient**) and may not tell the whole story.[12] Even with external audits, supposedly solid financial performance indicators can be misrepresented for extended periods. Just ask the folks at HealthSouth, who overstated earnings for almost 15 years without being caught by their auditor, Ernst and Young.[13] Despite these concerns, most HR professionals probably would prefer to work with quantitative data. Sometimes, especially at the individual level, performance isn't easily quantified. Either job output is not readily quantifiable or the components that are quantifiable do not reflect important job dimensions. As we noted earlier, a secretarial job could be reduced to words per minute and errors per page of keyboarding. But many secretaries, and their supervisors, would argue this captures only a small portion of the job. Courtesy in greeting clients and in answering phones, initiative in solving problems without running to the boss, dependability under deadlines—all of these intangible qualities can make the difference between a good secretary and a poor one. Such subjective goals are less easily measured. The end result, all too often, is a performance appraisal process that is plagued by errors.

One of the biggest attacks against appraisals in general, and subjective appraisals in particular, comes from top names in the total-quality-management area. Edward Deming, the grandfather of the quality movement here and in Japan, launched an attack on appraisals because, he contended, the work situation (not the individual) is the major determinant of performance.[14] Variation in performance arises many times because employees don't have the necessary information, technology, or control to adequately perform their jobs.[15] Further, Deming argued, individual work standards and performance ratings rob employees of pride and self-esteem.

Some experts argue that rather than throwing out the entire performance appraisal process, we should apply total-quality-management principles to improving it.[16] A first way to improve performance appraisals, then, would be to recognize that part of performance is influenced more by the work environment and system than by employee behaviors. For example, sometimes when a student says "The dog ate my paper" (latest version: "The computer ate my flash drive"), it really happened. When we tell teachers, or other raters, that the system sometimes does affect performance, raters are more sympathetic and rate higher.[17]

A second way to improve performance appraisal, one that involves most of the remainder of this chapter, concerns identifying strategies for understanding and measuring job performance better. This may help us reduce the number and types of rating errors illustrated later.

STRATEGIES FOR BETTER UNDERSTANDING AND MEASURING JOB PERFORMANCE

Efforts to improve the performance rating process take several forms.[18] First, researchers and compensation people alike devote considerable energy to defining job performance: What exactly should be measured when we evaluate employees? The answer depends on such factors as job level, type of occupation, the way work is organized, and the strategic goals of the organization.[19] Interestingly, managers can be grouped into one of three categories, based on the types of employee behaviors they focus on. One group looks strictly at task performance, how the employees perform the responsibilities of their jobs. A second group looks primarily at counterproductive performance, evaluating based on the negative behaviors employees show. The final group looks at both these types of behavior.[20] Studies that examine more specific factors focus on such performance dimensions as planning and organizing, training, coaching, developing subordinates, and technical proficiency.[21] As we noted earlier, one particularly good mega study found that much of performance can be accounted for by one general performance factor. Perhaps breaking performance ratings down into component performance dimensions may not be fruitful.[22] Countering this argument is the large amount of research and heavy adoption by industry of balanced scorecards.

The Balanced Scorecard Approach

A **balanced scorecard approach** is a way to look at what contributes value in an organization. Too often we just look at the bottom line, as measured by financial goals. The balanced scorecard acknowledges that bottom line success doesn't just happen. It depends on satisfied customers buying products and services from effective and satisfied employees who both serve the customers *and* produce goods (or deliver services) in the most operationally efficient way possible. If this is true, then we need to measure all four of the following dimensions and be prepared to say that success depends on high scores for each: customer satisfaction, employee internal growth and commitment, operational efficiency in internal processes, and financial measures. Besides the widespread enthusiasm in industry for this approach, data suggest that implementation of a balanced scorecard can have positive impacts on the bottom line and on rating accuracy.[23] Appendix 11-A shows a balanced scorecard used by the Department of Energy.

A second direction for performance research notes that the definition of performance and its components is expanding. Just consider the hugely successful company General Electric. In 1951 they began serious efforts to measure key performance indicators. More than a half century later they are still trying to achieve this goal.[24] Jobs are becoming more dynamic, and the need for employees to adapt and grow is increasingly stressed. This focus on individual characteristics, or personal competencies, is consistent with the whole trend toward measuring job competency.[25] Pizza Hut, for example, has five competencies that store managers must master: (1) sets high standards, (2) communicates well, (3) executes processes and routines, (4) holds self and others accountable, and (5) celebrates successes. Each of these competencies has specific behaviors a Pizza Hut general manager must show at three different levels of mastery.[26]

A third direction for improving the quality of performance ratings centers on identifying the best appraisal format. If only the ideal format could be found, so the argument goes, raters would use it to measure job performance better, that is, make more accurate ratings. As you might expect, there is little evidence that an ideal format exists.

Recent attention has focused less on the rating format and more on the raters themselves. This fourth direction identifies possible groups of raters (supervisor, peers, subordinates, customers, self) and examines whether a given group provides more or less accurate ratings. The fifth direction attempts to identify how raters process information about job performance and translate it into performance ratings. Such information, including an understanding of the role irrelevant information plays in the evaluation of employees, may yield strategies for reducing the flaws in the total process. Finally, data also suggest that raters can be trained to increase the accuracy of their ratings. The following sections focus on these last four approaches to better understanding and measuring performance: improving the format, selecting the right raters, understanding the way raters process information, and training raters to improve rating skills.

Strategy 1: Improve Appraisal Formats

Types of Formats

Evaluation formats can be divided into two general categories: **ranking** and **rating**.[27] **Ranking formats** require that the rater compare employees against each other to determine the relative ordering of the group on some performance measure (usually some measure of overall performance). Exhibit 11.2 illustrates three different methods of ranking employees:

- The **straight ranking** procedure is just that: employees are ranked relative to each other.
- **The alternation ranking** recognizes that raters are better at ranking people at extreme ends of the distribution. Raters are asked to indicate the best employee and then the worst employee. Working at the two extremes permits a rater to get more practice prior to making the harder distinctions in the vast middle ground of employees.

EXHIBIT 11.2
Three Ranking Formats

Straight Ranking Method	
Rank	**Employee's Name**
Best	1. _____
Next Best	2. _____
Next Best	3. _____
Etc.	

Alternation Ranking	
Rank	**Employee's Name**
Best performer	1. _____
Next best	2. _____
Next best	3. _____
Etc.	4. _____
Next worst	3. _____
Next worst	2. _____
Worst performer	1. _____

Paired Comparison Ranking Method					
	John	**Pete**	**Sam**	**Tom**	**Ranked Higher**
Bill	x	x	x	x	4
John		x	x	x	3
Pete			x	x	2
Sam				x	1

- The **paired-comparison ranking** method simplifies the ranking process by forcing raters to make ranking judgments about discrete pairs of people. Each individual is compared separately with all others in the work group. The person who "wins" the most paired comparisons is ranked top in the group, and so on. Unfortunately, when the size of the work group goes above 10 to 15 employees, the number of paired comparisons becomes unmanageable.

The second category of appraisal formats—ratings—is generally more popular than ranking systems. This popularity, though, is not accompanied by any evidence that rating formats are particularly valid.[28] Their use, especially when nonbehavioral anchors are employed (see Exhibit 11.3, for example), is more an issue of convenience than credibility.

The various **rating formats** have two elements in common. First, in contrast to ranking formats, rating formats require raters to evaluate employees on some absolute standard rather than relative to other employees. Second, each performance standard is measured on a scale whereby appraisers can check the point that best represents the employee's performance. In this way, performance variation is described along a continuum from good to bad. It is the types of descriptors used in anchoring this continuum that provide the major difference in rating scales.

EXHIBIT 11.3
Rating Scale
Using Absolute
Standards

Standard Rating Scale with Adjective Anchors					
Communications Skills	Written and oral ability to clearly and convincingly express thoughts, ideas, or facts in individual or group situations				
Circle the number that best describes the level of employee performance	1 well above average	2 above average	3 average	4 below average	5 well below average

These descriptors may be adjectives, behaviors, or outcomes. When adjectives are used as anchors, the format is called a **standard rating scale.** Exhibit 11.3 shows a typical rating scale with adjectives as anchors ("well above average" to "well below average"). Switching to behaviors as anchors, **Behaviorally Anchored Rating Scales (BARS)** seem to be the most common format using behaviors as descriptors. By anchoring scales with concrete behaviors, firms adopting a BARS format hope to make evaluations less subjective. When raters try to decide on a rating, they have a common definition (in the form of a behavioral example) for each of the performance levels. Consider, as an example, the following behaviors as recorded on a fictitious officer fitness report for the British Royal Navy. They are easily identifiable and, hopefully, humorous:

"This Officer reminds me very much of a gyroscope—always spinning around at a frantic pace, but not really going anywhere."
"He would be out of his depth in a car park puddle."
"Works well when under constant supervision and cornered like a rat in a trap."
"This man is depriving a village somewhere of an idiot."
"Only occasionally wets himself under pressure."[29]

A more serious behavioral scale for a similar occupation was developed by the Royal Canadian Mounted Police.[30] On the leadership dimension, the top and bottom ratings a mountie could get have behavioral descriptors that look like this:

Bottom rating—Ignores advice and views of other members: does not accept responsibility for own views and actions; blames others for own failures; provides others with incorrect information on policies and procedures.
Top rating—Takes charge of situations; consulted by other members for advice on operational and/or administrative policies and procedures.

This rating format directly addresses a major criticism of standard adjective rating scales: Different raters carry with them into the rating situation different definitions of the scale levels (e.g., different raters have different ideas about what "average work" is). Exhibit 11.4 illustrates a complete behaviorally anchored rating scale for teamwork.

In both the standard rating scale and the BARS, overall performance is calculated as some weighted average (weighted by the importance the organization attaches to each dimension) of the ratings on all dimensions. One way to derive an overall

EXHIBIT 11.4 **Standard Rating Scale with Behavioral Scale Anchors**

Teamwork:	Ability to contribute to group performance, to draw out the best from others, to foster activities building group morale, even under high-pressure situations.	
Exceeds Standards	1	Seeks out or is regularly requested for group assignments. Groups this person works with inevitably have high performance and high morale. Employee makes strong personal contribution and is able to identify strengths of many different types of group members and foster their participation. Wards off personality conflicts by positive attitude and ability to mediate unhealthy conflicts, sometimes even before they arise. Will make special effort to ensure credit for group performance is shared by all.
	2	Seen as a positive contributor in group assignments. Works well with all types of people and personalities, occasionally elevating group performance of others. Good ability to resolve unhealthy group conflicts that flare up. Will make special effort to ensure strong performers receive credit due them.
Meets Standards	3	Seen as a positive personal contributor in group assignments. Works well with most types of people and personalities. Is never a source of unhealthy group conflict and will encourage the same behavior in others.
	4	When group mission requires skill this person is strong in, employee seen as strong contributor. On other occasions will not hinder performance of others. Works well with most types of people and personalities and will not be the initiator of unhealthy group conflict. Will not participate in such conflict unless provoked on multiple occasions.
	5	Depending on the match of personal skill and group mission, this person will be seen as a positive contributor. Will not be a hindrance to performance of others and avoids unhealthy conflict unless provoked.
Does Not Meet Standards	6	Unlikely to be chosen for assignments requiring teamwork except on occasions where personal expertise is vital to group mission. Not responsive to group goals, but can be enticed to help when personal appeals are made. May not get along with other members and either withdraw or generate unhealthy conflict. Seeks personal recognition for team performance and/or may downplay efforts of others.
	7	Has reputation for noncontribution and for creating conflicts in groups. Cares little about group goals and is very hard to motivate toward goal completion unless personal rewards are guaranteed. May undermine group performance to further personal aims. Known to seek personal recognition and/or downplay efforts of others.
Rating:	Documentation of Rating (optional except for 6 and 7):	

evaluation from the dimensional ratings appears in Exhibit 11.5. The employee evaluated in Exhibit 11.5 is rated slightly above average. An alternative method for obtaining the overall rating would be to allow the rater discretion not only in rating performance on the individual dimensions but also in assigning the overall evaluation. The weights

EXHIBIT 11.5
An Example
of Employee
Appraisal

Employee: Kelsey T. Mahoney
Job Title: Supervisor, Shipping and Receiving

Performance Dimension	Dimension Rating					Dimension Weight
	Well Below Average 1	*Below Average* 2	*Average* 3	*Above Average* 4	*Well Above Average* 5	
Leadership Ability				×		0.2 (× 4) = 0.8
Job Knowledge					×	0.1 (× 5) = 0.5
Work Output				×		0.3 (× 4) = 1.2
Attendance			×			0.2 (× 3) = 0.6
Initiative			×			0.2 (× 3) = 0.6

Sum of Rating × Weight = 3.7
Overall Rating = 3.7

(shown in the far-right column of Exhibit 11.5) would not be used, and the overall evaluation would be based on a subjective and internal assessment by the rater.

Appendix 11-B for this chapter gives an example of the rating scale and appraisal form used by Pfizer Pharmaceutical to assess leadership, one of the competencies tracked by Pfizer. Pay attention to how long and involved Pfizer's form is—and this only covers one of four competencies. Considerable money went into its development.

In addition to adjectives and behaviors, outcomes also are used as a standard. The most common form is **Management By Objectives (MBO)**.[31] Management by objectives is both a planning and an appraisal tool that has many different variations across firms.[32] As a first step, organization objectives are identified from the strategic plan of the company. Each successively lower level in the organizational hierarchy is charged with identifying work objectives that will support attainment of organizational goals.[33] Exhibit 11.6 illustrates a common MBO objective. Notice that the emphasis is on outcomes achieved by em-ployees. At the beginning of a performance review period, the employee and supervisor discuss performance objectives (column 1).[34] Months

EXHIBIT 11.6
Example of
MBO Objective
for Communi-
cations Skill

1. Performance Objective	2. Results
By July 1 of this year, Bill will complete a report summarizing employee reactions to the new performance appraisal system. An oral presenta-tion will be prepared and delivered to all non-exempt employees in groups of 15–20. All oral presentations will be completed by August 31, and reactions of employees to this presentation will average at least 3.0 on a 5-point scale.	Written report completed by July 1. All but one oral presentation completed by August 31. Last report not completed until September 15 because of unavoid-able conflicts in vacation schedules. Average rating of employees (reaction to oral presentation) was 3.4, exceeding minimum expectations.

later, at the end of the review period, the two again meet to record results formally (of course, multiple informal discussions should have occurred before this time). Results are then compared against objectives, and a performance rating is determined based on how well the objectives were met.

Merck, the pharmaceutical giant, combines an MBO approach focusing on outcomes with a set of measures designed to assess how those outcomes were achieved— Merck calls this its multidimensional view of performance. The MBO portion of a performance review is regularly updated to ensure that individual objectives are aligned with corporate and department goals. At the end of the year, employees are reviewed both on goal performance and on five other measures: quality of work, resource utilization, timeliness of completing objectives, innovation, and leadership. Ratings on these latter measures must be accompanied by examples of behaviors shown by employees that justify particular ratings.

A review of firms using MBO indicates generally positive improvements in performance both for individuals and for the organization. This performance increase is accompanied by managerial attitudes toward MBO that become more positive over time, particularly when the system is revised periodically to reflect feedback of participants. Managers are especially pleased with the way MBO provides direction to work units, improves the planning process, and increases superior/subordinate communication. On the negative side, MBO appears to require more paperwork and to increase both performance pressure and stress.[36]

Exhibit 11.7 shows some of the common components of an MBO format and the percentage of experts who judge this component vital to a successful evaluation effort.

EXHIBIT 11.7
Components of a Successful MBO Program[35]

Source: From Mark L. McConkie, "A Clarification of the Goal Setting and Appraisal Process in MBO," *Academy of Management Review,* 1979, pp. 29–40.

	Total No. of Responses*	Percent of Authorities in Agreement
1. Goals and objectives should be specific.	37	97
2. Goals and objectives should be defined in terms of measurable results.	37	97
3. Individual goals should be linked to overall organization goals.	37	97
4. Objectives should be reviewed "periodically."	31	82
5. The time period for goal accomplishment should be specified.	27	71
6. Wherever possible, the indicator of the results should be quantifiable; otherwise, it should be at least verifiable.	26	68
7. Objectives should be flexible; changed as conditions warrant.	26	68
8. Objectives should include a plan of action for accomplishing the results.	21	55
9. Objectives should be assigned priorities of weights.	19	50

*In this table the total number of responses actually represents the total number of authorities responding; thus, percentages also represent the percent of authorities in agreement with the statements made.

A final type of appraisal format does not easily fall into any of the categories yet discussed. In an **essay format,** supervisors answer open-ended questions, in essay form, describing employee performance. Since the descriptors used could range from comparisons with other employees to the use of adjectives describing performance, types of behaviors, and goal accomplishments, the essay format can take on characteristics of all the formats discussed previously. Exhibit 11.8 illustrates the relative popularity of these formats in industry.

Evaluating Performance Appraisal Formats

What makes for a good appraisal format? Good ones score well on five dimensions: (1) employee development potential (amount of feedback about performance that the format offers), (2) administrative ease, (3) personnel research potential, (4) cost, and (5) validity. Admittedly, different organizations will attach different weights to these dimensions. For example, a small organization in its formative years is likely to be very cost-conscious. A large organization with pressing affirmative action commitments might place relatively high weight on validity and nondiscrimination and show less concern about cost issues. A progressive firm concerned with employee development might demand a format allowing substantial employee feedback. For example, some years ago Dow Chemical Company did away with performance ratings but kept performance reviews; stress was placed on using reviews to help develop employee skills. The five main criteria are explained below:[37]

1. *Employee development criterion:* Does the method communicate the goals and objectives of the organization? Is feedback to employees a natural outgrowth of the evaluation format, so that employee developmental needs are identified and can be attended to readily? We know that feedback has a positive impact on job performance.[38] There is also evidence that different kinds of feedback have different effects. Critical feedback that attacks the individual rather than focusing on the task has negative effects[39]. Employees respond better to feedback that tells them what went wrong on the task and how to improve.[40] Keep in mind, though, that the desire for feedback doesn't extend across all cultures. Lucent Technologies found that certain cultures are very reluctant to give feedback, either positive or negative. In most Asian cultures feedback is viewed with great suspicion, and only the most reckless executive would jeopardize his reputation by giving feedback, particularly in public.

2. *Administrative criterion:* How easily can evaluation results be used for administrative decisions concerning wage increases, promotions, demotions, terminations, and transfers? Comparisons among individuals for personnel action require some common denominator. Typically this is a numerical rating of performance. Evaluation forms that do not produce numerical ratings cause administrative headaches. So, for example, an essay format (solely a written explanation of what the employee did well and not so well), with no numerical evaluation, is difficult to evaluate relative to other essays. Who did better is an important question when giving out merit increases.

3. *Personnel research criterion:* Does the instrument lend itself well to validating employment tests? Can applicants predicted to perform well be monitored through

EXHIBIT 11.8   An Evaluation of Performance Appraisal Formats

	Employee Development Criterion	Administration Criterion	Personnel Research Criterion	Economic Criterion	Validity Criterion
Ranking	Poor—ranks typically based on overall performance, with little thought given to feedback on specific performance dimensions.	Poor—comparisons of ranks across work units to determine merit raises are meaningless. Other administrative actions similarly hindered.	Average—validation studies can be completed with rankings of performance.	Good—inexpensive source of performance data. Easy to develop and use in small organizations and in small units.	Average—good reliability but poor on rating errors, especially halo.
Standard rating scales	Average—general problem areas identified. Some information on extent of developmental need is available, but no feedback on necessary behaviors/outcomes.	Average—ratings valuable for merit increase decisions and others. Not easily defended if contested.	Average—validation studies can be completed, but level of measurement contamination unknown.	Good—inexpensive to develop and easy to use.	Average—content validity is suspect. Rating errors and reliability are average.
Behaviorally anchored rating scales	Good—extent of problem and behavioral needs are identified.	Good—BARS good for making administrative decisions. Useful for legal defense because job-relevant.	Good—validation studies can be completed and measurement problems on BARS less than many other criterion measures.	Average—expensive to develop but easy to use.	Good—high content validity. Some evidence of **interrater reliability** and reduced rating errors.
Management by objectives	Excellent—extent of problem and outcome deficiencies are identified.	Poor—MBO not suited to merit income decisions. Level of completion and difficulty of objectives hard to compare across employees.	Poor—nonstandard objectives across employees and no overall measures of performance make validity studies difficult.	Poor—expensive to develop and time-consuming to use.	Excellent—high content validity. Low rating errors.
Essay	Unknown—depends on guidelines or inclusions in essay as developed by organization or supervisors.	Poor—essays not comparable across different employees considered for merit or other administrative actions.	Poor—no quantitative indices to compare performance against employee test scores in validation studies.	Average—easy to develop but time-consuming to use.	Unknown—unstructured format makes studies of essay method difficult.

performance evaluation? Similarly, can the success of various employees and organizational development programs be traced to impacts on employee performance? As with the administrative criterion, evaluations typically need to be quantitative to permit the statistical tests so common in personnel research.

4. *Cost criterion:* Does the evaluation form initially require a long time to be developed? Is it time-consuming for supervisors to use the form in rating their employees? Is it expensive to use? All of these factors increase the format cost.

5. *Validity criterion:* By far the most research on formats in recent years has focused on reducing error and improving accuracy. Success in this pursuit would mean that decisions based on performance ratings (e.g., promotions, merit increases) could be made with increased confidence. In general, the search for the perfect format to eliminate rating errors and improve accuracy has been unsuccessful. The high acclaim, for example, accompanying the introduction of BARS has not been supported by research.[41]

Exhibit 11.8 provides a report card on the five most common rating formats relative to the criteria just discussed.

Which of these appraisal formats is the best? Unfortunately, the answer is a murky "It depends." Keeley suggests that the choice of an appraisal format is dependent on the type of tasks being performed.[42] He argues that tasks can be ordered along a continuum from those that are very routine to those for which the appropriate behavior for goal accomplishment is very uncertain. In Keeley's view, different appraisal formats require assumptions about the extent to which correct behavior for task accomplishment can be specified. The choice of an appraisal format requires a matching of formats with tasks that meet the assumptions for that format. At one extreme of the continuum are behavior-based evaluation procedures that define specific performance expectations against which employee performance is evaluated. Keeley argues that behaviorally anchored rating scales fall into this category. The behavioral anchors specify performance expectations representing the different levels of performance possible by an employee. Only for highly routine, mechanistic tasks is it appropriate to specify behavioral expectations. For these routine tasks it is possible to identify the single sequence of appropriate behaviors for accomplishing a goal. Consequently, it is possible to identify behavioral anchors for a performance scale that illustrate varying levels of attainment of the proper sequence of activities.

However, when tasks are less routine, it is more difficult to specify a single sequence of procedures that must be followed to accomplish a goal. Rather, multiple strategies are both feasible and appropriate to reach a final goal. Under these circumstances, the appraisal format should focus on evaluating the extent to which the final goal can be specified.[43] Thus, for less certain tasks an MBO strategy would be appropriate. As long as the final goal can be specified, performance can be evaluated in relation to that goal without specifying or evaluating the behavior used to reach that goal. The focus is exclusively on the degree of goal accomplishment.

At the other extreme of the continuum are tasks that are highly uncertain in nature. A relatively low consensus exists about the characteristics of successful performance. Moreover, the nature of the task is so uncertain that it may be difficult to specify expected goals. For this type of task, Keeley argues that judgment-based evaluation procedures—as exemplified by standard rating scales—may be the most appropriate. Raters make subjective estimates about the levels of employee performance on tasks for which neither the appropriate behavior nor the final goal is well specified. The extent of this uncertainty makes this type of appraisal very subjective and may well explain why trait rating scales are openly criticized for the number of errors that occur in performance evaluations.

Strategy 2: Select the Right Raters

A second way that firms have tried to improve the accuracy of performance ratings is by focusing on who might conduct the ratings and which of these sources is more likely to be accurate.[44] For example, recent evidence indicates raters who are not particularly conscientious and raters who are too agreeable tend to give artificially high evaluations of employees.[45] To lessen the impact of one reviewer, and to increase participation in the process, a method known as **360-degree feedback** has grown more popular in recent years. Generally, this system is used in conjunction with supervisory reviews.[46] The method assesses employee performance from five points of view: supervisor, peer, self, customer, and subordinate. The flexibility of the process makes it appealing to employees at all levels within an organization; most companies using the system report that their employees are satisfied with its results.[47] They feel that the 360-degree system has outperformed their old systems in improving employee understanding and self-awareness, promoting communication between supervisors and staff, and promoting better performance and results.[48] Hershey Foods, for example, uses a 360-degree process that identifies areas for leadership training, and employees have voiced support for continuation of the program.[49]

Regardless of the positive responses from those who have implemented the 360-degree feedback system, today most companies still use it only for evaluation of their top-level personnel and for employee development rather than for appraisal or pay decisions.[50] Some companies report frustration with the number of evaluation surveys each rater has to complete and the time necessary to complete the entire process.[51] More seriously, some research indicates that the different types of raters are very similar in their evaluations. Given the extra costs, then, why ask for multiple views the critics argue.[52] Responding to this criticism, recent research shows a distinct impact of rating source—raters do provide differing views.[53] As future HR professionals, you will face conflicting information daily. Part of your job will be to evaluate choices. Let's take a closer look at the role and benefit of each of the raters.

Supervisors as Raters

Who rates employees? Some estimates indicate that more than 80 percent of the input for performance ratings comes from supervisors.[54] There are good reasons why supervisors play such a dominant role. Supervisors assign (or jointly determine) what work employees are to perform. This makes a supervisor knowledgeable about the job and the dimensions to be rated. Also, supervisors frequently have considerable prior experience in rating employees, thus giving them some pretty firm ideas about what level of performance is required for any given level of performance rating.[55] Although there are some credible sources who question the validity of supervisory ratings,[56] the dominant view is that supervisors tend to provide accurate appraisals of their subordinates.[57] Supervisor ratings also tend to be more reliable than those from other sources.[58] On the negative side, though, supervisors are particularly prone to halo and leniency errors.[59]

Peers as Raters

One of the major strengths of using peers as raters is that they work more closely with the ratee and probably have an undistorted perspective of typical performance, particularly in group assignments (as opposed to what a supervisor might observe in a casual stroll around the work area). Balanced against this positive are at least two powerful negatives. First, peers may have little or no experience in conducting appraisals, leading to rather mixed evidence about the reliability of this rating source. Second, in a situation where teamwork is promoted, placing the burden of rating peers on co-workers can either create group tensions (in the case of low evaluations) or yield ratings second only to self-ratings in level of leniency.[60] One exception to this leniency effect comes from top performers, who it seems give the most objective evaluations of peers.[61] However, Motorola, one of the leaders in the use of teams and in peer ratings, reports that peer ratings help team members exert pressure on co-workers to perform better.[62]

Self as Rater

Some organizations have experimented with self-ratings. Obviously self-ratings are done by someone who has the most complete knowledge about the ratee's performance. Unfortunately, though, self-ratings are generally more lenient and possibly more unreliable than ratings from other sources.[63] One compromise in the use of self-ratings is to use them for developmental rather than administrative purposes. In addition, increasingly firms are asking employees to rate themselves as the first step in the appraisal process.[64] Forcing employees to think about their performance before they go into the formal appraisal with their boss may lead to more realistic assessments, ones that are also more in tune with a supervisor's own perceptions.

Customer as Rater

This is the era of the customer. The drive for quality means more companies are recognizing the importance of customers. One logical outcome of this increased interest is ratings from customers. For example, McDonald's surveys its customers, sets up 800 numbers to get feedback, and hires mystery customers to order food and report back on the service and treatment they receive. In a more personal example, Newman used to be a mystery shopper for the car wash company discussed several times in the book. He goes for a car wash, writes down the names of employees who do things out of the ordinary (either good or bad) and reports back to headquarters with a written report. For example, one time he asked for a new type of wax finish advertised on bill boards—the employee had no idea about this wash and "bluffed" that no such option was available. Bad boy! In exchange for regular reports on performance, Newman got car washes and oil changes for free. Yes, he's incredibly cheap!

Increasingly we can expect the boundaries between organizations and the outside world to fade. Although much of the customer rating movement is directed at performance of business units, we can expect some of this to distill down to individual workers. As another example, Home Depot prints its Web address on receipts and encourages feedback about specific employees. Great feedback can result in a $2,000 bonus.[65]

Subordinate as Rater

Historically, upward feedback has been viewed as countercultural, but the culture within organizations has undergone a revolution in the past 10 years and views are everchanging.[66] The notion of subordinates as raters is appealing since most superiors want to be successful with the people who report to them. Hearing how they are viewed by their subordinates gives them the chance to both see their strengths and their weaknesses as a leader and to modify their behavior.[67] The difficulty with this type of rating is in attaining candid reviews and also in counseling the ratee on how to deal with the feedback. Research shows that subordinates prefer, not surprisingly, to give their feedback to managers anonymously. If their identity is known, subordinates give artificially inflated ratings of their supervisors.[68]

---

e-Compensation

The American Compensation Association has an extensive website, including a bookstore. Go to *www.worldatwork.org/bookstore/* if you want information about other books on performance measurement, including books that talk about the advantages and disadvantages of using multiple raters.

Strategy 3: Understand How Raters Process Information

A third way to improve job performance ratings is to understand how raters think.[69] When we observe and evaluate performance, what else influences ratings besides an employee's performance?[70] We know, for example, that feelings, attitudes, and moods influence raters. If your supervisor likes you, then regardless of how well you perform, you are likely to get better ratings.[71] Your boss's general mood also influences performance ratings. Hope for a rater who is generally cheerful rather than grumpy; it could influence how you are evaluated![72]

Researchers continue to explore how raters process information about the performance of the people they rate. In general, we think the following kinds of processes occur:

1. The rater observes the behavior of a ratee.
2. The rater encodes this behavior as part of a total picture of the ratee (i.e., the rater forms stereotypes).
3. The rater stores this information in memory, which is subject to both short- and long-term decay. Simply put, raters forget things.
4. When it comes time to evaluate a ratee, the rater reviews the performance dimensions and retrieves stored observations/impressions to determine their relevance to the performance dimensions.

5. The information is reconsidered and integrated with other available information as the rater decides on the final ratings.[73]

Quite unintentionally, this process can produce errors, and they can occur at any stage.

Errors in the Rating Process

Ideally raters should notice only performance-related factors when they observe employee behavior. In fact, all of the processing stages should be guided by performance relevancy. Unless a behavior (or personality trait) affects performance, it should not influence performance ratings. Fortunately, studies show that performance actually does play an important role, perhaps the major role, in determining how a supervisor rates a subordinate.[74] Employees who are technically proficient and who do not create problems on the job tend to receive higher ratings than these who are weaker on these dimensions.[75] Indeed, political skill (amongst other things, your ability to ingratiate yourself—get in good—with your boss), pays off in a number of ways in performance ratings.[76] On the negative side, though, performance-irrelevant factors appear to influence ratings, and they can cause errors in the evaluation process.[77]

Common Errors in Appraising Performance: Criterion Contamination

Suppose you supervise 1,000 employees. How many would you expect to rate at the highest level? How many would be average or below? If you're tempted to argue that the distribution should look something like a normal curve, you might get an A in statistics but fail Reality 101. One of the authors had a consulting project once with a county department of social services. Part of the project required collecting performance ratings for the prior 10 years. With more than 10,000 performance reviews, guess how many times people were rated "average" or "below average"? Three times! Do you think that's just an aberration? **Criterion contamination,** or allowing non-performance factors to affect performance scores, occurs in every company and every job, and probably affects each of us at sometime during our careers. Sound a bit over the top? Consider the following: One survey of 1,816 organizations reported that only 4.6 percent of the managers were rated below average. See Exhibit 11.9; it looks like we all live in Lake Wobegone.

Now, we might argue that people who get to the managerial level do so because they are better-than-average performers.[78] So, of course, most of them rate average or better in their jobs. But the truth is that as raters we tend to make mistakes. Our ratings differ from those that would occur if we could somehow, in a moment of clarity, divine (and report!) the truth. We make errors in ratings. Recognizing and understanding the errors, such as those noted in Exhibit 11.10, are the first steps to communicating and building a more effective appraisal process.

EXHIBIT 11.9
Ratings of Managers

Rating	Percent of Managers Receiving Rating
Above average	46.4
Average	49.0
Below average	4.6

EXHIBIT 11.10
Common
Errors in the
Appraisal
Process

Halo error	An appraiser giving favorable ratings to all job duties based on impressive performance in just one job function. For example, a rater who hates tardiness rates a prompt subordinate high across all performance dimensions exclusively because of this one characteristic.
Horn error	The opposite of a halo error. Downgrading an employee across all performance dimensions exclusively because of poor performance on one dimension.
First impression error	Developing a negative or positive opinion of an employee early in the review period and allowing that to negatively or positively influence all later perceptions of performance.
Recency error	The opposite of first impression error. Allowing performance, either good or bad, at the end of the review period to play too large a role in determining an employee's rating for the entire period.
Leniency error	Consistently rating someone higher than is deserved.
Severity error	The opposite of leniency error. Rating individuals consistently lower than is deserved.
Central tendency error	Avoiding extremes in ratings across employees.
Clone error	Giving better ratings to individuals who are like the rater in behavior and/or personality.
Spillover error	Continuing to downgrade an employee for performance errors in prior rating periods.

Not surprisingly, the potential for errors causes employees to lose faith in the performance appraisal process. Employees, quite naturally, will be reluctant to have pay systems tied to such error-ridden performance ratings. At the very least, charges that the evaluation process is political will abound.[79] There are several factors that lead raters to give inaccurate appraisals: (1) guilt, (2) embarrassment about giving praise, (3) taking things for granted, (4) not noticing good or poor performance, (5) the halo effect (seeing one good attribute and leaping to positive impressions on remaining attributes), (6) dislike of confrontation, and (7) spending too little time on preparation of the appraisal. To counter such problems, companies and researchers alike have expended considerable time and money to identify ways job performance can be measured better.

Errors in Observation (Attention)

Generally, researchers have varied three types of input information to see what raters pay attention to when they are collecting information for performance appraisals. First, it appears that raters are influenced by general appearance characteristics of the ratees. Males are rated higher than females (other things being equal). A female ratee is observed not as a ratee but as a female ratee. A rater may form impressions based on stereotypic beliefs about women rather than the reality of the work situation and quite apart from any performance information. Females are rated less accurately when the rater has a traditional view of women's "proper" role; raters without traditional stereotypes of women are not prone to such errors.[80] Race also matters in performance ratings. Both in layoff decisions and in performance ratings, blacks are more likely to do worse than whites.[81]

Researchers also look at change in performance over time to see if this influences performance ratings. Both the pattern of performance (performance gets better versus worse over time) and the variability of performance (consistent versus erratic) influence performance ratings, even when the overall level (average) of performance is controlled.[82] Workers who start out high in performance and then get worse are rated lower than workers who remain consistently low.[83] Not surprisingly, workers whose performance improves over time are seen as more motivated, while those who are more variable in their performance are tagged as lower in motivation. All of us have seen examples of workers and students who intuitively recognize this type of error and use it to their advantage. The big surge of work at the end of an appraisal period is often designed to "color" a rater's perceptions.

Errors in Storage and Recall

Research suggests that raters store information in the form of traits.[84] More importantly, they tend to recall information in the form of trait categories. For example, a rater observes a specific behavior such as an employee resting during work hours. The rater stores this information not as the specific behavior but rather in the form of a trait, such as "That worker is lazy." Specific instructions to recall information about the ratee, as for a performance review, elicit the trait—lazy. Further, in the process of recalling information, a rater may remember events that didn't actually occur, simply because they are consistent with the trait category.[85] The entire rating process, then, may be heavily influenced by the trait categories that the rater adopts, regardless of their accuracy.

Errors in storage and recall also appear to arise from memory decay. At least one study indicates that rating accuracy is a function of the delay between performance and subsequent rating. The longer the delay, the less accurate the ratings.[86] Some research suggests that memory decay can be avoided if raters keep a diary and record information about employee performance as it occurs.[87] And should you ever have to go into court to defend your performance rating of an employee (e.g., discrimination charges sometimes come down to this), the judiciary likes witnesses who keep diaries documenting employee performance.

Errors in the Actual Evaluation

The context of the actual evaluation process also can influence evaluations.[88] Several researchers indicate that the purpose of an evaluation affects the rating process.[89] For example, performance appraisals sometimes serve a political end.[90] Supervisors have been known to deflate performance to send a signal to an employee—"You're not wanted here."[91] Supervisors also tend to weigh negative attributes more heavily than positive attributes: You are more likely to receive a much lower score if you do one task badly than you are to receive a proportionally higher score if you perform one task particularly well.[92]

If the purpose of evaluation is to divide up a fixed pot of merit increases, ratings also tend to be less accurate. Supervisors who know ratings will be used to determine merit increases are less likely to differentiate among subordinates than they are when the ratings will be used for other purposes.[93]

Rank and Yank: Good Idea or Bad?

Jack Welch, a hugely popular and successful former CEO of General Electric, popularized what came to be called **"rank and yank."** Estimates indicate rank and yank is used by about 60 percent of the Fortune 500, sometimes with more "gentle" names such as talent assessment.[94] Rank and yank requires managers to force-rank employees according to some preset distribution. McDonald's, GE, and Sun Microsystems, for example, use a 20–70–10 distribution (top 20 percent,[95] vital 70 percent, bottom 10 percent). Employees in the bottom 10 percent are given a chance to improve. Failure to move into the middle 70 percent usually results in termination. Some consultants and academics view forced ranking as the cure for inflated ratings and poor appraisal processes.[96] As a result, these supporters claim, company performance improves.[97] Some managers wonder, though, if there is a limit to this yank strategy. After a while, people ask, "Haven't you rid yourself of the deadwood?" and then you start cutting good employees. One simulation study, asking just this question, suggested as much as 16 percent average improvement over the first four years of rank and yank, but that benefits fall off dramatically after that.[98] This suggests the method has strong short-term benefits.

Also, being required to provide feedback to subordinates about their ratings yields less accuracy than a secrecy policy.[99] Presumably, anticipation of an unpleasant confrontation with the angry ratee persuades the rater to avoid confrontation by giving a rating higher than is justified. However, when raters must justify their scoring of subordinates in writing, the rating is more accurate.[100]

Strategy 4: Training Raters to Rate More Accurately

Although there is some evidence that training is not effective[101] or is less important in reducing errors than are other factors,[102] most research indicates rater training is an effective method for reducing appraisal errors.[103] Rater training programs can be divided into three distinct categories:[104] (1) **rater-error training,** in which the goal is to reduce psychometric errors (e.g., leniency, severity, central tendency, halo) by familiarizing raters with their existence; (2) **performance-dimension training,** which exposes supervisors to the performance dimensions to be used in rating (e.g., quality of work, job knowledge), thus making sure everyone is on the same page when thinking about a specific performance dimension; and (3) **performance-standard training,** which provides raters with a standard of comparison or frame of reference for making appraisals (what constitutes good, average, and bad). Several generalizations about ways to improve rater training can be summarized from this research:

1. Straightforward lecturing to ratees (the kind we professors are notorious for) about ways to improve the quality of their ratings generally is ineffective.
2. Individualized or small-group discussion sections are more effective in conveying proper rating procedures.
3. When these sessions are combined with extensive practice and feedback sessions, rating accuracy significantly improves.
4. Longer training programs (more than two hours) generally are more successful than shorter programs.
5. **Performance-dimension training** and **performance-standard training** generally work better than rater-error training, particularly when they are combined.
6. The greatest success has come from efforts to reduce halo errors and improve accuracy.

Leniency errors are the most difficult form of error to eliminate. This shouldn't be surprising. Think about the consequences to a supervisor of giving inflated ratings versus those of giving accurate or even deflated ratings. The latter two courses are certain to result in more complaints and possibly reduced employee morale. The easy way out is to artificially inflate ratings.[105] Unfortunately, this positive outcome for supervisors may come back to haunt them: With everyone receiving relatively high ratings there is less distinction between truly good and poor performers. Obviously, it is also harder to pay for real performance differences.

PUTTING IT ALL TOGETHER: THE PERFORMANCE EVALUATION PROCESS

A good performance evaluation doesn't begin on the day of the performance interview.[106] We outline here some of the key elements in the total process that from day one make for a good appraisal outcome.[107] First, figure out what your culture and strategy are. This should help you figure out what the key factors are that should be measured. Second, make sure your job descriptions are up to date and employees know what is expected of them. Third, periodically have informal discussions with employees about progress and any barriers that the supervisor needs to remove. Fourth, when evaluating performance, focus on behavior, not the person, in providing feedback employees don't know what you expect of them, how can they possibly please you?[108]

Second, we need to involve employees in every stage of developing performance dimensions and building scales to measure how well they perform on these dimensions. One extreme case of involvement is illustrated by Emmitt Smith, Hall of Fame football player. At age 21 Emmitt walked into Jerry Jones office (Dallas Cowboys owner). He handed him a slip of paper by which he wanted to be evaluated over his career. On that paper were five goals including win the Super Bowl more than once and become the NFL all-time leading rusher.[109] In cases where this occurs, employees have more positive reactions to ratings, regardless of how well they do. They are happier with the system's fairness and the appraisal accuracy. They give better evaluations of managers and indicate intentions to stay with their organization. Managers also respond well to this type of "due process" system. They feel they have a greater ability to resolve work problems. They have higher job satisfaction and less reason to distort appraisal results to further their own interests.[110] Employees also provide a unique perspective on what will or won't work. Consider the performance appraisal system developed by Alcatel-Lucent Technologies for its overseas operations. A performance dimension that worked well in Alcatel-Lucent U.S. operations was translated in local cultures as "obsession with serving our customers." It turns out that the word *obsession* in Saudi Arabia, Thailand, the Caribbean, and Latin America has very, very erotic and negative connotations. The problem was discovered only when managers reported employees speaking with one voice: "I don't care how important the customer is—I'm not doing this!"[111]

Third, we need to make sure raters are trained in use of the appraisal system and that all employees understand how the system operates and what it will be used for. A recent Harvard Business Review book talks about the importance of supervisors wearing both performance review and coaching hats.[112] Coaching addresses current performand and opportunities for growth through development of new skills. By fostering a creative environment and allowing employees to achieve goals using their unique individual skills, the Performance Review hat is easier to wear.

Fourth, we need to make sure raters are motivated to rate accurately. One way to achieve this is to ensure that managers are rated on how well they utilize and develop human resources. A big part of this would be evaluation and feedback to employees. Less than one-half of managers report that they provide feedback, and of those who do give feedback, most admit they are unsure if their feedback is worthwhile.[113] Almost one-half of employees agreed with this assessment, feeling performance reviews did little to guide performance.[114] Regardless of the quality of feedback one receives, don't assume that every review will improve performance![115]

Fifth, raters should maintain a diary of employee performance, both as documentation and to jog the memory.[116] This will help ensure that supervisors are knowledgeable about subordinates' performance and serve as an objective exhibit in any court-based allegation of discrimination.[117] Sixth, raters should attempt a performance diagnosis to determine in advance if performance problems arise because of motivation, skill deficiency, or external environmental constraints;[118] this process in turn tells the supervisor whether the problem requires motivation building, training, or efforts to remove external constraints.

And finally, feedback to employees should be timely. Recent research indicates "Millennials" like to have feedback frequently. Facebook's (the company) culture, for example, is such that feedback is encouraged after any meeting, presentation or project completion.[119] More companies are also trying to make the feedback developmental. A recent trend is to minimize negative feedback that can crush self-confidence. Such well-regarded firms as Boston Consulting Group have taken up the "accentuate the positive" movement.[120]

EQUAL EMPLOYMENT OPPORTUNITY AND PERFORMANCE EVALUATION

Equal employment opportunity (EEO) and **affirmative action** have influenced HR decision making for more than 40 years. While there are certainly critics of these programs, at least one important trend can be traced to the civil rights vigil in the workplace. Specifically, EEO has forced organizations to document decisions and to ensure they are firmly tied to performance or expected performance. For example, in a recent court case several female employees at Northern States Power Company in Minneapolis filed a lawsuit alleging that male workers in their job classification were paid more. While the case was dismissed, the problem of inequality remains.[121] This may well be the legacy of EEO. While it doesn't directly reduce segregation in the workforce, research shows that EEO affects HR practices and legal practices of companies that have been found guilty, and this in turn yields gradual positive changes in practices.[122] Nowhere is this more apparent than in the performance appraisal area. Just ask folks at the Social Security Administration, who settled an $8 million class action suit brought by black employees who successfully argued there was bias in the performance appraisal process.[123] Performance appraisals are subject to the same scrutiny as employment tests. Consider the use of performance ratings in making decisions about promotions. In this context, a performance appraisal takes on all the characteristics of a test used to make an initial employment decision. If employees pass the test—are rated highly in the performance evaluation process—they are predicted to do well at higher-level jobs. This interpretation of performance evaluation as a test, subject to validation requirements, was made in ***Brito v. Zia Company***.[124] In this case, Zia Company used performance evaluations based on a rating format to lay off employees. The layoffs resulted in a disproportionate number of minorities being discharged. The court held that:

> Zia, a government contractor, had failed to comply with the testing guidelines issued by the Secretary of Labor, and that Zia had not developed job-related criteria for evaluating employees' work performance to be used in determining employment promotion and discharges which is required to protect minority group applicants and employees from the discriminatory effects of such failure.[125]

Since the *Brito* case there has been growing evidence that the courts have very specific standards and requirements for performance appraisal.[126] The courts stress six issues in setting up a performance appraisal system.[127]

1. Courts are favorably disposed to appraisal systems that give specific written instructions on how to complete the appraisal. Presumably, more extensive training in other facets of evaluation would also be viewed favorably by the courts.
2. Organizations tend to be able to support their cases better when the appraisal system incorporates clear criteria for evaluating performance. Performance dimensions and scale levels that are written, objective, and clear tend to be viewed positively by courts in discrimination suits.[128] In part, this probably arises because behaviorally oriented appraisals have more potential to provide workers feedback about developmental needs.

3. As pointed out by every basic personnel book ever printed—and reinforced by this text—the presence of adequately developed job descriptions provides a rational foundation for personnel decisions. The courts reinforce this by ruling more consistently for defendants (companies) when their appraisal systems are based on sound job descriptions.

4. Courts also approve of appraisal systems that require supervisors to provide feedback about appraisal results to the employees affected. Absence of secrecy permits employees to identify weaknesses and to challenge undeserved appraisals.

5. The courts seem to like evaluation systems that incorporate a review of any performance rating by a higher-level supervisor.

6. Perhaps most importantly, the courts consistently suggest that the key to fair appraisals depends on consistent treatment across raters, regardless of race, color, religion, sex, or national origin.

The focal question then becomes: Are similarly situated individuals treated similarly? This standard is particularly evident in a court case involving performance appraisal and merit pay.[129] A black male filed suit against General Motors, claiming race discrimination in both the timing and the amount of a merit increase. The court found this case without merit. General Motors was able to show that the same set of rules was applied equally to all individuals. There also has been a recent jump in lawsuits challenging as discriminatory the practice of "rank and yank." Employees are arguing they've been "ranked and yanked" not because of performance, but because of age.[130] As a result, there has been a noticeable drop in the number of companies using this method.

A final word of caution about the role of equal employment and performance appraisal: Experts note that firms approaching performance appraisal primarily as a way to defend against discrimination claims may actually create more claims. Documentation of performance to discourage such claims only causes poor employee relations, and it can lead to solid employees feeling like plaintiffs themselves.[131] A better strategy is to follow the guidelines we developed earlier. They permit both effective performance reviews and a strong foundation in case legal issues arise.

TYING PAY TO SUBJECTIVELY APPRAISED PERFORMANCE

Think, for a moment, about what it really means to give employees merit increases. Bill Peterson makes $40,000 per year. He gets a merit increase of 3 percent, the approximate average increase over the past several decades. Bill's take-home increase (adjusted for taxes) is a measly $16 per week more than he used to make. Before we console Bill, though, consider Jane Krefting, who is a better performer than Bill and receives a 6 percent merit increase. Should she be thrilled by this pay-for-performance differential and be motivated to continue as a high achiever? Probably not. After taxes, her paycheck (assuming a base salary similar to Bill's) is only $15 dollars per week more than Bill's check.

The central issue involving merit pay is, "How do we get employees to view raises as a reward for performance?" Chapter 9 illustrated this difficulty in theoretical terms. Now it is addressed from a pragmatic perspective. Very simply, organizations frequently grant increases that are not designed or communicated to be related to performance. Perhaps the central reason for this is the way merit pay is managed. Many companies view raises not as motivational tools to shape behavior but as budgetary line items to control costs.[132] Frequently this results in **pay increase guidelines** with little motivational impact. Three pay increase guidelines that particularly fit the low-motivation scenario will be discussed briefly below before we outline standards that attempt to link pay to performance.

Two types of pay increase guidelines with low-motivation potential provide equal increases to all employees regardless of performance. The first type, a general increase, typically is found in unionized firms. A contract is negotiated that specifies an across-the-board, equal increase for each year of the contract. Similarly, in the second type, across-the-board increases often are linked to cost-of-living changes. When the Consumer Price Index (CPI) rises, some companies adjust base pay for all employees to reflect the rising costs. (This is discussed in more detail in Chapter 18.) The third form of guideline comes somewhat closer to tying pay to performance. **Seniority increases** tie pay increases to a preset progression pattern based on seniority. For example, a pay grade might be divided into 10 equal steps, with employees moving to higher steps based on seniority. To the extent that performance improves with time on the job, this method has the rudiments of paying for performance.

In practice, tying pay to performance requires three things. First, we need some definition of performance. One set of subjective measures, as we discussed in Chapter 6, involves the competencies that people possess or acquire. Increasingly companies assert that corporate performance depends on having employees who possess key competencies. Xerox identifies 17 core competencies. As a company with strong strategic objectives linked to customer satisfaction and quality, it's not surprising to find that Xerox values such competencies as quality orientation, customer care, dependability, and teamwork. Recent trends in compensation center on finding ways to build competencies in employees. Merit increases may be linked to employee ability and willingness to demonstrate key competencies. For example, showing more of the following behaviors might be tied to higher merit increases:

Competency: Customer Care

1. Follows through on commitments to customers in a timely manner
2. Defines and communicates customer requirements
3. Resolves customer issues in a timely manner
4. Demonstrates empathy for customer feelings
5. Presents a positive image to the customer
6. Displays a professional image at all times
7. Communicates a positive image of the company and individuals to customers

Whether we measure performance by behaviors, competencies, or traits, there must be agreement that higher levels of performance will have positive impacts on corporate strategic objectives. Second, we need some continuum that describes different levels from

EXHIBIT 11.11 Performance-Based Guideline

	Performance Level				
	1	**2**	**3**	**4**	**5**
	Outstanding	Very Satisfactory	Satisfactory	Marginally Unsatisfactory	Unsatisfactory
Merit Increase	5%	4%	3%	1%	0%

low to high on the performance measure. Third, we need to decide how much of a merit increase will be given for different levels of performance. Decisions about these three questions lead to some form of merit pay guide. In its simplest form a guideline specifies pay increases permissible for different levels of performance (see Exhibit 11.11).

A more complex guideline ties pay not only to performance but also to position in the pay range. Exhibit 11.12 illustrates such a system for a food market firm. The percentages in the cells of Exhibit 11.12 are changed yearly to reflect changing economic conditions. Two patterns are evident in this merit guideline. First, as would be expected in a pay-for-performance system, lower performance is tied to lower pay increases. In fact, in many organizations the poorest performers receive no merit increases. The second relationship is that pay increases at a decreasing rate as employees move through a pay range. For the same level of performance, employees low in the range receive higher percentage increases than employees who have progressed further through the range. In part this is designed to forestall the time when employees reach the salary maximum and have their salaries frozen. In part, though, it is also a cost-control mechanism tied to budgeting procedures, as discussed in Chapter 18.

Performance- and Position-Based Guidelines

Given a salary increase matrix, merit increases are relatively easy to determine. As Exhibit 11.12 indicates, an employee at the top of his or her pay grade who receives a "competent" rating would receive a 2 percent increase in base salary. A new trainee starting out below the minimum of a pay grade would receive an 8 percent increase for a "superior" performance rating.

EXHIBIT 11.12 Performance Rating Salary Increase Matrix

	Performance Rating				
Position in Range	**Not Satisfactory**	**Needs Improvement**	**Competent**	**Commendable**	**Superior**
Fourth quartile	0%	0%	2%	3%	4%
Third quartile	0	0	3	4	5
Second quartile	0	0	4	5	6
First quartile	0	1	5	6	7
Below minimum of range	0	2	6	7	8

Designing Merit Guidelines

Designing merit guidelines involves answering four questions. First, what should the poorest performer be paid as an increase? Notice that this figure is seldom negative. Base wages are, unfortunately, considered an entitlement. Wage cuts tied to poor performance are very rare. Most organizations, though, are willing to give no increases to very poor performers, perhaps as a prelude to termination if no improvements are shown.

The second question involves average performers: How much should they be paid as an increase? Most organizations try to ensure that average performers are kept whole (wages will still have the same purchasing power) relative to cost of living. This dictates that the midpoint of the merit guidelines equal the percentage change in the local or national consumer price index. Following this guideline, the 4 percent increase for an average performer in the second quartile of Exhibit 11.11 would reflect the change in CPI for that area. In a year with lower inflation, all the percentages in the matrix probably would be lower.

Third, how much should the top performers be paid? In part, budgetary considerations (Chapter 18) answer this question. But there is also growing evidence that employees do not agree on the size of increases that they consider meaningful (Chapter 8). Continuation of this research may help determine the approximate size of increases that is needed to make a difference in employee performance.

Finally, matrixes can differ in the size of the differential between different levels of performance. Exhibit 11.11 basically rewards successive levels of performance with 1 percent increases (at least in the portion of the matrix in which any increase is granted). A larger jump between levels would signal a stronger commitment to recognizing performance with higher pay increases. Most companies balance this, though, against cost considerations. Larger differentials cost more. When money is tight, this option is less attractive. Exhibit 11.13 shows how a merit grid is constructed when cost constraints (merit budget) are known. Finally, Exhibit 11.14 shows how Room & Board, a well-known and respected furniture and accessories firm, designs its pay-performance linkage.[133]

EXHIBIT 11.13 **Merit Grids**

Merit grids combine three variables: level of performance, distribution of employees within their job's pay range, and merit increase percentages.

Example

1. Assume a performance rating scale of A through D: 30 percent of employees get A, 35 percent get B, 20 percent get C, and 15 percent get D. Change the percents to decimals.

A	B	C	D
.30	.35	.20	.15

2. Assume a range distribution as follows: 10 percent of all employees are in the top (fourth) quartile of the pay range for their job, 35 percent in the third quartile, 30 percent in second quartile, and 25 percent in the lowest quartile. Change the percents to decimals.

1	.10
2	.35
3	.30
4	.25

(Continued)

EXHIBIT 11.13 (*Continued*)

3. Multiply the performance distribution by the range distribution to obtain the percent of employees in each cell. Cell entries = performance 3 range.

	A	B	C	D
1	.30 × .10 = .03	.35 × .20 = .037	.30 × .10 = .03	.15 × .10 = .015
2	.30 × .35 = .105	.35 × .35 = .1225	.20 × .35 = .07	.15 × .35 = .0525
3	.30 × .30 = .09	.35 × .30 = .105	.20 × .30 = .06	.15 × .30 = .045
4	.30 × .25 = .075	.35 × .25 = .1225	.20 × .25 = .05	.15 × .25 = .0375

Cell entries tell us that 3 percent of employees are in the top quartile of pay range *and* received an A performance rating, 10.5 percent of employees are in the second quartile of pay range *and* received an A performance rating, etc.

4. Distribute increase percentage among cells, varying the percentages according to performance and range distribution, for example, 6 percent to those employees in cell A1, 5 percent to those employees in B1.

5. Multiply increase percentages by the employee distribution for each cell. The sum of all cells should equal the total merit increase percentage.

Example:
$$6\% \times \text{cell A1} = .06 \times .03 = .0018$$
$$5\% \times \text{cell B1} = .05 \times .035 = .00175$$
$$\text{Etc.} \quad \underline{\qquad\qquad}$$
$$\text{Targeted merit increase percentage} = \text{Sum}$$

6. Adjust increase percentages among cells if needed in order to stay within budgeted increase.

EXHIBIT 11.14 Room & Board

As we begin our current business planning process we are targeting a 3% payroll increase. This is a guideline and is not meant as a template for you to apply to your team across the board. This range should be kept in mind as you work through your team to help assure we do not exceed our plan for payroll.

To determine salary increases for your team members this year you should take into account individuals' Priorities & Measures, your team assessment, scorecard data, as well as your market and location performance as a support to your individual decision making. Salaries should match one's contribution. We want to consider our long-term strategy of rewarding top performers and ensuring they get competitive increases each year. However, we do not want to be so aggressive in any given year that we do not leave ourselves room for competitive increases in future years.

Strong Contributor/Top Performer
Strong increases should be given to those individuals who have shown exemplary performance and have challenged themselves to grow and evolve with our business and gone above and beyond your expectations. (As a guide post it is our assumption that only a small number of your team may fit this definition.) Your criteria for performance should encompass both subjective and objective measures as well as the manner in which they performed. Staff members that have challenged themselves, improved their productivity and at the same time conducted themselves in a manner consistent with our culture should receive strong increases.

Strong Increase Example
Hourly Staff Member = $.75–$1.00

(For a staff member earning $18.00/hour this equates to an increase of 4.2%–5.6%)

EXHIBIT 11.14   (*Continued*)

Salaried individuals earning $40,000–$55,000 = $2,000 or $2,500

(At a $45,000 annual salary this represents an increase of 4.4%–5.5%)

Staff members earning in excess of $55,000 a year should receive approximately 4%

Solid, Core Contributor
Individuals that made a good contribution to the business yet are paid fairly for what they bring to our organization should see a moderate increase. Again, our assumption is that they are core, stable performers, immersed and learning every day and they are paid fairly. The vast majority of your team members should fit these criteria. This approach helps individuals keep pace with the market while reserving greater dollars for you to reward your key contributors. If you have core performers that you feel are not paid fairly for their role, you talk this through with your HR Partner to discuss this need for a stronger increase.

Moderate Increase Example:
Hourly Staff Member = $.50–$.75

(For a staff member earning $18.00/hour this equates to an increase of 2.8%–4.2%)

Salaried individuals earning $40,000–$55,000 = $1,000–$1,500

(At a $45,000 annual salary this represents an increase of 2.2%–3.3%)

Staff members earning in excess of $55,000 a year should receive approximately 3%

Non-Contributors
As in any year, those that have not contributed at a significant level and/or struggled in terms of their contribution and/or behavior should not be considered for an increase. Our expectation is that you have engaged these individuals in conversation throughout the year and your decision not to reward them with an annual increase will not come as a surprise.

It is also our expectation that those individuals not receiving an increase continue to be aggressively managed and will therefore either attain an acceptable level of contribution within a reasonable time period or be coached out of our organization.

Your **Turn**

Performance Appraisal at American Energy Development

Background

American Energy Development (AED) drills for oil using both vertical and horizontal ("fracking) drilling procedures. Financing for these operations in Pennsylvania and Texas comes largely through limited partnerships. The company identifies investors who become limited partners sharing in any successful drilling operations for the wells they have partially funded.

The founder of AED, Ron Robertson, recently passed away. His son John Robertson took over as CEO in 2014 and is steering a much more aggressive land acquisition strategy (for drilling wells) than was advocated by his father. Two hundred million dollars was raised last year to purchase land in Texas. Indeed, much of the operation is shifting to Texas and away from Pennsylvania because of the more lenient environmental laws governing fracking. Sixteen months ago six new employees were hired to help kick start the Texas operation. Additionally seven employees were voluntarily relocated to Dallas-Fort Worth (DFW) from the Buffalo, NY headquarters. John Robertson also relocated to DFW as a sign of his commitment to this new facility. Don Welch, Chief Operating Officer and President, remains behind in Buffalo to run that operation.

Present
John Robertson is a transplant from the aggressive, fast-moving trenches of Wall Street where as a broker he was weaned on tough performance appraisals and an incentive system that richly rewarded success stories and quickly discarded poor performers. He wants to instill a culture exactly like that in the DFW office. When he hired the six new key employees sixteen months ago, part of his early discussions with them was failure would not be accepted. No one was entitled to a job and it must be earned each day. Of the six new employees, two stand out for different reasons.

Billy Ray Jenson
Billy Ray is a petroleum engineer with 30 years' experience after graduating from the U. of Texas Petroleum Engineering program. He was hired in as senior engineer at a base wage of $216,000, a figure that matched the market rate. Market rate is a difficult figure to determine in Texas these days. Over 100,000 employees have been terminated in one of the worst downturns in the gas and oil economy in recent decades. Billy Ray is very grateful to get a job with a very competitive salary. He also is eligible for a 3 percent bonus on any wells that "hit" if he was the engineer of record for that field. As per agreement with John Robertson, Billy Ray will get his first full performance review in two weeks.

Elizabeth Andrews
Elizabeth also is a petroleum engineer. She has fourteen years' experience and is paid $165,000 with the same bonus arrangement as other petroleum engineers. Elizabeth is very bright and brimming over with initiative. She has made several suggestions for drilling procedures using a holographic technology that has cut down on the number of dry wells by 11 percent.

The Performance Appraisal System
John Robertson told the new employees when they were hired that they would be evaluated by him based on his perceptions of their performance. About one year ago he provided a performance appraisal form that had four performance dimensions rated on a five point scale. He also communicated base pay increases that would be associated with each rating. The factors and merit increases are as follows:

Performance Dimension	Performance Scale				
	Very Good	Good	Average	Not Good	Bad
	1	2	3	4	5
Merit increase (%)	8	5	3	1	0
Teamwork					
Productivity					
Quality					
Hard Working					

Teamwork: Someone who works well with fellow team players and values their efforts and contributions as much as his/her own.

Productivity: Amount of assigned work completed in an agreed upon time frame

Quality: Elimination of errors and absence of complaints

Hard Working: Shows up on time and works more hours than expected.

John Robertson's Concerns

John Robertson clearly has his dad's DNA. He purposely chose general performance dimensions because he believes the oil business is fast changing and demands people who are willing to work with a great deal of ambiguity. He doesn't want to be ties down to specific performance dimensions that employees can then use to "lawyer up" on him if they believe they didn't get a fair shake. Most of his employees he gave average or good ratings. Two employees, though, are causing him some problems. He likes to link ratings to performance. He's inclined to give Billy Ray Jenson a very good rating, and this would be associated with an 8 percent increase. John is reluctant to give Billy Ray this large an increase because he feels he overpaid the Petroleum Engineer to begin with. After all, there are hundreds of people who could fill his job in Texas, and all of them he believes would work for less. He can't rate Billy Ray Very Good and only give him a 3 percent increase. The merit pay guide is known to all employees. John has decided, therefore, to only rate Billy Ray Average. Billy Ray was great on the teamwork and hardworking dimensions. No question. So John has decided he'll downgrade Billy Ray on productivity and quality. Billy Ray has some promising wells that look like they might deliver and he is right on target with the number of wells sunk in a one year timeframe. But none of the wells have produced yet. So John figures he can rate Billy Ray lower on that. John also has decided to rate Billy Ray lower on quality. There aren't any hard and fast measures of quality, so John can justify whatever he wants to get an overall rating of average.

John has a different issue with Elizabeth Andrews. She is hard driving and aggressive. She shows great initiative but he has had many complaints from other engineers that she isn't a team player. They ask her for help using her holographic technology, claiming it will help them decide whether a well is worth pursuing. For the most part she turns these requests down, claiming that she is too busy exploring her own wells. She suggests that the others take them same online class at UT Dallas and this will guide them in use of holographic technology. On other dimensions Elizabeth is quite good. She works as hard as Billy Ray, has two wells that are producing already, far better than the industry standard for one year, and there have been no quality problems that he knows of. John is inclined to give Elizabeth an average rating because of complaints from other workers. The guys just don't think she is a team player.

John's action

John gives both workers an average rating. In the performance review Billy Ray takes the news and feedback stoically. However, six days later he tenders his letter of resignation, effective in one week. Two days after that, though, in a very bizarre move he asks to have the resignation revoked and return to his job. John accepts his change of heart and continues Billy Ray as an employee.

Elizabeth is far more confrontational. She maintains that she was indeed a good team player, and that others were taking advantage of her so much that she didn't have time to do her own job. She asserts that she took an online course on her own time and at her own initiative, so why couldn't others do that too. Plus, she says, in response to his rating of her on the quantity dimension, she has two producing wells in only one years' time. That is a phenomenal record, she maintains, and certainly better than any of the other Petro Engineers John hired for the new office. This statement is accurate. Elizabeth says nothing else during the meeting but leaves the office unhappy, perhaps unhappy enough to do something about it.

QUESTIONS FOR YOU

1. What problems do you see in the performance appraisal system and accompanying merit pay system? Did any of these problems contribute to the people problems John had with his two employees in the performance review process?
2. What might John have done differently in the early communications process to improve later performance review sessions?
3. Should Billy Ray have quit? Why? Should John have accepted his return? What other action might Billy Ray have taken that could have been hurtful to the company?
4. Was Elizabeth treated fairly? Should initiative be a performance dimension? What other action might she take? Could she make a case that she was discriminated against? What defense, if any, might the company have?

Summary   The process of appraising employee performance can be both time-consuming and stressful. These difficulties are compounded if the appraisal system is poorly developed or if a supervisor lacks the appropriate training to collect and evaluate performance data. Development of sound appraisal systems requires an understanding of organizational objectives balanced against the relative merits of each type of appraisal system. For example, despite its inherent weaknesses, an appraisal system based on ranking of employee performance may be appropriate in small organizations that, for a variety of reasons, choose not to tie pay to performance; a sophisticated MBO appraisal system may not be appropriate for such a company.

Training supervisors effectively to appraise performance requires an understanding of organizational objectives. We know relatively little about the ways raters process information and evaluate employee performance. However, a thorough understanding of organizational objectives combined with a knowledge of common errors in evaluation can make a significant difference in the quality of appraisals.

Review Questions

1. We talked in depth about four ways to improve performance ratings. Pick one that you think shows the most promise and defend your position.
2. You own a nonunion company with 93 nonexempt employees. All of these employees pack books into boxes for shipment to customers throughout the United States. Because of wide differences in performance, you have decided to try performance appraisal, something never done before. Until now, you have given every worker the same size increase. Now you want to measure performance and reward the best performers with bigger increases. Without any further information, which of the five types of appraisal formats do you think would be most appropriate? Justify your answer. Do you anticipate any complaints, or other comments, from employees after you implement your new system?

3. Think about the last group project you worked on. Describe that project and identify three performance criteria you think would be appropriate for evaluating the team members. Should every team member be able to rate one another on all these dimensions? Should the team-member ratings be used for feedback only or for feedback and part of the overall grade (with teacher approval, of course)? Should the teacher rate each team member on performance (all three criteria) in the group assignment? How are these questions relevant to setting up a 360° performance review?

4. Angela Lacy, an African American employee in your accounts receivable department, has filed a charge of discrimination, alleging she was unfairly passed over for promotion and regularly receives smaller pay increases than do employees who perform less well (she alleges). You have to go to your boss, the VP of HR, and explain what elements of your HR system can be used in your legal defense. What things do you hope you did in setting up and administering your systems to counter this discrimination charge?

Appendix **11-A**

Balanced Scorecard Example: Department of Energy (Federal Personal Property Management Program)

THE BSC PERSPECTIVE

Customer Perspective

The Customer Perspective enables organizations to align the core measure (customer satisfaction) to targeted customers. For this perspective, the primary objectives are to provide effective service to and establish effective partnerships with external and internal customers. Effective service and partnerships are key ingredients in assessing the health of any federal personal property management program.

Internal Business Processes Perspective

The objectives in the Internal Business Processes Perspective collectively assure that an effective federal personal property management program is established to (1) support customer needs; (2) provide efficient life cycle management (accountability, utilization and disposition) of direct operations personal property; and (3) maintain oversight of entities that have federal personal property management program responsibilities. Key processes in the federal personal property management program must be monitored to ensure that the outcomes satisfy program objectives. This perspective is important because it not only addresses the internal business processes that must be developed and maintained to meet customer and stakeholder requirements and expectations, but also the process results that lead to financial success and satisfied customers. Within any personal property management organization, there are a number of internal business processes that require focused management attention to ensure requirements and expectations are met as effectively as possible, while accommodating cost efficiency issues addressed in the Financial Perspective.

Learning and Growth

The two objectives under the Learning and Growth Perspective promote organizational and individual growth that will provide long-term benefits to the federal personal property management program. These objectives must be achieved if program performance is going to improve over time. While the objectives in the other perspectives identify where the program must excel to achieve breakthrough performance, the Learning and Growth objectives provide the infrastructure needed to enable the objectives in the other perspectives to be achieved. The Learning and Growth objectives are the drivers for achieving excellence in the other perspectives.

This perspective is important because it promotes individual and organizational growth—factors that are crucial to future success. Support for this perspective equates to recognition of the link between top-level strategic objectives and activities needed to re-skill and motivate employees; supply information; and align individuals, teams, and organizational units with the Department's strategy and long-term objectives. An analysis of the cause-and-effect relationships of the measures in this perspective clearly shows that employee satisfaction, employee alignment, and information availability are vital contributors to meeting the objectives stated in the other perspectives.

Financial Perspective

The objective of the Financial Perspective is to strive for optimum efficiency in the federal personal property management program. To achieve that, processes need to be analyzed to determine (1) cost and performance trends over time and (2) process changes that can be implemented to produce optimum efficiencies. Success for entities charged with federal personal property management program responsibilities should be measured by how effectively and efficiently these entities meet the needs of their constituencies. This perspective is important because optimizing the cost efficiency of the federal personal property management program ensures that the maximum amount of funds are available for accomplishing the primary missions of the Department and its field organizations. Managers must ensure that federal personal property management program operating costs are optimized in order to meet the challenge of creating business programs that work better and cost less.

OBJECTIVES, MEASURES, AND TARGETS

General

Each federal personal property BSC should contain both national and local performance objectives, measures, and targets. The national elements of the BSC are developed by the Department in support of the Departmental mission, vision, and strategy. The local elements of the BSC are developed locally, based on site-specific missions and needs.

National (Core) Measures

The core measures contained in the federal personal property BSC are measures that the Department expects all entities charged with federal personal property management program responsibilities to implement where applicable. The formulae and measuring methods should be maintained as standard as practicable from self assessment to self assessment. Some core measures may contain core and optional elements. Core elements are aspects of the federal personal property management program that the Department expects all entities to take into consideration, where applicable, when measuring. Optional elements are aspects of the federal personal property management program that the Department suggests, but does not require, for measurement where applicable.

Local Measures

The federal personal property BSC should also include local measures to track performance in areas of importance to the local site. The following measures are provided as examples of local measures that are currently in use throughout the DOE complex:

1. Customer Perspective

- Percent accuracy of key property data elements (e.g., property control number, nomenclature, part/model number, and serial number) where customers maintain or update databases.

2. Internal Business Processes Perspective

- Number of property system processes re-engineered during period.
- Percent and/or value (acquisition cost) of personal property items lost, damaged, destroyed, and/or stolen during the period.
- Value (acquisition cost) of personal property items found during the period.
- Percent of scheduled property management reviews conducted during period.
- Percent of scheduled management walk-throughs completed during period.
- Percent of excess or surplus property shipped within XX days of receipt of requisitions or transfer orders.
- Percent of usable property with sale value sold within XX days after completion of required screening.
- Extent to which reliable property, administrative, and financial systems are in place and integrated.
- Percent of government equipment issues resolved in a timely (defined locally) fashion.

3. Learning and Growth

- Number of classes/training sessions, supporting BSC objectives, provided to personal property custodians/representatives during the period.
- Percent of personal property custodians/representatives who attended the classes that were provided during the period in support of BSC objectives.

- Percent of personal property custodians/representatives who have been trained regarding their property management responsibilities.
- Percent of professional personal property employees who have attended a basic property administration course.
- Percent of professional personal property employees who have attended property management related training (e.g., demilitarization, high risk, NPMA).
- Number of employee suggestions, supporting BSC objectives, that were adopted during the period.
- Percent of personal property professional staff with professional certifications related to BSC objectives.

4. Financial Perspective

- Net proceeds from the sale of surplus assets as a percent of asset acquisition cost. Dollar value of site-generated excess property reutilized internally at the site.
- Dollar value of externally generated excess property (i.e., by other DOE sites and other federal agencies) utilized by the site.
- Reutilization screening transactions (number and dollar value) completed during period.

Appendix 11-B

Sample Appraisal Form for Leadership Dimension: Pfizer Pharmaceutical

PERFORMING FOR RESULTS

Reaching for the Future

District Manager/Regional Manager Capabilities

District Manager Baseline Capability Assessment

Employee Name:	Self Assessment: [ ]
Title:	(Select one)
	Manager Assessment: [ ]
District:	Manager's Name:

I. Strategic Capability Assessment	Unacceptable/ Needs Improvement	Stage I	Stage II	Stage III	Stage IV	Comments
1. Leadership						
2. Recruiting and Selection						
3. People Development						
4. Strategic Perspective						

Capabilities Cross-Reference Table

II. Core Behaviors Assessment	U	NI	S	RO	A	Comments
1. Planning & Organizing						
2. Impact						
3. Job Knowledge						
4. Problem Analysis						
5. Communication Ability						
6. Facilitation Skills						
7. Judgment						

8. Flexibility						
9. Political Savvy/Protocol						
10. Sensitivity						
11. Teamwork						

III. Employee Comments

Employee Signature:		Date:
Supervisor Signature:		Date:

	Key
U	"Unacceptable"
NI	"Needs Improvement"
S	"Sometimes"
RO	"Routinely"
A	"Always"

District Manager Strategic Capabilities

District Manager Strategic Capabilities (*Continued*)

Outlined below are four strategic capabilities for the District Manager (DM) role.

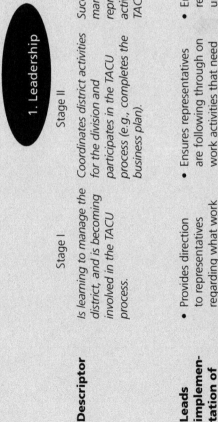

1. Leadership

	Stage I	Stage II	Stage III	Stage IV
Descriptor	Is learning to manage the district, and is becoming involved in the TACU process.	Coordinates district activities for the division and participates in the TACU process (e.g., completes the business plan).	Successfully leads and manages own representatives while actively contributing to the TACU process.	Emerges as a leader within the region, division, and TACU. Is willing to take on reasonable risk to push representatives/TACU/ district/region toward more forward thinking.
Leads implementation of sales strategy and tactics	• Provides direction to representatives regarding what work activities are important (e.g., communicates district standards to representatives).	• Ensures representatives are following through on work activities that need to be executed in the territory (e.g., physician calls, sample drops, computer data entry, etc.).	• Ensures that representatives understand how their activities affect district, regional, state, and U.S. Pharmaceuticals' objectives (e.g., regularly reviews territory, district, and regional results to reinforce line-of-sight).	• Takes a lead role in implementing and inspiring a vision of success for the district, region, and TACU (e.g., works with TACU members to clearly define outcomes based on what is best for the customer and Pfizer and develops innovative approaches that are adopted across U.S. Pharmaceuticals lines).

District Manager Strategic Capabilities (*Continued*)

Outlined below are four strategic capabilities for the District Manager (DM) role.

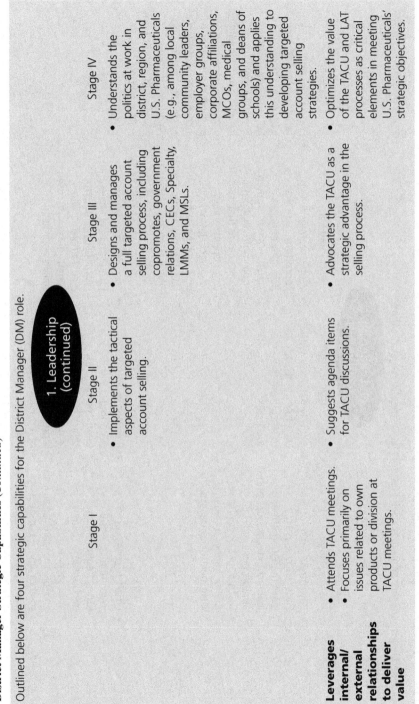

1. Leadership (continued)

	Stage I	Stage II	Stage III	Stage IV
		• Implements the tactical aspects of targeted account selling.	• Designs and manages a full targeted account selling process, including copromotes, government relations, CECs, Specialty, LMMs, and MSLs.	• Understands the politics at work in district, region, and U.S. Pharmaceuticals (e.g., among local community leaders, employer groups, corporate affiliations, MCOs, medical groups, and deans of schools) and applies this understanding to developing targeted account selling strategies.
Leverages internal/ external relationships to deliver value	• Attends TACU meetings. • Focuses primarily on issues related to own products or division at TACU meetings.	• Suggests agenda items for TACU discussions.	• Advocates the TACU as a strategic advantage in the selling process.	• Optimizes the value of the TACU and LAT processes as critical elements in meeting U.S. Pharmaceuticals' strategic objectives.

District Manager Strategic Capabilities (*Continued*)

Outlined below are four strategic capabilities for the District Manager (DM) role.

1. Leadership (continued)

Stage I

- Pays attention to other DMs' successes to learn management and leadership techniques and approaches.
- Discourages or confronts the exchange of negative disrespectful comments.

- Often focuses on individual contributors but is beginning to encourage a team approach (e.g., encourages representatives to coordinate business plan, goals, speakers, and call cycles).

Stage II

- Actively networks with DMs from other districts to learn from their successes.

- Recognizes and encourages a team approach to achieving results (e.g., acknowledges a representative's support of a priority copromote selling effort).

Stage III

- Works seamlessly with copromote partners. Regularly engages in activities to strengthen copromote relationships to maximize their benefits (e.g., openly shares resources, knowledge, and experience to facilitate representative/ DM mastery of market issues).

- Focuses on growing Pfizer's market share and profitability [e.g., adopts a customer-focused (versus division-focused) selling approach].

Stage IV

- Encourages and facilitates collaborating with CECs, MSLs, MSMs, Headquarters, and other field force members (e.g., identifies opportunities where a pooling of resources will increase the likelihood of success, matches up field force members who would benefit from collaboration).

District Manager Strategic Capabilities (*Continued*)

Outlined below are four strategic capabilities for the District Manager (DM) role.

1. Leadership (continued)

	Stage I	Stage II	Stage III	Stage IV
Raises performance in the field and develops high-performing teams	• Holds self to the same standards as representatives (e.g., is always punctual, files reports on time, willingly performs details, etc.). • Closely manages representative activities.	• Leads by example—personally demonstrates the core behaviors, skills, knowledge, and traits that representatives need to be successful. • Understands the principles of situational leadership and how it can improve performance (e.g., acknowledges individual differences but tends to rely on one preferred leadership style/approach). • Imparts a sense of responsibility among team members (e.g., requires representatives to assess their contributions and impact on district results, does not micromanage or under manage representatives, etc.).	• Raises performance of representatives by setting high performance standards that are perceived by representatives as being challenging but achievable. • Applies the principles of situational leadership (e.g., uses multiple leadership styles and adapts approach to individual needs/circumstances).	• Raises performance of the field beyond division, TACU, district, and regional lines. • Sought out by peers for advice on developing high-performing teams. • Recognized by representatives, peers, RM, and Sales VP as a situational leadership role model as measured by IMDI, EQ, 360 Degrees, and Situational Leadership surveys.

District Manager Strategic Capabilities (*Continued*)

Outlined below are four strategic capabilities for the District Manager (DM) role.

1. Leadership (continued)

Manages conflicts and makes tough decisions to position the district for success

Stage I
- Learning to surface and manage conflicts when dealing with individual representatives and at the TACU level (e.g., points out when representatives are making excuses).

Stage II
- Does not wait until problems arise before addressing performance issues (e.g., addresses significant work activity performance shortfalls early).

Stage III
- Recognizes opportunities to improve policies and/or practices and takes action to do so.
- Makes tough decisions within an appropriate time frame and with the appropriate documentation (e.g., places a representative on final probation after several performance discussions and demonstrates to the representative how to correct his/her behaviors).

Stage IV
- Sought out by peers, Headquarters, and sales leadership for advice, counsel, and assistance regarding business, customer, market, and people issues (e.g., is recommended by RM or Sales VP for various advisory panels).

District Manager Strategic Capabilities (*Continued*)

Outlined below are four strategic capabilities for the District Manager (DM) role.

1. Leadership (continued)

	Stage I	Stage II	Stage III	Stage IV
Capitalizes on the benefits of diversity (field force and customers)	• Understands that representatives and customers have individual needs and styles and respects these differences.	• Helps representatives respect and understand individual differences. • Hires diverse candidates to complement the current field force (e.g., works with minority recruiters to select top talent).	• Adapts management style to respond to individual and customer needs/styles. • Utilizes a diverse set of skills and perspectives to enhance the overall effectiveness of the team.	• Recognizes and draws on individual backgrounds, experiences, and strengths to optimize district performance. • Is considered to be a role model by representatives, peers, and RM for his/her commitment to using diversity to increase effectiveness (e.g., helps others develop relationships with minority recruiting centers). • Assesses individuals' backgrounds and strengths and matches them to specific initiatives to optimize district performance.

Note: DMs will be expected to maintain demonstration/mastery of behaviors from prior stages.

Endnotes

1. L. Landro, "Pay for Performance Reaches Out to Specialists," *The Wall Street Journal,* December 15, 2004, p. D3.

2. R. Heilbroner, *The Worldly Philosophers* (New York: Simon & Schuster, 1953).

3. K. Murphy and J. Cleveland, *Understanding Performance Appraisal* (Thousand Oaks, CA: Sage, 1995).

4. C. Viswesvaran, F. L. Schmidt, and D. Ones, "Is There a General Factor in Ratings of Job Performance? A Meta-Analytic Frame Disentangling Substantive and Error Influences," *Journal of Applied Psychology* 90(1), 2005, pp. 108–131.

5. Joo Hun Han, Kathryn M. Bartol, and Kim Seongsu, "Tightening Up the Performance-Pay Linkage: Roles of Contingent Reward Leadership and Profit-Sharing in the Cross-Level Influence of Individual Pay-For-Performance," *Journal of Applied Psychology*, 100(2), 2015, pp. 417–430.

6. Mercer homepage, *www.mercerhr.com,* April 24, 2003.

7. M. J. Ducharme, P. Singh, and M. Podolsky, "Exploring the Links between Performance Appraisals and Pay Satisfaction," *Compensation and Benefits Review,* September–October 2005, pp. 46–52; K. Murphy and J. Cleveland, *Understanding Performance Appraisal* (Thousand Oaks, CA: Sage, 1995).

8. Rachel Emma Silverman, "Are You Happy in Your Job? Bosses Push Weekly Surveys," *Wall Street Journal*, December 3, 2014, p. B1.

9. Joo Hun Han, Kathryn M. Bartol, and Kim Seongsu, "Tightening Up the Performance-Pay Linkage: Roles of Contingent Reward Leadership and Profit-Sharing in the Cross-Level Influence of Individual Pay-For-Performance," *Journal of Applied Psychology*, 100(2), 2015, pp. 417–430.

10. B. Gerhart and S. L. Rynes, *Compensation: Theory, Evidence, and Strategic Implications* (Thousand Oaks, CA: Sage, 2003).

11. Susan E. Jackson, Randall S. Schuler, and J. Carlos Rivero, "Organizational Characteristics as Predictors of Personnel Practices," *Personnel Psychology* 42 (1989), pp. 727–786.

12. Robert L. Cardy and Gregory H. Dobbins, *Performance Appraisal: Alternative Perspectives* (Cincinnati, OH: South-Western, 1994).

13. J. Weil, "HealthSouth Becomes Subject of a Congressional Probe," *The Wall Street Journal,* April 23, 2003, p. C1.

14. W. E. Deming, *Out of the Crisis* (Cambridge, MA: MIT Press, 1986).

15. David Waldman, "The Contributions of Total Quality Management to a Theory of Work Performance," *Academy of Management Review* 19 (1994), pp. 510–536.

16. David Antonioni, "Improve the Performance Management Process Before Discontinuing Performance Appraisals," *Compensation and Benefits Review,* May–June 1994, pp. 29–37.

17. R. L. Cardy, C. L. Sutton, K. P. Carson, and G. H. Dobbins, "Degree of Responsibility: An Empirical Examination of Person and System Effects on Performance Ratings," paper presented at the national meeting of the Academy of Management, San Francisco, 1990.

18. R. Arvey and K. Murphy, "Performance Evaluation in Work Settings," *Annual Review of Psychology* 49 (1998), pp. 141–168.

19. B. Gerhart, "Compensation Strategy and Organizational Performance, in S. L. Rynes and B. Gerhart (Eds.), *Compensation in Organizations* (San Francisco," CA: Jossey-Bass, 2000).

20. P. Gwynne, "How Consistent Are Performance Review Criteria," *MIT Sloan Management Review,* Summer 2002, pp. 15–22.

21. W. Borman and D. Brush, "More Progress Towards a Taxonomy of Managerial Performance Requirements," *Human Performance* 6(1), 1993, pp. 1–21.

22. C. Viswesvaran, F. L. Schmidt, and D. Ones, "Is There a General Factor in Ratings of Job Performance? A Meta-Analytic Frame Disentangling Substantive and Error Influences," *Journal of Applied Psychology* 90(1), 2005, pp. 108–131.

23. Shujun ding and Philip Beaulieu,"The Role of Financial Incentives in Balanced Scorecard-Based Performance Evaluations: Correcting Mood Congruency Biases." Journal of Accounting Research, 49(5), 2011, 1223–1247. Rachael Griffith and Andrew Neely, "Performance Pay and Managerial Experience in Multitask Teams: Evidence from within a Firm," *Journal of Labor Economics* 27(1), 2009, pp. 49–82.

24. Robert D. Austin, *Measuring and Managing Performance in Organizations* (New York: Dorsett Press, 1996).

25. D. Coleman, *Working With Emotional Intelligence* (New York: Bantam Books, 1998).

26. Based on a personal visit to Pizza Hut headquarters, March 2009.

27. Daniel Ilgen and Jack Feldman, "Performance Appraisal: A Process Focus," *Research in Organizational Behavior* 5 (1983), pp. 141–197.

28. Barry Gerhart, Sara L. Rynes, and Ingrid Smithey Fulmer, "Pay and Performance: Individuals, Groups and Executives," in *Academy of Management Annals,* vol. 3, A.P. Brief and J. P. Walsh, eds. (Newark, NJ: Lawrence Erlbaum, 2009).

29. Royal Navy and Marines fitness reports, Technical Report S206, Royal Navy Publications, 2004.

30. Victor M. Catano, Wendy Darr, and Catherine A. Campbell, "Performance Appraisal of Behavior Based Competencies," *Personnel Psychology* 60 (2007), pp. 201–230.

31. H. Levinson, "Management by Whose Objectives," *Harvard Business Review,* January 2003, pp. 1007–1016.

32. Mark L. McConkie, "A Clarification of the Goal Setting and Appraisal Processes in MBO," *Academy of Management Review* 4(1), 1979, pp. 29–40.

33. Chiara Mio, Andrea Venturelli, and Rossella Leopizzi, "Management by Objectives and Corporate Social Responsibility Disclosure," *Accounting, Auditing and Accountability Journal*, 28(3), 2015, pp. 325–364.

34. Mark L. McConkie, "A Clarification of the Goal Setting and Appraisal Processes in MBO," *Academy of Management Review* 4(1), 1979, pp. 29–40.

35. Mark L. McConkie, "A Clarification of the Goal Setting and Appraisal Process in MBO," *Academy of Management Review* 4(1), 1979, pp. 29–40. © 1979, Academy of Management Review.

36. J. S. Hodgson, "Management by Objectives: The Experiences of a Federal Government Department," *Canadian Public Administration* 16(4), 1973, pp. 422–431.

37. Bruce McAfee and Blake Green, "Selecting a Performance Appraisal Method," *Personnel Administrator* 22(5), 1977, pp. 61–65.

38. Abraham N. Kluger and Angelo DeNisi, "The Effects of Feedback Interventions on Performance: A Historical Review, A Meta-Analysis and A Preliminary Feedback Intervention Theory," *Psychological Bulletin* 119(2) (1996), pp. 254–284.

39. Rachel Feintzeig, "You're Awesome! Firms Scrap Negative Feedback," *Wall Street Journal*, February 11, 2015, p. B1.

40. Abraham N. Kluger and Angelo DeNisi, "The Effects of Feedback Interventions on Performance: A Historical Review, A Meta-Analysis and A Preliminary Feedback Intervention Theory," *Psychological Bulletin* 119(2) (1996), pp. 254–284.

41. H. John Bernardin, "Behavioral Expectation Scales v. Summated Ratings: A Fairer Comparison," *Journal of Applied Psychology* 62 (1977), pp. 422–427; H. John Bernardin, Kim Alvares, and C. J. Cranny, "A Recomparison of Behavioral Expectation Scales to Summated Scales," *Journal of Applied Psychology* 61 (1976), pp. 284–291; C. A.

Schriesheim and U. E. Gattiker, "A Study of the Abstract Desirability of Behavior-Based v. Trait-Oriented Performance Rating," *Proceedings of the Academy of Management* 43 (1982), pp. 307–311; F. S. Landy and J. L. Farr, "Performance Rating," *Psychological Bulletin* 87 (1980), pp. 72–107.

42. Michael Keeley, "A Contingency Framework for Performance Evaluation," *Academy of Management Review* 3 (1978), pp. 428–438.

43. H. Risher, "Refocusing Performance Management for High Performance," *Compensation and Benefits Review,* September–October 2003, pp. 20–30.

44. Harvard Business Review, *HBR Guide to Coaching Employees* (Boston, MA: Harvard Business Review Press, 2015).

45. H. J. Bernardin, K. Cooke, and P. Villanova, "Conscientiousness and Agreeableness as Predictors of Rating Leniency," *Journal of Applied Psychology* 85(2) (2000), pp. 232–234.

46. Mark R. Edwards and Ann J. Ewen, *360 Degree Feedback: The Powerful New Model for Employee Assessment and Performance Improvement* (Toronto: American Management Association, 1996).

47. Ibid.

48. Ibid.

49. IOMA, "Perils and Payoffs of Multi-Rater Feedback Programs," *Pay for Performance Report,* May 2003, p. 2.

50. Mark R. Edwards and Ann J. Ewen, *360 Degree Feedback: The Powerful New Model for Employee Assessment and Performance Improvement* (Toronto: American Management Association, 1996).

51. IOMA, "Perils and Payoffs of Multi-Rater Feedback Programs" (Newark, NJ: BNA Subsidiaries, 2007); D. Waldman, L. Atwater, and D. Antonioni, "Has 360 Degree Feedback Gone Amok?," *Academy of Management Executive* 12(2) (1998), pp. 86–94.

52. C. Viswesvaran, F. L. Schmidt, and D. S. Ones, "The moderating influence of job performance dimension on convergence of supervisory and peer ratings of job performance: Unconfounding construct-level convergence and rating difficulty," *Journal of Applied Psychology* 87, (2002), pp. 245–354.

53. Brian Hoffman, Charles E. Lance, Bethany Bynum, and William A. Gentry, "Rater Source Effects Are Alive and Well After All," *Personnel Psychology* 63, (2010), pp. 119–151.

54. Susan E. Jackson, Randall S. Schuller, and J. Carlos Rivero, "Organizational Characteristics as Predictors of Personnel Practices," *Personnel Psychology* 42 (1989), pp. 727–786.

55. E. Pulakos and W. Borman, *Developing the Basic Criterion Scores for Army-Wide and MOS-Specific Ratings* (Alexandria, VA: U.S. Army Research Institute, 1983).

56. K. R. Murphy, "Explaining the Weak Relationship between Job Performance and Ratings of Job Performance," *Industrial and Organizational Psychology: Perspectives on Science and Practice* 1, (2008), pp. 148–160.

57. Deniz S. Ones, Chockalingam Viswesvaran, and Frank L. Schmidt, "No New Terrain: Reliability and Construct Validity of Job Performance Ratings," *Industrial and Organizational Psychology* 1 (2008), pp. 174–179.

58. Deniz S. Ones, Frank L. Schmidt, and Chockalingam Viswesvaran, "Comparative Analysis of the Reliability of Job Performance Ratings," *Journal of Applied Psychology* 81(5), 1996, pp. 557–574.

59. F. S. Landy and J. L. Farr, "Performance Rating," *Psychological Bulletin* 87 (1980), pp. 72–107.

60. M. M. Harris and J. Schaubroeck, "A Meta Analysis of Self-Supervisor, Self-Peer, and Peer-Supervisor Ratings," *Personnel Psychology* 4 (1988), pp. 43–62.

61. R. Saavedra and S. Kwun, "Peer Evaluation in Self Managing Work Groups," *Journal of Applied Psychology* 78(3), 1993, pp. 450–462.

62. Conference on Performance Management, Center for Effective Organizations, April 23, 2003.

63. M. M. Harris and J. Schaubroeck, "A Meta Analysis of Self-Supervisor, Self-Peer, and Peer-Supervisor Ratings," *Personnel Psychology* 41(1), 1988, pp. 43–62.

64. C. Longenecker and L. Fink, "On Employee Self-Appraisals: Benefits and Opportunities," *Journal of Compensation and Benefits* 22(3), 2006, pp. 12–16.

65. Patti Bond, "Home Depot Uses Customer Ratings for Employee Incentives," Cox News Service, Wednesday, June 21, 2006; visited July 7, 2009 *http://www.statesman.com/news / content/shared/money/stories/coxnews/HOME_DEPOT_0621_COX.html.*

66. Mark R. Edwards and Ann J. Ewen, *360 Degree Feedback: The Powerful New Model for Employee Assessment and Performance Improvement* (Toronto: American Management Association, 1996).

67. William L. Bearly and John E. Jones, *360 Degree Feedback: Strategies, Tactics, and Techniques for Developing Leaders* (Amherst, MA: HRD Press, 1996).

68. D. Antonioni, "The Effects of Feedback Accountability on Upward Appraisal Ratings," *Personnel Psychology* 47 (1994), pp. 349–356.

69. Elena Belogolovsky and Peter A. Bamberger, "Signaling in Secret: Pay for Performance and the Incentive and Sorting Effects of Pay Secrecy," *Academy of Management Journal,* 57(6), 2014, pp. 1706–1733.

70. J. Schaubroeck and S. Lam, "How Similarity to Peers and Supervisor Influences Organizational Advancement in Different Cultures," *Academy of Management Journal,* 45(6), 2002, pp. 1125–1136; K. Murphy and J. Cleveland, *Understanding Performance Appraisal* (Thousand Oaks, CA: Sage, 1995).

71. J. Lefkowitz, "The Role of Interpersonal Affective Regard in Supervisory Performance Ratings: A Literature Review and Proposed Causal Model," *Journal of Occupational and Organizational Psychology* 73(1), 2000, pp. 61–85; R. L. Cardy and G. H. Dobbins, "Affect and Appraisal Accuracy: Liking as an Integral Dimension in Evaluating Performance," *Journal of Applied Psychology* 71 (1986), pp. 672–678; Robert C. Liden and Sandy J. Wayne, "Effect of Impression Management on Performance Ratings: A Longitudinal Study," *Academy of Management Journal* 38(1), 1995, pp. 232–260; Angelo S. DeNisi, Lawrence H. Peters, and Arup Varma, "Interpersonal Affect and Performance Appraisal: A Field Study," *Personnel Psychology* 49 (1996), pp. 341–360.

72. G. Alliger and K. J. Williams, "Affective Congruence and the Employment Interview," in *Advances in Information Processing in Organizations,* vol. 4, J. R. Meindl, R. L. Cardy, and S. M. Puffer, eds. (Greenwich, CT: JAI Press, 1986).

73. F. S. Landy and J. L. Farr, "Performance Rating," *Psychological Bulletin* 87 (1980), pp. 72–107; A. S. DeNisi, T. P. Cafferty, and B. M. Meglino, "A Cognitive View of the Performance Appraisal Process: A Model and Research Propositions," *Organizational Behavior and Human Performance* 33 (1984), pp. 360–396; Jack M. Feldman, "Beyond Attribution Theory: Cognitive Processes in Performance Appraisal," *Journal of Applied Psychology* 66(2), 1981, pp. 127–148; W. H. Cooper, "Ubiquitous Halo," *Psychological Bulletin* 90 (1981), pp. 218–244.

74. Angelo DeNisi and George Stevens, "Profiles of Performance, Performance Evaluations, and Personnel Decisions," *Academy of Management* 24(3), 1981, pp. 592–602; Wayne Cascio and Enzo Valtenzi, "Relations Among Criteria of Police Performance," *Journal of Applied Psychology* 63(1), 1978, pp. 22–28; William Bigoness, "Effects of Applicant's Sex, Race, and Performance on Employer Performance Ratings: Some Additional Findings,"

Journal of Applied Psychology 61(1), 1976, pp. 80–84; Dorothy P. Moore, "Evaluating In-Role and Out-of-Role Performers," *Academy of Management Journal* 27(3), 1984, pp. 603–618; W. Borman, L. White, E. Pulakos, and S. Oppler, "Models of Supervisory Job Performance Ratings," *Journal of Applied Psychology* 76(6), 1991, pp. 863–872.

75. W. Borman, L. White, E. Pulakos, and S. Oppler, "Models of Supervisory Job Performance Ratings," *Journal of Applied Psychology* 76(6) (1991), pp. 863–872.

76. Darren C. Treadway, Gerald R. Ferris, Allison B. Duke, et al., "The Moderating Role of Subordinate Political Skill on Supervisors' Impressions of Subordinate Ingratiation and Ratings of Subordinate Interpersonal Facilitation," *Journal of Applied Psychology* 92(3), 2007, pp. 848–855.

77. H. J. Bernardin and Richard Beatty, *Performance Appraisal: Assessing Human Behavior at Work* (Boston: Kent, 1984).

78. American Management Association, "Top Performers? Most Managers Rated Average or Better," *Compflash,* September 1992, p. 3.

79. Clinton Longnecker, Henry Sims, and Dennis Gioia, "Behind the Mask: The Politics of Employee Appraisal," *Academy of Management Executive* 1(3) (1987), pp. 183–193.

80. G. Dobbins, R. Cardy, and D. Truxillo, "The Effects of Purpose of Appraisal and Individual Differences in Stereotypes of Women on Sex Differences in Performance Ratings: A Laboratory and Field Study," *Journal of Applied Psychology* 73(3) (1988), pp. 551–558.

81. M. Elvira and C. Zatzick, "Who's Displaced First? The Role of Race in Layoff Decisions," *Industrial Relations* 49(2) (2002), pp. 329–361.

82. A. S. DeNisi and G. E. Stevens, "Profiles of Performance, Performance Evaluations, and Personnel Decisions," *Academy of Management Journal* 24(3), September 1981, pp. 592–602; William Scott and Clay Hamner, "The Influence of Variations in Performance Profiles on the Performance Evaluation Process: An Examination of the Validity of the Criterion," *Organizational Behavior and Human Performance* 14 (1975), pp. 360–370; Edward Jones, Leslie Rock, Kelly Shaver, George Goethals, and Laurence Ward, "Pattern of Performance and Ability Attributions: An Unexpected Primacy Effect," *Journal of Personality and Social Psychology* 10(4), 1968, pp. 317–340.

83. B. Gaugler and A. Rudolph, "The Influence of Assessee Performance Variation on Assessor's Judgments," *Personnel Psychology* 45 (1992), pp. 77–98.

84. F. J. Landy and J. L. Farr, "Performance Rating," *Psychological Bulletin* 87 (1980), pp. 72–107; H. J. Bernardin and R. W. Beatty, *Performance Appraisal: Assessing Human Behavior at Work* (Dallas: Scott, Foresman, 1984).

85. N. Cantor and W. Mischel, "Traits v. Prototypes: The Effects on Recognition and Memory," *Journal of Personality and Social Psychology* 35 (1977), pp. 38–48; R. J. Spiro, "Remembering Information From Text: The 'State of Schema' Approach," in R. C. Anderson, R. J. Spiro, and W. E. Montatague, eds., *Schooling and the Acquisition of Knowledge* (Hillsdale, CA: Erlbaum, 1977); T. K. Srull and R. S. Wyer, "Category Accessibility and Social Perception: Some Implications for the Study of Person Memory and Interpersonal Judgments," *Journal of Personality and Social Psychology* 38 (1980), pp. 841–856.

86. Robert Heneman and Kenneth Wexley, "The Effects of Time Delay in Rating and Amount of Information Observed on Performance Rating Accuracy," *Academy of Management Journal* 26(4), 1983, pp. 677–686.

87. B. P. Maroney and R. M. Buckley, "Does Research in Performance Appraisal Influence the Practice of Performance Appraisal? Regretfully Not," *Public Personnel Management* 21 (1992), pp. 185–196.

88. Robert Liden and Terence Mitchell, "The Effects of Group Interdependence on Supervisor Performance Evaluations," *Personnel Psychology* 36(2), 1983, pp. 289–299.

89. Dick Grote, *Forced Ranking: Making Performance Management Work* (Boston, MA: Harvard Business School Press, 2005); G. H. Dobbins, R. L. Cardy, and D. M. Truxillo, "The Effects of Purpose of Appraisal and Individual Differences in Stereotypes of Women on Sex Differences in Performance Ratings: A Laboratory and Field Study," *Journal of Applied Psychology* 73(33), 1986, pp. 551–558.

90. Samuel Y. Todd, Kenneth J. Harris, Ranida B. Harris, and Anthony R. Wheeler, "Career Success Implications of Political Skill," *Journal of Social Psychology* 149(3), June 2009, pp. 179–204.

91. G. R. Ferris and T. A. Judge, "Personnel/Human Resource Management: A Political Influence Perspective," *Journal of Management* 17 (1991), pp. 1–42.

92. Yoav Ganzach, "Negativity (and Positivity) in Performance Evaluation: Three Field Studies," *Journal of Applied Psychology* 80(4) (1995), pp. 491–499.

93. D. Winstanley, "How Accurate Are Performance Appraisals?" *Personnel Administrator* 25(8), 1980, pp. 55–58; F. S. Landy and J. L. Farr, "Performance Rating," *Psychological Bulletin* 87 (1980), pp. 72–107; R. L. Heneman and K. N. Wexley, "The Effects of Time Delay in Rating and Amount of Information Observed on Performance Rating Accuracy," *Academy of Management Journal* 26 (1983), pp. 677–686.

94. Leslie Kwoh, "'Rank and Yank' Retains Vocal Fans," *The Wall Street Journal,* January 31, 2012, p. B6.

95. Conversation between Jerry Newman and Lisa Emerson, VP Global Total Compensation, McDonalds, Fall 2008.

96. D. Grote, *Forced Ranking: Making Performance Management Work* (Boston, MA: Harvard Business School Press, 2005).

97. Ibid.

98. S. Scullen, P. Bergey, and L. Aiman-Smith, "Forced Distribution Rating Systems and the Improvement of Workforce Potential: A Baseline Simulation," *Personnel Psychology* 58(1), 2005, pp. 1–33.

99. L. Cummings and D. Schwab, *Performance in Organization* (Glenview, IL: Scott Foresman, 1973).

100. Neal P. Mero and Stephan J. Motowidlo, "Effects of Rater Accountability on the Accuracy and the Favorability of Performance Ratings," *Journal of Applied Psychology* 80(4), 1995, pp. 517–524.

101. H. J. Bernardin and E. C. Pence, "Effects of Rater Training: Creating New Response Sets and Decreasing Accuracy," *Journal of Applied Psychology* 6 (1980), pp. 60–66.

102. Sheldon Zedeck and Wayne Cascio, "Performance Appraisal Decision as a Function of Rater Training and Purpose of the Appraisal," *Journal of Applied Psychology* 67(6), 1982, pp. 752–758.

103. Erich C. Dierdorff, Eric A. Surface, and Kenneth G. Brown, "Frame-of-Reference Training Effectiveness: Effects of Goal Orientation and Self-Efficacy on Affective, Cognitive, Skill-Based, and Transfer Outcomes," *Journal of Applied Psychology* 6, vol. 95 (2010), pp. 1181–1191; E. Rogers, C. Rogers, and W. Metlay, "Improving the Payoff From 360-Degree Feedback," *Human Resource Planning,* 25(3), 2002, pp. 44–54; H. J. Bernardin and M. R. Buckley, "Strategies in Rater Training," *Academy of Management Review* 6(2), 1981, pp. 205–212; D. Smith, "Training Programs for Performance Appraisal: A Review," *Academy of Management Review* 11(1), 1986, pp. 22–40; B. Davis and M. Mount, "Effectiveness of Performance Appraisal Training Using Computer Assisted Instruction and Behavioral Modeling," *Personnel Psychology* 3 (1984), pp. 439–452; H. J. Bernardin, "Effects of Rater Training on Leniency and Halo Errors in Student Ratings of Instructors," *Journal of Applied Psychology* 63(3), 1978, pp. 301–308;

J. M. Ivancevich, "Longitudinal Study of the Effects of Rater Training on Psychometric Error in Ratings," *Journal of Applied Psychology* 64(5), 1979, pp. 502–508.

104. H. J. Bernardin and M. R. Buckley, "Strategies in Rater Training," *Academy of Management Review* 6 (1981), pp. 205–221.

105. C. O. Longnecker, H. P. Sims Jr., and D. A. Gioia, "Behind the Mask: The Politics of Employee Appraisal," *Academy of Management Executive* 1(3), August 1987, pp. 183–193.

106. S. Waugh, "Solid Performance Reviews," *Supervision* 67(5), 2006, pp. 16–17.

107. Doug Blizzard, "Effective Performance Management." *Journal of Accountancy*, 218(1), 2014, pp. 18–19.

108. Ann Podolske, "Creating a Review System that Works," *Pay for Performance Report,* March 1996, pp. 2–4.

109. Greg Bustin, *Accountability: The Key to Driving a High-Performance Culture* (New York: McGraw-Hill, 2014).

110. Stephen J. Carroll, J. Kline Harrison, Monika K. Renard, et al., "Due Process in Performance Appraisal: A Quasi-Experiment in Procedural Justice," *Administrative Science Quarterly* 40 (1995), pp. 495–523.

111. IOMA, *Pay for Performance Report* (Newark, NJ: BNA Subsidiaries, January 2002, p. 13).

112. Harvard Business Review, *HBR Guide to Coaching Employees* (Cambridge, MA: Harvard Business Review Press, 2014).

113. Ann Podolske, "Creating a Review System That Works," *Pay for Performance Report,* March 1996, pp. 2–4.

114. Mercer homepage, *www.mercerhr.com,* April 24, 2003.

115. Avraham N. Kluger and Angelo DeNisi, "The Effects of Feedback Interventions on Performance: A Historical Review, a Meta-Analysis, and a Preliminary Feedback Intervention Theory," *Psychological Bulletin* 119(2), 1996, pp. 254–284.

116. A. DeNisi, T. Robbins, and T. Cafferty, "Organization of Information Used for Performance Appraisals: Role of Diary-Keeping," *Journal of Applied Psychology* 74(1), 1989, pp. 124–129.

117. Angelo S. DeNisi, Lawrence H. Peters, and Arup Varma, "Interpersonal Affect and Performance Appraisal: A Field Study," *Personnel Psychology* 49 (1996), pp. 341–360; F. J. Landy, J. L. Barnes, and K. R. Murphy, "Correlates of Perceived Fairness and Accuracy of Performance Evaluations," *Journal of Applied Psychology* 63 (1978), pp. 751–754.

118. S. Snell and K. Wexley, "Performance Diagnosis: Identifying the Causes of Poor Performance," *Personnel Administrator,* April 1985, pp. 117–127.

119. Rachel Emma Silverman, "Yearly Reviews? Try Weekly," *The Wall Street Journal,* September 6, 2011, p. B6.

120. Rachel Feintzeig, "You're Awesome! Firms Scrap Negative Feedback." *Wall Street Journal*, February 11, 2015, p. B1.

121. HR Specialist, "Be Ready to Explain Male/Female Pay Differences," Minnesota Employment Law, 4(4), 2011, pp. 1–2.

122. Elizabeth C. Hirsh, "The Strength of Weak Enforcement: The Impact of Discrimination Charges, Legal Environments, and Organizational Conditions on Workplace Segregation," *American Sociological Review* 74(2), 2009, pp. 245–271.

123. LRP Publications, "Black SSA Employees Get 7.75 Million Settlement," *Federal Human Resources Week* 8(39), 2002, pp. 1, 3.

124. *Brito v. Zia Company,* 478 F.2d 1200 (1973).

125. Ibid.

126. G. L. Lubben, D. E. Thompson, and C. R. Klasson, "Performance Appraisal: The Legal Implications of Title VII," *Personnel* 57(3), 1980, pp. 11–21; H. Feild and W. Halley, "The

Relationship of Performance Appraisal System Characteristics to Verdicts in Selected Employment Discrimination Cases," *Academy of Management Journal* 25(2), 1982, pp. 392–406; *Albermarle Paper Company v. Moody,* U.S. Supreme Court, no. 74–389 and 74–428, 10 FEP Cases 1181 (1975); *Moody v. Albermarle Paper Company,* 474 F.3d. 134.

127.   H. S. Feild and W. H. Holley, "The Relationship of Performance Appraisal System Characteristics to Verdicts in Selected Employment Discrimination Cases," *Academy of Management Journal* 25(2), 1982, pp. 392–406; Gerald Barrett and Mary Kernan, "Performance Appraisal and Terminations: A Review of Court Decisions Since *Brito v. Zia* with Implications for Personnel Practices," *Personnel Psychology* 40 (1987), pp. 489–503.

128.   D. Martin and K. Bartol, "The Legal Ramifications of Performance Appraisal: An Update," *Employee Relations* 17(2), 1991, pp. 286–293.

129.   *Payne v. General Motors,* 53 FEP Cases 471 (D. C. Kan. 1990).

130.   J. McGregor, "The Struggle to Measure Performance," *BusinessWeek,* January 9, 2006, p. 26.

131.   C. Wood, "Measuring Progress, Avoiding Liability in Evaluating Employees," *Employment Law Weekly,* December 1999, pp. 1–9.

132.   George Milkovich and Carolyn Milkovich, "Strengthening the Pay-Performance Relationship: The Research," *Compensation and Benefits Review,* November–December 1992, pp. 22–31.

133.   Documents provided by Nancy McGough, Human Resource Director at Room & Board, April 7, 2011.

Part Five

Employee Benefits

Dig two holes in the ground. In the first, bury $9.60. In the second, put $15.78. Now every hour, Monday through Friday, 8 a.m. until 4 p.m., dig up those holes and add the corresponding amount.[1] Leave the money in these holes as very expensive fertilizer for your geraniums. Why these amounts, you ask? Why bury them in the backyard, you ask? Well, those dollar amounts are the cost of a full-time employee's benefits each hour of every workweek in, respectively, a private sector firm and in a state or local government job. Burying the money in the backyard is our way of saying it's not clear the money is any worse off in the ground than invested in employee benefits. A bit harsh? Especially since more than 75 percent of employees claim benefits are either extremely (33%) or very (45%) important in the decision to accept or reject a job.[2] But stop and think about what we know that is fact—not faith—in the benefits area. Which of the issues covered in the pay model (see Exhibit V.1), for example, can we answer with respect to benefits? Does effective employee benefit management facilitate organization performance? The answer is unclear. We do know that benefit costs can be cut, and this affects the bottom line (admittedly an important measure of organization performance). But what about other alignment and management efforts? Do benefits complement organization strategy and performance? We don't know. Or do employee benefits impact an organization's ability to attract, retain, and motivate employees? Conventional wisdom, says employee benefits can affect retention, but there is no definitive research to support this conclusion. A similar lack of research surrounds each of the other potential payoffs to a sound benefits program.

The only absolute reality is this: Employee benefits cost more than 10 trillion dollars per year. Maybe it's time we found out if this is a good way to spend corporate funds. Not surprisingly, firms are increasingly paying attention to this reward component. It represents a labor cost with no apparent returns.

Compounding this concern is the ever-present entitlement problem. Employees perceive benefits as a right, independent of how well they or the company perform. Efforts to reduce benefit levels or eliminate parts of the package altogether would meet with employee resistance and dissatisfaction. Just ask workers and retirees at GM, Ford, or Chrysler.[3] In an effort to stop the competitive bleeding, the auto industry is cutting benefits for both current and retired employees.

EXHIBIT V.1 The Pay Model

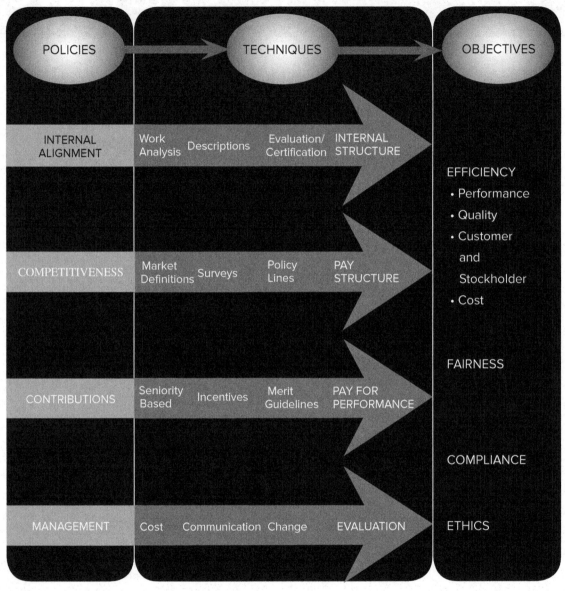

Assuming that organizations must find ways to control the costs of benefits wherever possible, this section of the book focuses on identifying ways to maximize the returns from benefit expenditures. As a first step in this direction, Chapter 12 identifies issues organizations should face in developing and maintaining a benefit program. A model of the benefit determination process is also presented, to provide a structure for thinking about employee benefits. Chapter 13 provides a summary of the state of employee benefits today. Hopefully this will provide the groundwork for the innovative and effective benefit packages of tomorrow.

Endnotes

1. Bureau of Labor Statistics, *www.data.bls.gov/cgi-bin/surveymost,* June 21, 2006.
2. The *McKinsey Quarterly* Chart Focus Newsletter, June 2006, Member Edition.
3. I. Watson, "GM Puts Salaried Staff in Firing Line," *Knight Ridder Tribune Business News,* March 26, 2006, p. 1.

The Benefit Determination Process

Chapter Outline

Why the Growth in Employee Benefits?
Wage and Price Controls
Unions
Employer Impetus
Cost Effectiveness of Benefits
Government Impetus

The Value of Employee Benefits

Key Issues in Benefit Planning, Design, and Administration

Benefit Planning and Design Issues
Benefit Administration Issues

Components of a Benefit Plan
Employer Factors
Employee Factors

Administering the Benefit Program
Employee Benefit Communication
Claims Processing
Cost Containment

Your Turn: World Measurement

What can you do with a few trillion dollars?[1] Help balance the budget? Buy a few new copies of this book? Well, the answer is, you can cover the cost of all employee benefits in the United States today. It's hard to believe that employee benefits cost this much. This is particularly hard to believe when we take a look at what used to pass as benefits in the not-too-distant past:

- A carriage shop published a set of rules for employees in 1880 that stated, in part: "Working hours shall be from 7 a.m. to 9 p.m. every day except the Sabbath. . . . After an employee has been with this firm for five years he shall receive an added payment of five cents per day, provided the firm has prospered in a manner to make it possible. . . . It is the bounden duty of each employee to put away at least 10 percent of his monthly wages for his declining years so he will not become a burden upon his betters."

- In 1915, employees in the iron and steel industry worked a standard 60 to 64 hours per week. By 1930 that schedule had been reduced to 54 hours.

- It was not until 1929 that the Blue Cross concept of prepaid medical costs was introduced.

- Prior to 1935, only one state (Wisconsin) had a program of unemployment compensation benefits for workers who lost their jobs through no fault of their own.

- Before World War II, very few companies paid hourly employees for holidays. In most companies, employees were told not to report for work on holidays and to enjoy the time off, but their paychecks were smaller the following week.[2]

EXHIBIT 12.1
Changes in
Benefit Costs
Over Time

	1959	1969	1991	2000	2010	2014
Percentage of Payroll	24.7	31.1	28.2	27.4	30.2	31.6

Source: U.S. Chamber
of Commerce,
Benefits Survey 2011
and 2014 data from
ncsinfor@bls.gov
civilian workers.

In comparison to these "benefits" from the past, today's reality seems staggering. Consider the kinds of things that are common in companies that made the *Fortune* magazine list of "100 Best Companies to Work For in America."[3] These companies recognize the importance of taking care of employees' needs as a key factor in attracting and retaining the best employees. A first-class benefit plan includes some mix of the following benefits: education reimbursement; on-site child care services, car cleaning, financial counseling, and concierge services; and retirement benefits.[4] Just consider some of the extra benefits beyond the norm at Google, this year's number-1 rated company to work at: The parental leave program has just been upgraded. New parents, regardless of gender now get up to twelve weeks of fully paid baby bonding time. This also included $500 "Baby Bonding Bucks." Along with this are liberal policies for volunteering, on-site fitness centers and medical care, lavish paid lunches daily, and college reimbursement for tuition. http://fortune.com/best-companies/google-1/.

Clearly Google would argue that these extra services are important benefits of employment, perhaps making attraction, retention, and motivation of employees just that much easier. But the truth is, we don't know if even ordinary benefits have positive payoffs. We do know that employees consistently rate benefits a key factor in job satisfaction even though less than one-half of employees are actually satisfied with their benefits.[5] Additionally, there is a mismatch between cost to employer and perceived value to employee: the cost is much higher than employees estimate.[6]

Until we can clearly identify the advantages of employee benefits, we need to find ways to control their costs or at least slow their growth. Exhibit 12.1 illustrates the rapid rise in employee benefit costs, moving from about 25 percent of payroll costs in 1959 to more than 40 percent by some calculations today.[7]

As Exhibit 12.1 illustrates, **employee benefits** can no longer realistically be called "fringe benefits." As an example, visualize a $20,000 car rolling down the assembly line at General Motors. A cost accountant would tell you that $1,200 of this cost is due to worker health insurance alone. Compare it to the cost of all the steel for the same car—$500—and the impact is evident. Now compare it to health insurance costs as low as $100 for foreign automakers in their U.S. factories (with their younger, healthier workers and hardly any retirees), and the global implications of benefit costs are all too frightening.[8]

Over one 20-year period (1955–1975), employee benefit costs rose at a rate almost four times greater than employee wages or the consumer price index.[9] A similar comparison for the period 1963–1987 showed that the rate of growth had slowed (benefit costs rose twice as fast as wage costs). And a still later comparison, for the

Employee benefits are that part of the total compensation package, other than pay for time worked, provided to employees in whole or in part by employer payments (e.g., life insurance, pension, workers' compensation, vacation).

period 1993–1999, the cost of benefits actually stabilized at about \$14,700 per full-time employee. Recently, though, benefit costs have begun to heat up again—with survey results from 2014 showing the average cost ranging from \$9.60–\$15.78 per hour worked for civilian and government workers.[10] For a standard 35-hour workweek, this translates into an average annual benefit cost of roughly \$16,800 to \$27,695. That translates into health-care costs that have more than doubled since 1990. Pension costs also are an area of concern. Just ask Delta Airlines or Sara Lee. Both companies face huge unfunded pension liabilities. When you are behind hundreds of millions in pension funding, it's difficult to interest anyone in buying your stock.[11] And problems may even be worse in the public sector, where state governments have regularly underfunded **pension plans**. With looming retirements of baby boomers, this could spell catastrophe for already burdened state budgets.[12] Estimates range from 0.7 to 2.5 trillion dollars for the amount pensions are underfunded in state and local governments. Part of that amount can be made up with belt-tightening efforts. But guess who is going to finance the rest through increased taxes. That's right—you![13]

WHY THE GROWTH IN EMPLOYEE BENEFITS?

Wage and Price Controls

During both World War II and the Korean War, the federal government instituted strict **wage and price controls.** The compliance agency charged with enforcing these controls was relatively lenient in permitting reasonable increases in benefits. With strict limitations on the size of wage increases, both unions and employers sought new and improved benefits to satisfy worker demands. This was the catalyst for growth in pensions, health-care coverage, time off, and the broad spectrum of benefits virtually unthinkable before 1950.

Unions

The climate fostered by wage and price controls created a perfect opportunity for unions to flex the muscles they had acquired under the Wagner Act of 1935. Several National Labor Relations Board rulings during the 1940s freed unions to negotiate over employee benefits. With little freedom to raise wages during the war, unions fought for the introduction of new benefits and the improvement of existing benefits. Success on this front during the war years led to further postwar demands. Largely through the efforts of unions, most notably the autoworkers and steelworkers, several benefits common today were given their initial impetus: pattern pension plans, supplementary unemployment compensation, extended vacation plans, and guaranteed annual wage plans.[14]

Employer Impetus

Many of the benefits in existence today were provided at employer initiative. Much of this initiative can be traced to pragmatic concerns about employee satisfaction and productivity. Rest breaks often were implemented in the belief that fatigue increased accidents and lowered productivity. Savings and profit sharing plans were implemented (e.g., Procter & Gamble's profit-sharing plan was initiated in 1885) to improve performance and provide increased security for worker retirement years. Indeed, many employer-initiated benefits were designed to create a climate in which employees perceived that management was genuinely concerned for their welfare. Notice, though, these supposed benefits were taken on faith. But their costs were quite real: Without hard data about payoffs, employee benefits slowly became a costly entitlement of the American workforce.

Cost Effectiveness of Benefits

Another important and sound impetus for the growth of employee benefits is their cost effectiveness in two situations. The first cost advantage is that most employee benefits are not taxable. Provision of a benefit rather than an equivalent increase in wages avoids payment of federal and state personal income tax. Remember, though, recurrent tax reform proposals continue to threaten the favorable tax status granted to many benefits.

A second cost-effectiveness component of benefits arises because many group-based benefits (e.g., life, health, and legal insurance) can be obtained at a lower rate than could be obtained by employees acting on their own. Group insurance also has relatively easy qualification standards, giving security to a set of employees who might not otherwise qualify.

Government Impetus

Obviously the government has played an important role in the growth of employee benefits. Three employee benefits are mandated by either the state or federal government: **workers' compensation** (state), **unemployment insurance** (federal), and **social security** (federal). In addition, most other employee benefits are affected by such laws as the **Employee Retirement Income Security Act** (**ERISA**), which affects pension administration, and various sections of the Internal Revenue Code. Most recently, the highly controversial Patient Protection and Affordable Care Act signed into law on March 23, 2010, by President Obama is currently impacting corporate practices dramatically, as we'll see in the next chapter.

THE VALUE OF EMPLOYEE BENEFITS

Exhibit 12.2 shows the relative importance employees attached to different types of benefits across five different studies.[15]

In general, the five studies reported in Exhibit 12.2 show remarkably consistent results over the past two decades. For example, medical benefits continue to be ranked tops in importance for most employee groups. These rankings have added significance when we note that today an employer pays on average $6025 for health coverage of a single employee. That figure jumps to $16,834 for a family.[16]

Again, The trillions of dollars employers spend on benefits each year would not seem nearly so outrageous if we had evidence that employees place high value on the benefits they receive. Unfortunately, there is evidence that employees frequently are not even aware of, or undervalue, the benefits provided by their organization. For example, in one study employees were asked to recall the benefits they received. The typical employee could recall less than 15 percent of them.[17]

EXHIBIT 12.2
Ranking of Employee Benefits

Note: × = indicates a benefit that was not rated in this study.

	Study				
	1	**2**	**3**	**4**	**5**
Medical	1	1	3	1	1
Pension	2	3	8	3	2
Paid vacations and holidays	3	2	×	2	3
Sickness	4	×	5	8	×
Dental	5	×	6	6	×
Long-term disability	7	×	7	9	6
Life insurance	8	×	4	×	5

For the past 20 years, we've argued here that benefits are taken for granted. Given their cost, that's not a good thing. Now, though, with companies cutting back benefits, or shifting costs to employees (or retirees!), the air of entitlement may be disappearing. A recent study by the Society of Human Resource Management indicates both employees and HR professionals see benefits as the top factor driving job satisfaction.[18]

One possible direction out of this money pit comes from recent reports of employees looking not necessarily for more benefits, but rather for greater choice in the benefits they receive.[19] In fact, up to 70 percent of employees in one study indicated they would be willing to pay more out of pocket for benefits if they were granted greater choice in designing their own benefit package. We do know, in support of this, that the perceived value of benefits rises when employers introduce choice through a flexible benefit package.[20] Maybe better benefit planning, design, and administration offer an opportunity to improve benefit effectiveness. Indeed, preliminary evidence indicates employers are making serious efforts to educate employees about benefits, with an outcome of increased employee awareness.[21] For example, the simple act of stating in an employment ad that benefits are generous leads to applicants' focusing on this characteristic and relying more heavily on it in job choice. Some experts speculate that a key element in reward attractiveness (and benefits in this example) may be their visibility. Not only do we have to plan and design effective benefit programs; we also need to communicate their value to employees.

KEY ISSUES IN BENEFIT PLANNING, DESIGN, AND ADMINISTRATION

Benefits Planning and Design Issues

What do you want—or expect—the role of benefits to be in your overall compensation package?[22] For example, if a major compensation objective is to attract good employees, we need to ask, "What is the best way to achieve this?" The answer is not always, or even frequently, "Let's add another benefit."

Put yourself in the following situation as the benefits manager. A casino opens up in the Niagara Falls area. The Seneca Indians own this casino, and they needed to fill thousands of entry-level jobs. The wages for a blackjack dealer were $4.60 per hour plus tips. The combination of the two exceeds minimum wage, but not by much.

How do we attract more dealers, and other applicants, given these low wages? One temptation might be to set up a day care center to attract more mothers of preschool children. Certainly this is a popular response today, judging from all the press business-sponsored day care centers are receiving. A more prudent compensation policy would ask the question: "Is day care the most effective way to achieve my compensation objective?" Sure, day care may be popular with working mothers, but can the necessary workers be attracted to the casino using some other compensation tool that better meets needs? If we went to compensation experts in the gaming industry, they might say (and we would be impressed if you said this along with them): "We target recruitment of young females for our entry-level jobs. Surveys of this group indicate day care is an extremely important factor in the decision to accept a job."

If you used this kind of logic in your arguments as benefits manager, we think you're well on the way to a successful career. As a second example, how do we deal with undesirable turnover? Rich Floersch, Sr. Vice President of HR at McDonald's, faced this very question. After looking at other alternatives to reduce turnover, Rich decided that the best strategy was to design a benefit package that improved progressively with seniority, thus providing a reward for continuing service. Keep in mind, though, Rich only made this decision after evaluating the effectiveness of other compensation tools (e.g., increasing wages, introducing incentive compensation).

In addition to integrating benefits with other compensation components, the planning process also should include strategies for ensuring external competitiveness and adequacy of benefits.[23] Competitiveness requires an understanding of what other firms in your product and labor markets offer as benefits. Firms conduct benefit surveys much as they conduct salary surveys. Either our firm must have a package comparable to that of survey participants or there should be a sound justification of why deviation makes sense for the firm.

In contrast, ensuring that benefits are adequate is a somewhat more difficult task. Most organizations evaluating adequacy consider the financial liability of employees with and without a particular benefit (e.g., employee medical expenses with and without medical expense benefits). There is no magic formula for defining benefit adequacy.[24] In part, the answer may lie in the relationship between benefit adequacy and the third plan objective: cost of effectiveness. More organizations need to consider whether employee benefits are cost justified. All sorts of ethical questions arise when we start asking this question. How far should we go with elder care? Can we justify paying for a $250,000 surgical procedure that will likely buy only a few more months of life? Companies face these impossible questions when designing a benefit system. And more frequently than ever before, companies are saying no to absorbing the cost increases of benefits. One survey shows that 59 percent of employers are shifting increased benefit costs to employees through higher deductibles and copays, for example.[25]

e-Compensation

Benefitslink, at *www.benefitslink.com/index.shtml,* provides a wealth of information about types of benefits, a message board for interacting in discussions with others interested in benefits, and an "Ask the Expert" question-and-answer column.

Benefit Administration Issues

Four major administration issues arise in setting up a benefit package: (1) Who should be protected or benefited?; (2) How much choice should employees have among an array of benefits?; (3) How should benefits be financed?[26]; and (4) Are your benefits legally defensible?[27]

The first issue—who should be covered—ought to be an easy question. The answer is *employees*, of course. But every organization has a variety of employees with different employment statuses. Should these individuals be treated equally with respect to benefits coverage? Historically companies have provided far fewer benefits for part-time workers.

As a second example, should retired automobile executives be permitted to continue purchasing cars at a discount price, a benefit that could be reserved solely for current employees or—given the state of the auto industry—perhaps eliminated entirely? In fact, a whole series of questions need to be answered:[28]

1. What probationary periods (for eligibility of benefits) should be used for various types of benefits? Does the employer want to cover employees and their dependents immediately upon employment or provide such coverage only for employees who have established more or less permanent employment with the employer? Is there a rationale for different probationary periods with different benefits?

2. Which dependents of active employees should be covered?

3. Should retirees (as well as their spouses and perhaps other dependents) be covered, and for which benefits?

4. Should survivors of deceased employees (and/or retirees) be covered? If so, for which benefits? Are benefits for surviving spouses appropriate?

5. What coverage, if any, should be extended to employees who are suffering from disabilities?

6. What coverage, if any, should be extended to employees during layoffs, leaves of absence, strikes, and so forth?

7. Should coverage be limited to full-time employees?[29]

The answers to these questions depend on the policy decisions regarding adequacy, competition, and cost effectiveness discussed in the last section.

The second administrative issue concerns choice (flexibility) in plan coverage. In the standard benefit package, employees typically have not been offered a choice among employee benefits. Rather, a package is designed with the average employee in mind, and any deviations in needs simply go unsatisfied. The other extreme (discussed in greater detail later) is represented by "cafeteria-style," or flexible, benefit plans. Under this concept employees are permitted great flexibility in choosing the benefit options of greatest value to them. Picture an individual allotted x dollars walking down a cafeteria line and choosing menu items (benefits) according to their attractiveness and cost. The flexibility in this type of plan is apparent. Exhibit 12.3 illustrates a typical choice among packages offered to employees under a flexible benefit system. Imagine an employee whose spouse works and already has family coverage for health, dental, and vision. The temptation might be to select package A.

EXHIBIT 12.3
Possible
Options in
a Flexible
Benefit
Package

* AE = average
earnings.

	Package			
	A	**B**	**C**	**D**
Health	No	No	Yes	Yes
Dental	No	No	No	Yes
Vision	No	Yes	Yes	Yes
Life insurance	1 × AE*	2 × AE	2 × AE	3 × AE
Dependent care	Yes	No	No	No
401(k) savings	No	Yes	No	No
Cash back	Yes	No	No	No

An employee with retirement in mind might select option B with its contributions to a **401(k)** pension plan. Exhibit 12.4 summarizes some of the major advantages and disadvantages of flexible benefits.

Even companies that are not considering a flexible benefit program are offering greater flexibility and choice. Such plans might provide, for example, (1) optional levels of group term life insurance; (2) the availability of death or disability benefits under pension or profit-sharing plans; (3) choices of covering dependents under group medical expense coverage; and (4) a variety of participation, cash distribution, and investment options under profit-sharing, thrift, and capital accumulation plans.[30]

The level at which an organization finally chooses to operate on this choice/ flexibility dimension really depends on its evaluation of the relative advantages and disadvantages of flexible plans, noted in Exhibit 12.4.[31] Many companies cite

EXHIBIT 12.4
Advantages
and
Disadvantages
of Flexible
Benefit
Programs

Advantages

1. Employees choose packages that best satisfy their unique needs.
2. Flexible benefits help firms meet the changing needs of a changing workforce.
3. Increased involvement of employees and families improves understanding of benefits.
4. Flexible plans make introduction of new benefits less costly. Any new option is added merely as one among a wide variety of elements from which to choose.
5. Cost containment: Organization sets dollar maximum; employee chooses within that constraint.

Disadvantages

1. Employees make bad choices and find themselves not covered for predictable emergencies.
2. Administrative burdens and expenses increase.
3. Adverse selection: Employees pick only benefits they will use; the subsequent high-benefit utilization increases its cost.
4. Flexible benefit plans are subject to nondiscrimination requirements in Section 125 of the Internal Revenue Code.

the cost savings from flexible benefits as a primary motivation. Companies also offer flexible plans in response to cost pressures related to the increasing diversity of the workforce. Flexible benefit plans, it is argued, increase employee awareness of the true costs of benefits and, therefore, increase employee recognition of benefit value.[32]

Another way to increase employee awareness, and probably the biggest trend today in health care, is to offer **market-based,** or **customer-driven**, health care. Although there are many variants on **consumer-driven health care,** here are the basic issues.[33]

- In a Consumer-driven or High Deductible plan an employee pays all health care costs up to some pre-determined rate. That rate can be as high as $3000–$6,000. After that amount the employee pays a rate of 10–35 percent of any additional medical services (called coinsurance). Each employer sets some out-of-pocket maximum, typically in the range of $6,000–$12,000 (single v. family). After that the employer pays.[34]

- The obvious inducement to an employee is to shop around for the lowest rate. Need an MRI? The cost can vary between $415 and $4530.[35] Before these High Deductible plans were implemented the employee had no motivation to choose a low cost provider. For the employer this yields a huge cost saving. Monthly premiums can dip to as low as $100. Of course, this can cause a health care crisis for the employee who foregoes the procedure because of cost.

The third administrative issue involves the question of how to finance benefit plans. Alternatives include:

1. Noncontributory (Employer pays total costs.)
2. Contributory (Costs are shared between employer and employee.)
3. Employee financed (Employee pays total costs for some benefits—by law the organization must bear the cost for certain benefits.)

In general, organizations prefer to make benefit options contributory, reasoning that a "free good," no matter how valuable, is less valuable to an employee. Furthermore, employees have no personal interest in controlling the cost of a free good. And with the cost of benefits rising considerably more than other goods and services, employers are increasingly turning to ways for cutting their costs.

Finally, benefits have to comply with hundreds of arcane sections of the tax code and other "devils" designed to turn any benefit administrator's hair gray. Because there are so many rules and regulations, benefit administrators should develop a compliance checklist and regularly conduct audits to ensure that they are complying with the avalanche of new and existing requirements.[36]

COMPONENTS OF A BENEFIT PLAN

Exhibit 12.5 outlines a model of the factors influencing benefit choice, from both the employer's and the employee's perspective. The remainder of this chapter briefly examines each of these factors.

EXHIBIT 12.5
Factors
Influencing
Choice of
Benefit
Package

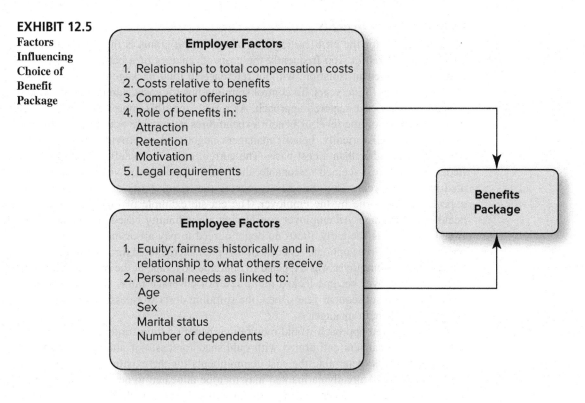

Employer Factors

1. Relationship to total compensation costs
2. Costs relative to benefits
3. Competitor offerings
4. Role of benefits in:
   Attraction
   Retention
   Motivation
5. Legal requirements

**Benefits
Package**

Employee Factors

1. Equity: fairness historically and in
   relationship to what others receive
2. Personal needs as linked to:
   Age
   Sex
   Marital status
   Number of dependents

Employer Factors

As Exhibit 12.5 indicates, a number of factors affect employer preference in determining desirable components of a benefit package.

Relationship to Total Compensation Costs

A good compensation manager considers employee benefit costs as part of a total package of compensation costs. Frequently employees think that just because an employee benefit is attractive, the company should provide it. A good compensation manager thinks somewhat differently: "Is there a better use for this money? Could we put the money into some other compensation component and achieve better results?" Benefit costs are only one part of a total compensation package. Decisions about outlays have to be considered from this perspective. Let's take a perfect example provided by former Governor of Tennessee Phillip Bredesen.[37] He argued that Tennessee could keep its employees whole with respect to health care and save the state $146 million. How, you ask? Under the Patient Protection and Affordable Care Act employees could purchase health insurance in part subsidized by the government. The governor calculated how much it would cost to keep state employees whole if they accepted this government support. By eliminating health coverage for state employees and providing an incentive keeping each worker whole, and paying the government-imposed fine of $2,000, the state saved $146 million. Even though Governor Bredesen's term ended several years ago, Tennessee still maintains its health insurance plan.

Costs Relative to Benefits

A major reason for the proliferating cost of benefit programs is the narrow focus of benefit administrators. Too frequently the costs/advantages of a particular benefit inclusion are viewed in isolation, without reference to total package costs or forecasts of rising costs in future years. To control spiraling benefit costs, administrators should adopt a broader, cost-centered approach. As a first step, this approach would require policy decisions on the level of benefit expenditures acceptable both in the short and the long runs. Historically, benefit managers negotiated or provided benefits on a package basis rather than a cost basis. The current cost of a benefit would be identified, and if the cost seemed reasonable, the benefit would be provided for or negotiated with employees. This failed to recognize that rising costs of this benefit were expected to be borne by the employer. The classic example of this phenomenon is health-care coverage. An employer considering a community-based medical plan like Blue Cross during the early 1960s no doubt agreed to pay all or most of the costs of one of the Blue Cross options. As costs of this plan skyrocketed throughout the rest of the century, the employer was expected to continue coverage at the historical level. In effect, the employer became locked into a level of coverage rather than negotiating a level of cost. In subsequent years, then, the spiraling costs were essentially out of the control of the benefit manager.

A cost-centered approach would require that benefit administrators, in cooperation with insurance carriers and armed with published forecasts of anticipated costs for particular benefits, determine the cost commitments for the existing benefit package. Budget dollars not already earmarked may then be allocated to new benefits that best satisfy organizational goals. Factors affecting this decision include an evaluation of benefits offered by other firms and the competitiveness of the existing package. Also important is compliance with various legal requirements as they change over time (Chapter 13). Finally, the actual benefit of a new option must be explored in relation to employee preferences. The benefits that top the list of employee preferences should be evaluated in relation to current and future costs. Because future cost estimates may be difficult to project, it is imperative that benefit administrators reduce uncertainty.

If a benefit forecast suggests future cost containment may be difficult, the benefit should be offered to employees only on a cost-sharing basis. Management determines what percentage of cost it can afford to bear within budget projections, and the option is offered to employees on a cost-sharing basis, with projected increases in both employer and employee costs communicated openly. In the negotiation process, then, employees or union representatives can evaluate their preference for the option against the forecasted cost burden. In effect, this approach defines in advance the contribution an employer is willing to make. And it avoids the constraints of a defined-benefit strategy that burdens the employer with continued provision of that defined-benefit level despite rapidly spiraling costs.

Competitor Offerings

Benefits must be externally equitable, too. This begs the question, what is the absolute level of benefit payments relative to important product and labor market competitors? A policy decision must be made about the position (market lead, market lag, or competitive) the organization wants to maintain in its absolute level of benefits relative to the competition. One of the best strategies for determining external equity is to conduct a benefit survey. Alternatively, many consulting organizations, professional associations, and interest groups collect benefit data that can be purchased. Perhaps the most widely used of these surveys is the annual benefit survey conducted by the U.S. Chamber of Commerce.[38] The Employee Benefits Research Institute is also a first-rate source for benefits information.[39]

Role of Benefits in Attraction, Retention, and Motivation

Given the rapid growth in benefits and the staggering cost implications, it seems only logical that employers would expect to derive a fair return on this investment. In fact, there is at best only anecdotal evidence that employee benefits are cost-justified.[40] This evidence falls into three categories.[41] First, employee benefits are widely claimed to help in the retention of workers. Benefit schedules are specifically designed to favor longer-term employees. For example, retirement benefits increase with years of service, and most plans do not provide for full employee eligibility until a specified number of years of service have been reached. Equally, the amount of vacation time increases with years of service, and employees' savings plans, profit-sharing plans, and stock purchase plans frequently provide for increased participation or benefits as seniority increases. By tying these benefits to seniority, it is assumed that workers are more reluctant to change jobs.

There is also some research to support this common assumption that benefits increase retention. Two studies found that higher benefits reduced mobility.[42] More detailed follow-up studies, though, found that only two specific benefits curtailed employee turnover: pensions and medical coverage.[43] Virtually no other employee benefit had a significant impact on turnover.

We've been assuming here that turnover is bad and stability is good. In fact, there are times when turnover may be good—something we may not want to discourage. For example, at one time or another 3 Americans in 10 have stayed in a job they wanted to leave simply because they could not give up their health-care coverage.[44] This "job lock" probably is not a desirable outcome for employers.

Employee benefits also might be valued if we could prove they increase employee satisfaction. A recent survey shows employees ranking employee benefits second,[45] behind only job security, in explaining job satisfaction. Trouble on the horizon, though. Another recent survey shows that 56 percent of employees are only somewhat satisfied (31%) or are dissatisfied (26%) with their benefits package.[46] Benefits also would be valuable if we could show a link to increased productivity. Unfortunately, no strong data exist linking benefits level and employee productivity. Perhaps as a result, companies are cutting benefits, especially medical insurance, as a cost reduction strategy. If we want to argue that benefits matter, first we need to show that benefits are well-designed—in part this means they must meet employee needs. Critics argue that benefits administrators haven't responded to long-term changes in the workforce. Ever-increasing numbers of women in the labor force, coupled with increasing numbers of dual-career families and higher educational attainments, suggest changing values of employees.[47] Changing values, in turn, necessitate a reevaluation of benefit packages.

One response to these workforce changes is increased interest in so-called work/life balance benefits. Things like day care, elder care, on-site fitness centers, and weight-loss programs foster a perception that the company cares about its employees. And in one well-constructed research study, this caring attitude led to greater worker involvement in suggesting ways to improve productivity and in helping others with their work.[48] Maybe benefits can pay off; we just need to document this better.

Legal Requirements

Employers obviously want a benefit package that complies with all aspects of the law. Exhibit 12.6 shows part of the increasingly complex web of legislation in the benefit area. Greater details on the three legally mandated benefits (workers' compensation, social security, and unemployment insurance) are provided in Chapter 13.

EXHIBIT 12.6   Impact of Legislation on Selected Benefits

Legislation	Impact on Employee Benefits
Fair Labor Standards Act 1938	Created time-and-a-half overtime pay. Benefits linked to pay (e.g., social security) increase correspondingly with those overtime hours.
Employee Retirement Income Security Act 1974	If an employer decides to provide a pension (it is not mandated), specific rules must be followed. Plan must vest (employee has right to both personal and company contributions into pension) after five years' employment. Pension Benefit Guaranty Corporation, as set up by this law, provides worker some financial coverage when a company and its pension plan go bankrupt.
Tax reforms—1982, 1986	Permit individual retirement accounts (IRAs) for eligible employees. Established 401(k) programs, a matched-contribution saving plan (employer matches part or all of employee contribution) that frequently serves as part of a retirement package.
Maintenance Act 1973	Required employers to offer alternative health coverage (e.g., **health maintenance organizations**) options to employees.
Discrimination legislation (Age Discrimination in Employment Act, Civil Rights Act, Pregnancy Disability Act, various state laws)	Benefits must be administered in a manner that does not discriminate against protected groups (on basis of race, color, religion, sex, national origin, age, pregnancy).
Consolidated Omnibus Budget Reconciliation Act (COBRA) 1984	Employees who resign or are laid off through no fault of their own are eligible to continue receiving health coverage under employer's plan at a cost borne by the employee.
Family Medical Leave Act (1993)	Mandates 12 weeks of leave for all workers at companies that employ 50 or more people.
The Patient Protection and Affordable Care Act (2010)	Requires individuals to maintain minimal essential health insurance coverage or pay a penalty unless exempted for religious beliefs or financial hardship. Employers must enroll new employees or face a levy.

Absolute and Relative Compensation Costs

Any evaluation of employee benefits must be placed in the context of total compensation costs. Cost competitiveness means the total package must be competitive—not just specific segments. Consequently, decisions on whether to adopt certain options must be considered in light of the impact on total costs and in relationship to expenditures of competitors (as determined in benefit surveys such as the Chamber of Commerce survey mentioned earlier in this chapter).

Employee Factors

Employee preferences for various benefit options are determined by individual needs. The benefits perceived to best satisfy individual needs are the most highly desired. In part, these needs arise out of feelings of perceived equity or inequity.

Equity

To illustrate the impact of equity, consider the example of government employees working in the same neighborhood as autoworkers. Imagine the dissatisfaction with government holidays that arises when government employees leave for work every morning, knowing that the autoworkers are home in bed for the whole week between Christmas and New Year's Day. The perceived unfairness of this difference need not be rational, especially considering the large number of layoffs in the auto industry in contrast to the relative job security in the public sector. But it is, nevertheless, a factor that must be considered in determining employee needs. Occasionally this comparison process leads to a "bandwagon" effect, in which new benefits offered by a competitor are adopted without careful consideration, simply because the employer wants to avoid hard feelings. This phenomenon is particularly apparent for employers with strong commitments to maintaining a totally or partially nonunion work force. Benefits obtained by a unionized competitor or a unionized segment of the firm's workforce are frequently passed along to nonunion employees. While the effectiveness of this strategy in thwarting unionization efforts has not been demonstrated, many nonunion firms would prefer to provide the benefit as a safety measure.

Personal Needs of Employees

One way to gauge employee preferences is to look at demographic differences. The demographic approach assumes that demographic groups (e.g., young versus old, married versus unmarried) can be identified for which benefit preferences are fairly consistent across members of the group. Furthermore, it assumes that meaningful differences exist between groups in terms of benefit preferences.

There is some evidence that these assumptions are only partially correct. In an extensive review of employee preference literature, Glueck traced patterns of group preferences for particular benefits.[49] As one might expect, older workers showed stronger preferences than younger workers for pension plans.[50] Also, families with dependents had stronger preferences for health/medical coverage than families with no dependents.[51] The big surprise in all these studies, though, is that many of the other demographic group breakdowns fail to result in differential benefit preferences. Traditionally, it has been assumed that benefit preferences ought to differ among males versus females, blue collar versus white collar, and married versus single. Few of these expectations have been born out by these studies. Rather, the studies have tended to be more valuable in showing preference trends that are characteristic of all employees. Among the benefits available, health/medical and stock plans are highly preferred benefits, while such options as early retirement, profit sharing, shorter hours, and counseling services rank among the least-preferred options (Note: by our definition several of these options don't really fall under the category of employee benefits). Beyond these conclusions, most preference studies have shown wide variation in individuals with respect to benefits desired.

The weakness of this demographic approach has led some organizations to undertake a second and more expensive empirical method of determining employee preference: surveying individuals about needs. One way of accomplishing this requires development of a questionnaire on which employees evaluate various benefits. For example, Exhibit 12.7 illustrates a questionnaire format.

EXHIBIT 12.7 **Questionnaire Format for Benefit Surveys**

Employee Benefit Questionnaire

1. In the space provided in front of the benefits listed below indicate how important each benefit is to you and your family. Indicate this by placing a "1" for the most important, and "2" for the next most important, etc. Therefore, if life insurance is the most important benefit to you and your family, place a "1" in front of it.

Importance		Improvement
_____	Dental insurance	_____
_____	Disability (pay while sick)	_____
_____	Educational assistance	_____
_____	Holidays	_____
_____	Life insurance	_____
_____	Medical insurance	_____
_____	Retirement annuity plan	_____
_____	Savings plan	_____
_____	Vacations	_____
_____	_____	_____
_____	_____	_____

Now, go back and in the space provided after each benefit, indicate the priority for improvement. For example, if the savings plan is the benefit you would most like to see improved, give it a "1," the next a priority "2," etc. Use the blank lines to add any benefits not listed.

2. Would you be willing to contribute a portion of your earnings for new or improved benefits beyond the level already provided by the Company?

❏ Yes   ❏ No

If yes, please indicate below in which area(s):

❏ Dental insurance   ❏ Medical insurance
❏ Disability benefits   ❏ Retirement annuity plan
❏ Life insurance   ❏ Savings plan

A third empirical method of identifying individual employee preferences is commonly known as a **flexible benefit plan** (also called a section 125 plan after the section of the Tax Code or a **cafeteria-style plan**). As previously noted, employees are allotted a fixed amount of money and permitted to spend that amount in the purchase of benefit options. From a theoretical perspective, this approach to benefit packaging is ideal. Employees directly identify the benefits of greatest value to them, and by constraining the dollars employees have to spend, benefit managers are able to control benefit costs. NCR has adopted a variant on flexible benefits that is part of its "customer-oriented" benefit push. Employees who wish can actually exchange some of their base salary for greater coverage on desired benefits.

ADMINISTERING THE BENEFIT PROGRAM

The job description for an employee benefit manager at Warner Brothers, shown in Exhibit 12.8, indicates that administrative time is spent on three functions requiring further discussion: (1) communicating about the benefits program, (2) claims processing, and (3) cost containment.[52]

EXHIBIT 12.8 **Entertainment Inc. Seeks an Employee Benefits Manager for the Compensation and Benefits Department.**	• General responsibility for health, welfare, and retirement questions from employees. • Oversees Executive Health, Medical Reimbursement, and Flexible Spending Account Programs. • Liaison for Appeals Committee and the Emergency Allocations Committee. • Will assume leadership role in special projects such as intranet communications system. • Charged with identification and maintenance of benefits' communications programs coming from a variety of different media (intranet, newsletter, computer-generated individual benefit accounts). • Performs and completes benefit surveys as required. • Evaluates performance of vendors and processes/facilitates employee complaints about delivery systems. • Resolves benefits administration problems emanating from MIS, finance, accounting, and legal departments. • Serves on committees to improve policies and processes in benefits strategy development and implementation. • Assists in Development of Strategic Benefits Survey, including identification of sample groups. • Provides input into design of benefits satisfaction survey and suggests format and conclusions for final report. • Attends benefits conferences to network with other benefits professionals. • Maintains working knowledge of new benefits studies, research, and practices. • Leads committee to evaluate benefits costs and reduction strategies. • Incorporates into benefits program relevant changes in state/federal law.

Employee Benefit Communication

Benefits communications revolves around four issues: What is communicated, to whom, how it's communicated, and how frequently. Much of the effort to achieve benefit goals today focuses on identifying methods (how) of communication. The most frequent method for communicating employee benefits today is probably still the employee benefit handbook.[53] A typical handbook contains a description of all benefits, including levels of coverage and eligibility requirements. To be most effective, the benefit manual should be accompanied by repetition of the message in multiple media: newsletters, e-mails, direct mailings, voice mail blasts, and social media (Facebook postings, Twitter, YouTube, Pinterest, and LinkedIn also).[54]

An effective communications package should match the message with the appropriate medium. Technological advances have made tremendous improvements in employee benefit communication. In the last 15 years, the Internet has become a major communication tool for benefits. Avaya, Inc., for example, has won awards for its portal hosted by Hay Consultants. Their site provides information on total reward policy, the role of benefits, and specific information on benefits costs with links to specific benefit options.[55]

Benefit administration over the Internet is also growing at a rapid pace. One report suggests that perhaps as many as 80 percent of the Fortune 1000 companies will utilize at least some form of Internet-based employee benefit application.[56] A wide range of applications will be offered, from online benefit information to annual benefit enrollment processing, personal data changes, 401(k) changes, and complete employee self-service.[57]

The Cedar Group estimates that the cost of a single hands-on HR-based benefits transaction is $35.65. The same transaction over the Internet or intranet is just $16.38.[58]

Companies also use intranets. An intranet is an internal organizational online Web through which all forms of communication within the organization can be streamlined. Advantages of an intranet include employee access to benefit information 24 hours a day, 7 days a week without added cost; employee's ability to directly post changes to their accounts without completing lengthy paperwork; and an increased ease of updating information.[59]

Employers are increasingly posting their employee benefit handbook components on their intranets.[60] This change is beneficial to employers because of the decreased cost and increased ease of making revisions in the employee benefit handbook components. More than 100,000 employees at IBM get benefit communications and enrollment data through the intranet, at savings estimated as $1 million per year. Joining IBM in this intranet-based enrollment process are such organizations as Alcatel-Lucent and Continental Airlines. Experts say **"e-benefits"** are a huge trend waiting to reinvent human resource practices.[61]

Another example of the recent advances in benefit communication is the streamlined call center operation that Kellogg Company launched in 1999 and that still operates today.[62] The call center decreased costs by as much as $105 million while improving service levels and maintaining close employee interaction. At a cost equal to approximately one-fifth of its paper-based predecessor, which required that specialists be located at every Kellogg's facility in the United States and Canada, the call center allows users to access benefit plan information, download and print documents, and retrieve basic information regarding Kellogg's benefit vendors. Annual cost savings of this system equal $500,000. Kellogg's anticipates that the future technological initiatives will include setting up kiosks, which will be Web-enabled personal computers that allow employees to access the information they presently access over the telephone and to contact specialists over the Internet in live chat rooms.

Despite these and other innovative plans to communicate employee benefit packages, failure to understand benefit components and their value is still one of the root causes of employee dissatisfaction with a benefit package. Information suggests less than 5 percent of employees fully understand their benefits package.[63] This can be remedied, though. One study of 500 employees in seven Canadian organizations found that perceived fairness of a plan was significantly higher when there was extensive communications and employee participation in plan design.[64] An organization must spell out its benefit objectives and it must ensure that any communications achieve these objectives. Exhibit 12.9 shows that employees who think company communications about benefits are effective are in turn more satisfied with those same benefits.

Claims Processing

As noted by one expert, **claims processing** arises when an employee asserts that a specific event (e.g., disability, hospitalization, unemployment) has occurred and demands that the employer fulfill a promise of payment.[65] As such, a claims processor must first determine whether the act has, in fact, occurred. We recently had lunch with an insurance agent who had a claim from a man asserting he had an on-the-job back injury. The injury allegedly was so severe that the employee's physical activities were

EXHIBIT 12.9   Employees Happy with Their Benefits versus Employees Happy with Communication about Their Benefits

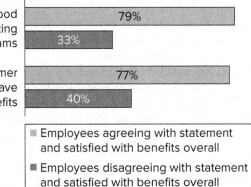

Source: "Rx for Rewards in the Downturn: Insights From Towers Perrin's Total Rewards Study," (New York: Towers Perrin, March 2009).

*Multiple responses permitted

drastically limited. The case was quickly dismissed when an insurance investigator caught the individual on tape lifting car engine blocks without a winch!

If the event did occur, the second step involves determining if the employee is eligible for the benefit. If payment is not denied at this stage, the claims processor calculates the payment level. It is particularly important at this stage to ensure coordination of benefits. If multiple insurance companies are liable for payment (e.g., working spouses covered by different insurers), a good claims processor can save from 10 to 15 percent of a claim's cost by ensuring that the liability is jointly paid.[66]

Cost Containment

Increasingly, employers are auditing their benefit options for **cost containment** opportunities. The most prevalent practices include:

1. **Probationary periods**—excluding new employees from benefit coverage until some term of employment (e.g., three months) is completed.
2. **Benefit limitations**—it is not uncommon to limit disability income payments to some maximum percentage of income and to limit medical/dental coverage for specific procedures to a certain fixed amount.
3. **Copay**—requiring that employees pay a fixed or percentage amount for coverage.
4. **Administrative cost containment**—controlling costs through policies such as seeking competitive bids for program delivery.
5. Deny Service for pre-existing conditions. (Note: in the not-to-distant-future we will face the ethical quandary about denying service to individuals with a genetic makeup that predicts future health problems.)
6. Negotiate lower fees by providers.
7. Develop programs that encourage wellness (e.g., smoking cessation).
8. Outsource benefits and administration.
9. Self insure
10. Provide accomodations for employees to return to work after illness or disability.

So prevalent is the cost issue today that the terminology of cost containment is becoming a part of every employee's vocabulary. Exhibit 12.10 provides definitions of some common cost containment terms.

Probably the biggest cost-containment strategy in recent years is the movement to **outsourcing**. By hiring vendors to administer their benefits programs, many companies, such as Tenneco, claim greater centralization, consistency, and control of costs and benefits.[67] Other companies, like Digital Equipment Corporation, outsource so that they may focus on their core businesses, "leaving benefits to the benefits experts."[68] In a related effort, companies are also cutting labor costs by using robots to do people jobs. It used to be that robots cost over one-hundred thousand dollars and could only do repetitive jobs (e.g., assembly line work at an auto company). Now though robots cost 20–50 thousand and can be set to do different works every day. Panek Precision, a machine shop in Illinois recently, bought 21 robots that do twice the work of a human—and they don't take coffee breaks![69]

EXHIBIT 12.10   Basic Primer of Cost Containment Terminology

Deductibles: An employee claim for insurance coverage is preceded by the requirement that the first $x be paid by the claimant.

Coinsurance: A proportion of insurance premiums are paid by the employee.

Benefit cutbacks: Corresponding to wage concessions, some employers are negotiating with employees to eliminate employer contributions or reduce them to selected options.

Defined contribution plans: Employers establish the limits of their responsibility for employee benefits in terms of a dollar contribution maximum.

Defined benefit plans: Employers establish the limits of their responsibility for employee benefits in terms of a specific benefit and the options included. As the cost of these options rises in future years, the employer is obligated to provide the benefit as negotiated, despite its increased cost.

Dual coverage: In families where both spouses work there is frequently coverage of specific claims from each employer's benefit package. Employers cut costs by specifying payment limitations under such conditions.

Benefit ceiling: Employers establish a maximum payout for specific claims (e.g., limiting liability for extended hospital stays to $150,000).

Your **Turn**   World Measurement

World Measurement is the global leader in product testing for safety. The recent problem with Chinese-made toy products (for example, Mattel recalled 19 million toys with evidence of lead paint) combined with the global recession has caused a 7 percent decline in sales and a 12 percent decline in net profits. The president of the company, Lewis Jacobs, is convinced that he must get concessions from the workers if World Measurement is to compete effectively with increasing foreign competition. In particular, Jacobs is displeased with the cost of employee benefits. He doesn't mind conceding a competitive wage increase (maximum 3 percent), but he wants the total compensation package to cost 3 percent less. The current costs are shown in Exhibit 1.

Your assistant has surveyed other companies that are obtaining concessions from employees. You also have data from a consulting firm that indicates employee preferences for different forms of benefits (Exhibit 2). Based on all this information, you have two possible concession packages that you can propose, labeled "Option 1" and "Option 2" (Exhibit 3).

1. Cost out these packages given the data in Exhibits 1 and the information obtained from various insurance carriers and other information sources (Exhibit 4).
2. Which package should you recommend to Jacobs? Why?
3. Which of the strategies do you think will require less input from employees in terms of their reactions?

EXHIBIT 1　　Current Compensation Costs

Average yearly wage	$26,769
Average hourly wage	$13.12
Dollar value of yearly benefits, per employee	$8,923
Total compensation (wages plus benefits)	$35,692
Daily average number of hours paid	8.0

Benefits (by Category)	Dollar Cost/Employee/Year
1. Legally required payments (employer's share only)	$2,141.00
a. Old-age, survivors, disability, and health insurance (FICA) taxes	$1,509.00
b. Unemployment compensation	$ 292.00
c. Workers' compensation (including estimated cost of self-insured)	$ 311.00
d. Railroad retirement tax, railroad unemployment and cash sickness insurance, state sickness benefits insurance, etc.	$ 29.00
2. Pension, insurance, and other agreed-upon payments (employer's share only)	$3,124.00
a. Pension plan premiums and pension payments not covered by insurance-type plan (net)	$1,460.00
b. Life insurance premiums; death benefits; hospital, surgical, medical, and major medical insurance premiums; etc. (net)	$1,427.00
c. Short-term disability	$ 83.00
d. Salary continuation or long-term disability	$ 57.00
e. Dental insurance premiums	$ 51.00
f. Discounts on goods and services purchased from company by employees	$ 27.00
g. Employee meals furnished by company	$ 0
h. Miscellaneous payments (compensation payments in excess of legal requirements, separation or termination pay allowances, moving expenses, etc.)	$ 24.00
3. Paid rest periods, lunch periods, wash-up time, travel time, clothes-change time, get-ready time, etc. (60 minutes)	$ 727.00
4. Payments for time not worked	$2,769.00
a. Paid vacations and payments in lieu of vacation (16 days average)	$1,558.00
b. Payments for holidays not worked (9 days)	$ 973.00
c. Paid sick leave (10 days maximum)	$ 172.00
d. Payments for state or national guard duty; jury, witness, and voting pay allowances; payments for time lost due to death in family or other personal reasons, etc.	$ 66.00
5. Other items	$ 157.00
a. Profit-sharing payments	$ 0
b. Contributions to employee thrift plans	$ 71.00
c. Christmas or other special bonuses, service awards, suggestion awards, etc.	$ 0
d. Employee education expenditures (tuition refunds, etc.)	$ 40.00
e. Special wage payments ordered by courts, payments to union stewards, etc.	$ 46.00
Total	$8,923.00

EXHIBIT 2   Benefit Preferences

Benefit Type or Method of Administering	Importance to Workers	Benefit Type or Method of Administering	Importance to Workers
Pensions	87	Paid rest periods, lunch periods, etc.	55
Hospitalization	86	Dental insurance	51
Life insurance	79	Christmas bonus	31
Paid vacation	82	Profit sharing	21
Holidays	82	Education expenditures	15
Long-term disability	72	Contributions to thrift plans	15
Short-term disability	69	Discount on goods	5
Paid sick leave	70	Fair treatment in administration	100

Note: 0 = unimportant; 100 = extremely important.

EXHIBIT 3
Two Possible
Packages for
Cutting Benefit
Costs

Option 1

Implement Copay for Benefit	Amount of Copay
Pension	$300.00
Hospital, surgical, medical, and major medical premiums	350.00
Dental insurance premiums	75.00

Reduction of Benefit

Eliminate 10-minute paid break (workers leave work 10 minutes earlier)
Eliminate one paid holiday per year
Coordination with **legally required benefit;** social security coordinated
with Lightning Industries pension plan

Option 2

Improved claims processing:
   Unemployment compensation
   Workers' compensation
   Long-term disability
Require probationary period (one year) before eligible for:
   Discounts on goods
   Employee meal paid by company
   Contributions to employee thrift plans
Deductible ($100 per incident):
   Life insurance, death benefits, hospital, etc.
   Dental insurance

Copay	Amount of Copay
Hospital, surgical, medical and major medical premiums	$350.00

EXHIBIT 4
Analysis
of Cost
Implications
for Different
Cost-Cutting
Strategies:
Lightning
Industries

Cost-Saving Strategy	Savings as Percent of Benefit-Type Cost
Copay	Dollar-for-dollar savings equal to amount of copay
Deductible ($100 per incident):	
Life insurance premiums, death benefits, hospital, etc.	10%
Dental insurance	15
Require probationary period before eligible (one year):	
Discount on goods and services	10
Employee meals furnished by company	15
Contributions to employee thrift plans	10
Improved claims processing:	
Unemployment compensation	8
Workers' compensation	3
Long-term disability	1
Coordination with legally required benefits:	
Coordinate social security with Lightning pension plan	15

Summary

Given the rapid escalation in the cost of employee benefits over the past 15 years, organizations would do well to evaluate the effectiveness of their benefit adoption, retention, and termination procedures. Specifically, how do organizations go about selecting appropriate employee benefits? Are the decisions based on sound evaluation of employee preferences balanced against organizational goals of legal compliance and competitiveness? Do the benefits chosen serve to attract, retain, and/or motivate employees? Or are organizations paying billions of dollars of **indirect compensation** without any tangible benefit? This chapter has outlined a benefit determination process that identifies major issues in selecting and evaluating particular benefit choices. The next chapter catalogs the various benefits available and discusses some of the decisions confronting a benefit administrator.

Review Questions

1. Early in this chapter, we identified reasons for the historical growth in the size of benefits packages. Which of these reasons still affect the growth of employee benefits today? Which actually might be current reasons for declines in the size of benefit packages?

2. Erinn Kelly, VP of Human Resources at Lawson Chemical, just purchased a local salary survey that has employee benefits data. She was shocked to see that Lawson has a larger benefits bill (38 percent of payroll) than the average in the

community (31 percent). In a memo to you, she demands an explanation for why our package is significantly bigger. What sound reasons might save you from getting fired?

3. You are the benefits manager in a firm metaphorically described as part of the rust belt, in Syracuse, NY. The average age of your 600-person workforce is 43. Eighty-eight percent of your workforce is male, and there is hardly any turnover. Not much is happening on the job front. How do these facts influence your decisions about designing an employee benefit program?

4. As HR director at Crangle Fixtures, your bonus this year is based on your ability to cut employee benefit costs. Your boss has said that it's okay to shift some of the costs over to employees (right now they pay nothing for their benefits) but that he doesn't want you to overdo it. In other words, at least one-half of your suggestions should not hurt the employee's pocket book. What alternatives do you want to explore, and why?

5. Google is famous for paying wages significantly above the market and also providing employee benefits that one might call lavish. Currently the European Union is suing Google for its monopolistic behavior, claiming that the company's internet search function systematically favors its own comparison shopping product in its search results pages (Their products turn up earlier in the search effort). Assume the European Union wins this antitrust case resulting in significant financial loss to Google. Speculate on what Google might change about its benefits package as a consequence of this ruling.

Endnotes

1. U.S. Department of Labor, Bureau of Labor Statistics, Employer Costs for Employee Compensation-USDL-15-0386, www.bls.gov/ect. March 11, 2015.

2. Society for Human Resource Management, "2010 Employee Benefits," February 2010, http://www.shrm.org/Research/SurveyFindings/Articles/Documents/10-0280%20 Employee%20Benefits%20Survey%20Report-FNL.pdf.

3. Pault Fronstin, "2013 Health and Voluntary Workplace Benefits Survey," Employee Benefits Research Institute, fronstin@ebri.org., 2013.

4. S. Bates, "Benefit Packages Nearing 40 Percent of Payroll," *HRMagazine*, March 2003, pp. 36–38, http://fortune.com/best-companies/google-1/.

5. Pault Fronstin, "2013 Health and Voluntary Workplace Benefits Survey," Employee Benefits Research Institute, fronstin@ebri.org., 2013.

6. Stephen Miller, "Survey: Employees Undervalue Benefits," *HR Magazine* 52(8), 2008, p. 7.

7. U.S. Chamber of Commerce, Benefits Survey 2011.

8. Rebecca Blumenstein, "Seeking a Cure: Auto Makers Attack High Health-Care Bills with a New Approach," *The Wall Street Journal,* December 9, 1996, p. A1.

9. John Hanna, "Can the Challenge of Escalating Benefits Costs Be Met?" *Personnel Administration* 27(9), 1977, pp. 50–57.

10. U.S. Bureau of Labor Statistics, Employer Costs for Employee Compensation – December 2014, http://data.bls.gov/cgi-bin/surveymost, accessed April 20, 2015.

11. J. Jargon, *Chicago Business,* March 2, 2006, *www.chicagobusiness.com,* June 26, 2006.

12. Douglas J. Elliott, "Potential Federal Roles in Dealing with State and Local Pension Problems," The Brookings Institution, 2012, www.brookings.edu/papers/2011/0512_pension_crisis_elliott.aspx.

13. R. McCaffery, *Managing the Employee Benefits Program* (New York: American Management Association, 1983).

14. Bashker D. Biswas, *A Guide to Employee Benefits Design and Planning* (Upper Saddle river, NJ: Pearson Education, 2014).

15. Exhibit 12.2 was compiled from five different sources. Some of the reward components rated in some of the studies were not traditional employee benefits and have been deleted from the rankings here. The five sources were: Employee Benefits Research Institute and Matthew Greenwald and Associates, "Worker Ranking of Employee Benefits," *www.ebri.org/pdf/publications/facts/fastfacts/fastfact062905.pdf,* June 26, 2006; "Employees Value Basic Benefits Most" (A on survey), *Best's Review* 103(4) (2002), pp. 1527–1591; "The Future Look of Employee Benefits" (Hewitt Associates survey), *The Wall Street Journal*, September 8, 1988, p. 23; Kermit Davis, William Giles, and Hubert Feild, *How Young Professionals Rank Employee Benefits:* Two Studies (Brookfield, WI: International Foundation of Employee Benefit Plans, 1988); Kenneth Shapiro and Jesse Sherman, "Employee Attitude Benefit Plan Designs," *Personnel Journal*, July 1987, pp. 49–58.

16. Kaiser Family Foundation, "2014 Employer Health Benefits," 2014 Annual Survey. KFF .org, accessed January 3, 2015.

17. M. L. Williams and E. Newman, "Employees' Definitions of and Knowledge of Employer-Provided Benefits," paper presented at Academy of Management meetings, Atlanta, GA, 1993; Richard Huseman, John Hatfield, and Richard Robinson, "The MBA and Fringe Benefits," *Personnel Administration* 23(7), 1978, pp. 57–60.

18. 2011 Job Satisfaction Survey, *www.shrm.org.*

19. Bashker D. Biswas, *A Guide to Employee Benefits Design and Planning* (Upper Saddle river, NJ: Pearson Education, 2014).

20. D. M. Cable and T. A. Judge, "Pay Preferences and Job Search Decisions: A Person-Organization Fit Perspective," *Personnel Psychology* 47 (1994), pp. 317–348.

21. Carol Danehower and John Lust, "How Aware Are Employees of Their Benefits?" *Benefits Quarterly* 12(4), 1996, pp. 57–61.

22. Burton Beam, Jr., and John J. McFadden, *Employee Benefits* (Chicago: Dearborn Financial Publishing, 1996).

23. Bashker D. Biswas, *A Guide to Employee Benefits Design and Planning* (Upper Saddle river, NJ: Pearson Education, 2014).

24. Ibid.

25. Laura Ungar and Jayne O'Donnell, "Dilemma over Deductibles," *USA Today,* January 2, 2015, p. A1. Rebecca Mazin, The Employee Benefits Answer Book (San Francisco: Pfeiffer, 2011).

26. Bashker D. Biswas, *A Guide to Employee Benefits Design and Planning* (Upper Saddle river, NJ: Pearson Education, 2014); E. Parmenter, "Employee Benefit Compliance Checklist," *Compensation and Benefits Review,* May/June 2002, pp. 29–39.

27. Bashker D. Biswas, *A Guide to Employee Benefits Design and Planning* (Upper Saddle river, NJ: Pearson Education, 2014).

28. E. Parmenter, "Employee Benefit Compliance Checklist," *Compensation and Benefits Review*, May/June 2002, pp. 29–39.

29. Rebecca Mazin, *The Employee Benefits Answer Book* (San Francisco: Pfeiffer, 2011).

30. Melissa W. Barringer and George T. Milkovich, "A Theoretical Exploration of the Adoption and Design of Flexible Benefit Plans: A Case of Human Resource Innovation," *Academy of Management Review* 23 (1998), pp. 306–308; Commerce Clearing House, "Flexible Benefits" (Chicago: Commerce Clearing House, 1983); American Can Company, "Do It Your Way" (Greenwich, CT: American Can Co., 1978); L. M. Baytos, "The Employee Benefit Smorgasbord: Its Potential and Limitations," *Compensation Review*, First Quarter 1970, pp. 86–90; "Flexible Benefit Plans Become More Popular," *The Wall Street Journal*, December 16, 1986, p. 1; Richard Johnson, *Flexible Benefits: A How-to Guide* (Brookfield, WI: International Foundation of Employee Benefit Plans, 1986).

31. EBRI, *Employee Benefits Research Institute Databook on Employee Benefits* (Washington, DC: Employee Benefits Research Institute, 1995).

32. Ibid.

33. Tara Siegel Bernard, "High Deductible Plans Projected to Grow," *Wall Street Journal*, September 2014, p. B1.

34. Kaiser Family Foundation, "2014 Employer Health Benefits," 2014 Annual Survey. KFF.org, accessed January 3, 2015.

35. Tara Siegel Bernard, "High Deductible plans projected to grow". *Wall Street Journal*, September 2014, p. B1.

36. E. Parmenter, "Employee Benefit Compliance Checklist," *Compensation and Benefits Review* 34(3), 2002, pp. 29–39.

37. Philip Bredesen, "ObamaCare's Incentive to Drop Insurance," *The Wall Street Journal* online, visited March 21, 2012 http://online.wsj.com/article/SB10001424052702304510704575562643804015252.html.

38. U.S. Chamber of Commerce, *Employee Benefits Annual Surveys, www.chamberofcommerce.com,* March 2012.

39. Paul Fronstin, "Offering Benefits Still Gives Employers a Competitive Advantage," fronstin@ebri.org., 2013.

40. Donald P. Crane, *The Management of Human Resources*, 2nd ed. (Belmont, CA: Wadsworth, 1979); J. Foegen, "Are Escalating Employee Benefits Self-Defeating?" *Pension World* 14(9), September 1978, pp. 83–84, 86.

41. Olivia Mitchell, "Fringe Benefits and Labor Mobility," *Journal of Human Resources* 17(2), 1982, pp. 286–298; Bradley Schiller and Randal Weiss, "The Impact of Private Pensions on Firm Attachment," *Review of Economics and Statistics* 61(3), 1979, pp. 369–380.

42. W. Even and D. Macpherson, "Employer Size and Labor Turnover: The Role of Pensions," *Industrial and Labor Relations Review* 49(4) (1996), pp. 707–729; Olivia Mitchell, "Fringe Benefits and the Cost of Changing Jobs," *Industrial and Labor Relations Review* 37(1), 1983, pp. 70–78.

43. Ibid.

44. *The New York Times* and CBS poll, as reported in *Human Resource Management News* (Chicago: Remy Publishing, 1991).

45. Society for Human Resources Management, "New SHRM Reports Highlight Trends in Employee Benefits, Job Satisfaction." visited October 20, 2012 http://www.reuters.com/article/2009/06/29/idUS117242+29-Jun-2009+PRN20090629.

46. Paul Fronstin, "Offering Benefits Still Gives Employers a Competitive Advantage," fronstin@ebri.org., 2013.

47. S. Lambert, "Added Benefits: The Link between Work-Life Benefits and Organizational Citizenship Behavior," *Academy of Management Journal* 43(5) (2000), pp. 801–815.

48. William F. Glueck, *Personnel: A Diagnostic Approach* (Plano, TX: Business Publications, 1978).

49. Ibid.

50. Ludwig Wagner and Theodore Bakerman, "Wage Earners' Opinions of Insurance Fringe Benefits," *Journal of Insurance*, June 1960, pp. 17–28; Brad Chapman and Robert Otterman, "Employee Preference for Various Compensation and Benefits Options," *Personnel Administrator* 25 (November 1975), pp. 31–36.

51. Stanley Nealy, "Pay and Benefit Preferences," *Industrial Relations*, October 1963, pp. 17–28.

52. Robert M. McCaffery, *Managing the Employee Benefits Program*, rev. ed. (New York: American Management Association, 1983).

53. See "Towers Perrin Survey Finds Dramatic Increase in Companies Utilizing the Web for HR Transactions: Two- to Threefold Increase Compared to 1999 Survey," *www.towers. /Users/f-com/towers/news*, October 20, 2000; Towers, Perrin, Forster, and Crosby, "Corporate Benefit Communication . . . Today and Tomorrow" (New York: Towers, Perrin, Forster, and Crosby, 1988).

54. Ellen Anreder, "Communicating the Value of Your Benefits," *Benefits Magazine*, 52(5), 2015, 28–33.

55. Ann Black, *Communicating Benefits.*

56. Ann Black, *Communicating Benefits.*

57. S. Simon and W. Mattle, "Rethinking Online Benefits," *Compensation and Benefits Review*, March/April 2002, pp. 80–84; "Towers Perrin Survey Finds Dramatic Increase in Companies Utilizing the Web for HR Transactions: Two- to Threefold Increase Compared to 1999 Survey," *www.towers.com/towers/news*, October 20, 2000.

58. T. Clifford, "Recognizing Maximum Return on Benefits Administration and Compensation Planning Technology Investments," *Employee Benefit Plan Review* 58(10), 2004, pp. 11–14.

59. S. Smith, "New Trends in Health Care Cost Control," *Compensation and Benefits Review*, January/February 2002, pp. 38–44; B. Ambrose, "Leveraging Technology via Knowledge Portals," *Compensation and Benefits Review*, May/June 2001, pp. 43–46; Frank E. Kuzmits, "Communicating Benefits: A Double-Click Away," *Compensation and Benefits Review* 61 (September/October 1998).

60. Ann Black, *Communicating Benefits.*

61. Stephanie Armour, "Workers Just Click to Enroll for Benefits," *USA Today*, November 8, 2000, p. B1.

62. Judith N. Mottl, "Cereal Killer," *Human Resources Executive*, May 2000, pp. 74–75.

63. Ibid.

64. Ibid.

65. Bennet Shaver, "The Claims Process," in *Employee Benefit Management*, H. Wayne Snider, ed. (New York: Warren, Gorham and Lamont, 1997), pp. 141–152.

66. Thomas Fannin and Theresa Fannin, "Coordination of Benefits: Uncovering Buried Treasure," *Personnel Journal*, May 1983, pp. 386–391.

67. G. McWilliams, "ACS Finds Profits in Business Outsourcing," *The Wall Street Journal*, May 3, 2001, p. B5; E. Scott Peterson, "From Those Who've Been There . . . Outsourcing Leaders Talk about Their Experiences," *Benefits Quarterly* 6(1), First Quarter 1997, pp. 6–13.

68. Bashker D. Biswas, *A Guide to Employee Benefits Design and Planning* (Upper Saddle river, NJ: Pearson Education, 2014).

69. Timothy Aeppel, "Robots Work Their Way into Small Factories," *Wall Street Journal*, September 18, 2014, p. B1.

Benefit Options

Chapter Outline

Legally Required Benefits

Retirement and Savings Plan Payments

Life Insurance

Medical and Medically Related Payments

Miscellaneous Benefits

Benefits for Contingent Workers

Your Turn: Adapting Benefits to a Changing Strategy

A Historical Perspective

The idea of employee benefits in the United States dates back to colonial days. Plymouth Colony settlers established a retirement program in 1636 for the military. American Express began the first private pension plan in 1875. Montgomery Ward, a now defunct competitor of JC Penneys, started the first group health and life insurance programs in 1910. In 1915, employees in the iron and steel industry worked a standard 60 to 64 hours per week. By 1930 that schedule had been reduced to 54 hours. It was not until 1929 that the Blue Cross concept of prepaid medical costs was introduced. Before that health care was the responsibility of the worker's family. Prior to 1935 only one state (Wisconsin) had a program of unemployment compensation benefits for workers who lost their jobs through no fault of their own. Before World War II very few companies paid hourly employees for holidays. In most companies employees were told not to report for work on holidays and to enjoy the time off, but their paychecks were smaller the following week.[1]

The biggest early push for benefits, though, came from Uncle Sam. In 1935 the federal government mandated retirement income protection under Social

Security. Coverage for the disabled and elderly followed in the 1950s and 1960s. Fast forward 50 years and companies are now reeling from the high cost of benefits, especially health care costs. And some of the measures to cut these costs are attracting public attention. For example, companies like PepsiCo, General Mills, and Northwest Airlines charge $20–$50 a month extra for smokers.[2] Twenty-one states even allow companies to discriminate against smokers in hiring. "You smoke? Sorry, no job for you."[3] The argument runs, if you're going to continue habits that raise our health insurance costs, we're going to charge you. Going even one giant step further, Walmart distributed an internal memo to the Board of Directors proposing that health care costs could be cut dramatically by discouraging unhealthy people from applying.[4] Illegal, you cry in dismay? What if Walmart, as suggested in the same internal memo, includes as a task in every job description that employees must take their turn at rounding up shopping carts in the parking lot?[5] If even a few unhealthy applicants are discouraged, Walmart could save untold millions. After all, health care provider WellPoint Inc says just 7 percent of its 29 million customers account for 63 percent of its medical costs. Add to these snippets of reality the explosion of ongoing research on the human genome, and we aren't very far away from a time when a company could test applicants for a disposition to contract fatal diseases—*years in the future!* Employers intent on reducing health care costs need only refuse to hire these future insurance risks.

All of these scenarios make the study of employee benefits far more interesting. Desperate to even slow the ever-growing cost of employee health insurance and other benefits, companies are experimenting with different, and sometimes radical, methods to entice, bribe, and even threaten. At the very least, this makes the study of benefits more exciting. Happy reading!

For years we've asked our students and HR professionals to rate different kinds of rewards in terms of importance. Usually, at least in the past, employee benefits lagged behind such rewards as pay, advancement opportunity, job security, and recognition. Recently, though, we've noticed a dramatic shift in this admittedly unscientific poll. As benefits costs, especially health care, have skyrocketed, so has their popularity. A recent survey listed the top four rewards contributing to employee satisfaction. In order, they are compensation, benefits, job security, and work/life balance.[6]

With this increased popularity comes a need for HR professionals to understand what benefits are important to employees. Just ask Rich Floersch, the executive vice president for human resources at McDonald's Corporation.[7] As we noted in Chapter 12, several years ago McDonald's unveiled a new benefits program for crew members. When we asked Rich why McDonald's was modifying its health care package as part of a total benefits upgrade, he cited the rising value of benefits to workers and the strategic importance of its 750,000 plus workers. Look at it from another perspective: The population (and your three favorite authors) are aging. This alone changes the pattern of preferences. We're not sure all companies are as attuned to changing preferences as McDonald's. For example, a McKinsey Survey reports 89 percent of CEOs think benefits are extremely or very important to attracting and retaining employees. However, less than one-half of these executives thought they understood what benefits employees

EXHIBIT 13.1   Employer Cost of Benefit per Hour Worked: Private Sector and State/Local Government

Benefit Type	Private Sector Average ($)	State and Local Government Avg ($)
Holiday	.63	.95
Vacation	1.08	1.19
Sick Leave	.28	.84
Personal leave	.11	.23
Life Insurance	.04	.06
Health Insurance	2.36	5.09
Short Term Disability	.06	.03
Long Term Disability	.05	.04
Retirement	1.15	4.42
Social Security & Medicare	1.75	1.95
Workers' Compensation	.42	.54
St/Fed Unemployment Insurance	.27	NA

Source: Employer Costs for Employee Compensation, December 2014. Bureau of Labor Statistics USDL-15-1386.

wanted. Moreover, almost 60 percent of these executives admitted they never assessed whether benefits were helping the company achieve its strategic goals.[8] Is it any wonder that daily news reports bring frequent alarms about the rising cost of benefits?

Our goal in this chapter is to give you a clearer appreciation of employee benefits. Let's start by comparing wages to benefits. In December of 2014 private industry wages averaged $21.72 (69.4%). Benefits Averaged $9.60 (30.6%). In the past four years benefits have risen as a percent of total compensation cost from 29.2 to 30.6 percent. While 1.4 percent rise doesn't seem like much, it highlights the continuing relative growth in benefits costs over the past several decades. Comparable figures for state and local government employees were $43.95 (68.4%) per hour for wages and $15.78 (31.6%) for benefits. Notice both wages and benefits are higher in the public sector jobs. it pays to work for the government! A breakdown of benefits in Exhibit 13.1 shows the relative costs.

Many students tell us they are struck by how low the Retirement and Health Insurance figures are for the private sector, especially in comparison to the Public Sector figures and also considering how much coverage the press devotes to these two benefits. The follow-up question we get is "doesn't everyone get a retirement package?" The answer is No! Many Americans work in jobs with no paid retirement. The same thing is true for health coverage. The insurance figures in this exhibit would be much higher if more organizations provided health-care insurance.

One way to get your attention is to show the dramatic increase in costs of benefits. Back about the time the first McDonalds opened (mid-1950s), benefits cost $18 billion. Today that figure is $5 trillion and change! If for no other reason than cost escalation, we need to understand the world of employee benefits. Let's begin by looking at a widely accepted categorization of employee benefits (Exhibit 13.2). The U.S. Chamber of Commerce issues an annual update of benefit expenditures.[9] This report identifies seven categories of benefits in a breakdown that is highly familiar to benefit

EXHIBIT 13.2 **Categorization of Employee Benefits**

Type of Benefit

1. Legally required payments (employers' share only)
   a. Old-age, survivors, disability, and health insurance (employer FICA taxes) and railroad retirement tax
   b. Unemployment compensation
   c. Workers' compensation (including estimated cost of self-insured)
   d. State sickness benefit insurance

2. Retirement and savings plan payments (employers' share only)
   a. Defined benefit pension plan contributions (401(k) type)
   b. Defined contribution plan payments
   c. Profit sharing
   d. Stock bonus and employee stock ownership plans (ESOPs)
   e. Pension plan premiums (net) under insurance and annuity contracts (insured and trusted)
   f. Administrative and other costs

3. Life insurance and death benefits (employers' share only)

4. Medical and medical-related benefit payments (employers' share only)
   a. Hospital, surgical, medical, and major medical insurance premiums (net)
   b. Retiree hospital, surgical, medical, and major medical insurance premiums (net)
   c. Short-term disability, sickness, or accident insurance (company plan or insured plan)
   d. Long-term disability or wage continuation (insured, self-administered, or trust)
   e. Dental insurance premiums
   f. Other (vision care, physical and mental fitness benefits for former employees)

5. Paid rest periods, coffee breaks, lunch periods, wash-up time, travel time, clothes-change time, get-ready time, etc.

6. Payments for time not worked
   a. Payments for or in lieu of vacations
   b. Payments for or in lieu of holidays
   c. **Sick leave pay**
   d. Parental leave (maternity and paternity leave payments)
   e. Other

7. Miscellaneous benefit payments
   a. Discounts on goods and services purchased from company by employees
   b. Employee meals furnished by company
   c. Employee education expenditures
   d. Child care
   e. Other

Source: U.S. Chamber of Commerce, Employee Benefits Study 2008, http://www.uschamber.com/research/benefits.htm. Reprinted with permission.

plan administrators. These seven categories will be used to organize this chapter and illustrate important principles affecting strategic and administrative concerns for each benefit type.

Exhibit 13.3 shows employee participation in selected benefit programs. As expected, the highest access is to health insurance and retirement benefits. With passage of the Affordable Care Act expect the access to health insurance to rise considerably.

EXHIBIT 13.3
Access to
Selected
Benefits

Source: 2014
National
Compensation
Survey, Bureau of
Labor Statistics.
http://www.bls.gov/
ncs/ebs/#data.

Benefit	Civilian Employees
Paid holiday	75%
Paid vacation	74
Paid sick leave	65
Short term disability	36
Health insurance	72
Life insurance	40
Retirement	68
Defined benefit plan	25
Defined contribution plan	56
Dental insurance	47
Vision care	26
Childcare	11
Wellness programs	39

LEGALLY REQUIRED BENEFITS

Virtually every employee benefit is somehow affected by statutory or common law (many of the limitations are imposed by tax laws). In this section the primary focus is on benefits that are required by statutory law: Workers' Compensation, Social Security, and Unemployment Compensation.

Workers' Compensation

What costs employers $83.2 billion a year and is a major cost of doing business? Answer: workers' compensation.[10] Of this total, $31.8 billion was for medical care and the remainder was paid as cash benefits.[11]

As a form of no-fault insurance (employees are eligible even if their actions caused the accident), workers' compensation covers injuries and diseases that arise out of, and while in the course of, employment. Benefits are given for:[12]

1. Medical care needed to treat the job injury or illness.
2. Temporary disability benefits to the employee to help replace lost wages.
3. Permanent disability payments to the employee to compensate for permanent effects of the injury.
4. Survivor death benefits.
5. Rehabilitation and training in most states, for those unable to return to their prior career.

Workers compensation costs vary over time. During the early years of this century, the costs rose. But as recently as 2005, the dollar costs began to decline. Costs in recent years have been the lowest since 1980.[13] Experts believe part of this stabilization relates to employer safety programs, with far fewer fatal accidents occurring and somewhat higher incidents of minor, less costly accidents.

States vary in the size of the payout for claims. New York State, for example, has a payout formula for totally or partially disabled that is based on his/her average weekly wage for the previous year. The following formula is used to calculate benefits:

2/3 × average weekly wage × % of disability = weekly benefit

Therefore, a claimant who was earning $400 per week and is totally (100%) disabled would receive $266.67 per week. A partially disabled claimant (50%) would receive $133.34 per week.[14]

Some states provide "second-injury funds." These funds relieve an employer's liability when a pre-employment injury combines with a work-related injury to produce a disability greater than that caused by the latter alone. For example, if a person with a known heart condition is hired and then breaks an arm in a fall triggered by a heart attack, medical treatments for the heart condition would not be paid from workers' compensation insurance; treatment for the broken arm would be compensated.

Workers' compensation is covered by state, not federal, laws. For details on each state's laws, go to the e-Compensation website below:

e-Compensation
Each state differs in its workers' compensation law. If you're a glutton for punishment, visit *www.workerscompensation.com/workers_comp_by_state.php* (visited April 22, 2015).

As Exhibit 13.4 shows, in general the states have fairly similar coverage, with differences occurring primarily in benefit levels and costs. In recent years states have made significant changes in Workers' Compensation (WC) designed to reduce costs. For example, Montana paid $3.22 per $100 of payroll cost, a figure much higher than most states. They and five other states passed major reforms attempting to control medical costs and rein in WC as a result.[15] In the following four years the per $100 of payroll cost dropped as follows: 3.06, 2.76, 2.54, 2.49.

e-Compensation
This website from the Department of Labor provides extensive information about legally required benefits and specific requirements for compliance: *http://www.dol.gov/dol/topic/*

EXHIBIT 13.4 Commonalities in State Workers' Compensation Laws

Issue	Most Common State Provision
Type of law	Compulsory (in 47 states)
	Elective (in 3 states)
Self-insurance coverage	Self-insurance permitted (in 48 states)
	All industrial employment
	Farm labor, domestic servants, and casual employees usually exempted
	Compulsory for all or most public sector employees (in 47 states)
Occupational diseases	Coverage for all diseases arising out of and in the course of employment
	No compensation for "ordinary diseases of life"

Source: *www.ncci.com.*

Social Security

When Social Security was introduced in 1937, only about 60 percent of all workers were eligible.[16] Today, nearly every American worker (96%) is covered.[17] Whether a worker retires, becomes disabled, or dies, Social Security benefits are paid to replace part of the lost family earnings. Ever since its passage, the Social Security Act has been designed and amended to provide a foundation of basic security for American workers and their families. Exhibit 13.5 outlines the initial provisions of the law and its subsequent broadening over the years.[18] In combination this law and its updates provide coverage in the form of: Retirement insurance; Survivors insurance; Disability insurance; Hospital and medical insurance for the aged, the disabled, and those with end-stage renal disease; Prescription Drug Benefit Extra Help with Medicare Prescription Drug Costs Supplemental security income; and Special Veterans Benefits.[19]

The money to pay these benefits comes from the Social Security contributions made by employees, their employers, and self-employed people during working years.

EXHIBIT 13.5 Changes in Social Security over the Years

1939	Survivor's insurance was added to provide monthly life insurance payments to the widow and dependent children of deceased workers.
1950–1954	Old-age and survivor's insurance was broadened.
1956	Disability insurance benefits were provided to workers and dependents of such employees.
1965	Medical insurance protection was provided for the aged, and later (1973) for the disabled under age 65 (Medicare).
1972	Cost-of-living escalator was tied to the consumer price index—guaranteed higher future benefits for all beneficiaries.
1974	Existing state programs of financial assistance to the aged, blind, and disabled were replaced by SSI (supplemental security income) administered by the Social Security Administration.
1983	Effective 1984, all new civilian federal employees were covered. All federal employees covered for purpose of Medicare.
1985	Social Security Administration (SSA) became an independent agency administered by a commissioner and a bipartisan advisory board.
1994	Amendments were enacted imposing severe restrictions on benefits paid to drug abusers and alcoholics (together with treatment requirements and a 36-month cap on the payment of benefits).
1996	Contract with America Advancement Act of 1996 (CWAAA) was enacted, eliminating substance abuse as a disabling impairment. Substance abuse may no longer be the basis for a finding of disability.
2000	Depression-era limits on amount of money that workers age 65 to 69 may earn without having their Social Security benefits reduced were eliminated—retroactive to January 1, 2000. The rules governing individuals who take early retirement at age 62 and the status of workers age 70 and over were not changed by the new law.
2003	**The Medicare Prescription Drug, Improvement and Modernization Act of 2003** (P.L.108-173) archive. Seniors must choose from among a variety of plans written in bureaucratic hieroglyphics.

Source: http://www.ssa.gov/OP_Home/handbook/handbook.01/handbook-toc01.html, June 10, 2009.

EXHIBIT 13.6   Trends in Social Security Taxes 1980–2009

| Year | OASI (All But Health) | | | Health Component | | Total Contribution | |
	Maximum Taxable Earnings	% OASI (Old Age Survivors)	% DI (Disability)	Maximum Taxable Earnings	% Health	%	$
1980	$25,900	4.52	0.56	$25,900	1.05	6.13	1,587.67
1990	51,300	5.6	0.6	51,300	1.45	7.65	3,924.45
1995	61,200	5.26	0.94	No max	1.45	7.65	No max because of uncapped health care
1997–1999	Increases with market wage movement	5.35	0.85	No max	1.45	7.65	No max, uncapped health
2000+	Increases with market wage movement— $117,000 in 2014.	5.3 In 2011 the total tax was reduced for one year from 6.2% to 4.2%	0.9	No max	1.45	7.65	No max, uncapped health

Source: U.S. Social Security Administration Office of Retirement and Disability Policy, *www.ssa.gov/policy/docs/quickfacts/prog_highlights/index.html*, April 6, 2015.

As contributions are paid in each year, they are immediately used to pay for the benefits to current beneficiaries. Herein lies a major problem with Social Security. While the number of retired workers continues to rise (because of earlier retirement and longer life spans), no corresponding increase in the number of contributors to Social Security has offset the costs. Combine the increase in beneficiaries with other cost stimulants (e.g., liberal cost-of-living adjustments) and the outcome is not surprising. To maintain solvency, there has been a dramatic increase in both the maximum earnings base and the rate at which that base is taxed. Exhibit 13.6 illustrates the trends in tax rate, maximum earnings base, and maximum tax for Social Security.

Several points immediately jump out from this exhibit. First, with the rapid rise in taxable earnings, you should get used to paying some amount of Social Security tax on every dollar you earn. This wasn't always true. Notice that in 1980 the maximum taxable earnings were $25,900. Every dollar earned over that amount was free of Social Security tax. Now the maximum is over $110,000, and for one part of Social Security (Medicare) there is no earnings maximum.[20] If Jordan Spieth makes $30 million this year, he will pay 7.65 percent social security tax on the first $117,000 and 1.45 percent (the health/Medicare portion) on all the rest of his income. For the super rich (even with royalties, textbook authors need not apply), this elimination of the cap is costly.

Second, remember that for every dollar deducted as an employees' share of social security, there is a matching amount paid by employers. For an employee with income in the $70,000 range, this means an employer contribution of just under $6,000. Because Social Security is retirement income to employees, employers should decrease private pension payouts by a corresponding amount.

Current funding levels produced a massive surplus throughout the 1990s. There is still, at least in accounting terms, a huge surplus (perhaps over two trillion dollars today). Unfortunately the surplus is something of a myth. The federal government doesn't put your contributions in a savings bank in anticipation of your retirement. Rather, they've continually used the fund to finance government spending. Baby boomers have reached their peak earnings potential, and their Social Security payments subsidize a much smaller generation born during the 1930s. The first of these boomers are now retired, and the impact of Social Security taxes lost and new benefits being paid spells big problems for the system. There are now almost 3.5 workers paying into the system for each person collecting benefits. Within the next 40 years this ratio will drop to about 2 to 1.[21] Many experts believe this statistic foreshadows the collapse of Social Security as we know it.

Benefits Under Social Security

The majority of benefits under Social Security fall into four categories: (1) old age or disability benefits, (2) benefits for dependents of retired or disabled workers, (3) benefits for surviving family members of a deceased worker, and (4) lump-sum death payments. To qualify for these benefits, a worker must work in covered employment and earn a specified amount of money (about $1250 today) for each quarter-year of coverage.[22] Forty quarters of coverage will insure any worker for life. The amount received under the four benefit categories noted above varies, but in general it is tied to the amount contributed during eligibility quarters. For example, a person who had maximum-taxable earnings in each year since age 22, and who retired this year at age 65 will earn $2452 per month in benefits.[23]

Unemployment Insurance

The earliest union efforts to cushion the effects of unemployment for their members (c. 1830s) were part of benevolent programs of self-help. Working members made contributions to their unemployed brethren. With passage of the unemployment insurance law (as part of the Social Security Act of 1935), this floor of security for unemployed workers became less dependent upon the philanthropy of co-workers (147 million workers are covered today). Since unemployment insurance laws vary by state, this review will cover some of the major characteristics of different state programs.

Financing

In the majority of states, unemployment compensation paid out to eligible workers is financed exclusively by employers that pay federal and state unemployment insurance tax. The federal tax amounts to 6.2 percent of the first $7,000 earned by each worker.[24] In addition, states impose a tax above the $7,000 figure. The extra amount a company pays depends on its **experience rating**—lower percentages are charged to employers who have terminated fewer employees. The tax rate may fall to almost 0 percent in some states for employers that have had no recent experience (hence the term "experience rating") with downsizing and may rise to 10 percent for organizations with large numbers of layoffs.

Coverage

All workers except a few agricultural and domestic workers are currently covered by unemployment insurance (UI) laws. These covered workers (97% of the workforce), though, must still meet eligibility requirements to receive benefits:

1. You must meet the state requirements for wages earned or time worked during an established (one year) period of time referred to as a "base period." [In most states, this is usually the first four out of the last five completed calendar quarters prior to the time that your claim is filed.]
2. You must be determined to be unemployed through no fault of your own [determined under state law], and meet other eligibility requirements of state law.[25]

Duration

Until 1958, the maximum number of weeks any claimant could collect UI was 26 weeks. However, the 1958 and 1960–61 recessions yielded large numbers of claimants who exhausted their benefits, leading many states temporarily to revise upward the maximum benefit duration. In 2008 Congress enacted the Emergency Unemployment Compensation program (EUC08). The program provided additional weeks of benefits to long term unemployed, extending benefits to as long as 53 weeks.[26]

This program expired in 2013 and maximum benefits duration returned to 26 weeks. Because unemployment has fallen to under 6 percent in many states, there has been some state legislation to reduce duration to as low as 20 weeks.[27]

Weekly Benefit Amount

In general, benefits are based on a percentage of an individual's earnings over a recent 52-week period—up to the state maximum amount.[28] For example, in many states, the compensation will be half your earnings, up to a maximum amount. For example, New York State recently increased its minimum benefit rate to $100 and the maximum to $420 with provisions for annual increases in these figures.[29]

Controlling Unemployment Taxes

Every unemployed worker's **unemployment benefits** are "charged" against the firm or firms most recently employing that currently unemployed worker. The more money paid out on behalf of a firm, the higher is the unemployment insurance rate for that firm. Efforts to control these costs quite logically should begin with a well-designed **human resource planning system.** Realistic estimates of human resource needs will reduce the pattern of hasty hiring followed by morale-breaking terminations. Additionally, a benefit administrator should attempt to audit pre-layoff behavior (e.g., lateness, gross misconduct, absenteeism, illness, leaves of absence) and compliance with UI requirements after termination (e.g., job refusals can disqualify an unemployed worker). The government can also play an important part in reducing unemployment expenses by decreasing the number of weeks that people are unemployed. Research shows that unemployment duration decreases by three weeks simply by stepping up enforcement of sanctions against fraudulent claims.[30]

Family and Medical Leave Act (FMLA)

The 1993 **Family and Medical Leave Act** applies to all employers having 50 or more employees and entitles all eligible employees to receive unpaid leave up to 12 weeks per year for specified family or medical reasons.[31] Common reasons for leave under FMLA include caring for a newborn or seriously ill spouse, child, or parent.[32] More state legislatures are now moving toward some form of paid family and medical leave for workers.

Consolidated Omnibus Budget Reconciliation Act (COBRA)

In 1985 Congress enacted this law to provide current and former employees and their spouses and dependents with a temporary extension of group health insurance when coverage is lost due to qualifying events (e.g., layoffs). All employers with 20 or more employees must comply with COBRA. An employer may charge individuals up to 102 percent of the premium for coverage (100% premium plus 2% administration fee), which can extend up to 36 months (standard 18 months), depending on the category of the qualifying event.[33] The biggest concern for individuals getting health insurance under COBRA is the relatively brief qualifying period. After 18 months you're not eligible. With passage of the Affordable Care Act COBRA participants can opt into the Health Insurance Marketplace discussed in a later section.[34]

Health Insurance Portability and Accountability Act (HIPAA)

The 1996 HIPAA is designed to (1) lessen an employer's ability to deny coverage for a preexisting condition and (2) prohibit discrimination on the basis of health-related status.[35] Perhaps the most significant element of HIPAA began in 2002, when stringent new privacy provisions added considerable compliance problems for both the HR people charged with enforcement and the information technology people delegated the task of building secure health information systems. Just watch next time you visit a new doctor. You will have to sign a HIPPA document that, should you choose to read it, will make your eyes glaze over.

RETIREMENT AND SAVINGS PLAN PAYMENTS

Pensions have been around for a long, long time. The first plan was established in 1759 to protect widows and children of Presbyterian ministers. After decades of steady growth in private pension plan coverage, today only 68 percent of workers have access to pension coverage, and only 53 percent actually participate.[36]

Blame competitive pressures from globalization, the recession, and paltry growth in productivity, but the reality is that more than half of the population will depend on Social Security for retirement income. That represents a problem because employees tend to rank pensions as one of the more important benefits.[37] Let's face it, baby boomers are a huge part of the working population now. The first baby boomer turned 66 on January 1, 2012. Every day for the next two decades another 10,000 will be applying for Social Security and dreaming about what they will do in retirement.[38] Pensions play a big role in this dream. The importance of employer-provided retirement plans is evidenced by a study showing that employees with employer-provided retirement plans are more likely to have sufficient savings for a comfortable retirement than those who do not have these plans.[39] Two generic types of pension plans are discussed below: **defined benefit plans** and **defined contribution plans.** As you read their descriptions, keep in mind that defined benefit plans may be a dying breed.[40] Prominent companies such as IBM, Verizon, and Sears have frozen their traditional defined benefit pension payouts. Workers still get their pensions, but there isn't any growth in the amount as a function of additional time on the job. Rather, many companies are shifting to 401(k) plans (a popular type of defined contribution plan) where the dollar contribution is known and controllable.[41] Today 92 percent of private sector employers with pension plans offer defined contribution plans, compared to only 21 percent offering defined benefit plans.[42] To understand why this rapid change is occurring, we have to explain the cost saving distinctions between the two types of plans.

Defined Benefit Plans

In a defined benefit plan an employer agrees to provide a specific level of retirement pension, which is expressed as either a fixed dollar or a percentage-of-earnings amount that may vary (increase) with years of seniority in the company. The firm finances this obligation by following an actuarially determined benefit formula and making current payments that will yield the future pension benefit for a retiring employee.[43]

The majority of defined benefit plans calculate average earnings over the last 3 to 5 years of service for a prospective retiree and offer a pension that is about one-half this amount (varying from 30% to 80% percent) adjusted for years of seniority.

So what is it about defined benefit (DB) plans that make them prime targets for cost cutting? The major complaints by chief financial officers (CFOs) center on funding. If I've got to pay Jim $40,000 a year at retirement, I have to start investing now to have that cash available. How much should I invest though? Given how volatile the stock market is, it's hard to predict how much is needed. CFOs report this is a drag on corporate financial health and a distraction from running the core business. As an example, GM recently eliminated its defined benefit plan for salaried employees. New hires already were covered by a defined contribution (DC) plan. Now all salaried employees are enrolled in DC pension plans. Why? GM has an $12 billion shortfall in funding its pension. As one step to eliminate their pension burden, GM paid Prudential $2.5 billon dollars to takeover 25 percent of GM's pension burden.[44] What companies do is purchase annuities with insurance companies. GM has a total of 25 billion in annuities with Prudential. Verizon has a 7.5 billion dollar annuity, also with Prudential. Motorola and Bristol Meyers Squibb paid a combined 4.5 billion to Prudential to takeover all pension payments. These companies buy the annuity at a premium (often 10%). When interest rates fluctuate in the future, now these companies won't have to worry about significantly higher pension costs. the annuity stabilized the cost of their pension obligation.[45]

Defined Contribution Plans

In a defined contribution (DC) plan the employer makes provisions for contributions to an account set up for each participating employee. Years later when employees retire, the pension is based on their contributions, employer contributions, and any gains (or losses) in stock investments. There are three popular forms of defined contribution plans. A **401(k) plan,** so named for the section of the Internal Revenue Code describing the requirements, is a savings plan in which employees are allowed to defer pretax income. Employers typically match employee savings at a rate of 50 cents on the dollar.[46] Defined contribution plans are more popular than defined benefit plans in both small and large companies. Expect this disparity to only grow with time! The number of traditional plans continues to drop at a rapid rate.[47] Interestingly, for younger employees this shift may be one of those rare win-win situations. Historically these plans are faster to vest (the companies matched share of the contribution permanently shifts over to employee ownership, and they are more portable—job hopping employees can take their pension accruals along to the next job). On the negative side, the recession of 2008–2010 destroyed many 401(k) portfolios. Poor investment decisions, either by employees or by a chosen financial advisor, reduced many retirement funds by half or more. Further, these plans have been plagued by low contribution rates. About 40 percent of all employees don't contribute enough to get the full employer match.[48] The end result of all this is predictable. About two-thirds of Americans ages 45–60 say they plan to delay retirement, up from 42 percent just two years earlier.[49]

The second type of plan is an **employee stock ownership plan (ESOP).** In a basic ESOP a company makes a tax-deductible contribution of stock shares or cash to a trust. The trust then allocates company stock (or stock bought with cash contributions) to participating employee accounts. The amount allocated is based on employee earnings. When an ESOP is used as a pension vehicle (as opposed to an incentive program), the employees receive cash at retirement based upon the stock value at that time. ESOPs have one major disadvantage, which limits their utility for pension accumulations. Many employees are reluctant to "bet" most of their future retirement income on just one investment source. If the company's stock takes a downturn, the result can be catastrophic for employees approaching retirement age. A classic example of this comes from Enron . . . yes, the same Enron linked to all the ethics problems. Under Enron's 401(k), employees could elect to defer a portion of their salaries. The employees were given 19 different investment choices, one of which was Enron common stock. Enron matched contributions, up to 6 percent of an employee's compensation. Enron's contributions were made in Enron stock and had to be held until the employee was at least age 50. This feature resulted in 60 percent of the total plan value being in Enron stock in 2001. Guess what? When Enron's shares went through the floor in 2001–2002, thousands of employees saw their retirement nest eggs destroyed. Recently 401(k) contributions have shifted away from company stock. The majority (53%) of companies allow less than 10 percent of assets in company stock.[50]

Finally, a *profit-sharing* **plan** can be considered a defined contribution pension plan if the distribution of profits is delayed until retirement. Chapter 10 explains the basics of profit sharing.

Not surprisingly, both DB and DC compensation plans are subject to stringent tax laws. For **deferred compensation** to be exempt from current taxation, specific requirements must be met. To qualify, an employer cannot freely choose who will participate in the plan (hence it is labeled a **"qualified" deferred compensation plan**). This requirement eliminated the common practice of building tax-friendly, extravagant pension packages for executives and other highly compensated employees. The major advantage of a qualified plan is that the employer receives an income tax deduction for contributions made to the plan even though employees may not yet have received any benefits. The disadvantage arises in recruitment of high-talent executives. A plan will not qualify for tax exemptions if an employer pays high levels of deferred compensation to entice executives to the firm unless proportionate contributions also are made to lower-level employees.

A hybrid of defined benefit and defined contribution plans has emerged in recent years. **Cash balance plans** are defined benefit plans that look like a defined contribution plan. Employees have a hypothetical account (like a 401[k]) into which is deposited what is typically a percentage of annual compensation. The dollar amount grows both from contributions by the employer and from some predetermined interest rate (e.g., often set equal to the rate given on 30-year treasury certificates).

In 2009, 401(k) contributions were suspended by many companies in the wake of the suffering U.S. economy. General Motors, FedEx, Sears Holdings, and Eastman Kodak are among companies who suspended contributions. One ancillary problem from all these suspensions of pension plans—less money is going into the Pension Benefit Guaranty Corporation (the PBGC charges companies with pensions $49 dollars per person per year). That means less money to cover future bankruptcies and pension deficits. The PBGC already is running a 27 billion dollar deficit. The numbers are likely to get larger.[51]

Individual Retirement Accounts (IRAs)

An **individual retirement account (IRA)** is a tax-favored retirement savings plan that individuals can establish themselves. That's right, unlike the other pension options, IRAs don't require an employer to set them up. Even people not in the workforce can establish an IRA. Currently, IRAs are used mostly to store wealth accumulated in other retirement vehicles, rather than as a way to build new wealth.[52]

Employee Retirement Income Security Act (ERISA)

The early 1970s were a public relations and economic disaster for private pension plans. Many people who thought they were covered were the victims of complicated rules, insufficient funding, irresponsible financial management, and employer bankruptcies. Some pension funds, including both employer-managed and union-managed funds, were mismanaged; other pension plans required long vesting periods. The result was a pension system that left far too many lifelong workers poverty stricken. Enter the Employee Retirement Income Security Act in 1974 as a response to these problems.

ERISA does not require that employers offer a pension plan. But if a company decides to have one, it is rigidly controlled by ERISA provisions.[53] These provisions were designed to achieve two goals: (1) to protect the interest of approximately 100 million active participants,[54] and (2) to stimulate the growth of such plans. The actual success of ERISA in achieving these goals has been mixed at best. In the first two full years of operation (1975 and 1976) more than 13,000 pension plans were terminated. A major factor in these terminations, along with the recession, was ERISA. Employers complained about the excessive costs and paperwork of living under ERISA. Some disgruntled employers even claimed ERISA was an acronym for "Every Ridiculous Idea Since Adam." To examine the merits of these claims, let us take a closer look at the major requirements of ERISA.

General Requirements

ERISA requires that employees be eligible for pension plans beginning at age 21. Employers may require 12 months of service as a precondition for participation. The service requirement may be extended to three years if the pension plan offers full and immediate vesting.

Vesting and Portability

These two concepts are sometimes confused but have very different meanings in practice. **Vesting** refers to the length of time an employee must work for an employer before he or she is entitled to employer payments made into the pension plan. The vesting concept has two components. First, any contributions made by the employee to a pension fund are immediately and irrevocably vested. The vesting right becomes questionable only with respect to the employer's contributions. The Economic Growth and Tax Relief Reconciliation Act of 2001 states that the employer's contribution must vest at least as quickly as one of the following two formulas: (1) full vesting after three years (down from five years previously) or (2) 20 percent after two years (down from three years) and 20 percent each year thereafter, resulting in full vesting after six years (down from seven years).

The vesting schedule an employer uses is often a function of the demographic makeup of the workforce. An employer who experiences high turnover may wish to use the three-year service schedule. By so doing, any employee with less than three years' service at time of termination receives no vested benefits. Or the employer may use the second schedule in the hopes that earlier benefit accrual will reduce undesired turnover. The strategy adopted is, therefore, dependent on organizational goals and workforce characteristics.

Portability of pension benefits becomes an issue for employees moving to new organizations. Should pension assets accompany the transferring employee in some fashion?[55] ERISA does not require mandatory portability of private pensions. On a voluntary basis, though, the employer may agree to let an employee's pension benefits transfer to the new employer. For an employer to permit portability, of course, the pension rights must be vested.

Pension Benefit Guaranty Corporation

Despite the wealth of constraints imposed by ERISA, the potential still exists for an organization to go bankrupt or in some way fail to meet its vested pension obligations. We guarantee you, there are many Eastman Kodak employees who lose sleep over this issue! To protect individuals confronted by this problem, employers are required to pay insurance premiums to the **Pension Benefit Guaranty Corporation (PBGC)** established by ERISA. In turn, the PBGC guarantees payment of vested benefits to employees formerly covered by terminated pension plans. Over 40 million people depend on the PBGC to protect 1.5 trillion dollars in pension benefits. In 2008 the PBGC had deficits of 11.2 billion dollars.[56] Today that deficit is 27 billion.[57]

Pension Protection Act of 2006 (PPA)

You remember Enron? Maybe you didn't know that many Enron employees lost more than their jobs. As we noted earlier, many employees had pension funds allocated to Enron stock. When the stock went through the floor, so did many retirement dreams. The PPA was passed by Congress in the wake of Enron and WorldCom. Its purpose was to protect employees' retirement income as well as transfer some responsibility for retirement savings from the employer to the employee. A key provision of the law allows employees in publicly traded companies the freedom to sell off any employer stock purchased through deferrals or after-tax contributions. We expect this provision will motivate employees toward investing in defined contribution plans and reduce some of the burden on employers. The law also aims at employers who fail to set aside enough reserves to cover current and future pension obligations by defining plans less than 70% funded as 'at risk' plans.

How Much Retirement Income to Provide?

The level of pension a company chooses to offer depends on the answers to five questions. First, what level of retirement compensation would a company like to set as a target, expressed in relation to pre-retirement earnings? Second, should Social Security payments be factored in when considering the level of income an employee should have during retirement? One integration approach reduces normal benefits by a percentage (usually 50%) of Social Security benefits.[58] Another feature employs a more liberal benefit formula on earnings that exceed the maximum income taxed by Social Security. Regardless of the formula used, about one-half of U.S. companies do not employ the cost-cutting strategy. Once a company has targeted the level of income it wants to provide employees in retirement, it makes sense to design a system that integrates private pension and social security to achieve that goal. Any other strategy is not cost-effective.

Third, should other postretirement income sources (e.g., savings plans that are partially funded by employer contributions) be integrated with the pension payment? Fourth, a company must decide how to factor seniority into the payout formula. The larger the role played by seniority, the more important pensions will be in retaining employees. Most companies believe that the maximum pension payout for a particular level of earnings should be achieved only by employees who have spent an entire career with the company (e.g., 30 to 35 years). As Exhibit 13.7 vividly illustrates, job hoppers are hurt financially by this type of strategy. In our example—a very plausible scenario—job hopping cuts final pension amounts in half.

Finally, companies must decide what they can afford. In recent years the press has printed dozens of stories about companies having a hard time funding their pension plans. Similar problems are on the public sector horizon. Between 2000 and 2004 average state and local benefit amounts grew 37 percent to $19,875. States also are allowing their employees to retire younger, often as early as 55. Estimates suggest

EXHIBIT 13.7 The High Cost of Job Hopping*

Career History	Years in Company	Percent of Salary for Pension		Salary at Company (Final)	Annual Pension
Sam					
Job 1	10	10%		$ 35,817	= $ 3,582
Job 2	10	10%	×	$ 64,143	= 6,414
Job 3	10	10%	×	$114,870	= 11,487
Job 4	10	10%	×	$205,714	= 20,571
Total pension					$42,054
Ann					
Job 1	40		×	$205,714	= $82,286
Total pension					$82,286

Source: Federal Reserve Bank of Boston.

*Assumptions: (1) Starting Salary of $20,000 with 6 percent annual inflation rate. (2) Both employees receive annual increases equal to inflation rate. (3) Pensions based on 1 percentage point (of salary) for each year of service multiplied by final salary at time of exit from company.

federal, state, and local governments are underfunding pensions by somewhere between .7 and 2.5 trillion dollars.[59] Don't count on your taxes being cut any time soon!

LIFE INSURANCE

Roughly three-fourths of all employees have access to paid life insurance, and this figure is about the same in both the private and public sectors.[60] Typical coverage would be a group term insurance policy with a face value of one to two times the employee's annual salary.[61] Most plan premiums are paid completely by the employer.[62] The cost is about ten cents per hour per employee.[63] Slightly over 30 percent include retiree coverage. To discourage turnover, almost all companies make this benefit forfeitable at the time of departure from the company.

Life insurance is one of the benefits heavily affected by movement to a flexible benefit program. Flexibility is introduced by providing a core of basic life coverage (e.g., $25,000). The option then exists to choose greater coverage (usually in increments of $10,000 to $25,000) as part of the optional package.

MEDICAL AND MEDICALLY RELATED PAYMENTS

General Health Care

Health-care costs continue to increase. Exhibit 13.8 shows the dollar increase over time. More costly technology, the explosion of lawsuits, the increased number of elderly people, and a system that does not encourage cost savings have all contributed to

EXHIBIT 13.8 Health-Care Costs per Employee 1999–2014

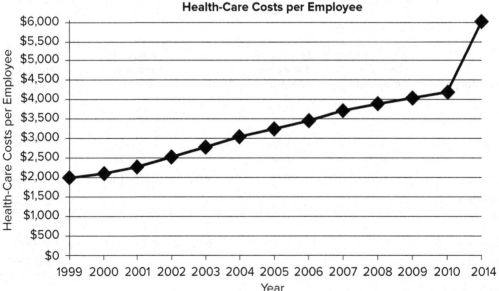

Source: U.S. Department of Labor, Bureau of Labor Statistics, www.bls.gov; Kaiser Family Foundation 2014 Employer Health Benefits 2014 annual survey.

the rapidly rising costs of medical insurance. In the past 15 years, though, employers have battled these rises. Despite these efforts, companies like GM figure about $1,500 toward the price of every car they manufacture comes from health-care costs. Comparatively, steel in the same cars costs less! Is it any wonder that companies across the country are seeking ways to cut healthcare costs or eliminate them completely from their benefits package. After a discussion of the types of health-care systems, these cost-cutting strategies will be discussed.

Before 1930 health care coverage essentially didn't exist. Health issues were the responsibility of the family. After the Great Depression, though, Blue Cross (BC) and Blue Shield (BS) appeared as the first institutional health care. Envious of the profits made by BC/BS, insurance companies began to offer plans for hospitalization along with doctor and surgical coverage. Then, of course, the government got involved. In the 1960s national health insurance emerged to cover the elderly (Medicare) and the poor (Medicaid). Then in 2012 the Affordable Care Act (ACA aka Obamacare) was instituted to target the uninsured with a goal of providing health care coverage to everyone. This controversial act isn't intended to change the way health care is delivered, but rather to provide both positive and negative incentives to make sure everyone is covered. Exhibit 13.9 outlines the ACA in 200 words or less. Here goes:

Some of the most dire predictions of "Obamacare" haven't occurred. First, it was predicted that large premium increases to employers would cause employers to decrease employment. Insurance premiums in the first full year of the plan rose only 3 percent, the lowest increase in 16 years.[65] It also was feared that many individuals would face the noncompliance fine. Actually, fewer than 10 percent

EXHIBIT 13.9 The Affordable Care Act in 200 Words or Less

1. If you have health coverage and it makes you smile, keep it.
2. If you don't have coverage you can use the new Health Insurance Marketplace to buy a private plan (like Blue Cross/Blue Shield or an HMO).
3. If you qualify (family size and income) you may get lower costs on premiums and out of pocket medical expenses.
4. You may also qualify for free or low cost coverage under Medicaid or Children's Health Insurance Program.
5. If you have coverage already and want to consider changing based on looking at Marketplace plans, you can. If, however, you have an offer of insurance from your employer, you may not be able to get lower costs based on your income. It depends on whether the employer coverage is considered affordable (costs less than 9.5% of an employee's household income) and meets minimum standards (covers more than 60% of plan cost).
6. A large employer who doesn't offer health care coverage for all full-time employees is taxed $2000 × N − 30 (N = number employees) per year.
7. Individuals must purchase a plan either through their employer, through private companies or through state-mandated insurance programs. Failure to do so results in a 2016 tax of $695 per adult (half that for children) up to a family maximum of $2085 (or 2.5% of family income, whichever is greater)
8. Any company with too good a plan (more than $10,200 individual or $27,500 family cost) pays a 40 percent "Cadillac tax" so named because the big three automakers are prime targets.[66]

of uninsured are likely to be fined, largely because the Obama administration has increased the number of exemptions permitted (e.g., exempt if electricity has been cut off for non payment).

The Affordable Care Act hasn't changed the basic underlying structure of health care delivery. The first method is through commercial insurance companies like Prudential, Aetna and Humana. Plans through these companies are called indemnity plans or so-called pay for service plans. Under these plans an employee can choose any health care provider. The second method of delivery is through a Health Maintenance Organization (HMO). An HMO pulls together a group of providers (e.g., hospitals and doctors) willing to provide services at an agreed upon rate in exchange for the employer limiting employees to these providers for health services. Employees make prepayments in exchange for guaranteed health care services on demand. Third, to provide employees with more options in selecting doctors and hospitals, Preferred Provider Organizations (PPOs) arose. Employers select certain providers who agree to provide price discounts and submit to strict utilization controls (e.g., strict standards on number of diagnostic tests that can be ordered). In turn, the employer influences employees to use these providers by charging higher fees if employees make selections outside the provider network. Finally, a **point-of-service plan (POS)** is a hybrid plan combining HMO and PPO benefits. The POS plan permits an individual to choose which plan to seek treatment from at the time that services are needed. POS plans, therefore, provide the economic benefits of the HMO with the freedom of the PPO. The HMO component of the POS plan requires office visits to an assigned primary care physician, with the alternative of receiving treatment through the PPO component. The PPO component does not require the individual to first contact the primary care physician but does require that in-network physicians be used. When POS plan participants receive all of their care from physicians in the network, they are fully covered, as they would be under a traditional HMO. Point-of-service plans also allow individuals to see a doctor outside the network, for which payment of an annual deductible ranging between $100 and $5,000 is required.[64]

Costs and participation rates of each type of plan are noted in Exhibit 13.10.

EXHIBIT 13.10
Cost and Participation Rates in Health care Plans

	Premium Paid	
	By Employee	**By Employer**
HMO	1182	5041
PPO	1134	5082
POS	984	5182

Enrollment by Plan Type	
PPO	58%
HMO	13
POS	8
Conventional (indemnity)	< 1

Health Care: Cost Control Strategies

There are three general strategies available to benefit managers for controlling the rapidly escalating costs of health care.[67] First, organizations can motivate employees to change their demand for health care, through changes in either the design or the administration of health insurance policies. Included in this category of control strategies are (1) deductibles, or the first x dollars of health-care cost are paid by the employee (at the extreme the state of Georgia recently told employees that certain name brand drugs will require a $100 copay, clearly signaling that enough is enough[68]); (2) coinsurance rates (premium payments are shared by the company and employee); (3) maximum benefits (defining a maximum payout schedule for specific health problems); (4) coordination of benefits (ensure no double payment when coverage exists under the employee's plan and a spouse's plan); (5) auditing of hospital charges for accuracy; (6) requiring preauthorization for selected visits to health-care facilities; (7) mandatory second opinion whenever surgery is recommended; (8) using intranet technology to allow employees access to online benefit information, saving some of the cost of benefit specialists[69]; (9) providing incentives to employees for using providers who meet certain high performance criteria.[70] The more questions answered online, the fewer specialists needed.

The second general cost control strategy involves changing the structure of healthcare delivery systems and participating in business coalitions (for data collection and dissemination). At the extreme are companies that simply decline to provide any health-care coverage whatsoever.

Less extreme are choices like HMOs, PPOs, POSs, and consumer-directed healthcare plans. Also called Consumer Driven Health Plans and High Deductible Plans, this increasingly popular option for companies cuts costs by shifting much of the burden of purchasing health care over to employees. Employees choose from any of the traditional providers (HMO, PPO, Indemnity Plans), but the employer sets its contribution equal to the lower cost of these three (usually HMO). If the employee wants a more expensive option, the extra cost is out-of-pocket. These plans usually are accompanied by high deductibles, sometimes reaching several thousand dollars.[71] Typically an employer helps lessen the cost of the deductible by setting up Health Savings (HSA) or Health Reimbursement (HRA) accounts. Funds in these accounts are either contributed by employees with pre-tax dollars (HSA) or by the employer up to some fixed dollar amount (HRA). All of this complexity is introduced simply to force employees to make choices in the most economical way while hopefully not neglecting important health issues.

A final category of cost control strategies links incentives to healthy behaviors. We know that preventable illnesses account for 70 percent of all health-care costs.[72] Obesity, for example, is preventable. Dieting, however, is not a favorite pastime. How, then, do we get people to lose weight? The answer may be health incentives. For example, Caesar's Casinos give a 40 dollar award to employees who get screened to measure cholesterol level and then work (e.g., lose weight) to lower levels. More than two-thirds of medium and large employers with wellness programs have incentives to get employees involved in wellness.[73] JetBlue provides a maximum of $400 in Health Reimbursement Accounts to be used by employees in roughly 45 activities (e.g., smoking cessation). On the negative incentive side, CVS drugstores charge employees $600 more in health premiums for not completing wellness assessment activities like annual checkups. In general, incentives are becoming much more popular. In 2009 only 57 percent of companies had any of these incentive. Now 75 percent use these motivational tools.[74]

> **e-Compensation**
> The Health Insurance Association of America provides research about a wide variety of specific health-related issues at its website, www.ahip.org/

Short- and Long-Term Disability

A number of benefit options provide some form of protection for disability. For example, workers' compensation covers disabilities that are work-related. Even Social Security has provisions for disability income to those who qualify. Beyond these two legally required sources, there are two private sources of disability income: employee **salary continuation plans** and **long-term disability plans.**[75]

Many companies have some form of salary continuation plan (we include here vacation days that might be used for sick leave as a last resort) that pays out varying levels of income depending on duration of illness (see Exhibit 13.11).

At one extreme is short-term illness covered by sick leave policy and typically reimbursed at a level equal to 100 percent of salary.[76] The most prevalent practice these days is to give paid time off (PTO) rather than sick days. This reduces the need for companies to "police" whether employees are indeed sick, and allows employees more flexibility in life planning. After such benefits run out, disability benefits become operative. **Short-term disability (STD)** pays a percentage of your salary (about 60% on average) for temporary disability because of sickness or injury (on-the-job injuries are covered by workers' compensation). Only about 37 percent of all employers provide this insurance after sick leave.[77] **Long-term disability plans (LTD),** if available, typically kick in after the short-term plan expires. Long-term disability is usually underwritten by insurance firms and provides 60 to 70 percent of pre-disability pay for a period varying between two years and life.[78] Estimates

EXHIBIT 13.11   Access to Leave Programs

Percent of Workers in Private Industry/State Local Government with Access to Different Leave Programs		
Type of Leave	**Private Industry %**	**State/Local Government %**
Paid Sick Leave	61	80
Paid Vacation	77	59
Short Term Disability	All workers 37	
Long Term Disability	All workers 34	

Source: National Compensation Survey, 2014. http://www.bls.gov/ncs/ebs/benefits/2014/ebbl0055.pdf.

indicate that only about 34 percent of all U.S. businesses provide long-term disability insurance.[79]

Dental Insurance

A rarity 30 years ago, dental insurance is now much more prevalent, with about 60 percent of all employers with more than 500 employees providing some level of coverage.[80] In many respects dental care coverage follows the model originated in health-care plans. The dental equivalent of HMOs and PPOs is the standard delivery system. For example, a dental HMO enlists a group of dentists who agree to treat company employees in return for a fixed monthly fee per employee.

At the start of the century, the typical cost for employee dental coverage was $219.[81] Annual cost increases now, though, are beginning to heat up. Employers battle these increases by requiring employee contributions—94 percent of employers require cost sharing now.[82] The relatively modest increase in dental care costs can be traced to stringent cost control strategies (e.g., plan maximum payouts are typically $1,000 or less per year) and an excess supply of dentists. As the excess turns into a predicted shortage in the coming years, we may expect dental benefit costs to grow at a faster rate.[83]

Vision Care

Vision care dates back only to the 1976 contract between the United States Auto Workers and the Big Three automakers. Since then, this benefit has spread to other auto-related industries and parts of the public sector. Seventy-eight percent of large employers offer a vision plan.[84] Most plans are noncontributory and usually cover partial costs of eye examination, lenses, and frames.

MISCELLANEOUS BENEFITS

Paid Time Off During Working Hours

Paid rest periods, lunch periods, wash-up time, travel time, clothes-change time, and get-ready time benefits are self-explanatory.

Payment for Time Not Worked

Included within this category are several self-explanatory benefits:

1. Paid vacations and payments in lieu of vacation
2. Payments for holidays not worked
3. Paid sick leave
4. Other (payments for National Guard, Army, or other reserve duty; jury duty and voting pay allowances; payments for time lost due to death in the family or other personal reasons).

Exhibit 13.12 shows what you can look forward to for vacations after you graduate. Stay in school!

Twenty years ago it was relatively rare to grant time off for anything but vacations, holidays, and sick leave. Now many organizations have a policy of ensuring payments

EXHIBIT 13.12 Employees Receiving Leave Time Benefits

Employee Benefits Paid Time Off	All Full-Time Employees	Professional, Technical, and Related Employees	Office and Administrative Employees	Blue Collar / Construction Employees
Holidays	75%	89%	79%	83%
Vacation	77	88	68	81

Source: Employee Benefits Survey, http://www.bls.gov/news.release/ebs2.t06.htm, visited April 29, 2015.

for civic responsibilities and other obligations. Any outside pay for such civic duties (e.g., jury duty) is usually nominal, so companies often supplement this pay, frequently to the level of 100 percent of wages lost. There is also increasing coverage for parental leaves. Maternity and, to a lesser extent, paternity leaves are much more common than they were 25 years ago. Indeed, passage of the Family and Medical Leave Act in 1993 provides up to 12 weeks of unpaid leave (with guaranteed job protection) for the birth or adoption of a child or for the care of a family member with a serious illness. The following sick policy, taken from Motley Fool's employee manual, shows just how far such policies have come:

> Unlike other companies, The Motley Fool doesn't make you wait for six months before accruing vacation or sick time. Heck, if you're infected with some disgusting virus—stay home! We like you, but don't really want to share in your personal anguish. In other words, if you're bleeding out your eyes and coughing up a lung—don't be a hero! Stay home. Out of simple Foolish courtesy, we expect you to call your supervisor and let him or her know you won't be in. And yes, you will get paid. So, pop quiz: You're feeling like you're going to snap any moment if you don't take some personal time off, you've made a small deposit on an M-16 rifle and are scoping out local clock towers, BUT you've only been a paid Fool for a short time . . . what do you do, what do you do?[85]

Many companies are switching from **traditional time-off plans (TTO),** as described above, to **paid-time-off (PTO) plans.** These lump all time off together into one total allotment and deduct any day missed from this bank. Not only is this administratively easier for companies to track, but it also eliminates the need for employees to lie and say they're sick when the reality is, for example, a scheduled dentist appointment.[86]

Child Care

Relatively few companies directly provide child care. However, it's becoming quite common for employers (96%) to offer flexible spending accounts with child care expenditures as a legitimate expense.[87] The employee, employer, or both pay into an account with pre-tax monies, and individuals can then use these funds to pay local child care providers.

Elder Care

With longer life expectancy than ever before and the aging of the baby-boom generation, one benefit that will become increasingly important is elder care assistance. Almost one-half of the companies offering child care assistance to employees also offer elder care assistance.[88]

Domestic Partner Benefits

Domestic partner benefits are benefits that are voluntarily offered by employers to an employee's unmarried partner, whether of the same or opposite sex. The major reasons motivating U.S. corporations to provide domestic partner benefits include fairness to all employees regardless of their sexual orientation or marital status.

Legal Insurance

Prior to the 1970s, prepaid legal insurance was practically nonexistent. Even though such coverage was offered only by approximately 7 percent of all employers in 1997, that percentage has more than tripled in the past decade (24%).[89] A majority of plans provide routine legal services (e.g., divorce, real estate matters, wills, traffic violations) but exclude provisions covering felony crimes, largely because of the expense and potential for bad publicity. Keep in mind, though, that most legal insurance premiums are paid by the employee, not the employer. Technically, then, this doesn't qualify as a traditional employee benefit.

BENEFITS FOR CONTINGENT WORKERS

Depending on what definition we use, **contingent workers** represent between 5 and 35 percent of the workforce. Ninety percent of all employers use some contingent workers.[90] Contingent work relationships include working through a temporary help agency, working for a contract company, working on call, and working as an independent contractor. Both to reduce costs (because benefits are reduced to 50% of what full-time workers receive) and to permit easier expansion and contraction of production/services, contracting offers a viable way to meet rapidly changing environmental conditions.

Your Turn   Adapting Benefits to a Changing Strategy

McDonald's is in the news quite a bit these days. As profits fall or fail to meet Wall Street expectations, senior management scrambles for answers to a changing environment: millennials are perceived to prefer products that are healthier; customers complain about long wait times in the drive thru; competitors offer burgers made to order that seem to resonate with today's customers. In response McDonald's has made a number of major changes. It is reducing the size of its menu to reduce the amount of preparation time. On the other hand, they have introduced a new kiosk environment where customers can build their own burger at the cost of a rise in wait time of several minutes. In addition, over the past years McDonald's has worked hard to reduce its turnover. Among other efforts they have moved their average employee age up to the high 20s. They recently announced wage increases and more paid time off for all its corporately owned stores. Given what we've told you here and what you can glean from news reports about McDonald's, what do you think is going on? Specifically, how do corporate strategy and wage/benefit decisions either support or conflict with each other?

Summary

Since the 1940s, employee benefits have been the most volatile area in the compensation field. From 1940 to 1980, dramatic changes came in the form of more and better types of employee benefits. The result should not have been unexpected. Employee benefits are now a major, and many believe prohibitive, component of doing business. Look for this century to be dominated by cost-saving efforts to improve the competitive position of American industry. A part of these cost savings will come from tighter administrative controls on existing benefit packages. But another part, as already seen in the auto industry, may come from a reduction in existing benefit packages. If this does evolve as a trend, benefit administrators will need to develop a mechanism for identifying employee preferences (in this case "least preferences") and use them as a guideline to meet agreed upon savings targets.

Review Questions

1. James A. Klingon has a mandate from his boss to cut employee benefit costs. In a company expanding by 10 percent in employees every year, Jim decides to control costs through his selection strategy. Is he crazy? Or crazy like a fox? Explain.

2. Explain the concept of experience rating using examples from unemployment insurance. Would the same concept apply to workers' compensation? Using the Internet, find out if experience rating plays a role in insurance coverage.

3. The CEO of Krinkle Forms Inc says there is a serious problem with turnover, with data for her observation provided below.

Seniority	Turnover Rate
0–2 yrs	61%
2–5 yrs	21%
5+yrs	9%

The CEO wants to use employee benefits to lessen this problem. Before agreeing to look at this as the solution, what should run through your mind as a trained professional? What might you do, specifically, in the areas of pension vesting, vacation and holiday allocation, and life insurance coverage in the effort to reduce turnover?

4. Why are defined contribution pension plans gaining in popularity in the United States and defined benefit plans losing popularity?

5. Some experts argue that consumer-directed health care is, amongst other things, a great communications tool for employee benefits. Defend this position.

Endnotes

1. R. McCaffery, *Managing the Employee Benefits Program* (New York: American Management Association, 1972), pp. 1–2.

2. Lisa Cornwell, "Some Employers Charge Smokers More for Health Insurance," *Buffalo News,* February 17, 2006, pp. D1, 8.

3. www.lung.org, visited April 6, 2012.

4. Ann Zimmerman, Robert Matthews, and Kris Hudson, "Can Employers Alter Hiring Policies to Cut Health Costs?" *The Wall Street Journal,* October 17, 2005, p. B1.

5. Ibid.

6. Stephen Miller, "HR, Employees Vary on Job Satisfaction," *HR Magazine* 52(8), August 2007, pp. 23–27.

7. www.mcdonalds.com, visited April 6, 2012.

8. Lydell Bridgeford, "CEOs in the Dark on Employees' Benefits Preferences," *Employee Benefits News,* September 1, 2006, pp. 12, 17.

9. U.S. Chamber of Commerce, *Employee Benefits,* 2014 edition (Washington, DC: Chamber of Commerce, 2014).

10. National Academy of Social Insurance, *Workers' Compensation: Benefits, Coverage and Costs* (Washington, DC: National Academy of Social Insurance, August 2014), p. 1.

11. National Academy of Social Insurance, Worker's Compensation: Benefits, Coverage, and Costs (Washington, DC: National Academy of Social Insurance, August 2014), p. 1.

12. http://www.wcb.ny.gov/content/main/Employers/getInsurance.jsp.

13. National Academy of Social Insurance, *Worker's Compensation: Benefits, Coverage, and Costs* (Washington, DC: National Academy of Social Insurance, August 2014), p. 1.

14. New York State Workers Compensation Board, *www.wcb.state.ny.us/content/main/onthejob/CashBenefits.jsp ,* visited April 22, 2015.

15. http://www.nasi.org/sites/default/files/research/NASI_Work_Comp_Year_2014.pdf, visited April 22, 2015.

16. Employee Benefit Research Institute, *Fundamentals of Employee Benefit Programs* (Washington, DC: EBRI, 2011).

17. www.ebri.org, visited April 22, 2015.

18. William J. Cohen, "The Evolution and Growth of Social Security," in *Federal Policies and Worker Status Since the Thirties,* J. P. Goldberg, E. Ahern, W. Haber, and R. A. Oswald, eds. (Madison, WI: Industrial Relations Research Association, 1976), p. 62.

19. http://www.ssa.gov/OP_Home/handbook/handbook.01/handbook-0100.html, visited April 22, 2015.

20. Social Security (Old-Age, Survivors, and Disability Insurance), *www.ssa.gov/policy/docs/statcomps/supplement/2002/oasdi.pdf,* May 15, 2003.

21. Thomas H. Paine, "Alternative Ways to Fix Social Security," *Benefits Quarterly,* Third Quarter 1997, pp. 14–18.

22. http://www.forbes.com/sites/kotlikoff/2015/04/14/social-security-qa-how-much-work-is-necessary-to-qualify-for-social-security/, visited April 24, 2015.

23. http://www.ssa.gov/OACT/COLA/examplemax.html, visited April 24, 2015.

24. http://www.workforcesecurity.doleta.gov/unemploy/uitaxtopic.asp, visited April 24, 2015.

25. Ibid.

26. Staff, "Introduction to Unemployment Insurance." Center on Budget and Policy Priorities, www.cbpp.org/cms/index.cfm?fa=view&id=1466.

27. Jake Grovum, "How Unemployment Benefit Cuts Will Affect Your State," *USA TODAY,* December 20, 2013. statehttp://www.usatoday.com/story/news/nation/2013/12/20/stateline-unemployment-benefit-cuts/4140761/, visited April 24, 2015. Unemployment-Extension.org., Some States Reducing Benefit Amounts Along with Duration of Benefits, http://www.unemployment-extension.org/more-states-cutting-unemployment-benefits-as-jobless-claims-edge-upward.php, visited April 24, 2015.

28. U.S. Department of Labor, www.workforcesecurity.doleta.gov/uitaxtopic.asp, visited May 15, 2003.

29. http://www.labor.ny.gov/formsdocs/ui/p823-english.pdf, visited April 24, 2015.

30. http://www.dol.gov/whd/fmla/, visited April 24, 2015.

31. Employee Benefit Research Institute, *Fundamentals of Employee Benefit Programs* (Washington, DC: EBRI, 2009).

32. http://www.dol.gov/whd/fmla/, visited April 24, 2015.

33. "Continuation of Health Coverage—COBRA," http://www.dol.gov/dol/topic/health-plans/cobra.htm.

34. U.S. Department of Labor, Employee Benefits Security Administration, *www.dol.gov/ebsa,* August 18, 2009.

35. U.S. Department of Health and Human Services, *http://www.hhs.gov/ocr/privacy/index.html,* February 5, 2009.

36. T. Harkin, "The Retirement Crisis and a Plan to Solve It," U.S. Senate Committee on Health, Education, Labor and Pensions, 2012.

37. Aon survey, "Employees Value Basic Benefits Most," *Best's Review,* 103(4), 2002, pp. 1527–1534.

38. http://crosscut.com/2012/04/06/econ-finance/22178/How-boomers-will-change-retirement-and-jobless-rates/, visited April 10, 2012.

39. IOMA, "Managing 401(k) Plans," Institute of Management & Administration (Newark, NJ: BNA Subsidiaries, August 2000).

40. Gordon Clark and Ashby Monk, "Conceptualizing the Defined Benefit Pension Promise," *Benefits Quarterly,* July 2007, pp. 7–26.

41. Ellen E. Schultz and Theo Francis, "How Safe Is Your Pension," *The Wall Street Journal,* January 12, 2006, pp. B1, B3.

42. Bashker D. Biswas, *A guide to Employee Benefits Design and Planning* (Upper Saddle river, NJ: Pearson Educaton, 2014). www.bls.gov/ncs/ebs/benefits/2011/ownership/civilian/table02a.pdf; visited April 10, 2012.

43. Employee Benefit Research Institute, *Fundamentals of Employee Benefit Programs* (Washington, DC: EBRI, 1997), pp. 69–73.

44. http://www.gurufocus.com/news/330501/thoughts-on-gms-2014 visited April 27, 2015.

45. Vipal Monga, "Pension Dropouts Cause Pinch," Wall Street Journal, October 7, 2014, p. B7.

46. "Employee Benefits News," *Benefits Marketplace* 22(16), 2009, pp. 19–22.

47. Jim Morris, "The Changing Pension Landscape," *Compensation & Benefits Review* 37(5), 2005, pp. 30–35.

48. www.401k.org/ visited April 11, 2012.

49. Lauren Weber, "Americans Rip Up Retirement Plans," *Wall Street Journal,* February 1, 2013, p. B1.

50. www.ebri.org/publications/benfaq/index.cfm?fa=retfaq14, visited April 11, 2012.

51. Vipal Monga, "Pension Dropouts Cause Pinch," *Wall Street Journal,* October 7, 2014, p. B7.

52. Employee Benefit Research Institute, "EBRI Research Highlights: Retirement Benefit," Special Report SR-42 (Washington, DC: EBRI, June 2003).

53. In 2001, the Economic Growth and Tax Relief Reconciliation Act of 2001 was passed. This act replaced some of the aspects of the original ERISA and came into effect for plans starting after December 31, 2001.

54. Employee Benefit Research Institute, *Fundamentals of Employee Benefit Programs* (Washington, DC: EBRI, 2009).

55. Stuart Dorsey, "Pension Portability and Labor Market Efficiency: A Survey of the Literature," *Industrial and Labor Relations Review,* January 1, 1995, pp. 43–58.

56. Amir Efrati and Jeffrey McCracken, "PBGC Stakes Claim in Bankruptcy Case," *The Wall Street Journal* 253(11), January 14, 2009, p. C3.

57. Vipal Monga, "Pension Dropouts Cause Pinch," *Wall Street Journal,* October 7, 2014, p. B7.

58. Burton T. Beam and John J. McFadden, *Employee Benefit 5* (Chicago, IL: Dearborn Financial Publishing, 1992).

59. Douglas J. Elliott, "Potential Federal Roles in Dealing with State and Local Pension Problems," The Brookings Institution, 2012, www.brookings.edu/papers/2011/0512_pension_crisis_elliott.aspx.

60. U.S. Department of Labor, Bureau of Labor Statistics, "Table 5: Life Insurance Benefits: Access, Participation, and Take-Up Rates," *www.bls.gov/news.release/ebs2.t05.htm,* April 11, 2014.

61. Ibid.

62. Employee Benefit Research Institute, *Fundamentals of Employee Benefit Programs* (Washington, DC: EBRI, 2009).

63. Bureau of Labor Statistics, "Employer Costs for Employee Compensation," December 2014, Bureau of Labor Statistics USDL-15-1386.

64. Bashker D. Biswas, *A Guide to Employee Benefits Design and Planning* (Upper Saddle river, NJ: Pearson Education, 2014).

65. Alex Wayne and Thomas Black, "Prediction That Health Care ACG Would Hurt Corporate America Doesn't Come True," Buffalo News, October 17, 2014, p. A6.

66. Christina Rogers, "Cadillac Tax Imperils UAW's Health Benefits," *Wall Street Journal,* March 25, 2015, p. B1.

67. S. Smith, "New Trends in Health Care Cost Control," *Compensation and Benefits Review,* January 2002, pp. 38–44; Regina Herzlinger and Jeffrey Schwartz, "How Companies Tackle Health Care Costs: Part I," *Harvard Business Review,* July–August 1985, pp. 69–81.

68. Tracey Walker, "Benefit Designs Continue to Evolve," *Managed Healthcare Executive* 15(9), 2005, p. 9.

69. "GE Workers Plan Strike over Benefit Cost-Shifting," *Business Insurance,* January 6, 2003, pp. 23–26.

70. Bashker D. Biswas, *A Guide to Employee Benefits Design and Planning* (Upper Saddle river, NJ: Pearson Educaton, 2014).

71. EBRI, "Characteristics of the Population with Consumer-Driven and High-Deductible Health Plans, 2005–2012," and "Retirement Plan Participation and Asset Allocation, 2010". Employee Benefits Research Institute, April 2013, Vol. 34, No. 4.

72. Barry Hall, "Health Incentives: The Science and Art of Motivating Healthy Behaviors," *Benefits Quarterly,* 2008 (second quarter), pp. 12–22.

73. Stephanie Armour, "CEO's Say Federal Limits Are Ailing Wellness Programs," *Wall Street Journal,* September, 4, 2014, p. B3.

74. Lauren Weber, "A Health Check for Wellness Programs," *Wall Street Journal,* October 8, 2014, p. B1.

75. The Health Insurance Association of America provides research about a wide variety of specific health-related issues at its website, *www.hiaa.org/pubs/.*

76. Employee Benefit Research Institute, *Fundamentals of Employee Benefit Programs* (Washington, DC: EBRI, 2009).

77. U.S. Department of Labor, *www.dol.gov/,* February 6, 2009.

78. Ibid.

79. U.S. Department of Labor, 2012, *www.dol.gov/* visited April 11, 2012.

80. Mercer Human Resources Consulting. *National Survey of Employer-Sponsored Health Plans: 2005 Survey Report* (New York: Mercer Human Resources Consulting, 2006).

81. U.S. Chamber of Commerce, "1999 Employee Benefits Survey," 2000, p. 10.

82. Hewitt Associates LLC, *Salaried Employee Benefits Provided by Major U.S. Employers 2005–2006* (Lincolnshire, IL: Hewitt Associates LLC, 2006).

83. T. Dolatowski, "Buying Dental Benefits," Delta Dental, *www.deltadental.com,* August 18, 2009.

84. Ibid.

85. The Motley Fool, "The Fool Rules! A Global Guide to Foolish Behavior," *Motley Fool Employees Manual* (Alexandria, VA: The Motley Fool, 1997), p. 14.

86. *www.cbsnews.com/stories/2009/05/28/eveningnews.*

87. Hewitt Associates LLC, *Spec.Summary: United States Salaried 2007–2008* (Lincolnshire, IL: Hewitt Associates LLC, 2008).

88. Ibid.

89. David Schlaifer, "Legal Benefit Plans Help Attract and Retain Employees," *HR Focus,* December 1999, pp. S7–S8.

90. P. Allan, "The Contingent Workforce: Challenges and New Directions," *American Business Review,* June 2002, pp. 103–110.

Extending the System

You've now read about three strategic policies in the pay model. The first, which focused on determining the structure of pay, dealt with internal alignment. The second examined determining pay level based on external competitiveness, and the third dealt with determining the pay for employees according to their performance. Strategic decisions regarding alignment, competitiveness, and performance are directed at achieving the objectives of the pay system. Specific objectives vary among organizations; helping achieve competitive advantage and treating employees fairly are basic ones.

We now extend the basic pay model to the strategic issue of execution. A number of employee groups require, because of their importance to strategic success, special consideration in the way we design their compensation packages. In fact, Chapter 14 is titled just that: "Compensation of Special Groups." Here we talk about employee groups that don't quite fit our basic model. Their special employment status, for reasons we will discuss in a moment, dictates the design of compensation administration programs that sometimes differ from the more traditional designs covered in Parts Two through Five.

In Chapter 15 we look at compensation in unionized firms. Although less than 15 percent of the workforce in the United States is unionized, the role of unions in wage determination extends far beyond the size of this small group. Firms looking to remain nonunion often pay considerable attention to the way rewards are distributed to union employees. As we shall see, the role of a compensation person in a unionized organization is, indeed, different.

Our final extension of the system focuses on international employees. Different cultures, different laws, and different economies all can lead to different strategic and administrative decisions for international employees. If we are truly to embrace the globalization of business, the globalization of compensation must be a key ingredient.

EXHIBIT VI.1 The Pay Model

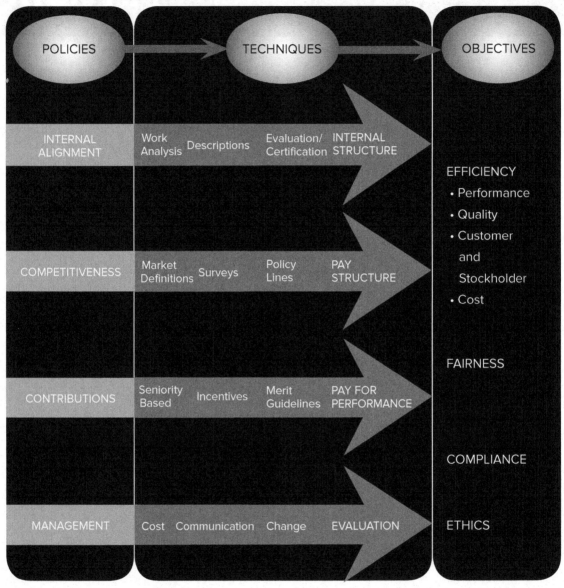

Compensation of Special Groups

Executives in the largest 100 public companies earn an average of roughly $14 million per year. Assuming two weeks of vacation and a 55-hour workweek, this translates into an hourly salary of almost $6000 dollars. In the amount of time it might take you to read this chapter (assuming you do read it), some executive is making $12,000 dollars. Most of us would be ecstatic if we made this much money in a week. We're even confident that most of you would be content with this as a starting wage every month (with appropriate bonuses, of course). Is it any wonder why so many news articles and blogs attack executive pay? We seem to fall further and futher behind as executives get richer.[1]

This chapter takes a look at groups that, for reasons we will discuss, receive compensation that is anything but common. Our goal is to show the logic, or illogic, of compensation practices for these special groups.

Some jobs simply don't fit the basic pay model. Something doesn't fit. Maybe the content of the job (from job evaluation) doesn't seem to match the pay that the job commands in the market. If you looked at the job description of a CEO, would you ever believe that the person in that job was paid $280 million (Base pay plus stock options) and change? That's what Les Moonves, CEO of CBS, was paid last year. Sure Big Bang Theory is good, but what the heck. Granted some CEOs make considerably less, but the mean is still over $1 million. Or take sales staff—their salaries also are hard to explain. Often sales employees are paid incentives that can amount to well over one-half their salaries. Our standard pay model up until now doesn't account for jobs that are outliers. This chapter looks at the compensation of these special groups.

WHO ARE SPECIAL GROUPS?

There is a pattern to the compensation of groups that we discuss in this chapter, a pattern that doesn't follow the pay model. Special treatment, either in the form of add-on packages not received by other employees or in the form of compensation components entirely unique in the organization, tends to focus on a few specific groups. This chapter argues that special groups share two characteristics. First, special groups tend to be strategically important to the company. If they don't succeed at their jobs, success for the whole organization is in jeopardy. Second, their positions tend to have built-in conflict, conflict that arises because different factions place incompatible demands on members of the group.

As the first characteristic explains, the work these employees perform is central to the strategic success of the company. As an example, consider the contrast in compensation treatment for engineers in two different organizations. One is a high-technology firm with a strong research and development component. The other organization employs a few engineers, but their role is not central to the mission of the organization. A survey of this type of difference in employee composition and organizational strategy found that research and development organizations with heavy concentrations of engineers had evolved unique compensation systems that were responsive to the special needs of the engineering contingent. Organizations with a different focus and with fewer engineers merged this group's compensation with the standard package offered to other employees.

Exhibit 14.1 describes the nature of the conflicts faced by such special groups as supervisors, top management, boards of directors, scientists and engineers, sales personnel, and contingent workers. When both of these characteristics are present, we tend to find distinctive compensation practices adopted to meet the needs of these special groups.

COMPENSATION STRATEGY FOR SPECIAL GROUPS

Supervisors

Remember, supervisors are caught between the demands of upper management to meet production goals and the needs of employees to receive rewards, reinforcements, and general counseling.[2] Conflict arises when management wants more output from workers and workers balk because the rewards don't increase. The major challenge in compensating supervisors centers on equity. Some incentive must be provided to entice nonexempt employees to accept the challenges of being a supervisor. Supervisor jobs often are classified as exempt, meaning they are exempt from overtime pay. If the job requires more than forty hours of work per week (a very common occurrence), every extra hour is either just part of the job with no extra pay or paid at straight time rather than time and a half. Picture a "recently promoted" supervisor working alongside a team member who collects overtime—and the financial incentive to be a supervisor quickly disappears. One of the authors (Newman) once worked undercover at fastfood restaurants as part of research for a book (My Secret Life on the McJob). On one of his jobs the Assistant Manager earned $32,000 per year. As an exempt employee he received nothing for the extra 15 or so hours he worked every week. The shift supervisor who reported to him was classified nonexempt. He received overtime pay and made more money than the Assistant Manager when the overtime was factored in. One day this inequity came to a head, ending in a profane screaming match over . . . tomatoes.

EXHIBIT 14.1 Conflicts Faced by Special Groups

Special Group	Type of Conflict Faced
Supervisors	Caught between upper management and employees. Must balance need to achieve organization's objectives with importance of helping employees satisfy personal needs. If unsuccessful, either corporate profit or employee morale suffers.
Top management	Stockholders want healthy return on investment. Government wants compliance with laws. Executives must decide between strategies that maximize short-run gains at expense of long run versus directions that focus on long run.
Boards of directors	Face possibility that disgruntled stockholders may sue over corporate strategies that don't "pan out."
Professional employees	May be torn between goals, objectives, and ethical standards of their profession (e.g., should an engineer leak information about a product flaw, even though that information may hurt corporate profits) and demands of an employer concerned more with the profit motive.
Sales staff	Often go for extended periods in the field with little supervision. Challenge is to stay motivated and continue making sales calls even in the face of limited contact or scrutiny from manager. Conflict is inevitable between customers who want product now and production facilities that can't deliver that quickly.
Contingent workers	Play an important "safety valve" role for companies. When demand is high, more are hired; when demand drops, they are the first workers downsized. Employment status is highly insecure and challenge is to find low-cost ways to motivate.

The Assistant Manager was tired of doing all the condiment stocking tasks for no extra money. He accused the shift supervisor of being a lazy who milked the job and never filled the tomato tray . . . until he was on overtime! More recently, organizations have devised several strategies to attract workers into supervisory jobs. The most popular method is to key the base salary of supervisors to some amount exceeding the top-paid subordinate in the unit (5% to 30% represents the typical size of the differential).

Another method for maintaining equitable differentials is simply to pay supervisors for scheduled overtime. Companies that do pay overtime are about evenly split between paying straight time and paying time-and-one-half for overtime hours.

The biggest trend in supervisory compensation centers on increased use of variable pay. Slightly more than half of all companies now have a variable pay component for supervisors, up from 16 percent in prior years.[3]

Corporate Directors

A board of directors comprises individuals from both inside and outside a firm who provide strategic advice on decision making. Because directors usually assume a major role in setting executive compensation, they are also a lightning rod for complaints about CEO pay. Most boards have between eight and eleven directors. Increasingly, these directors are expected to put in more hours on board activities such as cybersecurity (remember the breach on Target!) and risk oversight.[4]

Probably because of the increased attention to CEO pay and concerns about impartiality, companies are trying to populate their boards with outside directors who aren't beholding to a CEO who appointed them. Outside directors are harder to bring up to speed about a company's values and environment, but they are perceived to be less prone to bias than internal directors. CEOs influence the selection of directors, and often will favor people who have served on other boards with CEOs who are like-minded.[5] What used to be a "rubber stamp" process by internal board members beholden to the CEO is now a highly charged analysis of, among other things, CEO compensation. There is considerable risk in these jobs. Stockholders are prone to sue directors when CEOs receive large pay increases despite poor company performance on key financial measures.[6] In fact, if companies offer liability insurance to protect against these lawsuits (and vice versa), Director compensation is lower. We guess it pays to be uninsured?[7]

In exchange for assuming this risk, directors are well-rewarded. A typical member worked 30–40 hours per month last year.[8] In exchange, the median compensation was $240,000.[9] And as a reflection of greater concern about performance, the mix of compensation is shifting away from base pay toward incentives. Last year, for example, cash compensation was about $100,000 while incentive compensation (stock options) was $130,500.[10]

Executives

In an average 55-hour workweek a typical CEO spends 18 hours in meetings, 20 hours in travel/exercise/personal appointments, 4 hours in phone calls, 2 hours in public events, 5 hours in business meals, and 6 hours working alone.[11] Seems like a noncontroversial schedule, doesn't it? Like clockwork, though, every Spring controversy is renewed. That's when the major business publications (e.g., *Bloomberg Businessweek, The Wall Street Journal*) announce the top-paid executives in the country. Without fail this sparks a flurry of articles detailing stockholder disgust with CEO pay and vitriolic demands that something be done. Activists are directly responsible for significant changes in CEO pay practices in companies like Citigroup and Abbot Laboratories. For example, "companies are now reluctant to employ very controversial practices that increase CEO pay"? 1) Accelerating vesting of stock following a takeover, and 2) Implementing "Gross-Ups," the practice of covering taxes owed by executive for certain extravagant benefits.[12] Last year CEO pay rose 5 percent to 14.3 million. The biggest part of that was a gain in stocks, with options rising 72 percent to more than 9.6 million dollars.[13] CEOs strike it rich. On the positive front, we think, CEO compensation is one place women are actually earning more than men for the same job. Female CEO pay in the S&P 500 averaged 18.8 million compared to 12.7 for males.[14] How can anyone be worth tens of millions of dollars, the public demands. Especially infuriating, stockholders argue, is a reward package worth millions when, by all financial measures, the company is doing poorly. As one wag noted, apparently all CEOs live in Lake Wobegone where everyone is above average.[15] Even if the CEO is terminated for poor performance the outcome is often controversial. Most of us wouldn't expect to be rewarded when we do badly. Not CEOs, though. Exit compensation, often called "a Golden Parachute," is growing at staggering rates. Berkshire-Hathaway acquired H.J. Heinz resulting in approximately 200 million going to CEO William Johnson. 56 million of this is a Goldern Parachute. 57 million is for pension and deferred compensation.[16]

The disconnect between pay and performance of our nation's top executives has been a source of contention for over 30 years. We have reams of data indicating that executive compensation is badly in need of repair. For example, stock options are a big component of executive compensation. But we also know that paying executives with stock options increases the risks they are willing to take.[17] In fact, part of the global economy meltdown in 2008–2009 can be traced directly to executive compensation. Data are pretty clear that executives take more risks when they are paid more heavily in stock options. As evidence, some chief executives, such as Dick Fuld at Lehman Brothers and Jimmy Cayne at Bear Stearns, let their firms take huge risks and then paid the price when the value of their shareholdings evaporated. Who else paid the price? Yes, the shareholders took huge losses, but so also did the government, and ultimately the taxpayers. The public is understandably looking for someone to blame, and executive compensation is one legitimate target. Let's talk for a minute about standard executive compensation and then figure out what went wrong.

Components of an Executive Compensation Package

There are five basic elements of most executive compensation packages: (1) **base salary,** (2) short-term (annual) incentives or bonuses, (3) long-term incentives and capital appreciation plans, (4) employee benefits, and (5) perquisites.[18] Because of the changing nature of tax legislation and perceptions of the role an executive should play in guiding an organization, each of these at one time or another has received considerable attention in designing executive compensation packages. Over the past several decades companies used financial measures almost exclusively to incentivize executives. In this view stock price is the present value of future earnings. Stock options were the go to tool for this purpose. In this old economy view, if stock prices rise it's because executives have raised company value. More and more, lately, companies are saying that stock price is determined by things other than the present value of future earnings. If true, then the value of a CEO is more than what happens to financial measures during his tenure. New economy measures try to capture things beyond the bottom line. People assets, for example, in this view become more important. Companies start to measure customer satisfaction, environmental compliance, shareholder relations, and management cost ratios in relation to level of executive compensation.[19] Exhibit 14.2 shows changes in these components in recent years. Exhibit 14.3 shows overall compensation for the

EXHIBIT 14.2   Change in Executive Compensation Components

	Median Change	
	2012–2013	**2013–2014**
Salary	3.0%	2.9%
Bonus (target set at beginning of year)	3.9%	3.3%
Long Term Incentive (stock options and performance shares)	5.9%	7.1%

Source: Melissa Costa, Erik Nelson and Robert Newbury, Executive Compensation Bulletin 2015, Towers Watson, April 24, 2015, towerswatson.com.

EXHIBIT 14.3 Overall Compensation for the Top 5 of 2014

Executive	Company	Total Compensation
John Hammergren	McKesson	131.2 million
Ralph Lauren	Ralph Lauren	66.7 million
Michael Fascitelli	Vornado Realty	64.4 million
Richard Kinder	KinderMorgan	60.9 million
David Cote	Honeywell	55.8 million

Source: www.forbes.com/pictures/eggh45jef/highest-paid-bosses/.

top five executives in 2014. While these compensation levels may seem outrageously high to you, in comparison to years past when figures regularly topped 100 million, it appears compensation levels have indeed moderated. Roughly 40 percent of an executive's compensation package is equally split between base pay and short-term bonuses. The remaining 60 percent (note, benefits and perks aren't part of pay but do count in total rewards) is long-term incentives (e.g., stock options, performance shares). One obvious trend is apparent from these data. Companies continue to place more emphasis on incentives despite evidence they don't mirror actual CEO performance at all well.

Base Salary Although formalized job evaluation still plays an occasional role in determining executive **base pay,** other sources are much more important. Particularly important is the opinion of a compensation committee, composed usually of the company's board of directors or a subset of the board.[20] Frequently the compensation committee will take over some of the data analysis tasks previously performed by the chief personnel officer, even going so far as to analyze salary survey data and performance records for executives of comparably sized firms.[21] One empirical study suggests the most common approach (60% of the cases) of executive compensation committees is to identify major competitors and set the CEO's compensation at a level between the best and worst of these comparison groups.[22] Where pay fell in this range depends on a number of factors. CEOs who are particularly likely to be raided, or who have greater power over the wage setting process or successfully made strategic changes, were more likely to have higher compensation than peers.[23] Larger companies also tended to hit the high end of the compensation range by selecting "peer companies" to benchmark against that were tilted toward the high-paying end.[24]

Bonuses Annual bonuses often play a major role in executive compensation and are primarily designed to motivate better short-term performance. The first annual executive cash bonus may have been introduced by pharmaceutical giant Pfizer in 1901. The CEO got a five year contract with an annual bonus of 25 percent of company profits. In 1918 GM got a bit more complicated with a bonus of 10 percent less a deduction of 7 percent for capital employed.[25] Only 20 years ago, just 36 percent of companies gave annual bonuses. Today bonuses are given to 90 percent of executives, though the portion of executive compensation allotted to bonuses is smaller this decade than in the past (16% of total, down from 27% in the 1990s). Part of the explanation can be traced to the motivational impact of bonuses. They pay for good short-term results. This caused CEOs to approve decisions with great short-term payouts but clear long-term dire consequences. Less of this motivation is better, critics agreed. A second reason for lower portion of pay allocated to bonuses is their subjectivity. Perhaps to lessen this subjectivity, 65 percent of companies in a recent survey indicate they are introducing new financial measures for their annual incentive (bonus) schemes.[26] Part of this move is toward new objective measures that account for different aspects of performance. For example, some leading companies are linking executive bonuses to customer satisfaction. Both Motorola and Ford now link executive bonuses to performance on customer surveys or scorecards filled out by customers.[27] These performance measures are having dramatic impacts on the size of bonuses, even in years where total profits are way up. Nike had a 12 percent rise on net income recently, but CEO Mark Parker had a smaller bonus than in the previous year. Why? The company missed revenue and per share earnings targets set three years ago.[28] Same story for ConAgra Foods. Targets of 3 percent increase in revenue and 8 to 10 percent rise in per share earnings weren't met. So the maker of such iconic brands as Orville Redenbacher and Hunt's tomato sauce didn't give a healthy bonus to CEO Gary Rodkin. The board of directors refused to budge despite higher ingredient costs and increased competition.[29] Even with the enhanced interest in objective measures, though, 50 percent of companies are still exploring new nonfinancial measures.[30] Following the same logic as used with balanced scorecards, these companies reason that not all of a company's success is measureable with hard, objective outcomes.[31] As an example, a growth company might be interested in the level of innovation or progress in branding its products. Yes, we can track number of patents as a measure of innovation, but some of these issues are, of necessity, more subjective in nature.[32]

Long-Term Incentive and Capital Appreciation Plans   Bucking a trend toward ever-rising long-term incentives (e.g., stock options), both the dollar allocation and the portion of dollars allocated to long-term incentives has been declining recently.

So why the recent declines? Part of the reason is the furor over stock options' tax advantages. In just the last few years companies increasingly have been pressured to expense stock options in their annual reports, showing stockholders the real cost of options. Previously they received accounting treatment as if they were a free good. No more, say stockholders. So companies like Coca-Cola are increasingly volunteering to show the present cost of future stock options exercised. A second factor is stockholder dismay at the ease with which options are granted and exercised. We've just gone through some of the toughest stock market years in history, yet many executives in underperforming firms lined up for huge incentive payouts. Only public outcry and government intervention prevented this injustice. Passage of the 2010 Dodd-Frank Act is one signal that executive compensation will be monitored more closely. This act gives shareholders a nonbinding vote assessing the fairness of a CEO's compensation package. Even though the vote is non-binding, most companies view a no-vote as a public relations disaster.[33] A few companies like Oracle, Nabors industries and Cogent Communications dare to ignore the stockholder vote, but they tend to still be run by their founders, a group not likely to be voted out of office easily.

Of the two percent of companies that don't pass the "say on pay" vote, most try to overhaul their systems to obtain stockholder approval. For example, Abercrombie and Fitch split their Chairman and CEO jobs and restructured short and long term incentives to gain a positive vote.[34]

The vast majority of pay packages that were rejected by stockholders were traced to either stocks being issued despite poor CEO performance or because options were vesting based on time in job rather than performance.[35] The complaint, of course, is that stock options don't really link to performance of the executive.[36] Consider a rising stock market. If everyone's stock is going up, as often happens in a bull market, should CEOs be excessively rewarded because their stock also rises? It happens every day in boom markets. In a stock market that is rising on all fronts, executives can exercise options at much higher prices than the initial grant price—and the payouts are more appropriately attributed to general market increases than to any specific action by the executive. In a falling market stock options are underwater—the market price is below the exercise price. If I can exercise options at $23 per share, but they're valued at $18, I would be a fool to exercise. One frequent response by the corporate compensation committee is to issue new stock options with a lower exercise price, a practice perceived by many as inappropriate.[37] A final reason for the concern about stock options as an incentive tool is the ability to "game the system." For example, Safeway CEO Steven Burd recently received a stock award of $2.3 million dollars. Was it because he increased sales at this giant food chain? No, sales were basically flat. Rather, he led a 1.2 billion dollar stock buyback. That reduces the number of shares of stock outstanding. Shares just happen to be the denominator in an equation with profits as the numerator. Reducing the denominator makes the profits per share rise. This is an important metric for deciding executive bonuses. Can we spell manipulation?[38]

Companies are showing clear signs that the free lunch is over. Increased scrutiny means greater links of stock options to performance by CEOs and their companies.[39] About 40 percent of 300 corporations with more than $1 billion of revenues in a recent Hay Group survey link stock payouts to things like net income, total shareholder return, growth, and earnings per share.[40] A good example of this model is Tyson, the giant meatpacker. CEO John Tyson got 150,000 performance shares, so called because the shares are only granted if Mr. Tyson meets specific performance goals. Half of the shares depend on how Tyson stock performs against 12 other food companies. The more companies he beats, the more shares he keeps. Unless Mr. Tyson beats half the companies, he forfeits half the shares. The other half also evaporate unless Tyson's return on invested capital hits 13.25 percent.[41] Companies also are giving thought to the portion of compensation that must be carried in stock options. If the goal is to create a true incentive for CEOs to perform well, highly paid CEOs, it is argued, should have a greater portion of pay tied up in stock. Otherwise the rise or fall in stock isn't a significant motivator (think about the millionaire who bets at the five dollar blackjack table—winning or losing isn't really significant). For example, US Bancorp set a stock ownership rule in 2002 requiring the CEO to hold stock valued at five times salary. This standard is still enforced today. Other companies maintain a 4x salary rule.[42]

A third reason why traditional stock options may be declining in favor is linked to recent illegal backdating allegations. United Health Group and Caremark Rx, two large national health care companies, have been accused of backdating the granting of stock options to coincide with dates when share prices were particularly low.[43] When prices rebound, executives profit greatly. We think the decline in popularity masks an important reality. Executive decisions have an important impact on corporate success. Responsibly linking executive compensation to stock price is a very effective way to make sure executives are motivated to seek corporate successes. In comparison, **base wages** seem like an entitlement. As long as the executive doesn't get fired, wages are guaranteed. Bonuses also are flawed. They pay off for good short-term performance. What's good in the short

EXHIBIT 14.4   Description of Long-Term Incentives for Executives

Type	Description	Comments
Incentive stock options	Purchase of stock at a stipulated price, conforming with Internal Revenue Code (Section 422A).	No taxes at grant. Company may not deduct as expense.
Nonqualified stock options	Purchase of stock at a stipulated price, not conforming with Internal Revenue Code.	Excess over fair market value taxed as ordinary income. Company may deduct.
Phantom stock plans	Cash or stock award determined by increase in stock price at a fixed future date.	Taxed as ordinary income. Does not require executive financing.
Stock appreciation rights	Cash or stock award determined by increase in stock price during any time chosen (by the executive) in the option period.	Taxed as ordinary income. Does not require executive financing.
Restricted stock plans	Grant of stock at a reduced price with the condition that it may not be sold before a specified date.	Excess over fair market value taxed as ordinary income.
Performance share/unit plans	Cash or stock award earned through achieving specific goals.	Taxed as ordinary income. Does not require executive financing.

Source: From B. Ellig, *The Complete Guide to Executive Compensation*, 2014.

run isn't necessarily responsible in the long term. Stock options, which typically are vested (meaning they can't be exercised for a specified length of time, often three years), have a built-in incentive for executives to strive for long-term success. Exhibit 14.4 describes and comments on long-term incentives for executives.

Executive Benefits   Since many benefits are tied to income level (e.g., life insurance, disability insurance, pension plans), executives typically receive higher benefits than most other exempt employees. Beyond the typical benefits outlined in Chapter 13, however, many executives also receive additional life insurance, exclusions from deductibles for health-related costs, and supplementary pension income exceeding the maximum limits permissible under ERISA guidelines for qualified (eligible for tax deductions) pension plans.

Of course, various sections of ERISA and the tax code restrict employers' ability to provide benefits for executives that are too far above those of other workers. The assorted clauses require that a particular benefit plan (1) cover a broad cross-section of employees (generally 80%), (2) provide definitely determinable benefits, and (3) meet specific vesting (see Chapter 13) and nondiscrimination requirements. The nondiscrimination requirement specifies that the average value of benefits for low-paid employees must be at least 75 percent of the average value of those for highly paid employees.[44]

Executive Perquisites   Perquisites, or "perks," probably have the same genesis as the expression "rank has its privileges." Indeed, life at the top has its rewards, designed to satisfy unique needs and preferences. Since 1978, various tax and regulatory agency rulings have

EXHIBIT 14.5
Popular Perks
Offered to
Executives

Source: 1990 data from
Hewitt Associates;
2013 from Towers
Watson, Minha
Ahmed, "Despite the
Scrutiny, Perks Remain
a Key Component
of Executive
Rewards." Executive
Compensation Bulletin.
TowersWatson.com.

Perk	Percent of Fortune Fortune 500	1990 percentages
Automotive/parking	37	68
Executive physicals	32	91
Family spousal travel	21	47
Club dues	12	55
Match on charitable giving	5	*
Corporate housing	4	*

slowly been requiring companies to place a value on perks.[45] Despite this obstacle perks rose in value seven percent last year. Examples of interesting perks are the following:[46]

1. The most interesting perk pays for an executive's death. If the CEO of the Shaw group, James Bernhard, should die, the company will pay his family $18 million for him (the deceased) to not compete in Shaw's industry for two years. Is executive compensation insane, or what?

2. Seven percent of Fortune 500 firms give cash allowances, averaging $32,000 dollars. Explain why executives making millions of dollars need an allowance? Ken Chenault, CEO of American Express, gets 21 million in salary but still needs a $35,000 allowance for incidentals? Or Paul Murray, CEO of Calvin Klein needs a $20,000 clothing allowance?[47]

3. S.L. Green Realty spent $51,882 on a personal car for Chairman Stephen Green—plus another $119,050 for a chauffeur. Footnoted figures that work out to $468 a day, or enough to drive 233 miles a day for a year in a New York City cab.[48]

4. Our personal favorite, and now a classic of abuse: When Dennis Kozlowski's second wife hit the magic age of 40 in 2001, shortly after they wed, the then Tyco chief threw the party of parties. Guests were treated to a weeklong Roman-themed party on the island of Sardinia. Total cost? Over 2 million dollars, half paid by Tyco.[49]

Exhibit 14.5 shows common perks today in Fortune 100 companies and provides a loose comparison to perks in general for CEOs in 1990. Note the decline in numbers of companies offering perks. For example, between 2008 and 2009, executive perks dropped 28 percent. The biggest drop was in those receiving the greatest negative press: personal use of private jets declined 79 percent, and coverage of CEO personal taxes declined 10 percent.[50]

What's All the Furor over Executive Compensation?
What the Critics and Press Say

Let's first look at empirical data on executive compensation. Last year CEO pay averaged $14.3 million dollars.[51] Now, let's assume you accept that anyone can be worth that much money, will you grant that they should earn it? Our guess is that about 25 percent of the furor over executive compensation is from people who don't think anyone is worth $14 million per year. Many critics fall in this category—that this level of compensation can't be justified under any circumstances. Part of the argument includes comparisons to other countries. Wages in the European Union, for example, are much lower. Wages plus incentives for French CEOs, the highest-paid EU executives, average about $2 million in a sample of the 300 largest European companies. UK salaries for CEOs are about one-half that of their American counterparts, and other European executives fall even farther behind. Another part of the argument notes that the difference in pay between a CEO and the average worker has exploded. In 1980 an executive made 42 times as much as the typical worker. Today the differential is 331:1.[52] No shock that the average worker isn't a supporter of executive salary increases. The remainder of the furor, though, is over the rest of us who need to be convinced that someone is worth double-digit millions of dollars. Think about the job of the compensation directors sitting on an executive pay committee. How do they convince shareholders they are acting prudently? One argument could be that executive compensation is simply a reflection of changes in the market. Yes, executive compensation has risen dramatically since 1900, but so has the pay of other groups. Hedge fund, private equity, and venture capital investors have had fee increases multiply by a factor of 5–10 times what they were in the period 1994–2005.[53] The top 20 hedge fund managers earned more in 2005 than all 500 CEOs in the S&P 500.[54] Top professional ball players (football, baseball, and basketball) making more than $5 million in 1994 increased their wages by a factor of 10 over the next ten years. During the same period, the salaries of top lawyers increased by a factor of 2.5. Compare this, the supporters of executive pay, say, to the increase in CEO pay during the same period—a multiplier of 4–5.[55] Even if you don't buy these arguments—and many critics don't[56]—we can still fall back on a pay-for-performance argument. Maybe executives earn their increases. Increasingly boards are trying to make this very argument by linking pay to performance. Large pay can then be explained by great company performance. A typical argument would be as follows: If the company performance exceeds industry standards, big bonuses and stock payouts follow. Poor financial performance means much smaller pay packages. Examples of companies with at least 40 percent of executive compensation tied to performance targets include Briggs and Stratton, ConAgra Foods, and Intuit Inc.[57] Before the linkage to performance targets, executives were reaping huge payouts unrelated to their decision making and leadership skills. In a rising stock market, executives with stock options see an increase in their stock's value, even when their company might be lagging in financial performance. Stockholders rightly cry foul! Today, though, things may be changing. In a recent study the *Wall Street Journal* found CEO pay tracked stock prices much more closely than in the past. For each 1 percent increase in return to shareholders by a company, a CEO's salary changed by .6 percent. The two tracked nicely together last year.[58]

How did salaries get so high? Exhibit 14.6 gives a brief history of the path executive compensation took to reach these incredible heights. Pay attention to the way the granting of stock options has gradually played a bigger role in executive compensation.

Perhaps you can take small comfort in the fact that executives are sharing our pain. They too are seeing drops in compensation. Trying to lessen the public relations disaster trifecta of bankruptcy, record unemployment, *and* excessive executive compensation, many companies are making very public announcements about the cuts they are making in their top pay structure.[59] At the extreme, several CEOs have actually declared that

EXHIBIT 14.6 Brief History of Executive Compensation: The Key Event

1974	Michael Bergerac cracks the $1 million mark when recruited to Revlon.
1979	Chrysler's Lee Iacocca takes $1 million plus 400,000 option shares.
1983	William Bendix of Bendix becomes the first executive to collect a huge golden parachute (contract clause for payment in a takeover leading to termination) of $3.9 million over five years.
1984	Congress tries to limit excessive golden parachutes but gives rise to unintended consequences—the rules actually lead to larger amounts.
1986	New law gives favorable tax treatment to stock option awards. Sizes increase.
1987	Lee Iacocca receives first mega-grant of stock options: 820,000 option shares worth 15.3 times his salary and bonus that year.
1987	Junk bond expert Michael Milkin explodes through the $5 million mark in salary and bonus.
1987	Leon Hirsch of U.S. Surgical gets even larger megastock option award, worth 126 times his salary and bonus.
1992	Securities and Exchange Commission rules CEO salaries must be disclosed more often in proxy statements. Easier availability of peer compensation data serves to drive up the standard.
1992	Michael Eisner of Walt Disney exercises low-cost stock options for pretax profit of $126 million.
1993	New tax law sets upper limit on tax-deductible executive compensation at $1 million but has unintended effect of raising bar to that level.
2000	Charles Wang, Computer Associates Intl. executive, cracks two-thirds of billion-dollar mark.
2006	Steve Jobs lost the top-paid CEO position to Oracle's Lawrence J. Ellison, who was compensated $192.92 million in 2007.
2010	Dodd-Frank Act gives power to shareholders by giving them a nonbinding (but image important) vote on appropriateness of an executive's compensation.
2014	The top five paid executives average about 75 million dollars per year, less than the huge figures of pre-recession days; But the numbers are creeping up from immediate post-recession numbers.

Source: *BusinessWeek,* April 17, 2000, p. 100, April 23, 2003; *The Wall Street Journal,* April 10, 2006, pp. R1–R4; "Executive Pay," *BusinessWeek,* April 17, 2009, pp. 23–31, Forbes.com, visited May 5, 2015.

they would work for wages of one dollar per year! And they don't get stock options or bonuses either! KinderMorgan CEO Richard Kinder, one of the top paid executives in 2014, declared he would work for $1 per year with no bonus or perks. The same pledge was made by Whole Foods John Mackey. Topping this, watchmaker Fossil's CEO Kosta Kartsotis has worked three straight years for free.[60]

While these percentages aren't huge, at least symbolically they have important meaning. Wages don't usually fall for employees, especially executives.[61]

So far we've overwhelmed you with information about executive compensation in the private sector. The world of compensation is very different in not-for-profit organizations. It makes headlines when a CEO of a nonprofit makes more than one million dollars. Yes, you're right, if you want to get rich, don't work in a not-for-profit! Further, a large fraction of total compensation in the not-for-profit arena—much more than in the private sector—is allocated to expense accounts and employee benefits.[62]

Some experts today argue that executive compensation could be reined in by making sure the board of directors has explicit knowledge of how much CEOs receive each year. Sounds strange, doesn't it—why wouldn't the board know how much their CEO makes? Isn't that their job? Yes, but figuring out the worth of a compensation package in any given year isn't exactly easy. How do you value stock options that haven't been exercised yet? What's the value of unlimited use of a corporate jet? Only recently have companies begun to capture the true value of an entire compensation package, using a simple (at least in theory) tool called a **tally sheet**.[63] A tally sheet gives a comprehensive view on the true value of executive compensation. It's a simple concept that surprisingly only now is making its way into the executive board room: Tally up the value of base salary, annual incentives, long-term incentives, benefits, and perks. Part of this process includes estimating the current value of stock options (using something called the Black–Scholes model), stock appreciation rights, vested and unvested pensions, and payouts upon termination.[64] Experts argue that a tally sheet gives board members a single figure that they can then debate over: Is this competitive? Does performance justify this amount?

An alternative way to rein in executive compensation is to increase government regulation. In 1992 the Securities and Exchange Commission entered the controversy.[65] As we noted earlier, stockholders are now permitted to propose and vote on limits to executive compensation. And it appears these votes make a difference. The larger the portion of stockholders voting "No," the more likely the board is to respond by limiting CEO salary growth Extending this legislation, the SEC adopted a regulation in 2015 requiring most companies to report the differential between the CEO and a typical worker. Nothing raises stockholder ire more than finding out the CEO makes 300 times as much as the rest of the folks.[66] On another front, the 1993 Revenue Reconciliation Act limited employer deductions for executive compensation to $1 million and capped the amount of executive compensation used in computing contributions to and benefits from qualified retirement plans. Ironically, this very law may be contributing to the growth of executive compensation. The $1 million mark now serves as a new standard: Many executives who had been making less than $1 million are finding their pay quickly rising to this amount.

Although the 2008–2010 economic crisis brought many cries for more government controls on executive compensation, thus far President Obama has resisted popular pressure. His experts rightly point to history: Wage and price controls usually don't work effectively.

Are the critics right? Is CEO compensation excessive? A second way to answer the question is to look at the different ways executive compensation is determined and ask, "Does this seem reasonable?"

---

e-Compensation

For a union view of CEO wages, visit *www.aflcio.org/paywatch/*. This site is maintained by the AFL–CIO and is designed to monitor executive compensation. The union view is that CEOs are overpaid and that monitoring is the first step to curbing excess.

What's All the Furor over Executive Compensation? What Academics Say

Over the past 50 years behavioral scientists have tried to explain executive compensation excesses. One explanation for the extreme pay of executives involves *social comparisons*.[67] In this view, executive salaries bear a consistent relative relationship to compensation of lower-level employees. When salaries of lower-level employees rise in response to market forces, top executive salaries also rise to maintain the same relative relationship. In general, managers who are in the second level of a company earn about two-thirds of a CEO's salary, while the next level down earns slightly more than half of a CEO's salary.[68] Much of the criticism of this theory—and an important source of criticism about executive compensation in general—is the gradual increase in the spread between executives' compensation and the average salaries of the people they employ. In 1980, CEOs received about 42 times the average pay of lower-level workers. Now top executives are paid more than 300 times the pay of the average worker.[69] As a point of reference, the corresponding differential is less than 40:1 in France, Germany, Belgium, and Italy.[70] Although some of this difference is explainable by the higher degree of unionization and the presence of left-leaning governments, it still seems that a social comparison explanation is not sufficient to explain why executive wages are as high as they are.[71]

A second approach to understanding executive compensation focuses less on the difference in wages between executive and other jobs and more on explaining the level of executive wages.[72] The premise in this economic approach is that the worth of CEOs, or their subordinates, should correspond closely to some measure of company success, such as profitability or sales or firm size. Intuitively, this explanation makes sense. There is also empirical support. Numerous studies over the past 30 years have demonstrated that executive pay bears some relationship to company success, including the ability to make strategic changes and negotiate mergers/acquisitions successfully.[73] A recent article analyzing the results from over 100 executive pay studies found empirical evidence that firm size (sales or number of employees) is by far the best predictor of CEO compensation. Size variables are nine times better at explaining executive compensation than are performance measures. How big the firm is explains what the boss gets paid better than does how well he performs![74] A different economic perspective looks at labor markets. CEO salaries are strongly influenced by labor markets—competitor pay levels matter. CEOs who are in demand (their companies are performing well relative to competitors) are more likely to receive higher wages, or have pay tied less to annual performance (good long-term track records mean less reliance on yearly performance).[75]

Some evidence contradicts this, though. Research of pay packages at 702 publicly traded U.S. companies (1995–2004) showed a 1 percent increase in company value led to a 0.43 percent increase in compensation of senior executives. So far, so good. But what was troubling was the huge variations across the sample. Executive compensation in some firms was highly related to company value, while at others there was no relationship whatsoever. Worse yet, the present value of future compensation (mostly stock options, which account for about 75 percent of executive pay packages) shows very little sensitivity to company value.[76] Apparently a pure economic explanation for executive compensation isn't very successful. A variant on this argues that we should take into account environmental performance and social responsibility when measuring company value.[77] One interesting study found that environmental performance (e.g., pollution prevention) is an important determinant of CEO pay in polluting industries. This suggests that CEOs are rewarded for setting and working toward environmental goals. Remember it's still difficult to determine if these green goals have tangible benefits; they are not measured in typical bottom-line accounting.[78] Two other studies combined both social comparison and economic explanations to try to better understand CEO salaries.[79] Both of these explanations turned out to be significant. Size and profitability affected level of compensation, but so did social comparisons. In one study, the social comparison was between wages of CEOs and those of the board of directors. It seems that CEO salaries rose, on average, 51 percent for every $100,000 more that was earned by directors on the board.[80] Recognizing this, CEOs sometimes lobby to get a board loaded with directors who are highly paid in their primary jobs.

A third view of CEO salaries, called **agency theory,** incorporates the political motivations that are an inevitable part of the corporate world.[81] Sometimes, this argument runs, CEOs make decisions that aren't in the economic best interest of the firm and its shareholders. One variant on this view suggests that the normal behavior of a CEO is self-protective. CEOs will make decisions to solidify their positions and to maximize the rewards they personally receive.[82] For example, we argued earlier that CEOs are given stock options to encourage more risk in the expectation that risk positively affects option value. Classic agency theory prediction. But some would argue that CEOs are also protective of their current wealth, and taking risks could result in personal losses. The new variant on agency theory, called behavioral agency theory, suggests CEOs are conflicted about stock options, tempted to both be risky to accumulate future wealth but also tempted to be conservative to protect current wealth. The recommendation, if this view is correct, is to stop issuing stock options and rather give outright stock grants.[83] As further evidence of this self-motivated behavior, consider the following description of how executives ensure themselves high compensation.[84] The description comes from the experience of a well-known executive compensation consultant, now turned critic, who specialized for years in the design of executive compensation packages:

1. *If the CEO is truly underpaid:* A compensation consultant is hired to survey actual competitors of the company. The consultant reports to the board of directors that the CEO is truly underpaid. Salary is increased to a competitive or higher level.

2. *If the CEO is not underpaid and the company is doing well:* A compensation consultant is hired. Specific companies are recommended to the consultant as appropriate for surveying. The companies tend to be selected because they are on the top end in terms of executive compensation. The consultant reports back to the board that its CEO appears to be underpaid. Salary is increased.

3. *If the CEO is not underpaid and the company is doing poorly:* A compensation consultant is hired. The CEO laments with the consultant that wages are so low for

top management that there is a fear that good people will start leaving the company and going to competitors. Of course, no one ever asks why the company is under-performing if it has such a good management team. Anyway, the result is that the consultant recommends a wage increase to avoid future turnover.

In each of these scenarios CEO wages rise. Is it any surprise that executive compensation is under close scrutiny by an outraged public and, more importantly, angry stockholders?[85]

Despite this jaundiced view of the compensation determination process, agency theory argues that executive compensation should be designed to ensure that executives have the best interests of stockholders in mind when they make decisions.[86] The outcome has been to use some form of long-term incentive plan, most commonly stock options and stock grants. In the simplest form, an executive is given the option to purchase shares of the company stock at some future date for an amount equal to the fair market price at the time the option is granted. One view suggests this gives a built-in incentive for an executive to increase the value of the firm. Stock prices rise. The executive exercises the option to buy the stock at the agreed-upon price. Because the stock price has risen in the interim, the executive profits from the stock sale. Although this sounds like an effective tool for motivating executives, there are still many critics.[87] First, a number of studies offer contrary evidence that stock options don't align CEO interests with those of the firm. Second, critics argue, even the method for tying executives to the company is flawed. As we noted earlier, one major complaint is that stock options don't have a downside risk. If stock prices rise, the stock options are exercised. If stocks don't improve, or even decline, as was the case for much of the past four years, the executive suffers no out-of-pocket losses. Another complaint is that stocks can rise simply because the general market is rising, not because of some exceptional behavior by the CEO. To counter this argument about 30 percent of companies force CEOs to meet some financial performance target before they can exercise their options.[88] Some argue that executive compensation should move more toward requiring that executives own stock, rather than just have options to buy it.[89] With the threat of possible financial loss and the hope of possible substantial gains, motivation may be higher. Others advocate linking stock options to executive performance.[90] For example, if an executive doesn't lead his or her company to outperform other companies in the same industry, no stock options are granted.[91] Finally, there is growing recognition that the linkage between performance and pay is much more complex for executives than was previously thought. Current work focuses on firm risk, stock ownership versus stock options, and type of industry as possible additional factors explaining executive pay.[92]

Scientists and Engineers in High-Technology Industries

Scientists and engineers are classified as **professionals.** According to the Fair Labor Standards Act, this category includes any person who has received special training of a scientific or intellectual nature and whose job does not entail more than a 20 percent time allocation for lower-level duties. If you take a look at firms hiring scientists and engineers, they struggle to figure out what pay should be. For example, one of the authors recently worked with a company that recently purchased land in Texas and

Oklahoma for oil and gas exploration. This was the first venture south of the Mason-Dixon line. Should they pay Petroleum engineers like their engineers in the Marcellus shale in Pennsylvania? Should they pay the market rate in Texas or Oklahoma? But, given the layoff of over 100,000 employees in the Texas/Oklahoma oil industry because of falling gas prices, wouldn't wages reported on recent salary surveys be hugely overstated? You can begin to see the complexity. Some experts argue that salaries are beginning to lag compared to common comparisons like pharmacists, and this is causing drops in demand for engineering training.[93] To restore our lead in the generation of scientific knowledge, more attention needs to be paid to knowledge workers who should be paid for their special scientific or intellectual training. Here, though, lies one of the special compensation problems that scientists and engineers face. Consider the freshly minted electrical engineer who graduates with all the latest knowledge in the field. For the first few years after graduation this knowledge is a valuable resource on engineering projects where new applications of the latest theories are a primary objective. Gradually, though, this engineer's knowledge starts to become obsolete, and team leaders begin to look to newer graduates for fresh ideas. If you track the salaries of engineers and scientists, you will see a close parallel between pay increases and knowledge obsolescence (Exhibit 14.7). Early years bring larger-than-average increases (relative to employees in other occupations). After 10 years, increases drop below average, and they become downright puny in 15 to 20 years.

Partly because salary plateaus arise, many scientists and engineers make career changes such as moving into management or temporarily leaving business to update their technical knowledge. In recent years some firms have tried to deal with the plateau effect and also accommodate the different career motivations of mature scientists and engineers. The answer is something called **a dual-career ladder.** Exhibit 14.8 shows a typical dual career ladder.

Notice that dual ladders provide exactly that: two different ways of progressing in an organization, each reflecting different types of contributions to the organization's mission. The managerial ladder offers a promotion path with increasing responsibility for management of people. The professional track rises with increasing technical responsibility. At some point in a scientist's career, the choice to opt for one or the other track arises. The idea is that talented technical people shouldn't feel that they have to take management jobs in order to advance in their careers, that they can advance through the excellence of their technical work. The titles are different in each ladder, but pay and perquisites are supposed to be comparable across the rungs.[94]

A second problem in designing the compensation package of scientists and engineers centers on the question of equity. The very nature of technical knowledge and its dissemination requires the relatively close association of these employees across organizations. They mingle at trade association meetings. They keep in touch and cross-fertilize knowledge by discussing recent developments in the field. Scientists and engineers tend to compare themselves for equity purposes with graduates who entered the labor market when they did. Partially because of this and partially because of the volatile nature of both jobs and salaries in these occupations, organizations rely very heavily on external market data in pricing scientists' and engineers' base pay.[95] The result is the use of something called **maturity curves** (Exhibit 14.7 again).

EXHIBIT 14.7

Maturity Curve: Years Since Last Degree Relative to Salary

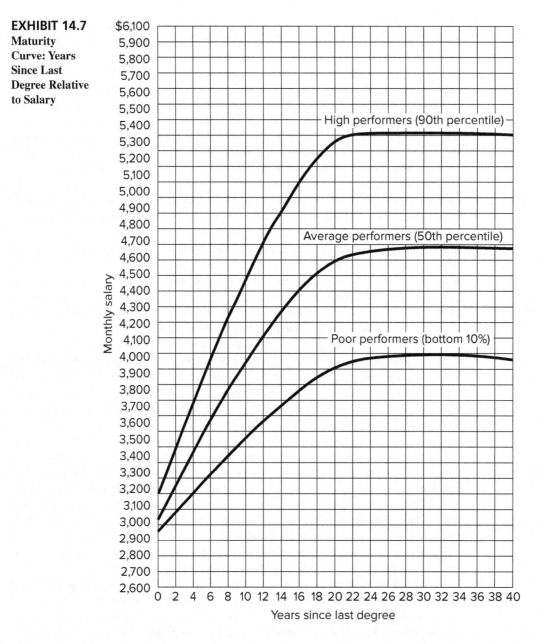

Maturity curves reflect the relationship between scientist/engineer compensation and years of experience in the labor market. Generally, surveying organizations ask for information about salaries as a function of years since the incumbent(s) last received a degree. This is intended to measure the half-life of technical obsolescence. In fact, a plot of this data, with appropriate smoothing to eliminate aberrations, typically shows

EXHIBIT 14.8
IBM Dual
Ladders

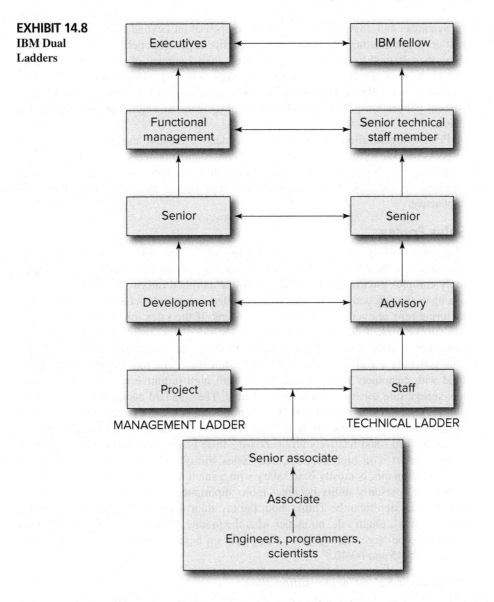

curves that are steep for the first 5 to 7 years and then rise more gradually as technical obsolescence erodes the value of jobs. Exhibit 14.7 illustrates such a graph with somewhat greater sophistication built into it, in that different graphs are constructed for different levels of performance. To construct such graphs, the surveying organization must also ask for data broken down by broad performance levels. Notice in the illustration that the high performers begin with somewhat higher salaries and the differential continues to broaden over the first few years.

Scientists and engineers also receive compensation beyond base pay. More than half get a bonus either linked to company profits or personal performance. The incentives, though, tend to be small, averaging less than 5 percent of pay. Other incentives link payment of specific cash amounts to completion of specific projects on or before agreed-upon deadlines. Post-hiring bonuses are also paid for such achievements as patents, publications, elections to professional societies, and attainment of professional licenses.[96]

Finally, organizations have devoted considerable creative energy to development of perks that satisfy the unique needs of scientists and engineers. These perks include flexible work schedules, large offices, campuslike environments, and lavish athletic facilities. The strategic importance of these groups dictates that both mind and body be kept active.

Sales Forces

The sales staff spans the all-important boundary between the organization and consumers of the organization's goods or services. To meet this need in an increasingly complex environment, the sales job has morphed into a variety of forms. For example, the job can be outsourced and called either indirect salesforce or manufacturing reps or even simply independent reps. If the sales job remains in-house it can still be broken down by inside or outside sales reps. Inside reps perform sales calls (the dreaded cold calls included in this) or sales support functions. Outside reps generally travel and visit potential customers.[97] The role of interacting in the field with customers requires individuals with high initiative who can work under low supervision for extended periods of time. The standard compensation system is not designed for this type of job. As you might expect, there is much more reliance on incentive payments tied to individual performance. Thus, even when salespeople are in the field—and relatively unsupervised—there is always a motivation to perform. If the product is in high demand, and "sales ability" isn't a difference maker, the compensation mix is mostly base salary with a small incentive component. However, as the sales person's ability becomes more important, the size of the incentive component rises significantly. Think about the last door-to-door salesperson you saw (if ever). That is a tough sale, no matter what the product. Here the incentive component is likely to be large. The typical sales job has a base/incentive ratio of somewhere between 55/45 and 60/40.[98]

Designing a Sales Compensation Plan

Six major factors influence the design of sales compensation packages: (1) the nature of people who enter the sales profession, (2) organizational strategy, (3) market maturity, (4) competitor practices, (5) economic environment, and (6) product to be sold.

The Nature of the People Popular stereotypes of salespeople characterize them as being heavily motivated by financial compensation.[99] One study supports this perception, with salespeople ranking pay significantly higher than five other forms of reward. In the study, 78 percent of the salespeople ranked money as the number-one motivator, with recognition and appreciation being ranked as the number-two motivator.[100]

EXHIBIT 14.9   Sales Strategy Matrix

		Sales Strategy Mix	
		Conversion Selling	*New Concept Selling*
	Prospects	**(grow base)**	**(develop markets)**
Buyers			
		Retention Selling	*Penetration Selling*
	Customers	(protect base)	(penetrate accounts)
		Existing	**New/Additional In-Line**
		Prospects	

Source: Jerome A. Colletti and Mary S. Fiss, "Sales Compensation," in Lance A. Berger and Dorothy R. Berger, eds., *The Compensation Handbook* (New York: McGraw-Hill, 2008), pp. 239–257.

Promotional opportunities, sense of accomplishment, personal growth, and job security were all less highly regarded. These values almost dictate that the primary focus of sales compensation should be on direct financial rewards (base pay plus incentives).

Organizational Strategy   A sales compensation plan should link desired behaviors of salespeople to organizational strategy.[101] This is particularly true in the Internet age. As more sales dollars are tied to computer-based transactions, the role of sales personnel will change.[102] Salespeople must know when to stress customer service and when to stress volume sales. And when volume sales are the goal, which products should be pushed hardest? Strategic plans signal which behaviors are important. For example, emphasis on customer service to build market share or movement into geographic areas with low potential may limit sales volume (see cell labeled New Concept Selling). Ordinarily, sales representatives under an incentive system will view customer service as an imposition, taking away from money-making sales opportunities. And woe be to the sales supervisor who assigns a commission-based salesperson to a market with low sales potential. Salespeople who are asked to forgo incentive income for low-sales tasks should be covered under a compensation system with a high base pay and small incentive component. Exhibit 14.9 outlines the strategy as a function of type of buyers.

Alternatively, an organization may want to motivate aggressive sales behavior. A straight commission-based incentive plan will focus sales efforts in this direction, to the possible exclusion of supportive tasks such as processing customer returns. Such incentive plans include both a statement about the size of the incentive and a discussion of the performance objective necessary to achieve the incentive.[103] Typical performance measures include overall territory volume, market share, number of product placements in retail stores, number of new accounts, gross profit, percentage of list-price attainment (relative to other salespeople in the organization), consistency of sales results, expense control, productivity per square foot (especially popular in retail stores), and bad debt generated by sales.[104] Each measure, of course, corresponds to a different business goal. For example, an organization might use a volume measure such as number of units, orders, invoices, or cash received if the business goal is to increase sales growth. Alternatively, if the goal is profit improvement, the appropriate measurement would be gross margin on sales or price per unit. Percentage account erosion would be stressed if improved account retention became a major focus of attention, while customer satisfaction indices are increasingly popular because of greater emphasis on quality. A good sales plan also factors in the KISS principle: Keep It Simple Stupid. Few plans have more than four sales objectives. The most common plan has three components (30%). Twenty-five percent of sales plans have two sales components.[105]

Generally, there are two types of sales compensation plans: (1) Unit rate plans and (2) add-on plans.[106] Unit rate plans differ by the amount they pay for each unit of sales. Flat commissions have the same rate for each unit sold (e.g., $8 dollars for each sale). Ramped commissions have one rate up to a target level, then a higher rate tied to more difficult "above-target" sales (e.g., 4% of the first $100,000 in sales, 6% thereafter). Declining commissions offer one rate up to a target level, then lesser rates thereafter. One of our authors bought a whole life insurance plan in 1972 (yes, he's very old). The agent got 100 percent of the first year residual and then declining amounts in following years. These declining amounts reflect the reduction in work the sales person must do in later years of the plan. Finally, with pooled commissions, a plan recognizes that a sales person works as part of a team. Your stockbrokers get a large chunk of the commission you pay to have them make investment decisions, but they also share with various assistants and market analysts who provide vital information on stock trends. Or, an organization can even have sales teams, individuals working together to sell services or products. There is evidence that sales teams shouldn't be any larger than two people, and they sell better when the team incentive component isn't too large relative to the individual component or base salary.[107] The second type of sales compensation plan tries to get sales staff to focus on specific types of sales. We've just introduced a new line of suits at a high-end men's clothing store. The sales staff gets an extra incentive for each sale of that line. Usually this stress on one product is short-lived, and then the focus turns to yet another sales item.[108]

Market Maturity   As the market of a product matures, the sales pattern for that product will change, and companies need to adapt the compensation for their sales force accordingly.[109] A recent study showed that with maturing markets, companies move toward a more conservative sales pattern, focusing even more on customer satisfaction and retention. This leads companies to employ more conservative, rather than aggressive, salespeople, who can comply with the companies' customer retention plans. In maturing markets, companies focus both on performance-based pay tied to customer satisfaction and on greater base salaries to retain conservative salespeople.[110]

Competitor Practices   In selecting an appropriate pay level, organizations should recognize that external competitiveness is essential. The very nature of sales positions means that competitors will cross paths, at least in their quest for potential customers.

This provides the opportunity to chat about relative compensation packages, an opportunity which salespeople will frequently take.

Economic Environment   The economic environment also affects the way a compensation package is structured. In good economic climates with roaring sales, companies can afford to hire mid- and low-level sales personnel to capture the extra sales. In a recession environment, however, companies need to react to the decreasing level of sales by focusing more on the top-level performers and rewarding those that achieve high levels of sales despite the economic downturn.

Product To Be Sold   The nature of the product or service to be sold may influence the design of a compensation system. For a product that, by its very technical nature, is difficult to understand, it will take time to fully develop an effective sales presentation. Such products are said to have high barriers to entry, meaning considerable training is needed to become effective in the field. Compensation in this situation usually includes a large base-pay component, thus minimizing the risk a sales representative will face, and an encouraging entry into the necessary training program. At the opposite extreme are products with lower barriers to entry, where the knowledge needed to make an effective sales presentation is relatively easy to acquire. These product lines are sold more often using a higher incentive component, thus paying more for actual sales than for taking the time to learn the necessary skills.

Products or services that sell themselves, where sales ability isn't as crucial, inspire different compensation packages than do opportunities where the salesperson is more prominent. Base compensation tends to be more important with easily sold products. Not surprisingly, incentives become more important when willingness to work hard may make the difference between success and failure. Clearly, figuring out what that sales target should be is a major challenge. Too easy a target and the sales staff receive undeserved compensation. An impossible target, in contrast, can be demotivating. One survey puts correct goal-setting as the number one challenge in program design (57% of respondents). The second biggest challenge is making the forecast of expected sales as accurate as possible (35%). The linkage between these two issues is clear. Bad forecasts lead to inaccurate goals. A local oil and gas company found this out the hard way. Salespeople received incentives for finding customers to become limited partners in oil and gas exploration. Sales quotas based on gas priced at $4.00 per gallon made sales easy. When gas dropped below three dollars the quotas became impossible to meet.[111]

Most jobs do not fit the ideal specifications for either of the two extremes represented by straight salary or straight commission plans. A combination plan is intended to capture the best of both these plans. A guaranteed straight salary can be linked to performance of nonsales functions such as customer service, while a commission for sales volume yields the incentive to sell. A plan combining these two features signals the intent of the organization to ensure that both types of activities occur in the organization.

A final caveat, though, in incentive system design. Salespeople are famous for finding loopholes in sales incentive plans and "milking'" them for personal profit. For example, if you design a sales plan based on unit sales, and don't prioritize sales, the staff will sell the easiest items at the expense of more profitable items that are harder to sell. Or beware the incentive plan that works too well: During Hurricane Sandy in 2012, Uber (car service) saw an opportunity to help stranded New Yorkers. They incentivized drivers to brave the horrible road conditions by doubling tolls. The plan worked—drivers went out. But the plan was also a PR nightmare. Customers blitzed social media with complaints about price gouging. Uber responded by dropping rates but bumping up base compensation to get drivers on the road. Beware of your incentive plan! It may not do what you want it to.

Contingent Workers

Explaining work classifications in the new economy is a challenge. Of course the largest-category is full-time workers, representing 86 percent of the workforce. Besides this group, there are other direct employees (part-time, on-call) who are paid directly by the employer. A second group of employees falls into a co-employment category (e.g, agency temp workers) paid by some external organization which is reimbursed by the employer. Third are contract workers such as independent contractors and day laborers. Of the 14 percent that aren't full-time employees, the largest group is part-timers at 7 percent. No other group is larger than 3 percent.[112] Workers in the first two of these categories (direct employment with part-time or on-call status and co-employment such as agency temps) typically earn less than workers in traditional arrangements; those in the contract work category earn more. For example, working through a temporary-help agency usually means low pay in administrative or day labor positions. In contrast, the wages for an independent contractor might be higher than those for a more permanently employed counterpart. Indeed, independent contractors often are people who have been downsized and then reemployed by the company. DuPont cut its workforce by 47,000 a while ago. About 14,000 of these workers were subsequently hired as vendors or contractors.[113] Because the employment status of contingent workers is temporary and employee benefits are less or nonexistent, wages at times tend to compensate by being somewhat higher. Be careful, though, in the way you define the status of your contingent workers. It simply isn't enough to declare them temporary or consultant status and, ipso facto, it's true. Just ask Microsoft. They classified a group of employees as consultants, thereby allowing them to skip paying overtime wages when hours exceeded 40 in a week. In *Vizcaino v. Microsoft* the court declared these workers common law employees. Before the case could go to the Supreme Court, Microsoft settled for $97 million. Sounds like Microsoft realized that not paying overtime was a mistake. More recently FedEx was guilty of the same infraction. They classified workers as independent contractors, and avoided paying 2 hours of overtime for the mandated 10-hour days. The government found them guilty.[114] In fact, since 2010 the Federal Department of Labor has recovered over one billion in illegally unpaid wages. Be sure to follow the rules about when workers are independent contractor/consultants and when they are common law employees.[115] What do you do though when the rules are in flux? McDonalds is being challenged right now because various agencies want to declare them as the employer of McDonald's franchise employees. McDonald's asserts that the franchise owner is the employer. The courts are still sorting this out.

Why the move to contingent workers? One answer may signal a permanent change in the way we do business. As we come out of the "Great Recession" companies are not hiring at the level we would expect. Rather, they are taking on temporary workers as a way to insulate themselves in a volatile economy. Temp workers afford a level of flexibility that allows expansion and contraction of the workforce in response to market changes. Recent labor market data show employers hired 93,000 part-time workers and 22,000 full-time workers. This is a marked shift to the prior year when employers hired only 31,000 part-timers and 171,000 full-timers.[116] Employers are being cautious. Their first move is to hire temps to satisfy greater customer demand. Of course, these temporary workers would rather be hired permanently. And this clearly could affect long-term loyalty and morale.[117] One summary of almost 100 studies of contingent workers showed lower levels of job satisfaction for part-timers and temps but levels comparable to full-time workers for contract employees.[118] But the arguments for hiring temps are persuasive. Usually the wages and benefits are lower and often the productivity is higher.[119] And terminating a temporary employee doesn't have the same moral strain attached to the decision.

A major compensation challenge for contingent workers, as with all our special-group employees, is identifying ways to deal with equity problems. Contingent workers may work alongside permanent workers yet often receive lower wages and benefits for the same work. Employers deal with this potential source of inequity on two fronts, one traditional and one that challenges the very way we think about employment and careers. One company response is to view contingent workers as a pool of candidates for more permanent hiring status. High performers may be moved off contingent status and afforded more employment stability. Cummins Engine, for example, is famous for its hiring of top-performing contingent workers. The traditional reward of a possible "promotion," then, becomes a motivation to perform. Another part of the equity challenge is to actually classify a worker correctly. Companies often prefer to classify workers as independent contractors to avoid overtime pay. Consider FedEx. It was found guilty of ordering 10 hour days from their "contract workers", and arguing as such they weren't responsible for two hours of overtime. The courts said these workers weren't independent contractors but rather full-time employees eligible for overtime payment. Since 2010 the Federal Department of Labor has recovered over one billion in illegally unpaid wages. Be careful how you classify your workers!

A second way to look at contingent workers is to champion the idea of boundary-less careers.[120] At least for high-skilled contingent workers, it is increasingly popular to view careers as a series of opportunities to acquire valuable increments in knowledge and skills. In this framework, contingent status isn't a penalty or cause of dissatisfaction. Rather, employees who accept the idea of boundaryless careers may view contingent status as part of a fast-track developmental sequence. Lower wages are offset by opportunities for rapid development of skills—opportunities that might not be so readily available in more traditional employment arrangements. Companies like General Electric that promote this reward—enhanced employability status through acquisition of highly demanded skills—may actually have tapped an underutilized reward dimension.

Your **Turn**

A Sports Sales Plan

The Buffalo Bisons are a Triple A affiliate of the Toronto Blue Jays. Players—on this team are one level below the Major Leagues where salaries can be huge. In the early days of the team's most recent incarnation, sell outs were very common. Filling almost 20,000 seats was fairly easy in the early 90's when the stadium was still new and the team was a perennial contender. In recent years the selling effort has become more difficult. Typical attendance is about 8,000 per game. (The following information is a fictional, but realistic, account of the sales plan used by the Bisons.)

The VP of Operations, Michael Salamone, wants to design a sales incentive plan that will reinvigorate the fan base for the Bisons. He recognizes several realities:

1. Three staff members serve as full-time sales agents. They have two major jobs:
   a. Sell tickets to games. Because the Bisons had a weak team last year, projections are that it will be difficult to exceed an average of 14,000 seats no matter what the plan design is. Further, architecture of the stadium makes sales above 12,000 more challenging because the seats are not as desirable. If last year is any indication, fans will buy less expensive seats, then switch to premium seats that are unoccupied after the game begins. For PR reasons, staff look the other way when this occurs, unless late-arriving fans find their seats occupied. The goal for Mike Salamone is to focus on sale of premium seats, thus reducing the "seat shifting" by fans buying standard and bleacher seats. Statistics for last year are as follows:

Type of Seat	Cost to Fan	Number of These Seats	Average Paid Occupancy
Premium	$12	6,000	1,500
Standard	$ 9	13,000	6,000
Bleacher	$ 7	1,900	500

   b. Sell advertising—Advertising dollars come from placement of product information throughout the stadium, including on billboards, outfield fences, scoreboards, even dugout roofs. The dollar amount sold last year was $908,013.
2. Increases in advertising sales are dependent on team performance. Team performance drives ticket sales. In turn, advertising depends on number of seats sold.
3. The three staff members are heavily dependent on the total administrative team (7 other individuals) for ancillary activities in the selling event (e.g., they send out brochures, answer phone queries, provide follow-up information after the initial sales contact, etc.). Mike Salamone wants to have a simple plan for advertising sales that rewards the total group yet still motivates the three sales staff.

QUESTIONS

1. Of the above information, what is most important in your design of a sales incentive plan for the three sales staff? How does this information affect your plan design?
2. Your book talks about unit rate plans. Which of these types of plan would you use for sales of tickets. Which plan might be appropriate for sales of advertising? Why?
3. What factors influence the dollar amount you can pay for increases in ticket sales?

Summary   Special groups are portrayed here as sharing two common characteristics: They all have jobs with high potential for conflict, and resolution of this conflict is central to the goals of the organization. Probably because of these characteristics, special groups receive compensation treatment that differs from the approach for other employees. Unfortunately, most of this compensation differentiation is prescriptive in nature (i.e., all we have is opinion to guide us, not hard data), and little is known about the specific roles assumed by special groups and the functions compensation should assume in motivating appropriate performance. Future practice and research should focus on answering these questions.

Review Questions

1. We read an article the other day that said it's getting harder to find good people willing to serve on a corporate board of directors. Given what you learned in this chapter, speculate on why it's hard to attract good people to this job.

2. What makes professional/scientist jobs different, such that they qualify for special group status in many companies? Why is the compensation of knowledge workers so frequently linked to the amount of time these workers have been out of school?

3. The differential between the salary of top executives and the lowest paid workers in the same country is quite small in Japan, at least in comparison to the United States. The same is true in unions (president of union versus union workers). Explain why the differential might be small in Japan and in U.S. unions but much larger in private U.S. corporations.

4. Romance Novels, Inc, located in Cheektowaga, NY, has gradually increased the number of contingent workers (full-time, temporary) from 10 percent of the workforce to about 28 percent today. Why might they do this? Also, what equity problems can arise from hiring contingent workers, especially when they work alongside regular employees?

5. Why is it easier to explain a $2 million payout to Jordan Spieth for working four days to win a Masters Championship than it is to explain why William Clay Ford made $30 million as CEO of Ford Motor Company?

Endnotes

1. M. Krantz and B. Hansen, "CEO Pay Soars While Workers' Pay Stalls," *USA Today,* April 1, 2011, p. B1–2.
2. P. Frost, "Handling the Pain of Others: The Hidden Role of Supervisors," *Canadian HR Reporter,* April 7, 2003, pp. 7–8.
3. IOMA, *Pay for Performance Report,* May 2000, p. 6.
4. Jesse Rhodes, "Historic Norms Return to Board Pay," 2013–14 Director Compensation Report. NACD Directorship March/April, 2014.
5. David Zhu and James Westpahl, "How Directors' Prior Experience with Other Demographically Similar CEOs Affects Their Appointments onto Corporate Boards and the Consequences for CEO Compensation," Academy of Management Journal 57(3), 2014, pp. 791–813.

6. G. Strauss, "$228,000 for a Part-Time Job? Apparently, That's Not Enough," *USA Today,* March 4, 2011, p. A1.

7. Iness Aguir, Natasha Burns, Sattar Mansi, and John Waki, "Liability Protection, Director Compensation, and Incentives," *Journal of Financial Intermediation* 23(4), October 2014, pp. 570–589.

8. Gary Strauss, "Part-Time Job Pays $240,000," http://www.usatoday.com/story/money/business/2014/09/23/big-company-director-pay-now-up-to-nearly-240000-a-year/16113497/, visited May 4, 2015; Emily Glazer and Joann Lublin, "Funds Get Active Over Director Pay," *Wall Street Journal,* May 21, 2013, p. B1.

9. Ibid.

10. Towers-Watson, "Compensation for U.S. Corporate Directors Increased 6%, Towers Watson 2014 Analysis Finds Increase in Stock-Based Portion Offset No Change to Cash Portion of Total Pay Package," http://www.towerswatson.com/en/Press/2014/09/compensation-for-us-corporate-directors-increased-6-percent, visited May 1, 2015.

11. Rachel E. Silverman, "Where's the Boss? Trapped in a Meeting," *The Wall Street Journal,* February 14, 2012, p. B1.

12. Joann S. Lublin, "Longstanding Pay Practices under Attack by Activists," *Wall Street Journal,* March 21, 2013, p. B1.

13. Gary Strauss "CEOs Strike It Even Richer in Record '14," *USA Today,* April 21, 2015, p. B1.

14. Matt Krantz, "Female CEO's Paychecks Fattest," *USA Today,* May 1, 2015, p. 4B.

15. Josh Boak, "CEOs Are 'Superstars' and Paid in Stock" Associated Press, *Buffalo News,* May 28, 2014, p. B1.

16. Julie Jargon and Scott Thurm, "Heinz CEO's Golden Exit Deal," *Wall Street Journal,* March 5, 2013, p. B1.

17. Yuval Deutsch, Thomas Keil, and Tom Laamanen, "A Dual Agency View of Board Compensation: The Joint Effects of Outside Director and CEO Stock Options on Firm Risk," *Strategic Management Journal* 32(2), 2011, pp. 212–227.

18. Joann S. Lublin, "Boards Tie CEO Pay More Tightly to Performance," *The Wall Street Journal,* February 11, 2006, p. A1.

19. Bruce R. Ellig, *The Complete Guide to Executive Compensation* (New York: McGraw-Hill, 2014).

20. Dan Lin and Lu Lin, "The Interplay Between Director Compensation and Ceo Compensation," *International Journal of Business & Finance Research* 8(3), 2014, pp. 11–26.

21. Gary Strauss and Barbar Hansen, "Median Pay for CEOs of 100 Largest Companies Rose 25%," *USA Today,* April 10, 2006, p. B1.

22. Ingrid Smithey Fulmer, "The Elephant in the Room: Labor Market Influences on CEO Compensation," *Personnel Psychology* 62, (2009), pp. 659–695.

23. Seemantini Pathak, Robert E. Hoskisson, and Richard A. Johnson, "Settling Up in CEO Compensation: The Impact of Divestiture Intensity and Contextual Factors in Refocusing Firms," *Strategic Management Journal* 35(8), August 2014, pp. 1124–1143; Marc Van Essen, Jordan Otten, and Edward J. Carberry, "Assessing Managerial Power Theory: A Meta-Analytic Approach to Understanding the Determinants of CEO Compensation," *Journal of Management* 41(1), 2015, pp. 164–202; J. Bizjak, M. Lemmon, M., and T Nguyen, T. (2011) Are all CEOs above average? An empirical analysis of compensation peer groups and pay design. *Journal of Financial Economics,* 100(3), 538–555.

24. Ibid.

25. Bruce R. Ellig, *The Complete Guide to Executive Compensation* (New York: McGraw-Hill, 2014).

26. Joanne Lublin, "Executive Bonuses bounce Back." Wall Street Journal Online, http://online.wsj.com/article/SB10001424052748703818204576206903329068840.html, visited March 21, 2012.

27. Mercer staff, "Organizations Are Focusing on Measuring Performance Aligned with Pay, Mercer Survey Shows" press release, January 2011.

28. Ibid.

29. Ibid.

30. Scott Thurm, "CEO pay lags behind 2011 results," *Wall Street Journal,* March 26, 2012, B1, B10.

31. Bruce R. Ellig, *The Complete Guide to Executive Compensation* (New York: McGraw-Hill, 2014).

32. Ram Charan, "14 Questions Every Board Member Needs to Ask," (Hoboken, NJ: Jossey-Bass, 2009).

33. Emily Chasan, "Companies Say 'No Way' to 'Say on Pay'," *Wall Street Journal,* August 26, 2014, p. B1.

34. Ibid.

35. Ram Charan, "14 Questions Every Board Member Needs to Ask," (Hoboken, NJ: Jossey-Bass, 2009).

36. Ryan Krause, Kimberly A. Whitler, and Matthew Semadeni, "Power to the Principals! An Experimental Look at Shareholder Say-on-Pay Voting," *Academy of Management Journal* 57(1), 2014, pp. 94–115.

37. Floyd Norris, "G. E. Is Latest to Reconfigure Stock Options," *New York Times,* August 1, 2002, *http://www.nytimes.com/2002/08/01/business/01PLAC.html,* October 7, 2009.

38. Scott Thurm and Serena Ng, "Stock Buybacks Propel Executive Bonuses," *Wall Street Journal,* May 6, 2013, p. B1.

39. Unknown author, January 2012, "The Pay for Performance Challenge," mercer, www.Mercer.com; visited March 27, 2012.

40. Hay Group, "The Rise of Performance Shares" *The Executive Edition,* October 2011, p.1 http://haygroupnews.com/ve/856171V60C96B9629x639/VT=0/page=1.

41. M. Langley, "Big Companies Get Low Marks for Lavish Executive Pay," *The Wall Street Journal,* June 9, 2003, p. C1; Graef S. Crystal, *In Search of Excess* (New York: Norton, 1991).

42. John E. Cor and Wayne R. Guay, "Is CEO Pay too High and Are Incentives too Low? A Wealth-Based Contracting Framework," *The Academy of Management Perspectives* 24(1), 2010, pp. 5–19.

43. Del Jones and Barbara Hansen, "Companies Get Creative to Boost CEOs' Pay," *USA Today,* May 4, 2009. p. 4B.

44. A. Henderson and J. Fredrickson, "Top Management Team Coordination Needs and the CEO Pay Gap: A Competitive Test of Economic and Behavioral Views," *Academy of Management Journal* 44(1), 2001, pp. 96–107; A. Simon, *Administrative Behavior,* 2nd ed. (New York: Macmillan, 1957); Conference Board, *Top Executive Compensation* (New York: Conference Board, 1996).

45. *United for a Fair Economy,* "Executive Excess 2007," 14th Annual Compensation Survey, *www.faireconomy.org/files/pdf/ExecutiveExcess2007.pdf,* August 29, 2007.

46. "Hard Times Haven't Cut What Some Execs Get," *USA Today,* April 12, 2011, pp. 1–2B.

47. Gary Strauss, "Some CEOs Get Cash Allowances," *Wall Street Journal,* May 28, 2014, p. B2.

48. Forbes Magazine, http://www.forbes.com/pictures/fhkd45jid/driving-in-style/, visited May 4, 2015.

49. Kathy Kristof, "8 Outrageous Executive Perks," 2011, http://us.lrd.yahoo.com /SIG=10ule8q1e/**http://www.kiplinger.com/.

50. Joe Mullich, "Executive Compensation Evolves," *The Wall Street Journal,* November 2, 2011, p. B8.

51. Gary Strauss, "CEOs Strike It Even Richer in Record '14," *USA Today,* April 21, 2015, p. B1.

52. Joann S. Lublin, "The Boss Makes How Much More Than You?" *Wall Street Journal*, November 26, 2014, p. B9.

53. Ibid.; Marc J. Wallace, "Type of Control, Industrial Concentration, and Executive Pay," *Academy of Management Proceedings,* 1977, pp. 284–288; W. Lewellan and B. Huntsman, "Managerial Pay and Corporate Performance," *American Economic Review* 60, 1977, pp. 710–720.

54. S. Kaplan and J. Rauh, "Wall Street and Main Street: What Contributes to The Rise in The Highest Incomes?" working paper, University of Chicago, 2008.

55. Steven N. Kaplan, "Are U.S. CEOs Overpaid?" *The Academy of Management Perspectives* 22(2), 2008, pp. 5–19.

56. Ibid.

57. John C. Bogle, "Reflections on CEO Compensation," *Academy of Management Perspectives* 22(2), 2008, pp. 21–25.

58. Joanne Lubin, "Ceo pay jumps 11%, "*Wall Street Journal,* May 9 2012, p. B6.

59. "ADP CEO Received 22 Percent Less in 2009," *BusinessWeek,* June 8, 2009, p. D48.

60. Matt Krantz, "Just $1 Will Pay These CEO's Salaries," *USA Today,* April 14, 2015, p. B1.

61. A. Henderson and J. Fredrickson, "Top Management Team Coordination Needs and the CEO Pay Gap: A Competitive Test of Economic and Behavioral Views," *Academy of Management Journal* 44(1), 2001, pp. 96–107; Charles O'Reilly, Brian Main, and Graef Crystal, "CEO Compensation as Tournament and Social Comparison: A Tale of Two Theories," *Administrative Science Quarterly* 33, 1988, pp. 257–274.

62. Kevin F. Hallock, "Managerial Pay and Governance in American Nonprofits," *Industrial Relations* 41(3), July 2002, pp. 377–406.

63. Hay Group, "Tally Sheets," *The Executive Edition,* (1), 2006, p. 7.

64. Ibid.

65. Julie Wernau, "CEO compensation: The $10 million-plus club" *Chicago Tribune,* May 23, 2010, p. 23.

66. Joann S. Lublin, "The Boss Makes How Much More Than You?" *Wall Street Journal,* November 26, 2014, p. B9.

67. Charles O'Reilly, Brian Main, and Graef Crystal, "CEO Compensation as Tournament and Social Comparison: A Tale of Two Theories," *Administrative Science Quarterly* 33, 1988, pp. 257–274.

68. Ibid.

69. James A. Martin, "Stacked Deck: Can governance structures explain CEO compensation differences across countries?" *Academy of Management Perspectives* 24(1), 2010, pp. 78–79.

70. Ibid.

71. O. Sjoberg, "Corporate Governance and Earnings Inequality in the OECD Countries 1979–2000," *European Sociological Review* 25, (2009), pp. 519–533.

72. Marc J. Wallace, "Type of Control, Industrial Concentration, and Executive Pay," *Academy of Management Proceedings* (1977), pp. 284–288; W. Lewellan and B. Huntsman, "Managerial Pay and Corporate Performance," *American Economic Review* 60, 1977, pp. 710–720.

73. Seemantini Pathak, Robert E. Hoskisson, and Richard A. Johnson, "Settling Up in CEO Compensation: The Impact of Divestiture Intensity and Contextual Factors in Refocusing Firms," *Strategic Management Journal,* 35(8), 2014, pp. 1124–1143; Eliezer M. Fich, Laura T. Starks, and Adam S. Yore, "CEO Deal-Making Activities and Compensation," *Journal of Financial Economics,* 114(3), 2014, pp. 471–492; H. L. Tosi, S. Werner, J. Katz, and L. Gomez–Mejia, "A Meta Analysis of CEO Pay Studies," *Journal of Management* 26(2), 2000, pp. 301–339.

74. Peter Kostiuk, "Firm size and Executive compensation," *Journal of Human Resources* 25(1), 2010, pp. 90–105.

75. Ingrid Smithey Fulmer, "The Elephant in the Room: Labor Market Influences on CEO Compensation," *Personnel Psychology* 62, 2009, pp. 659–695.

76. M. Makri, P. J. Lane, and L. R. Gomez-Mejia, "CEO Incentives, Innovation, and Performance in Technology–Intensive Firms: A Reconciliation of Outcome and Behavior–Based Incentive Schemes," working paper, 2006.

77. Michele Fabrizi, Christine Mallin, and Giovanna Michelon, "The Role of CEO's Personal Incentives in Driving Corporate Social Responsibility," *Journal of Business Ethics,* 124, 2014, pp. 311–326.

78. Pascual Berone and Luis R. Gomez-Mejia, "Environmental Performance and Executive Compensation: An Interated Agency-Institutional Perspective," *Academy of Management Journal* 52(9), 2009, pp. 103–126.

79. A. Henderson and J. Fredrickson, "Top Management Team Coordination Needs and the CEO Pay Gap: A Competitive Test of Economic and Behavioral Views," *Academy of Management Journal* 44(1) (2001), pp. 96–107; Charles O'Reilly, Brian Main, and Graef Crystal, "CEO Compensation as Tournament and Social Comparison: A Tale of Two Theories," *Administrative Science Quarterly* 33 (1988), pp. 257–274.

80. C. Daly, J. Johnson, A. Ellstrand, and D. Dalton, "Compensation Committee Composition as a Determinant of CEO Compensation," *Academy of Management Journal* 41(2), 1998, pp. 209–220.

81. B. Ellig, *The Complete Guide to Executive Compensation* (New York: McGraw–Hill, 2002).

82. Daniel J. Miller, "CEO Salary Increases May Be Rational After All: Referents and Contracts in CEO Pay," *Academy of Management Journal* 38(5), 1995, pp. 1361–1385.

83. R. M. Wiseman and L. R. Gomez-Mejia, "A Behavioral Agency Model of Managerial Risk-Taking," *Academy of Management Review,* 23, 1998, pp. 133–153.

84. Graef S. Crystal, *In Search of Excess: The Overcompensation of American Executives* (Hopewell, NJ: Ecco Press, 1991); L. Bebchuk and J. Fried, "Pay Without Performance," *Academy of Management Perspective,* February 2006, pp. 5–24.

85. Eric Dash, "A Bad Year for the Chief (But Not for the Bonus)," *The New York Times,* April 3, 2005, pp. 3, 13.

86. B. Ellig, *The Complete Guide to Executive Compensation* (New York: McGraw–Hill, 2002).

87. Hay Group, "2005 Executive Compensation Survey," *The Executive Edition* 5 (2006).

88. J. S. Lublin, "Boards Tie CEO Pay More Tightly to Performance," *The Wall Street Journal,* February 11, 2006, p. A1.

89. M. Taylor, "Stock Options Probe Grows," *Modern Healthcare* 36(21), May 22, 2006, p. 9.

90. Anthony J. Nyberg, Barry Gerhart, and Mason A. Carpenter, "Agency Theory Revisited: CEO Return and Shareholder Interest Alignment," *Academy of Management Journal* 53(5), 2010, pp. 1029–1049.

91. Dennis Blair and Mark Kimble, "Walking through the Discrimination Testing Wage for Welfare Plans," *Benefits Quarterly* 3(2), 1987, pp. 18–26.

92. Anthony J. Nyberg, Barry Gerhart, and Mason A. Carpenter, "Agency Theory Revisited: CEO Return and Shareholder Interest Alignment," *Academy of Management Journal,* 53(5), 2010, pp. 1029–1049.

93. Leland Teschler, "How to Get More Engineers? Pay Them!" *Machine Design,* 78(20), 2006, pp. 10–13.

94. Richard Demers, "Dual Career Ladders," *www.cincomsmalltalk.com/userblogs/rademers /blogView?showComments=true˜entry=3253517059,* June 16, 2006.

95. http://www.worldatwork.org/waw/community/discussions/discuss.jsp?did=19791, visited October 26, 2012.

96. Jo C. Kail, "Compensating Scientists and Engineers," in *New Perspectives on Compensation,* David B. Balkin and Luis R. Gomez-Mejia, eds. (Englewood Cliffs, NJ: Prentice–Hall, 1987), pp. 247–281.

97. Pankaj M. Madhani, "Managing Sales Compensation Across the Economic Cycle: Direct Sales Force Versus Independent Reps," *Compensation & Benefits Review* 46, 2014, pp. 16–24.

98. Ibid.

99. B. Davenport, "Now Is the Time to Redesign Your Sales Comp Plan," *Report on Salary Surveys 2006 Year book* (New York: IOMA, 2006), p. 10–12.

100. Charles Warner, "Recognition and Appreciation Is Vital for Salespeople," *www .charleswarner.us/recogsls.htm,* April 10, 2003.

101. David J. Cichelli, *Compensating the Sales Force,* (New York: McGraw-Hill), 2010.

102. Ibid.

103. V. Kumar, Sarang Sunder, and Robert P. Leone, "Measuring and Managing a Salesperson's Future Value to the Firm," *Journal of Marketing Research* 51(5), 2014, pp. 591–608.

104. David J. Chchelli (ed.) 2011 Sales Compensation Trends Survey© Results, Alexander Group, 2011.

105. Ibid.

106. Ibid.

107. Noah Lim and Hua Chen, "When Do Group Incentives for Salespeople Work?" *Journal of Marketing Research* 51, June 2014, pp. 320–334.

108. David J. Chchelli (ed.), 2011 Sales Compensation Trends Survey© Results, Alexander Group, 2011.

109. Pankaj M. Madhani, "Managing Sales Compensation Across the Economic Cycle: Direct Sales Force Versus Independent Reps," *Compensation & Benefits Review* 46, 2014, pp. 16–24.

110. Bill O'Connell, "Dead Solid Perfect: Achieving Sales Compensation Alignment," *Compensation and Benefits Review* March/April 1996, pp. 41–48.

111. Personal consulting assignment for Jerry Newman.

112. Peter Cappelli and JR Keller, "Classifying Work in the New Economy," *Academy of Management Review* 38(4), 2013, pp. 575–596.

113. Kim Clark, "Manufacturing's Hidden Asset: Temp Workers," *Fortune,* November 10, 1997, pp. 28–29.

114. Steven Greenhouse, "Suits Point to Increasing Wage Theft by Employers," *Wall Street Journal,* September, 2014, p. A1.

115. Rules for common law status can be found at: https://edisk.fandm.edu/prs/PDFs/FLSA. pdf, visited March 28, 2012.

116. Julie Jargon, Brenda Cronin, Sarah E. Needleman, "The Shift to Part-time," *Wall Street Journal,* July 15, 2013, p. B1.

117. Elizabeth G. Olson, "The Rise of the Permanently Temporary Worker," *Fortune,* May 5, 2011, http://management.fortune.cnn.com/2011/05/05/the-rise-of-the-permanently-temporary-worker/, visited online March 25, 2012.

118. Christa L. Wilkin, "I Can't Get No Job Satisfaction: Meta-analysis Comparing Permanent and Contingent Workers," *Journal of Organizational Behavior* 34(1), 2013, pp. 47–64.

119. Andrea Garnero, Stephan Kampelmann, and Francois Rycx, "Part-Time Work, Wages and Productivity: Evidence from Belgian Match Panel Data," *Industrial and Labor Relations Review* 67(3), 2014, pp. 926–955.

120. Jan Aylsworth, "Boundaryless and Protean Careers," Examiner.com, visited October 26, 2012.

Union Role in Wage and Salary Administration

Chapter Outline

The Impact of Unions in Wage Determination
- *Union Impact on General Wage Levels*
- *The Structure of Wage Packages*
- *Union Impact: The Spillover Effect*
- *Role of Unions in Wage and Salary Policies and Practices*

Unions and Alternative Reward Systems
- *Lump-Sum Awards*
- *Employee Stock Ownership Plans (ESOPs)*
- *Pay-for-Knowledge Plans*
- *Gain-Sharing Plans*
- *Profit-Sharing Plans*

Your Turn: Predicting a Contract's Clauses

Many experts believe that unions are facing their most critical challenge of the last 50 years.[1] In 1983 there were 17.7 million union workers, representing 20.1 percent of workers. In 2014, 31 years later, there were 14.6 million union members representing only 11.1 percent of workers. On the face, this decline is a serious problem for unions. But it gets worse. The numbers mask the fact that the public sector has seen union growth such that 35.7 percent of public sector workers are unionized. If we factor this out, only 6.6 percent of workers in the private sector are unionized.[2] The number of union certification elections for firms fell 85 percent from a high of 8,799 in 1973 to 1463 in 2014.[3] Out of these elections to unionize, those that swung in favor of unionization in 1950 were about 70 percent compared to 63 percent in 2014.[4] The overall trend from 1997 to present is an average 7 percent annual decrease in the number of union elections, yet a consistent 2 percent annual increase in elections decided in favor of unionization.[5] Today collective bargaining, except in the public sector, is not a major force. A recent study indicates unions peaked in the 1950s and 1960s and may well be no better off now than in their early days of struggle in the 1920s.[6] Recent efforts to buck this trend have taken unions into the fast food industry. The Service Employees International Union (SEIU) currently backs worker efforts in their massive demonstrations for a fair wage, defined by them as $15/hr.[7]

Four popular explanations are usually offered for this decline: (1) The structure of American industry is changing, and declining industries are most heavily unionized, while growing industries are less so. (While this is true, research suggests this isn't a primary explanation for union decline.) (2) Unionization may be declining because workers don't view unions as a solution to their problems. (3) There has been reduced intensity of union organizing efforts (frequently cited as a reason why several large and powerful unions, including the Teamsters, broke off from the AFL-CIO in 2005). And (4) management is taking an increasingly hard stance against unions in general and union demands in particular.[8] A classic example is management's increasing use of temps to combat unionization. Beyond the use of temps during strikes, they are now also used to prevent unions from forming and to weaken existing unions.[9] A large portion of this management opposition to unions is spurred by increasing pressure from both domestic and international competitors. Management more frequently resists wage increases that would give nonunion competitors, both domestic and foreign, a competitive price advantage. The end result of these competitive pressures is a declining union-nonunion wage differential. In fact, one study shows that a 10 percent rise in import share (a popular measure of international competition) has the effect of lowering the union wage differential (the difference between union and nonunion wages) by approximately 2 percent.[10]

Such competitive pressures, starting in the 1980s and continuing today, have triggered lower-than-normal wage increases in unionized firms and even some wage concessions. In general, though, the improved economy of late has stabilized labor contracts and even led to some union gains. One example is union attacks on two-tiered wage structures. As a cost cutting strategy in the early part of this century unions agreed to have two tiers of wages. New workers would be paid less, often as little as half as much, than existing workers. Unions like the Steelworkers have attacked these contract provisions with a vengeance. Recently this resulted in the elimination of two tiers in their contract with ArcelorMittal, the world's largest steel company.[11] Although the statistics indicate a decline in unionism, some of the issues that are important cornerstones of unionization continue to be important for workers. Fully 63 percent of employees say they want to have more influence in workday decisions. If need be, 40 percent of workers would vote union to achieve their needs. When workplace relations are bad, when management is not trustworthy, when workers feel they have little influence over decisions affecting them, the workers show strong interest in joining a union. You want to invite a unionization effort? Show little concern for employees' welfare and be unwilling to share power—over 70 percent of workers who see management acting this way claim they would vote for a union.[12] Just ask the physicians, nuclear engineers, psychologists, and judges who recently decided to unionize. Unions may be down but not out. One indication is the changing stance of unions on two-tier wages. One of the hallmarks of unionism is equality of treatment. Yet in recent years, to keep their wages whole, many unions have agreed to two-tier wages—new hires receive significantly lower wages. Within the UAW, for example, second-tier workers receive $19/hr today, compared to $28/hr for the first tier.[13] "hitting profit targets, autoworkers' hourly compensation is between $47/hr (Chrysler) and $58/hr (Ford). Workers hired after the second tier went into effect in 2007 average around $27/hr. The two-tier system causes discord between workers, often doing the same job on the same assembly line, and is targeted for elimination in the next contract talks.[14]

THE IMPACT OF UNIONS IN WAGE DETERMINATION

Despite strong management efforts to lessen the impact of unions, they still have an important effect on wages. Even in a nonunion firm, compensation managers will adjust rewards (usually upward) when there is a hint of nearby union activity. This section outlines four specific areas of union impact: (1) impact on general wage and benefit levels, (2) impact on the structure of wages, (3) impact on nonunion firms (also known as **spillover effect**), and (4) impact on wage and salary policies and practices in unionized firms. The chapter's concluding section focuses on union response to the changing economic environment of the 1980s and the alternative compensation systems that have evolved in response to these changes.

---

e-Compensation

This site gives detailed information about dozens of unions, including specifics of union contracts: http://www.irle.berkeley.edu/library/CBA.html.

Union Impact on General Wage Levels

Do unions raise wages? Are unionized employees better off than they would be if they were nonunion? Unfortunately, comparing "what is" to "what might have been" is no easy chore. Several measurement problems are difficult to overcome. The ideal situation would compare numerous organizations that were identical except for the presence or absence of a union.[15] Any wage differences among these organizations could then be attributed to unionization (a union wage premium). Unfortunately, few such situations exist. One alternative strategy that has been adopted is to identify organizations within the same industry that differ in level of unionization. For example, consider company A, which is unionized, and company B, which is not. Although they are in the same industry, it is still difficult to argue with assurance that wage differences between the two firms are attributable to the presence or absence of a union. First, the fact that the union has not organized the entire industry weakens its power base (strike efforts to shut down the entire industry could be thwarted by nonunion firms). Consequently, any union impact in this example might underestimate the role of unions in an industry where the percentage of unionization is greater. A second problem in measuring union impact is apparent from this example. What if company B grants concessions to employees as a strategy to avoid unionization? These concessions, indirectly attributable to the presence of a union, would lead to underestimation of union impact on wages.

Another strategy in estimating union impact on wages is to compare two different industries that vary dramatically in the level of unionization.[16] This strategy suffers because nonunionized industries (e.g., agriculture, service) are markedly different from unionized industries in the types of labor employed and their general availability. Such differences have a major impact on wages independent of the level of unionization and make any statements about union impact difficult to substantiate.

One source of continuing data on unionized and nonunionized firms is the Bureau of Labor Statistics. From 1969 to 1985, the union wage premium more than doubled, from 17.6 to 35.6 percent.[17] In 2003, the union wage premium declined a substantial amount to 24.5 percent.[18] In 2014, union members had median weekly earnings of $887 in the private sector ($994 public sector). Compare this to nonunion members with median weekly earnings of $739 in the private sector ($839 public sector).[19] The union/nonunion gap has declined to 12 percent recently because of an improving job market, bumping up nonunion wages faster than those of union workers who are tied to longer term labor contracts. These differences reflect a variety of influences, including variations in the distributions of union members and nonunion employees by occupation, industry, firm size, or geographic region. Historically, union wages have experienced multiple-year upswings followed by multiple-year downswings. The 1950s were characterized by a widening of the union wage premium, followed by a constriction in the 1960s, an enlargement from 1969 to 1983, and in general a constriction from 1983 into the new millennium.[20] Since 1983, the nonunion sector has been securing larger wage increases than the unionized sector, partially due to unions' acceptance of lump-sum payments in lieu of increases in base wage.[21]

Perhaps the best conclusion about union versus nonunion wage differences comes from a summary analysis of 114 different studies.[22] Two important points emerged:

1. *Unions do make a difference in wages, across all studies and all time periods.* Union workers earn between 8.9 and 12.4 percent more than their nonunion counterparts.

2. *The size of the gap varies from year to year.* During periods of higher unemployment, the impact of unions is larger. During strong economies the union-nonunion gap is smaller. Part of the explanation for this time-based phenomenon is related to union resistance to wage cuts during recessions and the relatively slow response of unions to wage increases during inflationary periods (because it's hard to respond quickly when a union is tied to a multiyear labor contract).

---

e-Compensation

These sites provide union employment and wage information: *www.unionstats.com http://stats.bls.gov/news.release/union2.nr0.htm*

Similar studies of union-nonunion wage differentials exist for employees in the public sector.[23] Union employees in the public sector earn, on average, about 22 percent more than their nonunion counterparts.[24] However, historically, this figure masks some large variations across unions, depending on the occupation(s) they represent. The largest gains for public sector employees are reported for firefighters. At the other extreme, however, teachers' unions (primarily affiliates of the National Education Association and the American Federation of Teachers) have not fared as well, with reported impacts generally in the range of 1 to 4 percent.[25]

In recent years, wage concessions have become more prominent. Some experts claim these concessions are more common in unionized firms and that this reduces the advantage union workers hold in wages, particularly during downturns in the economy. For example, in 1908 the glass-bottle blowers accepted a 20 percent wage cut in the hopes of fighting automation. During the 1930s, concessions were a regular feature in the construction, printing, and shoe industries. Concessions were also made in the apparel and textile industries during the 1950s. More recent trends in public sector legislation don't bode well for unions. In the past few years several strongholds of unionization have passed right to work laws. In 2012 Michigan, perhaps the birthplace of unionization, joined Wisconsin and Indiana in giving workers the right to not join unions as a condition of employment. Workers no longer have to support pro Democratic views of unions or support union endorsements that oppose their personal views. It's also easier to object to rules unions attempt to establish in contracts that might stifle their personal ambitions.[26]

The Structure of Wage Packages

The second compensation issue involves the structuring of wage packages. One dimension of this issue concerns the division between direct wages and employee benefits. In unionized firms, voluntary benefits (other than those legally required) amount to 36.9 percent of the total compensation package and 27.8 percent for nonunion employees.[27] So not only is the pie bigger in unionized companies, the share devoted to benefits is bigger too.[28] Research indicates that the presence of a union adds about 30 to 40 percent to employee benefits. Whether because of reduced management control, strong union-worker preference for benefits, or other reasons, unionized employees also have a greater percentage of their total wage bill allocated to employee benefits. Typically the higher costs show up in the form of higher pension expenditures or higher insurance benefits. One particularly well-controlled study found unionization associated with a 213 percent higher level of pension expenditures and 136 percent higher health insurance expenditures.[29]

A second dimension of the wage structure issue, as we noted briefly earlier, is the evolution of **two-tier pay plans.** Basically a phenomenon of the union sector, two-tier wage structures differentiate pay based upon hiring date. A contract is negotiated which specifies that employees hired after a given target date will receive lower wages than their higher-seniority peers working on the same or similar jobs. In 2008, the UAW and GM agreed to a two-tier wage system, with wages for 16,000 positions being cut to $14 per hour.[30] Three years earlier, the United Auto Workers ratified a new contract with Caterpillar Inc. to established a two-tier pay system for the next six years. New employees make $10 to $15 per hour upon hire whereas their veteran counterparts make about $20–$22 an hour.[31] New contracts seek to address these inequities. Workers sought and were granted larger increases for new workers to lessen the differentials.[32] From management's perspective, wage tiers represent a viable alternative compensation strategy. Tiers can be used as a cost control strategy to allow expansion or investment or as a cost-cutting device to allow economic survival.[33] Two-tier pay plans initially spread because unions viewed them as less painful than wage freezes and staff cuts among existing employees. The tradeoff, however, was a bargaining away of equivalent wage treatment for future employees. Recognize, this is a radical departure from the most basic precepts of unionization. Unions evolved and continue to endure, in part based on the belief that all members are equal. Two-tier plans are obviously at odds with this principle.

Lower-tier employees, those hired after the contract is ratified, receive wages 50 to 80 percent lower than employees in the higher tier.[34] The contract may specify that the wage differential may be permanent, or the lower tier may be scheduled ultimately to catch up with the upper tier. Eventually the inequity from receiving different pay for the same level may cause employee dissatisfaction.[35] Consider the Roman Emperor Carcalla who implemented a two-tier system for his army in AD 217.[36] He was assassinated by his disgruntled troops shortly thereafter. Although such expressions of dissatisfaction are unlikely today, unions are much more reluctant to accept a two-tier structure and may view it as a strategy of last resort.

Union Impact: The Spillover Effect

Although union wage settlements have declined in recent years, the impact of unions in general would be understated if we did not account for what is termed the *spillover effect*. Specifically, employers seek to avoid unionization by offering workers the wages, benefits, and working conditions won in rival unionized firms. The nonunion management continues to enjoy the freedom from union "interference" in decision making, and the workers receive the spillover of rewards already obtained by their unionized counterparts. Several studies document the existence of this phenomenon, although smaller as union power diminishes, providing further evidence of the continuing role played by unions in wage determination.[37]

Role of Unions in Wage and Salary Policies and Practices

Perhaps of greatest interest to current and future compensation administrators is the role unions play in administering wages. The role of unions in administering compensation is outlined primarily in the contract. The following illustrations of this role are taken from major collective bargaining agreements.

Basis of Pay

The vast majority of contracts specify that one or more jobs are to be compensated on an hourly basis and that overtime pay will be paid beyond a certain number of hours. Notice the specificity of the language in the following contract clause:

A. Overtime pay is to be paid at the rate of one and one-half (1 1/2) times the basic hourly straight-time rate.

B. Overtime shall be paid to employees for work performed only after eight (8) hours on duty in any one service day or forty (40) hours in any one service week. Nothing in this Section shall be construed by the parties or any reviewing authority to deny the payment of overtime to employees for time worked outside of their regularly scheduled work week at the request of the Employer.

C. Penalty overtime pay is to be paid at the rate of two (2) times the basic hourly straight-time rate. Penalty overtime pay will not be paid for any hours worked in the month of December.

D. Excluding December, part-time flexible employees will receive penalty overtime pay for all work in excess of ten (10) hours in a service day or fifty-six (56) hours in a service week.

Bargaining agreement between the American Postal Workers Union, AFL-CIO and U.S. Postal Service,

Further, many contracts specify a premium be paid above the worker's base wage for working nonstandard shifts:

> Double time will be paid as follows, except as provided in paragraph 4: (a) for time worked on a calendar Sunday (b) For time worked on a the calendar holidays designated in subparagraph (273). (Source: DaimlerChrysler Corporation and International Union, United Automobile Aerospace and Agricultural Implement Workers of America (UAW) Local 12 (Jeep Unit))

Alternatively, agreements may specify a fixed daily, weekly, biweekly, or monthly rate. In addition, agreements often indicate a specific day of the week as payday and sometimes require payment on or before a certain hour.

Much less frequently, contracts specify some form of incentive system as the basis for pay. The vast majority of clauses specifying incentive pay occur in manufacturing (as opposed to nonmanufacturing) industries:

> *Section 7. Establishment of Labor Standards.* The Company and the Union, being firmly committed to the principle that high wages can result only from high productivity, agree that the Company will establish Labor Standards that:
>
> a.   Are fair and equitable to both the Company and the workers; and
> b.   Are based on the working capacity of a normally qualified worker properly motivated and working at an incentive pace; and
> c.   Give due consideration to the quality of workmanship and product required; and
> d.   Provide proper allowances for fatigue, personal time, and normal delays, and
> e.   Provide for payment of incentive workers based on the earned hours produced onstandard (except when such Employees are working on a Preliminary Estimate, etc.), and for each one per cent (1%) increase in acceptable production over standard, such workers shall receive a one per cent (1%) increase in pay over the applicable incentive rate.
>
> The Company will, at its discretion as to the time and as to jobs to be placed on or removed from incentive, continue the earned-hour incentive system now in effect, and extend it to jobs in such other job classifications which, in the opinion of the Company, can properly be placed on incentive, with the objective of increasing productivity and providing an opportunity for workers to enjoy higher earnings thus made possible. The plan shall be maintained in accordance with the following principles.
> (Source: Maytag, Maytag and Admiral Products, and Auto Workers)

Occupation-Wage Differentials

Most contracts recognize that different occupations should receive different wage rates. Within occupations, though, a single wage rate prevails:

Occupational Code	Classification	Rate/hr
C5	Sheet and metal fabricator	$19.78
D1	Machinist grind, lap, and hone	20.45
D2	Machinist turn, drill, bore, and mill	20.45
F16	Spot welder	19.78
M26	Miscellaneous processor	18.63

Source: Agreement between John Deere and Company and Internation Union United Automobile Aerospace and Agricultural Implement Workers of America, October 2015.

Although rare, there are some contracts that do not recognize occupational/skill differentials. These contracts specify a single standard rate for all jobs covered by the agreements. Usually such contracts cover a narrow range of skilled groups.

Experience/Merit Differentials

Single rates are usually specified for workers within a particular job classification. Single-rate agreements do not differentiate wages on the basis of either seniority or merit. Workers with varying years of experience and output receive the same single rate. Alternatively, agreements may specify wage ranges. The following example is fairly typical:

Job Title	Years of Experience							
	None	**1**	**2**	**3**	**4**	**6**	**8**	**12**
Computer operators	$10.05	$10.30	$10.55	$10.80	$11.05	$11.55	$12.30	$14.05
QC inspectors	$12.30	$12.55	$12.80	$13.05	$13.30	$13.80	14.30	$16.30

Source: Negotiated agreement between District School Board of St. Johns County and St. Johns School Support Association.

The vast majority of contracts, as in the example above, specify seniority as the basis for movement through the range. *Automatic progression* is an appropriate name for this type of movement through the wage range, with the contract frequently specifying the time interval between movements. This type of progression is most appropriate when the necessary job skills are within the grasp of most employees. Denial of a raise is rare and frequently is accompanied by the right of the union to grieve the decision.

A second, and far less common, strategy for moving employees through wage ranges is based exclusively on merit. Employees who are evaluated more highly receive larger or more rapid increments than average or poor performers. Within these contracts, it is common to specify that disputed merit appraisals may be submitted to grievance. If the right to grieve is not explicitly excluded, the union also has the implicit right to grieve.

The third method for movement through a range combines automatic and merit progression in some manner. A frequent strategy is to grant automatic increases up to the midpoint of the range and permit subsequent increases only when merited on the basis of performance appraisal.

Other Differentials

There are a number of remaining contractual provisions that deal with differentials for reasons not yet covered. A first example deals with different pay to unionized employees who are employed by a firm in different geographic areas. Very few contracts provide for different wages under these circumstances, despite the problems that can arise in paying uniform wages across regions with markedly different costs of living.

A second category where differentials are mentioned in contracts deals with part-time and temporary employees. Few contracts specify special rates for these employees. Those that do, however, are about equally split between giving part-time and temporary employees wages above full-time workers (because they have been excluded from the employee benefit program) or below full-time workers.

Vacations and Holidays

Vacation and holiday entitlements are among the clauses frequently found in labor contracts. They, too, use very specific language, as the following example illustrates:

26.01 Observance
The following holidays will be observed:
New Year's Day—First Day in January;
Martin Luther King, Jr.'s Birthday—Third Monday in January;
President's Day—Third Monday in February;
Memorial Day—Last Monday in May;
Independence Day—Fourth day of July;
Labor Day—First Monday in September;
Columbus Day—Second Monday in October;
Veterans' Day—Eleventh day of November;
Thanksgiving Day—Fourth Thursday in November;
Christmas Day—Twenty-fifth day of December;
Any other day proclaimed by the Governor of the State of Ohio or the President of the United States.

When a holiday falls on a Sunday, the holiday is observed on the following Monday. When a holiday falls on a Saturday, the holiday is observed on the preceding Friday. For employees whose work assignment is to a seven (7) day operation, the holiday shall be celebrated on the day it actually falls. A holiday shall start at 12:01 A.M. or with the work shift that includes 12:01 A.M.

26.02 Work on Holidays
Employees required to work on a holiday will be compensated at their discretion either at the rate of one and one-half (1 1/2) times their regular rate of pay, or granted compensatory time at the rate of one and one-half (1 1/2) times, plus straight-time pay for the holiday. The choice of compensatory time or wages will be made by the employee. Holiday work beyond regularly scheduled work shall be distributed among employees by the provisions covered in Article 13. No employees' posted regular schedule or days off shall be changed to avoid holiday premium pay. Once posted, the employee's schedule shall not be changed, except that an employee who is scheduled to work on the holiday may be directed not to report to work on the holiday. The Agency reserves the right to determine the number of employees needed to work the holiday.
(Source: State of Ohio and Ohio Civil Service Employees Association (OCSEA) collective bargaining agreement.)

Wage Adjustment Provisions

Frequently in multiyear contracts some provision is made for wage adjustment during the term of the contract. There are three major ways these adjustments might be specified: (1) deferred wage increases, (2) **reopener clauses**, and (3) **cost-of-living**

adjustments (COLAs) or escalator clauses. A *deferred wage increase* is negotiated at the time of initial contract negotiations with the timing and amount specified in the contract. A *reopener clause* specifies that wages, and sometimes such nonwage items as pension and benefits, will be renegotiated at a specified time or under certain conditions. Finally, a *COLA clause,* as noted earlier, involves periodic adjustments based typically on changes in the consumer price index:

Section 4. Cost of Living Adjustment

A. Definitions

1. "Consumer Price Index" refers to the "National Consumer Price Index for Urban Wage Earners and Clerical Workers," published by the Bureau of Labor (1967 = 100) and referred to herein as the "Index."
2. "Consumer Price Index Base" refers to the Consumer Price Index for the month of October 2001 and is referred to herein as the "Base Index."

B. Effective Dates of Adjustment
Each employee covered by this Agreement shall receive cost-of-living adjustments, upward, in accordance with the formula in Section 4.C, below, effective on the following dates:
—the second full pay period after the release of the January 2002 Index
—the second full pay period after the release of the July 2002 Index
—the second full pay period after the release of the January 2003 Index
—the second full pay period after the release of the July 2003 Index

C. The basic salary schedules provided for in this Agreement shall be increased 1 cent per hour for each full 0.4 of a point increase in the applicable Index above the Base Index. For example, if the increase in the Index from October 2011 to January 2012 is 1.2 points, all pay scales for employees covered by this Agreement will be increased by 3 cents per hour. In no event will a decline in the Index below the Base Index result in a decrease in the pay scales provided for in this Agreement.
(Bargaining agreement between American Postal Workers Union, AFL-CIO, and U.S. Postal Service.)

UNIONS AND ALTERNATIVE REWARD SYSTEMS

International competition causes a fundamental problem for unions. If a unionized company settles a contract and raises prices to cover increased wage costs, there is always the threat that an overseas competitor with lower labor costs will capture market share. Eventually, enough market share erosion means the unionized company is out of business. To keep this from happening, unions have become much more receptive in recent years to alternative reward systems that link pay to performance. After all, if worker productivity rises, product prices can remain relatively stable even with wage increases.

About 20 percent of all U.S. collective bargaining agreements permit some alternative reward system (e.g., lump sum, piece rate, gain sharing, profit sharing, skill-based pay).[38] Willingness to try such plans is higher when the firm faces extreme competitive pressure.[39] In the unionized firms that do experiment with these alternative reward systems, though, the union usually insists on safeguards that protect both the union and its workers. The union insists on group-based performance measures with equal pay-outs to members. This equality principle cuts down strife and internal quarrels among the members and reinforces the principles of equity that are at the very foundation of union beliefs. To minimize bias by the company, performance measures more often tend to be objective in unionized companies. Most frequently the measures rely on past performance as a gauge of realistic targets rather than on some time study or other engineering standard that might appear more susceptible to tampering.[40] Below we offer specific feedback about union attitudes toward alternative reward concepts.

Lump-Sum Awards

As discussed in Chapter 10, **lump-sum awards** are one-time cash payments to employees that are not added to an employee's base wages. These awards are typically given in lieu of merit increases, which are more costly to the employer. This higher cost results both because merit increases are added on to base wages and because several employee benefits (e.g., life insurance and vacation pay) are figured as a percentage of base wages. Lump-sum payments are a reality of union contracts. For the past 10 years, a stable one-third of all major collective bargaining agreements in the private sector have contained a provision for lump-sum payouts. An example of lump sum awards between the UAW and General Motors is shown in Exhibit 15.1.

Employee Stock Ownership Plans (ESOPs)

An alternative strategy for organizations hurt by intense competition is to control base wages in exchange for giving employees part ownership in the company. For example, Southwest Airlines readily grants employee stock options as a key feature of its wage control strategy.[41]

Pay-for-Knowledge Plans

Pay-for-knowledge plans do just that: pay employees more for learning a variety of different jobs or skills. For example, the UAW negotiates provisions giving hourly-wage increases for learning new skills on different parts of the assembly process. By coupling this new wage system with drastic cuts in the number of job classifications, organizations have greater flexibility in moving employees quickly into high-demand areas. Unions also may favor pay-for-knowledge plans because they make each individual worker more valuable, and less expendable, to the firm. In turn, this also lessens the probability that work can be subcontracted out to nonunion organizations.

EXHIBIT 15.1 **Lump Sum, Quality Performance Bonus, and Profit Share Schedule: UAW and General Motors**

Date	Type	Amount
March 2014	Profit Share	As determined
June 2014	Lump Sum	$1,000
December 2014	Quality Performance Bonus	Up to $250
March 2015	Profit Share	As determined

Gain-Sharing Plans

Gain-sharing plans are designed to align workers and management in efforts to streamline operations and cut costs. Any cost savings resulting from employees' working more efficiently are split, according to some formula, between the organization and the workers. Some reports indicate gain sharing is more common in unionized than non-unionized firms.[42] In our experience, success is dependent on a willingness to include union members in designing the plan. Openness in sharing financial and production data, key elements of putting a gain-sharing plan in place, are important in building trust between the two parties.

While unions aren't always enthusiastic about gain sharing, they rarely directly oppose it, at least initially. Rather, the most common union strategy is to delay taking a stand until real costs and benefits are more apparent.[43] Politically, this may be the wisest choice for a union leader. As Exhibit 15.2 illustrates, there are numerous possible costs and benefits to union members for agreeing to a gain-sharing plan. Until the plan is actually implemented, though, it is unclear what the impact will be in any particular firm.

Profit-Sharing Plans

Unions have debated the advantages of profit-sharing plans for at least 80 years.[44] Walter Reuther, president of the CIO in 1948 (which became the AFL-CIO in 1955) championed the cause of profit sharing in the auto industry. In years past, the primary goal of unions was to secure sound, stable income levels for members. Coming out of the great recession, saving and creating jobs is rapidly becoming the top priority. Consider the auto industry. Foreign producers with U.S. plants (Volkswagen and Hyundai) have labor costs about one-half (27 dollars per hour) that of GM and Ford. Both U.S. companies seek greater profit sharing rather than wage increases as a way to become more competitive.[45]

EXHIBIT 15.2   Union Perceptions of Gain Sharing

The Top Nine Reasons for Unions Favoring Gain Sharing:	The Top Nine Reasons for Unions Opposing Gain Sharing:
1. Increased recognition	1. Management may try to substitute it for wages
2. Better job security	2. Management cannot be trusted
3. Increased involvement with job activities	3. Peer pressure to perform may increase
4. More money	4. Bonus calculations are not understood or trusted
5. Increased feeling of achievement or contributing to the organization	5. Union influence is undermined
6. Increased influence of union	6. Increased productivity may reduce need for jobs
7. Greater contributions to the nation's productivity	7. Grievances may go unprocessed
8. Compatibility with union goals	8. Gain sharing is incompatible with union goals
9. Fewer grievances	9. Employees really do not want more involvement

Source: http://www.bovino-consulting.com.

Your **Turn**

Predicting a Contract's Clauses

The Realities for General Motors

GM must remain competitive with global competitors who have much lower labor costs (in some instances because wages are lower, such as in Korea, and in some instances because the work-forces are younger and retirement/health costs aren't as high, as in the case of Japanese auto-makers who have plants in the United States). To cut labor costs, GM has made numerous moves over the past 20+ years:

1. Shifted from a straight automatic wage increase for every new contract to a clause more de-pendent on profit sharing. This allows the company to pay a bigger profit share during good years, yet protect themselves from high labor costs in bad profit years by giving low or no profit-sharing payout.
2. Introduced technologies that reduced the number of workers needed, both in the assembly line operations and in the skilled trades (e.g., pattern makers work in wood or metal to make models of future cars or future parts of cars—new technologies lead to lower demand for these pattern makers).
3. Introduced a two-tier wage plan in which new hires are paid substantially less than workers hired before the two-tier plan was initiated. In the past years, new workers received about $14/hour while their more senior counterparts—those hired before the plan was implemented—received about $28/hour in wages for doing essentially the same jobs.
4. Cut benefits costs, largely in the amount of health-care and pension expenses.

The Realities for the United Auto Workers

1. Unions preach fairness and equity. Workers are attracted to unions in part because they fight for fairness and equity.
2. Unions have faced catastrophic reductions in their membership. Companies, seeking to survive in a global environment, assert they can't afford the costs (and reduced freedom in decision making) that accompany unionization. To survive, unions have reluctantly become more ac-cepting of management demands.
3. The auto industry is a stronghold of unionization that unions cannot afford to lose. Further, Michigan is the historic birthplace of auto industry growth and industry unionization. As an ancillary goal, unions would like to preserve the Michigan stronghold.

Given all this information, explain why the following components of the current agreement are predictable outcomes.

a. The most recent agreement gives a $5,000 signing bonus to eligible UAW-represented GM employees, which could be worth as much as $242.5 million.
b. Entry-level assembly workers will be paid $2 to $3 more per hour, and more experienced Tier-2 employees (Tier 2 is the name for the tier of workers who were hired after the lower wage level for new hires was implemented) will see wages hiked to between $16 and $19 per hour.

c. The UAW negotiated a new profit-sharing formula based on GM's North American profits. Formerly profit-sharing checks issued to employees were based on a more global profit measure.

d. GM agreed to rehire laid-off workers, transfer jobs from overseas back to the United States, and give buyout offers to skilled trade workers for whom there are no longer job openings.

e. GM agreed to restart production at an idled plant in Spring Hill, Tennessee, and to start assembly of new products at factories in Michigan.

Summary

Other countries continue to make inroads in product areas traditionally the sole domain of American companies. The impact of this increased competition has been most pronounced in the compensation area. Labor costs must be cut to improve our competitive stance. Alternative compensation systems to achieve this end are regularly being devised. Unions face a difficult situation. How should they respond to these attacks on traditional compensation systems? Many unions believe that the crisis demands changing attitudes from both management and unions. Labor and management identify compensation packages that both parties can abide. Sometimes these packages include cuts in traditional forms of wages in exchange for compensation tied more closely to the success of the firm. We expect the beginning of the 21st century to be dominated by more innovation in compensation design and increased exploration between unions and management for ways to improve the competitive stance of American business.

Review Questions

1. What is spillover? How does it lead to underestimation of the impact unions have on wages?

2. Why don't many public sector unions have the right to strike, a weapon almost universally guaranteed in the private sector? Make your explanation based on compensation.

3. If merit pay is supposed to increase individual equity and unions are very concerned about equity, why do unions frequently oppose merit pay for their membership?

4. It is probably true that, if given a choice, unions would prefer to implement a skill-based pay system rather than some form of gain-sharing plan. Why?

Endnotes

1. Jack Fiorito, "Human Resource Management Practices and Worker Desires for Union Representation," *Journal of Labor Research* 22(2), Spring 2001, pp. 335–354; Thomas A. Kochan, Harry C. Katz, and Robert B. McKersie, *The Transformation of American Industrial Relations* (New York: Basic Books, 1986), pp. 221–223.

2. "Union Members Summary—Bureau of Labor Statistics," http://www.bls.gov/news.release/union2.nr0.htm, visited May 8, 2015.

3. http://www.nlrb.gov/sites/default/files/attachments/basic-page/node-4141/FY%202014. pdf, visited May 8, 2015.

4. Ibid.

5. USDOL, TED: The Editor's Desk, 2010, www.bls.gov/opub/ted/2010/ted_20100709_data.htm

6. John Pencavel, "How Successful Have Trade Unions Been? A Utility-Based Indicator of Union Well-Being," *Industrial & Labor Relations Review* 62(2), January 2009, pp. 147–156.

7. Julie Jargon, "Fast food Workers Take to Streets," *Wall Street Journal*, September 5, 2014, p. B3.

8. www.bls.gov/opub/ted/2008/feb/wk2/art01.htm; retrieved on September 9, 2008.

9. Erin Hatton, "Temporary Weapons: Employers' Use of Temps Against Organized Labor," *Industrial and Labor Relations Review* 67(1) 2014, pp. 86–111.

10. David A. Macpherson and James B. Steward, "The Effect of International Competition on Union and Non-Union Wages," *Industrial and Labor Relations Review* 43(4), 1990, pp. 434–446.

11. John W. Miller, "ArcelorMittal in Pact," *Wall Street Journal*, September 10, 2012, p. B3.

12. Robert J. Flanagan, "Has Management Strangled U.S. Unions?" *Journal of Labor Research* 26(1), 2005, pp. 33–98; Gail McCallion, "Union Membership Decline: Competing Theories and Economic Implications," CRS report for Congress, August 23, 1993, p. 13.

13. John D. Stoll, "UAW's Rands Press to Close Pay Gap," *Wall Street Journal*, March 23, 2015, p. B2.

14. John Stoll, "UAW, Detroit Prep for Talks," *Wall Street Journal*, December 8, 2014, p. B1.

15. Allan M. Carter and F. Ray Marshall, *Labor Economics* (Homewood, IL: Irwin, 1982).

16. Ibid.

17. David A. Macpherson and James B. Steward, "The Effect of International Competition on Union and Non-Union Wages," *Industrial and Labor Relations Review* 43(4), 1990, pp. 434–446.

18. Lawrence Mishel and Matthew Walters, "How Unions Help All Workers," Economic Policy Institute, www.epinet.org/content.cfm/briefingpapers_bp143; June 2, 2006.

19. http://www.bls.gov/news.release/union2.t04.htm.

20. Fehmida Sleemi, "Collective Bargaining Outlook for 1995," *Compensation and Working Conditions* 47(1), January 1995, pp. 19–39.

21. Ibid.

22. Stephen B. Jarrell and T. D. Stanley, "A Meta-Analysis of the Union–Non-Union Wage Gap," *Industrial and Labor Relations Review* 44(1), 1990, pp. 54–67.

23. David Lewin, "Public Sector Labor Relations: A Review Essay," in *Public Sector Labor Relations: Analysis and Readings,* David Lewin, Peter Feuille, and Thomas Kochan, eds. (Glen Ridge, NJ: Thomas Horton and Daughters, 1977), pp. 116–144.

24. The Labor Research Association, "Union v. Non-Union: Median Weekly Earnings in 2004," www.laborresearch.org/charts.php?id=34, June 3, 2006; John D. Bitzan, "The Effects of Unions on Wages by Occupation in the Public Sector," *International Business & Economics Research Journal* 9(7), 2010, pp. 107–119.

25. For a discussion on the reasons for this smaller public sector union impact, see Lewin et al., *Public Sector Labor Relations: Analysis and Readings* (Glen Ridge, N.J.: Thomas Horton and Daughters, 1977).

26. USA Today, "Right-to-Work Trend Bolsters Individual Rights," *USA Today*, March 17, 2015, 7A; Matthew Dolan and Kris Maher, "Unions Dealt Blow in UAW's Home State," *Wall Street Journal*, December 12, 2012, pp. A1, 4.

27. Bureau of Labor Statistics, "Employer Costs for Employee Compensation Summary," Table 7: Private industry, by region and bargaining status," stats.bls.gov/news.release/ecec .nr0.htm, March 28, 2006.

28. Bureau of Labor Statistics, "Employer Costs for Employee Compensation Summary, Table 7: Private industry, by major occupational group and bargaining status," December 2008, www.bls.gov/news.release/ecec.nr0.htm, retrieved on January 29, 2009; Bureau of Labor Statistics, "Employer Costs for Employee Compensation Summary, Table 5: Private industry, by major occupational group and bargaining status," December 2008, www.bls .gov/news.release/ecec.nr0.htm, January 29, 2009.

29. Loren Solnick, "Unionism and Fringe Benefits Expenditures," *Industrial Relations* 17(1), 1978, pp. 102–107.

30. Robert Snell, "Buyouts at GM Open Door for Hiring at Lower Wages," *Detroit News,* March 27, 2009, p. A1.

31. The Labor Research Association, "Two-Tier and Lump Sum Contracts Reappear," www .laborresearch.org/page_src.php?id=372˜src=Two%20tier, June 5, 2006.

32. Snavely, B., Thompson, C., and G. Gardner, "GM, UAW Deal Adds Jobs, Gives Bonus, Raises to Workers," *Buffalo News,* September 18, 2011, p. A1.

33. James E. Martin and Thomas D. Heetderks, *Two Tier Compensation Structures: Their Impact on Unions, Employers and Employees* (Kalamazoo, MI: Upjohn Institute for Employment Research, 1990).

34. Mollie Bowers and Roger Roderick, "Two-Tier Pay Systems: The Good, the Bad, and the Debatable," *Personnel Administrator* 32(6), 1987, pp. 101–112.

35. James Martin and Melanie Peterson, "Two-Tier Wage Structures: Implications for Equity Theory," *Academy of Management Journal* 30(2), 1987, pp. 297–315.

36. Ann C. Foster, "Union-Nonunion Wage Differences, 1997," *Compensation and Working Conditions,* 2006, p. 46.

37. Richard B. Freeman and Joel Rogers, *What Workers Want* (Ithaca, NY: ILR Press, 1999); David Neumark and Michael L. Wachter, "Union Effects on Nonunion Wages: Evidence from Panel Data on Industries and Cities," *Industrial and Labor Relations Review* 31(1), 1978, pp. 205–216.

38. J. L. McAdams and E. J. Hawk, *Organizational Performance and Reward: 663 Experiences in Making the Link* (Scottsdale, AZ: American Compensation Association, 1994).

39. L. B. Cardinal and I. B. Helbrun, "Union Versus Nonunion Attitudes Toward Share Agreements," in *Proceedings of the 39th Annual Meeting of the Industrial Relations Research Association* (Madison, WI: IRRA, 1987), pp. 167–173.

40. R. L. Heneman, C. von Hippel, D. E. Eskew, and D. B. Greenberger, "Alternative Rewards in Union Environments," *American Counseling Association Journal*, Summer 1997, pp. 42–55.

41. "Southwest Air, Agents' Union Reach an Accord," *The Wall Street Journal,* December 26, 2002.

42. R. L. Heneman and C. von Hippel, "Alternative Rewards in Unionized Environments," *ACA Journal* 6 (1995), pp. 42–55.

43. T. Ross and R. Ross, "Gainsharing and Unions: Current Trends," in *Gainsharing: Plans for Improving Performance,* B. Graham-Moore and T. Ross, eds. (Washington, DC: Bureau of National Affairs), pp. 200–213.

44. J. Zalusky, "Labor's Collective Bargaining Experience with Gainsharing and Profit Sharing," paper presented at the 39th Annual Meeting of the Industrial Relations Research Association, December 1986, pp. 175–182; William Shaw, "Can Labor Be Capitalized?" *American Federationist* 17 (June 1910), p. 517.

45. Matthew Dolan, "UAW Wants Union Jobs," *The Wall Street Journal,* July 25, 2011, pp. B1, 11.

International Pay Systems

All around the world, decentralized pay-setting competitive forces have changed the way people work and how they get paid.[1] Toyota and other Japanese companies have dismantled their seniority-based pay systems for managers and replaced them with merit-based systems.[2] Toshiba offers stock awards, which were not even legal in Japan only a few years ago.[3] Deutsche Bank, Nokia, Seimens, and other European companies are shifting to variable pay and performance-based (rather than personality-based) appraisal in their search for ways to improve productivity and control labor costs.[4] China's employment system has experienced a "fundamental transformation from stable and permanent employment with good benefits (often called the iron rice bowl) to a system characterized by highly precarious employment with no benefits for about 40 percent of the population."[5] In 1990, multinational companies employed 21.5 million people in their foreign affiliates. By 2010, it was 61.2 million and by 2013, it was 70.7 million.[6] Among the largest U.S. companies, about three-fourths of new jobs in recent years were added not in the United States, but rather overseas.[7] In 2000, General Motors produced 4.2 million vehicles in the United States and 30,000 vehicles in China. In 2013, by contrast, GM produced 2.0 million vehicles in the United States and 3.2 million vehicles in China.[8]

Global acquisitions of former competitors change pay systems. As part of its takeover and restructuring of Tungsram Electric in Poland, General Electric changed from a rigid seniority-based pay system to broad bands, market-based wage rates, and performance bonuses. India's leading software companies such as Tata Consulting Services, Wipro, and Infosystems all use performance-based bonus plans for their software engineers. Prior to Daimler's acquisition of Chrysler in 1998, the pay for Chrysler's CEO was equal to the combined total pay of the top 10 Daimler executives. As little as 25 percent of Chrysler managers' total compensation was in the form of base pay, whereas Daimler managers' base pay accounted for up to 60 percent of their total compensation. The merged DaimlerChrysler adopted a Chrysler-like approach to executive compensation. Some have even claimed that the attractive pay was the reason Daimler executives were eager to acquire Chrysler![9]

This merger, described by some as a "marriage made in hell," ended unhappily after 10 years (but presumably Daimler executives got to keep the "engagement ring" of higher pay).[10] One might also say that Daimler in particular had "hell to pay" to get out of the marriage. Daimler paid $36 billion for Chrysler in 1998, but received only $7.4 billion in 2006 when it sold 80.1 percent of Chrysler to Cerberus Capital Management.[11] As part of Chrysler's bankruptcy, Daimler appears to have received nothing for its remaining stake. Rather, it had to write off $1.5 billion in loans it made to Chrysler in 2008 and also had to make a payment of $600 million to Chrysler's pension plan.[12] Daimler will not be having bouts of nostalgia looking back at its marriage with Chrysler. Perhaps Daimler and Chrysler underestimated the challenges posed by the differences in contextual factors of the sort we highlight in this chapter. Any merger or acquisition, even between companies in the same country, has challenges. Adding an international component adds another layer of challenges.[13] Nevertheless, another suitor burst onto the scene. The Italian carmaker, Fiat, initially acquired 20 to 35 percent ownership in Chrysler and later increased it to 58.5 percent and then to 100 percent. Although Fiat is more similar (its product portfolio includes basic vehicles) than Daimler (high-end vehicles) to Chrysler in some ways, it is more similar to Daimler in its experience on a number of the other factors we will discuss in this chapter (ownership structure, regulation, trade union experience, social contract).[14] Thus, it was not clear whether things would work out better the second time around for a Chrysler merger with a European company that is used to operating in a different context.[15] Nevertheless, opinion seems to be that the Fiat-Chrysler merger is working.[16]

Sometimes changes in pay are directly tied to cataclysmic sociopolitical change, as in China, Russia, and Eastern Europe, where government authorities had long dictated pay rates.[17] Now companies in these countries face the challenge of devising pay systems responsive to business and market pressures while maintaining a sense of social justice among the people. In China, the only hope for profitability in many state-owned enterprises is to cut the massively bloated head count. Yet an army of unemployed people without social support is a threat to government survival.[18] Some state-owned enterprises, such as Baogang, the country's largest steelmaker, have moved to more "market- and performance-based" systems, even though labor markets are just emerging in many regions in China. Shanghai Shenyingwanguo Security Company and Shanghai Bank have implemented job-based structures to help them retain key employees and increase pay satisfaction. Most surprising of all is that some town-owned enterprises are using stock ownership as part of their employee compensation.[19] China may still be striving to become a worker's paradise, but the experimentation with compensation approaches might already qualify it as a pay pundit's paradise.

However, too much change and experimentation can have a dark side that threatens to create social unrest. Following the breakup of the USSR, workers in some of the formerly socialist countries reported going unpaid for months. At one point over half the Russian workers said they were owed back wages, with the average wait to be paid at 4.8 months.[20] A friend in Russia maintains that "the most effective pay delivery system is a brown bag under the table."

So it is a time of unprecedented global change. Or is it? Let's step back to gain some historical perspective:

> There [is] hardly a village or town anywhere on the globe whose wages are not influenced by distant foreign markets, whose infrastructure is not financed by foreign capital, whose engineering, manufacturing, and even business skills are not imported from abroad, or whose labor markets are not influenced by the absence of those who had emigrated or by the presence of strangers who had immigrated.[21]

This is not a description of the 21st century. Rather, it is from 100 years ago. In the late 1800s, trade barriers were being reduced, free trade was being promoted, and mass migration of people was underway. Thanks to transoceanic telegraphic cables, the speed of communication had increased dramatically, and investment capital flowed among nations. Yet by 1917 these global links had been replaced with a global war. Citizens desired security rather than face the greater risks and uncertainty of globalization. Nations began to raise tariffs to protect domestic companies hurt by foreign competitors. Immigrants were accused of "robbing jobs." Historians conclude that "globalization is neither unique nor irreversible; it has and can again sow seeds of its own destruction."[22]

THE GLOBAL CONTEXT

Understanding international compensation begins with recognizing differences and similarities and figuring out how best to manage them. How people get paid around the world depends on variations shown in Exhibit 16.1—*economic, institutional, organizational,* and *employee characteristics.* These factors have been discussed throughout the book; now they can be applied globally. But once we shift from a domestic to an international perspective, the discussion must necessarily broaden.

EXHIBIT 16.1 **The International Context of Compensation**

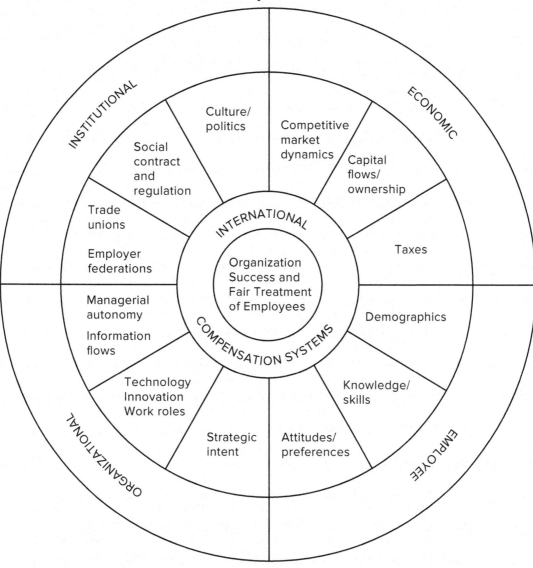

Source: © George T. Milkovich.

Organizations must first determine the degree to which each of these contextual factors constrain their compensation decisions and practices. Some constraints are regulatory (i.e., laws), while others may be more normative (national culture, the social contract).[23] In some cases (e.g., laws/regulations), there may be little room to exercise strategy.[24] On the other hand, in the case of other contextual factors (e.g., national culture), the constraint may be less than often believed.[25] So, to be sure, there are differences, on average, between organizations, depending on the country.[26] However, there is also evidence that different management approaches are used within the same country.[27] To the degree that strategy can be exercised, an organization must decide the degree to which it will choose compensation practices similar to those used by other organizations and the degree to which it will be different. Being the same is perhaps less risky, but, by necessity, following the pack means there is little chance to stand out from the pack and thus little chance to achieve anything better than average performance.[28] Also, in the international context, it is not always simple to follow the pack. A multinational corporation (MNC) having the United States as its home country may see a typical way of doing things there, but may see a different typical way of doing things in another country where it operates. If they want to play follow the pack or follow the leader, which do they follow? (There seem to be a lot of metaphors available here! Bonus points for you if you can name the group that sang "Leader of the Pack." Double bonus points if you can name the most well-known sound effect in the song's performance and in which country the song was banned from the airwaves.) Evidence indicates that MNCs are influenced by both the institutional pressures in their home country and in the local context.[29] To follow the (leader, pack, herd, lemmings, you choose), companies must balance pressures toward localization ("when in Rome . . .")— where compensation practice is tailored to each country—and standardization (where consistency, not with the local context, but instead with the organization's business strategy, is the objective).[30] Finally, organizations may weight the home and local country context differently for different jobs. For example, in higher level jobs, the local country context influence may be weaker.[31]

In the following discussion, we highlight five specific, contextual factors we feel are especially relevant in international compensation. These are variations in (1) social contracts, including the legal framework and regulation; (2) cultures; (3) trade unions; (4) ownership and financial markets; and (5) managers' autonomy. Although we separate the factors to clarify our discussion, they do not separate so easily in reality. Instead, they overlap and interact.

THE SOCIAL CONTRACT

Viewed as part of the social contract, the employment relationship is more than an exchange between an individual and an employer. It includes the government, all enterprise owners (sometimes acting individually and sometimes collectively through owner associations), and all employees (sometimes acting individually and sometimes in trade unions). The relationships and expectations of these parties form the social contract. As you think about how people get paid around the world, it will be clear that different people in different countries hold differing beliefs about the role of government, employees, unions, and employers. Understanding how to manage employee compensation in any country requires an understanding of the social contract in that country. Changing employee compensation systems—for example, to make them more responsive to customers, encourage innovative and quality service, or control costs— require changing the expectations of parties to the social contract.

The social contract evolves over time, sometimes very quickly. One need look no further than the United States for recent examples. Compared to many countries (e.g., those in the European Union), government has traditionally played a relatively modest role in the employment relationship. However, that role has recently greatly expanded, at least in two key sectors of the U.S. economy: automobiles and financial services. Consider that Chrysler and General Motors (GM) have recently gone through bankruptcy and upon their exit, major shareholders were the United Automobile Workers (UAW) union and the U.S. government (in return for the many billions in funds it has provided to stave off liquidation). In the financial services industry, the U.S. government also played a major role recently in saving firms, either by providing funds (e.g., Citibank, Goldman Sachs, Capital One, and many others) under the Troubled Assets Relief Program (TARP) or by actively facilitating mergers and acquisitions (e.g., Bank of America's acquisition of Merrill Lynch). The TARP program in the United States provided $700 billion (in return for warrants enabling the U.S. government to buy stock in the companies), an amount roughly the same as the total economic output (gross domestic product) of Turkey, the 17th largest economy in the world. As one of the "strings attached" to the TARP funds, the U.S. Treasury Department has issued special executive compensation regulations for firms while they have TARP funding (see Chapter 17). In summary, the social contract in the United States, known for the small role of government and the lack of a tripartite relationship between government, employees (and their representatives), and employers, has done a rapid "about face," at least in two of its major industries. While this government involvement and tripartism is seen as temporary, the question is whether this model will become the norm in the United States for handling future crises of this sort.

Centralized or Decentralized Pay-Setting

Perhaps the most striking example of the social contract's effects on pay systems is in Exhibit 16.2, which contrasts the degree of centralization of pay setting among countries.[32] Companies in the United States, United Kingdom, and some central European

EXHIBIT 16.2
The Social Contracts and Primary Bargaining Level in Selected European Union Countries and the United States

Source: European Industrial Relations Observatory Online, "Changes in National Collective Bargaining Systems Since 1990," 2005, http://www.eurofound.europa.eu/eiro/, June 30, 2009.

countries use highly decentralized approaches with little government involvement. In contrast, in western and northern European countries, wage bargaining is more likely to be centralized, taking place primarily at the industry or national level, with government involvement being typical in national-level bargaining countries.

Although understanding differences in wage bargaining levels is important, it should also be understood that things continue to evolve.[33] For example, not so long ago, countries like the Czech Republic and Sweden would have been placed in the national level bargaining group in Exhibit 16.2. Japan, not included in Exhibit 16.2, has become more decentralized in its wage bargaining.[34] Also, even where bargaining is primarily centralized, there is also typically bargaining at other levels.[35] Likewise, there may be exceptions, under particular circumstances, that permit companies to deviate from the centralized agreement. Thus, differences across countries in the degree of pay-setting centralization translate, but not perfectly, into differences in wage flexibility. Such flexibility is generally desirable to employers who do not want to be "locked in" to a particular wage level when product market conditions (i.e., level and growth of sales and profits) are in flux. Exhibit 16.3 shows judgments of wage flexibility gathered from an international sample of executives. We can see that countries with

EXHIBIT 16.3   Flexibility of Wage Determination

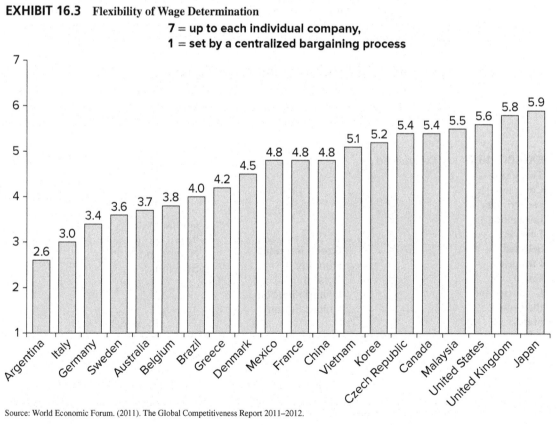

**7 = up to each individual company,
1 = set by a centralized bargaining process**

Source: World Economic Forum. (2011). The Global Competitiveness Report 2011–2012.

more centralized bargaining levels (e.g., Belgium, Germany, Sweden, Italy) generally have less wage flexibility, while countries with more decentralized bargaining (e.g., the United Kingdom, Czech Republic, United States) generally have higher wage flexibility, as do the Asian countries included.

Regulation

The social compact also relates to the legal/regulatory environment for human resource decisions in each country. The country differences in wage flexibility relate not only to degree of bargaining centralization, but also to regulatory restrictions such as maximum hours of work. The European Union Working Time Directive limits the workweek to no more than 48 hours. Countries such as France have experimented with a 35-hour workweek, which was in effect from 1998 until 2008.[36] In contrast, in countries like Japan and the United States, there is no maximum workweek and, as we saw, wage flexibility is high.

Another indicator of employment regulation (i.e., restriction on flexibility) is the degree of legal restriction in hiring and firing workers. As shown in Exhibit 16.4,

EXHIBIT 16.4 Flexibility in Hiring and Firing Workers

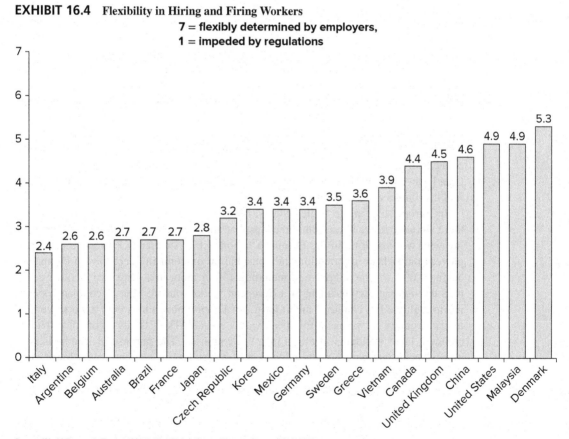

Source: World Economic Forum. (2011). The Global Competitiveness Report 2011–2012.

employers in the United States have more flexibility than employers in the European Union, South America, and Japan. Interestingly, Korea and China are not so different from the United States. As a final example of how the legal framework comes into play and affects employer flexibility, consider the role of works councils and co-determination in a European country like Germany.[37] A works council may be formed by employees in any business unit having five or more permanent employees. It operates separately from the trade union and collective bargaining process (although works council members are often union members) and may not, for example, call a strike. In general, the German works council deals with issues of a collective nature (i.e., that affect two or more employees). It has rights to information and consultation in these matters. In the area of compensation, consider that:

> the employer must obtain the consent of the Works Council on collective rules regarding criteria to be applied for determining wages and salaries of all employees, the implementation of systems that classify wages according to performance or time spent (e.g., bonus schemes), the mode of payment, and the method of determining criteria for pension rights.[38]

An employer must consult the Works Council and give it an opportunity to respond prior to taking actions in the area of compensation as well as in a wide range of other human resource and operational areas. The Works Council has "veto-rights and rights of consent" including "the right to block management decisions until an agreement is reached or a decision by the labour court is taken overruling the veto."[39]

In addition, the co-determination law in Germany requires that in companies with 500 to 2,000 employees, one-third of the supervisory board (akin to the board of directors in a United States company) must be employee representatives. In companies with over 2,000 employees, one-half of the board must be composed of employee representatives. However, there is not true parity here because shareholders elect the chairperson, who has the power to cast a tie-breaking vote.[40] By way of contrast, neither works councils or co-determination are legally required in the United States and are quite rare. Clearly, an employer from the United States that becomes an employer in Germany will find that things work very differently.

In Europe, like in the United States, laws can also vary within countries. Further, there are also, as we have seen, directives that apply across countries such as that dealing with working time in the European Union (EU). Another EU directive gives employees the right to information and consultation on company decisions in companies having 1,000 or more employees, including 150 or more in at least two member countries through the establishment of a European works council. Thus, a company operating in multiple EU countries might have consultation obligations with a works council in each country as well as a European works council. The EU has a goal of providing common labor standards in all its member countries. The purpose of standards is to avoid "social dumping," or the relocation of a business in a country with lower standards and labor costs. At present, average hourly labor costs vary substantially among the EU countries, sometimes in countries right next door, such as Germany, which, as we saw in Chapter 1, has much higher labor costs than Poland.

Finally, the social compact in Europe, with its regulatory and institutional limits on employer flexibility and protection of workers, comes at a cost. A longstanding literature seeks to determine whether more generous worker protection (e.g., unemployment benefits) undermines incentives for workers to put forth effort on the job (as efficiency wage theory would suggest) and look for work (thus resulting in higher unemployment rates and higher public expenditures). Here, we will simply look at how expenditures vary across countries, as well as how taxes, which of course are needed to fund such expenditure, also vary. Exhibit 16.5 shows that the tax burden in countries like Germany and France is more than 60 percent higher than in the United States, Canada, Australia, and Japan. One purpose of these higher taxes is to help insulate workers from income losses due to unemployment. As Exhibit 16.6 indicates, Germany, as well as some other EU countries, spends nearly 10 times as much as the United States on unemployment benefits. Consider that the gross domestic product of the United States in recent years has been around $17 trillion. Spending 0.24 percent of that on unemployment benefits works out to roughly $41 billion per year. If, however, it spent 2.16 percent, as in Germany, it would be about $367 billion per year.

EXHIBIT 16.5   Combined Employer-Employee Tax Rate on Wages

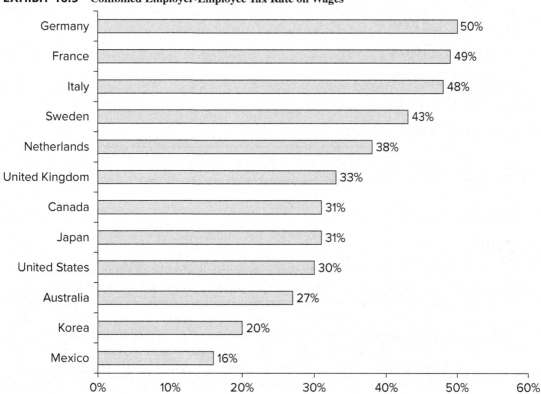

Source: Organization for Economic Cooperation and Development Taxing Wages. April 25, 2012. Table 0.1 Comparison of total tax wedge. As % of labour costs. Single individual without children at the income level of the average worker. Includes personal income tax, and unemployment disability, and health insurance, using income level of average worker.

EXHIBIT 16.6   **Expenditures on Unemployment Benefits as a Percent of Gross Domestic Product**

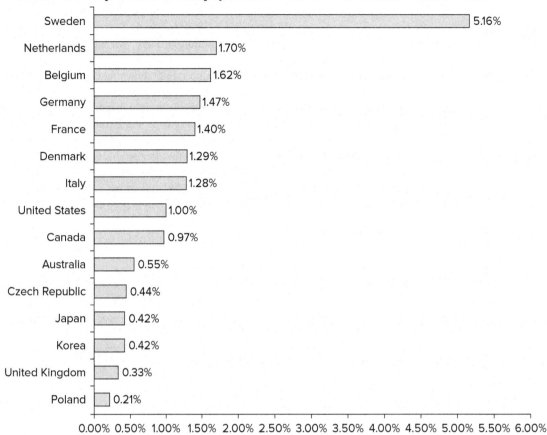

Source: Organisation for Economic Cooperation and Development. Employment Outlook 2011 Statistical Annex. Table K. "Out-of-Work Income Maintenance and Support." Brussels: OECD.

CULTURE

Culture is defined as shared mental programming which is rooted in the values, beliefs, and assumptions held in common by a group of people and which influences how information is processed.[41] The assumption that pay systems must be designed to fit different *national cultures* is based on the belief that most of a country's inhabitants share a national character. The job of the global manager, according to this assumption, is to define the national characteristics that influence pay systems. Typical of this thinking is the widely used list of national cultural attributes proposed by Hofstede (power distance, individualism–collectivism, uncertainty avoidance, and masculinity–femininity).[42] (See Exhibit 16.7.) Advocates of this view believe that "it is crucial that companies adjust their compensation practices to the cultural specifics of a particular host country."[43] Accordingly, in Malaysia and Mexico, where the culture is alleged to emphasize

EXHIBIT 16.7 Hofstede's National Culture Dimensions and Scores for Four Countries

Hofstede Culture Dimensions	United States	Germany	China	Japan
Power Distance The extent to which the less powerful members of organizations and institutions accept and expect that power is distributed unequally.	Low (40)	Low (35)	High (80)	Medium (54)
Uncertainty Avoidance The extent to which a culture programs its members to feel either uncomfortable or comfortable in unstructured situations. Unstructured situations are unknown, surprising, different from usual and societies differ in the degree to which they try to control the uncontrollable.	Low (46)	Medium (65)	Medium (60)	High (92)
Individualism On the one side versus its opposite, collectivism, it is the degree to which individuals are supposed to look after themselves or remain integrated into groups, usually around the family.	High (91)	High (67)	Low (20)	Medium (47)
Masculinity versus Femininity This refers to the distribution of emotional roles between the genders; it opposes 'tough' masculine to 'tender' feminine societies. Masculine societies emphasize assertiveness, performance, and competition.	High (62)	High (66)	Medium (50)	High (95)
Long-Term versus Short-term Orientation This refers to the extent to which a culture programs its members to accept delayed gratification of their material, social, and emotional needs.	Low (29)	Medium (31)	High (118)	High (80)

Source: G. Hofstede, "Cultural Constraints in Management Theories," *Academy of Management Executive,* 7 (1993) pp. 81–94; G. Hofstede, G., *Culture's Consequences: Comparing Values, Behaviors, Institutions, and Organizations Across Nations,* 2nd edition (Thousand Oaks, CA: Sage, 2001), pp. xix–xx.

respect for status and hierarchy (high power distance), hierarchical pay structures are appropriate. In low-power-distance nations such as Australia and the Netherlands, egalitarianism is a better approach.[44]

Advice can get even more specific. Companies operating in nations with supposedly "collectivistic" cultures, such as Singapore, Japan, Israel, and Korea, should use egalitarian pay structures, equal pay increases, and group-based rather than individual-based performance incentives. Employers in the more "individualistic" national cultures, such as the United States, United Kingdom, and Hong Kong, should use individual-based pay and performance-based increases.[45]

But such thinking risks stereotyping.[46] The question is not, What are the cultural differences among nations? Rather, the question is, Which culture matters?[47] Any group of people may exhibit a shared set of beliefs. Look around your college or workplace; engineers, lawyers, accountants, and technicians may each share some beliefs and values. Employees of organizations may, too. Your school's culture probably differs from Microsoft's, Toshiba's, or the London Symphony Orchestra's. You may even have chosen your school because of its culture. However, you are likely part of many cultures. You are not only part of your university but also part of your family, your social/political/interest groups, your region of the state or country, and so on. Cultures may be similar or different among all these categories.

Is National Culture a Major Constraint on Compensation?

In our view, theory and evidence increasingly say "no." At the very least, the importance of national culture in terms of how well employees accept pay for performance and in terms of how national culture influences the effectiveness of compensation and other human resource practices in different countries has been overstated. For example, research shows that respondents from what are seen as very different national cultures (e.g., China and the United States) have nearly identical beliefs in the importance of basing pay on performance (versus paying people equally or based on need).[48] Additionally, a meta-analysis of the effectiveness of "high performance work systems," (HPWSs) which typically include pay for performance, as well as worker involvement in decisions, use of teams, and abiity/performance-based hiring and advancement, found that such systems worked well in virtually every country and, in fact, some evidence suggested they worked better (not worse) in countries where they did not (according to conventional wisdom) fit the national culture as well. One explanation is that being out in front of within-country competitors in successfully implementing more effective management systems can be a source of competitive advantage. Deviating from what everyone else does carries a risk, but so does deviating from a global management practice standard that may be different from the domestic standard, but is more effective. That is especially true if a company competes not just domestically, but also in the global economy. It is also possible that organizations adapted/executed HPWS principles in different ways in different national contexts to reduce the possibility of misfit.[49]

Culture classifiers consider the United States a country of risk takers who rank high on the individualistic (rather than collectivistic) scale. In contrast, the country of Slovenia has been classified as more collectivistic and security-conscious (as opposed to risk taking).[50] Slovenia was the first country to break off from the former Yugoslavia. (How is that for taking a risk?) It has a population of less than 3 million and by most standards would be considered very homogeneous. So you might expect Slovenian managers to be very different from U.S. managers. However, a study found that Slovenian managers tended, on average, to be more risk taking and individualistic than U.S. managers. The most striking finding, as shown in Exhibit 16.8, was that the degree of variation among managers on cultural dimensions was virtually the same in both the Slovenian and the U.S. data. Thus, one can find employees with different values or personality traits (e.g., risk-averse collectivists and risk-taking individualists) in both nations.[51]

Indeed, re-analysis of data from Hofstede's seminal work on national differences in culture finds that the variance between individuals within countries is far larger than the variance between countries.[52] In other words, knowing what country someone is from tells us much less than the national culture literature seems to suggest.

So how useful is the notion of a *national* culture when managing international pay? In the absence of better data on variations such as those in Exhibit 16.8, it may offer a starting point. However, *it is only a starting point.*[53] National culture can be thought of as the "average" in Exhibit 16.8. It provides some information about what kinds of pay attitudes and beliefs you are likely to find in an area. But overreliance on the "average" can seriously mislead. This point is critical for managing international pay.

EXHIBIT 16.8
Understanding
the "Full
House" of
Variation
Within a
Culture

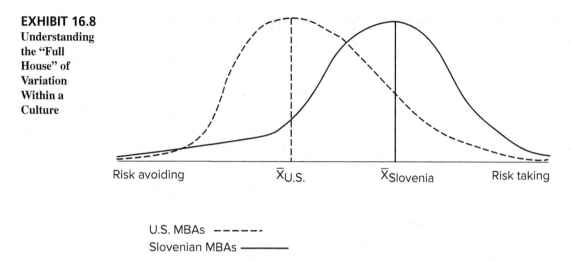

Risk avoiding $\overline{X}_{U.S.}$ $\overline{X}_{Slovenia}$ Risk taking

U.S. MBAs ------
Slovenian MBAs ————

To claim that all organizations and people within Germany or within China share a certain mind-set ignores variations and differences within each nation, and reviews of empirical work bear out the fact that differences in worker preferences across countries (including China and the United States) for the use of performance-based pay, for example, tend to be small in practical terms.[54] Again, country is just too rough of a proxy to use in making compensation decisions. Considerable diversity among companies and people within any country exists. The Chinese computer company Lenovo, which purchased IBM's PC division, illustrates the point. Throughout its short history, Lenovo has relied heavily upon government support. Yet Lenovo's approach to compensating employees does not reflect widely held beliefs about Chinese national culture. (Go to *geert-hofstede.international-business-center.com/* for Hofstede's description of Chinese national culture.) For example, the CEO uses 20 percent of the company's profits to award high-performing employees with "special merit" bonuses. Pay differentials among jobs, which in 1990 were 2 to 1, are now up to 30 to 1. Most amazing is a benefits plan in which individual employees select the specific benefits that best meet their personal preferences. All this diversity in a company in which the Chinese government still owns controlling interest!

So keep in mind our basic premise in this chapter: The interplay among economic, institutional, organizational, and individual conditions within each nation or region, taken as a whole, forms distinct contexts for determining compensation. Understanding these factors in the global guide is useful for managing employee compensation. However, do not assume uniformity (the average) within a country. Understanding the full range of individuals within nations is even more important.[55]

So how may understanding cultural diversity within a nation matter to global pay? Perhaps with an eye to attracting and motivating those risk-taking, entrepreneurial Slovenians, a multinational firm may use performance bonuses, stock awards, and hierarchical pay structures rather than simply matching the "average" Slovenian culture.

TRADE UNIONS AND EMPLOYEE INVOLVEMENT

Europe remains highly unionized: In Sweden, 71 percent of the workforce belongs to unions; in the United Kingdom, 28 percent; and in Italy, 33 percent. Asia is less heavily unionized. Japan's unionization rate is 18 percent, and South Korea's is around 10 percent. In some countries, workers' pay is set by collective agreements even though the workers may not be union members. In France, for example, more than 90 percent of workers are covered by collective agreements, even though fewer than 10 percent are union members.[56] In addition to having higher rates of unionization, as we have seen, workers in countries like Germany have the right to establish works councils, which must be involved in any changes to a pay plan.[57] In China, labor unions, although still closely linked to the Communist Party and thus not independent in the Western sense, are increasingly asserting themselves more strongly (especially at foreign companies with operations in China).[58]

OWNERSHIP AND FINANCIAL MARKETS

Ownership and financing of companies differ widely around the world. These differences are important to international pay. In the United States, corporate ownership and access to capital is far less concentrated than in most other countries. Fifty percent of American households own stock in companies either directly or indirectly through mutual funds and pension funds.[59] Direct stock ownership is only a few mouse clicks away. In Korea, six conglomerates control a significant portion of the Korean economy, and the six are closely linked with specific families. In Germany, the national Bundesbank and a small number of other influential banks have ownership interests in most major companies. These patterns of ownership make certain types of pay systems almost nonsensical because ownership in the companies is not readily available for individual investors. For example, linking performance bonuses to increased shareholder value or offering stock options to employees makes little sense in the large conglomerates in Germany, Korea, and Japan. However, ownership in small start-ups in the nations is outside the traditional channels, so these firms do offer stock options to attract new employees.[60] Recent tax law changes in many countries have made stock options more attractive, but limited ownership of many companies remains the rule.

The most vivid illustrations of the importance of ownership occur in China and in eastern Europe (Poland, Hungary, Slovenia, Czech Republic, and Slovakia), where a variety of forms are emerging. While state-owned enterprises still employ two-thirds of all workers in China, township enterprises, wholly privately owned enterprises, joint ventures with foreign companies, and wholly owned foreign enterprises (WOFEs) account for 50 percent of the profits. Chinese employees switching from government-owned enterprises to these newer organizations find that both the pay and the employer expectations (i.e., the social contract) are substantially different.[61] Individuals attracted to work in these various enterprises have different values and expectations. One study found that those working for local or town-owned enterprises prefer more performance-based pay than those working in federal-owned enterprises.[62]

Many families find it makes sense to have one wage earner working at a safe but low-paying government enterprise and another wage earner working at a private enterprise where expectations and pay are high. So it is clear that ownership differences may influence what forms of pay make sense. It is very misleading to assume that every place is like home.

MANAGERIAL AUTONOMY

Managerial autonomy, an organizational factor in the global guide in Exhibit 16.1, refers to the degree of discretion managers have to make total compensation a strategic tool. It is inversely related to the degree of centralization and regulatory intensity discussed earlier. Thus, most U.S.- and U.K.-based organizations have relatively greater freedom to change employee pay practices or to hire and downsize than do most European companies. As already noted, the centralized pay setting found in European Union countries limits organizations' autonomy to align pay to business strategies and changing market conditions.[63] Volkswagen AG, which is trying to reduce labor costs to better compete with Toyota and others, must negotiate changes with both IG Metall, a powerful trade union, and also with a federal labor agency.[64] Works councils also have information and consultation rights. In contrast, in Singapore the National Wage Council issues guidelines that are voluntary (e.g., "Wage freezes for most companies," "Emphasize variable and performance-based pay"). Most government organizations adhere to these guides, but private organizations do so to varying degrees.[65] Yet, even in countries with centralized bargaining, employers sometimes find ways to exercise autonomy. For example, subcontracting work seems to be one avenue for reducing the degree of constraint.[66] Also, even though Volkswagen must negotiate with IG Metall in Germany, it does not have to do so at its new (nonunion) plant in Chattanooga, TN.

---

e-Compensation

A good source of free information on labor laws throughout the world is the NATLEX database produced by the International Labor Organization (ILO): *natlex.ilo.org.*

Governments and trade unions are not the only institutions to limit managerial autonomy. Corporate policies often do so as well. Compensation decisions made in the home-country corporate offices and exported to subunits around the world may align with the corporate strategy but discount local economic and social conditions. While IBM corporate in Armonk, New York, expects all its worldwide operations to "differentiate people on performance" with total compensation, some IBM units in Tokyo remain convinced that Japanese IBMers in Japan prefer more egalitarian practices.[67] Nevertheless, managers are expected to comply with Armonk.

In sum, as the global guide depicts, international compensation is influenced by economic, institutional, organizational, and individual conditions. Globalization really means that these conditions are changing—hence international pay systems are changing as well.

COMPARING COSTS (AND PRODUCTIVITY)

In Chapter 8, we discussed the importance of obtaining accurate information on what competitors pay in domestic markets. Similar comparisons of total compensation among nations can be very misleading. Even if wage rates appear the same, expenses for health care, living costs, and other employer-provided allowances complicate the picture. Outside the United States, many nations offer some form of national health care. An organization may pay for it indirectly through payroll taxes, but since all people in a nation share similar coverage, its value as part of total compensation is diminished.

Comparisons between a specific U.S. firm and a specific foreign competitor may be even more misleading. Accurate data are usually difficult to obtain. While consulting firms are improving their global data collection, much of their data is still from U.S. companies' operations in global locations. Other foreign and local-national companies' data are often not available. Thus, international data may be biased toward U.S. companies' practices.[68]

Labor Costs and Productivity

Nevertheless, substantial differences in (average) labor costs do exist (see Exhibit 16.9) and companies may find that it makes sense to move or grow employment in lower cost countries if productivity can be maintained at a workable level. In Chapter 1, for example, we saw that hourly wages for Mexican manufacturing work ($6.82) are about 19 percent of those paid in the United States ($36.34). China's estimated $3.38 per hour is about 9 percent of the U.S. rate (up from 5 percent of the U.S. wage just a few years ago). Productivity in China is about 22 percent of that of U.S. workers (up from 15 percent of the U.S. figure just a few years ago), while Mexican worker productivity is 30 percent of the U.S. level. Based on those numbers, the average loss in productivity is more than offset by the labor cost savings. Exhibit 16.10 shows further information on wage rates in Asia. The top part of the exhibit reports estimates of actual monthly wages. (Keep in mind that the workweek often significantly exceeds 40 hours in these countries.) Note that China is not a low-wage country compared to several other Asian countries. The bottom part of the exhibit shows minimum monthly wages in China and Vietnam. Of note is that the minimum wage varies within these countries depending on location. Also of interest is how rapidly both the average wage in most of the countries and the minimum wage have risen. In China, minimum wage increases are part of its national 12th Five-Year Plan to increase minimum wages by an average of at least 13 percent annually from 2011 to 2015.[69] (Clearly, our Chapter 8 discussion of aging/updating salary survey data to account for market movement is highly relevant in countries such as China and Vietnam!)

Of course, most companies are not average and so each has to do its own analysis of the pros and cons of where to locate employment, as we discussed in Chapter 7.

EXHIBIT 16.9

Manufacturing Hourly Compensation Costs (in U.S. Dollars)

Source: The Conference Board. International Comparisons of Hourly Compensation Costs in Manufacturing, 2013. December 2014.

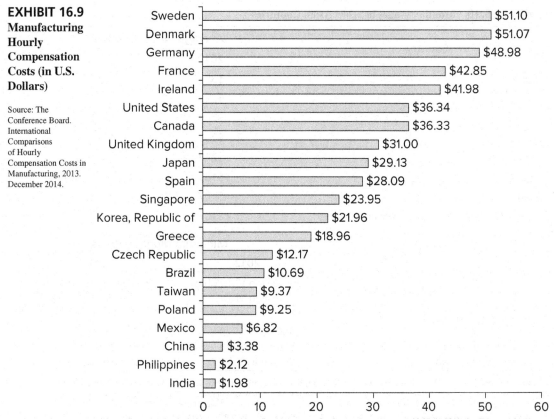

Notes: Compensation includes wages and benefits. Most recent Conference Board data was $3.07 (in 2012) for China and $1.59 (in 2011) for India. 2013 estimates for China and India were obtained by inflating the Conference Board estimates based on data from the National Bureau of Statistics of China, the Labour Bureau, Government of India, and Aon Hewitt's Annual Salary Increase Survey in India.

Also, while differences in labor costs are often the impetus to do the analysis, many other factors must be considered.

Consider the case of a small custom software company in the midwest that provides high end web applications to meet clients' core business needs (e.g., online registration or customer service). It sets up longstanding web development teams to provide client support on an ongoing basis. So, here we have a case involving knowledge work and customer responsiveness is key. The engineering work (software coding, architecture, testing, graphics production, database) is all done in a former Soviet Bloc country in Eastern Europe. Some employees work in teams that write HTML code (which tells web browsers how to present a page). New college graduates are hired at a rate of about $6,000 per year, with more senior team leads earning up to $15,000 per year. (We suspect that many readers of this book expect to make considerably more than that upon graduating from college.) Other employees, software engineers, with 2 to 4 years of experience, and writing applications in more complex languages, earn $10,000 per year, with the more senior and most highly skilled

EXHIBIT 16.10 Monthly Wages in Select Asian Countries

Country	Average Monthly Wage	
	2010	**2014**
China	$303	$403
Malaysia	$298	$453
India	$269	$239*
Thailand	$263	$369
Philippines	$212	$249
Indonesia	$182	$253
Vietnam	$107	$176
Cambodia, Bangladesh, Myanamar	<$107	<$127

Country	Minimum Monthly Wage	
	2012	**2015**
Vietnam		
First Zone (urban Hanoi & Ho Chi Minh City)	2.0 million VND/$103	3.1 million VND/$141
Fourth Zone (underdeveloped localities)	1.4 million VND/$72	2.15 million VND/$101
China (minimum wage)		
Shanghai (coast)	1450 yuan/$229	1820 yuan/$291
Shenzhen (coast)	1500 yuan/$236	1808 yuan/$259
Chongqing (inland)	870 yuan/$137	1250 yuan/$200

Sources: Average Monthly Wage: Japan External Trade Organization. Survey of Japanese-Affiliated Companies in Asia and Oceania, FY 2010 and FY 2014 Surveys. Minimum wage data from American Chamber of Commerce in Vietnam. Minimum Wage Adjustment for 2012 to be effective from Oct 5, 2011. *http://www.amchamvietnam.com/?id=4773* and from ChinaBriefing. Minimum Wage Levels Across China. February 22, 2012. *http://www.china-briefing.com/news/2012/02/22/minimum-wage-levels-across-china.html.* Extracted May 24, 2012. Vietnamnet. Minimum wage to increase from January, 2015. November 11, 2014. http://english.vietnamnet.vn/fms/society/116453/minimum-wage-to-increase-from-january–2015.html. Extracted February 3, 2015. Minimum Wages in China for the year 2014–15. http://www.wageindicator.org/main/salary/minimum-wage/china-custom. Extracted February 3, 2015.

*The Indian currency (rupee) weakened by roughly 21 percent against the U.S. dollar between 2010 and 2014.

engineers earning $22,000 to $30,000 per year. You may wish to compare these salaries to those we saw in Chapter 8 for engineers (and programmers). There, we saw that an engineer fresh out of college could expect about $60,000 per year and more senior engineers could advance to earning well over $100,000 per year. Thus, the labor cost savings for this midwest customer software company were too large to ignore. Of course, it is not quite that simple. In a global market, some of the very best engineering talent from Eastern Europe migrates to where it can command higher pay and be at the epicenter of the most exciting work being done (e.g., Silicon Valley in California). Thus, the productivity of the company's engineers in Eastern Europe is not as high. That is not necessarily a problem if the work to be done is relatively routine and not oriented toward innovation. What about setting up a team several time zones and a 16- to 20-hour roundtrip away? This company's experience has been that it can take 6 months to a year to get off the ground and fine tune. Other differences are harder to quantify. Former Soviet Bloc countries do not have the same consumer/marketing oriented culture as in the United States—until recently, you did not have

EXHIBIT 16.11   Drivers of Countries' Global Manufacturing Competitiveness

Rank	Component	Importance 10 = High, 1 = Low
1	Quality and availability of labor force	10.00
2	Cost competitiveness of materials	9.06
3	Cost competitiveness of labor	9.05
4	Health of economic and financial system	8.96
5	Quality and availability of scientists, researchers and engineers	8.85
6	Capacity for manufacturing innovation	8.82
7	Cost competitiveness of energy	8.23
8	Tax system	7.45
9	Quality of physical infrastructure	7.15
10	Legal and regulatory environment	7.13

Source: Deloitte and US Council on Competitiveness. 2010 Global Manufacturing Competitiveness Index. © Deloitte Touche Tohmatsu, 2010. Appendix Table A1.

multiple options when it came to toothpaste, apartments, cars, and so forth. So the underlying shared experiences and knowledge that you might find among U.S. engineers may not exist. Think of someone who has never had a credit card. How would a software engineer go about designing an online shopping experience without an inherent understanding of credit cards and comparison shopping?

Nevertheless, in some cases, especially in the manufacturing case, it can sometimes be all labor cost. As we saw in Chapter 7, by outsourcing assembly of the iPhone and iPad to Foxconn's plants in China, Apple, by some estimates, saves $8 billion to $15 billion per year in labor costs, or 24% to 44% of its operating income. Thus, even though wages are growing rapidly in China (including at Foxconn), eroding its labor cost advantage and leading some companies to look for lower labor cost countries,[70] labor costs remain much lower in China than in more advanced economies (e.g., the United States) and that appears to mean that other companies (e.g., Foxconn) will continue to manufacture in China. Exhibit 16.11, based on a survey of global manufacturing executives, provides the average importance of factors that go into location decisions. We see that labor cost, but also the quality of the labor available, are the most important factors. Taxes and the legal/regulatory environment, other factors addressed in the current chapter, are also important.

Cost of Living and Purchasing Power

If comparing total compensation is difficult, comparing living costs and standards across borders is even more complex. (Recall our discussion of the limitations of the CPI for wage setting in Chapter 8.) However, companies need such data to adjust pay for employees who transfer among countries. The objective is to maintain the same level of *purchasing* power.[71] Exhibit 16.12 provides several types of relevant data for this purpose. In the first three columns are earnings (based on multiple

EXHIBIT 16.12 Cost of Living, Domestic Purchasing Power, and Minutes of Working Time Required to Buy a Big Mac, Bread, and Rice

	Hourly Earnings (NYC = 100)		Price Level (NYC = 100)	Purchasing Power (NYC = 100)	Working time required to buy:			
	Gross	Net			1 Big Mac minutes	1 kilo bread minutes	1 kilo rice minutes	1 iPhone 6 hours
Amsterdam	65	55	65	85	16	7	7	50
Beijing	13	14	61	24	42	40	36	218
Buenos Aires	23	26	70	56	29	57	21	
Cairo	8	9	48	18	62	32	66	353
Chicago	85	85	84	101	11	10	6	28
Copenhagen	92	59	88	67	20	13	11	55
Dublin	69	64	70	93	15	6	8	43
Hong	49	51	73	70	9	18	13	52
Istanbul	26	26	65	40	34	22	23	132
Jakarta	6	7	53	13	67	70	58	468
Kuala Lumpur	18	20	41	39	23	17	13	136
London	76	72	85	85	12	6	16	41
Madrid	51	46	61	76	19	13	7	61
Manila	10	9	51	18	87	83	34	334
Mexico	12	13	55	24	78	46	22	218
Moscow	21	21	52	41	20	12	24	158
Mumbai	8	9	45	20	40	27	49	349
Munich	68	68	66	104	13	7	5	41
Nairobi	7	6	50	13	173	44	62	468
New York City (NYC)	100	100	100	100	11	12	16	24
Paris	63	67	73	92	15	10	9	42
Prague	20	20	46	35	30	11	15	143
Rio de Janeiro	27	30	58	50	32	18	9	140
Rome	60	54	67	81	18	10	14	54
Seoul	46	50	79	63	18	22	19	57
Shanghai	18	19	65	30	35	37	25	164

EXHIBIT 16.12 *(Continued)*

Stockholm	76	64	77	83	17	18	11	47
Sydney	90	84	81	104	11	10	5	34
Taipei	35	39	67	58	13	10	14	69
Tel Aviv	47	47	72	66	21	12	12	75
Tokyo	70	71	83	85	10	14	10	41
Toronto	72	69	78	89	15	12	7	37
Vienna	69	70	65	105	12	10	6	40
Warsaw	23	23	49	46	25	20	24	142
Zurich	132	142	109	131	11	5	5	21

Source: UBS. Prices and Earnings 2012. www.ubs.org. http://81.47.175.201/ETMS/rankings/2012_UBS_Prices_earnings.pdf

Notes:

Net Hourly Earnings earnings are calculated by removing taxes, social security and other special deductions from gross annual income
Price Level is based on prices for a basket of 122 goods and services
Purchasing Power is Net Hourly Earnings divided by Price Level

occupations), price level (i.e., cost of living), and purchasing power (basically earnings divided by price level and then standardized as a percentage of New York). Jakarta's cost of living is 53 percent of New York, whereas Zurich is 9 percent more expensive than New York. Thus, to maintain the purchas¬ing power of an expatriate from New York moving to Zurich, additional compensation must be provided beyond that paid in New York. In contrast, a move to Jakarta from New York at New York pay levels would provide an economic windfall. For the average person living in Jakarta, note that purchasing power is only 13 percent of that of the average person living in New York. Paying a New York–based expatriate in Jakarta at the local level would result in a serious decline in living standard. The final four columns take a slightly different approach to comparing purchasing power by estimating the amount of work time it takes, given the prevailing rate of pay and cost of living, to buy four different "staples." In the case of a Big Mac, a New Yorker must work 11 minutes. In sharp contrast, a person in Jakarta would have to work 67 minutes. The difference in working time required to buy an iPhone is also quite large: almost 3 months (468 hours) for the person in Jakarta versus less than 1 week (24 hours) for the person in New York.

COMPARING SYSTEMS

We have made the points that pay systems differ around the globe and that the differences relate to variations in economic pressures, sociopolitical institutions, and the diversity of organizations and employees. In this section we compare several compensation systems. The caution about stereotyping raised earlier applies here as well.

Even in nations described by some as homogeneous, pay systems differ from business to business. For example, two well-known Japanese companies, Toyota and Toshiba, have designed different pay systems. Toyota places greater emphasis on external market rates, uses far fewer levels in its structure, and places greater emphasis on individual-based merit and performance pay than does Toshiba. So as we discuss "typical" national systems, remember that differences exist and that change in these systems is occurring everywhere.

The Total Pay Model: Strategic Choices

The total pay model used throughout the book guides our discussion of pay systems in different countries. You will recognize the basic choices, which seem universal:

- Objectives of pay systems
- External competitiveness
- Internal alignment
- Employee contributions
- Management

While the choices may be universal, the results are not.

NATIONAL SYSTEMS: COMPARATIVE MIND-SET

A national system mind-set assumes that most employers in a country adopt similar pay practices. Understanding and managing international compensation then consists mainly of comparing the Japanese to the German to the U.S. or other national systems. This method may be useful in nations with centralized approaches (see Exhibit 16.8). Some even apply it to regional systems, as in the "European Way," the "Asian Way," or the "North American Way."[72] We describe the Japanese and German national systems below. But we cannot say this often enough: The national or regional mind-set overlooks variations among organizations within each nation. Thus, we refer to the national systems below as the "traditional" systems, to emphasize that this is one country model in each but not the only one.

Japanese Traditional National System

Traditionally, Japan's employment relationships were supported by "three pillars":

1. Lifetime security within the company.
2. Seniority-based pay and promotion systems.
3. Enterprise unions (decentralized unions that represent workers within a single company).

Japanese pay systems tend to emphasize the person rather than the job; seniority and skills possessed rather than job or work performed; promotions based on a combination of supervisory evaluation of trainability, skill/ability levels, and

EXHIBIT 16.13
Salary
Percentage
Differentials
and Age
Matrix for
General
Administration
Work in a
Traditional
Japanese
Company

Age*	Salary†	Age	Salary	Age	Salary	Age	Salary
22	100%	32	200%	42	300%	52	370%
23	110%	33	210%	43	310%	53	360%
24	120%	34	220%	44	320%	54	350%
25	130%	35	230%	45	330%	55	340%
26	140%	36	240%	46	340%	56	330%
27	150%	37	250%	47	350%	57	320%
28	160%	38	260%	48	360%	58	310%
29	170%	39	270%	49	370%	59	300%
30	180%	40	280%	50	380%	60	290%
31	190%	41	290%	51	380%		

*Age 22 is typical entry with college degree.
†Monthly salary (without bonus), converted to dollars.

performance rather than on performance alone; internal alignment over competitors' market rates; and employment security based on the performance of the organization and the individual (formerly lifetime security). Japanese pay systems can be described in terms of three basic components: base pay, bonuses, and allowances/ benefits.[73]

Base Pay

Base pay is not based on job evaluation or market pricing (as predominates in North America), nor is it attached to specific job titles. Rather, it is based on a combination of employee characteristics: career category, years of service, and skill/performance level.

Career   Five career categories prevail in Japan: (1) general administration, (2) engineer/ scientific, (3) secretary/office, (4) technician/blue-collar job, and (5) contingent.

Years of Service   Seniority remains a major factor in determining base pay. Management creates a matrix of pay and years of service for each career category. Exhibit 16.13 shows a matrix for general administration work. If starting annual salary (without bonus) at age 22 is 25,000 USD, then at age 50, the salary in this company would be 380 percent of 25,000, or 95,000 USD. Companies meet periodically to compare their matrixes, a practice that accounts for the similarity among companies. In general, salary increases with age until workers are 50 years old, when it is reduced. Employees can expect annual increases no matter what their performance level until age 50, although the amount of increase varies according to individual skills and performance.

Skills and Performance   Each skill is defined by its class (usually 7 to 13) and rank (1 to 9) within the class. Exhibit 16.14 illustrates a skill salary chart for the general administration career category. In this example, again assuming an annual starting (without bonus) salary of 25,000 USD for an Associate at the lowest rank/skill level, the

EXHIBIT 16.14 Salary Percentage Differentials by Job Level and Rank/Skill Level within Job Level, Traditional Japanese Company

	Job Level						
	Associate	**Senior Associate**	**Supervisor**		**Manager**	**General Director**	
	Class 1	Class 2	Class 3	Class 4	Class 5	Class 6	Class 7
Rank/Skill Level 1	100%	267%	433%	517%	600%	750%	917%
Rank/Skill Level 2	117%	283%	442%	525%	625%	783%	1000%
Rank/Skill Level 3	133%	300%	450%	533%	633%	817%	
Rank/Skill Level 4	150%	317%	458%	542%	650%	850%	
Rank/Skill Level 5	167%	333%	467%	550%	667%		
Rank/Skill Level 6	183%	350%	475%	558%	683%		
Rank/Skill Level 7	200%	367%	483%	567%			
Rank/Skill Level 8	217%	383%	492%	575%			
Rank/Skill Level 9	233%	400%	500%	583%			

*Age 22 is typical entry with college degree.
†Monthly salary (without bonus), converted to dollars.

salary for a General Director, Class 7, would be 250,000 USD. Classes 1 and 2 typically include associate (entry) and senior associate work; 2, 3, and 4, supervisor and managerial; 5, 6, and 7, managerial, general director, and so on. Employees advance in rank as a result of their supervisor's evaluation of their:

- Effort (e.g., enthusiasm, participation, responsiveness).
- Skills required for the work (e.g., analytical, decision making, leadership, planning, process improvement, teamwork).
- Performance (typical MBO-style ratings).

To illustrate how the system works, say you are a graduate fresh from college who enters at class 1, rank 1. After one year, you and all those hired at the same time are evaluated by your supervisors on their effort, abilities, and performance. Early in your career (the first three years) effort is more important; in later years abilities and performance receive more emphasis. The number of ranks you move each year (and therefore your increase in base pay) depends on this supervisory rating (e.g., receiving an A on an appraisal form lets you move up three ranks within the class, a B moves you two ranks, and so on).

Theoretically, a person with an A rating could move up three ranks in class each year and shift to the next class in three years. However, most companies require both minimum and maximum years of service within each class. So even if you receive four A ratings, you would still remain in class 1 for the minimum of six years. Conversely, if you receive four straight D grades, you would still get promoted to the next skill class after spending the maximum number of years in class 1. Setting a minimum time in each class helps ensure that the employee knows the work and returns value to the company. However, the system slows the progress of high-potential performers. Additionally, even the weakest performers eventually get to the top of the pay structure, though they do not get the accompanying job titles or responsibility. The system reflects the traditional Japanese saying, "A nail that is standing too high will be pounded down." An individual employee will not want to stand out. Employees work to advance the performance of the group or team rather than themselves.

Since the Japanese system is so seniority-based, labor costs increase as the average age of the workforce increases. In fact, a continuing problem facing Japanese employers is the increasing labor costs caused by the cumulative effects of annual increases and lifetime employment security. Early retirement incentives and "new jobs" with lower salaries are being used to contain these costs.[74]

Bonuses

Bonuses provide additional pay equivalent to 1 to 5 months of annual salary, depending on the level in the organization and often the financial results of the organization.[75] Generally, the higher up you are, the larger the percent of annual salary received as bonus. Typical Japanese companies pay bonuses twice a year (July and December). The bonuses are an *expectable* additional payment to be made twice a year, even in bad financial times. They are not necessarily related to performance.

---

e-Compensation

U.S. consulting firms are entering the Japanese market to provide HR consulting services for firms in Japan. For example, the Unifi Tokyo office has an English website *(www.unifinetwork.co.jp/html/index_eng.htm)*. Go to this website to see how it describes Japanese pay systems.

The amount of bonuses is calculated by multiplying employees' monthly base pay by a multiplier. The size of the multiplier is determined by collective bargaining between employers and unions in each company. Sometimes the multiplier may also vary according to an employee's performance evaluation. In a recent year, the average multiplier was 4.8 (2.3 in summer and 2.5 in winter) for white-collar workers. So an individual whose monthly base pay is $4,500 would receive a bonus of $10,350 in July and $11,250 in December.

According to the Japan Institute of Labour, for most employees (other than managers) bonuses are variable pay that help control the employer's cash flow and labor costs. They do not necessarily act as a motivator. Japanese labor laws encourage the use of bonuses to achieve cost savings by omitting bonuses from calculations of many other benefit costs (i.e., pension plan, overtime pay, severance pay, and early retirement allowances).

The timing of the bonuses is very important. In Japan both the summer festival and the new year are traditional gift-giving times; in addition, consumers tend to make major purchases during these periods. Employees use their bonuses to cover these expenses. Thus, the tradition of the bonus system is deeply rooted in Japanese life and is today considered an indispensable form of pay.

Benefits and Allowances

The third characteristic of Japanese pay systems, the allowance, comes in a variety of forms: family allowances, commuting allowances, housing and geographic differential allowances, and so on. Company housing in the form of dormitories for single employees or rent or mortgage subsidies is a substantial amount. Life-passage payments are made when an employee marries or experiences a death in the immediate family. Commuting allowances are also important. Family allowances vary with number of dependents. Some employers even provide matchmaking allowances for those who tire of life in company dorms.

Legally Mandated Benefits Legally mandated benefits in Japan include social security, unemployment, and workers' compensation. Although these three are similar to the benefits in the United States, Japanese employers also pay premiums for mandated health insurance, preschool child support, and employment of the handicapped.

German Traditional National System

Traditional German pay systems are embedded in a social partnership between business, labor, and government that creates a generous *vater staat,* or "nanny state."[76] *Vergutung* is the most common German word for "compensation." Pay decisions are highly regulated; over 90 different laws apply. Different **tariff agreements** (pay rates and structures) are negotiated for each industrial sector (e.g., banking, chemicals, metals, manufacturing) by the major employers and unions. Thus, the pay rates at Adam Opel AG, a major car company, are quite similar to those at Daimler, Volkswagen, and any other German car company. Methods for job evaluation and career progression are included in the tariff agreements. However, these agreements do not apply to managerial jobs. Even small organizations that are not legally bound by tariffs tend to use them as guidelines.

Base Pay

Base pay accounts for 70 to 80 percent of German employees' total compensation depending on their job level. Base pay is based on job descriptions, job evaluations, and employee age. The tariff agreement applicable to Adam Opel AG, for example, sets the following *tariff groups* (akin to job families and grades):

Wage earners	8 levels (L2–L9)
Salary earners	6 administrative levels (K1–K6)
	6 technical levels (T1–T6)
	4 supervisory levels (M1–M4)

Generally, a rate will be negotiated for one of the levels, for example, K2 and the other levels in that group will be calculated as a percentage of the negotiated rate.

> **e-Compensation**
>
> A number of web locations offer currency conversions to change euros into U.S. dollars, Canadian dollars, Hong Kong dollars, and any number of other currencies. Try *www.xe.com* or *www.globaldevelopment.org* over a period of several weeks to appreciate the complexity that currency conversion adds to managing compensation.

Bonuses

While there is a trend toward performance-based bonuses, they have not been part of a traditional German pay system for unionized workers. However, Adam Opel AG's tariff agreement stipulates that an average of 13 percent of the total base wages must be paid as "efficiency allowances." Systems for measuring this efficiency are negotiated with the works councils for each location. In reality, the efficiency allowances become expected annual bonuses. Performance bonuses for managerial positions not included in tariffs are based on company earnings and other company objectives. Currently only about one-third of top executives receive stock options.

Allowances and Benefits

As discussed, Germany's social contract includes generous social benefits.[77] These nationally mandated benefits, paid by taxes levied on employers and employees, include liberal social security, unemployment protection, health care, nursing care, and other programs. Employer and employee contributions to the social security system can add up to more than one-third of wages. Additionally, companies commonly provide other benefits and services such as pension plans, savings plans, building loans, and life insurance. Company cars are always popular. The make and model of the car and whether or not the company provides a cell phone are viewed as signs of status in an organization. German workers also receive 30 days of vacation plus about 13 national holidays annually (compared to an average of 11 holidays in the United States).

Strategic Comparisons: Traditional Systems in Japan, Germany, United States

As we have emphasized, speaking of *the* German, Japanese, or U.S. system is too simplistic, as there are important variations between firms within each country. Nevertheless, in looking at the average firm in each country, Japanese and German traditional systems reflect different approaches compared to U.S. pay systems. Exhibit 16.15 uses the basic choices outlined in the total pay model—objectives, internal alignment, competitiveness, and contributions—as a basis for comparisons. Both the Japanese and the German sociopolitical and culture systems constrain organizations' use of pay as a strategic tool. German companies face pay rates, job evaluation methods, and bonuses identical to those of their competitors, set by negotiated tariff agreements. The basic strategic premise, that competitive advantage is sustained by aligning with business strategy, is limited by laws and unions. Japanese companies do not face pay rates fixed industrywide; rather, they voluntarily meet to exchange detailed pay information. However, the end result appears to be the same: similar pay structures across companies

EXHIBIT 16.15 Strategic Similarities and Differences: An Illustrated Comparison

	Japan	United States	Germany
Objectives	Long-term focus High commitment Egalitarian—internal fairness Flexible workforce Control cash flow with bonuses	Short/intermediate focus High commitment Performance—market—meritocratic Flexible workforce Cost control; varies with performance	Long-term focus High commitment Egalitarian—fairness Highly trained Cost control through tariff negotiations
Internal alignment	Person based: age, ability, performance determines base pay Many levels Small pay differences	Work based: jobs, skills, accountabilities Fewer levels Larger pay differences	Work based: jobs and experience Many levels Small pay differences
External competitiveness	Monitor age-pay charts Consistent with competitors	Market determined Compete on variable and performance-based pay	Tariff based Same as competitors
Employee contribution	Bonuses vary with performance only at higher levels in organization Performance appraisal influences promotions and small portion of pay increases	Bonuses an increasing percentage of total pay Increases based on individual, unit, and corporate performance	Tariff negotiated bonuses Smaller performance bonuses for managers
Advantages	Supports commitment and security Greater predictability for companies and employees Flexibility—person based	Supports performance—competitor focus Costs vary with performance Focus on short-term payoffs (speed to market)	Supports commitment and security Greater predictability for companies and employees Companies do not compete with pay
Disadvantages	High cost of aging workforce Discourages unique contributors Discourages women and younger employees	Skeptical workers, less security Fosters "What's in it for me?" No reward for investing in long-term projects	Inflexible; bureaucratic High social and benefit costs Not a strategic tool

competing within an industry. In contrast, managers in U.S. companies possess considerable flexibility to align pay systems with business strategies. As a result, greater variability exists among companies within and across industries.

The pay objectives in traditional German systems include mutual long-term commitment, security, egalitarian pay structures, and cost control through tariff agreements, which apply to competitors' labor costs too. Japanese organizations set pay objectives that focus on the long term (age and security), support high commitment (seniority-based/ability-based), are also more egalitarian, signal the importance of company and individual performance, and encourage flexible workers (person-based pay). U.S. companies, in contrast, focus on the shorter term (less job security); are market-sensitive (competitive total pay); emphasize cost control (variable pay based on performance); reward performance improvement, meritocracy, and innovation (individual bonuses and stock, etc.); and encourage flexibility.

In Japan, person-based factors (seniority, ability, and performance) are used to set base pay. Market comparisons are monitored in Japan, but internal alignment based on seniority remains far more important. Job-based factors (job evaluation) and seniority are also used in Germany. Labor markets in Germany remain highly regulated, and tariff agreements set pay for union workers. So, like the Japanese system, the German system places much greater emphasis on internal alignment than on external markets.

Each approach has advantages and disadvantages. Clearly, the Japanese approach is consistent with low turnover/high commitment and high security, greater acceptance of change, and the need to be flexible. U.S. firms face higher turnover and greater skepticism about change. U.S. firms encourage innovation; they also recognize the contributions to be tapped from workforce diversity. German traditional systems tend to be more bureaucratic and rule-bound. Hence, they are more inflexible. However, they also offer more stability. Both the Japanese and the German national systems face challenges from the high costs associated with an aging workforce. Japan has taken very limited advantage of women's capabilities. The U.S. challenges include the impact of increased uncertainty that employees face, the system's short-term focus, and employees' skepticism about continuous change.

---

e-Compensation

Discussing national systems in other countries in the same detail as we do here for the Japanese and German systems would require another textbook. More information on these and other countries can be found easily on the web. Some useful websites for starting your search are provided by:

Economist Intelligence Unit (EIU):

countrydata.bvdep.com/ip (EIU country reports)

www.ebusinessforum.co (Ebusiness Forum)

Federation of European Employers:

www.euen.co.uk/condits.html (Report on Pay and Working Conditions across Europe)

Trak-it-Down: *www.trak-it-down.com/InterHR.htm* (list of international HR sites, updated regularly)

Evolution and Change in the Traditional Japanese and German Models

The slow economic growth that Japan has experienced combined with the emphasis in its traditional model on seniority-based pay creates a challenge in controlling labor costs. At the same time, cheaper labor in emerging Asian countries (e.g., China) puts further pressure on controlling labor costs and/or increasing productivity. Faced with these pressures, many companies are trying to maintain *long-time employment* (rather than **lifetime employment**) and are looking for other ways to reward less senior employees. These younger employees, who have been paid relatively poorly under the seniority-based pay system, are increasingly finding alternative job opportunities in non-Japanese firms operating in Japan, which have in the past rewarded individual ability and performance more strongly.[78] To compete, companies such as Toyota, Toshiba, and Mitsubishi are increasingly using performance-based pay. As a result, more variation in pay systems has emerged among traditional Japanese companies.[79] As Exhibit 16.16 shows, 41 percent of Japanese companies now report that they place a high emphasis on performance in compensation decisions.[80] Only 12 percent report that performance receives a low emphasis. Other evidence reports that 57 percent of Japanese firms now use merit pay and 21 percent have "eliminated" seniority-based pay and many more report that they "plan" to reduce its importance.[81] Likewise, Exhibit 16.17 shows that Japan is similar to other countries such as the United States in its degree of performance-based differentiation in the merit increase process. Also, national data indicate a decline in the role of seniority in pay in Japan, as well as less lifetime employment (as noted above).[82] Thus, the Japanese model has moved closer to the U.S. model in some key ways.[83] China too moved toward pay for (individual)

EXHIBIT 16.16
Use of Performance (versus Seniority) in Compensation Decisions

Source: From Markus Pudelko, "The Seniority Principle in Japanese Companies: A Relic of the Past?" *Asia Pacific Journal of Human Resources,* Vol. 44, No. 3, December 2006, pp. 276–294.

Use of Performance (versus Seniority) in Compensation Decisions

Legend: United States, Germany, Japan

High: 66%, 47%, 41%
Medium: 34%, 43%, 47%
Low: 0%, 9%, 12%

Emphasis on Performance (versus Seniority)

EXHIBIT 16.17   **Merit Pay Increase for Top Performer versus Average Performer, by Country**

Country	Number of Companies	Type of Employee	Top Performer	Average Performer	Top/Average Ratio[a]
United Kingdom	152	Professional/Technical	8.2%	4.1%	2.0
China	332	Junior Manager/Supervisor/Professional	17.8%	8.6%	2.1
Japan	115	Professional/Technical	6.4%	4.3%	1.5
Germany	127	Professional/Technical	8.3%	3.6%	2.3
United States	774	All Employees			1.0 to 1.5

Source: Hewitt Associates, Salary Increase Survey 2008 and 2009 for each country shown.

[a]Merit increase for top performers divided by merit increase for average performers for all countries but United States. For United States, merit increases not reported separately by performance. Instead, companies reported most typical ratio of merit increases for top and average performers.

performance many years ago.[84] Apparently, the fact that China, Korea, and Japan are medium high or high on collectivism and uncertainty avoidance, national culture characteristics thought to be inconsistent with individual pay for performance and lack of job security, did not prevent these countries from making major changes in these areas when faced with sufficiently strong competitive forces that called into question the sustainability of their traditional employment practices. We also know that there have been similar, perhaps even bigger changes in Korea, which had previously modeled its employment system on Japan.[85]

Turning to Germany, it is no longer all traditional manufacturing, machine tools, and BMW. It has over half of the top Internet companies in Europe. And nearly one in five German adults own stock—double the rate in the late 1990s. Many of the changes are the result of global competitive pressures and technological changes. Like many advanced economies, Germany, along with a number of other Western European countries, faces serious challenges. An aging population, low birth rates, earlier retirement ages, and high pension and unemployment benefits are pushing up the costs of the social support system. A relatively inflexible labor market means that employers are finding it easier to move to (or expand in) other EU countries (e.g., just across the border to countries like Poland where labor costs are much lower) as well as to China and India. All these factors are causing a rethinking of the traditional German social contract and the resulting total compensation systems. Companies are asking for greater autonomy in negotiating tariff agreements to better reflect each company's economic conditions, the use of performance-based pay, and ways to link job security to company performance.

A number of studies report substantial changes in the traditional German model, including greater use of pay for performance, similar to the shifts seen in Japan. Again, foreign multinationals have played some part.[86] As Exhibit 16.16 indicates, 47 percent of German companies now report that performance is highly emphasized in compensation decisions and only 9 percent report that it receives little emphasis. Exhibit 16.16

shows that performance is one of the most important factors in promotion decisions as well. Exhibit 16.17 demonstrates further that the magnitude of merit pay increases for top versus average performers is similar in Germany, China, the United States, and the United Kingdom, with Japan being somewhat different. Finally, the use of stock options in Germany has gone from near zero in 1990 (prior to the lifting of legal restrictions in 1998) to being commonplace in large firms.[87]

STRATEGIC MARKET MIND-SET

A global study of pay systems used by companies with worldwide operations identifies three general compensation strategies: (1) localizer, (2) exporter, and (3) globalizer.[88] These approaches reflect the company's business strategy.[89]

Localizer: "Think Global, Act Local"

If a localizer operates in 150 countries, it may have 150 different systems. The company's business strategy is to seek competitive advantage by providing products and services tailored to local customers. Localizers operate independently of the corporate headquarters. One manager compared his company's pay system this way: "It's as if McDonald's used a different recipe for hamburgers in every country. So, too, for our pay system." Another says, "We seek to be a good citizen in each nation in which we operate. So should our pay system." The pay system is consistent with local conditions.

Exporter: "Headquarters Knows Best"

Exporters are virtual opposites of localizers. Exporters design a total pay system at headquarters and "export" it worldwide for implementation at all locations. Exporting a basic system (with some adjustments for national laws and regulations) makes it easier to move managers and professionals among locations or countries without having to change how they are paid. It also communicates consistent corporatewide objectives. Managers say that "one plan from headquarters gives all managers around the world a common vocabulary and a clear message about what the leadership values." Common software used to support compensation decisions and deployed around the world makes uniform policies and practices feasible. However, not everyone likes the idea of simply implementing what others have designed. One manager complained that headquarters rarely consulted managers in the field: "There is no notion that ideas can go both ways. It's a one-way bridge."

Globalizer: "Think and Act Globally and Locally"

Similar to exporters, globalizers seek a common system that can be used as part of the "glue" to support consistency across all global locations. But headquarters and the operating units are heavily networked to share ideas and knowledge. Managers in these companies said:

> "No one has a corner on good ideas about how to pay people. We need to get them from all our locations."

> "'Home country' begins to lose its meaning; performance is measured where it makes sense for the business, and pay structures are designed to support the business."

"Compensation policy depends more on tax policies and the dynamics of our business than it does on 'national' culture. The culture argument is something politicians hide behind."

e-Compensation
Go to the Organization Resources Counselors' International website, *www. orcin.com,* to observe a state-of-the-art global market site. ORCI collects data from Azerbaijan, Belarus, and other central and eastern European locations as well as Latin America. How useful do you think its data would be for making pay decisions? What limitations exist? Compare the ORCI website with another consulting company's website. Critique each site.

Some believe the globalizer is the business model for the 21st century. IBM, for example, calls itself a "globally integrated enterprise." The aim is for all its operations, from production to marketing to R&D to be integrated around the world.[90] They continue to compete as multinationals. The point is that rather than emphasizing national pay systems as the key to international compensation, the three strategic **global approaches** focus first on the global business strategy and then adapt to local conditions. The upcoming "Your Turn" contrasts different perspectives on global corporations.

EXPATRIATE PAY

Multinationals operate, by definition, in many nations. Employees temporarily working and living in a foreign country are called **expatriates** (or "expats"). One key decision for companies is the degree of reliance on expatriates relative to local employees.[91]

- Expatriates who are citizens of the employer's parent or home country and living and working in another country (e.g., a Japanese citizen working for Toshiba in Toronto) are called parent-country nationals (PCNs).
- Expatriates who are citizens of neither the employer's parent country nor the foreign country where they are living and working (e.g., a German citizen working for Toshiba in Toronto) are called third-country nationals (TCNs).
- **Local country nationals (LCNs)** are citizens of a foreign country where the parent employer operates (e.g., a Canadian citizen working for Toshiba in Toronto).

Hiring LCNs has advantages. LCNs know local conditions and have relationships with local customers, suppliers, and government regulators. The company saves relocation expenses and the other often substantial expenses associated with the use of expatriates. It also avoids concerns about employees adapting to the local culture. Employment of LCNs satisfies nationalistic demands for hiring locals. Only rarely do organizations decide that hiring LCNs is inappropriate.

However, expats or TCNs may be brought in for a number of reasons.[92] The foreign assignment may represent an opportunity for selected employees to develop an international perspective; the position may be sufficiently confidential that information

EXHIBIT 16.18 Why Expatriates Are Selected

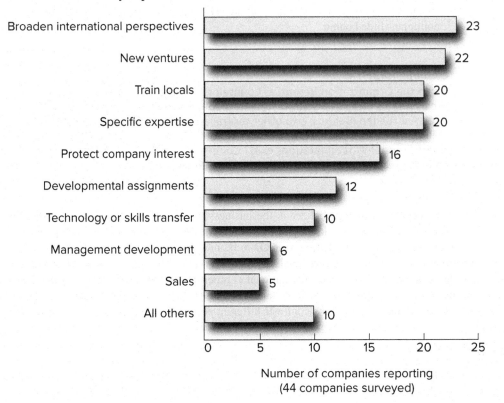

Number of companies reporting
(44 companies surveyed)

is entrusted only to a proven domestic veteran; or the particular skills required for a position may not be readily available in the local labor pool. Exhibit 16.18 catalogs a number of reasons for asking employees to take work assignments in another country.

Designing expatriate pay is a challenge. A company that sends a U.S. employee (base salary of $80,000) with a spouse and two children to London for three years can expect to spend $800,000 to $1,000,000. Obviously, the high cost of expatriate assignments must be offset by the value of the employee's contributions.

Elements of Expatriate Compensation

"(W)e are becalmed. There has been little real innovation in the expatriate compensation field in years," according to a leading consultant.[93] We would add, "So much money, going to so many people, with so little evidence of added value." Exhibit 16.19 is a shopping list of items that can make up expatriate compensation. The list includes everything from household furnishing allowances to language and culture training, spousal employment assistance, and rest and relaxation leaves for longer-term assignments. Usually such lists are organized into four major components: salary, taxes, housing, and allowances and premiums.[94]

EXHIBIT 16.19   Common Allowances in Expatriate Pay Packages

Financial Allowances	Social Adjustment Assistance
Reimbursement for tax return preparation	Emergency leave
Tax equalization	Home leave
Housing differential	Company car/driver
Children's education allowance	Assistance with locating new home
Temporary living allowance	Access to Western health care
Goods and services differential	Club membership
Transportation differential	General personal services (e.g., translation)
Foreign service premium	Personal security (manager and family)
Household furnishing allowance	General culture-transition training (manager)
Currency protection	Social events
Hardship premium	Career development and repatriation planning
Completion bonus	Training for local-culture customs (manager)
	Orientation to community (manager and family)
Family Support	Counseling services
Language training	Rest and relaxation leave
Assistance locating schools for children	Domestic staff (excluding child care)
Training for local culture's customs (family)	Use of company-owned vacation facilities
Child care providers	
Assistance locating spousal employment	

Salary

The base salary plus incentives (merit, eligibility for profit sharing, bonus plans, etc.) for expatriate jobs is usually determined via job evaluation or some system of "job leveling."[95] 3M applies a global job evaluation plan for its international assignments. Common factors describe different 3M jobs around the world. With this system, the work of a general manager in Brussels can be compared to the work of a manager in Austin, Texas, or in Singapore. General Mills has recently implemented a similar system.[96]

Beyond salaries and incentives, the intent of the other components is to help keep expatriate employees financially whole and minimize the disruptions of the move. This means maintaining a standard of living about equal to their peers in their home or base country. This is a broad standard that often results in very costly packages.

Taxes

Income earned in foreign countries has two potential sources of income tax liability.[97] With few exceptions (Saudi Arabia is one), foreign tax liabilities are incurred on income earned in foreign countries. For example, money earned in Japan is subject to Japanese income tax, whether earned by a Japanese or a Korean citizen. The other potential liability is the tax owed in the employee's home country. The United States has the dubious distinction of being the only developed country that taxes its citizens for income earned in another country, even though that income is taxed by the country in which it was earned. Most employers pay whatever income taxes are due to the host country and/or the home country via **tax equalization.**[98] Taxes are deducted from employees' earnings up to the same amount of taxes they would pay had they remained in their home country.

This allowance can be substantial. For example, the marginal tax rates in Belgium, the Netherlands, and Sweden can run between 70 and 90 percent. So if a Swedish expatriate is sent to a lower-tax country, say, Great Britain, the company keeps the difference. If a British expatriate goes to Sweden, the company makes up the difference in taxes. The logic here is that if the employee kept the windfall from being assigned to a low-tax country, then getting this person to accept assignments elsewhere would become difficult.

Housing

Appropriate housing has a major impact on an expatriate's success. Most international companies pay housing allowances or provide company-owned housing. **Expatriate colonies** often grow up in sections of major cities where many different international companies group their expatriates.

Allowances and Premiums

A friend in Moscow cautions that when we take the famed Moscow subway, we should pay the fare at the beginning of the ride. Inflation is so high there that if we wait to pay until the end of the ride, we won't be able to afford to get off! Cost-of-living allowances, club memberships, transportation assistance, child care and education, spousal employment, local culture training, and personal security are some of the many service allowances and premiums expatriates receive. The logic supporting these allowances is that foreign assignments require that the expatriate (1) work with less direct supervision than a domestic counterpart, (2) often live and work in strange and sometimes uncongenial surroundings, and (3) represent the employer in the host country. The size of the premium is a function of both the expected hardship and hazards in the host country and the type of job. An assignment in London will probably yield fewer allowances than one in Tehran, where the "National Day of Campaign against Global Arrogance" is observed every year on the anniversary of the takeover of the American Embassy in 1979.

The Balance Sheet Approach

Most North American, European, and Japanese global firms combine these elements of pay in a **balance sheet approach.**[99] The name stems from accounting, where credits and debits must balance. It is based on the premise that employees on overseas assignments should have the same spending power as they would in their home country. Therefore, the home country is the standard for all payments. The objective is to:

1. Ensure mobility of people to global assignments as cost-effectively as feasible.

2. Ensure that expatriates neither gain nor lose financially.

3. Minimize adjustments required of expatriates and their dependents.

EXHIBIT 16.20
Balance Sheet
Approach

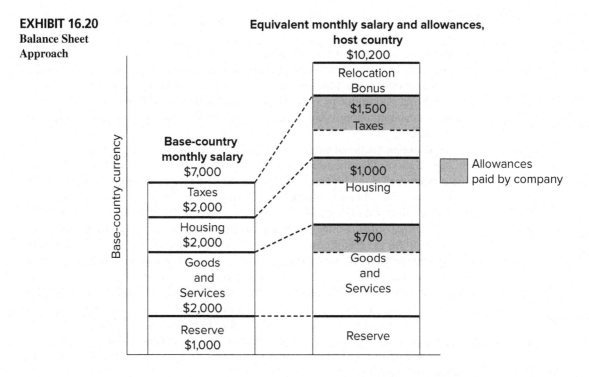

Equivalent monthly salary and allowances,
host country
$10,200

Base-country currency

Base-country
monthly salary
$7,000

Taxes
$2,000

Housing
$2,000

Goods
and
Services
$2,000

Reserve
$1,000

Relocation
Bonus

$1,500
Taxes

$1,000
Housing

$700

Goods
and
Services

Reserve

Allowances
paid by company

Notice that none of these objectives link (explicitly) to performance.

Exhibit 16.20 depicts the traditional balance sheet approach. Home-country salary is the first column. A person's salary (based on job evaluation, market surveys, merit, and incentives) must cover taxes, housing, and goods and services, plus other financial obligations (a "reserve").

The proportions set for each of the components in the exhibit are *norms* (i.e., assumed to be "normal" for the typical expatriate) set to reflect consumption patterns in the home country for a person at that salary level with that particular family pattern. They are not actual expenditures. These norms are based on surveys conducted by consulting firms. Using the norms is supposed to avoid negotiating with each individual, although substantial negotiation still occurs.

Let us assume that the norms suggest that a typical manager with a spouse and one child, earning $84,000 ($7,000 per month) in the United States, will spend $2,000 per month on housing, $2,000 on taxes, and $2,000 on goods and services and put away a reserve of $1,000 per month. The next building block is the equivalent costs in the host country where the assignment is located. For example, if similar housing costs $3,000 in the host country, the expatriate is expected to pay the same $2,000 paid in the United States and the company pays the employee the difference; in our example, an extra $1,000 per month. In the illustration, the taxes, housing, and goods and services components are all greater in the host country than in the home country. The expatriate bears the same level of costs (white area of right-hand column) as at home. The employer is responsible for the additional costs (shaded area). (Changing exchange rates among currencies complicates these allowance calculations.)

However, equalizing pay may not motivate an employee to move to another country, particularly if the new location has less personal appeal. Therefore, many employers also offer some form of financial incentive or bonus to encourage the move. The right-hand column in Exhibit 16.20 includes a relocation bonus. Most U.S. multinational corporations pay relocation bonuses to induce people to take expatriate assignments.

If gaining international experience is really one of the future competencies required by organizations, then the need for such bonuses ought to be reduced, since the expatriate experience should increase the likelihood of future promotions. Either the experience expatriates obtain is unique to each situation and therefore not transferable or companies simply do not know how to value it. Whatever the reason, research reveals that **U.S. expatriates** feel their U.S. organizations still do not value their international expertise.[100] So the rhetoric of the value of global competencies has yet to match the reality—hence the need for relocation incentives. Another way to look at it is that the employee takes a risk going overseas. Near-term promotion opportunities may be lost. While international experience could have a handsome payoff in later promotions for some, this payoff is not certain and not true for all. Moreover, a nontrivial share of expatriate assignments are cut short, due either to performance problems or family-related problems (e.g., spouse and/or children having difficulties adapting).[101] Thus, consistent with our earlier discussion of agency theory, a compensating differential for risk may be required.

Alternatives to Balance Sheet Approach

Employers continue to explore alternatives to the balance sheet, due primarily to the cost. Although in Exhibit 16.20 the expatriate premium was 46 percent ($10,200/$7,000 − 1), that premium can be much higher. For example, Exhibit 16.21 shows survey data on the cost of a manager (married plus one child/dependent) with a

EXHIBIT 16.21   **Manager Working in Singapore or United States ("Married Plus One" Situation)**

Type of Employee	Type of Approach	Net Pay (after taxes)	Percent Premium Relative to Pay in United States
Expatriate in Singapore	Balance Sheet Approach		
	Premium Package	$393,000	239%
	Standard Package	$312,000	169%
	Budget Package	$260,000	124%
Expatriate in Singapore	Local Plus Package	$247,000	113%
Local Employee in Singapore		$135,000	16%
Employee in United States		$116,000	

Source: Carole Mestre, Anne Rossier-Renaud, and Madeline Berger, "Better Benchmarks for Global Mobility," *Workspan,* April 2009.

U.S. salary of $116,000 posted to Singapore. The balance sheet approach cost ranged from a "budget package" cost of $260,000 to a "premium package" cost of $393,000, or a 239 percent premium. The "standard package" was $312,000, a 169 percent premium and had the following components:

Home Net Base Salary	$115,500
Cost of Living Adjustment	$ 16,570
Mobility Premium	$ 16,570
Accommodation/Housing	$115,500
Car Benefit	$ 14,400
Education Benefit	$ 33,600
Total	$312,140

Negotiation simply means the employer and employee find a mutually agreeable package. The arrangements tend to be relatively costly (or generous, depending on your point of view), create comparability problems when other employees are asked to locate overseas ("but Mike and Sarah got . . ."), and need to be renegotiated with each transfer.

Another alternative, *localization,* or *local plus,* ties salary to the host country's salary scales and provides some cost-of-living allowances for taxes, housing, and dependents. The allowances tend to be similar to those under the balance sheet, but the salary can vary with the location. As Exhibit 16.21 shows, in the case of Singapore, the localization approach would, on average, result in a cost of $247,000, a 113 percent premium, in contrast to the premium of as much as 239 percent for the balance sheet approach.

While the balance sheet approach ties salary to the home country, the *modified balance sheet* ties salary to a region (Asia-Pacific, Europe, North America, Central America, or South America). The logic is that if an employee of a global business who relocates from San Diego, California, to Portland, Maine, receives only a moving allowance, why should all the extras be paid for international moves of far less distance (e.g., from Germany to Spain)? In Europe, many companies no longer view European managers who work outside their home country as expats. Instead, they are Europeans running their European businesses. And the use of a common currency, the euro, makes this easier. In this vein, a study compared the over-base pay allowance provided by 17 multinational companies to an employee earning 100,000 euros being transferred from Frankfurt, Germany, to Paris, France.[102] The median premium was 23,000 euros, or 13 percent and the range was from as little as 5,000 euros, a 5 percent premium, to 45,000 euros, a 45 percent premium. Thus, in all 17 companies, the premium was modest relative to what we have seen.

Another common modification is to decrease allowances over time. The logic is that the longer the employee is in the host country, the closer the standard of living should come to that of a local employee. For example, if Americans eat a $10 pizza twice a week in the United States, should they eat a $30 pizza twice a week in Tokyo, at the employer's expense? More typically, after a couple of months, the expatriate will probably learn where the nationals find cheaper pizza or will switch to sushi. We had a friend posted to London by a U.S. company. The expatriate and spouse ate dinner out each night, leased a nice apartment in an upscale centrally located neighborhood, had a car, and the spouse went back to school. All this was paid for by the company, so the couple's entire paycheck went into the bank and investments. They were living in London with all expenses paid! When they had to eventually return to the United States, at the behest of the company, it was with great reluctance and after running out of extensions to the assignment.

The *lump-sum/cafeteria approach* offers expats more choices. This approach sets salaries according to the home-country system and simply offers employees lump sums of money to offset differences in standards of living. For example, a company will still calculate differences in cost of living, but instead of allocating them housing, transportation, goods and services, and so on, it simply gives the employee a total allowance. Perhaps one employee will trade less spacious housing for private schooling and tutors for the children; another employee will make different choices. We know of one expatriate who purchased a winery in Italy with his lump-sum allowance. He has been reassigned to Chicago but still owns and operates his winery.

Finally, a company can consider using fewer expatriates and more *local country nationals.* As we stated at the beginning of our discussion of expatriate pay, such a strategy has many advantages, including lower cost, and greater familiarity with the aspects of the business environment unique to that country. Another advantage is that such a strategy can be combined with a strategy of greater integration of talent into the career planning and development system. An increasing number of companies have foreign-born managers and executives in key posts. Some of these key people would not be where they are now making important contributions if they had not had the opportunity at some point to gain experience in key jobs in their home countries and then build on that to progress through the company's ranks.[103] Along these same lines, greater use of **third-country nationals (TCNs)** can also fit this strategy. In addition, TCNs can be less expensive if they come from countries having lower compensation levels. For example, whereas we saw in our earlier example that a U.S. expatriate earning $116,000 at home and posted to Singapore would cost $312,000, a comparable TCN from India posted to Singapore would cost $209,000.[104] In addition, given that the Indian TCN would earn $49,000 in India, the premium he or she would realize would be quite substantial and thus perhaps the assignment would have higher value than it would to a comparable expatriate from the United States.

Expatriate Systems → Objectives? *Quel dommage!*

Talk to experts in international compensation, and you soon get into complexities of taxes, exchange rates, housing differences, and the like. What you do not hear is how the expatriate pay system affects competitive advantage, customer satisfaction, quality, or other performance concerns. It does emphasize maintaining employee purchasing power and minimizing disruptions and inequities. But the lack of attention to aligning expatriate pay with organization objectives is glaring. Sadly, the major innovation in expat pay over the past decade seems to have been to relabel expats and TCNs as "international assignees."

Expatriate compensation systems are forever trying to be like Goldilocks' porridge: not too high, not too low, but just right. The expatriate pay must be sufficient to encourage the employee to take the assignment yet not be so attractive that local nationals will feel unfairly treated or that the expatriate will refuse any future reassignments. These systems also presume that expats will be repatriated to their home country. However, the relevant standard for judging fairness may not be home-country treatment. It may be the pay of other expats, that is, the expat community, or it may be local nationals. And how do local nationals feel about the allowances and pay levels of their expat co-workers? Very little research tells us how expats and those around them judge the fairness of expat pay.

Employee Preferences

Beyond work objectives, costs, and fairness, an additional consideration is employees' preferences for international assignments. For many Europeans, working in another country is just part of a career. Yet for many U.S. employees, leaving the United States means leaving the action. They may worry that expatriate experience sidetracks rather than enhances a career. Employees undoubtedly differ in their preferences for overseas jobs, and preferences can vary over time. Having children in high school or elderly parents to care for, divorce, working spouses, and other life factors exert a strong influence on whether an offer to work overseas is a positive or negative opportunity. Research does inform us of the following:

- 68 percent of expatriates do not know what their jobs will be when they return home.
- 54 percent return to lower-level jobs. Only 11 percent are promoted.
- Only 5 percent believe their company values overseas experience.
- 77 percent have less disposable income when they return home.
- Only 13 percent of U.S. expatriates are women. (Yet 49% of all U.S. managers and professionals are women.)
- More than half of returning expatriates leave their company within one year.[105] Unfortunately, while research does highlight the problem, it does not offer much guidance for designers of expat pay systems. Consequently, we are at the mercy of conjecture and beliefs.[106]

We should emphasize that, of course, some companies do a much better job of managing expatriates. Also, there is disagreement over what the evidence actually says on rates of success and failure of expatriates, especially those from the United States.[107]

BORDERLESS WORLD → BORDERLESS PAY? GLOBALISTS

Some corporations, particularly those attempting to become "globally integrated enterprises," are creating cadres of globalists: managers who operate anywhere in the world in a borderless manner. They expect that during their career, they will be located in and travel from country to country. According to a former CEO of General Electric, "The aim in a global business is to get the best ideas from everyone, everywhere." To support this global flow of ideas and people some companies are also designing borderless, or at least regionalized, pay systems. One testing ground for this approach is the European Union. As our global guide points out, one difficulty with borderless pay is that base pay levels and the other components depend too much on differences in each nation's laws and customs.

Focusing on expatriate compensation may blind companies to the issue of appropriate pay for employees who seek global career opportunities. Ignoring these employees causes them to focus only on the local operations, their home country pay, and devote less attention to integrating operations in global firms. It is naive to expect commitment to a long-term global strategy in which local managers have little input and receive limited benefits. Paradoxically, attempts to localize top management in subsidiaries may reinforce the differences in focus between local and global management.

Your Turn   IBM's Worldwide Business and Employment Strategies and Compensation

Read the description of IBM's worldwide business strategy in Exhibit 1. Next, in Exhibit 2, read the description of IBM's geographic breakdown of revenues and growth and its offer to North American employees being laid off to keep a job with IBM by moving overseas. Then, answer the following questions:

1. Think back to our discussion in Chapter 7 and in the current chapter regarding the labor cost difference between employing programmers in the United States versus overseas in locations like India and Eastern Europe. Is IBM's growth in employment in such countries inevitable given labor cost differences? How does this relate to Mr. Palmisano's comments in Exhibit 1?

2. Is the IBM offer typical of that offered to expatriates?

3. What is your reaction to the critical comments made by the Alliance@IBM spokesman, including the comment about asking employees to "offshore their citizenship"?

4. Review Exhibit 16.12 earlier in this chapter—The Cost of Living, Domestic Purchasing Power, and Minutes of Working Time Required to Buy a Big Mac, Bread, and Rice. How do the numbers for Indian cities like Delhi and Mumbai compare to those for U.S. cities like Chicago, Los Angeles, and New York? What are the implications of such differences?

5. Exhibit 2 gives examples of people who seem to enjoy living and working in India and also reports the opinion of an academic that this sort of move will become much more common. Do you believe that is likely? Why or why not?

EXHIBIT 1   Palmisano: Multinationals Have Been Superseded

Everyone, it seems, has a strongly felt position on globalization. . . . The emerging business model of the 21st century is not, in fact, "multinational." This new kind of organization—at IBM we call it "the globally integrated enterprise"—is very different in its structure and operations. Many parties to the globalization debate mistakenly project the 20th-century multinational on to 21st century global reality. . . .

In a multinational model, companies built local production capacity within key markets, while performing other tasks on a global basis. . . . As an example, American multinationals such as General Motors, Ford, and IBM built plants and established local workforce policies in Europe and Asia, but kept research and development and product design principally in the "home country."

The globally integrated enterprise, in contrast, fashions its strategy, management, and operations to integrate production—and deliver value to clients—worldwide. That has been made possible by shared technologies and shared business standards, built on top of a global information technology and communications infrastructure. . . .

These decisions are not simply a matter of offloading noncore activities, nor are they mere labor arbitrage—that is, shifting work to low-wage regions. Rather, they are about actively managing different operations, expertise, and capabilities to open the enterprise up in multiple ways, allowing it to connect more intimately with partners, suppliers, and customers and, most importantly, enabling it to engage in multifaceted, collaborative innovation.

This kind of innovation is much more than the creation of new products. It is also how services are delivered: three-quarters of most employment is in services. . . . Today, innovation is inherently global.

I believe the globally integrated enterprise is a better and more profitable way to organize business activities—and it can deliver enormous economic benefits to developed and developing nations. For example, integration of the workforce in developing countries into global production systems is already raising living standards, improving working conditions and creating more jobs in those countries. . . .

Source: Excerpt from Samuel Palmisano, "Multinationals Have Been Superseded," *Financial Times,* June 2006. Reprint Courtesy of International Business Machines Corporation, © 2006 International Business Machines Corporation.

EXHIBIT 2   IBM's Global Employment and Compensation

After 2008, IBM stopped reporting the number of employees it had in each country, perhaps because of media attention to its decline in U.S. employment and growth in overseas employment (e.g., in India). As of 2008, the majority of IBM's roughly 400,000 employees (71%) were outside of the United States, with over 70,000 of those in India. In 2012, Steve Lohr of the New York Times noted that "I.B.M. has hugely increased its employment in India in the last several years" and that "Some estimates place I.B.M.'s Indian work force at more than 100,000. That would probably place it on a par with I.B.M.'s employment
(Continued)

Source: Karina Frayter, "IBM to Laid-Off: Want a Job in India? Employees Who Would Otherwise Face Layoffs From Their North American Jobs at IBM Are Being Given the Chance to Work Abroad Through 'Project Match,'" *CNN.com,* February 5. 2009, retrieved 7/5/2009; William M. Bulkeley, "IBM to Cut U.S. Jobs, Expand in India: International Business Machines Corp. Plans to Lay Off About 5,000 U.S. Employees, With Many of the Jobs Being Transferred to India, According to People Familiar With the Situation," *Wall Street Journal,* March 26, 2009; Ben Arnoldy. "For Laid-Off IBM Workers, A Job in India? An IBM Program Offers Some Incentive to Relocate. Americans Who Have Migrated Overseas Find Less Pay—But a Good Lifestyle," *Christian Science Monitor,* March 26, 2009. Steve Lohr. Unboxed Extra: I.B.M. and America's Job Challenge. *New York Times.* January 1, 2012. Shamni Pande. Married to the job. Best companies to work for: Work culture continues to drive employees. *Business Today.* March 4, 2012. http://businesstoday. intoday.in. Extracted May 23, 2012. IBM Annual Reports. IBM lays off staff in India. The Times of India. February 13, 2014. IBM plans to invest $6 billion in India Country to play big role in advancing U.S. company's worldwide operation. International Herald Tribune. June 7, 2006. Patrick Thibodeau, In a symbolic shift, IBM's India workforce likely exceeds U.S. November 29, 2012. http://www.computerworld.com. Extracted February 3, 2015. 16-56. Paul McDougall, Amid Global Push, IBM Has Shrunk Its U.S. Workforce By Half Since 2000. International Business Times. October 2, 2014.

EXHIBIT 2 (*Continued*)

in the United States." Actually, as Exhibit 2 shows, recent data indicate that IBM employment in India now exceeds U.S. employment and that non-U.S. employment overall has continued to rapidly outpace U.S. employment. Likewise, as the following information from IBM annual reports and other sources shows, most of its revenue is outside of the Americas as well:

Revenue (in millions)	2013	2008	2000
Total	99,751	103,630	88,400
Americas	43,249	41,122	38,600
Europe/Middle East/Africa	31,628	34,699	24,300
Asia Pacific	22,923	19,501	17,700
Employment			
Total	431,212	398,455	316,303
United States	90,000*	115,000	153,857
Outside United States	341,212*	283,455	162,716
India	140,000*	70,000*	9,000*

*Estimate. Based on news reports.

One result of this shifting emphasis to overseas markets is that IBM employees who were being laid off in North America were given an alternative to joining the then growing ranks of the unemployed—work for the company abroad. IBM offered laid-off workers in the United States and Canada a chance to take an IBM job in India, Nigeria, Russia, or other countries, including Argentina, Brazil, China, Czech Republic, Hungary, Mexico, Poland, Romania, Slovakia, Slovenia, South Africa, Turkey, and United Arab Emirates.

The company also will help with moving costs and provide visa assistance, it says. Only "satisfactory performers" who are "willing to work on local terms and conditions" should pursue the jobs, the document says. IBM would not immediately confirm if it means that the workers would be paid local wages and would be subject to local labor laws.

Some of the jobs are being eliminated because customers have ended contracts or the company has automated tasks. But employees say in many cases, they have been training IBM workers from India to do work that will now be moved overseas.

A spokesman for Alliance@IBM, a workers' group that is affiliated with the Communications Workers of America but does not have official union status at IBM, slammed the initiative, saying that IBM has not only offshored jobs to countries that have low costs, but on top of that has asked employees "offshore themselves" and their citizenship.

IBM's cuts show that even companies that have so far navigated the global recession profitably are continuing to slash costs. The IBM offer hints at a future where it's not just skilled Indians who might have to travel halfway around the globe for a job. It's likely that more American job seekers will have to think globally, say analysts, and the experiences of Americans who have taken jobs with companies here say it's not something to fear.

"I was making six figures when I left the States. I'm making six figures here—in rupees," laughs Jeanne Heydecker, a marketing executive now living outside of Delhi and working at her third Indian company. The salary for this single mother actually translates to roughly $50,000 a year. But it would be a mistake to suppose her quality of life has gone down. Most everything she could want is available in Delhi. The health care, she says, has been top-notch and bottom-dollar. And like most Westerners and

(*Continued*)

EXHIBIT 2 (*Continued*)

wealthy Indians here, she is able to hire people to cook, clean, and drive for her. "You can come home from work and focus on your family, not on maintaining the car and the housework," she says. She left Chicago in 2007 after realizing that she was bored at work and didn't see companies nearby that were hiring "new people to do new things." Through the social-networking site Linkedin.com and Skype, Ms. Heydecker talked with the head of a Calcutta technology company who eventually hired her sight unseen.

Hers is not yet a well-worn path. But in the coming decades, it will be, says Arvind Panagariya, an expert on the Indian economy at Columbia University in New York. "Does the average American [worker] think globally? No. I don't think we're at that stage yet. But it will happen," he says. "Such a massive technological revolution will cause the borders to blur, if not disappear."

So far, there isn't much evidence of Americans expanding their search beyond places less like Peoria and more like Pune. In IBM's case, fewer than 20 people have taken up the offer for help in locating a new IBM job overseas, estimated company spokesman Doug Shelton. But the jobs in places like India are worth considering, Mr. Shelton suggested, saying that the cost of living is lower and international experience is highly prized in a global marketplace.

Moving beyond the IBM situation, in one of the new office high-rises, Mindcrest, a legal outsourcing firm, has recently hired three Americans—and has plans to hire more Westerners in the coming year. Like Heydecker in Delhi, the three women are mid-career and weren't sent here on a temporary foreign rotation by a multinational firm back home. Ms. Vega and her American counterparts Deirdre Byrne and Rana Rosen help the Indian attorneys understand what the Western clients want. None of them believe their work takes away American jobs, but say it instead frees young lawyers in the US from some early-career drudgery. Over lunch, the three women laugh about stashing pine nuts, manila folders, and lint-remover rolling pins in their luggage when they come back from visits home. There are other challenges: power cuts, the bureaucracy of setting up basic services like a cellphone, and the more pervasive scenes of deep poverty on the street here.

But Ms. Byrne, who has worked as a high-powered Manhattan attorney and a realtor for Sotheby's in the Hamptons, sums up the consensus: "We have a very nice life, and for a fraction of the costs at home"—even with smaller salaries. She stresses that the work is demanding "on the scale of a New York law firm," but comes with a "bonhomie" generally absent from Big Apple offices.

As for why more Americans are not considering work abroad, expatriates here admit it grows more complicated for those with more family ties. Heydecker's teenage son had to give up friends and skateboarding but has adjusted well, she says. She adds that the advantages to working abroad are often not communicated well.

She feels that her case is a success story. Although she admits that her overseas assignment was initially "isolating," once they got adjusted, they found life to be quite good and that it all depends how open you are to a new and interesting life experience.

Whatever relocated IBM employees may think of working in places like India, domestic Indian workers think highly of IBM, as indicated by it being ranked the 4th best employer in India (just ahead of 5th place Google and 7th place Microsoft, as reported by Business Today of India). TCS, Wipro, and Infosys finished ahead of IBM. Interestingly, however, IBM has not appeared on the 100 Best Places to Work in America list since 2004. Finally, although rapid IBM employment growth in India has been the story, things can change and they have for IBM in India. IBM has recently carried out workforce reductions worldwide, including in India.

Still Your **Turn**

Globalization of the Labor Market: The English Premier League

According to Forbes, the three most valuable sports teams in the world are football teams: Real Madrid ($3.4 billion), Barcelona ($3.2 billion), and Manchester United ($2.8 billion). As you can see, we are not talking about American football teams. We are talking about what some of us call soccer. Rounding out the top five most valuable teams are one baseball team, the New York Yankees ($2.5 billion) and one (American) football team, the Dallas Cowboys ($2.3 billion).

The English Premier League, where Manchester United plays, is the top soccer league in the world based on revenue generated. (La Liga in Spain, where Real Madrid and Barcelona play as well as the Bundesliga in Germany, where, for example, Bayern Munich plays, are other top leagues.) There are 500 players in the British Premier League (20 teams x 25 players each). The average salary is roughly $3.4 million. In 1992–93, the average player salary was about $210,000 (adjusted for inflation). Besides the salaries, one other thing that has changed is where the players come from. In 1992–93, 69 percent of the players were Englishmen. Today, it is 37 percent. Thus, the majority of players in the English Premier League are no longer English.

Some economists have noted the benefits of this globalization of the English Premier League and open borders/free movement of players ("workers"). Arguably, the quality of play in the League has improved because it draws the best talent from around the world rather than being mostly limited to local talent. That, in turn, has led to globalization of the product market. Specifically, English Premier League football is watched around the world, not only because of the elite quality of play and players, but also likely because many countries have players in the League, which probably increases interest in those countries. That brings in large amounts of revenue from outside of England in the form of television rights, jersey sales, and advertising. To help see the global reach of the League, one can look at the players' jerseys. One club, Tottenham, for example, carries the logo of AIA, an Asian-based insurance company, on its jerseys. (AIA has no offices in England.) The book, Soccernomics, refers to the League as "the most successful product in sporting history."

So, what's not to like? Greg Dyke, chairman of the Football Association, which governs English soccer, has asked "How many" English players are there in the English football academies who dream of playing football, but "who cannot get a first-team game?" Thus, he has proposed limits on the number of foreign players in the Premier League.

QUESTIONS:

1. Has the globalization of the English Premier League been a good thing? Who is better off as a result? Who is worse off? Think carefully about owners, fans/consumers, and players. Are there others who have been affected as well?

2. Consider the proposal by Mr. Dyke to limit the number of foreign players in the English Premier League. Take the perspective of owners, players, and fans/consumers. Who would benefit and who would lose under this proposal?

3. Do players from England play in elite leagues outside of England? Does that affect your evaluation of the proposal? If so, how?

4. One concern expressed by Mr. Dyke is that the English national team may be suffering because fewer English players can develop in the English Premier League. Jürgen Klinsmann, coach of the U.S. National time has criticized players who play in the Major League Soccer (MLS) league in the United States, rather than in one of the European elite leagues, because he feels MLS does not provide strong enough competition for the U.S. players to develop their full potential. Comment on the arguments by Mr. Dyke and Mr. Klinsmann. What would be best for the English national team?

Sources: Binyamin Appelbuam. Globalization under Attack, On the Soccer Field. New York Times, April 2, 2015. A3. Deloitte Football Money League 2015. Commercial breaks. Sports Business Group, Deloitte. January 2015. www .deloitte.com. Kurt Badenhausen. The World's 50 Most Valuable Sports Teams 2014. July 16, 2014. Forbes. www.forbes .com. Accessed April 5, 2015.

Summary

Studying employee compensation only in your neighborhood, city, or country is like being a horse with blinders. Removing the blinders by adopting an international perspective deepens your understanding of local issues. Anyone interested in compensation must adopt a worldwide perspective. The globalization of businesses, financial markets, trade agreements, and even labor markets is affecting every workplace and every employment relationship. And employee compensation, so central to the workplace, is embedded in the different political-socioeconomic arrangements found around the world. Examining employee compensation with the factors in the global pay model offers insights into managing total compensation internationally.

The basic premise of this book is that compensation systems have a profound impact on individual behavior, organization success, and social well-being. We believe this holds true within and across all national boundaries.

Review Questions

1. Rank the factors in the global guide according to your belief in their importance for understanding and managing compensation. How does your ranking differ from those of your peers? From those of international peers? Discuss how the rankings may change over time.

2. Distinguish between nationwide and industrywide pay determination. How do they compare to a business strategy–market approach?

3. Develop arguments for and against "typical" Japanese-style, "typical" German-style, and "typical" U.S.-style approaches to pay. Using the global guide, what factors are causing each approach to change?

4. Distinguish between global workers, expatriates, local nationals, and third-country nationals.

5. In the balance sheet approach to paying expats, most of total compensation is linked to costs of living. Some argue that expatriate pay resembles a traditional Japanese pay system. Evaluate this argument.

Endnotes

1. Ken Abosch, Jill Schermerhorn, and Lori Wisper, "Broad-Based Variable Pay Goes Global," *Workspan,* May 2008, pp. 57–62; Jie Shen, "HRM in Chinese Privately Owned Enterprises," *Thunderbird International Business Review* 50(2), 2008, pp. 91–101; Fay, C. H., "The Global Convergence of Compensation Practices," in *Global Compensation: Foundations and Perspectives*, L. R. Gomez-Mejia and S. Werner eds. (Oxon, UK: Routledge, 2008) pp. 32–141.

2. Hiroko Tabuchi, "Slacker Nation? Young Japanese Shun Promotions. 'Hodo-Hodo' Favor Humdrum Jobs Even as Recession Looms," *The Wall Street Journal,* November 1, 2008; Mitsuo Ishida, Akiko Ono, Naoki Mitani, Yoshinori Tomita, and Anja Kirsch, "The Automotive Industry in Japan," in Russell D. Lansbury, Nick Wailes, Jim Kitay, and Anja Kirsch, eds., *Globalization and Employment Relations in the Auto Assembly Industry. Bulletin of Comparative Labor Relations. Volume 64.* (Alphen aan den Rijn, Netherlands: Wolters Kluwer, 2008); Markus Pudelko, "The Seniority Principle in Japanese Companies: A Relic of the Past?" *Asia Pacific Journal of Human Resources* 44 (2006), pp. 276–294; T. Kono and S. Clegg, *Trends in Japanese Management: Continuing Strengths, Current Problems and Changing Priorities* (New York: Palgrave-Macmillan, 2001).

3. Interviews with Toshiba managers, included in M. Bloom, G. Milkovich, and A. Mitra, "Managing the Chaos of Global Pay Systems," *International Journal of Human Resource Management* 14 (2003), pp.1350–1367.

4. Geraldine Fabrikant, "U.S.-Style Pay Packages Are All the Rage in Europe," *The New York Times,* June 16, 2006; "New Equity Incentive Programs Gain Favor with Employers Around the World," *Towers Perrin Monitor,* July 22, 2005; *European Total Rewards Survey 2005, www.merhr.com/totalrewardseurope.*

5. Suruvilla, C.K. Lee, and M.E. Gallagher, eds., *From Iron Rice Bowl to Informalization: Markets, Workers, and the State in a Changing China* (Ithaca, NY: Cornell University Press, 2011).

6. United Nations, *World Investment Report 2011,* Table I.5 and *World Investment Report 2014.* Table 2.

7. Scott Thurm, "U.S. Firms Add Jobs, but Mostly Overseas," *The Wall Street Journal,* April 26, 2012.

8. International Association of Automobile Manufacturers, http://oica.net/category/production-statistics/; accessed June 6, 2012 and http://www.oica.net/wp-content/uploads//gm-2013.pdf, accessed February 3, 2015.

9. Geraldine Fabrikant, "U.S. Style Pay Packages Are All the Rage in Europe," *The New York Times,* June 16, 2006; Thomas Li Ping Tang, Toto Sutarso, Adebowale Akande, et al., "The Love of Money and Pay Level Satisfaction: Measurement and Functional Equivalence in 29 Geopolitical Entities Around the World," paper presented at the Annual Meeting of the Academy of Management, August 11–16, 2006, Atlanta, GA.

10. "Marriages Made in Hell," *The Economist,* May 20, 2009, *www.economist.com,* August 2009.

11. "Costs of Chrysler Sale Blamed in Daimler Loss," *The New York Times,* October 25, 2007, *www.nytimes.com,* August 2009.

12. Parmy Olson, "The Carmaker Finally Rids Itself of 19.9% Stake," *Forbes,* April 28, 2009, *www.forbes.com,* August 2009.

13. Torsten Kühlmann and Peter J. Dowling, "DaimlerChrysler: A Case Study of a Cross Border Merger," in *Mergers and Acquisitions: Managing Cultures and Human Resources,* Günther Stahl and Mark E. Mendenhall, eds. (Stanford, California: Stanford Business Books, 2005).

14. Carmelo Cennamo, "Shareholders' Value Maximization and Stakeholders' Interest," in *Global Compensation: Foundations and Perspectives,* Luis R. Gomez-Mejia and Steve Werner eds. (London: Routledge, 2008). See especially Table 8.1.

15. Mike Ramsey, "Chrysler Installs Fiat Production System before Plants Restart," *www.bloomberg.com,* 6/29/2009; "The Italian Solution: Fiat's Ambitions," *The Economist,* May 9, 2009, *www.economist.com,* August 2009; Serena Saitto, "Detroit Suburbs Beckon Fiat Executives with $1,595 Sandals," *www.bloomberg.com,* 6/29/2009.

16. Bill Vlasic, "A Merger Once Scoffed at Bears Fruit in Detroit," *The New York Times,* January 9, 2012; Jeremy Cato, "Chrysler and Fiat: The Odd Couple Triumphs," *The Globe and Mail,* May 3, 2012; Larry P. Vellequette, "How a Merger Made a Dart: First Test of Synergy Shows Chrysler, Fiat Can Listen, Communicate," *Automotive News,* May 14, 2012.

17. S. Basu, S. Estrin, and J. Svejnar, "Employment Determination in Enterprises under Communism and in Transition: Evidence from Central University," *Industrial and Labor Relations Review,* April 2005, pp. 353–369; J. Banister, "Manufacturing Compensation in China," *Monthly Labor Review,* November 2005, pp. 22–40; *Overview of the Chinese Economy,* Report by the Joint Economic Committee of United States Congress, July 2005; N. Zupan, "HRM in Slovenian Transitional Companies," presentation at CAHRS International Conference, Berlin, June 2002.

18. D. Dong, K. Goodall, and M. Warner, "The End of the Iron Rice Bowl," *International Journal of Human Resource Management,* April 2, 2000, pp. 217–236; Hesan A. Quazi, *Compensation and Benefits Practices in Selected Asian Countries* (Singapore: McGraw Hill, 2004).

19. Zhong-Ming Wang, presentation to Cornell University Global HRM Distance Learning seminar, Shanghai, China, March 2000; comments by Ningyu Tang, instructor in Shanghai for Global HRM Distance Learning seminar; Jing Zhou and J. J. Martocchio, "Chinese and American Managers' Compensation Award Decisions," *Personnel Psychology* 54 (Spring 2001), pp. 115–145; Mei Fong, "A Chinese Puzzle," *The Wall Street Journal,* August 16, 2005, p. B1; Zaohui Zhao, "Earnings Differentials between State and Non-State Enterprises in Urban China," *Pacific Economic Review* 7(1), 2002, pp. 181–197.

20. *Doing Business in the Russian Federation,* PricewaterhouseCoopers, April 2004; John S. Earle and Klara Sabirianova Peter, "Complementarity and Custom in Wage Contract Violation," Upjohn Institute Staff Working Paper 06-129, July 2006.

21. Kevin O'Rourke and J. G. Williamson, *Globalization and History: The Evolution of a 19th Century Atlantic Economy* (Cambridge, MA: MIT Press, 1999), p. 2.

22. Kevin O'Rourke and J. G. Williamson, *Globalization and History: The Evolution of a 19th Century Atlantic Economy* (Cambridge, MA: MIT Press, 1999), chap. 14. Also see W. Keller, L. Pauly, and S. Reich, *The Myth of the Global Corporation* (Princeton, NJ: Princeton University Press, 1998); B. Kogut, "What Makes a Company Global?" *Harvard Business Review,* January–February 1999, pp. 165–170.

23. T. Kostova, "Transnational Transfer of Strategic Organizational Practices: A Contextual Perspective," *Academy of Management Review* 24 (1999), pp. 308–324; W. R. Scott, *Institutions and Organizations* (Thousand Oaks, CA: Sage Publications, 2000); T. Kostova and K. Roth, "Adoption of Organizational Practice by Subsidiaries of Multinational Corporations: Institutional and Relational Effects," *Academy of Management Journal,* 45 (2002), pp. 215–233; R. Whitley, *Divergent Capitalisms: The Social Structuring and Change of Business Systems* (Oxford: Oxford University Press, 1999); Peter Hall and David Soskice, eds., *Varieties of Capitalism: The Institutional Foundations of Comparative Advantage* (New York: Oxford University Press, 2001); Tony Edwards and Sarosh Kuruvilla, "International HRM: National Business Systems, Organizational Politics and the International Division of Labour in MNCs," *International Journal of Human Resource Management,* 16 (2005), pp. 1–21; Luis R. Gomez-Mejia and Steve Werner, eds., *Global Compensation: Foundations and Perspectives* (London: Routledge, 2008); P. J. Dowling, M. Festing, and A. D. Engle, Sr., *International Human Resource Management,* 5th ed. (London: Thomson Learning, 2008); P. Evans, V. Pucik, and J. L. Barsoux, *The Global Challenge: International Human Resource Management* (New York: McGraw-Hill/Irwin, 2002); Gregory Jackson and Richard Deeg, "Comparing Capitalisms: Understanding Institutional Diversity and Its Implications for International Business," *Journal of International Business Studies,* 39 (2008), pp. 540–561; Chris Brewster, "Different Paradigms in Strategic HRM: Questions Raised by Comparative Research," in *Research in Personnel and Human Resources Management,* Supplement 4, Patrick Wright, Lee Dyer, John Boudreau, and George T. Milkovich, eds. (Greenwich, CT: JAI Press, 1999).

24. C. Oliver, "Strategic Responses to Institutional Processes," *Academy of Management Review* 16 (1991), pp. 145–179.

25. K. Y. Au, "Intra-Cultural Variation: Evidence and Implications for International Business," *Journal of International Business Studies,* 30 (1991), pp. 799–812; M. Bloom and G. T. Milkovich, "A SHRM Perspective on International Compensation and Rewards," in P. M. Wright, L. Dyer, J. W. Boudreau, and G. T. Milkovich, *Research in Personnel and Human Resources Management,* Supplement 4, (Stamford, CT: JAI Press, 1999), pp. 283–303; Barry Gerhart, "How Much Does National Culture Constrain Organization Culture?" *Management and Organization Review,* 5 (2009), pp. 244–259; Barry Gerhart, "Cross-Cultural Management Research: Assumptions, Evidence, and Suggested Directions," *International Journal of Cross Cultural Management,* 8 (2008), pp. 259–274; Barry Gerhart, and Meiyu Fang, "National Culture and Human Resource Management: Assumptions and Evidence," *International Journal of Human Resource Management,* 16 (2005), pp. 975–990; R. Nelson and S. Gopalan, "Do Organizational Cultures Replicate National Cultures? Isomorphism, Rejection, and Reciprocal Opposition in the Corporate Values of Three Countries," *Organization Studies,* 24 (2003), pp. 1115–1151; B. Gerhart, "Compensation and National Culture," in *Global Compensation: Foundations and Perspectives,* S. Werner and L. R. Gomez-Mejia, eds. (London, U.K.: Routledge, 2008); Barry Gerhart, "Does National Culture Constrain Organization Culture and Human Resource Strategy? The Role of Individual Mechanisms and Implications for Employee Selection," *Research in Personnel and Human Resources Management* 2009, 28, 1–48.

26. Russell D. Lansbury, Nick Wailes, Jim Kitay, and Anja Kirsch, eds., *Globalization and Employment Relations in the Auto Assembly Industry,* Bulletin of Comparative Labor Relations 64 (Alphen aan den Rijn, Netherlands: Wolters Kluwer, 2008).

27. H. C. Katz and O. Darbishire, *Converging Divergences: Worldwide Changes in Employment Systems* (Ithaca, NY: ILR Press/Cornell University Press, 2000); R. Batt and H. Nohara, "How Institutions and Business Strategies Affect Wages: A Cross-National Study of Call Centers," *Industrial and Labor Relations Review* 62 (2009) pp. 533–552.

28. J. B. Barney, "Organizational Culture: Can It Be a Source of Sustained Competitive Advantage?" *Academy of Management Review,* 11 (1986), pp. 656–665; J. B. Barney, "Firm Resources and Sustained Competitive Advantage," *Journal of Management,* 17 (1991), pp. 99–120; Barry Gerhart, "How Much Does National Culture Constrain Organization Culture?" *Management and Organization Review,* 5 (2009), pp. 244–259. J. Du and J.N. Choi, "Pay for Performance in Emerging Markets: Insights from China," *Journal of International Business Studies* 41, pp. 671–689.

29. M. Pudelko and A. W. K. Harzing, "The Golden Triangle for MNCs: Standardization Towards Headquarters Practices, Standardization Towards Global Best Practices and

Localization," *Organizational Dynamics,* 37(4), 2008, pp. 394–404; M. Pudelko and A. W. K. Harzing, "How European Is Management in Europe? An Analysis of Past, Present and Future Management Practices in Europe," *European Journal of International Management,* 1(3), 2007, pp. 206–224; M. Pudelko and A. W. K. Harzing, "Country-of-Origin, Localization or Dominance Effect? An Empirical Investigation of HRM Practices in Foreign Subsidiaries," *Human Resource Management,* 46 (2007), pp. 535–559; Anthony Ferner, "Country of Origin Effects and HRM in Multinational Companies," *Human Resource Management Journal* 7(1), 1997, pp. 19–37; Anthony Ferner and Javier Quintanilla, "Multinationals, National Business Systems and HRM: The Enduring Influence of National Identity or a Process of 'Anglo-Saxonization,'" *International Journal of Human Resource Management,* 9(4), 1998, pp. 710–731; Ingmar Björkman, Carl F. Fey, and Hyeon Jeong Park, "Institutional Theory and MNC Subsidiary HRM Practices: Evidence from a Three-Country Study," *Journal of International Business Studies,* 38 (2007), pp. 430–446.

30. Marion Festing, Judith Eidems, and Susanne Royer, "Strategic Issues and Local Constraints in Transnational Compensation Strategies: An Analysis of Cultural, Institutional and Political Processes," *European Management Journal* 25, (2007), pp. 118–131; Allen D. Engle, Sr., Peter J. Dowling, and Marion Festing, "State of Origin: Research in Global Performance Management: A Proposed Research Domain and Emerging Implications," *European Journal of International Management,* 2, (2008), pp. 153–169; C.A. Bartlett and S. Ghoshal, *Managing Across Borders: The Transnational Solution* (Boston: Harvard Business School Press, 1989); Matt Bloom, George T. Milkovich, and Atul Mitra, "International Compensation: Learning From How Managers Respond to Variations in Local Host Contexts," *International Journal of Human Resource Management* 14, (2008), pp. 1350–1367.

31. Y. Yanadori, "Paying Both Globally and Locally: An Examination of the Compensation Management of a U.S. Multinational Finance Firm in the Asia Pacific Region," *International Journal of Human Resource Management* 18, (2011), pp. 3867–3887. T. Greckhamer, "Cross-Cultural Differences in Compensation Level and Inequality across Occupations: A Set-theoretic Analysis," *Organization Studies* 32, pp. 85–115.

32. Fran Blau and Lawrence Kahn, *At Home and Abroad: U.S. Labor Market Performance in International Perspective* (New York: Russell Sage Foundation, 2002).

33. Harry C. Katz, Wonduck Lee, and Joohee Lee, eds., "The New Structure of Labor Relations," *Tripartism and Decentralization* (Ithaca, NY: Cornell University Press, 2004).

34. *World of Work Report* (Geneva, Switzerland: International Labour Organization, 2008). See especially Table 3.3.

35. Matthew M. C. Allen, Heinz-Joseph Tuselmann, Hamed El-Sa'id, and Paul Windrum, "Sectoral Collective Agreements: Remuneration Straitjackets for German Workplaces?" *Personnel Review* 36, (2006), pp. 963–967; European Industrial Relations Observatory Online, (2005), "Changes in National Collective Bargaining Systems Since 1990," *www.eurofound.europa.eu/eiro/* retrieved 6/30/2009.

36. Bruce Crumley, "Goodbye to France's 35-Hour Week," *Time,* July 24, 2008.

37. Baker & McKenzie LLP, "Worldwide Guide to Trade Unions and Works Councils," *www.gurn.info/en/,* June 30, 2009.

38. Ibid., p. 105.

39. Ibid., p. 104.

40. John W. Budd, *Labor Relations: Striking a Balance,* 2nd edition (New York: McGraw-Hill/Irwin, 2008).

41. G. Hofstede, *Culture's Consequences: International Differences in Work-Related Values* (Beverly Hills, CA: Sage, 1980); G. Hofstede, *Culture's Consequences: Comparing*

Values, Behaviors, Institutions, and Organizations Across Nations, 2nd edition (Thousand Oaks, CA: Sage, 2001); R. J. House, P. J. Hanges, M. Javidan, P. W. Dorfman, and V. Gupta, *Culture, Leadership, and Organizations: The Globe Study of 62 Societies* (Thousand Oaks, CA: Sage Publications, 2004); Trompenaars, *Riding the Waves of Culture: Understanding Diversity in Global Business* (Burr Ridge, IL: Irwin, 1995); H. C. Triandis, "Cross-Cultural Industrial and Organizational Psychology," in *Handbook of Industrial and Organizational Psychology,* M. D. Dunnette and L. M. Hough, eds. (Palo Alto, CA: Consulting Psychologists Press, 1994), pp. 103–172.

42. G. Hofstede, "The Cultural Relativity of Organizational Practices and Theories," *Journal of International Business Studies* 14, (1983), pp. 75–89; G. Hofstede, "Cultural Constraints in Management Theories," *Academy of Management Executive,* 7, (1993), pp. 81–94; G. Hofstede, *Culture's Consequences: International Differences in Work-Related Values* (Beverly Hills, CA: Sage, 1980); G. Hofstede, *Culture's Consequences: Comparing Values, Behaviors, Institutions, and Organizations Across Nations,* 2nd edition (Thousand Oaks, CA: Sage, 2001).

43. R. Schuler and N. Rogovsky, "Understanding Compensation Practice Variations Across Firms: The Impact of National Culture," *Journal of International Business Studies* 29 (1998), pp. 159–178.

44. L. R. Gomez-Mejia and T. Welbourne, "Compensation Strategies in a Global Context," *Human Resource Planning* 14, (1994), pp. 29–41; Sunny C. L. Fong and Margaret A. Shaffer, "The Dimensionality and Determinants of Pay Satisfaction: A Cross-Cultural Investigation of a Group Incentive Plan," *International Journal of Human Resource Management* 14(4), June 2003, pp. 559–580.

45. P. C. Early and M. Erez, *The Transplanted Executive: Why You Need to Understand How Workers in Other Countries See the World Differently* (New York: Oxford University Press, 1997).

46. G. Milkovich and M. Bloom, "Rethinking International Compensation: From Expatriates and National Cultures to Strategic Flexibility," *Compensation and Benefits Review,* April 1998; L. Markoczy, "Us and Them," *Across the Board,* February 1998, pp. 44–48; Brendan McSweeney, "Hofstede's Model of National Cultural Differences and Their Consequences: A Triumph of Faith, A Failure of Analysis," *Human Relations,* January 2002, pp. 89–118; Paul Gooderham and Odd Nordhaug, "Are Cultural Differences in Europe on the Decline?" *geert-hofstede.international-business-center.com.*

47. M. Bloom, G. Milkovich, and A. Mitra, "International Compensation: Learning from How Managers Respond to Variations in Local Host Contexts," *International Journal of Human Resource Management* special issue, 2003; Allen D. Engle, Sr., and Mark Mendenhall, "Transnational Roles and Transnational Rewards: Global Integration in Executive Compensation," presentation at international HR conference, Limerick, Ireland, June 2003; Paul Evans, Vlado Pucik, and Jean-Louis Barsoux, *The Global Challenge* (New York: McGraw-Hill, 2002); G. Hundley and J. Kim, "National Culture and the Factors Affecting Perceptions of Pay Fairness in Korea and the U.S.," *International Journal of Organization Analysis* 5(4), October 1997, pp. 325–341; David Landes, *Culture Matters: How Values Shape Human Progress* (New York: Basic Books, 2001).

48. B. Gerhart, "Compensation and National Culture," in *Global Compensation: Foundations and Perspectives,* S. Werner and L. R. Gomez-Mejia, eds. (London, U.K.: Routledge, 2008); Barry Gerhart, "Does National Culture Constrain Organization Culture and Human Resource Strategy? The Role of Individual Mechanisms and Implications for Employee Selection," *Research in Personnel and Human Resources Management* 2009, 28, pp. 1–48.

49. T. Rabl, M. Jayasinghe, B. Gerhart, and T. A. Kühlmann, "Meta-Analysis of Country Differences in the High Performance Work System-Business Performance Relationship: The Roles of National Culture and Managerial Discretion," *Journal of Applied Psychology* 99, 2014, pp. 1011–1041.

50. M. Bloom, G. Milkovich, and N. Zupan, "Contrasting Slovenian and U.S. Employment Relations: The Links between Social Contracts and Psychological Contracts," *CEMS Business Review,* no. 2 (1997), pp. S95–S109; Chun Hui, Cynthia Lee, and Denise Rousseau, "Psychological Contract and Organizational Citizenship Behavior in China: Investigating Generalizability and Instrumentality," *Journal of Applied Psychology* 89(2) (2004), pp. 311–321.

51. M. Bloom and G. T. Milkovich, "A SHRM Perspective on International Compensation and Rewards" in P.M. Wright, L. Dyer, J.W. Boudreau, and G.T. Milkovich, *Research in Personnel and Human Resources Management,* Supplement 4 (Stamford, CT: JAI Press, 1999), pp. 283–303; Barry Gerhart, "Does National Culture Constrain Organization Culture and Human Resource Strategy? The Role of Individual Mechanisms and Implications for Employee Selection," *Research in Personnel and Human Resources Management,* forthcoming; K. Y. Au, "Intra-Cultural Variation: Evidence and Implications for International Business," *Journal of International Business Studies* 30 (1999), pp. 799–812; D.V. Caprar, "Foreign Locals: A Cautionary Tale on the Culture of MNC Local Employees," *Journal of International Business* 42, pp. 608–628.

52. Barry Gerhart, "Cross-Cultural Management Research: Assumptions, Evidence, and Suggested Directions," *International Journal of Cross Cultural Management* 8 (2008), pp. 259–274; Barry Gerhart, and Meiyu Fang, "National Culture and Human Resource Management: Assumptions and Evidence," *International Journal of Human Resource Management* 16 (2005), pp. 975–990.

53. B. Gerhart, "Compensation and National Culture," in *Global Compensation: Foundations and Perspectives,* S. Werner & L.R. Gomez-Mejia, eds. (London, U.K.: Routledge, 2008); H. Yeganeh and Z. Su, "The Effects of Cultural Orientations on Preferred Compensation Policies," *International Journal of Human Resource Management* 22, 2011, pp. 2609–2628.

54. R. Fischer and P. Smith, "Reward Allocation and Culture: A Meta-Analysis," *Journal of Crosscultural Psychology* 34 (2003), pp. 251–268; B. Gerhart, "Compensation and National Culture," in *Global Compensation,* S. Werner and L. Gomez-Mejia, eds. (London, UK: Routledge, 2008).

55. Zhijun Ling and Martha Avery, *The Lenovo Affair: The Growth of China's Computer Giant and Its Takeover of IBM-PC* (New York: John Wiley & Sons, 2006). See especially pp. 266–273. Also see D. Z. Ding, S. Akhtar, and G. L. Ge, "Organizational Differences in Managerial Compensation and Benefits in Chinese Firms," *International Journal of Human Resource Management* 17(4), April 2006, pp. 693–715; and Wan Lixin, "The Student Job Crunch," *China International Business,* June 2006, pp. 18–25.

56. Organisation for Economic Co-operation and Development, "Trade Union Density, 1960–2007," *www.oecd.org/dataoecd/25/42/39891561.xls,* retrieved 6/29/2009; Jelle Visser, "Union Membership Statistics in 24 Countries," *Monthly Labor Review,* January 2006, pp. 38–49.

57. Baker & McKenzie LLP, "Worldwide Guide to Trade Unions and Works Councils," *www.gurn.info/en/,* 6/29/2009.

58. Elfstrom, M., and S. Kuruvilla, "The Changing Nature of Labor Unrest in China," *Industrial & Labor Relations Review* 67(2), 2014, pp. 453–480.

59. The website of the National Center for Employee Ownership (NCEO) has information and referrals concerning employee stock ownership plans (ESOPs) and other forms of

employee ownership: *www.esop.org.* Worker ownership around the world is discussed at *www.activistnet.org.*

60. Lowell Turner, ed., *Negotiating the New Germany: Can Social Partnership Survive?* (Ithaca, NY: Cornell University Press, 1998); Wolfgang Streeck, *Social Institutions and Economic Performance: Studies of Industrial Relations in Advanced Capitalist Economies* (London: Sage, 1992).

61. Wei He, Chao C. Chen, and Lihua Zhang, "Rewards Allocation Preferences in Chinese State-Owned Enterprises: A Revisit after a Decade's Radical Reform," in *The Management of Enterprises in the People's Republic of China,* Anne S. Tsui and Chung-Ming Lau, eds. (Boston: Kluwer Academic, 2002); Marshall Meyer, Yuan Lu, Hailin Lan, and Xiaohui Lu, "Decentralized Enterprise Reform: Notes on the Transformation of State-Owned Enterprises," in Anne S. Tsui and Shung-Ming Lau, eds., *The Management of Enterprises in the People's Republic of China* (Boston: Kluwer Academic, 2002); Chun Hui, Cynthia Lee, and Denise Rousseau, "Psychological Contract and Organizational Citizenship Behavior in China: Investigating Generalizability and Instrumentality," *Journal of Applied Psychology* 89(2), April 2004, pp. 311–321.

62. Jing Zhou and J. J. Martocchio, "Chinese and American Managers' Compensation Award Decisions," *Personnel Psychology* 54 (Spring 2001), pp. 115–145.

63. The European Trade Union Institute's website is at *www.etuc.org/etui/default.cf.*

64. Stephen Power and Guy Chazan, "Europe Auto Relations Get Testy," *The Wall Street Journal,* June 15, 2006, p. A8.

65. Hesan Ahmed Quazi, *Compensation and Benefits Practices in Selected Asian Countries* (Singapore: McGraw Hill, 2004).

66. R. Batt and H. Nohara, "How Institutions and Business Strategies Affect Wages: A Cross-National Study of Call Centers," *Industrial and Labor Relations Review* 62, pp. 533–552.

67. Samuel Palmisano, "Multinationals Have Been Superseded," *Financial Times,* June 11, 2006.

68. Mercer Human Resource Consulting, *2006 Worldwide Pay Survey* (London: October 3, 2005); Marie-Claire Guillard, "A Visual Essay: International Labor Market Comparisons," *Monthly Labor Review,* April 2006, pp. 33–37; Nic Paton, "Performance-Related Pay Becoming a Global Phenomenon," *www.management-issues.com,* accessed January 13, 2006; Chris Giles, "Moscow Is Now World's Costliest City for Expatriates," *Financial Times,* June 26, 2006, p. 2.

69. "Shanghai Raises Minimum Wage 13% as China Seeks to Boost Demand," *Bloomberg News,* February 27, 2012. www.bloomberg.com, accessed May 24, 2012.

70. John Gapper and Barney Jopson, "Coach to Cut Output in China," *Financial Times,* May 13, 2011; Ben Blanchard, "Foxconn to Raise Wages Again at China Plant," www.reuters. com, accessed October 19, 2010; Joe Manget and Pierre Mercier, "As Wages Rise, Time to Leave China?" *Bloomberg Businessweek,* December 1, 2010; and Shai Oster, "China's Rising Wages Propel U.S. Prices," *The Wall Street Journal,* May 9, 2011. Tim Worstall, "Apple's Foxconn to Double Wages Again," *Forbes,* May 28, 2012.

71. W. Lane and M. Schmidt, "Comparing U.S. and European COI and the HICP," *Monthly Labor Review* 129(5), May 2006, pp. 20–27; J. Abowd and M. Bognanno, "International Differences in Executive and Managerial Compensation," in *Differences and Changes in Wage Structures,* R. B. Freeman and L. Katz, eds. (Chicago: NBER, 1995), pp. 67–103; "Big Mac Index," *The Economist,* February 4, 2009, *www.economist.com.*

72. Duncan Brown, "The Third Way: The Future of Pay and Rewards in Europe," *WorldatWork,* Second Quarter 2000, pp. 15–25.

73. S. Jacoby, *The Embedded Corporation* (Princeton: Princeton University Press, 2005); J. Abegglen, *Twenty-First Century Japanese Management: New System, Lasting Values*

(New York: Palgrave-Macmillan, 2006); Toyo Keizai, *Japan Company Handbook* (Tokyo: Japan Labour Bureau, Summer 2001).

74. T. Kato, "The End of Lifetime Employment in Japan? Evidence from National Surveys and Field Research," *Journal of the Japanese and International Economies* 15 (2002), pp. 489–514; T. Kato and M. Rockell, "Experiences, Credentials, and Compensation in the Japanese and U.S. Managerial Labor Markets: Evidence from New Micro Data," *Journal of the Japanese and International Economies* 6 (1992), pp. 30–51; P. Evans, V. Pucik, and J. Barsoux, *The Global Challenge: Frameworks for International Human Resource Management* (New York: McGraw-Hill/Irwin, 2002).

75. B. D. Singh, *Industrial Relations: Emerging Paradigms.* 2nd edition (New Dehli: Excel Books. 2009) p. 448.

76. We thank Thomas Gresch and Elke Stadelmann, whose manuscript, *Traditional Pay System in Germany* (Ruesselsheim, Germany: Adam Opel AG, 2001), is the basis for this section of the chapter; Geoff Dyer, "A Tale of Two Corporate Cultures," *Financial Times,* May 23, 2006, p. 8; Paul DeGrauwe, "Germany's Pay Policy Points to a Eurozone Design Flaw," *Financial Times,* May 5, 2006, p. 13.

77. Bertrand Benoit, "Benefit Check: Why Germany Is Confronted with a Welfare State Fiasco," *Financial Times,* June 26, 2006.

78. Hiroshi Ono, "Careers in Foreign-Owned Firms in Japan," *American Sociological Review,* 72 (2007), pp. 267–290.

79. See S. Jacoby, *The Embedded Corporation* (Princeton: Princeton University Press, 2005), especially pp. 75–77; S. Strom, "In Japan, from Lifetime Job to No Job at All," *The New York Times* Online, February 3, 1999; M. Bloom, G. Milkovich, and A. Mitra, "International Compensation: Learning From How Managers Respond to Variations in Local Host Contexts," *International Journal of Human Resource Management,* special issue, 2003; T. Kato, "The End of Lifetime Employment in Japan? Evidence from National Surveys and Field Research," *Journal of Japanese and International Economies* 15 (2002), pp. 489–514; T. Kato and M. Rockell, "Experiences, Credentials, and Compensation in the Japanese and U.S. Managerial Labor Markets: Evidence from New Micro Data," *Journal of the Japanese and International Economies* 6 (1992), pp. 30–51; Hiromichi Shibata, "Wage and Performance Appraisal Systems in Flux: Japan-U.S. Comparison," *Industrial Relations* 41(4), 2002, pp. 629–652; National Personnel Authority, *Current Status of Private Firms' Remuneration Systems* (Tokyo: Japan Labour Bureau, 2006); D. Raj Adhikari, *National Factors in Employment Relations in Japan* (Tokyo: Japan Institute of Labor Policy, 2005).

80. Markus Pudelko, "The Seniority Principle in Japanese Companies: A Relic of the Past?" *Asia Pacific Journal of Human Resources* 44 (2006), pp. 276–294.

81. Gregory Jackson, "Employment Adjustment and Distributional Conflict in Japanese Firms," in *Corporate Governance in Japan: Institutional Change and Organizational Diversity,* M. Aoki, G. Jackson, and H. Miyajima, eds. (Oxford: Oxford University Press, 2007).

82. Hamaaki, J., Hori, M., Maeda, S., and Murata, K., "Changes in the Japanese Employment System in the Two Lost Decades," *Industrial & Labor Relations Review* 65(4), 2012, pp. 810–846.

83. "JapAnglo-Saxon Capitalism," *The Economist,* December 1, 2007.

84. Meng, X., *Labour Market Reform in China* (Cambridge University Press, 2000). Xiu, L., and Gunderson, M., "Performance Pay in China: Gender Aspects," *British Journal of Industrial Relations* 51(1), 2013, pp. 124–147.

85. Bae, J., and Lawler, J. J., "Organizational and HRM Strategies in Korea: Impact on Firm Performance in an Emerging Economy," *Academy of Management Journal* 43, 2000, pp. 502–517.

86. Antje Kurdelbusch, "Multinationals and the Rise of Variable Pay in Germany," *European Journal of Industrial Relations* 8 (2002), pp. 324–349; James Arrowsmith, Heidi Nicolaisen, Barbara Bechter, and Rosa Nonell, "The Management of Variable Pay in Banking: Forms and Rationale in Four European Countries," in *Challenges of European Employment Relations and Employment Regulation,* Roger Blanplain and Linda Dickens, eds. (The Netherlands: Kluwer Law International, 2008); Matthias Schmitt and Dieter Sadowski, "A Cost-Minimization Approach to the International Transfer of HRM/IR Practices: Anglo-Saxon Multinationals in the Federal Republic of Germany," *International Journal of Human Resource Management* 14 (2003), pp. 409–430.

87. William Gerard Sanders and Anja Tuschke, "The Adoption of Institutionally Contested Organizational Practices: The Emergence of Stock Option Pay in Germany," *Academy of Management Journal* 50 (2007), pp. 33–56.

88. M. Bloom, G. Milkovich, and A. Mitra, "International Compensation: Learning From How Managers Respond to Variations in Local Host Contexts," *International Journal of Human Resource Management,* special issue, 2003. See also N. Napier and Van Tuan Vu, "International HRM in Developing and Transitional Economy Context," *Human Resource Management Review* 8(1), 1998, pp. 39–71.

89. Thomas Friedman, *The World Is Flat: A Brief History of the Twenty-First Century* (New York: Farrar, Straus and Giroux, 2006); J. W. Walker, "Are We Global Yet?" *Human Resource Planning* (First Quarter 2000), pp. 7–8; R. Locke and K. Thelen, "Apples and Oranges Revisited: Contextualized Comparisons and Comparative Labor Policies," *Politics and Society* 23(2), 1996, pp. 337–367; M. Mendenhall and Gary Oddou, *Readings and Cases in International Human Resource Management* (Cincinnati: Southwestern, 2000).

90. Samuel Palmisano, "The Globally Integrated Enterprise," *Foreign Affairs,* May/June 2006.

91. P. J. Dowling, M. Festing, and A. D. Engle, Sr., *International Human Resource Management,* 5th ed. (London: Thomson Learning, 2008).

92. G. Latta, "The Future of Expatriate Compensation," *WorldatWork* (Second Quarter 2006), pp. 42–49; Geoffrey Latta, "Expatriate Policy and Practice: A 10-Year Comparison of Trends," *Compensation and Benefits Review* 31(4), 1999, pp. 35–39; C. Reynolds, "Global Compensation and Benefits in Transition," *Compensation and Benefits Review* 32(1), January/February 2000, pp. 27–37; J. Stewart Black and Hal B. Gregerson, "The Right Way to Manage Expats," *Harvard Business Review* (March–April 1999), pp. 52–62; Roger Heron, "The Cardinal Sins of Expatriate Policies," *Organization Resources Counselors: Innovations in International HR,* Fall 2001.

93. G. Latta, "The Future of Expatriate Compensation," *WorldatWork* (Second Quarter 2006), pp. 42–49; Cris Prystay and Tom Herman, "Tax Hike Hits Home for Americans Abroad," *The Wall Street Journal,* July 19, 2006, pp. D1, D5.

94. Runzheimer International, *www.runzheimer.com,* publishes monthly newsletters on the costs of relocation.

95. Bobby W. Watson, Jr., and Gangaram Singh, "Global Pay Systems: Compensation in Support of a Multinational Strategy," *Compensation and Benefits Review* 37(1), January/February 2005, pp. 33–36; Sherrie Webster Brown, "Spanning the Globe for Quality Pay Data," in *2003–2004 Survey Handbook and Directory* (Scottsdale, AZ: WorldatWork, 2002), pp. 95–100; Margaret A. Coil, "Salary Surveys in a Blended-Role World," in *2003–2004 Survey Handbook and Directory* (Scottsdale, AZ: WorldatWork, 2002), pp. 57–64.

96. Laura Johnson and Darrell Cira, "Taking the Best Path to Implementing a Global Pay Structure: The General Mill's Experience," World at Work Conference, Seattle, Washington, June 1, 2009.

97. W. Lane and M. Schmidt, "Comparing U.S. and European COI and the HICP," *Monthly Labor Review* (May 2006), pp. 20–27.

98. C. Reynolds, "Expatriate Compensation in Historical Perspective," *International Human Resource Journal* (Summer 1997), pp. 118–131.

99. *Global Rewards: A Collection of Articles From WorldatWork* (Scottsdale, AZ: WorldatWork, 2005); Cal Reynolds, "International Compensation," in *Compensation Guide,* William A. Caldwell, ed. (Boston: Warren, Gorham and Lamont, 1998).

100. Chun Hui, Cynthia Lee, and Denise Rousseau, "Psychological Contract and Organizational Citizenship Behavior in China: Investigating Generalizability and Instrumentality," *Journal of Applied Psychology* 89(2), April 2004, pp. 311–321; Richard A. Guzzo, Katherine A. Noonan, and Efrat Elron, "Expatriate Managers and the Psychological Contract," *Journal of Applied Psychology* 7(4), 1994, pp. 617–626; Steve Gross and Per Wingerup, "Global Pay? Maybe Not Yet!" *Compensation Benefits Review* 31 (1999), pp. 25–34.

101. P. J. Dowling, M. Festing, and A. D. Engle, Sr., *International Human Resource Management,* 5th ed. (London: Thomson Learning, 2008).

102. Carole Mestre, Anne Rossier-Renaud, and Madeline Berger, "Better Benchmarks for Global Mobility," *Workspan,* April 2009.

103. P. J. Dowling, M. Festing, and A. D. Engle, Sr., *International Human Resource Management,* 5th ed. (London: Thomson Learning, 2008).

104. Carole Mestre, Anne Rossier-Renaud, and Madeline Berger, "Better Benchmarks for Global Mobility," *Workspan,* April 2009.

105. Garry M. Wederspahn, "Costing Failures in Expatriate Human Resource Management," *Human Resource Planning* 15(3), pp. 27–35; Soo Min Toh and Angelo S. DeNissi, "Host Country National Reactions to Expatriate Pay Policies: A Model and Implications," *Academy of Management Review,* 28(4), 2003, pp. 606–621.

106. Paul Evans, Vlado Pucik, and Jean-Louis Barsoux, *The Global Challenge* (New York: McGraw-Hill, 2002); Allen D. Engle, Sr. and Peter Dowing, "Global Rewards: Strategic Patterns in Complexity," presentation at international HR conference, Ljubljana, Slovenia, June 2004.

107. For a very helpful review and analysis of this issue, see P. J. Dowling, M. Festing, and A. D. Engle, Sr., *International Human Resource Management,* 5th ed. (London: Thomson Learning, 2008). Also, see Claus Christensen and Anne-Wil Harzing, "Expatriate Failure: Time to Abandon the Concept?" *Career Development International* 9 (2004), pp. 616–626.

Managing the System

The last part of our total pay model is management. This means ensuring that the right people get the right pay for achieving the right objectives in the right way. We have touched on aspects of management already—the use of budgets in merit increase programs; the "message" that employees receive from their variable pay bonuses, communication, and cost control in benefits; and the importance of employee involvement in designing the total compensation system.

Several important issues remain. The first, already noted in Chapter 16's global guide, is the significant role that government plays in managing compensation. Laws and regulations are the most obvious government intervention. In the United States, minimum-wage legislation, the Equal Pay Act, and Title VII of the Civil Rights Act, among others, regulate pay decisions. Legal issues in compensation in the United States are covered in Chapter 17.

Government is more than a source of laws and regulations, however. As a major employer, as a consumer of goods and services, and through its fiscal and monetary policies, government affects the supply of and the demand for labor.

Chapter 18 covers several aspects of managing compensation: costs and added value, communication, and change. One of the key reasons for being systematic about pay decisions is to manage the costs associated with those decisions. As Chapter 18 will show, a total compensation system is really a device for allocating money in a way that is consistent with the organization's objectives. Recent developments in how to evaluate the value gained from compensation programs are discussed.

Communication and change are linked. What is to be communicated to whom is an important, ongoing issue. Compensation itself communicates. A pay increase tells people how they are doing. Changes in the pay system also communicate; they may signal change in business direction or even reinforce restructuring of the organization. Any system will founder if it is ineffectively communicated and managed.

Chapter 18 also discusses enterprise software that holds out the promise of helping users make pay decisions faster and smarter. Perhaps most critical of all, we return to look at ethics and the increasing importance of personal standards when no professional standards exist.

EXHIBIT VII.1 The Pay Model

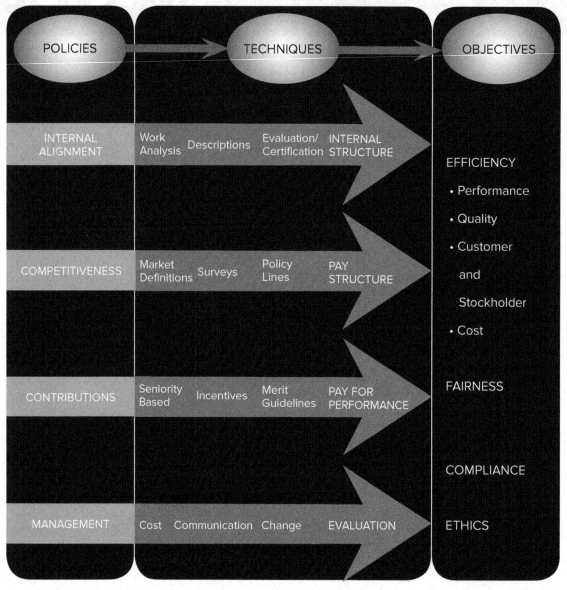

Government and Legal Issues in Compensation

A 1939 pay policy handbook for a major U.S. corporation outlines this justification for paying different wages to men and women working on the same jobs[1]:

> The . . . wage curve . . . is not the same for women as for men because of the more transient character of the former, the relative shortness of their activity in industry, the differences in environment required, the extra services that must be provided, overtime limitations, extra help needed for the occasional heavy work, and the general sociological factors not requiring discussion herein. Basically then we have another wage curve . . . for women below and not parallel with the men's curve.

The presumption that people should be paid different wages based on "general socio-logical factors" was still evident in the United States in the 1960s, in newspaper help-wanted ads that specified "perky gal Fridays" and in whites-only local unions. The 1960s civil rights movement and subsequent legislation were intended to end such practices.

Are you thinking you have stumbled into a history class by mistake? Not so. These historical practices and subsequent legislation still affect pay decisions. However, legislation does not always achieve what it intends nor intend what it achieves. Conse-quently, *compliance* and *fairness* are continuing compensation objectives.

In democratic societies, the legislative process begins when a problem is identified (not all citizens are receiving fair treatment in the workplace) and corrective legisla-tion is proposed (the Civil Rights Act). If enough support develops, often as a result of compromises and tradeoffs, the proposed legislation becomes law. Employers, along with other stakeholders, attempt to influence the form any legislation will take.

Once passed, laws are enforced by agencies through rulings, regulations, inspec-tions, and investigations. Companies respond to legislation by auditing and perhaps altering their practices, perhaps defending their practices before courts and agencies, and perhaps lobbying for still further legislative change. The laws and regulations is-sued by governmental agencies created to enforce the laws are a significant influence on compensation decisions throughout the world.

In the United States, there are three branches of *federal* government and each plays a role in the legal and regulatory framework in which employers work toward compliance objectives. The *legislative* branch (Congress) passes laws (or statutes). The *executive* branch, headed by the President, enforces laws through agencies and its other bodies (e.g., the Department of Labor), and the *judicial* branch interprets laws and considers their constitutionality. Over time, the legislative branch may change existing laws or pass new ones. The way that the judicial branch interprets laws can also change. The great interest in Supreme Court justice appointments and the difficulty sometimes encountered in gaining their confirmation is based on the belief that who the justices are will matter. Finally, enforcement priorities and intensity can vary from one presidential administra-tion to the next. Compliance efforts by employers must take that fact into account.

Of course, the regulatory environment is also a function of *state and local* laws, which often cover employers not covered by federal laws and/or include requirements that go be-yond federal laws. For example, Title VII of the (federal) Civil Rights Act, which prohibits employment (including pay) discrimination on the basis of race, color, religion, sex, or na-tional origin, covers employers with 15 or more employees. But, under the Wisconsin Fair Employment Act, all employers are covered and discrimination on the basis of some char-acteristics (e.g., sexual orientation) not included in Title VII is prohibited. As another ex-ample, in our discussion of minimum wage laws later in this chapter, we will see that some states have minimums greater than the federal minimum. We will also see that some cities have living wage laws. Finally, of course, as we saw in Chapter 16, laws differ by country.[2]

Our objective in this chapter is to help you become more familiar with the legal and regulatory framework of compensation. Importantly, however, you will not be an attor-ney after reading this chapter. Compliance will require legal advice.

To help motivate you to speak promptly to an attorney should you encounter legal compliance risks, consider Exhibit 17.1, which reports payments by employers to come

EXHIBIT 17.1 Payments by Employers to Settle Employment Discrimination and Wage and Hour Claims, Government Agency (EEOC, WHD) Enforcement Actions and Private Class Action Lawsuits

Year	Employment Discrimination		Private Plaintiff Class Action	Wage and Hour		Private Plaintiff Class Action
	EEOC Litigation Enforcement Activity Monetary Recovery From:		Lawsuit Settlements	WHD Enforcement Activity Back Wages Recovery from[4]		Lawsuit Settlements
	All Acts[1]	Title VII (only)[2]	10 Largest[3]	All Acts	FLSA (only)	10 Largest[3]
2014	$296,100,000	$220,000,000	$227,930,000	$240,831,606	$172,971,408	$215,300,000
2013	$372,100,000	$201,000,000	$234,100,000	$249,954,412	$169,173,322	$248,450,000
2012	$365,400,000	$214,000,000	$48,650,000	$280,697,546	$183,831,224	$292,000,000
2011	$364,700,000	$230,000,000		$224,844,870	$169,655,539	
2010	$319,400,000	$248,000,000		$176,005,043	$128,588,963	
Mean	$343,540,000	$222,600,000	$170,226,667	$234,466,695	$164,844,091	$251,916,667
5-Year Total	$1,717,700,000	$1,113,000,000		$1,172,333,477	$824,220,456	
5-Year Total (projected)			$851,133,333			$1,259,583,333

[1] U.S. Equal Employment Opportunity Commission. Title VII of the Civil Rights Act of 1964 Charges (includes concurrent charges with ADEA, ADA, and EPA).

[2] U.S. Equal Employment Opportunity Commission. Title VII of the Civil Rights Act of 1964 Charges (includes concurrent charges with ADEA, ADA, and EPA) FY 1997–FY 2014. http://www.eeoc.gov/eeoc/statistics/enforcement/titlevii.cfm.

[3] Annual Workplace Class Action Litigation Report, 2014 edition and 2015 edition. Published by Seyfarth Shaw LLP.

[4] United States Department of Labor. Wage and Hour Division. Fiscal Year Statistics for WHD. Fair Labor Standards Act Back Wages.

Notes: Title VII monetary recovery amounts include all Title VII related charges, not just those related to pay.

WHD = Wage and Hour Division, Department of Labor

EEOC = Equal Employment Opportunity Commission, Department of Labor

FLSA = Fair Labor Standards Act

into compliance with regulatory actions brought by two U.S. government agencies, the Department of Labor's Equal Employment Opportunity Commission (EEOC) and its Wage and Hour Division (WHD). Compliance issues fall into two corresponding areas: employment discrimination (especially Title VII of the Civil Rights Act) and wage and hour (especially the Fair Labor Standards Act, FLSA). Over the 5-year period of 2010 to 2014, the EEOC recovered over $1.7 billion from employers to resolve employment discrimination issues (some, but not all, having to do with compensation issues), with most of that relating to Title VII. During that same period, the WHD recovered over $1.1 billion in back wages payments (i.e., wages for work employees previously performed, but for which they were not fully paid) from employers. Employees may also bring private (i.e., without involving government agencies) lawsuits against employers. These are most costly when they are class action suits that include many similarly situated employees combining to bring a single joint lawsuit. In the area of employment discrimination, the 10 largest class action lawsuit settlements alone cost over $170 million per year, or about $850 million over a 5-year period at that rate. On the wage and hour side, the 10 largest class action lawsuit settlements cost almost $252 million per year, or almost $1.3 billion over a 5-year period at that rate. These, we think you will agree, are big numbers and it would be great if you could help your future employer comply with the law so as not to be paying out these very large amounts of money to settle lawsuits.

GOVERNMENT AS PART OF THE EMPLOYMENT RELATIONSHIP

Overview

People differ in their view of what role government should play in the contemporary workplace. Some call for organizations and the government to act in concert to carry out a public policy that protects the interests of employees.[3] Others believe that the best opportunities for employees are created by the constant change and reconfiguring that is inherent in market-based economies; the economy ought to be allowed to adapt and transform, undistorted by government actions.[4] All countries throughout the world must address these issues. However, as we will see, different countries take different approaches.[5]

Governments' usual interests in compensation decisions are whether procedures for determining pay are fair (e.g., pay discrimination), safety nets for the unemployed and/or those unable to work (e.g., unemployment compensation, workers compensation), and worker protection (e.g., overtime pay, minimum wage, child labor restrictions).

In addition to being a party to all employment relationships, government units are also employers and purchasers. Consequently, government decisions also affect conditions in the labor market. The U.S. federal government employs 2.73 million people; state and local governments employ 19.18 million. Overall, government employment is 21.9 million, representing 16 percent of the total U.S. nonfarm employment of 141.26 million.[6] In addition to being a big employer, and thus competing with private sector organizations for employees, government also indirectly affects labor demand in the private sector through its spending and purchases (military aircraft, computer systems, paper clips) and tax policy. In addition to government fiscal policy (i.e., total spending and budget, tax policy, taxes), the federal government influences overall economic growth/demand and business activity through its monetary policy (level of interest rates and money supply). Increased business activity translates into increased demand for labor and upward pressure on wages. In addition to being an employer, government affects labor supply through legislation. Laws aimed at protecting specific groups also tend to restrict those groups' participation in the labor market. Compulsory schooling laws restrict the supply of children available to sell hamburgers or to assemble soccer balls. Licensing requirements for certain occupations (plumbers, cosmetologists, attorneys, physicians, psychologists) restrict the number of people who can legally offer a service.[7] Immigration policy and how rigorously it is enforced is an increasingly important factor in labor supply.[8]

This chapter will examine the laws and regulations that most directly affect compensation in the United States. Exhibit 17.2 provides an overview of the regulatory

EXHIBIT 17.2 U.S. Federal Pay Regulations

1931	**Davis-Bacon Act**	Requires that mechanics and laborers on public construction projects be paid the "prevailing wage" in an area.
1934	**Securities Exchange Act**	Created the Securities and Exchange Commission (SEC). Currently, the SEC requires companies that have more than $10 million in assets and whose securities are publicly traded and held by more than 500 owners to periodically report information, which is available to the public. This includes disclosure of compensation received by the CEO, CFO, and three other highest paid executives.
1936	**Walsh-Healey Public Contracts Act**	Extends prevailing-wage concept to manufacturers or suppliers of goods for government contracts.
1938	**Fair Labor Standards Act (FLSA)**	Sets minimum wage, hours of work, overtime premiums; prohibits child labor.
1963	**Equal Pay Act**	Equal pay required for men and women doing "substantially similar" work in terms of skill, effort, responsibility, and working conditions.
1964	**Title VII of Civil Rights Act of 1964**	Prohibits discrimination in all employment practices on basis of race, sex, color, religion, or national origin.
1965	**Executive Order 11246**	Prohibits discrimination by federal contractors and subcontractors in all employment practices on basis of race, sex, color, religion, or national origin.
1967	**Age Discrimination in Employment Act (ADEA)**	Protects employees age 40 and over against age discrimination.
1978	**Pregnancy Discrimination Act (PDA)**	Pregnancy must be covered to same extent that other medical conditions are covered.
1990	**Americans with Disabilities Act (ADA)**	Requires that "essential elements" of a job be called out. If a person with a disability can perform these essential elements, reasonable accommodation must be provided.

EXHIBIT 17.2 *(Continued)*

1991	**Civil Rights Act of 1991**	Increases burden of proof on employers to rebut some discrimination claims. Stronger remedies available in cases of international discrimination
1993	**Family and Medical Leave Act (FMLA)**	Requires employers to provide up to 12 weeks' unpaid leave for family and medical emergencies.
1997	**Mental Health Act**	Mental illness must be covered to same extent that other medical conditions are covered.
2000	**Worker Economic Opportunity Act**	Income from most stock plans need not be included in calculating overtime pay.
2002	**Sarbanes-Oxley Act**	Executives cannot retain bonuses or profits from selling company stock if they mislead the public about the financial health of the company.
2004	**Financial Accounting Standards Board (FASB) Statement 123 R**	Value of all employee stock options must be expensed at estimates of fair value on financial statements.
2006	**Securities and Exchange Commission (SEC) rule change on executive compensation disclosure**	Adopts enhanced executive compensation disclosure requirements. For example, the Compensation Discussion and Analysis in the proxy statement must address the objectives and implementation of executive compensation programs.
2009	**Lilly Ledbetter Fair Pay Act**	Employers can be liable for current pay differences that are a result of discrimination (as defined under existing laws such as Title VII of the Civil Rights Act) that occurred many years earlier.
2009	**Troubled Asset Relief Program (TARP), American Recovery and Reinvestment Act of 2009 (ARRA)**	Financial institutions receiving funds from TARP have restrictions on compensation. Prohibits use of several compensation programs, including, but not limited to bonuses, retention awards, and incentive pay, except where part of a preexisting employment contract, during the period TARP funds are received. Restricted stock is permitted if one-third or less of annual compensation. In firms receiving the largest TARP assistance, restrictions cover senior executives and next 20 highest paid employees.
2010	**Dodd-Frank Wall Street Reform and Consumer Protection Act***	
	Nominating Directors	Gives SEC authority to grant shareholders proxy access to nominate directors.
	Independent Compensation Committees	Standards for listing a company on an exchange require that compensation committees include only independent directors and that the committee has authority to hire its own compensation consultants.

	Clawbacks	Requires public companies to set policies to allow executive compensation to be taken back if it was based on inaccurate financial statements that did not comply with accounting standards.
	Executive Compensation Disclosure	Requires reporting of the ratio of chief executive officer (CEO) pay to worker pay and the magnitude of the relationship between executive pay and corporate financial performance.
	Increased Oversight of Financial Industry	Directs regulators to develop rules specific to the financial industry.
	"Say on Pay"	Nonbinding vote by shareholders to approve or disapprove executive pay.
2014	**Executive Order 13665**	Prohibits federal contractors and subcontractors from having pay secrecy policies.
Ongoing	**SEC**	Executive compensation rules and enforcement.
	Internal Revenue Service (IRS)	Tax treatment of employee and executive compensation, including rules (e.g., nondiscrimination tests) for which compensation costs can be deducted. Also monitors employer decisions to classify workers as employees versus independent contractors (which has tax revenue implications).
	Financial Accounting Standards Board (FASB)	Engages in ongoing rule-making regarding accounting treatment of executive and employee compensation. FASB rules are given great deference by the SEC.
	Federal Trade Commission	Enforces antitrust laws, which includes prohibiting employers from collusion in fixing prices (i.e., pay) in compensation.
	Arbitration (deferral to)	Many employers now ask employees to sign agreements that require them to use arbitration systems to resolve individual employment disputes in lieu of filing a lawsuit or filing a complaint with a government agency. The employer must provide "consideration" (something of value) in return for employees giving up their right to sue in individual dispute cases.
	Noncompete Agreements	Many employers ask employees to agree not to work for a competitor within a certain time of leaving the employer. Consideration must be provided to the employee in return for waiving this right. Enforceability varies by state and typically as a function of the level of the employee and the degree to which the employee has access to valuable information or resources related to competitiveness.

EXHIBIT 17.2   *(Continued)*

Department of Labor (DOL)	The DOL's Wage and Hour Division (WHD) monitors and enforces compliance with the FLSA, FMLA, Davis-Bacon, Walsh-Healey, and other Acts. The DOL's Equal Employment Opportunity Commission (EEOC) monitors and enforces compliance with equal employment opportunity laws, including Title VII of the Civil Rights Act, ADA, ADEA, PDA, and the Equal Pact Act. The DOL's Office of Federal Contract Compliance (OFCCP) monitors and enforces compliance with equal employment opportunity laws, primarily Executive Order 11246, which applies to companies that do business (federal contractors and subcontractors) with the federal government.
Benefits	For further information on benefits-related regulation, see Chapters 12 and 13.

*The SEC is responsible for developing specific rules/policies for implementing the different provisions of Dodd-Frank. Rules for the provisions listed have been issued at various points in time since 2010.

framework, especially as it applies to wages and salaries and other forms of direct pay. Please see Chapters 12 and 13 for information on benefits-related regulations (e.g., the Employee Retirement Income Security Act, ERISA).

FAIR LABOR STANDARDS ACT OF 1938

The **Fair Labor Standards Act of 1938 (FLSA)** covers all employees (with some exceptions, discussed later) of companies engaged in interstate commerce or in the production of goods for interstate commerce. In spite of its age, this law remains a cornerstone of pay regulation in the United States. The FLSA's major provisions are:

1. Minimum wage
2. Hours of work (including overtime)
3. Child labor

An additional provision requires that records be kept of employees, their hours worked, and their pay. As noted earlier, in recent years, U.S. employers have paid out billions of dollars (see Exhibit 17.1) as a result of FLSA lawsuits and enforcement activity by the DOL Wage and Hour Division. Exhibit 17.3 provides a breakdown of the claim types covered in such settlements.

Minimum Wage

Minimum-wage legislation is intended to provide an income floor for workers in society's least productive jobs. When first enacted in 1938, the minimum wage was 25 cents an hour. It has been raised periodically; in 2009, it was raised to $7.25 and, at press time, remained there.

Forty-five states plus the District of Columbia have their own minimum wages to cover jobs omitted from federal legislation.[9] If state and federal laws cover the same

EXHIBIT 17.3
FLSA Wage and Hour Settlements, 2007 to 2011, by Type of Claim

Source: Denise Martin, Stephanie Plancich, and Janeen McIntosh, "Trends in Wage and Hour Settlements: 2013 Update," November 20, 2013, NERA Economic Consulting, www.nera.

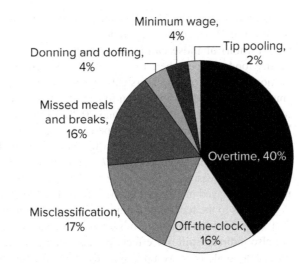

job, the higher rate prevails. Several states have minimums higher than the federal rate, with Washington being the highest at $9.47, closely followed by Oregon and District of Columbia at $9.25. San Francisco and Seattle have the highest minimum wage of any city, at $11.05 and $11.00, respectively. By 2018, San Francisco's minimum wage will be $15.00. Seattle's minimum wage will be $15 by 2019 for large employers and by 2021 for smaller employers. A lower minimum wage in Seattle exists for employers providing medical insurance.

Exhibit 17.4 shows the purchasing power of the federal minimum wage over time, adjusted for inflation. The decline in real purchasing power (especially prior to the recent increase in the minimum wage) could be used to argue for indexing the minimum wage to changes in the consumer price index.

EXHIBIT 17.4
Real (Inflation-Adjusted) Value of the Minimum Wage, by Year

Source: For 1938 to 2009 data, Kai Filion, "Minimum Wage Issue Guide" (Figure A), Economic Policy Institute, July 21, 2009, http://epi.3cdn.net/9f5a60cec02393cbe4_a4m6b5t1v.pdf. Estimates for 2010–2014 obtained using CPI-U from Bureau of Labor Statistics, U.S. Department of Labor.

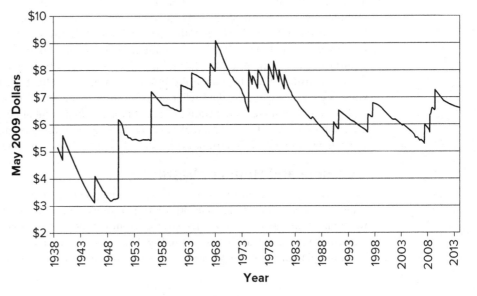

Estimates from the U.S. Bureau of Labor Statistics indicate that approximately 3.3 million U.S. workers are paid at or below the minimum wage. The majority (2.1 million) of those earning minimum wage or less are in service occupations, mostly food service, where tips supplement hourly wages for many workers. The proportion of hourly paid workers earning minimum wage or less has trended downward since 1979 when data first began to be collected systematically. In 1979, 13.4 percent of hourly workers (7.7% of men and 20.2% of women) earned at or below minimum. More recently, the figures are 4.3 percent of hourly workers (3.3% of men and 5.4% of women). As a percentage of all wage and salary workers, those earning at or below minimum wage has declined from 7.9 percent in 1979 to 2.6 percent more recently.[10] An important reason for the decline in those directly affected is that the federal minimum wage stayed unchanged at $5.15 from 1997 to 2007.

Changes to the federal minimum wage have direct effects (on workers having a current wage between any state minimum wage and the federal minimum wage). There are also indirect, spillover effects because as legislation forces pay rates at the lowest end of the scale to move up, pay rates above the minimum often increase in order to maintain differentials. This shift in pay structure does not affect all industries equally. The lowest rates paid in the software, chemical, oil, and pharmaceutical industries are already well above minimum; any legislative change has little direct impact on them. In contrast, retailing and hospitality firms tend to pay at or near minimum wage to many clerks, sales persons, and cleaning people.[11]

Why would anyone be opposed to a mandated minimum wage or making increases to it? The concern is that the resulting higher labor costs for affected firms may lead them to decrease their demand for workers and/or their hours worked. (See our discussion of supply and demand curves in Chapter 7.) In other words, a higher minimum wage, which is intended to help low wage workers, runs the risk of reducing employment opportunities for these very workers it is intended to help. So, whether a minimum wage "works" or not depends on whether the gains through higher wages are greater than the losses of jobs and/or hours.[12] Another consideration in evaluating minimum wage law effectiveness is whether wage gains go primarily to workers from low income families rather than going to workers from families with higher incomes.[13] Employers certainly have a stake in minimum wage public policy and thus may seek to influence it over time. In the shorter run, employers must be in compliance and will need to consider how changes to the minimum wage will affect their labor costs, to what degree they can pass the higher costs on to customers, and to what degree they will need to take some other action to control or offset higher labor costs.

Exhibit 17.5 provides an example of how an employer can run afoul of minimum wage, hours worked, and overtime provisions of the FLSA, as well as the consequences.

Overtime and Hours of Work

The overtime provision of the FLSA requires payment at one-and-a-half times the standard for working more than 40 hours per week. However, some of the largest wage and hour monetary settlements result from private class action suits brought by plaintiffs. Paying for all hours worked and/or for overtime are often central issues. For example, Bank of America paid $73 million to settle a nationwide class action

EXHIBIT 17.5   FLSA Wage and Hour Division Investigation Examples: LinkedIn and a Philadelphia
Sports Bar and Restaurant Chain

LinkedIn Corp. has paid $3,346,195 in overtime back wages and $2,509,646 in liquidated damages
to 359 former and current employees working at company branches in California, Illinois, Nebraska
and New York. An investigation by the U.S. Department of Labor's Wage and Hour Division found that
LinkedIn was in violation of the overtime and record-keeping provisions of the FLSA. LinkedIn failed
to record, account, and pay for all hours worked in a workweek, investigators found. The FLSA does
not allow unpaid "off the clock" hours are for employees covered by (nonexempt from) the FLSA.
LinkedIn agreed to pay all the overtime back wages due and take proactive steps to prevent repeat
violations.

Philadelphia sports bar and restaurant chain Chickie's & Pete's and its owner, Peter Ciarrocchi, Jr. have
signed a consent judgment agreeing to pay 1,159 current and former employees at nine locations more
than $6.8 million in back wages, plus damages (a $50,000 civil penalty) for improperly taking tips from
servers and violating federal minimum wage, overtime, and record-keeping requirements. The proposed
consent judgment has been filed in the U.S. District Court for the Eastern District of Pennsylvania and is
subject to the review and approval by the court.

Under the Fair Labor Standards Act, tips are the property of the employee who receives them;
however, restaurant operators can benefit by claiming a credit based on the tips toward their obligation
to pay those employees the full minimum wage. If an employee's tips combined with the employer's
direct wages do not equal the minimum wage, the employer must make up the difference during the
pay period. An employer that claims a tip credit is required to pay a tipped employee only $2.13 an hour
(unchanged since 1991) in direct wages provided that amount plus the tips received equals at least the
federal minimum wage of $7.25 an hour.

Investigators from the Wage and Hour Division found that the company required servers to contribute
a portion of their tips to an improper "tip pool," or tip-sharing arrangement, which was approximately
between 2 and 4 percent of the server's daily table sales. The owner illegally retained approximately
60 percent of the tip pool. This amount had come to be known as "Pete's Tax" and was required to be
paid to the manager in cash at the end of each shift.

Additionally, servers and bartenders were paid only a flat rate of $15 per shift at all locations except
for Chickie's and Pete's airport establishment—an amount that was not sufficient in all cases to even
cover the minimum cash wage of $2.13 per hour that must be paid to a tipped employee when an
employer claims a tip credit under federal law. Additionally, the employer failed to pay the required
overtime wages to these employees when they worked in excess of 40 hours in a week. Investigators also
determined that employees were not paid for time spent in mandatory meetings and training, and were
improperly required to pay for uniforms.

Under the provisions of the consent judgment the company will pay minimum wage and overtime
back wages and is required to return the improperly retained tips to the servers, as well as pay liquidated
damages. In addition, the company has agreed to enhanced compliance, including: External compliance
monitoring for an 18-month period; Internal compliance monitoring for an additional 18-month period;
Training for all employees on their rights under the FLSA; Providing a statement to any employee
required to contribute to a tip pool detailing the amounts that were contributed by the employee, the
job categories of workers included in the tip pool and the specific percentage each category receives;
Peter Ciarrocchi, Jr., the owner, will write an article for a restaurant trade publication that addresses an
employer's obligations under the FLSA; Chickie's & Pete's and Ciarrocchi are to be permanently enjoined
and restrained from violating the provisions of the FLSA in the future.

Source: U.S. Department of Labor, WHD News Release, Number 14-0940-SANI and WHD News Release, Number 13-0044-PHI. www.dol.gov/whd/.

lawsuit alleging that it had a company-wide policy that required nonexempt employees to perform off-the-clock work.[14] Walmart has settled or lost a number of lawsuits, including one for as much as $640 million (for allegedly not paying for all hours worked and for expecting workers to work through their breaks) and another for as much as $86 million (for not paying all wages due upon termination of employment). In another case, which it may appeal, a court ordered it to pay $188 million (for again expecting workers to skip or cut short rest and/or meal breaks).

One objective of the FLSA is to share available work by making the hiring of additional workers a less costly option than the scheduling of overtime for current employees. However, the conditions that inspired the legislation have changed since the law was passed. Contemporary employers face (1) an increasingly skilled workforce with higher training costs per employee and (2) higher benefits costs, the bulk of which are fixed per employee. These factors have lowered the break-even point at which it pays employers to schedule longer hours and pay the overtime premium, rather than hire, train, and pay benefits for more employees.

Again, state laws sometimes go beyond the FLSA. California, for example, requires time and a half pay for working more than 8 hours in a day and double time for working more than 12 hours in a day. It also requires premium pay for working a seventh day during a week.

Exemptions

The Wage and Hour Division of the Department of Labor, which is charged with enforcement of the FLSA, provides strict criteria that must be met in order for jobs to be **exempt** from minimum-wage and overtime provisions. These are summarized in Exhibit 17.6. Important update: President Obama has issued an executive order that instructed the Secretary of Labor to "update and modernize" the overtime exemption rules of the FLSA.[15] New regulations should be issued by the end of 2015. Thus, for example, the pay cutoff of $455/week shown in Exhibit 17.6 will be significantly increased. Specifically, the Wage and Hour Division has proposed increasing this salary "test" to $970 per week, which would greatly increase the number of U.S. employees who are nonexempt (i.e., covered by FLSA overtime provisions). Note also that the President has already issued an executive order to change the salary test amount and the only question that remains is whether the final salary test amount will be $970 exactly or something quite close to it. There may also be changes to the duties criteria shown in Exhibit 17.6. See the e-compensation box below.

Some employers try to get around the overtime requirement by classifying employees as executives, even though the work of these "executives" differs only slightly from that of their co-workers. However, in the eyes of the Department of Labor, the job title is not relevant. Rather, it is the actual nature of the work that matters.

Merrill Lynch reached a $37 million settlement with financial analysts in California regarding overtime pay. A Merrill Lynch financial analyst argued that because his salary was entirely from commissions, he did not meet the "salary basis" test for the administrative exemption. The plaintiff also successfully argued that he did not exercise sufficient discretion and independent judgment. Instead, the financial analyst's work was considered "production," Merrill Lynch's practices were standard in the financial industry, and the impact of this ruling rippled through other financial service companies and brought changes to Merrill Lynch's pay system for analysts.[16]

EXHIBIT 17.6   **Fact Sheet #17A: Exemption for Executive, Administrative, Professional, Computer & Outside Sales Employees under the Fair Labor Standards Act**

Executive Exemption

To qualify for the executive employee exemption, all of the following tests must be met:

- The employee must be compensated on a salary basis (as defined in the regulations) at a rate not less than $455 per week (new proposed rate is $970 per week);
- The employee's primary duty must be managing the enterprise, or managing a customarily recognized department or subdivision of the enterprise;
- The employee must customarily and regularly direct the work of at least two or more other full-time employees or their equivalent; and
- The employee must have the authority to hire or fire other employees, or the employee's suggestions and recommendations as to the hiring, firing, advancement, promotion or any other change of status of other employees must be given particular weight.

Administrative Exemptions

To qualify for the administrative employee exemption, all of the following tests must be met:

- The employee must be compensated on a salary or fee basis (as defined in the regulations) at a rate not less than $455 per week (new proposed rate is $970 per week);
- The employee's primary duty must be the performance of office or non-manual work directly related to the management or general business operations of the employer or the employer's customers; and
- The employee's primary duty includes the exercise of discretion and independent judgment with respect to matters of significance.

Professional Exemption

To qualify for the learned professional employee exemption, all of the following tests must be met:

- The employee must be compensated on a salary or fee basis (as defined in the regulations) at a rate not less than $455 per week (new proposed rate is $970 per week);
- The employee's primary duty must be the performance of work requiring advanced knowledge, defined as work which is predominantly intellectual in character and which includes work requiring the consistent exercise of discretion and judgment;
- The advanced knowledge must be in a field of science or learning; and
- The advanced knowledge must be customarily acquired by a prolonged course of specialized intellectual instruction.

To qualify for the creative professional employee exemption, all of the following tests must be met:

- The employee must be compensated on a salary or fee basis (as defined in the regulations) at a rate not less than $455 per week (new proposed rate is $970 per week);
- The employee's primary duty must be the performance of work requiring invention, imagination, originality or talent in a recognized field of artistic or creative endeavor.

EXHIBIT 17.6 *(Continued)*

Computer Employee Exemption

To qualify for the computer employee exemption, the following tests must be met:

- The employee must be compensated either on a salary or fee basis (as defined in the regulations) at a rate not less than $455 per week (new proposed rate is $970 per week) or, if compensated on an hourly basis, at a rate not less than $27.63 an hour;
- The employee must be employed as a computer systems analyst, computer programmer, software engineer or other similarly skilled worker in the computer field performing the duties described below;
- The employee's primary duty must consist of:
  1. The application of systems analysis techniques and procedures, including consulting with users, to determine hardware, software or system functional specifications;
  2. The design, development, documentation, analysis, creation, testing or modification of computer systems or programs, including prototypes, based on and related to user or system design specifications;
  3. The design, documentation, testing, creation or modification of computer programs related to machine operating systems; or
  4. A combination of the aforementioned duties, the performance of which requires the same level of skills.

Outside Sales Exemption

To qualify for the outside sales employee exemption, all of the following tests must be met:

- The employee's primary duty must be making sales (as defined in the FLSA), or obtaining orders or contracts for services or for the use of facilities for which a consideration will be paid by the client or customer; and
- The employee must be customarily and regularly engaged away from the employer's place or places of business.

Highly Compensated Employees

Highly compensated employees performing office or nonmanual work and paid total annual compensation of $100,000 or more (which must include at least $455 per week paid on a salary or fee basis) are exempt from the FLSA if they customarily and regularly perform at least one of the duties of an exempt executive, administrative or professional employee identified in the standard tests for exemption.

NOT Exempt

Blue-collar workers. The exemptions do not apply to manual laborers or other "blue collar" workers who perform work involving repetitive operations with their hands, physical skill and energy.
Police, fire fighters, paramedics, and other first responders.
These employee groups are not exempt, but rather are covered by the FLSA.

State Laws

When the state laws differ from the federal FLSA, an employer must comply with the standard most protective to employees.

Source: Excerpts from U.S. Department of Labor, Employment Standards Administration, Wage and Hour Division, http://www.dol.gov/whd/regs/compliance/fairpay/fs17a_overview.pdf. Accessed March 26, 2015.

Subsequently, Citigroup's Smith Barney brokerage unit settled an FLSA overtime lawsuit for $98 million, with UBS Financial Services and Morgan Stanley both also making substantial payments to settle similar suits. JPMorgan Chase & Co. reached a $42 million settlement with a class of 3,800 loan processors.[17] The U.S. Department of Labor ordered Walmart to pay $4.8 million in back wages and damages to 4,500 vision-center managers and asset-protection coordinators who worked at Walmart over a four-year period.[18] Insurance claims adjustors settled overtime lawsuits against Farmers Insurance for as much as $210 million and against State Farm Insurance for $135 million. Both of these lawsuits were brought under California law, under which it was more difficult than under federal law (i.e., the FLSA) to meet the administrative employee exemption. Indeed, similar lawsuits brought under FLSA have not succeeded.

e-Compensation
Go the website of the Wage and Hour Division, http://www.dol.gov/whd/overtime_pay.htm, and check for updates on the FLSA exemption criteria shown in Exhibit 17.6.

Another challenge in compliance is that "in an evolving, always-on workplace where employees routinely put in extra hours and shoot off e-mails late at night from mobile devices, when the workday begins and ends has become an issue for employers."[19] For example, writers at ABC News asked that they be paid overtime for using their smartphones for work purposes after business hours. As a result, ABC News asked writers to sign an agreement waiving rights to overtime for such activity. Writers who declined to sign had their smartphones taken away.[20] One survey reports that just over half of large firms have restricted the use of communications devices outside of the office and one-third have restricted telecommuting.[21]

In response to these types of lawsuits, some companies have reclassified some employees. For example, IBM voluntarily reclassified 7,000 technical and support employees after settling a class-action overtime lawsuit for $65 million. The employees, who had been earning an average of $77,000 per year, had their base salaries cut by 15 percent to account for the potential overtime that the company would need to pay them going forward.[22]

The impact of FLSA and other laws depends importantly on the degree to which they are enforced. A Government Accountability Office (GAO) report found that the Labor Department's Wage and Hour Division "mishandled" 9 of 10 cases brought by GAO undercover agents posing as workers who had experienced FLSA violations.[23] As one example, an agent posing as a dishwasher called four times to complain that he had not been paid overtime for almost five months. His calls were not returned until 4 months later and he was then told it would take another 8 to 10 months to begin an investigation. GAO also investigated existing files. In another case, an undercover agent posing as an employer who had violated the law appeared to escape any penalty by simply saying that business was bad, so he could not afford to pay anything. The Department of Labor investigator was quoted as saying "OK, so you're not in a position where you can pay?" and when the undercover agent said that was correct, the investigator seemed to give up and said that he would let the worker know that he could pursue the case on his own (i.e., need to hire an attorney). To increase enforcement of the FLSA, the Department of Labor since added wage-and-hour investigators.[24]

In Japan, unpaid overtime is (also) a major issue. The Japanese Trade Union Confederation reports that two-thirds of men work more than 20 hours of unpaid overtime each month.[25] Only in 2008 did Toyota begin to pay factory workers for participating in quality control programs that were held outside of normal work hours. Some large companies have introduced "no overtime" days on which employees are to leave at 5:30 p.m. However, the concern is that many employees just take the work home, which is referred to as *furoshiki,* or "cloaked overtime."[26] "Death by overwork" (*karoshi*) has resulted in lawsuits against companies in Japan.

What Time Is Covered?

As we have seen, employers are sometimes guilty of not paying employees for hours worked (i.e., of having them "work off the clock"). In addition to the FLSA, other laws come into play. Occupational Safety and Health Administration legislation specifies the number of breaks that must be provided in an eight-hour workday. The Portal-to-Portal Act provides that time spent on activities before beginning the "principal activity" is generally not compensable. The original issue that inspired the act was the time that miners were forced to spend traveling to and from the actual underground site where the mining was occurring. The meat processing industry has been the source of several cases defining time spent at work. Time spent sharpening knives and cutting tools is compensable time, as is the time spent donning protective gear and walking in this "integral" gear to the production area.[27]

The law is also relevant to "on-call employees" who must be available to respond outside the usual workday. Firefighters and emergency personnel are traditional examples. Today, telecommunications and software services personnel who must respond quickly to problems outside their regularly scheduled workday are newer categories of employees eligible for "beeper pay." (See also our ABC News example earlier.) In general, if employees can use this "on-call" time for their own purposes, there is no legal requirement to pay employees for such time, even if they are required to carry a beeper or must let their employer know where they can be reached. However, if they are required to stay on the employer's premises while on call, then they must be compensated for that time. Sometimes a flat rate is paid for the added inconvenience of being on call. These payments must be included when computing overtime pay.[28]

What Income Is Covered?

FLSA specifies one and a half times pay for overtime, but one and a half of what? As more employees became eligible for bonuses, there was an argument over whether bonus, gain-sharing, and stock option payments needed to be included for calculating overtime pay. A 1999 advisory from the Wage and Hour Division said they did. But the extra bookkeeping and calculations provided enough of a burden that employers simply did not offer these forms of pay to **nonexempt** employees. The Worker Economic Opportunity Act, a 2000 amendment to FLSA, allows stock options and bonuses to be exempt from inclusion in overtime pay calculations. Gifts or special-occasion bonuses have never needed to be included, because they are at the employer's discretion rather than a pay form promised to employees if certain conditions are met.

Compensatory Time Off

The changing nature of the workplace and of pay systems has led to calls to reform FLSA to allow for more flexible scheduling and easier administration of variable pay plans.

Federal legislation has been proposed (but not yet passed) that would give employees and employers the option of trading overtime pay for time off. Rather than being paid overtime after 8 hours for a 10-hour workday, an employee would have the option of taking 2 or more hours off at another time. Or, a 50-hour workweek could be banked against a future 30-hour workweek.[29] The employee would get more scheduling flexibility to attend to personal matters, and the employer would save money. This kind of change has a lot of appeal for employees who are also raising children and/or caring for elderly parents. One poll reported that 81 percent of women would prefer compensatory time off in lieu of overtime wages.[30]

Child Labor

Generally, persons under 18 cannot work in hazardous jobs such as meat packing and logging; persons under 16 cannot be employed in jobs involving interstate commerce except for nonhazardous work for a parent or guardian. Additional exceptions and limitations also exist.[31]

The union movement in the United States has taken a leading role in publicizing the extent of the use of child labor outside the United States to produce goods destined for U.S. consumers. Government guidelines help importers monitor the employment practices of subcontractors producing goods for the U.S. market. A recent International Labour Organization report finds that globally, child labor is declining, particularly in Latin America. Brazil and Mexico, where half the children in Latin America live, have made the greatest strides, which the study attributed to increased political will, awareness, poverty reduction, and education. The steepest declines were among children 14 and younger, and among hazardous occupations. The highest rates of child labor are in sub-Saharan Africa, where high population growth, grinding poverty, and the HIV/AIDS epidemic have left a lot of families in need of the income that children can provide.[32]

LIVING WAGE

Although living wage provisions are not part of the FLSA, we cover the topic here because of its similarity to FLSA minimum wage provisions.

Rather than (solely) push for changes in the FLSA, an alternative approach in recent years has been to push for a "living wage" at local levels that provides a minimum wage tailored to living costs in an area.[33] These laws have narrower coverage than minimum wage laws, as they cover only city (or state) employees and/or employers that do business with the city (i.e., contractors and subcontractors). Sometimes they cover only base wages, but more frequently they require health insurance, vacations, sick pay, job security, and provide incentives to unionize.

Maryland was the first to adopt a statewide **living wage** ordinance, effective in 2009.[34] The minimum ranges from $10.06 to $13.39, depending on location, compared to an $8.00 state minimum wage. More than 140 ordinances have been put into effect in the United States by cities, counties, universities, and other public entities. California has the most; it is followed by Michigan, New York, and Wisconsin.[35]

Los Angeles's law covers "contractors/subcontractors who have agreements with the city." The law mandates $11.03 an hour if health care benefits are offered by the employer, $12.28 an hour if not offered. The required wage rate is higher for airport workers and for large hotels, with the latter minimum being $15.37.[36]

An early study of the Los Angeles law's effects found that 7,735 of the covered employees got an average wage increase of 20 percent.[37] Another 149 noncovered employees got increases in order to maintain pay differentials. Employers adjusted to the law by making only very minor adjustments in employment—an estimated 112 jobs, or 1 percent of covered jobs, were lost. Benefits were cut for less than 5 percent of affected jobs, including cuts in health benefits, merit pay, bonuses, and employer-provided meals. Training for new hires stayed the same, but nonaffected firms were increasing their training. Firms benefited via reduced turnover and absenteeism. New hires tended to be better qualified, with higher levels of education and training than those hired before the law was passed. The new hires also included a higher proportion of males: 56 percent, compared to 45 percent of hires before the living wage. The study also found that 70 percent of the benefit of the law went to low-income families.

Living wage laws are increasingly popular. Coalitions of union members and church groups often support them. Because they are so narrowly tailored, there is some speculation that their real intention is to reduce any cost savings a municipality might receive from outsourcing. Reduced outsourcing means more government jobs, which generally translates into more union members.[38]

EMPLOYEE OR INDEPENDENT CONTRACTOR?

As we saw in Chapter 12, U.S. employers are legally obligated to pay Social Security, unemployment compensation, and workers compensation taxes on wages and salaries on behalf of their employees. As of 2015, the average total compensation per employee in private industry was $31.32 per hour, with $21.72 of that being in the form of wages and salaries and the remaining $9.60 being for benefits. Of the $9.60, $2.50 was for the legally required benefits just mentioned.[39] However, in the case of a worker who is an independent contractor rather than an employee, the employer is not obligated to pay the legally required benefits. In addition, independent contractors would also typically not receive other benefits. An independent contractor would not be eligible for overtime (time and a half). Thus, whether a worker is classified as an employee or an independent contractor can have substantial cost implications for an employer, which of course increases with the number of workers involved. Less obvious perhaps is that law-abiding employers are put at a disadvantage because complying with the law results in higher costs than those borne by employers that misclassify (unless those not in compliance are discovered). Finally, of course, workers suffer if they are denied access to benefits and legal protections that they should receive.

As with the FLSA exceptions discussed a few pages earlier, the decision of whether to classify a worker as an employee or independent contractor requires careful attention to compliance issues. Both tax law—enforced by the Internal Revenue Service (IRS)—and the Employee Retirement Income Security Act (ERISA)—enforced by the Department of Labor—are relevant. To get an idea of the potential revenue losses to government of misclassification of workers, consider that Ohio's attorney general estimates that Ohio alone at one point has 92,500 misclassified workers, estimated to cost the state up to $35 million in lost unemployment insurance taxes, up to $103 million in lost workers' compensation taxes, and up to $223 million in income tax revenue. (Note: some estimates suggest that misclassified independent contractors do not report 30% of their income.[40]) The most widely used classification criteria are provided by the IRS and shown in Exhibit 17.7. Two general criteria have to do with behavioral and financial control. The more control a firm is able to exercise, the more likely it is that the IRS will see the worker as an employee rather than an independent contractor. The IRS also considers the type of relationship, including its permanence. The Supreme Court, in *Nationwide v. Darden*, has applied similar criteria in deciding whether a worker is an employee under ERISA.[41] Among the most often misclassified are truck drivers, construction workers, home health aides, and high-tech engineers.[42]

Microsoft hired workers as independent contractors. It had these workers sign agreements acknowledging their independent contractor status. However, after an audit by the IRS concluded that these workers were actually employees, Microsoft agreed to begin paying legally required taxes (see above). Microsoft had used the workers on projects, often working on teams with regular employees, doing similar work, working similar hours, and being supervised by the same managers. Microsoft also required them to work onsite and they were given office equipment and supplies.[43]

Next, two separate suits *(Vizcaino v. Microsoft* and *Hughes v. Microsoft)* were filed against Microsoft to compel it to retroactively provide other benefits (e.g., a discounted stock purchase program) that it provided to its (other) employees. Some of the workers had been at Microsoft for several years with a few being there as long as 10 years. Microsoft eventually settled these suits for $97 million, which after attorneys' fees, will be divided between 8,000 and 12,000 people employed at Microsoft for at least 9 months during a several-year period.[44] Microsoft implemented new rules, including limiting independent contractor assignments to 12 months with at least 100 days between assignments. More recently, FedEx was ordered to pay $27 million to 203 drivers in California who were ruled *(Estrada v. FedEx Ground Package System, Inc.)* to have been wrongly classified as independent contractors.[45] And, that may not be the end of the compliance issue for FedEx. It announced that the IRS, upon tentatively deciding that FedEx has misclassified workers as contractors, was considering $319 million in tax and penalties for one year and that it was in the process of looking at other years also FedEx continues to deal with multiple lawsuits on this issue.[46]

EXHIBIT 17.7 Employee or Independent Contractor: Internal Revenue Service Tests

Behavioral control. Facts that show whether the business has a right to direct and control how the worker does the task for which the worker is hired include the type and degree of:

Instructions that the business gives to the worker. An employee is generally subject to the business' instructions about when, where, and how to work. Even if no instructions are given, sufficient behavioral control may exist if the employer has the right to control how the work results are achieved. Examples of types of instructions include: when and where to do the work, what tools or equipment to use, what workers to hire or to assist with the work, where to purchase supplies and services, what work must be performed by a specified individual, what order or sequence to follow.

Training that the business gives to the worker. An employee may be trained to perform services in a particular manner. Independent contractors ordinarily use their own methods.

Financial control. Facts that show whether the business has a right to control the business aspects of the worker's job include:

The extent to which the worker has unreimbursed business expenses. Independent contractors are more likely to have unreimbursed expenses than are employees.

The extent of the worker's investment. An independent contractor often has a significant investment in the facilities he or she uses in performing services for someone else.

The extent to which the worker makes his or her services available to the relevant market. An independent contractor is generally free to seek out business opportunities. Independent contractors often advertise, maintain a visible business location, and are available to work in the relevant market.

How the business pays the worker. An employee is generally guaranteed a regular wage amount for an hourly, weekly, or other period of time. An independent contractor is usually paid by a flat fee for the job. However, it is common in some professions, such as law, to pay independent contractors hourly.

The extent to which the worker can realize a profit or loss. An independent contractor can make a profit or loss.

Type of relationship. Facts that show the parties' type of relationship include:

Written contracts describing the relationship the parties intended to create.

Whether or not the business provides the worker with employee-type benefits, such as insurance, a pension plan, vacation pay, or sick pay.

The permanency of the relationship. If you engage a worker with the expectation that the relationship will continue indefinitely, rather than for a specific project or period, this is generally considered evidence that your intent was to create an employer-employee relationship.

The extent to which services performed by the worker are a key aspect of the regular business of the company. If a worker provides services that are a key aspect of your regular business activity, it is more likely that you will have the right to direct and control his or her activities. For example, if a law firm hires an attorney, it is likely that it will present the attorney's work as its own and would have the right to control or direct that work. This would indicate an employer-employee relationship.

Source: Adapted from *Publication 15-A (January 31, 2012)*, Internal Revenue Service, Department of U.S. Treasury. http://www.irs.gov/publications/p15a/ar02. html#en_US_publink100052199. Accessed May 28, 2012.

PREVAILING WAGE LAWS

Prevailing wage laws set pay for work done to produce goods and services contracted by the federal government. A *government-defined prevailing wage* is the minimum wage that must be paid for work done on covered government projects or purchases. Consider, for example, "The Big Dig," Boston's $15 billion taxpayer-financed project to put its freeways underground.[47] A construction project of such magnitude attracts workers from a very wide area and distorts the labor market. Prevailing-wage laws prevent contractors from using their size to drive down wages. The law was passed in response to conditions on projects such as the construction of the Hoover Dam during the Depression. Workers who collapsed from the July heat in Nevada or were killed in accidents were quickly replaced from a pool of unemployed men who were already camping near the job site.

To comply with the law, contractors must determine the "going rate" for construction labor in an area. As a practical matter, the "union rate" for labor becomes the going rate. That rate then becomes the mandated minimum wage on the government-financed project. One effect is to distort market wages and drive up the cost of government-financed projects. For example, a few years back, the market wage for plumbers in Kentucky was $18.15 an hour, according to the Bureau of Labor Statistics. Yet a wage survey for Owsley County, Kentucky, required that plumbers on public projects receive $23.75 an hour, more than 30 percent above the government's own market wage.[48]

A number of laws contain prevailing-wage provisions. They vary on the government expenditures they target for coverage. The main prevailing-wage laws include the Davis-Bacon Act, the Walsh-Healey Public Contracts Act, the Service Contract Act, and the National Foundation for the Arts and Humanities Act. A spate of new laws extends prevailing-wage coverage to new immigrants to the United States and to non-citizens who are working in the United States under special provisions. For example, the Nursing Relief for Disadvantaged Areas Act of 1999 allows qualified hospitals to employ temporary foreign workers as registered nurses for up to three years under a special visa program. The prevailing wage for registered nurses must be paid to these foreign workers. Similar acts target legal immigrants and farm workers.

Much of the legislation discussed so far was originally passed in the 1930s and 1940s in response to social issues of that time. While this legislation has continued to be extended up to the present, the Equal Rights movement in the 1960s pushed different social problems to the forefront. The Equal Pay Act and the Civil Rights Act were passed. Because of their substantial impact on human resource management and compensation, they are discussed at length below.

ANTITRUST ISSUES

In Chapter 8, we noted the need to avoid antitrust concerns in setting employee pay. A lawsuit representing 64,000 former software engineers and programmers at Apple Inc., Google, Inc., Intel Corp., and Adobe Systems alleged that these companies entered into an agreement between 2005 and 2009 that they would not poach (try to recruit away) each other's employees. Given that one of the main contributors to career earnings is advancement, either at one's present company or another company (typically with a higher salary), the companies' action to avoid a bidding war for talent (through using anticompetitive actions) is argued to have resulted in lost pay for their employees. The lawsuit alleges that the main mastermind of the no poaching agreement was the late Steve Jobs, the former head of Apple, Inc. (Indeed, according to one claim in the papers filed, when in 2007 a Google recruiter contacted an Apple employee about a job, Mr. Jobs complained and the Google recruiter was fired, purportedly within an hour.) The two sides in the lawsuit eventually agreed to settle the case by having the companies pay $324.5 million in back pay (and legal fees). However, a federal judge rejected the proposed settlement as being too small, saying that based on previous settlements by Intuit and Pixair around similar issues, a settlement of at least $380 million would be necessary. (Some of the plaintiffs made similar arguments.) Consequently, the parties were required to restart their negotiations with the aim of agreeing on a new settlement that would be acceptable to the federal judge.[49]

PAY DISCRIMINATION: WHAT IS IT?

Before we look at specific federal pay discrimination laws, which are summarized in Exhibit 17.8, let us address the more general question of how to legally define discrimination. The law recognizes two types of discrimination: access discrimination and valuation discrimination. The charges of discrimination and reverse discrimination that most often make the news involve **access discrimination:** the denial of particular jobs, promotions, or training opportunities to qualified women or minorities. The University of Michigan, for example, was accused of access discrimination for using differential standards among different racial groups to determine who is "qualified" for admission. Being a member of a minority group counted for 20 points, whereas the quality of the admission essay counted for 3 points. (Being an athlete also counted for 20 points.) In 2003, the Supreme Court ruled that while schools can take race into account for admission, this 20-point differential was illegal because it was applied in a mechanical way.[50] However, the admission process for Michigan's law school was upheld because it was narrowly tailored and more flexible. Minority candidates for the law school were interviewed and their entire record was examined, in contrast to the routine addition of 20 points that the undergraduate school used. (The court did not address the issue of the preferred treatment for athletes or children of alumni or big donors.[51]) Subsequently, however, the State of Michigan passed a constitutional amendment prohibiting race-conscious admission policies at the state's public universities.

A second legally recognized interpretation of discrimination is **valuation discrimination,** which looks at the pay women and minorities receive for the jobs they perform. This is the more salient definition for our purposes. The Equal Pay Act makes it clear that it is discriminatory to pay women less than males when they are performing equal work (i.e., working side by side, in the same plant, doing the same work, producing the same results). This definition of pay discrimination hinges on the standard of *equal pay for equal work.*

Many believe that this definition of valuation discrimination does not go far enough. They believe that valuation discrimination can also occur when men and

EXHIBIT 17.8   Federal Pay Discrimination Law and Enforcement

	Equal Pay Act	Title VII, Civil Rights Act	Executive Order 11246
Year	1963	1964	1965
Discrimination Prohibited on Basis of:	Sex	Race, color, religion, sex, or national origin	Race, color, religion, sex, or national origin
Type of Pay Discrimination Prohibited	"for equal work on jobs the performance of which requires equal skill, effort, and responsibility, and which are performed under similar working conditions, except where such payment is made pursuant to (i) a seniority system; (ii) a merit system; (iii) a system which measures earnings by quantity or quality of production; or (iv) a differential based on any other factor other than sex" (Equal Pay Act)	"[in] compensation, terms, conditions, or privileges of employment" (Title VII, Civil Rights Act)	"statistically significant compensation disparities between similarly situated employees . . . after taking into account legitimate factors which influence compensation." ("Systemic Compensation Discrimination," Federal Register, June 16, 2006)
Coverage	Same as FLSA. Virtually all employers.	Employers having 15 or more employees. Those with 100 or more employees must also file annual EEO-1 reports, which report the number of employees by race, ethnicity and gender for each of nine job categories. Over 600,000 employers covered.*	Government contractors and subcontractors with $10,000 or more in government contracts. Contractors with 50 or more employees and $50,000 or more in contracts must also file annual EEO-1 reports, which report the number of employees by race, ethnicity and gender for each of nine job categories. Over 116,000 employers covered.**
Enforcement Agency	Equal Employment Opportunity Commission (EEOC)	Equal Employment Opportunity Commission (EEOC)	Office of Federal Contract Compliance Programs (OFCCP), Department of Labor
Primary Enforcement Action Trigger	Employee Complaint-Driven	Employee Complaint-Driven	Regular Audits

*U.S. Government Accountability Office, "Federal Agencies Should Better Monitor Their Performance in Enforcing Anti-Discrimination Laws," GAO Reports, Report Number GAO-08-799. Washington, D.C., August 2008.

**Department of Labor. Office of Federal Contracts Compliance. Government Contractors, Requirement to Report Summary Data on Employee Compensation. Federal Register / Vol. 79, No. 153 / Friday, August 8, 2014 / Proposed Rules.

women hold entirely different jobs. For example, office and clerical jobs are typically staffed by women, and craft jobs (electricians, welders) are typically staffed by men. Is it illegal to pay employees in one job group less than employees in the other if the two job groups contain work that is not equal in content or results but is, in some sense, of **comparable worth** to the employer?[52]

In this case, the proposed definition of pay discrimination hinges on the standard of *equal pay for work of comparable worth* (also called **pay equity** or **gender pay equity**). Existing federal laws in the United States do not support this standard. However, several states have enacted laws that require a comparable-worth standard for state and local government employees. Significant pay equity adjustments have also been made in Canada (see our later discussion). For an understanding of the legal foundations for both the equal work and the comparable worth standard, let us turn to the legislation and key court cases.

THE EQUAL PAY ACT

The Equal Pay Act (EPA) of 1963 (which is part of the FLSA) forbids wage discrimination on the basis of gender if employees perform equal work in the same establishment. Jobs are considered equal if they require equal skill, effort, and responsibility and are performed under similar working conditions.

Differences in pay between men and women doing equal work are legal if these differences are based on any one of four criteria, called an *affirmative defense:*

- Seniority.
- Merit or quality of performance.
- Quality or quantity of production.
- Some factor other than sex.

These terms for comparison and permitted defenses seem deceptively simple. Yet numerous court cases have been required to clarify the act's provisions, particularly its definition of "equal."

Definition of Equal

The Supreme Court first established guidelines to define equal work in the *Schultz v. Wheaton Glass* case back in 1970. Wheaton Glass Company maintained two **job classifications** for selector-packers in its production department: male and female. The female job class carried a pay rate 10 percent below that of the male job class. The company claimed that the male job class included additional tasks such as shoveling broken glass, opening warehouse doors, and doing heavy lifting that justified the pay differential. The plaintiff claimed that the extra tasks were infrequently performed and not all men did them. Further, these extra tasks performed by some of the men were regularly performed by employees in another classification ("snap-up boys"), and these employees were paid only 2 cents an hour more than the women. Did the additional tasks sometimes performed by some members of one job class render the jobs unequal?

The Court decided they did not. It ruled that the equal work standard required only that jobs be *substantially* equal, not identical. Additionally, in several cases where the duties employees actually performed were different from those in the job descriptions, the courts held that the *actual work performed* must be used to decide whether jobs are substantially equal.

Definitions of Skill, Effort, Responsibility, Working Conditions

The Department of Labor provides these definitions of the four factors.

1. *Skill:* Experience, training, education, and ability as measured by the performance requirements of a particular job.
2. *Effort:* Mental or physical—the degree of effort (not type of effort) actually expended in the performance of a job.
3. *Responsibility:* The degree of accountability required in the performance of a job.
4. *Working conditions:* The physical surroundings and hazards of a job, including dimensions such as inside versus outside work, heat, cold, and poor ventilation.

Guidelines to clarify these definitions have evolved through court decisions. For an employer to support a claim of *unequal* work, the following conditions must be met:

1. The effort/skill/responsibility must be substantially greater in one of the jobs compared.
2. The tasks involving the extra effort/skill/responsibility must consume a *significant amount* of time for *all* employees whose additional wages are in question.
3. The extra effort/skill/responsibility must have a *value commensurate* with the questioned pay differential (as determined by the employer's own evaluation).

Time of day (e.g., working a night shift) does not constitute dissimilar working conditions. However, if a differential for working at night is paid, it must be separated from the base wage for the job.

Factors Other Than Sex

Of the four affirmative defenses for unequal pay for equal work, "a factor other than sex" has prompted the most court cases. Factors other than sex include shift differentials; temporary assignments; bona fide training programs; differences based on ability, training, or experience; and other reasons of "business necessity."

Factors other than sex have been interpreted as a broad exception that may include business reasons advanced by the employer. A practice will not automatically be prohibited simply because wage differences between men and women result. However, an employer is required to justify the business relatedness of the practice.[53] Usually a specific practice is not singled out; rather, the argument focuses on a "pattern of practices." That is what a group of female brokers at Merrill Lynch charged in their class action suit. They were concerned with how accounts from departing brokers, walk-ins, and referrals were being distributed. They felt that the top men brokers were given the most promising leads, while everyone else, including the 15 percent of brokers who were women, got the "crumbs." The women contended that Merrill Lynch discriminated against women in wages, promotions, account distributions, maternity leaves, and other areas. A negotiated settlement promised to establish a more open method for sharing leads and not to penalize brokers for time off in determining bonuses and production quotas.

Because such cases tend to be settled out of court, no legal clarification of a "factor other than sex" has ever been provided. It does seem that pay differences for equal work can be justified for demonstrably business-related reasons. But what is and is not demonstrably business-related has yet to be cataloged.

"Reverse" Discrimination

Many people dislike the term "reverse" discrimination, saying that it is still discrimination, even if the group penalized is white males. Several court cases deal with discrimination against men when pay for women is adjusted. The University of Nebraska created a model to calculate salaries based on estimated values for a faculty member's education, field of specialization, years of direct experience, years of related experience, and merit. Based on these qualifications, the university granted raises to 33 women whose salaries were less than the amount computed by the model. However, the university gave no such increases to 92 males whose salaries were also below the amount the model set for them based on their qualifications. The court found this system a violation of the Equal Pay Act. It held that, in effect, the university was using a new system to determine a salary schedule, based on specific criteria. To refuse to pay employees of one sex the minimum required by these criteria was illegal.

Viewed collectively, the courts have provided reasonably clear directions to interpret the Equal Pay Act. The design of pay systems must incorporate a policy of equal pay for substantially equal work. The determination of substantially equal work must be based on the actual work performed (the job content) and must reflect the skill, effort, responsibility, and working conditions involved. It is legal to pay men and women who perform substantially equal work differently if the pay system is designed to recognize differences in performance, seniority, quality, and quantity of results, or certain factors other than sex in a nondiscriminatory manner. Further, if a new pay system is designed, it must be equally applied to all employees.

But what does this tell us about discrimination on jobs that are *not substantially equal*—dissimilar jobs? Fifty-eight percent of all working women are not in jobs substantially equal to jobs of men, so they are not covered by the Equal Pay Act. Title VII of the Civil Rights Act extends protection to them.

TITLE VII OF THE CIVIL RIGHTS ACT OF 1964 AND RELATED LAWS

The Civil Rights Act is a far-reaching law that grew out of the civil rights movement of the 1950s and 1960s. **Title VII** of the act prohibits discrimination on the basis of sex, race, color, religion, or national origin in any employment condition, including hiring, firing, promotion, transfer, compensation, and admission to training programs. Title VII was amended in 1972, 1978, and 1990. The EEOC is responsible for Title VII enforcement. As we saw earlier in Exhibit 17.8, the cost to employers of equal employment opportunity (EEO) issues broadly (including Title VII) was about $2 billion over a 5-year period, taking into account both EEOC enforcement activity and private class action lawsuit settlements.

In addition to Title VII, other key EEO statutes, the 1967 **Age Discrimination in Employment Act (ADEA)** and the 1990 **Americans with Disabilities Act (ADA)** also prohibit discrimination based on age and disability, respectively. Compliance with the ADEA is typically a key concern when companies use workforce reduction programs. The ADEA pertains not only to age-related differences in pay and employment outcomes, but in addition, it was amended in 1990 to include the Older Workers Benefit Protection Act (OWBPA), which has detailed rules regarding how separation agreements (e.g., an early retirement incentive) involving older workers are used. As one example, at least 21 days must be given to consider the agreement.

Title VII cases of pay discrimination typically focus on differences in pay, promotions, pay raises, and performance reviews. Race-based differences in these areas were at the center of litigation against Merrill Lynch and gender-based differences were the issue at Bank of America. These companies settled with the plaintiffs for $160 million and $39 million, respectively.[54] Of course, these cases are very costly for the company not only in terms of legal expenses, but also in terms of, unfavorable publicity, employee relations, and the allocation of time away from the core business. Organizations that can successfully be proactive in maintaining compliance increase their chances of avoiding such litigation.

These types of settlements are the result of class action lawsuits. A class action lawsuit is "any civil case in which parties indicated their intent to sue on behalf of themselves as well as others not specifically named in the suit at some point prior to the final resolution of the matter."[55] Employment-related class action lawsuits such as those that pertain to EEO/discrimination can be very costly to employers because they can include large numbers of potential plaintiffs (employees, former employees, potential employees). These potential plaintiffs can potentially be included as part of the class without contacting them in advance. Instead, they can be given the opportunity to opt out in the event the lead plaintiffs prevail in court or reach a settlement with the employer. (FLSA lawsuits differ.)[56] Such settlements typically include back pay (pay that would have received absent discrimination) for each member of the class. The bigger the class, the bigger the potential cost to the employer. Clearly, a key issue in class actions is the definition of the class. The easier it is to include large numbers of potential plaintiffs, the more potential liability the employer faces and the bigger the potential payoff for plaintiffs (and their attorneys). Rule 23 of the Federal Rules of Civil Procedure and 29 U.S.C. § 216(b) provide the requirements for forming a class and one requirement is a commonality of interests.[57] A 2011 U.S. Supreme Court decision in Walmart Stores, Inc. v. Dukes, et al. made it more difficult for plaintiffs to certify a class of potential plaintiffs. The Supreme Court "reversed a class certification decision that joined the claims of 1.5 million female salaried and hourly employees who held any number of positions across Walmart's 3,400 stores because the plaintiffs could not articulate a common question that was capable of common answers as to the entire class. The Supreme Court ruled that the plaintiffs were required to demonstrate that Walmart operated under a 'general policy of discrimination,' which it concluded was 'entirely absent' [in the evidence presented in the case]."[58] Some experts believe the

Walmart ruling has already resulted in employers more aggressively challenging class action lawsuits and similarly in employers being less willing to settle such lawsuits to avoid litigation.[59] However, there is also evidence that plaintiffs and their attorneys are using new approaches to satisfy Rule 23 class action requirements and it is perhaps noteworthy that the Merrill Lynch settlement of a class action discrimination lawsuit for $160 million (see above) came after the Walmart decision.[60]

Another added impediment to bringing a class action lawsuit is a new strategy by employers to not only require employees to agree to resolve their individual employment discrimination complaints via arbitration (versus legal action), but to also require them to agree to give up their right to pursue their complaints as part of a class action lawsuit. (In return for waiving such a right, the employer must provide something in return referred to as "consideration.") Employers prefer arbitration because it is faster and cheaper, especially so if it can be used in lieu of costly class action litigation. At present, the law is not clear on whether such waivers are legal. The National Labor Relations Board has ruled that workers cannot be required to give up their right to be part of a class action lawsuit. However, another view is that a 2011 Supreme Court ruling (in a nonemployment context), AT&T Mobility v. Concepcion, can be applied to employment law to permit use of such waivers. Companies such as Sears, Nordstrom, Uber, and Haliburton are doing so and more generally, the use of such waivers is reported to have increased dramatically since the 2011 Supreme Court decision.[61]

Although class action lawsuits may provide more challenging to mount for plaintiffs, the passage in 2009 of the Lilly Ledbetter Fair Pay Act is expected to further increase the compliance challenge for employers. The statute of limitations for filing a claim of discrimination is within 180 days (300 days in states with their own equal employment opportunity agencies) of the date of the alleged discriminatory employment practice. Lilly Ledbetter's claim was made after she left her job as a supervisor in a tire plant and was based on the lasting effects of compensation decisions she alleged to be discriminatory that were made as much as 19 years earlier, far outside the 180 day period. In 2007, the Supreme Court ruled (*Ledbetter v. Goodyear Tire & Rubber Company*) that such decisions could not be litigated because they were outside the statute of limitations. However, the 2009 Act overturns this rule, instead stating that discrimination occurs—and starts the 180/300-day time period for filing a claim— "each time a discriminatory paycheck is issued, not just when the employer makes an adverse pay-setting decision."[62] According to the EEOC, "The Act restores the pre-Ledbetter position of the EEOC that each paycheck that delivers discriminatory compensation is a wrong which is actionable under the federal EEO statutes, regardless of when the discrimination began."[63] It has been argued that "employers will likely be called upon to defend against actions and decisions made by retired managers and supervisors that occurred years, and even decades, ago."[64]

Court cases have established two theories of discrimination behavior under Title VII: (1) **disparate treatment** and (2) **disparate impact.**

Disparate Treatment

Disparate or unequal treatment applies different standards to different employees: For example, asking women but not men if they plan to have children. In Japan, for example, women college students continue to report that recruiters ask them different questions than are asked of male college students. The mere fact of unequal treatment may be taken as evidence of the employer's intention to discriminate under U.S. law. In the pay context, an example would be requiring a woman to have higher performance than a man to be promoted to a higher paying job.

Disparate Impact

Practices that have a differential effect on members of protected groups are illegal, unless the differences are work-related. The major case that established this interpretation of Title VII is *Griggs v. Duke Power Co.*, which struck down employment tests and educational requirements that screened out a higher proportion of blacks than whites. Even though the practices were applied equally—both blacks and whites had to pass the tests—they were prohibited because (1) they had the consequence of excluding a protected group disproportionately and (2) the tests were not related to the jobs in question.

Under disparate impact, whether or not the employer intended to discriminate is irrelevant. A personnel decision can, on its face, seem neutral, but if its results are unequal, the employer must demonstrate that the decision is work-related. The two standards of discrimination—disparate treatment versus disparate impact—remain difficult to apply to pay issues, since pay differences are legal for dissimilar work. It is still not clear what constitutes pay discrimination in dissimilar jobs in the United States.[65]

EXECUTIVE ORDER 11246

Enforced by the Office of Federal Contracts Compliance Programs (OFCCP), Department of Labor, Executive Order 11246 (E.O. 11246) prohibits discrimination on the basis of race, color, religion, sex, or national origin. It requires covered government contractors to file affirmative action plans, which have three parts. First, utilization analysis compares the contractor's workforce to the available external workforce. Underutilization exists if a group (e.g., women) represents a significantly smaller percentage of the employer's workforce than of the external workforce. Second, goals and timetables are developed for achieving affirmative action. Third, action steps are developed for achieving these goals and timetables. As discussed below, the OFCCP conducts audits and seeks remedies where it finds insufficient compliance.

Here we focus specifically on the steps in the OFCCP's compliance review process as it applies to compensation.[66] It begins with a selection of contractors based, in part, on a mathematical model, called the Federal Contractor Selection System (FCSS), which is intended to predict the likelihood that a contractor is engaging in systemic (i.e., affecting a broad class of employees) discrimination. (Under a 1999 Memorandum of Understanding with the EEOC, individual complaints of compensation discrimination can be referred to the EEOC.) The OFCCP also selects contractors based on other factors (e.g., time since their previous review) and selects some contractors at random. In recent years, about 5 percent of all contractors have been selected for review.

If selected, the first step is a desk audit. The OFCCP will notify the employer that it is conducting an audit and will instruct the employer to provide complete information on its Affirmative Action Program and all supporting personnel activity (such as hiring, promotion decisions) and compensation data within 30 days. This is "analyzed for possible systemic discrimination indicators (i.e., a potential affected class of 10 or more applicants/workers)."[67] If such indicators are found, additional information for the desk audit will be requested. After the desk audit is completed, if the OFCCP decides the employer is in compliance, it ends the process by issuing a closure letter.

The OFCCP has also recently proposed an additional source of data for it to target its enforcement efforts. Currently, as Exhibit 17.7 indicates, employers who are federal contractors and subcontractors are required to file EEO-1 forms, which report the number of employees by sex, race, and ethnicity in each of nine job categories. The OFCCP has now proposed a new requirement requiring employers to additionally report compensation and hours worked in addition to the number of employees in those categories. It refers to the new report as the Equal Pay Report and it states that it will use this new report to help it target its compliance efforts.[68]

If the OFCCP believes systemic discrimination may be present, it conducts an onsite review, where it will delve deeper into statistical analyses of data (including using multiple regression analysis) and also conduct interviews with management and nonmanagement employees for "anecdotal evidence" to consider along with statistical evidence.[69] Based on its statistical analyses and anecdotal evidence, the OFCCP will decide whether there is evidence of systemic discrimination. If so, it will issue a Notice of Violation (NOV). Up until 2013, it would not, "except in unusual cases," rely *only* on statistical evidence.[70] However, that and other aspects of the investigative process have been revised (see below). If an NOV is issued, the OFCCP will seek to have the employer sign a conciliation agreement under which it agrees to stop and remedy practices identified as discriminatory. The employer may also be required to change its compensation levels for some employee groups to remedy disparities between similarly situated employees that the OFCCP judges to be the result of systemic discrimination. If the OFCCP cannot reach a settlement with the employer, it can refer the case to the Office of the Solicitor and disputes are addressed in a hearing in front of an administrative law judge. The OFCCP can also seek to disbar contractors from receiving future contracts from the government or to stop payments on current contracts.

In 2013, the OFCCP rescinded its previous (issued in 2006) standards for evaluating evidence of systemic pay discrimination, stating that these former standards "restrict[ed] OFCCP's ability to enforce the Executive Order's nondiscrimination mandate."[71] The OFCCP issued new standards (Directive 307)[72] giving it more "flexibility," which it argued was "critical because discrimination may be difficult to identify." Although some forms of pay discrimination "can be easy to spot," such as paying men and women in the same job and with the same performance differently, other forms may be more "complex." An example would be "a practice of discriminating against African-American sales workers in handing out territory assignments—so that no matter how well they perform, they can never have the same earnings opportunities as their white counterparts." The OFCCP goes on to state that "Title VII addresses all forms of compensation differences, including those that come from channeling a favored group into the better paying entry level jobs with better long-term opportunities, or where glass ceilings or other unfair promotion practices wrongly block advancement of talented workers on the basis of illegal criteria like race or gender. And even where base wages or salaries are fair, discrimination in access to overtime, or higher paying shifts, or bonuses, can add up to unequal take home pay in violation of federal civil rights law." Thus, under its new rules (Directive 307), the OFCCP will examine a broader range of employment practices than previously. See Exhibit 17.9 for more detailed examples of possible discriminatory practices that will receive increased scrutiny.

Most companies already have their hands full managing relationships with customers, investors, and suppliers. An onsite visit by an OFCCP compliance investigator can mean that at least some HR employees will be forced to put their work in managing employee relationships on hold and instead deal with the compliance review. Outside legal counsel may be necessary, which can be costly. If a NOV is issued, the company will face further challenges. So, what can a company do to avoid running afoul of E.O. 11246 and the OFCCP?

The simple answer is: Don't discriminate. The somewhat more complex answer is don't discriminate *and* collect and analyze data to document that you are not. In fact, self-evaluation by employers is actually required.[73] As with any analysis that can be seen as relevant to deciding whether an employer has engaged in or is engaging in discrimination, care must be taken to minimize legal risks. Obviously, obtaining prompt legal counsel is necessary. For the analyses to be privileged (and not open to discovery, for example, by a plaintiff's attorney in possible future litigation), they should be done under the direction of an attorney and strict communication protocols must be followed.[74]

EXHIBIT 17.9   Examples of Employment Discrimination to Avoid, Directive 307, OFCCP

Type of Difference	Basis for Comparison of Employees	Examples of Differences
Differences in Salary or Hourly Rate	Similar job, different pay	Hispanic customer service agents are paid less than white employees in the same or similar positions due to highly subjective salary system.
Differences in Job Assignment or Placement	Similar qualifications, different job	Women hired into entry-level grocery store positions are disproportionately assigned to the bakery department. Men are assigned to the meat department where pay and promotion opportunities are better.
Differences in Training or Advancement Opportunities	Similar job, different opportunities to increase skills	Employees may participate in a management training program on a recommendation by a manager. Certain managers are referring only white males resulting in disproportionate participation. Resulting promotions to management positions are disproportionately awarded to white males.
Differences in Earnings Opportunities	Similar job, different earnings	African-American sales workers are disproportionately assigned to territories with less potential.
Differences in Access to Increases and Add-Ons	Similar job, different opportunities to increase pay	Female lawyers who get exactly the same base pay as male counterparts earn less on annual bonuses.

PAY DISCRIMINATION AND DISSIMILAR JOBS

In 1981, the Supreme Court, in *Gunther v. County of Washington,* determined that pay differences for dissimilar jobs may reflect discrimination. In this case, four jail matrons in Washington County, Oregon, claimed that their work was comparable to that performed by male guards. The matrons also were assigned clerical duties, because guarding the smaller number of female prisoners did not occupy all of the work time.

Lower courts said the matrons had no grounds because the jobs did not meet the equal work requirement of the Equal Pay Act. But the Supreme Court stated that a Title VII pay case was not bound by the definitions in the Equal Pay Act. While the Supreme Court did not say that Washington County had discriminated, it did say that a claim of wage discrimination could also be brought under Title VII for situations where the jobs were not the same. Unfortunately, the Court did not say what might constitute evidence of pay discrimination in dissimilar jobs. The case was returned to a lower court for additional evidence of discrimination and was eventually settled out of court.

So if jobs are dissimilar and if no pattern of discrimination in hiring, promotion, or other personnel decisions exists, then what constitutes pay discrimination? Courts have ruled on the use of market data as well as the use of job evaluation. We will look at both of these possible standards in turn.

Evidence of Discrimination: Use of Market Data

In a landmark case regarding the use of market data, Denver nurse Mary Lemons claimed that her job, held predominantly by women, was illegally paid less than the city and county of Denver paid jobs held predominantly by men (tree trimmers, sign painters, tire servicemen, etc.). Lemons claimed that the nursing job required more education and skill. Therefore, to pay the male jobs more than the nurses' jobs simply because the male jobs commanded higher rates in the local labor market was discriminatory. She argued that the market reflected historical underpayment of "women's work." The court disagreed. The situation identified by *Lemons*—pay differences in dissimilar jobs—did not by itself constitute proof of intent to discriminate.

The courts continue to uphold use of market data to justify pay differences for different jobs. *Spaulding v. University of Washington* developed the argument in greatest detail. In this case, the predominantly female faculty members of the Department of Nursing claimed that they were illegally paid less than faculty in other departments. They presented a model of faculty pay comparisons in "comparable" departments that controlled for the effects of level of education, job tenure, and other factors. They asserted that any pay difference not accounted for in their model was discrimination.

But the courts have been dubious of this statistical approach. As the late Carl Sagan used to say, "Just because it's a light doesn't make it a spaceship." Far better to define discrimination directly, rather than concluding that it is "whatever is left." The judge in the *Spaulding* case criticized the statistical model presented, saying it "unrealistically assumed the equality of all master's degrees, ignored job experience prior to university employment, and ignored detailed analysis of day-to-day responsibilities." Without such data, "we have no meaningful way of determining just how much of the proposed wage differential was due to sex and how much was due to academic discipline." "Market prices," according to the judge, "are inherently job-related."

It is interesting to ask whether this judge's level of confidence in the objectivity of "the market" is justified. As you recall from Chapter 8, a lot of judgment goes into the wage survey process.[75] Which employers constitute the "relevant market"? Does the relevant market vary by occupation? Do different market definitions yield different wage patterns? Clearly, judgment is involved in answering these questions. Yet the courts have thus far largely neglected to examine those judgments for possible bias.

Evidence of Discrimination: Jobs of Comparable Worth

Comparable Worth: Overview

A second approach to determining pay discrimination on jobs of dissimilar content hinges on finding a standard by which to compare the value of jobs. The standard must do two things. First, it must permit jobs with dissimilar content to be declared equal or "in some sense comparable."[76] Second, it must permit pay differences for dissimilar jobs that are not comparable. Job evaluation has become that standard.[77] If an employer's own job evaluation study shows that jobs of dissimilar content are of equal value to the employer (equal total job evaluation points), then isn't failure to pay them equally proof of intent to discriminate? That was the issue considered in *AFSCME v. State of Washington,* where the state commissioned a study of the concept of comparable worth (discussed later in this chapter) and its projected effect on the state's pay system. The study concluded that by basing wages on the external market, the state was paying women approximately 20 percent less than it was paying men in jobs deemed of comparable value to the state. The state took no action on this finding, alleging it could not afford to adjust wages, so the American Federation of State, County, and Municipal Employees (AFSCME) sued the state. The union alleged that since the state was aware of the adverse effect of its present policy, failure to change the policy constituted discrimination.

But an appeals court ruled that the state was not obligated to correct the disparity. Even though the state had commissioned the study, it had not agreed to implement the study's results. Therefore, the employer had not, in the court's view, admitted that the jobs were equal or established a pay system that purported to pay on the basis of comparable worth rather than markets. Rather than appeal, the parties settled out of court. The state revamped its pay system and agreed to make more than $100 million in "pay equity" adjustments.

Since this case, many public employers have undertaken "pay equity studies" to assess the "gender neutrality" of pay systems. In states and cities which enacted comparable-worth legislation for public employees, the results of these studies are used to adjust pay for jobs held predominantly by woman. In other places the results become part of the give and take of collective bargaining. We return to issues of pay equity and comparable worth later in the chapter where we discuss the mechanics of implementing these policies.

The state of Washington conducted a study that concluded that the job of a licensed practical nurse required skill, effort, and responsibility equal to that of a campus police officer. The campus police officer was paid, on average, one-and-a-half times what the state paid the licensed practical nurse.[78]

In Ontario, Canada, jobs that were deemed comparable based on numerical scores displayed a similar disparity in pay. A chief librarian made $35,050, while a dairy herd improvement manager made $38,766. A computer operations supervisor made $20,193, while a forestry project supervisor made $26,947. A typist made $10,531, while a sailor made $14,097. It is this type of wage difference between jobs judged in some sense to be comparable that is controversial. The notion of comparable worth says that if jobs require comparable skill, effort, and responsibility, the pay must be comparable, no matter how dissimilar the job content may be. (In Canada and the European Union, comparable worth is called *gender equity*.) Consider the experience of Bell Canada and its unions. After lawyers spent over a decade disputing the quality and results of a pay equity study, Bell Canada agreed to a $104 million ($91.5 million American) settlement. The point job evaluation plan used in the study to determine pay equity is not being used in the contemporary workplace in Bell's operations.[79]

Comparable-worth proponents in the United States continue to lobby for either new legislation or voluntary action on the part of employers that would include the comparable-worth standard. A lot of this political activity is occurring in state and local governments. This is not surprising, since over half of all women in the workforce are employed in the public sector.

The Mechanics

Establishing a comparable-worth plan typically involves the following four basic steps:

1. *Adopt a single "gender neutral" point job evaluation plan for all jobs within a unit.* If employees are unionized, separate plans have been prepared for each bargaining unit and take precedence over previous agreements. The key to a comparable-worth system is a single job evaluation plan for jobs with dissimilar content. What a "gender neutral" point job evaluation plan is remains open to debate. Advocates of all persuasions offer often conflicting advice, and there is little research to provide guidance. Some advocates try to distinguish between "gender neutral" and "traditional" point job evaluation.[80] Close reading reveals that "traditional" refers to practices dating back 50 years that do not reflect contemporary point plan practices.

2. *All jobs with equal job evaluation results should be paid the same.* Although each factor in the job evaluation may not be equal, if the total points are equal, the wage rates must also be equal.

3. *Identify the percentages of male and female employees in each job group.* A job group is defined as a group of positions with similar duties and responsibilities that require similar qualifications, are filled by similar recruiting procedures, and are paid under the same pay schedule. Typically, a female-dominated job group is defined as having 60 percent or more female incumbents; a male-dominated job group has 70 percent or more male incumbents.

4. *The wage-to-job evaluation point ratio should be based on the wages paid for male-dominated jobs* since they are presumed to be the best estimate of nondiscriminatory wages.

EXHIBIT 17.10
Job Evaluation
Points and
Salary

• Female-dominated jobs
○ Male-dominated jobs

These steps are based on the state of Minnesota's law that mandates comparable worth for all public-sector employees (e.g., the state, cities, school districts, libraries). Canadian federal and provincial labour departments have also published detailed guidance on procedures.[81]

To understand the mechanics more clearly, consider Exhibit 17.10. The solid dots represent jobs held predominantly by women (i.e., 60% or more employees are female). The circles represent jobs held predominantly by men (i.e., 70% or more employees are men). The policy line (solid) for the women's jobs is below the policy line (dotted) for men's jobs. A comparable-worth policy uses the results of the single job evaluation plan and prices all jobs as if they were male-dominated jobs (dotted line). Thus, all jobs with 100 job points receive $600; all those with 200 points receive $800, and so on.

Market rates for male-dominated jobs are used to convert the job evaluation points to salaries. The point-to-salaries ratio of male-dominated jobs is then applied to female-dominated jobs.

However, a mandated job evaluation, especially a single point plan that specifies a hierarchy of all jobs, seems counter to the direction in which most organizations are moving today. A partner of Hay Associates observed:

> We, ourselves, do not know of a single case where a large and diverse organization in the private sector concluded that a single job evaluation method, with the same compensable factors and weightings, was appropriate for its factory, office, professional, management, technical, and executive personnel in all profit center divisions and all staff departments.[82]

People who advocate a point job evaluation plan as a vehicle for comparable worth credit the technique with more explanatory power than it possesses. Nevertheless, the comparable worth debate lives on.

Union Developments

The amount of union support for comparable worth appears to be related to its effects on the union's membership. AFSCME and the Communication Workers of America (CWA) actively support comparable worth and have negotiated comparable-worth-based pay increases, lobbied for legislation, filed legal suits, and attempted to educate their members and the public about comparable worth. The public sector faces little competition for its services and is frequently better able to absorb a wage increase, since public employees are in a better position to pressure lawmakers than are taxpayers. This probably accounts for the relative success of public employees' unions in bargaining comparable-worth pay adjustments. But tradeoffs between higher wages and fewer jobs make unions in industries facing stiff international competition (e.g., the International Ladies' Garment Workers' Union and the United Auto Workers) reluctant to aggressively support comparable worth.

The beauty of "equity adjustments," from a union's perspective, is that because they are a separate budget item, they do not appear to come at the expense of overall pay increases for all union members. Collective bargaining has produced more comparable-worth pay increases than any other approach.[83]

EARNINGS GAPS

Exhibit 17.11 shows that, across all races combined and limiting the analysis to full-time, year round workers, women's median annual earnings compared to men's has changed from about 60 percent to 78 percent from 1980 to 2013. The wage gap between men and women varies according to wage level, being relatively large at very high wages and even larger at very low wage levels. Since the 1990s, the gap at the top narrowed slightly, due mostly to education gains by women. The gap at the bottom narrowed more, mostly due to increases in overall years worked and years worked with current employer by women.[84]

EXHIBIT 17.11
Women's Median Earnings as a Percentage of Men's Median Earnings, Full-Time, Year-Round Workers, 1980–2010

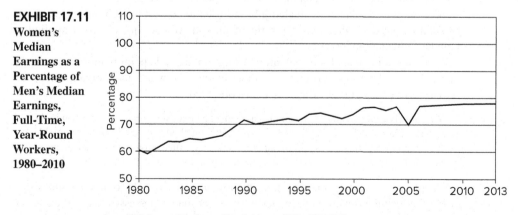

Source: U.S. Bureau of the Census, Historical Income Tables, Table P-40.

EXHIBIT 17.12
Asian, Black,
and Hispanic
Median Men's
Earnings as
a Percentage
of White,
Non-Hispanic
Median Men's
Earnings,
Full-time, Year-
Round Workers,
1987–2010

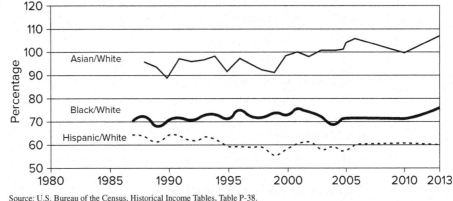

Source: U.S. Bureau of the Census, Historical Income Tables, Table P-38.

In 2013, median earnings of white, non-Hispanic men were $51,865 and of white, non-Hispanic women, $40,270. Exhibit 17.12 shows that Asian men's earnings compared to white men's varied between 89 and 107 percent during 1988 to 2013. Black to white men's earning ratios varied between about 68 to 76 percent, and the ratio of Hispanic to white men's earnings varied from about 55 to 61 percent. Exhibit 17.13 compares earnings of Asian, black, and Hispanic women to white women.

Hispanics are consistently at the bottom, for both men and women. Asian women earn more than white women (Exhibit 17.13), perhaps in part because a larger percentage of Asian women have a bachelor's degree or. The gap between black and white women is less than the gap between black and white men, again perhaps partly because of education differences, as black women are more likely than black men to have a college degree.[85]

EXHIBIT 17.13
Asian, Black,
and Hispanic
Median
Women's
Earnings as
a Percentage
of White,
Non-Hispanic
Median
Women's
Earnings,
Full-Time,
Year-Round
Workers,
1987–2010

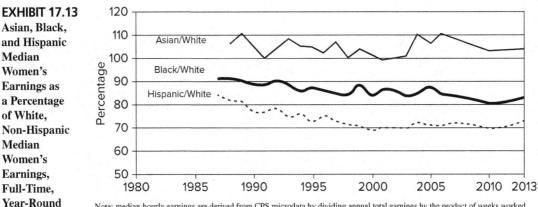

Note: median hourly earnings are derived from CPS microdata by dividing annual total earnings by the product of weeks worked during the year and hours usually worked per week. Earnings tabulations are restricted to those working at least 20 hours a week and 8 weeks a year.

Source: U.S. Bureau of the Census, Historical Income Tables, Table P-38.

What do we know about why these gaps exist? Some of the more important sources, shown in Exhibit 17.14, include the following:

- Work/occupation differences
- Work-related behavior
- Labor market conditions
- Firm/industry differences
- Union differences
- Discrimination

Let us first examine some data and then some conflicting beliefs.

Sources of the Earnings Gaps

Considerable research has examined the factors shown in Exhibit 17.14, which are the central sources of the wage differences between men and women and the racial/ethnic groups. The issue, especially any proposed remedies, continues to generate research and debate. Our reading of the recent research is that the primary sources contributing to the gender gap differ from the primary sources for the race/ethnic gaps. It appears that differences in the work/occupation (e.g., technician vs. clerical) and differences in work-related behaviors (e.g., work-life balance challenges) are central to understanding

EXHIBIT 17.14
Sources of
Earnings Gaps

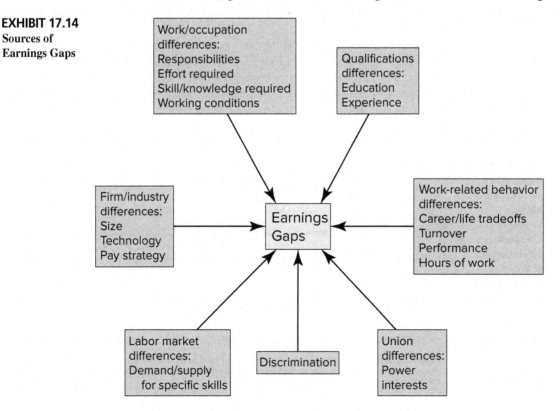

the remaining gender wage gaps.[86] In contrast, differences in qualifications, especially educational levels and work-related experience as well as differences in occupations, are important sources of the gaps for both blacks and Hispanics compared to white men.[87]

Differences in Occupations and Qualifications

There is evidence that women of all ethnic groups are more likely than men to seek part-time and flexible work arrangements and that they are more likely than men to interrupt their careers due to family responsibilities.[88] There is also evidence that gender differences in occupational choices and preferences continue to exist.[89] For every 100 women who earn bachelor's degrees today, 73 men do.[90] However, men are more likely to enroll, graduate, and continue working in engineering and certain scientific specialties, though women's enrollment and graduation rates exceed men's in the biological sciences.

In the early 1970s, 53 percent of women workers were in administrative support (including clerical) and service occupations, compared to only 15 percent of men. At that time, less than one in five managers were women; professional women were frequently employed in traditionally female professions, such as nurse, teacher, dietitian, or librarian. Women were also underrepresented in blue-collar jobs, including higher-paying precision production and craft occupations. In 1960, almost half of the women who graduated from college became teachers, while today less than 10 percent do so. Today, the number of women in managerial jobs is at parity with men. Despite progress, one notable concern (in addition to overall unexplained pay gaps) remains: lack of representation of women in executive and director level positions in organizations, sometimes referred to as the "Glass Ceiling" effect. Exhibit 17.15 shows how the representation of women declines at higher levels of organizations.

EXHIBIT 17.15
Representation of Women by Organization Level

Sources: Catalyst Research. Catalyst, *2011 Catalyst Census: Fortune 500 Women Executive Officers and Top Earners* (2011). Catalyst, *2011 Catalyst Census: Fortune 500 Women Board Directors* (2011). Bureau of Labor Statistics, "Table 18; Employed persons by detailed industry, sex, race, and Hispanic or Latino Ethnicity, 2011" (2012).

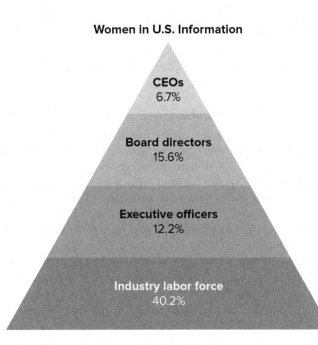

Women in U.S. Information

CEOs
6.7%

Board directors
15.6%

Executive officers
12.2%

Industry labor force
40.2%

Evidence of increased levels of occupational attainment does not automatically mean that the wage gap will close. A study of women in science and engineering finds that even though they have already cleared the hurdles of the occasional misguided high school guidance counselor and/or lack of peer support or role models, women scientists and engineers are almost twice as likely to leave these occupations as are males.[91]

For a variety of reasons, a relatively small wage gap among younger cohorts (i.e., recent college graduates) tends to increase as the cohort ages. Perhaps women continue to be more likely to drop out of the labor force at some point for family reasons, or perhaps the barriers to continued advancement become more substantial (the Glass Ceiling concept) at higher levels in the **job hierarchy**.[92]

One reviewer of all this research conjectures that some of the observed differences in wages paid in different occupations may be stuck due to inertia or, more poetically, "original sin."[93] Wage differences among occupations were determined decades ago. While a variety of reasons account for these original wage differences, an important one is the belief about gender roles and "women's work" that prevailed at the time. These pay differences have persisted and influence today's occupational wage structures even though attitudes have changed.[94]

Level of schooling and work-related experience appear to be primary sources of the pay gaps among both black and Hispanic men and women. Almost half of Hispanic men have not completed high school and only 9 percent are college graduates.[95] This may be due to the considerable differences in continuing immigration among Hispanics. Generally, the longer Hispanic immigrants stay in the United States, the better they do educationally and financially. However, the continuing inflow of poorly educated new immigrants holds down the average wage for the whole category. Black men's high school dropout rates match those of Hispanic men. In contrast, more than half of Asian men are college graduates or hold higher degrees. All this research and discussion about sources of the earnings gaps does not mean there are not any discriminatory pay practices; it does mean that important sources of the pay gaps reside in other productivity-related factors such as level and quality of education, work-life/career tradeoffs, and occupational choices.

Differences in Industries and Firms

Other factors that affect earnings differences among men and women and among race/ethnic groups are the industries and the firms in which they are employed. A study of middle-aged lawyers revealed large differences between men and women lawyers in the types of firms that employed them. Men were much more likely than women to be in private practice and to be at large firms (over 50 lawyers). They were much *less* likely than women to be in the lower-paying nonprofit sector. Clearly, these differences are related to pay: the most highly paid legal positions are in private-practice law firms; the larger the law firm, the greater the average rate of pay.[96] There also may be different promotion opportunities among firms within the same industry.[97]

Differences in the firm's compensation policies within a specific industry is another factor that accounts for some of the earnings gap.[98] As noted in Chapters 7 and 8, some firms within an industry adopt pay strategies that place them among the leaders in their industry; other firms adopt policies that may offer more work-life balance benefits compared to cash compensation. The unknown here is whether *within an industry* some firms are more likely to attract women or minorities than other firms because of these pay-mix differences and whether this has any effect on earnings gaps.

Within a firm, differences in policies for different jobs may even exist. For example, many firms tie pay for secretaries to the pay for the manager to whom the secretary is assigned. The rationale is that the secretary and the manager function as a team. When the manager gets promoted, the secretary also takes on additional responsibilities and therefore also gets a raise. However, this traditional approach breaks down when layers of management are cut. When IBM went through a major restructuring a few years back, it cut pay by up to 36 percent for secretaries who had been assigned to managerial levels that no longer existed. IBM justified the cuts by saying the rates were way above the market.

We also know that the size of a firm is systematically related to differences in wages. Female employment is more heavily concentrated in small firms. Wages of men in large firms are 54 percent higher than wages of men in small firms. The gap was 37 percent for women in small versus large firms. Hispanic men are concentrated in construction and service firms. Other studies report that employees in some jobs can get a pay increase of about 20 percent simply by switching industries in the same geographic area while performing basically similar jobs.[99] Nevertheless, a recent study concludes that this pay premium associated with changing jobs is enjoyed primarily by white males. Women and minorities who were MBA graduates from five universities did not obtain the same pay increases as their white male classmates when they switched jobs.[100]

To the extent that these differences in job setting are the result of an individual's preference or disposition, they are not evidence of discrimination. To the extent that these differences are the result of industry and firm practices that steer women and minorities into certain occupations and industries or lower-paying parts of a profession, they may reflect discrimination.

Challenges in Estimating Amount of Discrimination

We know that many factors affect pay and that discrimination can be one of them. Disagreement remains over what constitutes evidence of discrimination. Although the earnings gap is the most frequently cited example, closer inspection reveals the weaknesses in this statistic. Unfortunately, many studies of the earnings gap have little relevance to understanding discrimination in pay-setting practices within organizations. Some studies use aggregated data—for instance, treating all bachelor's degrees as the same, or defining an occupation too broadly (e.g., the U.S. Department of Labor categorizes LeBron James as well as the basketball game timekeeper in the same occupation—"sports professional"). Another problem is that mere possession of a qualification or skill does not mean it is work-related. Examples of cab drivers, secretaries, and house painters with college degrees are numerous.

A standard statistical approach for determining whether discrimination explains part of the gap is to try to relate pay differences to the factors discussed above (occupation, type of work, experience, education, and the like). The procedure typically regresses some measure of earnings on those factors thought to legitimately influence earnings. If the average wage of men with a given set of values for these factors is significantly different from the average wage of women with equal factors, then the residual portion of the gap is considered discrimination. Unfortunately, in a sample limited to white males, such an approach explained only 60 to 70 percent of their earnings. So statistical studies, by themselves, are not sufficient evidence of discrimination.[101]

---

e-Compensation

You can track legal issues and read transcripts of Supreme Court decisions at *www.law.cornell.edu*. Many states have their own web pages that include their compensation legislation. What information is available from your state? Compare the pay discrimination legislation in your state with another state's. What might explain these differences? Are there any unique characteristics of your state (e.g., unique industries, extent of unionization, etc.)?

Even if legitimate factors fully explain gender, ethnic, and racial group pay differences, discrimination still could have occurred. The factors shown in Exhibit 17.14 themselves may be tainted by discrimination. For example, construction laborers in California are mainly Hispanic males. A slowing of the housing market will disproportionately affect them. So, measurable factors may underestimate the effects of past discrimination. Statistical analysis needs to be treated as part of a pattern of evidence and needs to reflect the wage behaviors of specific firms.

Gaps Are Global

The gender wage gap is fairly universal. However, in a number of countries, the size of the gap is smaller than in the United States.[102] One analysis concludes that the difference can be found in narrower pay structures in European countries. In many countries, as the global guide in Chapter 16 suggests, rates negotiated by federations of employers, unions, and government agencies rather than individual companies and employees mean a narrower range of pay rates for each job, as well as smaller differences between jobs.[103]

Earlier chapters have emphasized the wide range of pay rates in the U.S. market for any job. More centralized wage decision making permits a pay gap to be closed by political/institutional fiat. Multinational companies operating in different nations face wide differences in how wages are influenced by varying social policies and regulations.

COMPLIANCE: A PROACTIVE APPROACH

Compliance with laws and regulations can be a constraint and/or an opportunity for a compensation manager. The regulatory environment certainly constrains the decisions that can be made. Once laws are passed and regulations published, employers must comply. But a proactive compensation manager can influence the nature of regulations and their interpretation. Astute professionals must be aware of legislative and judicial currents to protect both employers' and employees' interests and to ensure that compensation practices conform to judicial interpretation.

How can a compensation manager best undertake these efforts? First, join professional associations to stay informed on emerging issues and to act in concert to inform and influence public and legislative opinion. Second, constantly review compensation practices and their results. Be sure to consult with legal counsel in doing so, as attorney-client privilege and protection of work product are important issues to understand prior to conducting analyses on an organization's compliance. The fair treatment of all employees is the goal of a good pay system, and that is the same goal of legislation. When interpretations of what is fair treatment differ, informed public discussion is required. Such discussion cannot occur without the input of informed managers.

Your **Turn**   From Barista to Manager

You work at an upscale coffee shop that is part of a nationwide chain of 200 such stores. You started as a barista, but then you moved up. Your title is now store manager. You are expected to work 55 hours per week. Your boss says you need to be in the store to get to know the customers and because, well, you are the manager. It is up to you to make sure everything runs smoothly and that there is a great customer experience, which translates into growth in store sales volume and store profit. By the way, however many hours you work, you get paid for 40 hours only (and no overtime pay) because . . . that's right, you are the manager.

However, as you think about how you spend your time at the store, you can't help but feel that a lot of your time seems to be spent on things that don't seem much like "management" to you—making coffee drinks, checking supplies, and sometimes cleaning bathrooms. So, this is the life of a manager. It seems a lot like being a barista, except that you work a lot more hours, have more responsibility, and you don't get paid all that much more. You do spend some time on training other employees and you interview job applicants. But, the district manager is around a lot and she seems to have her own ideas on who to hire most of the time and how to run the store. Plus, there are pretty clear corporate guidelines to be followed on how to run many aspects of the store.

The more you think about it, the more you think that it sure would be nice to get paid for working 55 hours. In fact, you have friends who work in other businesses and when they work over 40 hours in a week, they get time and a half for the hours beyond 40. That sounds awfully good. If you are going to spend all of your time at work, it would be nice to at least get paid what you deserve for it.

Now, "switch hats" and look at it from the company point of view. Is this company running afoul of the Fair Labor Standards Act (FLSA)? Refer back to our discussion earlier in this chapter. Would this company be able to document that the store managers are exempt from the FLSA (not to mention similar state laws)? Also, what would it cost to re-classify your store managers as nonexempt? If managers feel overworked and underpaid, what do you project that they will do when the economy picks back up? Is that a concern for the company? Is the company in compliance with the FLSA? What would it cost to have a lawsuit filed against the company? Have other companies in your industry (e.g., Starbucks, Caribou, Peet's, etc.) had any FLSA issues? If so, what can you learn from their experiences? Would you advise meeting with corporate counsel? What facts and observations would you recommend be presented at such a meeting?

Still Your **Turn**

"I Was Gaga's Slave"

The above headline, "I was Gaga's slave," appeared in the *New York Post*. Pop superstar Lady Gaga, whose real name is Stefani Germanotta, employed Jennifer O'Neill as a personal assistant for 13 months. Ms. O'Neill is suing Gaga's touring company, Mermaid Touring, in the United States District Court for the Southern District of New York, alleging violations of the FLSA and New York State Labor Law (NYSLL).

Ms. O'Neill, 41, who was paid $75,000 per year, reported that she had to cater to the 25-year-old Gaga's every whim, whether it was related to schedule, finances, or food, at any hour of the day or night. Ms. O'Neill worked for Gaga both in New York City (at her Upper West Side duplex) and also on the Monster Ball world tour, where she assisted Gaga in a variety of settings, including "stadiums, private jets, fine hotel suites, yachts, ferries, trains and tour buses."

According to Court papers, Ms. O'Neill alleges that there were no breaks for meals "or, at times, even sleep," and that she was required to be on hand for anything the Grammy Award-winning singer needed, at her "earliest waking hour" or for "spontaneous, random matters in the middle of the night." One of Ms. O'Neill's tasks was "ensuring the availability of chosen outfits," a task of presumably considerable magnitude, given Gaga's unique approach to style (e.g., wearing a meat dress to the MTV Video Music Awards).

Ms. O'Neill alleges that she worked 6,656 hours of unpaid overtime over a period of 56 weeks. She is asking to be paid $359,956.48 for unpaid overtime. Along with this request for back pay, Ms. O'Neill, a graduate of American University, is also seeking unspecified damages.

A spokeswoman for Gaga branded the lawsuit "completely without merit."

QUESTIONS

1. Is Ms. O'Neill exempt or nonexempt under the Fair Labor Standards Act? Which exemption would be most relevant in this case? Conduct a search and describe how the lawsuit turned out.
2. Can you find any other examples in the news of similar lawsuits? If so, please again form an opinion on whether the plaintiff is exempt or not and which exemption is most relevant.[104]

Summary   Governments around the world play varying roles in the workplace. Legislation in any society reflects people's expectations about the role of government. Beyond direct regulation, government affects compensation through policies and purchases that affect labor supply and demand.

In the United States, legislation reflects the changing nature of work and the workforce. In the 1930s, legislation was concerned with correcting the harsh conditions and arbitrary treatment facing employees, including children. In the 1960s, legislation turned to the issue of equal opportunity. Such legislation has had a profound impact on all of U.S. society. Nevertheless, more progress to eliminate discrimination in the workplace, including pay discrimination, is required. Contemporary issues include treatment of the recent waves of immigrants. Recent attention has shifted to increasing the transparency of compensation for executives and accounting for stock options.

Pay discrimination laws require special attention for several reasons. First, these laws regulate the design and administration of pay systems. Second, the definition of pay discrimination and thus the approaches used to defend pay practices are in a state of flux, especially as employers increase their international operations. Many of the provisions of these laws simply require sound pay practices that should have been employed in the first place. Sound practices are those with three basic features:

1. They are work-related.
2. They are related to the mission of the enterprise.
3. They include an appeals process for employees who disagree with the results.

Achieving compliance with these laws rests in large measure on the shoulders of managers of compensation. It is their responsibility to ensure that the pay system is properly designed and managed.

The earnings gaps among various ethnic and racial groups for both women and men are attributable to many factors. The sources of the gender gap appear to center on differences in work/occupational attainment and work-life challenges. The sources for blacks and Hispanics center on differences in educational levels, work-related experience, occupational attainment, and qualifications. Discrimination, whether access or valuation, is another factor. Others include market forces, industry and employer differences, and union bargaining priorities. Compensation managers need to constantly monitor pay practices to be sure that they are complying with regulations and are not discriminatory.

Is all this detail on interpretation of pay discrimination really necessary? Yes. Without understanding the interpretation of pay discrimination legislation, compensation managers risk violating the law, exposing their employers to considerable liability and expense, and losing the confidence and respect of all employees when a few are forced to turn to the courts to gain nondiscriminatory treatment.

Review Questions

1. What is the nature of government's role in compensation?
2. Explain why changes in minimum wage can affect higher-paid employees as well.
3. What is the difference between access discrimination and valuation discrimination?
4. Consider contemporary practices such as skill-competency-based plans, broad banding, market pricing, and pay-for-performance plans. Discuss how they may affect the pay discrimination debate.
5. What factors help account for the pay gap?
6. What kinds of proactive activities can an employer undertake to enhance the regulatory environment?

Endnotes

1. The job evaluation manual was introduced as evidence in *Electrical Workers (IUE) v. Westinghouse Electric Corp.,* 632 F.2d 1094, 23 FEP Cases 588 (3rd Cir. 1980), *cert. denied,* 452 U.S. 967, 25 FEP Cases 1835 (1981).

2. Philip M. Berkowitz, Anders Etgen Reitz, Thomas Müller-Bonanni, eds., *International Labor and Employment Law,* 2nd edition (Chicago, IL: American Bar Association, 2008); Organisation for Economic Co-operation and Development, "The Price of Prejudice: Labour Market Discrimination on the Grounds of Gender and Ethnicity," *OECD Employment Outlook 2008* (Paris, France: OECD, 2008), includes a survey of equal employment opportunity regulation across OECD countries; Richard A. Posthuma, Mark V. Roehling, and Michael A. Campion, "Applying U.S. Employment Discrimination Laws to International Employers: Advice for Scientists and Practitioners," *Personnel Psychology,* 59(3), 2006, pp. 705–739; The U.S. Equal Employment Opportunity Commission, "The Equal Employment Opportunity Responsibilities of Multinational Employers," *www.eeoc.gov/facts/multiemployers. html;* The U.S. Equal Employment Opportunity Commission. Employee Rights When Working for Multinational Employers, *www.eeoc.gov/facts/multiemployees.html.*

3. Bruce Kaufman, ed., *Government Regulation of the Employment Relationship* (Ithaca, NY: Cornell University Press, 1998); Arthur Gutman, *EEO Law and Personnel Practices,* 2d edition (Thousand Oaks, CA: Sage, 2000).

4. Francine D. Blau and Lawrence M. Kahn, *At Home and Abroad: U.S. Labor Market Performance in International Perspective* (Thousand Oaks, CA: Sage, 2001).

5. Lindblom, C. E., *Politics and Markets: The World's Political Economic Systems* (New York: Basic Books. Hall, 1977) pp. 161–169; P. A., and Soskice, D. (eds.), *Varieties of Capitalism: The Institutional Foundations of Comparative Advantage* (Oxford University Press, 2001).

6. U.S. Bureau of Labor Statistics, "The Employment Situation—February 2015." March 6, 2015. Table B-1. March 6, 2015. www.bls.gov.

7. Morris Kleiner, *Licensing Requirements: Ensuring Quality or Restricting Competition?* (Kalamazoo, MI: Upjohn, 2006).

8. OECD, "Migration Policy Debates. Is Migration Good for the Economy?" May 2014. www.oecd.org/migration.

9. *www.dol.gov/esa/minwage/America.htm* has an interactive map of the United States. Click on a state to find their minimum wage requirements.

10. Bureau of Labor Statistics, U.S. Department of Labor, "Characteristics of Minimum Wage Workers: 2011" March 2, 2012.

11. Economic Policy Institute, "Issue Guide on Minimum Wage," *www.epi.org.*

12. David Neumark and William L. Wascher, *Minimum Wages* (Cambridge, MA: MIT Press, 2008); Economic Policy Institute, "Issue Guide on Minimum Wage," 2008, *www.epi .org;* David Card and Alan Krueger, "Minimum Wages and Employment: A Case Study of the Fast-Food Industry in New Jersey and Pennsylvania," *American Economic Review,* September 1994, pp. 772–793; Lawrence F. Katz and Alan B. Krueger, "The Effect of the Minimum Wage on the Fast-Food Industry," *Industrial and Labor Relations Review* 46(1), October 1992, pp. 6–21; K. I. Simon and R. Kaestner, "Do Minimum Wages Affect Non-Wage Job Attributes? Evidence on Fringe Benefits," *Industrial and Labor Relations Review* 58(1), October 2004, pp. 52–70; Joseph Sabia, "Identifying Minimum Wage Effects: New Evidence from Monthly CPS Data," *Industrial Relations* 48 (2009), pp. 311–328; Hristos Doucouliagos and T. D. Stanley, "Publication Selection Bias in Minimum-Wage Research? A Meta-Regression Analysis," *British Journal of Industrial*

Relations 47 (2009), pp. 406–428; "Hundreds of Economists Say: Raise the Minimum Wage," *Economic Policy Institute,* October 11, 2006.

13. Economic Policy Institute, Issue Guide on Minimum Wage. *www.epi.org,* 2008; David Neumark and William L. Wascher, *Minimum Wages* (Cambridge, MA: MIT Press, 2008); Richard V. Burkhauser and Joseph J. Sabia, "The Effectiveness of Minimum Wage Increases in Reducing Poverty: Past, Present and Future," *Contemporary Economic Policy* 25(2), April 2007, pp. 262–281.

14. Annual Workplace Class Action Litigation Report, 2014 edition and 2015 edition. Published by Seyfarth Shaw LLP. Miguel Bustillo, "Wal-Mart to Settle 63 Suits Over Wages," *The Wall Street Journal, December 24,* 2008; Wal-Mart must pay $188 million in workers' class action. Reuters. December 16, 2014. www.reuers.com. Extracted March 29, 2015.

15. "New FLSA Regulations Set to Be Released in First Quarter of 2015 Likely to Change America's Overtime Pay Landscape." *Cullen and Dykman LLP.* www.cdllpblogs.com. March 17, 2015. Accessed March 29, 2015.

16. Dale A. Hudson, "Plaintiff's Lawyers Bullish on Merrill Lynch: Brokerage Firm Agrees to Pay $37 Million to Settle Overtime Claims by Stockbroker," *Nixon Peabody Employment Law Alert,* August 26, 2005.

17. "Judge OKs $42 Million Settlement," *BNA Bulletin to Management,* October 18, 2011.

18. Ylan Q. Mui, "Walmart to Pay $4.8 million in Back Wages," *The Washington Post,* May 1, 2012.

19. Cindy Krischer Goodman, "Overtime under Fire: Workday Trends Blur Overtime Rules, Clogging Courts with Lawsuits," *Wisconsin State Journal,* August 17, 2008.

20. Ibid.

21. Paul Davidson, "More Americans Sue for Overtime Pay," *USA Today,* April 15, 2012.

22. Ibid.

23. Steven Greenhouse, "Labor Agency Is Failing Workers, Reports Says," *The New York Times,* March 25, 2009.

24. Paul Davidson, "More Americans Sue for Overtime Pay," *USA Today,* April 15, 2012.

25. Ian Rowley and Hiroko Tashiro, "Recession Puts More Pressure on Japan's Workers," *BusinessWeek,* January 5, 2009.

26. Ibid.

27. *IBP, Inc. v. Alvarez,* (03-1238) No. 03–1238, 339 F.3d 894, affirmed; No. 04–66, 360 F.3d 274, affirmed in part, reversed in part, and remanded.

28. Will Parsons, "On-Call Pay Premiums and Expenses," *Culpepper Pay Trends Survey e-Bulletin,* December 2005.

29. Peter Kuhn and Fernando Lozano, *The Expanding Workweek? Understanding Trends in Long Work Hours among U.S. Men, 1979–2004,* NBER Working Paper No. 11895, July 2006.

30. Kimberley Strassel, "Make My (Mother's) Day . . ." *The Wall Street Journal,* May 13, 2006, p. A11.

31. Douglas L. Kruse and Douglas Mahony, "Illegal Child Labor in the United States: Prevalence and Characteristics," *Industrial and Labor Relations Review* 54(1), October 2000, pp. 17–40; Faraaz Siddiqi and Harry Anthony Patrinos, "Child Labor: Issues, Causes, and Interventions," Human Capital Development and Operations Policy Working Paper 56, *www.worldbank.org/html/extdr/hnp/hddflash/workp/wp_00056.html;* Steven Greenhouse and Michael Barbaro, "An Ugly Side of Free Trade: Sweatshops in Jordan," *The New York Times,* May 3, 2006; B. Powell and D. Skarbek, "Sweatshops and Third World Living Standards: Are the Jobs Worth the Sweat?" *Journal of Labor Research* 27(2), Spring 2006, pp. 263–279.

32. *The End of Child Labour: Within Reach* (Geneva, Switzerland: International Labor Organization, 2006).

33. Jon Gertner, "What Is a Living Wage?" *The New York Times Magazine,* January 15, 2006.

34. www.dllr.state.md.us/labor/prev/livingwagefaqs.shtml#1; accessed May 28, 2012.

35. John G. Kilgour, "The Living Wage Ordinance Controversy," *Workspan,* First Quarter 2009, pp. 75–85.

36. http://bca.lacity.org/site/pdf/lwo/wage%20Rates%20Chart.pdf; accessed May 28, 2012.

37. David Fairris, David Runsten, Carolina Briones, and Jessica Goodheart, *Examining the Evidence: The Impact of the Los Angeles Living Wage Ordinance on Workers and Businesses, www.losangeleslivingwagestudy.org; accessed* June 2, 2005.

38. David Neumark, "Living Wages: Protection for or Protection From Low-Wage Workers?" *Industrial and Labor Relations Review* 58(1), October 2004, pp. 27–51.

39. Bureau of Labor Statistics, U.S. Department of Labor, "Employer Costs for Employee Compensation - December 2014," March 11, 2015.

40. Steven Greenhouse, "U.S. Cracks Down on 'Contractors' as a Tax Dodge," *The New York Times,* February 18, 2010.

41. *Nationwide Mutual Ins. v. Darden* (90-1802), 503 U.S. 318 (1992).

42. Steven Greenhouse, "U.S. Cracks Down on 'Contractors' as a Tax Dodge," *The New York Times,* February 18, 2010.

43. Dennis D. Grant (2000), "Employee or Independent Contractor? The Implications of Microsoft III," *http://library.findlaw.com/2000/Feb/1/127759.html.*

44. Bill Virgin, "Microsoft Settles 'Permatemp' Suits: Two $97 Million Cases Reshape Employment for Temps Nationwide," *Seattle Post-Intelligencer,* December 13, 2000.

45. Anne Freedman, "FedEx Agrees to Pay $27 Million in Misclassification Case," *Human Resource Executive,* January 21, 2009.

46. Ed Frauenheim, "IRS Deals Blow to Fedex on Use of Contractors," *Workforce Management,* January 14, 2008. Josh Eidelson, "FedEx Ground Says its Drivers Aren't Employees. The Courts Will Decide." *Bloomberg Businessweek.* October 16, 2014.

47. Rebecca Knight, "Politicians Shifting Blame Put Boston's Big Dig Back in News," *Financial Times,* July 16, 2006, p. 4.

48. Aaron Morris, "Prevailing-Wage Law: Noble Goal, Costly Projects," *Bluegrass Institute,* March 7, 2006, *www.bipps.org/ARTICLE.ASP?ID=535.*

49. David Streitfeld, "Engineers Allege Collusion in Silicon Valley." *New York Times.* March 1, 2014. A1; Jeff Elder, "Judge Rejects Settlement in Silicon Valley Wage Case." *Wall Street Journal,* August 8, 2014.

50. *Gratz v. Bollinger,* (02-516) 539 U.S. 244 (2003).

51. *Grutter v. Bollinger,* (02-241) 539 U.S. 306 (2003).

52. Paula England, *Comparable Worth: Theories and Evidence* (Hawthorne, NY: Aldine deGruyter, 1992); Ben A. Barres, "Does Gender Matter?" *Nature* 442 (July 13, 2006); Morley Gunderson, "The Evolution and Mechanics of Pay Equity in Ontario," *Canadian Public Policy* 28, suppl. 1 (2002).

53. Michael E. Gold, "Towards a Unified Theory of the Law of Employment Discrimination," *Berkeley Journal of Employment and Labor Law,* February 2001.

54. Davan Maharaj, "Coca-Cola to Settle Racial Bias Lawsuit," *Los Angeles Times,* November 17, 2000.

55. *Annual Workplace Class Action Litigation Report,* 2015 edition (Seyfarth Shaw LLP, 2015).

56. FLSA-based lawsuits representing similarly situated employees are "collective actions" rather than class actions and employees are required to "opt in" (rather than opt out) under FLSA Section 216(b).

57. The Rule 23(a) requirements, specifically, identify four criteria. Numerosity. The number of putative (potential) plaintiffs is so large that to identify all of them individually by name would not be practical. Commonality. The lawsuit issues must be common to the proposed class. Typicality. The lawsuit issues and claims must be typical of the those of putative class members. Adequacy of Representation. The lead plaintiffs and their attorneys must be able to fairly and adequately protect the interests of the putative class. Annual Workplace Class Action Litigation Report, 2015 edition. Published by Seyfarth Shaw LLP. January 2015.

58. Gerald L. Maatman Jr., Ada Dolph, and Annette Tyman. Wal-Mart Stores Inc. v. Dukes: Has It Lived Up to the Hype? January 24, 2014. http://www.shrm.org/legalissues/employmentlawareas/pages/walmart-dukes-class-action-fallout.aspx. Extracted March 30, 2014.

59. Annual Workplace Class Action Litigation Report, 2015 edition. Published by Seyfarth Shaw LLP. January 2015. Gerald L. Maatman Jr., Ada Dolph and Annette Tyman. Wal-Mart Stores Inc. v. Dukes: Has It Lived Up to the Hype? January 24, 2014. http://www.shrm.org/legalissues/employmentlawareas/pages/wal-mart-dukes-class-actionfallout.aspx. Extracted March 30, 2014.

60. Gerald L. Maatman Jr., Ada Dolph and Annette Tyman. Wal-Mart Stores Inc. v. Dukes: Has It Lived Up to the Hype? January 24, 2014. http://www.shrm.org/legalissues/employmentlawareas/pages/walmart-dukes-class-action-fallout.aspx. Extracted March 30, 2014.

61. Lauren Weber. More Companies Block Employees From Filing Suits Arbitration clauses with classaction waivers rise sharply after 2011 court ruling. Wall Street Journal. March 31, 2015. www.wsj.com.

62. U.S. Equal Employment Opportunity Commission, "Notice Concerning the Lilly Ledbetter Fair Pay Act of 2009," *www.eeoc.gov/epa/ledbetter.html*, June 22, 2009.

63. Ibid.

64. Brett A. Gorovsky, "Lilly Ledbetter Fair Pay Act of 2009: What's Next for Employers?" CCH Incorporated, *http://www.cch.com/Press/news/CCHWhitePaper_LedbetterFairPayAct.pdf*, June 22, 2009.

65. Michael E. Gold, "Towards a Unified Theory of the Law of Employment Discrimination," *Berkeley Journal of Employment and Labor Law*, February 2001.

66. U.S. Government Accountability Office, "Federal Agencies Should Better Monitor Their Performance in Enforcing Anti-Discrimination Laws," GAO Reports, Report Number GAO-08-799. Washington, D.C.; Debra Ann Millenson and David S. Fortney, "OFCCP Fundamentals," ABA Philadelphia Labor & Employment Conference, 2007, *www. abanet .org/labor/annualconference/2007/materials/data/papers/v1/009.pdf;* accessed June 12, 2009.

67. OFCCP Directive. Transmittal Number: 285, 09/17/2008, *www.dol.gov/esa/ofccp/ regs/compliance/directives/dir285.htm,* June 21, 2009.

68. Department of Labor. Office of Federal Contracts Compliance. Government Contractors, Requirement To Report Summary Data on Employee Compensation. Federal Register / Vol. 79, No. 153 / Friday, August 8, 2014 / Proposed Rules.

69. Office of Federal Contract Compliance Programs. Federal Contract Compliance Manual. Chapter 3—On-Site Review, *http://www.dol.gov/esa/ofccp/regs/compliance/fccm/ofcpch3 .htm,* June 21, 2009.

70. "OFCCP's New Systemic Compensation Discrimination Standards and Voluntary Guidelines for Compensation Self-Evaluation," Office of Federal Contract Compliance Programs, *http://www.dol.gov/esa/ofccp/regs/compliance/faqs/comstrds.htm,* June 21, 2009.

71. The previous standards required the use of multiple regression analysis (for any similarly situated group (SSEG) that had 30 or more total employees and at least five employees in each group to be compared (the 30/5 rule). An SSEG was defined as "a grouping of employees who perform similar work, and occupy positions with similar responsibility levels and involving similar skills and qualifications." The OFCCP had stated that the multiple regression "must include [as control variables] factors that are important to how the contractor in practice makes pay decisions" and gave as examples: education, work experience with previous employers, seniority, time in salary grade, and performance ratings. SSEG group was also to be controlled in the regression. Finally, anecdotal evidence (e.g., reports of discrimination from employees) was also necessary. It noted that under these now rescinded standards, the OFCCP could "only establish a systemic compensation violation of the Executive Order by testing narrowly defined groupings of employees... [and] OFCCP [had been required to] use multiple regression analysis to test for pay disparities and [to] have anecdotal evidence to establish a systemic compensation violation, 'except in unusual cases' [despite the fact that] employment discrimination comes in many forms." OFCCP further argued that the anecdotal evidence requirement was "particularly burdensome for workers who frequently lack meaningful access to information about pay." In summary, the OFCCP stated that "Fair and effective enforcement requires tailoring the compensation investigation and analytical procedures to the facts of the case based on Title VII principles." U.S. Department of Labor. Office of Federal Contract Compliance Programs (OFCCP). Advancing Equal Pay Enforcement. More Effective and Transparent Procedures for Investigating Pay Discrimination. http://www.dol.gov /ofccp/regs/compliance/CompGuidance/index.htm.

72. Under the new standards, the OFCCP (and employers performing self-evaluations) are to form "Pay Analysis Groups", defined as "A group of employees (potentially from multiple job titles, units, categories and/or job groups) who are comparable for purposes of the contractor's pay practices." In data analysis, "Regression analysis may be performed on different types of pay analysis groups. A pay analysis group may be limited to a single job or title, or may include multiple distinct units or categories of workers. A pay analysis group may combine employees in different jobs or groups, with statistical controls to ensure that workers are similarly situated." However, use of multiple regression is no longer mandated. In forming Pay Analysis Groups, "similarly situated" employees are used. "For purposes of evaluating compensation differences, employees are similarly situated where it is reasonable to expect they should be receiving equivalent compensation absent discrimination. Relevant factors in determining similarity may include tasks performed, skills, effort, level of responsibility, working conditions, job difficulty, minimum qualifications, and other objective factors. In some cases, employees are similarly situated where they are comparable on some of these factors, even if they are not similar on others." U.S. Department of Labor. Office of Federal Contract Compliance Programs (OFCCP). Directive. U.S. Department Of Labor Office of Federal Contract Compliance Programs. Number: 307 Date: February 28, 2013 ADM. Notice/ Compensation.

73. Ibid. The OFCCP until 2013 offered what it described as an "incentive" do so in that it "will coordinate its compliance monitoring activities with the contractor's self-evaluation approach." If the self-evaluation approach "reasonably meets the general standards outline in the Voluntary Guidelines, OFCCP will consider the contractor's compensation practices to be in compliance with Executive Order 11246." In other words, if the self-evaluation follows the standards and shows no disparities between similarly situated employee

groups, the OFCCP would conclude the employer was in compliance. Again, as noted, this is no longer the case since 2013.

74. Murray S. Simpson, "Analyzing Pay Equity in an Uncertain Regulatory Environment," *Compensation & Benefits Review,* November/December, pp. 29–39.

75. Sara L. Rynes and George T. Milkovich, "Wage Surveys: Dispelling Some Myths about the 'Market Wage,'" *Personnel Psychology,* Spring 1986, pp. 71–90; Charlie Trevor and Mary E. Graham, "Deriving the Market Wage: Three Decision Areas in the Compensation Survey Process," *WorldatWork Journal,* Fourth Quarter 2000, pp. 69–76; Judith K. Hellerstein, David Neumark, and Kenneth R. Troske, "Market Forces and Sex Discrimination," *Journal of Human Resources* 37(2), Spring 2002, pp. 353–380.

76. H. Remick, ed., *Comparable Worth and Wage Discrimination* (Philadelphia: Temple University Press, 1984); B. F. Reskin and H. I. Hartmann, eds., *Women's Work, Men's Work: Segregation on the Job* (Washington, DC: National Academy Press, 1986); Morley Gunderson, *Women and the Labour Market: Transitions towards the Future* (Toronto: ITP Nelson Publishing, 1998); Morley Gunderson and Nan Weiner, *Pay Equity: Issues, Options and Experiences* (Toronto: Butterworths, 1990).

77. *Job Evaluation: A Tool for Pay Equity* (Washington, DC: National Committee on Pay Equity, November 1987); Morley Gunderson, "The Evolution and Mechanics of Pay Equity in Ontario," *Canadian Public Policy* 28, suppl. 1 (2002).

78. Sharon Toffey-Shepela and Ann T. Viviano, "Some Psychological Factors Affecting Job Segregation and Wages," *Comparable Worth and Wage Discrimination,* in H. Remick, ed. (Philadelphia: Temple University Press, 1984); Helen Remick, "Beyond Equal Pay for Equal Work: Comparable Worth in the State of Washington," in Ronnie Steinber-Ratner, ed., *Equal Employment Policy for Women,* (Philadelphia: Temple University Press, 1980), pp. 405–448; "Supreme Court Decision a Victory for Pay Equity and Human Rights," press release from Public Service Alliance of Canada, June 26, 2003; Theresa Glomb, John Kammeyer-Mueller, and Maria Rotundo, "Emotional Labor Demands and Compensating Wage Differentials," *Journal of Applied Psychology* 89(4), 2004, pp. 700–714.

79. "Bell Canada Operators Accept Pay Equity Deal," *Canadian Employment Law Today* June 20, 2006, *www.employmentlawtoday.com;* Judy Fudge, "The Paradoxes of Pay Equity: Reflections on the Law and the Market in Bell Canada and the Public Service Alliance of Canada," *Canadian Journal of Women and the Law* 12 (2000), pp. 312–344.

80. Ronnie Steinberg, "Emotional Labor in Job Evaluation: Redesigning Compensation Practices," *Annals of the American Academy of Political and Social Science* 561(1), 1999, pp. 142–157.

81. Kenneth Kovach, "An Overview and Assessment of Comparable Worth Based on a Large Scale Implementation," *Public Personnel Management* 26(1), 1997, pp. 109–122; Judith McDonald and Robert Thornton, "Private Sector Experience with Pay Equity in Ontario," *Canadian Public Policy* 24(2), 1998, pp. 227–241; Nan Weiner and Morley Gunderson, *Pay Equity: Issues, Options, and Experiences* (Toronto: Butterworths, 1990); Lynda Ames, "Fixing Women's Wages: The Effectiveness of Comparable Worth Policies," *Industrial and Labour Relations Review* 48(4), 1995, pp. 709–725.

82. Alvin O. Bellak, "Comparable Worth: A Practitioner's View," in *Comparable Worth: Issue for the 80s,* vol. 1 (Washington, DC: Equal Employment Advisory Council, 1980).

83. Unions are becoming more adept at using the web to share information.The AFSCME website has a section called "LaborLinks," and within that is a section called "Classification and Compensation." Here the AFSCME provides links to private wage

survey sites such as *salary.com,* Wageweb, and the Executive Pay Watch, as well as links to BLS, DOT/ONET, and a few state and local government sites. In another section, it provides information on how to research companies using the web. Unite and the SEIU provide links to the BLS. The Steelworkers Union provides information on its wage policy statement. The UAW provides detailed information on its bargaining strategies and gains, all the way down to the locals. Most unions also have newsletters that provide helpful information, and you can search the old issues to find relevant information.

84. Sonja C. Kassenboehmer and Mathias G. Sinning, "Distributional Changes in the Gender Wage Gap," *Industrial and Labor Relations Review*, 67, 335–361.

85. U.S. Bureau of Census, "Educational Attainment in the United States: 2011—Detailed Tables," www.census.gov/hhes/socdemo/education/data/cps/2011/tables.html; accessed May 30, 2012.

86. U.S. Department of Labor, Bureau of Labor Statistics, "Highlights of Women's Earnings in 2007," Report 1008, October 2008; Francine D. Blau and Lawrence M. Kahn, "The Gender Pay Gap: Have Women Gone as Far as They Can?" *Academy of Management Perspectives;* D. A. Black, A. M. Haviland, S. G. Sanders, and L. J. Taylor, "Gender Wage Disparities among the Highly Educated," *Journal of Human Resources* 42 (2008), pp. 630–659. Cheri Ostroff and Leanne Atwater, "Does Whom You Work with Matter? Effects of Referent Group Gender and Age Composition on Managers' Compensation," *Journal of Applied Psychology,* August 2003, pp. 725–740; Paula England, "The Gender System: What's Changing? What's Not?" Alice Cook Memorial Lecture, Cornell University, Ithaca, NY, March 22, 2006; Nabanita Datta Gupta, Ronald L. Oaxaca, and Nina Smith, "Swimming Upstream, Floating Downstream: Comparing Women's Relative Wage Progress In the United States and Denmark," *Industrial and Labor Relations Review,* January 2006, pp. 243–266; Warren Farrell, *Why Men Earn More: The Startling Truth behind the Pay Gap—and What Women Can Do About It* (New York: Amacom, 2005); Gerrit Mueller and Erik Plug, "Estimating the Effect of Personality on Male and Female Earnings," *Industrial and Labor Relations Review,* October 2006, pp. 3–22.

87. June O'Neill and Dave O'Neill, *What Do Wage Differentials Tell Us about Labor Market Discrimination?* NBER Working Paper W11240, April 2005.

88. Croson, Rachel, and Uri Gneezy. 2009. "Gender Differences in Preferences." Journal of Economic Literature, 47: 448–74. D. Anderson, M. Binder, and K. Krause, "The Motherhood Wage Penalty Revisited: Experience, Heterogeneity, Work Effort and Work-Schedule Flexibility," *Industrial and Labor Relations Review* 56(2), January 2003, pp. 273–295; Andrew M. Gill and Duane E. Leigh, "Community College Enrollment, College Major, and the Gender Wage Gap," *Industrial and Labor Relations Review* 54(1), October 2000, pp. 163–181; C. Brown and M. Corcoran, "Sex-Based Differences in School Content and the Male-Female Wage Gap," *Journal of Labor Economics* 15(3), 1997, pp. 431–465; M. Montgomery and I. Powell, "Does an Advanced Degree Reduce the Gender Wage Gap? Evidence From MBAs," *Industrial Relations* 42(3), July 2003, pp. 396–418.

89. Laurie A. Morgan, "Major Matters: The Within-Major Gender Pay Gap for Early-Career College Graduates," *Industrial Relations* 47 (2008) pp. 625–650; Nicole M. Fortin, "The Gender Gap among Young Adults in the United States: The Importance of Money versus People," *Journal of Human Resources* 43 (2008), p. 884; C. A. Karlin, P. England, and Mary Richardson, "Why Do 'Women's Jobs' Have Low Pay for Their Educational Level?" *Gender Issues* 20(4), Fall 2002, pp. 3–22; Stephanie Boraas and William M. Rodgers III, "How Does Gender Play a Role in the Earnings Gap? An Update," *Monthly Labor Review,* March 2003, pp. 9–15.

90. Tamar Lewin, "At Colleges, Women Are Leaving Men in the Dust," *The New York Times,* July 9, 2006, p. 1; Francine Blau and Marianne Ferber, "Career Plans and Expectations of Young Women and Men," *Journal of Human Resources* 26(4), 1998, pp. 581–607; Greg Hundley, "Male/Female Earnings Differences in Self-Employment: The Effects of Marriage, Children, and the Household Division of Labor," *Industrial and Labor Relations Review* 54(1), October 2000, pp. 95–114.

91. Anne E. Preston, "Why Have All the Women Gone? A Study of Exit of Women from the Science and Engineering Professions," *American Economic Review,* December 1994, pp. 1446–1462; Joy A. Schneer and Frieda Reitman, "The Importance of Gender in Mid-Career: A Longitudinal Study of MBAs," *Journal of Organizational Behavior* 15 (1994), pp. 199–207.

92. Eduardo Porter, "Stretched to Limit, Women Stall March to Work," *The New York Times,* March 2, 2006, p. 1.

93. Paula England, Paul Allison, Yuxiao Wu, and Mary Ross, "Does Bad Pay Cause Occupations to Feminize, Does Feminization Reduce Pay, and How Can We Tell with Longitudinal Data?" presented at annual meeting of the American Sociological Association, August 2004, San Francisco.

94. Yet another reviewer of the same research evidence emphasizes limitations in data sources and research methods, disagreements over variables to include in the studies, and randomness. T. Tam, "Sex Segregation and Occupational Gender Inequality: Devaluation or Specialized Training," *American Journal of Sociology* 102 (1997), pp. 1652–1692.

95. June O'Neill and Dave O'Neill, *What Do Wage Differentials Tell Us about Labor Market Discrimination?* NBER Working Paper W11240, April 2005; Finis Welch, "Catching Up: Wages of Black Men," American Economic Association Papers and Proceedings, May 2003, pp. 320–322; J. Heckman, "Detecting Discrimination," *Journal of Economic Perspectives* 12(2), 1998, pp. 101–116.

96. Dan Black, Amelia Haviland, Seth Sanders, and Lowell Taylor, "Why Do Minority Men Earn Less? A Study of Wage Differentials among the Highly Educated," *Review of Economics and Statistics,* May 2006, pp. 300–313; Robert G. Wood, Mary E. Corcoran, and Paul N. Courant, "Pay Differences among the Highly Paid: The Male-Female Earnings Gap in Lawyers' Salaries," *Journal of Labor Economics* 11(3), 1993, pp. 417–441.

97. Barry A. Gerhart and George T. Milkovich, "Salaries, Salary Growth, and Promotions of Men and Women in a Large, Private Firm," *Pay Equity: Empirical Inquiries* (Arlington, VA: National Science Foundation, 1989); Francine Blau and Jed DeVaro, *New Evidence on Gender Difference in Promotion Rates: An Empirical Analysis of a Sample of New Hires,* NBER Working Paper No. 12321, June 2006.

98. Mary E. Graham, Julie L. Hotchkiss, and Barry Gerhart, "Discrimination by Parts: A Fixed Effects Analysis of Starting Pay Differences across Gender," *Eastern Economic Journal,* 26 (2000), pp. 9–27; Erica L. Groshen, "Sources of Intra-Industry Wage Dispersion: How Much Do Employers Matter?" *The Quarterly Journal of Economics* 106 (1991) pp. 869–884; Kimberly Bayard, Judith Hellerstein, David Neumark, and Kenneth Troske, "New Evidence on Sex Segregation and Sex Differences in Wages From Matched Employee-Employer Data," *Journal of Labor Economics* 21 (2003), pp. 887–922; George Johnson and Gary Solon, "Estimates of the Direct Effects of Comparable Worth Policy," *American Economic Review,* 76 (1986), pp. 1117–1125; Barry Gerhart, "Gender Differences in Current and Starting Salaries: The Role of Performance, College Major, and Job Title," *Industrial and Labor Relations Review* 43 (1990), pp. 418–433.

99. George F. Dreher and Taylor H. Cox, Jr., "Labor Market Mobility and Cash Compensation: The Moderating Effects of Race and Gender," *Academy of Management Journal* 43(5), 2000, pp. 890–900; J. M. Brett and L. K. Stroh, "Jumping Ship: Who Benefits from an External Labor Market Career Strategy?" *Journal of Applied Psychology* 82 (1997), pp. 331–341; G. F. Dreher and T. H. Cox, Jr., "Race, Gender, and Opportunity: A Study of Compensation Attainment and the Establishment of Mentoring Relationships," *Journal of Applied Psychology* 81 (1996), pp. 297–308.

100. George F. Dreher and Taylor H. Cox, Jr., "Labor Market Mobility and Cash Compensation: The Moderating Effects of Race and Gender," *Academy of Management Journal* 43(5), 2000, pp. 890–900.

101. D. Weichselbaumer and R. Winter-Ebmer, "Rhetoric in Economic Research: The Case of Gender Wage Differentials," *Industrial Relations* 45(3), 2006, pp. 416–436.

102. Organisation for Economic Co-operation and Development, "The Price of Prejudice: Labour Market Discrimination on the Grounds of Gender and Ethnicity," *OECD Employment Outlook* 2008, chapter 3 (Paris: OECD, 2008).

103. Francine D. Blau and Lawrence M. Kahn, *The Sources of International Differences in Wage Inequality* (ILR Impact Brief #10), (Ithaca, NY: School of Industrial and Labor Relations, Cornell University, 2006); H. C. Jain, P. J. Sloane, and F. Horwitz, *Employment Equity and Affirmative Action: An International Comparison* (Armonk, NY: ME Sharpe, 2003); Janet C. Gornick, Marcia K. Meyers, and Katherine E. Ross, "Supporting the Employment of Mothers: Policy Variation across Fourteen Welfare States," *Journal of European Social Policy* 7(1), 1997, pp. 45–70.

104. www.nypost.com/p/news/local/manhattan/was_gaga_slave_IyvXjE3n412CoMqKQnyS1L #ixzz1wTpq5Gaz; accessed May 31, 2012. www.employmentlawattorneyoh.com/2012/01 /lady-gaga-subject-to-fair-labor-standards-act.shtml; accessed May 31, 2012.

Management: Making It Work

Chapter Outline

This chapter is about making it work: ensuring that the right people get the right pay for achieving the right objectives in the right way. The greatest pay system design in the world is useless without competent management. So why bother with a formal system at all? If management is that important, why not simply let every manager pay whatever works best? Such total decentralization of decision making could create a chaotic array of rates. Managers could use pay to motivate behaviors that achieved their own immediate objectives, not necessarily those of the organization. Employees could be treated inconsistently and unfairly.

This was the situation in the United States in the early 1900s. The "contract system" made highly skilled workers managers as well as workers. The employer agreed to provide the "contractor" with floor space, light, power, and the necessary raw or semifinished materials. The contractor hired *and* paid labor.[1] Pay inconsistencies for the same work were common. Some contractors demanded kickbacks from employees' paychecks; many hired their relatives and friends. Dissatisfaction and grievances were widespread, eventually resulting in legislation that outlawed the arrangement.

Corruption and financial malfeasance were also part of decentralized decision making in the early 1900s. Some see parallels today. To help avoid history repeating itself and to redeem HR (and compensation) vice presidents from the image of unindicted coconspirators, the compensation system should be managed to achieve the objectives in the pay model: efficiency, fairness, and compliance.

Any discussion of managing pay must again raise the basic questions: So what is the impact of the decision or technique? Does it help the organization achieve its objectives? How?

Although many pay management issues have been discussed throughout the book, a few remain to be called out explicitly. These include (1) managing labor costs, (2) managing revenues, (3) communication, and (4) designing the compensation department.

MANAGING LABOR COSTS AND REVENUES

Financial planning is integral to managing compensation. As we noted in Chapter 1, compensation decisions influence organization's performance by influencing costs and/or revenues. The cost implications of actions such as updating the pay structure, increasing merit pay, or instituting gain sharing are critical for making sound decisions. Budgets account for these costs. Creating a compensation budget requires tradeoffs, such as how much of an increase should be allocated according to employee contributions versus across-the-board increases versus company performance. Tradeoffs also occur over short- versus long-term incentives, over pay increases contingent on performance versus seniority, and over cash compensation compared to benefits.

Financial planning also requires understanding the revenues (or returns) gained from the allocation.[2] Total compensation makes up at least 50 percent of operating expenses in many organizations. Yet, most companies have not tried to analyze the returns from their compensation decisions.[3] As we noted in Chapter 2, compensation strategy influences effectiveness not only by its influence on (labor) costs, but through its influence in helping increase revenues or returns as well. Returns might be the productivity increases expected from a new gain-sharing or profit-sharing plan, or the expected value added by boosting merit increases to the top performers.[4] In the past, financial planning in compensation was only about costs.[5] This is perhaps because costs are tangible and easy to measure, whereas the returns generated by compensation strategy may often be intangible and harder to quantify. It is important to keep in mind, however, that how easy or difficult it is to quantify something has little to do with how important it is. Fortunately, analysis of the expected returns compared to costs is becoming more common.[6] More on this later.

EXHIBIT 18.1
Managing
Labor Costs

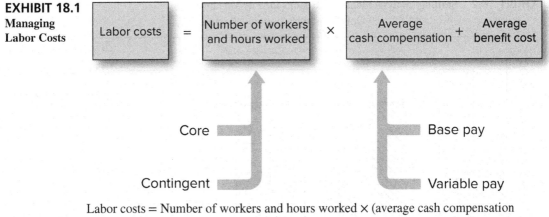

Labor costs = Number of workers and hours worked × (average cash compensation + average benefit cost)

MANAGING LABOR COSTS

You already know many of the factors that affect labor costs. Exhibit 18.1 shows a simple labor cost model. Using this model, there are three main factors to control in order to manage labor costs: employment (e.g., number of workers and the hours they work), average cash compensation (e.g., wages, bonuses), and average benefit costs. Cash compensation and benefits have been this book's focus. However, if our objective is to better manage labor costs, then all three factors require attention.

Number of Employees (a.k.a.: Staffing Levels or Headcount)

Using information about competitors' average pay helps improve understanding of labor costs. Exhibit 18.2A shows how one organization pays its engineers relative to its competitors at each of five job levels, E5–E1. The pay for each position is the cross-hatched bar. Market pay is the shaded bar, with the average falling in the middle of the unshaded part of the bar. So the organization meets competition by paying E5, E3, and E2 engineers at about the median. But the company leads competition at E4 and lags at the entry-level E1.

Exhibit 18.2B provides more insight into the organization's labor costs. This part of the exhibit compares the organization's distribution of engineers among the five job levels to its competitors' distributions. A larger percentage of the organization's engineers are at higher levels, E4 and E5, than its competitors. So even though the organization pays above market for only one of the five job levels, its labor costs may be higher than its competitors due to its staffing pattern. So what? Looking only at total headcount, as suggested in Exhibit 18.1, may mislead since the total employment level

EXHIBIT 18.2 **Staffing Analysis Identifies Reasons for Pay Variances**

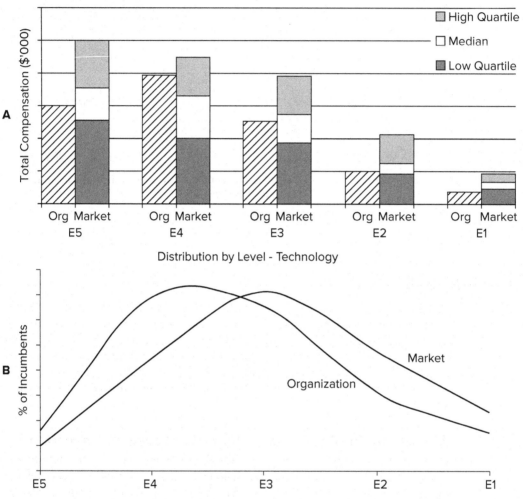

could be identical to competitors' but deployment among job levels may vary. Here, the organization differs from its competitors most at E4, where it employs a larger percent of engineering talent and also pays them more. Something is going on at E4. More information is required to better understand what underlies these differences. Are the organization's engineers more experienced and thus promoted into E4? Does the company do more sophisticated work that requires more experienced engineers? Absent some sound business-related rationale, labor costs can be reduced by redeploying staffing levels and wages at E4.[7] Obviously, paying the same wages (e.g., meeting competition) to fewer employees is less expensive. The effects on all pay objectives—efficiency and fairness—also need to be considered before taking any action.

Reducing Headcount

As is apparent from following the business news during any recession, organizations often reduce headcount to cut labor costs. Such cuts may take the form of layoffs (often with severance benefits that depend on length of service) or exit incentives that are designed to encourage employees to leave "by choice." A major advantage of a reduction in force (RIF) is that it also reduces benefits costs, something that a pay cut, furlough, or reduction in hours ordinarily does not achieve. (An exception would be Lincoln Electric, which has a very lean, low-cost benefits package.) To the degree that headcount reductions can be targeted based on performance, it can also be an opportunity for an organization to reshape its workforce in a way that creates positive sorting effects. Under such a scenario, stronger performers are unaffected (e.g., their pay is not cut) and the organization has an opportunity to maintain good employee relations with this important group.

There are, however, several potential problems with headcount reductions. First, regulatory requirements make it difficult to make targeted cuts. The Age Discrimination in Employment Act (ADEA) often comes into play if organizations target reductions among higher paid employees (to maximize labor cost savings) because higher paid employees also tend to be older employees. In addition, the Older Worker Benefits Protection Act, part of the ADEA, requires that exit incentive programs be structured in very specific ways. For example, a program must give workers 40 years old and older 21 days to consider the offer and 7 days to change their mind if they accept the offer. These and other provisions tend to make it difficult to single out high-wage and/or poor-performing workers. If exit incentives cannot be effectively targeted and all employees are eligible, which employees do you think would be most likely to take the incentive and leave? Probably those most employable and most able to find another good job, right? That is indeed what a number of organizations have experienced. Thus, you may end up, in essence, paying your top performers to leave—a very undesirable sorting effect! Second, workforce reductions, especially if not handled well, can harm employee relations. Regulatory restrictions on headcount reductions can be quite stringent outside the United States. (See our discussion of works councils, for example, in Chapter 16.)[8] Third, organizations that make greater (involuntary) workforce reductions also experience greater voluntary turnover.[9] Fourth, RIFs, while reducing costs over time, are very costly in tangible terms up front due to increases in unemployment insurance tax rates, disruption of work processes and serving customers, and administrative costs of handling exits. Exit incentives, if provided, further drive up costs. Fifth, some companies have learned to run so "lean" (i.e., very few employees on manufacturing lines), and have controlled hiring so successfully, that there may be little room to cut headcount.[10] Finally, where cuts can be made, if the cuts are too deep, an organization will be poorly positioned to generate revenue if business picks up again.[11] An organization may spend a lot of money reducing headcount and then spend a lot more a short time later to hire new employees to handle increased product demand. If other firms increase hiring at the same time, costs will be even greater. Announcements of layoffs and plant closings often have favorable short-run effects on stock prices as investors anticipate improved cash flow and lower costs. However, in the

EXHIBIT 18.3
Core and
Contingent
Employees

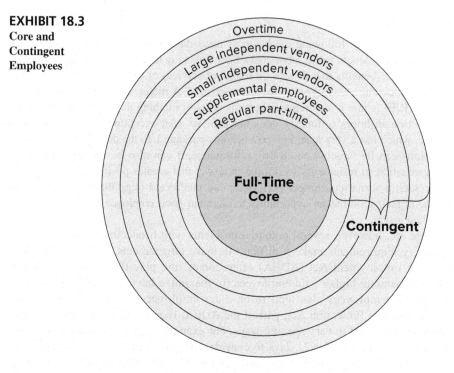

longer term, adverse effects such as loss of trained employees, unrealized productivity, and lowered morale often translate into lower financial gains than anticipated. Some evidence indicates that close attention to process and employee relations during workforce reductions can help financial results.[12]

In addition, as we saw in Chapter 17, the regulatory environment differs from country to country. Many European countries have legislation as part of their social contracts that makes it very difficult to reduce headcount or wages. Managing labor costs is a greater struggle in such circumstances.

Many employers seek to buffer themselves from getting into a position where layoffs are necessary. As discussed below, use of overtime is part of this strategy. In addition, organizations establish different relationships with different groups of workers. As Exhibit 18.3 depicts, the two groups are commonly referred to as **core employees,** with whom a long-term relationship is desired, and *contingent workers,* whose employment agreements may cover only short, specific time periods. Contingent workers can be employees, but can also be independent contractors/vendors or may be employed by staffing services firms/vendors. Rather than expand or contract the core workforce, many employers achieve flexibility and control labor costs by expanding or contracting the contingent workforce. Toyota, for example, while not cutting regular employees in either the United States or Japan during the recent recession, has cut its contract worker headcount.

The segmented supply of nurses at St. Luke's Hospital, discussed in Chapter 7 and shown in Exhibit 18.4, illustrates the variable costs from use of different sources of

EXHIBIT 18.4
Segmented Supplies: St. Luke's Labor Cost Model

Source: © George T. Milkovich.

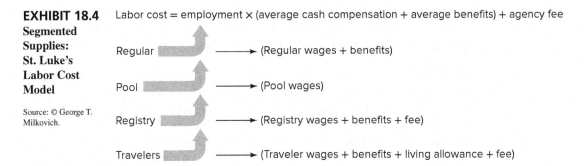

Labor cost = employment × (average cash compensation + average benefits) + agency fee

Regular ⟶ (Regular wages + benefits)

Pool ⟶ (Pool wages)

Registry ⟶ (Registry wages + benefits + fee)

Travelers ⟶ (Traveler wages + benefits + living allowance + fee)

nurses. Regular, pool, registry, and traveler nurses are paid differently. Some have benefits from St. Luke's, others have them from the contracting agencies, and still others must purchase their own benefits (pool nurses). The tradeoffs in managing costs include balancing patient loads, nurse-to-patient ratios, costs of alternative sources, and quality of care.[13]

Hours

Rather than define employment as number of employees, hours of work is often used. For nonexempt employees in the United States, hours over 40 per week are more expensive (one-and-a-half times regular wage). Hence, another way to manage labor costs is to examine overtime hours versus hiring more employees. St. Luke's may guarantee its regular nurses a specific number of hours, but contract nurses (pool, registry, or travelers) are "on call."

The four factors in the labor cost model—number of employees, hours worked, cash compensation, and benefit costs—are not independent. Overtime hours require higher wages but the incremental benefits cost is substantially lower than that incurred in hiring an additional regular nurse. The higher the fixed benefits costs, the more viable is the option to add overtime (even with the time and a half premium) rather than hiring another nurse. By not hiring, the organization avoids recruitment/selection costs. It also gains more flexibility to reduce labor costs if demand for its health care services declines in the future. In that case, rather than cutting headcount, it can reduce hours worked, which helps avoid employee relations problems as well as the monetary costs of reducing headcount.

During the most recent recession, a number of firms reduced hours and costs through the use of mandatory unpaid leave or furloughs to cut hours and thus labor costs. For example, state employees in California were required to take two furlough days off per month, resulting in a 10 percent pay cut. Wendy Roberson, one such employee, partly as a joke, founded the "Fun Furlough Fridays Club." Nobody wants a pay cut, but if you are going to get some extra time off, you might as well make the best of it and enjoy it, right? Well, as it turns out, although the pay cut was real, the time off in many cases was not. The amount of work to be done did not decrease, so many "furloughed" employees found themselves at work, rather than having Fun Furlough Fridays.[14] Nevertheless, reducing hours and pay does mean that fewer headcount reductions are necessary and by avoiding these, there will be less disruption and private sector organizations should be better positioned to respond when business picks up again, at least so long as top performers don't find greener pastures in the meantime.[15]

Benefits

One of the most common approaches to reducing benefits costs recently has been for employers to suspend matching (made when employees contribute) to 401(k) retirement plans. Survey data show about one in four companies either have already suspended their matching contributions or are considering doing so. Even the American Association for Retired Persons (AARP) decided it needed to suspend its 401(k) retirement plan match, a decision that was presumably not taken lightly![16] The average company match is 50 cents on the dollar up to 6 percent of pay. More companies may move to a model that makes matching contributions dependent on profits.[17] Another action we have seen is organizations eliminating benefits such as defined benefit (pension) plans as part of seeking bankruptcy protection from creditors. Examples include several airlines (e.g., United, Delta, USAir, Northwest), automobile companies (General Motors, Chrysler), and automobile parts companies (e.g., Delphi). As noted in Chapter 13, the Pension Benefit Guaranty Corporation (PBGC) provides benefits to employees who were covered under such plans. However, the maximum monthly retirement benefit from the PBGC is $5,011 at age 65, meaning that more highly paid employees (e.g., airline pilots) can experience a significant loss in pension benefits after bankruptcy. Other, more typical, ways of controlling or reducing benefits costs have to do with efforts by companies in the area of health care (as discussed in Chapters 12 and 13).

Average Cash Compensation (Fixed and Variable Components)

Average cash compensation includes average salary (fixed payments) level plus variable compensation payments such as bonuses, gain sharing, stock plans, and/or profit sharing. The fixed component is typically paid regardless of business performance. In contrast, the variable component of compensation, in theory, will rise and fall in line with business performance. For example, a profit-sharing plan will ordinarily have lower than normal profit-sharing payouts in years when profits are lower than normal. If other firms are experiencing similar profit declines, then there may be less danger of losing employees through turnover when this happens and the full advantage of "automatic" labor cost flexibility can be experienced.

During the most recent recession (in 2009) almost one-half of firms froze salaries, giving no annual increase,[18] resulting in an average salary increase budget across companies of just 1.9 percent. As Exhibit 18.5 indicates, salary increase budgets have increased since 2009. In addition, only 5 percent of firms froze salary increase budgets in 2011 (and in subsequent years), down from 21 percent in 2010, and 48 percent in 2009.[19] Another major tool used by organizations to control salary costs, in both good and bad times, is variable pay (See Chapters 8 and 10.) As Exhibit 18.6 shows, while the size of the merit increase budget has come down over time, the size of the variable pay (e.g., lump sum merit increases, profit sharing) budget has gone up very significantly. Unlike base salary increases, variable pay does not become a permanent part of base salary. Thus, the variable aspect allows companies to reduce labor costs when times are tough and to share

EXHIBIT 18.5 Base Salary Increases in Recent Years, as Percentage of Payroll, Salaried Exempt Employees

2007	2008	2009	2010	2011	2012	2013	2014	2015
3.6%	3.7%	1.9%	2.4%	2.7%	2.9%	2.9%	2.9%	3.0%*

Source: Aon Hewitt, 2014 *Annual Salary Increase Survey*, August 2014. Percentage increase each year is based on average for salaried exempt, salaried nonexempt, and nonunion hourly employee groups.

*Projected

EXHIBIT 18.6 Traditional Base Salary Increases and Variable Pay, as Percentage of Payroll, Salaried Exempt Employees, Changes over Time

	1991	2015*
Base salary increase budget	5.0%	3.0%*
Variable pay budget	3.8%	12.7%*

Source: Ken Abosch. Ensuring Effective Broad-Based Variable Pay. Total Rewards 2014 Conference, WorldatWork. Aon Hewitt, *2014 Annual Salary Increase Survey*, August 2014.

* Projected

success with (and reward) employees when times are good. As we saw earlier, the Big Three U.S. automobile companies have followed this strategy in recent years.

Adjustments to average cash compensation level (here, to simplify, we focus primarily on the salary component) can be made (1) *top down,* in which top management determines the amount of money to be spent on pay and allocates it "down" to each subunit for the plan year, and (2) *bottom up,* in which individual employees' pay for the plan year is forecasted and summed to create an organization-wide salary budget.

Budget Controls: Top Down

Top-down budgeting begins with an estimate from top management of the pay increase budget for the entire organization. Once the total budget is determined, it is then allocated to each manager, who plans how to distribute it among subordinates. There are many approaches to top-down budgeting. A typical one, **planned pay-level rise,** is simply the percentage increase in average pay for the unit that is planned to occur. Several factors influence the decision on how much to increase the average pay level for the next period: how much the average level was increased this period, ability to pay, competitive market pressures, turnover effects, and cost of living.

Current Year's Rise

This is the percentage by which the average wage changed in the past year; mathematically:

$$\text{Percent pay-level rise} =$$
$$100 \times \frac{\text{average pay at year-end} - \text{average pay at year beginning}}{\text{average pay at year beginning}}$$

Ability to Pay

Any decision to increase the average pay level is in part a function of the organization's financial circumstances. Financially healthy employers may wish to maintain their competitive positions in the labor market or share financial success through bonuses and profit sharing. Conversely, financially troubled employers may not be able to maintain competitive market positions. As noted, the conventional response has been to reduce employment. As shown earlier, by analyzing pay and staffing at each level, potential cost savings can be discovered. Other options are to reduce the rate of increase in average pay by controlling adjustments in base pay and/or variable pay. Raising employees' copays and deductibles for benefits is another. Often as a last resort, firms decrease base wages (as well as variable pay). Airline pilots and mechanics have taken highly publicized pay cuts in recent years. Other alternatives also exist. Look again at the cost model for St. Luke's and its segmented labor supply. The hospital can reduce costs by reducing the different sources of contract nurses.

Competitive Market Pressures

In Chapter 8, we discussed how managers determine an organization's competitive position in relation to its competitors. Recall that a distribution of market rates for benchmark jobs was collected and analyzed into a single average wage for each benchmark. This "average market wage" becomes the "going market rate," and this market rate changes each year in response to a variety of factors in the external market.

Turnover Effects

Sometimes referred to as **"churn"** or "slippage," the **turnover effect** recognizes the fact that when people leave (through layoffs, quitting, retiring), they typically are replaced by employees who earn a lower wage. Exhibit 18.2 illustrates where an organization is overstaffed compared to competitors. Reducing levels at E5 and E4 and replacing them with E1s and E2s will reduce labor costs. However, keep in mind the potential impact on revenues and customer satisfaction, as well as possible violation of the Age Discrimination in Employment Act.

The turnover effect can be calculated as annual turnover multiplied by the planned average increase. For example, assume that an organization whose labor costs equal $1 million a year has a turnover rate of 15 percent and a planned average increase of 6 percent. The turnover effect is $.15 \times .06 = 0.9\%$, or $9,000 ($.009 \times $1,000,000$). So instead of budgeting an additional $60,000 to fund a 6 percent increase, only $51,000 is needed. The turnover effect will also reduce benefit costs linked to base pay, such as pensions.[20]

Cost of Living

Although there is little research to support **cost of living increases,** employees undoubtedly compare their pay increases to changes in their living costs. Unions consistently argue that increasing living costs justify increasing pay.

It is important to distinguish among three related concepts: the *cost of living, changes in prices in the product and service markets,* and *changes in wages in labor markets.* As Exhibit 18.7 shows, changes in wages in labor markets are measured

EXHIBIT 18.7   Three Distinct but Related Concepts and Their Measures

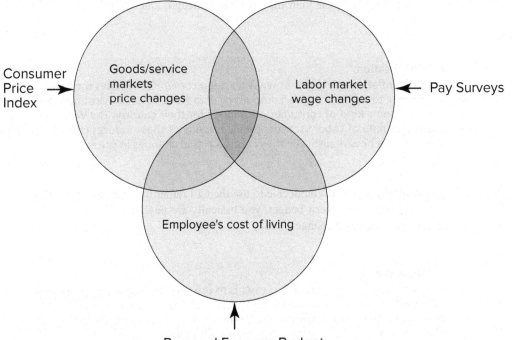

through pay surveys. These changes are incorporated into the system through market adjustments in the budget and updates of the policy line and range structure. Price changes for goods and services in the product and service markets are measured by several government indexes, one of which is the consumer price index (CPI). The third concept, the cost of living, refers to the expenditure patterns of individuals for goods and services. The cost of living is more difficult to measure because employees' expenditures depend on many things: marital status, number of dependents and ages, personal preferences, location, and so on. Different employees experience different costs of living, and the only accurate way to measure them is to examine the personal expenditures of each employee.

The three concepts are interrelated. Wages in the labor market are part of the cost of producing goods and services, and changes in wages create pressures on prices. Similarly, changes in the prices of goods and services create the need for increased wages in order to maintain the same lifestyle.

Many people refer to the CPI as a "cost-of-living" index, and many employers choose, as a matter of pay policy or in response to union pressures, to tie wages to it. However, the CPI does not necessarily reflect an individual employee's cost of living. Instead, it measures *changes in prices over time.* Changes in the CPI indicate whether prices have increased more or less rapidly in an area since the base period. For example, a CPI of 110 in Chicago and 140 in Atlanta does not necessarily mean that it costs more to live in Atlanta. It does mean that prices have risen faster in Atlanta since the base year than they have in Chicago, since both cities started with bases of 100.

---

e-Compensation

A simple inflation calculator at *www.westegg.com/inflation/* uses the consumer price index to adjust any given amount of data from 1800 on. Most governments calculate some kind of consumer price index for their country. The Web page for the U.S. Bureau of Labor Statistics provides many of these indexes (*stats.bls.gov*). They vary on how realistically they capture actual changes in prices.

A word of caution: If you decide to use the CPI rather than labor market salary surveys to determine the merit budget, you basically are paying for inflation rather than performance or market changes.

---

e-Compensation

A quicker way to compare living costs is to use the "relocation salary calculator" at *www.homefair.com/homefair/calc/salcalc.html*. Enter your current city and potential new city to see what salary you need in the new city based on cost-of-living differences. How accurate is this website's information?

The CPI is of public interest because changes in it trigger changes in labor contracts, social security payments, federal and military pensions, and food stamp eligibility. Tying budgets or payments to the CPI is called *indexing.*

Rolling It All Together

Let us assume that the managers take into account all these factors—current year's rise, ability to pay, market adjustments, turnover effects, changes in the cost of living, and **geographic differentials**—and decide that the planned rise in average salary for the next period is 6.3 percent. This means that the organization has set a target of 6.3 percent as the increase in *average* salary that will occur in the next budget period. It does not mean that everyone's increase will be 6.3 percent. It means that at the end of the budget year, the average salary calculated to include all employees will be 6.3 percent higher than it is now.

The next question is, How do we distribute that 6.3 percent budget in a way that accomplishes management's objectives for the pay system and meets the organization's goals?

Distributing the Budget to Subunits

A variety of methods exist for determining what percentage of the salary budget each manager should receive. Some use a uniform percentage, in which each manager gets an equal percentage of the budget based on the salaries of each sub-unit's employees. Others vary the percentage allocated to each manager based on pay-related issues—such as turnover or performance—that have been identified in that subunit.

Once salary budgets are allocated to each subunit manager, they become a constraint: a limited fund of money that each manager has to allocate to subordinates. Typically, **merit increase guidelines** are used to help managers make these allocation decisions. Merit increase grids help ensure that different managers grant consistent increases to employees with similar performance ratings and in the same position in their ranges. Additionally, grids help control costs. Chapter 11 provides examples of merit increase grids. To limit the number of employees placed in high performance categories (and thus the number of employees receiving the largest merit increases), some companies used forced distribution approaches.

Budget Controls: Bottom Up

In contrast to top-down budgeting, where managers are told what their salary budget will be, bottom-up budgeting begins with managers' pay increase recommendations for the upcoming plan year. Exhibit 18.8 shows the process involved.

1. *Instruct managers in compensation policies and techniques.* Train managers in the concepts of a sound pay-for-performance policy and in standard company compensation techniques such as the use of pay-increase guidelines and budgeting techniques. Communicate market data and the salary ranges.

2. *Distribute forecasting instructions and worksheets.* Furnish managers with the forms and instructions necessary to preplan increases. Most firms offer managers computer software to support these analyses and to enter information and perform what-if analyses.[21] Adjustments for each individual are fed into the summary merit budget, promotion budget, equity adjustment budget, and so on, on a summary screen. These recommendations are then submitted electronically.

   The type of information available to each supervisor to guide him or her in making recommendations might include performance rating history, past raises, training background, and stock allocations are all included. Guidelines for increases based on merit, promotion, and equity adjustments are provided, and all the worksheets are linked so that the manager can model pay adjustments for employees and see the budgetary effects of those adjustments immediately.

   Some argue that providing such detailed data and recommendations to operating managers makes the process biased. How would you like your instructor to look at your overall GPA before giving you a grade in this course? Pay histories, however, ensure that managers are at least aware of this information and that pay increases for any one period are part of a continuing message to individual employees, not some ad-hoc response to short-term changes.

3. *Provide consultation to managers.* Offer advice and salary information services to managers upon request. Dell's online approach makes it much easier to request and apply such guidance.

EXHIBIT 18.8
Compensation
Forecasting
and Budgeting
Cycle

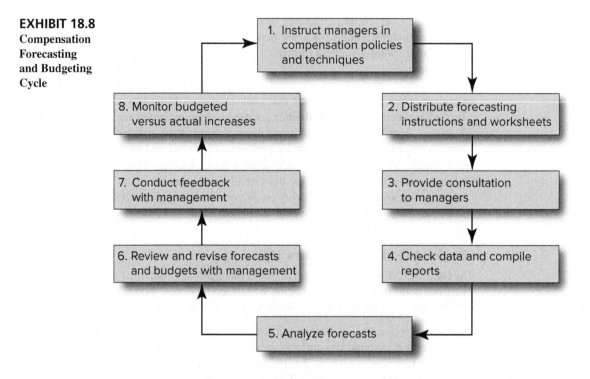

4. *Check data and compile reports.* Audit the increases forecasted to ensure that they do not exceed the pay guidelines and are consistent with appropriate ranges. Then use the data to feed back the outcomes of pay forecasts and budgets.

5. *Analyze forecasts.* Examine each manager's forecast, and recommend changes based on noted inequities among different managers.

6. *Review and revise forecasts and budgets with management.* Consult with managers regarding the analysis and any recommended changes. Obtain top-management approval of forecasts.

7. *Conduct feedback with management.* Present statistical summaries of the forecasting data by department, and establish unit goals.

8. *Monitor budgeted versus actual increases.* Control the forecasted increases versus the actual increases by tracking and reporting periodic status to management.

The result of the forecasting cycle is a budget for the upcoming plan year for each organization's unit as well as estimated pay treatment for each employee. The budget does not lock in the manager to the exact pay change recommended for each employee. Rather, it represents a plan, and deviations due to unforeseen changes such as performance improvements and unanticipated promotions are common. The approach places responsibility for pay management on the managers by requiring them to plan the pay treatment for each of their employees. The compensation manager takes on the role of advisor to operating management's use of the system.[22]

Embedded (Design) Controls

Controls on managers' pay decisions come from two different aspects of the compensation process: (1) controls that are inherent in the design of the techniques, and (2) the formal **budgeting** process discussed above. Think back to the many techniques already discussed: job analysis and evaluation, skill- and competency-based plans, policy lines, **range minimums and maximums,** broad bands, performance evaluation, gain sharing, and salary-increase guidelines. In addition to their primary purposes, these techniques also regulate managers' pay decisions by guiding what managers can and cannot do. Controls are built into these techniques to direct them toward the pay system objectives. A few of these controls are examined below.

Range Maximums and Minimums

Ranges set the maximum and minimum dollars to be paid for specific work. The maximum is an important cost control. Ideally, it represents the highest value the organization places on the output of the work. With job-based structures, skills and knowledge possessed by employees may be more valuable in another job, but the range maximum represents the maximum worth to an organization of work performed in a particular job. When Walmart installed range maximums and minimums for its jobs, its critics accused the company of "capping wages" of its workers. Those readers who recall Chapter 8's discussion on designing ranges recognize that specific jobs may have a maximum rate (a cap) but individuals may still be able to increase their pay through promotions, profit sharing, and so on.[23]

When employees are paid above the range maximum, these rates are called **red circle rates.** Most employers "freeze" red circle rates until the ranges are shifted upward by market update adjustments so that the rate is back within the range again. An organization also has the option to combine a salary freeze with the use of merit bonuses, which unlike merit increases, do not become part of base salary. If red circle rates become common throughout an organization, then the design of the ranges and the evaluation of the jobs should be reexamined. **Green circle rates** refer to instances where employees are paid below the minimum. As with red circle rates, organizations typically take steps to make sure these are temporary.

Range minimums are just that: the minimum value placed on the work. Often rates below the minimum are used for trainees. Pay below minimum may also occur if outstanding employees receive a number of rapid promotions and pay increases have not kept up.

Broad Bands

Broad bands are intended to offer managers greater flexibility compared to a grade-range design. Usually broad bands are accompanied by external market "reference rates" and "shadow ranges" that guide managers' decisions. Bands may be more about career management than pay decisions. Rather, the control is in the salary budgets given to managers. The manager has flexibility in pay decisions, as long as the total pay comes in under the budget.

Promotions and External versus Internal Hires

Promotion-based pay increases are often substantial, meaning that cost control efforts must monitor both rates of promotion and the salary increase that is given with promotions. Some organizations limit the number of promotions permitted within a time period and some also limit the number of grades/levels that an employee can advance as well as the size of the promotion salary increase.[24] Another, more strategic issue concerns the degree to which positions are filled from the inside via promotion versus the use of outside hires.[25] Outside hires often command a pay premium and, to the degree that their higher pay is known to other employees, internal equity pressures may, in some cases, result in higher pay for current employees as a means to preserve current norms regarding relative pay.

Compa-Ratios

Range midpoints reflect the pay policy line of the employer in relationship to external competition. To assess how managers actually pay employees in relation to the midpoint, an index called a **compa-ratio** is often calculated:

$$\text{Compa - ratio} = \frac{\text{average rate actual paid}}{\text{range midpoint}}$$

A compa-ratio of less than 1 means that, on average, employees in a range are paid below the midpoint. That is, managers are paying less than the intended policy. There may be several valid reasons for such a situation. The majority of employees may be new or recent hires; they may be poor performers; or promotion may be so rapid that few employees stay in the job long enough to get into the high end of the range.

A compa-ratio greater than 1 means that, on average, the rates exceed the intended policy. The reasons for this are the reverse of those mentioned above: a majority of workers with high seniority, high performance, low turnover, few new hires, or low promotion rates. Compa-ratios may be calculated for individual employees, for each range, for organization units, or for functions.

Other examples of controls designed into the pay techniques include the mutual sign-offs on job descriptions required of supervisors and subordinates. Another is slotting new jobs into the pay structure via job evaluation, which helps ensure that jobs are compared on the same factors. Similarly, an organization-wide performance management system is intended to ensure that all employees are evaluated on similar factors.

Variable Pay

The essence of variable pay is that it must be re-earned each period, in contrast to conventional merit pay increases or across-the-board increases that increase the base on which the following year's increase is calculated. We have distinguished between fixed and variable pay and noted multiple times that organizations have moved toward greater reliance on variable pay. It is important enough that it bears repeating again. As we saw in Exhibit 18.6, organizations have increased their use of variable pay relative to traditional base pay increases.

Increases added into base pay have compounding effects on costs, and these costs are significant. For example, a $15-a-week take-home pay added onto a $40,000 base compounds into a cash flow of $503,116 over 10 years. In addition, costs for some benefits also increase. By comparison, the organization could use that same $503,000 to keep base pay at $40,000 a year and pay a 26.8 percent bonus every single year. As the example shows, the greater the ratio of variable pay to base pay, the more flexible the organization's labor costs.

Apply this flexibility to the general labor cost model in Exhibit 18.1. The greater the ratios of contingent to core workers and variable to base pay, the greater the variable component of labor costs and the greater the options available to managers to control these costs. A caution: Although variability in pay and employment may be an advantage for managing labor costs, it may be less appealing from the standpoint of managing effective treatment of employees. The inherent financial insecurity built into variable plans may adversely affect employees' financial well-being, especially for lower-paid workers. Managing labor costs is only one objective for managing compensation.

Analyzing Costs

Costing out wage proposals is commonly done prior to recommending pay increases, especially for collective bargaining. For example, it is useful to bear in mind the dollar impact of a 1-cent-per-hour wage change or a 1 percent change in payroll as one goes into bargaining. Knowing these figures, negotiators can quickly compute the impact of a request for a 9 percent wage increase.

Commercial compensation software is available to analyze almost every aspect of compensation information. Software can easily compare past estimates to what actually occurred (e.g., the percentage of employees that actually did receive a merit increase and the amount). It can simulate alternate wage proposals and compare their potential effects. It can also help evaluate salary survey data and simulate the cost impact of incentive and gain-sharing options.

MANAGING REVENUES

Although the cost of compensation is most easily measured (and managed/controlled), we cannot forget that compensation, via its incentive and sorting effects on the workforce and its central role in supporting strategy execution, is also central to driving future revenues. According to one study, only about one-third of organizations actually calculate the cost and value added by their pay programs.[26] Not surprisingly, another survey reports that assessment of the impact of compensation on revenues falls especially short, with about 70 percent of the compensation specialists reporting their tools as "ineffective" to determine the value added. However, a handful of companies, supported by consultants and researchers, are beginning to analyze the value added (or return on investments) of pay decisions and how that influences revenues.[27] This analysis requires a shift in how compensation is viewed. Compensation becomes an investment as well as an expense. Decisions are based on analysis of the return on this investment. The hope is to answer questions such as, "So what" returns are expected from spending more on the offensive team (as do the Seattle Seahawks), or showering rewards on the top performers (as does General Electric), or on a new incentive plan based on a balanced scorecard (as does Citigroup)?[28]

Exhibit 18.9 illustrates the approach to assessing value gained in different ways, which directly or indirectly influence revenues. The company in this exhibit has already done an analysis that suggests that the top 10 percent of employees improve returns by about 2 to 5 percent of their average salary. Now the company is considering two actions:

1. Implement a bonus plan based on balanced scorecards for individual managers.
2. Increase the differentiation between top performers and average performers.

The exhibit shows the analysis of potential value added by these two options. The returns are grouped into four types: recruiting and retaining top talent, reducing turnover of top performers, revenue enhancement, and productivity gains. The logic, assumptions, measures, and estimates of gains are described in the exhibit. The cautious reader will immediately see that the assumptions are critical and based on research evidence, best estimates, and judgments.

The practice of analyzing the returns from compensation decisions is in its early stages. The promise is that it will direct thinking beyond treating compensation as only an expense to considering the returns gained as well. Our discussion of utility analysis in the Appendix to Chapter 7 is an example of one approach.[29] Advocates want to develop compensation managers' *analytical literacy*. Readers will recognize the similarity to topics in their finance and operations management classes. Nevertheless, managers still must use their heads as well as their models. Treating compensation as an investment and employees as human capital risks losing sight of them as people.[30] The fairness objective must not get lost in the search for ROI.

Using Compensation to Retain (and Recruit) Top Employees

Recall that one aspect of the sorting effect is that high performers will tend to move from organizations that do not adequately compensate them for the high value they create to organizations that do. Some in this group will be "pushed" to look for another job because of their perception that they are not equitably paid. However, a substantial share of employees, especially high performers, leave their jobs because of being "pulled" by opportunities elsewhere. They leave not as a result of being dissatisfied with their current job and/or as a result of looking for a new job, but rather because an unsolicited opportunity from a proactive organization came their way.[31] Indeed, Google's top human resources executive takes the view that the best people are doing well where they are and that it is important to invest resources to learn who they are. They may not actively search or apply for jobs at Google, but Google wants to cultivate these "passive job seekers," even if it takes years because Google sees successfully hiring such people as a path to higher revenues.[32] The implication is that their current employer would do well to keep compensation current and competitive (given their skills and value/revenues generated) because other (proactive) organizations will eventually find them. It also means that organizations can be proactive too not just in terms of keeping valuable employees they already have, but in looking for people employed elsewhere who can come and create value and higher revenues.

EXHIBIT 18.9 Examples of How Compensation Can Influence Revenues (directly or indirectly)

Description of Value	Assumptions	Measure	Value Added	
			Low Estimate	High Estimate
Recruiting/Retaining Top Talent				
Increase pool of top people applying; Increase percent accepting offers; Decrease time to fill position	Top performers improve returns by 2% to 5% of average salary ($68,000)	Increase top talent yield ratios and turnover rates	Increases revenues by $1,400/top person	Improves revenues by $3,400/top person
Reduced Turnover/Replacement Costs				
Reduction of recruiting costs due to lower turnover of top performers	Reduction in turnover of one top performer results in a savings of $25,000 (based on an average salary of $68,000)	Savings of $25,000/top performer	$100,000 for a reduction of four "resigned" top employees	$500,000 for a reduction of 10 "resigned" top employees
Revenue Enhancers				
Reduced loss of revenue due to faster time to fill key customer-facing (sales, technical support) and other key positions	Revenue will increase by some percentage (e.g., 5%) Headcount remains constant	Productivity savings reflected in "loss of revenue" section Revenue increase Assume current revenue of $2 billion	2% or $40 million	5% or $100 million
Greater revenue because of focus on revenue and customer goals as driven by the balanced scorecard				
Increased revenue because of stronger and longer-lasting customer relationships due to retention of key/top performers through market competitiveness and pay differentiation				
Productivity Gains				
Increased productivity by retaining top performers through significant pay differentiation and market-competitive base pay	Retaining and engaging more of the top employees results in significant productivity gains and revenue generation because top employees are 25% to 50% more productive than the average employee	Increased revenue (reflected in revenue gains-above)	A reduction in 10 headcount results in a savings of $900,000 ($68,000 employee + benefit cost)	A reduction in 50 headcount results in a savings of $4.5-million
	Increasing the productivity of all results in increased revenue, customer satisfaction, or fewer headcount	Headcount reduction (need fewer employees or grow slower)		
Increased productivity of all employees because of greater perception of "internal alignment" and "market competitiveness" resulting from paying competitive with the market and common programs	Terminating low-productivity employees and replacing them with high-productivity employees result in significant productivity gains and revenue generation	Headcount reduction because fewer top performers achieve the same results as more lower performers	A reduction in 1 headcount results in a savings of $90,000	A reduction in 5 headcount results in a savings of $450,000

683

MANAGING PAY TO SUPPORT STRATEGY AND CHANGE

In Chapter 2, we noted the important role of pay in supporting the business strategy and the HR strategy. We saw that organizations with different business strategies often have correspondingly different compensation strategies. We also saw, using the ability-motivation-opportunity (AMO) framework that pay plays a crucial role. These alignment issues must be managed successfully to drive future revenues (and control costs). Compensation often plays a singular role when organizations restructure. Strategic changes in the business strategy mean the compensation strategy must be realigned as well. Looking back again to Chapter 2, pay's incentive effects can help redirect and reenergize employee efforts. Its sorting effects can help replace current employees who fit the old system, but not the new system, with new employees who do fit. The bigger the change, the bigger the sorting effects and the more likely that there will a difficult period of adjustment as part of the change. The question is whether the short-term pain will be worth it to reposition the organization to better succeed going forward in terms of achieving the goals of stakeholders (owners, employees, customers, and so forth).

Pay is a powerful signal of change; changing people's pay captures their attention. At a broader level, pay changes can play two roles in any restructuring. Pay can be a *leading catalyst* for change or a *follower* of change. Shifts from conventional across-the-board annual increases to profit sharing or from narrow job descriptions and ranges to broad roles and bands signal major change to employees. Determining the role pay plays is an important part of a strategic perspective, as you will recall from the Chapter 2 discussion of strategic mapping.

Microsoft's shift from its uniquely aggressive stock options to less risky stock awards illustrates the point. Microsoft used its change in the pay mix to communicate a shift from a "workaholic—get rich quick" to a "work hard—get paid well" approach. Whether this shift acts as a catalyst or a support is open to debate. As a catalyst, it communicates change more strongly and vividly than any rhetoric could. It helps drive recruiting and retention. Yet it may be that Microsoft had already changed as an organization. Faced with murmuring employees (their options were underwater) and external conditions (an accounting rule change that required options to be treated as an expense) the shift in pay mix merely confirmed reality—that Microsoft had changed.

Whether pay is a leading catalyst for change or a follower of change, compensation managers must learn how to implement and manage change. Not only must they know the strategic and technical aspects of compensation, they also must know how to bargain, resolve disputes, empower employees, and develop teams. Being able to grab bullets in midflight doesn't hurt, either.[33]

COMMUNICATION: MANAGING THE MESSAGE

Compensation communicates. It signals what is important and what is not. If you receive a pay increase for one more year of experience on your job, then one more year is important. If the pay increase is equal to any change in the CPI, then the CPI and its real meaning is important. If the increase is for moving to a bigger job or for outstanding performance, then a bigger job or outstanding performance is important. Changes in a pay system also send a powerful message. Microsoft's shift from stock options to grants tells everyone (current and future employees and stockholders) to expect lower risks and lower returns.

Earlier in this book, we stressed that employees must understand the pay system. Their understanding is shaped indirectly through the paychecks they receive and directly via formal communication about their pay, their performance, and the markets in which the organization competes. An argument for employee involvement in the design of pay systems is that it increases understanding. Two surveys are revealing. A Watson Wyatt survey of 13,000 employees reported that about only 35 percent of them understood the link between their job performance and the pay they receive. (Watson Wyatt failed to point out that some workers may simply believe that in their organizations there is no real link!)[34] WorldatWork did a second survey of 6,000 employees. Only about one-third of them said they understood how pay ranges are determined or had a reasonable idea of what their increase would be if they were promoted. Fewer than half understood how their own pay increases are calculated.[35] Exhibit 18.10 provides further insight into employee (lack of) pay knowledge. Of note is that only 8 and 4 percent, respectively, of compensation professionals strongly agree that employees know their own pay range (e.g., the maximum they can earn without getting promoted), the pay range above them (so, how much they could earn if they were promoted). By contrast, 15 and 20 percent, respectively, strongly disagree that employees have this information, which presumably is relevant to their work motivation. Finally, only a minority of respondents agree that pay-related information is "shared openly" in their organizations.

Two reasons are usually given for communicating pay information. The first is that considerable resources have been devoted to designing a fair and equitable system that is intended to attract and retain qualified people and motivate performance. For managers and employees to gain an accurate view of the pay system—one that perhaps influences their attitudes about it—they need to be informed. Of course, one might observe that increasing the accuracy of employee perceptions through pay openness is most useful in cases where the compensation system is well-designed and will be perceived as fair and credible by employees. In that case, from a motivational point of view, it would certainly make sense to communicate and demonstrate to employees that those with consistently high performance receive higher compensation (including via more promotions) than others.[36] Thus, it is quite interesting (see Exhibit 18.10) that most (25% + 41% = 66%) U.S. private sector employees report working in organizations where pay secrecy is the policy and few (17%) report that pay information is made public. The lack of pay knowledge among employees discussed above now becomes easier to understand. As Exhibit 18.10 also shows, there is much more pay openness in the public sector (both because of higher union coverage and because taxpayers wish to know how their tax dollars are spent).

Finally, it is important to keep in mind that a pay secrecy policy in private sector organizations may be illegal. Under the National Labor Relations Act, it is illegal if it interferes with "concerted action" by employees. In addition, Executive Order 13665, "Non-Retaliation for Disclosure of Compensation Information," prohibits federal contractors or subcontractors from "discharging or discriminating in any other way

EXHIBIT 18.10 Pay Communication and Employee Knowledge of Pay

	Strongly Disagree	Disagree	Neither Agree nor Disagree	Agree	Strongly Agree
Employees know the pay ranges for their [*own*] pay grade or position	15%	26%	18%	33%	8%
Employees know what the pay ranges are for the grade or the positions *immediately above their own*	20%	40%	19%	17%	4%
Compensation program information is shared openly by the organization	12%	35%	17%	29%	7%

Source: Dow Scott, Tom McMullen, Bill Bowbin, and John Shields. Alignment of Business Strategies, Organization Structures and Reward Programs: A Survey of Policies, Practices and Effectiveness. WorldatWork, May 2009. N = 442 to 446 responses from compensation professionals.

against employees or applicants who inquire about, discuss, or disclose their own compensation or the compensation of another employee or applicant."[37] It serves to modify existing Executive Order 11246 with the aim of making it more effective. A major rationale given is that to the degree discrimination explains why men and women are paid differently, "strictures against revealing compensation can conceal compensation disparities among employees. This makes it impossible for an employee to know he or she is being underpaid compared to his or her peers. If compensation remains hidden, employees who are being unfairly paid less because of their gender or race will remain unaware of the problem and will be unable to exercise their rights by filing a complaint pursuant to the Executive Order."

The second (and related) reason for communicating pay information is that, according to some research, employees seem to misperceive the pay system. For example, they tend to overestimate the pay of those in lower-level jobs and to underestimate the pay of those in higher-level jobs. They assume that the pay structure is more compressed than it actually is. If differentials are underestimated, their motivational value is, as noted above, diminished, because they underestimate the payoff to high performance.

Further, there is some evidence to suggest that the goodwill engendered by the act of being open about pay may also affect perceptions of pay equity. Interestingly, the research also shows that employees in companies with open pay communication policies are as inaccurate in estimating pay differentials as those in companies in which pay secrecy prevails.[38] (Caution: Most of this research was done over 20 years ago.) However, employers in companies with open pay policies tend to express higher satisfaction with their pay and with the pay system.[39] Other research indicates that employee reactions to pay secrecy versus pay openness depend on equity sensitivity, with those more sensitive to whether pay is fair given inputs like performance being most likely to respond favorably (higher performance, stronger perceived performance—pay instrumentality) to pay openness.[40] Other research, in a university setting, found that making pay information on other employees in the university systems more explicitly available resulted in more pay comparisons by employees (especially with peers in the same department) and lower satisfaction and greater search intentions among

EXHIBIT 18.11

Pay Secrecy
Policies,
Private and
Public Sector

	Private Sector Workers	Public Sector Workers
The discussion of wages and salaries at work is **formally prohibited,** and/or employees caught discussing wage and salary information could be punished	25%	6%
The discussion of wages and salaries at work is **discouraged by managers**	41%	9%
Wage and salary information **can be discussed** in the workplace	17%	15%
Wage and salary information is **public**	17%	70%

Source: Adapted from Institute for Women's Policy Research, *Pay Secrecy and Wage Discrimination. Fact Sheet* IWPR #C382, June 2011, www.ipr.org.; accessed June 5, 2012. Data from national (U.S.) survey of 2,700 adults (18 and over). Percentages differ slightly from source because categories constrained here to sum to 100%.

employees paid below the median for their department and occupation. This finding led the study authors to conclude that "employers have a strong incentive to impose pay secrecy rules," but also noted that another result could be a change in the composition of the workforce.[41] Another way to put it is that being more open with pay information will decrease the satisfaction of some employees. So, an employer must be prepared to address that consequence. However, an employer will also want to consider who is dissatisfied and why. To the degree that pay is based on performance, being more open with pay could result in positive sorting effects over time to the extent that it is low performers who are dissatisfied and they leave and are replaced by higher performing employees. A laboratory study found some evidence that more open pay not only had positive incentive effects on performance (especially when performance was measured in relative terms), but also that there were positive sorting effects of the type just suggested.[42]

In the case of benefits too, communication plays a potentially important role. We know that employees greatly underestimate the value of their benefits, which is a major concern given that benefits add roughly 40 cents on top of every dollar spent on cash compensation.[43]

WorldatWork recommends a six-stage process of communication, similar to that shown in Exhibit 18.12.[44]

Step 1 is, not surprisingly, defining the objectives of the communication program. Is it to ensure that employees fully understand all the components of the compensation system? Is it to change performance expectations? Or is it to help employees make informed health care choices? While specifying objectives as a first step seems obvious, doing so is often overlooked in the rush to design an attractive brochure, website, or CD.

Step 2 is to collect information from executives, managers, and employees to assess their current perceptions, attitudes, and understanding of the subject. Information may be gathered through online opinion surveys and focus groups to identify problems in understanding the compensation system.

EXHIBIT 18.12
The Compensation Communication Cycle

1. Define Objectives of the Employee Communication Program

2. Collect Information and Identify the Facts

3. Choose Communication Tools and Media

4. Conduct the Communication Sessions with Employees

5. Evaluate the Success of the Communication Program

Step 3 is a communication program that will convey the information needed to accomplish the original objectives. There is no standard approach on what to communicate to individuals about their own pay or that of their colleagues. Some organizations adopt a *marketing approach.* That includes consumer attitude surveys about the product, snappy advertising about the pay policies, and elaborate websites expounding policies and rationale. The objective is to manage expectations and attitudes about pay. In contrast, the *communication approach* tends to focus on explaining practices, details, and the way pay is determined. The marketing approach focuses on the strategy, values, and advantages of overall policies and may be silent on specifics such as range maximums, increase guides, and the like.

Steps 4 and 5 of the communication process are to determine the most effective media, in light of the message and the audience, and to conduct the campaign. The message can be fine-tuned, depending on the audience. Executives, for example, should be interested in how the compensation programs fit the business strategy. Managers need to know how to use the development and motivation aspects of the compensation program for the people they supervise. Employees may want to know the processes and policies as well as specifics about how their pay is determined. The danger is overload—information is so detailed that employees get snowed under sorting through it.

Step 6 of the communication process suggests that the program be evaluated. Did it accomplish its goals? Pay communication often has unintended consequences.[45] For example, improving employees' knowledge about pay may cause some initial short-term concerns. Over the years, employees may have rationalized a set of relationships between their pay and the perceived pay and efforts of others. Receiving accurate information may require that those perceptions be adjusted.

e-Compensation
One compensation manager reports having a great deal of difficulty with an employee who used the homefair website *www.homefair.com* to determine that he should receive a 30 percent pay differential to accompany his transfer from one office to another. In contrast, the manager's information showed a differential of around 12 to 15 percent. How can you judge the accuracy of information obtained on the Web? How would you deal with the unhappy employee?

Say What? (Or, What to Say?)

As noted above, if the pay system is not based on work-related or business-related logic, then the wisest course is probably to avoid formal communication until the system is put in order. However, avoiding *formal* communication is not synonymous with avoiding communication. Employees are constantly getting intended and unintended messages through the pay treatment they receive.

Some employers communicate the range for an incumbent's present job and for all the jobs in a typical career path or progression to which employees can logically aspire. Some also communicate the typical pay increases that can be expected for poor, satisfactory, and top performance. The rationale given is that employees exchange data (not always factual) and/or guess at normal treatment and that the rumor mills are probably incorrect. However, as we saw just above, employee pay knowledge is often quite limited.

How people process information and make decisions, as shown in Exhibit 18.13, offers some new ideas when contemplating compensation communications.[46]

Opening the Books

There are some who advocate going beyond the sharing of pay information to the sharing of all financial information with employees.[47] Employees at engine rebuilder Springfield Remanufacturing receive weekly peeks at everything from revenues to labor costs. The employees, who own 31 percent of the company stock, believe that this "open-book" approach results in high commitment and an understanding of how to maintain competitiveness. Whole Foods' open-paybook approach was described in Chapter 1. Most employers don't share information with such gusto, but they are increasingly disclosing more to their employees. Some are even providing basic business and financial training to help employees better understand the information. Devotees of opening the books and providing financial training believe these methods will improve attitudes and performance, but there is no research to support this. With salary data available on the Internet (albeit often inaccurate and misleading), developing in-house compensation portals has appeal.

EXHIBIT 18.13 Guidance from the Research on Pay Communication

Behavior	What Is It?	So What?
Persistence of beliefs	Reluctance to accept evidence that contradicts existing beliefs.	Changing existing beliefs requires actively engaging employees in pay system design and communication.
Anchoring/framing	Initial data strongly affect decisions/beliefs.	First data matters, e.g., market data swamps job-evaluation results. Previous bonus sets expectation for future bonus.
Herding	Following fashions in programs/techniques.	Benchmark selectively. Use pilot programs and test trials to guide.
Pattern recognition	People "discover" patterns in random events. They believe correlation means causation.	Higher pay may not mean higher performance; higher performance may not mean higher pay.

At the minimum, the most important information to be communicated is the work-related and business-related rationales on which pay systems are based. Some employees may not agree with these rationales or the results, but at least it will be clear that pay is determined by something other than the whims of their supervisors.

STRUCTURING THE COMPENSATION FUNCTION AND ITS ROLES

Compensation professionals seem to be constantly reevaluating where within the organization the responsibility for the design and administration of pay systems should be located. The organizational arrangements of the compensation function vary widely.[48] Other key issues include the use of enterprise information systems and ethics issues for compensation professionals.

Centralization–Decentralization (and/or Outsourcing)

An important issue related to structuring the function revolves around the degree of decentralization (or centralization) in the overall organization structure. *Decentralized* refers to a management strategy of giving separate business units the responsibility of designing and administering their own systems. This contrasts with a *centralized* strategy, which locates the design and administration responsibility at corporate headquarters. A centralized compensation strategy and function is more likely to be found in smaller and/or single line of business organizations. This "one size fits all" approach is more likely to make sense when the entire company mostly competes in a single product market. Examples include Herman Miller (furniture) and McDonald's (quick service food).[49] However, in organizations (e.g., IBM) that are larger and/or compete in different product (or geographic) markets, human resource and compensation strategies are more likely to need to be tailored to fit those different contexts. In such cases, compensation professionals are increasingly likely to be embedded in each business unit. Typically, corporate will retain some number of compensation professionals, perhaps in what is known as a center for expertise. This group provides an internal consulting capability that human resource professionals in the business units, who are often human resource generalists, can be drawn on to assist in the design of compensation strategies. The mix of corporate and business unit compensation expertise is a balancing act. Too big of a corporate group risks becoming out of touch with specific business unit needs. Too many staff in the business units risks reinventing the wheel, duplication/redundancy of expertise, and higher costs. Over time, it is not unusual to see the pendulum swing within companies back and forth between more or less centralization.

Other, more decentralized organizations, such as Eaton and GE, have relatively small corporate compensation staffs. Sometimes, their primary responsibility is to manage the systems by which executives and the corporate staff are paid (although GE corporate compensation drives the salary planning process company-wide). These professionals may operate in a purely advisory capacity to other organization sub-units. The subunits, in turn, may employ their own compensation specialists. Or the subunits may choose to employ only personnel generalists rather than compensation specialists and may turn to outside compensation consultants to purchase the expertise required on specific compensation issues.

AES, an electric power company, has no compensation unit at all. They don't even have an HR department. Compensation functions are handled by teams of managers. Decentralizing certain aspects of pay design and administration has considerable appeal. Pushing these responsibilities (and expenses) close to the units, managers, and employees affected by them may help ensure that decisions are business-related. However, decentralization is not without dilemmas. For example, it may be difficult to transfer employees from one business unit to another. A pay system may support a subunit's objectives but run counter to the overall corporate objectives. Also, we have seen time and again that decentralization, which by definition includes less direct control of what managers do, can contribute to legal problems. As noted in Chapter 17, for example, Walmart is facing sex-discrimination claims in what would be the largest class action discrimination suit to date (1.6 million or more claimants). Interestingly, Walmart has argued that "establishing a national class is unwarranted because its store managers acted with discretion" in their decisions regarding promotion and pay of workers. So, in effect, Walmart's defense is that if its managers discriminated, it was because Walmart did not have centralized control over their decisions.[50]

Flexibility within Corporatewide Principles

The answers to these and related problems of decentralization can be found in developing a set of corporatewide principles or guidelines that all must meet. The principles may differ for each major pay technique. For example, GE's business units worldwide have the flexibility to design incentive plans tailored to each unique business unit's strategies and cultures. The only guidance is to ensure that the plans adhere to GE's basic beliefs, improve financial and business objectives, and maintain or enhance GE's reputation.

Keep in mind that the pay system is one of many management systems used in the organization. Consequently, it must be congruent with these other systems. For example, it may be appealing, on paper at least, to decentralize some of the compensation functions. However, if financial data and other management systems are not also decentralized, the pay system may be at odds with other systems.

Reengineering and Outsourcing

Value chain analysis and Six Sigma are processes used to improve quality and ensure that value is added by each technique and at each stage in a process. For the compensation system, the basic question to ask is, "Does each specific activity (technique) directly contribute to our objectives?" If some added value isn't apparent, then the question is, "How should it be redesigned? Or should it be dropped?" Of those activities that do add value, the next question is, "Who should do it?" "Should the activity be done in-house, or can others do it more effectively? That is, should it be outsourced?"

Outsourcing is a viable alternative as organizations struggle with activities that do not directly contribute to objectives. These are often referred to as transactional activities, which are not unique to the organization and might be done cheaper (and perhaps also better) by an outside provider. On the other hand, more transformational or strategic activities (e.g., what pay-for-performance strategy would best align with the business strategy) are less likely to be outsourced.[51]

Cost savings are the major potential advantage of outsourcing. All those compensation pros can be laid off and/or retrained and reassigned to other work. Sometimes, the quality of the service provided may increase also. A firm that does nothing but administer retirement benefits may be able to do a better job than a firm whose primary business is something else (e.g., making furniture or cars, selling quick service food). Major potential disadvantages include less responsiveness to unique employee–manager problems, less control over decisions that are often critical to all employees (i.e., their pay), and information leaks to rivals and competitors. In addition, as with any contract, while an agreement may be signed stating that an outsourcing firm will provide a certain set of services and at a certain level, either side may subsequently find that their vision of the agreement and their experience of what is actually delivered may end up being different.[52]

Balancing Flexibility and Control

One of the major attacks on traditional compensation plans is that they often degenerate into bureaucratic nightmares that hinder the organization's ability to respond to competitive pressures. Some recommend reducing the controls and guidelines inherent in any pay plan. Hence, banding eliminates or at least reduces the impact of range maximums and minimums. Replacing merit grids with bonuses eliminates the link between the pay increase and the employees' salary position in the range and performance rating. Replacing job evaluation with skill- or competency-based plans permits assigning employees to a variety of work, regardless of their pay.

Such approaches are consistent with the oft-heard plea that managers should be free to manage pay. Or, as some more bluntly claim, pay decisions are too important to be left to compensation professionals. Yet, permitting managers to be free to pay employees as they judge best rests on a basic premise: Managers will use pay to achieve the organization's objectives—efficiency, fairness, and compliance with regulations—rather than their own objectives. But the ongoing leadership scandals in some corporations and public agencies casts doubt on this premise.

Clearly, some balance between hidebound controls and chaos is required to ensure that pay decisions are directed at the organization's goals yet permit sufficient flexibility to respond to unique situations. Achieving the balance becomes the art of managing compensation.

A final issue related to pay design and administration is the skills and competencies required in compensation managers. The grandest strategy and structure may seem well designed, well thought out in the abstract, but could be a disaster if people qualified to carry it out are not part of the staff. In view of the importance of a well-trained staff, both WorldatWork and the Society of Human Resource Managers (SHRM) have professional development programs to entice readers into the compensation field.

Making Information Useful—Compensation Enterprise Systems

A friend of ours e-mailed from Shanghai that "six months after we have acquired this operation from the government, I still cannot get an accurate headcount. I do not know how many people we actually employ or who should get paychecks!" That manager clearly needs more information. But most managers find themselves overwhelmed with too much information. The challenge is to make the information useful.

Compensation software transforms data into useful information and guides decision making. Many software packages that serve a variety of purposes are available.[53] Some of them support *employee self-service,* by which employees can access their personal information, make choices about which health care coverage they prefer, allocate savings between growth or value investment funds, access vacation schedules, or check out a list of child or elder care service providers. *Manager self-service* helps managers pay their employees appropriately. *Communication portals,* designed for employees or managers, explain compensation policies and practices, answer frequently asked questions, and explain how these systems affect their pay.[54] Other software *processes transactions.* It standardizes forms, performs some analysis, and creates reports at the click of the mouse. The advantage is that all employees at all locations are on the same system.

While compensation software is proliferating, what remains a scarcer resource is the intellectual capital: the compensation knowledge and judgment required to understand which information, analyses, and reports are useful. Part of this intellectual capital includes analytical (read "statistical and math") skills. Another part is knowledge of the business. A shortage of this knowledge among compensation managers not only limits the usefulness of compensation software but also limits the contribution of compensation management.

Computers inevitably bring up the issue of confidentiality. If personal compensation data are accessible to employees and managers, privacy and security issues as well as ethical and legal issues emerge. Regulations vary around the world. The European Union has issued the Data Privacy Directive, which is significantly stronger than U.S. regulations.[55] Unauthorized users, both inside and outside the corporation, remain a threat.

Ethics: Managing or Manipulating?

Compensation ethics is not an oxymoron. But absent a professional code of behaviors and values, it is a challenge for compensation managers to ensure that their actions *are* ethical. The Web page for the compensation society, WorldatWork, includes the topic of ethics. Public discussion of ethics in compensation topics such as executive pay or backdating option grants benefits from the voices of informed compensation practitioners.

Managing compensation ethically is increasingly complicated for several reasons. First, pay really matters; it is important to all of us. Second is the fierce pressure to achieve results. The increased use of pay for performance, which is based on results achieved and exceeding targets, can contribute to these pressures. However, assessing results sometimes has a "smoke and mirrors" feel to it. At an organization's compensation strategy session that we attended, the chief financial officer observed that it was possible to "manage our reported earnings within several percentage points of the target. We can exceed analysts' and shareholder expectations by 1 to 10 percent." This was relatively easy for this particular company since about one-third of its earnings came from liquid investments in other companies. The remainder was revenue from its products and services. The implication of managing earnings for employees' profit-sharing payouts and executive stock valuations were not ignored. The point is that measures of financial performance do not provide an immutable gold standard. They can be "managed."[56]

Where Is the Compensation Professional?

Performance-based pay is not the only area that presents ethical dilemmas. Misusing and even failing to understand survey statistics, manipulating job evaluations, peer-company competitive data, masking overtime and pay discrimination violations, failure to understand that correlation does not mean causation, and recommending pay programs without addressing their expected costs and returns should force us to take a hard look at what we are doing.[57]

Stephen Landry, the former HR director at Sycamore Networks, reports that the company's chief financial officer pressured him to change the hiring dates of some employees to make their stock option grants worth more money. These actions were to be kept hidden from the company auditors. Instead, Landry told executives these actions were unethical and probably illegal. He was fired. Internal memos from the company reveal a "risk assessment" of the action becoming exposed. Changing the date on documents was judged a low risk since the original grant "has been deleted from the system in its entirety." Landry is suing and the SEC is investigating. If Mr. Landry's experience is not enough for the professional compensation community, over at Cablevision, they backdated stock grants to a dead executive.[58]

A starting point to judge the ethics of our behavior may be our compensation model, presented with the advice: "Strive to achieve both efficiency and fairness."

Your **Turn**   Communication by Copier

Deb Allen's life-altering discovery at work really "communicated" her company's pay practices. Swamped with work at an asset-management firm, she went into the office over the weekend and found a document abandoned on the copy machine. The document contained the base compensation, raises, performance ratings, and bonus information for 80 of her colleagues.

Ms. Allen was outraged that a noted screw-up was making $65,000 a year more than more competent colleagues, while some new hires were earning almost $200,000 more than their counterparts with more experience. The discovery led her to question why she was working weekends for less pay than others were getting. "I just couldn't stand the inequity of it," she says. Three months later she quit.

But Ms. Allen couldn't bring herself to share the information with her colleagues. "I would have been better off not knowing any of that," she explains. "I couldn't give it to people who were still working there because it would make them depressed, like it made me depressed."

1. How would you have reacted if you were Ms. Allen? Explain why.
2. Put yourself in the place of the compensation director at Ms. Allen's company. Based on the pay model and what you now know about compensation, are there any possible business- and work-related explanations for what Ms. Allen observed (i.e., the screw-up getting $65,000 more; new hires earning $200,000 more than more-experienced employees; and Ms. Allen making less pay than others)?
3. As the compensation director, what would you do if Ms. Allen had brought you this document, and asked for your help in understanding what was going on. (Firing the person who left it on the copier is not an option. It may have been you.)

Still Your **Turn**   Managing Compensation Costs, Headcount, and Participation/Communication Issues

Cisco Systems, Hewlett-Packard, American Airlines, and General Motors are examples of companies that have cut employment or cut wages and/or benefits to reduce labor costs in hopes of becoming more competitive and more profitable. Indeed, American and GM went through bankruptcy in part to gain control over labor costs. In contrast, some companies— Southwest Airlines, Nucor, and Lincoln Electric—have a no-layoff practice and do not appear to have cut wages or benefits even in years when sales have declined significantly (They have also not gone through bankruptcy). What is the difference between these two sets of companies? Is it simply that one set of companies cares more about its employees than the other set of companies cares about its employees? Or, is it also the case that Southwest, Nucor, and Lincoln Electric have set up their compensation strategies in a way that makes them more able (than Cisco, HP, American, and GM) to cut labor costs when times are tough? (For more background, go to google.com or another search engine and conduct a separate search for each company using its name and the term "layoff.") What about protecting investment in employees and employee relations?

What can an employer do to make labor costs flexible so that profits do not take as much of a beating during difficult economic times and so that fewer employees need to be laid off? If you were in charge of designing a compensation system for a company that is fairly new but is now reaching a stage and size where it needs a formal compensation system, how would you design the compensation system to have labor cost flexibility? To what degree would you have others at the company participate in the design of the new compensation system? Who would participate? Would you follow a policy of pay openness in communicating your compensation system? Provide a rationale for your decisions.

Summary

We have now completed the discussion of the pay management process. Management includes control: control of the way managers decide individual employees' pay as well as control of overall costs of labor. As we noted, some controls are designed into the fabric of the pay system (embedded controls). The salary budgeting and forecasting processes impose additional controls. The formal budgeting process focuses on controlling labor costs and generating the financial plan for the pay system. The budget sets the limits within which the rest of the system operates.

We also noted that with the continuous change in organizations, compensation managers must understand how to manage change and be knowledgeable business partners. They are responsible for communicating information about pay in a way that treats employees fairly and honestly. The basic point is that pay systems are tools, and like any tools they need to be evaluated in terms of usefulness in achieving an organization's objectives.

Review Questions

1. How can employers control labor costs?
2. How does the management of the pay system affect pay objectives?
3. Why is the structure of the compensation function important?
4. Give some examples of how employers use inherent controls.
5. What activities in managing the pay system are likely candidates to be outsourced? Why?
6. Use Exhibit 18.13 to explain how the research on individual decision making can be used in pay communication.

Endnotes

1. Sanford Jacoby, *The Embedded Corporation* (Princeton: Princeton University Press, 2005).

2. Felix Barber and Rainer Strack, "The Surprising Economics of a 'People Business'," *Harvard Business Review,* June 2005, pp. 81–90.

3. D. Scott, D. Morajda, T. McMullen, and R. Sperling, "Evaluating Pay Program Effectiveness," *WorldatWork Journal,* 15(2), Second Quarter 2006, pp. 50–59.

4. Lindsay Scott, "Managing Labor Costs Using Pay-for-Performance," Lindsay Scott & Associates, Inc., *www.npktools.com.*

5. *Reward Transformation: Turning Rewards from Costs into an Investment* (New York: Deloitte, 2006), *www.deloitte.com.*

6. Personal communication from B. Dunn, president, McLagan Partners; D. Scott, D. Morajda, T. McMullen, and R. Sperling, "Evaluating Pay Program Effectiveness," *WorldatWork Journal* 15(2), Second Quarter 2006, pp. 50–59; John Boudreau and Peter Ramstad, "From 'Professional Business Partner' to 'Strategic Talent Leader:' What's Next for Human Resource Management," CAHRS Working Paper 02–10, Ithaca, NY.

7. B. Dunn, president, McLagan Partners; *The Lake Wobegon Salary Survey, Lindsay Scott & Associates, Inc., www.npktools.com,* 2006.

8. Allen Smith, "Layoffs in Europe: Deal or No Deal?" *HR Magazine,* January 2009, pp. 71–73.

9. Charlie O. Trevor and Anthony J. Nyberg, "Keeping Your Headcount When All About You Are Losing Theirs: Downsizing, Voluntary Turnover Rates, and the Moderating Role of HR Practices," *Academy of Management Journal* 51 (2008), pp. 259–276.

10. Timothy Aeppel and Justin Lahart, "Lean Factories Find It Hard to Cut Jobs Even in Slump," *The Wall Street Journal,* March 9, 2009, p. A1.

11. Erin White, "Retaining Employees before an Upturn Hits," *The Wall Street Journal,* May 8, 2009, *http://online.wsj.com/article/SB124178707883900633.html,* September 14, 2009; Gray Yohe, "A Delicate Balance," *Human Resource Executive,* March 2, 2009, *www. hreonline.com/HRE/story.jsp?storyId=1815633178query=morale,* September 14, 2009.

12. Clint Chadwick, Larry W. Hunter, and Stephen Walston, "Effects of Downsizing Practices on the Performance of Hospitals," *Strategic Management Journal* 25 (2004), pp. 405–427.

13. Charles Duhigg, "Hospital Clients Nurture Firm's Scheduling Software," *Los Angeles Times,* June 21, 2006, p. C1.

14. Susan Saulny and Robbie Brown, "On a Furlough, but Never Leaving the Cubicle," *The New York Times,* June 15, 2009; Jonathan Buck, "British Airways Urges Staff to Work without Pay," *The Wall Street Journal,* June 16, 2009; "The Quiet Americans: Employees Are Social in the Face of Pay Cuts and Compulsory Unpaid Leave," *The Economist,* June 25, 2009, *www.economist.com/world/unitedstates/displaystory.cfm?story_id=13915822,* September 14, 2009.

15. Riva Richmond, "How to Cut Payroll Without Layoffs," *BusinessWeek*, April 3, 2009, *www.businessweek.com/magazine/content/09_64/s0904048707309.htm,* September 14, 2009; Matthew Boyle, "Cutting Work Hours Without Cutting Staff," *BusinessWeek,* February 25, 2009, *www.businessweek.com/magazine/content/09_10/b4122055789445. htm,* September 14, 2009.

16. Ron Lieber, "Et Tu, AARP? Good Guys Cut 401(k)s, Too," *The New York Times,* June 27, 2009, p. B1.

17. Sandra Block, "Companies Rethink 401(k) Plan Contributions for Employees," *USA Today,* June 24, 2009, *www.usatoday.com/money/perfi/retirement/2009-06-24-401kcontributions-economy_N.htm,* September 14, 2009.

18. Michael Sanserino, "Pay Raises Are the Smallest in Decades, Surveys Show," *The Wall Street Journal,* July 21, 2009; Aon Hewitt, *Annual Salary Increase Survey,* September 2011.

19. Aon Hewitt, *Annual Salary Increase Survey,* September 2011.

20. Carlos Tejada and Gary McWilliams, "New Recipe for Cost Savings: Replace Expensive Workers," *The Wall Street Journal,* June 11, 2003, pp. 1, A12.

21. John Watson, "Delivering Total Compensation Online at Dell," *ACA News* 42(4), April 1999, pp. 14–19.

22. Ronald T. Albright and Bridge R. Compton, *Internal Consulting Basics* (Scottsdale, AZ: American Compensation Association, 1996); John Watson, "Delivering Total Compensation Online at Dell," *ACA News* 42(4), April 1999, pp. 14–19.

23. Jennifer Hicks, an Oklahoma State University student, has coined the term "yellow circle rates" while working as a compensation specialist for FastCat. Yellow circle rates result where if you give an employee the percent raise indicated by the merit increase grid, that employee would become red circled. For Walmart information, see Steven Greenhouse and Michael Barbaro, "Wal-Mart to Add Caps and Part-Timers," *The New York Times,* October 2, 2006, p. B1.

24. WorldatWork. Promotional Guidelines 2010. December 2010. www.worldatwork.org /waw/adimLink?id=45914; accessed June 22, 2012.

25. M.J. Bidwell and J.R. Keller, "Promote or Hire? Comparing Make or Buy and Competing Process Views in a Professional Service Firm," working paper, Wharton School, University of Pennsylvania. See the related article: Rachel Emma Silverman and Lauren Weber, "An Inside Job: More Firms Opt to Recruit From Within," *The Wall Street Journal,* May 29, 2012.

26. *Reward Transformation: Turning Rewards from Costs Into an Investment* (New York: Deloitte, 2006), *www.deloitte.com;* D. Scott, D. Morajda, T. McMullen, and R. Sperling, "Evaluating Pay Program Effectiveness," *WorldatWork Journal* 15(2), Second Quarter 2006, pp. 50–59.

27. Wayne Cascio, *Responsible Restructuring: Creative and Profitable Alternatives to Layoffs* (San Francisco: Berrett-Koehler, 2002); John Boudreau and Peter Ramstad, "Beyond Cost per Hire and Time to Fill: Supply-Chain Measurements for Staffing" (Los Angeles: Center for Effective Organizations, 2006); Jaap deJonge, *Watson Wyatt Human Capital Index* (New York: Watson Wyatt, 2003); S. Raza, *Optimizing Human Capital Investments for Superior Shareholder Returns* (New York: Hewitt Associates, 2006); M. Huselid and B. Becker, "Improving HR Analytical Literacy: Lessons from Moneyball," chapter 32 in M. Losey, S. Meisinger, and D. Ulrich, *The Future of Human Resource Management* (Hoboken, NJ: Wiley, 2005); J. Burton and S. Pollack, "ROI of Human Capital: The United States and Europe," *Workspan,* November 2006, pp. 28–27.

28. Ibid.

29. M. C. Sturman, C. O. Trevor, J. W. Boudreau, and B. Gerhart, "Is It Worth It to Win the Talent War? Evaluating the Utility of Performance-Based Pay," *Personnel Psychology* 56 (2003), pp. 997–1035; Wayne Cascio and John Boudreau, *Investing in People* (Saddle River, NJ: Pearson Education, 2008); Mark A. Huselid, Brian E. Becker, and Richard W. Beatty, *The Workforce Scorecard* (Boston: Harvard Business School Press, 2005).

30. Peter F. Drucker, "They're Not Employees, They're People," *Harvard Business Review,* February 2002, pp. 70–77.

31. Lee, T. H., B. Gerhart, I. Weller, and C. O. Trevor, "Understanding Voluntary Turnover: Path-Specific Job Satisfaction Effects and the Importance of Unsolicited Job Offers," *Academy of Management Journal,* 51 (2008), 651–671.

32. Laszlo Bock, *Work Rules!* (Twelve, 2015). Daniel, Freedman, "Silicon Valley Star Search." *Wall Street Journal,* April 7, 2015., p. A11. Call, M. L., Nyberg, A. J., &

Thatcher, S. M. B. (2015, March 30). Stargazing: An Integrative Conceptual Review, Theoretical Reconciliation, and Extension for Star Employee Research. Journal of Applied Psychology. Advance online publication.

33. Michael Beer and Mitin Nohria, "Cracking the Code of Change," *Harvard Business Review,* May–June 2000, pp. 133–141; Dave Ulrich, "A New Mandate for Human Resources," *Harvard Business Review,* January–February 1998, pp. 125–134.

34. "Growing Worker Confusion about Corporate Goals Complicates Recovery, Watson Wyatt WorkUSA Study Finds," Watson Wyatt news release, September 9, 2002.

35. Robert L. Heneman, Paul W. Mulvey, and Peter V. LeBlanc, "Improve Base Pay ROI by Increasing Employee Knowledge," *WorldatWork Journal* 11(4), Fourth Quarter 2002, pp. 22–27.

36. A. Bandura, *Social Learning Theory* (New York: General Learning Press, 1977); E.E. Lawler, *Pay and Organizational Effectiveness: A Psychological View* (New York: McGraw-Hill, 1977).

37. Federal Register/Vol. 79, No. 180/Wednesday, September 17, 2014/Proposed Rules. Department of Labor, Office of Federal Contract Compliance Programs, 41 CFR Part 60–1 RIN 1250–AA06. Government Contractors, Prohibitions Against Pay Secrecy Policies and Actions. Notice of proposed rulemaking.

38. Thomas A. Mahoney and William Weitzel, "Secrecy and Managerial Compensation," *Industrial Relations* 17(2), 1978, pp. 245–251; Julio D. Burroughs, "Pay Secrecy and Performance: The Psychological Research," *Compensation Review,* Third Quarter 1982, pp. 44–54; George Milkovich and P. H. Anderson, "Management Compensation and Secrecy Policies," *Personnel Psychology* 25 (1972), pp. 293–302.

39. Adrienne Colella, Ramona Paetzold, Asghar Zardkoohi, and Michael Wesson, "Exposing Pay Secrecy," *Academy of Management Review* 32 (2007), pp. 55–71; Renae Broderick and Barry Gerhart, "Non-Wage Compensation," in *The Human Resource Management Handbook,* Part 3; David Lewin, Daniel J. B. Mitchell, and Mahmood A. Zaidi, eds. (Greenwich, CT: JAI Press, 1997), pp. 95–135.

40. P. Bamberger and E. Belogolovsky, "The Impact of Pay Secrecy on Individual Task Performance," *Personnel Psychology* 63, 2010, pp. 965–966.

41. Card, David, et al., "Inequality at Work: The Effect of Peer Salaries on Job Satisfaction," *The American Economic Review* 102(6), (2012): 2981–3003.

42. Belogolovsky, Elena, and Peter A. Bamberger, "Signaling in Secret: Pay for Performance and the Incentive and Sorting Effects of Pay Secrecy," *Academy of Management Journal* 57(6), (2014): 1706–1733.

43. M. Wilson, G. B. Northcraft, and M. A. Neale, "The Perceived Value of Fringe Benefits," *Personnel Psychology* 38 (1985), pp. 309–320.

44. John A. Rubino, *Communicating Compensation Programs* (Scottsdale, AZ: American Compensation Association, 1997).

45. Jared Sandberg, "Why You May Regret Looking at Papers Left on the Office Copier," *The Wall Street Journal,* June 20, 2006, p. B1; John Case, "When Salaries Aren't Secret," case study, *Harvard Business Review,* May 2001.

46. A. Tversky and D. Kahneman, "The Framing of Decisions and the Psychology of Choice," *Science* 211 (1981), pp. 453–458; C. F. Camerer and U. Malmendier, "Behavioral Organizational Economics," July 8, 2006, working paper available from *www.hss.caltech.edu/camerer/SS200/SS200.html;* Sharla A. Stewart, "Can Behavioral Economics Save Us From Ourselves?" *University of Chicago Magazine* 97(3), February 2005, *www.magazine.uchicago.edu/0502/features/economics.shtml.*

47. Dori Meinert, "An Open Book: Involving Employees in Business Decisions Can Improve the Bottom Line. That's Why Fans of Open-Book Management Are So Dedicated to the Approach," *HR Magazine*, April 2013, pp. 43–46. "Rethinking Ways to Present Financial Information to Employees," *Employee Ownership Report,* March/April 2000, pp. 7, 10; Jack Stack and Bo Burlingham, *The Great Game of Business* (New York: Currency Doubleday, 1992); Jack Stack and Bo Burlingham, *A Stake in the Outcome* (New York: Currency Doubleday, 2002); John Case, "Opening the Books," *Harvard Business Review,* March–April, 1996, pp. 118–127.

48. *HR Services Delivery Research Report,* Towers Perrin, 2005, *www.towersperrin.com;* "The Psychology of Change Management," *McKinsey Quarterly,* July 2006.

49. Dave Ulrich, Jon Younger, and Wayne Brockbank, "The Next Evolution of the HR Organization," in *The Routledge Companion to Strategic Human Resource Management,* John Storey, Patrick M. Wright, and Dave Ulrich, eds. (London and New York: Routledge, 2009), pp. 182–203.

50. Alexandria Sage, "Wal-Mart Sex Discrimination Case Back in Court," Reuters, March 25, 2009, *www.reuters.com/article/topNews/idUSTRE52O0P820090325.*

51. Stephen Miller, "Companies Continue to Selectively Outsource HR Programs," *HRMagazine* (2009), p. 76; Dave Ulrich and Wayne Brockbank, *The HR Value Proposition* (Boston, MA: Harvard Business School Press, 2005); Brian S. Klaas, "Outsourcing and the HR Function: An Examination of Trends and Developments Within North American Firms," *International Journal of Human Resource Management* 19 (2008), pp. 1500–1514.

52. Michael Skapinker, "Much to Question on Outsourcing," *Financial Times,* June 30, 2003, p. 4.

53. A useful guide on selecting HR software is James G. Meade, *The Human Resources Software Handbook* (San Francisco: Jossey-Bass/Pfeiffer, 2003); Mark L. Lengnick-Hall and Steve Moritz, "The Impact of e-HR on the Human Resource Management Function," *Journal of Labor Research,* Summer 2003, pp. 365–379.

54. Diane Palframan, *HR Technology Strategies* (New York: Conference Board, 2003); James H. Dulebohn and Janet H. Marler, "e-Compensation: The Potential to Transform Practice?" in *Brave New World of e-HR: Human Resources in the Digital Age,* H. Gueutal and D. Stone, eds. (San Francisco: Jossey Bass, 2005), pp. 138–165.

55. Privacilla, *www.privacilla.org/business/eudirective.html.*

56. Flora Guidry, Andrew J. Leon, and Steve Rock, "Earnings-Based Bonus Plans and Earnings Management by Business-Unit Managers," *Journal of Accounting and Economics* 26 (1999), pp. 113–142.

57. Joseph P. O'Connor, Jr., Richard L. Priem, Joseph E. Coombs, and K. Matthew Gilley, "Do CEO Stock Options Prevent or Promote Fraudulent Financial Reporting?" *Academy of Management Journal,* June 2006, pp. 483–500; Frederic W. Cook, "Compensation Ethics: An Oxymoron or Valid Area for Debate?" Featured speech at ACA International Conference Workshop, 1999; Barrie Litzky, Kimberly Eddleston, and Deborah Kidder, "The Good, the Bad, and the Misguided: How Managers Inadvertently Encourage Deviant Behaviors," *Academy of Management Perspectives,* February 2006, pp. 91–102; Gretchen Morgenson, "Advice on Boss's Pay May Not Be So Independent," *The New York Times,* April 10, 2006, p. B1. The WorldatWork Ethics Initiative is described on their website, *www.worldatwork.org.* Also see their WorldatWork Standards of Professional Practice.

58. John Hechinger and James Bandler, "In Sycamore Suite, Memo Points to Backdating Claims," *The Wall Street Journal,* July 12, 2006, p. A3. Also see C. Forelle, J. Bandler, and Steve Stecklaw, "Brocade Ex-CEO, 2 Others Charged in Options Probe," *The Wall Street Journal,* July 21, 2006, p. A1, A8; Peter Grant, James Bandler, and Charles Forelle, "Cablevision Gave Backdated Grant to Dead Official," *The Wall Street Journal,* September 22, 2006, pp. A1, A8; Della Bradshaw, "MBA Students 'Cheat the Most,'" *Financial Times,* September 21, 2006, p. 8.

Glossary

ability   An individual's capability to engage in a specific behavior.

ability to pay   The ability of a firm to meet employee wage demands while remaining profitable; a frequent issue in contract negotiations with unions. A firm's ability to pay is constrained by its ability to compete in its product market.

access discrimination   Discrimination that focuses on the staffing and allocation decisions made by employers. It denies particular jobs, promotions, or training opportunities to qualified women or minorities. This type of discrimination is illegal under Title VII of the Civil Rights Act of 1964.

across-the-board increases   A general adjustment that provides equal increases to all employees.

affirmative action   Firms with government contracts must take affirmative steps to hire women and minorities in proportion to their presence in the labor force.

affordable Care Act   *See* Patient Protection and Affordable Care Act.

Age Discrimination in Employment Act (ADEA) of 1967 (amended 1978, 1986, and 1990)   Legislation that makes nonfederal employees age 40 and over a protected class relative to their treatment in pay, benefits, and other personnel actions. The 1990 amendment is called the Older Workers Benefit Protection Act.

agency theory   A theory of motivation that depicts exchange relationships in terms of two parties: agents and principals. According to this theory, both sides of the exchange will seek the most favorable exchange possible and will act opportunistically if given a chance. As applied to executive compensation, agency theory would place part of the executive's pay at risk to motivate the executive (agent) to act in the best interests of the shareholders (principals) rather than in the executive's own self-interests.

all-salaried workforce   Pay approach in which not only exempt employees (exempt from provisions of the Fair Labor Standards Act), who traditionally are paid a salary rather than an hourly rate, but also nonexempt employees receive a prescribed amount of money each pay period that does not primarily depend on the number of hours worked.

alternation ranking   A job evaluation method that involves ordering the job description alternately at each extreme. All the jobs are considered. Agreement is reached on which is the most valuable and then the least valuable. Evaluators alternate between the next most valued and next least valued and so on until the jobs have been ordered.

Americans with Disabilities Act   Legislation passed in 1990 that requires that reasonable accommodations be provided to permit employees with disabilities to perform the essential elements of a job.

appeals processes   Mechanisms are created to handle pay disagreements. They provide a forum for employees and managers to voice their complaints and receive a hearing.

balance sheet approach   A method for compensating expatriates based upon the belief that the employee should not suffer financially for accepting a foreign-based assignment. The expatriate's pay is adjusted so that the amounts of the financial responsibilities the expatriate had prior to the assignment are kept at about the same level while on assignment—the company pays for the difference.

balanced scorecard   A corporatewide, overall performance measure typically incorporating financial results, process improvements, customer service, and innovation.

base pay   *See* base wage.

base salary   *See* base wage.

base wage   The basic cash compensation that an employer pays for the work performed. Tends to reflect the value of the work itself and ignore differences in individual contributions.

Bedeaux plan   Individual incentive plan that provides a variation on straight piecework and standard hour plans. Instead of timing an entire task, a Bedeaux plan requires determination of the time required to complete each simple action of a task. Workers receive a wage incentive for completing a task in less than the standard time.

behaviorally anchored rating scales (BARS) Variants on standard rating scales in which the various scale levels are anchored with behavioral descriptions directly applicable to jobs being evaluated.

benchmark conversion Process of matching survey jobs by applying the employer's plan to the external jobs and then comparing the worth of the external job with its internal "match."

benchmark (key) job A prototypical job, or group of jobs, used as a reference point for making pay comparisons within or without the organization. Benchmark jobs have well-known and stable contents; their current pay rates are generally acceptable, and the pay differentials among them are relatively stable. A group of benchmark jobs, taken together, contains the entire range of compensable factors and is accepted in the external labor market for setting wages.

benefit ceiling A maximum payout for specific benefit claims (e.g., limiting liability for extended hospital stays to $150,000).

benefit limitation Limit of disability income payments to some maximum percentage of income and limit of medical/dental coverage for specific procedures to a certain fixed amount.

best-pay practices Compensation practices that allow employers to gain preferential access to superior human resource talent and competencies (i.e., valued assets), which in turn influence the strategies the organization adopts.

BLS *See* Bureau of Labor Statistics.

bonus A lump-sum payment to an employee in recognition of goal achievement.

bottom-up approach to pay budgeting Approach in which individual employees' pay rates for the next plan year are forecasted and summed to create an organization's total budget.

bourse market A market that allows haggling over terms and conditions until an agreement is reached.

branding Establishing an image or reputation associated with a product or service. As related to total compensation systems, it seeks to establish a reputation that will influence employees' and the public's perceptions about how an organization pays its employees.

Brito v. Zia Company Benchmark case that interpreted performance evaluation as a test, subject to validation requirements, and used these evaluations based on a rating format to lay off employees, resulting in a disproportionate number of minorities being discharged.

broad banding Collapsing a number of salary grades into a smaller number of broad grades with wide ranges.

broad-based option plans (BBOPs) Stock grants: A company gives employees shares of stock over a designated time period.

budgeting A part of the organization's planning process; helps to ensure that future financial expenditures are coordinated and controlled. It involves forecasting the total expenditures required by the pay system during the next period as well as the amount of the pay increases. Bottom up and top down are the two typical approaches to the process.

Bureau of Labor Statistics (BLS) A major source of publicly available pay data. It also calculates the consumer price index.

Cafeteria-style compensation Like in a cafeteria line, employees have a fixed dollar amount to choose from among many benefit choices.

cafeteria (flexible) benefit plan A benefit plan in which employees have a choice as to the benefits they receive within some dollar limit. Usually a common core benefit package is required (e.g., specific minimum levels of health, disability, retirement, and death benefits) plus elective programs from which the employee may select a set dollar amount. Additional coverage may be available through employee contributions.

capital appreciation plans *See* long-term incentives.

career path A progression of jobs within an organization.

cash balance plan A defined benefit plan that looks like a defined contribution plan. Employees have a hypothetical account, such as a 401(k), into which is deposited what is typically a percentage of annual compensation. The dollar amount grows both from contributions by the employer and by some predetermined interest rate (e.g., often set equal to the rate given on 30-year treasury certificates).

central tendency A midpoint in a group of measures.

central tendency error A rating error that occurs when a rater consistently rates a group of employees at or close to the midpoint of a scale irrespective of the true score performance of ratees. Avoiding extremes (both high and low) in ratings across employees.

churn   *See* turnover effect.

Civil Rights Act of 1964   Legislation that prohibits, under Title VII, discrimination in terms and conditions of employment (including benefits) that is based on race, color, religion, sex, or national origin.

Civil Rights Act of 1991   Legislation that clarifies the standards for proving discrimination. Allows jury trials and damage awards.

claims processing   Procedure that begins when an employee asserts that a specific event (e.g., disablement, hospitalization, unemployment) has occurred and demands that the employer fulfill a promise for payment. As such, a claims processor must first determine whether the act has, in fact, occurred.

classification   Job evaluation method that involves slotting job descriptions into a series of classes or grades that cover the range of jobs and that serve as a standard against which the job descriptions are compared.

clone error   A rating error that occurs when a rater gives better ratings to individuals who are like the rater in behavior or personality.

coinsurance   Benefit option whereby employees share in the cost of a benefit provided to them.

commission   Payment tied directly to achievement of performance standards. Commissions are directly tied to a profit index (sales, production level) and employee costs; thus, they rise and fall in line with revenues.

committee a priori judgment approach   Compensable factor importance weights are assigned by a committee based on judgment.

community rating   When insurance rates are based on the medical experience of that entire community. Higher use of medical facilities and services results in higher premiums.

comparable worth   A policy that women performing jobs judged to be equal on some measure of inherent worth should be paid the same as men, excepting allowable differences, such as seniority, merit, production-based pay plans, and other non-sex-related factors. Objective is to eliminate use of the market in setting wages for jobs held by women.

compa-ratio   An index that helps assess how managers actually pay employees in relation to the midpoint of the pay range established for jobs. It estimates how well actual practices correspond to

intended policy. Calculated as average rates actually paid divided by range midpoint.

compensable factor   Job attributes that provide the basis for evaluating the relative worth of jobs inside an organization. A compensable factor must be work-related, business-related, and acceptable to the parties involved.

compensating differentials   Economic theory that attributes the variety of pay rates in the external labor market to differences in attractive as well as negative characteristics in jobs. Pay differences must overcome negative characteristics to attract employees.

compensation   All forms of financial returns and tangible services and benefits employees receive as part of an employment relationship.

compensation at risk   *See* risk sharing.

compensation differentials   Differentials in pay among jobs across and within organizations, and differences among individuals in the same job in an organization.

compensation objectives   The desired results of the pay system. The basic pay objectives include efficiency, fairness, and compliance with laws and regulations. Objectives shape the design of the pay system and serve as the standard against which the success of the pay system is evaluated.

competency   Basic knowledge and abilities employees must acquire or demonstrate in a competency-based plan in order to successfully perform the work, satisfy customers, and achieve business objectives.

competency analysis   A systematic process to identify and collect information about the competencies required for the person and the organization to be successful.

competency-based system   Compensation approach that links pay to the depth and scope of competencies that are relevant to doing the work. Typically used in managerial and professional work where what is accomplished may be difficult to identify.

competitive intelligence   The collection and analysis of information about external conditions and competitors that will enable an organization to be more competitive.

competitive position   The comparison of the compensation offered by one employer relative to that paid by its competitors.

compliance Compliance as a pay objective means conforming to federal and state compensation laws and regulations.

compression The existence of very narrow pay differentials among jobs at different organization levels as a result of wages for jobs filled from the outside (frequently these are entry-level jobs) increasing faster than the internal pay structure.

congruency The degree of consistency or "fit" between the compensation system and other organizational components such as strategy, product-market stage, culture and values, employee needs, and union status.

Consolidated Omnibus Budget Reconciliation Act (COBRA) Legislation that provides that employees who resign or are laid off through no fault of their own are eligible to continue receiving health coverage under the employer's plan at a cost borne by the employee.

consumer-directed health care plans Costs link consumer choice of more or less expensive options to higher or lower individual costs.

consumer-driven health care benefits *See* consumer-directed health care plans.

Consumer Price Index (CPI) A measure of the changes in prices in a fixed market basket of goods and services purchased by a hypothetical average family. *Not* an absolute measure of living costs; rather, a measure of how fast costs are changing. Published by the Bureau of Labor Statistics, U.S. Department of Labor.

content The work performed in a job and how it gets done (tasks, behaviors, knowledge required, etc.).

content theories Motivation theories that focus on what motivates people rather than on how people are motivated. Maslow's need hierarchy theory and Herzberg's two-factor theory are in this category.

contingent employees A growing workforce that includes flexible workers, temporaries, part-time employees, and independent contractors whose employment is of a limited duration.

contingent workers *See* contingent employees.

conventional job analysis Methods (e.g., functional job analysis) that typically involve an analyst using a questionnaire in conjunction with structured interviews of job incumbents and supervisors. The methods place considerable reliance on analysts' ability to understand the work performed and to accurately describe it.

coordination of benefits Process of ensuring that employer coverage of an employee does not "double pay" because of identical protection offered by the government (private pension and social security coordination) or a spouse's employer.

copay Copay requires that employees pay a fixed or percentage amount for coverage.

core employees Workers with whom a long-term, full-time work relationship is anticipated.

correlation coefficient A common measure of association that indicates how changes in one variable are related to changes in another.

cost containment An attempt made by organizations to contain benefit costs, such as imposing deductibles and coinsurance on health benefits or replacing defined benefit pension plans with defined contribution plans.

cost cutter The cost cutter's efficiency-focused strategy stresses doing more with less by minimizing costs, encouraging productivity increases, and specifying in greater detail exactly how jobs should be performed.

cost of living Actual individual expenditures on goods and services. The only way to measure it accurately is to examine the expense budget of each employee.

cost-of-living adjustments (COLAs) Across-the-board wage and salary increases or supplemental payments based on changes in some index of prices, usually the consumer price index (CPI). If included in a union contract, COLAs are designed to increase wages automatically during the life of the contract as a function of changes in the CPI.

cost-of-living increase Same as across-the-board increase, except magnitude based on change in cost of living (e.g., as measured by the consumer price index [CPI]).

CPI *See* Consumer Price Index.

criterion contamination Allowing nonperformance factors to affect performance scores.

criterion deficiency A criterion is deficient if it fails to include all of the dimensions relevant to job performance (e.g., excluding keyboarding skills for a secretary's job performance).

criterion pay structure A pay structure to be duplicated with a point plan.

culture The informal rules, rituals, and value systems that influence how people behave.

customer-driven health care Medical care package where the employer finances the cost up to a dollar maximum and the employees search for options that best fit their specific needs.

customer-focused business strategy   The customer-focused business strategy stresses delighting customers and bases employee pay on how well they achieve this.

Davis-Bacon Act   Legislation that requires that most federal contractors pay wage rates prevailing in the area.

deductibles   Employees cost-saving tool by which the employee pays the first *x* number of dollars when a benefit is used (e.g., hospitalization). The employer pays subsequent costs up to some predetermined maximum.

deferred compensation   Pay approach that provides income to an employee at some future time as compensation for work performed now. Types of deferred compensation programs include stock option plans and pension plans.

defined benefit plan   A benefit option or package in which the employer agrees to give the specified benefit without regard to cost maximum. Opposite of defined contribution plan.

defined contribution plan   A benefit option or package in which the employer negotiates a dollar maximum payout. Any change in benefit costs over time reduces the amount of coverage unless new dollar limits are negotiated.

delayering   Eliminating some layers or job levels in the pay structure.

differentials   Pay differences among levels within the organization, such as the difference in pay between adjacent levels in a career path, between supervisors and subordinates, between union and nonunion employees, and between executives and regular employees.

direct compensation   Pay received directly in the form of cash (e.g., wages, bonuses, incentives).

disparate impact   Discrimination theory that outlaws the application of pay practices that may appear to be neutral but have a negative effect on females or minorities unless those practices can be shown to be business-related.

disparate treatment   Discrimination theory that outlaws the application of different standards to different classes of employees unless the standards can be shown to be business-related.

distributive justice   Fairness in the amount of reward distributed to employees.

Dodd-Frank Act   Requires reporting by all public companies on the ratio of CEO pay relative to the median pay of employees.

double-track system   A framework for professional employees in an organization whereby at least two general tracks of ascending compensation steps are available: (1) a managerial track to be ascended through increasing responsibility for supervision of people and (2) a professional track to be ascended through increasing contributions of a professional nature.

drive theory   A motivational theory that assumes that all behavior is induced by drives (i.e., energizers such as thirst, hunger, sex) and that present behavior is based in large part on the consequences or rewards of past behavior.

dual-career ladders   Presence of two different ways to progress in an organization, each reflecting different types of contribution to the organization's mission. The managerial ladder ascends through increasing responsibility for supervision or direction of people. The professional track ascends through increasing contributions of a professional nature that do not mainly entail the supervision of employees.

dual coverage   In families in which both spouses work, the coverage of specific claims from each spouse's employment benefit package. Employers cut costs by specifying payment limitations under such conditions.

earnings-at-risk plans   *See* risk sharing.

e-benefits   Employee benefits, from information to applications, posted on company intranet by employer, which allows employee access 24/7 and employer to update easily.

economic rent   Confusingly, rent has two different meanings for economists. The first is the commonplace definition: the income your landlord receives from your apartment. The second, also known as economic rent, is the difference between what a factor of production is paid and how much it would need to be paid to remain in its current use. If an employee is paid $10,000 a week but would be willing to work for only $1,000, that employee's economic rent is $9,000 a week.

efficiency wage theory   A theory that explains why firms are rational in offering higher-than-necessary wages.

employee benefits   The parts of the total compensation package, other than pay for time worked, provided to employees in whole or in part by employer payments (e.g., life insurance, pension, workers' compensation, vacation).

employee contributions   Comparisons among individuals doing the same job for the same organization.

Employee Retirement Income Security Act (ERISA) For employers who choose to have a retirement plan, this act sets some formidable rules that must be followed to be in compliance.

employee stock ownership plan (ESOP) A retirement plan in which the company contributes its stock as the retirement benefit.

employer of choice The view that a firm's external wage competitiveness is just one facet of its overall human resource policy and that competitiveness is more properly judged on overall policies. Challenging work, great colleagues, or an organization's prestige must be factored into an overall consideration of attractiveness.

entitlement Employee belief that returns and/or rewards are due regardless of individual or company performance.

entry jobs Jobs that are filled from the external labor market and whose pay tends to reflect external economic factors rather than an organization's culture and traditions.

equal employment opportunity A mandate that all firms make employment decisions that are "blind" to minority/gender status.

Equal Pay Act (EPA) of 1963 An amendment to the Fair Labor Standards Act of 1938 that prohibits pay differentials on jobs that are substantially equal in terms of skills, efforts, responsibility, and working conditions, except when they are the result of bona fide seniority, merit, production-based systems, or any other job-related factor other than sex.

equity theory A theory proposing that in an exchange relationship (such as employment) the equality of outcome/input ratios between a person and a comparison other (a standard or relevant person/group) will determine fairness or equity. If the ratios diverge from each other, the person will experience reactions of unfairness and inequity.

ESOP (employee stock ownership plan) A plan in which a company borrows money from a financial institution by using its stock as a collateral for the loan. Principal and interest loan repayments are tax-deductible. With each loan repayment, the lending institution releases a certain amount of stock being held as security. The stock is then placed into an employee stock ownership trust (ESOT) for distribution at no cost to all employees.

The employees receive the stock upon retirement or separation from the company. TRASOPs and PAYSOPs are variants of ESOPs.

essay format An open-ended performance appraisal format. The descriptors used can range from comparisons with other employees to adjectives, behaviors, and goal accomplishment.

essential elements The parts of a job that cannot be assigned to another employee. The Americans with Disabilities Act requires that if applicants with disabilities can perform the essential elements of a job, reasonable accommodations must then be made to enable the qualified individuals to perform the job.

exchange value The price of labor (the wage) determined in a competitive market; in other words, labor's worth (the price) is whatever the buyer and seller agree upon.

Executive Order 11246 Law signed in 1965 that prohibits discrimination by federal contractors and subcontractors in all employment practices on basis of race, sex, color, religion, or national origin.

executive perquisites (perks) Special benefits made available to top executives (and sometimes other managerial employees). May be taxable income to the receiver. Company-related perks may include luxury offices; special parking; and company-paid membership in clubs/associations, hotels, and resorts. Personal perks include low-cost loans, personal and legal counseling, free home repairs and improvements, and so on. Since 1978, various tax and agency rulings have slowly been requiring that companies place a value on perks, thus increasing the taxable income of executives.

exempt jobs Jobs not subject to provisions of the Fair Labor Standards Act with respect to minimum wage and overtime. Exempt employees include most executives, administrators, professionals, and outside sales representatives.

exercise period Time during which, or after which, an individual who has been granted stock options is permitted to exercise them.

expatriate colony A section of a large city where expatriates tend to locate and form a community that takes on some of the cultural flavor of their home country.

expatriates Employees assigned outside their base country for any period of time in excess of one year.

expectancy theory   A motivation theory that proposes that individuals will select an alternative based on how this choice relates to outcomes such as rewards. The choice made is based on the strength or value of the outcome and on the perceived probability that this choice will lead to the desired outcome.

experience rating   Rating system in which insurance premiums vary directly with the number of claims filed. An experience rating is applied to unemployment insurance and workers' compensation and may be applied to commercial health insurance premiums. In a *community rating system,* insurance rates are based on the medical experience of the entire community.

external competitiveness   The pay relationships among organizations; focuses attention on the competitive positions reflected in these relationships.

extrinsic rewards   Rewards that a person receives from sources other than the job itself. They include compensation, supervision, promotions, vacations, friendships, and all other important outcomes apart from the job itself.

face validity   The determination of the relevance of a measuring device on the basis of "appearance" only.

factor scales   Measures that reflect different degrees within each compensable factor. Most commonly five to seven degrees are defined. Each degree may be anchored by typical skills, tasks and behaviors, or key job titles.

factor weights   Measures that indicate the importance of each compensable factor in a job evaluation system. Weights can be derived through either a committee judgment or a statistical analysis.

Fair Labor Standards Act of 1938 (FLSA)   A federal law governing minimum wage, overtime pay, equal pay for men and women in the same types of jobs, child labor, and record-keeping requirements.

Family and Medical Leave Act   Legislation passed in 1993 that entitles eligible employees to receive unpaid leave up to 12 weeks per year for specified family or medical reasons, such as caring for ill family members or adopting a child.

Federal Insurance Contribution Act (FICA)   The source of social security contribution withholding requirements. The FICA deduction is paid by both employer and employee.

first impression error   Rating error in which the rater develops a negative (positive) opinion of an employee early in the review period and allows it to negatively (positively) color all subsequent perceptions of performance.

flat rate   A single rate, rather than a range of rates, for all individuals performing a certain job. Ignores seniority and performance differences.

flexible benefit plan   Benefit package in which employees are given a core of critical benefits (necessary for minimum security) and permitted to expend the remainder of their benefit allotment on options that they find most attractive.

flexible benefits   *See* cafeteria (flexible) benefit plan.

flexible compensation   The allocation of employee compensation in a variety of forms tailored to organization pay objectives and/or the needs of individual employees.

forms of compensation   The various types of pay, which may be received directly in the form of cash (e.g., wages, bonuses, incentives) or indirectly through series and benefits (e.g., pensions, health insurance, vacations). This definition excludes other forms of rewards or returns that employees may receive, such as promotion, recognition for outstanding work behavior, and the like.

forms of pay   *See* forms of compensation.

401(k)   A 401(k) plan, so named for the section of the Internal Revenue Code describing the requirements, is a savings plan in which employees are allowed to defer pretax income.

gain-sharing (group incentive) plans   Incentive plans that are based on some measure of group performance rather than individual performance. Taking data on a past year as a base, group incentive plans may focus on cost savings (e.g., the Scanlon, Rucker, and Improshare plans) or on profit increases (profit-sharing plans) as the standard for distributing a portion of the accrued funds among relevant employees.

Gantt plan   Individual incentive plan that provides for variable incentives as a function of a standard expressed as time period per unit of production. Under this plan, a standard time for a task is purposely set at a level requiring high effort to complete.

gender pay equity   *See* comparable worth.

General Schedule (GS)   A job structure used by the U.S. Office of Personnel Management for white-collar employees. It has 15 "grades" (classes) plus 5 more levels on an Executive Schedule.

geographic differentials   Local conditions that employees in a specific geographic area encounter, such as labor shortages and differences in housing costs.

global approach   Substitution of a particular skill and experience level for job descriptions in determining external market rates. Includes rates for all individuals who possess that skill.

golden parachute   A contract clause that calls for the payment of a large lump sum in specified circumstances of an executive's termination, for example, following the company's acquisition by another firm.

Green Circle Rate   Pay rate that is below the minimum rate for a job or pay range for a grade

group incentive plans   *See* gain-sharing (group incentive) plans.

halo error   Rating error in which an appraiser gives favorable ratings to all job duties based on impressive performance in just one job function. For example, a rater who hates tardiness rates a prompt subordinate high across all performance dimensions exclusively because of this one characteristic.

Halsey 50–50 method   Individual incentive method that provides for variable incentives as a function of a standard expressed as time period per unit of production. This plan derives its name from the shared split between worker and employer of any savings in direct costs.

Hay job evaluation system   A point factor system that evaluates jobs with respect to know-how, problem solving, and accountability. It is used primarily for exempt (managerial/professional) jobs.

Health Maintenance Act of 1973   Legislation that requires that employers offer alternative health coverage options (e.g., health maintenance organizations) to employees.

health maintenance organization (HMO)   A nontraditional health care delivery system. HMOs offer comprehensive benefits and outpatient services, as well as hospital coverage, for a fixed monthly prepaid fee.

health reimbursement arrangements (HRAs)   The employer sets up an account for a specified amount. When an employee has qualified medical costs, they're submitted for reimbursement until the account is depleted.

health savings accounts (HSA)   An HSA is a tax-exempt account built up through contributions of the employee or the employer, or both, that can be used to pay for health care.

hierarchies (job structures)   Jobs ordered according to their relative content and/or value.

high-commitment practices   Factors such as high base pay, sharing successes only (not risks), guaranteed employment security, promotions from within, training and skill development, employee ownership, and long-term perspective. High-commitment practices are believed to attract and retain a high-committed workforce that will become the source of competitive advantage.

hit rate   The ability of a job evaluation plan to replicate a predetermined, agreed-upon job structure.

horn error   The opposite of halo error; downgrading an employee across all performance dimensions exclusively because of poor performance on one dimension.

human capital theory   An economic theory proposing that the investment one is willing to make to enter an occupation is related to the returns one expects to earn over time in the form of compensation.

human resource planning system   Put in place by the benefit administrator to make realistic estimates of human resource needs and avoid a pattern of hasty hiring and morale-breaking terminations.

Improshare (IMproved PROductivity through SHARing)   A gain-sharing plan in which a standard is developed to identify the expected hours required to produce an acceptable level of output. Any savings arising from production of agreed-upon output in fewer-than-expected hours are shared by the firm and the worker.

incentive   Inducement offered in advance to influence future performance (e.g., sales commissions).

incentive effect   The degree to which pay influences individual and aggregate motivation among employees at any point in time.

incentive stock options (ISO)   A form of deferred compensation designed to influence long-term performance. Gives an executive the right to pay today's market price for a block of shares in the company at a future time. No tax is due until the shares are sold.

increase guidelines   Inherent compensation system controls. They specify the amount and timing of pay increases on an organizationwide basis.

indirect compensation   Noncash benefits provided to an employee.

individual incentive plans Incentive compensation that is tied directly to objective measures of individual production (e.g., sales commissions).

individual retirement accounts (IRAs) Tax-favored retirement savings plans that individuals can establish themselves.

innovator The innovator stresses new products and short response time to market trends.

instrumentality The perceived contingency that an outcome (performing well) has another outcome (a reward such as pay).

internal alignment The pay relationships among jobs or skill levels within a single organization; focuses attention on employee and management acceptance of those relationships. It involves establishing equal pay for jobs of equal worth and acceptable pay differentials for jobs of unequal worth.

interrater reliability The extent of agreement among raters rating the same individual, group, or phenomena.

interval scaling A particular numerical point difference has the same meaning on all parts of a scale.

inventories Questionnaires in which tasks, behaviors, and abilities are listed. The core of all quantitative job analysis.

job analysis The systematic process of collecting information related to the nature of a specific job. It provides the knowledge needed to define jobs and conduct job evaluation.

job-based structure Structure that relies on work content—tasks, behaviors, responsibilities.

job-based systems Systems that focus on jobs as the basic unit of analysis to determine the pay structure; hence, job analysis is required.

job classification (grade) A grouping of jobs that are considered substantially similar for pay purposes.

job content Information that describes a job. May include responsibility assumed and/or the tasks performed.

job description A summary of the most important features of a job. It identifies the job and describes the general nature of the work, specific task responsibilities, outcomes, and the employee characteristics required to perform the job.

job evaluation A systematic procedure designed to aid in establishing pay differentials among jobs within a single company. It includes classification, comparison of the relative worth of jobs, blending internal and external market forces, measurement, negotiation, and judgment.

job evaluation committee Group that may be charged with the responsibility of (1) selecting a job evaluation system, (2) carrying out or at least supervising the process of job evaluation, and (3) evaluating the success with which the job evaluation has been conducted. Its role may vary among organizations, but its members usually represent all important constituencies within the organization.

job evaluation manual Handbook that contains information on the job evaluation plan and is used as a "yardstick" in evaluating jobs. It includes a description of the job evaluation method used, descriptions of all jobs, and, if relevant, a description of compensable factors, numerical degree scales, and weights; may also contain a description of the available review or appeals procedure.

job family A group of jobs involving work of the same nature but requiring different skill and responsibility levels (e.g., computing and account recording are a job family; bookkeeper, accounting clerk, and teller are jobs within that family).

job grade *See* pay grade.

job hierarchy A grouping of jobs based on their job-related similarities and differences and on their value to the organization's objectives.

job pricing The process of assigning pay to jobs, based on thorough job analysis and job evaluation.

job specifications The job specifications that can be used as a basis for hiring are knowledge, skills, and abilities required to adequately perform the tasks.

job structure Relationship among jobs inside an organization, based on work content and each job's relative contribution to achieving the organization's objectives.

just wage doctrine A theory of job value that posits a "just" or equitable wage for any occupation based on that occupation's place in the larger social hierarchy. According to this doctrine, pay structures should be designed on the basis of societal norms, customs, and tradition, not on the basis of economic and market forces.

key jobs *See* benchmark (key) job.

labor demand The employment level organizations require. An increase in wage rates will reduce the demand for labor, other factors constant. Thus, the labor demand curve (the relationship between employment levels and wage rates) is downward-sloping.

labor supply The different numbers of employees available at different pay rates.

lag pay-level policy A wage structure that is set to match market rates at the beginning of the plan year only. The rest of the plan year, internal rates will lag behind market rates. Its objective is to offset labor costs, but it may hinder a firm's ability to attract and retain quality employees.

lead pay-level policy A wage structure that is set to lead the market throughout the plan year. Its aim is to maximize a firm's ability to attract and retain quality employees and to minimize employee dissatisfaction with pay.

legally required benefits Benefits that are required by statutory law: workers' compensation, social security, and unemployment compensation are required in the United States. Required benefits vary among countries. Companies operating in foreign countries must comply with host-country compensation and benefit mandates.

leniency error Rating error in which the rater consistently rates someone higher than is deserved.

leveling Weighting market survey data according to the closeness of the job matches.

lifetime employment Most prevalent in Japanese companies, the notion of employees' staying with the same company for their entire career, despite possible poor performance on the part of either an employee or the company.

line of sight An employee's ability to see how individual performance affects incentive payout. Employees on a straight piecework pay system have a clear line of sight—their pay is a direct function of the number of units they produce; employees covered by profit sharing have a fuzzier line of sight—their payouts are a function of many forces, only one of which is individual performance.

living wage Pay legislation in some U.S. cities that requires wages well above the federal minimum wage. Often applies only to city government employees.

local country nationals (LCNs) Citizens of a country in which a U.S. foreign subsidiary is located. LCNs' compensation is tied either to local wage rates or to the rates of U.S. expatriates performing the same job.

long-term disability (LTD) plan An insurance plan that provides payments to replace income lost through an inability to work that is not covered by other legally required disability income plans.

long-term incentives Inducements offered in advance to influence longer-rate (multiyear) results. Usually offered to top managers and professionals to get them to focus on long-term organization objectives.

low-high approach Use of the lowest- and highest-paid benchmark job in the external market to anchor an entire skill-based structure.

lump-sum award Payment of entire increase (typically merit-based) at one time. Because amount is not factored into base pay, any benefits tied to base pay do not increase.

lump-sum bonus *See* lump-sum award.

managed care Steps taken to contain health care and workers' compensation costs, such as switching to preferred provider organizations for health care delivery, utilization-review procedures, and medical bill audits.

management by objectives (MBO) An employee planning, development, and appraisal procedure in which a supervisor and a subordinate, or group of subordinates, jointly identify and establish common performance goals. Employee performance on the absolute standards is evaluated at the end of the specified period.

managing compensation The fourth dimension in the pay model: ensuring the right people get the right pay for achieving the right objectives in the right way.

marginal product of labor The additional output associated with the employment of one additional human resource unit, with other factors held constant.

marginal productivity theory (MPT) In contrast to Marxist "surplus value" theory, a theory that focuses on labor demand rather than supply and argues that employers will pay a wage to a unit of labor that equals that unit's use (not exchange) value. That is, work is compensated in proportion to its contribution to the organization's production objectives.

marginal revenue of labor The additional revenue generated when the firm employs one additional unit of human resources, with other factors held constant.

market-based health care *See* customer-driven health care.

market pay line Using key/benchmark jobs, a market pay policy line can be constructed that shows external market pay survey data as a function of internal job evaluation points. In many cases, the market pay policy line is obtained by using regression analysis, which yields an equation of the form "market pay = intercept +

slope × job evaluation points." By plugging the job evaluation points for any job (both benchmark and non-benchmark jobs) into the equation, the predicted pay for each job can be obtained.

market pricing   Setting pay structures almost exclusively through matching pay for a very large percentage of jobs with the rates paid in the external market.

maturity curve   A plot of the empirical relationship between current pay and years since a professional has last received a degree (YSLD), thus allowing organizations to determine a competitive wage level for specific professional employees with varying levels of experience.

Medicare Prescription Drug, Improvement and Modernization Act of 2003   Seniors must choose among a variety of plans written in bureaucratic hieroglyphics.

Mental Health Act   Law passed in 1997 that stipulates that mental illness must be covered to same extent that other medical conditions are covered.

merit Bonus   *See* lump-sum bonus.

merit increase guidelines   Specifications that tie pay increases to performance. They may take one of two forms: The simplest version specifies pay increases permissible for different levels of performance. More complex guidelines tie pay not only to performance but also to position in the pay range.

merit pay   A reward that recognizes outstanding past performance. It can be given in the form of lump-sum payments or as increments to the base pay. Merit programs are commonly designed to pay different amounts (often at different times) depending on the level of performance.

Merrick plan   Individual incentive plan that provides for variable incentives as a function of units of production per time period. It works like the Taylor plan, but three piecework rates are set: (1) high—for production exceeding 100 percent of standard; (2) medium—for production between 83 and 100 percent of standard; and (3) low—for production less than 83 percent of standard.

minimum wage   A minimum-wage level for most Americans established by Congress as part of the Fair Labor Standards Act of 1938.

motivation   An individual's willingness to engage in some behavior. Primarily concerned with (1) what energizes human behavior, (2) what directs or channels such behavior, and (3) how this behavior is maintained or sustained.

multiskill systems   Systems that link pay to the number of different jobs (breadth) an employee is certified to do, regardless of the specific job he or she is doing.

National Electrical Manufacturers Association (NEMA) plan   A point factor job evaluation system that evolved into the National Position Evaluation Plan sponsored by NMTA associates.

National Metal Trades Association (NMTA) plan   A point factor job evaluation plan for production, maintenance, and service personnel.

noncontributory financing   Benefit option in which an employee benefit is fully paid for by the employer.

nonexempt employees   Employees who are subject to the provisions of the Fair Labor Standards Act.

nonexempt jobs   Jobs subject to provisions of the Fair Labor Standards Act with respect to minimum wage and overtime. Exempt employees include most executives, administrators, professionals, and outside sales representatives.

nonqualified deferred compensation plans   A plan does not qualify for tax exemption if an employer who pays high levels of deferred compensation to executives does not make proportionate contributions to lower-level employees.

nonqualified stock options   Form of compensation that gives an executive the right to purchase stock at a stipulated price; the excess over fair market value is taxed as ordinary income.

Obamacare   *See* Patient Protection and Affordable Care Act.

objective performance-based pay systems   Pay approach that focuses on objective performance standards (e.g., counting output) derived from organizational objectives and a thorough analysis of the job (e.g., incentive and gain-sharing plans).

occupational diseases   Diseases that arise out of the course of employment, not including "ordinary diseases of life," for which workers' compensation claims can be filed.

offshoring   Offshoring refers to the movement of jobs to locations beyond a country's borders.

on-call employees   Employees who must respond to work-related assignments/problems 24 hours a day. Firefighters, SPCA humane officers, and other emergency personnel are traditional examples. Increasingly, this group includes technical workers such as software service personnel.

organizational culture   The composite of shared values, symbols, and cognitive schemes that ties people together in the organization.

outlier   An extreme value that may distort some measures of central tendency.

outsourcing   The practice of hiring outside vendors to perform functions that do not directly contribute to business objectives and in which the organization does not have a comparative advantage.

paid-time-off (PTO) plan   Eliminates the distinction between sick days and other paid days off, thus eliminating the incentive to "fake" illness.

paired comparison ranking   A ranking job evaluation method that involves comparing all possible pairs of jobs under study.

Patient Protection and Affordable Care Act   Enacted by Congress and survivor of a Supreme Court Test, this law requires the vast majority of Americans to either have health insurance or to pay a tax for not doing so.

pay discrimination   Discrimination usually defined as including (1) access discrimination, which occurs when qualified women and minorities are denied access to particular jobs, promotions, or training opportunities; and (2) valuation discrimination, which takes place when minorities or women are paid less than white males for performing substantially equal work. Both types of discrimination are illegal under Title VII of the Civil Rights Act of 1964. Some argue that valuation discrimination can also occur when men and women hold entirely different jobs (in content or results) that are of comparable worth to the employer. Existing federal laws do not support the "equal pay for work of comparable worth" standard.

pay equity (also **gender pay equity**)   *See* comparable worth.

pay-for-knowledge plans   A compensation practice whereby employees are paid for the number of different jobs they can adequately perform or the amount of knowledge they possess.

pay-for-performance plans   Pay that varies with some measure of individual or organizational performance, such as merit pay, lump-sum bonus plans, skill-based pay, incentive plans, variable pay plans, risk sharing, and success sharing.

pay forms   The various types of payments, or pay mix, that make up total compensation.

pay grade   One of the classes, levels, or groups into which jobs of the same or similar values are grouped for compensation purposes. All jobs in a pay grade have the same pay range—maximum, minimum, and midpoint.

pay increase guidelines   The mechanisms through which levels are translated into pay increases and, therefore, dictate the size and time of the pay reward for good performance.

pay level   An average of the array of rates paid by an employer.

pay-level policies   Decisions concerning a firm's level of pay vis-à-vis product and labor market competitors. There are three classes of pay-level policies: to lead, to match, or to follow competition.

pay-level rise   The percentage increase in the average wage rate paid. Calculated as: $100 \times$ [(Average pay-year end − average pay at year beginning)/Average pay at year beginning].

pay mix (or pay forms)   Relative emphasis among compensation components such as base pay, merit, incentives, and benefits.

pay objectives   *See* compensation objectives.

pay-policy line   Representation of the organization's pay-level policy relative to what competitors pay for similar jobs.

pay ranges   The range of pay rates from minimum to maximum set for a pay grade or class. It puts limits on the rates an employer will pay for a particular job.

pay satisfaction   A function of the discrepancy between employees' perceptions of how much pay they should receive and how much pay they do receive. If these perceptions are equal, an employee is said to experience pay satisfaction.

pay structures   The array of pay rates for different jobs within a single organization; they focus attention on differential compensation paid for work of unequal worth.

pay (wage) survey   The systematic process of collecting information and making judgments about the compensation paid by other employers. Pay (wage) survey data are useful in designing pay levels and structures.

pay techniques   Mechanisms or technologies of compensation management, such as job analysis, job descriptions, market surveys, job evaluation, and the like, that tie the four basic pay policies to the pay objectives.

pay-with-competition policy   Policy that tries to ensure that a firm's labor costs are approximately equal to those of its competitors. It seeks to avoid placing an employer at a disadvantage in pricing products or in maintaining a qualified workforce.

pension benefit guaranty corporation (PBGC)   Agency to which employers are required to pay insurance premiums to protect individuals from bankrupt companies (and pension plans!). In turn, the PBGC guarantees payment of vested benefits to employees formerly covered by terminated pension plans.

pension plan   A form of deferred compensation. All pension plans usually have four common characteristics: They (1) involve deferred payments to a former employee (or surviving spouse) for past services rendered; (2) specify a normal retirement age, at which time benefits begin to accrue to the employee; (3) specify a formula for calculating benefits, and (4) provide for integration with social security benefits.

performance-dimension training   Training that gives performance appraisers an understanding of the dimensions on which to evaluate employee performance.

performance evaluation (performance appraisal)   A process to determine correspondence between worker behavior/task outcomes and employer expectations (performance standards).

performance metrics   Quantitative measures of job performance.

performance share/unit plans   Cash or stock awards earned through achieving specific goals.

performance standard   An explicit statement of what work output is expected from employees in exchange for compensation.

performance-standard training   Training that gives performance appraisers a frame of reference for making ratee appraisals.

perquisites (perks)   The extras bestowed on top management, such as private dining rooms, company cars, and first-class airfare.

person-based structure   A person-based structure shifts the focus to the employee: the skills, knowledge, or competencies the employee possesses, whether or not they are used in the employee's particular job.

personal care account (PCA)   A tool used by employers to gain some control over health care costs while still providing health security to workers. The employer establishes a high deductible paid by employees but cushions the blow by setting up a PCA to cover part of the deductible cost.

phantom stock plan   Stock plan in which an increase in stock price at a fixed future date determines the cash or stock award. It is called a phantom plan because the organization in question is not publicly traded. Stock price, therefore, is an illusion. The "phantom price" is derived from standard financial accounting procedures.

planned pay-level rise   The percentage increase in average pay that is planned to occur after considering such factors as anticipated rates of change in market data, changes in cost of living, the employer's ability to pay, and the efforts of turnover and promotions. This index may be used in top-down budgeting to control compensation costs.

point (factor) method   A job evaluation method that employs (1) compensable factors, (2) factor degrees numerically scaled, and (3) weights reflecting the relative importance of each factor. Once scaled degrees and weights are established for each factor, each job is measured against each compensable factor and a total score is calculated for each job. The total points assigned to a job determine the job's relative value and hence its location in the pay structure.

point-of-service plan (POS)   A point-of-service plan is a hybrid plan combining health maintenance organization (HMO) and preferred provider organization (PPO) benefits.

policy capturing   Compensable factor importance weights are inferred using statistical methods such as regression analysis.

policy line   A pay line that reflects the organization's policy with respect to the external labor market.

portability   Transferability of pension benefits for employees moving to a new organization. ERISA does not require mandatory portability of private pensions. On a voluntary basis, the employer may agree to let an employee's pension benefit transfer to an individual retirement account (IRA) or, in a reciprocating arrangement, to the new employer.

Position Analysis Questionnaire (PAQ)   A structured job analysis technique that classifies job information into seven basic factors: information input, mental processes, work output, relationships with other persons, job context, other job characteristics, and general dimensions. The PAQ analyzes jobs in terms of worker-oriented data.

preferred provider organization (PPO) Health care delivery system in which there is a direct contractual relationship between and among employers, health care providers, and third-party payers. An employer is able to select providers (e.g., selected doctors) who agree to provide price discounts and submit to strict utilization controls.

Pregnancy Discrimination Act of 1978 An amendment to Title VII of the Civil Rights Act. It requires employers to extend to pregnant employees or spouses the same disability and medical benefits provided to other employees or spouses of employees.

prevailing-wage laws Legislation that provides for a government-defined prevailing wage as the minimum wage that must be paid for work done on covered government projects or purchases. In practice, these prevailing rates have been union rates paid in various geographic areas.

probationary period Period during which new employees are excluded from benefits coverage, usually until some term of employment (e.g., 3 months) is completed.

procedural justice/fairness Concept concerned with the process used to make and implement decisions about pay. It suggests that the way pay decisions are made and implemented may be as important to employees as the results of the decisions.

professional An employee who has specialized training of a scientific or intellectual nature and whose major duties do not entail the supervision of people.

profit-sharing plan A plan that focuses on profitability as the standard for group incentive. These plans typically involve one of three distributions: (1) Cash or current distribution plans provide full payment to participants soon after profits have been determined (quarterly or annually); (2) deferred plans have a portion of current profits credited to employee accounts, with cash payments made at time of retirement, disability, severance, or death; and (3) combination plans that incorporate aspects of both current and deferred options.

purchasing power The ability to buy goods and services in a certain currency, determined by exchange rates and availability of goods. Companies must determine purchasing power when allocating allowances to expatriates.

qualified deferred compensation plan A deferred compensation program that qualities for tax exemption.

It must provide contributions or benefits for employees other than executives that are proportionate to contributions provided to executives.

quantitative job analysis (QJA) Job analysis method that relies on scaled questionnaires and inventories that produce job-related data that are documentable, can be statistically analyzed, and may be more objective than other analyses.

quoted price market Stores that label each item's price or ads that list a job's opening starting wage are examples of quoted-price markets.

range maximums The maximum values to be paid for a job grade, representing the top value the organization places on the output of the work.

range midpoint The salary midway between the minimum and maximum rates of a salary range. The midpoint rate for each range is usually set to correspond to the pay-policy line and represents the rate paid for satisfactory performance on the job.

range minimums The minimum values to be paid for a job grade, representing the minimum value the organization places on the work. Often, rates below the minimum are used for trainees.

range overlap The degree of overlap between adjoining grade ranges is determined by the differences in midpoints among ranges and the range spread. A high degree of overlap and narrow midpoint differentials indicate small differences in the value of jobs in the adjoining grades and permit promotions without much change in the rates paid. By contrast, a small degree of overlap and wide midpoint differentials allow the manager to reinforce a promotion with a large salary increase.

ranges *See* pay ranges.

rank and yank Requires managers to complete performance appraisals by ranking employees into a preset distribution of top, middle, and needs improvement categories. Often this latter category has employees who are "yanked" or terminated from the organization.

ranking format A type of performance appraisal format that requires that the rater compare employees against each other to determine the relative ordering of the group on some performance measure.

rater error training Training that enables performance appraisers to identify and suppress psychometric errors such as leniency, severity, central tendency, and halo errors when evaluating employee performance.

rating errors Errors in judgment that occur in a systematic manner when an individual observes and evaluates a person, group, or phenomenon. The most frequently described rating errors include halo, leniency, severity, and central tendency errors.

rating format A type of performance appraisal format that requires that raters evaluate employees on absolute measurement scales that indicate varying levels of performance.

recency error The opposite of first-impression error. Performance (either good or bad) at the end of the review period plays too large a role in determining an employee's rating for the entire period.

red circle rates Pay rates that are above the maximum rate for a job or pay range for a grade.

reengineering Making changes in the way work is designed to include external customer focus. Usually includes organizational delayering and job restructuring.

regression A statistical technique for relating present-pay differentials to some criterion, that is, pay rates in the external market, rates for jobs held predominantly by men, or factor weights that duplicate present rates for all jobs in the organization.

regression analysis One output from a regression analysis is the R2. The R2 is much like a correlation in that it tells us what percentage of the variation is accounted for by the variables we are using to predict or explain.

relational returns The nonquantifiable returns employees get from employment, such as social satisfaction, friendship, feeling of belonging, or accomplishment.

relative value of jobs The relative contribution of jobs to organizational goals, to their external market rates, or to some other agreed-upon rates.

relevant markets Those employers with which an organization competes for skills and products/services. Three factors commonly used to determine the relevant markets are the occupation or skills required, the geography (willingness to relocate and/or commute), and employers that compete in the product market.

reliability The consistency of the results obtained, that is, the extent to which any measuring procedure yields the same results on repeated trials. Reliable job information does not mean that it is accurate (valid), comprehensive, or free from bias.

rent *See* economic rent.

reopener clause A provision in an employment contract that specifies that wages, and sometimes such nonwage items as pension/benefits, will be renegotiated under certain conditions (changes in cost of living, organization, profitability, and so on).

reservation wage A theoretical minimum standard below which a job seeker will not accept an offer, no matter how attractive the other job attributes.

restricted stock plan Plan that grants stock at a reduced price with the condition that it not be sold before a specified date.

reverse incentive plan A plan where there is penalty for poor performance rather than reward for good.

reward system The composite of all organizational mechanisms and strategies used to formally acknowledge employee behaviors and performance. It includes all forms of compensation, promotions, and assignments; nonmonetary awards and recognitions; training opportunities; job design and analysis; organizational design and working conditions; the supervisor; social networks; performance standards and reward criteria; performance evaluation; and the like.

risk sharing An incentive plan in which employees' base wages are set below a specified level (e.g., 80% of the market wage) and incentive earnings are used to raise wages above the base. In good years an employee's incentive pay will more than make up for the 20 percent shortfall, giving the employee a pay premium. Because employees assume some of the risk, risk-sharing plans pay more generously than success-sharing plans in good years.

Roth IRA For employees who meet certain requirements, all earnings are tax free when withdrawn. However, no income tax deductions are allowed for contributions.

Rowan plan Individual incentive plan that provides for variable incentives as a function of a standard expressed as time period per unit of production. It is similar to the Halsey plan, but in this plan a worker's bonus increases as the time required to complete the task decreases.

Rucker plan A group cost savings plan in which cost reductions due to employee efforts are shared with the employees. It involves a somewhat more complex formula than a Scanlon plan for determining employee incentive bonuses.

salary Pay given to employees who are exempt from regulations of the Fair Labor Standards Act and hence do not receive overtime pay (e.g., managers and professionals). Exempt pay is calculated at an annual or monthly rate rather than hourly.

salary continuation plans   Benefit options that provide some form of protection for disability. Some are legally required, such as workers' compensation provisions for work-related disability and social security disability income provisions for those who qualify.

sales compensation   Any form of compensation paid to sales representatives. Sales compensation formulas usually attempt to establish direct incentives for sales outcomes.

sales value of production (SVOP)   An incentive metric that calculates the dollar value of goods produced and in inventory.

Sarbanes-Oxley Act   Legislation passed in 2002 that prohibits executives from retaining bonuses or profits from selling company stock if they mislead the public about the financial health of the company.

say on pay   Sarbanes-Oxley Act of 2002 and subsequent legislation gives shareholders the right to exercise a nonbinding vote favoring or disapproving of an executive's compensation package.

scaling   Determining the intervals on a measurement instrument.

Scanlon plan   A group cost-savings plan designed to lower labor costs without lowering the level of a firm's activity. Incentives are derived as the ratio between labor costs and sales value of production (SVOP).

Securities Exchange Act   Legislative act passed in 1934 that created the Securities and Exchange Commission (SEC).

segmented labor supply   A labor supply that comes from multiple markets. Some employees may come from different global locations, may receive different pay forms, and may have varied employment relationships.

self-determination theory   Belief that people are motivated not only by extrinsic rewards like pay but also by intrinsic rewards that promote sense of autonomy, self-worth, and relatedness.

self-funding plans   These plans specify that payouts only occur after the company reaches a certain profit target. Then variable payouts for individual, team, and company performance are triggered.

self-insurance compensation   System in which an organization funds its own insurance claims, for either health or life insurance or workers' compensation.

seniority increases   Pay increases tied to a progression pattern based on seniority. To the extent

performance improves with time on the job, this method has the rudiments of paying for performance.

severity error   The opposite of leniency error. Rating someone consistently lower than is deserved.

shared choice   An external competitiveness policy that offers employees substantial choice among their pay forms.

shirking behavior   The propensity of employees to allow the marginal revenue product of their labor to be less than its marginal cost; to be lax.

short-term disability (STD)   *See* workers' compensation.

short-term incentives   Inducements offered in advance to influence future short-range (annual) results. Usually very specific performance standards are established.

sick leave   Paid time when an employee is not working due to illness or injury.

simplified employee pension (SEP)   A retirement income arrangement intended to markedly reduce the paperwork for regular pension plans.

single-rate pay system   A compensation policy under which all employees in a given job are paid at the same rate instead of being placed in a pay grade. Generally applies to situations in which there is little room for variation in job performance, such as an assembly line.

skill analysis   A systematic process to identify and collect information about the skills required to perform work in an organization.

skill-based pay system   *See* pay-for-knowledge plan.

skill-based structure   Pay structure that links pay to the depth or breadth of the skills, abilities, and knowledge a person acquires that are relevant to the work.

skill-based system   Compensation approach that links pay to the depth and/or breadth of the skills, abilities, and knowledge a person acquires/demonstrates that are relevant to the work. Typically applies to operators, technicians, and office workers where the work is relatively specific and defined. The criterion chosen can influence employee behaviors by describing what is required to get higher pay.

skill blocks   Basic units of knowledge employees must master to perform the work, satisfy customers, and achieve business objectives.

skill requirement   Composite of experience, training, and ability as measured by the performance requirements of a particular job.

slippage *See* turnover effect.

sorting effect The effect that pay can have on the composition of the workforce. Different types of pay strategies may cause different types of people to apply to and stay with an organization.

special groups Employee groups for whom compensation practices diverge from typical company procedures (e.g., supervisors, middle and upper management, nonsupervisory professionals, sales, and personnel in foreign subsidiaries).

spillover effect The fact that improvements obtained in unionized firms "spill over" to nonunion firms seeking ways to lessen workers' incentives for organizing a union.

spillover error Rating error in which the rater continues to downgrade an employee for performance errors in prior rating periods.

spot award One-time award for exceptional performance; also called a spot bonus.

standard hour plan Individual incentive plan in which rate determination is based on time period per unit of production and wages vary directly as a constant function of product level. In this context, the incentive rate in standard hour plans is set based on completion of a task in some expected time period.

standard rating scales Appraisal system characterized by (1) one or more performance standards being developed and defined for the appraiser and (2) each performance standard having a measurement scale indicating varying levels of performance on that dimension. Appraisers rate the appraisee by checking the point on the scale that best represents the appraisee's performance level. Rating scales vary in the extent to which anchors along the scale are defined.

stock appreciation rights (SARs) Rights that permit an executive to receive all the potential capital gain of a stock incentive option (ISO) without having to purchase the stock; thus, they reduce an executive's cash commitment. Payment is provided on demand for the difference between the stock option price and the current market price.

stock grant Issue of a share(s) of stock at no cost to the recipient which, in turn, can be sold at some agreed upon time at market rate.

stock option A right to purchase, at market price, a share(s) of stock at some future point in time for a rate agreed upon at the time the option is granted.

stock purchase plan (nonqualified) A plan that is, in effect, a management stock purchase plan. It allows senior management or other key personnel to buy stock in the business. This plan has certain restrictions: (1) The stockholder must be employed for a certain period of time, (2) the business has the right to buy back the stock, and (3) stockholders cannot sell the stock for a defined period.

stock purchase plan (qualified) A program under which employees buy shares in the company's stock, with the company contributing a specific amount for each unit of employee contribution. Also, stock may be offered at a fixed price (usually below market) and paid for in full by the employees.

straight piecework system Individual incentive plan in which rate determination is based on units of production per time period; wages vary directly as a constant function of production level.

straight ranking procedure A type of performance appraisal format in which the rater compares or ranks each employee relative to each other employee.

strategy The fundamental direction of the organization. It guides the deployment of all resources, including compensation.

strategic perspective A strategic perspective focuses on those compensation choices that help the organization gain and sustain competitive advantage.

strike price Price an individual is permitted to buy a stock at by the company granting the stock.

subjective performance-based pay systems Pay approach that focuses on subjective performance standards (e.g., achieving agreed-upon objectives) derived from organizational objectives and a thorough analysis of the job.

success sharing An incentive plan (e.g., profit sharing or gain sharing) in which an employee's base wage matches the market wage and variable pay adds on during successful years. Because base pay is not reduced in bad years, employees bear little risk.

supermarket plan *See* cafeteria (flexible) benefit plan.

supplemental unemployment benefits (SUB) plan Employer-funded plan that supplements state unemployment insurance payments to workers during temporary periods of layoffs. Largely concentrated in the automobile, steel, and related industries.

supply chain analysis As applied to work flow analysis, supply chain analysis looks at how an organization does its work: activities pursued to accomplish specific objectives for specific customers.

surplus value The difference between labor's use and exchange values. According to Marx, under capitalism wages are based on labor's exchange value—which is lower than its use value—and thus provide only a subsistence wage.

survey The systematic process of collecting and making judgments about the compensation paid by other employers.

tacit work Complex work (as compared to transactional, or routine, work).

tally sheet A tally sheet gives a comprehensive view on the true value of executive compensation. Add up the value of base salary, annual incentives, long-term incentives, benefits, and perks. Part of this process includes estimating the current value of stock options (using something called the Black–Scholes model), stock appreciation rights, vested and unvested pensions, and payouts upon termination.

tariff agreements In some European countries, the wage rates negotiated by employer associations and trade union federations for all wage earners for all companies in an industry group.

task (work) data Information on the elemental units of work (tasks), with emphasis on the purpose of each task, collected for job analysis. Work data describe the job in terms of actual tasks performed and their output.

tax equalization A method whereby an expatriate pays neither more nor less tax than the assumed home-country tax on base remuneration.

Taylor plan Individual incentive plan that provides for variable incentives as a function of units of production per time period. It provides two piecework rates that are established for production above and below standard, and these rates are higher and lower than the regular wage incentive level.

team incentive Group incentive restricted to team members with payout usually based on improvements in productivity, customer satisfaction, financial performance, or quality of goods and services directly attributable to the team.

third-country nationals (TCNs) Employees of a U.S. foreign subsidiary who maintain citizenship in a country other than the United States or the host country. TCNs' compensation is tied to comparative wages in the local country, the United States, or the country of citizenship.

360-degree feedback A rating method that assesses employee performance from five points of view: supervisor, peer, self, customer, and subordinate.

Title VII of the Civil Rights Act of 1964 A major piece of legislation prohibiting pay discrimination.

It is much broader in intent than the Equal Pay Act, forbidding discrimination on the basis of race, color, religion, sex, pregnancy, or national origin.

top-down approach to pay budgeting Also known as *unit-level budgeting,* an approach in which a total pay budget for the organization (or unit) is determined and allocated "down" to individual employees during the plan year. There are many kinds of unit-level budgeting. They differ in the type of financial index used as a control measure. Controlling to a planned level rise and controlling to a planned compa-ratio are two typical approaches.

topping out Situation in which employees in a skill-based compensation plan attain the top pay rate in a job category by accumulating and/or becoming certified for the top-paid skill block(s).

total cash Base wage plus cash bonus; does not include benefits or stock options.

total compensation The complete pay package for employees, including all forms of money, bonuses, benefits, services, and stock.

total returns All returns to an employee, including financial compensation, benefits, opportunities for social interaction, security, status and recognition, work variety, appropriate workload, importance of work, authority/control/autonomy, advancement opportunities, feedback, hazard-free working conditions, and opportunities for personal and professional development. An effective compensation system will utilize many of these returns.

total rewards *See* total returns.

tournament theory The notion that larger differences in pay are more motivating than smaller differences. Like prize awards in a golf tournament, pay increases should get successively greater as one moves up the job hierarchy. Differences between the top job and the second-highest job should be the largest.

traditional time-off (TTO) plan Paid vacations, holidays (or pay if worked), sick leave, and personal leave, tracked separately.

transactional work Routine work.

turnover effect The downward pressure on average wage that results from the replacement of high-wage-earning employees with workers earning a lower wage.

two-tier pay plans Wage structures that differentiate pay for the same jobs based on hiring date. A contract is negotiated that specifies that employees hired after a stated day will receive lower wages than their higher-seniority peers working on the same or similar jobs.

underwater stock option A stock option with a market price lower than the original offer price. Fairly common during a market downturn, these options are of no value to someone who has received them as an incentive.

unemployment benefits   *See* unemployment insurance.

unemployment compensation   *See* unemployment insurance.

unemployment insurance (UI)   State-administered program that provides financial security for workers during periods of joblessness.

unequal treatment   *See* disparate treatment.

use value   The value or price ascribed to the use or consumption of labor in the production of goods or services.

U.S. expatriates (USEs)   American citizens working for a U.S. subsidiary in a foreign country. Main compensation concerns are to "keep the expatriates whole" relative to their U.S.-based counterparts and to provide expatriates with an incentive wage for accepting the foreign assignment.

utility theory   The analysis of utility, the dollar value created by increasing revenues and/or decreasing costs by changing one or more human resource practices. It has most typically been used to analyze the payoff to making more valid employee hiring/selection decisions.

valence   The amount of positive or negative value placed on specific outcomes by an individual.

validity   The accuracy of the results obtained; that is, the extent to which any measuring device measures what it purports to measure.

value   The worth of the work; its relative contribution to organization objectives.

valuation discrimination   Discrimination that focuses on the pay women and minorities receive for the work they perform. Discrimination occurs when members of these groups are paid less than white males for performing substantially equal work. This definition of pay discrimination is based on the standard of "equal pay for equal work." Many believe that this definition is limited and that valuation discrimination can also occur when men and women hold entirely different jobs (in content or results) that are of comparable worth to the employer. Existing federal laws do not support the "equal pay for work of comparable worth" standard.

variable pay   Pay tied to productivity or some measure that can vary with the firm's profitability.

vesting   A benefit plan provision that guarantees that participants will, after meeting certain requirements, retain a right to the benefits they have accrued, or some portion of them, even if employment under their plan terminates before retirement.

wage   Pay given to employees who are covered by overtime and reporting provisions of the Fair Labor Standards Act. Nonexempts usually have their pay calculated at an hourly rate rather than a monthly or annual rate.

wage adjustment provisions   Clauses in a multilayer union contract that specify the types of wage adjustments that have to be implemented during the life of the contract. These adjustments might be specified in three major ways: (1) deferred wage increases—negotiated at the time of contract negotiation, with the time and amount specified in the contract; (2) cost-of-living adjustments (COLAs) or escalator clauses; and (3) reopener clauses.

wage and price controls   Government regulations that aim at maintaining low inflation and low levels of unemployment. They frequently focus on "cost-push" inflation, limiting the size of pay raises and the rate of increases in prices charged for goods and services. Used for limited time periods only.

wage survey   *See* pay (wage) survey.

Walsh-Healey Public Contracts Act of 1936   A federal law requiring certain employers holding federal contracts for the manufacture or provision of materials, supplies, and equipment to pay industry prevailing-wage rates.

Worker Economic Opportunity Act   Law passed in 2000 that provides that income from most stock plans need not be included in calculating overtime pay.

work flow   The process by which goods and services are delivered to the customer.

work/life balance benefits   Benefits that increase the perception that the company cares about the employee as a whole person (e.g., fitness centers, eldercare programs).

zones   Ranges of pay used as controls or guidelines within pay bands that can keep the system more structurally intact. Maximums, midpoints, and minimums provide guides to appropriate pay for certain levels of work. Without zones employees may float to the maximum pay, which for many jobs in the band is higher than market value.

Name Index

Subject Index